IMPACT
CALIFORNIA SOCIAL STUDIES

U.S. History
Making a New Nation

TEACHER'S EDITION

McGraw-Hill Education

Mc
Graw
Hill
Education

mheducation.com/prek-12

Copyright © 2019 McGraw-Hill Education

Send all inquiries to:
McGraw-Hill Education
303 East Wacker Drive, Suite 2000
Chicago, IL 60601

ISBN: 978-0-07-899310-7
MHID: 0-07-899310-5

Printed in the United States of America.

2 3 4 5 6 7 8 9 LMN 22 21 20 19 18 17

Welcome to

IMPACT
CALIFORNIA SOCIAL STUDIES
from your partners at McGraw-Hill Education

*We created **IMPACT**: California Social Studies around the philosophy that social studies is both engaging and essential. Captivating stories, immersive hands-on activities, and dynamic digital content will spark students' curiosity and readiness for learning. These experiences open the door for students to engage in meaningful and relevant inquiries about their world. This is where, together, we can make an IMPACT on the next generation of informed and engaged citizens.*

*Designed specifically to the California History-Social Science Standards and Framework, **IMPACT**: California Social Studies takes a fresh approach to standards-based curriculum. Our instructional model builds inquiry skills through active engagement with a rich variety of primary sources, informational texts, and media, and participation in activities with real-world application. We also know the challenges you face as an elementary teacher, given the demands of teaching many subject areas and limited time. **IMPACT**: California Social Studies was designed as a solution to these challenges by integrating social studies content, analysis skills, and ELA requirements into lessons that you can confidently implement to build your students' thinking, reading, and writing skills. The program thus supports the deep interconnectedness of content, inquiry, literacy, and citizenship that is reflected in the History-Social Science Framework.*

> ❝ *This is where, together, we can make an IMPACT on the next generation of informed and engaged citizens.* ❞

Democratic citizens don't grow on trees; they have to be educated. Social studies is important from the earliest grades because it creates "intellectual capital." Research shows that children who begin learning social studies early are able to learn more later. Children who are fortunate enough to get strong history, geography, economic, and civic education in each grade are thus given a key advantage— a gift that will keep on giving for the rest of their lives.

Are you ready to make an IMPACT?

IMPACT
CALIFORNIA SOCIAL STUDIES

Program Authors

James Banks, Ph.D.
Kerry and Linda Killinger Endowed Chair
in Diversity Studies
Director, Center for Multicultural Education
University of Washington
Seattle, Washington

Kevin P. Colleary, Ed.D.
Curriculum and Teaching Department
Graduate School of Education
Fordham University
New York, New York

William Deverell, Ph.D.
Director of the Huntington-USC Institute
on California and the West
Professor of History, University of
Southern California
Los Angeles, California

Daniel Lewis, Ph.D.
Dibner Senior Curator
The Huntington Library
Los Angeles, California

Elizabeth Logan Ph.D., J.D.
Associate Director of the Huntington-USC
Institute on California and the West
Los Angeles, California

Walter C. Parker, Ph.D.
Professor of Social Studies Education
Adjunct Professor of Political Science
University of Washington
Seattle, Washington

Emily M. Schell, Ed.D.
Professor, Teacher Education
San Diego State University
San Diego, California

IMPACT
CALIFORNIA
SOCIAL STUDIES

Table of Contents

Be a Social Studies Detective

Reference Sources

  Reinforce and extend classroom instruction with chapter specific From School to Home letters.

(t)Fred Smith/EyeEm/Getty Images, (b)JordiDelgado/iStock/Getty Images

Chapter
1

The Land and People Before Columbus

 EQ **Where and How Did American Indians Live Before the Arrival of Europeans?**

Chapter Planning

Chapter Lessons

Chapter Wrap Up

 HOMEWORK Consider assigning these activities as student homework.

 Go Digital!  Reinforce and extend classroom instruction with
chapter specific From School to Home letters.

Chapter 2

The Age of Exploration

EQ **What Happened When Diverse Cultures Crossed Paths?**

Go Digital! Reinforce and extend classroom instruction with chapter specific From School to Home letters.

Chapter 3

A Changing Continent

EQ How Did European Settlements Impact
North America?

Chapter Planning

Chapter Lessons

Chapter Wrap Up

Chapter 4

The Road to War

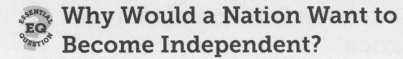

Why Would a Nation Want to Become Independent?

Chapter Planning

Chapter Lessons

Chapter Wrap Up

Go Digital! ✉ Reinforce and extend classroom instruction with chapter specific From School to Home letters.

Chapter 5

The American Revolution

What Does the Revolutionary Era Tell Us About Our Nation Today?

Chapter Planning

Chapter Lessons

Chapter Wrap Up

Chapter 6

Forming a New Government

 How Does the Constitution Help Us Understand What It Means to Be an American?

Chapter Planning

Chapter Lessons

Chapter Wrap Up

(*Go Digital!*) 🏠✉ Reinforce and extend classroom instruction with chapter specific From School to Home letters.

Chapter 7 — Life in the Young Republic

How Were the Early Years of the United States Transformative for the Nation?

Chapter Planning

Chapter Lessons

Chapter Wrap Up

Chapter 8

The Westward Expansion

 What Does the Westward Expansion Reveal About the Character of Our Nation?

Chapter Planning

Chapter Lessons

Chapter Wrap Up

  Reinforce and extend classroom instruction with chapter specific From School to Home letters.

SKILLS AND FEATURES

All page numbers shown here are from the student Research Companion.

Contents **xv**

James Forten. *Black History: More Than Just a Month.* Mike Henry. Lanham, MD: Rowman & Littlefield Education, 2013. p. 6. 234

Washington, George. George Washington to General Lord Charles Cornwallis. 17 October 1781. George Washington Papers at the Library of Congress, 1741-1799: Series 3e Varick Transcripts. 239

Charles James Fox. "American Revolution." *Encyclopedia of North Carolina.* http://www.ncpedia. org/american-revolution-part-5-gen-nath. 240

Marie Joseph Marquis de Lafayette. *Lafayette in the Age of the American Revolution.* Ed. by Stanley J. Idzerda, Roger E. Smith, et al. Ithaca: Cornell University Press, 1979. 241

Treaties and Other International Acts of the United States of America. Edited by Hunter Miller, Volume 2 Documents 1-40 : 1776-1818. Washington: Government Printing Office, 1931. 245

Hall, Prince. "Petition for Equal Educational Facilities," (October 17, 1787). Quoted in Herbert Aptheker, ed., A *Documentary History of the Negro People in the United States: From Colonial Times through the Civil War, Volume 1.* (New York: Citadel Press, 1951), 19–20 247

Chapter 6

Henry Lee, Jr. Letter to George Washington from Henry Lee, Jr, 8 September 1786. https://founders.archives. gov/documents/Washington/04-04-02-0229 264

Thomas Jefferson. From Thomas Jefferson Foundation website: https://www.monticello.org/site/jefferson/little-rebellionquotation. 265

Samuel Adams. From Calvin Coolidge Memorial Foundation website: https://coolidgefoundation.org/ resources/speeches-as-governor-of-mass-1919-1920-10/ 265

The Constitution. Article I. Legal Information Institute, Cornell University. https://www.law.cornell.edu/anncon/ html/artIfrag26_user.html 277

James Madison. The Federalist, number 51. In *The Federalist Papers.* Ed. by Ian Shapiro. Copyright © 2009 by Yale University. 278

George Mason. "Federalists and Antifederalists Debate a Bill of Rights," by Gordon Lloyd. http://teaching americanhistory.org/bor/fed-antifed-debate 280

Elbridge Gerry. "Elbridge Gerry's Reasons for Not Signing the Federal Constitution." http://www.loc. gov/teachers/classroommaterials/presentations andactivities/presentations/timeline/newnatn/ usconst/egerry.html 280

Patrick Henry, speaking before the Virginia Ratifying Convention, June 1788. 280

William Tyler Page. "'American's Creed' by Future Clerk of the House William Tyler Page." http://history.house. gov/HistoricalHighlight/Detail/35813?ret=True 286

Chapter 7

Louisiana Purchase: Treaty between the United States of America and the French Republic, art. 3. April 30, 1803. National Archives and Records Administration. 304

Dolley Madison to her sister, Anna Cutts, August 23, 1814. In *Dolly Madison,* by Maud Wilder Goodwin, pp. 173–175. New York: C. Scribner's Sons, 1896. 307

Samuel F. B. Morse. "Today in History—May 24." Library of Congress. https://www.loc.gov/item/today-in-history/ may-24/ 316

Daniel Boone. *Missouri: A Guide to the "Show Me" State.* Works Progress Administration. New York: Duell, Sloan and Pearce, 1941. 320

A Treaty of Peace between the United States of America and the Tribes of Indians..., art. 3." In The Public Statutes at Large of the United States of America, Vol. 7, edited by Richard Peters, 49. Boston: Charles C. Little and James Brown, 1848. 321

Tecumseh. In a speech to William Henry Harrison. Vincennes, Indiana Territory. 12 August 1810. 322

Chapter 8

Sarah L. Byrd, interview by Sara B. Wrenn, March 1, 1939, Portland, Oregon. Library of Congress, Manuscript Division, WPA Federal Writers' Project Collection, Folklore Project, Life Histories, 1936-39, MS55715: BOX A729. 344

"Resistance in the Courts." Digital History, University of Houston. http://www.digitalhistory.uh.edu/disp_ textbook.cfm?smtID=3&psid=691 350

Chief John Ross. "The Papers of Chief John Ross, vol 1, 1807-1839." Translated by Gary E. Moulton Norman OK: University of Oklahoma Press, 1985 350

Worcester v. Georgia, 31 U.S. 515 (1832). https://www. law.cornell.edu/supremecourt/text/31/515 351

Sequoyah. *Sequoyah: Inventor of Written Cherokee.* Roberta Basel. Minneapolis: Compass Point, 2007. p. 37 352

Edwin Bryant. *What I Saw in California.* New York: D. Appleton, 1848. p. 68 361

 Teacher Notes

Make an IMPACT!

ENGAGE > **INVESTIGATE** > **REPORT AND TAKE ACTION**

IMPACT: California Social Studies is a student-centered, comprehensive, and coherent knowledge-building program that promotes students' understanding of the world and their individual place in it.

Empowering great teaching is something McGraw Hill Education stands behind. We know California teachers are strong, passionate, and dedicated to teaching that makes an impact on students. We want to be your partner in delivering interactive, engaging, and meaningful social studies content in an efficient manner so that your time in the classroom is honored.

Built for the California History-Social Science Framework and Standards, IMPACT Social Studies was intentionally written with a focus on

Inquiry, Literacy, Content, and Citizenship.

IMPACT: California Social Studies offers educators the flexibility of easily integrating social studies into the literacy block or devoting time specifically to social studies content. Regardless of the path educators take, instruction starts with engaging content that fosters collaboration through thinking, talking, and considering multiple perspectives. Enabling students to think critically and design solutions to the problems in their world is a program priority.

⌕ ENGAGE

Learning begins with curiosity.

Learning begins with curiousity, asking the essential questions that encourage students to wonder about the world, our history, and how it all impacts their lives. At all grade levels, *IMPACT*: California Social Studies inquiry-based chapters of study have been designed to help you spark students' interest and empower them to ask more questions, think more critically and inspire them to make a difference. By taking an active role in their learning, students will enrich and deepen their content-specific knowledge and skills, and improve their attitudes toward learning and their ability to see clearly the world around them. By teaching students to read and write for specific purposes rather than memorizing discrete pieces of information, they become more engaged in learning and can form connections between chapter concepts, their own communities, and the larger world.

A Word from the Author

"Grounding in social studies education knows no grade-level restrictions. Social studies teaches us about ourselves: where we came from, who we are, where we are going. Children of all ages can wrestle with the problems and mysteries we all wrestle with, and inviting them to do so in appropriate grade-level fashion is what great curriculum and great teaching is all about"

William Deverell , Ph.D.

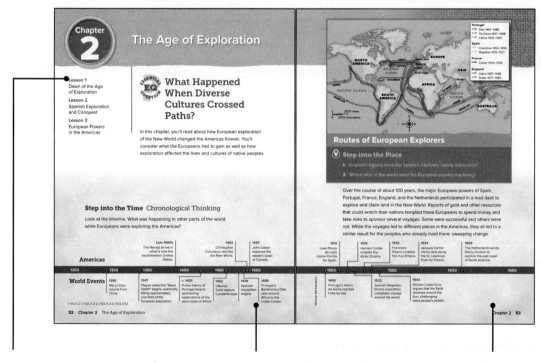

Lesson Question lets you think about how the lesson connects to the chapter EQ.

Lesson Outcomes help you think about what you will be learning and how it applies to the EQ.

Images and text provide opportunities to explore the lesson topic.

Essential Questions guide students toward unpacking concepts.

Teaching the art and strategy of inquiry and critical thinking is at the heart of our program. Each lesson, organized around a chapter-level **Essential Question**, guides students toward unpacking the concepts, and information, and discovering unique perspectives.

Developing student literacy, inspiring participation in democracy, helping students explore the past to understand how it shapes the present and the future, and learning to develop evidenced-based conclusions are critical aspects of instruction in *IMPACT*: California Social Studies.

A Word from the Author

❝The important reciprocal relationship that exists between the California History-Social Science Framework and the California Common Core State Standards for English Language Arts challenges us to think anew about how we teach reading and content areas in the elementary classroom❞

Kevin Colleary, Ed.D.

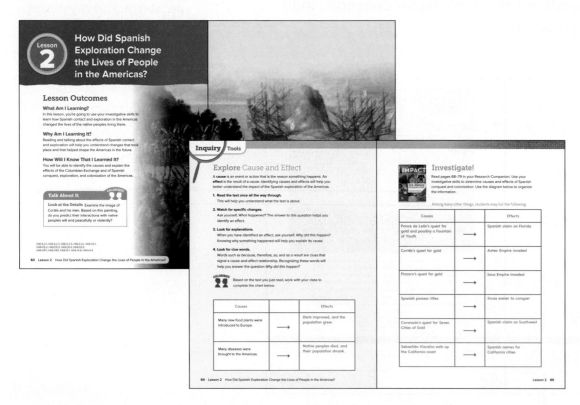

Daily instruction is built on text-based decisions, collaborative presentations, debates, questioning, and games. Students investigate and analyze primary and secondary sources, explore connections to art and literary sources, and examine texts written from a variety of perspectives.

⌕REPORT AND TAKE ACTION

Today's students are tomorrow's leaders.

Today's students are tomorrow's leaders, and that means they need to be prepared. Globally, we want our students to think about their IMPACT on their communities, their nation and the world.

By stretching students' thinking to take informed action, we can work to promote inclusion, critical thinking, and investigation.

By learning from the past and applying that knowledge to our ever-changing world, students will develop the skills necessary for college, career, and civic life. Preparing California students for college, career and civic life is at the core of the *IMPACT*: California Social Studies.

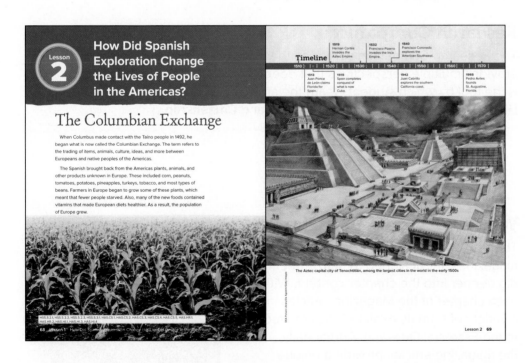

We need to help our students become human. We need to teach our students how to know, how to care and how to act. *IMPACT*: California Social Studies was built to help you do this by addressing important questions, by helping students think critically, and to offer opportunities for students to create evidence-based opinions.

A Word from the Author

"Today's students are both witnesses to and participants in an ever-changing world. Access to modern technologies provides a constant flow of information from near and far. Our challenge is to help students understand themselves better by investigating the world, recognizing perspectives, communicating ideas, and taking action. Success will be found when students realize their potential as concerned and active community members who use evidence-based arguments to inspire change"

Emily Schell, Ed.D.

Tools to enhance the Knowledge-Building Journey!

Student Materials

IMPACT: California Social Studies is an inquiry-based program, with a rich array of print and digital resources that make learning active and engaging. Along the way, students will witness new people, places, and ideas. They will hear and evaluate multiple perspectives, as they participate in activities with real-world applications.

Inquiry Journal

The Inquiry Journal is built on the premise that deep knowledge begins by capturing students' attention and sparking their curiosity by integrating what is known with what is new. The Journal introduces the overarching concepts required to unpack each chapter of study through critical review and close reading of multiple sources of information.

Research Companion

The Research Companion serves as the primary source of information and provides multiple perspectives that deepen understanding of knowledge. It is the tool by which students learn the art of research and critical analysis of **History, Geography, Civics, Economics,** and **Citizenship.**

A Word from the Author

❝ The Explorer Magazine is an excellent resource that provides students with accessible and interesting social studies information. It can be used as a supplement during the literacy block or as a collaborative task during social studies. The magazine provides students with engaging, grade-level content that fosters critical thinking and deeper understanding of the content standards ❞

Douglas Fisher, Ph.D.

Weekly Explorer Magazine

The grade-level **Weekly Explorer** magazines are designed to help students dig deeper into the chapter content. Within each chapter of the Magazine, articles in a variety of formats explore ideas related to the Essential Question. Additionally, the magazine articles provide a unique perspective for students to use in their overall research of the chapter-level concepts and ideas to enhance and extend the learning experience.

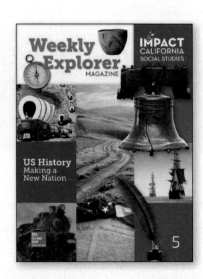

Teacher Materials

Instructional Planning and Teacher Support

IMPACT: California Social Studies teacher materials provide a road map for teachers to follow as they plan what to teach, how to teach, and when to teach social studies lessons. The teacher materials also allow flexibility to organize and expand the chapter content based around student inquiry.

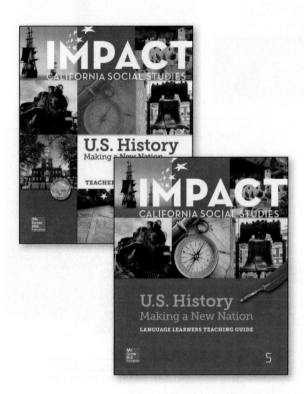

Teacher Edition

IMPACT: California Social Studies Teacher's Edition includes:

- instructional support and practices based on the content in the standards and framework

- pacing guides for 180 days of instruction

- well-organized content

- background information about important events, people, places, and ideas appearing in the standards and framework

- suggestions for teachers on how to differentiate instruction to meet the needs of all learners

- opportunities for all students to achieve essential knowledge and skills.

- point-of-use instructional notes designed to scaffold instruction to meet the needs of all students, including advanced learners, below-grade level, and special-needs students.

- support for the development of domain-specific and academic vocabulary for all students

- point-of-use integrated ELD scaffolds that are tiered and focused, oral, written, and collaborative.

Language Learners Teaching Guide

The Language Learners Teaching Guide provides a focused language study designed to support language learners and help them gain content knowledge in the complex literacy-based history-social science discipline. The instructional model is focused on language development while building content knowledge.

Go *Digital!*

Weekly Explorer Magazine Teaching Guide

The Online Weekly Explorer Teaching Guide follows a three-step lesson format for guiding students through the reading and analysis of the articles. The flexible lesson plans provide focused instruction. The teaching guide provides support for a variety of classroom situations and instructional approaches.

A Word from the Author

" Providing access to social studies content for English learners requires attention to their language needs. Lessons should include a number of features to enhance their comprehension including clear, student-friendly definitions of terms, use of visuals, questions that are differentiated by proficiency level, and opportunities to discuss ideas with peers. Remember that these students are learning new content in a language they are still in the process of acquiring." "

Jana Echevarria, Ph.D.

Go Digital!

Online Student Center

The **Online Student Center** delivers learning resources that support whole-class presentations and individual research on most devices. In addition to the complete content from the Inquiry Journal and Research Companion in HTML and .pdf formats, the Online Student Center provides learning resources connected to each chapter's Essential Question and to each lesson inquiry investigation.

IMPACT Chapter Videos

Engage with Rich Chapter Resources

Learning Resources provide options for evidence-gathering through videos and a variety of interactive features, including maps, timelines, graphic organizers, and activities.

Investigate and Deepen Understanding

This wide variety of assets has been developed to help students use inquiry beyond the social studies classroom to better understand the world around them.

Report Findings and Take Action

Formative discussion, writing prompts, and lesson-specific rubrics measure student application of the core content, application of the Inquiry Tools, and engagement.

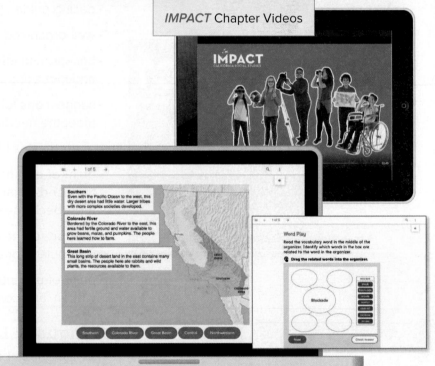

Online Teacher Center

A simple, easy-to-access teacher site for the digital resources provides teachers with a means to organize and sort resources, personalize their classroom instruction, and upload their personal resources. Teachers can initiate and monitor group projects through the online collaboration tools. They can also easily develop and deliver assignments and assessments to the whole class, small groups, or individual students.

The Online Teacher Center also includes *IMPACT News*, our current events blogsite. This feature helps students understand the world around them by reading, viewing, and discussing current events.

McGraw-Hill Education

Incorporate Foldables into Your Instruction

What are Foldables?

Foldables are student-directed, three-dimensional, interactive graphic organizers that can be used to enhance vocabulary, strengthen note-taking skills, outline main ideas, encourage questioning, sequence events, and reinforce skills such as making comparisons, finding similarities, and determining cause and effect. Foldables can be made using blank sheets of paper. The folds that form them make tabs or layers that students raise and lower as they interact with the manipulative. Foldables can also begin with a duplicated template that provides a graphic or map before being folded to make a kinesthetic activity.

IMPACT: California Social Studies Foldables Templates

In *IMPACT*: California Social Studies, you will find a variety of Foldables templates with graphics or maps. Duplicate these to use with your students to strengthen note taking skills while forming chapter study aids. Even though these are made using only one sheet of paper, they provide hours of interactions during a chapter study. Don't forget to use backs and insides of folded sheets, too! You might find it advantageous to use more than one template in some chapters. For example, you might use the Flag Shutterfold for part of a chapter and then add a map template later. All Foldables used in *IMPACT*: California Social Studies can be glued into notebooks, placed in notebook pockets, or stored in portfolios.

Assessment Tools

You can also duplicate and use a clean version of the chapter template as an assessment tool. Have students summarize an event, predict an outcome, apply what they have learned to a different situation or time period, justify or question an action, or mark things on a map without looking at their original note-taking tool.

SAY Vocabulary Charts

Note that my new SAY Vocabulary Chart can be used with three or six terms and can be completed by individual students or enlarged 133% to make an 11" x 17" version for small or large group discussion. Either size can be folded in half (with the chart as the book cover) to form a half-book that provides a clean page for making lists and recording student questions for follow up.

For more on Foldables, go to **Go Digital!**

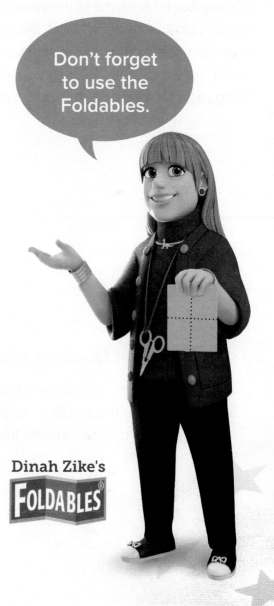

Don't forget to use the Foldables.

Dinah Zike's
FOLDABLES®

Know What Your Students Know!

Frequent and measurable assessment is the cornerstone of effective teaching by shining a light on areas of mastery and, more importantly, to inform instruction. An effective social studies programs provides daily opportunities for students to gain new knowledge, produce questions and ideas, and receive feedback to keep them immersed in a productive cycle of learning. The flexible formal and informal paths included in the *IMPACT*: California Social Studies program are built on the understanding that students thrive on feedback from their teachers and peers.

The *IMPACT*: California Social Studies assessment of student learning in history-social science is informed by 1) the History–Social Science Standards for California Public Schools (HSS), which include both the grade level content expectations and analysis skill sections, 2) California Common Core State Standards for English Language Arts and Literacy, and 3) California English Language Development Standards (CA ELD Standards).

BEFORE
PRE-TEST

Chapter-Level Quick Check

Measure students' content knowledge, including domain-specific vocabulary. The results can be used to inform instruction.

EVERY LESSON
ONGOING ASSESSMENT

☑ Stop and Check

Teachers can use the quick questions to monitor students' comprehension of the lesson content. The Stop and Check questions prompt students to make connections to their world today, engage in discourse designed to deepen their understanding of the content, and to look at different perspectives.

◌ Report Your Findings

The lesson tasks can be used to measure student understanding of the lesson content, reading, writing, and students' ability to effectively express their understanding. Lesson task-specific rubrics are included for ease in evaluation.

A Word from the Author

" Students gather facts and information to develop knowledge about society, issues, events, and systems. They form opinions, ideas, and questions based on that knowledge, which leads to greater understanding. This is the on-going cycle of inquiry that we want for our students, which we promote through continuous and consistent formative assessments. Informal assessments help students stay "on track" with their investigations and formal assessments provide opportunities for students to showcase their newfound understandings, skills, and ideas in a variety of formats. "

Emily Schell, Ed.D

EVERY CHAPTER POST TEST

Post Assessments are used to evaluate students' understanding of core chapter content and learning objectives.

Connections in Action

Teachers can use these to evaluate students' understanding of core chapter content through discussion.

Essential Question Inquiry Project

Measure student understanding of the chapter content and students' ability to effectively express their understanding. A task-specific evaluation rubric has been included in both print and digital formats.

Go Digital!

Lesson Assessment

Use the Lesson Assessment to monitor students' understanding of the lesson content aligned to SBAC claims and targets

Online Chapter Benchmark Assessment

Teachers can use the chapter tests to monitor students' understanding of the chapter History-Social Science standards and content. All assessments are aligned to the California Smarter Balanced Assessment claims and targets.

	CHAPTER 1	CHAPTER 2
	The Land and People Before Columbus Weeks 1 - 6	**The Age of Exploration** Weeks 7 - 10
ESSENTIAL QUESTION	**EQ** Where and How Did American Indians Live Before the Arrival of Europeans?	**EQ** What Happened When Diverse Cultures Crossed Paths?
INQUIRY PROJECT	**EQ** Show what life was like … A museum has asked students to design a display case for an American Indian group of their choice. Students will create a poster or diorama to showcase this group's daily life, including how the group obtained water, food, tools, clothing, and shelter. Display cases will include depictions of the group's religious and/or cultural traditions, government, and economy. Include a museum plaque to describe the visual and then prepare a two-minute presentation.	**EQ** European Explorers: Collect Them All! Students will choose a European explorer discussed in this chapter to research in depth, other than Christopher Columbus. They will create a trading card for this explorer that includes an image of the explorer on the front. On the back, they will include important statistics, such as where and when he was born, what led him to explore the Americas, and how his expedition impacted his country and the native peoples with whom he interacted. Then students will write a conclusion evaluating whether his actions were mostly positive or mostly negative.
CHAPTER FOCUS CONTENT STANDARD	**HSS** **HSS 5.1** Students describe the major pre-Columbian settlements, including the cliff dwellers and pueblo people of the desert Southwest, the American Indians of the Pacific Northwest, the nomadic nations of the Great Plains, and the woodland peoples east of the Mississippi River.	**HSS** **HSS 5.2** Students trace the routes of early explorers and describe the early explorations of the Americas.
ASSESSMENT TOOLS	*Go Digital!* **Benchmark Assessment** **Connections In Action** Discussion based assessment of core chapter content. **Evaluation Rubric**	*Go Digital!* **Chapter Benchmark Assessment** **Connections In Action** Discussion based assessment of core chapter content. **Evaluation Rubric**
School to Home	**School to Home** Reinforce and extend classroom instruction with chapter specific From School to Home letters.	**School to Home** Reinforce and extend classroom instruction with chapter specific From School to Home letters.

* See page T786 for a California History-Social Science Content Standards correlation.

PACING GUIDE AND OVERVIEW

CHAPTER 3

A Changing Continent
Weeks 11 - 14

EQ ESSENTIAL QUESTION How Did European Settlements Impact North America?

EQ ESSENTIAL QUESTION Tell Both Sides of the Story

Students will write a short narrative that illustrates the relations between a specific group of European settlers and the American Indians they encountered. Students will describe events clearly from both sides, using effective dialogue and descriptions. They will identify the effects of relations on the American Indians' way of life as well as the benefits or setbacks the Europeans experienced. Working with a small group, students will read each other's stories aloud.

(HSS) **HSS 5.3** Students describe the cooperation and conflict that existed among the American Indians and between the Indian nations and the new settlers.

(HSS) **HSS 5.4** Students understand the political, religious, social, and economic institutions that evolved in the colonial era.

Go Digital!

Benchmark Assessment

Connections In Action Discussion based assessment of core chapter content.

Evaluation Rubric

School to Home Reinforce and extend classroom instruction with chapter specific From School to Home letters.

CHAPTER 4

The Road to War
Weeks 15 - 18

EQ ESSENTIAL QUESTION Why Would a Nation Want to Become Independent?

EQ ESSENTIAL QUESTION Which Side Will You Choose?

Students will write an essay from the perspective of a Patriot, Loyalist, African American, or American Indian, outlining his or her reasons for wanting or not wanting a war with Britain. They will use evidence from the chapter and outside research. Students will form small groups that contain multiple perspectives and debate whether the colonies should go to war. They will then hold a vote and present their conclusions to the class.

(HSS) **HSS 5.4** Students explain the causes of the American Revolution.

Go Digital!

Chapter Benchmark Assessment

Connections In Action Discussion based assessment of core chapter content.

Evaluation Rubric

School to Home Reinforce and extend classroom instruction with chapter specific From School to Home letters.

CHAPTER 5	CHAPTER 6
The American Revolution Weeks 19 - 22	**Forming a New Government** Weeks 23 - 26

ESSENTIAL QUESTION

EQ What Does the Revolutionary Era Tell Us About Our Nation Today?

EQ How Does the Constitution Help Us Understand?
What It Means to Be an American?

INQUIRY PROJECT

EQ How Would Our Lives Have Been Impacted If . . . ?

Working together, students will research people, ideas, and events that had an impact during the American Revolution. They will each choose one for which they will develop a timeline card. They'll evaluate the information in the classroom timeline and choose what they think are the five most important people, ideas, or events. Then students will take one item from the timeline and consider how our country would be different today if it had never happened.

EQ Which Side Will You Choose?

As a class, students will propose a new amendment to the Constitution that has a good case for and against it. Then, divided into two groups, one in favor of it and one opposed, they will debate the issue. On a class website, students will write a series of letters or editorials for and against the amendment, making references to points made in one another's writings.

CHAPTER FOCUS CONTENT STANDARD

(HSS) **HSS 5.5** Students explain the causes of the American Revolution.

(HSS) **HSS 5.6** Students understand the course and consequences of the American Revolution.

(HSS) **HSS 5.7** Students describe the people and events associated with the development of the U.S. Constitution and analyze the Constitution's significance as the foundation of the American republic.

ASSESSMENT TOOLS

Go Digital!

Benchmark Assessment

Connections In Action   Discussion based assessment of core chapter content.

Evaluation Rubric

Go Digital!

Chapter Benchmark Assessment

Connections In Action   Discussion based assessment of core chapter content.

Evaluation Rubric

School to Home

School to Home   Reinforce and extend classroom instruction with chapter specific From School to Home letters.

School to Home   Reinforce and extend classroom instruction with chapter specific From School to Home letters.

* See page T786 for a California History-Social Science Content Standards correlation.

PACING GUIDE AND OVERVIEW

CHAPTER 7	CHAPTER 8
Life in the Young Republic Weeks 27 - 31	**The Westward Expansion** Weeks 32 - 36

 How Were the Early Years of the United States Transformative for the Nation?

 What Does the Westward Expansion Reveal about the Character of Our Nation?

 Which Change Will You Choose?

Create a Museum Gallery

Students will take a stand by choosing which change during the early years of the United States had the biggest impact on the nation. They will make a slideshow presentation on that change using images, video clips, songs, or other media. Students will explain what the change was, who was involved, who was using evidence from the text and outside sources.

Students will create a gallery (print or digital) of three paintings that depict Westward Expansion. They will write a museum card for each picture, including the title, the name of the artist, the year it was painted, and a brief description of what the painting shows. Discuss as a group how the paintings work together to tell a story of how the United States grew and expanded west.

(HSS) **HSS 5.8** Students trace the colonization, immigration, and settlement patterns of the American people from 1789 to the mid-1800s, with emphasis on the role of economic incentives, effects of the physical and political geography, and transportation systems.

(HSS) **HSS 5.9** Students know the location of the current 50 states and the names of their capitals.

(HSS) **HSS 5.8** Students trace the colonization, immigration, and settlement patterns of the American people from 1789 to the mid-1800s, with emphasis on the role of economic incentives, effects of the physical and political geography, and transportation systems.

(HSS) **HSS 5.9** Students know the location of the current 50 states and the names of their capitals.

(**Go** *Digital!*)

Benchmark Assessment

Connections In Action   Discussion based assessment of core chapter content.

Evaluation Rubric

(**Go** *Digital!*)

Chapter Benchmark Assessment

Connections In Action   Discussion based assessment of core chapter content.

Evaluation Rubric

School to Home   Reinforce and extend classroom instruction with chapter specific From School to Home letters.

School to Home   Reinforce and extend classroom instruction with chapter specific From School to Home letters.

When Minutes Count

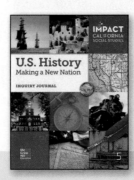

DAY 1

Suggested Pacing

45 Minutes

Inquiry Journal

- Discuss Lesson Outcomes.
- Explore the Essential Question.
- Introduce the Inquiry Tools.

Explorer Magazine

Introduce the magazine.

 Inquiry: Introduce the chapter project.

Short on Time?

Use this path to teach core content in less time.

30 Minutes

Inquiry Journal

- Discuss Lesson Outcomes.
- Explore the Essential Question.
- Introduce the Inquiry Tools.

Explorer Magazine

Use the magazine during your English/Language Arts block.

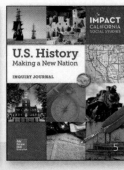
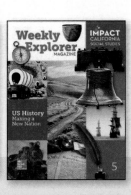
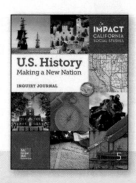

DAYS 2 - 4

Research Companion

- Analyze the source.
- Inspect: Explore the inquiry articles.
- Find Evidence: Analyze, critique, and synthesize the text.
- Make Connections: Assess understanding.

Inquiry Journal

Investigate: Add notes to the graphic organizer

Explorer Magazine

Read the magazine

 Inquiry: **Begin work on the chapter project.**

Research Companion

- Analyze the source.
- Inspect: Explore the inquiry articles.
- Find Evidence: Analyze, critique, and synthesize the text.
- Make Connections: Assess understanding.

Inquiry Journal

Investigate: notes to the graphic organizer

Explorer Magazine

Use the magazine during your English/Language Arts block.

DAY 5

Inquiry Journal

- Report Your Findings
- Think About It: Review research and connect to lesson focus.
- Talk About It: Collaborate with other students to discuss and assess learning.
- Write About It: Respond to the prompt.

Connect to the EQ

Explore connections between the lesson focus and the EQ.

 Inquiry: **Make notes and assess project progress.**

Inquiry Journal

- Report Your Findings
- Think About It: Review research and connect to lesson focus.
- Talk About It: Collaborate with other students to discuss and assess learning.
- Write About It: Respond to the prompt.

Connect to the EQ

Explore connections between the lesson focus and the EQ.

EXPLORE AND INVESTIGATE

Primary Sources

- Discuss with students the concept of primary sources. Point out that a primary source is a piece of evidence from the time period that they are studying.

- Talk about other examples of primary sources, such as scrapbooks, photo albums, autobiographies, audio and video recordings, household appliances and gadgets, clothing, and furniture. Discuss why these are examples of primary sources. These are artifacts from a certain time period that can tell us more about that time.

Secondary Sources

- Review the information in the Did You Know? box. Make sure the difference between primary and secondary sources is clear.

- Talk about other examples of secondary sources, such as encyclopedias, textbooks, and biographies. Discuss how these are different from primary sources. These sources provide information about people and events. They also tell us how people lived. However, they aren't first-hand accounts from the time period.

Social Studies Detective Strategies

- Review the strategies with students. Discuss how these strategies can help us investigate a primary source.

- Work with students to use the Social Studies Detective Strategies to examine the photograph on page 9a. If students need additional information about the photograph, tell them it is a newsboy on a London street in April 1912.

A Word from the Author

" The task of using—and understanding—primary sources lies at the center of the social studies endeavor. To see and apply the undistilled stuff of history is to gain direct insight into social, cultural, economic, and political life as it played out in the past. Engagement with primary sources leads to understanding, which leads to direct action in our democratic processes. "

Daniel Lewis, Ph.D.

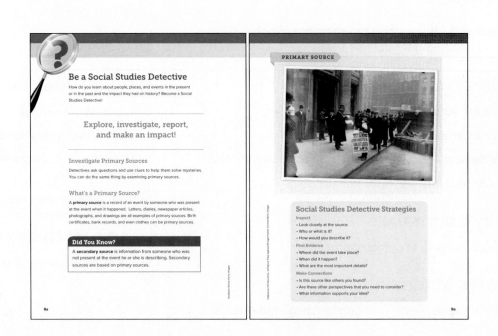

A Word from the Author

66 "The discipline of social studies forms the foundation of our collective goals for K-5 education by providing students a toolbox of skills to frame and address the questions of their age. By engaging with primary sources, students start multi-generational conversations. As students learn about how their communities, state, and country work, they begin to imagine their roles in creating our future and understand how to become more actively engaged. 99

Elizabeth Logan, Ph.D. , J.D.

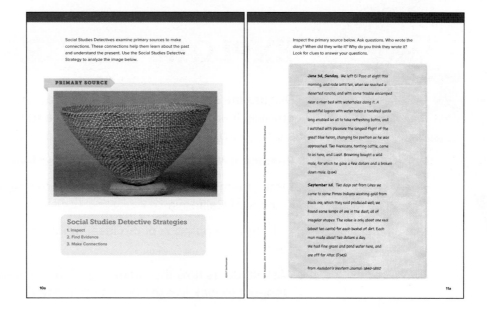

Have students work in pairs or small groups to investigate the primary sources on pp. 10a and 11a. Refer them to the steps on p. 9a for more information about the Social Studies Detective Strategies. Instruct students to take notes for each step in the Strategies as they review each primary source.

If students have difficulty identifying item in the photo on p. 10a, explain that it is a basket made by a member of an American Indian tribe. The excerpt from the journal entry on p. 11a is from John Woodhouse Audubon's *Western Journal: 1849-1850*. Audubon was the son of the famous naturalist, John James Audubon.

REPORT

Have groups report their findings to the class. Since students may not have used every step in the Social Studies Detective Strategies, discuss the steps they used and how these helped them analyze the photo and text. Then discuss the similarities and differences in the information each group found.

EXPLORE GEOGRAPHY

Discuss the study of geography with students. Explain that geographers study the physical features of the earth, such as land forms and bodies of water. They also study how humans impact the earth and its atmosphere.

Reading a Map Discuss the various map features with students.

- Have them use the Map Key to locate the capital of the United States and the capital of California.

- Discuss the purpose of the inset maps and the locator on the map of the United States.

- Ask students how they think the term "compass rose" originated. (The points were thought to look like the petals on a rose.)

- Challenge students to use the Map Scale to estimate the distance across the United States from the Pacific Ocean to the Atlantic Ocean in miles and kilometers. Distances will vary depending on the points students use to measure, but it should be between 2800 and 3000 miles (4480-4800 kilometers).

A Word from the Author

" We teach students to read the word and the world. To read the word, students need basic knowledge and skills. Reading the world requires students to question assumptions and paradigms and to use knowledge to make the world more just and humane. This is a critical goal of social studies education. "

James Banks, Ph.D.

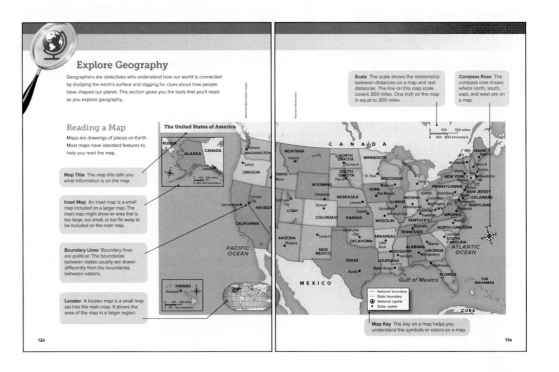

StasKhom/iStock/Getty Images

Special Purpose Maps Explain that special purpose maps show specific kinds of information. Road maps, climate maps, landform maps, and elevation maps are examples of special purpose maps. Special purpose maps often use different symbols and colors to provide information.

Primary Source Explain that the historical map was drawn by Samuel Lewis after Lewis and Clark completed their journey. The map was published in 1814 and was based on information that they brought back with them. Discuss with students how this map would have been helpful to others who were heading west.

Looking at Earth Discuss the various features of a globe shown in the images on p. 15, including the equator, the prime meridian, the four hemispheres, and the North and South Poles. Tell students that the prime meridian is also called the Greenwich Meridian because it is based at the Royal Observatory located in Greenwich Park, London. If there's a globe in the classroom, have students locate these features on the globe.

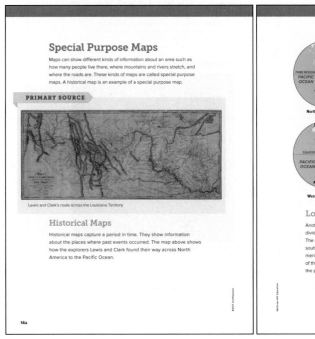

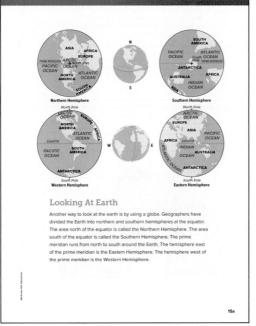

EXPLORE ECONOMICS

Define and Discuss Discuss the concept of costs and benefits with students. Explain that costs can involve money, but costs can also involve other things that might be given up to achieve a benefit. Use this example of studying for a test with students. The cost of studying might be that we can't do something else we'd like to do, such as go to a movie with friends. However, the benefit is that we do well on the test.

Talk About It Have students consider the list of Costs and Benefits in the chart on p. 16a in order to inform their decision.

Primary Source Provide additional information about the currency pictured. This is a Fugio Cent and was the first official one-cent piece of the United States currency. The word "fugio" means "I flee." Also on the coin is a sun and sundial and the motto "Mind Your Business." Discuss which of these types of elements are still on our currency today (Latin terms, motto, and images).

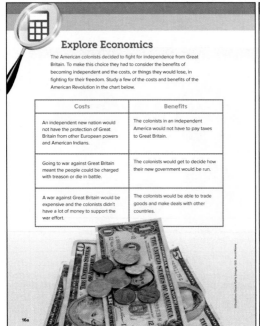

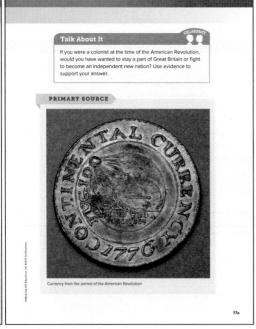

EXPLORE CITIZENSHIP

Define and Discuss Explain that citizenship means belonging to a community. We can be citizens of a country, a state, a city or town, or even a school. Discuss the qualities of good citizens on p. 19a with students. Ask students how they might embody those qualities at home, in school, or in the community.

Primary Source Have students examine the primary source photograph on p. 18a and discuss details they notice in the photo. For additional background, explain to students that Antietam, Maryland, was the sight of a significant battle of the Civil War in September 1862.

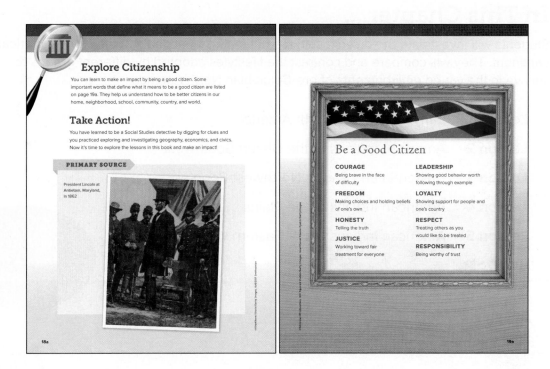

Explore Citizenship

You can learn to make an impact by being a good citizen. Some important words that define what it means to be a good citizen are listed on page 19a. They help us understand how to be better citizens in our home, neighborhood, school, community, country, and world.

Take Action!

You have learned to be a Social Studies detective by digging for clues and you practiced exploring and investigating geography, economics, and civics. Now it's time to explore the lessons in this book and make an impact!

PRIMARY SOURCE

President Lincoln at Antietam, Maryland, in 1862

Be a Good Citizen

COURAGE
Being brave in the face of difficulty

FREEDOM
Making choices and holding beliefs of one's own

HONESTY
Telling the truth

JUSTICE
Working toward fair treatment for everyone

LEADERSHIP
Showing good behavior worth following through example

LOYALTY
Showing support for people and one's country

RESPECT
Treating others as you would like to be treated

RESPONSIBILITY
Being worthy of trust

18a

19a

Where and How Did American Indians Live Before the Arrival of Europeans?

In This Chapter ...

Students will investigate the diverse cultures of the first inhabitants of the North American continent. They will compare and contrast the lifestyles adopted by different groups to survive in the varied environments of pre-Columbian North America.

Lesson 1   Early Peoples of North America

Lesson 2   American Indians of the Desert Southwest

Lesson 3   California and Pacific Northwest Peoples

Lesson 4   American Indians of the Plains

Lesson 5   American Indians of the Eastern Woodlands

 CHAPTER STANDARDS

✔ Students describe the major pre-Columbian settlements, including the cliff dwellers and pueblo of the desert Southwest, the American Indians of the Pacific Northwest, the nomadic nations of the Great Plains, and the woodland peoples east of the Mississippi River. **HSS.5.1**

Don't forget to use the Foldables.

Dinah Zike's

FOLDABLES®

1 ENGAGE

Inquiry Journal
pp. 2–5

 Inquiry Project

Show what life was like . . .

- **Explore Words**

- *Go Digital!*
  - IMPACT Chapter Video: The Land and People Before Columbus

2 INVESTIGATE

Research Companion
pp. 2–7

- **Step Into Time and Place**

- **Connect Through Literature**
  The Legend of the Wishpoosh
  Retold by Elizabeth M. Tenney

Weekly Explorer Magazine pp. 2–13

3 REPORT

Inquiry Journal
pp. 46–47

 **Inquiry Project**

Show what life was like . . .

 Short on Time? Look for the clock to teach core content in less time.

CULTIVATE MEANING AND SUPPORT LANGUAGE

Language Learner Teaching Guide,
pp. 2–3

Content Objectives

- Describe how early American Indian groups from different regions developed special characteristics.
- Explore the traditions of early American Indian.

Language Objectives

- Analyze information and explain meaning.
- Analyze comparison and contrasts in texts.
- Use compare and contrast words to identify text structure.

CONNECT TO Wonders

Unit 4, Week 4
Consider Our Resources

Read Aloud
"Minerals"

Reading/Writing Workshop
"Power from Nature"

Literature Anthology/Paired Selection
One Well
"The Dirt on Dirt"

Leveled Readers
The Delta and "Get Rich with Compost"

CONNECT TO SCIENCE

Explore the different biomes that can be found in North America. Understanding the climate, flora and fauna, and geography of these ecosystems will provide context to help students better understand the lifestyles of the various American Indian groups.

CONNECT TO MATH

Study demographics. Show students how to calculate percentages and make pie charts to help them compare things like population and territory.

Choose the assessment options that work best for you and your students.

BEFORE
PRE-TEST

1. Begin the Chapter

Measure students' content knowledge before you begin the chapter with the following questions.

🕐 Quick Check

✔ What are the names of American Indian individuals and groups?

✔ What did they wear and what possessions did they have?

✔ What kinds of building did they live in?

✔ How did they get food?

✔ What as their culture like?

1. Afterwards, have students circle all the information from media that they think is accurate, and cross out everything they think is inaccurate.

2. When all students have responded, ask them to rate how confident they are in their answers on a scale from 1 – not very confident to 5 – very confident.

3. Ask students to compare their responses. Determine what are commonly held beliefs about American Indians. Ask students to keep these in mind as they progress through the chapter.

4. **Don't Forget!** Revisit students' quick check responses with them. If students change their response, ask them to support the change with text evidence. You may wish to have students respond to a different prompt to measure students' content knowledge, such as *What are the unique traits of this group of American Indians?*

EVERY LESSON
ONGOING ASSESSMENT

Use the lesson tools to monitor the IMPACT of your instruction.

☑ Stop and Check

Use the quick quesetion prompts to monitor student comprehension of the content. The **Stop and Check** questions prompt students to make connections to their world today, engage in discussions to deepen their understanding of the content, and to look at different perspectives.

🔎 Report Your Findings

The lesson task, **Report Your Findings**, can be used to measure student understanding of the lesson content and ability to effectively express their understanding. See the Lesson Assessment pp. T32, T52, T72, T90, and T112 for task-specific evaluation rubrics.

(*Go Digital!*) Lesson Assessment

Use the **Lesson Assessment** to monitor student understanding of the lesson content. Have students complete the assessment online. See pp. T33, T53, T73, T91, and T113 for California Smarter Balanced Assessments Connections.

EVERY CHAPTER POST TEST

Evaluate student understanding of core chapter content with one or more of the following assessment options.

Connections in Action
Use the **Connections in Action** to evaluate student understanding of core chapter content through discussion.

Inquiry Project
Use the **EQ Inquiry Project** to measure student understanding of the chapter content and ability to effectively express their understanding. See the EQ Inquiry Project Wrap Up below for a task-specific evaluation rubric.

	4	3	2	1
Historical Understanding	Strong understanding of the cultures of American Indian groups	Adequate understanding of the cultures of American Indian groups	Uneven understanding of the cultures of American Indian groups	No understanding of the cultures of American Indian groups
Present Information	Clearly states a thesis	Adequately states a thesis	Somewhat clear or unclear thesis	No thesis or student does not show understanding of the task
Support with Details	Key details well supported with relevant information cited from credible sources	Key details adequately supported with relevant information and cited from credible sources	Key details unevenly supported or poorly cited	Key details are missing or unsupported
Presentation	Speaks clearly and at an understandable pace Provides informative and interesting visuals	Speaks clearly during most of the presentation Provides generic or uninteresting visuals	At times speaker is unclear Provides flawed or misleading visuals	Does not use complete sentences Does not provide visuals

(Go *Digital!*) Chapter Benchmark Assessments

Use the chapter tests to monitor student understanding of the chapter History-Social Science standards and content. Have students complete the assessment online.

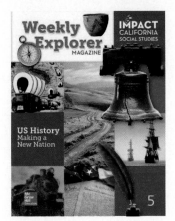

pp. 2–13

 Short on Time?

Use the Weekly Explorer Magazine during your reading block.

Go *Digital!*

Look online for the Weekly Explorer Magazine Teaching Guide.

WordBlast

Remind students to look for the Word Blasts as they read the Explorer Magazine.

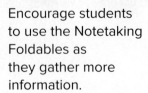

FOLDABLES

Encourage students to use the Notetaking Foldables as they gather more information.

Weekly Explorer Magazine

The Weekly Explorer Magazine is designed to provide students with more information to use as they dig deeper into the **cultures of American Indians**. The articles in a variety of formats explore the Essential Question and support the Inquiry Project.

Engage

Build background for students and share any information needed to provide a context for the chapter topic. Have students read the Essential Question and the Table of Contents.

Analyze the Visual Discuss the opening visual (photograph, photo essay, artwork) on the second page of the Magazine chapter. Help students connect the visual to the chapter topic and the Essential Question.

Analyze the Sources

Students will read and analyze the articles, graphic novel, poems, songs, literature excerpts, primary sources, and infographics.

Read and Analyze Before reading, provide any additional information you think students will need about the topics. Then guide students through the three-step process to read and analyze the articles.

1 Inspect Have students skim the article or articles on a page or multiple pages. Ask questions to help students recall and retell key ideas.

- What is this article mostly about?
- Who is _____?

2 Find Evidence Have students reread the articles and look for details they might have missed. Ask additional questions to help them read more closely.

- What details do you notice in the photographs?
- Why was _____ important?

3 Make Connections Have students work in pairs or small groups to discuss prompts that help them connect the article(s) to other texts, their own lives, current ideas and issues, and other topics.

- How is _____ similar to what we do today?
- How do you think _____ felt about what happened?
- What do you think about _____?

Bibliography

The following suggested resources may help students' investigation of the chapter content.

EXPLORE PEOPLE, PLACES, AND EVENTS

▶ **Arrow to the Sun: A Pueblo Indian Tale**
by Gerald McDermott; Dutton Books, 1998.

▶ **Buffalo Hunt**
by Russell Freedman; Scholastic, 1992.

Perspectives
▶ **Children of the Longhouse**
by Joseph Bruchac; Puffin Books, 1998.

▶ **Hiawatha: Messenger of Peace**
by Dennis Brindell Fradin;

▶ **A History of Us**
by Joy Hakim; Oxford University Press, 2007.

Perspectives
▶ **If You Lived with the Cherokee**
By Connie and Peter Roop; Scholastic, 1998.

Perspectives
▶ **The Inland Whale: Nine Stories Retold from California Indian Legends**
by Theodora Kroeber; University of California Press, 1989.

▶ **The People with Five Fingers: A Native Californian Creation Tale**
by John Bierhorst; Marshall Cavendish, 2000.

▶ **The Wampanoag: American Indians**
by Kevin Cunningham; Scholastic, 2011.

EXPLORE MUSIC

Did you know? There is no written record of music in North and South America before the arrival of Europeans. However, archaeologists and anthropologists have found many different types of drums, flutes, and other percussion and wind instruments that predate the arrival of European explorers. From this, we can assume that music was part of the everyday life of the native peoples of the Americas.

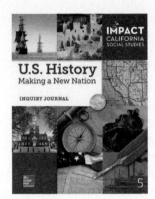

Inquiry Journal
pp. 2–5

IMPACT
CALIFORNIA
SOCIAL STUDIES

U.S. History
Making a New Nation

INQUIRY JOURNAL

 STANDARDS

Describe how geography and climate influenced the way various nations lived and adjusted to the natural environment, including locations of villages, the distinct structures that they built, and how they obtained food, clothing, tools, and utensils. **HSS.5.1.1**

Describe their varied customs and folklore traditions. **HSS.5.1.2**

Explain their varied economies and systems of government. **HSS.5.1.3**

Go Digital!

Explore Words: Interactive vocabulary activities support students as they explore the chapter words.

 See the **Language Learner Teaching Guide** pp. 2–3 for support strategies.

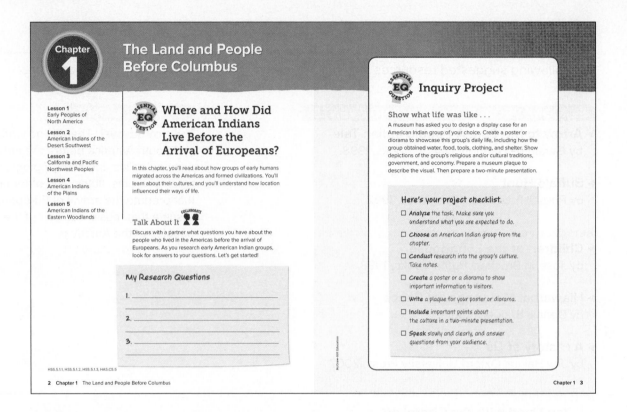

Chapter 1

The Land and People Before Columbus

Lesson 1
Early Peoples of North America

Lesson 2
American Indians of the Desert Southwest

Lesson 3
California and Pacific Northwest Peoples

Lesson 4
American Indians of the Plains

Lesson 5
American Indians of the Eastern Woodlands

Where and How Did American Indians Live Before the Arrival of Europeans?

In this chapter, you'll read about how groups of early humans migrated across the Americas and formed civilizations. You'll learn about their cultures, and you'll understand how location influenced their ways of life.

Talk About It

Discuss with a partner what questions you have about the people who lived in the Americas before the arrival of Europeans. As you research early American Indian groups, look for answers to your questions. Let's get started!

My Research Questions

1. _____
2. _____
3. _____

HSS.5.1.1, HSS.5.1.2, HSS.5.1.3, HAS.CS.5

2 Chapter 1 The Land and People Before Columbus

Inquiry Project

Show what life was like . . .

A museum has asked you to design a display case for an American Indian group of your choice. Create a poster or diorama to showcase this group's daily life, including how the group obtained water, food, tools, clothing, and shelter. Show depictions of the group's religious and/or cultural traditions, government, and economy. Prepare a museum plaque to describe the visual. Then prepare a two-minute presentation.

Here's your project checklist.

☐ **Analyze** the task. Make sure you understand what you are expected to do.

☐ **Choose** an American Indian group from the chapter.

☐ **Conduct** research into the group's culture. Take notes.

☐ **Create** a poster or a diorama to show important information to visitors.

☐ **Write** a plaque for your poster or diorama.

☐ **Include** important points about the culture in a two-minute presentation.

☐ **Speak** slowly and clearly, and answer questions from your audience.

Chapter 1 3

Where and how did American Indians live before the arrival of Europeans?

Have students read the Chapter Essential Question on p. 2.

Talk About It

- Prompt students to write what they would like to learn about American Indians.

- After jotting down their questions, have students discuss their questions with partners.

Inquiry Project
Show What Life was Like . . .

- Have students read aloud the EQ Inquiry Project.

- Tell students that they will use information gathered from the chapter and from independent research to complete the project.

- Make certain students understand the task by reviewing each step of the project.

Complete this chapter's Word Rater. Write notes
as you learn more about each word.

endeavor   My Notes
- ☐ Know It!
- ☐ Heard It!
- ☐ Don't Know It!

harvest   My Notes
- ☐ Know It!
- ☐ Heard It!
- ☐ Don't Know It!

hieroglyph   My Notes
- ☐ Know It!
- ☐ Heard It!
- ☐ Don't Know It!

hunter-gatherer   My Notes
- ☐ Know It!
- ☐ Heard It!
- ☐ Don't Know It!

mesa   My Notes
- ☐ Know It!
- ☐ Heard It!
- ☐ Don't Know It!

oral history   My Notes
- ☐ Know It!
- ☐ Heard It!
- ☐ Don't Know It!

potlatch   My Notes
- ☐ Know It!
- ☐ Heard It!
- ☐ Don't Know It!

prairie   My Notes
- ☐ Know It!
- ☐ Heard It!
- ☐ Don't Know It!

slash-and-burn   My Notes
- ☐ Know It!
- ☐ Heard It!
- ☐ Don't Know It!

totem pole   My Notes
- ☐ Know It!
- ☐ Heard It!
- ☐ Don't Know It!

4   Chapter 1   The Land and People Before Columbus

Chapter 1   5

McGraw-Hill Education

Explore Words

- **Academic/Domain-Specific Vocabulary** Read the words aloud to students. Explain to students that these are words they will learn more about in the chapter.

- **Word Rater** Have students place a checkmark in one of the three boxes below each word, indicating that they "Know It," "Heard It," or "Don't Know It."

  ✓ **Know It** Tell students that if they know the word, they should write its meaning on the lines provided.

  ✓ **Heard It** Tell students that if they have heard, or are familiar with the word, they should write what they know about it on the lines provided. Remind them to take notes about the word as they encounter it.

  ✓ **Don't Know It** If they do not know the word's meaning, tell them to write down its meaning when they encounter the word in the chapter.

🔍 Explore Words Routine

Remind students that when they come to an unfamiliar word or phrase in their research, they should follow these steps to determine its meaning.

1. Look around the word or phrase for clues to unlock its meaning.

2. Look inside the word or phrase for word part clues.

3. Look up the word in other resources.

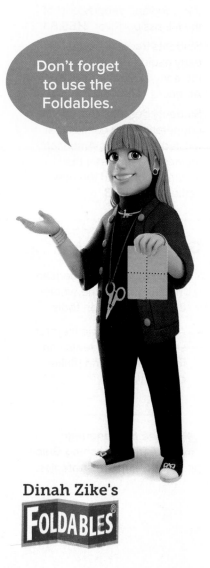

Don't forget to use the Foldables.

Dinah Zike's
FOLDABLES®

2 INVESTIGATE

The Land and People Before Columbus

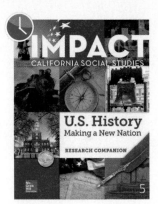

U.S. History
Making a New Nation

RESEARCH COMPANION

Research Companion
pp. 2–7

 STANDARDS

Students describe the major pre-Columbian settlements, including the cliff dwellers and pueblo people of the desert Southwest, the American Indians of the Pacific Northwest, the nomadic nations of the Great Plains, and the woodland peoples east of the Mississippi River. **HSS.5.1**

Students trace the routes of early explorers and describe the early explorations of the Americas. **HSS.5.2**

Students describe the cooperation and conflict that existed among the American Indians and between the Indian nations and the new settlers. **HSS.5.3**

Go Digital!

• Investigate early American Indians with online whole-class presentation tools.

• Analyze the online literature selection so students can find evidence and make connections.

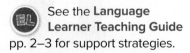
See the **Language Learner Teaching Guide** pp. 2–3 for support strategies.

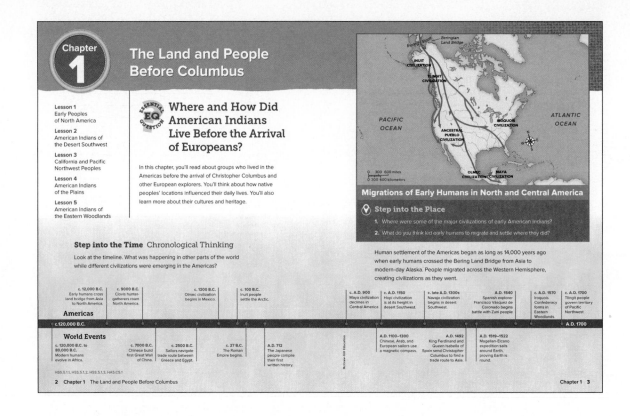

Step Into the Time

• Have students read over the events on the timeline, first examining the events from the Americas and then the events from around the world.

• Which named groups are older than the Great Wall? (The Clovis and the Olmec)

• While the desert Southwest was being settled, what else has happening in the world? (Sailors began using magnetic compasses.)

Step Into the Place

In partners or in small groups, have students examine the map on p. 3 and answer the questions beneath it.

1. Where were some of the major civilizations of early American Indians? (Central America (present-day Mexico), the Southwest of the United States, the Great Plains, the Pacific Northwest, and the East Coast)

2. What do you think led early humans to migrate and settle where they did? (Possible responses: They settled near bodies of water or rivers. Fresh water is necessary for farming and drinking.)

Background Information

This folktale is a retelling of a story told by pre-Columbian Indians of the Pacific Northwest. The American Indians of this region believed a great flood had taken place, which is explained by the events in the story. Many of the locations in the tale can be found on a map of present-day Washington state.

GENRE Folktale *"The Legend of Wishpoosh" is a folktale. A Folktale is a story passed down through generations.*

Analyze the Source

Inspect Have students read the selection on pp. 4–7 together to determine the general meaning of the text.

1. How are the Speelyei and Wishpoosh alike? (they are both very powerful animal spirits) How are they different? (Wishpoosh is destructive, while Speelyei tries to protect his region)

Find Evidence Have students reread the selection and ask:

2. Why did the two characters fight? (Wishpoosh's appetite was out of control and he would destroy all of creation.)

Make Connections

3. Why was this story told? (explains the origins and distinctions of various people)

Perspectives What conclusions about American Indian civilization can you draw from this story? (responses will vary, but could include their connection to nature, reverence for animals, and the importance of stories to them)

How Did the Characteristic of Early American Indian Groups Develop?

Background Information

Explain to students that in this lesson they will learn that location plays a key role in the development of a civilization. They will track how some of the first groups of American Indians grew and created their own cultures.

Community Connections

To enrich what students have learned about early American Indian groups, plan a virtual field trip to a museum that houses artifacts and information about one of the groups discussed in the lesson. You can also use detailed online digital maps to show ruins and burial mounds across North America.

LESSON STANDARDS

✓ Describe how geography and climate influenced the way various nations lived and adjusted to the natural environment, including locations of villages, the distinct structures that they built, and how they obtained food, clothing, tools, and utensils. **HSS.5.1.1**

✓ Students use map and globe skills to determine the absolute locations of places and interpret information available through a map's or globe's legend, scale, and symbolic representations. **HAS.CS.4**

✓ Students judge the significance of the relative location of a place (e.g., proximity to a harbor, on trade routes) and analyze how relative advantages or disadvantages can change over time. **HAS.CS.5**

Connect to the Essential Question

Chapter 1, pp. 2–13

The **Weekly Explorer Magazine** supports students' exploration of the Essential Question and provides additional resources for the EQ Inquiry Project.

Inquiry Project

What was life like in the Americas before Columbus?

Remind students to use the information they learn in this lesson and other resources to complete their EQ Inquiry Project!

Dinah Zike's

In this lesson you will use Foldables.

When Minutes Count!

Suggested Lesson Pacing

1 ENGAGE
One Day

- Lesson Opener
- Analyze the Source
- Inquiry Tools

Go Digital

- **Video**: The Iroquois Confederacy
- **iMap:** Settling the Americas
- **iMap:** The Maya, 300–900 CE
- **iMap:** The Aztec Empire
- **iMap:** The Inuit, c. 1500 CE

2 INVESTIGATE
Two to Three Days

 Short on Time? Look for the clock to teach core content in less time.

- The First Hunter-Gatherers
- The Olmec
- The Maya
- Early Desert Peoples
- The Mound Builders

3 REPORT
One Day

- Take a Stand
- Write and Cite Evidence
- Compare Your Groups

Make Connections!

(CCSS) CONNECT TO ELA

Reading

Draw on information from multiple print or digital sources, demonstrating the ability to locate an answer to a question quickly or to solve a problem efficiently. **RI.5.7**

Integrate information from several texts on the same topic in order to write or speak about the subject knowledgeably. **RI.5.9**

Research

Conduct short research projects that use several sources to build knowledge through investigation of different aspects of a topic. **W.5.7**

Writing

Write informative/explanatory texts to examine a topic and convey ideas and information clearly. **W.5.2**

Draw evidence from literary or informational texts to support analysis, reflection, and research. **W.5.9**

Speaking and Listening

Report on a topic or text or present an opinion, sequencing ideas logically and using appropriate facts and relevant, descriptive details to support main ideas or themes; speak clearly at an understandable pace. **SL.5.4**

Classroom Resources

Search for additional resources using the following key words.

Adena

Ancestral Pueblo

Clovis people

Hohokam

Hopewell

Maya

Mississippian people

Olmec

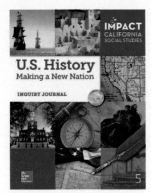

Inquiry Journal,
pp. 6–7

 **STANDARDS**

Describe how geography
and climate influenced the
way various nations lived
and adjusted to the natural
environment, including
locations of villages, the distinct
structures that they built,
and how they obtained food,
clothing, tools, and utensils.
HSS.5.1.1

Go Digital!

Explore the lesson content
with online whole-class
presentation tools.

* **Video:** The Iroquois
  Confederacy
* **iMap:** Settling the Americas
* **iMap:** The Maya,
  300–900 CE
* **iMap:** The Aztec Empire
* **iMap:** The Inuit, c. 1500 CE

How Did the Characteristics of Early American Indian Groups Develop?

Bellringer

Prompt students to make some learning goals for this course. Say: *What do you want to learn about the early history of the United States? Discuss with a partner what you expect to learn in this class.* (Responses will vary, but students should identify that they want to learn about the history and peoples of the United States.)

Lesson Outcomes

What Am I Learning? Have students read the Lesson Question and Lesson Outcomes on page 6.

Why Am I Learning It? Make sure students understand the term *characteristics*. Characteristics are specific traits. To help students understand the word in context, have them identify characteristics of a group of people, such as fifth graders. Students may say that most fifth graders are 10 or 11 years old, and they go to elementary school.

How Will I Know That I Learned It? Ask students the following questions.

* What will you be able to identify? (characteristics of early American groups)

* What is the purpose of this task? (to state an opinion)

* How will you support your opinion? (with evidence from the text)

Talk About It

Explain that when we look at images of ruins, we try to learn more about the civilization that created them. Guide students to look at the image, read the caption, and answer the questions to better understand what the image shows. Provide sentence frames as needed as students complete the activity.

* *The image shows _____.*

* *_____ or _____ created the ruin.*

* *I think the structure was originally used for _____ or _____.*

Collaborative Conversations

Add New Ideas As students engage in partner, small-group, and whole-class discussions, encourage them to

* first read the material carefully.

* be respectful of the opinions of others.

* use evidence from the text to support their conclusions or to provide counterclaims to another group member's conclusions.

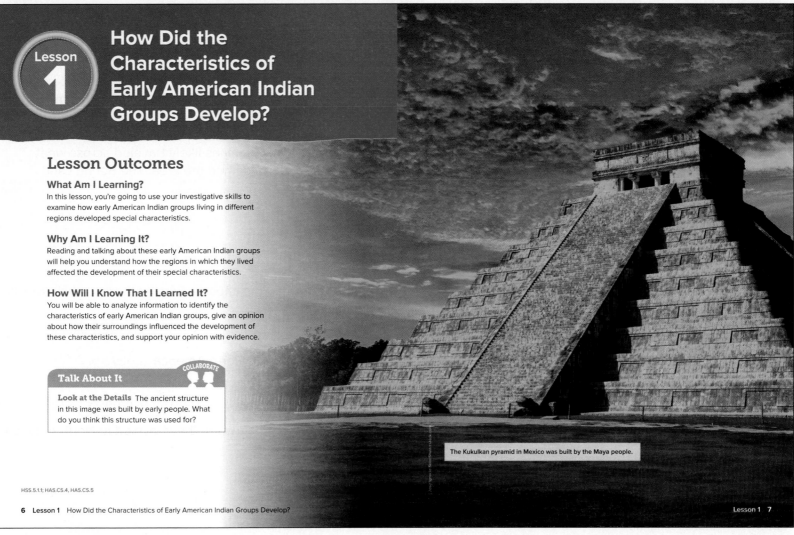

Lesson 1

How Did the Characteristics of Early American Indian Groups Develop?

Lesson Outcomes

What Am I Learning?
In this lesson, you're going to use your investigative skills to examine how early American Indian groups living in different regions developed special characteristics.

Why Am I Learning It?
Reading and talking about these early American Indian groups will help you understand how the regions in which they lived affected the development of their special characteristics.

How Will I Know That I Learned It?
You will be able to analyze information to identify the characteristics of early American Indian groups, give an opinion about how their surroundings influenced the development of these characteristics, and support your opinion with evidence.

Talk About It COLLABORATE

Look at the Details The ancient structure in this image was built by early people. What do you think this structure was used for?

The Kukulkan pyramid in Mexico was built by the Maya people.

HSS.5.1.1; HAS.CS.4, HAS.CS.5

6 Lesson 1 How Did the Characteristics of Early American Indian Groups Develop?

Lesson 1 **7**

Inquiry Journal, pp. 6–7

 ENGLISH LEARNERS SCAFFOLD

ELD.PI.5.2 Interacting with others in written English in various communicative forms (print, communicative technology, and multimedia)

Emerging	Expanding	Bridging
Identify Features Work with students to identify features of the ruin in the photograph.	**Describe Features** Have small groups create a list of words that describe the features of the ruin. Encourage them to share what they think the structure was originally used for.	**Apply Language** Have students work together to explain what they think the structure was originally used for. Guide them to describe the features of the ruin that helped them come to those conclusions.

See the **Language Learner Teaching Guide** for more language support strategies.

Monitor and Differentiate

REACHING ALL LEARNERS

Approaching Level

Have students work together to describe what they see in the photograph, including shapes and structures.

On Level

Have students look for more details in the photograph, such as location and landscape. Have them think about what life might have been like for the people who used the structure.

Beyond Level

Have students identify possible ways the civilization that created the structure used it in daily life.

INQUIRY JOURNAL
Analyze the Source

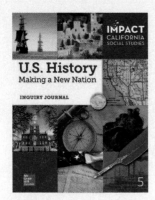

Inquiry Journal,
pp. 8–9

 STANDARDS

Describe how geography
and climate influenced the
way various nations lived
and adjusted to the natural
environment, including
locations of villages, the
distinct structures that they
built, and how they obtained
food, clothing, tools, and
utensils. **HSS.5.1.1**

CCSS Draw on information from
multiple print or digital
sources, demonstrating the
ability to locate an answer to a
question quickly or to solve a
problem efficiently.
CCSS.ELA.RI.5.7

___

Go Digital!

Model how to inspect and find
evidence with online whole-
class presentation tools.

Background Information

Bering Land Bridge Scientists believe that the Bering Land Bridge, which once
connected North America and Asia, was one of the principal ways in which humans
migrated from Asia to the Americas. During Earth's many Ice Ages, ocean levels fell,
exposing the sea floor. During the most recent Ice Age, between 30,000 to 12,000
years ago, sea levels fell as much as 400 feet. Humans likely traveled across what
is now the Bering Strait in pursuit of game that roamed the area. The Bering Land
Bridge is sometimes called Beringia.

1 Inspect

Look Have students look at the map and read the caption. Remind them to circle words
in the text with which they are unfamiliar.

- What does the map show? (migration routes across the Bering Land Bridge, or Beringia)
- Circle details about when humans first arrived in North America. (between 30,000 and
  12,000 years ago)
- Explain what the pink area shows. (the area of land that is now covered by water)
- Circle details about the options early humans had when they traveled to North America.
  (walking or going by boat)
- Where did these humans start from? (Asia)

2 Find Evidence

Look Again Ask students to look again at the map.

Analyze the Related Text Reread the text that explains the importance of the
Beringia.

- Underline details about how the spread of glaciers during the last Ice Age caused
  Beringia to develop. (So much water was caught up in glaciers that sea level dropped
  enough to expose more of the sea floor. People and animals were able to cross from
  Asia to North America using this land, later called Beringia, or the Bering Land Bridge.)
- How does the map show the boundary of Beringia? (the pink area)
- How does the map show the outline of current landmasses? (yellow areas)

COLLABORATE
3 Make Connections

Collaborate Encourage students to work with a partner to make inferences about the
hunting skills of early humans. Guide them to identify how the symbols on the map can
help them make inferences. (Students should use the symbols to identify such animals as
mammoths and bison. They should infer that hunting such animals shows a high degree of
skill.)

Analyze the Source

1 Inspect

Look Read the caption below the map. What do you think the term "land bridge" means?

- **Circle** words on the map that identify land areas and bodies of water.
- **Trace** possible migration routes followed by early humans.
- **Discuss** with a partner how the last Ice Age caused early humans to migrate into North America.

My Notes

_____

_____

_____

_____

_____

_____

_____

_____

_____

_____

_____

_____

_____

_____

Early Humans in North America

Many major ice ages have taken place in Earth's history. During these periods, sheets of ice thousands of feet thick covered vast areas of land. With so much seawater trapped in ice sheets, or *glaciers*, sea levels dropped. Dry land appeared in some places. During the last major Ice Age, from about 30,000 to 12,000 years ago, sea levels dropped very low. A land bridge formed between the northeast tip of Asia and the northwest tip of North America. Scientists refer to this area as the Bering Land Bridge, or *Beringia*. Herds of Ice Age animals moved from Asia to North America across Beringia, looking for food. Many scientists think that early humans from Asia followed the animals they hunted across this land bridge.

Sometimes a hunting trip could take many days. The hunters had to gather plants to eat until they were able to kill an animal. The plants they gathered included berries, grasses, and mushrooms. This is why we call these people hunter-gatherers.

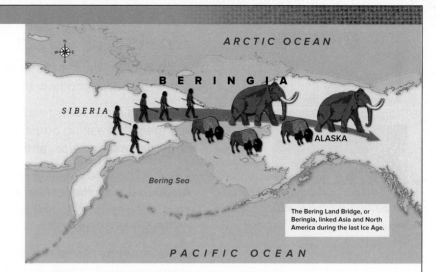

The Bering Land Bridge, or Beringia, linked Asia and North America during the last Ice Age.

Scientists think that humans first reached North America sometime between 30,000 and 12,000 years ago. Once in North America, these early humans may have migrated southward on land. Another possibility is that they avoided the ice by traveling in boats along the Pacific Coast.

2 Find Evidence

Look Again Underline words in the text that explain how the spread of glaciers during the last Ice Age caused Beringia to develop.

Examine Look back at the map. How does the map show the outline of Beringia? How does it show the outline of current landmasses?

3 Make Connections

Talk Using the symbols on the map, discuss with a partner the types of Ice Age animals that early human hunters followed into North America. What does this tell you about the hunting skills of these early humans?

8 Lesson 1 How Did the Characteristics of Early American Indian Groups Develop?

Lesson 1 **9**

Inquiry Journal, pp. 8–9

(EL) ENGLISH LEARNERS SCAFFOLD

ELD.PI.5.5 Listening actively to spoken English in a range of social and academic contexts

Emerging

Develop Language Work with students to unpack the sentence, "Once in North America, these early humans may have migrated southward along an inland route that was ice-free." Students should understand that the early humans migrated along a specific route after they got to America. They chose a route that had no ice on it. Guide students to use the map to describe how the early humans moved across North America.

Expanding and Bridging

Develop Language Guide students to describe why the humans took a route that was ice-free, or not covered by ice. Have them explain whether they would have chosen to migrate over land or by boat and what the challenges of each method might have been.

See the **Language Learner Teaching Guide** for more language support strategies.

Monitor **and Differentiate**

REACHING ALL LEARNERS

Approaching Level

Have students discuss what they see on the map. Have them find details in the text that explain what the map shows. Guide them to analyze how the map and the text support one another, and then have them share their findings with the class.

Beyond Level

Have students choose a route and state why it would have been the best way to travel. Encourage them to imagine that they are early humans, facing the long trek across the continent. Guide them to be creative, but make sure they base their opinions on details in the map and the text.

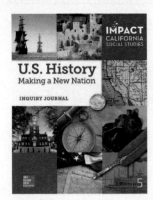

Inquiry Journal,
pp. 10–11

 STANDARDS

Describe how geography and climate influenced the way various nations lived and adjusted to the natural environment, including locations of villages, the distinct structures that they built, and how they obtained food, clothing, tools, and utensils. **HSS.5.1.1**

Draw on information from multiple print or digital sources, demonstrating the ability to locate an answer to a question quickly or to solve a problem efficiently. **CCSS.ELA.RI.5.7**

Write informative/explanatory texts to examine a topic and convey ideas and information clearly. **CCSS.ELA.W.5.2**

Go Digital!

- Model how to explore and investigate with online whole-class tools.

- Students can access the online graphic organizer to use the inquiry tools as they read.

Analyze Information

Explain Tell students that to analyze information means to break it down into parts in order to understand how the parts fit together.

Read Have students read the step-by-step instructions about how to analyze information. Tell them that asking questions about what is happening in the text will help them to find patterns, relationships, and trends.

Guide Practice Guide students through the following model. *Beringia and North America during the last Ice Age was an important location. The area would have been cold, but passable, which would have allowed people to travel pretty easily from one continent to another.*

Explain that by identifying details about where a group of early Americans lived, their surroundings, and their way of life, students can understand how the group developed.

Investigate!

Have students read pages 8–17 in the Research Companion. Tell them the information will help them answer the lesson question **How Did the Characteristics of Early American Indian Groups Develop?**

Take Notes Tell students that they should take notes of the key characteristics of each group of native peoples in the graphic organizer on page 9 of the Inquiry Journal. Explain to students that they will take notes as they read each section. Remind them that taking notes will help them understand and remember what they read.

Remind students that good note taking is about finding the most important information and writing key words or phrases about it. Note takers do not rewrite every word from the text unless they plan to quote an author later on.

Inspect Guide students to read the text in each section to determine what the text says. Encourage them to make note of words they don't understand and look for answers to questions, such as *who? what? where? when? why?* and *how?*

Find Evidence Encourage students to reread the text to develop a deeper understanding of the content. Remind students that after they read and take notes, they should review and think about how the facts and details will help them answer the lesson question.

Collaborative Conversations

Text-Based Discussion Remind students that discussing the text with partners can help students

- discover a new point of view.
- find evidence.
- benefit from someone else's understanding of the text.

Inquiry Tools

Analyze Information

To analyze information means to break the information down into parts and then look at how those parts fit together. Analyzing information will help you determine what information means and how it will be useful.

1. **Read the text once all the way through.**
   This will give you a general idea of the subject, what kind of information is available, and how it might fit together.

2. **Look closely at the sources of information.**
   Do you trust that source will provide accurate information?

3. **Ask questions about what you are reading.**
   Questions such as *who, what, where, when,* and *why* can help you break the information down into parts.

4. **Note important patterns, relationships, and trends.**
   Taking note of important information in a graphic organizer can help you better interpret information.

 COLLABORATE Based on what you have just read about Beringia, work with your class to complete the chart below.

Location	Surroundings	Way of Life
Beringia and North America during the last Ice Age	Thick sheets of ice cover vast areas of the land. Herds of animals roam the region.	People take long hunting trips and gather plants to eat when they are not able to kill animals.

Investigate!

Read pages 8–17 in your Research Companion. Use your investigative skills to find information in the maps, images, and text that will help you understand the early American Indian groups living in one geographical area mentioned in the lesson. Use the chart to organize information.

Location	Surroundings	Way of Life
Students should choose a single geographic area discussed in the text and provide in the chart for that area only.		

Inquiry Journal, pp. 10–11

(EL) ENGLISH LEARNERS SCAFFOLD

ELD.PI.5.11 Supporting own opinions and evaluating others' opinions in speaking and writing

Emerging	Expanding	Bridging
Develop Language Encourage students to point out words in the text that describe people, places, and events.	**Cite Evidence** Have students point out words in the text that describe people, places, and events. Then have them use two of those words in sentences of their own.	**Summarize** Have students use descriptive words from the text in sentences of their own as they summarize important details. Have them compare their summaries in small groups.

See the **Language Learner Teaching Guide** for more language support strategies.

Monitor and Differentiate

REACHING ALL LEARNERS

Approaching Level

Have students ask and answer more detailed questions to guide their reading, such as *What is the most important, interesting, or surprising information in this section? Why might I need to know this information to understand how early American Indian groups developed?*

Beyond Level

Have a small group of students discuss why it is important to analyze information when learning about historical events. They should discuss why knowing what happened, to whom it happened, and when it happened helps them have a better understanding of an event.

Research Companion
pp. 8–9

 STANDARDS

Describe how geography and climate influenced the way various nations lived and adjusted to the natural environment, including locations of villages, the distinct structures that they built, and how they obtained food, clothing, tools, and utensils. **HSS.5.1.1**

Students place key events and people of the historical era they are studying in a chronological sequence and within a spatial context; they interpret time lines **HAS.CR.1**

Draw on information from multiple print or digital sources, demonstrating the ability to locate an answer to a question quickly or to solve a problem efficiently. **CCSS.ELA.RI.5.7**

Go Digital!

Investigate the lesson content with online whole-class presentation tools.

- **Video:** The Iroquois Confederacy

- **iMap:** Settling the Americas

- **iMap:** The Maya, 300–900 CE

- **iMap:** The Aztec Empire

- **iMap:** The Inuit, c. 1500 CE

Background Information

End of Beringia The Bering Land Bridge, or Beringia, was likely last accessible between 30,000 and 12,000 years ago, during the last major Ice Age. When the Ice Age ended, the land bridge disappeared beneath a body of water that is now known as the Bering Strait. Beneath the strait, scientists have found fossilized remains of plants and animals to support this theory of early human migration.

| TIMELINE | Invite students to look at the timeline at the top of page 9.

Analyze What is the first event on the timeline that does not have a B.C. date? (Hohokam settle in American Southwest.) **HAS.CS.1**

Analyze the Source

Inspect Have students read pp. 8–9

Find Evidence Use the questions below to check comprehension. Remind students to support their answers with text evidence.

Identify What geographical feature allowed humans to migrate from Asia to North America? (the Bering Land Bridge, or Beringia) **DOK 1**

Vocabulary What was a hunter-gatherer? (a person who gathered plants and hunted animals for food) **DOK 2**

Analyze How does the image help you understand about mammoths? (They were enormous animals.) **DOK 3**

Apply Using what you know about Beringia from Inquiry Journal pages 8–9, explain why the land bridge was accessible during the Ice Age. (So much seawater had frozen into glaciers that the level of the oceans dropped enough to expose parts of the sea floor.) **DOK 3**

Consider Location Why might early humans have wanted to travel from Asia to North America? Do you think they knew that they were traveling to an entirely different continent? (Answers may include that they needed to hunt animals and gather plants for food. They followed herds of animals from one place to another. They didn't have maps, so they probably didn't know they were making such an important trip. They were simply trying to feed themselves.) **DOK 3**

Make Connections

Point of View If you were an early human traveling across Beringia, would you choose to keep going toward North America, or would you have turned back to more familiar territory? (Responses will vary, but some students may say they would prefer to go back because of the risks and challenges of going to an unknown land.) **DOK 3**

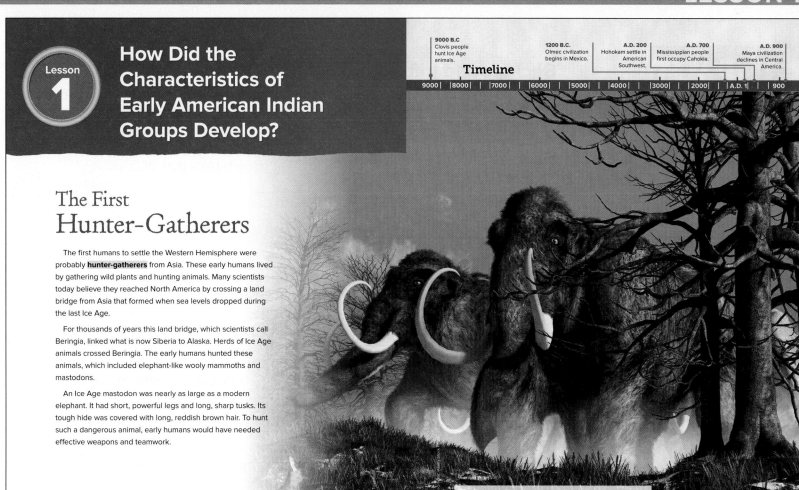

Lesson 1

How Did the Characteristics of Early American Indian Groups Develop?

Timeline

9000 B.C
Clovis people hunt Ice Age animals.

1200 B.C.
Olmec civilization begins in Mexico.

A.D. 200
Hohokam settle in American Southwest.

A.D. 700
Mississippian people first occupy Cahokia.

A.D. 900
Maya civilization declines in Central America.

| 9000 | 8000 | 7000 | 6000 | 5000 | 4000 | 3000 | 2000 | A.D. 1 | 900 |

The First Hunter-Gatherers

The first humans to settle the Western Hemisphere were probably **hunter-gatherers** from Asia. These early humans lived by gathering wild plants and hunting animals. Many scientists today believe they reached North America by crossing a land bridge from Asia that formed when sea levels dropped during the last Ice Age.

For thousands of years this land bridge, which scientists call Beringia, linked what is now Siberia to Alaska. Herds of Ice Age animals crossed Beringia. The early humans hunted these animals, which included elephant-like wooly mammoths and mastodons.

An Ice Age mastodon was nearly as large as a modern elephant. It had short, powerful legs and long, sharp tusks. Its tough hide was covered with long, reddish brown hair. To hunt such a dangerous animal, early humans would have needed effective weapons and teamwork.

Ice Age hunters followed woolly mammoths across land bridges.

HSS.5.1, HSS.5.1.1, HSS.5.1.2, HSS.5.1.3, HAS.CS.4

8 Lesson 1 How Did the Characteristics of Early American Indian Groups Develop?

Lesson 1 9

Research Companion, pp. 8–9

ENGLISH LEARNERS SCAFFOLD

ELD.PI.5.1 Exchanging information and ideas with others through oral collaborative discussions on a range of social and academic topics

Emerging

Organize Information As students look at the timeline, have them identify words, including proper nouns, with which they are unfamiliar. Have students keep a list of these words as a reference as they read the lesson. Have them write, draw on, or annotate the list as they learn about each term.

Expanding and Bridging

Collaborate Have students use information from the timeline to discuss what they think they will learn during Lesson 1. Have them write or share a few predictions that they can return to at the end of the lesson. Ask them to discuss what event or events they are most interested in learning about.

See the **Language Learner Teaching Guide** for more language support strategies.

Monitor and Differentiate

REACHING ALL LEARNERS

Special Needs

To help students understand prehistoric dating, assign each student a year, such as 10,000 B.C., 5,200 B.C., 1 B.C., 0, A.D. 1, and so on. Have students line up in chronological order.

Approaching Level

Encourage students to look at the timeline. Point out that 9,000 B.C. was more than 11,000 years ago. Ask them to consider where on the timeline an entry about humans crossing Beringia would fit. Remind students that B.C. years count down to the year 1 B.C, and A.D. years count up from the year 1 A.D.

RESEARCH COMPANION
The Olmec

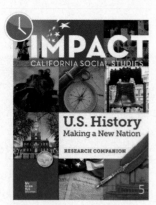

Research Companion
pp. 10–11

 STANDARDS

Describe how geography and climate influenced the way various nations lived and adjusted to the natural environment, including locations of villages, the distinct structures that they built, and how they obtained food, clothing, tools, and utensils. **HSS.5.1.1**

 Draw on information from multiple print or digital sources, demonstrating the ability to locate an answer to a question quickly or to solve a problem efficiently. **CCSS.ELA.RI.5.7**

___

Go Digital!

Investigate the lesson content with online whole-class presentation tools.

Background Information

The Olmec were the first major civilization in Mesoamerica, influencing later groups such as the Maya and Aztec. The Olmec got their name from the Aztec word for the rubber plants the Olmec grew. The extant artifacts from the Olmec culture include huge stone heads with full faces and helmets. They had a system of writing, which has been deciphered with the help of several stone tablets that still survive.

Analyze the Source

Inspect Have students read pp. 10–11.

Find Evidence Use the questions below to check comprehension. Remind students to support their answers with text evidence.

Identify What is a scientist who studies the tools and artifacts of people who lived long ago? (archaeologist) **DOK 1**

Explain How do archaeologists know that people first reached the tip of South American by about 10,500 B.C.? (They have found artifacts and other evidence.) **DOK 2**

Identify What group was the first to start a civilization in North America? (the Olmec) **DOK 1**

Explain According to the text, how does a civilization develop? (A group of people makes more food than it needs, which frees up some people to develop artwork, language, writing, and other pieces of cultural heritage.) **DOK 2**

Generate Based on the details you read about the Olmec civilization, how would you define the word *civilization*? (Answers may include that a civilization is a group of people who have a shared history, language, culture, and way of life.) **DOK 3**

Make Connections

Analyze Why does a civilization need a system of writing and a calendar? (Possible response: so they can keep records about important events and create a written history) **DOK 3**

Map Skills

Project a large version of the map on p. 9. Guide students to identify why the Olmec and Maya settled near water. (Students should identify that settling near the ocean would allow for fishing and easy trade.)

☑ Stop and Check

Think Encourage students to use text evidence and what they learned from the map in their response. Remind students that to be valid, their opinion must be supported by evidence. (Students should understand that early humans needed to find ice-free areas that would provide sources of food for them on their migrations.)

Find Details Explain to students that after they read and take notes, they should review and think about how the facts and details will help them answer the Essential Question.

Archaeologists are people who study the tools and other artifacts of people who lived long ago. Using such evidence, they reach conclusions about how ancient people lived. Archaeologists have different views about exactly when early humans first reached North America. They have evidence that these people had migrated all the way to the tip of southern South America by about 10,500 B.C. The people's migrations must have taken place a long time. So their arrival likely occurred centuries earlier.

Archaeologists also have different views about which route (or routes) these early American Indian groups might have used in their migrations throughout North and South America. Some scientists think they used an ice-free inland route. Others think early humans traveled by boat along the Pacific Coast.

Did You Know?

Beginning in the 1930s, archaeologists started to find evidence that early American Indians may have hunted large Ice Age animals. Mixed in with the bones of extinct animals, such as mammoths, scientists found slim, beautifully crafted stone spear points. The first site where these spear points were found was near present-day Clovis, New Mexico. So the early humans who made them became known as the Clovis people. Clovis sites date back to about 9000 B.C.

Archaeologists use special tools when uncovering artifacts.

✓ Stop and Check

Think Consider the routes that archaeologists believe early humans took when migrating into North America. What probably caused these people to select these routes?

Find Details As you read, add additional information to the graphic organizer on page 11 in your Inquiry Journal.

10 Lesson 1 How Did the Characteristics of Early American Indian Groups Develop?

The Olmec

About 11,500 years ago, the last Ice Age ended. The climate of the Western Hemisphere slowly grew warmer and drier. Many of the Ice Age animals that the early American Indians had hunted became extinct. These hunter-gatherer cultures had to adapt to survive. Instead of gathering wild plants, they began to grow their own food. By about 4000 B.C., farmers in Mexico and Central America were raising three crops: maize (also called corn), beans, and squash.

One of the most important effects of farming is that a community can raise more food than it needs to feed itself. This food surplus allows some people in the community to focus on the arts and religion that help to create a civilization.

The first civilization to develop in the Western Hemisphere was started by the Olmec people. It developed in the hot rain forests of southern Mexico about 1200 B.C. The Olmec built temples, carved huge stone statues, played ball games, and created a calendar and a writing system. They spread their culture across Mexico and Central America through an effective trade network.

The Olmec and the Maya

⊙ **Map Skills** Why might the two areas shown on the map inhabited by early peoples have included many coastal areas?

✓ Stop and Check

Think Why is a food surplus so important to the growth of a civilization?

Lesson 1 11

Research Companion, pp. 10–11

ⒺⓁ ENGLISH LEARNERS SCAFFOLD

ELD.PI.5.2 Interacting with others in written English in various communicative forms (print, communicative technology, and multimedia).

Emerging

Use Visuals Encourage students to use the map to understand where the Olmec civilization was. Ask them to write a sentence that explains which nation or cities are in the same area today. Have them compare their sentences with a partner's.

Expanding and Bridging

Collaborate Have students read the map to identify where the Olmec civilization was. Put students in pairs and have them write sentences that explain why the Olmec chose to build their civilization where they did. Encourage students to use language in their sentences that describes the area.

See the **Language Learner Teaching Guide** for more language support strategies.

Monitor and Differentiate

REACHING ALL LEARNERS

Approaching Level

Guide students to identify the causes that led to the rise of the Olmec civilization. Have a small group of students work together to create a graphic organizer that identifies causes such as farming, food surplus, writing system, and culture.

Beyond Level

Encourage students to do more research into the Olmec way of life, including its religion, writing system, city of San Lorenzo, art and artifacts, or sports. Have students present their findings to the whole class.

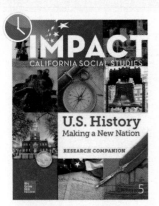

Research Companion
pp. 12–13

 STANDARDS

Describe how geography and climate influenced the way various nations lived and adjusted to the natural environment, including locations of villages, the distinct structures that they built, and how they obtained food, clothing, tools, and utensils. **HSS.5.1.1**

Draw on information from multiple print or digital sources, demonstrating the ability to locate an answer to a question quickly or to solve a problem efficiently. **CCSS.ELA.RI.5.7**

Engage effectively in a range of collaborative discussions (one-on-one, in groups, and teacher-led) with diverse partners on *grade 5 topics and texts*, building on others' ideas and expressing their own clearly. **CCSS.ELA.SL.5.1**

Go Digital!

Investigate the lesson content with online whole-class presentation tools.

Background Information

The Maya civilization was once the largest in North America. Unlike many other Mesoamerican civilizations, however, people who speak Mayan languages are still living in Mexico and Guatemala today. The Maya built pyramids and used a form of hieroglyphic writing. At their height, A.D. 250–900, the Maya built large cities. Their population may have reached 2 million before war and overpopulation caused the empire to decline.

Analyze the Source

Inspect Have students read pages 12–13.

Find Evidence Use the questions below to check comprehension. Remind students to support their answers with text evidence.

> **Recall** Where did the Olmec and Maya civilizations develop? (southern Mexico) **DOK 1**
>
> **Interpret** What does it mean that the Maya had a "Classic Period"? What happened during this time? (Answers may include that the Maya culture reached its peak at that time, which is what "Classic Period" means. During the Classic Period, they built cities, temples, and developed their culture.) **DOK 2**
>
> **Explain** What was the government of the Maya Empire? (The cities in the empire were ruled by kings who commanded the army and started building projects.) **DOK 2**
>
> **Describe** What happened to the Maya? Use text evidence in your response. (Their civilization declined, possibly because of overpopulation. However, millions of Maya still live in Mexico, Belize, and Guatemala today.) **DOK 3**

Make Connections

> **Draw Conclusions** How did the Maya Communicate? How can we understand their writing today? (They had a writing system made up of heiroglyphs. They were translated in the mid-1990s.) **DOK 3**

✓ **Stop and Check**

Evaluate Encourage students to consider why cultural characteristics spread from one early American culture to another and how shifts in culture spread within our culture today. Guide them to make inferences based on the text and what they know about our world. (Students should express the idea that early American Indian groups such as the Olmec and Maya spread the characteristics of their culture to their neighbors though trade.)

Called the "Pyramid of the Magician," this thousand-year-old structure rises more than 90 feet above the Maya city of Uxmal in Mexico.

The Maya

The Maya developed their culture in the same part of Mexico as the Olmec. They traded with their Olmec neighbors and were influenced by their culture. Between about A.D. 250 and 900, Maya culture reached its peak. Archaeologists call this the "Classic Period" of Maya civilization.

During the Classic Period, the Maya world grew to more than 40 cities, each with a population between 5,000 and 50,000. In cities such as Uxmal, Tikal, and Copan, the Maya built great palaces for their rulers and huge pyramid temples to honor their gods. These structures were covered with elaborate carvings and inscriptions in their system of picture writing. Scholars often refer to such inscriptions as **hieroglyphs**. The meaning of these inscriptions was unknown for centuries after Maya civilization collapsed. Thorough translations appeared in the mid-1900s.

Did You Know?

The Maya were fascinated with time. They created a 365-day calendar. The year was divided into 18 months of 20 days each. The Maya believed that the remaining five days were very unlucky. To show when historical events took place, they used a system of dating called the "Long Count." Translated to today's calendar, the Maya's Long Count suggests the world was created about 3113 B.C.

Mayan influence is seen in the design of this Aztec stone calendar.

Maya cities were ruled by kings who claimed that Maya gods had chosen them. These rulers directed huge building projects and commanded the army. To form alliances and strengthen trade, Maya rulers often married members of the royal families of other cities.

Maya civilization declined rapidly after A.D. 900. Archaeologists have looked for explanations in the environment. They think that as time passed, the population of the Maya cities outgrew their food supply. Rulers fought over farmland. People began to abandon the Maya cities in search of food. Drought may also have led to their decline. However, the Maya did not disappear. Today, more than six million descendants of the ancient Maya still live in Mexico, Belize, and Guatemala.

✓ Stop and Check

COLLABORATE

Talk How did cultural characteristics spread from one early American Indian group to another?

Image Source

Frank van Bergh/Getty Images

Research Companion, pp. 12–13

(EL) ENGLISH LEARNERS SCAFFOLD

ELD.PII.5.1 Understanding text structure

Emerging

Identify Text Structure Work with students to ensure they understand the chronological text structure used in this section. Begin by reviewing the meaning of the word *chronological*. Then have them identify and highlight signal words that show time order, such as "Between about A.D. 250 and 900," "During the Classic Period," and "Maya civilization declined rapidly after A.D. 900."

Expanding and Bridging

Use Text Structure Encourage students to make a list of the transitions and signal words that indicate the text structure used in this section. Have students discuss why the chronological text structure is useful to helping them understand what happened during the Maya Empire.

See the **Language Learner Teaching Guide** for more language support strategies.

Monitor and Differentiate

REACHING ALL LEARNERS

Approaching Level

Work with students to understand the text structure used in this section. Help them to understand the signal words and transitions that indicate a chronological text structure.

On Level

Work with students to create a timeline of the rise and fall of the Maya. Have students make inferences about how major events are connected.

Beyond Level

Encourage students to conduct further research into any aspect of the Maya Empire that interests them. Have them share their findings with the whole class.

2 INVESTIGATE / Early Desert Peoples

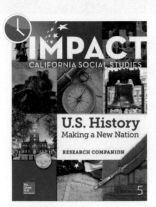

Research Companion
pp. 14–15

Describe how geography and climate influenced the way various nations lived and adjusted to the natural environment, including locations of villages, the distinct structures that they built, and how they obtained food, clothing, tools, and utensils. **HSS.5.1.1**

CCSS Draw on information from multiple print or digital sources, demonstrating the ability to locate an answer to a question quickly or to solve a problem efficiently. **CCSS.ELA.RI.5.7**

Engage effectively in a range of collaborative discussions (one-on-one, in groups, and teacher-led) with diverse partners on *grade 5 topics and texts*, building on others' ideas and expressing their own clearly. **CCSS.ELA.SL.5.1**

Go *Digital!*

Investigate the lesson content with online whole-class presentation tools.

Background Information

The **Ancestral Pueblo** people were once called the Anasazi. This name, however, is a Navajo word, which means "ancestor of the enemy," because the Ancestral Pueblo people were enemies of the Navajo. The Ancestral Pueblo are made up of several tribes including the Hopi, the Laguna, and the Zuni.

Analyze the Source

Inspect Have students read pages 14–15.

Find Evidence Use the questions below to check comprehension. Remind students to support their answers with text evidence.

Describe In what ways were the settlements of the Hohokam and the Olmec and Maya different? (The Olmec and Maya lived in the tropical rain forest of southern Mexico, while the Hohokam settled in the desert of the American southwest. The Hohokam would have had a much more difficult time farming than the Olmec and the Maya.) **DOK 2**

Interpret What might have led the Hohokam to settle in the area between the Salt River and the Gila River? (Answers may include that they knew they would need to water their crops somehow, and so they would need to live near rivers to have access to water.) **DOK 3**

Explain How did the Hohokam water their crops? (They built irrigation ditches to bring water to their fields.) **DOK 2**

Explain How did the Ancestral Pueblo people water their crops? (They collected rainwater and irrigated their fields through a system of shallow drains.) **DOK 2**

Make Connections

Cite Evidence What were the advantages of the cliff dwellings of the Ancestral Pueblo people? (Answers may include that cliff dwellings were easy to defend against enemies. The building material, adobe, made the buildings warm at night and cool during the day.) **DOK 3**

Map Skills

Guide students to identify rivers in Hohokam territory. (Gila River, Salt River)

COLLABORATE

✓ Stop and Check

Defend In your partner discussion, state an opinion about which features of the societies of the early desert people modern society should imitate. Use evidence from the text to defend your opinion. (Whichever opinion students express, they should support it with evidence from the text.)

Early Desert Peoples

The early American Indian groups of the Southwest developed in an environment very different from the rain forests of Mexico and Central America. About A.D. 200, a group known as the Hohokam moved from a part of the Sonoran Desert in northern Mexico to present-day Arizona, between the Salt River and Gila River. At that time, the area received only about three inches of rain a year. Yet the settlers discovered ways to turn the desert into fields of corn, beans, squash, and cotton.

The Hohokam built a complex irrigation system to bring water to their fields. With simple tools such as sharpened sticks and stone blades, they dug shallow canals that stretched for hundreds of miles. Hohokam farmers used small gates to direct water from these canals into their fields. The Hohokam irrigation canals were built so well that some of them are still used today.

Hohokam farmers lived in small villages. They built their houses by digging a shallow pit and covering it with a wooden frame, roofed with plant material called thatch. Building underground helped to keep Hohokam houses cool during the day and warm at night. The Hohokam wove cotton into cloth for clothing. They made baskets and pottery for storage. Hohokam jewelry was crafted from turquoise mined in the desert and from shells. Shell jewelry was especially prized. Hohokam traders traveled long distances to trade cotton cloth and pottery for shells gathered by people on the Gulf of California and the Pacific Coast.

The Ancestral Pueblo people built the Cliff Palace at Mesa Verde, in what is now Colorado.

The Ancestral Pueblo were another of the American Indian groups to settle in the deserts of the Southwest. They are also known as the Anasazi. In about A.D. 700, the Ancestral Pueblo people settled in the "Four Corners" area where Utah, Colorado, Arizona, and New Mexico meet today. Like the Hohokam, the Ancestral Pueblo planted squash, corn, and beans. The high desert plateaus where they lived were not suited to the use of canals for irrigation, however. Instead, the Ancestral Pueblo developed a method called dry farming. They channeled rainwater and snowmelt into catch basins. Then this water was slowly released into narrow, pebbled-lined drains to the crops.

The Ancestral Pueblo are known as the first "cliff dwellers." They lived in huge apartment-like dwellings built along the steep sides of the cliffs. Living in cliff dwellings, such as Mesa Verde, made it easier for the Ancestral Pueblo to defend themselves against enemies. These dwellings were made of finely carved stone and logs that were plastered with adobe. Adobe is a mixture of mud and straw that dries into a hard clay. An adobe house stays cool during the heat of the day and warm during cold desert nights.

The Hohokam and Ancestral Pueblo

Map Skills What sources of water might the Hohokam have used?

✓ Stop and Check

COLLABORATE

Connect to Now Are there any features of the societies of the early desert peoples that modern American society should imitate? Why or why not? Discuss your opinion with a partner.

14   Lesson 1   How Did the Characteristics of Early American Indian Groups Develop?   Lesson 1   15

Research Companion, pp. 14–15

 ENGLISH LEARNERS SCAFFOLD

ELD.PI.5.8 Analyzing how writers and speakers use vocabulary and other language resources for specific purposes (to explain, persuade, entertain, etc.) depending on modality, text type, purpose, audience, topic, and content area

Emerging

Draw Unfamiliar Words Encourage students to identify unfamiliar words that the author uses to describe the culture of the Hohokam and Ancestral Pueblo peoples. Have students make drawings to illustrate their understanding.

Expanding and Bridging

Use Unfamiliar Words Make sure students understand the language used to describe the cultures of the early desert peoples. Have students retell an important detail about the Hohokam or the Ancestral Pueblo way of life.

See the **Language Learner Teaching Guide** for more language support strategies.

Monitor and Differentiate

REACHING ALL LEARNERS

Special Needs

Work with students to understand the importance of irrigation to the early desert peoples. Project the map. Ask students to point to the settlements of the Hohokam and the Ancestral Pueblo people on a map. Discuss as a group the features of a desert climate.

Beyond Level

Have students conduct further research into the cliff dwellings of the Ancestral Pueblo people. Encourage them to visit the website of Mesa Verde National Park to learn more about the area. Have students put their findings into a brochure or travel guide and share it with the rest of the class.

2 INVESTIGATE

RESEARCH COMPANION

The Mound Builders

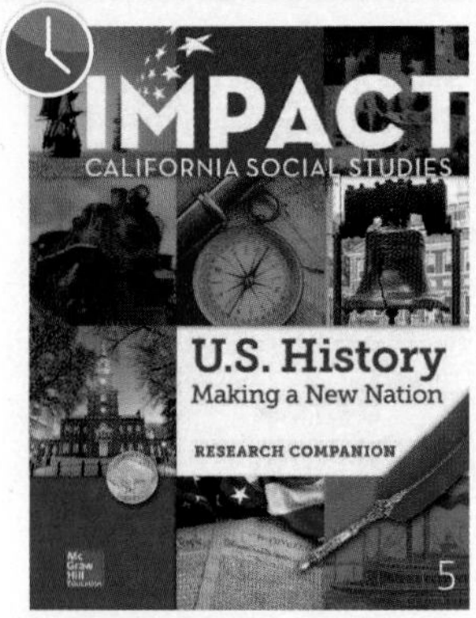

Research Companion
pp. 16–17

STANDARDS

Describe how geography and climate influenced the way various nations lived and adjusted to the natural environment, including locations of villages, the distinct structures that they built, and how they obtained food, clothing, tools, and utensils. **HSS.5.1.1**

Draw on information from multiple print or digital sources, demonstrating the ability to locate an answer to a question quickly or to solve a problem efficiently. **CCSS.ELA.RI.5.7**

Go Digital!

Investigate the lesson content with online whole-class presentation tools.

Background Information

Once known as the "Mound Builders," the **Adena** and **Hopewell** peoples were actually two among many cultures to build mounds. The mounds served several purposes, including burials, bases of buildings, and fortifications. Within the mounds, archaeologists have found pottery, tools, and metalwork. Goods that originated from the East Coast, the Rocky Mountains, and the Gulf of Mexico have also been found on Hopewell sites, indicating that the civilization had well developed systems of trade.

Analyze the Text

Inspect Have students read pages 16–17.

Find Evidence Use the questions below to check comprehension. Remind students to support their answers with text evidence.

Analyze What is similar about the series of events that led to the rise of the Olmec, the Hopewell, and the Mississippian cultures? (Answers may include that the cultures arose once there was a food surplus.) **DOK 3**

Describe What did an Adena village look like? (groups of round log houses surrounded by farms) **DOK 1**

Compare How were Hopewell and Adena cultures similar? (They occupied the same region in the southern Ohio River Valley; they created objects made of copper, obsidian, and mica; and they had a strong trade network.) **DOK 2**

Make Inferences How do archaeologists know that the Adena and Hopewell benefited from trading networks? (They have found objects that could only have come from faraway places.) **DOK 2**

Make Connections

Cite Evidence To which early American Indian settlement would you have wanted to belong? Use evidence from the text to support your opinion. (Answers may include that the Ancestral Pueblo cliff dwellings seemed comfortable and easy to defend from enemies. Even though they were in the desert, the people were able to grow plenty of food and make beautiful objects.) **DOK 3**

Stop and Check

COLLABORATE

Think What was successful about each culture? What evidence found by archaeologists supports your critique? Discuss your opinion with a partner. (Students should able to identify such characteristics as farming, trade, crafts, and the construction of mounds as common to these three cultures.)

The Mound Builders

As Europeans began to settle the Ohio and Mississippi river valleys in the 1700s, they encountered a variety of earthen mounds. Some were cone-shaped hills. Others were earthen walls. A few even had the shapes of animals. The most amazing of these is the Great Serpent Mound in southern Ohio, which is more than 1,300 feet long. The people who built these mysterious structures and then left were once referred to simply as "Mound Builders." Archaeologists have identified several different Mound Builder cultures.

The earliest of these cultures is known as the Adena, after a site in Ohio where archaeologists first studied their mounds. The Adena culture lasted from about 500 B.C. to A.D. 100. These people lived in villages of round houses built from logs and roofed with bark. Originally hunter-gatherers, the Adena people later began to farm. Their crops included gourds and sunflowers.

The Adena used stone to craft both simple tools and complex objects such as smoking pipes used in rituals. They fashioned ornaments from copper, mica, and shells—materials that they obtained through trade with distant peoples. What is known about Adena culture comes from such objects, which the Adena people placed in the burial mounds they built for their dead.

Between about 200 B.C. and A.D. 500, another mound-building culture called the Hopewell occupied the same region as the Adena culture. The Hopewell people were also named for a site in southern Ohio where archaeologists first studied their culture. The Hopewell people shared many features of the Adena culture. Hopewell artists created objects from copper, mica, and obsidian, a volcanic glass. Like the Adena people, the Hopewell obtained these materials through a far-flung trade network.

The Adena people built the Great Serpent Mound.

Tony Linck/SuperStock

Then and Now

Archaeologists have been studying the Cahokia mounds since the late 1800s, but only a small part of the site has been excavated. Seventy of the original 120 mounds are preserved today in Illinois's Cahokia Mounds State Historic Park (established in 1979). Cahokia was named a World Heritage Site in 1982, meaning it deserves special protection.

An artist's depiction of Cahokia about A.D. 1100

One of the last major American Indian groups to develop before the arrival of Europeans was the Mississippian culture. Mississippian culture developed in the Mississippi River valley between A.D. 700 and 900.

Large-scale farming of corn, beans, squash, and other crops produced food surpluses. This encouraged the growth of large populations in Mississippian towns and cities. Priest-kings ruled Mississippian society. Each town or city controlled a group of outlying villages. High fences of sharpened logs defended these villages from attack. Warfare seems to have been frequent.

The greatest Mississippian city is the site known today as Cahokia. Built in what is now southern Illinois, Cahokia at its peak was home to more than 20,000 people. A plaza for holding ceremonies was the center of a Mississippian city. Around this plaza were groups of mounds on top of which might have been a temple or a chief's dwelling. Monk's Mound at Cahokia was 100 feet high and covered 14 acres. It was the largest pre-Columbian earthen structure in the Western Hemisphere.

✓ Stop and Check

COLLABORATE

Talk Which characteristics did the Adena, Hopewell, and Mississippian cultures share?

16 Lesson 1 How Did the Characteristics of Early American Indian Groups Develop?

Lesson 1 17

Research Companion, pp. 16–17

(EL) ENGLISH LEARNERS SCAFFOLD

ELD.PI.5.11 Supporting own opinions and evaluating others' opinions in speaking and writing

Emerging	Expanding	Bridging
State an Opinion Encourage students to make a claim about which early American Indian culture they would want to be a part of. Guide them to refer to the text as they make their claim.	**Support an Opinion** Guide students to paraphrase information from the text as they make a claim. Remind students that when they paraphrase, they restate the text in their own words.	**Defend an Opinion** Have students quote accurately from the text as they give their opinion about which early American Indian culture they would like to be a part of.

See the **Language Learner Teaching Guide** for more language support strategies.

Monitor and Differentiate

REACHING ALL LEARNERS

Approaching Level

Work with students to understand the importance of trade to the mound builder cultures of the Ohio and Mississippi river valleys. Show images of Adena or Hopewell artifacts that came from the Atlantic or Gulf Coast, and lead a discussion about how such artifacts traveled thousands of miles to the central part of the United States.

Beyond Level

Have students conduct additional research into the cultures of the Hopewell, Adena, or Mississippian cultures. Have them share their findings with the whole class.

3 REPORT

Report Your Findings

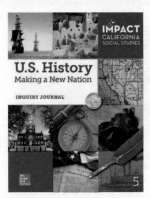

Inquiry Journal
pp. 12–13

 STANDARDS

Describe how geography and climate influenced the way various nations lived and adjusted to the natural environment, including locations of villages, the distinct structures that they built, and how they obtained food, clothing, tools, and utensils. **HSS.5.1.1**

Draw on information from multiple print or digital sources, demonstrating the ability to locate an answer to a question quickly or to solve a problem efficiently. **CCSS.ELA.RI.5.7**

Write informative/explanatory texts to examine a topic and convey ideas and information clearly. **CCSS.ELA.W.5.2**

Engage effectively in a range of collaborative discussions (one-on-one, in groups, and teacher-led) with diverse partners on *grade 5 topics and texts*, building on others' ideas and expressing their own clearly. **CCSS.ELA.SL.5.1**

Go Digital!

- Students can go online to report their findings. Assess their responses online.

- Students can access the online graphic organizer to capture ideas from their investigation.

Think About It

Students will review their research and consider how the characteristics of early American Indian groups developed. Remind students to review the information about the group they chose that they have included in their graphic organizer. Direct students back to pages 8–17 of their Research Companion if they need more information.

Write About It

Take a Stand Read the Write About It prompt aloud to students. Remind students that they should have chosen one group and included details in their graphic organizer about how its location influenced the development of its culture. If necessary, remind students that they must use text evidence to support their explanation.

Remind students to include the following elements as they craft their response from their notes:

- Introduce the American Indian group they have chosen to write about.

- Organize key details about its location.

- Draw a strong conclusion about how its location influenced the development of its culture.

- Use chapter vocabulary as appropriate.

- Include page references when citing text evidence.

Use the rubric on p. T32 to evaluate students' work.

Talk About It

Compare Your Groups Help students pair up with a classmate who chose a different American Indian group. Explain that they should take turns discussing the details about where the group lived and how its location helped to shape its culture. Each student should listen respectfully while the partner talks about his or her findings.

Connect to the Essential Question

Read the prompt aloud to students. If necessary, ask them the following guiding questions: Who were the groups you learned about in this lesson? Where did each group live? What was the culture of each group like? What kinds of objects did each group create? How did they communicate with each other and with other groups? What led them to create a civilization? What led to their eventual decline? Remind students to use the space provided in their journal to jot down notes. (Responses will vary, but students should indicate facts about groups they learned about in this lesson, using text evidence to support their response.)

Report Your Findings

Think About It

Based on your research, how do you think the location and surroundings of the American Indian group you picked affected the way the people lived?

Write About It

Take a Stand

Write and Cite Evidence Write a brief, three-paragraph informational essay describing how the location and surroundings of the American Indian group you chose influenced the way the people lived.

Students should be able to use evidence from the text to identify the geographic area in which an American Indian group lived and how that area affected the development of the specific characteristics of the group.

Talk About It

Compare Your Groups

Talk to a classmate who chose a different American Indian group. What was similar about the ways your two groups lived? What was different?

Connect to the EQ

Geography

Pull It Together

Think about the people you have learned about in this lesson. How would you describe the way American Indians lived before the arrival of the Europeans?

Students should be able to understand how the geography of the Western Hemisphere affected the development of the various early American Indian groups that first settled there.

EQ Inquiry Project Notes

12 Lesson 1 How Did the Characteristics of Early American Indian Groups Develop?

Lesson 1 13

Inquiry Journal, pp. 12–13

EL ENGLISH LEARNERS SCAFFOLD

ELD.PI.5.10 Writing literary and informational texts to present, describe, and explain ideas and information, using appropriate technology

Emerging	Expanding	Bridging
Write Complete Sentences Encourage students to use descriptive words and phrases as they explain how location influenced the culture of the American Indian group of their choice. Work with students to help them create complete sentences, providing sentence frames as needed: *The _____ group lived near present-day _____.* *They built their way of life by _____.*	**Organize Ideas** Work with students to organize their writing. Have students consider using words that show time order or cause and effect. Provide signal words as needed, such as *First, second, third; because, as a result, then.*	**Use Details** Encourage students to use descriptive details. Remind them to consider language that is appropriate for their audience and purpose.

See the **Language Learner Teaching Guide** for more language support strategies.

Monitor and Differentiate

REACHING ALL LEARNERS

Approaching Level

Work with students to organize their writing based on the text structure that works best for the information they present. Review chronological order and cause-and-effect structure. If needed, provide a list of signal words for students to use.

Beyond Level

Have students use this writing project as a starting point for a larger project in which they compare and contrast more early American Indian groups. They may choose groups discussed in this lesson, or they may conduct their own research into other groups.

Know what your students know!

Lesson Task
Report Your Findings

Use this rubric to evaluate students' response.

Take a Stand Students write a brief, three-paragraph informational essay describing how the location and surroundings of the American Indian group they chose influenced the way the people lived.

Compare Your Groups Students work with a partner who chose a different group. They compare and contrast how the characteristics of the two groups were influenced by location.

Performance Task Evaluation Rubric

	4	3	2	1
Historical Understanding	Strong understanding of how the characteristics of the group were influenced by geography	Adequate understanding of how the characteristics of the group were influenced by geography	Uneven understanding of how the characteristics of the group were influenced by geography	No understanding of how the characteristics of the group were influenced by geography
Explanation	Clearly explains main idea and key details	Adequately explains main idea and key details	Somewhat clear or unclear explanation of main idea and key details	No explanation or student does not show understanding of the task
Support with Evidence	Reasons contain thorough and convincing evidence	Reasons contain adequate evidence	Reasons contain uneven or only somewhat convincing evidence	Reasons are missing or contain no supporting evidence
Defend Your Claim	Speaks clearly and at an understandable pace Speaks in complete sentences throughout the presentation	Speaks clearly during most of the presentation Speaks in complete sentences through most of the presentation	At times speaker is unclear Mixes complete and incomplete sentences	Speaks unclearly throughout the presentation Does not use complete sentences

Lesson Assessment

Go Digital!

- Have students complete the Chapter 1 Lesson 1 Assessment online to monitor their understanding of the lesson content.

ONLINE ASSESSMENT

California Smarter Balanced Assessment Connections!

Standards Covered	Lesson Task	Lesson Assessment	Alignment with California Smarter Balanced Assessment
History Social Science Content 5.1.1	✓	✓	Claim 1 Targets 8, 9, 10
History Social Science Analysis Skills Chronological and Spatial Thinking 5.4; 5.5	✓	✓	Claim 1 Targets 11, 12
Writing W.5.2	✓	✓	Claim 2 Targets 3, 4, 5
Research and Inquiry W.5.7; W.5.9	✓	✓	Claim 4 Targets 2, 3, 4
Reading RI.5.7	✓	✓	Claim 1 Target 8
Speaking and Listening SL.5.1	✓		Claim 3 Target 3

LESSON QUESTION

How Did the People of the Desert Southwest Meet Their Needs?

Background Information

Explain to students that in this lesson they will learn about some of the different cultures living in the deserts of the American Southwest. They will compare and contrast the different lifestyles of these groups.

Community Connections

To enrich what students have learned about the peoples of the Southwest, plan a field trip to local American Indian history museum.

LESSON STANDARDS

✓ Describe how geography and climate influenced the way various nations lived and adjusted to the natural environment, including locations of villages, the distinct structures that they built, and how they obtained food, clothing, tools, and utensils. **HSS.5.1.1**

✓ Describe their varied customs and folklore traditions. **HSS.5.1.2**

✓ Students use map and globe skills to determine the absolute locations of places and interpret information available through a map's or globe's legend, scale, and symbolic representations. **HAS.CS.4**

✓ Students identify the human and physical characteristics of the places they are studying and explain how those features form the unique character of those places. **HAS.HI.2**

Connect to the Essential Question

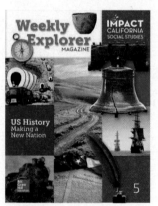

Chapter 1, pp. 2–13

The **Weekly Explorer Magazine** supports students' exploration of the Essential Question and provides additional resources for the EQ Inquiry Project.

Inquiry Project

What was life like in America before Columbus?

Remind students to use the information they learn in this lesson and other resources to complete their EQ Inquiry Project!

Dinah Zike's

In this lesson you will use Foldables.

When Minutes Count!

Suggested Lesson Pacing

1 ENGAGE
One Day

- Lesson Opener
- Analyze the Source
- Inquiry Tools

Go Digital
- **Video:** Native Americans of the Southwest
- **iMap:** Native Americans of the Southwest, 1700s

2 INVESTIGATE
Two to Three Days

🕐 **Short on Time?** Look for the clock to teach core content in less time.

- The Pueblo People
- The Navajo
- The Apache

3 REPORT
One Day

- Think About It
- Write from Another's Perspective
- Discuss

Make Connections!

ⒸⓈⓈ CONNECT TO ELA

Reading

Explain the relationships or interactions between two or more individuals, events, ideas, or concepts in a historical, scientific, or technical text based on specific information in the text. **RI.5.3**

Compare and contrast the overall structure (e.g., chronology, comparison, cause/effect, problem/solution) of events, ideas, concepts, or information in two or more texts. **RI.5.5**

Research

Recall relevant information from experiences or gather relevant information from print and digital sources; summarize or paraphrase information in notes and finished work, and provide a list of sources. **W.5.8**

Writing

Write narratives to develop real or imagined experiences or events using effective technique, descriptive details and clear event sequences. **W.5.3**

Draw evidence from literary or informational texts to support analysis, reflection, and research. **W.5.9**

Speaking and Listening

Engage effectively in a range of collaborative discussions (one-on-one, in groups, and teacher-led) with diverse partners on *grade 5 topics and texts*, building on others' ideas and expressing their own clearly. **SL.5.1**

Classroom Resources

🔍 Search for additional resources using the following key words.

Apache

Hopi

mesas

Navajo

oral history

Pueblo

Zuni

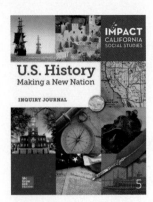

Inquiry Journal,
pp. 14–15

 STANDARDS

Describe how geography and climate influenced the way various nations lived and adjusted to the natural environment, including locations of villages, the distinct structures that they built, and how they obtained food, clothing, tools, and utensils.
HSS.5.1.1

Describe their varied customs and folklore traditions.
HSS.5.1.2

Go Digital!

Explore the lesson content with online whole-class presentation tools.

- **Video:** Native Americans of the Southwest

- **iMap:** Native Americans of the Southwest, 1700s

How Did the People of the Desert Southwest Meet Their Needs?

Bellringer

Prompt students to retrieve information from the previous lesson. Say: *Remember the early American Indians from the previous lesson.* Ask: *Which of these peoples lived in the southwestern deserts? What did they do that allowed them to live in the desert?* (The Hohokam and Ancestral Pueblo people lived in the deserts of the Southwest. They farmed using canals and dry farming. They built homes underground or in cliff faces.)

Lesson Outcomes

What Am I Learning? Have students read the Lesson Question and Lesson Outcomes on p. 14.

Why Am I Learning It? Ensure students understand how to compare and contrast. Demonstrate comparing by asking students to give examples of similarities between cats and dogs. Then ask them to give differences to demonstrate contrasting.

How Will I Know That I Learned It? Ask students the following questions.

- What will you identify? (lifestyles of different groups of Southwestern American Indians)

- What is the purpose of your task? (to understand how they were able to live in the desert southwest)

- How will you support your comparison and contrast? (with text evidence)

Talk About It

Explain *petroglyphs* to the students. The word comes from the Greek words for "rock" and "carved." Petroglyphs are picture messages carved into stone. Allow students to guess at the meaning of the petroglyphs. Explain that their meaning is unknown, but some researchers believe it depicts the Crab Supernova, an exploding star that was visible in the night sky for two years beginning in A.D. 1054. Have students discuss in small groups whether or not they believe the petroglyphs depict an astronomical event. Have them come up with and consider alternative explanations.

- *The supernova explanation is supported by* _____.

- *The* _____ *doesn't fit that explanation.*

Collaborative Conversations

Support Claims As students take part in the discussion, encourage them to

- Think of reasons and evidence to support their claim.
- Check their reasons for logical fallacies. Are they making unsupported assumptions?

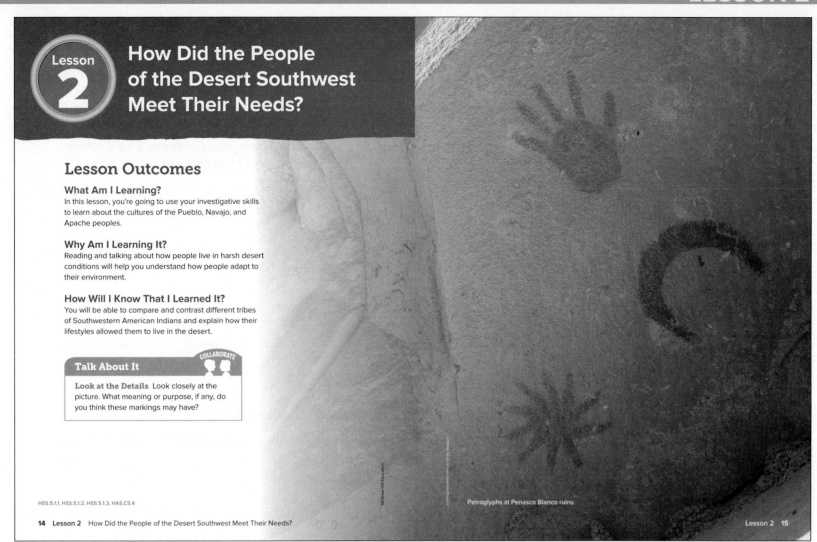

Lesson 2

How Did the People of the Desert Southwest Meet Their Needs?

Lesson Outcomes

What Am I Learning?
In this lesson, you're going to use your investigative skills to learn about the cultures of the Pueblo, Navajo, and Apache peoples.

Why Am I Learning It?
Reading and talking about how people live in harsh desert conditions will help you understand how people adapt to their environment.

How Will I Know That I Learned It?
You will be able to compare and contrast different tribes of Southwestern American Indians and explain how their lifestyles allowed them to live in the desert.

Talk About It
COLLABORATE

Look at the Details Look closely at the picture. What meaning or purpose, if any, do you think these markings may have?

HSS.5.1.1, HSS.5.1.2, HSS.5.1.3, HAS.CS.4

Petroglyphs at Penasco Blanco ruins

14 Lesson 2 How Did the People of the Desert Southwest Meet Their Needs?

Lesson 2 **15**

Inquiry Journal, pp. 14–15

ENGLISH LEARNERS SCAFFOLD

ELD.PI.5.3 Offering and supporting opinions and negotiating with others in communicative exchanges

Emerging	Expanding	Bridging
Use Persuasion Words Work with students to state their opinions with phrases like "I think . . ." or "I agree/disagree because . . ."	**Make Claims** Help students state specifically what they agree and disagree with. "I agree with X, but . . ." Also encourage them to create counterarguments.	**Provide Support** Help students use more complex phrases to state their opinions and elaborate on ideas. "Although this could be X, I think it is actually Y because . . ."

See the **Language Learner Teaching Guide** for more language support strategies.

Monitor and Differentiate

REACHING ALL LEARNERS

Approaching Level

Work with students to understand symbolism. Provide sentence frames such as "This petroglyph represents . . ."

On Level

Have students support their claims for what the petroglyphs represent.

Beyond Level

Encourage students to research other examples of petroglyphs. What kinds of similarities can be found between these and the artwork of other cultures?

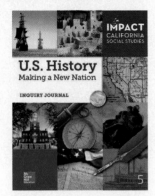

Inquiry Journal,
pp. 16–17

 STANDARDS

Describe how geography and climate influenced the way various nations lived and adjusted to the natural environment, including locations of villages, the distinct structures that they built, and how they obtained food, clothing, tools, and utensils. **HSS.5.1.1**

Interpret figurative language, including similes and metaphors, in context. **CCSS.ELA.L.5.5a**

Go Digital!

Model how to inspect and find evidence with online whole-class presentation tools.

Background Information

Traditional Medicine Most people associate medicine with pills and shots, but music and art are among the most ancient treatments. Today, music therapy and art therapy continue to be used to reduce stress and anxiety. Their effectiveness in calming troubled psyches may be the reason ceremonial songs and dances play such an important role in Navajo culture, both in the past and the present.

1 Inspect

Read Have students skim the text and read the lyrics.

- Whom were these ceremonies for? (people who were ill or returning from battle)
- Why were these ceremonies performed? (to help people recover from their problems)
- What words would you use to describe the song? (welcoming, peaceful)

2 Find Evidence

Look Again Have students reread the song lyrics and text.

Analyze the Primary Source Reread the song lyrics and discuss them as a class.

- What words in "Jó Ashilá" hint at its meaning? (traveling together, happy, beauty, beautiful)
- What is the literal meaning of the song? (Two people have arrived and it is a good thing.)
- What could be another meaning? (The recipient of the song is welcome.)

3 Make Connections

Talk Why do the Navajo perform these rituals? (to help relax those who have suffered)

Collaborative Conversations

Talk Tell students to study the image that accompanies the song lyrics. Ask them how the image supports the main ideas of the texts. Play a recording of "Jó Ashilá" for the class. How does the music support the main ideas?

Connect to Now Have students consider the actions that are involved in the ritual, such as singing, dancing, and making art. How do the students feel when they do these things?

Analyze the Source

Navajo Ceremonies

1 Inspect

Read Study the translation of the Navajo song "Jó Ashílá." Then read the description of Navajo Ceremonies.

- **Discuss** with a partner why songs and ceremonies like "Jó Ashílá" and Enemyway are important to people.
- **Listen** to a recording of "Jó Ashílá." How would you describe the sound?

My Notes

_____
_____
_____
_____
_____
_____
_____
_____
_____
_____
_____
_____
_____
_____

"Jó Ashílá" is part of the Enemyway ceremony, a three-day-long ceremony meant to bring balance to the lives of the Navajo people. It can be performed for people who are ill or for individuals who have returned from war.

Singing and dancing are important parts of this and other ceremonies. There are more than sixty major ceremonies, including the Enemyway, the Blessingway, and the Navajo Night Chant. Some ceremonies can last more than a week and may contain more than five hundred songs. Dancers in masks help by representing various spirits in the ceremony. Sandpaintings, designs using brightly colored sands, are made specifically for each ceremony. The ceremonies are long and complex. So the singers who are qualified to lead them are highly respected.

Jó Ashílá

Hee yée' yaa' a', hee yée' yaa' a', Jó a-shí-lá,

jó a-shí-lá, jó a- shí-lá, hee yée' yaa' a',

T'óó-gá ni-zhó-ní-go baa hó-zhó lá, hee ya hèe hee yá,

Jó a-shí-lá, jó a-shí-lá, jó a-shí-lá,

Hee yée' yaa' ya', T'óó-gá ni-zhó-ní-go

łįį' gá N-dáá gi béézh ní'-áázh lá, hee ya hèe hee ya',

T'óó-gá ni-zhó-ní-go N-dáá gi łįį' gá béézh ní'-áázh lá,

hee ya hèe hee ya', Jó a-shí-lá, jó a-shí-lá,

jó a-shí-lá, hee yée' ya wèi yaa' ya'.

English Translation:

Traveling together, Happy about beauty. It is beautiful that they both came on a horse at the Enemyway.

From We'll be in Your Mountains, We'll be in Your Songs: A Navajo Woman Sings by Brian McCullough. Edited and Music Help. Copyright © 2001 University of New Mexico Press, 2001.

Special items used in an Enemyway ceremony

Doug Scottage fotostock/Getty Images

2 Find Evidence

Reread What is the song "Jó Ashílá" about? Circle words that help support this.

Examine Are the lyrics of the song meant to be taken exactly as it says? What else could this song mean? Why do you think this?

3 Make Connections

Talk Why do the Navajo perform these rituals?

16 Lesson 2 How Did the People of the Desert Southwest Meet Their Needs?

Lesson 2 **17**

Inquiry Journal, pp. 16–17

ENGLISH LEARNERS SCAFFOLD

ELD.PI.5.6 Reading closely literary and informational texts and viewing multimedia to determine how meaning is conveyed explicitly and implicitly through language

Emerging	Expanding	Bridging
Connect Ideas Ask students to think of a favorite song in their first language. Have them say the first two lines of the song and give a basic English translation of the lines.	**Select Vocabulary** Ask students to look up and print out the lyrics to their favorite song in English. Have them underline words and phrases that give the main idea of the song.	**Use Descriptive Language** Ask students to explain why they like their favorite song. Encourage them to use descriptive words.

See the **Language Learner Teaching Guide** for more language support strategies.

Monitor and Differentiate

REACHING ALL LEARNERS

Approaching Level

Have students look through the primary source and text. Ask them to mark words with similar or related meanings (for example, *performed, singing, dancing*).

Beyond Level

Ask students to choose 3–5 words and make a web graphic organizer. Have the students choose a central word and surround it with related words from the text and then add two or three related words from outside the texts.

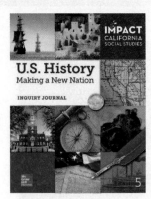

Inquiry Journal,
pp. 18–19

 STANDARDS

Describe how geography and climate influenced the way various nations lived and adjusted to the natural environment, including locations of villages, the distinct structures that they built, and how they obtained food, clothing, tools, and utensils. **HSS.5.1.1**

Compare and contrast the overall structure (e.g., chronology, comparison, cause/effect, problem/solution) of events, ideas, concepts, or information in two or more texts. **CCSS.ELA.RI.5.5**

Go *Digital!*

• Model how to explore and investigate with online whole-class tools.

• Students can access the online graphic organizer to use the inquiry tools as they read.

Explore Compare and Contrast

Explain Tell students that one way to learn about something is to use something else for context. Comparing to find similarities may indicate similar functions or causes. Likewise, contrasting to find differences will indicate differences in origins or purposes.

Read Have students read through the step-by-step instructions on comparing and contrasting. Suggest students use word webs to make a list of keywords to search for in the texts.

Guide Practice Model the process for students. Draw their attention to the graphic organizer. Note that the topic is "Rituals and Ceremonies." Have students list words with related meanings. Ask them to think of examples in their lives when they have encountered these words. Then ask them to look through their texts and notes for these words to find information about Navajo rituals and ceremonies. Have them choose one example from their lives and a Navajo example. Then have them compare and contrast these examples.

Investigate!

Instruct students to come up with words to look for to find information on housing, culture, religion, and economy for the Pueblo, Navajo, and Apache peoples.

Take Notes Have students write short notes in the graphic organizer on page 19 of their Inquiry Journals to keep track of what they find. Remind students that notes do not need to be complete sentences but rather should be simple words and phrases to help them recall information.

Inspect Guide students to read the text in each section to determine what the text says. Encourage them to make note of words they don't understand and to look for answers to questions, such as *who? what? when? where? why?* and *how?*

Find Evidence When the students have completed their discussions and noted possible reasons for the similarities and differences, encourage them to do further research to confirm or disprove their hypotheses. Direct them to reread their notes and the texts for details they may have missed, look in additional books in the classroom or library, and search the Internet.

Collaborative Conversations

Text-Based Discussion After students have identified similarities and differences between the Southwest American Indian cultures, have them discuss their findings with others—either partners or small groups. Ask them to brainstorm explanations for the similarities and differences.

Inquiry Tools

Explore Compare and Contrast

To **compare** is to find the similarities between two things. To **contrast** is to find their differences.

Similarities and differences can be linked. Two cultures may have similarities because they both came from the same group or they both live in similar environments. A difference in culture, however, could mean that one group has an advantage or hardship that the other group does not.

To compare and contrast:

1. Read the text all the way through.
This will help you understand what the text is about.

2. Look for keywords related to the information you want.
If you are looking for information about housing, look for words like *house*, *home*, and *build*, or materials like *wood* and *stone*.

3. Summarize the information.
Make quick, simple answers to your questions.

4. Review your answers.
Ask yourself, "*Which are the same?*" "*Which are different?*" "*Why?*"

COLLABORATE Based on the text you just read, work with your class to complete the chart below comparing rituals and ceremonies.

	People in Your Community	Navajo
Rituals and Ceremonies	weddings, funerals, religious services	sixty major ceremonies include singing, dancing, and sandpainting

IMPACT U.S. History Making a New Nation

Investigate!

Read pages 18–25 in your Research Companion. Use your investigative skills to look for text evidence that tells you about the lifestyles of different American Indian groups of the Southwest. Then, think about what is similar and what is different and why.

	Pueblo	Navajo	Apache
Housing	stone buildings resemble small, stepped pyramids; underground rooms called kivas	dome-shaped structures called *hogans* were made from logs or stones and covered in dirt	dome-shaped *wikiups* had a frame of wood poles covered with animal skins or reed mats
Culture/Religion	rituals and ceremonies held in kivas; kachina spirits part of Hopi culture	*hozho* beliefs involve staying in balance with nature; ceremonies include singing and dancing	trace ancestry through mothers; community divided into small groups of extended families
Economy	farmed crops, such as corn and beans; Hopi crafts included cotton cloth and pottery	crops grown with irrigation; rode horses to herd sheep and cattle; crafts included cloth and jewelry	hunter-gatherers; hunted bison and deer, and gathered agave, cactus, berries, and nuts

Inquiry Journal, pp. 18–19

(EL) ENGLISH LEARNERS SCAFFOLD

ELD.PI.5.1 Exchanging information and ideas with others through oral collaborative discussions on a range of social and academic topics

Emerging

Identify Key Details
Provide students with sentence frames to help them describe the similarities and differences they have found.

Examples: **Ceremonies that are similar are _____.**

Ceremonies that are different are _____.

Expanding

Cite Evidence Provide sentence frames to help students explain the reasons for the similarities and differences between the American Indians.

Examples: **The _____ ceremonies are similar because _____.**

The _____ ceremonies are different because _____.

Bridging

Evaluate findings
Encourage students to offer feedback to one another. They should say what they agree or disagree with and maintain a positive tone.

See the **Language Learner Teaching Guide** for more language support strategies.

Monitor and Differentiate

REACHING ALL LEARNERS

Special Needs

Put students in two groups. They will act out comparing and contrasting important details. When the two groups have details in common, they should step to the center, between the two groups.

Beyond Level

Encourage students to do a similar compare and contrast activity using another American Indian group, such as the Anasazi, or the Athabaskans from whom the Apache apparently originated.

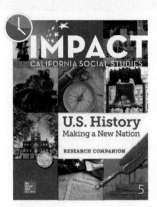

Research Companion
pp. 18–19

STANDARDS

Describe how geography and climate influenced the way various nations lived and adjusted to the natural environment, including locations of villages, the distinct structures that they built, and how they obtained food, clothing, tools, and utensils. **HSS.5.1.1**

Quote accurately from a text when explaining what the text says explicitly and when drawing inferences from the text. **CCSS.ELA.RI.5.1**

Go *Digital!*

Investigate the lesson content with online whole-class presentation tools.

- **Video:** Native Americans of the Southwest

- **iMap:** Native Americans of the Southwest, 1700

Background Information

The Pueblo people are descended from the Ancestral Pueblo people. They live in New Mexico and northeastern Arizona. Unlike many other American Indian groups, they have never been forced completely out of their homelands.They are named for their pueblo homes, which resemble boxes stacked in a roughly pyramidal fashion. These buildings offered good protection from both enemies and the elements, and aspects of the architectural style continue to be used today.

| TIMELINE | Invite students to look at the timeline at the top on page. 19.

Analyze What event happened between the Great Draught and Francisco Vásquez de Coronado's battle with the Zuni? (The Navajo arrived in the Southwest.) **HAS.CS.3**

Analyze the Source

Inspect Have students read about the Pueblo people on pp. 18–19.

Find Evidence Use the questions below to check comprehension. Remind students to support their answers with text evidence.

Identify Why are these people called Pueblo? (They were named after their homes.) **DOK 1**

Infer How do you know religion was important to the Southwest peoples? (Pueblo homes contained kivas; fighting broke out when Spanish interrupted a Zuni ceremony) **DOK 3**

Cite Evidence Are the Navajo likely related to the Pueblo? (No, the Navajo didn't arrive in the area until the late 1300s.) **DOK 2**

Analyze How long did the Great Drought last? (23 years) **DOK 2**

Make Connections

Compare and Contrast What advantage do Pueblo homes have over the cliff homes of the Ancestral Pueblo people? (They can be built in many more locations.) **DOK 2**

Analyze the Image How does the illustration support the text? (It shows the structure of the pueblo buildings, including ladders and kivas.) **DOK 3**

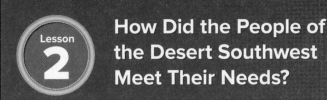

Lesson 2
How Did the People of the Desert Southwest Meet Their Needs?

1150	1276–1299	Late 1300s	1540
The Hopi build Oraibi, the oldest continuously occupied settlement in the United States.	The Great Drought causes cultural shift in Ancestral Pueblo peoples.	The Navajo arrive in the Southwest.	Spanish explorer Francisco Vásquez de Coronado interrupts a sacred Zuni ceremony and causes a battle.

1150 | 1300 | 1540

The Pueblo People

The Pueblo peoples of the American Southwest have inhabited the area for more than a thousand years. They mostly farmed crops such as corn and beans, and they built permanent homes out of stone and adobe clay. The Spanish word for these homes is *pueblo*, and that is how these people got their name.

Pueblo homes were modeled after the cliff dwellings of the Ancestral Pueblo. They are cube-like rooms stacked on top of each other. The largest rooms are at the bottom, while the smaller rooms are near the top. There are also fewer rooms near the top. So the entire house does not look like a big square or rectangle but more like a small, stepped pyramid. Wooden ladders outside of the rooms were usually used to get from one floor to another. Sometimes the bottom floor would have no doors or windows, and a person could get in only by climbing a ladder. This made the structure easy to defend because the ladder could be pulled up.

Pueblo buildings were usually home to several families and had connecting shared rooms. They also contained *kivas*, special below-ground rooms used for rituals and ceremonies.

A Southwest pueblo

HSS.5.1.1, HSS.5.1.2, HSS.5.1.3, HAS.CS.4

18   Lesson 2   How Did the People of the Desert Southwest Meet Their Needs?

Lesson 2   19

Research Companion, pp. 18–19

ENGLISH LEARNERS SCAFFOLD

ELD.PI.5.11 Supporting own opinions and evaluating others' opinions in speaking and writing

Emerging	Expanding	Bridging
Identify Ask students, *"What activities do you see the Pueblo people doing in the picture?"* Allow them to answer with single words. Then ask, *"Why do they do these activities?"*	**Analyze** Have students study the picture of the pueblo. Ask them if the pueblo buildings are good for life in the desert. Have students give reasons why or why not. Have them use evidence from the text and the picture.	**Support Opinions** Have students study the picture and explain whether they think pueblo buildings are good for life in the desert. Ask them to share their thoughts with partners. Ask them to critique their partner's responses, saying whether they agree or disagree and what they think is the strongest piece of evidence their partner presented.

See the **Language Learner Teaching Guide** for more language support strategies.

Monitor and Differentiate

REACHING ALL LEARNERS

Approaching Level

Ask students to examine the picture of the pueblo. Have them explain what kinds of information is included in the illustration.

On Level

Ask students to explain how the features in the illustration help them understand more about pueblos.

Beyond Level

Ask students to think of ways to improve the illustration by adding, expanding, or removing text features, or in other ways.

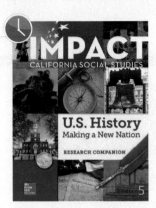

Research Companion
pp. 20–21

 STANDARDS

Describe how geography and climate influenced the way various nations lived and adjusted to the natural environment, including locations of villages, the distinct structures that they built, and how they obtained food, clothing, tools, and utensils. **HSS.5.1.1**

Describe their varied customs and folklore traditions. **HSS.5.1.2**

CCSS Students use map and globe skills to determine the absolute locations of places and interpret information available through a map's or globe's legend, scale, and symbolic representations. **HAS.CS.4**

Go Digital!

Investigate the lesson content with online whole-class presentation tools.

Background Information

The Pueblo are not a single group of people. Rather, they are numerous communities who share similarities in culture and language. The Zuni is one of those communities. They call themselves *Ashiwi* (AH-shee-wee), or "the people," and the name *Zuni* is how they are known by the Acoma Pueblo people.

The Hopi are another group of Pueblo people. Their culture is more than a thousand years old, and the Hopi have been called "the oldest of the people" by other American Indians.

Analyze the Source

Inspect Have students continue reading about Pueblo peoples, specifically the Zuni and the Hopi, on pp. 20–21.

Find Evidence Use the questions below to check comprehension. Remind students to support their answers with text evidence.

Identify What is the purpose of kachina dolls? (to help children learn about kachinas) **DOK 1**

Identify Were men or women responsible for getting food? Were men or women responsible for making things? (Both. Men hunted and farmed; women gathered. Men wove; women made baskets, jewelry, and pottery.) **DOK 1**

Cite Evidence How is the idea that the Hopi is an old culture supported? (The village of Oraibi is nearly one thousand years old.) **DOK 2**

Make Connections

Infer Why were the kachinas important? (The Hopi believed they brought rain and the growing season, which is important for a desert community.) **DOK 3**

Map Skills

Instruct students to study the map on p. 21.

* What does the orange area represent? (Pueblo lands)

* What does the yellow area represent? (Non-Pueblo lands)

* What is significant about the features of the eastern part of the orange area? (The eastern Pueblo territory follows the Rio Grande. It shows the value of water in the desert.)

* Which rivers are on or near the Puebo lands? (Rio Grande and Pecos River)

COLLABORATE

Stop and Check

Talk Have students list the advantages of pueblo buildings. Guide them in determining and discussing what makes them ideal for the Hopi and Zuni lifestyles. (Students should be able to give advantages of pueblos, such as: They are strong and easy to defend, they allow the community to live and work together, they have spaces for rituals, the roofs allow workspace for crafting.)

Find Details Explain to students that after they read and take notes, they should review them and ask themselves if they need more information.

There are many groups that make up the Pueblo people. Two of these are the Zuni and the Hopi.

The Zuni occupy their ancestral land in the Zuni River valley, though their territory is not as large as it was in the past. Attacks by Spanish treasure hunters and, later, settlers from the United States caused the Zuni to abandon some of their villages. They gathered into a single village to better protect themselves. This village was called Halona and is now called Zuni.

Another Pueblo group is the Hopi. The Hopi people are believed to be one of the oldest desert peoples. Their village of Oraibi is believed to be nearly nine hundred years old. They used dams and irrigation to grow crops such as corn, cotton, beans, and squash. They also took advantage of the sand dunes that formed against the sides of **mesas**. These dunes would trap moisture, and so the Hopi would plant crops in them.

Hopi men and women had different jobs. The men farmed and hunted. They also wove cloth from cotton. The women gathered food like nuts and berries. They also made baskets and pottery to store their food. The Hopi were among the first people to fire, or strengthen by heating, their pottery, using coal.

Kachina dolls

Chuck Place/Alamy Stock Photo

Important parts of Hopi culture include *kachinas*. According to Hopi beliefs, kachinas are spirits who live in sacred places for half of the year. During the other half, they live near the Hopi villages and bring with them rain and the growing season. The kachinas are represented by masked dancers who perform in the villages when the kachinas visit. There are hundreds of kachinas, so the dancers often give small carved kachina dolls to children to help them learn about the spirits.

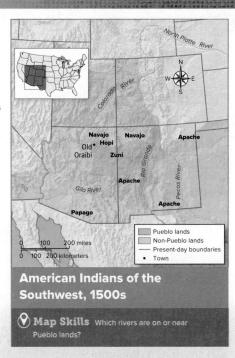

American Indians of the Southwest, 1500s

Pueblo lands
Non-Pueblo lands
— Present-day boundaries
• Town

0   100   200 miles
0   100   200 kilometers

Navajo   Navajo   Apache
Old ● Hopi
Oraibi   Zuni
        Apache
    Gila River
        Apache
Papago

Map Skills Which rivers are on or near Pueblo lands?

✓ **Stop and Check**

Talk With a small group, list the advantages of the pueblo buildings. What makes them ideal for the Hopi and Zuni lifestyles?

Find Details As you read, add additional information to the graphic organizer on page 19 in your Inquiry Journal.

20   Lesson 2   How Did the People of the Desert Southwest Meet Their Needs?   Lesson 2   21

Research Companion, pp. 20–21

ELD.PII.5.6 Connecting ideas

Emerging	Expanding	Bridging
Provide Details Provide sentence frames to help students explain characteristics of Pueblo culture, such as "The buildings have _____ because _____."	**Provide Details** Help students support ideas with more complex sentence frames, such as "In order to _____, the Hopi have _____."	**Analyze** Encourage students to compare cultures, showing how some differences are linked. For example, the students may point out that the Zuni don't have villages as old as Oraibi because they had to abandon some of their villages due to pressure from European explorers and settlers.

See the **Language Learner Teaching Guide** for more language support strategies.

Monitor and Differentiate

REACHING ALL LEARNERS

Special Needs

Encourage students to find more images of kachina dolls to help them illustrate why the kachinas were important to Pueblo culture.

Approaching Level

Ask students to identify the main ideas in the section on kachinas and kachina dolls.

Beyond Level

Ask students to research a kachina. Ask them to give a summary of who the kachina is and why it is important. Assist the students in searching the internet or looking for information in a library.

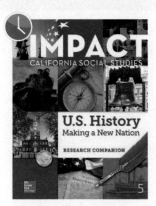

Research Companion
pp. 22–23

 STANDARDS

Describe how geography and climate influenced the way various nations lived and adjusted to the natural environment, including locations of villages, the distinct structures that they built, and how they obtained food, clothing, tools, and utensils. **HSS.5.1.1**

CCSS Explain the relationships or interactions between two or more individuals, events, ideas, or concepts in a historical, scientific, or technical text based on specific information in the text. **CCSS.ELA.RI.5.3**

Go *Digital!*

Investigate the lesson content with online whole-class presentation tools.

Background Information

One of the largest groups of American Indians, the **Navajo** constitute more than a quarter of a million people. The Navajo Nation reservation is the largest in the United States, covering about 26,000 square miles in Arizona, New Mexico, and Utah. In addition to the hunting and gathering techniques of their ancestors, the Navajo learned farming and crafting from the Pueblo. They also learned how to raise horses and herd cattle after making contact with the Spanish in the late 1600s.

DID YOU KNOW?

Explain that often, the common name of a group or place doesn't come from the people who live there, but by people who explored it. This is why so many American Indian peoples and places have Spanish- or French-sounding names.

Analyze the Source

Inspect Have students read about the Navajo on pp. 22–23.

Find Evidence Use the questions below to check comprehension. Remind students to support their answers with text evidence.

> **Vocabulary** Ask students to write words from the text that they do not understand. Have them guess the meanings from context and then look up the words to check if they were correct. **DOK 1**
>
> **Analyze** What type of text structure is used to discuss the Pueblo and the Navajo? (compare and contrast) **DOK 3**
>
> **Cite Evidence** What are some of the examples of the Navajo being adaptable? (changing food sources, learning from Pueblo and Spanish) **DOK 2**

Make Connections

> **Compare and Contrast** What do hogans have in common with pueblos? (They use earth as a building material; they have a hole in the roof (though for different purposes); they are intended to be permanent and sturdy.) **DOK 3**
>
> **Photograph** What details about hogans are in the text but cannot be seen in the photograph? (blanket in doorway, hole in roof) **DOK 3**

Map Skills

Ask students to look at the map on p. 23, and have them think about what people look for when finding a new home (opportunities, near resources, good neighbors, weather, etc.) (Students should identify that having resources such as fresh water and animals to hunt for food impact a people's decision on where to live.)

☑ Stop and Check

Think Have students think about the changes the Navajo had to make. (Students should be able to explain that the Navajo transitioned from nomadic hunter-gatherers to farmers and herdsmen. They planted crops from the Pueblo, raised animals from the Spanish, and built homes that had aspects of the Plains and the Southwest Indians combined.)

The Navajo

The Navajo were neighbors to the Pueblo and borrowed some of their ideas. They used irrigation to grow crops, made clothes with cotton, and were skilled in making jewelry and pottery. Despite these similarities, the Navajo were not related to the Pueblo. The Navajo were related to the Athabaskans of Alaska and Canada. Scholars think the Navajo migrated from the northern tundra to the southwestern deserts in the late 1200s.

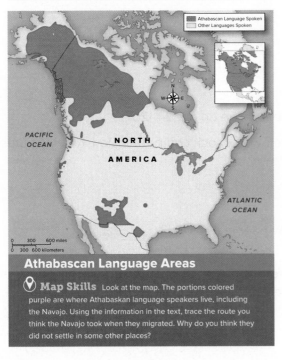

Athabascan Language Spoken
Other Languages Spoken

PACIFIC OCEAN

NORTH AMERICA

ATLANTIC OCEAN

0 300 600 miles
0 300 600 kilometers

Athabascan Language Areas

📍 **Map Skills** Look at the map. The portions colored purple are where Athabaskan language speakers live, including the Navajo. Using the information in the text, trace the route you think the Navajo took when they migrated. Why do you think they did not settle in some other places?

The Navajo were originally hunter-gatherers but quickly adopted new techniques for surviving in the desert. In addition to learning farming from the Pueblo, the Navajo also learned from Spanish settlers when they arrived in the 1500s. They were interested in the animals the Spanish brought with them. The Navajo soon became skilled at herding sheep and cattle, as well as at riding horses. Their relationship with the Spanish was otherwise hostile. The culture of the Spanish clashed with several of the American Indian groups. The Navajo became close allies with the Pueblo and the Apache in fighting the Spanish.

The Navajo lived in *hogans*, large dome-shaped buildings. Hogans were made of logs or stone and covered in mud and dirt. They had one entrance, usually facing east and covered with a blanket. Hogans had no windows, only a hole in the roof so that smoke from the fire could escape.

A hogan

Traditionally, the Navajo believed in *hozho*, or "walking in beauty." This means maintaining balance with the earth. They believed that being out of harmony with the earth was the cause of illness and suffering. In order to restore harmony, they took part in long ceremonies involving singing and dancing. Many of these rituals are still practiced today.

✓ Stop and Check

Think What changes did the Navajo have to make when they moved from the North to the South?

Find Details As you read, add additional information to the graphic organizer on page 19 in your Inquiry Journal.

Research Companion, pp. 22–23

(EL) ENGLISH LEARNERS SCAFFOLD

ELD.PII.5.5 Modifying to add details

Emerging	Expanding	Bridging
Identify Ask students to read through the texts and write words and phrases that describe the activities of the Pueblo and Navajo.	**Identify** Ask students to read through the text and write adverbs, adverb phrases, and prepositional phrases. Review the functions of adverbs and prepositions.	**Describe** Ask students to use adjectives and adverbs to compare Pueblos and Navajos.

See the **Language Learner Teaching Guide** for more language support strategies.

Monitor and Differentiate

REACHING ALL LEARNERS

Approaching Level

Ask students to describe hogans in their own words.

On Level

Ask students to describe *hozho* in their own words. Encourage them to compare it with concepts more familiar to them.

Beyond Level

Ask students to give their opinion about whether contact with the Spanish was overall beneficial or detrimental to the Navajo.

2 INVESTIGATE > The Apache

Research Companion
pp. 24–25

(HSS) STANDARDS

Describe how geography and climate influenced the way various nations lived and adjusted to the natural environment, including locations of villages, the distinct structures that they built, and how they obtained food, clothing, tools, and utensils. **HSS.5.1.1**

(CCSS) Compare and contrast the overall structure (e.g., chronology, comparison, cause/effect, problem/solution) of events, ideas, concepts, or information in two or more texts. **CCSS.ELA.RI.5.5**

Go *Digital!*

Investigate the lesson content with online whole-class presentation tools.

Background Information

The **Apache** have spent their history wandering in small family groups and were not unified under a single government until recently. Treaties had to be made with each group individually; no one spoke for all Apaches. They moved frequently, making them hard to find. For these reasons, Apaches were the last American Indians to surrender to the U.S. government.

Analyze the Source

Inspect Have students read about the Apache on pp. 24–25.

Find Evidence Use the questions below to check comprehension. Remind students to support their answers with text evidence.

Identify What is the advantage of wikiups? (They can be taken apart and moved easily.) **DOK 1**

Infer How are homes related to how people get food? (Farmers have permanent homes; hunters have small, easy to move homes.) **DOK 2**

Infer The Apache were eventually forced to live on reservations. Why might this have been a terrible hardship for the Apache? (Apaches were used to wandering and hunting, so staying in one place and trying to farm was a very different lifestyle from what they were used to.) **DOK 3**

Make Connections

Compare and Contrast Are the Apache more similar to the Pueblo or to Navajo? (Answers may vary, but Apache language, homes, and hunting lifestyle are more similar to Navajos.) **DOK 3**

Illustration Why is a step-by-step diagram used rather than just a picture of the finished wikiup? (It provides information about the internal structure and how easily it is put together.) **DOK 3**

COLLABORATE

☑ Stop and Check

Write Have students discuss why the Apache are different among Southwestern peoples. (Students should be able to explain that Apaches were not primarily farmers who stayed in one place like the other Southwestern American Indians. Rather than growing food, they hunted and raided, and they were frequently on the move. Their culture was also more independent.)

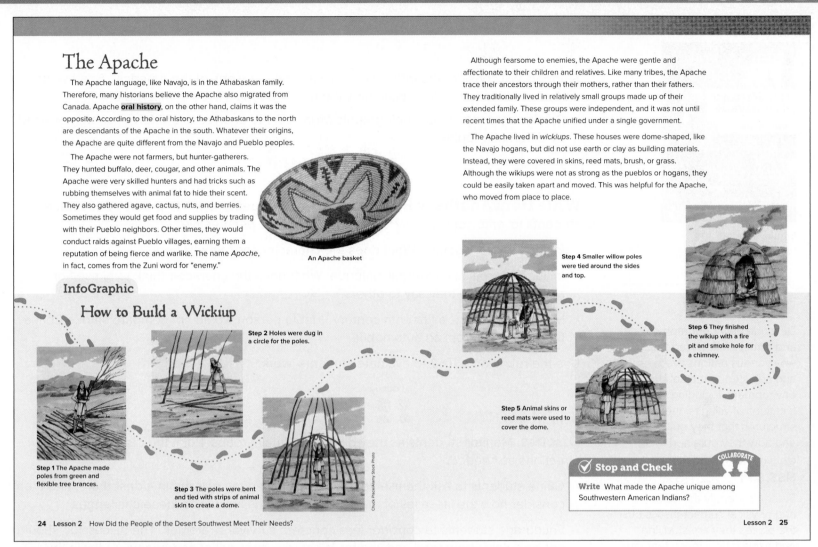

The Apache

The Apache language, like Navajo, is in the Athabaskan family. Therefore, many historians believe the Apache also migrated from Canada. Apache **oral history**, on the other hand, claims it was the opposite. According to the oral history, the Athabaskans to the north are descendants of the Apache in the south. Whatever their origins, the Apache are quite different from the Navajo and Pueblo peoples.

The Apache were not farmers, but hunter-gatherers. They hunted buffalo, deer, cougar, and other animals. The Apache were very skilled hunters and had tricks such as rubbing themselves with animal fat to hide their scent. They also gathered agave, cactus, nuts, and berries. Sometimes they would get food and supplies by trading with their Pueblo neighbors. Other times, they would conduct raids against Pueblo villages, earning them a reputation of being fierce and warlike. The name *Apache*, in fact, comes from the Zuni word for "enemy."

An Apache basket

Although fearsome to enemies, the Apache were gentle and affectionate to their children and relatives. Like many tribes, the Apache trace their ancestors through their mothers, rather than their fathers. They traditionally lived in relatively small groups made up of their extended family. These groups were independent, and it was not until recent times that the Apache unified under a single government.

The Apache lived in *wickiups*. These houses were dome-shaped, like the Navajo hogans, but did not use earth or clay as building materials. Instead, they were covered in skins, reed mats, brush, or grass. Although the wikiups were not as strong as the pueblos or hogans, they could be easily taken apart and moved. This was helpful for the Apache, who moved from place to place.

InfoGraphic

How to Build a Wickiup

Step 1 The Apache made poles from green and flexible tree brances.

Step 2 Holes were dug in a circle for the poles.

Step 3 The poles were bent and tied with strips of animal skin to create a dome.

Step 4 Smaller willow poles were tied around the sides and top.

Step 5 Animal skins or reed mats were used to cover the dome.

Step 6 They finished the wikiup with a fire pit and smoke hole for a chimney.

✓ Stop and Check
COLLABORATE

Write What made the Apache unique among Southwestern American Indians?

24 Lesson 2 How Did the People of the Desert Southwest Meet Their Needs?

Lesson 2 25

Research Companion, pp. 24–25

(EL) ENGLISH LEARNERS SCAFFOLD

ELD.PI.5.3 Offering and supporting opinions and negotiating with others in communicative exchanges

Emerging	Expanding	Bridging
Make Claims Would it be better to live as an Apache or a Pueblo? Have students state their preference and explain why.	**Support Opinions** Have students explain whether they would prefer the lifestyle of an Apache or a Pueblo. They should use facts from the texts to support their preference.	**Support Opinions** Have students explain why the Pueblo or Apache lifestyle would be preferable for them personally, explaining which of their personal traits are best suited for that type of life.

See the **Language Learner Teaching Guide** for more language support strategies.

Monitor and Differentiate

REACHING ALL LEARNERS

Approaching Level

Have students describe how to build a *wikiup* using their own words and transitions such as *first, next,* and so on.

Beyond Level

Did the Apache deserve the Zuni name "enemy"? Have students support their opinion using information from the text.

3 REPORT

Report Your Findings

Inquiry Journal
pp. 20–21

Go Digital!

- Students can go online to report their findings. Assess their responses online.

- Students can access the online graphic organizer to capture ideas from their investigation.

Think About It

Students will consider the difficulties of living in the deserts of the American Southwest and use their research to explain how the native peoples lived in that region.

- Remind students to use their graphic organizers to analyze the different strategies used by different peoples.

Write About It

Write from Another's Perspective Have students read the prompt. Encourage students to write convincingly from their character's perspective.

- Include sensory details: What does the character see? Smell? Feel?

- Include internal and external dialogue: What does the character think to himself or herself? What do they say to others?

- Maintain accuracy: a fifteenth century Pueblo person would not compare smoke from a fire to exhaust from an automobile.

Use the rubric on p. T52 to evaluate students' work.

Talk About It
COLLABORATE

Discuss Monitor students as they discuss in small groups. Point the discussions in new directions as needed.

- Guide students to ask themselves what the challenges of living in a desert are, and then consider how the lifestyles of the American Indians answered these challenges.

- Encourage students to consider less concrete survival strategies. The discussion should not be solely about food and shelter. What role does belief and behavior play in the American Indians' survival?

- Remind students to follow the rules of appropriate classroom conversation.

Connect to the
Essential Question

Read the prompt aloud to students. Ask them the following guiding questions:

- Are any of the traditions similar to things you and your family do?

- How is life today different for American Indians than it was for their ancestors? How is it the same? (Answers will vary, but students may indicate that many customs and practices are still the same because American Indians try to hold on to their heritage.)

Remind students to use the space provided in their journal to jot down notes.

Report Your Findings

Think About It

Review your research. Based on the information you have gathered, how did native peoples live in the deserts of the American Southwest?

Write About It

Write from Another's Perspective

Write a diary entry from the viewpoint of a Pueblo, Navajo, or Apache person. Be sure to include details about where you live, what you eat, what chores or jobs you do, and what possessions you have.

Students should include in their diary entry details from the text about food, chores, and possessions of a Pueblo, Navajo, or Apache person.

Talk About It

Discuss

In small groups, consider what you have learned about the American Indians of the Southwest. How have they adapted to life in the desert?

Connect to the EQ

Pull It Together

Think about what you have learned about the lifestyles of the Southwest American Indians. What traditions continue to be used today? Why have these traditions continued?

Pueblo-style houses are still in use, though slightly modernized. These homes are good for the desert and so have not needed to change much. Many rituals also continue, out of a desire for American Indians to hold on to their heritage.

Inquiry Project Notes

Inquiry Journal, pp. 20–21

 ## ENGLISH LEARNERS SCAFFOLD

ELD.PI.5.1 Exchanging information and ideas with others through oral collaborative discussions on a range of social and academic topics

Emerging	Expanding	Bridging
Model Provide a sample of narrative writing from historical fiction for students to study so they have examples of sentences they could modify and use.	**Use Varied Language** Ask students to use a variety of verb tenses appropriately in their narratives. Review some of the more difficult tenses, such as the present perfect and the progressive.	**Discuss Writing** Have students share and critique each other's work. Remind them to maintain a positive and helpful tone.

See the **Language Learner Teaching Guide** for more language support strategies.

Monitor and Differentiate

REACHING ALL LEARNERS

Approaching Level

Encourage students to incorporate domain specific vocabulary in their narratives, using Pueblo, Navajo, and Apache terms appropriately.

Beyond Level

Encourage students to do further research on the American Indians they are writing about and to incorporate some of the additional information into their writing.

Know what your students know!

Lesson Task
Report Your Findings

Use this rubric to evaluate students' response.

Take a Stand Students write a diary entry from the viewpoint of a Pueblo, Navajo, or Apache person. They include details about where the person lives, what he or she eats, what chores or jobs he or she does, and what possessions he or she has.

Compare Your Groups Students work in small groups to discuss how the American Indians of the Southwest adapted to life in the desert.

Performance Task Evaluation Rubric

	4	3	2	1
Historical Understanding	Strong understanding of the lifestyle of an American Indian group living in the Southwest	Adequate understanding of the lifestyle of an American Indian group living in the Southwest	Uneven understanding of the lifestyle of an American Indian group living in the Southwest	No understanding of the lifestyle of an American Indian group living in the Southwest
Write a Diary Entry	Diary entry is creative and full of details about the daily life of the character	Diary entry is adequate and includes facts about the daily life of the character	Diary entry is missing details about the daily life of the character	No details given or student does not show understanding of the task
Support with Evidence	Diary entry is fully supported by facts and details about the lifestyle of the American Indian group	Diary entry is adequately supported by facts and details about the lifestyle of the American Indian group	Diary entry is unevenly supported by facts and details about the lifestyle of the American Indian group	Facts and details are missing or contain no supporting evidence
Defend Your Claim	Speaks clearly and at an understandable pace Provides supporting details and facts during discussion	Speaks clearly during most of the presentation Provides some supporting details and facts during discussion	At times speaker is unclear Provides few supporting details and facts during discussion	Speaks unclearly throughout the presentation Does not provide supporting details and facts during discussion

Lesson Assessment

Go Digital!

- Have students complete the Chapter 1 Lesson 2 Assessment online to monitor their understanding of the lesson content.

California Smarter Balanced Assessment Connections!

Standards Covered	Lesson Task	Lesson Assessment	Alignment with California Smarter Balanced Assessment
History Social Science Content 5.1.1; 5.1.2	✔	✔	Claim 1 Targets 8, 9, 10
History Social Science Analysis Skills Chronological and Spatial Thinking 5.4 Historical Interpretation 5.2	✔	✔	Claim 1 Targets 11, 12
Writing W.5.3	✔	✔	Claim 2 Targets 1, 3, 5
Research and Inquiry W.5.9	✔	✔	Claim 4 Targets 2, 3, 4
Reading RI.5.3; RI.5.5	✔	✔	Claim 1 Targets 11, 12, 13
Speaking and Listening SL.5.1	✔		Claim 3 Target 3

How Are the California and Pacific Northwest Peoples Shaped by Their Surroundings?

Background Information

Explain to students that in this lesson they will learn about the environmental features that shaped the lives of American Indians in California and the Pacific Northwest.

Community Connections

To enrich what students have learned about California and Pacific Northwest peoples, have groups of students each explore a different official website of one of the groups discussed in the lesson. They can find such websites by doing Internet searches that use the word *official* before the name of a group.

LESSON STANDARDS

- ✓ Describe how geography and climate influenced the way various nations lived and adjusted to the natural environment, including locations of villages, the distinct structure that they built, and how they obtained food, clothing, tools, and utensils. **HSS.5.1.1**
- ✓ Describe their varied customs and folklore traditions. **HSS.5.1.2**
- ✓ Explain their varied economies and systems of government. **HSS.5.1.3**
- ✓ Students judge the significance of the relative location of a place (e.g., proximity to a harbor, on trade routes) and analyze how relative advantages and disadvantages can change over time. **HAS.CS.5**
- ✓ Students pose relevant questions about events they encounter in historical documents, eyewitness accounts, oral histories, letters, diaries, artifacts, photographs, maps, artworks, and architecture. **HAS.HR.2**

 Connect to the
Essential Question

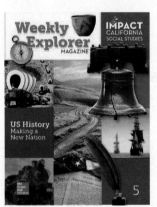

Chapter 1, pp. 2–13

The **Weekly Explorer Magazine** supports students' exploration of the Essential Question and provides additional resources for the EQ Inquiry Project.

 ## Inquiry Project

What was life like in America before Columbus?

Remind students to use the information they learn in this lesson and other resources to complete their EQ Inquiry Project!

Dinah Zike's

In this lesson you will use Foldables.

When Minutes Count!

Suggested Lesson Pacing

1 ENGAGE
One Day

2 INVESTIGATE
Two to Three Days

🕐 **Short on Time?** Look for the clock to teach core content in less time.

3 REPORT
One Day

- Lesson Opener
- Analyze the Source
- Inquiry Tools

Go Digital

- **Video:** Native Americans of the Pacific Northwest
- **iMap:** Native Americans of the Pacific Northwest

- A Variety of Landscapes
- American Indians of California
- American Indians of the Pacific Northwest
- **Then and Now** Totem Poles of the Pacific Northwest

- Think About It
- Take a Stand
- Defend Your Claim

Make Connections!

CONNECT TO ELA

Reading

Draw on information from multiple print or digital sources, demonstrating the ability to locate an answer to a question quickly or to solve a problem efficiently. **RI.5.7**

Research

Conduct short research projects that use several sources to build knowledge through investigation of different aspects of a topic. **W.5.7**

Recall relevant information from experiences or gather relevant information from print and digital sources; summarize or paraphrase information in notes and finished work, and provide a list of sources. **W.5.8**

Writing

Write opinion pieces on topics or texts, supporting a point of view with reasons and information. **W.5.1**

Draw evidence from literary or informational texts to support analysis, reflection, and research. **W.5.9**

Speaking and Listening

Engage effectively in a range of collaborative discussions (one-on-one, in groups, and teacher-led) with diverse partners on grade 5 topics and texts, building on others' ideas and expressing their own clearly. **SL.5.1**

Classroom Resources

🔍 Search for additional resources using the following key words.

American Indians of California

American Indians of the Pacific Northwest

Cahuilla

Chemehuevi

Inuit

Miwok

Native Peoples of Alaska

Makah

Pomo

potlatch

Chief Seattle

Serrano

Tlingit

totem pole

Yurok

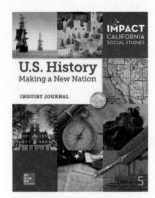

Inquiry Journal,
pp. 22–23

 STANDARDS

Describe how geography and climate influenced the way various nations lived and adjusted to the natural environment, including locations of villages, the distinct structures that they built, and how they obtained food, clothing, tools, and utensils. **HSS.5.1.1**

Engage effectively in a range of collaborative discussions (one-on-one, in groups, and teacher-led) with diverse partners on *grade 5 topics and texts*, building on others' ideas and expressing their own clearly. **CCSS.ELA.SL.5.1**

Go Digital!

Explore the lesson content with online whole-class presentation tools.

- **Video:** Native Americans of the Pacific Northwest

- **iMap:** Native Americans of the Pacific Northwest

How Are the California and Pacific Northwest Peoples Shaped by Their Surroundings?

Bellringer

Prompt students to retrieve information from the previous lessons. Ask: How did each group of American Indians obtain their food? What was different about the shelters in which they lived? (Some native peoples hunted animals and gathered plants for food. Others grew crops. Shelters ranged from cubelike rock structures stacked on top of each other to domelike buildings with walls of logs, stones, or animal skins.)

Lesson Outcomes

What Am I Learning? Have students read the Lesson Question and Lesson Outcomes on p. 22.

Why Am I Learning It? Confirm that students understand the word *environment*. Say: *Environment* is a word used often in social studies. It refers to the surroundings in which people live.

How Will I Know That I Learned It? Ask students the following questions.

- What will you identify? (the geographic features of California)

- What is the purpose of your task? (to explain how these geographic features influenced the cultures of the American Indians who lived there)

- How will you support your explanation? (with text evidence)

Talk About It

Explain that when we analyze an image, we examine its parts and interpret what they show or signify. Guide students to look at all of the parts of the photograph, to read the caption, and to answer the questions to help them understand what the image shows.

Collaborative Conversations

Set Discussion Goals As students engage in partner, small-group, and whole-class discussions, encourage them to

- Stay on topic.
- Connect their own ideas to things their peers have said.
- Look for ways to connect their personal experiences or prior knowledge to the conversation.

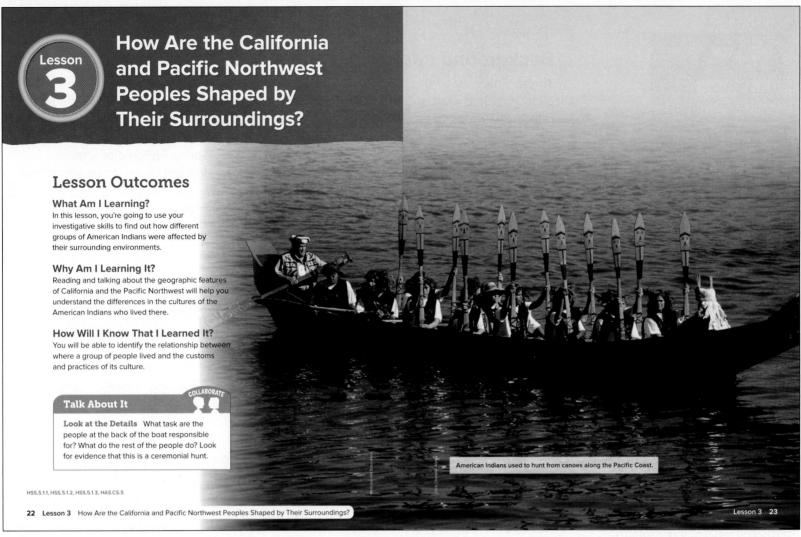

Lesson 3

How Are the California and Pacific Northwest Peoples Shaped by Their Surroundings?

Lesson Outcomes

What Am I Learning?
In this lesson, you're going to use your investigative skills to find out how different groups of American Indians were affected by their surrounding environments.

Why Am I Learning It?
Reading and talking about the geographic features of California and the Pacific Northwest will help you understand the differences in the cultures of the American Indians who lived there.

How Will I Know That I Learned It?
You will be able to identify the relationship between where a group of people lived and the customs and practices of its culture.

Talk About It COLLABORATE

Look at the Details What task are the people at the back of the boat responsible for? What do the rest of the people do? Look for evidence that this is a ceremonial hunt.

American Indians used to hunt from canoes along the Pacific Coast.

HSS.5.1.1, HSS.5.1.2, HSS.5.1.3, HAS.CS.5

22 Lesson 3 How Are the California and Pacific Northwest Peoples Shaped by Their Surroundings?

Lesson 3 23

Inquiry Journal, pp. 22–23

EL ENGLISH LEARNERS SCAFFOLD

ELD.PI.5.2 Interacting with others in written English in various communicative forms (print, communicative technology, and multimedia)

Emerging	Expanding	Bridging
Identify Features Work with students individually to recognize and name details in the image. Provide specific words as needed.	**Describe Features** Have students work with partners to create a list of words and phrases that describe the image. Encourage them to consider what the people in the photograph are thinking or feeling as well as what they are doing.	**Apply Language** Encourage students to describe the cultural factors that the picture conveys about the American Indians it depicts—living near the coast, hunting in groups, building canoes, and so on.

See the **Language Learner Teaching Guide** for more language support strategies.

Monitor and Differentiate

REACHING ALL LEARNERS

Special Needs

Work with students to use correct spatial terms for their descriptions of the image. Encourage them to act out terms such as *foreground* and *background*.

On Level

Have students speculate about other foods besides whales and fish that would be available to American Indians who live on the coast.

Beyond Level

Have students conduct research to identify how American Indians living on the coast use the ocean as a resource. Encourage students to confirm and supplement their ideas with online research.

1 ENGAGE

Analyze the Source

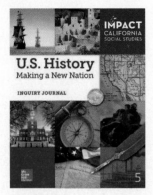

Inquiry Journal,
pp. 24–25

 STANDARDS

Describe the varied customs and folklore traditions of American Indians. **HSS.5.1.2**

Pose and respond to specific questions by making comments that contribute to the discussion and elaborate on the remarks of others. **CCSS.ELA.SL.5.1c**

Summarize a written text read aloud or information presented in diverse media formats, including visually, quantitatively, and orally. **CSS.ELA.SL.5.2**

Go *Digital!*

Model how to inspect and find evidence with online whole-class presentation tools.

Background Information

Totem Poles Used throughout the Pacific Northwest, totem poles comprise a pictographic means of chronicling information. Genealogy poles placed outside a residence trace the history of the family that lives inside. Memorial poles honor the achievements of a deceased clan member or the significance of an important event. Mortuary poles provide the history of a person buried nearby. Ridicule or shame poles mock someone who has done something wrong and are taken down when that person atones.

1 Inspect

Look Have students examine the totem pole and circle the figures it depicts, or shows. Be sure students understand that each symbol on the totem pole is called a totem.

- What does the first totem show? (an eagle or other bird)

- What does the second totem show? (many different eyes)

- What does the third totem show? (an upside-down face, meaning "ridicule" or "shame")

2 Find Evidence

Look Again Have students reexamine the image and reread the labels.

- What type of story might this totem pole be telling? (Answers will vary, but students should use the details in the image to support their interpretation.)

- How do the totems and their order help tell the story? (Answers will vary, but students should use details from the image to draw a conclusion.)

- Some totems tell the story of a family; some tell the story of a person being honored or a person who has died; some shame a person. From the story on this totem pole, what do you think its main purpose is? Why? (Answers will vary, but students should use the details in the image to support their interpretation.)

3 Make Connections
COLLABORATE

Encourage students to discuss with partners their ideas for a school totem pole. Tell them not only to pose and respond to the questions in the text (e.g., *Which symbols would you include as totems?*) but also to ask and answer questions that get at the reasons for their responses (e.g., *Why would you include those symbols?*). Remind students that they can convey their ideas in speech, writing, or drawings. (Responses will vary, but students should justify their choices for symbols to include on their totems.)

Analyze the Source

1 Inspect

Look Examine the image of a totem pole.

- **Circle** the figures depicted on the pole.
- **Discuss** with a partner what order the totems appear in and what they might represent.

My Notes

_____
_____
_____
_____
_____
_____
_____
_____
_____
_____
_____
_____
_____
_____
_____
_____
_____

"Ridicule" totems, often used to shame individuals, appear upside down.

Bob Corson/Alamy

Totem Poles

The images carved on totem poles are often human, animal, or spiritual forms that represent something important to a family. For example, some American Indians have used wolves, eagles, and grizzly bears as symbols for their families. Totem poles have also been carved in honor of an important person or event. Today, these structures are associated with American Indians across the Pacific Northwest, but they originate with groups in southeastern Alaska such as the Tlingit and the Tsimshian.

Totem poles vary in height, but most are 10–50 feet tall. They can be placed in front of a family's home or beside a gravesite. Shorter ones may be kept inside the home. Totem pole carving nearly died out in the late 1800s when the U.S. government banned a number of American Indian ceremonies. American Indians revived the practice in the 1950s and continue to make totem poles today.

Totem-pole carvers usually make the poles from the wood of red cedar trees. Before a tree is cut down, native peoples may hold a ceremony of respect and thanks for the use of the tree.

On a pole the top totem, called a crest, often shows which clan the family belongs to. An upside-down totem is sometimes included to make fun of an enemy. Most totems have oval shapes. The carver may use colors or patterns in the wood to help determine designs.

2 Find Evidence

Infer What type of story might this totem pole tell? How do the totems and their order help tell that story?

Think Where would you place this totem pole in a village so that its message would be best delivered?

3 Make Connections

Talk Look again COLLABORATE at the totem pole on the previous page. Pretend that your school is planning to build a totem pole outside the front doors. Like the Pacific Northwest peoples, your school wants the animals and people on the totem pole to welcome visitors and tell a story about the school's history. Which symbols would you include as totems? Which totems should be the highest on your pole? What story would you want visitors to know about your school?

Inquiry Journal, pp. 24–25

(EL) ENGLISH LEARNERS SCAFFOLD

ELD.PI.5.12 Selecting and applying varied and precise vocabulary and language structures to effectively convey ideas

Emerging	Expanding	Bridging
Identify Features Work with students individually to identify the different parts of the totem pole. Help them pronounce and understand unfamiliar words.	**Develop Language** Guide students to work with partners to identify the parts of the totem pole. Encourage them to use specific words to describe the position and appearance of different parts of the totem pole.	**Exchange Ideas** Encourage students to describe the important cultural information the totem pole conveys about the American Indians who use it.

See the **Language Learner Teaching Guide** for more language support strategies.

Monitor and Differentiate

REACHING ALL LEARNERS

Approaching Level

Work with students to use correct spatial terms for their descriptions of the totem pole. Have them complete sentence frames, such as *At the top, the totem pole shows ____. At the bottom, there is _____.*

On Level

Have students summarize what the totem pole shows about the people who made it.

Beyond Level

Encourage students to find out more about the way in which totem poles are carved. Students may report their findings to the class in a series of sketches accompanying an oral or written report.

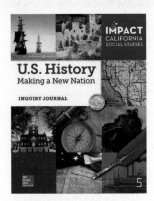

Inquiry Journal,
pp. 26–27

 STANDARDS

Describe how geography and climate influenced the way various nations lived and adjusted to the natural environment, including locations of villages, the distinct structures that they built, and how they obtained food, clothing, tools, and utensils. **HSS.5.1.1**

Describe the varied customs and folklore traditions of American Indians. **HSS.5.1.2**

Explain the relationships or interactions between two or more individuals, events, ideas, or concepts in a historical, scientific, or technical text based on specific information in the text. **CCSS.ELA.RI.5.3**

Go Digital!

- Model how to explore and investigate with online whole-class tools.

- Students can access the online graphic organizer to use the inquiry tools as they read.

Explore Compare and Contrast

Explain Clarify for students that to compare is to look for similarities and that to contrast is to focus on differences. Point out that students will often understand something better if they see how it is like and unlike other things.

Read Have students read the step-by-step instructions about how to compare and contrast. Tell students that in addition to examining text organization to help themselves compare and contrast, they should look for words and phrases that signal similarities and differences.

- Similarities: same, similarly, both, like, alike, also, too, in the same way

- Differences: but, although, however, unlike, different, in contrast

Guide Practice Model the strategy by briefly describing two activities, such as attending a sports event and watching one on TV, and then having students identify the similarities and differences. Include signal words or phrases in the descriptions.

Investigate!

Have students read pp. 26–33 in the Research Companion. Tell them the information will help them answer the lesson question *How Are the California and Pacific Northwest Peoples Shaped by Their Surroundings?*

Take Notes Ask students to keep track of similarities and differences between different groups of American Indians by filling out the graphic organizer on p. 27 of the Inquiry Journal. Be sure they understand where to put similarities and where to put differences in the Venn diagram. Explain to students that they will take notes as they read each section. Point out that taking notes will help them understand and remember the information they learn. Remind them of the importance of paraphrasing, or using their own words, when they take notes.

Inspect Guide students to read the text in each section to determine what the text says. Encourage them to make note of words they don't understand and to look for answers to questions, such as *who? what? when? where? why?* and *how?*

Find Details Encourage students to reread the text to find more points of comparison and contrast.

Collaborative Conversations

Text-Based Discussion Remind students that, in discussing the text with a partner, they should

- listen and respond to the partner's points
- ask for evidence from the text
- build on each other's ideas
- see the text from a different point of view.

Inquiry Tools

Explore Compare and Contrast

You can better understand the ideas in a text if you **compare and contrast** the details the author provides.

1. Read the text.
This will help you understand what the text is about.

2. Think about how the text is organized.
If the text is divided into sections that each focus on a place or a group of people, look for topics that the author mentions in every section—for example, housing and customs. The author may be expecting you draw comparisons.

3. Reread and look for text features.
Authors often use text features when they want to call attention to the similarities and differences between ideas. Analyze text features, looking at headings, bulleted texts, and images.

4. Make notes in a chart.
You can use these notes later to help you remember what you read.

 COLLABORATE With the class, work to fill in one circle of the Venn diagram on page 27 using information about the Tlingit people from the previous page.

 ## Investigate!

Read pages 26–33 in your Research Companion. Use your investigative skills to compare the Tlingit people with two other American Indian groups from this lesson. Consider where each group lived, its customs, and its artifacts. Write your findings in the diagram.

Tlingit People

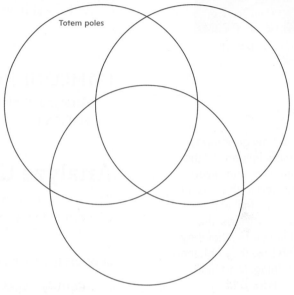
Totem poles

Students should be able to fill out the Venn Diagram with details about the Tlingit people as well as two other groups from the lesson.

26 Lesson 3 How Are the California and Pacific Northwest Peoples Shaped by Their Surroundings?

Lesson 3 27

Inquiry Journal, pp. 26–27

EL ENGLISH LEARNERS SCAFFOLD

ELD.PI.5.11 Supporting own opinions and evaluating others' opinions in speaking and writing

Emerging

Organize Information
Work with students individually to identify the different parts of the Venn diagram. Help them see where they should put details that apply to just one group, details that apply to two groups, and details that apply to all three groups.

Expanding

Develop Language Have students work in pairs to identify similarities and differences between the Indian groups. Encourage students to identify the details by taking turns posing and answering questions, such as *Where in North America does this group live? How did the group traditionally obtain food?*

Bridging

Classify Information
Remind students to compare and contrast details that fall into the same category of information—details about each group's type of shelter, for example, or details about the way each group obtains food.

See the **Language Learner Teaching Guide** for more language support strategies.

Monitor and Differentiate

REACHING ALL LEARNERS

Approaching Level

Work with students to make statements of comparison and contrast. Have them complete sentences frames, such as *Both the Pomo and the Miwok ____* or *While the Tlingit ____, the Miwok ____.*

Beyond Level

Encourage students to do online research to find out more about the three groups they compare and contrast and then, based on their research, to add appropriate details to the Venn diagram.

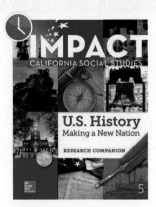

Research Companion
pp. 26–27

 STANDARDS

Describe how geography and climate influenced the way various nations lived and adjusted to the natural environment, including locations of villages, the distinct structures that they built, and how they obtained food, clothing, tools, and utensils. **HSS.5.1.1**

Students place key events and people of the historical era they are studying in a chronological sequence and within a spatial context; they interpret time lines. **HAS.CS.1**

Students use map and globe skills to determine the absolute locations of places and interpret information available through a map's or globe's legend, scale, and symbolic representation. **HAS.CS.5**

Go Digital!

Investigate the lesson content with online whole-class presentation tools.

- **Video:** Native Americans of the Pacific Northwest

- **iMap:** Native Americans of the Pacific Northwest

Background Information

Many languages of Pacific Northwestern peoples, including Tlingit, Haida, and the Athabascan language family, are part of the Na-Dené language superfamily. So too are the Athabascan languages of the Navajo and Apache peoples of the American Southwest. In many of these languages, including Navajo, *dené* is in fact the word for "human being" or "people." Despite their common linguistic ancestry, however, Indians in the vastly different environments of the Pacific Northwest and American Southwest have very different customs and practices.

| TIMELINE | Invite students to look at the timeline at the top of page 27.

Analyze Which native people were the first to occupy California? (The Miwok) **HAS.CS.1**

Analyze the Source

Inspect Have students read about the landscapes of the Pacific Northwest and California on pages 26–27. Use the questions below to check comprehension.

Find Evidence Use the questions below to check comprehension. Remind students to support their answers with text evidence.

Identify What type of environment is associated with southern California? (desert) **DOK 1**

Compare and Contrast Based on the information in the text, which part of the Pacific Northwest probably has the most snow? (Alaska) **DOK 1**

Infer What detail in the text shows that the coastal regions of Oregon and Washington are NOT arid, or dry? (They have forests.) **DOK 2**

Identify Using the map, identify at least three Indian groups in California. (Pomo, Miwok, Yokuts) **DOK 2**

Explain According to the text, what caused the American Indians of California and the Pacific Northwest to develop different ways of life? (different natural environments) **DOK 2**

Analyze What common element shows that the Tlingit people of the Pacific Northwest are related to the Navajo and Apache of the Southwest? (language) **DOK 2**

Make Connections

Speculate What skills would you expect to find among the American Indians of the Pacific Northwest that you would not expect to find among the American Indians of southern California? (Possible answers include making wooden canoes, carving and other woodworking, and forestry skills such as taking down tall trees.) **DOK 3**

How Are the California and Pacific Northwest Peoples Shaped by Their Surroundings?

Lesson 3

Timeline

100 B.C.
Inuit settle the Arctic.

circa A.D. 1700
Tlingit people govern a large territory in the Pacific Northwest.

A.D. 1855
Chief Seattle and other Pacific Northwest Indian chiefs sign the Port Elliott Treaty, granting their land to the U.S. government.

100 B.C. A.D. 1 | | | | | | | 1700   1800 | | | | |

A.D. 1
Miwok begin occupying lowlands of California.

A Variety of Landscapes

American Indians settled in a number of vastly different natural environments in the American West. American Indians established settlements in the snowy Arctic regions of Alaska, the forested coasts of Oregon and Washington, and the arid deserts of southern California. Surviving in each of these climates required very specific skills, and, as a result, American Indians across the American West developed unique ways of life.

Ancestors of the Navajo and Apache people may have reached the Pacific Northwest about 5000 B.C. Eventually, some of the ancestors of these people migrated south, but others remained in the region. The Tlingit people belong to the same language family as the Navajo and Apache—meaning the groups share a common ancestor—but their surroundings have caused them to develop a very different way of life.

Hand-woven baskets were an important tool in Pomo life.

The Pacific Northwest and California were home to many groups of American Indians.

Inuit
Koyukon
Inuit
Ingalik
Tanana
Inuit
Tlingit
Haida
Tsimshian
Kwakiutl
Nootka
Makah
Chinook
Tillamook
Tolowa
Yurok
Hupa Medoc Shoshone
Yuki Nisenan Shoshone Cheyenne
Pomo Shoshone
Miwok Washo Paiute
Yokuts
Chumash Mojave
Cahuilla
Luiseño Kumeyaay

0   300   600 miles
0   300   600 kilometers

American Indians of Alaska
American Indians of the West

HSS.5.1.1, HSS.5.1.2, HSS.5.1.3, HAS.CS.5

26   Lesson 3   How Are the California and Pacific Northwest Peoples Shaped by Their Surroundings?

Lesson 3   **27**

Research Companion, pp. 26–27

ⒺⓁ ENGLISH LEARNERS SCAFFOLD

ELD.PII.5.4 Using nouns and noun phrases

Emerging

Develop Language As students read the text, help them use context clues to determine the meaning of unfamiliar modifiers. For example, note that *arid* modifies or describes *deserts*, which have very little rainfall, so *arid* may mean "dry." *Vastly* modifies *different* in the phrase "vastly different natural environments," and the next sentences give examples of greatly different environments, so *vastly probably* means "greatly."

Expanding and Bridging

Make Predictions Have students speculate about the ways in which life would be different for the Americans Indians living in the different environments mentioned in the opening paragraph—snowy Arctic, forested coasts, and arid deserts. Ask students to consider which of the three environments would probably present the most problems for people trying to meet their basic needs of food, clothing, and shelter.

See the **Language Learner Teaching Guide** for more language support strategies.

Monitor and Differentiate

REACHING ALL LEARNERS

Approaching Level

Go over the timeline with students. Explain that the Arctic is the most northern part of the Earth, north of what is called the Arctic Circle. Elicit or explain that the Inuit, Miwok, and Tlingit are different native peoples, and help students pronounce each name. Clarify that *circa* means "around" or "about" and is used when a precise date is not known.

Beyond Level

Encourage students to do additional research about American Indian peoples in the Pacific Northwest and California in order to find more important events to add to the timeline. Have them share their additions in a new timeline that they post online or in the classroom.

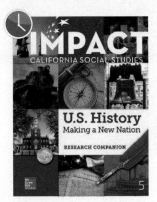

Research Companion
pp. 28–29

STANDARDS

Describe how geography and climate influenced the way various nations lived and adjusted to the natural environment, including locations of villages, the distinct structures that they built, and how they obtained food, clothing, tools, and utensils. **HSS.5.1.1**

Describe the varied customs and folklore traditions of American Indians. **HSS.5.1.2**

Students differentiate between primary and secondary sources. **HAS.HR.1**

Engage effectively in a range of collaborative discussions (one-on-one, in groups, and teacher-led) with diverse partners on *grade 5 topics and texts*, building on others' ideas and expressing their own clearly. **CCSS.ELA.SL.5.1**

Go Digital!

Investigate the lesson content with online whole-class presentation tools.

Background Information

American Indian groups in California display great linguistic diversity. But while the Karok, Hupa, and Yurok are remarkably similar in their ceremonies and other practices, their languages come from California, other areas of the Pacific Northwest, and the Northeastern United States, respectively.

Analyze the Source

Inspect Have students read about the American Indians of California on pages 28–29.

Find Evidence Use the questions below to check comprehension. Remind students to support their answers with text evidence.

Identify For what craft are the Pomo Indians famous? (basket weaving) **DOK 1**

Explain Why are the six regions of American Indians in California called cultural regions? (The peoples of each region share many cultural practices.) **DOK 1**

Analyze What details about the Pomo show that they lived near water? (They fished with nets and traps, and they decorated their baskets with shells.) **DOK 2**

Compare and Contrast In what way is the land of the Pomo and Miwok like that of the groups of the Pacific Northwest that you read about at the beginning of the lesson? (It has forests.) **DOK 2**

Make Connections

Speculate Of the Pomo, the Miwok, and the Serrano, which group probably had the most problems in obtaining food? Why? (the Serrano; because they live in a desert) **DOK 3**

Map Skills

Help students mark off the edge of a piece of paper to match that of the map scale and then use it to measure each area. They should recognize that the largest area is about 20 times bigger than the smallest. (largest: central; smallest: Colorado River)

Analyze the Primary Source Have students read the passage from the Miwok legend, or read it aloud to them.

Identify What does the passage show about the Miwok relationship with nature? (The details show a strong and careful observation of nature.) **DOK 1**

COLLABORATE
Stop and Check

Think Encourage students to think about natural resources that were available to both groups. (The Miwok lived in marshes, where the ground was already wet, or rain came often.)

Find Details Explain to students that after they read and take notes, they should review and think about how the facts and details will help them answer the Essential Question.

American Indians of California

The American Indians of California can be divided into at least six distinct cultural regions—Northwestern, Northeastern, Central, Great Basin, Southern, and Colorado River. Groups in each area share cultural similarities. Some of the peoples living in the Central region, for instance, speak similar languages.

The location of each group directly affects their culture and way of life. The Cahuilla, for example, built irrigation systems to raise crops in the desert basins in the south, while the Yurok, living along the northern coast, fished for most of their food.

American Indian Groups of California

 Map Skills Working with a partner, determine which of California's American Indian cultural areas was the largest and which was the smallest. Using the scale, measure the lengths of both the largest and smallest cultural areas from north to south.

The Pomo are part of the Central California cultural area. Before encountering Europeans, the Pomo thrived by making use of the plentiful natural resources available in their region. The Pomo collected acorns, fished with nets and traps, and hunted deer, birds, and other small game. Roundhouses made from wood, earth, and grass functioned as homes and gathering places.

Basket weaving played a large role in Pomo life and traditions. Pomo baskets, often decorated with feathers and shells, are well known around the world for quality among art collectors. Baskets served a purpose in a number of aspects of Pomo life, including cooking and childcare. Museums collect Pomo baskets as valuable works of art.

Farther to the south, in the Central Valley, pre-Columbian groups including the Miwok built their cultures around the region's resources. In the valley, Miwok hunters stalked deer, elk, and antelope. In the marshes, they set traps for otters and beavers.

Forests may have been the most pivotal source of the Miwok way of life. Oak trees provided the Miwok with their staple product, the acorn. Children would shake loose acorns from the oaks' upper branches, while women collected the fallen acorns in large baskets. The Miwok women ground the acorns into flour to make bread, biscuits, and soup.

Southern California's deserts do not have this same wealth of resources. There, groups such as the Cahuilla (kuh WEE uh), the Serrano, and the Chemehuevi (cheh mih HWEY vee) adapted to use the few plants that grow in the desert. The Cahuilla also developed irrigation systems to raise crops including corn, squash, beans, and melons. By digging ditches to feed into small lakes, the Cahuilla made use of the limited precipitation to sustain a vibrant culture.

PRIMARY SOURCE

How the World Grew... Miwok Legend

In the beginning the world was rock. Every year the rains came and fell on the rock and washed off a little; this made earth. By and by plants grew on the earth and their leaves fell and made more earth. Then pine trees grew and their needles and cones fell every year and with the other leaves and bark made more earth and covered more of the rock.

If you look closely at the ground in the woods you will see how the top is leaves and bark and pine needles and cones, and how a little below the top these are matted together, and a little deeper are rotting and breaking up into earth. This is the way the world grew—and it is growing still.

— translation of a Northern Miwok legend by C. Hart Merriam, published in 1910

Merriam, C. Hart, ed. The Dawn of the World. Cleveland: The Arthur H. Clark Company, 1910.

 Stop and Check

Talk Why are the Miwok not known for building irrigation systems like the Cahuilla?

Find Details As you read, add additional information to your graphic organizer on page 27 in your Inquiry Journal.

28 Lesson 3 How Are the California and Pacific Northwest Peoples Shaped by Their Surroundings?

Lesson 3 29

Research Companion, pp. 28–29

(EL) ENGLISH LEARNERS SCAFFOLD

ELD.PI.5.12 Selecting and applying varied and precise vocabulary and language structures to effectively convey ideas

Emerging	Expanding	Bridging
Develop Domain-Specific Vocabulary Remind student that *pre-Columbian* refers to the period of American history before the arrival of Christopher Columbus and other Europeans. Help students with other domain-specific language in the text, such as *natural resources, staple product,* and *irrigation.*	**Write** Have students show their mastery of domain-specific vocabulary by writing their own sentences for such terms as *pre-Columbian, natural resources, staple product,* and *irrigation.* Students should discuss with a partner whether they have used the terms correctly.	**Research** Have students do research to expand their knowledge of domain-specific vocabulary. For example, they might investigate other staple products—such as corn, wheat, or rice—among different cultural groups.

See the **Language Learner Teaching Guide** for more language support strategies.

Monitor and Differentiate

REACHING ALL LEARNERS

Special Needs

Encourage students to use the map to understand where the different cultural regions of California Indians were located.

On Level

Have students compare the map with a map of present-day California and identify cities in the same area as each of the six cultural regions.

Beyond Level

Have students compare the map on page 27 with the map on page 29. Ask them to consider which of the cultural regions of California Indians probably has the most in common with the Pacific Northwest, and have them explain their answer.

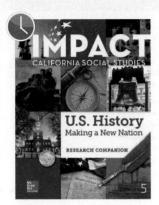

Research Companion
pp. 30–31

 STANDARDS

Describe how geography and climate influenced the way various nations lived and adjusted to the natural environment, including locations of villages, the distinct structures that they built, and how they obtained food, clothing, tools, and utensils. **HSS.5.1.1**

Describe the varied customs and folklore traditions of Native Americans. **HSS.5.1.2**

___

Go Digital!

Investigate the lesson content with online whole-class presentation tools.

Background Information

The Suquamish and Duwamish are Puget Sound Salish Indians, speaking a language in the Salish family known as Lushootseed. Chief Seattle was chief of the Suquamish and Duwamish. Seattle is often credited with a famous speech about preserving the environment. Most scholars believe that the text of that speech was heavily edited when first written and has changed even more over the years. Nevertheless, the sentiments it expresses are important to Pacific Northwest peoples.

Analyze the Source

Inspect Have students read about the American Indians of the Pacific Northwest on pp. 30–31.

Find Evidence Use the questions below to check comprehension. Remind students to support their answers with text evidence.

Identify For whom is the city of Seattle, Washington, named? (Chief Seattle, leader of the Suquamish and Duwamish people) **DOK 1**

Define What is a totem pole? (a pole that has been carved into a series of vertical symbols, or totems, that usually tell a story) **DOK 1**

Consider Location Remind students of the map of the Pacific Northwest that appears on p. 27. Ask them to identify, based on that map and the information in this section of the text, the two things that the Tlingit lived near that were most important to their way of life. (ocean and forests) **DOK 2**

Point of View Do you think you might want to host a potlatch? Why or why not? (Responses will vary, but some students may say that they would enjoy the respect they could earn, the pleasure of being generous, or the opportunity to rid themselves of the clutter of too many possessions.) **DOK 2**

Speculate Why might Chief Seattle have decided to give over his people's land? (Responses will vary, but some students may say that he believed in peace or that he realized fighting was useless and would result only in greater land loss.) **DOK 3**

Make Connections

Analyze What are two specific examples from the text that show the importance that American Indians of the Pacific Northwest placed on preserving the environment? (In using trees, they were careful to cut down only as many trees as they needed. In hunting whales, the Makah used every part of each whale they killed.) **DOK 3**

Stop and Check

Write Have students list the items made of wood and then discuss their ideas about an equally important material of today. (Students should list homes, canoes, masks, dishes, spoons, and other household items. They may identify materials such as plastic and metal.)

American Indians of the Pacific Northwest

Native peoples of this region reside in communities along the Pacific Coast from what is now British Columbia to northern California. The ocean supplies seafood and plants for the groups of American Indians living in the Pacific Northwest.

Long ago, wood from the area's forests allowed these people to construct homes, carve canoes and masks, and fashion household items including dishes and spoons. The Pacific Northwest peoples believed that all living things, including plants and animals, had rights that should be respected. They were careful to cut down only as many trees as they needed to continue their way of life.

Did You Know?

Chief Seattle (circa 1790–1866) was the leader of the Suquamish and Duwamish people who lived in what is now northwestern Washington state. Seattle wanted to work with European settlers to coexist with the groups of American Indians living in the area. In 1855, Seattle agreed to give over his people's land to the U.S. government and move to a reservation. When groups of American Indians tried to take back their land by force, Chief Seattle protected the Europeans. The settlers later named their new city after him.

Chief Seattle

Pacific Northwest groups such as the Tlingit carved **totem poles** as a way of chronicling their family histories. Totem poles are made from long logs that are carved and decorated to represent people or animals. Each totem pole is made up of a series of these symbols, called totems. The totems and their order often reflect the stories of the family.

These families often mark major life events, such as a wedding or a change of leader, with a ceremony known as a **potlatch**. At a potlatch, guests of the family receive gifts and enjoy feasting and music. The host is responsible for gift giving and sometimes can offer more than a hundred presents at a single potlatch. The host receives respect and standing among the community as a result of his or her generosity. Pacific Northwest peoples still hold potlatches today, and they are an important source of cultural identity for many people who live in the region.

The Makah people made their home on the shores of the Pacific Ocean and the Strait of Juan de Fuca. Though the Makah hunted many kinds of sea animals, including seals, porpoises, and sea otters, whale hunting held a special place in Makah life.

Makah canoes carrying as many as sixty hunters at a time would set out in search of whales. After a successful hunt, the Makah gave thanks for their triumph. Every part of a whale was used in different Makah activities.

A modern-day potlatch ceremony

Harris/Alamy Stock Photo

✓ Stop and Check

Write Reread the text and make a list of all of the ways that American Indians of the Pacific Northwest used wood. Is there a material that is as important to Americans today as wood was to these groups of American Indians?

Research Companion, pp. 30–31

(EL) ENGLISH LEARNERS SCAFFOLD

ELD.PI.5.11 Supporting own opinions and evaluating others' opinions in speaking and writing

Emerging	Expanding	Bridging
State Opinions Have students explain how they would feel about participating in a potlatch. Would they prefer to be a host or a guest? Why?	**Evaluate** Ask students their opinion of the view of the environment held by many American Indians of the Pacific Northwest. Encourage them to give reasons and examples to support their opinions.	**Collaborate** Have students discuss in small groups their views of Chief Seattle's decisions mentioned in the text. Remind them to use evidence to support their own ideas and to refute those of classmates with which they disagree.

See the **Language Learner Teaching Guide** for more language support strategies.

Monitor and Differentiate

REACHING ALL LEARNERS

Approaching Level

Offer students simpler synonyms for some of the more difficult vocabulary in text, such as *live* for *reside*, *build* for *construct*, *live together* for *coexist*, and *writing about* for *chronicling*.

On Level

Have students look up the meanings of multiple-meaning words used in the text, such as *fashion* ("to fashion household items") and *standing* ("the host receives respect and standing"). Ask them to use context clues to figure out which meaning of the word applies.

Research Companion
pp. 32–33

 STANDARDS

Describe the varied customs and folklore traditions of Native Americans. **HSS.5.1.2**

Students explain how the present is connected to the past, identifying both similarities and differences between the two, and how some things change over time and some things stay the same. **HAS.CS.3**

Go Digital!

Investigate the lesson content with online whole-class presentation tools.

Background Information

In the late nineteenth and early twentieth centuries, American Indian traditions were on the decline, often repressed by U.S. government laws and practices that encouraged assimilation. The middle of the twentieth century, however, saw an upsurge of interest in those traditions, coming from outside scholars and artists as well as the American Indian communities themselves. The revival of totem poles that began in the 1950s was part of that broader revival of American Indian traditions.

Analyze the Feature

Inspect Have students read about the comparison of past and present Pacific Northwest Indians on pp. 32–33.

Find Evidence Use the questions below to check comprehension. Remind students to support their answers with text evidence.

Explain According to the text, what must a person have to fully understand a totem pole? (deep cultural knowledge) **DOK 1**

Identify When in the twentieth century was the art of totem pole carving revived? (around 1950) **DOK 1**

Explain By what method did Pacific Northwest peoples learn to "read" totem poles? (oral tradition, in which the stories behind the totem poles were passed down from one generation to the next) **DOK 2**

Analyze What two main types of artistic skills are employed to create a totem pole? (carving and painting) **DOK 2**

Speculate Why do you think Europeans in the 1700s recorded seeing totem poles when they first came to the Pacific Northwest? (Answers may vary, but students should recognize that the totem poles were impressive.) **DOK 2**

Make Connections

Describe Compare and contrast the images of the traditional totem and modern totem poles. How are modern totem poles different from those of past centuries? (Responses will vary, but students may include that modern totem poles use several different styles of carving.) **DOK 3**

Then and Now: Totem Poles of the Pacific Northwest

Then

Historians can only speculate when the first totem poles were erected. Europeans recorded seeing them in the 1700s, when they first landed on the coast of the Pacific Northwest. Though immediately impressive in their size and detail, totem poles can be fully understood only with a deep knowledge of the culture that built them. The order of a pole's totems tells a story. The only way to read the pole is to first know the story. Each generation of Pacific Northwest people passed down the stories expressed in totem poles to the younger generation.

A traditional totem pole

Now

At the start of the twentieth century, very few American Indians still practiced the art of totem-pole making. In about 1950, however, more Indians began to learn the traditional methods of carving and painting the poles. Totem poles today can be found in their traditional place in front of houses of gathering and celebration for Indian communities. Modern totem-pole carvers tend to combine many different styles and methods of carving on the same pole.

A totem pole designed in a more modern art style

32 Lesson 3 How Are the California and Pacific Northwest Peoples Shaped by Their Surroundings?

Lesson 3 33

Research Companion, pp. 32–33

 ## ENGLISH LEARNERS SCAFFOLD

ELD.PI.5.7 Evaluating how well writers and speakers use language to support ideas and opinions with details or reasons depending on modality, text type, purpose, audience, topic, and content area

Emerging

Chronology Use a chart or another visual aid to help students understand the terminology used for centuries. Explain that the 1700s, mentioned in the text, can also be called the eighteenth century, and that the twentieth century, mentioned in the text, can also be called the 1900s.

Expanding and Bridging

Discuss Lead a class discussion on the ways in which monuments and other works of art from the past can be dated. Explain that art can often be dated from its style. Sometimes the material that is used can give some idea of the timing; for example, works made of bronze cannot have been created before the ability to make bronze was introduced.

See the **Language Learner Teaching Guide** for more language support strategies.

Monitor and Differentiate

REACHING ALL LEARNERS

Approaching Level

To help students discuss totem poles then and now, provide sentence frame with signal words for comparison and contrast. For example, **Both traditional totem poles and modern totem poles show _____. While early totem poles usually used _____, modern totem poles tend to use _____.**

On Level

Have students work in pairs, discussing the similarities and differences between traditional and modern totem poles. Remind them to cite details from the text and from the images to support their observations.

3 REPORT

Report Your Findings

Inquiry Journal
pp. 28–29

IMPACT
CALIFORNIA
SOCIAL STUDIES

U.S. History
Making a New Nation

INQUIRY JOURNAL

5

(HSS) STANDARDS

Describe how geography and climate influenced the way various nations lived and adjusted to the natural environment, including locations of villages, the distinct structures that they built, and how they obtained food, clothing, tools, and utensils. **HSS.5.1.1**

Describe the varied customs and folklore traditions of Native Americans. **HSS.5.1.2**

(CCSS) Explain the relationships or interactions between two or more individuals, events, ideas, or concepts in a historical, scientific, or technical text based on specific information in the text. **CCSS.ELA.RI.5.3**

Write opinion pieces on topics or texts, supporting a point of view with reasons and information. **CCSS.ELA.W.5.1**

Go Digital!

• Students can go online to report their findings. Assess their responses online.

• Students can access the online graphic organizer to capture ideas from their investigation.

Think About It

Students will review their research and consider the effect of plentiful resources on California and Pacific Northwest Indian cultures. Remind them to review the information on their graphic organizer. Direct them back to pages 26–33 of their Research Companion if they need more information.

Write About It

Take a Stand Read the Write About It prompt aloud to students. Remind them that they should have compared and contrasted three groups, including the Tlingit, in their graphic organizer, and tell them to choose two of those groups for this assignment. Remind students to use details from the graphic organizer as evidence in their response. Offer these guidelines for writing the response:

• Introduce the two groups.

• Describe key details about the artifacts and housing of each group.

• Draw a strong conclusion about which group best handles its surroundings.

• Use text evidence and logical reasons to support this conclusion.

• Use chapter vocabulary as appropriate.

• Include page references when citing text evidence.

Use the rubric on p. T72 to evaluate students' work.

Talk About It

Defend Your Claim Tell students to review what they learned in Lesson 2 about Southwestern groups who live in the desert. Encourage them to create a Venn diagram with two interlocking circles to compare and contrast details about the desert groups' ways of life and that of the groups in the temperate rainforests of the Pacific Northwest. Then help students form small groups for their discussion. Tell them to use the details they gathered in their new Venn diagrams as evidence to support their ideas about each group. Explain that students should take turns comparing and contrasting the two groups and listen respectfully when other group members talk.

Connect to the Essential Question

Read the prompt aloud to students. Work with them to list elements of the environment that seem to benefit the American Indians of California and the Pacific Northwest—coastal location, ample rainfall, nearby food sources, nearby forests, and so on. Elicit that one or more of these factors also help determine the locations of major cities throughout the world—for example, coastal location is important to San Francisco, New York, Hong Kong, Shanghai, Tokyo, Mumbai, Amsterdam, and Rio de Janeiro, and many other cities. Have students pull this information together to make statements about environmental factors that determine where large cities have been settled and why they have grown.

Report / Your Findings

Think About It

Based on your research, what effect did plentiful resources have on the culture of American Indians in California and the Pacific Northwest?

Write About It

Take a Stand

Write and Cite Evidence Compare the artifacts and housing of two American Indian groups discussed in this lesson. In one paragraph, write an opinion about which group you think was best equipped to handle its surroundings and why.

Student paragraphs should identify one of two native peoples as being best equipped for its surrounding and provide text evidence to support the claim.

Talk About It

Defend Your Claim

In small groups, compare and contrast the American Indians you learned about this week with the groups from the Southwest deserts in Lesson 2. How does life in a desert and life in the Pacific Northwest affect culture?

 Geography

Connect to the EQ

Pull It Together

Think about what you have learned about the American Indians of California and the Pacific Northwest. Consider the locations of major cities throughout the world. Explain why people tend to gather in certain areas using what you know about how American Indians of California and the Pacific Northwest were affected by their surroundings.

California Indians needed irrigation to farm their dry land; Pacific Northwest Indians made use of wood from forests and hunted in the oceans.

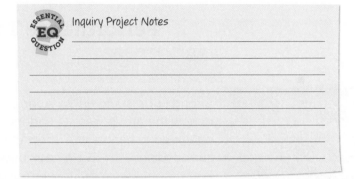

Inquiry Project Notes

28 Lesson 3 How Are the California and Pacific Northwest Peoples Shaped by Their Surroundings?

Lesson 3 29

Inquiry Journal, pp. 28–29

(EL) ENGLISH LEARNERS SCAFFOLD

ELD.PI.5.4 Adapting language choices to various contexts (based on task, purpose, audience, and text type)

Emerging	Expanding	Bridging
Develop Vocabulary Help students understand unfamiliar words in the directions, such as *plentiful* (in large amounts), *artifacts* (any objects made by humans), and *equipped* (able). Clarify that a temperate rainforest is a region with a mild climate.	**Cite Evidence** Have students share ideas about details they might use as evidence to complete each of the four assignments.	**Extend** As students work on the Connect to the Essential Question assignment, have them consider how new technology might change city settlement patterns. As an example, mention or elicit that air conditioning has made settlement in hot locations more attractive.

See the **Language Learner Teaching Guide** for more language support strategies.

Monitor and Differentiate

REACHING ALL LEARNERS

Approaching Level

Help students with signal words and phrases (*because, since, as a result,* etc.) when they discuss causes and effects of the activities. Also remind them of signal words to use for their comparisons and contrasts as they write, such as *similarly, too, although, in contrast,* and so on.

Beyond Level

Encourage students to do additional research for more evidence they can use to complete the four assignments. In particular, they might research settlement patterns of world cities to find evidence.

Know what your students know!

Lesson Task
Report Your Findings

Use this rubric to evaluate students' response.

Compare and Contrast Students compare the artifacts and housing of two American Indian groups discussed in this lesson. In one paragraph, they write an opinion about which group they think was best equipped to handle its surroundings and why.

Compare Your Groups Students work in small groups to compare and contrast the American Indian groups in this lesson with those in Lesson 2. They discuss how life in a desert and life in a temperate rainforest affect culture.

Performance Task Evaluation Rubric

	4	3	2	1
Historical Understanding	Strong understanding of how the group was equipped to handle its surroundings	Adequate understanding of how the group was equipped to handle its surroundings	Uneven understanding of how the group was equipped to handle its surroundings	No understanding of how the group was equipped to handle its surroundings
Take a Stand	Clearly states opinions and provides reasons	Adequately states opinions and provides some reasons	Somewhat clear or unclear opinion and reasons	No opinion stated or student does not show understanding of the task
Support with Evidence	Reasons contain thorough evidence	Reasons contain adequate evidence	Reasons contain uneven evidence	Reasons are missing or contain no supporting evidence
Defend Your Claim	Carefully compares and contrasts details Speaks in complete sentences throughout the discussion	Adequately compares and contrasts details Speaks in complete sentences through most of the discussion	Inconsistently compares and contrasts details Mixes complete and incomplete sentences	Does not compare or contrast details Does not use complete sentences

Lesson Assessment

Go Digital!

- Have students complete the Chapter 1 Lesson 3 Assessment online to monitor their understanding of the lesson content.

California Smarter Balanced Assessment Connections!

Standards Covered	Lesson Task	Lesson Assessment	Alignment with California Smarter Balanced Assessment
History Social Science Content 5.1.1; 5.1.2; 5.1.3	✔	✔	Claim 1 Targets 8, 9, 10
History Social Science Analysis Skills Chronological and Spatial Thinking 5.1; 5.3; 5.5 Research, Evidence, Point of View 5.2	✔	✔	Claim 1 Targets 11, 12
Writing W.5.1	✔	✔	Claim 2 Target 6b
Research and Inquiry W.5.9	✔	✔	Claim 4 Targets 2, 3, 4, 7
Reading RI.5.3; RI.5.7	✔	✔	Claim 1 Targets 8, 11
Speaking and Listening SL.5.1; SL.5.4	✔		Claim 3 Target 3

How Did the Great Plains Influence the Traditions of the People Living There?

Background Information

Explain to students that the term *Great Plains* refers to a large expanse of land east of the Rocky Mountains in the United States and southern Canada. In this lesson, students will learn how environmental features of that area shaped the lives of the American Indians living there.

Community Connections

To enrich what students have learned about Plains peoples, have them visit the website of a museum. Students can use the search words *Plains American Indian museum* to find an appropriate website.

LESSON STANDARDS

✓ Describe how geography and climate influenced the way various nations lived and adjusted to the natural environment, including locations of villages, the distinct structures that they built, and how they obtained food, clothing, tools, and utensils. **HSS.5.1.1**

✓ Describe their varied customs and folklore traditions. **HSS.5.1.2**

✓ Explain their varied economies and systems of government. **HSS.5.1.3**

✓ Students use map and globe skills to determine the absolute locations of places and interpret information available through a map's or globe's legend, scale, and symbolic representation. **HAS.CS.4**

✓ Students identify the human and physical characteristics of the places they are studying and explain how those features form the unique character of those places. **HAS.HI.2**

Connect to the
Essential Question

The **Weekly Explorer Magazine** supports students' exploration of the Essential Question and provides additional resources for the EQ Inquiry Project.

Chapter 1, pp. 2–13

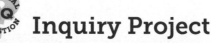
Inquiry Project

What was life like in America before Columbus?

Remind students to use the information they learn in this lesson and other resources to complete their EQ Inquiry Project!

Dinah Zike's

In this lesson you will use Foldables.

When Minutes Count!

Suggested Lesson Pacing

1 ENGAGE
One Day

2 INVESTIGATE
Two to Three Days

🕐 **Short on Time?** Look for the clock to teach core content in less time.

3 REPORT
One Day

- Lesson Opener
- Analyze the Source
- Inquiry Tools

Go Digital

- **Video:** Native Americans of the Great Plains
- **iMap:** Native Americans of the Great Plains, 1700s

- Grass and Sky for Miles
- Peoples of the Plains
- Life on the Plains

- Think About It
- Compare and Contrast
- Explain Your Thinking

Make Connections!

(CCSS) CONNECT TO ELA

Reading

Quote accurately from a text when explaining what the text says explicitly and when drawing inferences from the text. **RI.5.1**

Explain the relationship or interactions between two or more individuals, events, ideas, or concepts in a historical, scientific, or technical text based on specific information in the text. **RI.5.3**

Research

Conduct short research projects that use several sources to build knowledge through investigation of different aspects of a topic. **W.5.7**

Writing

Write informative/explanatory texts to examine a topic and convey ideas and information clearly. **W.5.2**

Draw evidence from literary or informational texts to support analysis, reflection, and research. **W.5.9**

Speaking and Listening

Engage effectively in a range of collaborative discussions (one-on-one, in groups, and teacher-led) with diverse partners on grade 5 topics and texts, building on others' ideas and expressing their own clearly.. **SL.5.1**

Classroom Resources

 Search for additional resources using the following key words.

bison

buffalo

Cheyenne

Crow

Great Plains

Kiowa

Lakota

Pawnee

Plains Indians

Sioux

winter count

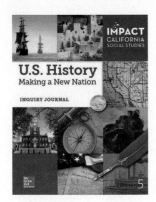

Inquiry Journal,
pp. 30–31

 STANDARDS

Describe how geography and climate influenced the way various nations lived and adjusted to the natural environment, including locations of villages, the distinct structures that they built, and how they obtained food, clothing, tools, and utensils. **HSS.5.1.1**

CCSS Summarize a written text read aloud or information presented in diverse media formats, including visually, quantitatively, and orally. **CCSS.ELA.SL.5.2**

Go Digital!

Explore the lesson content with online whole-class presentation tools.

- **Video:** Native Americans of the Great Plains
- **iMap:** Native Americans of the Great Plains, 1700s

How Did the Great Plains Influence the Traditions of the People Living There?

Bellringer COLLABORATE

Prompt students to retrieve information from the previous lesson. Ask: *How did American Indians' locations help determine what they hunted and gathered?* (Living near the ocean, they hunted whales and other seafood. Living near forests, they not only hunted and fished but also gathered plant products like acorns, which they ground into flour.)

Lesson Outcomes

What Am I Learning? Have students read the Lesson Question on p. 30.

Why Am I Learning It? Be sure students understand that *traditions* are long-time practices that are part of a people's culture. Ask students to use the word in a sentence that names a tradition in their home, school, or neighborhood.

How Will I Know That I Learned It? Ask students the following questions:

- What will you be able to identify? (the relationship between where Great Plains groups lived and their traditions and ways of life)
- What is the purpose of the task? (to explain information)
- How will you support your analysis? (with evidence from the text)

Talk About It COLLABORATE

Analyze the Image Explain that students will better understand art if they analyze it, or examine its parts and interpret what they show or mean. Guide students to look at all the parts of the art, read the caption, and answer the questions in the text.

- *The image shows Indians who are _____.*
- *For these Indians, buffalo probably _____ .)*

Collaborative Conversations COLLABORATE

Add New Ideas As students engage in partner, small group, and whole-class discussions, encourage them to

- Stay on topic.
- Connect their own ideas to things their peers have said.
- Look for ways to connect their personal experiences or prior knowledge to the conversation.

Lesson 4

How Did the Great Plains Influence the Traditions of the People Living There?

Lesson Outcomes

What Am I Learning?
In this lesson, you're going to use your investigative skills to explore the traditions of the native peoples of the Great Plains.

Why Am I Learning It?
Reading and talking about where and how the people of the Great Plains lived will help you understand their traditions and ways of life.

How Will I Know That I Learned It?
You will be able to compare and contrast the roles of men and women in Great Plains groups to explain their traditions and ways of life.

Talk About It
COLLABORATE

Look at the Details What does the painting show? What role do you think the buffalo played in the lives of the Great Plains people?

The people of the Plains depended on buffalo, more accurately called bison. Once horses came to the Americas, Plains hunters could move as fast as the buffalo could run.

HSS.5.1.1, HSS.5.1.2, HSS.5.1.3, HAS.HI.2

McGraw-Hill Education

Yale University Art Gallery

30 Lesson 4   How Did the Great Plains Influence the Traditions of the People Living There?

Lesson 4   31

Inquiry Journal, pp. 30–31

EL ENGLISH LEARNERS SCAFFOLD

ELD.PI.5.6 Reading closely literary and informational texts and viewing multimedia to determine how meaning is conveyed explicitly and implicitly through language

Emerging	Expanding	Bridging
Identify Details Work with students individually to recognize and name details in the painting. Provide specific words as needed.	**Describe Details** Have students work with partners to create a list of words and phrases that describe the painting. Encourage them to consider what the person in the painting is thinking or feeling as well as what he is doing.	**Use Language** Encourage students to describe the cultural factors that the picture conveys about the American Indians it depicts.

See the **Language Learner Teaching Guide** for more language support strategies.

Monitor and Differentiate

REACHING ALL LEARNERS

Approaching Level

Work with students to use correct spatial terms to describe the painting. Have them complete sentence frames, such as *In the background, _____. On the left, _____.*

On Level

Have students discuss for what besides food Plains Indians may have used buffalo.

Beyond Level

Explain that horses were brought to the Americas by the Spanish in the 1500s, and have students speculate about how Plains Indians may have hunted buffalo before they had horses.

Lesson 4   **Lesson Outcomes**   T77

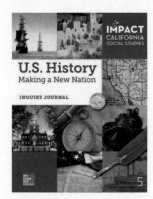

Inquiry Journal,
pp. 32–33

 STANDARDS

Describe how geography and climate influenced the way various nations lived and adjusted to the natural environment, including locations of villages, the distinct structures that they built, and how they obtained food, clothing, tools, and utensils. **HSS.5.1.1**

Describe their varied customs and folklore traditions. **HSS.5.1.2**

CCSS Come to discussions prepared, having read or studied required material; explicitly draw on that preparation and other information known about the topic to explore ideas under discussion. **CCSS.ELA.SL.5.1a**

Go Digital!

Model how to inspect and find evidence with online whole-class presentation tools.

Background Information

The Lakota The Lakota are one of several groups of Plains Indians collectively known as the Sioux. Once hunters and gatherers in the Great Lakes area, they moved west in part to escape their enemies and with the acquisition of horses became nomadic, following the buffalo herds they hunted. In the nineteenth century, the Sioux united under Lakota chief Sitting Bull to resist white encroachment but after initial success at the Battle of Little Big Horn were eventually defeated.

1 Inspect

Look Have students examine the image of the winter count and read the caption and text about it. Clarify that an *artifact* is an object that is made by human beings and shows something about the culture that produced it. Be sure students understand that a *spiral* begins at a center point and keeps curling around. Then have students read and discuss their answers to the questions in the text.

- Who made the artifact? (Lone Dog of the Lakota people)

- What is the artifact made of? (animal hide)

- How was the artifact used? (to keep track of passing years and record important events)

2 Find Evidence

Take Another Look Have students reexamine the winter count and the text about it and then respond to the questions in the text.

Analyze the Artifact

- How is the winter count organized? (in chronological order, starting with the center of the spiral)

- How does this organization help you understand the calendar? (You know to start in the center and count one year, or winter, for each pictograph.)

- Would you have wanted to serve as the keeper of the winter count? (Responses will vary, but students should recognize that the job was an important one.)

- Why was this an important job? (Students should recognize that the winter count was a tribal history recording major events. Some may say it is important to remember the past in order to learn from it.)

3 Make Connections COLLABORATE

Draw Encourage students to work with partners on their own "winter counts," counting weeks, not winters. Tell them to design a different pictograph, or picture symbol, to represent an important event in each past week and to speculate about likely events to represent through the end of the school year—tests, sports events, class projects, celebrations, and so on. (Responses will vary, but students should be able to support their use of symbols with reasons.)

Analyze the Source

Lakota Winter Count

1 Inspect

Look Examine the artifact on the next page. What can it tell you about the traditions of the Lakota people?

Discuss Talk about clues that answer these questions:

- Who made the artifact?
- What is the artifact made of?
- How was the artifact used?

My Notes

_____
_____
_____
_____
_____
_____
_____
_____
_____
_____
_____
_____
_____

The winter count shown on the next page is an illustrated calendar created by the Lakota people of the Great Plains. Each year, Lakota leaders met to discuss the memorable events of the year. A pictograph, or symbol, that describes the most memorable event was then painted on an animal hide. Leaders would name the year based on that event. In this way, the Lakota could reference events by the name of a year. A keeper, who served as the band's historian, kept the winter count safe, year after year. Keepers were usually men. Women tended to have other responsibilities, such as making clothing and constructing teepees.

The artifact is called a "winter count" because the Lakota measured years from the first snowfall of one winter to the first snowfall of the next. This winter count recalls events that occurred between 1800 and 1871. The pictographs appear chronologically, starting at the center of the spiral. Some of the images depict events related to food and hunting, while others show battles with or visits from Europeans. For example,

- The first image on this page shows that Europeans brought striped blankets to the Lakota people in 1853–1854.
- The second image, at the bottom left, shows that the Lakota had plenty of buffalo meat in 1845–1846.
- The third image shows that 30 Lakota were killed by Crow Indians in 1800–1801.

Winter Count by Lone Dog, 1801–1876

2 Find Evidence

Take Another Look How is the winter count organized? How does this organization help you understand the calendar?

3 Make Connections

Draw Work with a partner. Begin your own winter count that includes pictographs that show important events that have happened at your school over the past two or three weeks. Why did you include the events you did?

VCG Wilson/Fine Art/Corbis Historical/Getty Images

Inquiry Journal, pp. 32–33

(EL) ENGLISH LEARNERS SCAFFOLD

ELD.PI.5.6 Reading closely literary and informational texts and viewing multimedia to determine how meaning is conveyed explicitly and implicitly through language

Emerging

Understand Symbols Be sure students understand that a pictograph is a picture used as a symbol to represent, or mean, something. Go over the meaning of the three pictographs from the winter count that are discussed in the text.

Expanding

Explain Symbols Have students discuss the pictographs from the winter count, explaining how the images convey meaning.

Bridging

Expand Symbols Encourage students to describe the cultural information that the images on the winter count convey about the American Indians who created it.

See the **Language Learner Teaching Guide** for more language support strategies.

Monitor and Differentiate

REACHING ALL LEARNERS

Special Needs

Have students describe each of the pictographs that make up the winter count.

Approaching Level

To help them describe the winter count, offer students sentence frames, such as **At the center of the spiral is _____. The next pictograph shows _____.**

Beyond Level

Encourage students to find out more about the process for making winter counts. Students may report their findings in a series of sketches accompanying an oral or written report.

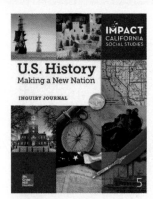

1 ENGAGE

Inquiry Journal,
pp. 34–35

 STANDARDS

Describe their varied customs and folklore traditions.
HSS.5.1.2

Explain the relationships or interactions between two or more individuals, events, ideas, or concepts in a historical, scientific, or technical text based on specific information in the text.
CCSS.ELA.RI.5.3

Draw evidence from literary or informational texts to support analysis, reflection, and research. **CCSS.ELA.W.5.9**

Go *Digital!*

- Model how to explore and investigate with online whole-class tools.

- Students can access the online graphic organizer to use the inquiry tools as they read.

Explore Compare and Contrast

Explain Clarify for students that to compare is to look for similarities; to contrast is to look for differences. Point out that students will often understand something better if they see how it is like and unlike other things.

Read Have students read aloud the step-by-step instructions about how to compare and contrast. Discuss graphic features that sometimes show comparisons and contrasts—charts, for example, and Venn diagrams like the ones in the previous lesson. Remind students to look for terms that signal similarities (such as *same, similarly, both, alike, also*) and differences (such as *but, although, however, unlike, in contrast*).

Guide Practice To help students understand the process, provide the following model for students: *I read in the text that men serve as keeper of the winter count, while women set up teepees. Those are some of the specific roles for men and for women. If I keep reading, I will find other examples of gender roles.*

Investigate!

Have students read pages 34–39 in the Research Companion. Tell them to look for information that will answer the lesson question *How did the Great Plains Influence the Traditions of the People Living There?*

Take Notes Tell students that they will take notes as they read each section. Remind them that taking notes will help them understand and remember the information they learn. Explain the importance of paraphrasing, or using their own words, when they take notes.

Inspect Guide students to read the text in each section to see what it says about the role of men and women. Encourage them to make note of words they don't understand and to look for answers to questions such as *who? what? when? where? why?* and *how?*

Find Evidence Encourage students to reread the text to find more points of comparison and contrast. Remind them that after they read and take notes, they should review and think about how the facts and details help them answer the lesson question.

Collaborative Conversations

Text-Based Discussion Remind students of the goals of discussing the text with others.

- to better understand what they read
- to ask for evidence from the text
- to understand someone else's point of view

Inquiry Tools

Explore Compare and Contrast

You can better understand the ideas in a text if you **compare and contrast** the details the author provides.

1. Read the text.
This will help you understand what the text is about.

2. Think about what the author wants you to know.
When you compare two things, you tell how they are the same. When you contrast things, you tell how they are different. Consider what the author wants you to know about similarities and differences between the roles of men, women, and children in Plains culture.

3. Reread and look for text features.
Authors often use text features when they want to call attention to the similarities and differences between ideas. Analyze text features, looking at headings, bulleted texts, and images.

4. Make notes in a chart.
You can use these notes later to help you remember what you read.

COLLABORATE Based on the text you have read so far, work with your class to fill in some information in the chart below.

Roles for Plains Men	Roles for Plains Women
Men serve as keeper of winter count.	Women set up teepees and make clothes.

IMPACT U.S. History Making a New Nation

Investigate!

Read pages 34–39 in your Research Companion. Use your investigative skills to look for text evidence that tells you about traditional roles for Great Plains men and women. This chart will help you organize your notes.

Roles for Plains Men	Roles for Plains Women
hunt animals	cook meals
fight in battles	clean hides
educate boys	educate girls
serve as keeper	grow crops

Inquiry Journal, pp. 34–35

(EL) ENGLISH LEARNERS SCAFFOLD

ELD.PI.5.11 Supporting own opinions and evaluating others' opinions in speaking and writing

Emerging

Organize Information
Work with students individually to identify details that go in each column of the chart. Help them put comparisons or contrasts involving the same categories of information (such as educating children) side by side.

Expanding

Ask and Answer Questions Have students work in pairs, identifying similarities and differences between men and women in Plains culture by taking turns posing and answering questions, such as *What did the men hunt? Who cooked the meals?*

Bridging

Interpret Information Ask students to consider what the division of labor shows about similarities and differences in lifestyle between the men and women of the Plains. For example, *Who was away from the teepee more? Who was more likely to develop or display skill in crafts?*

See the **Language Learner Teaching Guide** for more language support strategies.

Monitor and Differentiate

REACHING ALL LEARNERS

Approaching Level

To help students state comparisons and contrasts, offer sentences frames such as *Among Plains Indians, both men and women _____* or *While the men of the Plains _____, the women _____.*

Beyond Level

Encourage students to conduct online research to find out more about the roles of men and women in Plains Indian culture. Then, based on their research, have them add appropriate details to their charts women in Plains Indian culture. Then, based on their research, have them add appropriate detai

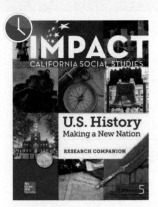

Research Companion
pp. 34–35

 STANDARDS

Describe how geography and climate influenced the way various nations lived and adjusted to the natural environment, including locations of villages, the distinct structures that they built, and how they obtained food, clothing, tools, and utensils. **HSS.5.1.1**

Students identify the human and physical characteristics of the places they are studying and explain how those features form the unique character of those places. **HAS.HI.2**

Quote accurately from a text when explaining what the text says explicitly and when drawing inferences from the text. **CCSS.ELA.RI.5.1**

Go Digital!

Investigate the lesson content with online whole-class presentation tools.

- **Video:** Native Americans of the Great Plains

- **iMap:** Native Americans of the Great Plains, 1700s

Background Information

The American Bison Like cattle and sheep, the American bison, or "buffalo," typically grazes on grass and other small plants, chewing its cud twice. In 1800, as many as 60 million roamed the Plains. It then became U.S. government policy to kill them off, mainly to destroy the Indian culture that depended on them. By 1900, less than 200 wild bison remained. Today, conservation efforts have increased their number to about 30,000, with the largest herd in Yellowstone National Park.

| TIMELINE | Invite students to look at the timeline on the top of p. 35.

> **Analyze** How many years after American Indians settled the plains did they begin to use horses? (about 200 years) **HAS.CS.1**

Analyze the Source

Inspect Have students read pages 34–35. Use the questions below to check comprehension.

Find Evidence Use the questions below to check comprehension. Remind students to support their answers with text evidence.

> **Describe** What two main forms of land are found in the Great Plains? (hills and flat, grassy stretches called *prairie*) **DOK 1**

> **Infer** The text says, "Except near rivers, it is difficult to grow crops in the Great Plains." What does this statement suggest about the reason growing crops is so difficult? (There is too little water and the soil is poor.) **DOK 3**

> **Explain** Why did Plains Indians develop a lifestyle in which they did not live in one place? (They could not live by farming so instead hunted buffalo, roaming from place to place, following the herds.) **DOK 2**

> **Identify** Technically, what is the correct term for the buffalo that roamed the Great Plains? (bison) **DOK 1**

> **Apply** During the 1800s, white settlers and the U.S. government killed off many of the buffalo on the Great Plains. What effect do you think this had on the Plains Indians? (It destroyed their way of life.) **DOK 2**

Make Connections

> **Analyze Images** Look at the picture of the buffalo, and think about what you have read about them. Why do you think Plains Indians had so much respect for these animals? (They were large and impressive, and they supplied many of the things that the Indians needed to live. Also, native peoples had great respect for the natural world in general.) **DOK 3**

> **Compare and Contrast** The text says that buffalo are "cattle-like" animals. In what way are they probably "cattle-like"? (They probably feed by grazing on grass, supply humans with food and other needs, and travel in groups.) **DOK 3**

How Did the Great Plains Influence the Traditions of the People Living There?

Lesson 4

| 1300 American Indians settle the Plains | 1500 Horses first come to North America. | 1600s The Lakota are pushed westward by competing tribes | **Timeline** |

1300 | | | 1400 | | | 1500 | | | 1600 | | | 1700

Buffalo were part of the spiritual practice of the Plains people. They prepared for each hunt with special ceremonies, and they believed they needed the support of the spirit for the hunt to be successful. Buffalo roamed from place to place, so many Plains people developed a lifestyle that allowed them to follow the herds.

Grass and Sky for Miles

The Great Plains region covers a huge area of land that spreads from Canada south to Texas, and from the Rocky Mountains east to North Dakota, South Dakota, Nebraska, Kansas, and Oklahoma. It is mainly made up of hills and flat, grassy stretches of land called **prairies**. Except near rivers, it is difficult to grow crops in the Great Plains. Most native peoples who lived there could not depend on farming for food. Instead, they followed and hunted the huge herds of buffalo that roamed the prairies. (These animals were first called "buffalo" by early American settlers. The name stuck, but these large, cattle-like animals are actually bison.)

Plains people depended on the buffalo for more than just food. Buffalo hides were used to make clothes and shelter. Plains people made ropes, bowls, needles, thread, and tools from other parts of the buffalo. In fact, they had a use for every part of the buffalo.

Buffalo on the Great Plains

HSS.5.1.1, HSS.5.1.2, HSS.5.1.3, HAS.HI.2

34 Lesson 4 How Did the Great Plains Influence the Traditions of the People Living There?

Lesson 4 **35**

Research Companion, pp. 34–35

ENGLISH LEARNERS SCAFFOLD

ELD.PII.5.4 Using nouns and noun phrases

Emerging	Expanding	Bridging
Use Context As students read the text, help them use context clues to determine the meanings of unfamiliar nouns. For example, *herds* are described as "huge," or very large, and are said to roam the prairie, so the context suggests that a herd is a large group of animals traveling together.	**Clarify Multiple-Meaning Words** Have students look up *crop* and *hide* in a dictionary and use context clues to determine which meaning applies in the text. (to farm plants; animal skins)	**Understand Origins** Have students investigate the origins of the word *prairie*. Then have them explain where it comes from and what its origin suggests about the history of the Great Plains.

See the **Language Learner Teaching Guide** for more language support strategies.

Monitor and Differentiate

REACHING ALL LEARNERS

Approaching Level

Review cause-and-effect relationships in the text: Because crops did not grow well on the Plains, Plains Indians hunted buffalo for food. Because buffalo roamed the prairie, Plains Indians followed the herds. Because they respected buffalo, Plains Indians held ceremonies before hunting them.

Beyond Level

Ask students to conduct research to find out why the buffalo, once so plentiful on the Great Plains, came to be so scarce.

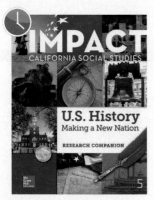

Research Companion
pp. 36–37

 STANDARDS

Describe how geography and climate influenced the way various nations lived and adjusted to the natural environment, including locations of villages, the distinct structures that they built, and how they obtained food, clothing, tools, and utensils. **HSS.5.1.1**

Describe their varied customs and folklore traditions. **HSS.5.1.2**

Explain their varied economies and systems of government. **HSS.5.1.3**

Students use map and globe skills to determine the absolute locations of places and interpret information available through a map's or globe's legend, scale, and symbolic representation. **HAS.CS.4**

Go Digital!

Investigate the lesson content with online whole-class presentation tools.

Analyze the Source

Inspect Have students read pages 36–37.

Find Evidence Use the questions below to check comprehension. Remind students to support their answers with text evidence.

Identify Besides the Sioux, what are four other native peoples who are considered Plains Indians? (Pawnee, Cheyenne, Crow, and Kiowa) **DOK 1**

Speculate What is another reason besides drought that could have led some Indians to move to the Plains? (warfare) **DOK 2**

Explain The text says that rivers provided fertile land for some Plains Indians to farm. How might rivers help make land fertile? (Water from the rivers can be used to irrigate the land, and floodwaters wash up nutrients, substances that help plants grow, into the soil.) **DOK 3**

Describe What is the difference between teepees and lodges? (Teepees are made of hide and are portable, or able to be moved; lodges are made of logs and are more permanent.) **DOK 2**

Make Connections

Analyze How do you think Plains Indians carried their teepees and poles when they traveled? (They probably carried them on a sled pulled by dogs or horses.) **DOK 3**

Map Skills

Project a larger version of the map on p. 36. Ask students these questions about it.

- Of the Lakota, Osage, and Mandan, which group is westernmost? (Mandan)

- What is one group of Plains Indians in present-day Oklahoma? (Seminole)

- Who is farther north, the Kiowa or the Crow? (Crow)

- In what present-day state are the Cheyenne? (Wyoming)

DID YOU KNOW?

Common Misconception Many people think that because the Spanish brought horses to the Americas, the horse was native to the Old World. In fact, fossil evidence shows that the modern horse evolved in the Americas. From there, horses probably crossed the Bering land bridge into Asia and beyond. Horses then became extinct in the Americas about 10,000 years ago. So the Spanish actually reintroduced them.

COLLABORATE

Stop and Check

Talk Have students read and answer the question. (They allowed people to move and hunt more efficiently.)

Find Evidence Explain to students that after they read and take notes, they should review and think about how the facts and details will help them answer the Essential Question.

Peoples of the Plains

American Indians began settling the Great Plains as early as A.D. 1300. By the 1700s, groups included the Lakota, Dakota, and Nakota Sioux as well as the Pawnee, Cheyenne, Crow, Kiowa, and several others. Some people moved to the region because of drought, or a long period without rain, in the place where they used to live. Many people lived near rivers, which provided fertile land for them to farm. Others who followed the buffalo were nomads, or people who move from place to place with no fixed residence.

Plains Indians who traveled usually lived in cone-shaped homes called teepees. These structures consisted of buffalo hide spread across long poles. When the buffalo moved, women collapsed the teepees and set them back up in a new place. Those who lived near rivers set up more permanent homes called lodges made of logs, grasses, and dirt. But they also used teepees when they needed to travel to hunt.

Bands and Tribes of the Great Plains

Did You Know?

Horses

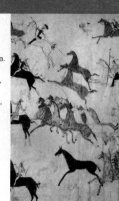

You may have thought that people in the Great Plains region have been riding horses for thousands of years. Before the 1500s, however, nobody had ridden a horse in North America. Explorers from Spain brought horses to the Americas, and some of the horses escaped. After about one hundred years, the horses had traveled up to the Great Plains. There the Lakota caught and tamed them. After another hundred years, most American Indians on the Plains were using horses to help them hunt buffalo and move their camps.

The introduction of horses completely changed the way of life for the Plains people. Before they had horses, Plains people followed the buffalo on foot. They trained dogs to pull belongings on a special sled called a *hupak'in*. After the introduction of horses, a person's wealth was measured by the number of horses owned.

✓ Stop and Check

Talk How did the introduction of horses completely change the way of life for the Plains people?

Find Evidence As you read, add additional information to the graphic organizer on page 35 in your Inquiry Journal.

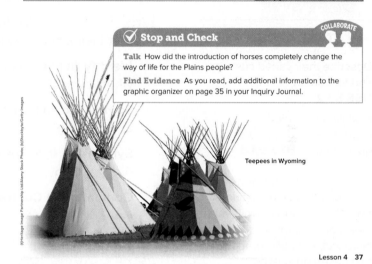

Teepees in Wyoming

36 Lesson 4 How Did the Great Plains Influence the Traditions of the People Living There?

Lesson 4 37

Research Companion, pp. 36–37

ⓔⓛ ENGLISH LEARNERS SCAFFOLD

ELD.PI.5.12 Selecting and applying varied and precise vocabulary and language structures to effectively convey ideas

Emerging	Expanding	Bridging
Develop Vocabulary Go over the domain-specific terms *nomads, teepees, lodges,* and *hupak'in.* Encourage students to give their own explanations of the terms, based on the definitions in the text.	**Define Vocabulary** Have students define the words *drought, fertile,* and *permanent*, which all appear in the text, and use them in sentences.	**Understand Origins** Have students look up and share information about the special sled called the *hupak'in.* Encourage students to give a description as well as other examples of sleds used around the world that are pulled by dogs or horses.

See the **Language Learner Teaching Guide** for more language support strategies.

Monitor and Differentiate

REACHING ALL LEARNERS

Special Needs

Help students use the visuals to understand what a teepee looks like and what cone-*shaped* means. Encourage them to use a sheet of paper and craft sticks or straws to create a miniature teepee.

Beyond Level

Have students compare the map on page 36 with a map of the present-day United States that shows cities. Ask them identify at least two states and two cities that take their names from the names of Plains peoples. (Examples include Iowa, North Dakota, South Dakota, Omaha, and Cheyenne.)

Life on the Plains

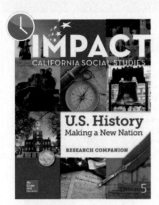

Research Companion
pp. 38–39

 STANDARDS

Describe their varied customs and folklore traditions.
HSS.5.1.2

Explain their varied economies and systems of government. **HSS.5.1.3**

CCSS Explain the relationships or interactions between two or more individuals, events, ideas, or concepts in a historical, scientific, or technical text based on specific information in the text. **CCSS.ELA.RI.5.3**

Go Digital!

Investigate the lesson content with online whole-class presentation tools.

Background Information

Warfare was frequent among the Plains peoples. When fought mainly with bows and arrows, casualties were light, although greater violence did place take in raids on enemy camps. European introduction of horses and guns greatly escalated the violence. The coming of the Europeans also caused many groups to migrate further west, resulting in more warfare when they encroached on the territory of others.

Analyze the Source

Inspect Have students read pages 38–39.

Find Evidence Use the questions below to check comprehension. Remind students to support their answers with text evidence.

Identify In Plains culture, who was responsible for packing and unpacking belongings when it was time to move? (women) **DOK 1**

Summarize In Plains culture, what one thing helped provide the necessities of shelter and clothing? (buffalo hides) **DOK 1**

Synthesize In Plains culture, who was responsible for educating children? (Men educated boys; women educated girls.) **DOK 2**

Compare and Contrast What did both men and women do to fulfill the need for food? (Men hunted buffalo and other game; women cooked the food and sometimes also grew food crops like corn, beans, and squash.) **DOK 2**

Make Connections

Speculate Why do you think Plains peoples sometimes grew sunflowers? (They used them for food. Students will likely recognize that sunflower seeds are edible; some may also mention sunflower oil.) **DOK 3**

Evaluate How separate were the roles of men and women in Plains culture? (Men and women each had very clearly defined tasks; they all worked together for the well-being of the group.) **DOK 3**

Explain In Plains culture, what was the chief purpose of the toys and games for youngsters? (to train them in the skills they would need to know as adults) **DOK 3**

Stop and Check

Think Have students compare their own experiences to those of the children of Plains peoples. Remind them to look for similarities as well as differences. (Responses will vary, but students may include that today they go to traditional schools, but they still learn valuable skills from the adults around them.)

What Do You Think?

Support Opinions Encourage students to use text evidence to respond to the What Do You Think? prompt. Note that they may also support their opinions with logical reasons or examples from their own knowledge or experiences.

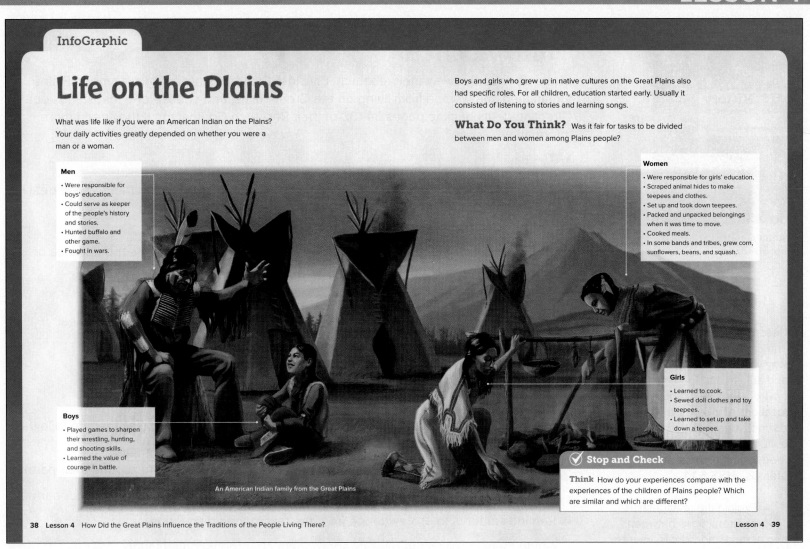

InfoGraphic

Life on the Plains

What was life like if you were an American Indian on the Plains? Your daily activities greatly depended on whether you were a man or a woman.

Boys and girls who grew up in native cultures on the Great Plains also had specific roles. For all children, education started early. Usually it consisted of listening to stories and learning songs.

What Do You Think? Was it fair for tasks to be divided between men and women among Plains people?

Men
- Were responsible for boys' education.
- Could serve as keeper of the people's history and stories.
- Hunted buffalo and other game.
- Fought in wars.

Women
- Were responsible for girls' education.
- Scraped animal hides to make teepees and clothes.
- Set up and took down teepees.
- Packed and unpacked belongings when it was time to move.
- Cooked meals.
- In some bands and tribes, grew corn, sunflowers, beans, and squash.

Boys
- Played games to sharpen their wrestling, hunting, and shooting skills.
- Learned the value of courage in battle.

Girls
- Learned to cook.
- Sewed doll clothes and toy teepees.
- Learned to set up and take down a teepee.

An American Indian family from the Great Plains

✓ **Stop and Check**

Think How do your experiences compare with the experiences of the children of Plains people? Which are similar and which are different?

38 Lesson 4 How Did the Great Plains Influence the Traditions of the People Living There?

Lesson 4 39

Research Companion, pp. 38–39

 # ENGLISH LEARNERS SCAFFOLD

ELD.PI.5.11 Supporting own opinions and evaluating others' opinions in speaking and writing

Emerging	Expanding	Bridging
State Opinions Ask students whether they would rather have been a Plains man or a Plains woman. Have them explain why, citing text evidence in their explanations.	**Evaluate** Have students consider in what ways both men and women could express themselves artistically. Encourage students to state why they would have liked expressing themselves in these ways.	**Evaluate** Have students discuss the childhood games they played, or toys with which they played, that they think have best prepared them for their lives as adults.

See the **Language Learner Teaching Guide** for more language support strategies.

Monitor and Differentiate

REACHING ALL LEARNERS

Approaching Level

To help students compare and contrast the roles of men and women, have them complete sentences frames such as *Both the men and women of the Plains ___* or *The men of the Plains ___, while the women ___.*

Beyond Level

Have students consider in what ways the lives of Plains peoples were free and in what ways they were restrictive.

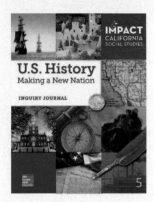

Inquiry Journal
pp. 36–37

 STANDARDS

Describe how geography and climate influenced the way various nations lived and adjusted to the natural environment, including locations of villages, the distinct structures that they built, and how they obtained food, clothing, tools, and utensils. **HSS.5.1.1**

CCSS Explain the relationships or interactions between two or more individuals, events, ideas, or concepts in a historical, scientific, or technical text based on specific information in the text. **CCSS.ELA.RI.5.3**

Write informative/explanatory texts to examine a topic and convey ideas and information clearly. **CCSS.ELA.W.5.2**

Go Digital!

- Students can go online to report their findings. Assess their responses online.

- Students can access the online graphic organizer to capture ideas from their investigation.

Think About It

Students should review their research, consider the traditions that arose among Plains Indian men and women from living on the Great Plains, and choose one that stands out. Direct students back to pages 34–39 of their Research Companion if they need more information.

Write About It

Compare and Contrast Have students read the prompt. Remind them to use details from the graphic organizer as evidence in their response. Tell them to follow these guidelines in their response.

- Introduce the two groups in a general statement about the similarity or difference of their traditions.

- Support the statement in a series of specific comparisons and contrasts.

- Use terms that signal comparisons and contrasts to make their relationship clear.

Use the rubric on p. T90 to evaluate students' work.

Talk About It

Explain Your Thinking Help students pair up with classmates. Tell them to follow these guidelines in their discussion.

- Remind students to take turns during the discussion and avoid interrupting their partner.

- Encourage students to listen carefully and be respectful of the opinions of their partner.

- Remind students to use evidence from the text in their discussion.

- Guide them to follow the rules of appropriate classroom conversation.

Connect to the
Essential Question

Read the prompt aloud to students. Ask them the following guiding questions:

- What was the landscape like where the Plains Indians lived? (prairie)

- How did that affect their traditions? (They farmed if they lived near a river, or they roamed after buffalo herds.)

Remind students to use the space provided in their journal to jot down notes.

Report *Your Findings*

Think About It

Review your research, and imagine that you are a blogger researching the Plains people. What were the most memorable things you learned about the Plains people?

Write About It

Compare and Contrast

Write an informative blogpost about the various activities and responsibilities of men and women in American Indian groups of the Plains.

Students' blogposts should cover activities of both men and women and should be based on details from the text.

Talk About It

Explain Your Thinking

Talk to a classmate about your findings. Take turns discussing how the activity helped you understand the differences between the roles of men and women among the Plains people.

 **Connect to the**

Geography

Pull It Together

Think about the people you studied in this lesson. How were their lives shaped by geography?

Sample Response: Geography played an important role in the lives of Plains people. If they lived near a river, they were likely to be farmers and stay in permanent houses. Otherwise, they lived in teepees and followed herds of buffalo across the prairie.

EQ Inquiry Project Notes

36 Lesson 4 How Did the Great Plains Influence the Traditions of the People Living There?

Lesson 4 **37**

Inquiry Journal, pp. 36–37

(EL) ENGLISH LEARNERS SCAFFOLD

ELD.PI.5.12 Selecting and applying varied and precise vocabulary and language structures to effectively convey ideas

Emerging	Expanding	Bridging
Develop Vocabulary Help students understand difficult vocabulary in the four assignments, such as *memorable* ("standing out in one's mind") and *responsibilities* ("duties; assigned tasks"). Be sure students know what a blogpost is.	**Collaborate** Have students share ideas about details from the lesson that they might use as evidence to complete each of the four assignments.	**Extend** As students compare and contrast the roles of men and women of the Great Plains, have them consider why gender-based roles like those of the Plains peoples are less necessary in modern life. Encourage them to include phrases that explain those reasons in their writing.

See the **Language Learner Teaching Guide** for more language support strategies.

Monitor and Differentiate

REACHING ALL LEARNERS

Approaching Level

Help students use signal words and phrases, such as *similarly, too, like, although, but,* and *in contrast,* when they state their comparisons and contrasts.

Beyond Level

Encourage students to conduct additional research for more evidence they can use to complete the four assignments.

Know what your students know!

Lesson Task
Report Your Findings

Use this rubric to evaluate students' response.

Compare and Contrast Students write an informative blogpost about the various activities and responsibilities of men and women in American Indian groups of the Plains.

Explain Your Thinking   Students talk to classmates about their findings. They take turns discussing how the activity helped them understand the roles of Plains men and women.

Performance Task Evaluation Rubric

	4	3	2	1
Historical Understanding	Strong understanding of activities of the men and women of the Plains peoples	Adequate understanding of activities of the men and women of the Plains peoples	Uneven understanding of activities of the men and women of the Plains peoples	No understanding of activities of the men and women of the Plains peoples
Take a Stand	Clearly explains main idea and key details.	Adequately explains main idea and key details.	Somewhat clear or unclear explanation of main idea and key details.	No explanation or student does not show understanding of the task.
Support with Evidence	Blogpost contains thorough text evidence	Blogpost contains adequate text evidence	Blogpost contains uneven text evidence	Evidence is missing
Defend Your Claim	Speaks clearly and at an understandable pace Speaks in complete sentences throughout the presentation	Speaks clearly during most of the presentation Speaks mostly in complete sentences	At times speaker is unclear Mixes complete and incomplete sentences	Speaks unclearly throughout the presentation Does not use complete sentences

Lesson Assessment

Go Digital!

- Have students complete the Chapter 1 Lesson 4 Assessment online to monitor their understanding of the lesson content.

California Smarter Balanced Assessment Connections!

Standards Covered	Lesson Task	Lesson Assessment	Alignment with California Smarter Balanced Assessment
History Social Science Content 5.1.1; 5.1.2; 5.1.3	✓	✓	Claim 1 Targets 8, 9, 10
History Social Science Analysis Skills Chronological and Spatial Thinking 5.4 Historical Interpretation 5.2	✓	✓	Claim 1 Targets 11, 12
Writing W.5.2	✓	✓	Claim 2 Targets 3b, 5
Research and Inquiry W.5.9	✓	✓	Claim 4 Targets 2, 3, 4
Reading RI.5.1; RI.5.3; RI.5.7	✓	✓	Claim 1 Targets 8, 9, 10, 11, 12
Speaking and Listening SL.5.1; SL.5.2	✓		Claim 3 Targets 3, 4

How Did the Eastern Woodlands Impact the Lives of Early People?

Background Information

Explain to students that in this lesson they will learn about the environmental features and terrain that shaped the lives of American Indians in the Northeast and Southeast Woodlands.

Community Connections

To enrich what students have learned about Eastern Woodland peoples, have groups of students look for online videos that provide cultural information about one of the groups of American Indians discussed in the lesson.

 LESSON STANDARDS

✓ Describe how geography and climate influenced the way various nations lived and adjusted to the natural environment, including locations of villages, the distinct structures that they built, and how they obtained food, clothing, tools, and utensils. **HSS.5.1.1**

✓ Describe their varied customs and folklore traditions. **HSS.5.1.2**

✓ Explain their varied economies and systems of government. **HSS.5.1.3**

✓ Students pose relevant questions about events they encounter in historical documents, eyewitness accounts, oral histories, letters, diaries, artifacts, photographs, maps, artworks, and architecture. **HAS.HR.2**

✓ Students judge the significance of the relative location of a place (e.g., proximity to a harbor, on trade routes) and analyze how relative advantages or disadvantages can change over time. **HAS.CS.5**

 Connect to the
Essential Question

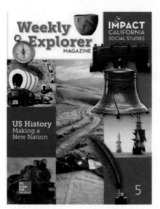

The **Weekly Explorer Magazine** supports students' exploration of the Essential Question and provides additional resources for the EQ Inquiry Project.

Chapter 1, pp. 2–13

 ## Inquiry Project

What was life like in America before Columbus?

Remind students to use the information they learn in this lesson and other resources to complete their EQ Inquiry Project!

Dinah Zike's

In this lesson you will use Foldables.

When Minutes Count!

Suggested Lesson Pacing

1 ENGAGE
One Day

- Lesson Opener
- Analyze the Source
- Inquiry Tools

Go Digital

- **Video:** Native Americans of the Southern Woodlands
- **iMap:** Native Americans of the Eastern Woodlands, 1600s
- **iMap:** Settling of the Americas

2 INVESTIGATE
Two to Three Days

🕐 **Short on Time?** Look to the clock to teach core content in less time.

- Terrain and Climate of Eastern Woodlands
- People of the Southeast Woodlands
- People of the Northeast Woodlands
- Government in the Woodlands
- Citizenship

3 REPORT
One Day

- Think About It
- Take a Stand
- Defend Your Claim

Make Connections!

(CCSS) **CONNECT TO ELA**

Reading

Explain the relationships or interactions between two or more individuals, events, ideas, or concepts in a historical, scientific, or technical text based on specific information in the text. **RI.5.3**

Research

Conduct short research projects that use several sources to build knowledge through investigation of different aspects of a topic. **W.5.7**

Recall relevant information from experiences or gather relevant information from print and digital sources; summarize or paraphrase information in notes and finished work, and provide a list of sources. **W.5.8**

Writing

Write opinion pieces on topics or texts, supporting a point of view with reasons and information. **W.5.1**

Draw evidence from literary or informational texts to support analysis, reflection, and research. **W.5.9**

Speaking and Listening

Engage effectively in a range of collaborative discussions (one-on-one, in groups, and teacher-led) with diverse partners on grade 5 topics and texts, building on others' ideas and expressing their own clearly. **SL.5.1**

Classroom Resources

🔍 Search for additional resources using the following key words.

American Indians of the Eastern Woodlands

Catawba

Cherokee

Chickasaw

Choctaw

Creek

Iroquois

longhouse

Mohawk

Narragansett

Natchez

Oneida

Pequot

Senecea

slash-and-burn

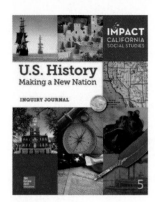

Inquiry Journal,
pp. 38–39

Go Digital!

Explore the lesson content
with online whole-class
presentation tools.

- **Video:** Native Americans of
  the Southern Woodlands

- **iMap:** Native Americans
  of the Eastern Woodlands,
  1600s

- **iMap:** Settling of the
  Americas

How Did the Eastern Woodlands Impact the Lives of Early People?

Bellringer
COLLABORATE

Prompt students to retrieve information from the previous lessons. Ask: *How were the lives of the Great Plains people shaped by geography?* (The geography is not well suited to growing crops, so many early peoples focused on hunting buffalo on the Plains.)

Lesson Outcomes

What Am I Learning? Have students read the Lesson Question and Lesson Outcomes on p. 38.

Why Am I Learning It? Check that students understand the word *opinion*. Ask them to tell you something about which they have a strong opinion. Say: *Opinion is an academic word that means a personal belief or judgment. For example: If you tell about what you did or did not like about a book or movie, you are giving an* opinion.

How Will I Know That I Learned It? Ask students the following questions.

- What will you be able to identify? (the problem-solving skills of American Indians living in the Eastern Woodlands)

- What is the purpose of the task? (to state an opinion about the most significant example of problem-solving skills)

- How will you support your opinion? (with text evidence)

Talk About It
COLLABORATE

Analyze the Image Explain that when we talk about a photograph, we describe, analyze, and interpret it and present our ideas in our own words. Provide sentence frames to help students talk about the photograph of the longhouse.

- *The photograph shows _____.*

- *I can tell that several families lived in the longhouse because _____.*

Collaborative Conversations
COLLABORATE

Add New Ideas As students engage in partner, small group, and whole-class discussions, encourage them to

- Stay on topic.
- Connect their own ideas to things their peers have said.
- Look for ways to connect their personal experiences or prior knowledge to the conversation.

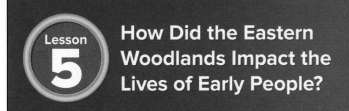

Lesson 5

How Did the Eastern Woodlands Impact the Lives of Early People?

Lesson Outcomes

What Am I Learning?
In this lesson, you're going to use your investigative skills to explore how the American Indians of the Eastern Woodlands survived and lived.

Why Am I Learning It?
Reading and talking about the lives of American Indians living in this area will help you understand the problem-solving skills that allowed them to survive and thrive.

How Will I Know That I Learned It?
You will be able to describe the problem-solving skills of the American Indians living in the Eastern Woodlands, state an opinion about the most significant example of problem solving in the region, and support your opinion with evidence.

Talk About It

Look at the Details Examine the image and read the caption. Based on the image, what do you think the advantages of the longhouse were? Support your answer with details.

The Iroquois lived in large homes called longhouses that held several families.

HSS.5.1.1, HSS.5.1.3, HAS.CS.4

38 Lesson 5 How Did the Eastern Woodlands Impact the Lives of Early People?

Lesson 5 **39**

Inquiry Journal, pp. 38–39

ENGLISH LEARNERS SCAFFOLD

ELD.PI.5.6 Reading closely literary and informational texts and viewing multimedia to determine how meaning is conveyed explicitly and implicitly through language

Emerging	Expanding	Bridging
Identify Details Work with students individually to identify and name details in the image. Provide specific words as needed.	**Describe Details** Guide students to work with partners to describe details in the image. Encourage them to use specific words to describe what they see.	**Use Language** Encourage students to describe what they find the most interesting or surprising about the longhouse.

See the **Language Learner Teaching Guide** for more language support strategies.

Monitor and Differentiate

REACHING ALL LEARNERS

Approaching Level
Work with students to understand the following terms: *Iroquois village, longhouse*. Have them complete sentence frames such as **The longhouse was the place where _____.**

On Level
Have students identify more details in the image. Encourage them to share with the whole class the details they have noticed.

Beyond Level
Encourage students to do additional research on Iroquois villages. Have students share their findings with the rest of the class.

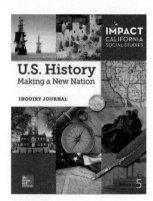

Inquiry Journal,
pp. 40–41

 STANDARDS

Describe their varied customs
and folklore traditions.
HSS.5.1.2

Summarize a written text
read aloud or information
presented in diverse media
formats, including visually,
quantitatively, and orally.
CCSS.ELA.SL.5.2

Go *Digital!*

Model how to inspect and find
evidence with online whole-
class presentation tools.

Background Information

The Longhouse The center of Iroquois life was the longhouse. A small Iroquois village might have only four or five longhouses. Larger villages could have as many as 100. In the longhouse two families shared the same fire pit, or hearth. Families lived in compartments with an aisle separating each family. The longhouse had a door on either end made of animal hide or bark. Over the front door hung a carved or painted panel that showed the clan symbols of the families living there.

1 Inspect

Look Examine the illustration of the outside and inside of an Iroquois longhouse. Remind students to circle unknown words they encounter.

- What is the outside of the longhouse made of? (saplings, flexible young trees that curve to make the rafters, poles to make the framework, bark used as shingles)

- What features did the inside of the longhouse have? (built-in shelves, a shared hearth, doors at each end, family compartments, smoke flaps)

Collaborate Have partners discuss how the longhouse made life easier for the Iroquois. What needs did the structure and organization of the longhouse provide for? (safety, shelter, shared life together)

2 Find Evidence

Look Again Have students reread the text and review the illustration. Provide support for vocabulary as needed.

Examine Analyze the illustration of the longhouse as a class.

- Ask partners to take turns explaining to each other how the compartments and the hallway are organized. Have partners discuss how the structure of the longhouse provides both shared space and privacy. (Answers will vary. Students should note that families live together in one house, but that they still have privacy in their own compartment.)

- What is the purpose of the longhouse? (to provide shelter and safety)

- What does the word *hearth* mean? (fire pit or fireplace)

Analyze the Illustration Guide students to discuss what problems the structure and organization of the longhouse solved for the Iroquois.

3 Make Connections

Talk Have students discuss with a partner the different parts of the longhouse and the problems that each of these parts solve. (Answers will vary, but students should note the sturdy outside structure, family compartments, common hallways, built-in shelves, shared hearth, smoke flaps. Problems that these parts solve include shelter, privacy, storage space, warmth, place for the smoke to escape,)

Write Have students describe what they like best about the design of the longhouse. Remind them to give details from the illustration to support their opinion.

Analyze the Source

1 Inspect

Look Examine the illustration showing the outside and inside of an Iroquois longhouse.

- **Describe** the shape of the longhouse.
- **Identify** the material used to make the longhouse.
- **Discuss** with a partner why the Iroquois would have chosen to live in longhouses.

My Notes

_____

_____

_____

_____

_____

_____

_____

_____

_____

_____

_____

_____

_____

The Iroquois Longhouse

While men sometimes built small wigwams while they were away hunting, the main type of housing for the Iroquois was the longhouse. These large houses took time to build. However, they were built from strong materials so that the Iroquois could live in permanent villages near the land they farmed. The walls were often made with saplings, which are strong and flexible trees that could curve to make the rafters. Large pieces of bark were used for the shingles.

The average Iroquois longhouse was 16 feet wide, 15 feet tall, and 60 feet long, but some houses could be as long as 300 feet. The longhouses had different compartments for different families. When a man married, he moved into his wife's longhouse to live with her extended family. These families were known as clans. As a clan grew, it could add compartments to its longhouse.

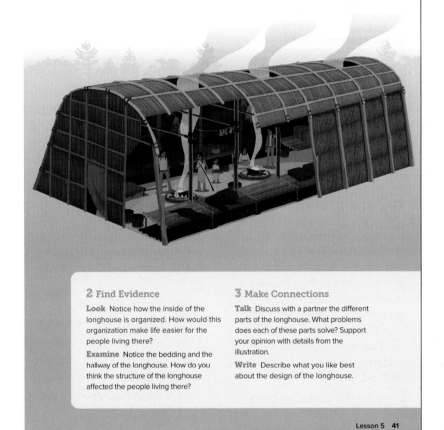

2 Find Evidence

Look Notice how the inside of the longhouse is organized. How would this organization make life easier for the people living there?

Examine Notice the bedding and the hallway of the longhouse. How do you think the structure of the longhouse affected the people living there?

3 Make Connections

Talk Discuss with a partner the different parts of the longhouse. What problems does each of these parts solve? Support your opinion with details from the illustration.

Write Describe what you like best about the design of the longhouse.

40 Lesson 5 How Did the Eastern Woodlands Impact the Lives of Early People?

Lesson 5 41

Inquiry Journal, pp. 40–41

(EL) ENGLISH LEARNERS SCAFFOLD

ELD.PI.5.6 Reading closely literary and informational texts and viewing multimedia to determine how meaning is conveyed explicitly and implicitly through language

Emerging	Expanding	Bridging
Describe Work with students individually to help them find words to describe what they see in the illustration.	**Describe** Have students work with partners to find words to describe what they see.	**Use Language** Encourage students to use specific vocabulary, such as _smoke flaps, hearth,_ and _compartments_ to describe what they see in the illustration.

See the **Language Learner Teaching Guide** for more language support strategies.

Monitor and Differentiate

REACHING ALL LEARNERS

Approaching Level

Work with students to help them understand and define the words _rafters, framework,_ and _shingles._ Have them complete sentence frames, such as **The first thing that needs to be built on any house is its _____.**

On Level

Have students examine closely the inside of the longhouse. Encourage them to share what they notice with the whole class.

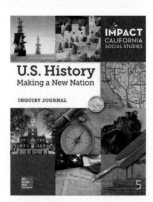

Inquiry Journal,
pp. 42–43

 STANDARDS

Describe how geography
and climate influenced the
way various nations lived
and adjusted to the natural
environment, including
locations of villages, the distinct
structures that they built,
and how they obtained food,
clothing, tools, and utensils. .
HSS.5.1.1

Describe the varied customs
and folklore traditions of
American Indians. **HSS.5.1.2**

(CCSS) Draw evidence from
literary or informational
texts to support analysis,
reflection, and research.
CCSS.ELA.W.5.9

Go *Digital!*

• Model how to explore and
  investigate with online
  whole-class tools.

• Students can access the
  online graphic organizer to
  use the inquiry tools as they
  read.

Explore Problem and Solution

Explain Tell students that problem and solution is one kind of text structure that authors use to organize information in a historical text.

Read Have students read aloud the step-by-step instructions about how to identify problem and solution structure. Tell students to look for problems that the people you are reading about faced. In addition, look for information about what made these problems difficult to solve.

Guide Practice Model identifying a problem and its solution for students: *One of the problems the people of the Eastern Woodlands faced was how best to provide shelter. They decided that the longhouse was a good fit for their lifestyle, so they made it out of wood and created a shared hearth inside.*

Investigate!

Have students read pages 40–49 in the Research Companion. Tell them the information that will help them answer the lesson question ***How Did the Eastern Woodlands Impact the Lives of Early People?***

Take Notes Ask students to keep track of problems and solutions experienced by Eastern Woodland peoples by filling out the graphic organizer on page 43 of the Inquiry Journal. Be sure they understand that they need to include details from the text for each problem and solution that they identify. Point out that taking notes will help them understand and remember the information they learn. Remind students of the importance of paraphrasing—using their own words—when they take notes.

Inspect Guide students to read the text in each section to determine what the text says. Encourage them to make note of words they don't understand and look for answers to questions, such as *who? what? when? where? why?* and *how?*

Find Evidence Encourage students to reread the text to develop a deeper understanding of the content. Remind students that after they read and take notes, they should review and think about how the facts and details will help them answer the lesson question.

Collaborative Conversations

Text-Based Discussion Remind students of the goals of discussing the text with others.

• to listen attentively and respond respectfully to their partners' points

• to ask for evidence from the text

• to build on each other's ideas

• to see the text from a point of view that is different from their own

Inquiry Tools

Explore Problem and Solution

Identifying **problems and solutions** in what you read will help you understand the people you are studying and evaluate their ability to overcome challenges.

1. **Read the text all the way through.**
   This will help you understand what the text is about.

2. **Look at the illustrations and diagrams as well as section titles.**
   This will help you locate and understand important concepts.

3. **Think of the problems faced by the people you are reading about.**
   This will help you recognize solutions when you see them.

4. **Find key facts about the problems and the solutions.**
   While reading, ask yourself, *What details make this problem difficult to solve? What details about the solution make it work well?*

 COLLABORATE Based on the text you just read as well as illustrations and diagrams, work with your class to complete the chart below.

Problem	Solution	Key Details
How best to provide shelter	Longhouse	Strong saplings were curved to make rafters for roof; shared hearth for warmth.

 IMPACT U.S. History Making a New Nation

Investigate!

Read pages 40–49 in your Research Companion. Use your investigative skills to identify problems American Indians in the Eastern Woodlands faced and the solutions they devised. Use the chart to organize your information.

Problem	Solution	Key Details
Weather changes during the seasons in the Eastern Woodlands.	People do different activities during the seasons.	Hunt in winter; plant crops in spring; build homes and gather berries in summer; gather crops in fall
In Northeast Woodlands, forests make farming difficult.	People cut down and burn trees so that they can turn forests into farmland.	In slash-and-burn agriculture, ash from trees that have been cut down and burned is used to fertilize soil
In Southeast Woodlands, resources such as fish, rice, and bison are not available.	People focus on growing crops.	Cherokee grow crops called Three Sisters: corn, beans, and squash
Climate in the Northeast Woodlands is sometimes very cold.	People wear special clothing when it is cold.	People wear heavier leggings, furs, and snowshoes as necessary.

Inquiry Journal, pp. 42–43

EL ENGLISH LEARNERS SCAFFOLD

ELD.PI.5.1 Exchanging information and ideas with others through oral collaborative discussions on a range of social and academic topics

Emerging

Organize Information
Point to the table on p. 43. Explain to students that each box indicates information they will need to find and fill in. Check that students understand the meaning of the words *problem* and *solution*. Work individually with students, using sentence frames such as **Getting to school on time was a big ___ for William. His ___ was to set three alarm clocks.**

Expanding

Develop Language
Guide students to refer to information from the text as they discuss the chart with a partner. Supply key vocabulary words as needed.

Bridging

Cite Evidence Guide students to cite evidence from the text and explain how it connects with the problem listed in its row of the graphic organizer as they discuss the text with a partner.

See the **Language Learner Teaching Guide** for more language support strategies.

Monitor and Differentiate

REACHING ALL LEARNERS

Special Needs

Have students work with a partner to determine the problems different groups of native people living in the Eastern Woodlands faced and the solutions they devised. Have students act out how the people of the Eastern Woodlands solved these problems.

On Level

Have students work with a partner to determine key details supporting the problems and solutions they have listed.

Lesson 5 **Inquiry Tools** T99

Slash-and-burn was an agricultural method practiced by the native people living in the Northeast part of the Eastern Woodlands. The process consisted of several steps. Before planting, all trees and vegetation in a given area are cut down and burned. The ash from the burning produced a rich layer of nutrients that made the soil fertile. The crops were then planted and harvested in the autumn.

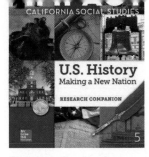

Research Companion
pp. 40–41

 STANDARDS

Describe how geography and climate influenced the way various nations lived and adjusted to the natural environment, including locations of villages, the distinct structures that they built, and how they obtained food, clothing, tools, and utensils. **HSS.5.1.1**

Students judge the significance of the relative location of a place (e.g., proximity to a harbor, on trade routes) and analyze how relative advantages or disadvantages can change over time. **HAS.CS.5**

Go Digital!

Investigate the lesson content with online whole-class presentation tools.

- **Video:** Native Americans of the Southern Woodlands

- **iMap:** Native Americans of the Eastern Woodlands, 1600s

- **iMap:** Settling of the Americas

| TIMELINE | Invite students to look at the timeline at the top on page 41.

Analyze What two events happened between c. 1570 and c. 1722? (The Iroquois Confederacy was formed and Tuscora joined the Iroquois Confederacy) **HAS.CS.1**

Analyze the Source

Inspect Have students read about the terrain and climate of the Eastern Woodlands on pages 40–41. Use the questions below to check comprehension.

Find Evidence Use the questions below to check comprehension. Remind students to support their answers with text evidence.

Infer Why did the men of the Eastern Woodlands spend the winter hunting game? (because they were not farming during the winter) **DOK 2**

Compare Compare and contrast the terrain and climate of the Northeast and Southeast regions of the Eastern Woodlands. (The Southeast was thinly wooded with a mild climate and long growing season. The Northeast had thicker forests and a cooler climate.) **DOK 2**

Cite Evidence Cite evidence showing that the native peoples of the Northeast region used slash-and-burn agriculture because farming in the Northeast was more difficult than in the Southeast region. (The text says that because of the thick forests in the Northeast, farming was "more difficult." Slash-and-burn gave farmers a way to make their soil more fertile.) **DOK 3**

Make Connections

Spatial Thinking Based on what you read, in what ways was life in the Northeast region of the Eastern Woodlands more difficult than it was in the Southeast region? (Answers may vary, but students should note that because of the thick forests farming was more difficult in the Northeast region.) **DOK 3**

Ⓥ Map Skills

Project a large version of the map on p. 41. Guide students to identify the groups of American Indians who lived in the Eastern Woodlands.

- Where did the Mohawk mainly live? (Massachusetts and New York)

- Where did the Huron live? (in modern-day Canada)

- Did the Narragansett and the Seneca people have to share territory? (No, they are on opposite sides of New England.)

How Did the Eastern Woodlands Impact the Lives of Early People?

Timeline

A.D. 700 The Mississippian culture arises in the Southeast Woodlands.

1600 The Iroquois Confederacy is formed.

1700 Tuscarora join the Iroquois Confederacy.

700 · 1600 · 1700

Terrain and Climate of the Eastern Woodlands

The Eastern Woodlands stretch from the Mississippi River to the Atlantic Ocean. In the past, most of this area was covered in thick forests. Since the Eastern Woodlands cover a large area, the early peoples of the region were often very different from one another.

The seasons often guided how the people of the Eastern Woodlands lived. During the winter, men hunted game such as deer, bear, rabbits, beavers, and wild turkeys. During spring, the soil was ideal for growing crops. In summer, men fished, carved canoes, and built homes while women gathered berries and wild plants. In autumn, the tribes gathered, dried, and stored the crops for the winter. After the **harvest**, they let the land rest for several years before replanting the crops. They used different land the next year.

The large area of the Eastern Woodlands can be divided into two regions: the Northeast and the Southeast. The Southeast was more thinly wooded and had a mild climate and a long growing season. These conditions were good for farming. The thicker forests of the Northeast made farming more challenging. There, many early peoples practiced a type of farming called **slash-and-burn**. They cut down and burned the trees in the forest, and ash from the burned vegetation helped make the soil fertile.

McGraw-Hill Education

HSS.5.1.1, HSS.5.1.2, HSS 5.1.3, HA.CS.4, HA.HI.2

40 Lesson 5 How Did the Eastern Woodlands Impact the Lives of Early People?

Great Lakes
Penobscot
Huron · Oneida · Hudson River
Cayuga · Mohawk · Wampanoag
Seneca · Onondaga · Narragansett
Pequot
Mohegan
Shawnee
Ohio River
Cherokee · Tuscarora
Chickasaw · Catawba · Atlantic Ocean
Tennessee River · Creek
Choctaw
Natchez
Timucua
Seminole
Gulf of Mexico
Mississippi River

American Indians of the Eastern Woodlands, 1600s
International border
State border
Present-day borders shown

0   150   300 miles
0   150 300 kilometers

American Indians of the Eastern Woodlands, 1600s

Lesson 5 41

Research Companion, pp. 40–41

ENGLISH LEARNERS SCAFFOLD

ELD.PI.5.6 Reading closely literary and informational texts and viewing multimedia to determine how meaning is conveyed explicitly and implicitly through language

Emerging

Establish a Purpose Working with students individually have them look at the map on page 41. Explain that the map shows the names of peoples living in the Northeast Woodlands. Point to and pronounce the name of each tribe. Then have students pronounce the names with you.

Expanding/Bridging

Understand Have student pairs look at the map on page 41. Point out and explain the meaning of the rose compass and the key. Ask: *What information can you learn from this map?*

See the **Language Learner Teaching Guide** for more language support strategies.

Monitor and Differentiate

REACHING ALL LEARNERS

Approaching Level

Have students identify the major bodies of water shown on the map on page 41.

Beyond Level

Have students explain the meaning of the key shown at the bottom of the map on page 41.

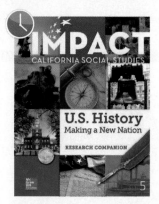

Research Companion
pp. 42–43

 STANDARDS

Describe how geography and climate influenced the way various nations lived and adjusted to the natural environment, including locations of villages, the distinct structures that they built, and how they obtained food, clothing, tools, and utensils. **HSS.5.1.1**

Students judge the significance of the relative location of a place (e.g., proximity to a harbor, on trade routes) and analyze how relative advantages or disadvantages can change over time. **HAS.CS.5**

CCSS Draw evidence from literary or informational texts to support analysis, reflection, and research. **CCSS.ELA.W.5.9**

Go *Digital!*

Investigate the lesson content with online whole-class presentation tools.

Background Information

People in the Eastern Woodlands believed that spirits were involved in everyday life. They believed that good spirits helped those in need, and that evil spirits caused sickness and conflict. They conducted ceremonies to communicate with spirits. Dancing, singing, and playing instruments played an important part in these ceremonies.

Analyze the Source

Inspect Have students read about the people of the Southeastern Woodlands on pp. 42–43.

Find Evidence Use the questions below to check comprehension. Remind students to support their answers with text evidence.

Identify What are the names some of the tribes who lived in the Southeast Woodlands? (the Creek, Cherokee, Natchez, and Choctaw) **DOK 1**

Infer Based on what you read, how did the American Indians of the Southeast Woodlands get the material from which they made their clothing? (from the pelts of animals they hunted) **DOK 2**

Analyze How did the climate and geography in which the native people of the Southeast Woodlands lived affect what they ate? (Answers may vary, but students should note that people in both regions ate according to what food sources were available. These food sources were dependent on climate and geography.) **DOK 3**

Compare Compare and contrast the housing of the Cherokee and the Creek. (Answers will vary, but students should note things such as that the Cherokee built their houses with wattle and daub and had fences around their villages; the Creek built their houses out of grass, mud, or thatch and arranged their town around a central plaza.) **DOK 3**

Make Connections

Support an Opinion Based on what you have read about how the people of the Southeast Woodland fed, clothed, and housed themselves, what is your opinion of their resourcefulness, or ability to adapt to situations? What evidence can you use to support your opinion? (Answers will vary, but students should note the native peoples made excellent use of the resources available to them.) **DOK 4**

✓ Stop and Check

Talk Encourage students to discuss how climate and terrain affected the diet and clothing of American Indians in the Southeast Woodlands. (Answers will vary, but students should note that people used what was available for food and clothing.)

Find Details Explain to students that after they read and take notes, they should review and think about how the facts and details will help them answer the Essential Question.

People of the Southeast Woodlands

Among the American Indian tribes that lived in the Southeast Woodlands were the Creek, Cherokee, Chickasaw, Catawba, Natchez, and Choctaw. Each tribe had its own unique customs and traditions.

In both the Southeast and the Northeast, people ate a variety of farmed, hunted, and gathered foods, including beans, corn, deer, nuts, and maple syrup. However, in the Southeast Woodlands, many wild resources such as rice and bison were unavailable. The tribes relied more heavily on crops. The Cherokee in the Southeast, for example, grew the "Three Sisters" of corn, beans, and squash.

People of the Southeast Woodlands wore clothing that could be adjusted depending on the weather. Men wore a breechcloth, which is a long rectangular piece of deerskin, cloth, or animal fur. It is worn between the legs and tucked over a belt. Men in the Southeast Woodlands also wore leggings, or leg pants, usually made from buckskin or some other soft leather. Women generally wore a deerskin top and a skirt to which they might add leggings, a cape, or a robe. Both men and women wore moccasins—soft-soled and heelless shoes. In hotter areas of the Southeast, men wore little clothing and often tattooed their bodies.

Moccasins—soft-soled, heelless shoes—made by American Indians of the Eastern Woodlands

Ways of life varied from tribe to tribe in the Southeast. The Cherokee, who lived mainly in what is now Tennessee and Georgia, constructed fairly large villages, with each having 20 to 60 houses and a large meeting building. Cherokee homes were usually made of wattle—twigs and branches woven together to make the house's frame—and daub, which is a sticky substance like mud or clay. The Cherokee covered the wattle frame with daub, which held it all together. This created the look of an upside-down basket. The Cherokee also placed fences around their villages for protection against enemies. Each Cherokee village had its own leaders and made its own decisions. However, during times of celebration or war, villages came together. One celebration, called the Green Corn Festival, honored the summer's first corn crop with dances and games.

Like the Cherokee, the Natchez built homes from wattle and daub. The Natchez lived in permanent villages in what today is Mississippi. They were successful farmers, but they also hunted, fished, and gathered food from plants. Like the Hopewell and Mississippian people before them, the Natchez built ceremonial mounds.

The Creek arranged their towns around a central town plaza, used for religious ceremonies and games. Surrounding the plaza were family homes built out of poles and covered with grass, mud, or thatch. Like the Cherokee, the Creek relied on the "Three Sisters" of corns, beans, and squash for food. In addition, they hunted small animals and gathered plants.

> **✓ Stop and Check**
>
> **Talk** How did climate and terrain affect the diet and clothing of the Americans Indians in the Southeast Woodlands?
>
> **Find Details** As you read, add additional information to the graphic organizer on page 43 in your Inquiry Journal.

The "Three Sisters" crops: corn, squash, and beans

Research Companion, pp. 42–43

(EL) ENGLISH LEARNERS SCAFFOLD

ELD.PI.5.1 Exchanging information and ideas with others through oral collaborative discussions on a range of social and academic topics

Emerging	Bridging	Expanding
Build Meaning Work individually with students to make sure they understand how people in the Southeast Woodlands housed themselves. Help students to draw the housing arrangements of the Cherokee and to label their drawings.	**Describe** Have students work in pairs to draw and label the housing arrangement of the Cherokee, Natchez, or Creek.	**Develop Language** Encourage students to use specific language, such as *wattle, daub, and thatch* to describe the housing of the Cherokee, Natchez, and Creek.

See the **Language Learner Teaching Guide** for more language support strategies.

Monitor and Differentiate

REACHING ALL LEARNERS

Approaching Level

Have students use a two-column chart to list the similarities and differences among the people of the Southeast Woodlands.

On Level   **Beyond Level**

Have students conduct additional research on customs the Cherokee, Natchez, or Creek. Have them share their findings with the whole class.

Longhouses were often built along the shores of rivers and streams, as this gave people a fresh supply of water for drinking and other needs. Being close to water also made it easy to travel by boat. Longhouses in a village were arranged in a random pattern in order to prevent the spread of fire. An Iroquois longhouse village could be small (four or five longhouses) or large (more than a hundred longhouses). The size of a longhouse depended on how much food was available in the area.

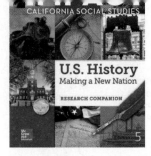

Research Companion
pp. 44–45

 STANDARDS

Describe how geography and climate influenced the way various nations lived and adjusted to the natural environment, including locations of villages, the distinct structures that they built, and how they obtained food, clothing, tools, and utensils. **HSS.5.1.1**

CCSS Draw evidence from literary or informational texts to support analysis, reflection, and research. **CCSS.ELA.W.5.9**

Go Digital!

Investigate the lesson content with online whole-class presentation tools.

Analyze the Source

Inspect Have students read about the people of the Northeastern Woodlands on pp. 44–45

Find Evidence Use the questions below to check comprehension. Remind students to support their answers with text evidence.

Compare How did the food eaten by the people of the Northeast Woodlands differ from that eaten in the Southeast Woodlands? (People in the Northeast Woodlands ate food unavailable to the people in the Southeast Woodlands, such as salmon and shellfish.) **DOK 2**

Infer What does the creation of the snowshoe by the people of the Northeast Woodlands tell you about their lives? (It tells you that they had to deal with cold winters and had to find a way to walk in heavy snow.) **DOK 2**

Compare What is the difference between a wigwam and a longhouse? (Wigwams were much smaller than longhouses; wigwams did not house multiple families.) **DOK 2**

Define What is a clan? (a group of families that shared the same ancestor) **DOK 2**

Assess Assess the Iroquois's attitude toward women. (Answers will vary, but students should note that their attitude was quite positive as evidenced by women's controlling the land and who would use it, overseeing all important decisions, and giving their names to their children.) **DOK 3**

Make Connections

Analyze Based on what you have read, what do you think about the prominent position given to women in Iroquois society? How does it differ from the position of women in other societies and cultures? (Answers will vary, but students should note that the Iroquois culture gave women quite a bit of power while most other cultures and societies did not.) **DOK 4**

COLLABORATE

 Stop and Check

Talk Guide students to discuss how groups of American Indians found different ways to organize themselves and their members. (Tribe organization was important to keep order and guide the people.)

Find Details Explain to students that after they read and take notes, they should review and think about how the facts and details will help them answer the Essential Question.

People of the Northeast Woodlands

Like the Southeast Woodlands, the Northeast Woodlands area was populated by different tribes, each with their unique customs and traditions. The Mohawk, Narragansett, Seneca, Pequot, Iroquois, and Oneida tribes lived in the Northeast Woodlands.

Because of differences in climate and terrain, people in the Northeast ate food unavailable to people in the Southeast. Rivers in the Northeast, for example, had annual runs of fish, like salmon, that moved up rivers from the sea. In the North, people often had to rely more on fish than on crops because frost frequently destroyed crops. On the Atlantic coast and along major rivers, shellfish were plentiful and provided a major source of food for the people living there.

Because of the colder climate, the clothing worn by people in the Northeast differed from what people in the Southeast wore. While the basics—breechcloth and leggings for men and deerskin tops and skirts for women—remained the same, people in the Northeast wore heavier and warmer leggings and various furs. Northeast tribes also used snowshoes for walking in the snow. Snowshoes work by distributing a person's weight over a larger area so that the person does not sink in the snow.

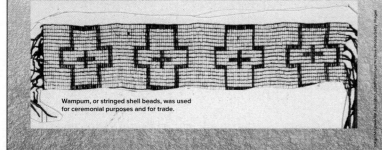

Wampum, or stringed shell beads, was used for ceremonial purposes and for trade.

In the 1500s, the Iroquois lived mostly in what is now upstate New York. Historians call this group the Iroquois because they spoke languages in the Iroquoian language family. However, the Iroquois call themselves Haudenosaunee (hoe dee noh SHOH nee). In Iroquoian, this means "people of the longhouse."

For housing, the Iroquois depended on wigwams and longhouses. The Iroquois made wigwams by bending young trees to form the round shape of a dome. Then, over this basic shape, they wrapped pieces of tree bark to protect against bad weather. Over the bark layer they added thatch, or dried grass. A small hole at the top allowed smoke from the fire to escape.

Longhouses were long, rectangular homes. The Iroquois made their longhouses by building a frame from saplings, or young trees. They covered the frame with bark sewn together. Inside, they built a long hallway with rooms on both sides. Then they lined the walls with sleeping platforms, covered with deerskin. They also built in shelves for storing baskets, pots, and pelts (the skins of animals with the fur attached). Several families lived in the same longhouse.

Almost all Iroquois property was controlled by clans—groups of families who shared the same ancestor. Women were the leaders of their clans. Among the Iroquois, it was women who decided how the land would be used and who would use it. When a man married, he moved into his wife's longhouse and lived with her family. Children took their clan name from their mother. No important decision could be made without the approval of the clan mother. Although the leaders of each village were men, it was the clan mother who chose them.

> ✓ **Stop and Check**
>
> **Talk** American Indian tribes found different ways to organize themselves and their members. Why was it important that the tribes organized themselves?

Research Companion, pp. 44–45

 ## ENGLISH LEARNERS SCAFFOLD

ELD.PI.5.1 Exchanging information and ideas with others through oral collaborative discussions on a range of social and academic topics

Emerging

Build Meaning Make sure students understand the word *custom*. Tell them that a custom is an accepted way of behaving. Say: *In many families it is a custom to give gifts on someone's birthday.* Have students complete sentence frames such as: *It is the ____ in my family to thank people for gifts.*

Bridging

Describe Have students work in pairs to tell why people in the Northeast Woodlands ate more fish than crops. Supply pertinent vocabulary as needed.

Expanding

Develop Language Encourage students to use specific language, such as *climate* and *terrain*, to describe the environment of the people of the Northeast Woodlands.

See the **Language Learner Teaching Guide** for more language support strategies.

Monitor and Differentiate

REACHING ALL LEARNERS

Special Needs

Work with students to provide examples of resources available in different types of terrain. Compare these examples with the resources of the Eastern Woodlands. Bring in, or encourage students to bring in, examples of these resources or products made from them.

On Level   Beyond Level

Have students do research on how the Iroquois people of today celebrate their traditions. Have them share their findings with the whole class.

Lesson 5   **People of the Northeast Woodlands**   T105

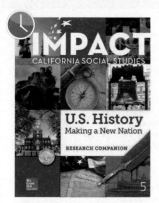

Research Companion
pp. 46–47

(HSS) STANDARDS

Explain their varied economies and systems of government. **HSS.5.1.3**

Students pose relevant questions about events they encounter in historical documents, eyewitness accounts, oral histories, letters, diaries, artifacts, photographs, maps, artworks, and architecture. **HAS.HR.2**

Students use map and globe skills to determine the absolute locations of places and interpret information available through a map's or globe's legend, scale, and symbolic representations. **HAS.CS.4**

(CCSS) Explain the relationships or interactions between two or more individuals, events, ideas, or concepts in a historical, scientific, or technical text based on specific information in the text. **CCSS.ELA.RI.5.3**

Go Digital!

Investigate the lesson content with online whole-class presentation tools.

Background Information

In 1995, Cayuga Clan Mother Carol Jacobs spoke to the United Nations. She explained that, in her tradition, women have a special responsibility to protect the earth. In addition, when making a law, chiefs must consider its effects on peace, the natural world, and seven generations in the future. She invited all nations to adopt these principles and work together to protect the planet.

Analyze the Source

Inspect Have students read about government in the Woodlands on pp. 46-47.

Find Evidence Use the questions below to check comprehension. Remind students to support their answers with text evidence.

Identify What were the Creek peace (white) towns and war (red) towns? (The red towns declared war, planned military actions, and held meetings with enemy groups. The white towns passed laws and held conquered groups. However, during a war peace towns joined in the fighting.) **DOK 1**

Explain By the year 1300, fighting was increasingly breaking out among the Iroquois. Why was this? (When the Iroquois had been a small group, they cooperated on many matters. But as their numbers increased, arguments arose and fighting broke out.) **DOK 2**

Analyze the Primary Source Reread the excerpt from *The Constitution of the Iroquois* People aloud and then analyze the excerpt together as a class. Provide support for the vocabulary as needed.

Use Context Ask partners to take turns explaining to each other what such phrases as "such a nation or nations shall be deemed guilty of treason" mean. (such a nation would be considered guilty of betraying the Iroquois nation) **DOK 2**

Analyze What is the purpose of the excerpt? (to say what will happen to any person or nation that tries to destroy the peace) **DOK4**

Use Context What does the word endeavor mean? (It means "try.") **DOK 2**

Make Connections

Draw Conclusions Have students discuss why the penalty was so strict for nations that did anything to threaten the peace. (The penalties were strict because the authors understood that only strict penalties would make people behave.) **DOK4**

(⊙) Map Skills

Which group of Iroquois lived the farthest east? (the Mohawk)

(✓) Stop and Check  COLLABORATE

Talk Encourage students to discuss why the Iroquois felt the need to form a confederacy. (to protect themselves and prevent war)

Government in the Woodlands

To help protect themselves, the Creek formed a confederacy. A confederacy is a group of people formed for a common purpose. The Creek Confederacy divided its towns into peace (white) towns and war (red) towns. Red towns declared war, planned military actions, and met with enemies. White towns passed laws and held conquered groups. However, during war, people in peace towns joined in the fighting.

Farther north, the Iroquois also had a system of government. When they were a small group, they cooperated on many matters. By about A.D. 1300, their numbers had grown, and their communities were crowded. Arguments arose and fighting broke out. The Iroquois believed that if one person was wronged, it hurt the whole clan. For this reason, wrongs had to be punished. The Iroquois also fought with other Eastern Woodlands peoples, often over hunting grounds. Warfare soon became a constant problem for the Iroquois.

According to Iroquois history, two Iroquois leaders, Deganawida and Hiawatha, saw that fighting was destroying their people. In the 1500s, these two leaders urged the Iroquois to join together to make peace. In about 1570, five separate Iroquois tribes joined together to form the Iroquois Confederacy, also known as the Iroquois League. The Confederacy is still active today.

PRIMARY SOURCE

Constitution of the Iroquois Nations

"If a nation, part of a nation, or more than one nation within the Five Nations should in any way endeavor to destroy the Great Peace by neglect or violating its laws and resolve to dissolve the Confederacy, such a nation or such nations shall be deemed guilty of treason and called enemies of the Great Peace."

"They [the offending people] shall be warned once and if a second warning is necessary they shall be driven from the territory of the Confederacy. . . ."

PHOTO: Constitution of the Iroquois Nations, Art. 95. Prepared by Arthur C. Parker and adopted (1915) by the New York State Museum and the Iroquois and the Constitution Society. PHOTO: Adam Aczel/EyeEm/Getty Images

The Iroquois Confederacy, 1500

Hodenosaunee Trail
Present-day boundaries

St. Lawrence River · Lake Champlain · Lake Ontario · Oneida · Mohawk · Cayuga · Lake Erie · Seneca · Onondaga · Hudson River

0   50   100 miles
0   50   100 kilometers

🧭 **Place** Which group of Iroquois lived the farthest east?

✓ **Stop and Check** COLLABORATE

Talk What was the major reason the Iroquois formed a confederacy?

Find Details As you read, add additional information to the graphic organizer on page 43 of your Inquiry Journal.

46   Lesson 5   How Did the Eastern Woodlands Impact the Lives of Early People?

Lesson 5   47

Research Companion, pp. 46–47

ENGLISH LEARNERS SCAFFOLD

ELD.PI.5.6 Reading closely literary and informational texts and viewing multimedia to determine how meaning is conveyed explicitly and implicitly through language

Emerging	Bridging	Bridging
Build Meaning Work with students to locate and name important places on the map, such as the inset map of the entire United States, Lake Ontario, Lake Champlain, and the Hudson River. Pronounce the name of each group. Have students say the names with you.	**Describe** Have students work with a partner to identify important names and locations on the map.	**Develop Language** Encourage students to use the words *key* and *compass rose* as they describe the map.

See the **Language Learner Teaching Guide** for more language support strategies.

Monitor and Differentiate

REACHING ALL LEARNERS

Approaching Level

Work with students to understand how the Creek Confederacy functioned and how its purpose differed from the purpose of the Iroquois Confederacy.

Beyond Level

A form of the Iroquois Confederacy still exists today, but it is known as the Six Nations. Have students conduct additional research on the Iroquois Confederacy. Have them share their findings with the whole class.

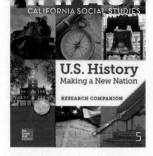

Research Companion
pp. 48–49

(HSS) STANDARDS

Explain their varied economies and systems of government. **HSS.5.1.3**

Students explain how the present is connected to the past, identifying both similarities and differences between the two, and how some things change over time and some things stay the same. **HAS.CS.3**

(CCSS) Draw evidence from literary or informational texts to support analysis, reflection, and research. **CCSS.ELA.W.5.9**

Go Digital!

Investigate the lesson content with online whole-class presentation tools.

Find Evidence Use the questions below to check comprehension. Remind students to support their answers with text evidence.

> **Describe** What was the Great Law? (the set of rules by which the Iroquois people lived) **DOK 2**
>
> **Explain** How were each of the groups represented in the Iroquois Confederacy? (Representatives from all the clans, chosen by the clan mothers, met at the Grand Council. The Grand Council made decisions through discussion and compromise.) **DOK 2**

Make Connections

Analyze the Primary Source Reread the excerpt from the concurrent resolution, or official opinion of Congress on an issue, and then analyze the excerpt together as a class.

> **Infer** What is the opinion being expressed in the primary source? (that the original framers of the Constitution greatly admired Iroquois concepts as expressed by the Iroquois Confederacy) **DOK 3**
>
> **Context** What does the word *reaffirm* mean? (to state again for emphasis) **DOK 2**

Build Citizenship

Justice

1. List the ways the U.S. Government is like the Iroquois Council. (Like the Iroquois government, the U.S. Government has officials who represent the people.)

2. List the ways the U.S. Government is different from the Iroquois Council. (The U.S. Government has two rule-making bodies: the Senate and the House of Representatives. The Iroquois government has only one: the Iroquois Council.)

3. Do you think the Iroquois Confederacy had more similarities or more differences with our government? (Answers will vary, but students should support their answers with evidence.)

Think About It

Perspectives Ensure that students follow the rules of appropriate classroom conversation.

Write About It

Encourage students to consider what makes a democracy. (Answers will vary, but students should support their opinion with evidence from the text.)

Citizenship

Does the Iroquois Confederacy Resemble
Our Government?

In order to keep the Great Peace, the Iroquois people developed the Great Law. This was a set of rules by which the Iroquois people lived. They also set up a way for each of the tribes in the Iroquois Confederacy to have a voice in making decisions. Representatives from all of the clans met at the Grand Council. These representatives were chosen by the clan mothers. The Grand Council made decisions through discussion and compromise, or settled a dispute by each side agreeing to give up part of what it wanted. The Grand Council continues to make decisions for the Iroquois today.

Some historians believe the Iroquois government influenced the plan of the American government. In fact, in 1988 the U.S. Senate passed a resolution acknowledging the influence of the Iroquois Confederacy on the U.S. Constitution. But just how much did the Iroquois Confederacy influence our government? How democratic was the Iroquois Confederacy?

PRIMARY SOURCE

In Their Words...   Concurrent Resolution 331

To acknowledge the contribution of the Iroquois Confederacy of Nations to the development of the United States Constitution and to reaffirm the continuing government-to-government relationship between Indian tribes and the United States established in the Constitution.

Whereas the original framers of the Constitution, including, most notably, George Washington and Benjamin Franklin, are known to have greatly admired the concepts of the Six Nations of the Iroquois Confederacy . . .

—U.S. Senate, October 21, 1988

Build Citizenship
Justice

1. List ways the American government is like the Iroquois Council.
2. List ways the American government is different from the Iroquois Council.
3. Do you think the Iroquois Confederacy had more similarities or more differences with our government?

Think About It
Perspectives

1. Find a classmate that answered the question differently than you.
2. Take turns giving your perspective and supporting it with reasons and evidence.
3. Discuss with your classmate whether or not you think the Iroquois Confederacy was a democracy.

An 18th century French engraving of Deganawida meeting with the Iroquois Confederacy

Write About It

Think about how you described the Iroquois government. Write a paragraph answering the following questions. What makes a government a democracy? Is it the way leaders are chosen, or is it the way the government makes decisions?

Research Companion, pp. 48–49

 ENGLISH LEARNERS SCAFFOLD

ELD.PI.5.1 Exchanging information and ideas with others through oral collaborative discussions on a range of social and academic topics

Emerging	Bridging	Expanding
Build Meaning Make sure students understand *compromise* and *democracy*. Tell students that a compromise is a way of reaching an agreement in which each person gives up something. Democracy is a kind of government that is ruled by the people. Provide sentence frames: **The form of government we have in the United States is a ___. The two sisters reached a ___ and decided to share the toy.**	**Describe** Have students work with a partner to define the words *compromise* and *democracy*. Provide vocabulary help as needed.	**Develop Language** Encourage students to use the words *compromise* and *democracy* as they describe the U.S. and Iroquois forms of government.

See the **Language Learner Teaching Guide** for more language support strategies.

Monitor **and Differentiate**

REACHING ALL LEARNERS

Approaching Level

Work with students to understand how the Iroquois and U.S. forms of government are alike and different. Review the structure and role of Congress in the U.S. government.

On Level   Beyond Level

Have students conduct additional research on the similarities between the Iroquois Confederacy and the U.S. Government, focusing on the U.S. Constitution.

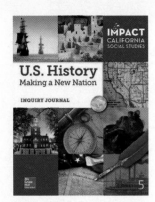

Inquiry Journal
pp. 44–45

 STANDARDS

Describe how geography and climate influenced the way various nations lived and adjusted to the natural environment, including locations of villages, the distinct structures that they built, and how they obtained food, clothing, tools, and utensils. **HSS.5.1.1**

CCSS Write opinion pieces on topics or texts, supporting a point of view with reasons and information. **CCSS.ELA.W.5.1**

Go Digital!

- Students can go online to report their findings. Assess their responses online.

- Students can access the online graphic organizer to capture ideas from their investigation.

Think About It

Students will review their research and consider how well the native peoples of the Eastern Woodlands solved their problems.

- Remind students to review the problems and solutions they have listed in their graphic organizer and the key details associated with these problems and solutions. Direct students back to pages 40–49 of their Research Companion if they need more information.

Write About It

Take a Stand Have students read the prompt. Explain to students that an effective opinion essay includes a claim and evidence that supports it. Remind students to include the following elements in their response.

- Introductory topic sentences that include a clearly stated claim

- Logical reasons supported by facts and details

- Transition words to link opinions and evidence

Use the rubric on p. T112 to evaluate students' work.

COLLABORATE
Talk About It

Defend Your Claim Help students pair up with a classmate who chose a different example of problem-solving.

- Explain that they should take turns discussing their opinions and the reasons that helped them form that opinion.

- Students should discuss whether they agree or disagree with their partner's opinion and explain why.

- Remind students to follow the rules of appropriate classroom conversation.

Connect to the
EQ
Essential Question

Read the prompt aloud to students. Ask them the following guiding questions:

- Which information from this lesson has most helped you to understand how the Eastern Woodland lived? (Responses will vary, but students may identify that the information on how they farmed was helpful.)

- What information has most helped you to understand the importance of problem-solving skills? (Responses will vary, but students should point to specific evidence from the text.)

Remind students to use the space provided in their journal to jot down notes.

Report Your Findings

Think About It

Based on your research, how well did the American Indians of the Eastern Woodlands solve their problems?

Write About It

Take a Stand

Write and Cite Evidence In your opinion, what was the most significant example of problem solving in the Eastern Woodlands? List three reasons that support your opinion. Include page references.

Students should be able to state an opinion about the most significant example of problem solving in the Eastern Woodlands and give three reasons from their research that support their opinion.

Talk About It

Defend Your Claim

Talk with a classmate who chose a different example of problem solving. Take turns discussing your opinions and supporting evidence. Do you agree or disagree with your partner's opinion?

 Geography

Connect to the EQ

Pull It Together

Think about the people and events that you have read and talked about in this lesson. How did they solve problems posed by their environment?

Students may respond that peoples in the Northeast used slash-and-burn agriculture, and peoples in the Southeast grew the Three Sisters crops.

Inquiry Project Notes

44 Lesson 5 How Did the Eastern Woodlands Impact the Lives of Early People?

Lesson 5 **45**

Inquiry Journal, pp. 44–45

EL ENGLISH LEARNERS SCAFFOLD

ELD.PI.5.11 Supporting own opinions and evaluating others' opinions in speaking and writing

Emerging

Organize Information Make sure students understand *claim* and *evidence*. Tell students that in opinion writing your *claim* is the sentence that clearly states your opinion—or what you think or believe. *Evidence* is the facts and examples you use to support your opinion. Say: *In an opinion essay about dogs versus cats, the sentence "I think that dogs make much better pets than cats" is a claim.*

Expanding/Bridging

Organizing Information Have students work with a partner to be sure they understand the words *claim* and *evidence*. Say: *In an opinion essay about dogs vs. cats, the sentence "I think that dogs are much better pets than cats" is a claim. The facts and examples you give to defend your opinion about dogs are evidence.* Have students practice stating and supporting opinions.

See the **Language Learner Teaching Guide** for more language support strategies.

Monitor and Differentiate

REACHING ALL LEARNERS

Approaching Level

Review with students that a claim is a sentence that clearly states an opinion. Remind students that a good opinion essay contains evidence that is strong enough to convince others of your point of view.

Beyond Level

Have students lists the reasons that support their opinion. Guide them to rank the reasons in order from least to most convincing. Have students try to strengthen their least convincing reasons.

Know what your students know!

Lesson Task
Report Your Findings

Use this rubric to evaluate students' response.

Take a Stand Students write an opinion essay about the most significant example of problem solving among the early peoples of the Eastern Woodlands.

Defend Your Claim Students talk to classmates about their findings. They take turns discussing how the activity helped them understand how the people of the Eastern Woodlands solved problems involving climate and terrain.

Performance Task Evaluation Rubric

	4	3	2	1
Historical Understanding	Strong understanding of problem solving by the peoples of the Eastern Woodlands	Adequate understanding of problem solving by the peoples of the Eastern Woodlands	Uneven understanding of problem solving by the peoples of the Eastern Woodlands	No understanding of problem solving by the peoples of the Eastern Woodlands
Take a Stand	Clearly explains opinion and reasons	Adequately explains opinion and reasons	Somewhat clear or unclear opinion or reasons	No opinion or student does not show understanding of the task
Support With Evidence	Reasons contain thorough evidence	Reasons contain adequate evidence	Reasons contain uneven evidence	Reasons are missing or contain no supporting evidence
Defend Your Claim	Provides plenty of reasons and evidence for opinion Is always respectful of partner's opinions	Provides adequate reasons and evidence for opinion Is usually respectful about partner's opinions	Provides few reasons or evidence for opinion Is sometimes disrespectful of partner's opinions	Provides no reasons or evidence for opinion Does not respect partner's opinions

Lesson Assessment

Go *Digital!*

- Have students complete the Chapter 1 Lesson 5 Assessment online to monitor their understanding of the lesson content.

California Smarter Balanced Assessment Connections!

Standards Covered	Lesson Task	Lesson Assessment	Alignment with California Smarter Balanced Assessment
History Social Science Content 5.1.1; 5.1.2; 5.1.3	✔	✔	Claim 1 Targets 8, 9, 10
History Social Science Analysis Skills Chronological and Spatial Thinking 5.4; 5.5 Research, Evidence, and Point of View 5.2 Historical Interpretation 5.2	✔	✔	Claim 1 Targets 11, 12
Writing W.5.1	✔	✔	Claim 2 Target 6a
Research and Inquiry W.5.9	✔	✔	Claim 4 Targets 2, 3, 4
Reading RI.5.3	✔	✔	Claim 1 Targets 11, 12
Speaking and Listening SL.5.1; SL.5.2	✔		Claim 3 Targets 3, 4

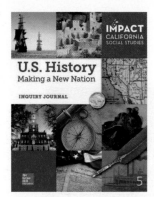

Inquiry Journal
pp. 46–47

 STANDARDS

STANDARDS

Students describe the major pre-Columbian settlements, including the cliff dwellers and pueblo people of the desert Southwest, the American Indians of the Pacific Northwest, the nomadic nations of the Great Plains, and the woodland peoples east of the Mississippi River. **HSS.5.1**

CCSS Integrate information from several texts on the same topic in order to write or speak about the subject knowledgably. **CCSS.ELA.RI.5.9**

Write narratives to develop real or imagined experiences or events using effective technique, descriptive details, and clear event sequences. **CCSS.ELA.W.5.3**

Go Digital!

Look online for the EQ Inquiry Project rubric.

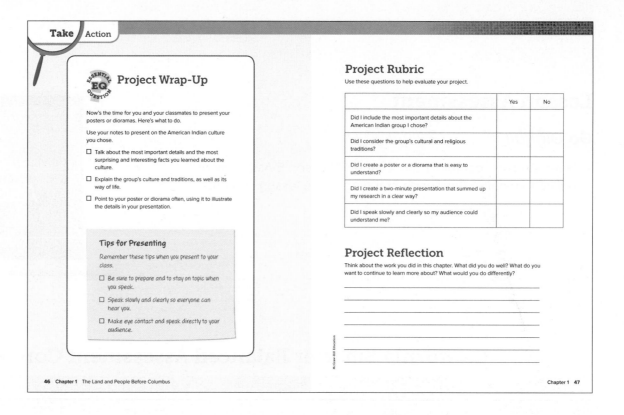

 Inquiry Project Wrap-Up

Have students share their inquiry projects by presenting their displays.

- Before students present their displays, discuss the wrap-up steps with them, making sure they know what's expected in their presentations.

- Allow time after each presentation for a Q-and-A session.

Tips for Presenting

Discuss the tips for presenting with students and the importance of communicating effectively with their audience. Remind students to integrate the visual aids into their spoken presentation.

Project Rubric

Discuss each question in the Project Rubric with students. If students have worked as part of a group to develop their projects, you might want to have them work as a group to address each question in the rubric.

Project Reflection

Student reflections can focus on the work they did as part of the group or their individual performance on the project. Give groups time to discuss each phase of their projects and reflect on their work.

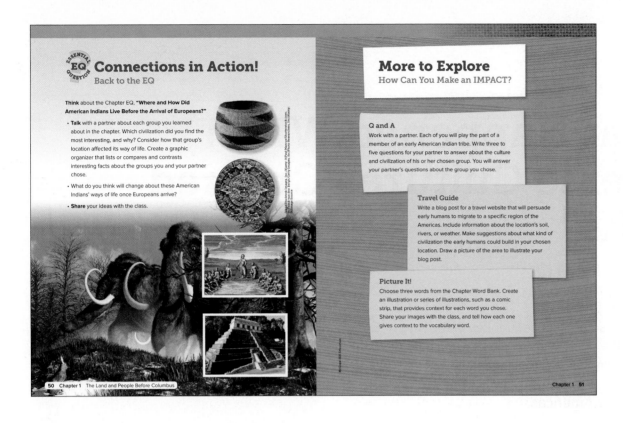

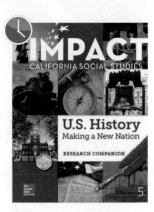

Research Companion
pp. 50–51

Connections in Action

To help focus students' conversations, you may want to discuss the EQ with the entire class before students discuss their ideas with a partner. Remind students to think about evidence they can provide that will support their ideas. After students present, allow time for others to ask questions.

More to Explore

Q and A Encourage students to work with a partner to develop questions and answers for a member of an early American Indian group.

Travel Guide Guide students to write posts for a travel website that persuade people to move to a specific region of the Americas. Remind students to use language that persuades and pictures that inspire.

Picture It! Have students create illustrations that provide context for three words from the chapter Word Bank. Post illustrations around the classroom.

Chapter 2

ESSENTIAL EQ QUESTION

What Happened When Diverse Cultures Crossed Paths?

In This Chapter ...

Students will investigate the course and consequences of the Age of Exploration in North America. They will learn about the European explorers who came to North America, why they came, what they did, and what the consequences of their expeditions were.

Lesson 1   Columbus in the Americas

Lesson 2   Spanish Exploration and Conquest

Lesson 3   European Powers in the Americas

"Don't forget to use the Foldables."

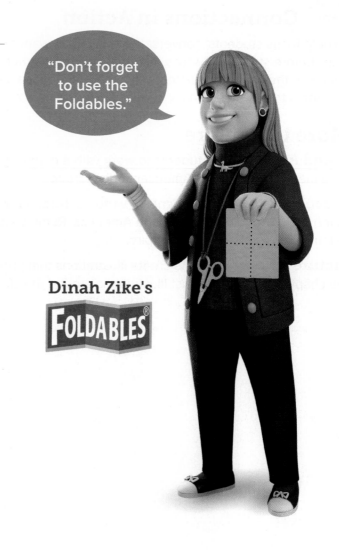

Dinah Zike's
FOLDABLES®

HSS   CHAPTER STANDARDS

✔ Students trace the routes of early explorers and describe the early exploration of the Americas. **HSS.5.2**

✔ Students describe the cooperation and conflict that existed among the American Indians and between the Indian nations and the new settlers. **HSS.5.3**

✔ Students understand the political, religious, social, and economic institutions that evolved in the colonial era. **HSS.5.4**

1 ENGAGE

Inquiry Journal
pp. 48–51

 Inquiry Project

European Explorers: Collect Them All!

- **Explore Words**

- *Go Digital!*
  - IMPACT Chapter Video: The Age of Exploration

2 INVESTIGATE

Research Companion
pp. 52–57

- **Step Into Time and Place**

- **Connect Through Literature**
  Cabin Boy Aboard the Buena Estrella by Jennifer Buchet

- **People You Should Know**

Weekly Explorer Magazine pp. 14–29

3 REPORT

Inquiry Journal
pp. 76–77

Inquiry Project

European Explorers: Collect Them All!

🕐 **Short on Time?** Look for the clock to teach core content in less time.

CULTIVATE MEANING AND SUPPORT LANGUAGE

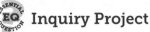

Language Learner Teaching Guide,
pp. 34–35

Content Objectives

- Explore how and why Spanish explorers first came to the Americas, and what they achieved.
- Understand how the colonial period began and how native peoples were impacted.

Language Objectives

- Talk and write about cause and effect relationships.
- Identify and use prepositions and prepositional phrases

CONNECT TO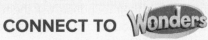

Unit 3, Week 1
Cultural Exchange

Read Aloud
"Foods for Thought"

Reading/Writing Workshop
"A Reluctant Traveler"

Literature Anthology/Paired Selection
They Don't Mean It!
"Where Did That Come From?!"

Leveled Readers
All the Way from Europe, Dancing the Flamenco, A Vacation in Minnesota, "A Sporting Gift," "Flamenco," and "The Scandinavian State?"

Unit 3, Week 5
Into the Past

Read Aloud
"Stonehenge: Puzzle from the Past"

Reading/Writing Workshop
"What was the Purpose of the Inca's Strange Strings?"

Literature Anthology/Paired Selection
Machu Picchu: Ancient City
"Dig This Technology!"

Leveled Readers
The Anasazi and "The Anasazi Were Astronomers"

Choose the assessment options that work best for you and your students.

BEFORE
PRE-TEST

Measure students' content knowledge before you begin the chapter with the following questions.

 Quick Check

✔ Who are the most famous explorers?

✔ Why do people explore?

✔ What are the risks and rewards of being an explorer?

1. Provide a large card for each student. Ask students to write their responses to the questions on the card.

2. When all students have responded, ask them to rate how confident they are in their answers on a scale from 1 – not very confident to 5 – very confident.

3. Collect the cards and review them for misconceptions, factual errors, and to inform instruction. You may wish to hang the cards in the classroom. Revisit their responses as students Investigate chapter 2.

4. **Don't Forget!** Revisit students' quick check responses with them. If students change their response, ask them to support the change with text evidence. You may wish to have students respond to a different prompt to measure students' content knowledge, such as *What were the goals of European explorers?*

EVERY LESSON
ONGOING ASSESSMENT

Use the lesson tools to monitor the IMPACT of your instruction.

 Stop and Check

Use the quick question prompts to monitor student comprehension of the content. The **Stop and Check** questions prompt students to make connections to their world today, engage in discussions to deepen their understanding of the content, and to look at different perspectives.

Report Your Findings

The lesson task, **Report Your Findings**, can be used to measure student understanding of the lesson content and ability to effectively express their understanding. See the Lesson Assessment pp. T148, T172, and T194 for task-specific evaluation rubrics.

(*Go Digital!*) **Lesson Assessment**

Use the **Lesson Assessment** to monitor student understanding of the lesson content. Have students complete the assessment online. See pp. T149, T173, and T195 for California Smarter Balanced Assessments Connections.

EVERY CHAPTER
POST TEST

Evaluate student understanding of core chapter content with one or more of the following assessment options.

Connections in Action

Use the **Connections in Action** to evaluate student understanding of core chapter content through discussion.

Inquiry Project

Use the **EQ Inquiry Project** to measure student understanding of the chapter content and ability to effectively express their understanding. See the EQ Inquiry Project Wrap Up below for a task-specific evaluation rubric.

	4	3	2	1
Historical Understanding	Strong understanding of the Age of Exploration	Adequate understanding of the Age of Exploration	Uneven understanding of the Age of Exploration	No understanding of the Age of Exploration
Take a Stand	Clearly states opinion	Adequately states opinion	Somewhat clear or unclear opinion	No opinion or student does not show understanding of the task
Support with Evidence	Reasons contain thorough and convincing evidence	Reasons contain adequate evidence	Reasons contain uneven or only somewhat convincing evidence	Reasons are missing or contain no supporting evidence
Present Your Project	Trading card is well made and informative Provides a concluding statement that relates to the student's position	Trading card is adequately made and informative Provides a concluding statement that mostly relates to the student's position	Trading card is confusing and poorly made Loosely links reasons to the student's opinion	Student did not understand assignment Does not link reasons to the student's opinion

(Go Digital!) ## Chapter Benchmark Assessments

Use the chapter tests to monitor student understanding of the chapter History-Social Science standards and content. Have students complete the assessment online.

ONLINE
ASSESSMENT

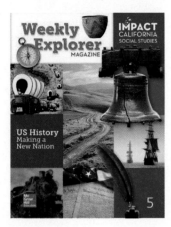

pp. 14–29

 Short on Time?

Use the Weekly Explorer Magazine during your reading block.

Go *Digital!*

Look online for the Weekly Explorer Magazine Teaching Guide.

WordBlast

Remind students to look for the Word Blasts as they read the Explorer Magazine.

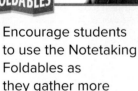

FOLDABLES

Encourage students to use the Notetaking Foldables as they gather more information.

Weekly Explorer Magazine

The Weekly Explorer Magazine is designed to provide students with more information to use as they dig deeper into the **Age of Exploration**. The articles in a variety of formats explore the Essential Question and support the Inquiry Project.

Engage

Build background for students and share any information needed to provide a context for the chapter topic. Have students read the Essential Question and the Table of Contents.

Analyze the Visual Discuss the opening visual (photograph, photo essay, artwork) on the second page of the Magazine chapter. Help students connect the visual to the chapter topic and the Essential Question.

Analyze the Sources

Students will read and analyze the articles, graphic novel, poems, songs, literature excerpts, primary sources, and infographics.

Read and Analyze Before reading, provide any additional information you think students will need about the topics. Then guide students through the three-step process to read and analyze the articles.

1 Inspect Have students skim the article or articles on a page or multiple pages. Ask questions to help students recall and retell key ideas.

- What is this article mostly about?
- Who is _____?

2 Find Evidence Have students reread the articles and look for details they might have missed. Ask additional questions to help them read more closely.

- What details do you notice in the photographs?
- Why was _____ important?

3 Make Connections Have students work in pairs or small groups to discuss prompts that help them connect the article(s) to other texts, their own lives, current ideas and issues, and other topics.

- How is _____ similar to what we do today?
- How do you think _____ felt about what happened?
- What do you think about _____?

Bibliography

The following suggested resources may help students' investigation of the chapter content.

EXPLORE PEOPLE, PLACES, AND EVENTS

▶ **Age of Exploration, 1492 to 1600**
by Gill Davies: National Geographic, 2007.

▶ **Carlota**
by Scott O'Dell; Laurel-Leaf Books, 2006.

▶ **Encounter**
by Jane Yolen; Voyager Books, 1996.

▶ **Explorers of North America**
by Christine Taylor-Butler; Children's Press, 2007.

▶ **"Hernando De Soto"**
by Rosemary and Stephen Vincent Benét (poem)
from **A Book of Americans;** Henry Holt (Macmillan), 1933.

▶ **Pedro's Journal: A Voyage with Christopher Columbus, August 3, 1492–February 14, 1493**
by Pam Conrad; Scholastic, 1992.

▶ **Smallpox in the New World**
by Stephanie True Peters; Benchmark Books, 2005.

Perspectives
▶ **You Wouldn't Want to Sail with Christopher Columbus**
by Fiona MacDonald; Children's Press, 2014.

EXPLORE MUSIC

Did you know? During the Age of Exploration, songs like **Ayo visto lo mappamundi** were common. This song, popular in the court of Naples around 1450 tells of the explorers navigating the unknown (to them) world. The opening lines are: "Ayo visto lo mappamundi é la carta dei naviguari, ma Sicilia me pari la più bella d'aquesto mundi." (I have seen the world map and the navigational charts, but Sicily is to me the most beautiful in all this world.)

Did you know? Like the languages, religions, and goods that explorers carried with them, they also brought the music of their homelands to these new lands. The four-part song **En Memoria D'Alixandre** tells of the fall of the Spanish city of Baza in 1489 after a long siege. This took place during the war between the Spanish monarchy and the Islamic Emirate of Granada.

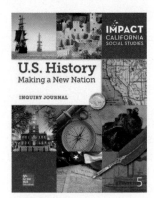

Inquiry Journal
pp. 48–51

 HSS STANDARDS

Students trace the routes of early explorers and describe the early explorations of the Americas. **HSS.5.2**

CCSS Write opinion pieces on topics or texts, supporting a point of view with reasons and information. **CCSS.ELA.W.5.1**

Draw evidence from literary or informational texts to support analysis, reflection, and research. **CCSS.ELA.W.5.9**

Go *Digital!*

Explore Words: Interactive vocabulary activities support students as they explore the chapter words.

See the **Language Learner Teaching Guide** pp. 34–35 for support strategies.

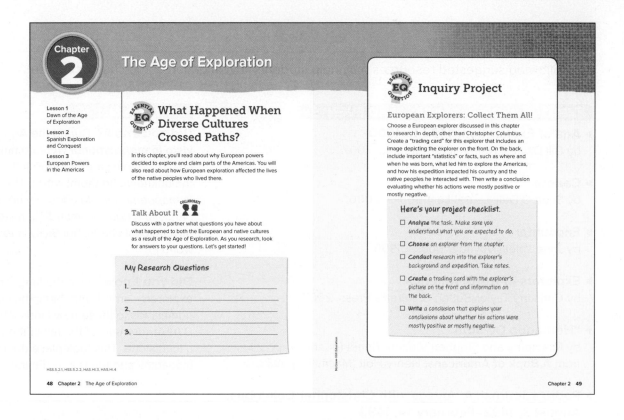

Chapter 2 The Age of Exploration

Inquiry Project
European Explorers: Collect Them All!

 # What Happened When Diverse Cultures Crossed Paths?

Have students read the Chapter Essential Question on p. 48.

Talk About It

- Prompt students to write three questions they would like to know the answers to after reading about the Age of Exploration.

- After jotting down their questions, have students discuss their questions with partners.

 # Inquiry Project

European Explorers: Collect Them All!

- Have students read aloud the EQ Inquiry Project.

- Tell students that they will use information gathered from the chapter and from independent research to complete the project.

- Make certain students understand the task by reviewing each step of the project.

Explore Words Worksheet

Complete this chapter's Word Rater. Write notes as you learn more about each word.

charter
- ☐ Know It!
- ☐ Heard It!
- ☐ Don't Know It!

My Notes
_____

claim
- ☐ Know It!
- ☐ Heard It!
- ☐ Don't Know It!

My Notes
_____

colony
- ☐ Know It!
- ☐ Heard It!
- ☐ Don't Know It!

My Notes
_____

conquest
- ☐ Know It!
- ☐ Heard It!
- ☐ Don't Know It!

My Notes
_____

diverse
- ☐ Know It!
- ☐ Heard It!
- ☐ Don't Know It!

My Notes
_____

merchants
- ☐ Know It!
- ☐ Heard It!
- ☐ Don't Know It!

My Notes
_____

navigation
- ☐ Know It!
- ☐ Heard It!
- ☐ Don't Know It!

My Notes
_____

resistance
- ☐ Know It!
- ☐ Heard It!
- ☐ Don't Know It!

My Notes
_____

settlement
- ☐ Know It!
- ☐ Heard It!
- ☐ Don't Know It!

My Notes
_____

warship
- ☐ Know It!
- ☐ Heard It!
- ☐ Don't Know It!

My Notes
_____

50　Chapter 2　The Age of Exploration

Chapter 2　51

Explore Words

- **Academic/Domain-Specific Vocabulary** Read the words aloud to students. Explain to students that these are words they will learn more about in the chapter.

- **Word Rater** Have students place a checkmark in one of the three boxes below each word, indicating that they "Know It," "Heard It," or "Don't Know It."

  - ✔ **Know It** Tell students that if they know the word, they should write its meaning on the lines provided.

  - ✔ **Heard It** Tell students that if they have heard, or are familiar with the word, they should write what they know about it on the lines provided. Remind them to take notes about the word as they encounter it.

  - ✔ **Don't Know It** If they do not know the word's meaning, tell them to write down its meaning when they encounter the word in the chapter.

🔍 Explore Words Routine

Remind students that when they come to an unfamiliar word or phrase in their research, they should follow these steps to determine its meaning.

1. Look around the word or phrase for clues to unlock its meaning.

2. Look inside the word or phrase for word part clues.

3. Look up the word in other resources.

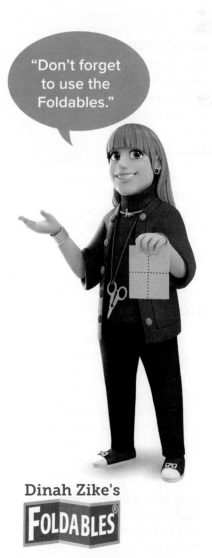

"Don't forget to use the Foldables."

Dinah Zike's
FOLDABLES®

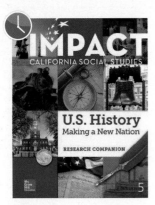

Research Companion
pp. 52–55

 STANDARDS

Students trace the routes of early explorers and describe the early exploration of the Americas. **HSS.5.2**

Students describe the cooperation and conflict that existed among the American Indians and between the Indian nations and the new settlers. **HSS.5.3**

Students understand the political, religious, social, and economic institutions that evolved in the colonial era. **HSS.5.4**

CCSS Explain the relationships or interactions between two or more individuals, events, ideas, or concepts in a historical, scientific, or technical text based on specific information in the text. **CCSS.ELA.RI.5.3**

Go Digital!

- Investigate the Age of Exploration with online whole-class presentation tools.

- Analyze the online literature selection so students can find evidence and make connections.

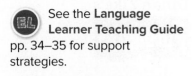 See the **Language Learner Teaching Guide** pp. 34–35 for support strategies.

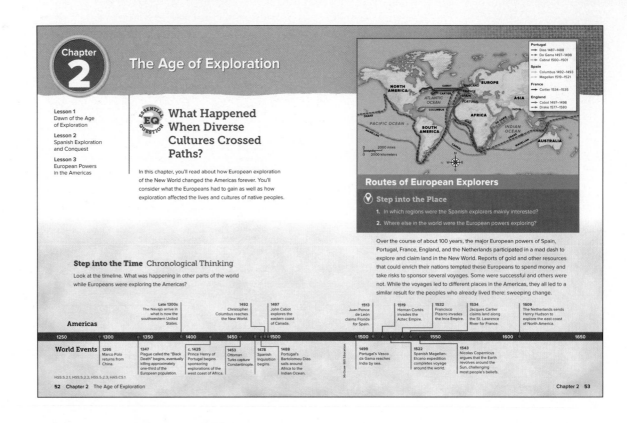

Step Into the Time

- Have students read over the events on the timeline, first examining the events from the Americas and then the events from around the world.

- Aside from North America, what other areas were being explored during the Age of Exploration? (China, parts of Africa, India)

- How much time elapsed between the discovery of the New World and the first journey around the world? (30 years)

Step Into the Place

In partners or in small groups, have students examine the map on p. 53 and answer the questions beneath it.

1. In which regions were the Spanish explorers mainly interested? (Central and South America, and the southeastern part of North America)

2. Where else in the world were the European powers exploring? (Possible responses: Africa, India, and all the way around the world)

Connect Through Literature

Cabin Boy
Aboard the Buena Estrella

From the Journal of Dominic Raimundo, Age 10

by Jennifer Buchet
illustrated by Shelley Jackson

What if you could have sailed with an explorer 400 years ago? This is what your days might have been like.

August 5, 1524 At last, the winds are with us. I'm anxious to reach New Spain¹ and discover my fortune! Every day, I rise at 3 a.m. to wake the crew. I sing the morning hymns. Cook and I then lay out salted pork and ale for everyone. Afterward, I help the captain with the logbooks that record everything that is happening. And then I walk the ship, working wherever I'm needed. Yesterday, I helped stop up a small leak. I still smell the awful odor of tar on me. Perhaps tomorrow, I can bathe with a bucket of seawater.

August 15 I miss my bed at home! I didn't have enough money to buy a hammock before we left Spain. So I sleep against sacks of grain or with the horses. But it really smells down below, and the rats bite. When the nights are clear, I sleep topside and stargaze. The clanging of the rigging (the ropes and metal fixtures) and the whoosh of the waves are my lullaby.

August 22 The sky has been darkening all day. The air is heavy. Captain Padilla ordered us to batten down the hatches (to cover up the entrances to go below deck) and secure all the lines. Even the dolphins have gone. I'm afraid . . .

¹In the 1500s, Spain had claimed a huge area of land in North America. The land was called New Spain.

August 26 Dios mío, I'm alive! These last few days have been the worst of my life. I feared a giant sea monster was trying to devour us all! I couldn't tell if it was day or night, so dark was the sky. The ship bucked and pitched in the merciless waves. Twice we nearly capsized! Sadly, three sailors fell into the churning seas. Water was everywhere, including below deck. I helped pump the bilge, trying to ignore the horses' terrified cries. My arms still ache, but at least I'm alive.

August 28 We limp toward Havana for repairs. Captain Padilla says our expedition is delayed by at least three weeks! Food supplies are low and tempers are high. We couldn't collect rainwater during the storm, and now our barrels are filled with algae scum. The remaining cheese is moldy, and sometimes it hurts to bite into what's left of the hardtack. Hard is the right word for those biscuits! I remind myself that gold and glory await me.

September 8 At last, dry land! Some sailors talk of staying in Cuba, finding work in the gold mines or on the sugarcane farms. But I'll continue; after that hurricane, I don't even fear the Indians!²

²Because Columbus thought he had reached the Indies in Asia, he called the people of the Caribbean "Indians." Later explorers used the same name.

Think About It

1. What motivated Dominic travel to the New Spain?

2. How would you describe the journey from Spain to New Spain?

3. Think about Dominic's character. What characteristics does he show that are necessary for survival in the journey to the New World?

54 Chapter 2 The Age of Exploration

Chapter 2 55

GENRE Historical Fiction *"Cabin Boy Aboard the Buena Estrella" is a piece of historical fiction. Fiction tells a story about something that happened in history. While many people took Dominic Raimundo's journey, this is a story and not an authentic journal.*

Analyze the Source

Inspect Have students read the selection on pp. 54–55 together to determine the general meaning of the text.

1. What motivated Dominic to travel to the New Spain? (Dominic believes he will find gold and glory in New Spain.)

Find Evidence Have students reread the selection and ask

2. How would you describe the journey from Spain to New Spain? Cite examples from the text. (Responses will vary, but students should include details about dangers such as the storm, and hardships such as the cramped living quarters and low food supplies.)

Make Connections

3. Think about Dominic's character. What characteristics does he show that are necessary for survival in the journey to the New World? (Answers will vary.)

Perspectives Would you want to be an explorer? Why or why not? (Answers will vary.)

Research Companion
pp. 56–57

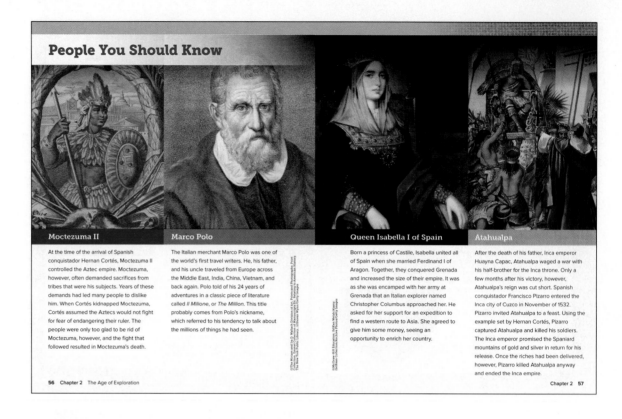

People You Should Know

Moctezuma II

At the time of the arrival of Spanish conquistador Hernan Cortés, Moctezuma II controlled the Aztec empire. Moctezuma, however, often demanded sacrifices from tribes that were his subjects. Years of these demands had led many people to dislike him. When Cortés kidnapped Moctezuma, Cortés assumed the Aztecs would not fight for fear of endangering their ruler. The people were only too glad to be rid of Moctezuma, however, and the fight that followed resulted in Moctezuma's death.

Marco Polo

The Italian merchant Marco Polo was one of the world's first travel writers. He, his father, and his uncle traveled from Europe across the Middle East, India, China, Vietnam, and back again. Polo told of his 24 years of adventures in a classic piece of literature called *Il Milione*, or *The Million*. This title probably comes from Polo's nickname, which referred to his tendency to talk about the millions of things he had seen.

Queen Isabella I of Spain

Born a princess of Castile, Isabella united all of Spain when she married Ferdinand I of Aragon. Together, they conquered Grenada and increased the size of their empire. It was as she was encamped with her army at Grenada that an Italian explorer named Christopher Columbus approached her. He asked for her support for an expedition to find a western route to Asia. She agreed to give him some money, seeing an opportunity to enrich her country.

Atahualpa

After the death of his father, Inca emperor Huayna Capac, Atahualpa waged a war with his half-brother for the Inca throne. Only a few months after his victory, however, Atahualpa's reign was cut short. Spanish conquistador Francisco Pizarro entered the Inca city of Cuzco in November of 1532. Pizarro invited Atahualpa to a feast. Using the example set by Hernan Cortés, Pizarro captured Atahualpa and killed his soldiers. The Inca emperor promised the Spaniard mountains of gold and silver in return for his release. Once the riches had been delivered, however, Pizarro killed Atahualpa anyway and ended the Inca empire.

56   Chapter 2   The Age of Exploration

Chapter 2   57

STANDARDS

Students trace the routes of early explorers and describe the early exploration of the Americas. **HSS 5.2**

Students describe the cooperation and conflict that existed among the American Indians and between the Indian nations and the new settlers. **HSS.5.3**

Students understand the political, religious, social, and economic institutions that evolved in the colonial era. **HSS.5.4**

 Determine two or more main ideas of a text and explain how they are supported by key details; summarize the text. **CCSS.ELA.RI.5.2**

Explain the relationships or interactions between two or more individuals, events, ideas, or concepts in a historical, scientific, or technical text based on specific information in the text. **CCSS.ELA.RI.5.3**

People You Should Know

How do personal stories IMPACT our understanding of the Age of Exploration?

- Have students read aloud the biographies.

- Tell them that they will learn about these people and others throughout the chapter.

- In groups or as a class, have students create an infographic map. Have them make a map and mark locations of significant events for one or more figure discussed in the chapter or associated with the Age of Exploration. Each location should be accompanied by a short description of what occurred, when it happened, and why it was important. Figures may include:

  ▷ Moctezuma II
  ▷ Marco Polo
  ▷ Queen Isabella and King Ferdinand
  ▷ Ponce de Leon
  ▷ Hernán Cortés
  ▷ Cabeza de Vaca
  ▷ Francisco Pizarro

  ▷ Hernando de Soto
  ▷ Francisco Vázquez de Coronado
  ▷ John Cabot
  ▷ Jacques Cartier
  ▷ Samuel de Champlain
  ▷ Giovanni da Verrazzano
  ▷ Henry Hudson

Go Digital!

Investigate chapter content with the online teaching plan.

See the **Language Learner Teacher Guide** pp. 34–35 for support strategies.

Teacher Notes

Why Did the Spanish Explore the Americas?

Background Information

Tell students that in this lesson, they will learn why early Spanish explorers, such as Columbus, sailed to the Americas and how technological advances made their long voyages possible.

Community Connections

To enrich students' understanding of sea travel in Columbus's day, plan a field trip to a replica of an early sailing ship at a maritime museum or special exhibit in your area. The Columbus Foundation, for example, has public displays of its replicas of the *Niña* and *Pinta* at over 30 locations in the U.S. each year.

 LESSON STANDARDS

- ✓ Describe the entrepreneurial characteristics of early explorers (e.g., ChristopherColumbus, Francisco Vásquez de Coronado) and the technological developmentsthat made sea exploration by latitude and longitude possible (e.g., compass, sextant,astrolabe, seaworthy ships, chronometers, gunpowder). **HSS.5.2.1**

- ✓ Explain the aims, obstacles, and accomplishments of the explorers, sponsors, andleaders of key European expeditions and the reasons Europeans chose to explore andcolonize the world (e.g., the Spanish Reconquista, the Protestant Reformation, theCounter Reformation). **HSS.5.2.2**

- ✓ Students place key events and people of the historical era they are studying in a chronological sequence and spatial context; they interpret time lines. **HAS.CS.1**

- ✓ Students use map and globe skills to determine the absolute locations of places and interpret information available through a map's or globe's legend, scale, and symbolic representations. **HAS.CS.4**

- ✓ Students differentiate between primary and secondary sources. **HAS.HR.1**

- ✓ Students identify and interpret the multiple causes and effects of historical events. **HAS.HI.3**

 Connect to the
Essential Question

The **Weekly Explorer Magazine** supports students' exploration of the Essential Question and provides additional resources for the EQ Inquiry Project.

Chapter 2, pp. 14–29

 ## Inquiry Project

What happened when diverse cultures crossed paths?

Remind students to use the information they learn in this lesson and other resources to complete their Big Idea Inquiry Project.

In this lesson you will use Foldables.

When Minutes Count!
Suggested Lesson Pacing

1 ENGAGE
One Day

- Lesson Opener
- Analyze the Source
- Inquiry Tools

Go Digital
- **Video:** Columbus Sails
- **iMap:** Explorer Routes
- **iMap:** Voyages of Columbus, 1492–1502
- **iMap:** Trade Routes of the Ancient World

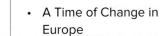

2 INVESTIGATE
Two to Three Days

🕐 **Short on Time?** Look to the clock to teach core content in less time.

- A Time of Change in Europe
- **Infographic** Technological Advances
- A Sea Route to the Indies

3 REPORT
One Day

- Think About It
- Be Persuasive
- Defend Your Choice

Make Connections!

(CCSS) CONNECT TO ELA

Reading

Explain the relationships or interactions between two or more individuals, events, ideas, or concepts in a historical, scientific, or technical text based on specific information in the text. **RI.5.3**

Compare and contrast the overall structure (e.g., chronology, comparison, cause/effect, problem/solution) of events, ideas, concepts, or information in two or more texts. **RI.5.5**

Research

Recall relevant information from experiences or gather relevant information from print and digital sources; summarize or paraphrase information in notes and finished work, and provide a list of sources. **W.5.8**

Writing

Write opinion pieces on topics or texts, supporting a point of view with reasons and information. **W.5.1**

Speaking and Listening

Engage effectively in a range of collaborative discussions (one-on-one, in groups, and teacher-led) with diverse partners on grade 5 topics and texts, building on others' ideas and expressing their own clearly. **SL.5.1**

Summarize a written text read aloud or information presented in diverse media and formats, including visually, quantitatively, and orally. **SL.5.2**

Classroom Resources

🔍 Search for additional resources using the following key words.

Vasco Núñez de Balboa

caravel

Christopher Columbus

Ferdinand and Isabella

Ferdinand Magellan

Prince Henry the Navigator

Silk Road

Taíno

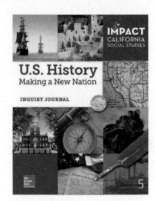

Inquiry Journal,
pp. 52–53

Why Did the Spanish Explore the Americas?

Bellringer

COLLABORATE

Prompt students to retrieve information from the previous lessons. Say: *In 1492, many native peoples were living in the lands that would become known as the Americas. How do you think the coming of Europeans would change their way of life?* (Responses will vary, but students should recognize that the change would be drastic.)

Lesson Outcomes

What Am I Learning? Have students read the Lesson Question and Lesson Outcomes on p. 52.

Why Am I Learning It? Check that students are familiar with the term *technological* ("related to practical uses of science") and with the nation of Spain and its location in Western Europe. Clarify that while Columbus himself was Italian, he is called a Spanish explorer because he was hired by the rulers of Spain to explore for Spain's benefit.

How Will I Know That I Learned It? Ask students the following questions.

- What will you identify? (the developments that encouraged Spanish explorers to sail to the Americas)

- What is the purpose of the task? (to write an advertisement for an invention)

- How will you support your claims? (with evidence from the text)

Talk About It

COLLABORATE

Explain that letters written by historical figures can show us why they did what they did and what they thought about it. Provide sentence frames to help students talk about the letter Columbus sent when he returned from his first voyage to America.

- *Columbus gave the native people ____ in order to ____.* (beautiful things; win them over to Christianity and support for Spain)

- *He hoped that the people would give him ____.* (things they had a lot of that the Spanish needed)

HSS STANDARDS

Describe the entrepreneurial characteristics of early explorers (e.g., ChristopherColumbus, Francisco Vásquez de Coronado) and the technological developmentsthat made sea exploration by latitude and longitude possible (e.g., compass, sextant,astrolabe, seaworthy ships, chronometers, gunpowder). **HSS.5.2.1**

Explain the aims, obstacles, and accomplishments of the explorers, sponsors, andleaders of key European expeditions and the reasons Europeans chose to explore andcolonize the world (e.g., the Spanish Reconquista, the Protestant Reformation, theCounter Reformation). **HSS.5.2.2**

Students differentiate between primary and secondary sources. **HAS.HR.1**

Go Digital!

Explore the lesson content with online whole-class presentation tools.

- **Video:** Columbus Sails

- **iMap:** Explorer Routes

- **iMap:** Voyages of Columbus, 1492–1502

- **iMap:** Trade Routes of the Ancient World

Collaborative Conversations

COLLABORATE

Add New Ideas As students engage in partner, small group, and whole-class discussions, encourage them to

- Stay on topic.

- Connect their own ideas to things their peers have said.

- Look for ways to connect their personal experiences or prior knowledge to the conversation.

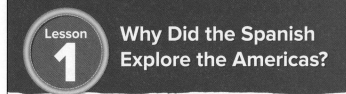

Lesson 1
Why Did the Spanish Explore the Americas?

Lesson Outcomes

What Am I Learning?
In this lesson, you're going to use your investigative skills to learn how and why Spanish explorers first came to the Americas.

Why Am I Learning It?
Reading and talking about the lesson will help you understand the achievements of early Spanish explorers, such as Christopher Columbus, and how they affected the development of colonial America.

How Will I Know That I Learned It?
You will be able to use cause and effect to understand the developments that encouraged early Spanish explorers, such as Columbus, to sail to the Americas. You will be able to write an advertisement describing one of these technological developments and explaining how it would help an explorer on their voyage.

Talk About It · COLLABORATE

Examine the Details Read Columbus's letter that is translated into English. What does it show you about the goals or motives of the Spanish explorers who first came to the Americas?

Primary Source

In Their Words ... Christopher Columbus

. . . I gave [the inhabitants] many beautiful and pleasing things, which I had brought with me, for no return whatever, in order to win their affection, and that they might become Christians and inclined to love our King and Queen and Princes and all the people of Spain; and that they might be eager to search for and gather and give to us what they abound in and we greatly need.

—from a letter Columbus wrote to Queen Isabella and King Ferdinand as soon as he returned from his first voyage in 1493

TEXT: Christopher Columbus to King Ferdinand and Queen Isabella, March 14, 1493, Lisbon, Gilder Lehrman Collection # GLC01427, Gilder Lehrman Institute of American History; PHOTO: GL Archive/Alamy

HSS.5.2.1, HSS.5.2.2, HAS.HR.1, HAS.HR.2, HAS.HI.3.

52 Lesson 1 Why Did the Spanish Explore the Americas?

Lesson 1 **53**

Inquiry Journal, pp. 52–53

ENGLISH LEARNERS SCAFFOLD

ELD.PI.5.12 Selecting and applying varied and precise vocabulary and language structures to effectively convey ideas

Emerging	Expanding	Bridging
Develop Vocabulary Help students read Columbus's letter by going over more difficult vocabulary, such as *inhabitants* ("people who live in an area"), *affection* ("liking"), *inclined* ("tending to"), and *abound* ("are found in large numbers").	**Paraphrase** Have students paraphrase Columbus's letter in more modern language. Example: *I gave the inhabitants things I had brought, getting nothing in return, to win them over to our religion and nation and get them to give us what we needed that they had a lot of.*	**Discuss Idioms** Have students discuss Columbus's phrase "for no return whatever" and whether or not it is true.

See the **Language Learner Teaching Guide** for more language support strategies.

Monitor and Differentiate

REACHING ALL LEARNERS

Approaching Level

Read the credit of Columbus's letter, which tells to whom it was written. Clarify that Isabella and Ferdinand were the king and queen of Spain.

On Level

Have students clarify which inhabitants the letter is about and what Columbus wants them to provide in future.

Beyond Level

Discuss whether Columbus would be completely honest in a letter to Spain's rulers.

1 ENGAGE

Analyze the Source

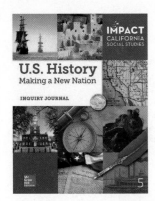

Inquiry Journal,
pp. 54–55

 STANDARDS

Describe the entrepreneurial characteristics of early explorers (e.g., ChristopherColumbus, Francisco Vásquez de Coronado) and the technological developmentsthat made sea exploration by latitude and longitude possible (e.g., compass, sextant,astrolabe, seaworthy ships, chronometers, gunpowder). **HSS.5.2.1**

Students identify and interpret the multiple causes and effects of historical events. **HAS.HI.3**

CCSS Students summarize information presented in diverse media and formats, including visually, quantitatively, and orally. **CCSS.ELA.SL.5.1.2**

Go Digital!

Model how to inspect and find evidence with online whole-class presentation tools.

Background Information

The Caravel Developed by the Portuguese, the caravel changed its design over time as modifications made it lighter and speedier. Portuguese voyages sponsored by Prince Henry in the 1440s used caravels to explore the coast of West Africa. Columbus is said to have praised his favorite caravel, the *Niña*, for its safety, speed, and maneuverability.

1 Inspect

Look Tell students to examine the image and read the labels.

- What kind of ship does the image depict? (a caravel)
- What kind of sails does it have? (lateen (triangular), main, and square topsails)
- Where is the rudder for steering the ship located? (in the stern, or back)

Collaborate Have partners discuss their impressions of the caravel. (Students should recognize that the ship, though top-of-the-line for its time, is still fairly simple.)

2 Find Evidence

Look Again Have students reexamine the diagram of the caravel.

Analyze the Image Read aloud the text that accompanies the diagram, with students studying the diagram as you describe its features.

- Have partners discuss the advantages that the caravel has over other ships. (It is fast, easy to steer, able to go close to shore, and can hold a large cargo.)
- Guide students to discuss why it would be an advantage for the ship to go closer to shore. (It made it easier to see what the shore looked like so the sailor could map the new land.)
- Have students discuss why the ship had so many different types of sails. (to catch as much wind as possible to move swiftly)
- Ask students which of Columbus's ships were caravels. (the *Niña* and the *Pinta*)
- **Context Clues** Have students use the context clues to determine the meaning of the term *cargo hold*. (the area of the ship where goods are stored)

3 Make Connections
COLLABORATE

Talk Have students discuss the reasons that the caravel helped make Spanish exploration possible. (Its speed allowed Spanish explorers to reach the Americas faster, its cargo hold could carry the supplies needed on the long voyage, and its shallow keel, or bottom, made it easier to explore and map the new lands.)

Connect to Now Have partners discuss how the explorers' achievements still affect the Americas today.

Analyze the Source

1 Inspect

Look Examine this image. What does it depict?

- **Underline** words you don't know that are used as labels.
- **Circle** parts of the image that show you what those labels indicate.
- **Discuss** with a partner the kind of ship that Columbus sailed to the New World.

My Notes

_____

_____

_____

_____

_____

_____

_____

_____

_____

_____

_____

_____

_____

_____

Diagram of a Caravel

The caravel was a small, light sailing ship. It was designed by the Portuguese and used by the Spanish in the late 1400s. Its lateen (triangular) and square sails caught the wind to help the ship travel faster. The caravel had a stern, or rear, rudder that helped it steer easily. It had a shallow keel, or bottom, that allowed it to go closer to shore than most other ships. It also had a large cargo hold to store supplies that were needed for a long journey. The *Niña* and the *Pinta*, two of the ships Columbus used to sail to the New World, were caravels.

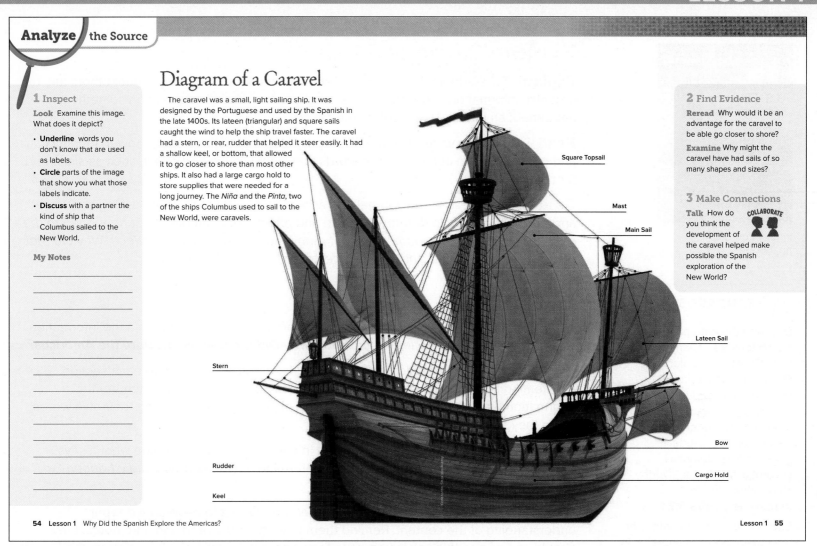

Square Topsail

Mast

Main Sail

Lateen Sail

Bow

Cargo Hold

Stern

Rudder

Keel

2 Find Evidence

Reread Why would it be an advantage for the caravel to be able go closer to shore?

Examine Why might the caravel have had sails of so many shapes and sizes?

3 Make Connections

Talk How do you think the development of the caravel helped make possible the Spanish exploration of the New World?

COLLABORATE

54 Lesson 1 Why Did the Spanish Explore the Americas?

Lesson 1 55

Inquiry Journal, pp. 54-55

ENGLISH LEARNERS SCAFFOLD

ELD.PI.5.12 Selecting and applying varied and precise vocabulary and language structures to effectively convey ideas

Emerging	Expanding	Bridging
Develop Vocabulary Have students examine the diagram and provide the technical terms for the front, back, and bottom of the caravel. (bow, stern, keel)	**Use Vocabulary** Have students write sentences for the labels on the diagram to show understanding of what the terms mean. (Example: We stored the goods in the *cargo hold*.)	**Explain** Have students study the diagram and accompanying text and then explain how the caravel sailed. (Example: Driven by winds caught in the sails, the ship moved forward. A rudder in the stern helped steer it.)

See the **Language Learner Teaching Guide** for more language support strategies.

Monitor and Differentiate

REACHING ALL LEARNERS

Approaching Level

Have students discuss the importance of the large cargo hold to early explorers.

Beyond Level

Ask students to compare overseas travel in Columbus's day to travel today.

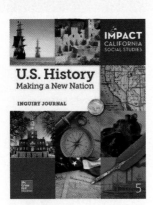

Inquiry Journal,
pp. 56–57

 STANDARDS

Describe the entrepreneurial characteristics of early explorers (e.g., ChristopherColumbus, Francisco Vásquez de Coronado) and the technological developmentsthat made sea exploration by latitude and longitude possible (e.g., compass, sextant,astrolabe, seaworthy ships, chronometers, gunpowder). **HSS.5.2.1**

Students identify and interpret the multiple causes and effects of historical events. **HAS.HI.3**

(CCSS) Draw evidence from literary or informational texts to support analysis, reflection, and research. **CCSS.ELA.W.5.9**

Go Digital!

- Model how to explore and investigate with online whole-class tools.

- Students can access the online graphic organizer to use the inquiry tools as they read.

Explore Cause and Effect

Explain Tell students that cause and effect is one kind of structure that authors use to organize information in historical texts. Clarify that a cause is the reason something has happened; an effect is the result of the cause.

Read Have students read aloud the step-by-step instructions about how to identify cause and effect. Mention additional clue words that signal cause and effect, such as *since* and *for that reason*.

Guide Practice Use the Journal text about the caravel to illustrate asking and answering questions to determine cause and effect. For example: *What happened to the caravel? It made a long journey without running out of supplies (the effect). Why did that happen? It traveled fast and had a large cargo hold (the cause).*

Investigate!

Have students read pages 58–67 in the Research Companion. Tell them the information will help them answer the lesson question **Why Did the Spanish Explore the Americas?**

Take Notes Tell students that they will take notes as they read each section. Remind them that taking notes will help them understand and remember the information they learn. Stress the importance of paraphrasing, or using their own words, when they take notes.

Inspect Guide students to read the text in each section to determine what it says. Remind them to ask *What happened?* to determine effects and *Why did it happen?* to determine causes.

Find Evidence Encourage students to reread the text to develop a deeper understanding of the content. Remind them that after they read and take notes, they should review and think about how the facts and details will help them answer the lesson question.

Collaborative Conversations

Text-Based Discussion Remind students of the goals of discussing the text with others.

- to listen and respond to their partners' points
- to ask for evidence from the text
- to build on each other's ideas
- to see the text from a different point of view

Inquiry Tools

Explore Cause and Effect

Identifying **cause and effect** will help you understand why events in history happened.

1. **Read the text once all the way through.**
   This will help you understand what the text is about.

2. **As you read a passage, ask yourself, What happened?**
   The answer to this question helps you identify an effect.

3. **Then ask yourself, Why did that happen?**
   This is the cause.

4. **Look for clue words.**
   Words such as *because, so,* and *as a result* are clues that point to a cause-and-effect relationship.

 COLLABORATE Based on the text you read, work with your class to complete the chart below.

Cause	Effect
The caravel's sails allowed the ship to go faster, and its large cargo hold could store enough supplies for long journeys.	The caravel made long journeys and exploration of far-off lands possible.

Investigate!

Read pages 58–67 in your Research Companion. Use your investigative skills to identify the developments that helped cause Spanish exploration of the New World. Use the chart below to organize the information.

Cause		Effects
astrolabe, introduced to Europeans in the 1100s	⟶	helped sailors determine their position
the compass, introduced to Europeans in the 1200s	⟶	helped sailors determined their direction
the stern rudder, adopted by Europeans by the 1400s	⟶	helped sailors steer ships
the printing press, invented in 1436	⟶	helped spread news about explorers' discoveries and encouraged further exploration
the caravel, developed in the 1400s	⟶	useful for making long voyages and exploring new coastlines

Inquiry Journal, pp. 56–57

(EL) ENGLISH LEARNERS SCAFFOLD

ELD.PII.5.1 Understanding text structure

Emerging

Understand Cause and Effect Illustrate the use of clue words to signal cause-and-effect relationships. For example, *Because* of its sails, the caravel went fast. It could sail close to shore *since* it had a shallow keel, or bottom. It had a large cargo hold, *so* it could carry the supplies needed for a long voyage.

Expanding

Identify Cause and Effect Ask students to identify cause-and-effect relationships about the caravel on pages 54–55.

Bridging

Synthesize Cause and Effect Have students consider all the specific details and then identify the *key* cause and effect about the caravel and its relationship to Spanish exploration. (Because of its design, the caravel allowed Spanish explorers like Columbus to reach and explore the Americas.)

See the **Language Learner Teaching Guide** for more language support strategies.

Monitor and Differentiate

REACHING ALL LEARNERS

Approaching Level

Have students identify simple cause-and-effect relationships in daily life. Offer this example: *Because of bad weather, the bus was late.*

On Level

Discuss why cause and effect is a common way of organizing historical writing. Elicit or explain that in studying history, we often want to know what happened and why it happened.

Beyond Level

Have students consider the general reasons, or causes, of exploration of foreign lands and the results, or effects, of such exploration.

Research Companion
pp. 58–59

 STANDARDS

Describe the entrepreneurial characteristics of early explorers (e.g., ChristopherColumbus, Francisco Vásquez de Coronado) and the technological developmentsthat made sea exploration by latitude and longitude possible (e.g., compass, sextant,astrolabe, seaworthy ships, chronometers, gunpowder). **HSS.5.2.1**

Students place key events and people of the historical era they are studying in a chronological sequence and spatial context; they interpret time lines. **HAS.CS.1**

Students identify and interpret the multiple causes and effects of historical events. **HAS.HI.3**

Go Digital!

Investigate the lesson content with online whole-class presentation tools.

- **Video:** Columbus Sails

- **iMap:** Explorer Routes

- **iMap:** Voyages of Columbus, 1492–1502

- **iMap:** Trade Routes of the Ancient World

Background Information

Marco Polo probably did not bring pasta back from China, as legend has it, but his book did give details of other Chinese practices, such as the use of paper money and coal, that Europeans would eventually adopt. Among those probably inspired by his adventures was Christopher Columbus, believed to have had a copy of Polo's *Travels*.

| TIMELINE | Invite students to look at the timeline at the top on page 59.

Analyze In what decades did Bartolomeu Dias, Vasco da Gama, and Christopher Columbus all make their famous voyages? (the 1480s and 1490s) **HAS.CS.1**

Analyze the Source

Inspect Have students read pp. 58–59.

Find Evidence Use the questions below to check comprehension. Remind students to support their answers with text evidence.

Analyze Cause and Effect According to the text, what two experiences stirred European interest in foreign travel? (going on pilgrimages to the Holy Land and reading *The Travels of Marco Polo*) **DOK 2**

Define What is a merchant? (someone who makes a living buying and selling goods) **DOK 2**

Infer Why were Europeans interested in China and the East Indies? (They wanted gems, silks, spices, and other products from those lands.) **DOK 2**

Identify To which Chinese ruler's court did Marco Polo and his family travel? (Kublai Khan's) **DOK 1**

Make Connections

Analyze Based on what you read, explain why Europeans of the Middle Ages became interested in travel. (They wanted to make religious pilgrimages, trade for unusual goods from foreign lands, and see the world as Marco Polo had.) **DOK 3**

Analyze the Image Direct students to the image of the atlas and the caption that explains it. Say: *The atlas shows a map of the east and west hemispheres.*

- What does the view at the top of the page show? (the world seen from the top of the North Pole)

- How was exploration of the fifteenth and sixteenth centuries important in creating maps like this one? (Students should recognize that because the explorers brought back information about foreign places, map makers were able to make more accurate maps.)

Lesson 1
Why Did the Spanish Explore the Americas?

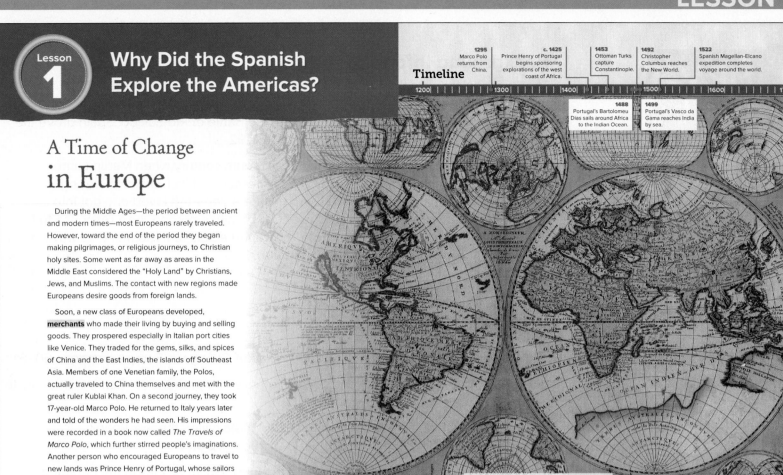

Timeline

1295	c. 1425	1453	1492	1522
Marco Polo returns from China.	Prince Henry of Portugal begins sponsoring explorations of the west coast of Africa.	Ottoman Turks capture Constantinople.	Christopher Columbus reaches the New World.	Spanish Magellan-Elcano expedition completes voyage around the world.

1200 | 1300 | 1400 | 1500 | 1600 | 1700

1488 Portugal's Bartolomeu Dias sails around Africa to the Indian Ocean.

1499 Portugal's Vasco da Gama reaches India by sea.

A Time of Change in Europe

During the Middle Ages—the period between ancient and modern times—most Europeans rarely traveled. However, toward the end of the period they began making pilgrimages, or religious journeys, to Christian holy sites. Some went as far away as areas in the Middle East considered the "Holy Land" by Christians, Jews, and Muslims. The contact with new regions made Europeans desire goods from foreign lands.

Soon, a new class of Europeans developed, **merchants** who made their living by buying and selling goods. They prospered especially in Italian port cities like Venice. They traded for the gems, silks, and spices of China and the East Indies, the islands off Southeast Asia. Members of one Venetian family, the Polos, actually traveled to China themselves and met with the great ruler Kublai Khan. On a second journey, they took 17-year-old Marco Polo. He returned to Italy years later and told of the wonders he had seen. His impressions were recorded in a book now called *The Travels of Marco Polo*, which further stirred people's imaginations. Another person who encouraged Europeans to travel to new lands was Prince Henry of Portugal, whose sailors explored the west coast of Africa in the early 1400s.

HSS.5.2.1, HSS.5.2.2, HSS.5.2.3, HAS.CS.1, HAS.CS.2, HAS.CS.4, HAS.CS.5, HAS.HR.1, HAS.HR.2, HAS.HR.3, HAS.HI.1, HAS.HI.3.

58 Lesson 1 Why Did the Spanish Explore the Americas?

This historical map, circa 1700, shows the east and west hemispheres of the earth.

Lesson 1 59

Research Companion, pp. 58–59

EL ENGLISH LEARNERS SCAFFOLD

ELD.PII.5.5 Modifying to add details

Emerging

Identify Proper Adjectives Explain that *Venetian* is the adjective form of *Venice* and also a noun for a person from Venice: *The Polos were a Venetian family; Marco Polo was a Venetian.* Have students identify another adjective that is formed from a place name and appears in the same paragraph as *Venetian*.

Expanding

Use History-Related Adjectives Tell students that the adjective used to describe something or someone from the Middle Ages is *medieval*, and have them use *medieval* in sentences based on the text. (Examples: Medieval Europeans rarely traveled. In late medieval times, some Europeans made pilgrimages to holy places.)

Bridging

Use Adjectives Have students use adjectives to describe medieval Europeans' likely feelings about the gems, silks, and spices from China and the East Indies.(Example: The bright gems, soft silk, and fragrant spices seemed rare and wonderful.)

See the **Language Learner Teaching Guide** for more language support strategies.

Monitor and Differentiate

REACHING ALL LEARNERS

Approaching Level

Clarify that *Holy Land* refers to the area around the city of Jerusalem in present-day Israel. Medieval Christians made pilgrimages, or holy trips, there because it is where Christ once lived.

On Level

Have pairs of students read excerpts from *The Travels of Marco Polo* online and discuss the experiences the author describes.

Beyond Level

Ask students to research and report on different aspects of the cultural and military achievements of Kublai Khan and China in his era.

A Time of Change in Europe

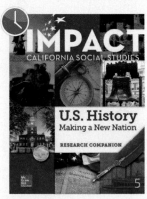

Research Companion
pp. 60–61

STANDARDS

Describe the entrepreneurial characteristics of early explorers (e.g., ChristopherColumbus, Francisco Vásquez de Coronado) and the technological developmentsthat made sea exploration by latitude and longitude possible (e.g., compass, sextant,astrolabe, seaworthy ships, chronometers, gunpowder). **HSS.5.2.1**

Explain the aims, obstacles, and accomplishments of the explorers, sponsors, andleaders of key European expeditions and the reasons Europeans chose to explore andcolonize the world (e.g., the Spanish Reconquista, the Protestant Reformation, theCounter Reformation). **HSS.5.2.2**

Students use map and globe skills to determine the absolute locations of places and interpret information available through a map's or globe's legend, scale, and symbolic representations. **HAS.CS.4**

Go Digital!

Investigate the lesson content with online whole-class presentation tools.

Background Information

The Reconquista was the Christian effort to retake the Iberian Peninsula from the North African Muslims known as Moors. It met with setbacks until 1340, when Portuguese and Spanish forces triumphed at the Battle of Río Salado. Spain drove the Moors from their last stronghold of Granada in 1492.

The Protestant Reformation began in the sixteenth century when Martin Luther criticized the Roman Catholic Church for its excesses and its practice of selling indulgences, which a person could buy to ensure a departed loved one got into heaven. As a result, protestant divisions of Christianity emerged. As a response to the Protestant Reformation, the Catholic Church issued edicts to try to mend its ways, a movement known as the **Counter-Reformation**.

Analyze the Source

Inspect Have students continue reading A Time of Change in Europe on pages 60–61.

Find Evidence Use the questions below to check comprehension. Remind students to support their answers with text evidence.

Explain Why was the trade route with eastern Asia called the Silk Road? (Silk from China was a highly valued product that was traded.) **DOK 1**

Identify Cause and Effect What role did the Ottoman Turks play in encouraging Europeans to seek trade routes that did not go through the Middle East? (After getting control of Constantinople, they cut off most European trade through the Middle East.) **DOK 2**

Define For the Spanish, what was the goal of the Reconquista? (to recapture Spanish land lost to the Moors) **DOK 1**

Make Connections

Analyze What role did religion play in Spanish involvement in the Age of Exploration? (It drove Spain to compete with other countries in claiming new land.) **DOK 3**

Map Skills

Project a large version of the map on page 61. Guide students to identify the trade routes between Venice and Khanbalik, China. Ask:

- Through what body of water do all routes go at the end? (Mediterranean Sea)

- Across what continent do the all-land routes, or Silk Road, go? (Asia)

Stop and Check

COLLABORATE

Discuss Encourage students to consider how Marco Polo and Prince Henry of Portugal helped to encourage the growth of trade. (Polo's book interested people in trading there. Prince Henry sponsored explorers, encouraging them to find new trade routes.)

Find Details Explain to students that after they read and take notes, they should review and think about how the facts and details will help them answer the Essential Question.

Trade with Asia usually moved along a route called the Silk Road. It was named for a product much in demand—Chinese silk. Sometimes, goods from China came by sea, because the Chinese had made many advances in sailing. Goods from the East Indies also came partly by sea. But whether entirely or only partly over land, the trade from Asia had to pass through the Middle East to reach the Mediterranean Sea and Italy.

In 1453, the Ottoman Turks captured Constantinople (now Istanbul, Turkey). They cut off most European trade through the Middle East. European leaders began to sponsor, or pay for, voyages of exploration. They hoped to make their countries rich by finding new trade routes that did not go through the Middle East. Important advances in **navigation**, or the science of guiding a boat, made this possible.

During the Age of Exploration, Europe was bursting with religious conflict and change. Spain wished to become an even more powerful country after recapturing land it had lost to invading peoples from North Africa. Spaniards called this violent recapturing of territory the *Reconquista*. The Protestant Reformation caused many people who were upset with the Roman Catholic Church to break away and form new churches. Some people wished to stay and improve the Catholic Church—an effort called the Counter-Reformation. Competing religions, ideas, and countries would become key drivers of the Age of Exploration.

Merchants trading in Venice, Italy

The Travels of Marco Polo, 1271–1295

Map Skills With a classmate, trace the different routes between Venice and Khanbalik, China. Which go entirely over land in Asia? Which go partly by sea?

Stop and Check

Talk How did Marco Polo and Prince Henry of Portugal each help encourage the growth of trade?

Find Details As you read, add additional information to the graphic organizer on page 57 in your Inquiry Journal.

Research Companion, pp. 60–61

ENGLISH LEARNERS SCAFFOLD

ELD.PI.5.8 Analyzing how writers and speakers use vocabulary and other language resources for specific purposes (to explain, persuade, entertain, etc.) depending on modality, text type, purpose, audience, topic, and content are.

Emerging	Expanding	Bridging
Clarify Cultural Terms Clarify that *Moor* refers to a North African Muslim and that *Muslims* are those who practice the religion of Islam.	**Understand Historical Terms** Note that *Reconquista* is a Spanish (and Portuguese) word. Then have non-Spanish, non-Portuguese speaking students guess what it literally means in English, based on the English word it resembles and the events it describes.	**Explain Historical Terms** Define *nationalism* as strong feelings for one's country, often with the view that it is better than others. Discuss why nationalism during the Reconquista would encourage Spain to explore new lands.

See the **Language Learner Teaching Guide** for more language support strategies.

Monitor and Differentiate

REACHING ALL LEARNERS

Special Needs

Help students use the map to appreciate the great distance between China and Italian ports like Venice and Genoa. Note that Spain and Portugal were even farther, well west of Genoa.

Beyond Level

Have students research and report on Prince Henry's pioneering role in the Age of Exploration and in European involvement in the African slave trade. Tell students to use Henry's nickname, *Henry the Navigator*, in online searches.

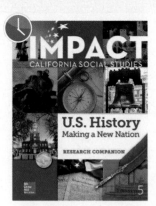

Research Companion
pp. 62–63

 STANDARDS

Describe the entrepreneurial characteristics of early explorers (e.g., ChristopherColumbus, Francisco Vásquez de Coronado) and the technological developmentsthat made sea exploration by latitude and longitude possible (e.g., compass, sextant,astrolabe, seaworthy ships, chronometers, gunpowder). **HSS.5.2.1**

Students identify and interpret the multiple causes and effects of historical events. **HAS.HI.3**

Go Digital!

Investigate the lesson content with online whole-class presentation tools.

Background Information

Chronometer Calculating latitude is easy—it can be done simply by observing the sky. Calculating longitude is much harder. John Harrison solved the problem in the 1700s by creating a timepiece called a chronometer that, despite conditions at sea, kept totally accurate time, enabling computation of distance or amount of longitude traveled. This helped explorers to produce accurate maps.

Analyze the Source

Inspect Have students read about Technological Advances on pages 62–63 and study the accompanying illustrations.

Find Evidence Use the questions below to check comprehension. Remind students to support their answers with text evidence.

Synthesize What did the astrolabe and the later inventions of the sextant and chronometer all help sailors determine? (their location at sea) **DOK 2**

Identify What did the compass help sailors determine? (the direction in which they were going) **DOK 1**

Compare and Contrast Where were the first compass and the stern rudder invented? (China) **DOK 1**

Identify Cause and Effect How did the printing press encourage the Age of Exploration? (Printed materials helped spread news about explorers' discoveries and encourage more exploration.) **DOK 2**

Draw Conclusions What made the carrack suitable for long voyages? (It was very strong.) **DOK 3**

Compare and Contrast How was the carrack different from the caravels you read about earlier? (It was bigger and heavier.) **DOK 3**

Make Connections

Analyze How did contact with people from other cultures encourage Europe's Age of Exploration? (Europeans learned of technological advances like the astrolabe and compass from Arab traders and improved upon the stern rudder, invented in China. These technological advances helped make Europe's Age of Exploration possible.) **DOK 3**

COLLABORATE

☑ Stop and Check

Think Students should discuss with a partner the importance of technology in encouraging explorers of the day. Explain that they can cite reasons as well as examples from the text as support for their opinions. (Responses will vary, but students should support their explanations with text evidence.)

InfoGraphic

Technological Advances

The Spanish explored the Americas in a time of adventure and discovery. A number of technological advances helped make their adventures and Portugal's explorations possible.

The Astrolabe

An astrolabe measures the position of the stars in the sky. It helps sailors determine a ship's latitude, or how far north or south of the Equator they are. Europeans learned of the astrolabe from Arab traders in the 1100s.

The Compass

A compass has a magnetic arrow that points north so that people can figure out in which direction they are going. The compass was invented in China and introduced to Europeans in the 1200s, probably by Arab sailors.

The Stern Rudder

Chinese sailors used an oar that hung off the stern, or back of the boat, to help control its direction. This evolved into the stern-mounted rudder, which directed the flow of water passing over it to help steer a ship. By the 1400s, European shipbuilders had adopted and improved the stern-mounted rudder.

The Printing Press

Around 1450, German inventor Johannes Gutenberg built Europe's first printing press that used movable type to print the text. Printed materials could be mass-produced far more easily and cheaply than handwritten documents. They helped spread news about explorers' discoveries and encouraged others to take to the seas.

The Carrack

The carrack was a three- or four-masted sailing ship developed in the Italian city of Genoa in the late 1400s. It was very strong and useful on long voyages. The *Santa Maria*, the ship on which Columbus sailed to the New World, was a carrack.

Sextant and Chronometer

In 1759, John Bird invented the sextant. This tool uses two mirrors and a movable arm to measure the angles of stars in the sky. Also invented in the middle of the 18th century, the chronometer is a device that helps keep accurate time at sea. These two devices finally allowed sailors to determine longitude, or the distance east or west of the Prime Meridian. Measuring longitude as well as latitude made navigation and mapmaking more accurate.

✓ **Stop and Check**

COLLABORATE

Talk Based on what you've just read, how important do you think technology was in encouraging the explorers of the day? Discuss your opinion with a partner.

Research Companion, pp. 62–63

ⓔⓛ ENGLISH LEARNERS SCAFFOLD

ELD.PI.5.6 Reading closely literary and informational texts and viewing multimedia to determine how meaning is conveyed explicitly and implicitly through language

Emerging

Clarify Terms Note that the Equator, an imaginary circle around the earth's center, is 0 degrees latitude; the Prime Meridian is 0 degrees longitude. Latitude measures how far north or south a point is from the Equator, longitude, how far east or west it is from the Prime Meridian.

Expanding/Bridging

Understand a Process
Clarify that the movable type on the printing press consisted of individual letters and other symbols moved into place to spell out words and sentences. Once the type was in place, the press could print many copies of the same page. Ask why this is an advance. (It is much quicker than making each copy by hand.)

See the **Language Learner Teaching Guide** for more language support strategies.

Monitor and Differentiate

REACHING ALL LEARNERS

Special Needs

Ask students to choose one of the technological advances pictured on these pages and use classroom materials to make a model of it.

Approaching Level

Have students study the timeline on page 59 and state which technological advances on these pages came too late to help the early Spanish explorers. (the sextant and chronometer)

Beyond Level

Have students research and report on modern advances in navigation, such as radar, Loran, or the Global Positioning System (GPS).

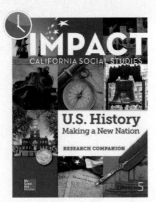

Research Companion
pp. 64–65

 STANDARDS

Describe the entrepreneurial characteristics of early explorers (e.g., ChristopherColumbus, Francisco Vásquez de Coronado) and the technological developmentsthat made sea exploration by latitude and longitude possible (e.g., compass, sextant,astrolabe, seaworthy ships, chronometers, gunpowder). **HSS.5.2.1**

Explain the aims, obstacles, and accomplishments of the explorers, sponsors, andleaders of key European expeditions and the reasons Europeans chose to explore andcolonize the world (e.g., the Spanish Reconquista, the Protestant Reformation, theCounter Reformation). **HSS.5.2.2**

Students use map and globe skills to determine the absolute locations of places and interpret information available through a map's or globe's legend, scale, and symbolic representations. **HAS.CS.4**

Go Digital!

Investigate the lesson content with online whole-class presentation tools.

Background Information

Santa María While experts call the *Santa María*, a carrack, Columbus simply called it a *nao*, Spanish for "ship." He made the trip west on the *Santa María* but, after it wrecked on a coral reef, he went home on the *Niña*. With just two ships, 39 crew members stayed behind; they and the fort they built were gone when Columbus returned. Claims that a shipwreck found off Haiti's coast in 2014 was the Santa *María* were later disproven.

Analyze the Source

Inspect Have students begin reading A Sea Route to the Indies on pages 64–65.

Find Evidence Use the questions below to check comprehension. Remind students to support their answers with text evidence.

Explain By what route did Portuguese explorers try to reach China and the East Indies? (sailing around the southern tip of Africa and then crossing the Indian Ocean) **DOK 1**

Explain What route to China and the East Indies did Columbus propose? (sailing west to reach them) **DOK 2**

Analyze What do the details in the text suggest was one reason that Ferdinand and Isabella agreed to sponsor Columbus? (They wanted to outdo their rival, Portugal, by finding a better way to reach China and the East Indies.) **DOK 3**

Analyze the Primary Source Point out phrases showing Columbus's impression of the Taíno's welcome—"took much pleasure," "so much our friends," "very willingly." Ask:

Compare and Contrast Which sentences in the text above the primary source does the primary source support? ("A native people called the Taíno warmly greeted his crew. The two groups exchanged gifts.") **DOK 2**

Make Connections

Draw Conclusions Ask students how they think Columbus and his crew felt when they reached land. Have them cite evidence for their opinions. (Possible responses include overjoyed, relieved, nervous, and/or exhausted. Evidence might include the length of the voyage, its unknown nature, and the welcome they received.) **DOK 4**

📍 Map Skills

Project a large version of the map on page 65. Guide students to work with a partner to respond to the prompts about Columbus's trips to the Americas.

- List five islands or island groups that Columbus explored. (Bahama Islands (including San Salvador), Cuba, Hispaniola, Puerto Rico, Jamaica)

- On which voyage did he go to South America? (third)

- On which did he sail along the coast of Central America? (fourth)

A Sea Route to the Indies

By the late 1400s, Europeans knew that China and the islands off Southeast Asia held great riches. Explorers from Portugal, such as Bartolomeu Dias and Vasco da Gama, were trying to reach these lands. They wanted to sail around the southern tip of Africa and then across the Indian Ocean. Christopher Columbus, a sailor from Genoa, Italy, had a different idea. He believed that he could reach the East Indies more quickly by sailing west across the Atlantic Ocean, known then as the Ocean Sea. He did not know the North and South American continents would get in the way. He persuaded King Ferdinand and Queen Isabella of Spain, Portugal's neighbor and rival, to pay for his voyage. In return, he would **claim** lands and open valuable trade for Spain.

On August 3, 1492, Columbus sailed from Spain with three ships—the *Niña*, the *Pinta*, and the *Santa Maria*. For weeks, the ships traveled across unknown waters. Finally, on October 12, a member of the crew, called the lookout, spotted land. Columbus would call the island he had reached San Salvador. Today, we know it as part of the Bahama Islands. A native people called the Taíno warmly greeted his crew. The two groups exchanged gifts.

PRIMARY SOURCE

In Their Words... Christopher Columbus

"... to some of them I gave red caps, and glass beads which they put on their chests, and many other things of small value, in which they took much pleasure and became so much our friends that it was a marvel. Later they came swimming to the ships' launches where we were and brought us parrots and cotton thread in balls and javelins and many other things, and they traded them to us for other things which we gave them, such as small glass beads and bells. In sum, they took everything and gave of what they had very willingly."

—from the journal of Christopher Columbus, October 12, 1492

TEXT: Olson, Julius E., and Edward Gaylord Bourne, eds. The Northmen, Columbus and Cabot, 985–1503. New York: Charles Scribner's Sons, 1906. PHOTO: GL Archive/Alamy

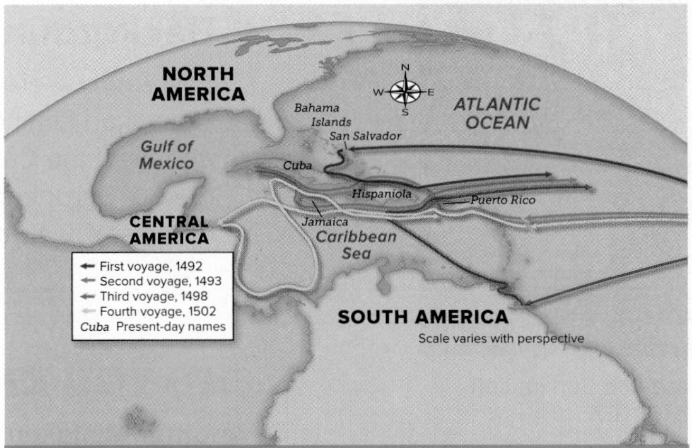

The Voyages of Columbus

Map key:
- First voyage, 1492
- Second voyage, 1493
- Third voyage, 1498
- Fourth voyage, 1502
- *Cuba* Present-day names

Map labels: NORTH AMERICA, CENTRAL AMERICA, SOUTH AMERICA, Bahama Islands, San Salvador, ATLANTIC OCEAN, Gulf of Mexico, Cuba, Hispaniola, Puerto Rico, Jamaica, Caribbean Sea, Scale varies with perspective

Map Skills Working with a partner, list five islands or island groups that Columbus explored. On which voyage did he go to South America? On which did he sail along the coast of Central America?

Did You Know?

Because he thought he had reached the East Indies, Columbus called the people he encountered *Indios*, Spanish for *Indians*. The name stuck, even though it was an error. The people Columbus actually met, the Taíno, did not survive long after the coming of the Spanish, mainly because of the diseases the Spanish brought. However, some of their culture is still evident in certain English and Spanish words such as *barbecue* and *hurricane*.

Research Companion, pp. 64–65

ENGLISH LEARNERS SCAFFOLD

ELD.PI.5.6 Reading closely literary and informational texts and viewing multimedia to determine how meaning is conveyed explicitly and implicitly through language

Emerging

Understand Maps Use the key to explain what the differently colored arrows mean, and trace Columbus's four voyages. Note that two nations, Haiti and the Dominican Republic, today share the island of Hispaniola. Be sure students understand that Spain, where Columbus began his trip, is east of the area shown on the map, across the Atlantic Ocean.

Expanding

Understand Geography Use a world map to illustrate the three basic routes of Europeans trying to reach China and the East Indies: (1) Italians traveled across the Mediterranean Sea and Middle East then went by land; (2) Portuguese explorers tried to sail around Africa and then across the Indian Ocean; and (3) Columbus sailed west from Spain, thinking the trip would be shorter than going around Africa.

See the **Language Learner Teaching Guide** for more language support strategies.

Monitor and Differentiate

REACHING ALL LEARNERS

Approaching Level

Clarify difficult terms in the primary source, explaining that *launches* are small boats attached to ships, used for going ashore, and *javelins* are light spears thrown by hand, typically used for hunting.

On Level

Mention that before approaching Ferdinand and Isabella, Columbus tried to convince Portugal's rulers to support his idea of sailing west to Asia. Have students investigate why they refused. (They rightly thought the distance much farther than Columbus estimated.)

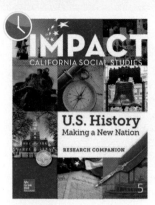

Research Companion
pp. 66–67

 STANDARDS

Describe the entrepreneurial characteristics of early explorers (e.g., ChristopherColumbus, Francisco Vásquez de Coronado) and the technological developmentsthat made sea exploration by latitude and longitude possible (e.g., compass, sextant,astrolabe, seaworthy ships, chronometers, gunpowder). **HSS.5.2.1**

Explain the aims, obstacles, and accomplishments of the explorers, sponsors, andleaders of key European expeditions and the reasons Europeans chose to explore andcolonize the world (e.g., the Spanish Reconquista, the Protestant Reformation, theCounter Reformation). **HSS.5.2.2**

Students use map and globe skills to determine the absolute locations of places and interpret information available through a map's or globe's legend, scale, and symbolic representations. **HAS.CS.4**

Go Digital!

Investigate the lesson content with online whole-class presentation tools.

Background Information

The Taíno were a subgroup of Arawakan Indians, their language part of the Arawakan family. In 1511, forced into labor by the Spanish, they joined their former enemies, the Caribs, in an unsuccessful revolt against Spanish rule. The majority died of European diseases such as smallpox. By 1550, virtually all the Taíno had disappeared.

DID YOU KNOW?

Another Mistaken Term Tell students that the name *West Indies* for the islands in the Caribbean Sea also comes from Columbus's mistaken belief that he had reached the *Indies*, the islands off the coast of Southeast Asia. A distinction was later made between the *East Indies* in Asia and *West Indies* in the Americas.

Analyze the Source

Inspect Have students continue reading A Sea Route to the Indies on pages 66–67.

Find Evidence Use the questions below to check comprehension. Remind students to support their answers with text evidence.

Analyze What most disappointed Columbus about the lands he had reached? (They did not contain the riches of the (East) Indies.) **DOK 3**

Identify Cause and Effect On his second voyage, what did Columbus do to establish Spanish claims in the New World? (He established a colony.) **DOK 2**

Explain How did the lands Columbus reached come to be called the Americas? (They were named after another explorer, Amerigo Vespucci.) **DOK 2**

Identify Who was the first Spanish explorer to record seeing what is now called the Pacific Ocean? (Vasco Núñez de Balboa) **DOK 1**

Make Connections

Compare and Contrast To whom was the area Columbus reached a "New World"? To whom was it not a "New World"? (It was a "New World" to the Europeans but not to the people who already lived there.) **DOK 3**

Map Skills

Project a large version of the map on page 67. Guide students to work with a partner, identifying the islands inhabited by the Taíno and the bodies of water around them. Ask:

- What three bodies of water surround the Taíno islands? (the Gulf of Mexico, the Atlantic Ocean, and the Caribbean Sea)

- Which island inhabited by the Taíno was farthest west? (Cuba)

COLLABORATE

Stop and Check

Think Encourage students to consider how Columbus was right and wrong about what he would find on his voyages. (He was right to think Asia could be reached by sailing west. He was wrong about the distance and length of time the trip would take, and he did not expect the great body of land in between.)

On his first voyage, Columbus sailed to several neighboring islands in addition to the Bahamas. He still believed he had landed in the East Indies. But nowhere did he find the "riches of the Indies." Claiming the islands for Spain, he reported his discoveries to Ferdinand and Isabella when he returned home. The king and queen soon sent him back on a second voyage to extend Spanish claims. This time he brought enough settlers and supplies to establish a Spanish **colony** on the island he named Hispaniola. In all, Columbus made four voyages to the area.

Other explorers soon followed. By now, they knew that the islands were not the East Indies but part of a mass of lands between Europe and Asia—a New World, as they called it. The name *Americas* began to be used for these lands in honor of Amerigo Vespucci, who sailed one of Columbus's routes in 1499. In 1513, Vasco Núñez de Balboa became the first Spanish explorer to record seeing the great waters to the west of these lands. Another explorer, Ferdinand Magellan, named those waters the Pacific Ocean. Magellan died as he attempted to sail around the world. His voyage was completed in 1522 by his crew under the command of Juan Sebastián Elcano. The voyage took three years.

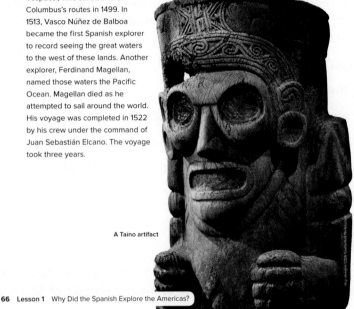

A Taíno artifact

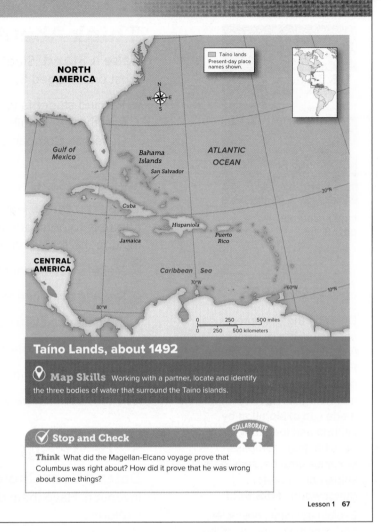

Taíno lands
Present-day place names shown.

NORTH AMERICA

Gulf of Mexico

Bahama Islands

San Salvador

ATLANTIC OCEAN

Cuba

Hispaniola

Jamaica

Puerto Rico

CENTRAL AMERICA

Caribbean Sea

0   250   500 miles
0   250   500 kilometers

Taíno Lands, about 1492

Map Skills Working with a partner, locate and identify the three bodies of water that surround the Taíno islands.

> ✓ **Stop and Check**   COLLABORATE
>
> **Think** What did the Magellan-Elcano voyage prove that Columbus was right about? How did it prove that he was wrong about some things?

Research Companion, pp. 66–67

 ENGLISH LEARNERS SCAFFOLD

ELD.PI.5.8 Analyzing how writers and speakers use vocabulary and other language resources for specific purposes (to explain, persuade, entertain, etc.) depending on modality, text type, purpose, audience, topic, and content area

Emerging	Expanding	Bridging
Interpret Word Origins Point out the word *colony*, and encourage students to think about why it was important that Columbus established a European colony in the New World.	**Apply Vocabulary** Explain that the word *pacific—pacífico* in Spanish—means "peaceful." Have students speculate about why Magellan used that word to name the Pacific Ocean.	**Recognize Word Origins** Note that while the Americas are named for Amerigo Vespucci, Columbus is also honored in many place names. Have students cite examples.

See the **Language Learner Teaching Guide** for more language support strategies.

Monitor and Differentiate

REACHING ALL LEARNERS

On Level

Have small groups of students use online sources to find out more about Balboa's explorations or the Magellan-Elcano voyage. Ask them to share their findings in short reports that include simple maps they photocopy or draw.

Beyond Level

Have pairs of students research and report on other explorers believed to have reached the Americas before Columbus, such as Leif Eriksson or Zheng He. Ask: *What evidence supports the claim, and how reliable is it?*

Report Your Findings

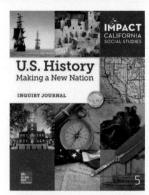

Inquiry Journal
pp. 58–59

 STANDARDS

Describe the entrepreneurial characteristics of early explorers (e.g., ChristopherColumbus, Francisco Vásquez de Coronado) and the technological developmentsthat made sea exploration by latitude and longitude possible (e.g., compass, sextant,astrolabe, seaworthy ships, chronometers, gunpowder). **HSS.5.2.1**

Explain the aims, obstacles, and accomplishments of the explorers, sponsors, andleaders of key European expeditions and the reasons Europeans chose to explore andcolonize the world (e.g., the Spanish Reconquista, the Protestant Reformation, theCounter Reformation). **HSS.5.2.2**

Students write opinion pieces, supporting a point of view with reasons and information. **CCSS.ELA.W.5.1**

Go Digital!

- Students can go online to report their findings. Assess their responses online.

- Students can access the online graphic organizer to capture ideas from their investigation.

Think About It

Take a Stand Students will review their research and consider which of the inventions most encouraged Spanish exploration of the New World.

- Remind students to review each invention they have listed in their graphic organizer and the key details associated with it. Direct students back to pages 58–67 of their Research Companion if they need more information.

Write About It

Be Persuasive Have students read the prompt. Explain that an effective advertisement attempts to persuade a particular audience to think or do something. Remind students to include the following elements in their response.

- Make a claim about the product you are advertising.

- Provide evidence to support the claim.

- Indicate what you want your audience to do with the product.

- Provide logical reasons to show why your audience should do it.

- Use language and emotional appeals designed to persuade your audience.

Use the rubric on page T148 to evaluate students' work.

Talk About It

Defend Your Choice Help students pair up with a classmate who chose a different invention. Have them discuss how each invention would help meet the goals of Spanish explorers.

- Tell students to take turns discussing their opinions and the reasons that helped them form those opinions.

- Ask students to discuss whether they agree or disagree with their partner's opinions and to explain why.

- Remind students to follow the rules of appropriate classroom conversation.

Connect to the Essential Question

Read the prompt aloud to students. Ask them the following guiding questions:

- Which inventions from this lesson most helped Spanish explorers achieve their goals? (Responses will vary, but students should explain why they chose the invention they did.)

- How did the help those inventions gave Spanish explorers affect the development of colonial America? (Responses will vary, but students should support their conclusions with text evidence.)

Remind students to use the space provided in their journal to jot down notes.

Report / Your Findings

Think About It

Review your research about the developments that encouraged Spanish exploration of the New World. Which invention do you think was the most important? Why?

Write About It

Be Persuasive
Write an Advertisement Write an advertisement describing how the invention you chose works and why an explorer would find it useful. Find an image on the Internet to illustrate your ad.

Students' ads should describe one of the inventions in the text and use persuasion to show how it is useful. The ad should include an online image.

Talk About It

Defend Your Choice
Review the goals of Spanish explorers. Then discuss how the invention you chose would help them achieve these goals.

History Connect to the

Pull It Together
Explain how the invention you chose helped Spanish explorers like Christopher Columbus and how it might have affected the exploration and development of colonial America.

Student responses should explain how the invention made a difference to Spanish explorers and how colonial America might have been affected by it.

> **EQ** Inquiry Project Notes

Inquiry Journal, pp. 58–59

EL ENGLISH LEARNERS SCAFFOLD

ELD.PI.5.11 Supporting own opinions and evaluating others' opinions in speaking and writing

Emerging	Expanding	Bridging
State and Support Opinions Provide this sentence frame to help students state and support opinions: *In my opinion, ___ was the most important technological advance because ___.*	**State and Support Opinions** Provide this sentence frame to help students state and support opinions: *In my opinion, ___ was the most important technological advance because ___, ___, and ___.*	**State and Support Opinions** Check students' understanding by asking these questions: *What do you think was the most important invention in the era of Columbus? How did it help Spanish explorers achieve their goals?*

See the **Language Learner Teaching Guide** for more language support strategies.

Monitor and Differentiate

REACHING ALL LEARNERS

Approaching Level

Review with students that an advertisement makes a claim about a product and then tries to get the audience to buy or use that product. Point out that the claim, or opinion, needs to be supported by evidence and that the argument to get the audience to use the product needs logical reasons or strong emotional appeals.

On Level

Note that a good advertisement takes into account the audience it is trying to reach. It uses language that audience will understand and makes emotional appeals designed to persuade the audience. For instance, it might appeal to the audience's patriotism or competitive spirit.

Know what your students know!

Lesson Task
Report Your Findings

Use this rubric to evaluate students' response.

Write an Advertisement Students write an advertisement describing how the invention they chose works and why it would be useful to the Spanish explorers they have been reading about.

Defend Your Choice Students defend the idea that the invention they chose would be useful to the Spanish explorers.

Performance Task Evaluation Rubric

	4	3	2	1
Historical Understanding	Displays strong understanding of the goals, challenges, and achievements of early Spanish explorers	Displays adequate understanding of the goals, challenges, and achievements of early Spanish explorers	Displays uneven understanding of the goals, challenges, and achievements of early Spanish explorers	Displays no understanding of the goals, challenges, and achievements of early Spanish explorers
Explanation	Provides a clear explanation of how the invention works	Provides an adequate explanation of how the invention works	Provides a somewhat unclear explanation of how the invention works	Provides no explanation or shows no understanding of how the invention works
Supporting Evidence and Language	Supports claims or reasons with thorough and convincing evidence Uses language that would appeal to the audience of the advertisement	Supports claims or reasons with adequate evidence Uses some language that would appeal to the audience of the advertisement	Supports claims or reasons with too little convincing evidence Uses little language that would appeal to the audience of the advertisement	Supplies no claims or reasons or no supporting evidence Uses no language that would appeal to the audience of the advertisement
Presentation	Speaks clearly and at an understandable pace Uses complete sentences throughout the discussion	Speaks clearly during most of the discussion Speaks in complete sentences through most of the discussion	Speaks unclearly at times Mixes complete and incomplete sentences during the discussion	Speaks unclearly throughout the discussion Does not use complete sentences in the discussion

Lesson Assessment

Go *Digital!*

- Have students complete the Chapter 2 Lesson 1 Assessment online to monitor their understanding of the lesson content.

California Smarter Balanced Assessment Connections!

Standards Covered	Lesson Task	Lesson Assessment	Alignment with California Smarter Balanced Assessment
History Social Science Content 5.2.1; 5.2.2	✔	✔	Claim 1 Targets 8, 9, 10
History Social Science Analysis Skills Chronological and Spatial Thinking 5.1; 5.4 Research, Evidence, and Point of View 5.4	✔	✔	Claim 1 Targets 11, 12
Writing W.5.1	✔	✔	Claim 2 Target 3a
Research and Inquiry W.5.7; W.5.9	✔	✔	Claim 4 Targets 2, 3, 4
Reading RI.5.7	✔	✔	Claim 1 Target 8
Speaking and Listening SL.5.1	✔		Claim 3 Target 3

How Did Spanish Exploration Change the Lives of People in the Americas?

Background Information

Tell students that in this lesson, they will learn how contact with the Spanish changed the Americas and the lives of native peoples living there.

Community Connections

To enrich students' understanding of native cultures of the Americas, have them visit your local library to find resources about Aztec, Inca, or other pre-Columbian artifacts and culture.

 HSS **LESSON STANDARDS**

- ✔ Describe the entrepreneurial characteristics of early explorers (e.g., Christopher Columbus, Francisco Vásquez de Coronado). **HSS.5.2.1**
- ✔ Explain the aims, obstacles, and accomplishments of the explorers, sponsors, and leaders of key European expeditions and the reasons Europeans chose to explore and colonize the world. **HSS.5.2.2**
- ✔ Trace the routes of the major land explorers of the United States, the distances traveled by explorers, and the Atlantic trade routes. **HSS.5.2.3**
- ✔ Students place key events and people of the historical era they are studying in a chronological sequence and spatial context; they interpret time lines. **HAS.CS.1**
- ✔ Students use map and globe skills to determine the absolute locations of places and interpret information available through a map's or globe's legend, scale, and symbolic representations. **HAS.CS.4**
- ✔ Students differentiate between primary and secondary sources. **HAS.HR.1**
- ✔ Students identify the human and physical characteristics of the places they are studying and explain how those features form the unique character of those places. **HAS.HI.1**
- ✔ Students identify and interpret the multiple causes and effects of historical events. **HAS.HI.3**

 Connect to the
Essential Question

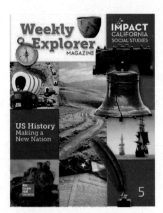

Chapter 2, pp. 14–29

The **Weekly Explorer Magazine** supports students' exploration of the Essential Question and provides additional resources for the EQ Inquiry Project.

 Inquiry Project

What happened when diverse cultures crossed paths?

Remind students to use the information they learn in this lesson and other resources to complete their EQ Inquiry Project!

Dinah Zike's

In this lesson you will use Foldables.

When Minutes Count!

Suggested Lesson Pacing

1 ENGAGE
One Day

- Lesson Opener
- Analyze the Source
- Inquiry Tools

Go Digital

- **iMap:** Spanish Exploration Routes
- **iMap:** Aztec and Inca Empires, 1519

2 INVESTIGATE
Two to Three Days

🕐 **Short on Time?** Look for the clock to teach core content in less time.

- The Columbian Exchange
- Spanish Exploration and Conquest in the Americas
- New Spain Expands
- Field Trip to St. Augustine, Florida

3 REPORT
One Day

- Think About It
- Write an Essay
- Share Your Ideas

Make Connections!

(ccss) CONNECT TO ELA

Reading
Quote accurately from a text when explaining what the text says explicitly and when drawing inferences from the text. **RI.5.1**

Research
Draw evidence from literary or informational texts to support analysis, reflection, and research. **W.5.9**

Writing
Write informative/explanatory texts to examine a topic and convey ideas and information clearly. **W.5.2**

Speaking and Listening
Engage effectively in a range of collaborative discussions (one-on-one, in groups, and teacher-led) with diverse partners on grade 5 topics and texts, building on others' ideas and expressing their own clearly. **SL.5.1**

Classroom Resources

🔍 Search for additional resources using the following key words.

Aztecs

Juan Rodríguez Cabrillo

Columbian Exchange

Francisco Vásquez de Coronado

Hernan Cortés

Incas

Juan Ponce de León

Francisco Pizarro

Hernando de Soto

Alvar Nuñez Cabeza de Vaca

Sebastián Vizcaíno

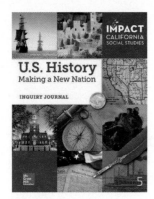

Inquiry Journal,
pp. 60–61

 STANDARDS

Explain the aims, obstacles, and accomplishments of the explorers, sponsors, and leaders of key European expeditions and the reasons Europeans chose to explore and colonize the world. **HSS.5.2.2**

Come to discussions prepared, having read or studied required material, to explore ideas under discussion. **CCSS.ELA.SL.5.1.a**

Summarize information presented in diverse media and formats, including visually, quantitatively, and orally. **CCSS.ELA.SL.5.2**

Go *Digital!*

Explore the lesson content with online whole-class presentation tools.

- **iMap:** Spanish Exploration Routes

- **iMap:** Aztec and Inca Empires, 1519

How Did Spanish Exploration Change the Lives of People in the Americas?

Bellringer

Prompt students to retrieve information from the previous lessons. Say: *Columbus began Spanish exploration and settlement in the New World. What plans did he have for the native peoples like the Taíno?* (to convert them to Christianity, win their loyalty to Spain, and obtain their natural resources for Spain's benefit)

Lesson Outcomes

What Am I Learning? Have students read the Lesson Question and Lesson Outcomes.

Why Am I Learning It? Check that students are familiar with the term *contact*. Call on volunteers to define the term, eliciting that it can mean "coming together" or "being in touch." For example: *When you have contact with someone who has a cold, you may catch a cold too.*

How Will I Know That I Learned It? Remind students that *Columbian* refers to the activities or era of Columbus.

- What will you identify? (the Columbian Exchange and the Spanish conquest, exploration, and colonization of the Americas)

- What is the purpose of the task? (to explain the impact of an explorer on the New World)

- How will you support your explanation? (with text evidence)

Talk About It

Explain that when we talk about artwork, we describe, analyze, and interpret it and present out ideas in our own words. Provide sentence frames to help students form sentences as they talk about the artwork.

- Coronado and his men are wearing _____ and are carrying _____. (armor, swords)

- Their battle dress seems _____ for a hot climate. (too hot and heavy; inappropriate)

Collaborative Conversations

Add New Ideas As students engage in partner, small group, and whole-class discussions, encourage them to

- Stay on topic.
- Connect their own ideas to things their peers have said.
- Look for ways to connect their personal experiences or prior knowledge to the conversation.

Lesson 2

How Did Spanish Exploration Change the Lives of People in the Americas?

Lesson Outcomes

What Am I Learning?
In this lesson, you're going to use your investigative skills to learn how Spanish contact and exploration in the Americas changed the lives of the native peoples living there.

Why Am I Learning It?
Reading and talking about the effects of Spanish contact and exploration will help you understand changes that took place and that helped shape the Americas in the future.

How Will I Know That I Learned It?
You will be able to identify the causes and explain the effects of the Columbian Exchange and of Spanish conquest, exploration, and colonization of the Americas.

Talk About It

Look at the Details Examine the image of Cortés and his men. Based on this painting, do you predict their interactions with native peoples will end peacefully or violently?

HSS.5.2.1, HSS.5.2.2, HSS.5.2.3, HSS.5.3.1, HAS.CS.1,
HAS.CS.2, HAS.CS.3, HAS.CS.4, HAS.CS.5,
HAS.HR.1, HAS.HR2, HAS.HI.1, HAS.HI.3, HAS.HI.4

Hernan Cortés at Vera Cruz in 1519, where he decided to found a village.

60 Lesson 2 How Did Spanish Exploration Change the Lives of People in the Americas?

Lesson 2 **61**

Inquiry Journal, pp. 60–61

ENGLISH LEARNERS SCAFFOLD

ELD.PI.5.12 Selecting and applying varied and precise vocabulary and language structures to effectively convey ideas

Emerging	Expanding	Bridging
Understand Vocabulary Explain to students that the suffix *-ation* turns verbs into nouns and usually means "the act of." Then elicit or explain that *exploration* in the lesson question means "the act of exploring." Be sure students know that to *explore* is "to travel and search through an area."	**Develop Vocabulary** Explain that the suffix *-ize* turns nouns into verbs and often means "to make"; *-ation* turns verbs into nouns and often means "the act of." Then have students define *colonize* and *colonization*. Remind them that a colony is a place ruled by a distant land.	**Use Vocabulary** Ask students to use precise terms to describe how Cortés and his men are dressed for battle. Students may mention lances as well as swords, helmets as well as armor, or even more specific parts of body armor, such as breastplates.

See the **Language Learner Teaching Guide** for more language support strategies.

Monitor and Differentiate

REACHING ALL LEARNERS

Special Needs

Before they answer the question in Talk About It, ask students to make a drawing to describe the typical tropical climate.

Approaching Level

As students study the painting and caption, clarify that to found means "to begin or establish."

Beyond Level

As students discuss the painting, elicit that despite their heavy armor, Cortés' men may triumph in battle because of their horses and weapons.

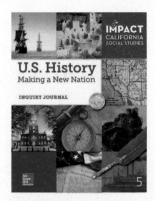

Inquiry Journal,
pp. 62–63

 STANDARDS

Describe the entrepreneurial characteristics of early explorers (e.g., Christopher Columbus, Francisco Vásquez de Coronado). **HSS.5.2.1**

Explain the aims, obstacles, and accomplishments of the explorers, sponsors, and leaders of key European expeditions and the reasons Europeans chose to explore and colonize the world. **HSS.5.2.2**

Students identify and interpret the multiple causes and effects of historical events. **HAS.HI.3**

Summarize information presented in diverse media and formats, including visually, quantitatively, and orally. **CCSS.ELA.SL.5.2**

Go Digital!

Model how to inspect and find evidence with online whole-class presentation tools.

Background Information

American Animals Not all animals native to the Americas were part of the Columbian Exchange; many did not make it overseas until much later. The raccoon, for example, was not exported until the 20th century, although since that time it has done quite well in Germany, Russia, and Japan, among other places. The muskrat, introduced to Europe for its pelts in the early 1900s, has become something of a pest there.

1 Inspect

Look Tell students to examine the image and read the labels. Ask:

- What are five vegetables that came from the Americas in the Columbian Exchange? (Vegetables include corn, potatoes, tomatoes, most beans, pumpkins, squash, sweet potatoes, and chili and bell peppers.)

- What are three animals that came to the Americas in the Columbian Exchange? (Animals include cattle, goats, horses, sheep, and pigs.)

Collaborate Have partners consider the likely health benefits of the Columbian Exchange. (American vegetables could add vitamins to European diets; European farm animals could add more sources of protein to American diets.)

2 Find Evidence

Look Again Have students reexamine the map illustrating the Columbian Exchange.

Analyze the Map Read aloud the caption that accompanies the map, and have volunteers read the items listed in the Columbian Exchange.

- Have students speculate about why so many new animals were brought from Europe. (The animals came with settlers, who brought with them their valuable possessions, including farm animals they planned to use and breed.)

- Ask students why they think so many more plants than animals were brought from North America. (Plants are much easier to transport, and settlers were not going to Europe and bringing all their valuable possessions.)

3 Make Connections

Talk Have students discuss the items they think have the biggest effect on the lives of peoples of the Americas. (Students are likely to mention wheat and farm animals that would be valuable new food sources; plows and wheels, which would improve farming and other activities; horses that would improve hunting and warfare (after being used by the Spanish to aid in their conquest); and swords and diseases that would kill them.)

Connect to Now Have partners discuss how the items brought to the Americas in the Columbian Exchange still affect life here today.

Analyze the Source

The Columbian Exchange

1 Inspect

Look Examine this map. What types of items does it show?

- **Underline** plants that traveled between the Americas and Europe.
- **Circle** animals that traveled between the Americas and Europe.
- **Discuss** with a partner the effects that these items might have had on the peoples involved in the exchange.

My Notes

_____
_____
_____
_____
_____
_____
_____
_____
_____
_____
_____
_____
_____
_____

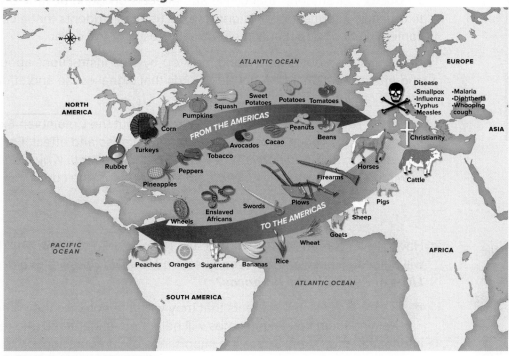

The Columbian Exchange changed life on both sides of the Atlantic Ocean. People in the Americas now had access to livestock, and Europeans were exposed to new food plants. The population in Europe grew, but many people in the Americas died as a result of diseases from Europe.

2 Find Evidence

Look Again Beyond items such as food and technology, what other things were exchanged? Were all of them beneficial?

3 Make Connections

Talk Which items do you think had the biggest effect on the lives of natives of the Americas? Why?

COLLABORATE

Inquiry Journal, pp. 62–63

 ## ENGLISH LEARNERS SCAFFOLD

ELD.PI.5.8 Analyzing how writers and speakers use vocabulary and other language resources for specific purposes (to explain, persuade, entertain, etc.) depending on modality, text type, purpose, audience, topic, and content area

Emerging

Understand Origins Be sure students understand all terms listed in the Columbian Exchange, including *squash, avocados, cattle, plows,* and *firearms.* Using a dictionary, explain that terms that come originally from languages of the Americas, such as *squash and avocado,* name items native to the Americas.

Expanding

Use Origins Explain that words for items native to the Americas often go back to languages of the Americas. Those naming items that were part of the Columbian Exchange often came to English through Spanish. Have students identify which of these are from languages native to the Americas, based on dictionary word origins: *avocado, chocolate, coyote, potato, raccoon, squash, tobacco, tomato.* all

See the **Language Learner Teaching Guide** for more language support strategies.

Monitor and Differentiate

REACHING ALL LEARNERS

On Level

Have students find out how the turkey, native to the Americas, came to share its name with the nation of Turkey. It was associated with an African bird, called the *turkey* or *guinea* fowl, imported to Europe via Turkey.

Beyond Level

Explain that American corn was originally called *maize,* while the English word corn was used for the main grain in an area, whatever it was. For example, the corn of England was wheat; of Scotland, oats; of parts of Germany, rye. Ask why students think maize came to be called corn. It was the main grain of North America.

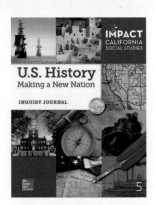

Inquiry Journal,
pp. 64–65

 STANDARDS

Describe the entrepreneurial characteristics of early explorers (e.g., Christopher Columbus, Francisco Vásquez de Coronado). **HSS.5.2.1**

Explain the aims, obstacles, and accomplishments of the explorers, sponsors, and leaders of key European expeditions and the reasons Europeans chose to explore and colonize the world. **HSS.5.2.2**

Identify and interpret the multiple causes and effects of historical events. **HAS.HI.3**

Recall or gather relevant information from sources; summarize or paraphrase information in notes and finished work. **CCSS.ELA.W.5.8**

Come to discussions prepared, having read or studied required material, to explore ideas under discussion. **CCSS.ELA.SL.5.1a**

Go Digital!

- Model how to explore and investigate with online whole-class tools.

- Students can access the online graphic organizer to use the inquiry tools as they read.

Explore Cause and Effect

Explain Tell students that cause and effect is one kind of structure that authors use to organize information in historical texts. Remind students that a cause is the reason something has happened; an effect is the result of the cause.

Read Have students read aloud the step-by-step instructions about how to identify cause and effect. Mention additional clue words that signal cause and effect, such as *since* and *for that reason*.

Guide Practice Use the previous pages about the Columbian Exchange to illustrate asking and answering questions to determine cause and effect. For example: *What happened to European diets? They improved (the effect). Why did that happen? Many new food plants were introduced from the Americas (the cause).*

Investigate!

Have students read pages 68–79 in the Research Companion. Tell them the information will help them answer the lesson question *How Did Spanish Exploration Change the Lives of People in the Americas?*

Take Notes Tell students that they will take notes as they read each section. Remind them that taking notes will help them understand and remember the information they learn. Stress the importance of paraphrasing, or using their own words, when they take notes.

Inspect Guide students to read the text in each section to determine what it says. Remind them to ask *What happened?* to determine effects and *Why did it happen?* to determine causes.

Find Evidence Encourage students to reread the text to develop a deeper understanding of the content. Remind them that after they read and take notes, they should review and think about how the facts and details will help them answer the lesson question.

Collaborative Conversations

Text-Based Discussion Remind students of the goals of discussing the text with others.

- to listen and respond to their partners' points
- to ask for evidence from the text
- to build on each other's ideas
- to see the text from a different point of view

Inquiry Tools

Explore Cause and Effect

A **cause** is an event or action that is the reason something happens. An **effect** is the result of a cause. Identifying causes and effects will help you better understand the impact of the Spanish exploration of the Americas.

1. Read the text once all the way through.
This will help you understand what the text is about.

2. Watch for specific changes.
Ask yourself, *What happened?* The answer to this question helps you identify an effect.

3. Look for explanations.
When you have identified an effect, ask yourself, *Why did this happen?* Knowing why something happened will help you explain its cause.

4. Look for clue words.
Words such as *because, therefore, so,* and *as a result* are clues that signal a cause-and-effect relationship. Recognizing these words will help you answer the question *Why did this happen?*

 COLLABORATE
Based on the text you just read, work with your class to complete the chart below.

Causes		Effects
Many new food plants were introduced to Europe.	→	Diets improved, and the population grew.
Many diseases were brought to the Americas.	→	Native peoples died, and their population shrank.

 IMPACT U.S. History Making a New Nation

Investigate!

Read pages 68–79 in your Research Companion. Use your investigative skills to determine causes and effects of Spanish conquest and colonization. Use the diagram below to organize the information.

Among many other things, students may list the following:

Causes		Effects
Ponce de León's quest for gold and possibly a Fountain of Youth	→	Spanish claim on Florida
Cortés's quest for gold	→	Aztec Empire invaded
Pizzaro's quest for gold	→	Inca Empire invaded
Spanish possess rifles	→	Incas easier to conquer
Coronado's quest for Seven Cities of Gold	→	Spanish claim on Southwest
Sebastián Vizcaíno sails up the California coast	→	Spanish names for California cities

Inquiry Journal, pp. 64–65

(EL) ENGLISH LEARNERS SCAFFOLD

ELD.PII.5.1 Understanding text structure

Emerging	Expanding	Bridging
Understand Cause and Effect Illustrate the use of clue words to signal cause-and-effect relationships. For example, *Because Europeans brought new diseases to the Americas, many natives died. The native labor force shrank, so Europeans brought African slaves as replacements.*	**Identify Cause and Effect** Ask students to identify cause-and-effect relationships about the Columbian Exchange on pages 62–63. Example: *Europeans improved their diet because of new vegetables from the Americas.*	**Synthesize Cause and Effect** Have students consider all the specific details and then identify the *key* cause and effect about the Columbian Exchange. *European explorers' reaching the Americas resulted in the movement of plants, animals, and other things from one part of the globe to another.*

See the **Language Learner Teaching Guide** for more language support strategies.

Monitor and Differentiate

REACHING ALL LEARNERS

Approaching Level
Have students identify simple cause-and-effect relationships in daily life. Offer this example: *Because it was cold, I wore a warm hat.*

On Level
Discuss why history books often use cause-and-effect organization. Elicit that in studying history, we learn what happened and why it happened.

Beyond Level
Have students consider the general reasons that the Europeans coming to the Americas brought items with them and sent items home.

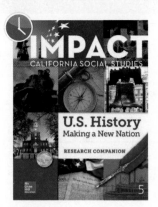

Research Companion
pp. 68–69

 STANDARDS

Describe the entrepreneurial characteristics of early explorers (e.g., Christopher Columbus, Francisco Vásquez de Coronado). **HSS.5.2.1**

Explain the aims, obstacles, and accomplishments of the explorers, sponsors, and leaders of key European expeditions and the reasons Europeans chose to explore and colonize the world. **HSS.5.2.2**

Students place key events and people of the historical era they are studying in a chronological sequence and spatial context; they interpret time lines. **HAS.CS.1**

Students identify and interpret the multiple causes and effects of historical events. **HAS.HI.3**

Quote accurately from a text when explaining what the text says explicitly and when drawing inferences from the text. **CCSS.ELA.RI.5.1**

Go Digital!

Investigate the lesson content with online whole-class presentation tools.

• **iMap:** Spanish Exploration Routes

• **iMap:** Aztec and Inca Empires, 1519

Background Information

Beans Although the Old World had other kinds of legumes, most beans are native to the Americas. These include green beans, kidney beans, navy beans, white beans, runner beans, and lima beans. The main variety of bean in Europe before 1492 was the broad bean, also called a fava bean, which came originally from North Africa.

| TIMELINE | Invite students to look at the timeline at the top on page 69.

Analyze Which part of the present-day United States did the Spanish explore first? (Florida) **HAS.CS.1**

Analyze the Source

Inspect Have students read pages 68–69.

Find Evidence Use the questions below to check comprehension. Remind students to support their answers with text evidence.

Define What is the Columbian Exchange? (the trading of items between Europe and the Americas after 1492) **DOK 1**

Identify Which of these plants or animals were found in Europe before the Columbian Exchange—turkeys, pineapples, peanuts, tomatoes, potatoes? (none of them) **DOK 2**

Generalize In the Columbian Exchange, what were most of the things brought to Europe? (plants, especially those used for food) **DOK 3**

Analyze Cause and Effect What effect did the introduction of American foods have on European diets? (It made them more healthful.) **DOK 2**

Make Connections

Analyze Cause and Effect Consider the items the text says were part of the Columbian Exchange. Why do you think the Spanish brought most of them back to Europe? (Students should mention the appealing taste of some of the foods and a likely desire to diversity farming and diet.) **DOK 3**

Analyze the Image Direct students to the image of Tenochtitlán and the caption that explains it. Say: *The Aztecs ruled a large area in what is now Mexico, with Tenochtitlán as their capital.*

• What words would you use to describe Tenochtitlán? (Possibilities include *huge, magnificent, and impressive.)*

• What do you think seems unique about Tenochtitlán? (Answers may include that it is built over water.)

Lesson 2

How Did Spanish Exploration Change the Lives of People in the Americas?

The Columbian Exchange

When Columbus made contact with the Taíno people in 1492, he began what is now called the Columbian Exchange. The term refers to the trading of items, animals, culture, ideas, and more between Europeans and native peoples of the Americas.

The Spanish brought back from the Americas plants, animals, and other products unknown in Europe. These included corn, peanuts, tomatoes, potatoes, pineapples, turkeys, tobacco, and most types of beans. Farmers in Europe began to grow some of these plants, which meant that fewer people starved. Also, many of the new foods contained vitamins that made European diets healthier. As a result, the population of Europe grew.

Timeline

1519 Hernan Cortés invades the Aztec Empire.
1532 Francisco Pizarro invades the Inca Empire.
1540 Francisco Coronado explores the American Southwest.

1510 | 1520 | 1530 | 1540 | 1550 | 1560 | 1570

1513 Juan Ponce de León claims Florida for Spain.
1515 Spain completes conquest of what is now Cuba.
1542 Juan Cabrillo explores the southern California coast.
1565 Pedro Aviles founds St. Augustine, Florida.

The Aztec capital city of Tenochtitlán, among the largest cities in the world in the early 1500s

DEA Picture Library/De Agostini/Getty Images

HSS.5.2.1, HSS.5.2.2, HSS.5.2.3, HSS.5.3.1, HAS.CS.1, HAS.CS.2, HAS.CS.3, HAS.CS.4, HAS.CS.5, HAS.HR.1, HAS.HR.2, HAS.HI.1, HAS.HI.3, HAS.HI.4

68 Lesson 1 How Did Spanish Exploration Change the Lives of People in the Americas?

Lesson 2 69

Research Companion, pp. 68–69

ENGLISH LEARNERS SCAFFOLD

ELD.PI.5.8 Analyzing how writers and speakers use vocabulary and other language resources for specific purposes (to explain, persuade, entertain, etc.) depending on modality, text type, purpose, audience, topic, and content area

Emerging

Clarify and Pronounce Words Clarify verbs such as *invades* ("enters by force") and *founds* ("starts a settlement"). Help students pronounce the Spanish names: HWÄN PÄN-sā dā lā-ŌN, är-NÄN kōr-TÄS, frän-SĒS-kō pē-SÄR-ō, frän-SĒS-kō kōr-ō-NÄ-dō.

Expanding

Pronounce Names Explain that a Spanish *j* is like an English *h*; an *h* is silent; a double *l* is like a *y*; an *a* sounds like *ah*; an *e* has a long *a* sound; an *i* has a long *e* sound; an *o* has a long *o* sound. Then have students pronounce the names on the timeline.

Bridging

Explain Pronunciations Pair students familiar with Spanish with classmates who are not. Then have the students familiar with Spanish explain to their partners how to pronounce the names on the timeline and the Aztec capital of *Tenochtitlán*.

See the **Language Learner Teaching Guide** for more language support strategies.

Monitor and Differentiate

REACHING ALL LEARNERS

Approaching Level

Discuss the information on nutrition in the text, making clear that *diets* refers not to what people eat to lose weight but simply to what people eat. Explain, if necessary, what vitamins are and how they help people grow strong and healthy.

On Level

Have students study the dates and events on the timeline. Ask: *How long after the Spanish claimed Florida was St. Augustine, Florida, settled? 52 years How many years after Cortés invaded the Aztec Empire did Pizarro invade the Inca Empire? 13 years*

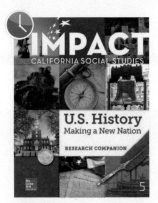

Research Companion
pp. 70–71

 STANDARDS

Describe the entrepreneurial characteristics of early explorers (e.g., Christopher Columbus, Francisco Vásquez de Coronado). **HSS.5.2.1**

Explain the aims, obstacles, and accomplishments of the explorers, sponsors, and leaders of key European expeditions and the reasons Europeans chose to explore and colonize the world. **HSS.5.2.2**

Students identify and interpret the multiple causes and effects of historical events. **HAS.HI.3**

CCSS Quote accurately from a text when explaining what the text says explicitly and when drawing inferences from the text. **CCSS.ELA.RI.5.1**

Go Digital!

Investigate the lesson content with online whole-class presentation tools.

Background Information

New Crops Many of the plants brought to the Americas in the Columbian Exchange became cash crops: sugar in the Caribbean, oranges in Florida and California, and bananas in Central America, for example. At the same time, New World plants took root overseas. The potato, introduced to Ireland by Sir Walter Raleigh, became such a staple there that a great famine resulted when blight struck the potato crop in 1845.

Analyze the Source

Inspect Have students pages 70–71.

Find Evidence Evidence Use the questions below to check comprehension. Remind students to support their answers with text evidence.

Infer How did the introduction of horses change the way American Indians on the Great Plains hunted for buffalo? (They rode the horses when they hunted for buffalo.) **DOK 2**

Identify From where did the chili peppers used in Asian foods originally come? (the Americas) **DOK 1**

Analyze Cause and Effect What was the main effect of the Columbian Exchange on the Taíno people? (It destroyed them, mostly by bringing diseases for which they had no resistance.) **DOK 3**

Infer What did Ponce de León's name for Florida suggest about it? (It had many plants.) **DOK 3**

Analyze Cause and Effect What similar motives, or reasons, did Ponce de León and Hernan Cortés have for exploring? (seeking riches; looking for gold) **DOK 2**

Make Connections

Analyze What were the main reasons that the Spanish participated in the Columbian Exchange? (to do what would benefit them financially and make their lives easier in the New World) **DOK 4**

COLLABORATE

✓ **Stop and Check**

Talk What positive effects did the Columbian Exchange have on people native to the Americas? What negative effects did the Columbian Exchange have on them and on others? (Positive effects were the new plants to grow, animals to raise as food, and horses to use for hunting. Negative effects were diseases that killed them and slavery that also helped kill them and brought misery to many Africans.)

Find Details Explain to students that after they read and take notes, they should review and think about how the facts and details will help them answer the Essential Question.

The Spanish also brought new products to the Americas. These included wheat, sugar, oranges, peaches, bananas, cattle, goats, sheep, pigs, and horses. Many of these items changed the way of life for native peoples of the Americas. Horses, for example, changed the way in which American Indians hunted buffalo on the Great Plains.

The Columbian Exchange did not involve just Europe and the Americas. It transformed the whole planet. Some of the plants Europeans brought to the Americas originally came from Asia and Africa. Many American plants traveled around the world as well. Chili peppers, for instance, were brought to Asia by European sailors and became popular ingredients in many Asian dishes.

Not all things traded in the Columbian Exchange were useful. The Europeans also brought diseases such as smallpox and measles to the Americas. Because these diseases were new to the natives, they had not developed any **resistance** to them. As a result, they died in very large numbers.

The Spanish also forced many natives to work as enslaved persons and even shipped some back to Spain on voyages during which many died. By 1550, few Taíno survived. African slaves were brought to the islands to replace them. This forced relocation of peoples was also part of the Columbian Exchange.

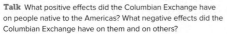

✓ Stop and Check

COLLABORATE

Talk What positive effects did the Columbian Exchange have on people native to the Americas? What negative effects did the Columbian Exchange have on them and on others?

Find Details As you read, add additional information to the graphic organizer on page 65 in your Inquiry Journal.

Spanish Exploration and Conquest in the Americas

By 1515, Spain had spread its control to several islands in the Caribbean Sea. Spain's **conquests** gave them land to settle and people to enslave, but they did not bring the riches the Spanish sought. Sometimes they saw bits of gold in the hands of the island natives. The Spanish wondered, *Where did this gold come from?*

Juan Ponce de León was a Spanish explorer who came to the Americas on Columbus's second voyage. Later he was governor of the island that would come to be known as Puerto Rico. In 1513, Ponce de León became the first Spanish explorer to land in what is now part of the United States. He called the area *La Florida* (Spanish for "full of flowers") and claimed it for Spain. He was looking for gold, although legend says that he was also seeking a Fountain of Youth—a place where magical waters could restore one's youth. But Ponce de León found no gold in Florida, and no Fountain of Youth, either. When he returned there in 1521 to establish a Spanish **settlement**, he was wounded in fighting with the Calusa people of the area. He returned to Cuba and died there of his wounds.

Hernan Cortés, another Spanish explorer, was more successful in his search for riches. In fact, he is called a *conquistador*, Spanish for "conqueror." Like Ponce de León, Cortés was very interested in finding gold. Having heard stories from the native people, he decided there must be a great empire rich in gold to the west of the Caribbean islands. He was right.

Ponce de Léon became the first Spanish explorer to claim land in what is now the United States.

Research Companion, pp. 70–71

(EL) ENGLISH LEARNERS SCAFFOLD

ELD.PI.5.8 Analyzing how writers and speakers use vocabulary and other language resources for specific purposes (to explain, persuade, entertain, etc.) depending on modality, text type, purpose, audience, topic, and content area

Emerging	Expanding	Bridging
Understand Vocabulary Help students understand academic vocabulary by explaining that *positive* effects are good and *negative* effects are bad. Clarify other possibly unfamiliar words in the text, such as *transformed* ("changed") and *relocation* ("settlement in another place").	**Understand Suffixes** Note that the historical term *conquistador* uses the Spanish suffix *-dor* for "one who," while English words use *-er* or *-or* to turn verbs into nouns meaning "one who": *explore + -er = explorer,* "one who explores"; *conquer + -or = conqueror,* "one who conquers."	**Understand Terms** Distinguish the domain-specific term *legend* from *history*, clarifying that a legend is a story handed down over the years that seems like history but may not be true. Mention that there were legends about a Fountain of Youth.

See the **Language Learner Teaching Guide** for more language support strategies.

Monitor and Differentiate

REACHING ALL LEARNERS

Special Needs

Encourage students to recall and describe what they saw in the diagram of the Columbian Exchsange on pp. 62–63 of the Inquiry Journal.

On Level

Have students investigate which animals before the Columbian Exchange were domesticated, or tamed and raised, by people in the Americas. (dogs, llamas, alpacas, guinea pigs, some birds)

Beyond Level

Explain that honeybees were rare in the Americas before 1620. Have students research what native peoples used as a sweetener instead of sugar or honey. (tree (maple) syrup and its crystallized form)

Research Companion
pp. 72–73

 STANDARDS

Describe the entrepreneurial characteristics of early explorers (e.g., Christopher Columbus, Francisco Vásquez de Coronado). **HSS.5.2.1**

Explain the aims, obstacles, and accomplishments of the explorers, sponsors, and leaders of key European expeditions and the reasons Europeans chose to explore and colonize the world. **HSS.5.2.2**

Students identify and interpret the multiple causes and effects of historical events. **HAS.HI.3**

Go Digital!

Investigate the lesson content with online whole-class presentation tools.

Background Information

Fall of the Aztecs Many details about the fall of the Aztecs are disputed. For example, some sources cite an Aztec legend predicting the white-bearded god Quetzalcoatl would rule the empire and say that Cortés, with his white beard, took advantage of the situation. Some say that Cortés took Moctezuma prisoner because he suspected a trap and that the riots were not in support of the emperor but in anger at his weakness.

Analyze the Source

Inspect Have students continue reading about Spanish Exploration and Conquest in the Americas on pages 72–73.

Find Evidence Use the questions below to check comprehension. Remind students to support their answers with text evidence.

Define What is an empire? (a large area in which different groups are controlled by one ruler) **DOK 1**

Infer What sort of city was Tenochtitlán? (large and impressive) **DOK 2**

Compare and Contrast For how long had Moctezuma ruled before Cortés appeared on the scene? (17 years) **DOK 2**

Summarize What are three reasons the Spanish were able to defeat the Aztecs (They had excellent swords, horses for fighting on horseback, and help from natives unhappy with Aztec rule.) **DOK 2**

Explain What happened to Tenochtitlán? (The Spanish destroyed it and built their own capital, Mexico City, on its ruins.) **DOK 1**

Make Connections

Analyze What main problem did Moctezuma face because he ruled an empire? (Many of the different groups he ruled did not like being under his control.) **DOK 3**

DID YOU KNOW?

COMMON MISCONCEPTION Though generally described as floating gardens, the chinampas were not really floating, since they were actually filled mud. A useful form of agriculture in a swampy area, the chinampas helped feed the large Aztec population.

Analyze the Painting Direct students' attention to the painting of the Battle of Otumba. Encourage students to use images in the text to understand events. Ask:

• Which warriors are on horseback? (the Spanish)

• What weapons are they using? (swords)

• What weapons are their opponents using? (clubs or sticks)

• What words would you use to describe the scene? (Possibilities include *violent, hectic, and confusing.*)

An empire is a large area in which different groups are controlled by one ruler. Since the 1430s, the Aztec Empire had ruled over several native groups in what is now central Mexico. The Aztecs built a magnificent capital, Tenochtitlán, where more than 300,000 people lived. In 1502, Moctezuma II became the emperor, or ruler of the empire. However, many native peoples under his rule had started to rebel against the Aztecs.

In 1519, Hernan Cortés left Cuba seeking the great riches he had heard about. After landing in what is today the coastal city of Veracruz, Mexico, he and his soldiers moved inland. When he arrived at Tenochtitlán, Moctezuma met with him. He offered Cortés gifts of gold and precious jewels. These were not enough for Cortés, however. He took Moctezuma prisoner, causing a riot in which the emperor was killed.

Statue of an Aztec eagle knight warrior found at the main temple in Tenochtitlán

Did You Know?

Tenochtitlán was built on watery, swampy land. The Aztecs developed floating gardens called *chinampas*. They stuck rows of thick posts into the swamp. Then, they filled spaces between the posts with mud.

72   Lesson 2   How Did Spanish Exploration Change the Lives of People in the Americas?

The Aztecs then drove Cortés and his troops from the city. They battled on the plains of Otumba, where Cortés and his troops killed the Aztec commander. The Spanish then retreated to a friendlier area.

A few months later, Cortés returned with a larger force to fight the Aztecs. Along the way, his army was joined by a number of native fighters unhappy with Aztec rule.

This help from native allies was just one reason the Spanish were able to defeat the Aztecs. The Spanish soldiers also had two things that the Aztecs did not: fine swords and horses. These gave the Spanish a clear fighting advantage. In fact, even when outnumbered, forces with swords and lances fighting on horseback usually won the day.

After 75 days of battle, Cortés and his army destroyed the Aztec capital. On its ruins, the Spanish built Mexico City. It would be the capital of a colony the Spanish called *Nueva España*, or New Spain.

Spanish and Aztec warriors fighting at the Battle of Otumba

Lesson 2   73

Research Companion, pp. 72–73

(EL) ENGLISH LEARNERS SCAFFOLD

ELD.PI.5.6 Reading closely literary and informational texts and viewing multimedia to determine how meaning is conveyed explicitly and implicitly through language

Emerging	Expanding	Bridging
Describe Images Clarify that a *warrior* is someone who fights in wars. Then offer students sentence frames to describe the art on these pages: **The Aztec warrior is ____. The Spanish warriors are ____.**	**Describe a Place** Have students describe the floating gardens based on the text and accompanying image.	**Describe a Person** Ask students for sentences describing Hernan Cortés based on what they have read.

See the **Language Learner Teaching Guide** for more language support strategies.

Monitor and Differentiate

REACHING ALL LEARNERS

Approaching Level

Help students summarize the events leading up to the Spanish victory over the Aztecs.

On Level

To help them recount the events in the text, offer students signal words showing time or sequence, such as *first, then, next,* and *after.*

Beyond Level

Have students create their own timeline of events leading up to the Spanish victory over the Aztecs, doing research to supplement the events from the text that they include.

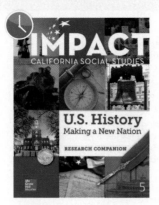

Research Companion,
pp. 74–75

 STANDARDS

Describe the entrepreneurial characteristics of early explorers (e.g., Christopher Columbus, Francisco Vásquez de Coronado). **HSS.5.2.1**

Explain the aims, obstacles, and accomplishments of the explorers, sponsors, and leaders of key European expeditions and the reasons Europeans chose to explore and colonize the world. **HSS.5.2.2**

Students use map and globe skills to determine the absolute locations of places and interpret information available through a map's or globe's legend, scale, and symbolic representations. **HAS.CS.4**

Quote accurately from a **CCSS** text when explaining what the text says explicitly and when drawing inferences from the text. **CCSS.ELA.RI.5.1**

Go Digital!

Investigate the lesson content with online whole-class presentation tools.

Background Information

The Incas had the largest of the Americas' pre-Columbian empires, ruling over 100 different ethnic groups, which were connected by an excellent road system. They also mastered the terrain agriculturally, using sophisticated terracing and irrigation systems to grow crops including potatoes, quinoa, and corn. Domesticated llamas not only provided food and clothing but also served as beasts of burden.

Analyze the Source

Inspect Have students continue reading Spanish Exploration and Conquest in the Americas on pages 74–75.

Find Evidence Use the questions below to check comprehension. Remind students to support their answers with text evidence.

> **Explain** Why did the Incas feel safe from the Spanish? (They lived high in the mountains in thick stone cities.) **DOK 1**

> **Explain** Why were the Incas not safe from the Spanish? (The Spanish had guns; the Incas did not.) **DOK 2**

Make Connections

> **Compare and Contrast** Have students identify the main similarities between Cortés and Pizarro. (Both were Spanish conquistadors seeking riches who defeated large empires in the Americas.) **DOK 3**

Analyze the Image Direct students' attention to the photograph of Machu Picchu on page 74. Encourage students to use the image to help them understand the text. Ask:

- What does the photograph show about Inca skills? (They were skillful builders.)

- What information in the text on the page does the illustration help support? ("Because they lived in thick stone cities high in the mountains, . . .")

⊙ Map Skills

Project a large version of the map on page 75. Use these questions to guide students as they respond to the prompts about the information on the map.

- What does red indicate on the map? (Aztec Empire)

- What does green indicate on the map? (Inca Empire)

- About how many Aztec Empires could fit inside the Inca Empire? (about 8)

COLLABORATE

☑ Stop and Check

Talk Guide students to discuss the strongest motive, or reason, for Spanish exploration and conquest. (desire for riches, especially gold) Then have them talk about Spanish advantages over the Aztec and the Incas. (more effective weapons (swords and firearms), horses, and the unhappiness of some of the native groups the Aztecs ruled)

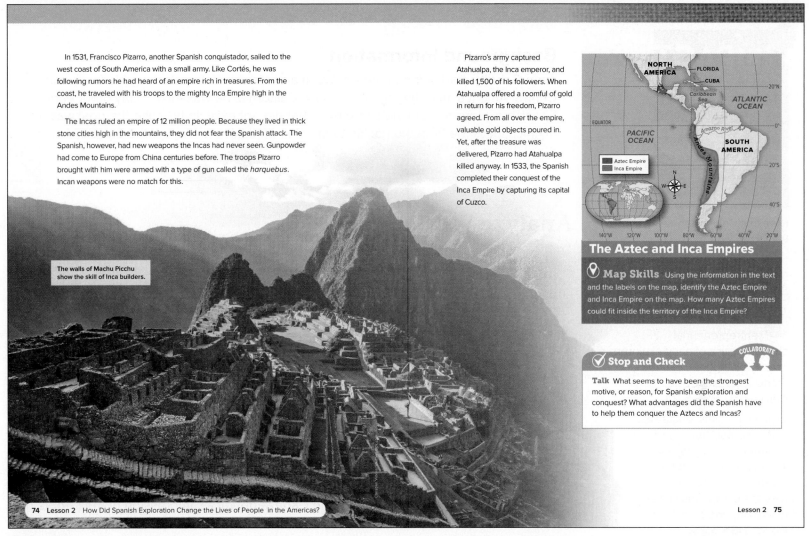

In 1531, Francisco Pizarro, another Spanish conquistador, sailed to the west coast of South America with a small army. Like Cortés, he was following rumors he had heard of an empire rich in treasures. From the coast, he traveled with his troops to the mighty Inca Empire high in the Andes Mountains.

The Incas ruled an empire of 12 million people. Because they lived in thick stone cities high in the mountains, they did not fear the Spanish attack. The Spanish, however, had new weapons the Incas had never seen. Gunpowder had come to Europe from China centuries before. The troops Pizarro brought with him were armed with a type of gun called the *harquebus*. Incan weapons were no match for this.

Pizarro's army captured Atahualpa, the Inca emperor, and killed 1,500 of his followers. When Atahualpa offered a roomful of gold in return for his freedom, Pizarro agreed. From all over the empire, valuable gold objects poured in. Yet, after the treasure was delivered, Pizarro had Atahualpa killed anyway. In 1533, the Spanish completed their conquest of the Inca Empire by capturing its capital of Cuzco.

The walls of Machu Picchu show the skill of Inca builders.

The Aztec and Inca Empires

Map Skills Using the information in the text and the labels on the map, identify the Aztec Empire and Inca Empire on the map. How many Aztec Empires could fit inside the territory of the Inca Empire?

✓ Stop and Check

Talk What seems to have been the strongest motive, or reason, for Spanish exploration and conquest? What advantages did the Spanish have to help them conquer the Aztecs and Incas?

74 Lesson 2 How Did Spanish Exploration Change the Lives of People in the Americas?

Lesson 2 75

Research Companion, pp. 74–75

 ENGLISH LEARNERS SCAFFOLD

ELD.PI.5.6 Reading closely literary and informational texts and viewing multimedia to determine how meaning is conveyed explicitly and implicitly through language

Emerging	Expanding	Bridging
Understand Maps Help students figure out the missing labels on the map key by reminding them that the Aztec Empire was located in Mexico and the Inca Empire was located in the Andes Mountains of South America.	**Understand Maps** Show students how to mark off the edge of a piece of paper with the measurements from the map's scale and then use the marked-out paper to measure the approximate distance of the Inca Empire from north to south.	**Understand Maps** Have pairs of students check online to find out from where Pizarro set sail for the Inca Empire. Then have them point out his route on the map on page 75.

See the **Language Learner Teaching Guide** for more language support strategies.

Monitor and Differentiate

REACHING ALL LEARNERS

On Level

Have students create a template with labels for listing key information about the Aztec and Inca Empires. Labels might include Location, Capital, Last Emperor, Spanish Conquistador, and Dates of Conquest. Students should use the template twice, filling in details for each empire.

Beyond Level

Have students research what happened to Pizarro after conquering the Incas and discuss their findings with classmates. He was governor of Peru, founding Lima, but was assassinated by rival conquistadors who felt he had cheated them of profits conquering the Incas.

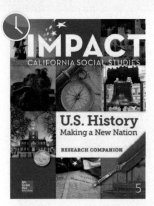

Research Companion
pp. 76–77

STANDARDS

CCSS Describe the entrepreneurial characteristics of early explorers (e.g., Christopher Columbus, Francisco Vásquez de Coronado). **HSS.5.2.1**

Explain the aims, obstacles, and accomplishments of the explorers, sponsors, and leaders of key European expeditions and the reasons Europeans chose to explore and colonize the world. **HSS.5.2.2**

Students use map and globe skills to determine the absolute locations of places and interpret information available through a map's or globe's legend, scale, and symbolic representations. **HAS.CS.4**

HSS Quote accurately from a text when explaining what the text says explicitly and when drawing inferences from the text. **CCSS.ELA.RI.5.1**

Go Digital!

Investigate the lesson content with online whole-class presentation tools.

Background Information

Juan Cabrillo had helped conquer Cuba and Mexico before making his fortune in Central America. In sailing to what is now California, he was—like many other early Spanish explorers—seeking something that did not exist. In his case the goal was a mythical passage from the Pacific to the Gulf of Mexico known as the Strait of Anian.

Analyze the Source

Inspect Have students read New Spain Expands on pages 76–77.

Find Evidence Use the questions below to check comprehension. Remind students to support their answers with text evidence.

Compare and Contrast How was Cabeza de Vaca's attitude toward native peoples different from that of many other Spanish explorers and conquistadors? (Instead of exploiting native peoples, he tried to convince the king of Spain to treat them better.) **DOK 3**

Compare and Contrast For what similar motives, or reasons, did De Soto and Coronado explore North America? (They sought riches, particularly gold.) **DOK 2**

Identify Whose explorations were the basis for Spanish claims on California? (Juan Cabrillo's) **DOK 1**

Analyze the Primary Source Explain that the Mariames were American Indians in present-day Texas. Note phrases showing Cabeza de Vaca's impression of the people he met, such as "received us well," "appeared to be pleased." Ask:

Compare and Contrast Which sentence in the text above the primary source does the primary source help to support and explain? ("His experiences made him sympathetic to native peoples, and he urged the king of Spain to treat them better.") **DOK 3**

Make Connections

Generalize Compare the goals of each explorer with the outcome of his journey. What generalization can you make? (Answers may include that many Spanish explorers did not achieve what they hoped to achieve.) **DOK 4**

⦿ Map Skills

Project a large version of the map on page 77. Guide students respond to the prompts.

- Which explorer started his journey in Puerto Rico? (Ponce de León)

- Which once went the farthest north? (Vizcaíno)

✓ Stop and Check

Think Guide students to consider which parts of the United States the Spanish explored. (They mainly explored the southern part of the United States. Several of them found something other than what they were looking for; for example, De Soto was hunting for riches but found the Mississippi River.)

New Spain Expands

By 1525, the Spanish territory of New Spain included most of present-day Mexico and Central America. Despite its size, Spanish explorers and conquistadors continued looking for rich new lands for Spain to control.

In 1528, Alvar Nuñez Cabeza de Vaca was exploring the coast along the Gulf of Mexico. He was shipwrecked by a hurricane and landed in what is now Texas. There he and his crew lived among American Indians for four years. Eventually they left on foot. They walked through parts of what are now New Mexico and Arizona to return to Mexico. His experiences made him sympathetic to native peoples, and he urged the king of Spain to treat them better.

Hunting for riches, Hernando de Soto began an expedition in 1538 through what is now the southeastern United States. De Soto found no riches. But he and his group did become the first Europeans to see the Mississippi River. Then, in 1542, De Soto became ill and died not far from the river.

In 1540, Francisco Vásquez de Coronado, having heard tales of Seven Cities of Gold, went searching to find them. He discovered no such cities. He and his group did, however, become the first Europeans to see the Grand Canyon. They also claimed for Spain large areas of what is now the American Southwest.

PRIMARY SOURCE

In Their Words... Alvar Nuñez Cabeza de Vaca

At sunset we came in sight of the lodges, and [the length of] two crossbow shots before reaching them met four Indians waiting for us, and they received us well. We told them in the language of the Mariames that we had come to see them. They appeared to be pleased with our company and took us to their homes.

—from the journal of Alvar Nuñez Cabeza de Vaca

Nuñez Cabeza de Vaca, Alvar. *The Journey of Alvar Nuñez Cabeza de Vaca and his Companions from Florida to the Pacific, 1528-1536.* Edited by Ad. F. Bandelier. Translated by Fanny Bandelier. New York: A.S. Barnes & Company, 1905.

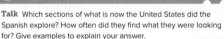

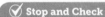

Routes of Spanish Explorers, 1513–1603

Lands claimed by Spain in 1513
Lands claimed by Spain in 1536
Lands claimed by Spain in 1575

Routes of Exploration
Ponce de León, 1513
Cabeza de Vaca, 1529–1536
De Soto, 1539–1542
Coronado, 1540–1542
Cabrillo, 1542
Vizcaino, 1602–1603

Map Skills Which explorer started his journey in Puerto Rico? Which one went the farthest north?

Spanish claims on what is now California began with Juan Rodríguez Cabrillo, who explored the coast around present-day San Diego in 1542. Sixty years later, Sebastián Vizcaíno sailed up the California coast, giving many places the Spanish names we still use today. Spain also continued to pursue its claims in what is now Florida. After several failed attempts at a settlement there, Pedro Menéndez de Aviles in 1565 built a fort in an area on the east coast that he named St. Augustine.

✓ Stop and Check

COLLABORATE

Talk Which sections of what is now the United States did the Spanish explore? How often did they find what they were looking for? Give examples to explain your answer.

Research Companion, pp. 76–77

 ENGLISH LEARNERS SCAFFOLD

ELD.PI.5.6 Reading closely literary and informational texts and viewing multimedia to determine how meaning is conveyed explicitly and implicitly through language

Emerging	Expanding	Bridging
Understand Primary Sources Help students read the primary source. Remind them that a *journal* is a record of events or experiences kept daily, or nearly daily, by the person writing it.	**Distinguish Multiple Meanings** Mention different meanings of *lodges*—"lives or stays in," "small houses," "gives a place to stay," "comes to rest firmly"—and *company*—"visitors," "a group," a business"—and have students use the context to determine which meaning applies.	**Understand Measurements** Discuss the phrase "the length of two crossbow shots" in the primary source. Have a volunteer use the context clues to help him or her explain what it most likely means. Twice the distance an arrow flies when it is shot from a crossbow.

See the **Language Learner Teaching Guide** for more language support strategies.

Monitor and Differentiate

REACHING ALL LEARNERS

Approaching Level

Help students use the map to identify the specific areas in the present-day United States explored by Ponce de León, Cabeza de Vaca, Coronado, Cabrillo, and Vizcaíno.

On Level

Have students work in pairs, quizzing each other on the different areas in the present-day United States explored by Ponce de León, Cabeza de Vaca, Coronado, Cabrillo, and Vizcaíno.

Beyond Level

Have groups research the places in California explored by Cabrillo or named by Vizcaíno and present their findings on simple maps.

Research Companion
pp. 78–79

 STANDARDS

Explain the aims, obstacles, and accomplishments of the explorers, sponsors, and leaders of key European expeditions and the reasons Europeans chose to explore and colonize the world. **HSS.5.2.2**

Students use map and globe skills to determine the absolute locations of places and interpret information available through a map's or globe's legend, scale, and symbolic representations. **HAS.CS.4**

Students identify the human and physical characteristics of the places they are studying and explain how those features form the unique character of those places. **HAS.HI.2**

 Produce clear and coherent writing in which the development and organization are appropriate to task, purpose, and audience. **CCSS.ELA.W.5.4**

Go Digital!

Investigate the lesson content with online whole-class presentation tools.

Background Information

Spanish–French Conflict In 1564 a group of French Protestants established a colony called Fort Caroline near present-day Jacksonville, Florida, or perhaps further north. A year later, insisting on Spanish claims to the area, King Phillip sent Pedro Menéndez de Avilés to remove the French. After skirmishing with them, he landed in St Augustine and built his fort there. The French sailed to attack it, but a hurricane wrecked their ships. In their absence, Menéndez was able to attack and destroy Fort Caroline. Returning to his fort, he killed the French stranded nearby by the hurricane. The waters just off St. Augustine thus came to be called Matanzas Bay—*matanzas* is Spanish for "slaughters."

Analyze the Source

Inspect Have students read Field Trip to St. Augustine on pages 78–79 and study the accompanying photographs and map.

Find Evidence Use the questions below to check comprehension. Remind students to support their answers with text evidence.

Identify What special place does St. Augustine, Florida, hold in United States history? (It is the oldest permanent European settlement in the United States.) **DOK 1**

Explain What is the significance of the Mission Nombre de Dios? (It marks the spot where the Spanish came ashore.) **DOK 1**

Infer Study the map of St. Augustine. Based on the location of the fort (the building with points on the corners) known as the Castillo San Marcos, from where did the Spanish expect to be attacked? (from the sea) **DOK 2**

Make Connections

Analyze Based on the details in the text, what main danger can you conclude colonial St. Augustine faced? (attacks from the British and the French) **DOK 2**

✓ Stop and Check

Write Tell students to compose a speech that begins with an introduction and then describes the different sites in St. Augustine. Remind them to take into account the audience of tourists listening to the speech. (Speeches will vary but should sound like something a tour guide might say and should accurately describe each of the four numbered sites.)

What Do You Think?

Do you think you would like to visit St. Augustine? Why or why not? Encourage students to use text evidence from the whole lesson as they respond to the prompt.

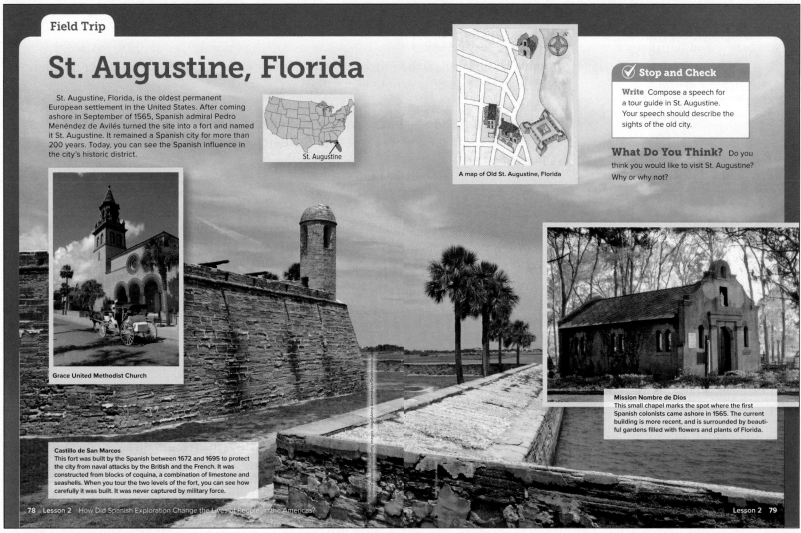

Field Trip

St. Augustine, Florida

St. Augustine, Florida, is the oldest permanent European settlement in the United States. After coming ashore in September of 1565, Spanish admiral Pedro Menéndez de Avilés turned the site into a fort and named it St. Augustine. It remained a Spanish city for more than 200 years. Today, you can see the Spanish influence in the city's historic district.

St. Augustine

A map of Old St. Augustine, Florida

✓ Stop and Check

Write Compose a speech for a tour guide in St. Augustine. Your speech should describe the sights of the old city.

What Do You Think? Do you think you would like to visit St. Augustine? Why or why not?

Grace United Methodist Church

Castillo de San Marcos
This fort was built by the Spanish between 1672 and 1695 to protect the city from naval attacks by the British and the French. It was constructed from blocks of coquina, a combination of limestone and seashells. When you tour the two levels of the fort, you can see how carefully it was built. It was never captured by military force.

Mission Nombre de Dios
This small chapel marks the spot where the first Spanish colonists came ashore in 1565. The current building is more recent, and is surrounded by beautiful gardens filled with flowers and plants of Florida.

78 Lesson 2 How Did Spanish Exploration Change the Lives of People in the Americas?

Lesson 2 79

Research Companion, pp. 78–79

 ENGLISH LEARNERS SCAFFOLD

ELD.PI.5.8 Analyzing how writers and speakers use vocabulary and other language resources for specific purposes (to explain, persuade, entertain, etc.) depending on modality, text type, purpose, audience, topic, and content area

Emerging

Understand Vocabulary
Clarify unfamiliar terms in the opening description of St. Augustine, such as permanent ("lasting") and admiral ("navy commander"). Point out the relationship between the words *fort* and *fortified*, and ask what a fortified site is.

Expanding/Bridging

Interpret Description Point out that the text describes the Mission Nombre de Dios as a *chapel*, or small house of worship. Ask what building it at the site of the original Spanish colonists' landing shows about colonial St. Augustine.

See the **Language Learner Teaching Guide** for more language support strategies.

Monitor and Differentiate

REACHING ALL LEARNERS

Approaching Level

Help students use the street map of St. Augustine and its images to understand the locations of the tourist attractions.

Beyond Level

Have a group of students research Santa Fe, New Mexico, another early Spanish settlement in the present-day United States, and create a pictographic report similar to the one on St. Augustine in their texts.

3 REPORT

Report Your Findings

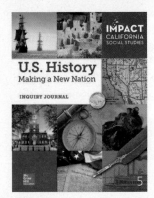

Inquiry Journal
pp. 66–67

 STANDARDS

Describe the entrepreneurial characteristics of early explorers (e.g., Christopher Columbus, Francisco Vásquez de Coronado). **HSS.5.2.1**

Explain the aims, obstacles, and accomplishments of the explorers, sponsors, and leaders of key European expeditions and the reasons Europeans chose to explore and colonize the world. **HSS.5.2.2**

HSS Write informative/explanatory texts to examine a topic and convey ideas and information clearly. **CCSS.ELA.W.5.2**

Engage effectively in discussions, building on others' ideas and expressing their own clearly. **CCSS.ELA.SL.5.1**

Go Digital!

- Students can go online to report their findings. Assess their responses online.

- Students can access the online graphic organizer to capture ideas from their investigation.

Think About It

Students should review their research and consider in what ways the explorer they have been assigned was or was not successful.

- Remind students to review the causes and effects in their graphic organizer. Direct students back to pages 68–79 of their Research Companion if they need more information.

Write About It

Write an Essay Have students read the prompt. Stress that an effective informational essay provides information in a clear, organized way. Remind students to include the following elements in their response.

- An introduction that states their topic and their main point about it.

- Evidence, including facts and reasons, that supports the main point.

- Words that signal cause and effect or other relationships.

Use the rubric on page T172 to evaluate students' work.

Talk About It

Share Your Ideas Help students form groups. Then have them discuss what was most significant about the achievements of the explorer or conquistador they wrote about.

- Tell students to take turns discussing their main points and the facts and reasons that support those points.

- Ask students to discuss whether they agree or disagree with other group members' assessments and to explain why.

- Remind students to follow the rules of appropriate classroom conversation.

Connect to the
Essential Question

Read the prompt aloud to students. Ask them the following guiding questions:

- What happened when they crossed paths with native peoples of the Americas? (Many native peoples died.)

- How do you imagine native peoples' lives would have been different if the Spanish had not arrived? (They would have had more freedom and kept their independence.)

- Would the native peoples have been better off without the Spanish? Why or why not? (Responses will vary, but students should support their answers with text evidence.)

Remind students to use the space provided in their journal to jot down notes.

Report Your Findings

Think About It

Your teacher will assign one of these explorers or conquistadors that you read about: Juan Ponce de Léon, Hernan Cortés, Francisco Pizarro, Alvar Nuñez Cabeza de Vaca, Hernando de Soto, or Francisco Vásquez de Coronado. Based on what you have read, how successful do you think the person was?

Write About It

Write an Essay

Choose a *different* explorer or conquistador than the one you were assigned. Write a three-paragraph informational essay about the impact the explorer or conquistador had on the native peoples of the Americas.

Students should discuss an explorer other than the one they talked about in the previous activity. The essay should focus on the impact of the Spanish explorer on native peoples.

Talk About It

Share Your Ideas

Form a group with other students who wrote about the same Spanish explorer or conquistador. Discuss what was most significant about his achievements.

 **Connect to the EQ**

Consider a Different Outcome

Think about the details in the material you have read. From those details, how do you imagine native people's lives would have been different had the Spanish not arrived in the Americas? Would they have been better off?

There would have been many more native peoples in the Americas if the Spanish had not arrived. The Spanish killed many of the native people and took away the freedom of many others.

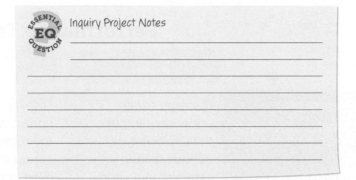
Inquiry Project Notes

Inquiry Journal, pp. 66–67

(EL) ENGLISH LEARNERS SCAFFOLD

ELD.PI.5.11 Supporting own opinions and evaluating others' opinions in speaking and writing

Emerging	Expanding	Bridging
State a Topic Provide this sentence frame to help students state the topic of their essay. ____*was a Spanish explorer (or conquistador) who* ____.	**State a Topic** Provide these sentence frames to students. Have them choose one to help them express their ideas. *(1)* ____*was a Spanish explorer who set out to* ____ *but instead* ____. *(2)* ____*was a Spanish conquistador whose goal was to* ____, *and he did achieve that goal when he* ____.	**Explore a Topic** Tell students to develop their ideas for the text assignments by asking and answering these questions: *Did the explorer or conquistador achieve his goals? For what is he most remembered today? How did his activities affect the lives of native peoples in the Americas?*

See the **Language Learner Teaching Guide** for more language support strategies.

Monitor and Differentiate

REACHING ALL LEARNERS

Approaching Level

List with students the vocabulary they are likely to use in the text assignments: *explore, conquer, successful, achievement, goal,* and so on.

On Level

Remind students to make the ideas in their essays clear by using words that signal cause and effect or other relationships, such as *because, therefore, but, however,* and *after*.

Beyond Level

Have students exchange papers to check if their classmates' essays provide enough supporting evidence and if the relationship between their ideas and evidence is clear.

Know what your students know!

Lesson Task
Report Your Findings

Use this rubric to evaluate students' response.

Write an Essay Students chose a different explorer or conquistador than the one they were assigned and write a three-paragraph informational essay about his impact on native peoples of the Americas.

Share Your Ideas Students discuss the significance of the achievements of the explorer or conquistador with other students who wrote their essays about him.

Performance Task Evaluation Rubric

	4	3	2	1
Historical Understanding	Displays strong understanding of the explorer's or conquistador's achievements and impact, including on native peoples	Displays adequate understanding of the explorer's or conquistador's achievements and impact, including on native peoples	Displays uneven understanding of the explorer's or conquistador's achievements and impact, including on native peoples	Displays no understanding of the explorer's or conquistador's achievements and impact, including on native peoples
Informative Essay	Provides a clear explanation of the explorer's or conquistador's goals and actions	Provides an adequate explanation of the explorer's or conquistador's goals and actions	Provides a somewhat clear or unclear explanation of the explorer's or conquistador's goals and actions	Provides no explanation or shows no understanding of the explorer's or conquistador's goals and actions
Support with Evidence	Supports main ideas with thorough and convincing evidence	Supports main ideas with adequate evidence	Supports main ideas with too little or only somewhat convincing evidence	Supplies no main ideas or no supporting evidence
Share Your Ideas	Discusses significance of explorer, including most important facts and details Speaks in complete sentences throughout the discussion	Discusses significance of explorer, including some important facts and details Speaks in complete sentences through most of the discussion	Discusses significance of explorer, including few important facts and details Mixes complete and incomplete sentences during the discussion	Does not discuss significance of explorer Does not use complete sentences in the discussion

Lesson Assessment

Go *Digital!*

- Have students complete the Chapter 2 Lesson 2 Assessment online to monitor their understanding of the lesson content.

California Smarter Balanced Assessment Connections!

Standards Covered	Lesson Task	Lesson Assessment	Alignment with California Smarter Balanced Assessment
History Social Science Content 5.1; 5.2; 5.3	✔	✔	Claim 1 Targets 8, 9, 10
History Social Science Analysis Skills Chronological and Spatial Thinking 5.4 Historical Interpretation 5.2	✔	✔	Claim 1 Targets 11, 12
Writing W.5.2	✔	✔	Claim 2 Targets 3b, 5
Research and Inquiry W.5.9	✔	✔	Claim 4 Targets 2, 3, 4
Reading RI.5.1; RI.5.3; RI.5.4	✔	✔	Claim 1 Targets 8, 9, 10, 11, 12
Speaking and Listening SL.5.1	✔		Claim 3 Target 3

How Did European Exploration Affect the Americas?

Background Information

Tell students that in this lesson, they will learn how contact with European nations other than Spain changed the Americas and the lives of native peoples living there.

Community Connections

To enrich students' understanding of the different European cultures of the Americas, have them visit a local museum that specializes in early American art.

 HSS **LESSON STANDARDS**

✓ Explain the aims, obstacles, and accomplishments of the explorers, sponsors, and leaders of key European expeditions and the reasons Europeans chose to explore and colonize the world. **HSS.5.2.2**

✓ Trace the routes of the major land explorers of the United States, the distances traveled by explorers, and the Atlantic trade routes. **HSS.5.2.3**

✓ Locate on maps of North and South America land claimed by Spain, France, England, Portugal, the Netherlands, Sweden, and Russia. **HSS.5.2.4**

✓ Describe the competition among the English, French, Spanish, Dutch, and Indian nations for control of North America. **HSS.5.3.1**

✓ Describe the cooperation that existed between the colonists and Indians during the 1600s and 1700s (e.g., in agriculture, the fur trade, military alliances, treaties, cultural interchanges). **HSS.5.3.2**

✓ Students explain how the present is connected to the past, identifying both similarities and differences between the two, and how some things change over time and some things stay the same. **HAS.CS.3**

✓ Students use map and globe skills to determine the absolute locations of places and interpret information available through a map's or globe's legend, scale, and symbolic representations. **HAS.CS.4.**

✓ Students differentiate between primary and secondary sources. **HAS.HR.1**

 Connect to the
Essential Question

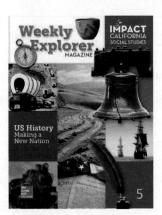

The **Weekly Explorer Magazine** supports students' exploration of the Essential Question and provides additional resources for the EQ Inquiry Project.

Chapter2, pp. 14–29

 Inquiry Project

What happened when diverse cultures crossed paths?

Remind students to use the information they learn in this lesson and other resources to complete their EQ Inquiry Project!

Dinah Zike's

In this lesson you will use Foldables.

When Minutes Count!

Suggested Lesson Pacing

1 ENGAGE
One Day

- Lesson Opener
- Analyze the Source
- Inquiry Tools

Go Digital

- **Video:** New Amsterdam
- **iMap:** European Control in North America
- **iMap:** The Search for a Northwest Passage

2 INVESTIGATE
Two to Three Days

🕐 **Short on Time?** Look for the clock to teach core content in less time.

- The Search for a Northwest Passage
- New Netherland
- The Founding of New France
- The Lost English Colony

3 REPORT
One Day

- Think About It
- Talk About It
- Write a Narrative

Make Connections!

(CCSS) CONNECT TO ELA

Reading

Quote accurately from a text when explaining what the text says explicitly and when drawing inferences from the text. **RI.5.1**

Research

Recall relevant information from experiences or gather relevant information from print and digital sources; summarize or paraphrase information in notes and finished work, and provide a list of sources. **W.5.8**

Draw evidence from literary or informational texts to support analysis, reflection, and research. **W.5.9**

Writing

Write narratives to develop real or imagined experiences or events using effective technique, descriptive details, and clear event sequences. **W.5.3**

Produce clear and coherent writing in which the development and organization are appropriate to task, purpose, and audience. **W.5.4**

Speaking and Listening

Engage effectively in a range of collaborative discussions (one-on-one, in groups, and teacher-led) with diverse partners on grade 5 topics and texts, building on others' ideas and expressing their own clearly. **SL.5.1**

Summarize information presented in diverse media and formats, including visually, quantitatively, and orally. **SL.5.2**

Classroom Resources

 Search for additional resources using the following key words.

John Cabot

Jacques Cartier

Samuel de Champlain

Henry Hudson

New France

New Netherland

Northwest Passage

Roanoke Island

Giovanni da Verrazzano

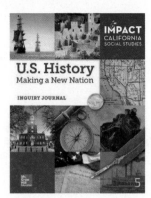

Inquiry Journal,
pp. 68–69

How Did European Exploration Affect the Americas?

 STANDARDS

Explain the aims, obstacles, and accomplishments of the explorers, sponsors, and leaders of key European expeditions and the reasons Europeans chose to explore and colonize the world. **HSS.5.2.2**

Describe the cooperation that existed between the colonists and Indians during the 1600s and 1700s (e.g., in agriculture, the fur trade, military alliances, treaties, cultural interchanges). **HSS.5.3.2**

CCSS Come to discussions prepared, having read or studied required material, to explore ideas under discussion. **CCSS.ELA.SL.5.1a**

Go Digital!

Explore the lesson content with online whole-class presentation tools.

- **Video:** New Amsterdam
- **iMap:** European Control in North America
- **iMap:** The Search for a Northwest Passage

Bellringer
COLLABORATE

Prompt students to retrieve information from the previous lessons. Say: *Columbus was trying to find a shortcut to the riches of Asia when he stumbled on the Americas. After that, Spanish exploration and settlement had enormous effects on the native peoples. What were some of the changes they faced?* (land taken over and empires destroyed; diseases, warfare, and slavery led to many deaths and end of some tribes; way of life changed by new items brought to Americas, such as horses)

Lesson Outcomes

What Am I Learning? Have students read the Lesson Question and Lesson Outcomes.

Why Am I Learning It? Discuss the term *colonial period,* making sure students understand that it refers to the time when the Americas were colonies of European nations. If necessary, remind students that a *colony* is a place settled and governed by another place some distance away.

How Will I Know That I Learned It? Ask students the following questions:

- What will you identify? (how Europeans interacted with native groups)
- What is the purpose of the task? (to write a narrative from the point of view of a European explorer or a native person)
- How will you support the details in your narrative? (with evidence from the text)

Talk About It
COLLABORATE

- Explain that when we talk about artwork, we describe, analyze, and interpret it and present our ideas in our own words. Provide sentence frames to help students form sentences as they talk about the artwork.

- *Cartier and the American Indians are* _____.
- *The relationship between them seems to be* _____ .

Collaborative Conversations
COLLABORATE

Add New Ideas As students engage in partner, small group, and whole-class discussions, encourage them to

- Stay on topic.
- Connect their own ideas to things their peers have said.
- Look for ways to connect their personal experiences or prior knowledge to the conversation.

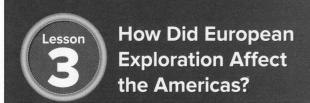

Lesson 3
How Did European Exploration Affect the Americas?

Jacques Cartier meets American Indians in what is now Montreal, Canada.

Lesson Outcomes

What Am I Learning?
In this lesson, you're going to use your investigative skills to explore how European exploration and settlement affected the Americas.

Why Am I Learning It?
Reading and talking about European exploration and settlement in the Americas will help you understand how the colonial period began and how native peoples were impacted.

How Will I Know That I Learned It?
You will be able to show an understanding of how Europeans affected the Americas by examining maps, and you will be able to demonstrate an understanding of how Europeans interacted with native peoples by writing about those encounters.

Talk About It COLLABORATE

Look at the Details What seems to be happening? How do the people in the picture seem to feel about each other?

HSS.5.2.2, HSS.5.2.3, HSS.5.2.4, HSS.5.3.1, HSS.5.3.2, HAS.CS.4

68 Lesson 3   How Did European Exploration Affect the Americas?

Lesson 3   69

Inquiry Journal, pp. 68–69

 ENGLISH LEARNERS SCAFFOLD

ELD.PI.5.12 Selecting and applying varied and precise vocabulary and language structures to effectively convey ideas

Emerging	Expanding	Bridging
Distinguish Homophones Discuss the academic vocabulary word *affected* in the lesson question and its meaning ("changed; had an impact on"). Note that it is a form of *affect,* which is a verb; the noun form, which has the same sound, is *effect.* Clarify with these examples: *Sad songs affect me. They have an effect on me.*	**Understand Multiple-Meaning Words** Clarify that *settle* means "to establish residence in." Explain that *settlement* can mean "the act of settling" or "a place where people settle." Help students recognize that in the text after What Am I Learning? and Why Am I Learning It? *settlement* means "the act of settling."	**Use Vocabulary** Ask students to use precise nouns and adjectives to describe the appearance and attitudes of the people in the painting of Cartier and the American Indians.

See the **Language Learner Teaching Guide** for more language support strategies.

Monitor and Differentiate

REACHING ALL LEARNERS

Special Needs

Point out that the painting shows a meeting in what is now Montreal, Canada. Help students pinpoint the location on the map on page 71.

On Level

Explain that the French language has many silent letters. Help students pronounce the name of French explorer Jacques Cartier: ZHÄK kärt-YĀ.

Beyond Level

Discuss what the maps mentioned in How Will I Know That I Learned It? are likely to show. (routes of explorers for different European nations and areas of the Americas those nations colonized)

1 ENGAGE

Analyze the Source

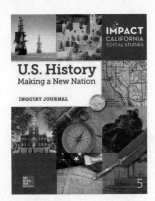

Inquiry Journal,
pp. 70–71

 STANDARDS

Explain the aims, obstacles, and accomplishments of the explorers, sponsors, and leaders of key European expeditions and the reasons Europeans chose to explore and colonize the world. **HSS.5.2.2**

Trace the routes of the major land explorers of the United States, the distances traveled by explorers, and the Atlantic trade routes. **HSS.5.2.3**

Locate on maps of North and South America land claimed by Spain, France, England, Portugal, the Netherlands, Sweden, and Russia. **HSS.5.2.4**

Describe the competition among the English, French, Spanish, Dutch, and Indian nations for control of North America. **HSS.5.3.1**

Go *Digital!*

Model how to inspect and find evidence with online whole-class presentation tools.

Background Information

The Northwest Passage was the topic of an influential 1566 treatise by Humphrey Gilbert, half-brother of Walter Raleigh, who argued that the English should seek a route to Asia not dominated by the Spanish or Portuguese. English explorers Martin Frobisher and John Davis tried to find it in the 1500s; William Baffin, Thomas James, and Luke Foxe, in the 1600s; and even James Cook, in the late 1700s, explored the Pacific coast in an effort to find an all-water route across the continent.

1 Inspect

Look Tell students to examine the map, read the title and key, and circle important words and dates, names of explorers, and labels on the map or in the text. Ask:

- What part of the world does the map show? (North America)

- What is the map about? (European voyages in North America from 1497 to 1611)

- What do the colored lines represent? (different voyages)

Collaborate Have small groups discuss what the Northwest Passage was and whether the explorers succeeded in finding it. (an all-water route through northwestern North America to Asia; no)

2 Find Evidence

Look Closely Have students reexamine the map and reread the text that accompanies it. Ask which explorer spent the longest time searching for the Northwest Passage. (Hudson)

Analyze Ask what makes the routes of Cartier in 1523 and Hudson in 1620 different from the other four routes. (They went beyond coastal areas to the interior of North America.)

3 Make Connections

Discuss Have students discuss which explorer came closest to finding a Northwest Passage. (Students are likely to name Jacques Cartier, since he did travel farther into the continent on the St. Lawrence River; or Hudson, since he went north toward where a Northwest Passage actually is.)

Analyze the Source

A Shortcut to Asia

Many of the European explorers who reached North America between the late 1400s and early 1600s were really trying to get to Asia. Trade with Asia could be very profitable, especially when spices were involved. However, getting to Asia by sailing around Africa was difficult and dangerous. European rulers wanted to see if there was another way there.

The voyages shown on the map on the next page were paid for by the governments of England, France, and the Netherlands. The voyages took place between the years 1497 and 1611.

Europeans Search for a Northwest Passage, 1497-1611

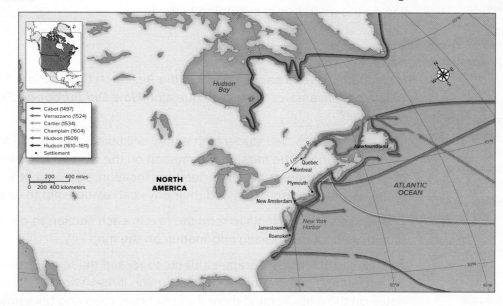

Cabot (1497)
Verrazzano (1524)
Cartier (1534)
Champlain (1604)
Hudson (1609)
Hudson (1610–1611)
• Settlement

0 200 400 miles
0 200 400 kilometers

NORTH AMERICA

Hudson Bay

St. Lawrence R.
Quebec
Montreal
Plymouth
New Amsterdam
Jamestown
Roanoke
New York Harbor
Newfoundland
ATLANTIC OCEAN

Inquiry Journal, pp. 70–71

ENGLISH LEARNERS SCAFFOLD

ELD.PI.5.6 Reading closely literary and informational texts and viewing multimedia to determine how meaning is conveyed explicitly and implicitly through language

Emerging	Expanding	Bridging
Understand Maps Help students trace on the map the rivers on which Cartier and Hudson sailed into the interior of North America. Mention that Hudson did not name the river after himself; it got that name decades later.	**Use Maps** Have students trace on the map Cartier's route up the St. Lawrence River. Ask: *To what large body of water does the St. Lawrence lead? Did Cartier sail that far? If not, how far did he sail?* It leads to Lake Ontario, but Cartier sailed only as far as present-day Montreal, Canada.	**Discuss Maps** Have students consider the St. Lawrence as a means of reaching the interior of North America.

See the **Language Learner Teaching Guide** for more language support strategies.

Monitor and Differentiate

REACHING ALL LEARNERS

On Level

Clarify that *profitable* in the text means "able to make money." Be sure students understand why explorers wanted to find the Northwest Passage: They were looking for a shortcut to Asia so that they could make money from trading for the spices and other valuable goods there.

Beyond Level

Elicit or explain that there were, far north in the Arctic, all-water passages across North America. Ask students why they think explorers between 1497 and 1611 could not find one. (Any passage was too far north and icy for their ships to cross.)

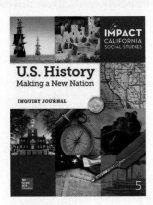

Inquiry Journal,
pp. 72–73

 STANDARDS

Explain the aims, obstacles, and accomplishments of the explorers, sponsors, and leaders of key European expeditions and the reasons Europeans chose to explore and colonize the world. **HSS.5.2.2**

Trace the routes of the major land explorers of the United States, the distances traveled by explorers, and the Atlantic trade routes. **HSS.5.2.3**

Describe the competition among the English, French, Spanish, Dutch, and Indian nations for control of North America. **HSS.5.3.1**

Students use map and globe skills to determine the absolute locations of places and interpret information available through a map's or globe's legend, scale, and symbolic representations. **HAS.CS.4**

Go Digital!

- Model how to explore and investigate with online whole-class tools.

- Students can access the online graphic organizer to use the inquiry tools as they read.

Explore Maps

Explain Tell students that maps provide information about places in visual form. They clarify, highlight, or add details to the information in the text they accompany.

Read Project a large version of the map on page 73. As students read aloud the step-by-step instructions about how to analyze a map, point out the different parts of the map that each step discusses.

Guide Practice Discuss the specific details on the map in conjunction with the step-by step instructions. Have students work as a class to explain what each differently colored line on the map shows, according to the key.

Investigate!

Have students read pages 80–89 in the Research Companion. Tell them the information will help them answer the lesson question *How Did European Exploration Affect the Americas?*

Take Notes Tell students that they will take notes on the incomplete map on page 73 by filling in the missing information on the map key. Point out that taking notes on a map will help students better understand location, size, and other physical details about the places under discussion and their physical relationship to one another.

Inspect Guide students to read the text in each section to determine what information it provides about the missing information on the map key.

Find Evidence Encourage students to reread the text to develop a deeper understanding of the content and determine if they should add more information to their notes on the map. Remind them that after they read and take notes, they should review and think about how the facts and details will help them answer the lesson question.

Collaborative Conversations

Text-Based Discussion Remind students of the goals of discussing with others the text and its accompanying maps or other graphics.

- to listen and respond to their partners' points
- to ask for evidence from the text or graphics
- to build on each other's ideas
- to see the text or graphics from a different point of view

Inquiry Tools

Reading Maps

Maps can provide many types of information. Look at the map on the following page, and think about what information is being provided.

To analyze a map, follow these steps:

1. Read the title of the map.

This should give you a good idea of the most important information the mapmaker is trying to provide.

2. Read the labels on the map.

Note any differences in the size or style of the type. Larger labels may show major regions. Italic type may show bodies of water or other land features.

3. Look for any places on the map shown with dots or other markers.

For example, mapmakers often use large dots to show the locations of major cities.

4. Identify the compass rose and scale of the map.

The compass rose shows the directions north, south, east, and west. On almost all maps, the top of the map is north. The map scale shows the lengths used to represent miles or kilometers. You may need to use a ruler to determine the scale.

5. Look for a map key.

This is a box that provides information about the special features of a map, such as color coding, dashed lines, or icons.

COLLABORATE As a class, use the map key on page 71 to match each colored route with its explorer. Write the name of each explorer close to the colored line that shows his route.

Investigate!

Read pages 80–89 in your Research Companion. Use your investigative skills to look for text evidence that helps you fill in the missing information in the map key. Write the name of the country that claimed the territory shown by each color on the map.

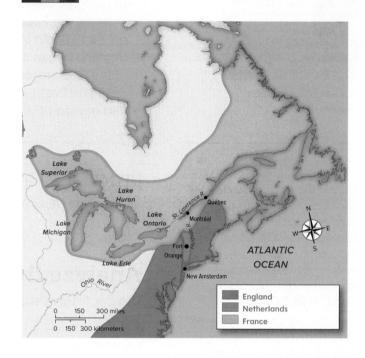

72 Lesson 3 How Did European Exploration Affect the Americas?

Lesson 3 73

Inquiry Journal, pp. 72–73

(EL) ENGLISH LEARNERS SCAFFOLD

ELD.PI.5.6 Reading closely literary and informational texts and viewing multimedia to determine how meaning is conveyed explicitly and implicitly through language

Emerging

Understand Maps Be sure students understand the terms *color coding, dashed lines,* and *icons* in the discussion of map keys. Clarify that the colored lines on the map on page 71 are like a code, with each color representing a different explorer's voyages. The key gives the clues to the code.

Expanding/Bridging

Use Maps Tell students that they do not need a ruler to use a map scale to measure distances. Instead, they can create their own ruler by putting the edge of a piece of paper along the map scale and marking off the measures three or four times. Demonstrate the procedure by helping students create a hand-drawn ruler of the scale of the map and then use it to measure approximate distances of various explorers' voyages shown on the map.

See the **Language Learner Teaching Guide** for more language support strategies.

Monitor and Differentiate

REACHING ALL LEARNERS

Approaching Level

Clarify the unchanging relationship between north, east, south, and west. Note that if a map simply shows north instead of using a compass rose, students can figure out the other directions.

On Level

Tell students that maps often use larger, darker, or special colored print to indicate larger cities or other locations and often use stars for capitals.

Beyond Level

Point out that since maps are flat and the earth is round, maps of large areas are never completely accurate. On some maps, lands farther north, like Canada, look bigger than they actually are.

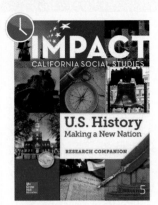

Research Companion
pp. 80–81

STANDARDS

Explain the aims, obstacles, and accomplishments of the explorers, sponsors, and leaders of key European expeditions and the reasons Europeans chose to explore and colonize the world. **HSS.5.2.2**

Describe the competition among the English, French, Spanish, Dutch, and Indian nations for control of North America. **HSS.5.3.1**

Students place key events and people of the historical era they are studying in a chronological sequence and spatial context; they interpret time lines. **HAS.CS.1**

Go Digital!

Investigate the lesson content with online whole-class presentation tools.

- **Video:** New Amsterdam
- **iMap:** European Control in North America
- **iMap:** The Search for a Northwest Passage

Background Information

Competing in the South While Spain dominated South America and the southern part of North America, other European nations made claims there as well. Portugal first claimed Brazil in 1500, when Pedro Álvarez Cabral sailed off course while trying to navigate the west coast of Africa. The claim fit in with the 1494 Treaty of Tordesillas, in which the Pope officially divided Columbus's "discoveries" between Portugal in the east and Spain in the west. Then, in the early 1600s, France, the Netherlands, and England began claiming Caribbean islands that Spain was not protecting and portions of the Guianas on the nearby South American coast. In most of these colonies, including Brazil, African slaves were brought in, usually to replace natives who either fled or died off from disease, fighting, or ill treatment.

| TIMELINE | Invite students to look at the timeline at the top on page 81.

Analyze Ask: What shift in activity does the timeline show in the entry for 1585? (a shift from exploring and claiming land to actually establishing colonies) **HAS.CS.1**

Analyze the Source

Inspect Have students read pages 80–81.

Find Evidence Use the questions below to check comprehension. Remind students to support their answers with text evidence.

Identify What are five European nations other than Spain that sent explorers to the Americas in the Age of Exploration? (Portugal, France, England, the Netherlands, and Sweden) **DOK 1**

Analyze Why do you think these nations sent many of their explorers to the northeastern part of North America instead of further south? (They were exploring and claiming areas different from those Spain had already claimed.) **DOK 3**

Define What was the Northwest Passage so many explorers were looking for? (an all-water route to Asia through northwestern North America) **DOK 2**

Make Connections

Analyze Cause and Effect Why were so many countries hoping to find the Northwest Passage? (They wanted a shorter way to reach the riches of Asia.) **DOK 3**

Analyze the Image Explain to students that the painting shows Henry Hudson entering the Hudson River.

- Who is in the large ship, *The Half Moon*? (Hudson and his men)
- Who is in the smaller ships? (American Indians)
- What are the people in the smaller ships doing? (rowing out to meet the large ship)

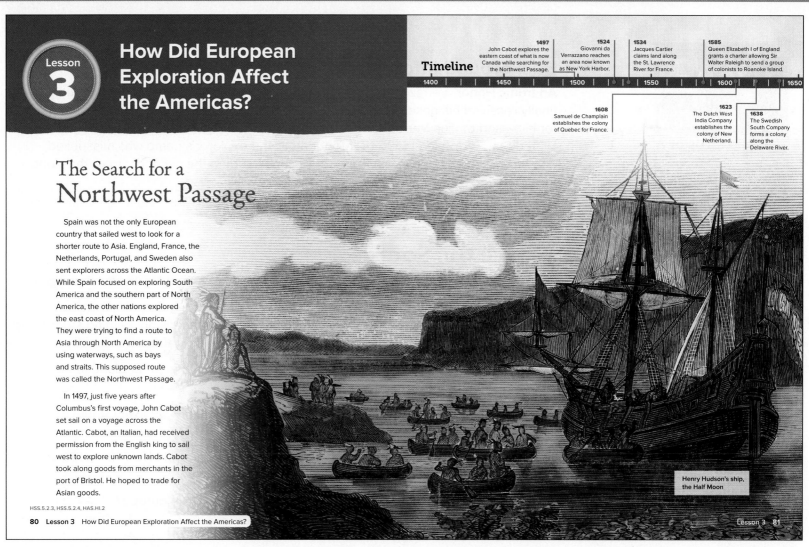

How Did European Exploration Affect the Americas?

Timeline

1497 John Cabot explores the eastern coast of what is now Canada while searching for the Northwest Passage.

1524 Giovanni da Verrazzano reaches an area now known as New York Harbor.

1534 Jacques Cartier claims land along the St. Lawrence River for France.

1585 Queen Elizabeth I of England grants a charter allowing Sir Walter Raleigh to send a group of colonists to Roanoke Island.

1400 | 1450 | 1500 | 1550 | 1600 | 1650

1608 Samuel de Champlain establishes the colony of Quebec for France.

1623 The Dutch West India Company establishes the colony of New Netherland.

1638 The Swedish South Company forms a colony along the Delaware River.

The Search for a Northwest Passage

Spain was not the only European country that sailed west to look for a shorter route to Asia. England, France, the Netherlands, Portugal, and Sweden also sent explorers across the Atlantic Ocean. While Spain focused on exploring South America and the southern part of North America, the other nations explored the east coast of North America. They were trying to find a route to Asia through North America by using waterways, such as bays and straits. This supposed route was called the Northwest Passage.

In 1497, just five years after Columbus's first voyage, John Cabot set sail on a voyage across the Atlantic. Cabot, an Italian, had received permission from the English king to sail west to explore unknown lands. Cabot took along goods from merchants in the port of Bristol. He hoped to trade for Asian goods.

HSS.5.2.3, HSS.5.2.4, HAS.HI.2

80 Lesson 3 How Did European Exploration Affect the Americas?

Henry Hudson's ship, the Half Moon

Lesson 3 81

Research Companion, pp. 80–81

 ENGLISH LEARNERS SCAFFOLD

ELD.PI.5.8 Analyzing how writers and speakers use vocabulary and other language resources for specific purposes (to explain, persuade, entertain, etc.) depending on modality, text type, purpose, audience, topic, and content area

Emerging	Expanding	Bridging
Clarify Terms Discuss the domain-specific terms *route* and *passage,* which both refer to ways of traveling. Define *route* as "a regularly traveled way to reach a place." Mention its two pronunciations: it may rhyme with *doubt* (rowt) or *boot* (rōōt).	**Use Context Clues** Have students use the context of the paragraph to get an idea of the meanings of the domain-specific terms *bays* and *straits.* (Both are bodies of water.) Ask which word in the paragraph is a context clue for these terms. (waterways)	**Explain Domain-Specific Words** Discuss the domain-specific word *charter,* which appears in the timeline. Elicit or explain that a charter is a document usually issued by a government that grants specific rights to a person or a group.

See the **Language Learner Teaching Guide** for more language support strategies.

Monitor and Differentiate

REACHING ALL LEARNERS

Approaching Level

Using a map of Europe, show students the different European countries mentioned on this page. Elicit or point out that all the countries are on the Atlantic Coast of Europe and so would be more interested in sea travel to the Americas than an inland nation would be.

On Level

Explain that *Netherlands* means "low-lying lands," a suitable name for a nation where much of the land is below sea level. Clarify that the Netherlands is sometimes called Holland and its people and language are known as Dutch.

Research Companion
pp. 82–83

 STANDARDS

Explain the aims, obstacles, and accomplishments of the explorers, sponsors, and leaders of key European expeditions and the reasons Europeans chose to explore and colonize the world. **HSS.5.2.2**

Describe the competition among the English, French, Spanish, Dutch, and Indian nations for control of North America. **HSS.5.3.1**

ccss Quote accurately from a text when explaining what the text says explicitly and when drawing inferences from the text. **CCSS.ELA.RI.5.1**

Summarize information presented in diverse media and formats, including visually, quantitatively, and orally. **CCSS.ELA.SL.5.2**

Go Digital!

Investigate the lesson content with online whole-class presentation tools.

Background Information

An Ironic Honor Verrazzano's role in New York history was long neglected, but he finally received his deserved honors when a bridge in New York Harbor was named for him—sort of. The Verrazano Narrows Bridge, the longest suspension bridge in the United States, opened in 1964. Unfortunately, the explorer's name was misspelled, and officials decided to retain the error because adding the second z to all the signs for the bridge would have been too expensive.

Analyze the Source

Inspect Have students continue reading about the search for a Northwest Passage on pages 82–83.

Find Evidence Use the questions below to check comprehension. Remind students to support their answers with text evidence.

Infer What continent did John Cabot hope to reach when he left England in 1497? (Asia) **DOK 3**

Analyze Cause and Effect Why were English merchants pleased with Cabot's discoveries? (He had found waters excellent for fishing.) **DOK 2**

Identify Which two explorers led the first European voyages in New York Harbor? (Verrazzano and Hudson) **DOK 1**

Evaluate Why did Verrazzano's voyages have little impact in Europe? (They occurred at about the same time that the Spanish conquered the Aztecs, and Europeans were interested in obtaining gold like the Aztecs had, not in exploring northern waters.) **DOK 3**

Make Connections

Draw Conclusions Why do you think Henry Hudson's last crew turned against him? (Answers will vary, but students should recognize that he had brought them on a failed mission and had to eat food that made them ill.) **DOK 4**

Compare and Contrast What did the voyages of Cabot, Verrazzano, and Hudson all have in common? (They were made for nations other than Spain, sought to find a Northwest Passage, and found something else instead.) **DOK 3**

COLLABORATE

 Stop and Check

Think Guide students to discuss why European explorers wanted to find a Northwest Passage. (They were looking for a short cut to the riches of eastern Asia.)

What Do You Think?

In your opinion, why were the explorers unable to find a Northwest Passage? Encourage students to use text evidence from the whole lesson as they respond to the prompt.

Cabot reached the North American coast somewhere in the region of what is now Newfoundland, an area in Canada. He could not find any people to trade with. What he did find were huge quantities of fish in the coastal waters. The English merchants were interested in this discovery. Dried fish was an important source of food at the time. Unfortunately, Cabot disappeared during his next voyage, probably the victim of a huge storm. Following Cabot's lead, Portugal sent sailors to the Newfoundland area. It established a small colony there as a base for fishing ships.

An oil painting of John and Sebastian Cabot

Another Italian, Giovanni da Verrazzano, obtained the support of the king of France. Verrazzano traveled up the Atlantic Coast. He explored areas including what are now New York Harbor and the mouth of the Hudson River. He had friendly encounters with American Indians on this voyage.

Verrazzano's next voyage was to Brazil, where he found a type of wood that is valuable in creating dyes for textiles. Verrazzano's voyages were overlooked in Europe, however. They occurred during the same decade that Spain conquered the Aztec Empire and brought large amounts of gold home to Europe.

Giovanni da Verrazzano

The Hudson River, named for the English explorer Henry Hudson.

Henry Hudson's voyages to the area that is now New York occurred in the early 1600s. Hudson was from England, but he worked for both England and the Netherlands. The Dutch East India Company hired Hudson in 1608 to try to find a shorter route to Asia. This company had been set up to increase Dutch trade with what is now Indonesia.

In 1609, Hudson's ships reached the same area near New York that Verrazzano had visited. Hudson sailed far up a river that was later named after him, the Hudson River. He concluded that it did not lead to a Northwest Passage because it became shallow as he moved north; also, it contained fresh water, not saltwater.

Hudson returned to Europe and then began exploring for England in 1610. This time his effort to find the Northwest Passage ended in disaster. He sailed into a bay in northern Canada now called Hudson Bay. He became stuck in the ice and spent the winter there. He and his crew had to eat spoiled food. When spring came and the ice melted, the crew took over the ship and put Hudson and his son in a rowboat with a few other crew members. They were never heard from again. The crew was arrested when it returned to England.

During his second voyage to North America, Henry Hudson, his son, and others were abandoned in a rowboat after most of his crew rebelled.

✓ Stop and Check

COLLABORATE

Talk Why did European explorers want to find a Northwest Passage?

Find Details As you read, add additional information to the graphic organizer on page 73 in your Inquiry Journal.

What Do You Think? In your opinion, why were the explorers unable to find a Northwest Passage?

Research Companion, pp. 82–83

ENGLISH LEARNERS SCAFFOLD

ELD.PI.5.8 Analyzing how writers and speakers use vocabulary and other language resources for specific purposes (to explain, persuade, entertain, etc.) depending on modality, text type, purpose, audience, topic, and content area

Emerging	Expanding	Bridging
Understand Vocabulary Help students understand possibly unfamiliar terms in the text and captions, such as *encounters* ("meetings"), *textiles* ("woven fabrics"), *abandoned* ("left behind"), and *rebelled* ("rose up against authority").	**Clarify Text** Note the distinction between saltwater, found in oceans, and fresh water, found in mountain streams and lakes. Clarify that Hudson knew he was not on a passage to the Pacific Ocean when the water of the river up which he was sailing turned fresh.	**Clarify Text** Note that the area near Newfoundland where Cabot found plenty of fish is called the Grand Banks and that the fish was mostly cod. Clarify the mention of dried fish—the fish had to be dried to bring it back to England for sale, since fresh fish would spoil on the trip.

See the **Language Learner Teaching Guide** for more language support strategies.

Monitor and Differentiate

REACHING ALL LEARNERS

Special Needs

Have students begin charts of the explorers discussed in this lesson, listing each along with what he was looking for, what he found, and when he found it, if mentioned in the text.

Approaching Level

Students may be puzzled by John Cabot's name, since the text says he was Italian. Explain that his name was actually Giovanni Caboto but he is known in English as John Cabot.

Beyond Level

Have small groups research and report on the native peoples of Newfoundland, the island's Viking past, its early European explorers, or its importance as a fishery.

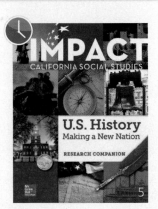

Research Companion
pp. 84–85

 STANDARDS

Explain the aims, obstacles, and accomplishments of the explorers, sponsors, and leaders of key European expeditions and the reasons Europeans chose to explore and colonize the world. **HSS.5.2.2**

Describe the competition among the English, French, Spanish, Dutch, and Indian nations for control of North America. **HSS.5.3.1**

Describe the cooperation that existed between the colonists and Indians during the 1600s and 1700s (e.g., in agriculture, the fur trade, military alliances, treaties, cultural interchanges). **HSS.5.3.2**

Students explain how the present is connected to the past, identifying both similarities and differences between the two, and how some things change over time and some things stay the same. **HAS.CS.3**

Go Digital!

Investigate the lesson content with online whole-class presentation tools.

Background Information

The Hudson River was known to Algonquian tribes as *Mahicantuck,* meaning "river that is never still" or "river that flows two ways." That is because fresh water flows down the river to the sea but the lower river is a tidal estuary, with saltwater flowing in. The name also means "Mohicans' river" since the Mohicans, or Mahicans, were "the people of the river that is never still." In the Dutch colony of New Netherland, the river was usually called the North River. Today that name is still used for its lower portion, particularly by those who do business on the river.

Analyze the Source

Inspect Have students read about New Netherland on pages 84–85.

Find Evidence Use the questions below to check comprehension. Remind students to support their answers with text evidence.

> **Define** What was New Netherland, and when was it established? (the colony in what is now New York State that the Dutch West India Company established in 1623) **DOK 1**
>
> **Infer** Why do you think the first settlements in New Netherland were established on the Hudson River? (The Dutch arrived by water and used water transportation for travel and trade.) **DOK 3**
>
> **Summarize** How did the misunderstanding about buying versus sharing the land lead to later problems between the Dutch and native peoples? (The native peoples came into the colony, thinking they had agreed only to share it; but the Dutch thought they had bought it and fought to keep them out.) **DOK 2**
>
> **Explain** In what way did Peter Stuyvesant expand New Netherland? (He took over a Swedish colony along the Delaware River.) **DOK 2**

Make Connections

> **Analyze** About twelve years after Henry Hudson sailed for the Dutch *East* India Company, Dutch merchants formed the Dutch *West* India Company. What does the new company show about the interests of Dutch merchants? (They were now expanding their interests, trying to make money in the Americas as well as Asia.) **DOK 4**

THEN AND NOW

Two routes qualify as a Northwest Passage, both far north in the Arctic. Taking the more southerly of these, Roald Amundsen—the Norwegian explorer best known for being the first to reach the South Pole—became the first to make a complete transit of the Northwest Passage on a three-year voyage that ended in 1906. Since the late 2000s, the melting of the polar ice cap has made the southerly passage more accessible.

Stop and Check

Think Encourage students to think about why Dutch settlers choose to settle in what is now New York State. (They hoped to benefit from trade and had a claim on the area based on Hudson's exploration.)

New Netherland

In 1621, a group of Dutch merchants formed the Dutch West India Company. This company established the colony of New Netherland in 1623. This colony was the earliest European settlement in what is now New York state. The Dutch West India Company established the colony in that location because Henry Hudson had claimed the land for the Netherlands in 1609.

The first settlements in New Netherland were established along the Hudson River. The Dutch colonists benefited from the rich resources in the area, particularly fur obtained by trading with native peoples. In 1626, Peter Minuit became the colony's governor. Some Dutch settlers established a profitable trading post on the southern tip of Manhattan Island. Minuit negotiated with native peoples there to recognize and accept the Dutch settlement, called New Amsterdam.

Minuit offered the native peoples weapons, tools, and other supplies as part of the agreement. These goods were worth about 60 guilders, or about 700 dollars in today's money. But the native peoples did not believe that they were selling Manhattan. Because of communication difficulties, they thought they were agreeing only to share the land.

New Netherland was one of the most **diverse** European colonies in North America. People of different religious and ethnic backgrounds were allowed to settle there. However, New Netherland was also one of the first colonies to bring African slaves to North America. Fighting occurred between the colonists and native peoples in the early 1640s. The governor of New Netherland, Willem Kieft, was unhappy that native peoples were moving into the northern part of New Netherland.

Dutch West India House was built in the Netherlands in 1623.

These peoples were trying to escape attacks by other Northeast Woodlands tribes that were seeking to expand their territories. Against the advice of other colonial leaders, Kieft sent Dutch soldiers to attack native villages. The result was a series of attacks by both sides that left hundreds dead. Many Dutch settlers returned to Europe because of the violence.

In 1647, Peter Stuyvesant became the leader of New Netherland. He had a conflict with a Swedish colony along the Delaware River. He believed the colony was on Dutch territory. He had a fort built in the area. When the Swedes took over the fort, Stuyvesant sent a force to take over the Swedish colony, which had log cabins that were later widely copied.

As English colonies in North America grew, some English leaders became interested in New Netherland. England and the Netherlands fought wars in Europe in the 1600s. In 1664, the brother of the King of England sent four **warships** to New Amsterdam harbor. His troops demanded that Stuyvesant surrender the entire Dutch colony. Stuyvesant wanted to fight, but his colonists instead surrendered. Most stayed in North America, living under British rule.

Then and Now

The Northwest Passage

Although there is a Northwest Passage from the Atlantic Ocean to the Pacific Ocean, it was nearly impossible to pass through during the age of European exploration. This is because the passage lies far to the north and was usually covered by Arctic ice. The illustration at the upper right shows a Dutch explorer stuck in this ice in the 1500s.

But with the gradual melting of the Arctic ice cap in recent years, the Northwest Passage is now nearly ice-free during the summer. Ships are able to travel through the passage in warmer months. The photograph at the lower right shows the Northwest Passage in August 2016.

✓ Stop and Check

Think Why did Dutch settlers choose to settle in what is now New York state?

84 Lesson 3 How Did European Exploration Affect the Americas?

Lesson 3 85

Research Companion, pp. 84–85

Ⓔ ENGLISH LEARNERS SCAFFOLD

ELD.PI.5.6 Reading closely literary and informational texts and viewing multimedia to determine how meaning is conveyed explicitly and implicitly through language

Emerging	Expanding	Bridging
Summarize Have students sum up the information about the relationship between the native peoples and the Dutch in New Netherland. Offer these sentence frames to help them: *The Dutch thought they were ____. The Indians thought they were just ____.*	**Contrast Images** Have students describe the contrasting images in the Then and Now feature and the relationship between them.	**Draw Conclusions** Ask students what the text suggests *guilders* are. (the Dutch form of money) Then ask: Where do you think Amsterdam is located? Why?

See the **Language Learner Teaching Guide** for more language support strategies.

Monitor and Differentiate

REACHING ALL LEARNERS

On Level

Have students sum up the information about the governors of New Netherland on a timeline that lists their activities mentioned in the text.

Beyond Level

Help students use enlarged online maps to study the Hudson River, which the Dutch called the North River, and the Delaware River, which the Dutch called the South River. Point out their similar advantages: Both empty into bays that create protected harbors, and both provide water access to the interior for trade with the American Indians.

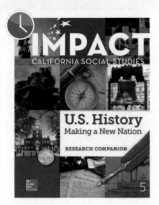

Research Companion
pp. 86–87

 STANDARDS

Explain the aims, obstacles, and accomplishments of the explorers, sponsors, and leaders of key European expeditions and the reasons Europeans chose to explore and colonize the world. **HSS.5.2.2**

Locate on maps of North and South America land claimed by Spain, France, England, Portugal, the Netherlands, Sweden, and Russia. **HSS.5.2.4**

Describe the competition among the English, French, Spanish, Dutch, and Indian nations for control of North America. **HSS.5.3.1**

Describe the cooperation that existed between the colonists and Indians during the 1600s and 1700s (e.g., in agriculture, the fur trade, military alliances, treaties, cultural interchanges). **HSS.5.3.2**

Go Digital!

Investigate the lesson content with online whole-class presentation tools.

Background Information

Fur Trade Though neither Asian spices nor Aztec gold, fur did bring a tidy profit to Europeans merchants. Popular European hats were made of felt, and the best felt came from the underfur of beavers. In North America, beaver was abundant, and the natives were eager to trade beaver fur for products the Europeans could supply that they did not have before—including guns they could use in warfare.

Analyze the Source

Inspect Have students read The Founding of New France on pages 86–87.

Find Evidence Use the questions below to check comprehension. Remind students to support their answers with text evidence.

> **Infer** What does the name *Canada* suggest about the kinds of communities found there in these early times? (They were small villages.) **DOK 3**
>
> **Identify** Which French explorer founded the city of Quebec? (Samuel de Champlain) **DOK 1**
>
> **Compare and Contrast** How did Brûlé and Nicolet expand Cartier's efforts as an explorer? (Cartier explored only the St Lawrence River in his search for the Northwest Passage, but they traveled farther in searching for it, exploring the Great Lakes.) **DOK 2**

Make Connections

> **Draw Conclusions** Why do you think the French would try to maintain good relations with the native peoples? (They were interested in trading for furs with them.) **DOK 2**

Analyze the Primary Source Point out the word *savages* in the primary source, and discuss its meaning and negative connotations. Ask:

> **Infer** What do Cartier's language and actions show about his opinion of native peoples and their ways? (He has a poor opinion of them and wants to impose his own cultural practices.) **DOK 3**

Map Skills

Project a large version of the map on page 87. Use these questions to guide students as they respond to the prompts about the information on the map. Ask:

- On what river did Champlain establish the city of Quebec? (the St. Lawrence)

- Which river did Nicolet use to search for the Northwest Passage? (the Ottawa River)

- What lake does the map show is the source of the St. Lawrence River? (Lake Ontario)

☑ Stop and Check

Think Guide students to consider why French rulers did not make a greater effort to expand the size of the colonies in New France. (The French became interested in the fur trade, which did not require large settlements.)

The Founding of New France

After Giovanni da Verrazzano failed to find the Northwest Passage for France, the king of France sent Jacques Cartier in 1534 to continue the search. Cartier explored what is now Canada, sailing up the St. Lawrence River. The French adapted the name *Canada* from the Huron group of native peoples. In the Huron language, *kanata* means "village."

This map shows France's first fort in Quebec, Canada.

PRIMARY SOURCE

In Their Words... Jacques Cartier

July 24 – We had a cross made thirty feet high, which was put together in the presence of a number of savages on the point at the entrance to this harbor, [and on it] was written LONG LIVE THE KING OF FRANCE. When we had returned to our ships, the chief, dressed in an old black bearskin, arrived in a canoe with three of his sons and his brother ... And pointing to the cross he made us a long harangue, making the sign of the cross with two of his fingers, and then he pointed to the land all around about, as if he wished to say that all this region belonged to him, and that we ought not to have set up the cross without his permission.

—from the journal of Jacques Cartier, 1534

TEXT: Jacques Cartier. 1534. Quoted in H.P. Biggar, trans., A Collection of Documents Relating to Jacques Cartier and the Sieur de Roberval (Public Archives of Canada, 1924), 26.; PHOTO: (b) Library of Congress Geography and Map Division [G3454 Q452 1670. All Vault]; (b)The Miriam and Ira D. Wallach Division of Art, Prints and Photographs; Point Collection, Emmet Collection of Manuscripts Etc. Relating to American History,The New York Public Library

The French Explore New France, 1617–1673

Map Skills The map shows the routes of French explorers. Which river did Nicollet use to search for the Northwest Passage?

The next important French explorer in Canada was Samuel de Champlain. King Henry VI of France appointed him governor of French settlements in North America, called New France. Champlain made four voyages to North America. On one voyage, he established a colony in what is now Quebec City. Champlain was on friendly terms with native peoples. This allowed the French to expand their fur trade.

On another voyage, Champlain brought along a young explorer named Étienne Brûlé. In 1615, he sent Brûlé to continue the search for a passage to Asia. Brûlé was unable to find it, but he did explore what are now Lake Ontario, Lake Erie, and Lake Superior. In 1634, a French explorer named Jean Nicollet explored what is now Lake Michigan.

Although some French people moved to Canada, growth was slow. French rulers were disappointed that Cartier could find neither gold nor a Northwest Passage. The focus of New France's economy continued to be the fur trade, and only a few large settlements thrived.

✓ Stop and Check

Think In your opinion, why did French rulers not make a greater effort to expand the size of the colonies in New France?

Research Companion, pp. 86–87

(EL) ENGLISH LEARNERS SCAFFOLD

ELD.PI.5.6 Reading closely literary and informational texts and viewing multimedia to determine how meaning is conveyed explicitly and implicitly through language

Emerging

Discuss Maps Have students complete these sentence frames about the French explorers shown on the map:
The explorer ___ was looking for ___. Instead, he found ___.

Expanding

Understand Maps Use the map to clarify that Lake Ontario, Lake Erie, and Lake Superior, all mentioned in the text, are three of the five Great Lakes. Point out that the St. Lawrence River has its source in Lake Ontario.

Bridging

Understand Maps Explain that Champlain also searched for a Northwest Passage and on one trip found the lake that bears his name. Have students pinpoint Lake Champlain on a map and explain its location.

See the **Language Learner Teaching Guide** for more language support strategies.

Monitor and Differentiate

REACHING ALL LEARNERS

Special Needs

Have students continue the charts of explorers they began earlier in the lesson, adding any details the text provides about each French explorer's goals and achievements.

Beyond Level

Have students research and report on early French exploration and settlement of the Great Lakes area of what is now the United States, such as Sault Saint Marie, Michigan, and Green Bay, Wisconsin. What role did the fur trade and the lakes themselves play in their history?

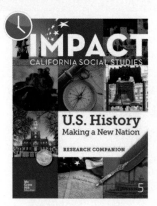

Research Companion
pp. 88–89

 STANDARDS

Explain the aims, obstacles, and accomplishments of the explorers, sponsors, and leaders of key European expeditions and the reasons Europeans chose to explore and colonize the world. **HSS.5.2.2**

Locate on maps of North and South America land claimed by Spain, France, England, Portugal, the Netherlands, Sweden, and Russia. **HSS.5.2.4**

Describe the competition among the English, French, Spanish, Dutch, and Indian nations for control of North America. **HSS.5.3.1**

Describe the cooperation that existed between the colonists and Indians during the 1600s and 1700s (e.g., in agriculture, the fur trade, military alliances, treaties, cultural interchanges). **HSS.5.3.2**

Go Digital!

Investigate the lesson content with online whole-class presentation tools.

Background Information

England vs. Spain Though England and Spain were not yet at war, Queen Elizabeth I turned a blind eye to the exploits of English adventurers, like Francis Drake and Walter Raleigh, who were robbing Spain's ships returning from its colonies laden with gold. The queen signed letters of marque granting these "privateers" the right to engage in what would otherwise be considered piracy. Yet she could still disavow their actions, since they were technically private citizens. Raleigh's interest in establishing Roanoke was primarily as a way to launch attacks on Spanish ships.

Analyze the Source

Inspect Have students read The Lost English Colony on pages 88–89.

Find Evidence Use the questions below to check comprehension. Remind students to support their answers with text evidence.

Identify Where was the English colony of Roanoke? (on an island off what is now North Carolina) **DOK 1**

Explain What were Walter Raleigh's main reasons for wanting an English colony in North America? (to explore for treasure and to attack ships of Spain) **DOK 2**

Summarize How did the first settlers of Roanoke treat the native people? (The settlers traded with the natives at first but later stole from them.) **DOK 2**

Explain What happened to the second group of settlers on Roanoke? (no one knows) **DOK 2**

Make Connections

Evaluate Based on the experiences of the settlers of Roanoke, what suggestions would you make for future settlements? (Suggestions might include having settlers who know how to farm and live off the land and who treat the natives respectfully.) **DOK 4**

Map Skills

Project a large version of the map on page 89. Guide students to respond to the prompts.

- Which landforms were near English settlements? (the Atlantic Ocean; the James River)

- Why do you think settlements were located near bodies of water? (The English came by ship and used water transportation for travel and trade; they needed to be near a place where they could be resupplied.)

COLLABORATE
☑ Stop and Check

Think Guide students to consider why the colony at Roanoke failed. (Responses will vary, but students should use text evidence to support their reasoning.)

The Lost English Colony

After the voyages of John Cabot and Henry Hudson, England did little to explore North America until the 1580s. Then, an English noble named Sir Walter Raleigh asked Queen Elizabeth I for permission to establish a colony in North America. Raleigh wanted to create settlements that would serve as bases to explore for treasure and to attack the ships of Spain, an enemy of England.

The English queen granted Raleigh a **charter**, a document that allowed him to found a colony. In 1585, Raleigh sent a group of men to North America to start the colony. They chose an island called Roanoke in what is now North Carolina. The colonists were not skilled at farming, and so they tried to get goods by trading with native peoples. The native peoples lost interest in trading, and the colonists decided they had to steal food from them. This led to fighting. After a difficult winter, the colonists returned to England in 1586.

Sir Walter Raleigh

John White arrives in Roanoke to find the colony abandoned.

88   Lesson 3 · How Did European Exploration Affect the Americas?

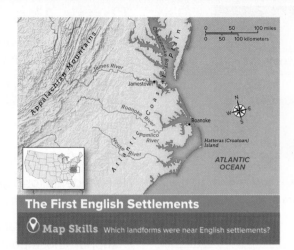

The First English Settlements

Map Skills Which landforms were near English settlements?

In 1587, another group of colonists led by John White returned to Roanoke. This time the group included women and children. The colony again had difficulty finding enough food. White sailed back to England to get supplies. But while he was there, war broke out between England and Spain. England needed all of its ships for the war. By the time White returned to the colony three years later, it had been abandoned. The only clue was the word *Croatoan* carved on a tree. The Croatoan were a native people in the area. What happened to the English settlers has never been determined.

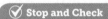
✓ **Stop and Check**

Talk In your opinion, why did the Roanoke Colony fail?

What Do You Think? What do you think happened to the people in the "lost colony"?

Lesson 3   89

Research Companion, pp. 88–89

ENGLISH LEARNERS SCAFFOLD

ELD.PI.5.3 Offering and supporting opinions and negotiating with others in communicative exchanges

Emerging

Summarize Text Have students work in small groups to tell the story of the lost colony of Roanoke. Remind them to use signal words that show the order of events in time, such as *first, next, then,* and *later.*

Expanding

Compare and Contrast Text Details Have students compare and contrast the first and second groups of settlers on Roanoke. Students might use a Venn diagram to gather the details from the text that show similarities and differences between the two groups.

Bridging

Discuss Text Have students hold small-group discussions about what they think may have happened to the second group of settlers at Roanoke. Encourage students to do online research to supplement information in the text that they use to support their opinions.

See the **Language Learner Teaching Guide** for more language support strategies.

Monitor and Differentiate

REACHING ALL LEARNERS

On Level

Have students do simple online research to find out some of Walter Raleigh's other achievements besides founding Roanoke and then share their findings with classmates. Note that his name is sometimes spelled *Ralegh.*

Beyond Level

Have students write brief stories about the lost colony of Roanoke, including their speculations about what happened to the second group of settlers. Encourage students to share their stories aloud or post them to the class website.

Report Your Findings

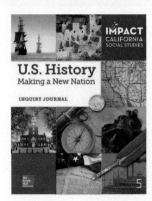

Inquiry Journal
pp. 74–75

HSS STANDARDS

Explain the aims, obstacles, and accomplishments of the explorers, sponsors, and leaders of key European expeditions and the reasons Europeans chose to explore and colonize the world. **HSS.5.2.2**

Describe the competition among the English, French, Spanish, Dutch, and Indian nations for control of North America. **HSS.5.3.1**

Describe the cooperation that existed between the colonists and Indians during the 1600s and 1700s (e.g., in agriculture, the fur trade, military alliances, treaties, cultural interchanges). **HSS.5.3.2**

CCSS Write narratives to develop real or imagined experiences or events using effective technique, descriptive details, and clear event sequences. **CCSS.ELA.W.5.3**

Go Digital!

- Students can go online to report their findings. Assess their responses online.

- Students can access the online graphic organizer to capture ideas from their investigation.

Think About It

Students should review their research and consider in what ways each European nation's goals of exploration were met.

- Remind students to review the details they gathered on their map. Direct them to pages 80–89 of their Research Companion if they need more information.

Talk About It

Help students form groups. Then have students discuss the native groups Dutch, French, and English settlers most likely encountered and how they interacted with those groups.

- Tell students to take turns discussing their main points and the facts and reasons that support those points.

- Ask students to discuss whether they agree or disagree with other group members' assessments and to explain why.

- Remind students to follow the rules of appropriate classroom conversation.

Write About It

Narrative Have students read the prompt. Discuss how the point of view or impressions of events would be different for a European explorer than a native person. Remind students to include the following elements in their response.

- a series of events in chronological order, the order of time

- clear information about the setting, or time and place in which the events occur

- clear information about the real or imaginary people involved in the events

Use the rubric on page T194 to evaluate students' work.

Connect to the Essential Question

Read the prompt aloud to students. Ask them the following guiding questions:

- What happened when the European settlers crossed paths with native peoples of the Americas? (Sometimes there was peace, but often there were clashes.)

- How do you imagine native peoples' lives would have been different if the Dutch, French, and English had not arrived? (Responses will vary but should be based on text evidence.)

- Would the natives have been better off without the Europeans? Why or why not? (Responses will vary.)

Remind students to use the space provided in their journal to jot down notes.

Report / Your Findings

Think About It

Review your research. Based on what you have read, what were the exploration goals in the Americas of the Netherlands, France, and England?

Talk About It COLLABORATE

Compare the maps of European settlements in this lesson with the map on page 41 in your Research Companion. Which native groups might the Europeans have encountered? How did the Dutch, French, and English interact with native peoples?

Write About It

Narrative

Write a narrative from the point of view of either a European explorer mentioned in this lesson or a native person describing a first encounter with a European. Consider how the goals of the explorer or the experiences of the native person might have affected this encounter.

Students should write in a narrative form from the point of view of either a non-Spanish European explorer or a native person. The narrative should describe an encounter with someone from the other side.

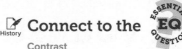 History **Connect to the EQ**

Contrast

Looking back over the chapter, discuss how the relationships between American Indians and the various European explorers differed.

Students who discuss American Indians may emphasize how native people tried to live in balance with nature and adapt to their environments. Students discussing Europeans may emphasize how explorers were seeking riches.

EQ Inquiry Project Notes

Inquiry Journal, pp. 74–75

EL ENGLISH LEARNERS SCAFFOLD

ELD.PI.5.1 Exchanging information and ideas with others through oral collaborative discussions on a range of social and academic topics

Emerging	Expanding	Bridging
Explore Point of View Have students discuss how a narrative written by an explorer would be most likely differ from one written by a native of the Americas. Offer these sentence frames to help them express their ideas: **The explorer would probably ___. A native person would probably ___.**	**Outline Plot** Tell students to number and list the events in their narrative before they actually write it. Remind them to use chronological order, the order of time.	**Develop Setting** Note that the setting of a narrative is the time and place in which it occurs. Tell students to develop the settings of their narratives with specific details based on the text. Ask them to work on their setting descriptions to make them as realistic, or real-seeming, as possible.

See the **Language Learner Teaching Guide** for more language support strategies.

Monitor and Differentiate

REACHING ALL LEARNERS

Approaching Level

Remind students to make the sequence of events in their narratives clear by using words that signal time, such as _first, next, the following year,_ and _three years later._

Beyond Level

As they explore the Essential Question, have students discuss similarities and differences in the way the Dutch, French, and English seem to have treated native peoples in the settlements described in the text. Ask them to consider how participating in the fur trade may have encouraged better treatment of the American Indians, and why.

Know what your students know!

Lesson Task
Report Your Findings

Use this rubric to evaluate students' response.

Talk About It After comparing the maps of European settlements in the lesson with the maps of American Indian groups in Chapter 1, Lesson 5, students discuss which native groups the Europeans might have encountered and how the Dutch, French, and English interacted with native peoples.

Write a Narrative Students write from the point of view of either a European explorer mentioned in the lesson or a native person having his or her first encounter with a European.

Performance Task Evaluation Rubric

	4	3	2	1
Historical Understanding	Displays strong understanding of the goals and achievements of explorers and of their interaction with native peoples	Displays adequate understanding of the goals and achievements of explorers and of their interaction with native peoples	Displays uneven understanding of the goals and achievements of explorers and of their interaction with native peoples	Displays no understanding of the goals and achievements of explorers and of their interaction with native peoples
Compare and Contrast	Creatively uses details from all maps to support discussion Speaks clearly and at an understandable pace	Adequately uses details from all maps to support discussion Speaks clearly during most of the discussion	Sometimes omits details from maps during discussion Speaks unclearly at times	Does not use details from maps during discussion Speaks unclearly throughout the discussion
Write a Narrative	Provides a clear explanation of the actions and reactions of one or more native people or explorers	Provides an adequate explanation of the actions and reactions of one or more native people or explorers	Provides a somewhat clear or unclear explanation of the actions and reactions of one or more native people or explorers	Provides no explanation or shows no understanding of the actions and reactions of one or more native people or explorers
Support with Details	Supports ideas with sufficient accurate details	Supports ideas with fairly sufficient and fairly accurate details	Supports ideas with too many inaccurate details	Supplies far too few details or details with many inaccuracies

Lesson Assessment

***Go** Digital!*

- Have students complete the Chapter 2 Lesson 3 Assessment online to monitor their understanding of the lesson content.

California Smarter Balanced Assessment Connections!

Standards Covered	Lesson Task	Lesson Assessment	Alignment with California Smarter Balanced Assessment
History Social Science Content 5.2; 5.3	✔	✔	Claim 1 Targets 8, 9, 10
History Social Science Analysis Skills Chronological and Spatial Thinking 5.4; 5.5	✔	✔	Claim 1 Targets 11, 12
Writing W.5.3	✔	✔	Claim 2 Targets 2, 1
Research and Inquiry W.5.9	✔	✔	Claim 4 Targets 2, 3, 4
Reading RI.5.1	✔	✔	Claim 1 Target 8, 9, 11
Speaking and Listening SL.5.1	✔		Claim 3 Target 3

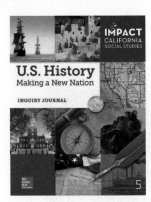

U.S. History
Making a New Nation

INQUIRY JOURNAL

Inquiry Journal
pp. 76–77

 STANDARDS

Students trace the routes of early explorers and describe the early explorations of the Americas. **HSS.5.2**

 Explain the relationships or interactions between two or more individuals, events, ideas, or concepts in a historical, scientific, or technical text based on specific information in the text. **CCSS.ELA.RI.5.3**

Write opinion pieces on topics or texts, supporting a point of view with reasons and information. **CCSS.ELA.W.5.1**

Engage effectively in a range of collaborative discussion (one-on-one, in groups, and teacher-led) with diverse partners on *grade 5 topics and texts*, building on others' ideas and expressing their own clearly. **CCSS.ELA.SL.5.1**

Go Digital!

Look online for the EQ Inquiry Project rubric.

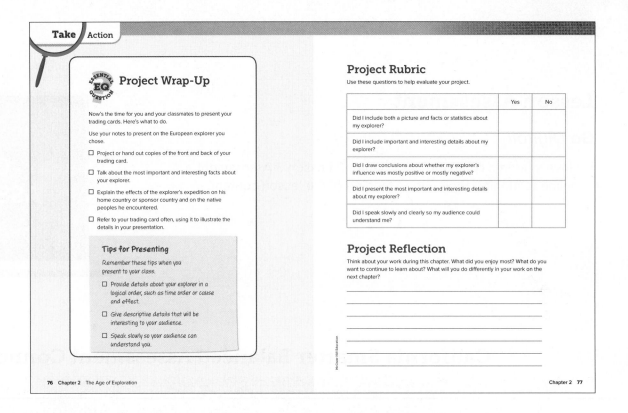

Take Action

Project Wrap-Up

Now's the time for you and your classmates to present your trading cards. Here's what to do.

Use your notes to present on the European explorer you chose.

☐ Project or hand out copies of the front and back of your trading card.

☐ Talk about the most important and interesting facts about your explorer.

☐ Explain the effects of the explorer's expedition on his home country or sponsor country and on the native peoples he encountered.

☐ Refer to your trading card often, using it to illustrate the details in your presentation.

Tips for Presenting

Remember these tips when you present to your class.

☐ Provide details about your explorer in a logical order, such as time order or cause and effect.

☐ Give descriptive details that will be interesting to your audience.

☐ Speak slowly so your audience can understand you.

Project Rubric

Use these questions to help evaluate your project.

	Yes	No
Did I include both a picture and facts or statistics about my explorer?		
Did I include important and interesting details about my explorer?		
Did I draw conclusions about whether my explorer's influence was mostly positive or mostly negative?		
Did I present the most important and interesting details about my explorer?		
Did I speak slowly and clearly so my audience could understand me?		

Project Reflection

Think about your work during this chapter. What did you enjoy most? What do you want to continue to learn about? What will you do differently in your work on the next chapter?

_____

_____

_____

_____

_____

76 Chapter 2 The Age of Exploration

Chapter 2 77

 Inquiry Project Wrap-Up

Have students share their inquiry projects by presenting their trading cards.

- Before students present their trading cards, discuss the wrap-up steps with them, making sure they know what's expected in their presentations.

- Allow time after each presentation for a Q-and-A session.

Tips for Presenting

Discuss the tips for presenting with students and the importance of communicating effectively with their audience. Remind students that it's also important to be a good listener.

Project Rubric

Discuss each question in the Project Rubric with students. If students have worked as part of a group to develop their projects, you might want to have them work as a group to address each question in the rubric.

Project Reflection

Student reflections can focus on the work they did as part of the group or their individual performance designing and producing a trading card. Give groups time to discuss each phase of their projects and reflect on their work.

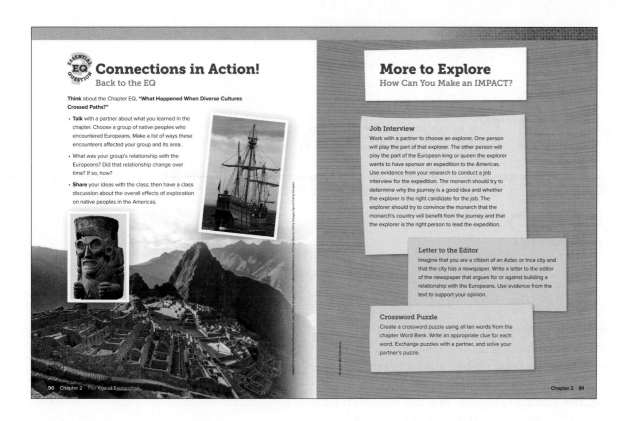

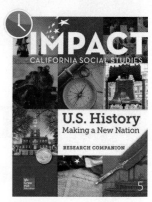
 Connections in Action

To help focus students' conversations, you may want to discuss the EQ with the entire class before students discuss their ideas with a partner. Remind students to think about evidence they can provide that will support their opinions. After students present, allow time for others to ask questions.

More to Explore

Job Interview In pairs, one student will play the role of an explorer while the other plays the role of a sponsoring monarch. Partners will act out a job interview in which the explorer asks the monarch to fund and support an expedition to the New World. Encourage students to be creative while grounding their quesitons and responses in text evidence.

Letter to the Editor Students write letters to the editor of an Aztec or Inca city newspaper. They argue for or against building a relationship with the Europeans. Encourage students to end with a call to action.

Crossword Puzzle Have students create crossword puzzles that use all of the terms in the chapter Word Bank. Guide them to switch papers with a partner then complete each other's puzzles.

ESSENTIAL EQ QUESTION

How Did European Settlements Impact North America?

In This Chapter ...

Students will investigate the relationships between early European settlers and the American Indians with whom they came in contact. They will also analyze how competition for land and resources in North America led to conflicts and alliances among Europeans and American Indian groups. Students will learn more about what life was like in early settlements in New England, the Middle Colonies, and the Southern Colonies, including how religion and economics shaped culture and customs.

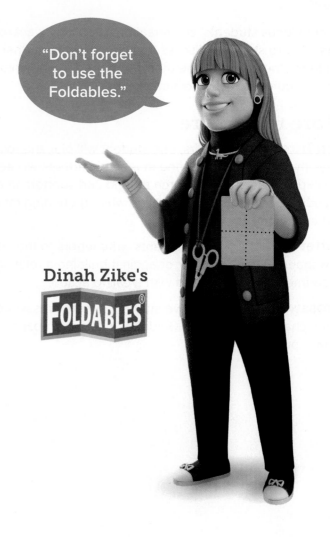

"Don't forget to use the Foldables."

Dinah Zike's

FOLDABLES®

HSS   **CHAPTER STANDARDS**

✔ Students describe the cooperation and conflict that existed among the American Indians and between the Indian nations and the new settlers. **HSS.5.3**

✔ Students understand the political, religious, social, and economic institutions that evolved in the colonial era. **HSS.5.4**

1 ENGAGE

Inquiry Journal
pp. 78–81

 Inquiry Project

Tell Both Sides of the Story

- **Explore Words**

- *Go Digital!*
  - IMPACT Chapter Video: A
    Changing Continent

2 INVESTIGATE

Research Companion
pp. 92–99

- **Step Into Time and Place**

- **Connect Through Literature**
  The Whistle
  by Benjamin Franklin

- **People You Should Know**

**Weekly Explorer
Magazine** pp. 30-43

3 REPORT

Inquiry Journal
pp. 122–123

 Inquiry Project

Tell Both Sides of the Story

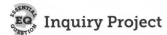 **Short on Time?** Look for the clock to teach core content in less time.

CULTIVATE MEANING AND SUPPORT LANGUAGE

**Language Learner
Teaching Guide,**
pp. 54–55

Content Objectives

- Demonstrate an understanding of how and why the different groups attempted to gain power over one another in North America.
- Explore what life was like for settlers and American Indians.

Language Objectives

- Demonstrate an understanding of gerunds as adjectives
- Use summarization techniques to report.

CONNECT TO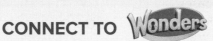

Unit 2 Week 1
Reaching a Compromise

Read Aloud
"The Mayflower Compact"

Reading/Writing Workshop
"Creating a Nation"

Literature Anthology/Paired Selection
Who Wrote the Constitution?
"Parchment and Ink"

Leveled Readers
The Bill of Rights and "Having Your Say"

CONNECT TO SCIENCE

Explore how climate, faming, and agriculture affected the success and failure of the early European settlements in North America.

CONNECT TO MATH

Use measurement to understand how to calculate distance using a map's scale.

ASSESSMENT

Monitor Progress to
Know What Your Students Know

Choose the assessment options that work best for you and your students.

BEFORE
PRE-TEST

Measure students' content knowledge before you begin the chapter with the following questions.

 Quick Check

✔ Would it be impossible for American Indians and European settlers to get along?

✔ What would be one of the biggest challenges in starting a settlement from nothing?

✔ How might freedom of religion be an important motivation for settling in North America?

1. When all students have responded, ask them to rate how confident they are in their answers on a scale from 1 – not very confident to 5 – very confident.

2. Collect students' responses and review them for misconceptions, factual errors, and to inform instruction. You may wish to return to these questions as students investigate chapter 3.

3. **Don't Forget!** Revisit students' quick check responses with them. If students change their response, ask them to support the change with text evidence. You may wish to have students respond to a different prompt to measure students' content knowledge, such as *How did the French and English compete for land in North America?*

EVERY LESSON
ONGOING ASSESSMENT

Use the lesson tools to monitor the IMPACT of your instruction.

 Stop and Check

Use the quick question prompts to monitor student comprehension of the content. The **Stop and Check** questions prompt students to make connections to their world today, engage in discussions to deepen their understanding of the content, and to look at different perspectives.

Report Your Findings

The lesson task, **Report Your Findings**, can be used to measure student understanding of the lesson content and ability to effectively express their understanding. See the Lesson Assessment pp. T230, T254, T278, T300, and T324 for task-specific evaluation rubrics.

(*Go Digital!*) **Lesson Assessment**

Use the **Lesson Assessment** to monitor student understanding of the lesson content. Have students complete the assessment online. See pp. T231, T255, T279, T301, and T325 for California Smarter Balanced Assessments Connections.

EVERY CHAPTER POST TEST

Evaluate student understanding of core chapter content with one or more of the following assessment options.

Connections in Action

Use the **Connections in Action** to evaluate student understanding of core chapter content through discussion.

Inquiry Project

Use the **EQ Inquiry Project** to measure student understanding of the chapter content and ability to effectively express their understanding. See the EQ Inquiry Project Wrap Up below for a task-specific evaluation rubric.

	4	3	2	1
Historical Understanding	Strong understanding of the relationship between the American Indians and the first European settlers in North America	Adequate understanding of the relationship between the American Indians and the first European settlers in North America	Uneven understanding of the relationship between the American Indians and the first European settlers in North America	No understanding of the relationship between the American Indians and the first European settlers in North America
Tells a Story	Cleverly uses descriptive details to tell an interesting story that is based on facts	Adequately uses details to tell a story that is based on facts	Somewhat clear or descriptive details	No details given or student does not show understanding of the task
Support with Details	Includes relevant details from text in story	Includes some details from text in story	Includes few details from text in story	Includes no details from text in story
Read Your Story	Speaks clearly and at an understandable pace Reads in character and uses appropriate emphasis and inflection	Speaks clearly during most of the reading Reads clearly with some emotion	At times speaker is unclear Reads without proper emphasis or emotion	Does not use complete sentences Does not read or remain in character during reading

(Go Digital!) Chapter Benchmark Assessments

Use the chapter tests to monitor student understanding of the chapter History-Social Science standards and content. Have students complete the assessment online.

ONLINE ASSESSMENT

Weekly Explorer Magazine

The Weekly Explorer Magazine is designed to provide students with more information to use as they dig deeper into the **first European settlements in North America**. The articles in a variety of formats explore the Essential Question and support the Inquiry Project.

pp. 30–43

Engage

Build background for students and share any information needed to provide a context for the chapter topic. Have students read the Essential Question and the Table of Contents.

Analyze the Visual Discuss the opening visual (photograph, photo essay, artwork) on the second page of the Magazine chapter. Help students connect the visual to the chapter topic and the Essential Question.

Analyze the Sources

Students will read and analyze the articles, graphic novel, poems, songs, literature excerpts, primary sources, and infographics.

Read and Analyze Before reading, provide any additional information you think students will need about the topics. Then guide students through the three-step process to read and analyze the articles.

1 Inspect Have students skim the article or articles on a page or multiple pages. Ask questions to help students recall and retell key ideas.

- What is this article mostly about?
- Who is _____?

2 Find Evidence Have students reread the articles and look for details they might have missed. Ask additional questions to help them read more closely.

- What details do you notice in the photographs?
- Why was _____ important?

3 Make Connections Have students work in pairs or small groups to discuss prompts that help them connect the article(s) to other texts, their own lives, current ideas and issues, and other topics.

- How is _____ similar to what we do today?
- How do you think _____ felt about what happened?
- What do you think about _____?

Short on Time?

Use the Weekly Explorer Magazine during your reading block.

Go Digital!

Look online for the Weekly Explorer Magazine Teaching Guide.

WordBlast

Remind students to look for the Word Blasts as they read the Explorer Magazine.

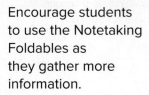

FOLDABLES®

Encourage students to use the Notetaking Foldables as they gather more information.

Bibliography

The following suggested resources may help students' investigation of the chapter content.

EXPLORE PEOPLE, PLACES, AND EVENTS

Perspectives
▶ **1607: A New Look at Jamestown**
by Karen Lange; National Geographic, 2007.

▶ **Adventurous Life of Myles Standish and the Amazing-But-True Survival Story of Plymouth Colony**
by Cheryl Harness; National Geographic, 2006.

Perspectives
▶ **A Break with Charity: A Story About the Salem Witch Trials**
by Ann Rinaldi; HMH Books for Young Readers; 2003.

▶ **Fort Mose: And the Story of the Man Who Built the First Free Settlement in Colonial America**
by Glennette Tilley Turner; Abrams Books for Young Readers, 2010.

Perspectives
▶ **"Indian"**
by Rosemary and Stephen Vincent Benét (poem)
from **A Book of Americans;** Henry Holt (Macmillan), 1933.

▶ **John Smith Escapes Again!**
by Rosalyn Schanzer; National Geographic, 2006.

▶ **The Mayflower and the Pilgrims' New World**
by Nathaniel Philbrick; G. P. Putnam's Sons, 2008.

▶ **Pocahontas: Princess of the New World**
by Kathleen Krull; Walker Publishing Company, 2007.

▶ **Raleigh's Page**
by Alan Armstrong; Random House, 2007.

Perspectives
▶ **Roanoke: The Lost Colony—An Unsolved Mystery from History**
by Heidi E. Y. Semple; Simon & Schuster Books for Young Readers, 2003.

Perspectives
▶ **You Wouldn't Want to Sail on the Mayflower!: A Trip that Took Entirely Too Long**
by Peter Cook; Franklin Watts, 2013.

EXPLORE MUSIC

Did you know? Just as the explorers of the fifteenth century brought their cultures with them, so did the European settlers carry their own customs with them to the New World. Of course, this included music. Colonists brought music church music, popular songs, music for the theater, and music for dancing. **The Beggar's Opera** premiered in London in 1728 and had its first performance in the colonies 1750.

Did you know? Dance music from the British Isles: jigs, reels, and hornpipes were popular throughout the colonies. Also, popular songs, like the well-known **Barbara Allen** crossed the Atlantic with the new Americans.

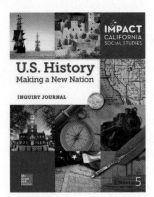

Inquiry Journal
pp. 78–81

1 ENGAGE

 STANDARDS

Students describe the cooperation and conflict that existed among the American Indians and between the Indian nations and the new settlers. **HSS.5.3**

CCSS Write narratives to develop real or imagined experiences or events using effective technique, descriptive details, and clear event sequences. **CCSS.ELA.W.5.3**

Draw evidence from literary or informational texts to support analysis, reflection, and research. **CCSS.ELA.W.5.9**

Go Digital!

Explore Words: Interactive vocabulary activities support students as they explore the chapter words.

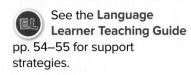 See the **Language Learner Teaching Guide** pp. 54–55 for support strategies.

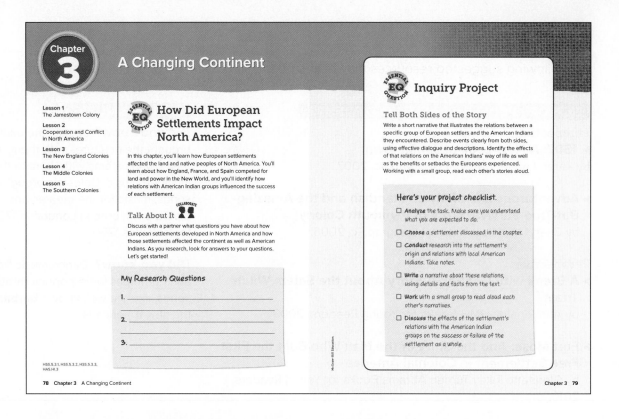

How Did European Settlements Impact North America?

Have students read the Chapter Essential Question on p. 78.

Talk About It

- Prompt students to write what they would like to know about European settlements in North America after reading the chapter.

- After jotting down their questions, have students discuss their questions with partners.

Inquiry Project

Tell Both Sides of the Story

- Have students read aloud the EQ Inquiry Project.

- Tell students that they will use information gathered from the chapter and from independent research to complete the project.

- Make certain students understand the task by reviewing each step of the project.

Explore Words

Complete this chapter's Word Rater. Write notes as you learn more about each word.

The worksheet contains a Word Rater with the following vocabulary words, each with "My Notes" and checkboxes for "Know It!", "Heard It!", and "Don't Know It!":

- assembly
- cash crop
- commerce
- covenant
- demand
- dissension
- encomiendas
- environment
- missionary
- proprietor

80 Chapter 3 A Changing Continent

Chapter 3 81

Explore Words

- **Academic/Domain-Specific Vocabulary** Read the words aloud to students. Explain to students that these are words they will learn more about in the chapter.

- **Word Rater** Have students place a checkmark in one of the three boxes below each word, indicating that they "Know It," "Heard It," or "Don't Know It."

  ✓ **Know It** Tell students that if they know the word, they should write its meaning on the lines provided.

  ✓ **Heard It** Tell students that if they have heard, or are familiar with the word, they should write what they know about it on the lines provided. Remind them to take notes about the word as they encounter it.

  ✓ **Don't Know It** If they do not know the word's meaning, tell them to write down its meaning when they encounter the word in the chapter.

🔍 Explore Words Routine

Remind students that when they come to an unfamiliar word or phrase in their research, they should follow these steps to determine its meaning.

1. Look around the word or phrase for clues to unlock its meaning.

2. Look inside the word or phrase for word part clues.

3. Look up the word in other resources.

"Don't forget to use the Foldables."

Dinah Zike's
FOLDABLES®

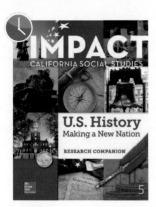

Research Companion
pp. 92–97

(HSS) **STANDARDS**

Students describe the cooperation and conflict that existed among the American Indians and between the Indian nations and the new settlers. **HSS.5.3**

Students understand the political, religious, social, and economic institutions that evolved in the colonial era. **HSS.5.4**

(CCSS) Explain the relationships or interactions between two or more individuals, events, ideas, or concepts in a historical, scientific, or technical text based on specific information in the text. **CCSS.ELA.RI.5.3**

Go Digital!

• Investigate the changing continent with online whole-class presentation tools.

• Analyze the online literature selection so students can find evidence and make connections.

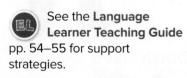 See the **Language Learner Teaching Guide** pp. 54–55 for support strategies.

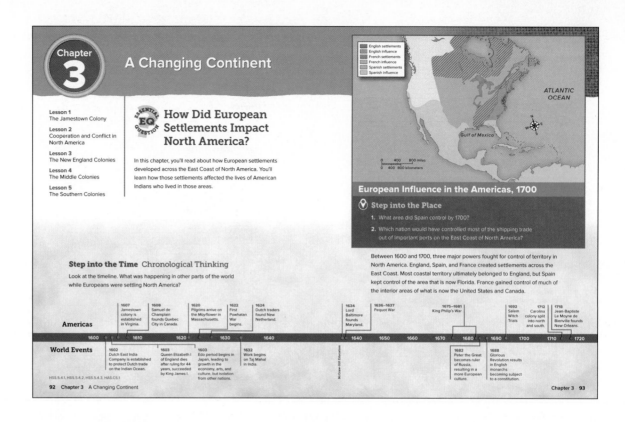

Step Into Time

• Have students read over the events on the timeline, first examining the events from the Americas and then the events from around the world.

• What important events happened in 1603 across the world from each other? (Queen Elizabeth I dies in England while the Edo period in Japan is beginning.)

• How many years did it take for the Dutch to settle North America after building their trading empire with the Dutch East India Company? (about 22 years)

Step Into Place

In partners or in small groups, have students examine the map on p. 93 and answer the questions beneath it.

1. What area did Spain control by 1700? (The area that is now Florida and part of Georgia and Alabama.)

2. Which nation would have controlled most of the shipping trade out of important ports such as New York, Boston, and Norfolk? (England)

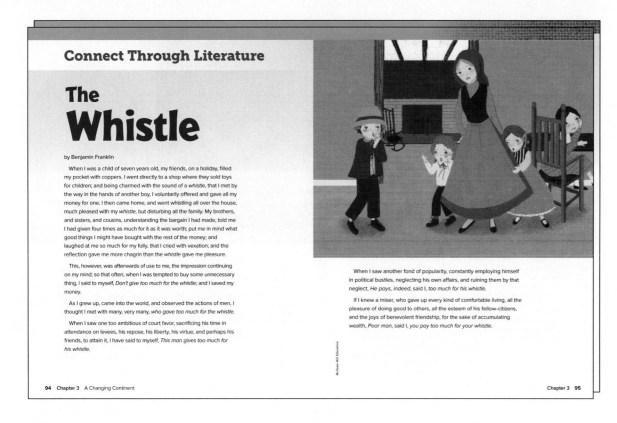

Connect Through Literature

The Whistle

by Benjamin Franklin

When I was a child of seven years old, my friends, on a holiday, filled my pocket with coppers. I went directly to a shop where they sold toys for children; and being charmed with the sound of a *whistle*, that I met by the way in the hands of another boy, I voluntarily offered and gave all my money for one. I then came home, and went whistling all over the house, much pleased with my *whistle*, but disturbing all the family. My brothers, and sisters, and cousins, understanding the bargain I had made, told me I had given four times as much for it as it was worth; put me in mind what good things I might have bought with the rest of the money; and laughed at me so much for my folly, that I cried with vexation; and the reflection gave me more chagrin than the *whistle* gave me pleasure.

This, however, was afterwards of use to me, the impression continuing on my mind; so that often, when I was tempted to buy some unnecessary thing, I said to myself, *Don't give too much for the whistle;* and I saved my money.

As I grew up, came into the world, and observed the actions of men, I thought I met with many, very many, *who gave too much for the whistle.*

When I saw one too ambitious of court favor, sacrificing his time in attendance on levees, his repose, his liberty, his virtue, and perhaps his friends, to attain it, I have said to myself, *This man gives too much for his whistle.*

When I saw another fond of popularity, constantly employing himself in political bustles, neglecting his own affairs, and ruining them by that neglect, *He pays, indeed,* said I, *too much for his whistle.*

If I knew a miser, who gave up every kind of comfortable living, all the pleasure of doing good to others, all the esteem of his fellow-citizens, and the joys of benevolent friendship, for the sake of accumulating wealth, *Poor man,* said I, *you pay too much for your whistle.*

GENRE Memoir *A memoir is an essay based on the personal recollection of the author.*

Analyze the Source

Inspect Have students read the selection on pp. 94–97 together to determine the general meaning of the text.

1. Based on the text, what does the word *levee* mean? (Students should be able to infer that this is a social occasion for important people.)

Find Evidence Have students reread the selection and ask:

2. What does Ben Franklin mean when says someone pays too much for a whistle? (giving more time, money, value, or effort for something than it should deserves)

Make Connections

3. What are some situations today that you think cause people to "give too much for their whistle? (Responses will vary.)

Perspectives Can you think of a time when you "gave too much for your whistle"? Describe it. (Responses will vary.)

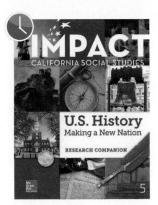

Research Companion
pp. 98–99

 STANDARDS

Students describe the cooperation and conflict that existed among the American Indians and between the Indian nations and the new settlers. **HSS.5.3**

Students understand the political, religious, social, and economic institutions that evolved in the colonial era. **HSS.5.4**

CCSS Explain the relationships or interactions between two or more individuals, events, ideas, or concepts in a historical, scientific, or technical text based on specific information in the text. **CCSS.ELA.RI.5.3**

Go Digital!

Investigate chapter content with the online teaching plan.

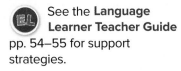 See the **Language Learner Teacher Guide** pp. 54–55 for support strategies.

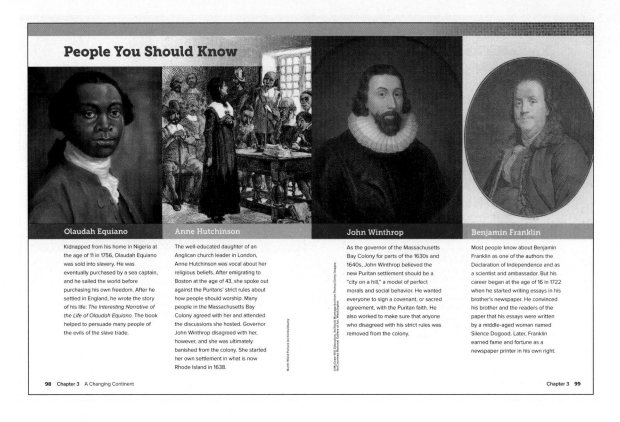

People You Should Know

Olaudah Equiano
Kidnapped from his home in Nigeria at the age of 11 in 1756, Olaudah Equiano was sold into slavery. He was eventually purchased by a sea captain, and he sailed the world before purchasing his own freedom. After he settled in England, he wrote the story of his life: *The Interesting Narrative of the Life of Olaudah Equiano*. The book helped to persuade many people of the evils of the slave trade.

Anne Hutchinson
The well-educated daughter of an Anglican church leader in London, Anne Hutchinson was vocal about her religious beliefs. After emigrating to Boston at the age of 43, she spoke out against the Puritans' strict rules about how people should worship. Many people in the Massachusetts Bay Colony agreed with her and attended the discussions she hosted. Governor John Winthrop disagreed with her, however, and she was ultimately banished from the colony. She started her own settlement in what is now Rhode Island in 1638.

John Winthrop
As the governor of the Massachusetts Bay Colony for parts of the 1630s and 1640s, John Winthrop believed the new Puritan settlement should be a "city on a hill," a model of perfect morals and social behavior. He wanted everyone to sign a covenant, or sacred agreement, with the Puritan faith. He also worked to make sure that anyone who disagreed with his strict rules was removed from the colony.

Benjamin Franklin
Most people know about Benjamin Franklin as one of the authors the Declaration of Independence and as a scientist and ambassador. But his career began at the age of 16 in 1722 when he started writing essays in his brother's newspaper. He convinced his brother and the readers of the paper that his essays were written by a middle-aged woman named Silence Dogood. Later, Franklin earned fame and fortune as a newspaper printer in his own right.

98   Chapter 3   A Changing Continent

Chapter 3   99

People You Should Know

How do personal stories IMPACT our understanding of how North America changed as a result of European settlement?

- Have students read aloud the biographies.

- Tell them that they will learn about these people and others throughout the chapter.

- Prompt students to create a timeline that includes major events in the lives of these individuals. Encourage students to add to the timeline information they learn about other important historical figures as they read the chapter. Other people they encounter will include:

▷ Captain John Smith

▷ Pocahontas

▷ Powhatan

▷ Bartolomé de Las Casas

▷ Samuel de Champlain

▷ Jacques Marquette

▷ Louis Jolliet

▷ René-Robert Cavelier Sieur de La Salle

▷ William Bradford

▷ Squanto

▷ Massasoit

▷ Roger Williams

▷ Metacomet

▷ Peter Stuyvesant

▷ William Penn

▷ Benjamin Franklin

▷ George Calvert

▷ Chief Hancock

Teacher Notes

How Did Early English Settlers Cooperate and Clash with American Indians?

Background Information

Most students will likely have heard the story of the first Thanksgiving, but most interactions between early settlers and American Indians were, at best, more complicated. Jamestown is an excellent example of the tense and paranoid relationship between colonists and American Indians.

Community Connections

To enrich what students will learn about early English settlers, provide a list of suggested movie clips on Jamestown, Pocahontas, and similar subjects. The clips may be fictionalized accounts or historical documentaries. If possible, invite a local expert on American history to discuss the clips with students.

HSS **LESSON STANDARDS**

✓ Explain the aims, obstacles, and accomplishments of the explorers, sponsors, and leaders of key European expeditions and the reasons Europeans chose to explore and colonize the world (e.g., the Spanish Reconquista, the Protestant Reformation, the Counter Reformation). **HSS.5.2.2**

✓ Describe the cooperation that existed between the colonists and Indians during the 1600s and 1700s (e.g., in agriculture, the fur trade, military alliances, treaties, cultural interchanges). **HSS.5.3.2**

✓ Examine the conflicts before the Revolutionary War (e.g., the Pequot and King Philip's Wars in New England, the Powhatan Wars in Virginia, the French and Indian War). **HSS.5.3.3**

✓ Explain the influence and achievements of significant leaders of the time (e.g., John Marshall, Andrew Jackson, Chief Tecumseh, Chief Logan, Chief John Ross, Sequoyah). **HSS.5.3.6**

✓ Understand the influence of location and physical setting on the founding of the original 13 colonies, and identify on a map the locations of the colonies and of the American Indian nations already inhabiting these areas. **HSS.5.4.1**

✓ Identify the major individuals and groups responsible for the founding of the various colonies and the reasons for their founding (e.g., John Smith, Virginia; Roger Williams, Rhode Island; William Penn, Pennsylvania; Lord Baltimore, Maryland; William Bradford, Plymouth; John Winthrop, Massachusetts). **HSS.5.4.2**

 Connect to the
Essential Question

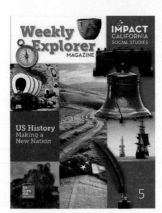

Chapter 3, pp. 30–43

The **Weekly Explorer Magazine** supports students' exploration of the Essential Question and provides additional resources for the EQ Inquiry Project.

 Inquiry Project

Tell Both Sides of the Story

Remind students to use the information they learn in this lesson and other resources to complete their EQ Inquiry Project!

Dinah Zike's

In this lesson you will use Foldables.

When Minutes Count!
Suggested Lesson Pacing

1 ENGAGE
One Day

- Lesson Opener
- Analyze the Source
- Inquiry Tools

Go Digital
- **iMap:** Early English Settlements
- **iMap:** Colonia Settlement by 1760

2 INVESTIGATE
Two to Three Days

 Short on Time? Look for the clock to teach core content in less time.

- England's First Permanent Colony in North America
- Relations Between the Powhatan and the Colonists
- Biography: The Real Story of Pocahontas
- Legacy of the Colony

3 REPORT
One Day

- Think About It
- Take a Stand
- Defend Your Claim

Make Connections!

(ccss) CONNECT TO ELA

Reading
Explain the relationships or interactions between two or more individuals, events, ideas, or concepts in a historical, scientific, or technical text based on specific information in the text. **RI.5.3**

Determine the meaning of words and phrases as they are used in a text, including figurative language such as metaphors and similes. **RL.5.4**

Research
Draw evidence from literary or informational texts to support analysis, reflection, and research. **W.5.9**

Writing
Write opinion pieces on topics or texts, supporting a point of view with reasons and information. **W.5.1**

Produce clear and coherent writing (including multiple-paragraph texts) in which the development and organization are appropriate to task, purpose, and audience. **W.5.4**

Speaking and Listening
Engage effectively in a range of collaborative discussions (one-on-one, in groups, and teacher-let) with diverse partners on *grade 5 topics and texts,* building on others' ideas and expressing their own clearly. **SL.5.1**

Report on a topic or text or present an opinion, sequencing ideas logically and using appropriate facts and relevant, descriptive details to support main ideas or themes; speak clearly at an understandable pace. **SL.5.4**

Classroom Resources
🔍 Search for additional resources using the following key words.

cash crops

House of Burgesses

King James I

Jamestown

Pocahontas

Chief Powhatan

Roanoke

John Smith

1 ENGAGE

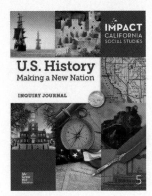

Inquiry Journal
pp. 82–83

 STANDARDS

Understand the influence of location and physical setting on the founding of the original 13 colonies, and identify on a map the locations of the colonies and of the American Indian nations already inhabiting these areas. **HSS.5.4.1**

Students use map and globe skills to determine the absolute locations of places and interpret information available through a map's or globe's legend, scale, and symbolic representations. **HAS.CS.4**

Go Digital!

Explore the lesson content with online whole-class presentation tools.

- **iMap:** Early English Settlements

- **iMap:** Colonial Settlement by 1760

How Did Early English Settlers Cooperate and Clash with American Indians?

Bellringer

Prompt students to retrieve information from previous lessons. Say: *In the previous lesson, you learned about the failed colony of Roanoke. In this lesson, you will learn about the next attempt at an English colony, Jamestown. What should Jamestown do differently to be successful?* (Answers could include: ensure colony is regularly supplied and avoid conflict with the American Indians.)

Lesson Outcomes

What Am I Learning? Have students read the Lesson Question and Lesson Outcomes on p. 82.

Why Am I Learning It? Check that students understand the word *interact*. Ask them for examples of person-to-person interactions, and then expand to examples of community-to-community or culture-to-culture interactions.

How Will I Know That I Learned It? Ask students the following questions.

- What will you identify? (the causes and effects of Jamestown's successes and failures)

- What is the purpose of your task? (to better understand the relationship between Jamestown settlers and American Indians)

- How will you support your analysis? (with evidence from the text)

Talk About It

- Point to features of the illustration and ask students to identify them.

- Use frames such as: **The fort had buildings for _____, _____, and _____.**

- **Because it was located on the James River, it also had _____.**

Collaborative Conversations

Adapt Speech As students engage in partner, small group, and whole-class discussions, encourage them to

- Use cardinal directions. Instead of saying "above the fort," say "to the north."

- Use geographic terms, such as *coast* or *bay* instead of *water*.

Lesson 1

How Did Early English Settlers Cooperate and Clash with American Indians?

James Fort at Jamestown settlement

Lesson Outcomes

What Am I Learning?
In this lesson, you're going to use your investigative skills to understand the history of England's first permanent colony in North America and how the colonists affected and were affected by American Indians.

Why Am I Learning It?
Reading and talking about the Jamestown colony will help you learn how different cultures interact and how actions and decisions are connected.

How Will I Know That I Learned It?
You will be able to explain the causes and effects of Jamestown's failures and successes.

Talk About It

Look at the Map What features do you notice about the settlement? What is the importance of these features?

HSS.5.3.1, HSS.5.3.2, HSS.5.3.3, HSS.5.4.1, HAS.HR.2

82 Lesson 1 How Did Early English Settlers Cooperate and Clash with American Indians?

Lesson 1 **83**

Inquiry Journal, pp. 82–83

 ENGLISH LEARNERS SCAFFOLD

ELD.PI.5.4 Adapting language choices to various contexts (based on task, purpose, audience, and text type)

Emerging	Bridging
Domain-Specific Language Teach students the cardinal directions. Be sure to point out that north/south go before east/west (i.e., northeast, not eastnorth). Provide sentence frames such as _____ *is north of* _____.	**Apply Language** Have students work with partners. One student chooses two landmarks on the map. The student should give directions to help the other student navigate from one landmark to the other, using cardinal directions and prepositions.

See the **Language Learner Teaching Guide** for more language support strategies.

Monitor and Differentiate

REACHING ALL LEARNERS

Approaching Level

Have students consider what a settlement needs to succeed. As a class, make a list. If students are stalled, provide suggestions, some good and some bad, and ask them to decide whether or not it is necessary.

On Level

Ask students to study the map and guess what life would have been like for the settlers. For example, what did they eat? How did they travel?

Beyond Level

Have students look online for additional maps of the Jamestown settlement. Ask them to look for maps with labels so they can find out what kinds of buildings were in the settlement. Help them with new words they may encounter.

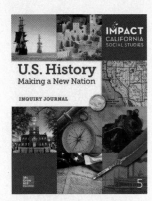

Inquiry Journal
pp. 84–85

 STANDARDS

Examine the conflicts before the Revolutionary War (e.g., the Pequot and King Philip's Wars in New England, the Powhatan Wars in Virginia, the French and Indian War). **HSS.5.3.3**

(ccss) Explain the relationships or interactions between two or more individuals, events, ideas, or concepts in a historical, scientific, or technical text based on specific information in the text. **CCSS.ELA.RI.5.3**

Demonstrate understanding of figurative language, word relationships, and nuances in word meanings. **CCSS.ELA.L.5.5**

Go Digital!

Model how to inspect and find evidence with online whole-class presentation tools.

Background Information

Jamestown Among the archaeological finds of the Jamestown Rediscovery Project were fragments of a skeleton belonging to an English teenage girl. There were tool marks on the skull and leg bone, and they were found in the cellar alongside animal bones and other food remains. These remains were the first piece of physical evidence of cannibalism that occurred during the "Starving Time." Her remains highlight just how desperate the colonists were when their food ran out and the Powhatans refused to trade with them—or even allow them to leave the fort.

1 Inspect

Read Have students read the entire text, including the Primary Source, to focus on understanding the overall meaning. Remind them to circle unfamiliar words.

- Who was John Smith? George Percy? Chief Powhatan? (John Smith was the leader of Jamestown. George Percy replaced Smith after he was injured. Chief Powhatan was the leader of the Powhatan people.)

- Why did the Powhatan refuse to help the settlers? (They felt the settlers were disrespectful and they had trouble with the drought as well.)

- What did the settlers do to survive the Starving Time? (They ate animals that were not normally used for food; they ate leather; they attempted to get food from the forest despite danger from the Powhatan.)

2 Find Evidence

Reread Have students reread the text.

Analyze the Primary Source Reread George Percy's account of the Starving Time. Explain to students that figurative language refers to words and phrases used in ways that do not match their dictionary definitions. Figurative language may be used to explain something more clearly or to add meaning or emotion.

- Ask students to find examples of figurative language in the primary source. (sharp prick of hunger, a world of miseries, all was fish that came to net)

- What is the effect of figurative language on George Percy's writing? (it strengthens the sense of suffering that he and the other settlers experienced.)

3 Make Connections
COLLABORATE

Talk Working individually, have students list the reasons they found for the Starving Time, and ask them to put them in order from "Most Influential" to "Least Influential." Then have them share their list with one or two partners. Ask students to support their decision for which reason they chose as "Most Influential." (Responses will vary.)

When the students have finished discussing, ask them to raise their hand if they changed their mind as a result of their partners' arguments.

Analyze the Source

The Starving Time

1 Inspect

Read First read the introductory text, and then read the quotation in the Primary Source box. How are they related?

- **Circle** words used in ways that are different from the ways they are most often used. Try to determine their meaning from context.

- **Discuss** with a group whether the starving time could have been prevented if John Smith had not been injured.

My Notes

_____

_____

_____

_____

_____

_____

_____

_____

_____

_____

_____

George Percy

In 1609, Captain John Smith was wounded in a gunpowder accident. His injuries forced him to return to England, and a noble named George Percy took his place as the leader of the Jamestown colony. Smith had played a key role in improving relations with the Powhatan Indians and ensuring the colonists worked hard. Without him, they were unprepared for a drought later that year, and Chief Powhatan refused to help them. Although Chief Powhatan had liked and respected Smith, he did not feel the same about other settlers. In fact, he was insulted when the Virginia Company gifted him with a crown to mark him as a prince under the rule of King James. Furthermore, his own people were hurt by the drought. Seeing the colony as weak and vulnerable, the Powhatan leader decided to starve the settlers into abandoning their colony, ordering his men to kill any colonist attempting to hunt or gather food outside of the fort. By the spring of 1610, only 60 colonists remained at Jamestown.

PRIMARY SOURCE

In Their Words… George Percy

Jamestown "Starving Time"

Now all of us at James Town, beginning to feel that sharp prick of hunger which no man truly describe but he which has tasted the bitterness thereof, a world of miseries ensued as the sequel will express unto you, in so much that some to satisfy their hunger have robbed the store for the which I caused them to be executed.

Then having fed upon horses and other beasts as long as they lasted, we were glad to make shift with vermin as dogs, cats, rats, and mice. All was fish that came to net to satisfy cruel hunger as to eat boots, shoes, or any other leather some could come by, and, those being spent and devoured, some were enforced to search the woods and to feed upon serpents and snakes and to dig the earth for wild and unknown roots, where many of our men were cut off of and slain by the savages.

—from George Percy's *A True Relation—A Trewe Relacyon*, written in the mid-1620s.

TEXT: Percy, George. "Jamestown: 1609-10, The Starving Time." In *A True Relation*. London, 1624.. PHOTO: McGraw-Hill Education

2 Find Evidence

Reread What details does George Percy include in his account to support the idea that the colony was starving? Why are these details effective?

What is meant by the statement "All was fish that came to net to satisfy cruel hunger"? Is Percy referring to actual fish?

3 Make Connections

Talk What was the main cause of the Starving Time? Discuss and defend your opinion with your group.

COLLABORATE

What long-term effects do you think the Starving Time had on the colony?

Inquiry Journal, pp. 84–85

ENGLISH LEARNERS SCAFFOLD

ELD.PI.5.6 Reading closely literary and informational texts and viewing multimedia to determine how meaning is conveyed explicitly and implicitly through language

Emerging	Expanding	Bridging
Identify Figurative Language Explain that students can use similes and metaphors to compare unlike things. Point out that similes use *like* or *as* and metaphors do not. Ask students to complete sentence frames like: **Chocolate is _____. Cats are like _____.**	**Use Figurative Language** Explain that figurative language is not always saying one thing is or is like another. It can also give non-literal actions. A red sunset could be described by saying "the sky burns." Have students use figurative words, such as **_____ flew past.**	**Apply Figurative Language** Ask students to look at the text preceding the primary source, which introduces and describes the Starving Time. Ask students to choose an event from that text and describe it using figurative language of their own creation.

See the **Language Learner Teaching Guide** for more language support strategies.

Monitor and Differentiate

REACHING ALL LEARNERS

Approaching Level

Provide examples of common idioms, such as *to pitch in* or *to be on the ball*. Then guide students in unpacking and interpreting them. Help them make the connection between the literal and the figurative meaning.

On Level

Ask each student to choose an idiom that they do not understand. Have them look up the idiom to find out the meaning and the origin of the phrase.

Beyond Level

Ask students to listen for and make note of idioms and other examples of figurative language they encounter throughout the day, whether while reading or listening.

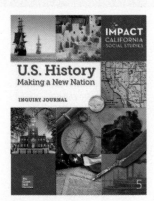

Inquiry Journal
pp. 86–87

 STANDARDS

Describe the cooperation that existed between the colonists and Indians during the1600s and 1700s (e.g., in agriculture, the fur trade, military alliances, treaties, cultural interchanges) **HSS.5.3.2**

Students identify and interpret the multiple causes and effects of historical events. **HAS.HI.3**

(CCSS) Explain the relationships or interactions between two or more individuals, events, ideas, or concepts in a historical, scientific, or technical text based on specific information in the text. **CCSS.ELA.RI.5.3**

Go Digital!

- Model how to explore and investigate with online whole-class tools.

- Students can access the online graphic organizer to use the inquiry tools as they read.

Explore Cause and Effect

Explain Tell students that writers sometimes use cause-and-effect structure in writing. Cause-and-effect emphasizes the links between events, helping readers understand why things happen.

Read Have students read the instructions on analyzing cause and effect. Remind students that transitions often appear at the beginning of sentences, so they can quickly search for cause-and-effect statements by reading only the first few words of each sentence.

Guide Practice Help students analyze events. Make sure the students ask themselves the questions in "Analyze the events." Explain that such questions are important for avoiding mistakes. Provide the following examples:

1. *John reads the newspaper. Then he eats a sandwich.* Students must be careful not to mistake correlation with causation. Reading the newspaper is not the cause of eating. They are unrelated.

2. *Stephanie opens her umbrella. It is raining.* The umbrella does not cause the rain. This example will seem obvious to students, but other cases may not be so easily seen.

3. *The dog barked at the door. Jeremy went to the door.* It may seem that Jeremy went to the door because the dog was barking at it, but both events may actually be effects of an overlooked cause: the doorbell was rung.

Investigate!

Have students read 100–109 in the Research Companion. Tell them the information will help them answer the lesson question *How Did Early English Settlers Cooperate and Clash with American Indians?*

Take Notes Tell students they should use the graphic organizer on page 87 to take notes on the relationship of the Jamestown colonists and the Powhatan. Encourage them to find examples events that improved the relationship and events that worsened it. Remind the students to ensure they are placing the events into the correct columns.

Inspect Guide students to read the text in each section to determine what the text says. Encourage them to make note of words they don't understand and look for answers to questions, such as *who? what? when? where? why?* and *how?*

Find Evidence Encourage students to reread the text to develop a deeper understanding of the content. Remind students that after they read and take notes, they should review and think about how the details will help them answer the lesson question.

Collaborative Conversations

Constructive Criticism Students may disagree on the extent to which one event influences another. Remind students that the goal in discussions is not to win; the goal is to examine and debate points so they can be improved. Make sure the conversation does not get too heated and that all criticism is given with the intent of fostering improvement.

Inquiry Tools

Explore Cause and Effect

Some of the events you will read about in this lesson have cause-and-effect relationships. To better understand history, it is important to know about cause and effect. The causes of historical events explain why things happened, and the effects of events show why the events are important to people afterwards.

1. Look for transitions related to causes and effects.
Because, therefore, as a result, in order to, and similar transitional words and phrases can indicate cause-and-effect relationships.

2. Take note of chronology.
Texts will often present cause-and-effect relationships in the order that the two events happen. This is not always true, though, so be careful.

3. Analyze the events.
Would an event have happened without this particular cause? Would the effect have been the same if the earlier event had never happened? Ask yourself questions like these to determine how strong the relationship between two events is.

4. Note that an event may have more than one cause or effect.

COLLABORATE Based on the text you just read, work with your class to complete the chart below.

Cause		Effect
John Smith returned to England.	→	Chief Powhatan refused to help the settlers.

Investigate!

Read pages 100–109 in your Research Companion. Use your investigative skills to identify cause-and-effect relationships in the text. Find events in the text that led to improved or worsened relations between the colonists and the Powhatan. Each event will be the "cause," while what happened as a result of each event is the "effect." Use this information to fill in the graphic organizer below.

Cause		Effect
John Smith and Chief Powhatan respect each other.	→	Jamestown colonists are able to get food by trading with the Powhatan.
Chief Powhatan dies.	→	Chief Opechancanough wages war against Jamestown.
Pocahontas marries John Rolfe.	→	Relations between Jamestown and the Powhatan become more peaceful.
John Rolfe introduces tobacco as a crop in the colony.	→	Colonists become wealthy enough to protect themselves.

Inquiry Journal, pp. 86–87

ⓔⓛ ENGLISH LEARNERS SCAFFOLD

ELD.PII.5.3 Using verbs and verb phrases

Emerging	Expanding	Bridging
Use Past Tense Remind students that verbs in the simple past tense often end in *–ed.* Guide students in describing cause-and-effect relationships using sentence frames with simple past tense verbs.	**Use Was and Were** Remind students that *was* and *were* are the past tense forms of *be.* *Was* is used for first person singular and third person singular. *Were* is used for second person singular and all plural subjects.	**Use Passive Voice** The passive voice is used when the focus of the sentence is on the recipient of an action. The past tense of the passive voice is the past form of *be* followed by the past participle.
_____ *caused* _____. _____ *resulted in* _____. _____ *led to* _____.	_____ *was a cause of* _____. _____ *were effects of* _____.	_____ *was caused by* _____. _____ *were caused by* _____.

See the **Language Learner Teaching Guide** for more language support strategies.

Monitor and Differentiate

REACHING ALL LEARNERS

Special Needs
Ask students to imagine what their life would have been like in Jamestown. Have them close their eyes and visualize the good and bad parts of living there.

On Level
In groups or as a class, have students discuss ways the Jamestown colony might have avoided some of their hardships. What actions could they have taken instead? Then, have students consider the possible effects of these new actions.

Beyond Level
Have students write a short letter to a new colony following in Jamestown's footsteps. Have them give the new colonists advice based on Jamestown's experiences. Make sure they include the reasons to take or avoid certain actions.

Research Companion
pp. 100–101

 STANDARDS

Describe the competition among the English, French, Spanish, Dutch, and Indian nations for control of North America. **HSS.5.3.1**

Students place key events and people of the historical era they are studying in a chronological sequence and within a spatial context; they interpret time lines. **HAS.CS.1**

CCSS Explain the relationships or interactions between two or more individuals, events, ideas, or concepts in a historical, scientific, or technical text based on specific information in the text. **CCSS.ELA.RI.5.3**

Go Digital!

Investigate the lesson content with online whole-class presentation tools.

- **iMap:** Early English Settlements

- **iMap:** Colonial Settlement by 1760

Background Information

The Lost Colony of Roanoke The lost colony of Roanoke was established in 1587. The Jamestown Company was given a charter in 1606. This gap of nearly twenty years was due to the realization that establishing a colony in the New World was expensive and difficult, especially when trying to get past the Spanish Armada. It was with the signing of a peace treaty with Spain in 1604 that England was able to turn its attention once again to colonization.

| TIMELINE | Invite students to look at the timeline at the top of page 101.

> **Analyze** Study the timeline and the picture. Where on the timeline does this picture most likely occur? Why? (The picture shows colonists building, so most likely it is depicting the start of the colony in 1607.) **HAS.CS.1 DOK 2**

Analyze the Source

Inspect Have students read pp. 100–101.

Find Evidence Use the questions below to check comprehension. Remind students to support their answers with text evidence.

> **Identify** Who founded Jamestown? (105 men and boys working for the Virginia Company) **DOK 1**

> **Infer** How did Jamestown get its name? (from King James I, who gave the Virginia Company a charter) **DOK 3**

Make Connections

> **Draw Conclusions** How might the failure of Roanoke have led to the poorly chosen location of Jamestown? (Roanoke failed in part because it could not receive supplies. Thus, the founders may have prioritized being close to shore, where ships could resupply them.) **DOK 3**

> **Analyze** From the timeline, does the relationship between the English settlers and the American Indians appear to improve, worsen, or remain the same over time? (The Powhatan Wars suggest the relationship worsened.) **DOK 3**

Analyze the Image From the image, what can you learn about the way the Jamestown colony was built? (Responses will vary, but students should identify that the settlers had to build the colony themselves using only the tools they brought with them on the ships.) **DOK 3**

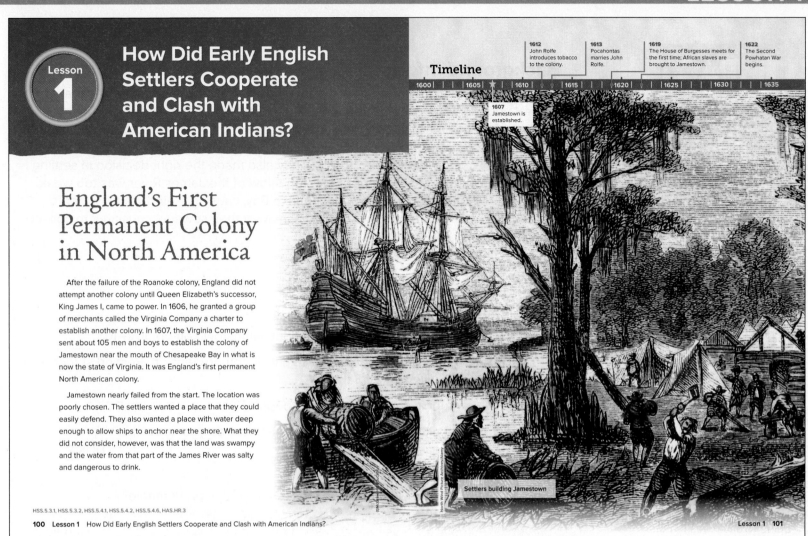

Lesson 1

How Did Early English Settlers Cooperate and Clash with American Indians?

England's First Permanent Colony in North America

After the failure of the Roanoke colony, England did not attempt another colony until Queen Elizabeth's successor, King James I, came to power. In 1606, he granted a group of merchants called the Virginia Company a charter to establish another colony. In 1607, the Virginia Company sent about 105 men and boys to establish the colony of Jamestown near the mouth of Chesapeake Bay in what is now the state of Virginia. It was England's first permanent North American colony.

Jamestown nearly failed from the start. The location was poorly chosen. The settlers wanted a place that they could easily defend. They also wanted a place with water deep enough to allow ships to anchor near the shore. What they did not consider, however, was that the land was swampy and the water from that part of the James River was salty and dangerous to drink.

Timeline

1607 Jamestown is established.

1612 John Rolfe introduces tobacco to the colony.

1613 Pocahontas marries John Rolfe.

1619 The House of Burgesses meets for the first time; African slaves are brought to Jamestown.

1622 The Second Powhatan War begins.

1600 | 1605 ★ | 1610 | 1615 | 1620 | 1625 | 1630 | 1635

Settlers building Jamestown

HSS.5.3.1, HSS.5.3.2, HSS.5.4.1, HSS.5.4.2, HSS.5.4.6, HAS.HR.3

100 Lesson 1 How Did Early English Settlers Cooperate and Clash with American Indians?

Lesson 1 101

Research Companion, pp. 100–101

ENGLISH LEARNERS SCAFFOLD

ELD.PII.5.5 Modifying to add details

Emerging

Identify Modifiers Have students read the passage and identify all the adjectives and adverbs. Then ask them to change the adjectives into adverbs and the adverbs into adjectives.

Expanding/Bridging

Use Modifiers Instruct students to come up with 2–3 sentences to describe the picture on p. 101. Each sentence must contain at least one adjective and one adverb.

See the **Language Learner Teaching Guide** for more language support strategies.

Monitor and Differentiate

REACHING ALL LEARNERS

Approaching Level

Ask students to imagine they are one of the 105 colonists sent to establish Jamestown. How would they feel upon arrival at the chosen location? Have students explain the reasons for their feelings.

Beyond Level

Ask students to compare and contrast colonizing a new land in 1607 to moving to a new home today. Have them discuss in small groups the similarities and differences in these two situations.

U.S. History
Making a New Nation

RESEARCH COMPANION

5

Research Companion
pp. 102–103

 STANDARDS

Identify the major individuals and groups responsible for the founding of the various colonies and the reasons for their founding (e.g., John Smith, Virginia; Roger Williams, Rhode Island; William Penn, Pennsylvania; Lord Baltimore, Maryland; William Bradford, Plymouth; John Winthrop, Massachusetts). **HSS.5.4.2**

Students judge the significance of the relative location of a place (e.g., proximity to a harbor, on trade routes) and analyze how relative advantages or disadvantages can change over time. **HAS.CS.5**

Determine the meaning of general academic and domin-specific words and phrases in a text relevant to a *grade 5 topic or subject area.* **CCSS.ELA.RI.5.4**

Go Digital!

Investigate the lesson content with online whole-class presentation tools.

Background Information

Although it would be untrue to depict the colonists as incompetent, they did make several poor decisions that compounded their hardships as time went on. The location of the fort was in a secure place, where cannon fire from Spanish ships could not reach them. They constructed their fort very quickly to protect themselves from the Powhatan, who were initially hostile. They also made the right decision in settling near a river for fresh water. Unfortunately, the flow of the James River was too weak to compete with tidal forces from Chesapeake Bay, causing their drinking water to be salty. The river was also too weak to wash away their sewage, causing it to collect just like the salt.

Analyze the Source

Inspect Have students continue reading about Jamestown on pp. 102–103.

Find Evidence Use the question below to check comprehension. Remind students to support their answers with text evidence.

Identify Which supply ship brought more people? (the Third Supply) **DOK 1**

Infer Was John Smith important to the colony? How do you know this? (Yes; colony was saved by his leadership and nearly failed again with his departure.) **DOK 2**

Make Connections

Opinion Were the most serious problems of the colony preventable? (Answers may vary. Some problems, such as poor leadership and work ethic, could have been prevented. Others, such as the hurricane that delayed the third supply ship, could not be foreseen.) **DOK 3**

Map Skills

Have students study the map on p. 103 of their Research Companion.

- What settlements are shown on the map? (Werowocomo, Jamestown, and Roanoke)
- What American Indian groups lived near Jamestown? (Chiskiack)
- How did the land make Roanoke and Jamestown desirable areas for settlements? (They were both near water so they could get supplies and food easily.)
- What new information is presented in the map? (information on the Werowocomo colony)

Have students use the scale to estimate distances on the map, such as the distance from Roanoke to Jamestown, or the length of one of the rivers.

Many of the colonists were not prepared for the challenges of Jamestown. Many came from the upper class and were interested in finding treasure. They had little experience or desire to do hard outdoor work, such as building or farming. They did not plan to stay permanently but wanted to find gold and return to England. Their participation did little to help. Also, the seven men on the council selected to lead the colony were distrustful of one another and did not cooperate well.

The poor conditions at Jamestown led to starvation and disease. After two-thirds of the colony had died, Captain John Smith took over as leader. He understood the importance of hard work, especially in a survival situation. He required every person to work four to six hours every day. According to some sources, he told the colonists, "Those who don't work, don't eat." His firm leadership saved the colony, but its troubles weren't over yet.

The Virginia Company continued to support the colony. It would send supply ships with food, tools, goods for trading, and additional settlers. These ships did not come often, however. The "First Supply" arrived in January 1608. It carried about 100 new settlers. The "Second Supply" did not come until October of that year. It carried 70 new settlers, including the first two women of the colony, Martha Forest and her maid, Anne Burras. The "Third Supply" was hit by a hurricane. Some of the ships arrived in August 1609 with about 300 men, women, and children. Much of their food, however, was on the other ships, which were sent off course in the storm and wrecked in Bermuda. This disaster was one of the causes of what became known as the "Starving Time."

Jamestown men wore chest plates in battle.

Daniella Nowitz/National Geographic/Getty Images

MATTAPONI	Native American group
●	Settlement

Native Peoples and the English, 1607

Map Skills What information in the map is also found in the text? What new information is presented in the map? Compare the area surrounding Jamestown with the area surrounding Roanoke. What do they have in common? What makes those locations desirable?

The "Starving Time" occurred when Captain John Smith left the colony in 1609 and it nearly collapsed. Tensions with the Powhatan Indians and lack of leadership caused the majority of the colonists to die of starvation and disease. When the group of settlers who had been shipwrecked in Bermuda reached Jamestown in May 1610, they found the colony in such poor condition that they considered abandoning it. They received news that more ships bringing supplies and people would be arriving, so they stayed and rebuilt the colony with the survivors. Among the shipwrecked settlers was John Rolfe, who would end up helping to save the colony.

McGraw-Hill Education

Research Companion, pp. 102–103

ⒺⓁ ENGLISH LEARNERS SCAFFOLD

ELD.PI.5.12 Selecting and applying varied and precise vocabulary and language structures to effectively convey ideas

Emerging	Expanding	Bridging
Identify Domain-Specific Language Check that students understand basic geographic terms by having them identify features such as rivers, oceans, islands, and land on p. 103 of the research companion.	**Use Domain-Specific Language** Teach more specific geographic terms, such as *bay*, *inlet*, *coast*, *peninsula*, and any others you feel are appropriate. Ask students to demonstrate their understanding by locating examples of these features on the map on page 103.	**Apply Domain-Specific Language** Tell students that Captain John Smith has asked them to go on an expedition to the lost colony of Roanoke. The students cannot take the map, so they must write instructions for how to make the journey by boat. Have them use geographic terms.

See the **Language Learner Teaching Guide** for more language support strategies.

Monitor and Differentiate

REACHING ALL LEARNERS

Special Needs

Have students close their eyes and use their pencils to point to a random location on the map on p. 103 of their Research Companion. If students point to somewhere in water, have them go to the nearest point of dry land. Tell them to evaluate this location as a potential site for a new colony. Ask them to compare and contrast it with Jamestown.

On Level

Have students work in groups to propose a location for a new colony, Jamestown II (or the students may choose their own name). As a group, they should make a list of pros and cons for the location. They should be able to explain why the benefits of their location outweigh any drawbacks.

Lesson 1 **England's First Permanent Colony in North America** T221

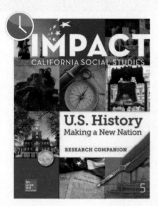

Research Companion
pp. 104–105

 STANDARDS

Explain the influence and achievements of significant leaders of the time (e.g., John Marshall, Andrew Jackson, Chief Tecumseh, Chief Logan, Chief John Ross, Sequoyah). **HSS.5.3.6**

Students correctly apply terms related to time, including past, present, future, decade, century, and generation. **HAS.CS.2**

Students explain how the present is connected to the past, identifying both similarities and differences between the two, and how some things change over time and some things stay the same. **HAS.CS.3**

 Explain the relationships or interactions between two or more individuals, events, ideas, or concepts in a historical, scientific, or technical text based on specific information in the text. **CCSS.ELA.RI.5.3**

Go Digital!

Investigate the lesson content with online whole-class presentation tools.

Background Information

Chief Wahunsonacock Chief Wahunsonacock (*He Makes an Offering by Crushing with a Falling Weight* or *He Knows How to Crush Them* in Algonquin) was a shrewd and powerful leader. He was born around 1548 in what is now Richmond, Virginia. He inherited a handful of small groups from his parents and, taking the name of his group, Powhatan, to signify his authority. He steadily expanded his power through a combination of warfare and diplomacy. At its peak, the Powhatan Confederacy consisted of 30 groups, 14,000 people, and 8,500 square miles of territory. He tolerated the presence of the Jamestown Colony in the hope of developing a beneficial relationship: territory and food for the colonists in exchange for their metal weapons, which would give the Powhatan an advantage over their enemies.

Then and Now

Explain to students that knowledge of Jamestown comes from written records and archaeological discoveries, such as what is shown on p. 104. Lead students in a discussion of the strengths and weaknesses of each method of learning about the past.

Stop and Check

Write Encourage students to consider the challenges the settlers at Jamestown faced. (Responses will vary, but students should identify that the settlers had to solve problems such as food shortages and bad weather.)

Find Details Explain to students that after they read and take notes, they should review and think about how the facts and details will help them answer the Essential Question.

Analyze the Source

Inspect Have students read p. 105, Relations Between the Powhatan and the Colonists.

Find Evidence Use the questions below to check comprehension. Remind students to support their answers with text evidence.

Identify Who are the notable leaders of the Powhatan and colonists? (Chief Powhatan/Wahunsonacock and Chief Opechancanough; Captain John Smith.) **DOK 1**

Analyze What do the Powhatan and the English have in common? (Both wanted to expand their territory, and both maintained peace through strong leadership.) **DOK 2**

Infer Ask students to identify details that indicate Jamestown's growth. ("Jamestown could not survive a full-force attack from the Powhatan . . ."; Opechancanough "waged wars against the colony for the next several decades.") **DOK 2**

Make Connections Using Captain John Smith and Chief Powhatan as examples, discuss as a class what characteristics make a good leader. **DOK 4**

Stop and Check

Think Guide students to consider the relationship between the Powhatan and the settlers. (Responses will vary, but students should identify that John Smith and Chief Powhatan were reasonable leaders who wanted to avoid conflict when possible.)

Then and Now

Jamestown may have looked like this at its peak.

Archaeologists study the remains of old Jamestown.

As the Jamestown colony grew, the original fort was eventually abandoned. Over time, the wood rotted away and the foundations became buried in mud. For a while, the location was forgotten. A graduate student, William Kelso, eventually found the original location by studying writings left by the colonists. Kelso started the Jamestown Rediscovery Project in 1994. He and others began to uncover, study, and preserve the original fort. Visitors can now visit the site of Jamestown.

✓ Stop and Check

Write What problems did the Jamestown colony face? What recommendations would you give to solve these problems?

Find Details As you read, add additional information to the graphic organizer on page 87 in your Inquiry Journal.

Relations between the Powhatan and the Colonists

In addition to being a salty swamp, the location of Jamestown was also in Powhatan territory. The Powhatan Confederacy was an alliance of about thirty tribes. They were led by Chief Wahunsonacock (wah hun SAHN uh kahk), also called Chief Powhatan. He was an intelligent leader who had been successfully increasing the strength and territory of his people when the colonists arrived. Historians are not sure exactly how many tribes Chief Powhatan ruled, but he had thousands of warriors at his command. For the struggling Jamestown colony, the Powhatan could be much-needed allies or dangerous enemies.

As an experienced soldier, Captain John Smith knew Jamestown could not survive a full-force attack from the Powhatan, so he wisely chose to avoid conflict as much as possible. He and Chief Powhatan respected one another. Although there were a few conflicts, the relationship was mostly peaceful, and the Jamestown colony was able to get food through trade with the Powhatan.

Unfortunately, Smith was injured in a gunpowder accident. His injury forced him to return to England. Then, in 1618, Chief Powhatan died. Power passed to one of his brothers, who ruled briefly before passing the title again to another brother, named Opechancanough (oh pun CHAN kun awf). He was angry about the growth of the Jamestown colony into native lands, and he waged wars against the colony for the next several decades.

Colonists traded with the Powhatan for food.

✓ Stop and Check

Think What made it possible for the colonists to trade with the Powhatan?

Research Companion, pp. 104–105

EL ENGLISH LEARNERS SCAFFOLD

ELD.PI.5.4 Adapting language choices to various contexts (based on task, purpose, audience, and text type)

Emerging	Expanding	Bridging
Consider Language Guide students in describing what the Powhatan and Jamestown colonists want and why. Provide sentence frames such as *The colonists want _____ because _____.*	**Create an Argument** Help students write persuasive arguments to answer the question "Should the colonists and the Powhatan fight or make peace?" Remind students that arguments based on fact are best supported with concrete data.	**Support an Argument** Divide the class into an even number of groups. Pair off the groups and designate one as representing the Powhatan and the other as the colonists. Have the pairs of groups negotiate a treaty. Each group should provide appropriate support for their arguments.

See the **Language Learner Teaching Guide** for more language support strategies.

Monitor and Differentiate

REACHING ALL LEARNERS

Approaching Level

Make cards with "resources" such as food, fur, metal, tools, weapons, soldiers, and so on. Distribute these among students so that all have the same number of resource cards but not the same amount of each resource. Then have students trade. If desired, make additional rules involving alliances. Every few turns, make announcements like "A new mine is discovered. Anyone with more than X tool cards gets additional metal cards."

Beyond Level

Ask students to develop opinion statements comparing and contrasting Chief Powhatan and Captain John Smith. Then, have students research these figures in outside sources to further support or refute their opinions.

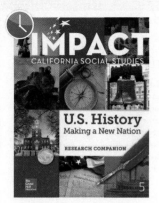

Research Companion
pp. 106–107

STANDARDS

Describe the cooperation that existed between the colonists and Indians during the 1600s and 1700s (e.g., in agriculture, the fur trade, military alliances, treaties, cultural interchanges). **HSS.5.3.2**

Students distinguish fact from fiction by comparing documentary sources on historical figures and events with fictionalized characters and events. **HAS.HR.3**

CCSS Explain the relationships or interactions between two or more individuals, events, ideas, or concepts in a historical, scientific, or technical text based on specific information in the text. **CCSS.ELA.RI.5.3**

Go Digital!

Investigate the lesson content with online whole-class presentation tools.

Background Information

Pocahontas Due to popular depictions of the daughter of Chief Powhatan, students may have many misconceptions about the story of Pocahontas. What cannot be doubted, however, is the importance of her diplomacy between the Powhatan and the colonists. Time and time again, she acted as an ambassador and negotiator for her people. She de-escalated tensions, secured trade deals, and even gained freedom for hostages of both sides.

The introduction of tobacco changed Jamestown from a settlement struggling to survive into a thriving colony. It jumpstarted the growth that would eventually create the United States. Unfortunately, it also brought with it misfortune for the American Indians and slavery for Africans.

Analyze the Sources

Inspect Have students read "The Real Story of Pocahontas" and "The Legacy of the Colony."

Find Evidence Use the questions below to check comprehension. Remind students to support their answers with text evidence.

Identify Who was John Rolfe and why was he important? (He married Pocahontas and introduced tobacco to the colony.) **DOK 1**

Main Ideas What happened to Pocahontas after she married John Rolfe? (She went to England, where she later died.) **DOK 1**

Vocabulary What is a cash crop? (a crop grown to make money rather than provide direct sustenance for the grower) **DOK 2**

Cause and Effect How did tobacco lead to growing tensions between the Powhatan and the settlers? (The tobacco required a lot of land, and the colonists gradually encroached upon Powhatan territory more and more.) **DOK 2**

Make Connections

Opinion Was the introduction of tobacco overall a positive or negative thing? (Answers will vary, but students should defend their opinion with evidence from the text.) **DOK 4**

Connect to Now Consider the people you have learned about so far this lesson: John Smith, Powhatan, Pocahontas, and John Rolfe. Who had the greatest impact on history? Support your answer. (Answers will vary, but students should support their opinion with text evidence.) **DOK 4**

☑ Stop and Check

COLLABORATE

List Encourage students to look beyond their textbooks for information. Guide them in using the internet to separate fictional from factual details. Help them recognize signs of reliable and unreliable sources. (Responses will vary, but students should identify that Pocohontas' role was important, but her real story differs from modern interpretations of her life.)

Biography

The Real Story of Pocahontas

The most famous story about Jamestown and the Powhatan is the story about Chief Powhatan's daughter, Pocahontas. Her real name was Matoaka; Pocahontas was her nickname and meant "the playful one." According to legend, when she was around 13 years old, her father captured Captain John Smith and planned to execute him. Pocahontas saved Smith's life by convincing Powhatan to let him go.

Historians are uncertain if these events happened at all. Captain Smith was known to exaggerate stories. Some historians suggest that the incident was not an attempted execution and that Smith misunderstood a ceremony making him a sub-chief under Powhatan. What is more certain is that Pocahontas was curious and friendly toward the colonists. This improved relations between the two groups. She later married John Rolfe, a successful Jamestown farmer. This marriage brought peace between the settlers and the Powhatan, who had been growing more hostile since Captain Smith returned to England. Pocahontas died of illness in 1617 while visiting England with her husband.

Pocahontas saving John Smith

Pocahontas

[bsg/McGraw-Hill Education; (t)Library of Congress Prints and Photographs Division LC-USZC4-3368]; BrWilliams, S.M., ed. "Pocahontas." Page 183 in Queerly Women, Crowned and Uncrowned. Cincinnati: Cranston and Stowe, 1885.

✓ Stop and Check

COLLABORATE

List Make a list of facts and myths about Pocahontas. Compare your list with a partner's list.

Find Details As you read, add additional information to the graphic organizer on page 87 in your Inquiry Journal.

106 Lesson 1 How Did Early English Settlers Cooperate and Clash with American Indians?

The Legacy of the Colony

In 1612, John Rolfe introduced tobacco to the colony. It grew well in Virginia and quickly became a **cash crop**. The colony would grow in population and size due to the wealth gained from the new crop. Unfortunately, tobacco is hard on the soil, and so the colonists needed more and more land to grow it. This caused conflicts with the Powhatan and was one of the reasons for the Powhatan Wars. The value of tobacco, however, made the colony strong and the colonists wealthy enough to protect themselves.

Tobacco required a lot of labor, so indentured servants were brought from England to work. Their employers paid for them to travel there, and the indentured servants worked under contract for five to seven years until they repaid their debt. The colonists wanted even more expansion, however, and eventually began purchasing African slaves to work on tobacco farms.

(t)McGraw-Hill Education; (b)North Wind Picture Archives/Alamy

Tobacco farming

Lesson 1 107

Research Companion, pp. 106–107

(EL) ENGLISH LEARNERS SCAFFOLD

ELD.PII.5.7 Condensing ideas

Emerging	Expanding	Bridging
Combine Sentences Ask students to write two simple sentences about one of the figures discussed in this chapter. Then, walk them through combining the sentences using *who, which,* or *that.*	**Use Commas and Dependent Clauses** Have students write two simple sentences about one of the figures discussed in this chapter. Then, walk them through combining the sentences using commas and dependent clauses.	**Use Relative Clauses** Have students describe the relationship between two figures from this chapter using relative and dependent clauses. For example: *Pocahontas, the daughter of Powhatan, married John Rolfe, who introduced tobacco to the colony.*

See the **Language Learner Teaching Guide** for more language support strategies.

Monitor and Differentiate

REACHING ALL LEARNERS

Approaching Level

Have students compare and contrast the real Pocahontas with one or more fictional depictions of Pocahontas. Encourage them to use additional sources for research.

Beyond Level

Pocahontas, Johnny Appleseed, and other real, historical figures have become heavily fictionalized characters in popular media. Lead a class discussion on why this happens and whether or not it is a good thing.

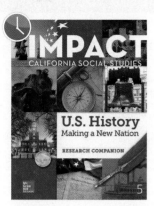

Research Companion
pp. 108–109

 STANDARDS

Describe the introduction of slavery into America, the responses of slave families to their condition, the ongoing struggle between proponents and opponents of slavery, and the gradual institutionalization of slavery in the South. **HSS.5.4.6**

Explain the early democratic ideas and practices that emerged during the colonial period, including the significance of representative assemblies and town meetings. **HSS.5.4.7**

CCSS Explain the relationships or interactions between two or more individuals, events, ideas, or concepts in a historical, scientific, or technical text based on specific information in the text. **CCSS.ELA.RI.5.3**

Go Digital!

Investigate the lesson content with online whole-class presentation tools.

Background Information

Two things happened in Jamestown that would shape the future of America. The first was slavery. The first enslaved Africans to arrive in Jamestown were likely pirated by the Dutch from a Portuguese ship leaving Angola. Portugal had been purchasing enslaved people there for some time, so these Africans likely knew European languages and were Christian converts. This, combined with the lack of a slaving culture in England at the time, led to these people being accepted as indentured servants equal to someone of European descent. Eventually, however, favoritism began to be shown toward white indentured servants, and race-based slavery began in earnest.

The other institution to originate in Jamestown was more positive. The House of Burgesses was the first representative government created by Europeans in the Americas. The House of Burgesses consisted of two burgesses from every settlement, as well as the Virginian governor and a council. Only the burgesses were elected; the Virginia Company selected the governor and the council. As a result, this government wasn't particularly empowering to the colonies. It served more to organize than to lead. Even so, having elected people involved in governance was the first step towards democracy.

Analyze the Source

Inspect Have students read text on pp. 108–109

Find Evidence Use the questions below to check comprehension.

Compare What is the difference between indentured servitude and slavery? (Indentured servitude is unpaid labor for a predetermined length of time; it is an agreement. Slavery makes one person the property of another.) **DOK 3**

Summarize How did Africans come to be enslaved in North America? (Slaves may first have come as indentured servants. As demand for tobacco grew, so did the demand for cheap or slave labor. The number of slaves continued to rise.) **DOK 3**

Explain What is the significance of the House of Burgesses? (first representational government in the Americas by Europeans; predecessor of the US democracy) **DOK 2**

Identify Where was the colonial capital after 1698? (Williamsburg) **DOK 1**

Make Connections

Analyze How did the introduction of tobacco lead to both slavery and democracy? (The rapid growth of the colony due to the cash crop created demand for inexpensive labor and for better governmental organization.) **DOK 3**

Stop and Check

Think Guide students to consider what they have read about Jamestown in this lesson and in their own research. (Responses will vary, but should include information about the first representative government by Europeans in America, the roots of slavery in America, and the introduction of tobacco as a cash crop in America.)

What do you think?

If you had been in charge of Jamestown, what would you have done differently? Remind students to explain the reasoning for their answers to the prompt, using evidence from the text.

Slavery in the English colonies began in the early 1600s.

This means that the cruel practice of slavery in North America has its roots in England's first permanent colony. The slave trade had already been established by other countries, and in 1619, a Dutch ship entered the port of Jamestown carrying African slaves. Twenty of them were exchanged for food. Since slavery had not yet been established in the colony, these first Africans may have been treated more like indentured servants. Records at the time listed them as servants, not slaves. Some apparently gained freedom after working a certain number of years.

This situation would not last. As the contracts on indentured servants ended and the **demand** for tobacco and other crops grew, planters needed more workers. Some planters attempted to enslave American Indians, since the relationship had become much worse after the departure of Captain John Smith and the death of Chief Powhatan. The American Indians knew the land well and had friends and family to help them, so attempts to enslave them were unsuccessful. African slaves, however, did not have the same networks of friends or family in the unfamiliar land of North America. Escaping was more difficult. By 1650, the number of slaves in the Virginia colony had grown to about 300.

The House of Burgesses

Another important legacy of Jamestown was the first representative government set up by Europeans in the Americas. In 1619, the Virginia Company had the colonists establish their own government, the House of Burgesses. By this time, the Virginia colony had expanded into eleven settlements. Each was allowed to elect two representatives, or burgesses, to speak for them when the House met in Jamestown. Since most of the burgesses were wealthy white tobacco growers, one of their first laws was simply to settle the price of tobacco.

The House of Burgesses had been around for only five years when King James took control of the colony from the Virginia Company. The company had been losing money, and the increasing attacks by the Powhatan, led by Chief Opechancanough, made King James think the colony needed more direct control. He sent royal governors to represent him in leading the colony. Despite this, the House of Burgesses continued to meet every year. Even if the burgesses were no longer in control, they liked being able to discuss what needed to be done and to be united when dealing with the royal government.

Jamestown remained the capital of the Virginia colony until 1698, when the statehouse burned down. By this time, many of the people had moved to other settlements, so they decided to rebuild in a better location. Williamsburg became the new capital, and Jamestown was eventually abandoned.

✓ Stop and Check

Think Aside from being the first successful English colony in America, what other "firsts" can be traced back to Jamestown?

What Do You Think? If you had been in charge of Jamestown, what would you have done differently?

108 Lesson 1 How Did Early English Settlers Cooperate and Clash with American Indians?

Lesson 1 109

Library of Congress Prints and Photographs Division [LC-USZ62-76385]

(l)McGraw-Hill Education; (b)Matt Purciel/Alamy

Research Companion, pp. 108–109

(EL) ENGLISH LEARNERS SCAFFOLD

ELD.PI.5.2 Interacting with others in written English in various communicative forms (print, communicative technology, and multimedia)

Emerging

Use Visuals Have students make a relationship map of the various important people and concepts discussed in the chapter. The lines connecting the people and concepts should include a short description of how they are related. Encourage students to use different colored lines to indicate positive, negative, or neutral relationships.

Expanding

Organize Events Point out to students that the information in this chapter of the Research Companion has been primarily organized by topic. Have them reorganize the events chronologically by constructing a timeline. Have them use complete sentences to describe each event. Encourage them to use additional resources to fill in missing dates and information.

See the **Language Learner Teaching Guide** for more language support strategies.

Monitor and Differentiate

REACHING ALL LEARNERS

Approaching Level

Explain to students that the members of the House of Burgesses were chosen by either the Virginia Company or by the colony (the burgesses). Have students list what the members might have disagreed about based on what the Virginia Company wanted versus what the colonists wanted.

On Level

Divide the class into large groups. Each group will role-play as a House of Burgesses member. Half of each group will represent the governor and council, and the other will be the burgesses. Have each group choose a topic (such as higher profits for the colonists). Keeping in mind the goals of each side, groups should negotiate an agreement.

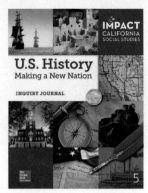

Inquiry Journal
pp. 88–89

 STANDARDS

Students describe the cooperation and conflict that existed among the American Indians and between the Indian nations and the new settlers. **HSS.5.3**

Students summarize the key events of the era they are studying and explain the historical contexts of those events. **HAS.HI.1**

(CCSS) Write opinion pieces on topics or texts, supporting a point of view with reasons and information. **CCSS.ELA.RI.5.1**

Go Digital!

• Students can go online to report their findings.

• Students can access the online graphic organizer to capture ideas from their investigation.

Think About It

Students will review their research and consider whether the settlers' relationship with American Indians ultimately helped or hurt the Jamestown Colony.

• Remind students to review the causes and effects they have listed in their graphic organizer and other key details from the text. Direct students back to pages 100–109 of their Research Companion if they need more information.

Write About It

Take a Stand Have students read the prompt. Encourage them to prewrite with a graphic organizer or outline before they begin their opinion essay. Make sure they include the following elements:

• An introduction that states their opinion

• Three reasons the relationship was positive or negative

• Support for each reason, including examples cited from the text

Use the rubric on p. T230 to evaluate students' work.

Talk About It

Defend Your Claim Have students find partners who had the opposite opinion. The partners should discuss and attempt to persuade one another.

• Remind them to be polite and take turns. A disagreement is not a personal attack.

• Encourage students to consider their opponent's opinions with an open mind.

Connect to the Essential Question

Read the prompt aloud to students. Ask them the following guiding questions:

• What were the most memorable and influential events? (Responses will vary, but students should use evidence from the text.)

• Which events had short-term consequences? Which events had long-term consequences? (Responses will vary.)

• What are the effects of these events from a political perspective? A cultural perspective? An economic perspective? (Responses may include that future interaction at all levels was affected by the conflicts that arose between the settlers and the American Indians.)

Remind students to use the space provided in their journal to jot down notes.

Report / Your Findings

Think About It

Review your research. Based on the information you have gathered, did the settlers' relationship with American Indians ultimately help or hurt the Jamestown Colony?

Write About It

Take a Stand

Write and Cite Evidence Defend your idea by identifying at least three examples from Jamestown's history that indicate whether the relationship with American Indians helped or harmed the Jamestown settlement. Use evidence from the text to support your opinion.

<u>Students should clearly state their opinion on the topic of Jamestown-Powhatan relations and support it using examples from the text.</u>

Talk About It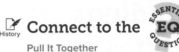

Defend Your Claim

Choose a partner who disagrees with you about the relationship between the Powhatan and the settlers. Work together to outline your difference of opinion. Did your partner's claim change your thinking about your own claim?

Connect to the ESSENTIAL QUESTION

Pull It Together

Think about the changing relationship between the English settlers and the Powhatan people. How might this relationship have shaped future interaction between English colonists and American Indians?

<u>Students should put forth an opinion and support it. Answers could include: "The hostility between both groups led to distrust and later conflicts throughout much of American history."</u>

Inquiry Project Notes

Inquiry Journal, pp. 88–89

EL ENGLISH LEARNERS SCAFFOLD

ELD.PI.5.3 Offering and supporting opinions and negotiating with others in communicative exchanges

Emerging	Expanding	Bridging
State an Opinion Make sure students are expressing their opinions using phrases like *I think* or *I believe*. Suggest additional phrases, such as *In my opinion* or *It seems to me that.*	**Support an Opinion** Provide statements to help students agree or disagree with their partners. *I agree that _____, but I think _____. I disagree with you opinion that _____ because _____.*	**Summarize an Opinion** Check on students by asking them to summarize both their own and their partner's opinions. They should be able to point out the similarities and the differences.

See the **Language Learner Teaching Guide** for more language support strategies.

Monitor and Differentiate

REACHING ALL LEARNERS

Approaching Level

Have students write a short summary of what they learned in this lesson. Ask them to focus on information that was new to them or that changed their perspective on history.

On Level

Have students compare and contrast Jamestown with some of the other settlements they have learned about. How are they similar and different in terms of purpose, relationship with American Indians, and degree of success?

Beyond Level

Have students do further research on a person they learned about this lesson. Ask them to write a short biography of that person that describes their influence on history.

Know what your students know!

Lesson Task
Report Your Findings

Use this rubric to evaluate students' response.

Take a Stand Did the settlers' relationship with American Indians ultimately help or hurt the Jamestown Colony? Make sure students provide three examples to support their opinion.

Defend Your Claim Students should find a partner who disagrees with them and attempt to persuade them to change their mind.

Lesson Task Evaluation Rubric

	4	3	2	1
Historical Understanding	Strong understanding of the relationship between the colonists and the Powhatan	Adequate understanding of the relationship between the colonists and the Powhatan	Uneven understanding of the relationship between the colonists and the Powhatan	No understanding of the relationship between the colonists and the Powhatan
Take a Stand	Clearly states opinion	Adequately states opinion	Somewhat clear or unclear opinion	No opinion or student does not show understanding of the task
Support with Evidence	Reasons contain thorough and connecting evidence	Reasons contain adequate evidence	Reasons contain uneven of only somewhat convincing evidence	Reasons are missing or contain no supporting evidence
Defend Your Claim	Speaks clearly and at an understandable pace Provides a concluding statement that relates to the speaker's position	Speaks clearly during most of the presentation Provides a concluding statement that mostly relates to the speaker's position	At times speaker is unclear Loosely links reasons to the speaker's opinion	Does not use complete sentences Does not link reasons to speaker's opinion

Lesson Assessment

Go Digital!

- Have students complete the Chapter 3 Lesson 1 Assessment online to monitor their understanding of the lesson content.

California Smarter Balanced Assessment Connections!

Standards Covered	Lesson Task	Lesson Assessment	Alignment with California Smarter Balanced Assessment
History Social Science Content 5.3.1; 5.3.2; 5.3.3	✔	✔	Claim 1 Targets 2, 4
History Social Science Analysis Skills Chronological and Spatial Thinking 5.3 Research, Evidence, and Point of View 5.2 Historical Interpretation 5.3; 5.4	✔	✔	Claim 1 Targets 8, 11
Writing W.5.1; W.5.4	✔		Claim 2 Targets 6a, 7
Research and Inquiry W.5.7; W.5.9.b	✔		Claim 4 Targets 1, 3, 4,
Reading RI.5.3; RI.5.9	✔	✔	Claim 1 Targets 9, 11, 12
Speaking and Listening SL.5.1; SL.5.2; SL.5.4a	✔		Claim 3 Targets 3, 4

How and Why Did Early European Settlers Compete with One Another and American Indians?

Background Information

In this lesson, students will learn about the colonization of North America by other European countries—specifically, Spain and France. Students will discover the different approaches and results of these countries' colonization efforts.

Community Connections

To enrich what students have learned about colonization, encourage students to look around their community for examples of French or Spanish influence and to research the historical background of these examples.

 LESSON OBJECTIVES

✔ Explain the aims, obstacles, and accomplishments of the explorers, sponsors, and leaders of key European expeditions and the reasons Europeans chose to explore and colonize the world (e.g., the Spanish Reconquista, the Protestant Reformation, the Counter Reformation). **HSS.5.2.2**

✔ Describe the competition among the English, French, Spanish, Dutch, and Indian nations for control of North America. **HSS.5.3.1**

✔ Describe the cooperation that existed between the colonists and Indians during the 1600s and 1700s (e.g., in agriculture, the fur trade, military alliances, treaties, cultural interchanges). **HSS.5.3.2**

✔ Examine the conflicts before the Revolutionary War (e.g., the Pequot and King Philip's Wars in New England, the Powhatan Wars in Virginia, the French and Indian War). **HSS.5.3.3**

✔ Describe the internecine Indian conflicts, including the competing claims for control of lands (e.g., actions of the Iroquois, Huron, Lakota [Sioux]). **HSS.5.3.5**

✔ Explain the influence and achievements of significant leaders of the time (e.g., John Marshall, Andrew Jackson, Chief Tecumseh, Chief Logan, Chief John Ross, Sequoyah). **HSS.5.3.6**

✔ Describe the introduction of slavery into America, the responses of slave families to their condition, the ongoing struggle between proponents and opponents of slavery, and the gradual institutionalization of slavery in the South. **HSS.5.4.6**

 Connect to the
Essential Question

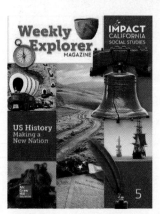

The **Weekly Explorer Magazine** supports students' exploration of the Essential Question and provides additional resources for the EQ Inquiry Project.

Chapter 3, pp. 30–43

 ## Inquiry Project

How have European settlements shaped modern America?

Remind students to use the information they learn in this lesson and other resources to complete their EQ Inquiry Project!

Dinah Zike's

In this lesson you will use Foldables.

When Minutes Count!

Suggested Lesson Pacing

1 ENGAGE
One Day

2 INVESTIGATE
Two to Three Days

🕐 **Short on Time?** Look for the clock to teach core content in less time.

3 REPORT
One Day

- Lesson Opener
- Analyze the Source
- Inquiry Tools

Go Digital
- iMap: The New England Colonies

- Competition Among European Nations
- French Trappers and Traders
- New Alliances, New Conflict
- Around the World

- Think About It
- Write a Story
- Compare Your Accounts

Make Connections!

ⒸⒸⓈⓈ CONNECT TO ELA

Reading
Explain the relationships or interactions between two or more individuals, events, ideas, or concepts in a historical, scientific, or technical text based on specific information in the text. **RI.5.3**

Research
Conduct short research projects that use several sources to build knowledge through investigation of different aspects of a topic. **W.5.7**

Writing
Write narratives to develop real or imagined experiences or events using effective technique, descriptive details, and clear event sequences. **W.5.3**

Speaking and Listening
Engage effectively in a range of collaborative discussion (one-on-one, in groups, and teacher-led) with diverse partners on *grade 5 topics and texts,* building on others' ideas and expressing their own clearly. **SL.5.1**

Classroom Resources
🔍 Search for additional resources using the following key words.

criollos

drainage basin

encomiendas

felt

hydrographer

mestizos

peninsulares

tributaries

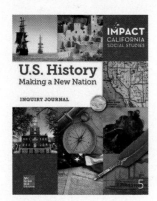

Inquiry Journal
pp. 90–91

 STANDARDS

Describe the competition among the English, French, Spanish, Dutch, and Indian nations for control of North America. **HSS.5.3.1**

Students pose relevant questions about events they encounter in historical documents, eyewitness accounts, oral histories, letters, diaries, artifacts, photographs, maps, artworks, and architecture. **HAS.HR.2**

Go Digital!

Explore the lesson content with online whole-class presentation tools.

- **iMap:** The New England Colonies

How and Why Did Early European Settlers Compete with One Another and American Indians?

Bellringer

Prompt students to retrieve information from the previous lessons. Say: *Aside from the search for a Northwest passage, what other reasons were there to colonize North America?* (Students may give answers such as *searching for freedom* or *desire for land*. Direct their attention to answers focusing on the acquisition of natural resources.)

Lesson Outcomes

What Am I Learning? Have students read the Lesson Question and Lesson Outcomes on p. 90.

Why Am I Learning It? Point out to students that resources are limited. Throughout history, conflict and cooperation have been driven by the desire to fulfill the needs and desires of nations. Prompt students to list things a country needs to thrive.

How Will I know That I Learned It? Ask students the following questions.

- What will you identify? (the strategies used by people, both American Indian and European settlers who occupy North America, in the search for resources)

- What is the purpose of the task? (to identify main ideas and key details)

- How will you support your understanding? (with evidence from the text)

Talk About It

- Have students read and answer the prompt. Ask them further questions such as *Which group is attacking and which is defending? Who is winning?* Provide sentence frames:

- *I know the _____ are _____ because _____.*

- *The person in the top/bottom right/left is _____ which shows that _____.*

Collaborative Conversations

Look at the Details Have students practice sharing details by describing pictures. This can be made into a game.

- Have a student choose a person in the picture and identify them to others by describing their actions, physical appearance, and location in reference to other figures or elements of the picture. The goal is to get the class to correctly identify the figure in the fewest sentences.

- Have a student choose a figure. Other students will guess the identity by asking yes-or-no questions.

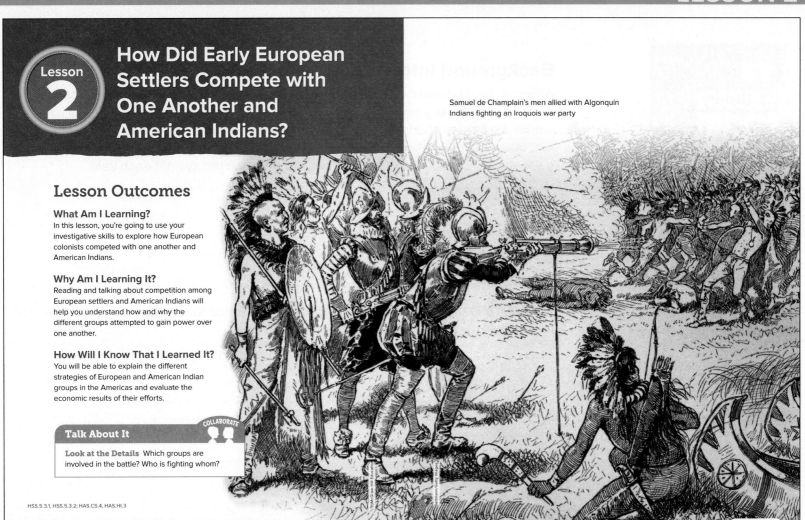

Lesson 2
How Did Early European Settlers Compete with One Another and American Indians?

Samuel de Champlain's men allied with Algonquin Indians fighting an Iroquois war party

Lesson Outcomes

What Am I Learning?
In this lesson, you're going to use your investigative skills to explore how European colonists competed with one another and American Indians.

Why Am I Learning It?
Reading and talking about competition among European settlers and American Indians will help you understand how and why the different groups attempted to gain power over one another.

How Will I Know That I Learned It?
You will be able to explain the different strategies of European and American Indian groups in the Americas and evaluate the economic results of their efforts.

Talk About It COLLABORATE

Look at the Details Which groups are involved in the battle? Who is fighting whom?

HSS.5.3.1, HSS.5.3.2; HAS.CS.4, HAS.HI.3

90 Lesson 2 How Did Early European Settlers Compete with One Another and American Indians?

Lesson 2 **91**

Inquiry Journal, pp. 90–91

 ENGLISH LEARNERS SCAFFOLD

ELD.PII.5.5 Modifying to add details

Emerging	Bridging
Use Prepositions Encourage students to use prepositions when describing a picture. Provide examples such as *above, below, next to, to the right/left of,* and so on. Demonstrate their use if needed.	**Use Modifiers** Have students combine multiple prepositions and adjectives to describe a figure in a picture with more detail. *Look at the (adjective) person in the top/bottom left/right of the picture (preposition) (noun).*

See the **Language Learner Teaching Guide** for more language support strategies.

Monitor and Differentiate

REACHING ALL LEARNERS

Approaching Level

Remind students that this lesson will mostly focus on Spanish and French colonization. Ask students: Do you think they will be more or less successful than the English?

On Level

Ask students to think back to the previous chapter about the Age of Exploration. Discuss what the explorers found that made them decide to start colonizing.

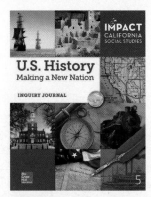

Inquiry Journal
pp. 92–93

 STANDARDS

Identify the major individuals and groups responsible for the founding of the various colonies and the reasons for their founding (e.g., John Smith, Virginia; Roger Williams, Rhode Island; William Penn, Pennsylvania; Lord Baltimore, Maryland; William Bradford, Plymouth; John Winthrop, Massachusetts). **HSS.5.4.2**

Students judge the significance of the relative location of a place (e.g., proximity to a harbor, on trade routes) and analyze how relative advantages or disadvantages can change over time. **HAS.CS.5**

CCSS Include multimedia components (e.g., graphics, sound) and visual displays in presentation when appropriate to enhance the development of main ideas or themes. **CCSS.ELA.SL.5.5**

Go *Digital!*

Model how to inspect and find evidence with online whole-class presentation tools.

Background Information

Although the St. Lawrence River did not become the Northwest Passage, as hoped by explorers, it was a route into the heart of the North American continent. Furs, lumber, and other goods could be moved with considerable speed to the East Coast and taken to Europe. Today, it remains one of the most heavily used international trade routes: 35–40 million tons of cargo go through the system each year.

1 Inspect

Read Have students read the text.

- Who was one of the early explorers of the St. Lawrence River and when did he explore it? (Samuel de Champlain, 1603)

- How do we know about what Champlain encountered? (He published a report about his travels.)

- What did the French use the river for? (to transport furs and other goods)

- To where does the St. Lawrence River flow? (from the Great Lakes to the Atlantic Ocean)

2 Find Evidence

Reread Have students reread the text.

Analyze the Source After students have reread the text, ask them to closely study the picture on p. 93.

- Which paragraph of the text would this picture best be paired with? What pictures would be appropriate for the other paragraphs? (The third paragraph, since it covers traveling the river and encountering American Indians. Possible pairs for the first and second paragraphs could be a map and a portrait of Champlain, respectively.)

3 Make Connections

COLLABORATE

Talk Encourage students to think about whether American Indians likely benefitted or suffered as a result of the Saint Lawrence trade network. Engage in a class discussion on this topic, using a graphic organizer drawn on the board to keep track of supporting details given by students. (Answers will vary, but students may identify that American Indians probably benefitted from trade relations with Europe.)

Have students describe, in detail, what they see in the picture. Who is in it, what are they wearing, what kind of boat and equipment can be seen, etc.

Analyze the Source

(0)McGraw-Hill Education, (b)Library and Archives Canada/George Agnew Reid fonds/c010015k

1 Inspect

Read Look at the title. What do you think this text will be about?

- **Circle** words you don't know.
- **Underline** clues that help answer these questions:
  - Where is the Saint Lawrence River?
  - Who used the river?
  - Why was it important?

My Notes

_____
_____
_____
_____
_____
_____
_____
_____
_____
_____
_____
_____
_____
_____
_____
_____

The Saint Lawrence: At the Heart of New France

The Saint Lawrence River connects the Great Lakes to the Atlantic Ocean. French explorers hoped that the Saint Lawrence could take them all the way across North America. The river did not do so. However, it did supply a route for trade and exploration of Canada and what is now the northern United States.

Samuel de Champlain was one of the first Europeans to sail the river in 1603. At the time, he called it the River of Canada. Champlain published a report of his travels in France. Champlain's writings inspired more support for the exploration of the Saint Lawrence. In 1608, Champlain and a group of colonists settled along the river, naming the region Quebec.

The colony of New France used this lengthy waterway to transport furs and other trade goods. From trading posts as far inland as Chicago and Detroit, the colonists could easily move goods to and across the Atlantic Ocean. Since people tend to live close to water, the Saint Lawrence also allowed the French to establish relationships with many of the American Indian groups of the region. This Saint Lawrence trade network played a major role in the economy of New France.

Samuel de Champlain arrives at the site of Quebec City along the Saint Lawrence River.

2 Find Evidence

Reread List three reasons why the Saint Lawrence River was important to New France.

Underline the names of places connected by the Saint Lawrence River.

3 Make Connections

Talk Do you think American Indians likely benefited or suffered as a result of the Saint Lawrence trade network?

How does the picture help you understand how French sailors navigated the Saint Lawrence?

92 Lesson 2 How Did Early European Settlers Compete with One Another and American Indians?

Lesson 2 93

Inquiry Journal, pp. 92–93

ENGLISH LEARNERS SCAFFOLD

ELD.PII.5.6 Connecting ideas

Emerging

Understand Cause and Effect Provide sentence frames to help students talk about the effect of the Saint Lawrence trade network. _The Saint Lawrence trade network was beneficial/harmful because _____._

Expanding/Bridging

Use Cause and Effect Encourage students make more complex sentences. For example, _The Saint Lawrence River allowed the French/ the American Indians to _____, which was beneficial because _____._

See the **Language Learner Teaching Guide** for more language support strategies.

Monitor and Differentiate

REACHING ALL LEARNERS

Special Needs

Explain to students that this lesson will have several names and phrases in Spanish and French. Pronunciation for these languages can be quite different from American English. Have each student make a Pronunciation Journal. It will be a two-column graphic organizer, with one column to list words and the next to contain instructions for pronunciation, such as phonetic spellings or words that rhyme.

On Level

Print out copies of phonetic characters for American English. Explain the symbols and how they are said. Show the students that these symbols can be found in dictionaries and encyclopedias to show how a word is pronounced.

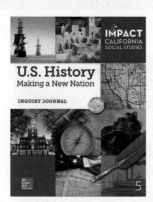

Inquiry Journal
pp. 94–95

Explain the aims, obstacles, and accomplishments of the explorers, sponsors, and leaders of key European expeditions and the reasons Europeans chose to explore and colonize the world (e.g., the Spanish Reconquista, the Protestant Reformation, the Counter Reformation). **HSS.5.2.2**

Students summarize the key events of the era they are studying and explain the historical contexts of those events. **HAS.HI.1**

CCSS Determine two or more main ideas of a text and explain how they are supported by key details; summarize the text. **CCSS.ELA.RI.5.2**

Draw evidence from literary or informational texts to support analysis, reflection, and research. **CCSS.ELA.W.5.9**

Go *Digital!*

- Model how to explore and investigate with online whole-class tools.

- Students can access the online graphic organizer to use the inquiry tools as they read.

Explore Main Idea and Details

Explain Tell students that the main idea is the primary point of the text. To express a main idea is the reason the author writes. A good writer supports the main idea with details to help the reader understand the topic.

Read Have students read the step-by-step instructions on identifying the main idea and details. Explain that a good writer will stay focused on the main idea and not wander too far from it.

Guided Practice Explain that newspapers usually use the main idea as the headline of articles. Read a short newspaper article to students without showing them the headline. Ask students to guess what the headline is. Next, read another headline. Ask them what questions they would like to have answered after hearing that headline. The answers to those questions would be key details.

Investigate!

Have students read pages 110–121 in the Research Companion. Tell them the information will help them answer the lesson question *How and Why Did Early European Settlers Compete With One Another and American Indians?*

Take Notes Tell students that they should take notes on the main reasons the European nations wanted to colonize the New World in the graphic organizer on page 95 of their Inquiry Journal. They should then add some key details for each main idea.

Inspect Guide students to read the text in each section to determine what the text says about European colonization. Encourage them to make note of words they don't understand and to look for answers to questions, such as *who? what? when? where? why?* and *how?*

Find Evidence Encourage students to reread the text to find key details they may have missed. Also encourage them to look over the details they have to make sure they are integral to meaning. If any detail can be omitted without significantly affecting the student's understanding, then it may not be a key detail.

Collaborative Conversations

Text-Based Discussion Remind students that, in discussing the text with the class, they should

- Avoid whispering or making distracting movements while another student is speaking

- Raise their hand and speak in a clear and loud voice

- Consider what every student has to say, even if they disagree

Inquiry Tools

Explore Main Ideas and Details

The author's point is the **main idea** of a text. This is what the author wants readers to understand. He or she supports the main idea with **details**. Sometimes a text has more than one main idea. Details are facts and evidence about the topic.

To understand main ideas and details:

1. Read the text all the way through.
This will help you understand what the text is about.

2. Look at section titles.
These can be clues to how the text is organized and can help you understand what each section is mostly about.

3. Reread the first and last paragraphs in each section.
These paragraphs may state the main idea or give you clues about what the main idea is.

4. Identify key details.
Look for important information, facts, or evidence that seem to support the main idea.

 Based on the text you just read, work with your class to complete the chart below.

Main Idea	Details
The Saint Lawrence River played a major role in the development of New France.	The river helped traders move goods to the ocean; it made exploration of North America easier; it helped colonists build good relations with American Indians.

Investigate!

Read pages 110–121 in your Research Companion. Use your investigative skills to look for text evidence that tells you about the goals or motivations of the European nations for colonizing the New World. This chart will help you organize your notes.

Main Idea	Details
The Spanish wanted to enrich their empire by mining silver and gold.	"Spanish settlers quickly learned to use the many resources of their new colony."
The Spanish wanted to convert American Indians to Catholicism.	". . . Spain's relationship with the American Indians was based on conquest. The Spanish also wanted to convert all native peoples to Catholicism."
The French wanted to enrich their empire through trapping animals and trading furs.	"The money raised through the fur trade helped pay for more expeditions into North America."
The French wanted to expand their control in North America by settling in Louisiana and Mississippi.	"Successful plantations brought in more money from trade with American Indians, which allowed the farmers to increase the size of the plantations."

McGraw-Hill Education

Inquiry Journal, pp. 94–95

(EL) ENGLISH LEARNERS SCAFFOLD

ELD.PI.5.5 Listening actively to spoken English in a range of social and academic contexts

Emerging

Participate in Discussion Observe students while others are talking. Ensure they are being polite and paying attention. Ask students questions about what the speaker said to check comprehension.

Expanding

Ask and Answer Questions Encourage students to ask questions or offer counterarguments to the speaker once they are finished.

See the **Language Learner Teaching Guide** for more language support strategies.

Monitor and Differentiate

REACHING ALL LEARNERS

Special Needs

Have the class work in groups. Hand out one blank web graphic organizer to each group. Also give each group some cards. One will have a main idea written on it, and the others will have key details. Ask students to arrange the cards on the web GO correctly.

Beyond Level

Have students imagine they are journalists in New France. Have them write a short news article on some event in the text, such as giving up on finding the Northwest Passage or the founding of Quebec. Remind students to have the main idea in the headline and to organize the paragraphs around the key details. Encourage students to do extra research to find more details.

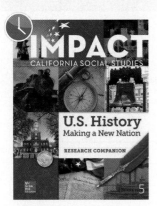

Research Companion
pp. 110–111

 STANDARDS

Explain the aims, obstacles, and accomplishments of the explorers, sponsors, and leaders of key European expeditions and the reasons Europeans chose to explore and colonize the world (e.g., the Spanish Reconquista, the Protestant Reformation, the Counter Reformation). **HSS.5.2.2**

Students place key events and people of the historical era they are studying in a chronological sequence and within a spatial context; they interpret time lines. **HAS.CS.1**

(ccss) Analyze multiple accounts of the same event or topic, noting important similarities and differences in the point of view they represent. **CCSS.ELA.RI.5.5**

Go Digital!

Investigate the lesson content with online whole-class presentation tools.

- **iMap:** The New England Colonies

Background Information

England, Spain, and France were primary colonizers of North America. Italy had been dominant for centuries thanks to their position in the Mediterranean sea; they had become gatekeeper from Europe to Asia and Africa. Many of the early explorers of North America were Italian, such as Christopher Columbus and John Cabot. However, with the development of long-distance ships, the discovery of a sea route around Africa, and the discovery of the New World, trade was no longer confined to the Mediterranean. The peninsular countries of western Europe became the best suited for exploration and trade.

| TIMELINE | Invite students to look at the timeline at the top of p. 111.

Analyze According to the timeline, who founded a city? (Samuel de Champlain and Jean-Baptiste Le Moyne de Bienville each founded a city.) **HAS.CS.1 DOK 1**

Analyze the Source

Inspect Have students read pages 110–111. Use the questions below to check comprehension.

Identify What were the goals of Spain, France, and England? (wealth through land and trade, spreading religion) **DOK 1**

Compare and Contrast How do Spain and France differ from England? (they spread Catholicism; colonies governed by people selected by monarchy) **DOK 1**

Draw Conclusions How does the timeline support the assertion that these European countries desired wealth? (The timeline mentions Spain finding silver.) **DOK 2**

Make Connections

Speculate How do you think Spain, France, and England viewed one another? (Answers will vary. They were competitors, but had some common goals, and they could learn from each other.) **DOK 3**

Analyze the Painting Direct students' attention to the early map of Quebec City. Encourage students to use images to help them understand the text.

- Describe what you see in the image. (Students should note that ships, the river, and the buildings indicate a large, thriving settlement.)

- What does the picture tell you about the St. Lawrence River? (Students should note that the city of Quebec is on the river and can be reached by ship.)

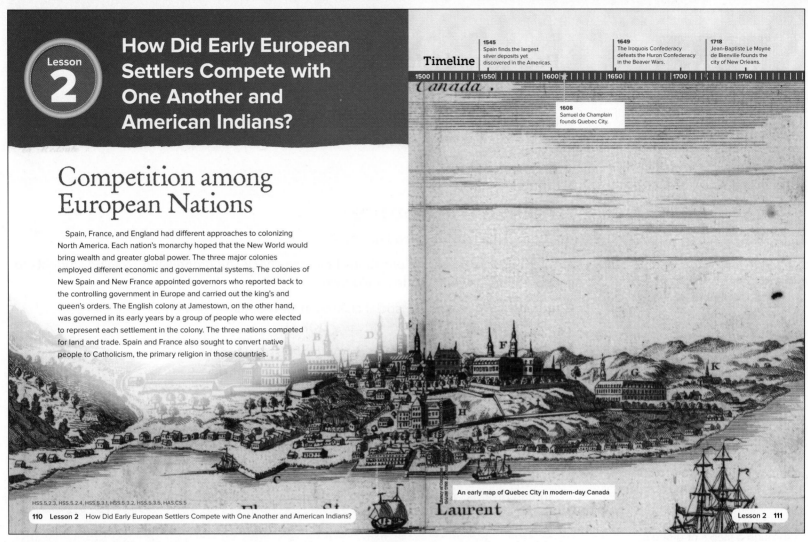

Lesson 2

How Did Early European Settlers Compete with One Another and American Indians?

Competition among European Nations

Spain, France, and England had different approaches to colonizing North America. Each nation's monarchy hoped that the New World would bring wealth and greater global power. The three major colonies employed different economic and governmental systems. The colonies of New Spain and New France appointed governors who reported back to the controlling government in Europe and carried out the king's and queen's orders. The English colony at Jamestown, on the other hand, was governed in its early years by a group of people who were elected to represent each settlement in the colony. The three nations competed for land and trade. Spain and France also sought to convert native people to Catholicism, the primary religion in those countries.

Timeline

1545 Spain finds the largest silver deposits yet discovered in the Americas.

1608 Samuel de Champlain founds Quebec City.

1649 The Iroquois Confederacy defeats the Huron Confederacy in the Beaver Wars.

1718 Jean-Baptiste Le Moyne de Bienville founds the city of New Orleans.

1500 1550 1600 1650 1700 1750

An early map of Quebec City in modern-day Canada

HSS.5.2.3, HSS.5.2.4, HSS.5.3.1, HSS.5.3.2, HSS.5.3.5, HAS.CS.5

110 Lesson 2 How Did Early European Settlers Compete with One Another and American Indians?

Lesson 2 **111**

Research Companion, pp. 110–111

ENGLISH LEARNERS SCAFFOLD

ELD.PI.5.5 Listening actively to spoken English in a range of social and academic contexts

Emerging	Expanding	Bridging
Describe Have students write sentences to describe the timeline using prepositions such as *before* and *after*.	**Use Chronology** Have students write sentences to describe the timeline using phrases like *In _____* or *_____ years later, . . .*	**Analyze Chronology** Have students write a short paragraph describing the timeline.

See the **Language Learner Teaching Guide** for more language support strategies.

Monitor and Differentiate

REACHING ALL LEARNERS

Approaching Level

Have students recall the problems of Jamestown. If they were Jamestown colonists, what advice might they give to Spain or France?

On Level

Tell students they have been appointed governors for a small settlement for New Spain or New France. They need twenty people to go with them. Ask who they will bring (how many farmers, how many doctors, and so on.). Have them write a short classified ad explaining who they need and why.

Beyond Level

Ask students: *Is colonialism good or bad?* Have students write a short paragraph describing their opinion.

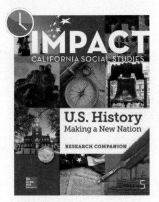

Research Companion
pp. 112–113

HSS STANDARDS

Describe the introduction of slavery into America, the responses of slave families to their condition, the ongoing struggle between proponents and opponents of slavery, and the gradual institutionalization of slavery in the South. **HSS.5.4.6**

Students use map and globe skills to determine the absolute locations of places and interpret information available through a map's or globe's legend, scale, and symbolic representations. **HAS.CS.4**

CCSS Determine the meaning of general academic and domain-specific words and phrases in a text relevant to a *grade 5 topic or subject area.* **CCSS.ELA.RI.5.4**

Go *Digital!*

Investigate the lesson content with online whole-class presentation tools.

Background Information

Spain's reputation for cruelty in colonial America is not entirely deserved. The *encomiendas* were disastrous in terms of human rights, but the Spanish government intended for them to protect the American Indian groups. These intentions, however, often did not reach the governors in the New World.

Analyze the Source

Inspect Have students read pp. 112–113.

Find Evidence Use the questions below to check comprehension. Remind students to support their answers with text evidence.

> **Identify** What were the social classes in New Spain? (Peninsulares, Criollos, Mestizos, and American Indians and Africans) **DOK 1**
>
> **Infer** Why were Peninsulares on top of the social order? (They were "purest" since they were Spanish born in Spain.) **DOK 2**
>
> **Draw Conclusions** How did the social structure of the Spanish colonies influence race relations for future societies in North America? (The social hierarchy was based on race and on slavery, which endured and had lasting effects on later centuries.) **DOK 3**

Make Connections

> **Recall** Have students look over previous chapters and their notes on American Indian groups. Which groups did New Spain interact with? New France? The English colonies? (New Spain would have interacted with the Mexican and Southwest American groups, such as the Aztec, Pueblo, and Navajo. New France would have dealt with Plains Indians, such as the Lakota and Pawnee. The English colonists would have encountered Eastern Woodlands Indians, such as Penobscot and Creek.) **DOK 3**

ⓥ Map Skills

Project a large version of the map on p. 113, or ask students to follow along with the map in their Research Companion. Use the following questions to guide the students' understanding.

- Which country controls the green portion? The red? The orange? (France, England, Spain.)

- What is the population of each colony? (New France: 15,000. The Thirteen Colonies: 250,000. New Spain: 5–7 million.)

- Which colony had the smallest population per square mile? (New France)

Explain to the students that population density is the number of people in a given amount of space. In this map, the Thirteen Colonies had the highest density because the population was high even though the territory was small.

☑ Stop and Check

Think Guide students to discuss how New Spain treated American Indians. (Responses will vary, but make sure students support their answer with evidence from the text.)

Find Details Explain to students that after they read and take notes, they should review and think about how the facts and details will help them answer the Essential Question.

Spain established territories in South America, the Caribbean, Central America and Mexico, as well as the southern and western United States. Spanish settlers quickly learned to use the resources of their new colony to increase the wealth of Spain. The Spanish did not want land in the Americas to be taken by the French or the English. So, to further expand, Spanish rulers offered large portions of land to those willing to move to New Spain. These areas, called **encomiendas**, included any American Indian villages on the land. The American Indians living in an encomienda were forced to work for its owner in exchange for housing and food.

While the early English relationship with the Powhatan in the Jamestown colony involved some instances of cooperation, Spain's relationship with the American Indians was based on conquest. The Spanish also wanted to convert all native peoples to Catholicism.

New Spain's wealth and power came in part from its gold and silver mines. Spanish settlers also built ranches and sugar cane plantations. Many of the workers in the mines and on the plantations were American Indians. Disease, mistreatment, and dangerous working conditions resulted in the deaths of 24 million American Indians in just one hundred years. To replace the shrinking workforce, the Spanish brought slaves to New Spain. By 1570, more than 200,000 Africans were enslaved on the plantations of New Spain.

One Spanish colonist named Bartolomé de Las Casas was so upset at how colonists were treating American Indians that he decided to help them. He became a **missionary**, or a person who teaches his or her religious beliefs to people with different beliefs.

Eventually, many more missionaries from Spain came to the Americas to teach the native peoples about Catholicism. But rather than helping the native peoples, the Spanish missionaries forced them to work and give up their own religion. These native peoples and Spanish missionaries lived in settlements called missions. As Spain began claiming the West Coast, these missions became part of their strategy to prevent Russia and England from settling land in present-day California.

A mission was a common type of settlement in New Spain.

North America in 1700

British lands
French lands
Spanish lands
Disputed or unclaimed by Europeans

NEW FRANCE

Population 15,000

LOUISIANA

THE THIRTEEN COLONIES

Population 250,000

NEW SPAIN

FLORIDA

ATLANTIC OCEAN

Population 5–7 million

Gulf of Mexico

West Indies

PACIFIC OCEAN

Caribbean Sea

⦿ Map Skills Compare each colony's population with its approximate size. Which colony had the smallest population per square mile?

✓ **Stop and Check**

Think How did New Spain treat American Indians?

Find Details As you read, add new information to the graphic organizer on page 95 in your Inquiry Journal.

112 Lesson 2 How Did Early European Settlers Compete with One Another and American Indians?

Lesson 2 113

Research Companion, pp. 112–113

(EL) ENGLISH LEARNERS SCAFFOLD

ELD.PII.5.5 Modifying to add details.

Emerging	Expanding	Bridging
Identify Adjectives Explain comparative adjectives to students: by adding *–er* or *more* to an adjective, it can be used to compare things. Have students look for examples of adjectives in the text of the Research Companion. Then, ask them to correctly make the comparative forms of the adjectives.	**Use Adjectives** Have students compare rural and urban areas using comparative adjectives. Have each student make five sentences with comparisons.	**Use Adjectives** Ask students to explain, verbally, whether they prefer to live in the country or the city using comparative adjectives.

See the **Language Learner Teaching Guide** for more language support strategies.

Monitor and Differentiate

REACHING ALL LEARNERS

Approaching Level

Explain to students that cities have high population density and rural areas have low population density. Ask students which they prefer and why.

On Level

As a class, have students consider and discuss the strengths and weakness of areas with high population density and low population density.

Beyond Level

Have students search the internet to find population density maps for the state of their choice. Have students analyze the maps and explain why some areas are higher density than others.

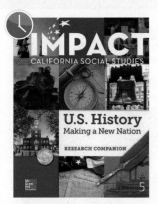

 IMPACT
CALIFORNIA SOCIAL STUDIES

U.S. History
Making a New Nation

RESEARCH COMPANION

5

Research Companion
pp. 114–115

(HSS) **STANDARDS**

Describe the cooperation that existed between the colonists and Indians during the 1600s and 1700s (e.g., in agriculture, the fur trade, military alliances, treaties, cultural interchanges). **HSS.5.3.2**

Students differentiate between primary and secondary sources. **HAS.HR.1**

(CCSS) Analyze multiple accounts of the same event or topic, noting important similarities and differences in the point of view they represent. **CCSS.ELA.RI.5.6**

___

Go Digital!

Investigate the lesson content with online whole-class presentation tools.

Background Information

While Spain was extremely controlling of its territory, New France used a light touch. In many ways, the region didn't really stop being American Indian territory. The French population was never very high, and they "controlled" the region through alliances. The French didn't need workers and religious conversion wasn't very profitable. There was little need for conquest, so the relationship between the French and the American Indians was generally amicable.

Analyze the Source

Inspect Have students read pp. 114–115.

Find Evidence Use the questions below to check comprehension. Remind students to support their answers with text evidence.

> **Infer** Why did Champlain learn to speak Huron? (To improve relations with the Huron people.) **DOK 2**
>
> **Analyze** How does control of the Mississippi River benefit New France? (gives them access to New Spain's territory, which could be useful if the two countries fight) **DOK 3**
>
> **Analyze** Why would a study of waterways be important to the French? (They shipped goods by river, so needed to know how to navigate waterways.) **DOK 3**

Analyze the Primary Source Have students reread the Primary Source from Samuel de Champlain.

> **Analyze** What is the main idea of the passage? (There is a lot of wildlife there.) **DOK 3**
>
> **Analyze** Why would or wouldn't he be interested in this place? (There are plenty of animals to hunt, though he makes no mention of beaver, which is most desirable.) **DOK 2**

Make Connections Compare and contrast the canoes, pictured on p. 115, to the other ships shown previously in this chapter. Why are canoes advantageous for life in New France? (They were easy to carry over land, but sturdy enough to travel on the ocean or rivers.)

 COLLABORATE

☑ Stop and Check

Talk Have students read and answer the prompt. Then ask them to give their opinion as to whether Champlain was right to act as he did. (Responses will vary, but students should support their opinion with reasons and evidence.)

French Trappers and Traders

When French settlers began to colonize North America, they were interested in finding gold and a route to Asia. Their settlements along the St. Lawrence River in Canada would not help them with either of those goals. What Canada did offer was many fur-bearing animals. The forests of Europe had been overhunted, but Europeans still desired hats made from beaver fur. To meet European demand, French settlers began to export beaver pelts across the Atlantic. The money raised through the fur trade helped pay for more expeditions into North America.

As French explorers continued to explore Canada, the king of France wanted to organize the colony to ensure it made money. He chose Samuel de Champlain (sham PLAYN) to lead New France. In 1604, Champlain sailed to New France as its first governor. Champlain's strategy in North America differed greatly from that of the Spanish conquistadors. He felt that building friendly relationships with groups of American Indians would lead to successful trade. He believed these alliances would allow him to travel freely and keep the French settlements safe from attack. Within his first year in New France, Champlain learned to speak the Huron language. New France and the nearby Huron and Algonquin groups traded with each other and maintained friendly relations.

PRIMARY SOURCE

In Their Words... Samuel de Champlain

We departed on the following day, pursuing our way up the river as far as the entrance to the lake. In it are many beautiful low islands covered with very fine woods and meadows with much wild fowl and animals to hunt, such as stags, fallow deer, fawns, roebucks, bears, and other kinds of animals which come from the mainland to these islands.

—from a diary entry of Samuel de Champlain, 1609

114 **Lesson 2** How Did Early European Settlers Compete with One Another and American Indians?

Marquette and Jolliet

French explorers' efforts to find the Northwest Passage led them to further explore North America's waterways. In 1673, Jacques Marquette and Louis Jolliet headed south in a canoe on the uncharted Mississippi River. They encountered many groups of American Indians living on the banks of the Mississippi. While some American Indians were hostile, the Illinois and other groups helped Marquette and Jolliet.

Marquette and Jolliet claimed the land drained by the Mississippi River for France. Marquette later set up a mission in present-day Illinois, and Jolliet continued to explore North America.

La Salle and Louisiana

In 1682, René-Robert Cavelier Sieur de La Salle led an expedition down the Mississippi River. La Salle claimed the Mississippi and its tributaries, or smaller branching rivers and streams, for France. He named the region *Louisiana* after the French king, Louis XIV. La Salle wanted to build a fort at the mouth of the Mississippi and attack the Spanish in northern Mexico. La Salle and several hundred settlers, however, got lost and ended up in present-day Texas. By 1687, only 36 of La Salle's settlers remained alive.

Bark canoes were sturdy enough to withstand ocean waves and light enough to be carried.

✓ Stop and Check

COLLABORATE

Talk Why did Champlain develop friendly relationships with American Indians he encountered in New France?

Lesson 2 **115**

Research Companion, pp. 114–115

(EL) ENGLISH LEARNERS SCAFFOLD

ELD.PI.5.8 Analyzing how writers and speakers use vocabulary and other language resources for specific purposes (to explain, persuade, entertain, etc.) depending on modality, text type, purpose, audience, topic, and content area

Emerging	Expanding	Bridging
Identify Words Have students reread the Primary Source. Ask them to identify words related to wildlife.	**Analyze Words** Ask students what was Samuel de Champlain's purpose in writing the diary entry. Who was he writing for and what did he want them to think?	**Use Descriptive Words** Ask students to briefly describe a place they have been where they experienced wildlife. They should use vocabulary appropriate to the task and audience.

See the **Language Learner Teaching Guide** for more language support strategies.

Monitor and Differentiate

REACHING ALL LEARNERS

Approaching Level

Have students imagine that New France decided have elections for governor. Students should pretend to be Samule de Champlain, who needs to run for re-election. Guide students to write a short speech highlighting Champlain's accomplishments. Have students practice giving their speech with a partner.

Beyond Level

Have students research a figure from the lesson. Have them write three facts and one false fact about the person. Then, put the students in groups. Have each read their "facts" to the group. The group will attempt to identify the false fact.

Research Companion
pp. 116–117

 STANDARDS

Describe the competition among the English, French, Spanish, Dutch, and Indian nations for control of North America. **HSS.5.3.1**

Students identify the human and physical characteristics of the places they are studying and explain how those features form the unique character of those places. **HAS.HI.2**

CCSS Engage effectively in a range of collaborative discussion (one-on-one, in groups, and teacher-led) with diverse partners on *grade 5 topics and texts*, building on others' ideas and expressing their own clearly. **CCSS.ELA.SL.5.1**

Go Digital!

Investigate the lesson content with online whole-class presentation tools.

Background Information

New Orleans is a one-of-a-kind city that blends American, French, Spanish, African, and Caribbean influences in its history, architecture, music, food, and language—the Cajun dialect. This unique combination is the byproduct of its position as a port city that has attracted diverse groups of people and has changed hands numerous times over its history.

Analyze the Source

Inspect Have students read pp. 116-117.

Find Evidence Use the questions below to check comprehension. Remind students to support their answers with text evidence.

Identify What was New Orleans originally? (It was originally a group of forts meant to protect the Mouth of the Mississippi from Spain and England.) **DOK 1**

Infer Why do you think New Orleans, but not the rest of New France, engaged in slavery? (New Orleans was better for farming than the rest of New France; slavery was mostly used for farm labor.) **DOK 3**

Make Connections

Draw Conclusions Return to the map on p. 113. Notice that New France controls the St. Lawrence River and the Mississippi River. Which route did they most likely use to transport furs back to France? Why? (The St. Lawrence appears to be more direct and doesn't pass through as much Spanish and English territory, making it a safer choice.)

Analyze the Image Direct students to the image on p. 116.

• Describe the image. (Answers will vary, but students may point to the importance of ships in the image, the time period, and details such as the smaller ships moving transporting people in the harbor.)

• What does the image tell you about the port of New Orleans? (Students should note it is very busy and full of ships, underscoring the city's dependence on trade.)

Analyze the Primary Source Read aloud the primary source on p. 117.

Analyze What does d'Iberville say was the point of settling Louisiana? (to have a larger population and more control than England in North America) **DOK 3**

✓ Stop and Check COLLABORATE

Talk Have students explain why it was important that France built forts in Mississippi and Louisiana. As a follow-up, ask why diplomacy and alliances, as used with the American Indians, would have been less effective with the Spanish and English. (Answers may include that they wanted a permanent presence there, with land that was protected from the English and Spanish.)

New Orleans

French colonists slowly began to settle parts of the Louisiana Territory. They built forts in strategic locations to protect new settlements from the Spanish and English. Louis XIV instructed a Canadian naval officer, Pierre Le Moyne Sieur d'Iberville, to build forts at the mouth of the Mississippi. The series of forts he built in present-day Mississippi and Louisiana further established Louisiana as a French possession. One such fort, Fort La Boulaye, lay just south of the future site of the city of New Orleans. When he died of yellow fever, Iberville's younger brother, Jean-Baptiste Le Moyne Sieur de Bienville, continued his work.

FORT OF NEW ORLEANS.

Ships anchored at the Port of New Orleans, about 1800

Kean Collection/Archive Photos/Getty Images

PRIMARY SOURCE

In Their Words... Pierre Le Moyne Sieur d'Iberville

If France does not take possession of this part of America, which is the finest, to have a colony strong enough to resist those that England possesses... these colonies which are becoming very extensive, will increase to such an extent that in less than a century, they will be strong enough to seize upon the whole continent of America, and to expel all other nations.

—from *The Argument to Settle Louisiana*, 1698

TEXT: Pierre le Moyne Sieur d'Iberville, 1698. Quoted in Parliamentary Debates on the Subject of the Confederation of the British North American Provinces, 3rd Session, 8th Provincial Parliament of Canada (Quebec: Hunter, Rose & Company, parliamentary printers, 1865), 324.; PHOTO: ©McGraw-Hill Education; ©North Wind Picture Archives/Alamy

In 1701, Bienville became governor of Louisiana at the age of 21. He built Fort Louis on Mobile Bay and lived there until 1711. In 1718, Bienville founded New Orleans. The Louisiana Territory was much easier to farm than the rest of New France. Settlers built plantations on the fertile soil and grew indigo, rice, and tobacco. Successful plantations brought in more money from trade with American Indians, which allowed the farmers to increase the size of the plantations. The growing plantations required more and more workers. In 1720, a ship carrying about 200 slaves landed in New Orleans. In the decade that followed, the colony imported more than six thousand slaves. Eventually, more than half of the people of New Orleans were slaves.

 Stop and Check

Talk Why was it important that France built forts in Mississippi and Louisiana?

COLLABORATE

116 Lesson 2 How Did Early European Settlers Compete with One Another and American Indians?

Lesson 2 **117**

Research Companion, pp. 116–117

 ENGLISH LEARNERS SCAFFOLD

ELD.PI.5.9 Expressing information and ideas in formal oral presentations on academic topics

Emerging	Bridging
Research Have students research New Orleans and briefly present their findings to a partner. It should cover basic information about the city. Afterwards, have the partner offer feedback.	**Research** Have students do more in-depth research of a specific aspect of New Orleans or Cajun culture. It could be on the French Quarter, Jazz Music, Cajun cuisine, or any other topic that interests them. Encourage students to present visual aids. Students will present their topic to a group, who will evaluate and offer feedback.

See the **Language Learner Teaching Guide** for more language support strategies.

Monitor and Differentiate

REACHING ALL LEARNERS

Special Needs

Write details about Canadian New France and New Orleans on cards. Distribute the cards to the students. Draw a large Venn Diagram on the board and have the students tape their card to the correct area.

On Level

Ask: *Would you rather live in New France in the north, or New Orleans?* Have students explain why.

Beyond Level

Have students imagine they are a New French trapper who decided to stop trapping and move to New Orleans. Have them write a letter to a friend in New France saying how life in New Orleans is different.

2 INVESTIGATE / New Alliances, New Conflict

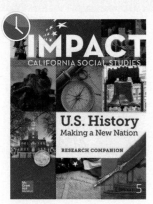

Research Companion
pp. 118–119

 STANDARDS

Describe the internecine Indian conflicts, including the competing claims for control of lands (e.g., actions of the Iroquois, Huron, Lakota [Sioux]). **HSS.5.3.5**

Students conduct cost-benefit analyses of historical and current events. **HAS.HI.4**

CCSS Explain the relationships or interactions between two or more individuals, events, ideas, or concepts in a historical, scientific, or technical text based on specific information in the text. **CCSS.ELA.RI.5.3**

Go *Digital!*

Investigate the lesson content with online whole-class presentation tools.

Background Information

The Wendat Confederacy, also known as the Huron, was an alliance of four bands: the Rock, Bear, Cord, and Deer. The Iroquois Confederacy, or Five Nations, contained the Mohawk, Oneida, Onondaga, Cayuga, and Seneca. Both confederacies share a similar language and appear to have shared roots. Their conflict seems to have been spurred by competition for resources.

Analyze the Source

Inspect Have students read pp. 118–119, New Alliances, New Conflict.

Find Evidence Use the questions below to check comprehension. Remind students to support their answers with text evidence.

Explain Why did the arrival of the French complicate the American Indians' relationships? (They disrupted trade and territorial agreements.) **DOK 2**

Identify Which groups allied with the French? (the Huron and the Algonquin) **DOK 1**

Summarize What caused the downfall of the Huron? (Illness reduced their numbers, then the Iroquois blocked their trade routes to weaken them further.) **DOK 2**

Analyze How was the alliance between the French and the American Indians beneficial to both? How was it detrimental? (They gained allies against the Iroquois and trading partners. The French likely brought smallpox.) **DOK 3**

Make Connections

Compare and contrast How were the motives and actions of the French and the Spanish similar and different? (The Spanish were much more interested in converting native peoples to Christianity than the French were. Both wanted riches from the New World.) **DOK 3**

COLLABORATE
✓ Stop and Check

Think Have students think about why the Huron and the Algonquin sided with Champlain in 1609. Then, ask students to consider: did they regret the alliance? (They wanted to use Champlain's strength to fight the Iroquois.)

What Do You Think?

Encourage students to use text evidence from the whole lesson as they respond to the prompt.

New Alliances, New Conflict

As European colonial powers sought to rapidly expand in North America, they came into contact with more and more native peoples. Reactions to the Europeans varied. Some groups of American Indians were friendly, and some were hostile. Before the Europeans arrived, the people living in North America already traded with one another, had military agreements, and shared cultures. The settlers' arrival often complicated the existing relationships between groups of American Indians.

In 1609, Huron and Algonquin leaders approached Samuel de Champlain asking to form a military alliance. The Huron and Algonquin had long been enemies of the Iroquois. Eventually, Algonquin commanders convinced Champlain to lend them French troops in their fight with the Iroquois.

Iroquois armies did not yet have guns and gunpowder. As a result, Champlain's men easily defeated the Iroquois. To thank the French, the Huron and Algonquin helped grow French fur traders' business in the region. After the battle with the Iroquois, France formed a permanent alliance with the Huron and Algonquin. The Iroquois confederacy, meanwhile, sought revenge.

A colonial trading post

French soldiers fight alongside Huron warriors.

The Iroquois' chance came in 1634, when a smallpox outbreak weakened the Huron confederacy. Smallpox was a disease brought to North America by Europeans. At the same time, beaver populations in Canada dropped significantly. Historians believe that this was the effect of the overhunting of the animal by fur traders. Because of the beavers' role in the conflict, the war between the Iroquois, the French, and the Huron and Algonquin confederacies is called the Beaver Wars.

In 1642, the Iroquois blocked the Huron from accessing the rivers they used to trade with the French and other native peoples. The Huron economy had become dependent on trade. The Huron nearly starved as a result of the Iroquois blockade. By 1649, the Iroquois had defeated the Huron. The Iroquois' conflicts with the French and Algonquin would continue well into the 18th century.

✓ Stop and Check

COLLABORATE

Talk Why did the Huron and the Algonquin side with Champlain in 1609?

What Do You Think? Did the relationships France and Spain had with the American Indians they encountered make a difference in the outcomes of their settlements?

Research Companion, pp. 118–119

ELD.PII.5.3 Using verbs and verb phrases

Emerging	Expanding	Bridging
Use Verb Forms Have students take the role of either a French person or a Huron/Algonquin person. Instruct students to write a letter to the other group thanking them for their support. Have students pay attention to the verb forms they are using.	**Use Descriptive Verbs** Have students write a letter as described in the Emerging activity. Encourage them to use gerunds and infinitives multiple times in their writing.	**Use Gerunds** Have students write a letter as described in the Emerging activity. Encourage them to use gerunds as the subject of sentences.

See the **Language Learner Teaching Guide** for more language support strategies.

Monitor and Differentiate

REACHING ALL LEARNERS

Approaching Level

Have students discuss in groups the advantages and disadvantages of forming alliances.

On Level

Ask students to consider the saying *"The enemy of my enemy is my friend."* Do they agree or disagree? Discuss as a class, having students explaining and supporting their opinion.

Beyond Level

Ask: *Should France have sided with the Huron and the Algonquin, have made peace between them and the Iroquois, or simply have stayed neutral and left the American Indians alone?* Have the students discuss this in groups.

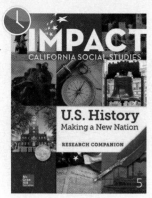

Research Companion
pp. 120–121

Explain the aims, obstacles, and accomplishments of the explorers, sponsors, and leaders of key European expeditions and the reasons Europeans chose to explore and colonize the world (e.g., the Spanish Reconquista, the Protestant Reformation, the Counter Reformation). **HSS.5.2.2**

Students identify and interpret the multiple causes and effects of historical events. **HAS.HI.3**

Go Digital!

Investigate the lesson content with online whole-class presentation tools.

Background Information

American beavers (*Castor canadensis*) are the largest rodents in North America. Today they are famed for their architectural abilities. Their dams and lodges can remake the landscape, flooding portions of forest and driving out or attracting different species of flora and fauna. In previous centuries, however, they were known for their fur and other products. Their double layer of thick, waterproof fur made highly desirable clothing material. They were nearly hunted to extinction. Conservation efforts, however, have allowed them to make a comeback.

Analyze the Source

Inspect Have students read pp. 120–121, Around the World.

Find Evidence Use the questions below to check comprehension. Remind students to support their answers with text evidence.

Identify Why were beavers important? (Their fur made popular hats, and an oil they produced could be used in perfumes.) **DOK 1**

Summarize What eventually saved the beavers? (The hats fell out of fashion when silk prices dropped.) **DOK 2**

Infer This period of time was also considered the Golden Age of Piracy. Why? (This period had a huge increase in trading, with ships crossing the ocean carrying gold and other valuables.) **DOK 3**

Draw Conclusions How did France's and Spain's success also cause them problems? (The French almost hunted the beaver to extinction, and the Spanish mined so much gold and silver that their money lost value.) **DOK 3**

Make Connections

Speculate Have students imagine being either a French or a Spanish colonist. What advice would they give to the other colony to solve their problems? (Responses will vary.) **DOK 4**

COLLABORATE

☑ Stop and Check

Think Explain to students that Supply and Demand are basic economic principles. Supply is the amount of something you have. Demand is how much people want it. Guide students to conclude that France stopped hunting so much beaver when the Demand changed: people wanted silk hats instead of felt. Have them discuss how Supply and Demand apply to the loss of Spanish power. (The Spanish made too great a Supply of gold and silver, and so Demand dropped.)

Around the World

Resources from the New World Enrich Europe

Though many French explorers were disappointed not to find gold in Canada, they did discover another valuable resource. People across Europe were fond of hats made from pelts, or the skins of animals with the fur still on it. Unlike North America, parts of Europe were overpopulated. Some of the continent's forests had been cleared to expand cities. The larger animals that lived there became rare.

Meanwhile, large animals thrived in North America. The French colony made money by hunting and trapping mammals such as moose, elk, deer, and caribou. Beaver fur held special value. European clothing makers used the beaver's thick fur to make felt, which is a smooth, leathery fabric. Beaver hats were especially popular in the cold winters of Northern Europe. An oil naturally produced by beavers was even used to make perfumes. Hat makers had long used the fur of the European beaver to make hats, but overhunting and habitat destruction caused that species to become scarce by the 17th century. French traders were able to replace European beaver fur with an American version.

Just as in Europe, American beaver numbers decreased significantly as a result of overhunting. The animal was eventually saved by a change in fashion trends. Silk prices dropped at the beginning of the 19th century, and Europeans exchanged their beaver hats for silk ones. This allowed the beaver population to make a comeback. Today, beavers are one of the most important national symbols of Canada.

European clothes makers regarded beaver fur as a fashionable and useful material.

In the 1500s, Spain rose to become one of the world's most powerful empires. Its American colonies were key to the empire's growth. Spanish colonists mined large amounts of silver and gold in South America and Mexico. In 1545, Spanish colonists exploring in the mountains of Peru found the largest silver deposit yet discovered in the Americas. From American gold and silver, the Spanish made coins. Silver and gold coins were important to Spain's economic success because Spain produced very few goods that could be sold to other countries. Spanish traders exchanged coins for foreign goods. With this new wealth, the Spanish built ships and armies to further expand the Spanish Empire.

Other European powers tried to prevent the growth of Spain's territories. French leaders hired private sea captains to attack Spanish treasure ships as they returned to Spain. Eventually, Spain's dominance came to an end. The value of gold and silver was based on the fact that these metals were very rare. As more and more gold became available, Spanish coins were not as valuable as before. Nations that produced goods began to catch up with Spain economically. Without the ability to buy armies to protect and expand its empire, Spain's influence in the world shrank. In the 1700s, England, France, and the Netherlands fought to take Spain's place as Europe's most powerful nation.

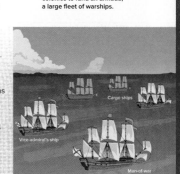

Spain used profits from the colonies to fund an armada, a large fleet of warships.

✓ Stop and Check

Talk What caused Spain's power to decrease?

Research Companion, pp. 120–121

 ENGLISH LEARNERS SCAFFOLD

ELD.PI.5.11 Supporting own opinions and evaluating others' opinions in speaking and writing

Emerging	Expanding	Bridging
Make an Argument Ask students to write a persuasive paragraph in favor of or against the beaver fur trade. Instruct them to cite evidence in the text.	**Participate in a Debate** Instruct students to debate a partner in favor of or against the beaver fur trade. Students should support their arguments with text evidence. Students should respond to their partner with counter arguments.	**Participate in a Debate** Have students debate in favor of or against the beaver fur trade. In addition to text evidence, students should make a prediction of what would happen if the beaver trade is stopped/continues. Encourage them to use modal expressions like *probably* or *definitely*.

See the **Language Learner Teaching Guide** for more language support strategies.

Monitor and Differentiate

REACHING ALL LEARNERS

Special Needs

Have students draw a map illustrating the trade between the New World and Europe. They should include pictures of what products were being moved and arrows to show where they were going.

On Level

How have supply and demand influenced the colonization of North America? Have students answer this question with examples from this lesson and previous lessons.

Beyond Level

Ask students to create a pamphlet informing the French public of the problems in the beaver fur trade and encouraging them to stop wearing it.

3 REPORT

Report Your Findings

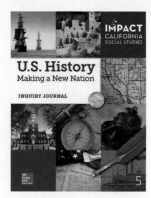

Inquiry Journal
pp. 96–97

HSS STANDARDS

Describe the competition among the English, French, Spanish, Dutch, and Indian nations for control of North America. **HSS.5.3.1**

 Write narratives to develop real or imagined experiences or events using effective technique, descriptive details, and clear event sequences. **CCSS.ELA.W.5.3**

Engage effectively in a range of collaborative discussions (one-on-one, in groups, and teacher-led) with diverse partners on *grade 5 topics and texts*, building on others' ideas and expressing their own clearly. **CCSS.ELA.SL.5.1**

Go *Digital!*

- Students can go online to report their findings. Assess their responses online.

- Students can access the online graphic organizer to capture ideas from their investigation.

Think About It

Have students review their research and consider what the main causes and effects of European colonization were. Remind them to review the information on their graphic organizers. Direct them to pages 110-121 of their Research Companion if they need more information.

Write About It

Write a Story Have students read the prompt and check to make sure they understand what is expected of them. They should explain who they are and how the colonization has affected their life. Encourage students to not only describe what is happening, but how they feel about it.

Use the rubric on p. T254 to evaluate students' work.

Talk About It

Compare Your Accounts Have students work with a partner who wrote from a different perspective. Have them compare their accounts. Make sure students are not simply reading their work. They should discuss their accounts in depth, looking for similarities and differences. Ask them to list the costs and benefits of French and Spanish settlement based on their combined accounts.

Connect to the Essential Question

Read the prompt aloud to students. Ask them the following guiding questions.

- What are the short-term effects of settlement? (Relations between American Indians and the French were positive.)

- What are the long-term effects of settlement? (subjugation and war)

Remind students to use the space provided in their journal to jot down notes.

Report Your Findings

Think About It

Review your research. Based on the information you have gathered, what do you think European powers wanted most from North America? How did that affect the people who already lived in North America?

Write About It

Write a Story
Write a short story from the point of view of an American Indian or a colonist. Explain who you are, where you come from, and how your life was affected by European colonization of the New World. Use details from the text in your story.

Students' responses will vary, but they should include details from the text to support the descriptions and dialogue in their short stories with a first-person American Indian or European narrator.

Talk About It

Compare Your Accounts
Work with a partner who has chosen to write from a different point of view. What were the costs of European settlement of North America? What were the benefits?

 Connect to the EQ
Economics

Compare
Think about the lasting effects of European settlement of North America. How did trade affect the relationship between Europeans and American Indians?

Possible response: At first, the relationship between the French settlers and some of the American Indians was positive, leading to trade and cooperation. The relationship between the Spanish and the American Indians was one of subjugation. The Spanish caused the deaths of millions of American Indians in their pursuit of gold and other riches.

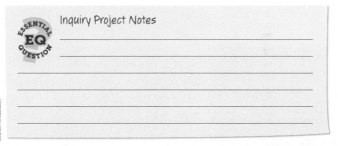

Inquiry Project Notes

96   Lesson 2   How Did Early European Settlers Compete with One Another and American Indians?

Lesson 2   97

Inquiry Journal, pp. 96–97

(EL) ENGLISH LEARNERS SCAFFOLD

ELD.PI.5.1 Exchanging information and ideas with others through oral collaborative discussions on a range of social and academic topics

Emerging	Expanding	Bridging
Ask and Answer Questions While working with partners in the Talk About It activity, encourage students to ask questions about why they chose that point of view.	**Explain Your Views** While students are working with a partner, encourage them to agree or disagree with the partner's views and explain why.	**Research to Refute** After students complete the Talk About It activity, encourage them to look up more information to support a written rebuttal.

See the **Language Learner Teaching Guide** for more language support strategies.

Monitor and Differentiate

REACHING ALL LEARNERS

Approaching Level

Discuss with students the strengths and weakness of colonization. Encourage them to think from the perspectives of the country creating the colony and of the people who live where the colony is being created.

On Level

Have students compare and contrast the colonies of England, France, and Spain. Discussion can take place in groups or as a class.

Know what your students know!

Lesson Task
Report Your Findings

Use this rubric to evaluate students' response.

Write a Story Students write a narrative from the point of view of a colonist or an American Indian, telling how colonization of the New World affected his or her life.

Compare Your Accounts Students compare their understanding of the costs and benefits of European settlement in North America.

Lesson Task Evaluation Rubric

	4	3	2	1
Historical Understanding	Strong understanding of European colonization of North America	Adequate understanding of European colonization of North America	Uneven understanding of the European colonization of North America	No understanding of the European colonization of North America
Point of View	Clearly expresses point of view of subject	Adequately expresses point of view of subject	Shows difficulty in expressing point of view of subject	Student does not show understanding of the task
Support with Details	Includes accurate and believable details	Includes some details	Includes few or inaccurate details	Lacks significant details
Compare	Engages in lively conversation with partner Answers questions in detail	Expresses own account well but does not offer significant feedback to partner Answers questions	Has trouble engaging partner and expressing ideas Does not answer some of the questions	Unable to express ideas or respond to partner Cannot answer questions

Lesson Assessment

***Go** Digital!*

- Have students complete the Chapter 3 Lesson 2 Assessment online to monitor their understanding of the lesson content.

California Smarter Balanced Assessment Connections!

Standards Covered	Lesson Task	Lesson Assessment	Alignment with California Smarter Balanced Assessment
History Social Science Content 5.2.2; 5.3.1; 5.3.2; 5.3.3; 5.3.5; 5.3.6; 5.4.6	✔	✔	Claim 1 Targets 2, 3, 5, 10
History Social Science Analysis Skills Chronological and Spatial Thinking 5.1; 5.2; 5.4; 5.5 Research, Evidence, and Point of View 5.1; 5.2 Historical Interpretation 5.1; 5.3; 5.4	✔	✔	Claim 1 Targets 5, 8, 9, 10
Writing W.5.3	✔	✔	Claim 2 Targets 2, 8, 9
Research and Inquiry W.5.7; W.5.9	✔	✔	Claim 4 Targets 2, 3, 4
Reading RI.5.1; RI.5.2; RI.5.3; RI.5.8	✔	✔	Claim 1 Targets 1, 5, 8, 9
Speaking and Listening SL.5.1	✔		Claim 3 Targets 2, 4

What Was Life Like for People in New England?

Background Information

In this lesson, students learn about how the first English colonies in New England developed. They study the Pilgrims and the Puritans, and they analyze how relationships with the American Indians living in the area shaped the colonies.

Community Connections

To enrich what students have learned about the New England colonies, plan a field trip to a local museum that has early American art in its collection.

LESSON STANDARDS

✓ Describe the cooperation that existed between the colonists and Indians during the 1600s and 1700s (e.g., in agriculture, the fur trade, military alliances, treaties, cultural interchanges). **HSS.5.3.2**

✓ Describe the internecine Indian conflicts, including the competing claims for control of lands (e.g., actions of the Iroquois, Huron, Lakota [Sioux]). **HSS.5.3.5**

✓ Identify the major individuals and groups responsible for the founding of the various colonies and the reasons for their founding (e.g., John Smith, Virginia; Roger Williams, Rhode Island; William Penn, Pennsylvania; Lord Baltimore, Maryland; William Bradford, Plymouth; John Winthrop, Massachusetts). **HSS.5.4.2**

✓ Describe the religious aspects of the earliest colonies (e.g., Puritanism in Massachusetts, Anglicanism in Virginia, Catholicism in Maryland, Quakerism in Pennsylvania). **HSS.5.4.3**

✓ Identify the significance and leaders of the First Great Awakening, which marked a shift in religious ideas, practices, and allegiances in the colonial period, the growth of religious toleration, and free exercise of religion. **HSS.5.4.4**

✓ Understand how the British colonial period created the basis for the development of political self-government and a free-market economic system and the differences between the British, Spanish, and French colonial systems. **HSS.5.4.5**

✓ Explain the early democratic ideas and practices that emerged during the colonial period, including the significance of representative assemblies and town meetings. **HSS.5.4.7**

Connect to the Essential Question

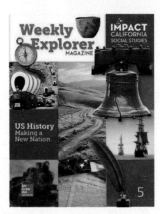

The **Weekly Explorer Magazine** supports the students' exploration of the Essential Question and provides additional resources for the EQ Inquiry Project.

Chapter 3, pp. 30–43

Inquiry Project

Tell Both Sides of the Story

Remind students to use the information they learn in this lesson and other resources to complete the EQ Inquiry Project.

Dinah Zike's

Remind students to use their notetaking Foldables.

When Minutes Count!
Suggested Lesson Pacing

1 ENGAGE
One Day

- Lesson Opener
- Analyze the Source
- Inquiry Tools

Go Digital
- **Video** The History of Massachusetts

2 INVESTIGATE
Two to Three Days

Short on Time? Look for the clock to teach core content in less time.

- Seeking Religious Freedom
- The Pilgrims
- **Citizenship** The Mayflower Compact
- The Puritans
- American Indian Relations

3 REPORT
One Day

- Think About It
- Write and Cite Evidence
- Explain Your Thinking

Make Connections!

CCSS CONNECT TO ELA

Reading
Quote accurately from a text when explaining what the text says explicitly and when drawing inferences from the text. **RI.5.1**

Determine two or more main ideas of a text and explain how they are supported by key details; summarize the text. RI.5.2

Research
Conduct short research projects that use several sources to build knowledge through investigation of different aspects of a topic. **W.5.7**

Recall relevant information from experiences or gather relevant information from print and digital sources; summarize or paraphrase information in notes and finished work, and provide a list of sources. **W.5.8**

Writing
Write informative/explanatory texts to examine a topic and convey ideas and information clearly. **W.5.2**

Speaking and Listening
Engage effectively in a range of collaborative discussions (one-on-one, in groups, and teacher-led) with diverse partners on *grade 5 topics and texts*, building on others' ideas and expressing their own clearly. **SL.5.1**

Classroom Resources

Search for additional resources using the following key words.

Anne Hutchinson

King Philip's War

Metacomet

Pequot War

Pilgrims

Plymouth Rock

Puritans

Squanto

Wampanoag

Inquiry Journal
pp. 98–99

(HSS) STANDARDS

Describe the cooperation that existed between the colonists and Indians during the 1600s and 1700s (e.g., in agriculture, the fur trade, military alliances, treaties, cultural interchanges). **HSS.5.3.2**

Describe the religious aspects of the earliest colonies (e.g., Puritanism in Massachusetts, Anglicanism in Virginia, Catholicism in Maryland, Quakerism in Pennsylvania). **HSS.5.4.3**

Go Digital!

Explore the lesson content with online whole-class presentation tools.

- **Video:** The History of Massachusetts

What Was Life Like for People in New England?

Bellringer

Prompt students to retrieve information from the previous lessons. Say: *Spain, France, and England had differing approaches to colonizing the New World. How did their approaches to governing vary? How did that affect the colonies they were creating?* (Spain and France created governorships that reported back to the governments in Europe. England established a representative form of government at Jamestown.)

Lesson Outcomes

What Am I Learning? Have students read the Lesson Outcomes.

Why Am I Learning It? Check that students understand the word *interact*. Guide them to understand from context that the word *interacted* refers to something that happens between two or more people. Ask them to pick out the root word *act*. Explain that the prefix *–inter* changes the word to mean "to act with each other." When people interact, they talk or communicate in some way.

How Will I Know That I Learned It? Ask students the following questions.

- What will you identify? (main idea and key details about challenges facing the colonists and American Indians)

- What is the purpose of the task? (to write an essay)

- How will you support your opinion? (with text evidence)

Talk About It
COLLABORATE

Provide some scaffolding for students to use as they discuss the picture. Provide background information as needed.

- *The painting shows* _____ *and* _____.
- *It looks like they are* _____.
- *The people in the painting seem* _____ *with each other.*

COLLABORATE

Collaborative Conversations

Add New Ideas As students engage in partner, small group, and whole-class discussions, encourage them to

- Think carefully about the subject.
- Ask and answer questions that are on topic.
- Draw or modify conclusions that are based on the discussion.

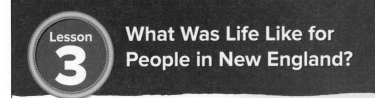

What Was Life Like for People in New England?

Lesson Outcomes

What Am I Learning?
In this lesson, you're going to use your investigative skills to explore what life was like in New England for settlers and American Indians.

Why Am I Learning It?
Reading and talking about what life was like in New England will help you learn more about how people interacted in colonial times.

How Will I Know That I Learned It?
You will be able to identify the main idea and key details about the challenges facing colonists and American Indians in New England and then write an essay about the two biggest challenges facing those peoples.

Talk About It COLLABORATE

Look at the Details Who are these people? How are they interacting with each other? How do you know?

The First Thanksgiving at Plymouth
by Jennie Augusta Brownscombe

HSS.5.3.2, HSS.5.3.3, HSS.5.4.2, HSS.5.4.3, HAS.CS.5

98 Lesson 3 What Was Life Like for People in New England?

Lesson 3 99

Inquiry Journal, pp. 98–99

 ENGLISH LEARNERS SCAFFOLD

ELD.PI.5.6 Reading closely literary and informational texts and viewing multimedia to determine how meaning is conveyed explicitly and implicitly through language

Emerging	Expanding	Bridging
Identify Details Guide students to identify the groups shown in the painting by picking out details. Help them understand the American holiday of Thanksgiving if it is unfamiliar to them.	**Describe Details** Work with students to describe what they see in the painting. Guide them to use words that they have learned from studying other lessons in the chapter. Have them work in pairs to discuss what they see in the picture.	**Use Language** Encourage students to identify and discuss what the picture says about the origins of the Thanksgiving holiday. Remind them to use language that describes the groups and setting of the event shown in the picture.

See the **Language Learner Teaching Guide** for more language support strategies.

Monitor and Differentiate

REACHING ALL LEARNERS

Special Needs

Work with students to identify the groups shown in the painting. Have them identify what the painting says about the relationship between the groups.

On Level

Encourage students to describe the events in the painting. Encourage them to discuss their ideas with a partner. Have groups discuss how the first Thanksgiving and modern Thanksgivings are similar and different.

Beyond Level

Guide students to look for more details in the painting. Ask them to identify some reasons the artist might have made these decisions. Have them share their thoughts with the class.

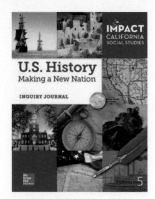

Inquiry Journal
pp. 100–101

 STANDARDS

Describe the religious aspects of the earliest colonies (e.g., Puritanism in Massachusetts, Anglicanism in Virginia, Catholicism in Maryland, Quakerism in Pennsylvania). **HSS.5.4.3**

Engage effectively in a range of collaborative discussions (one-on-one, in groups, and teacher-led) with diverse partners on *grade 5 topics and texts*, building on others' ideas and expressing their own clearly. **CCSS.ELA.SL.5.1**

Go Digital!

Model how to inspect and find evidence with online whole-class presentation tools.

Build Background

Plymouth The Plymouth colony in Massachusetts was the first permanent European settlement in New England. After reaching Cape Cod in November 1620, the Pilgrims floated around the bay for nearly a month before moving toward Plymouth and making a landing there. The famous "Plymouth Rock" marks the spot where they finally landed.

1 Inspect

Read Ask students to skim the text, including the Primary Source, to focus on understanding the overall meaning. Remind them to circle unknown words they encounter.

- Who was William Hilton? (an English colonist)

- What is the primary source? (a letter to Hilton's cousin back in England)

- What did Hilton think of the colony? (He thought it was full of good food, friendly American Indians, and devout colonists. He seems to be enjoying himself.)

Collaborate Have partners take turns discussing what Hilton's reasons for liking the colony are. Make a list of the good things he names. (friendly American Indians, pleasant country, plenty of fruits and vegetables, good timber, lots of animals, plenty of seafood, natural resources, religious company)

2 Find Evidence

Reread Have students reread the text.

Analyze the Primary Source Reread Hilton's letter aloud then analyze the excerpt together as a class.

- Guide students to take turns explaining the statement "There is likewise walnuts, chestnuts, small nuts and plums, with much variety of flowers and herbs, no less pleasant than wholesome and profitable." (There is so much here that is not only good for you and nice to look at, but also useful and potentially a source of income.)

- What does Hilton want his cousin to do with this information? (to send Hilton's family to Plymouth from England)

- **Context Clues** What does the word *divers* mean? (many types, diverse)

3 Make Connections

Talk Hilton presents a very positive portrait of the colony. Ask students to consider whether they think it was really this good. What might have been his motivations for telling his cousin only the good things and leaving out dangerous or frightening details? (Responses may include that maybe he was so afraid of what he would find upon arriving at Plymouth that he was overjoyed to be able to create a life there.)

Connect to Now Have partners discuss what they would write home if they moved to an new place. Guide them to draft short letters explaining their experiences, thinking carefully about what they would want their families to understand and think.

Analyze the Source

1 Inspect

Read Look at the text. What is the purpose of this text?

- **Circle** words you don't know.
- **Underline** clues that tell you about the purpose of the letter.
- **Discuss** why William Hilton wrote this letter. What did he hope his cousin would do?

My Notes

_____
_____
_____
_____
_____
_____
_____
_____
_____
_____
_____
_____
_____
_____

The Bounty of the New World

Colonists like William Hilton faced many hardships on their journey to North America. They traveled for two months on a cramped ship across a rough and stormy ocean. They endured disease, hunger, and seasickness. With luck, they were able to build a settlement without encountering more dangers. Often, however, their worst fears became reality when they clashed with American Indians or failed to grow food. Luckily, Hilton managed to make a good start at his new life.

PRIMARY SOURCE

Loving Cousin,

At our arrival in New Plymouth, in New England, we found all our friends and planters in good health, though they were left sick and weak, with very small means; the Indians round about us peaceable and friendly; the country very pleasant and temperate, yielding naturally, of itself, great store of fruits, as vines of divers sorts in great abundance.

There is likewise walnuts, chestnuts, small nuts and plums, with much variety of flowers, roots and herbs, no less pleasant than wholesome and profitable. No place hath more gooseberries and strawberries, nor better. Timber of all sorts you have in England doth cover the land, that affords beasts of divers sorts, and great flocks of turkey, quails, pigeons and partridges; many great lakes abounding with fish, fowl, beavers, and otters.

The sea affords us great plenty of all excellent sorts of sea-fish, as the rivers and isles doth variety of wild fowl of most useful sorts. Mines we find, to our thinking; but neither the goodness nor quality we know. Better grain cannot be than the Indian corn, if we will plant it upon as good ground as a man need desire. We are all freeholders; the rent-day doth not trouble us; and all those good blessings we have, of which and what we list in their seasons for taking.

Our company are, for most part, very religious, honest people; the word of God sincerely taught us every Sabbath; so that I know not any thing a contented mind can here want. I desire your friendly care to send my wife and children to me, where I wish all the friends I have in England; and so I rest

Your loving kinsman,

William Hilton

From Alexander Young's *Chronicles of the Pilgrim Fathers of the Colony of Plymouth, from 1602–1625.* Boston: Charles C. Little and James Brown, 1841.

TEXT: Hilton, William. William Hilton to his Cousin, November 1621, in *Chronicles of the Pilgrim Fathers of the Colony of Plymouth, from 1602–1625,* collected by Alexander Young. Boston: C. C. Little and J. Brown, 1841.
PHOTO: McGraw-Hill Education

2 Find Evidence

Reread the statement "We are all freeholders." What is a context clue for the meaning of the word "freeholder"? Why does being a freeholder mean so much to Hilton?

Underline the details that illustrate why this new status is important to Hilton. How does this help you understand why some people made the long and dangerous journey to settle New England?

3 Make Connections

Talk Could a letter like Hilton's have inspired others in England to move to North America? Would it have persuaded you to make such a long journey?

Inquiry Journal, pp. 100–101

EL ENGLISH LEARNERS SCAFFOLD

ELD.PI.5.7 Evaluating how well writers and speakers use language to support ideas and opinions with details or reasons depending on modality, text type, purpose, audience, topic, and content area

Emerging

Identify Details Work with students to identify how the author supports his main idea that the Plymouth colony is a good place. Encourage students to use the list of the examples Hilton gives.

Expanding and Bridging

Analyze Primary Sources Encourage students to consider why letters like Hilton's are valuable historical documents. Guide students to use language they have learned about primary sources in their discussions. Students should understand that the letter gives modern readers a brief snapshot of that moment in time. While the letter does not explain what the entire situation in the New England colonies was like, it does help provide some context for other types of facts and figures.

See the **Language Learner Teaching Guide** for more language support strategies.

Monitor and Differentiate

REACHING ALL LEARNERS

Approaching Level

Work with students to grasp some of the archaic language Hilton uses in the letter. Provide frame sentences that allow students to use words like *hath* (has), *divers* (different), and *doth* (does).

The boy _____ a red hat.

The grocery story has ____ fruits.

Our friend _____ not like blueberries.

Beyond Level

Have students discuss what the letter tells them about life in the New England colonies. Guide them to conduct research into the colony. They may choose to look for other first-hand accounts of life there. Have them share their findings with the whole class.

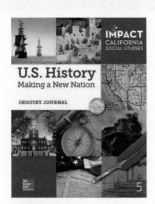

Inquiry Journal
pp. 102–103

 STANDARDS

Describe the religious aspects of the earliest colonies (e.g., Puritanism in Massachusetts, Anglicanism in Virginia, Catholicism in Maryland, Quakerism in Pennsylvania). **HSS.5.4.3**

CCSS Determine two or more main ideas of a text and explain how they are supported by key details; summarize the text. **CCSS.ELA.RI.5.1**

Go Digital!

- Model how to explore and investigate with online whole-class tools.

- Students can access the online graphic organizer to use the inquiry tools as they read.

Explore Main Ideas and Details

Explain Tell students that main ideas are the most important points an author makes. The author supports the main ideas with details about the topic. Those details may be facts, evidence, or reasons that support his or her opinion.

Read Have students read aloud the step-by-step instructions about how to identify main ideas and details. Tell students that they can use information found in section heads, as well as names, dates, and places as clues for finding main ideas and details.

Guide Practice Present a brief model of a main idea in the primary source by William Hilton that is supported by details: *One of the main ideas in the letter is that the area is a great place to settle. The details Hilton includes help us understand that this is his main idea; for example, "No place hath more gooseberries and strawberries, nor better."*

Investigate!

Have students read pages 122–133 in the Research Companion. Tell them the information that will help them answer the lesson question **What Was Life Like for People in New England?**

✎ **Take Notes** Tell students that they will take notes as they read each section. Remind them that taking notes will help them understand and remember the information they learn. Explain to students that they should gather relevant information, or information that is important to understanding the topic.

Inspect Guide students to read the text in each section to determine what the text says. Encourage them to work to find answers to important questions and to try to fit important people and events into the larger context of what was happening at the time.

Find Evidence Encourage students to reread the text to develop a deeper understanding. Remind students that they should think about how the facts and details will help them answer the lesson question.

Collaborative Conversations

Text-Based Discussion Remind students that discussing the text with others can help them

- find evidence in the text
- form new ideas
- understand someone else's perspective

Inquiry Tools

Explore Main Idea and Details

The **main idea** of a text is what the author most wants readers to know about the topic. The author uses **key details** to support the main idea. Sometimes the main idea is stated in the text, but readers often must infer the main idea from the key details.

To find the main idea and key details:

1. Read the text all the way through.
This will help you understand what the text is about.

2. Look at section titles.
These can be clues to how the text is organized and can help you understand what each section is mostly about.

3. Reread the first and last paragraphs in each section.
These paragraphs may state the main idea or give you clues about what the main idea is.

4. Identify key details.
Look for important information, facts, or evidence that seem to support the main idea.

 COLLABORATE Based on the text you just read, work with your class to complete the chart below.

"No place hath more gooseberries and strawberries, nor better."

Detail

The main idea is that the land they were in was a great place to settle.

Main Idea

Investigate!

Read pages 122–133 in your Research Companion. Use your investigative skills to look for text evidence that tells you key details and the main idea. Think about the challenges facing the American Indians and the English settlers in New England.

The Pilgrims nearly died of starvation during their first year, but Squanto and other American Indians taught them how to survive.

Detail

In Connecticut, the Narragansett and Mohegan people allied with the English in the Pequot War to defeat the Pequot, who had controlled trade in the area for years.

Detail

As more Pilgrims arrived, they encroached on the Wampanoag land, leading to conflict and ultimately King Philip's War and the end of American Indian resistance to English colonization.

Detail

The American Indians and English settlers had reasons to cooperate, but disputes over land eventually led to war and paved the way for English domination of New England.

Main Idea

McGraw-Hill Education

Inquiry Journal, pp. 102–103

(EL) ENGLISH LEARNERS SCAFFOLD

ELD.PI.5.1 Exchanging information and ideas with others through oral collaborative discussions on a range of social and academic topics

Emerging

Discuss the Text
Encourage students to discuss what specific sections of the text are mostly about. Have them work together to distill their notes into main ideas.

Expanding

Identify Main Ideas
Have students talk with a partner about specific sections of the text. Have them identify the main ideas and then work together to find details that support those main ideas. Remind them that only important information should be included as a key detail.

Bridging

Organize Main Ideas
Guide students to work together to identify main ideas and details to include in their graphic organizers. Have them share their ideas with the class.

See the **Language Learner Teaching Guide** for more language support strategies.

Monitor and Differentiate

REACHING ALL LEARNERS

Approaching Level

Encourage students to think about what makes an important detail different from an unimportant detail. Have them use this information as they decide what details to include in their graphic organizers.

Beyond Level

Have students expand on their graphic organizers, using their own paper if needed. Ask them to go into more depth, finding all the important main ideas and details they could use to answer the Lesson Question. Have them share their information with the class.

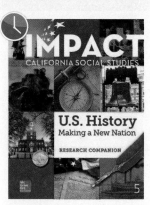

Research Companion
pp. 122–123

 STANDARDS

Understand the influence of location and physical setting on the founding of the original 13 colonies, and identify on a map the locations of the colonies and of the American Indian nations already inhabiting these areas. **HSS.5.4.1**

Describe the religious aspects of the earliest colonies (e.g., Puritanism in Massachusetts, Anglicanism in Virginia, Catholicism in Maryland, Quakerism in Pennsylvania). **HSS.5.4.3**

Students place key events and people of the historical era they are studying in a chronological sequence and within a spatial context; they interpret time lines. **HAS.CS.1**

Students use map and globe skills to determine the absolute locations of places and interpret information available through a map's or globe's legend, scale, and symbolic representations. **HAS.CS.4**

Go Digital!

Investigate the lesson content with online whole-class presentation tools.

- **Video:** The History of Massachusetts

Background Information

Separatists The Pilgrims were only one group of people known as Separatists. *Separatists* described any group that split from the Church of England in the sixteenth and seventeenth centuries. Most separatists viewed the church as having become corrupt. They wanted a fresh start.

DID YOU KNOW?

Common Misconception Students might think that all the Pilgrims came to the New World aboard the *Mayflower*, but there were several ships that made this journey over the course of several years.

| TIMELINE | Invite students to look at the timeline at the top on p. 123.

Analyze What events happened between 1620 and 1636? (The Pilgrims arrived on the *Mayflower*, the Puritans settled Boston, and Rhode Island colony was established.) **HAS.CS.1 DOK 3**

Analyze the Source

Inspect Have students read pp. 122–123.

Find Evidence Use the questions below to check comprehension. Remind students to support their answers with text evidence.

Identify Who were the Pilgrims? (a group of people who disagreed with the Church of England) **DOK 1**

Infer Why did the Pilgrims leave England for the Netherlands? (because they needed to escape persecution for their beliefs) **DOK 2**

Cite Evidence Why did the London Company agree to pay for the Pilgrims' trip? (because the Pilgrims agreed to send back resources for the London Company to sell) **DOK 3**

Make Connections

Point of View What would it have been like to be a Pilgrim or another Separatist living in England in the 1600s? Why might they have wanted to make a new life elsewhere? (Answers may include that life would have been difficult because it was a crime to go against the Church of England. Life in a new place would give them freedom.) **DOK 3**

Analyze the Map Direct students' attention to the map of the New England colonies. Encourage them to find information in the map based on what they already know.

- What are three colonies that you can find on the map? (Massachusetts, Rhode Island, Connecticut) Encourage students to use the gray outlines to help them.

- Who were the Pequot and where did they live? (an American Indian group; between Boston and Providence)

- Where were the main New England settlements? (Boston, Plymouth, Providence, Portsmouth, and Hartford)

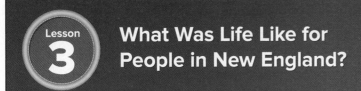

Lesson 3

What Was Life Like for People in New England?

Timeline

1620 Pilgrims on the *Mayflower* arrive at Plymouth in what is now Massachusetts.

1630 Puritans establish settlement at Boston.

1636 Providence colony is established in what is now Rhode Island.

1675-1671 King Philip's War

1692 Salem Witch Trials

1637 Pequot War

1700 First Great Awakening

1620 | 1640 | 1660 | 1680 | 1700

Seeking Religious Freedom

In England in the 1600s, it was a crime to belong to any church other than the Church of England. Members of the church called Separatists, however, wanted to set up their own churches and make their own rules. As a consequence, many members of the church were arrested and fined.

In the early 1600s, a group of Separatists decided to move to the Netherlands to escape persecution. This group called itself the Pilgrims. Eventually, the Pilgrims decided to leave the Netherlands. Historians disagree over exactly why the Pilgrims left, but some reasons include Pilgrim parents' concerns that their children would lose their English identity and fear of war breaking out between Spain and the Netherlands.

The Pilgrims decided to venture to the New World, not to enrich themselves or to explore, but to find a safe place to practice their religion. They asked the English government permission to settle in Virginia, and the London Company agreed to pay for their passage. In return, the Pilgrims had to send resources such as timber, fish, and furs back to the company.

Pilgrims departing on the *Mayflower* in 1620

HSS.5.3.1, HSS.5.3.2, HSS.5.3.3, HSS.5.4.1, HSS.5.4.2, HSS.5.4.3, HSS.5.4.4, HSS.5.4.5, HSS.5.4.6, HSS.5.4.7

122 Lesson 3 What Was Life Like for People in New England?

MAINE (PART OF MASSACHUSETTS)

VERMONT (CLAIMED BY NEW HAMPSHIRE AND NEW YORK)

ATLANTIC OCEAN

Boston

Pequot

Providence • Plymouth

Hartford • Wampanoag

Narragansett • Portsmouth

Long Island Sound

Settlement

Pequot Native American group

New England Colonies

0   50   100 miles
0   50   100 kilometers

The New England colonies were the northernmost English colonies.

Lesson 3 **123**

Research Companion, pp. 122–123

ENGLISH LEARNERS SCAFFOLD

ELD.PI.5.6 Reading closely literary and informational texts and viewing multimedia to determine how meaning is conveyed explicitly and implicitly through language

Emerging

Use Visuals Encourage students to use the map to help them understand where the Pilgrims landed. Ask them to work together to identify the settlement.

Expanding and Bridging

Analyze Visuals Have students use descriptive language to explain why the Pilgrims may have landed where they did. Guide students to use the map to describe the location of the Plymouth colony, and have them remember what William Hilton said about the location in his letter on pp 100–101 of the Inquiry Journal.

See the **Language Learner Teaching Guide** for more language support strategies.

Monitor and Differentiate

REACHING ALL LEARNERS

Approaching Level

Explain to students that the map shows the colonies before they had the same boundaries the states do today. Have students read the captions beneath Maine and Vermont. Explain that these territories were originally claimed by other colonies.

Beyond Level

Have students conduct research into the Pilgrims, including what drove them to disagree with the Church of England, what made them decide to emigrate to North America, and how they developed their settlement at Plymouth. Have them share their findings with the class.

2 INVESTIGATE

The Pilgrims

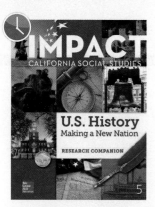

Research Companion
pp. 124–125

 STANDARDS

Describe the cooperation that existed between the colonists and Indians during the 1600s and 1700s (e.g., in agriculture, the fur trade, military alliances, treaties, cultural interchanges). **HSS.5.3.2**

Describe the religious aspects of the earliest colonies (e.g., Puritanism in Massachusetts, Anglicanism in Virginia, Catholicism in Maryland, Quakerism in Pennsylvania). **HSS.5.4.3**

Understand how the British colonial period created the basis for the development of political self-government and a free-market economic system and the differences between the British, Spanish, and French colonial systems. **HSS.5.4.5**

Explain the early democratic ideas and practices that emerged during the colonial period, including the significance of representative assemblies and town meetings. **HSS.5.4.7**

Go *Digital!*

Investigate the lesson content with online whole-class presentation tools.

Background Information

Squanto At a young age, Squanto was kidnapped and sold into slavery by one of Captain John Smith's men. He escaped and traveled to England, where he eventually boarded a ship back to Massachusetts. When he arrived, however, he found that all his people, the Pawtuxet had died. He lived instead with the nearby Wampanoag before befriending the Pilgrims.

Analyze the Source

Inspect Have students read The Pilgrims on pp. 124–125.

Find Evidence Use the questions below to check comprehension. Remind students to support their answers with text evidence.

Identify How did the Pilgrims come to North America? (on the *Mayflower*) **DOK 1**

Cite Evidence Why did the colonists create the Mayflower Compact? (They wanted to create a new agreement since they were going to settle somewhere they hadn't planned to.) **DOK 2**

Explain How did Squanto help the Pilgrims survive at Plymouth? (by teaching them what crops to plant and how to catch animals) **DOK 2**

Analyze the Primary Source Read aloud the primary source with students.

Summarize What did the colonists agree to in the Mayflower Compact? (to pledge themselves to work for the good of the colony) **DOK 3**

Make Connections

Draw Conclusions What did William Bradford mean when he said that Squanto was "a special instrument sent from God for their good"? Why is this important? (Responses will vary, but students may say that he meant that Squanto was a blessing because he helped the Pilgrims survive. It shows the good relationship the Pilgrims had with the American Indians at the beginning of the colony.)

COLLABORATE

✅ Stop and Check

Talk Have students reread the text to determine why the Pilgrims felt a new agreement was needed. Guide them to discuss the significance of the Mayflower Compact in small groups. (Responses will vary, but students should identify that the Pilgrims felt that the original agreement was no longer valid because they were going to be settling in a different place than they had intended.)

Find Details Explain to students that after they read and take notes, they should think about how the information can help them answer the Essential Question.

The Pilgrims

In September of 1620, 102 men, women, and children set sail from Plymouth, England, on a ship named the *Mayflower*. These Pilgrims faced a number of hardships on their 66-day voyage across the Atlantic Ocean, including storms and rough seas, disease, and hunger.

When they finally caught sight of land, they realized that they had not landed in Virginia as they had planned. Instead, they were hundreds of miles north, at Provincetown in northern Cape Cod, Massachusetts. The Pilgrims were changing the rules of their original agreement by settling in a different area. Led by William Bradford, the colonists drew up a new contract for their community. This document, called the Mayflower Compact, provided the outline of a new government. This was one of the first steps toward self-government in colonial North America.

The Pilgrims did not decide on a location for their settlement right away. In the early days, they lived on board the *Mayflower*. They eventually chose Plymouth, named by Captain John Smith a few years earlier. They arrived in late December, at the start of a brutal winter. They were without experience, low on supplies, and utterly unprepared for the weather. Half of the Pilgrims died that winter due to starvation, disease, and the cold.

PRIMARY SOURCE

In Their Words...
Mayflower Compact, 1620

Having undertaken, for the glory of God, and advancement of the Christian faith, and honor of our king and country, a voyage to plant the first colony in the northern parts of Virginia, do by these presents solemnly and mutually in the presence of God and one of another . . . [we] combine ourselves together . . . for the general good of the colony: unto which we promise all due submission and obedience. . . .

William Bradford

"The Mayflower Compact." In *The Signers of the Mayflower Compact*, by Henry Whittemore, p. 5. New York: Mayflower Publishing Co., 1899.

124 Lesson 3   What Was Life Like for People in New England?

The new colony seemed doomed. But in the spring, they befriended a Pawtuxet man named Squanto, who had been living with the Wampanoag people. Squanto spoke English and taught the Pilgrims how to survive. He showed them how to plant corn and use fish to fertilize the soil. He taught them how to trap animals, catch fish, and find oysters. William Bradford called Squanto "a special instrument sent from God." The Pilgrim settlement thrived and grew.

An artist's interpretation of what the *Mayflower* looked like

McGraw-Hill Education

✓ Stop and Check

COLLABORATE

Talk Why did the Pilgrims draft a new formal agreement about how their colony would be run?

Find Details As you read, add new information to the graphic organizer on page 103 in your Inquiry Journal.

Lesson 3   125

Research Companion, pp. 124–125

ENGLISH LEARNERS SCAFFOLD

ELD.PI.5.11 Supporting own opinions and evaluating others' opinions in speaking and writing

Emerging/Expanding

State and Support an Opinon Provide a written translation of the primary source into modern English.

Even though we did not land in Virginia, we have made this journey, and we are going to pledge to make our new colony a success. We will work together, and we will work hard, and we commit to being governed by this agreement.

Encourage students to discuss what it would mean to sign this agreement. Would it provide protection? Limit freedom? Make life easier or harder?

See the **Language Learner Teaching Guide** for more language support strategies.

Monitor and Differentiate

REACHING ALL LEARNERS

Approaching Level

Encourage students to underline unfamiliar words in the primary source. Have them work together to define the words or identify synonyms. Then have them write a version of the primary source in more modern English.

Beyond Level

Encourage students to read the full transcript of the Mayflower Compact, summarize the entire document, and present more information about it to the whole class.

Research Companion
pp. 126–127

 STANDARDS

Understand how the British colonial period created the basis for the development of political self-government and a free-market economic system and the differences between the British, Spanish, and French colonial systems. **HSS.5.4.5**

Students understand the political, religious, social, and economic institutions that evolved in the colonial era. **HSS.5.5.4**

Go Digital!

Investigate the lesson content with online whole-class presentation tools.

Analyze the Source

Inspect Have students read about the Mayflower Compact on pp. 126–127.

Find Evidence Use the questions below to check comprehension. Remind students to support their answers with text evidence.

Identify Why is the Mayflower Compact an important document? (It was the first government framework written in North America.) **DOK 1**

Cite Evidence Why were women not allowed to participate in government? (Only men were allowed to make important decisions and laws.) **DOK 2**

Explain What were you agreeing to if you signed the Mayflower Compact? (You were pledging to follow laws that would be written later on.) **DOK 2**

Analyze Visuals How does the illustration help you understand the events surrounding the signing of the Mayflower Compact? (It shows the document being signed inside a ship. It also shows only men participating in the process. A woman stands off to the side, watching what is happening.) **DOK 3**

Make Connections

Speculate Would society in North America have been different through the years if women and minorities had a chance to help govern? Why or why not? (Responses will vary, but students may identify that participation by women and minorities in government may have come easier and earlier if the societies of the original settlers had begun with those structures in place.)

COLLABORATE
✓ Stop and Check

Think Have students carefully consider what a society is like when only one part of it makes the rules. Remind them to use their experience creating a colony as a guide for their responses. (Responses will vary, but students may recognize that an official document of this kind would be different if different groups of people were involved.)

What Do You Think?

Work with students to complete the activity on p. 127. Encourage them to be creative when developing their colony. Have each small group present its colony to the whole class.

Citizenship

Perspectives
The Mayflower Compact

When the Pilgrims wrote the Mayflower Compact, it was the first government framework written in the land that is now the United States. It was signed by only some of the colonists—the men. At the time, women rarely held positions of authority in civic or religious life. As a result, they did not have the opportunity to sign such important documents. The purpose of the document was to bind the Pilgrims together. However, the Mayflower Compact did not include any laws. Instead, those who signed it were pledging to follow the laws that would later be enacted by the Pilgrims' small system of self-government.

The Pilgrims signing the Mayflower Compact

You Decide

Working in small groups, you will establish a new settlement.
- Give your settlement a name.
- Tell the location of your settlement.
- Indicate why you are moving to the settlement.

Work together to develop a system of laws for the settlement.
- Consider what principles are most important to your group.
- Think about the kinds of rights and protections you need.
- Write your new laws as a compact, and give the document an official title.
- Sign the compact.

Reflect

What did developing a plan for your new community teach you about the importance of self-government?
- Who helped make the decisions about the settlement's laws and rules?
- How did you come to an agreement about the laws?
- How did you resolve conflicts with other members of your group?

Make Connections

Consider how the development of your settlement compares with the development of Plymouth settlement. What was similar, and what was different?

✓ **Stop and Check**

COLLABORATE

Talk Do you think the Pilgrims would have written a different compact if women had been included in the drafting? Would this have been better for the colony as a whole?

What Do You Think? Should women have been allowed to help set up the Pilgrims' community and make laws?

Research Companion, pp. 126–127

ENGLISH LEARNERS SCAFFOLD

ELD.PI.5.9 Expressing information and ideas in formal oral presentations on academic topics

Emerging	Expanding	Bridging
Give Information Work with students to understand the assignment. Encourage them to use information from the text as well as their own opinions when they work in groups.	**Paraphrase Evidence** Encourage students to paraphrase evidence from the text to support their opinions when they work with the group to develop a new colony. Remind them to use relevant reasons to make a strong argument.	**Support an Argument** Encourage students to make their cases forcefully, using evidence from the text when appropriate.

See the **Language Learner Teaching Guide** for more language support strategies.

Monitor and Differentiate

REACHING ALL LEARNERS

Approaching Level

Encourage students to consider what makes a society diverse. Ask them to decide whether having different groups of people helping to make rules would lead to a better society.

Beyond Level

Have students write the entire history of the colony they created. Encourage them to consider what their relationship with any native peoples was like, how they got food, whether they traded or sold goods, and so on. Students may even write about what happened to eventually cause the decline or end of the colony. Have students present their histories to the class.

2 INVESTIGATE

The Puritans

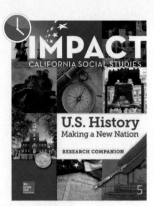

Research Companion
pp. 128–129

 STANDARDS

Identify the major individuals and groups responsible for the founding of the various colonies and the reasons for their founding (e.g., John Smith, Virginia; Roger Williams, Rhode Island; William Penn, Pennsylvania; Lord Baltimore, Maryland; William Bradford, Plymouth; John Winthrop, Massachusetts). **HSS.5.4.2**

Describe the religious aspects of the earliest colonies (e.g., Puritanism in Massachusetts, Anglicanism in Virginia, Catholicism in Maryland, Quakerism in Pennsylvania). **HSS.5.4.3**

Go Digital!

Investigate the lesson content with online whole-class presentation tools.

Background Information

City on a Hill The idea of the "city on a hill" comes from the Bible. The first governor the Massachusetts Bay Colony, John Winthrop, used the analogy in his treatise "A Model of Christian Charity." He explained that the eyes of the world would be on the colony, and that if it failed, the world would take that as a sign that such a religious community would always be doomed. However, if they succeeded, the world would see that God had blessed their colony.

Analyze the Source

Inspect Have students continue reading about the Puritans on pp. 128–129.

Find Evidence Use the questions below to check comprehension. Remind students to support their answers with text evidence.

Identify Who were the Puritans? (a group of people who believed God had called them to work hard to create a pure society) **DOK 1**

Outline How did the Puritans support themselves? (by selling New England lumber and by producing what they needed) **DOK 1**

Cite Evidence Why did the Puritans require members of the colony to sign a covenant with the church? (They needed a way to enforce their strict morals and rules. If someone broke the covenant, they could be thrown out of the colony.) **DOK 2**

Infer Did the Puritans believe in equal rights for men and women? (No; Puritans believed that each had a role to fulfill.) **DOK 3**

Predict How might the early Puritan focus on education have affected the education system in the United States today? (They put a focus on education and creating schools, which is still an important part of American society today.) **DOK 3**

Analyze Visuals What was life like in a Puritan home? (It centered around one main room where the family did their work, such as churning butter and spinning wool.) **DOK 3**

Compare and Contrast What was life like for a Puritan boy? For a Puritan girl? (Boys did chores, but they also went to school. Girls stopped going to school after they learned basic reading, writing, and math skills.) **DOK 3**

Make Connections

Compare and Contrast How were women's rights different in Pilgrim society and Puritan society? (Women had fewer rights than men in both societies. They were not allowed to help govern, and they were expected to keep to their roles as wives and mothers.) **DOK 3**

The Puritans

The Pilgrims were not the only group to flee religious persecution in England. A group of Puritans made their own journey to North America in 1629. Unlike the Pilgrims, the Puritans planned to land in Massachusetts. When they arrived in 1630, they founded the Massachusetts Bay Colony. They named their first settlement Boston. Another difference between the Pilgrims and the Puritans was that the Puritans had not separated from the Church of England.

The Puritans believed God had chosen them to create a religious community that was purer than the ones in England. The Puritans worked hard to show that their community was a success. They also worked hard just to survive. While most Puritans were farmers, they also made most of what they needed, however, such as flour, barrels, horseshoes, cabinets, saddles, and shoes.

Because of the abundance of good lumber in New England, shipbuilding eventually became an important part of the economy. The industry was successful in part because of slave labor. Slaves were also put to work in shops and on farms. Massachusetts was the first colony to legalize slavery in 1641. By 1750, it was legal across all of the original thirteen colonies. Massachusetts did not outlaw slavery until 1783.

A saltbox house was a common type of home in Puritan villages.

The Puritans organized their villages so that each one had a school and a common building that served as both meeting house and church.

Puritan leaders wanted each settlement to be "a city upon a hill," which meant its residents had to live up to high moral standards. In an effort to enforce their rules, Puritan leaders required each family to sign a covenant with the church. If a family broke the **covenant**, it had to leave the settlement.

Puritan children were taught the value of hard work from an early age. Young children were expected to work around the house. They also learned to read, because the Puritans believed everyone should be able to read the Bible.

By age twelve, girls did the same chores as women, such as churning butter, spinning and dyeing cloth, and making soap and candles. Girls usually did not get any additional schooling.

Boys helped with the farm animals, chopped wood, and picked vegetables before going to school. At school, some had the chance to learn another language, such as Latin or Greek. Boys also began to learn a trade, such as blacksmithing or printing.

Life for Puritan women consisted mostly of managing the home and raising children. Most women were not allowed to own property, and they were supposed to be obedient to men. They were not allowed to participate in town government. Only men could vote in town meetings, in which they decided issues and made laws.

McGraw-Hill Education

128   Lesson 3   What Was Life Like for People in New England?

Lesson 3   129

Research Companion, pp. 128–129

(EL) ENGLISH LEARNERS SCAFFOLD

ELD.PI.5.9 Expressing information and ideas in formal oral presentations on academic topics

Emerging

Express an Opinion Encourage students to discuss the Puritans' views on the roles of men and women. Have students share their thoughts about having to follow gender rules about what they could and could not do. Remind students to refer to the text as needed.

Expanding/Bridging

Support an Opinion Have students use information from the text to support their opinions about the Puritans' views on the roles of men and women. Remind students to discuss the issue using language they have read in this lesson.

See the **Language Learner Teaching Guide** for more language support strategies.

Monitor and Differentiate

REACHING ALL LEARNERS

Approaching Level

Encourage students to consider why a society has rules. First, have them name some rules that people in our society practice. This can include both written and unwritten laws. Then have them compare and contrast the rules of modern society with the Puritans' rules about morals and gender roles.

Beyond Level

Encourage students to identify an element of Puritan society that they want to learn more about. Students may choose to research a major settlement, such as Boston, or they may choose to research the Puritan economy, their religious beliefs, or major figures in the group. Have them share their findings with the whole class.

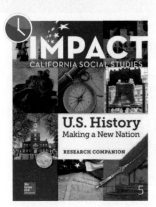

Research Companion
pp. 130–131

 STANDARDS

Describe the cooperation that existed between the colonists and Indians during the 1600s and 1700s (e.g., in agriculture, the fur trade, military alliances, treaties, cultural interchanges). **HSS.5.3.2**

Identify the major individuals and groups responsible for the founding of the various colonies and the reasons for their founding (e.g., John Smith, Virginia; Roger Williams, Rhode Island; William Penn, Pennsylvania; Lord Baltimore, Maryland; William Bradford, Plymouth; John Winthrop, Massachusetts). **HSS.5.4.2**

Identify the significance and leaders of the First Great Awakening, which marked a shift in religious ideas, practices, and allegiances in the colonial period, the growth of religious toleration, and free exercise of religion. **HSS.5.4.4**

Go Digital!

Investigate the lesson content with online whole-class presentation tools.

Background Information

The First Great Awakening Tired of formal religious practices and rules, members of several groups of protestants became interested in the teachings of preachers such as John Wesley and Jonathan Edwards. From informal settings such as fields, these men preached that people did not have to work hard to gain God's grace. This often irritated the local clergy.

Analyze the Source

Inspect Have students continue reading about the Puritans on pp. 130–131.

Find Evidence Use the questions below to check comprehension. Remind students to support their answers with text evidence.

Identify Why did Roger Williams disagree with the Puritans in the Massachusetts Bay Colony? (He thought the Puritans should be more tolerant of other religions, and he thought they should stop taking land from the American Indians.) **DOK 1**

Identify Why did Anne Hutchinson disagree with the Puritans? (She believed that people should be allowed to interpret the Bible for themselves.) **DOK 1**

Explain Why did Williams and Hutchinson get in trouble with the Puritans? (The Puritans did not want anyone to disagree with their teachings, and Williams and Hutchinson did so publically.) **DOK 2**

Infer Why did the Puritans dislike disagreement within the congregation? (They believed their community had to look like the "city on a hill" to outsiders so it would be seen as a success. They believed disobedience could be seen as weakness.) **DOK 3**

Analyze Cause and Effect Why did the words of the preachers of the First Great Awakening seem attractive to many Puritans? (Those preachers taught that following a strict set of morals and rules was not the way to gain favor with God. This more relaxed approach to worship appealed to many people who were tired of the strictness of the Puritans.) **DOK 3**

Identify How did the Pilgrims give thanks for surviving the first winter? (By celebrating the First Thanksgiving with Squanto and the Wampanoag people.) **DOK 1**

Explain Why did other settlers clash with groups of American Indians? (The settlers encorached upon American Indians' lands.) **DOK 2**

Make Connections

Justify If you were a member of the Puritan religion, and you started to disagree with their teachings, would you have stayed and tried to change their beliefs, or would you have left to follow a different group? (Students' responses will vary, but they should use information from the text to justify their responses.) **DOK 3**

COLLABORATE

✓ Stop and Check

Talk Encourage students to discuss whether the Puritans were unfair in their intolerance of other religions. Remind students to use information from the text in their discussions. (Responses will vary, but students should identify the double standard.)

Although the Puritans founded the Massachusetts Bay Colony on the principles of religious freedom, they were not tolerant of **dissension** among their own members. Roger Williams told leaders they should not take land that belonged to the American Indians. He also thought that the colony should allow other religions to be practiced. Believing Williams's ideas were dangerous, Puritan leaders banished him. In 1636, Williams founded Providence, now the capital of Rhode Island.

In 1638, Anne Hutchinson was put on trial for arguing that people should be allowed to interpret the Bible themselves. Hutchinson was forced to leave Massachusetts. She founded a new settlement, now Portsmouth, Rhode Island.

Anne Hutchinson on trial

In 1692, the Puritans' strict moral codes led to one of the darkest episodes in their history. Three girls in Salem fell mysteriously ill. They blamed three women for using witchcraft on them, and other accusations soon followed. From June to September, the Puritans tried and hanged 19 people for witchcraft. Finally, a higher court stepped in to stop the trials.

Events like these left some Puritans yearning for more independence from the church. In the 1700s, ministers like John Wesley, Jonathan Edwards, and George Whitefield began to preach in a dramatic, emotional style. They emphasized the importance of faith over actions. They and their followers created the Baptist and Methodist churches, which focused on ordinary people who had not been attending church regularly. This movement, called the First Great Awakening, led many away from Puritanism.

✓ Stop and Check

COLLABORATE

Talk If the Puritans left England because people were intolerant of their religion, why didn't the Puritans tolerate other religious views in their colony?

130   Lesson 3   What Was Life Like for People in New England?

North Wind Picture Archives/Alamy

American Indian Relations

The New England colonists had both positive and negative encounters with local American Indians. The Pilgrims' relationship with Squanto and the Wampanoag people made the difference between the survival and extinction of their new colony.

Squanto teaches the Pilgrims to farm.

To give thanks for their survival, the Pilgrims and Wampanoag had a three-day festival to celebrate the good harvest. This feast would later be called the first "thanksgiving." The Wampanoag brought deer, and the Pilgrims brought turkey, goose, duck, and a variety of vegetables and fruits.

Not all relationships between New England colonists and local American Indians were friendly, however. In 1637, the Pequot people of Connecticut and the English settlers went to war over trade disputes. The settlers were allied with the Narragansett and Mohegan people. These two peoples disliked the Pequot for their strict control of trade in the previous decades. At first, the two sides seemed evenly matched in what came to be called the Pequot War. The English had superior weapons, but the Pequot had knowledge of the land. In the end, however, the English defeated the Pequot. Many of the Pequot people taken prisoner by the English were sold into slavery.

©McGraw-Hill Education; ©JCCI ARCHIVES/SCIENCE PHOTO LIBRARY/Getty Images

Lesson 3   131

Research Companion, pp. 130–131

ELD.PI.5.1 Exchanging information and ideas with others through oral collaborative discussions on a range of social and academic topics

Emerging

Summarize Guide students to discuss what they have learned about the Puritans. Provide support as needed with archaic terms or language that is specific to religion. Have students summarize in a few sentences what they have learned.

Expanding and Bridging

Discuss and Summarize Have students discuss the problems that the Puritans faced. Students should identify that the group's challenges came from sources both within their group and from the outside, but that these issues were mostly a result of the Puritans' strict views and rules. Guide students to use descriptive language to summarize what they have learned.

See the **Language Learner Teaching Guide** for more language support strategies.

Monitor and Differentiate

REACHING ALL LEARNERS

Special Needs

Have students reread the paragraph on the Salem Witch Trials. Encourage students to create a cause and effect chart that explains how the trials began and what happened as a result, and states a conclusion about why it was a dark time for the Puritans.

On Level

Have students create a timeline of the Puritans in New England. Students may conduct additional research. Encourage students to summarize the important events that shaped both the group and the colony.

2 INVESTIGATE American Indian Relations

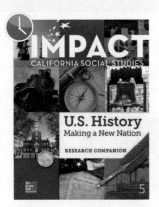

Research Companion
pp. 132–133

Describe the cooperation that existed between the colonists and Indians during the 1600s and 1700s (e.g., in agriculture, the fur trade, military alliances, treaties, cultural interchanges). **HSS.5.3.2**

Describe the internecine Indian conflicts, including the competing claims for control of lands (e.g., actions of the Iroquois, Huron, Lakota [Sioux]). **HSS.5.3.5**

Understand the influence of location and physical setting on the founding of the original 13 colonies, and identify on a map the locations of the colonies and of the American Indian nations already inhabiting these areas. **HSS.5.4.1**

___

Go Digital!

Investigate the lesson content with online whole-class presentation tools.

Background Information

Pequot War While the Pequot War was the first major conflict between white settlers and American Indians, it was mostly a struggle for supremacy over trade routes between the allied Narragansett and Mohegan people against the Pequot. The white settlers fought on the side of the Narragansett and Mohegan and eventually defeated the Pequot. This opened up trade with Europe to the Narragansett and Mohegan that had previously been controlled by the Pequot.

Analyze the Source

Inspect Have students continue reading about American Indian relations on pp. 132–133.

Find Evidence Use the questions below to check comprehension. Remind students to support their answers with text evidence.

Identify What American Indian groups were initially friendly with the English settlers? (the Wampanoag, Narragansett, and Mohegan peoples) **DOK 1**

Infer What went wrong with the relationship between the Wampanoag and the Pilgrims? (More settlers arrived, taking land from the American Indians.) **DOK 2**

Explain What were the causes of the Pequot War? (competition between American Indian groups over trade with Europe and land disputes with white settlers) **DOK 2**

Analyze Sequence of Events What events happened before, during, and after King Philip's War? (The white settlers wanted more land. Fighting broke out. The settlers eventually captured Metacomet, the chief of the Wampanoag. After that, resistance to English settlement of New England was basically over.) **DOK 3**

Make Connections

Assess If you could go back and change the way the English settlers behaved to the Wampanoag, what would you change? Be specific about the actions you would take. (Students' responses will vary, but they should use information from the text to justify their responses.) **DOK 3**

✓ Stop and Check COLLABORATE

Talk Encourage students to discuss why King Philip's War marked the end of resistance to English settlement of New England. Remind students to use information from the text in their discussions. (Students should identify that English settlers encroached upon American Indian lands, which led to increased tensions.)

What Do You Think?

Encourage students to use text evidence from the whole lesson as they respond to the prompt.

Despite the promising beginning to the Pilgrims' relationship with the Wampanoag, Narragansett, and Mohegan peoples, the colonists soon became enemies with these groups. The American Indians were angered by the increasing number of new colonists who were settling on their lands. By 1675, these tensions resulted in a bloody conflict called King Philip's War.

"King Philip" was the name that English settlers gave to the Wampanoag leader, Metacomet. Metacomet's father, Massasoit, had helped the Pilgrims survive their first harsh winters. However, the colonists' desire for more and more territory changed their relationship with the Wampanoag for the worse.

Thousands of people died in King Philip's War. Metacomet was eventually killed, and his family was sold into slavery. In their brutal conquest of the American Indians, the English showed they were capable of seizing land and maintaining power. The war marked the end of any resistance to English colonization of New England.

Metacomet, also called King Philip, of the Wampanoag people

Did You Know?

You might have thought that the English Pilgrims and the Wampanoag celebrated the first Thanksgiving in Plymouth, Massachusetts. Many historians, however, believe that it was actually French settlers who began this tradition. The French had colonized the area that is now Jacksonville, Florida. They held a Thanksgiving service in 1564, which was 57 years before the Pilgrims arrived. Spanish colonists in El Paso, Texas, also celebrated Thanksgiving services in 1598. In 1619, English colonists first held the feast we know best today.

✓ Stop and Check
COLLABORATE

Talk What caused the tensions that led to King Philip's War?

What Do You Think? Why did King Philip's War mark the end of resistance to English settlement of New England?

The First Thanksgiving at Plymouth by Jennie Augusta Brownscombe

Research Companion, pp. 132–133

EL ENGLISH LEARNERS SCAFFOLD

ELD.PI.5.6 Reading closely literary and informational texts and viewing multimedia to determine how meaning is conveyed explicitly and implicitly through language

Emerging

Identify Signal Words Have students underline the words in the paragraphs about King Philip's War that help them put the events in order. Point out words such as *by 1675* and *eventually*.

Expanding and Bridging

Use Signal Words Encourage students to summarize the events of King Philip's War using language they have learned in the lesson. Remind them to use details from the text in their discussions. Have them identify words that signal time order and important events. Encourage them to share their summaries.

See the **Language Learner Teaching Guide** for more language support strategies.

Monitor and Differentiate

REACHING ALL LEARNERS

Approaching Level

Guide students to think about the word *relationship* and whether it can have a positive or negative meaning. Guide them to discuss how the relationship between the American Indians and the settlers changed over time.

Beyond Level

Have students make predictions about how King Philip's War and the end of resistance to English settlement of New England will affect the colonies going forward. Guide them to consider what the settlers will gain as well as what they will lose because of the breakdown of the relationship with the American Indians.

3 REPORT

Report Your Findings

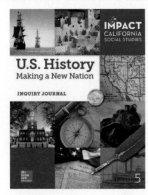

U.S. History
Making a New Nation

Inquiry Journal
pp. 104–105

 STANDARDS

Describe the cooperation that existed between the colonists and Indians during the 1600s and 1700s (e.g., in agriculture, the fur trade, military alliances, treaties, cultural interchanges). **HSS.5.3.2**

Explain how an author uses reasons and evidence to support particular points in a text, identifying which reasons and evidence support which point(s). **CCSS.ELA.RI.5.8**

Write informative/explanatory texts to examine a topic and convey ideas and information clearly. **CCSS.ELA.W.5.2**

Engage effectively in a range of collaborative discussions (one-on-one, in groups, and teacher-led) with diverse partners on *grade 5 topics and texts*, building on others' ideas and expressing their own clearly. **CCSS.ELA.SL.5.1**

Go *Digital!*

- Students can go online to report their findings. Assess their responses online.

- Students can access the online graphic organizer to capture ideas from their investigation.

Think About It

Students will review their research and consider what life was like for people living in New England.

- Remind students to review the details about challenges they have listed in their graphic organizer. Direct students back to pages 122–133 of their Research Companion if they need more information.

Write About It

Write and Cite Evidence Have students read the prompt. Explain that an effective informative essay includes facts and details that support the main ideas.

Remind students to include the following elements in their response.

- Introduce a Topic.

- Use concrete facts and details to support the topic.

- Use transition words to link ideas and details.

Use the rubric on p. T278 to evaluate students' work.

Talk About It

Explain Your Thinking Help students pair up with a classmate and determine whether they wrote about the same or different events.

- Explain that they should take turns discussing their opinions and the reasons for choosing the challenges they did.

- Students should discuss whether they agree or disagree with their partner's choices and explain why.

- Remind students to follow the rules of appropriate classroom conversation.

Connect to the Essential Question

Read the prompt aloud to students. Ask them the following guiding questions:

- What were the goals of the Pilgrims in settling North America? The Puritans? (The Pilgrims and Puritans both wanted religious freedom.)

- How do you think their successes and failures influenced future settlers? What evidence from the text makes you think that? (Their successes at establishing a functioning society may have set a good example for future settlers, but their inflexibility and their failure to tolerate other religions could have been a warning to future colonists.)

Remind students to use the space provided in their journal to jot down notes.

Report Your Findings

Think About It

Review your research. Based on the information you have gathered, what do you think were the two greatest challenges facing New England settlers and American Indians?

Write About It

Write and Cite Evidence

Write an informative essay about the two greatest challenges facing the New England settlers and American Indians. Use facts and details from the text to support your response.

Sample response: The two greatest challenges facing American Indians and English settlers in the New England colonies were tensions over land and war. In the early 1620s, the Pilgrims befriended Squanto and Massasoit and the Wampanoag people. The Pilgrims learned how to farm, hunt, trap, and fish. They survived because of this help. In later years, however, new settlers began to take Wampanoag lands. After years of tensions, the two sides fought a bloody war called King Philip's War. The English, forgetting their debt to the Wampanoag, brutally put down Wampanoag resistance.

Talk About It

Explain Your Thinking

Tell a partner about your essay. Did you write about the same issues? Do you agree with what your partner chose?

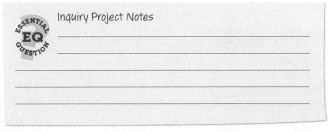

Make Connections

How did the goals of the Pilgrims and the Puritans in settling North America influence future settlers?

Sample response: The Pilgrims and the Puritans were different from other settlers because they came to the New World not for trade or precious metals, but for religious freedom. That principle survived and became part of what the United States stands for today.

Inquiry Project Notes

104 Lesson 3   What Was Life Like for People in New England?

Lesson 3   **105**

Inquiry Journal, pp. 104–105

ENGLISH LEARNERS SCAFFOLD

ELD.PII.5.1 Understanding text structure

Emerging	Expanding	Bridging
Organize Ideas Encourage students to apply basic text structuring to their informative essay. Have students identify an order of events. Encourage them to use some of the signal words they learned in the lesson to show the progression of their main ideas.	**Use Logical Order** Guide students to structure their texts in a logical and cohesive way, using reasons and evidence to support their opinions about the greatest challenges that faced people living in New England.	**Use Signal Words** Encourage students to use chronological order or cause and effect to structure their writing. Students should use any signal words that help to clarify their thinking. Have students share their work with a partner, offer feedback, and revise for clarity.

See the **Language Learner Teaching Guide** for more language support strategies.

Monitor and Differentiate

REACHING ALL LEARNERS

Approaching Level

Have students think about the terms they have learned in this lesson. Have them describe the important challenges people in New England faced. They should try to use the words from the chapter Word Bank if possible.

Beyond Level

Encourage students to conduct further research into the events they have chosen. Have them include those additional details in their writing and share them during discussions.

Know what your students know!

Lesson Task
Report Your Findings

Use the rubric to evaluate students' responses.

Write and Cite Evidence Students write an informative essay about the two greatest challenges facing the New England settlers and American Indians. They use facts and details from the text to support their response.

Explain Your Thinking Students tell a partner about their essay. They discuss whether they wrote about the same issues and whether they agree with what their partner chose.

Lesson Task Evaluation Rubric

	4	3	2	1
Historical Understanding	Strong understanding of the challenges facing early settlers and American Indians in New England	Adequate understanding of the challenges facing early settlers and American Indians in New England	Uneven understanding of the challenges facing early settlers and American Indians in New England	No understanding of the challenges facing early settlers and American Indians in New England
Write an Informative Essay	Clearly states main ideas	Adequately states main ideas	Somewhat clear or unclear main ideas	No main ideas or student does not show understanding of the task
Support with Evidence	Topic developed with many facts and details	Topic developed with adequate facts and details	Topic developed with uneven or few facts and details	Facts and details are missing or irrelevant
Explain Your Thinking	Sequences ideas logically throughout discussion Includes descriptive details to develop topic	Mostly sequences ideas logically Includes some details to develop topic	At times does not sequence ideas logically Includes few details to develop topic	Ideas do not follow a logical order Does not include enough details to develop topic

Lesson Assessment

Go Digital!

- Have students complete the Chapter 3 Lesson 3 Assessment online to monitor their understanding of the lesson content.

ONLINE ASSESSMENT

California Smarter Balanced Assessment Connections!

Standards Covered	Lesson Task	Lesson Assessment	Alignment with California Smarter Balanced Assessment
History Social Science Content 5.3.2; 5.3.5; 5.4.1; 5.4.2; 5.4.3; 5.4.4; 5.4.5; 5.4.7	✔	✔	Claim 1 Targets 8, 9, 11
History Social Science Analysis Skills Chronological and Spatial Thinking 5.1; 5.2; 5.4; 5.5 Research, Evidence, and Point of View 5.1; 5.2 Historical Interpretation 5.1; 5.2; 5.3; 5.4	✔	✔	Claim 1 Targets 8, 9, 11
Writing W.5.2	✔	✔	Claim 2 Targets 3b, 5
Research and Inquiry W.5.7; W.5.9	✔	✔	Claim 4 Targets 1, 2, 3, 4
Reading RI.5.1; RI.5.2	✔	✔	Claim 1 Targets 8, 9, 11 Claim 4 Target 4
Speaking and Listening SL.5.1	✔		Claim 3 Target 3 Claim 4 Target 1

What Shaped Life in the Middle Colonies?

Background Information

In this lesson, students will learn about life in the Middle Colonies. They will learn how victory over the Dutch resulted in England's acquisition of what became New York and New Jersey and how William Penn came to acquire Pennsylvania and Delaware.

Community Connections

To enrich students' understanding of colonial history in the Middle Colonies, have them visit the website of a colonial-era historical site in New York, New Jersey, Pennsylvania, or Delaware, such as Elfreth's Alley or Franklin's Print Shop in Philadelphia, Historic New Castle in Delaware, or the Stockade Historic District in Schenectady, New York.

 LESSON STANDARDS

✔ Describe the competition among the English, French, Spanish, Dutch, and Indian nations for control of North America. **HSS.5.3.1**

✔ Describe the cooperation that existed between the colonists and Indians during the 1600s and 1700s (e.g., in agriculture, the fur trade, military alliances, treaties, cultural interchanges). **HSS.5.3.2**

✔ Students understand the political, religious, social, and economic institutions that evolved in the colonial era. **HSS.5.4**

✔ Identify the major individuals and groups responsible for the founding of the various colonies and the reasons for their founding (e.g, William Penn, Pennsylvania). **HSS.5.4.2**

✔ Describe the religious aspects of the earliest colonies (e.g., Quakerism in Pennsylvania). **HSS.5.4.3**

✔ Identify the significance and leaders of the First Great Awakening. **HSS.5.4.4**

✔ Understand how the British colonial period created the basis for the development of political self-government and a free market system. **HSS.5.4.5**

✔ Explain the early democratic ideas and practices that emerged during the colonial period. **HSS.5.4.7**

✔ Students place key events and people of the historical era they are studying in a chronological sequence and spatial context; they interpret time lines. **HAS.CS.1**

 Connect to the
Essential Question

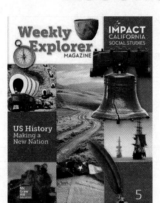

Chapter 3, pp. 30–43

The **Weekly Explorer Magazine** supports students' exploration of the Essential Question and provides additional resources for the EQ Inquiry Project

 Inquiry Project

Tell Both Sides of the Story

Remind students to use the information they learn in this lesson and other resources to complete their EQ Inquiry Project!

Dinah Zike's

In this lesson you will use Foldables.

When Minutes Count!

Suggested Lesson Pacing

1 ENGAGE
One Day

2 INVESTIGATE
Two to Three Days

 Short on Time? Look for the clock to teach core content in less time.

3 REPORT
One Day

- Lesson Opener
- Analyze the Source
- Inquiry Tools

Go Digital

- **Video:** The Founding of Pennsylvania
- **iMap:** The Middle Colonies

- A Region of Diversity
- New York and New Jersey
- Pennsylvania and Delaware
- Life in the Middle Colonies

- Think About It
- Write an Essayt
- Defend Your Claim

Make Connections!

(CCSS) CONNECT TO ELA

Reading

Quote accurately from a text when explaining what the text says explicitly and when drawing inferences from the text. **RI.5.1**

Research

Recall or gather relevant information from sources; summarize or paraphrase information in notes and finished work. **W.5.8**

Draw evidence from literary or informational texts to support analysis, reflection, and research. **W.5.9**

Writing

Students write opinion pieces, supporting a point of view with reasons and information. **W.5.1**

Produce clear and coherent writing in which the development and organization are appropriate to task, purpose, and audience. **W.5.4**

Speaking and Listening

Engage effectively in discussions, building on others' ideas and expressing their own clearly. **SL.5.1**

Come to discussions prepared, having read or studied required material, to explore ideas under discussion. **SL.5.1.a**

Summarize information presented in diverse media and formats, including visually, quantitatively, and orally. **SL.5.2**

Classroom Resources

Search for additional resources using the following key words.

Middle Colonies

New York Colony

New Jersey Colony

Pennsylvania Colony

Delaware Colony

John Peter Zenger Trial

William Penn

Lenape

First Great Awakening

Benjamin Franklin

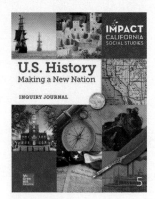

Inquiry Journal
pp. 106–107

 STANDARDS

Describe the cooperation that existed between the colonists and Indians during the 1600s and 1700s (e.g., in agriculture, the fur trade, military alliances, treaties, cultural interchanges). **HSS.5.3.2**

Identify the major individuals and groups responsible for the founding of the various colonies and the reasons for their founding (e.g, William Penn, Pennsylvania). **HSS.5.4.2**

CCSS Summarize information presented in diverse media and formats, including visually, quantitatively, and orally. **CCSS.ELA.SL.5.2**

Go Digital!

Explore the lesson content with online whole-class presentation tools.

- **Video:** The Founding of Pennsylvania
- **iMap:** The Middle Colonies

What Shaped Life in the Middle Colonies?

Bellringer

Prompt students to retrieve information from the previous lessons. Say: *What colony in what is now the United States was established by the Dutch? For what qualities was it known?* (New Netherland; commerce and ethnic and religious diversity)

Lesson Outcomes

What Am I Learning? Have students read the Lesson Question and Lesson Outcomes.

Why Am I Learning It? Discuss the term *colonial times,* making sure students understand that it refers to the period when the present-day states in the United States were colonies of European nations. Clarify that the thirteen English colonies on the Atlantic coast were separately governed and had different policies and practices.

How Will I Know That I Learned It? Ask students the following questions:

- What will you be able to describe for each of the Middle Colonies? (its important qualities, the people who lived there, and the way they lived)

- What will you point out about two or more of the colonies? (their similarities and differences)

COLLABORATE
Talk About It

Explain that when we talk about artwork, we describe, analyze, and interpret it and present our ideas in our own words. Provide sentence frames to help students form sentences as they talk about the artwork.

- ***Penn and the Indians are*** __(signing a treaty)__.

- ***The relationship between them seems to be*** __(friendly; respectful)__.

Collaborative Conversations

Add New Ideas As students engage in partner, small group, and whole-class discussions, encourage them to

- Stay on topic.
- Connect their own ideas to things their peers have said.
- Look for ways to connect their personal experiences or prior knowledge to the conversation.

Lesson 4

What Shaped Life in the Middle Colonies?

Lesson Outcomes

What Am I Learning?
In this lesson, you're going to use your investigative skills to learn about life in the English Middle Colonies—New York, New Jersey, Pennsylvania, and Delaware.

Why Am I Learning It?
Reading and talking about the Middle Colonies will help you better understand colonial times and how the past still affects life in the area today.

How Will I Know That I Learned It?
You will be able to describe important characteristics of the Middle Colonies, the people who lived there, the way they lived, and the similarities and differences between the colonies.

Talk About It

Look at the Details What positive qualities does the painting convey about William Penn and his treaty?

HSS.5.3.2, HSS.5.4.2, HSS.5.4.3, HAS.HI.1

106 Lesson 4 What Shaped Life in the Middle Colonies?

Artist Benjamin West created this painting, *William Penn's Treaty with the Indians*, more than 100 years after the event.

Lesson 4 **107**

Inquiry Journal, pp. 106–107

ENGLISH LEARNERS SCAFFOLD

ELD.PI.5.8 Analyzing how writers and speakers use vocabulary and other language resources for specific purposes

Emerging	Expanding	Bridging
Understand Academic Vocabulary Help students recognize similarities and differences. If necessary, clarify that *similarities* are ways in which two or more things are alike or nearly alike; *differences* are the ways they are unalike, or different.	**Distinguish Homophones** Discuss the meaning of the academic vocabulary word *affects* ("changed; had an impact on") in the sentence after *Why Am I Learning It?* Note that it is a verb; the noun form, which has the same sound, is *effects.* Clarify with examples: *The weather affects what we do. Different weather has different effects.*	**Use Synonyms** Point out the term *characteristics* in the sentence after *How Will I Know That I Learned It?* Ask students for words that mean the same or nearly the same thing as *characteristics.* (Possibilities include *qualities* and *traits.*)

See the **Language Learner Teaching Guide** for more language support strategies.

Monitor and Differentiate

REACHING ALL LEARNERS

Approaching Level

Clarify that a treaty may be signed to end a war or officially seal a land deal. Explain that it is for the second reason that Penn and the Indians are signing a treaty in the painting on page 107.

On Level

Ask students to use precise language to describe the appearance and attitudes of the people in the painting on page 107.

Beyond Level

Have small groups research artist Benjamin West, whose painting is reproduced on page 107, and prepare a multimedia report using graphics of West's paintings available online.

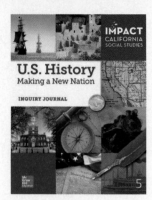

Inquiry Journal
pp. 108–109

STANDARDS

Students understand the political, religious, social, and economic institutions that evolved in the colonial era. **HSS.5.4**

Describe the religious aspects of the earliest colonies (e.g., Quakerism in Pennsylvania). **HSS.5.4.3**

Students differentiate between primary and secondary sources. **HAS.HR.1**

Students pose relevant questions about events they encounter in historical documents, eyewitness accounts, oral histories, letters, diaries, artifacts, photographs, maps, artworks, and architecture. **HAS.HR.2**

Come to discussions prepared, having read or studied required material, to explore ideas under discussion. **CCSS.ELA.SL.5.1a**

Go Digital!

Model how to inspect and find evidence with online whole-class presentation tools.

Background Information

Franklin's autobiography, in tracing his progress from poverty on arrival in Philadelphia to his great success there, was a landmark work on the American theme of the self-made, self-reliant individual. It painted a picture of a place where, unlike Europe, birth did not determine one's station in life. Nor was it just a rags-to-riches tale; Franklin's self-reliance includes spiritual development, an idea expanded later by writers like Ralph Waldo Emerson and Henry David Thoreau.

1 Inspect

Read Have students read the entire text, including the primary source. Ask:

- What does the word *autobiography* show about the source? (It is about the writer's life.)

- Who is the text about? (Benjamin Franklin)

- What did that person do in the text? (left home and went to a new city)

- Where did he go? (Philadelphia)

- When did he go there, and how was he? (in 1723, when he was 17)

Collaborate Have partners discuss what the text shows them about Ben Franklin. (He is observant, able to adjust to different situations, able to take care of himself, and easily satisfied with simple things.)

2 Find Evidence

Reread Have students reread the text.

Analyze the Primary Source Read aloud the excerpt from Franklin's autobiography.

- Ask what sort of first impression Ben Franklin seems to have of Philadelphia and its people. (He finds the city attractive and its people welcoming and generous.)

- Have students cite details to support their answer. (Details include the low price of bread and being allowed to sleep in the Quaker meeting-house.)

COLLABORATE
3 Make Connections

Talk Have students discuss with a partner the things they learn about colonial Philadelphia from reading the text. (Students may mention that the city had numbered streets [Second Street], freshly baked goods sold at a bakeshop, rolls sold at a reasonable price, and a market with a large Quaker meeting-house nearby.)

Analyze the Source

1 Inspect

Read the text from the primary source and the sentences that introduce it. What does the word *autobiography* in the source's title suggest about its content?

- **Circle** words you don't know.
- **Underline** clues that tell you *whom* the text is about, *what* that person did, and *where* and *when* that person did it.
- **Discuss** with a partner what the text shows you about Benjamin Franklin.

My Notes

_____

_____

_____

_____

_____

_____

_____

_____

_____

_____

Young Ben Franklin Arrives in Philadelphia

Benjamin Franklin grew up in Boston, where he was an apprentice in his brother's print shop. Then he argued with his brother when things he wrote got his brother's newspaper in trouble with authorities. So Franklin, who was just seventeen, left Boston for Philadelphia. On the next page is his account of his arrival in Philadelphia in 1723.

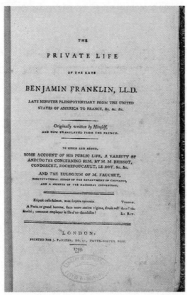

A printed page from Benjamin Franklin's autobiography

The Library of Congress/Benjamin Franklin: In His Own Words, Printer and Writer

PRIMARY SOURCE

In Their Words... Benjamin Franklin

I walked up the street, gazing about till near the market-house I met a boy with bread. I had made many a meal on bread, and, inquiring where he got it, I went immediately to the baker's he directed me to, in Second Street, and asked for biscuit, intending such as we had in Boston; but they, it seems, were not made in Philadelphia. Then I asked for a three-penny loaf, and was told they had none such. So not considering or knowing the difference of money, and the greater cheapness nor the names of his bread, I bade him give me three-penny worth of any sort. He gave me, accordingly, three great puffy rolls. I was surprised at the quantity, but took it, and, having no room in my pockets, walked off with a roll under each arm, and eating the other. . . .

Thus refreshed, I walked again up the street, which by this time had many clean-dressed people in it, who were all walking the same way. I joined them, and thereby was led into the great meeting-house of the Quakers near the market. I sat down among them, and, after looking round awhile and hearing nothing said, being very drowsy through labor and want of rest the preceding night, I fell fast asleep, and continued so till the meeting broke up, when one was kind enough to rouse me. This was, therefore, the first house I was in, or slept in, in Philadelphia.

—from *The Autobiography of Benjamin Franklin*

TEXT: Franklin, Benjamin. The Autobiography of Benjamin Franklin. Edited by Frank Woodworth Pine. New York: Henry Holt and Company, 1916.; PHOTO: McGraw-Hill Education

2 Find Evidence

Reread the text from Franklin's autobiography. What first impression does Philadelphia make on Ben Franklin? Cite details to support your answer.

3 Make Connections

Talk Discuss with a partner the things you learn about colonial Philadelphia from reading the text from Franklin's autobiography.

COLLABORATE

Inquiry Journal, pp. 108–109

EL ENGLISH LEARNERS SCAFFOLD

ELD.PI.5.6 Reading closely literary and informational texts

Emerging	Expanding	Bridging
Clarify Vocabulary Clarify possibly unfamiliar words in the primary source and the sentences introducing it, such as *apprentice* ("trainee"), *authorities* ("people in charge"), *gazing* ("looking"), *refreshed* ("renewed"), *market-house* ("shopping area"), *drowsy* ("sleepy"), *labor* ("work"), and *rouse* ("wake").	**Clarify Archaic Language** Point out that Franklin uses some wordings rarely used today. Explain how these phrases would be said today: "intending such as we had in Boston" ("meaning what we had in Boston"), "I bade him" ("I asked him"), "want of rest" ("lack of rest"), and "and continued so" ("and kept doing it").	**Interpret Details** Have students consider what young Ben Franklin's reactions to his experiences in Philadelphia show about specific differences in the colonies. (Money is different in different colonies; foods and the way they are sold also seem to be different.)

See the **Language Learner Teaching Guide** for more language support strategies.

Monitor and Differentiate

REACHING ALL LEARNERS

Approaching Level

Remind students that a primary source is an eyewitness account or a document, photograph, or other source from the time events happened.

On Level

Explain that the silence Franklin encounters in the meeting-house is the silent worship typical of Quaker services. Elicit that the older Franklin finds it is amusing that he fell asleep then.

Beyond Level

Have students read more about Franklin's arrival in Philadelphia in Chapter 3 of his autobiography (available online) and report on what it shows about colonial life.

Lesson 4 **Analyze the Source** T285

Inquiry Journal
pp. 110–111

IMPACT
CALIFORNIA
SOCIAL STUDIES

U.S. History
Making a New Nation

INQUIRY JOURNAL

5

STANDARDS

Students understand the political, religious, social, and economic institutions that evolved in the colonial era. **HSS.5.4**

Identify the major individuals and groups responsible for the founding of the various colonies and the reasons for their founding (e.g, William Penn, Pennsylvania). **HSS.5.4.2**

Understand how the British colonial period created the basis for the development of political self-government and a free market system. **HSS.5.4.5**

Explain the early democratic ideas and practices that emerged during the colonial period. **HSS.5.4.7**

Recall or gather relevant information from sources; summarize or paraphrase information in notes and finished work.
CCSS.ELA.W.5.8

Go Digital!

- Model how to explore and investigate with online whole-class tools.

- Students can access the online graphic organizer to use the inquiry tools as they read.

Explore Compare and Contrast

Explain Tell students that compare and contrast is one kind of text structure that authors use to organize information in historical texts. Showing how events, places, people, or other things are alike or different makes them easier to understand and helps give readers an idea of what things were like in general.

Read Have students read aloud the step-by-step instructions about how to identify comparisons and contrasts. Tell students to look for clue words that signal similarities, such as *both, similar, like,* and *in the same way,* and contrasts or differences, such as *although, but, however,* and *on the other hand*.

Guided Practice Present two familiar things to students, such as fourth and fifth grade or two nearby places, in order to model the strategy. Show them how the Venn diagram works—differences go in the non-overlapping parts labeled with the things being contrasted; similarities go in the overlapping part.

Investigate!

Have students read pages 134–143 in the Research Companion. Tell them the information will help them answer the lesson question **What Shaped Life in the Middle Colonies?**

Take Notes Tell students that they should take notes in the Venn diagram on page 111 of the Inquiry Journal. Point out that taking notes will help them better understand and remember the information. Explain to students the importance of paraphrasing, or using their own words, when they take notes.

Inspect Guide students to read the text in each section to determine what it says about the colonies and how they are alike and different.

Find Evidence Encourage students to reread the text to develop a deeper understanding of the content and determine if they should add more information to their notes. Remind them that after they read and take notes, they should review and think about how the facts and details will help them answer the lesson question.

Collaborative Conversations

Text-Based Discussion Remind students of the goals of discussing with others.

- to listen and respond to their partner's points
- to ask for evidence from the text
- to build on each other's ideas
- to see the text from a different point of view

Inquiry Tools

Explore Compare and Contrast

You can better understand the ideas in a text if you compare and contrast the details the author provides.

1. Read the text once all the way through.
This will help you understand what the text is about.

2. Look at the section titles to see how the text is organized.
Do the titles offer any clues about which important qualities or characteristics are discussed in the text?

3. Think about what the author wants you to know.
When you **compare** two things, you tell how they are the same. When you **contrast** things, you tell how they are different. Consider what the author wants you to know about similarities and differences between colonial Pennsylvania and New York?

4. Find specific similarities and differences.
While reading, ask yourself in what specific ways colonial New York and Pennsylvania were alike. Then ask yourself in what specific ways they were different.

COLLABORATE Based on the primary source you just read, work as a class to compare Philadelphia and Boston. List one similarity and one difference in the Venn diagram below.

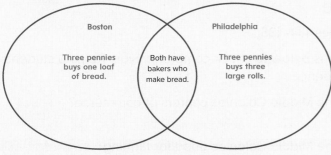

Boston — Three pennies buys one loaf of bread.

Both have bakers who make bread.

Philadelphia — Three pennies buys three large rolls.

110 Lesson 4 What Shaped Life in the Middle Colonies?

U.S. History
Making a New Nation

Investigate!

Read pages 134–143. Then add details to the Venn diagram about the similarities and differences between the New York and Pennsylvania colonies. Add at least five similarities and six differences (three for each colony).

Comparing and Contrasting New York and Pennsylvania

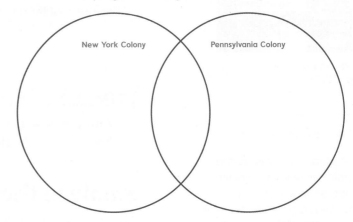

New York Colony   Pennsylvania Colony

Among many things, students may list the following similarities in the overlapping section: colonists of diverse backgrounds and religions, tolerance of diversity; commercial center; prosperous farming; trial by jury. They may list these differences for New York: begun as Dutch colony; begun for commercial reasons; freedom of the press; path to freedom for slaves at first, later less so. They may list these differences for Pennsylvania: begun as English colony; begun for religious reasons; limited elected assembly; capital has wide, tree-lined streets; moral laws restrict some personal activities; respectful treatment of American Indians at first, later less so.

McGraw-Hill Education

Lesson 4 111

Inquiry Journal, pp. 110–111

EL ENGLISH LEARNERS SCAFFOLD

ELD.PII.5.1 Understanding text structure

Emerging

Organize Information Work with students individually to identify details to go in each section of the Venn diagram. Be sure students understand the way in which a Venn diagram shows comparisons and contrasts.

Expanding

State Comparisons and Contrasts To help students state comparisons and contrasts, offer sentences frames such as: *In both the New York and Pennsylvania colonies ___* or *While the New York colony was ___, the Pennsylvania colony was ___.*

Bridging

Generalize Have students use the similarities they list for New York and Pennsylvania to make statements about life in the English Middle Colonies in general.

See the **Language Learner Teaching Guide** for more language support strategies.

Monitor and Differentiate

REACHING ALL LEARNERS

Approaching Level

Have students work in pairs, identifying similarities and differences between the New York and Pennsylvania colonies by taking turns posing and answering questions, such as *Who got the colony from the English king? What democratic ideas were established there?*

Beyond Level

Have students do additional research about colonial New York and Pennsylvania and add details to their Venn diagram. Remind them that information about the history of New York may also be found earlier in Chapter 3 of the Research Companion.

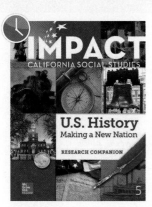

Research Companion
pp. 134–135

 STANDARDS

Students understand the political, religious, social, and economic institutions that evolved in the colonial era. **HSS.5.4**

Understand how the British colonial period created the basis for the development of political self-government and a free market system. **HSS.5.4.5**

Explain the early democratic ideas and practices that emerged during the colonial period. **HSS.5.4.7**

CCSS Quote accurately from a text when explaining what the text says explicitly and when drawing inferences from the text. **CCSS.ELA.RI.5.1**

Summarize information presented in diverse media and formats, including visually, quantitatively, and orally. **CCSS.ELA.SL.5.2**

Go Digital!

Investigate the lesson content with online whole-class presentation tools.

- **Video:** The Founding of Pennsylvania
- **iMap:** The Middle Colonies

Background Information

Farms in the Middle Colonies were generally of moderate size. The Dutch West India Company had granted some large tracts to investing landowners called patroons, some of whose holdings were still intact when New Netherland became New York; nevertheless, most farms in the colony had been and continued to be smaller. In Pennsylvania, William Penn encouraged farms of moderate size by keeping the price of land low, although he did try to charge an annual fee called a quitrents.

| TIMELINE | Invite students to look at the timeline at the top on page 135.

Analyze Ask: How long did the Dutch control New Netherland before it became New York? (40 years) **HAS.CS.1 DOK 2**

Analyze the Source

Inspect Have students read pages 134–135.

Find Evidence Use the questions below to check comprehension. Remind students to support their answers with text evidence.

Explain What qualities made the Middle Colonies centers of commerce? (central location, good ports) **DOK 2**

Explain What qualities made the Middle Colonies good for farming? (fertile soil, mild climate) **DOK 2**

Identify What are two democratic principles that the Middle Colonies helped establish? (trial by jury, freedom of the press) **DOK 1**

Analyze In what ways were the Middle Colonies successful? (in commerce, in farming, in the exchange of ideas, and in establishing democratic principles) **DOK 3**

Make Connections

Evaluate Why do you think tolerance was important in the Middle Colonies? (They had people of different religions and ethnic backgrounds who needed to get along so that the colonies could prosper.) **DOK 4**

Map Skills

Project a large version of the map on page 135. Ask:

- Which four colonial cities are shown? (New York, Trenton, Philadelphia, and Dover)
- Which three rivers are shown? (Hudson, Delaware, and Susquehanna)
- What areas were the settlements near? (the coast and rivers)

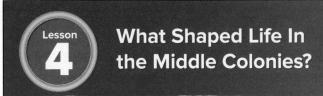

Lesson 4

What Shaped Life In the Middle Colonies?

Timeline

1624 Dutch traders found New Netherland.

1664 English take New Netherland from the Dutch, renaming it New York.

1732 Benjamin Franklin begins publishing *Poor Richard's Almanack*.

| 1600 | 1650 | 1700 | 1750 |

1638 Swedish and other traders found New Sweden.

1682 William Penn comes to Pennsylvania.

1735 John Peter Zenger found not guilty of libel.

1738 First Great Awakening begins.

A Region of Diversity

The English Middle Colonies—New York, New Jersey, Pennsylvania, and Delaware—were quite diverse, or varied. These colonies were home to people of many different ethnic backgrounds and religions. They became known for tolerance of these differences. They also became known as centers of **commerce**. Their central location and fine ports made them ideal for trading and distributing goods both north and south. Outside the port cities, fertile soil and a mild climate encouraged farming of wheat, corn, and other grains. Farming was so successful that growers were usually able to produce a surplus, or more than they needed. They could sell the surplus to the other colonies. For this reason, the Middle Colonies were sometimes called the "breadbasket" of colonial America.

A crossroads of ideas as well as trade, these successful colonies helped establish important American principles such as trial by jury and freedom of the press. They were also home to some of the most influential colonial figures. Among them was author, inventor, and thinker Benjamin Franklin.

HSS.5.3.1, HSS.5.4.1, HSS.5.4.2, HSS.5.4.3, HSS.5.4.4, HSS.5.4.5, HSS.5.4.6, HSS.5.4.7, HAS CS.5

134 Lesson 4 What Shaped Life In the Middle Colonies?

Lake Ontario

NEW YORK

MOHAWK

Hudson R.

APPALACHIAN MOUNTAINS

Susquehanna R.

Delaware R.

Long Island Sound

New York City MANAHATES MONTAUK

PENNSYLVANIA

NEW JERSEY

Philadelphia Trenton

LENNI LENAPE

ATLANTIC OCEAN

Dover

DELAWARE

· Settlement
MOHAWK Native American group
Middle Colonies

0   50   100 miles
0   50   100 kilometers

Located between New England and the Southern Colonies, the Middle Colonies became the commercial center of colonial America.

Lesson 4   135

Research Companion, pp. 134–135

ENGLISH LEARNERS SCAFFOLD

ELD.PI.5.8 Help students understand domain-specific and other vocabulary.

Emerging

Clarify Terms Explain domain-specific terms such as *ethnic* ("referring to cultural backgrounds"), *tolerance* ("respecting those who are different"), and *fertile* ("rich in what is needed to grow things"). Note that *surplus,* another domain-specific term, is explained in the text, and ask what it means. ("more than is needed")

Expanding

Use Context Clues Point out that the first paragraph explains that *diverse* means "varied." Then ask the meaning of the section heading "A Region of Diversity," based on the meaning of *diverse* and the details in the text. (an area in which people of varied backgrounds all live and varied activities are performed)

Bridging

Understand Figurative Language Explain that *breadbasket* is a figure of speech—the Middle Colonies were not really a basket of bread— and ask what the term indicates. (They supplied a lot of grain.) Ask what *crossroads of ideas* in the second paragraph means. (a place where different ideas meet)

See the **Language Learner Teaching Guide** for more language support strategies.

Monitor and Differentiate

REACHING ALL LEARNERS

On Level

Have students compare the map on page 135 with a map of the area today. Ask: How does the area of colonial settlement compare to the states of New York, New Jersey, Pennsylvania, and Delaware today? (It is smaller.)

Beyond Level

Remind students that Benjamin Franklin came to Philadelphia in 1723. Then refer students to the timeline. Ask: About how long was it before he published *Poor Richard's Almanac?* (9 years) Elicit that the answer shows he was fairly successful in a short time.

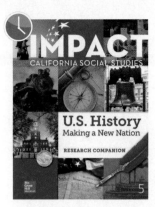

Research Companion
pp. 136–137

 STANDARDS

Describe the competition among the English, French, Spanish, Dutch, and Indian nations for control of North America. **HSS.5.3.1**

Students understand the political, religious, social, and economic institutions that evolved in the colonial era. **HSS.5.4**

Understand how the British colonial period created the basis for the development of political self-government and a free market system. **HSS.5.4.5**

Explain the early democratic ideas and practices that emerged during the colonial period. **HSS.5.4.7**

CCSS Quote accurately from a text when explaining what the text says explicitly and when drawing inferences from the text. **CCSS.ELA.RI.5.1**

Summarize information presented in diverse media and formats, including visually, quantitatively, and orally. **CCSS.ELA.SL.5.2**

Go Digital!

Investigate the lesson content with online whole-class presentation tools.

Background Information

James, Duke of York, was also Duke of Albany; Albany, New York, which the Dutch had called Fort Orange and then Beverwyck, is named for him. Despite all the renaming, James was not popular in his colony. The governors he appointed levied high property taxes and grew increasingly repressive; after he succeeded his brother as king, colonists lost even privileges they had enjoyed when he was duke. Most colonists thus welcomed England's Glorious Revolution of 1688, which replaced James II with his daughter Mary and her husband, William.

Analyze the Source

Inspect Have students start reading about New York and New Jersey on pages 136–137.

Find Evidence Use the questions below to check comprehension. Remind students to support their answers with text evidence.

> **Explain** How did New Netherland come to be called New York? (It was renamed to honor the Duke of York, brother of the king of England, who sent a fleet of warships to seize it from the Dutch.) **DOK 3**
>
> **Infer** What did the New Netherland colonists think would happen if they joined Peter Stuyvesant in fighting the English? (They would lose and have to accept much worse terms of surrender.) **DOK 3**
>
> **Identify** What colony was New Jersey part of before the Duke of York gave it to his friends? (New Netherland) **DOK 2**
>
> **Generalize** How were the lives of women in New Netherland different from those of most other women of the day? (They had more rights.) **DOK 2**
>
> **Explain** What was "half-freedom" for African slaves? (It was freedom for only part of the year.) **DOK 1**

Make Connections

> **Generalize** How much did life change for most New Netherland colonists when the English took over the colony? (not that much) **DOK 3**

Analyze the Image Encourage students to analyze the image of Peter Stuyvesant surrendering to the English. Ask:

- Who seems to be accompanying Peter Stuyvesant as he surrenders? (soldiers; militia)

- Why do you think he is wearing a red sash? (He sees the surrender as a serious ceremony, and the sash is probably something the governor wears in ceremonies.)

New York and New Jersey

England and the Netherlands were at war in Europe for much of the late 1600s. In 1664, English king Charles II decided to try to gain control of New Netherland to expand his colonies in North America. He put his brother the Duke of York in charge of seizing the Dutch colony and putting it under English rule.

The Duke of York sent a fleet of English warships to New Netherland. English troops reached the colony in August 1664. The English commander, Colonel Richard Nicolls, demanded that the Dutch leaders in New Netherland surrender the colony immediately. Peter Stuyvesant, the Dutch governor, wanted to fight the English. The Dutch colonists refused. They saw no chance of victory against the powerful English navy. They thought it best to surrender on reasonable terms. Nicolls became the governor of England's new colony. England changed the name from New Netherland to New York, in honor of the Duke of York. New Amsterdam became New York City.

The Duke of York soon granted some of the colony's land to two friends. The friends, Lord John Berkeley and Sir George Carteret, received the land west of the Hudson River. Their holdings became New Jersey, named for an island between England and France that Carteret had previously governed.

Dutch governor Peter Stuyvesant (in the yellow sash) surrenders New Netherland to the English.

Colonial New York City was a bustling port and center of trade.

Under English rule, the colonists in what had been New Netherland were allowed to live much as before. People continued to speak Dutch, particularly north of New York City. They could continue worshipping in their own churches. Most of those who held land were allowed to keep it. The practice of granting farmland to settlers continued. The English also agreed not to place troops in people's houses without paying for them.

People had come to the colony from all over Europe because the colony was tolerant of religious and ethnic differences. Women, too, had more rights here than elsewhere. They could own property, keep shops, and engage in the fur trade. The Dutch had also been active in the African slave trade and brought slaves to the colony to build the settlements or help farm the land. Though slaves had few rights, under the Dutch they did have a path through which many could become free. Those working directly for the Dutch West India Company could gain what was called "half-freedom," supplying slave labor only at certain times of the year.

136 Lesson 4 What Shaped Life In the Middle Colonies?

Lesson 4 137

Research Companion, pp. 136–137

ⒺⓁ ENGLISH LEARNERS SCAFFOLD

ELD.PI.5.7 Evaluating how well writers and speakers use language to support ideas and opinions with details or reasons

Emerging	Expanding	Bridging
Identify Support Help students find and list the three details in the text that support the idea that women in New Netherland enjoyed more rights than most other women of the day: (own property, keep shops, engage in the fur trade) Clarify that *engage in* means "be active in."	**Provide Support** Have students provide examples that support the idea that life in New Netherland did not change much when it became New York. (Colonists mostly kept their land; they continued worshipping in their own churches; they continued speaking Dutch, especially in the northern part of the colony.)	**State and Support** Have students make a general statement about slaves' lives in New Netherland and then support it with details from the text. (They had few rights but still had more rights than most other slaves, since they had a path to freedom or at least had half freedom, in which they were slaves for only part of the year.)

See the **Language Learner Teaching Guide** for more language support strategies.

Monitor and Differentiate

REACHING ALL LEARNERS

Approaching Level

Help students use context clues to determine meanings of unfamiliar words. For example, in the second paragraph on page 136, *They saw no chance of victory* is a clue that *surrender* means "to give up."

On Level

Pair students to help each other use the context to determine simpler synonyms for possibly unfamiliar words in the text, such as *seizing* ("taking"), *granting* ("giving"), and *labor* ("work").

Beyond Level

Ask small groups to research and report on the New Jersey colony and how the two sections that the Duke of York granted to friends eventually became one colony.

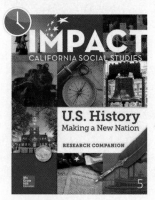

Research Companion
pp. 138–139

Students understand the political, religious, social, and economic institutions that evolved in the colonial era. **HSS.5.4**

Identify the major individuals and groups responsible for the founding of the various colonies and the reasons for their founding (e.g, William Penn, Pennsylvania). **HSS.5.4.2**

Describe the religious aspects of the earliest colonies (e.g., Quakerism in Pennsylvania). **HSS.5.4.3**

Understand how the British colonial period created the basis for the development of political self-government and a free market system. **HSS.5.4.5**

Explain the early democratic ideas and practices that emerged during the colonial period. **HSS.5.4.7**

CCSS Quote accurately from a text when explaining what the text says explicitly and when drawing inferences from the text. **CCSS.ELA.RI.5.1**

Go *Digital!*

Investigate the lesson content with online whole-class presentation tools.

Background Information

Royal and Proprietary Colonies New York was a *royal colony* under direct control of the crown, with a royal governor appointed to run it. Pennsylvania (with Delaware) was a *proprietary colony* under control of the person or family (William Penn and later his sons) to whom the crown had granted the land. New Jersey began as two proprietary colonies, resold a few times, and in 1702 united as a royal colony under Queen Anne.

Analyze the Source

Inspect Have students read pp. 138–139.

Find Evidence Use the questions below to check comprehension.

Explain Why did the English pass laws cutting back slaves' rights? (They feared rebellion.) **DOK 2**

Draw Conclusions What does the text show about the number of slaves in New York? (It was increasing.) **DOK 3**

Generalize What two democratic ideas did the John Peter Zenger trial help establish? (trial by jury and freedom of the press) **DOK 2**

Summarize Why did the king of England give William Penn the land that became Pennsylvania? (to pay back a debt) **DOK 2**

Explain Why was it important to Penn for people to practice their religion freely in his colony? (He has been persecuted in England for his religion.) **DOK 3**

Make Connections

Infer What do the details about the Zenger trial show about colonists' views of the royal governor's authority? (They resented it.) **DOK 4**

Analyze the Primary Source Note that a primary source can support, make clearer, or add information to the information in a secondary source. Ask:

Synthesize Which sentence in the text above it does the primary source give more information about? ("He then argued that newspapers must have the freedom to print material critical of the government.") **DOK 3**

✓ Stop and Check

Think What main characteristics of the New York colony dated back to the Dutch and continued after the colony became English? (diversity, tolerance, stress on commerce)

Find Details Explain to students that after they read and take notes, they should review and think about how the facts and details will help them answer the Essential Question.

One way in which the English differed from the Dutch was in their treatment of slaves. This was partly because English authorities feared rebellion from the growing number of slaves. They passed a law preventing slaves from gathering in groups of more than two. They also made it more difficult for slaves to win freedom and much easier to force freed slaves back into slavery.

English authorities also feared criticism, which they said might lead to unrest. In 1733, a colonist named John Peter Zenger printed newspaper articles that strongly criticized the governor of New York. Arrested and put on trial, Zenger was defended by a well-known lawyer named Andrew Hamilton. Hamilton insisted on a trial by jury, which is a group of peers who decide if someone is innocent or guilty. He then argued that newspapers must have the freedom to print material critical of the government. The judge disagreed, but the jury did not, and Zenger was found not guilty. The trial helped establish two important American principles: the right to a trial by jury and freedom of the press.

PRIMARY SOURCE

In Their Words... Andrew Hamilton

The question before the Court and you, Gentlemen of the jury, is not of small or private concern. It is not the cause of one poor printer, nor of New York alone, which you are now trying. No! . . . It is the cause of liberty.

—from his speech at the trial of John Peter Zenger, 1733

✓ Stop and Check

COLLABORATE

Talk What main characteristics of the Middle Colonies dated back to the Dutch and continued after the colony became English? Discuss your ideas with a partner.

Find Details As you read, add additional information to the graphic organizer on page 111 in your Inquiry Journal.

138 Lesson 4 What Shaped Life In the Middle Colonies?

Zenger, John Peter. The Tryal of John Peter Zenger, of New-York, Printer, Who was Lately Try'd and Acquitted for Printing and Publishing a Libel Against the Government : With the Pleadings and Arguments on Both Sides. London: Printed for J. Wilford, 1738.

(b)McGraw-Hill Education; (b)The Miriam and Ira D. Wallach Division of Art, Prints and Photographic Print Collection, Emmet Collection of Manuscripts Etc. Relating to American History, The New York Public Library.

Pennsylvania and Delaware

William Penn came from a wealthy English family. His father had even lent the King of England a large sum of money. In 1681, the king repaid the debt by granting land in North America to Penn. The land was called Pennsylvania in his father's honor.

Some years before, Penn had joined the Society of Friends, or Quakers. Some of the members of this Christian group had been jailed and even killed for their beliefs. They believed that each person could have a direct relationship with God. They also thought that all people should be treated fairly. They believed women were equal to men in God's eyes and allowed them to take on roles much larger than those in other religions. Quakers were against war and refused to join the military. In time, they would become strong opponents of slavery.

Penn himself had been jailed more than once for his beliefs. He wanted a place where Quakers and others could worship without fear. He called his colony a "Holy Experiment" to prove that people of many faiths and backgrounds could live together peacefully. Penn explained his plans in his publication *Frame of Government* and made them part of the Charter of Privileges under which the Pennsylvania colony was governed. In addition to freedom of religion and trial by jury, the charter set up an elected **assembly** that could propose and pass laws. However, not all colonists had the right to vote. In addition, a strict moral code limited some personal activities; for example, the performance of plays was banned.

William Penn

Lesson 4 **139**

Research Companion, pp. 138–139

EL ENGLISH LEARNERS SCAFFOLD

ELD.PI.5.8 Analyzing how writers and speakers use vocabulary

Emerging

Understand Domain-Specific Terms Clarify that *freedom of the press* is the right of newspapers and other publications to criticize, or find fault with, the government without being punished by that government; *trial by jury* is having a court case decided by a group of peers, or equals—that is, by fellow citizens.

Expanding

Define a Domain-Specific Term Work with students on a definition of *freedom of religion,* such as "people's right to worship as they choose with no government interference." Clarify that England and most other European nations of the day had laws against practicing some religions, and people were fined or put in jail for breaking those laws.

Bridging

Compare and Contrast Have students list in two columns the democratic ideas that emerged in the New Netherland or New York colony and those that emerged in the Pennsylvania colony. Ask them to compare and contrast the two columns to get a better picture of democratic ideas brewing in the colonies.

See the **Language Learner Teaching Guide** for more language support strategies.

Monitor and Differentiate

REACHING ALL LEARNERS

Approaching Level

Have student pairs discuss how William Penn was treated back in England because of his Quaker faith. Remind them to cite details from the text to support their observations.

On Level

Explain that *sylvan* means "relating to woods or forests" and that *Pennsylvania* means "Penn's woods." Ask what the name shows about the colony. (It was had a lot of woodland, or forests.)

Beyond Level

Have small groups discuss the treatment of African slaves in New Netherland and New York. Ask them to consider what the worsening treatment suggests about slavery.

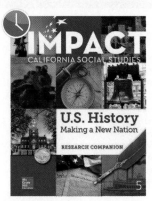

Research Companion
pp. 140–141

 STANDARDS

Describe the cooperation that existed between the colonists and Indians during the 1600s and 1700s (e.g., in agriculture, the fur trade, military alliances, treaties, cultural interchanges). **HSS.5.3.2**

Identify the major individuals and groups responsible for the founding of the various colonies and the reasons for their founding (e.g, William Penn, Pennsylvania). **HSS.5.4.2**

Describe the religious aspects of the earliest colonies (e.g., Quakerism in Pennsylvania). **HSS.5.4.3**

Explain the early democratic ideas and practices that emerged during the colonial period. **HSS.5.4.7**

CCSS Quote accurately from a text when explaining what the text says explicitly and when drawing inferences from the text. **CCSS.ELA.RI.5.1**

Go *Digital!*

Investigate the lesson content with online whole-class presentation tools.

Background Information

The Lenape, pronounced LEN-ä-pē, are an Algonquian-speaking people also known as the Lenni Lenape or the Delaware, since they originally lived in and around the Delaware River in present-day New York, New Jersey, Pennsylvania, and Delaware. Forced by the Walking Purchase to move to Iroquois lands, they over the years drifted farther and farther west; the majority today now live in Oklahoma. The name *Lenape* means "the people"; *Lenni Lenape,* "the true people."

Analyze the Sources

Inspect Have students continue reading about Philadelphia and Delaware on pages 140–141.

Find Evidence Use the questions below to check comprehension. Remind students to support their answers with text evidence.

> **Infer** What do you think happened to the Lenape after the Walking Purchase? (They had to move beyond the new borders of Pennsylvania.) **DOK 4**
>
> **Explain** What was Penn's main reason for having wide, tree-lined streets in Philadelphia? (to stop the spread of fire and disease) **DOK 2**
>
> **Analyze Cause and Effect** Why did Penn want a coast on the Atlantic Ocean? (He wanted a port that was ice-free in winter.) **DOK 3**
>
> **Compare and Contrast** What was similar about Penn's treatment of the Lenape and of the Delaware colonists? (He tried to be fair.) **DOK 3**

Make Connections

> **Synthesize** How did Penn's experiences in England affect decisions he made about Pennsylvania? (They made him try to be fair and welcoming to people of different religions and backgrounds, including Indians, and they made him try to avoid the problems of London in planning Philadelphia.) **DOK 3**

Analyze the Image Direct students' attention to the illustration of Philadelphia and its caption on page 141. Have them scan that page and the one before it for information about Philadelphia. Ask:

• What information does the text reveal about the port of Philadelphia? (It is located where the Schuylkill and Delaware rivers meet, and ships must sail down the Delaware to reach the Atlantic Ocean.)

• What information about the port of Philadelphia does the illustration add? (It was a busy port in colonial times and one of the largest cities in the English colonies.)

COLLABORATE

☑ **Stop and Check**

Think In what ways did government in Pennsylvania support people's rights and freedoms? In what ways did it fail to support them? (It granted the right of trial by jury, freedom of religion, and some self-government, including in Delaware. However, not all colonists could vote, a moral code restricted some personal activities, and the government cheated the Lenape after Penn died.)

When the king gave Penn the land for his colony, a native people called the Lenape were living on it. Penn insisted on paying the Lenape for the land. He believed that American Indians should be treated justly. His sons, however, did not share those views. After he died in 1737, they used a false document to claim that the colony was entitled to a "Walking Purchase" of more Lenape land—the distance a man could walk in one-and-a-half days. They then hired the fastest runners in the colony to cover twice as much land as the Lenape had thought they would.

When Penn founded Pennsylvania, he planned its main "towne," or capital city. He called it *Philadelphia*, Greek for "city of brotherly love." He located it where the Schuylkill (pronounced SKOOL kil) River and Delaware River meet. This seemed like a good spot for a trading port, since ships could sail down the Delaware into the Atlantic Ocean or northwest on the Schuylkill to the interior part of the colony. Penn had lived through some terrible disasters in London, and so he wanted a city where disease and fire could not spread so easily. He created a grid of wide, tree-lined streets with many small parks and gardens. On them, he planned brick and stone buildings that would not burn.

People from all over Europe came to Philadelphia. Many came because they could earn a living much more easily than in their native lands. They also appreciated the rights they could enjoy there. As trade grew, the city prospered. People who specialized in different goods and crafts—butchers, bakers, silversmiths, cabinetmakers, and blacksmiths—opened busy shops.

Outside Philadelphia, many immigrants came to farm the land. Among them were German settlers who practiced the Mennonite religion. Some belonged to a strict set of Mennonites called the Amish. These people dressed plainly and lived very simple lives. Their descendants are sometimes called the Pennsylvania Dutch, but that does not mean they are from the Netherlands. It refers to their German background and the language they spoke; *deutsch* (pronounced DOYCH) is the German word for "German."

A man dressed as a colonial-era blacksmith

140 Lesson 4 What Shaped Life In the Middle Colonies?

South of Philadelphia along the Atlantic coast was the area known as Delaware. Swedish traders had come there in 1638 and claimed it as part of their colony of New Sweden. They built a settlement called Fort Christina near what is now the city of Wilmington, Delaware. Insisting that the Swedes took Dutch lands, Peter Stuyvesant had captured New Sweden in 1654 and made it part of New Netherland. Ten years later, it became an English possession along with the rest of New Netherland.

When the English king granted Pennsylvania to William Penn, Penn was worried because the land had no Atlantic coastline. Ships sailing from the port of Philadelphia had to go down the Delaware River to reach the ocean, and the river sometimes froze in winter. Penn asked the Duke of York to sell him the area we now call Delaware, which did have an Atlantic coastline. The Duke agreed. However, the Swedish, Dutch, and Finnish colonists who already lived in the area did not like the idea of being controlled by Pennsylvania. They wanted to make laws for themselves. So in 1702, Penn allowed Delaware to create its own lawmaking assembly.

✓ Stop and Check

COLLABORATE

Talk In what ways did government in Pennsylvania support people's rights and freedoms? In what way did it fail to support them? Discuss your views with a partner.

By the 1700s, Philadelphia had become a busy port and one of the largest cities in the English colonies.

Lesson 4 141

Research Companion, pp. 140–141

(EL) ENGLISH LEARNERS SCAFFOLD

ELD.PI.5.3 Offering and supporting opinions and negotiating with others in communicative exchanges

Emerging	Expanding	Bridging
State Opinions Help students express their opinions of Penn's and his sons' different treatment of the Lenape. Offer these sentence frames to help them express their opinions : *William Penn ___ the Lenape. Penn's sons ___ the Lenape.*	**State and Support Opinions** Have students state opinions of Penn's and his sons' different treatment of the Lenape and support their opinions with text details. (Most students will find Penn fair in paying the Lenape for their land and his sons unfair in using a false document and fast runners to get more land.)	**State and Support Opinions** Have students state and support an opinion about the kind of person William Penn was. (Students are likely to have a positive opinion of Penn, supported by his treatment of the Lenape and his treatment of the colonists in Delaware,)

See the **Language Learner Teaching Guide** for more language support strategies.

Monitor and Differentiate

REACHING ALL LEARNERS

Special Needs

Identify five words that students may have difficulty spelling (for example: *justly, prospered, descendants, coastline.*) Explain spelling rules as necessary and have students copy the words.

On Level

Use maps to illustrate geographic points in the text: the location of Philadelphia between the Schuylkill and Delaware rivers; the need to sail down the Delaware River from Philadelphia to reach the Atlantic Ocean; the Atlantic coastline that Delaware has and Pennsylvania does not.

Beyond Level

Have students generalize, from text details, the importance of water transportation at the time Pennsylvania was settled. (It was very important.)

Lesson 4 **Pennsylvania and Delaware** T295

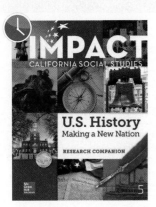

Research Companion
pp. 142–143

Students understand the political, religious, social, and economic institutions that evolved in the colonial era. **HSS.5.4**

Describe the religious aspects of the earliest colonies (e.g., Quakerism in Pennsylvania). **HSS.5.4.3**

Identify the significance and leaders of the First Great Awakening. **HSS.5.4.4**

Understand how the British colonial period created the basis for the development of political self-government and a free market system. **HSS.5.4.5**

Explain the early democratic ideas and practices that emerged during the colonial period. **HSS.5.4.7**

Students correctly apply terms related to time, including past, present, future, decade, century, and generation. **HAS.CS.2**

Go Digital!

Investigate the lesson content with online whole-class pres-entation tools.

Background Information

Abolitionism, the movement to abolish slavery, did not gain momentum until around the time of the American Revolution. However, doubts about the morality of owning slaves began to be voiced earlier, particularly by Quakers. In 1688, a group of Quakers in Germantown, now part of Philadelphia, issued the first written protest against slavery in the Americas. In 1758, the Philadelphia Quaker Yearly Meeting took an official stand against slavery, persuaded by a local teacher named Anthony Benezet who would go on to found the first abolitionist society in the colonies.

Analyze the Source

Inspect Have students read Life in the Middle Colonies on pages 142–143.

Find Evidence Use the questions below to check comprehension. Remind students to support their answers with text evidence.

> **Compare and Contrast** In the Middle Colonies, how did most people who were not servants or slaves earn a living? (They earned a living as shopkeepers, craft workers, and small farmers.) **DOK 1**
>
> **Identify** With whom did an apprentice sign up for training? (a master craftsman) **DOK 3**
>
> **Summarize** What basic agreement did indentured servants make? (to work as servants for a time in exchange for getting their trip to the colonies paid for) **DOK 2**
>
> **Define** What was the First Great Awakening? (a colonial religious movement that began in 1738) **DOK 1**
>
> **Infer** What did the content of Middle Colony newspapers suggest about colonists' attitude toward government authority? (They were often critical.) **DOK 3**

Make Connections

> **Summarize** What are two subjects besides social studies in which you might study Benjamin Franklin's achievements? Why? (science, because Franklin was a scientist and inventor; and English, because Franklin wrote literary works such as *Poor Richard's Almanac* and his autobiography) **DOK 4**

DID YOU KNOW?

Franklin's experiment proved that lightning and electricity were related. He was not the only scientist to prove this, but he did prove it in the most famous way.

Connect to Science Students should do brief Internet research to find an invention of Franklin's, such as the Franklin stove or bifocal glasses. Have them explain what it is.

COLLABORATE

☑ Stop and Check

Think What do the details about Benjamin Franklin show about life in the Middle Colonies? (People were versatile; a person could achieve a lot through hard work; ideas and writing were important.)

Life in the Middle Colonies

The English may have claimed the Middle Colonies, but the people who settled there came from many places besides England. The diversity of backgrounds and religions helped make the Middle Colonies unique. Only a small number of colonists were wealthy landowners and traders. Many more were shopkeepers, craft workers, and small farmers. They had to work hard, but there were often great opportunities if they did. Farming was especially difficult, with land to clear and weather to worry about. Yet even small farmers could become prosperous in the Middle Colonies.

Many endured difficulties hoping for a brighter future. In the cities, young boys often signed up as apprentices, or trainees learning a craft. They had to promise to work for several years with the master training them. To get to America, some people signed indenture agreements. They promised to work as servants for a certain number of years in exchange for having the cost of their trip to America paid. At the end of that period, they usually got a piece of land, a suit of clothes, or a set of tools—and their freedom. African slaves found it harder and harder to become free. However, the movement to end slavery was growing.

Religion was important in most colonists' lives. Some, like Quakers, Jews, and Mennonites, came to the colonies to practice their religion more freely. Others were attracted to new religious movements. In 1738, George Whitefield, an English preacher, arrived to lead a Protestant movement known as the First Great Awakening, because it awakened strong religious feelings. Traveling through the colonies, Whitefield drew huge crowds of people from many different churches and backgrounds.

George Whitefield's dramatic sermons drew large crowds.

Preachers were not the only public speakers that colonists went to hear. Political speeches were also well attended. And by the 1700s, printers were distributing newspapers that often contained political news—and criticism. *The New York Gazette*, New York's first newspaper, began publication in 1725. It was put out by a master printer that William Penn originally brought to Pennsylvania to print religious materials.

Colonists attending a political discussion

Words were central to the life of Philadelphia's most famous resident, Benjamin Franklin. Franklin opened his Philadelphia print shop in 1728. He married a woman who ran a bookshop. In 1731, he helped found America's first library. A year later, he began publishing *Poor Richard's Almanack*, a magazine famous for its proverbs, or wise sayings—such as "There are no gains without pains" and "Well done is better than well said." Franklin also wrote many other works, including his autobiography.

Did You Know?

Ben Franklin was also a scientist and an inventor. You may have heard about his experiment with a kite in a lightning storm, which helped us understand how electricity works. Franklin was also the first person to use the terms "battery," "conductor," "positive charge," and "negative charge."

Connect to Science Do Internet research to find out one thing that Benjamin Franklin invented.

✓ Stop and Check

Talk What do the details about Benjamin Franklin show about life in the Middle Colonies? Discuss your ideas with a classmate.

COLLABORATE

Research Companion, pp. 142–143

(EL) ENGLISH LEARNERS SCAFFOLD

ELD.PI.5.8 Analyzing how writers and speakers use vocabulary and other language resources for specific purposes

Emerging	Expanding	Bridging
Recognize Context Definitions Show students how the second paragraph in the section makes clear that an *apprentice* was a trainee who signed up for years of work in order to learn a craft and the *master* was the craftsman with whom he signed up for training.	**Define Terms from Context** Have students study the second paragraph of the section and then provide a definition of the term *indenture agreements.* (Arrangements in which people agreed to work as servants for a set number of years in exchange for having the cost of coming to the colonies paid by their employer.)	**Use Terms Defined in Context** Have students explain to each other what the First Great Awakening was, using details from the context to obtain a complete definition. (The First Great Awakening was a religious movement that began in 1738 and aroused strong religious feelings in colonial America.)

See the **Language Learner Teaching Guide** for more language support strategies.

Monitor and Differentiate

REACHING ALL LEARNERS

On Level

Ask students to paraphrase the two sayings from *Poor Richard's Almanac* and then explain what they show about Franklin's attitude. (For example: You cannot get ahead in life without working very hard; It is more important to do something well than to make a good speech about it. The sayings show that Franklin believed in hard work and effective action.)

Beyond Level

Have students discuss the popularity in colonial times of public speakers and of newspapers and other printed material. Students should consider the need for live speech and printed material in order to exchange news and ideas in an era before electronic communication.

3 REPORT

Report Your Findings

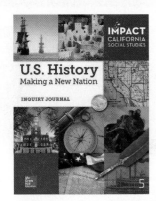

Inquiry Journal
pp. 112–113

 STANDARDS

Identify the major individuals and groups responsible for the founding of the various colonies and the reasons for their founding (e.g, William Penn, Pennsylvania). **HSS.5.4.2**

Describe the religious aspects of the earliest colonies (e.g., Quakerism in Pennsylvania). **HSS.5.4.3**

Understand how the British colonial period created the basis for the development of political self-government and a free market system. **HSS.5.4.5**

Write opinion pieces on topics or texts, supporting a point of view with reasons and information. **CCSS.ELA.W.5.1**

Draw evidence from literary or informational texts to support analysis, reflection, and research. **CCSS.ELA.W.5.9**

Go Digital!

- Students can go online to report their findings. Assess their responses online.

- Students can access the online graphic organizer to capture ideas from their investigation.

Think About It

Students should review their research and consider similarities and differences between the New York and Pennsylvania colonies.

- Remind students to review the details they gathered on their Venn diagram. Direct them to pages 134–143 of their Research Companion if they need more information.

Write About It

Write an Essay Have students read the prompt. Explain to students that an effective opinion essay includes a claim and evidence that supports it. Remind students to include the following elements in their response:

- a statement that introduces the topic

- logical reasons supported by facts and details

- words that clearly signal comparison or contrast, such as *both, alike, different, although,* and *on the other hand.*

Use the rubric on p. T300 to evaluate students' work.

Talk About It

Defend Your Claim Help students pair up with classmates who chose a different colony to write about.

- Tell students to take turns discussing their main points and the facts and reasons that support those points.

- Ask students to discuss whether they agree or disagree with their partners' assessments and to explain why.

- Remind students to follow the rules of appropriate classroom conversation.

Connect to the Essential Question

Read the prompt aloud to students. Ask them the following guiding questions:

- What role did diversity play in the growth of the Middle colonies? (It resulted in tolerance for ethnicity and religion)

- How did diversity affect life in these colonies? (Women had more rights than in other colonies.)

- What problems did slaves have as these colonies grew? (Demand for labor grew, making slavery more rampant.)

- Remind students to use the space provided in their journal to jot down notes.

Report Your Findings

Think About It

Review your research. Based on the information you have gathered, how was life in Pennsylvania similar to life in New York? How was it different?

Write About It

Write an Essay
Would you rather be a Quaker settler in the Pennsylvania colony or an English settler in the New York colony? Explain your preference, supporting your opinions with facts and details from the text.

Student essays should express a preference between a Quaker Pennsylvania settler or a English New York settler, explain the preference, and provide support from the text.

Talk About It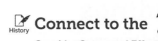

Defend Your Claim
Work with a partner who preferred to live in a different colony. Discuss the reasons for your preference. Did your partner make any good points that might change your mind?

Connect to the EQ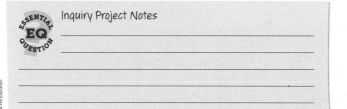

Consider Cause and Effect
Think about the diversity of ethnic backgrounds, religions, and economic opportunities in the Middle Colonies. How did the diversity affect life in these colonies?

The diversity of the Middle Colonies resulted in tolerance for differences in ethnicity and religion. Women had more rights than they did in other colonial regions.

Inquiry Project Notes

112 Lesson 4   What Shaped Life in the Middle Colonies?

Lesson 4   113

Inquiry Journal, pp. 112–113

ENGLISH LEARNERS SCAFFOLD

ELD.PI.5.11 Supporting own opinions and evaluating others' opinions in speaking and writing

Emerging	Expanding	Bridging
State and Support Opinions Provide this sentence frame to help students state and support their opinion: *I would rather be a ___ in ___ than a ___ in ___ because ___.*	**State and Support Opinions** Provide this sentence frame to help students state and support opinions: *In my opinion, ___ was a better place to live because of ____, ___, and ___.*	**State and Support Opinions** Check students' understanding by asking these questions: *What were the benefits of living in colonial New York or Pennsylvania? What problems did these colonies have?*

See the **Language Learner Teaching Guide** for more language support strategies.

Monitor and Differentiate

REACHING ALL LEARNERS

Special Needs

Have students use manipulatives representing Quaker Pennsylvania settlers and English New York settlers to express which they prefer. Then have student describe how they chose.

Approaching Level

Be sure students understand that in expressing a *preference*, they need to explain not only what is good about one colony but also why they would choose it over the other.

On Level

To help students organize supporting details in their responses, have them categorize details in their notes as (a) details that relate to diversity, (b) details that relate to economic opportunity, and (c) details that relate to other issues.

Know what your students know!

Lesson Task
Report Your Findings

Use this rubric to evaluate students' response.

Write an Essay Students state whether they would rather be a Quaker settler in the Pennsylvania colony or an English settler in the New York colony and explain their preference, supporting their opinions with facts and details from the text.

Defend Your Claim Students discuss with a partner who preferred the other colony the reasons for their preference and consider whether points their partner makes might change their mind.

Performance Task Evaluation Rubric

	4	3	2	1
Historical Understanding	Displays strong understanding of events and conditions in the Pennsylvania and New York colonies	Displays adequate understanding of events and conditions in the Pennsylvania and New York colonies	Displays uneven understanding of events and conditions in the Pennsylvania and New York colonies	Displays no understanding of events and conditions in the Pennsylvania and New York colonies
Take a Stand	Provides a clear explanation of the student's preference	Provides an adequate explanation of the student's preference	Provides a somewhat clear or unclear explanation of the student's preference	Provides no statement or no explanation of the student's preference
Support with Evidence	Supports claims and reasons with thorough and convincing evidence	Supports claims and reasons with adequate evidence	Supports claims and reasons with too little or only somewhat convincing evidence	Supplies no claims or reasons or no supporting evidence
Defend Your Claim	Speaks clearly and at an understandable pace Speaks in complete sentences throughout the discussion	Speaks clearly during most of the discussion Speaks in complete sentences through most of the discussion	Speaks unclearly at times Mixes complete and incomplete sentences during the discussion	Speaks unclearly throughout the discussion Does not use complete sentences in the discussion

Lesson Assessment

Go Digital!

- Have students complete the Chapter 3 Lesson 4 Assessment online to monitor their understanding of the lesson content.

California Smarter Balanced Assessment Connections!

Standards Covered	Lesson Task	Lesson Assessment	Alignment with California Smarter Balanced Assessment
History Social Science Content 5.3.1; 5.3.2; 5.4; 5.4.2; 5.4.3; 5.4.4; 5.4.5; 5.4.7	✔	✔	Claim 1 Targets 8, 9, 11
History and Social Science Analysis Skills Chronological and Spatial Thinking 5.1; 5.4 Research, Evidence, and Point of View 5.1; 5.2	✔	✔	Claim 1 Targets 8, 9, 11
Writing W.5.1; W.5.4	✔	✔	Claim 2 Targets 3, 8
Research and Inquiry W.5.8; W.5.9	✔	✔	Claim 4 Targets 1, 2
Reading RI.5.1	✔	✔	Claim 1 Targets 8, 9, 11 Claim 4 Target 4
Speaking and Listening SL.5.1; SL.5.1.a; SL.5.2	✔		Claim 3 Target 3 Claim 4 Target 1

How Did Economics Impact the People in the Southern Colonies?

Background Information

Explain to students that in this lesson they will learn about who settled the Southern Colonies, the economy of the southern colonies, and the rise of slavery in the South.

Community Connections

To enrich what students have learned about the economy and the people of the Southern Colonies, have groups of students look for online videos that trace the rise of slavery in the South.

LESSON STANDARDS

✓ Describe the cooperation that existed between the colonists and Indians during the 1600s and 1700s (e.g., in agriculture, the fur trade, military alliances, treaties, cultural interchanges). **HSS.5.3.2**

✓ Understand the influence of location and physical setting on the founding of the original 13 colonies, and identify on a map the locations of the colonies and of the American Indian nations already inhabiting these areas. **HSS.5.4.1**

✓ Identify the major individuals and groups responsible for the founding of the various colonies and the reasons for their founding (e.g., John Smith, Virginia; Roger Williams, Rhode Island; William Penn, Pennsylvania; Lord Baltimore, Maryland; William Bradford, Plymouth; John Winthrop, Massachusetts). **HSS.5.4.2**

✓ Describe the religious aspects of the earliest colonies (e.g., Puritanism in Massachusetts, Anglicanism in Virginia, Catholicism in Maryland, Quakerism in Pennsylvania). **HSS.5.4.3**

✓ Identify the major individuals and groups responsible for the founding of the various colonies and the reasons for their founding (e.g., John Smith, Virginia; Roger Williams, Rhode Island; William Penn, Pennsylvania; Lord Baltimore, Maryland; William Bradford, Plymouth; John Winthrop, Massachusetts). **HSS.5.4.2**

✓ Describe the introduction of slavery into America, the responses of slave families to their condition, the ongoing struggle between proponents and opponents of slavery, and the gradual institutionalization of slavery in the South. **HSS.5.4.6**

 Connect to the
Essential Question

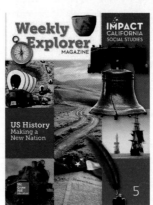

The **Weekly Explorer Magazine** supports students' exploration of the Essential Question and provides additional resources for the EQ Inquiry Project.

Chapter 3, pp. 30–43

 Inquiry Project

Tell Both Sides of the Story

Remind students to use the information they learn in this lesson and other resources to complete their EQ Inquiry Project!

Dinah Zike's

In this lesson you will use Foldables.

When Minutes Count!

Suggested Lesson Pacing

1 ENGAGE
One Day

- Lesson Opener
- Analyze the Source
- Inquiry Tools

Go Digital

- **Video:** Slavery In Charleston
- **iMap:** The Southern Colonies
- **iMap:** Triangular Trade Routes
- **iMap:** Northeast United States

2 INVESTIGATE
Two to Three Days

 Short on Time? Look for the clock to teach core content in less time.

- An Agricultural Economy
- Virginia and Maryland
- The Carolinas and Georgia
- An Inhumane System
- Triangle Trade and Slavery

3 REPORT
One Day

- Think About It
- Explain What Happened
- Share Your Thinking

Make Connections!

(ccss) CONNECT TO ELA

Reading
Quote accurately from a text when explaining what the text says explicitly and when drawing inferences from the text. **RI.5.1**

Research
Conduct short research projects that use several sources to build knowledge through investigation of different aspects of a topic. **W.5.7**

Recall relevant information from experiences or gather relevant information from print and digital sources; summarize or paraphrase information in notes and finished work, and provide a list of sources. **W.5.8**

Writing
Write informative/explanatory texts to examine a topic and convey ideas and information clearly. **W.5.2**

Draw evidence from literary or informational texts to support analysis, reflection, and research. **W.5.9**

Speaking and Listening
Engage effectively in a range of collaborative discussions (one-on-one, in groups, and teacher-led) with diverse partners on grade 5 topics and texts, building on others' ideas and expressing their own clearly. **SL.5.1**

Summarize a written text read aloud or information presented in diverse media and formats, including visually, quantitatively, and orally. **SL.5.2**

Classroom Resources

Search for additional resources using the following key words.

agricultural economics

Brown Fellowship of South Carolina

early African-American churches

economies of the early colonies

families of enslaved people

harbors and trade

Oglethorpe, James

slave codes

slave revolts

slave owners

southern food

plantations

spirituals

triangle trade

Tuscarosas

work songs

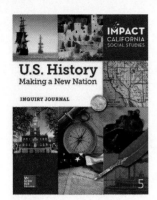

Inquiry Journal
pp. 114–115

IMPACT CALIFORNIA SOCIAL STUDIES
U.S. History
Making a New Nation
INQUIRY JOURNAL
5

 STANDARDS

Describe the introduction of slavery into America, the responses of slave families to their condition, the ongoing struggle between proponents and opponents of slavery, and the gradual institutionalization of slavery in the South.
HSS.5.4.6

(CCSS) Explain the relationships or interactions between two or more individuals, events, ideas, or concepts in a historical, scientific, or technical text based on specific information in the text.
CCSS.ELA.RI.5.3

Go Digital!

Explore the lesson content with online whole-class presentation tools.

- **Video:** Slavery In Charleston
- **iMap:** The Southern Colonies
- **iMap:** Triangular Trade Routes
- **iMap:** Northeast United States

How Did Economics Impact the People in the Southern Colonies?

Bellringer

Prompt students to retrieve information from previous lessons. Say: *Name the modern states that form the Middle Colonies; then, describe how freedom of the press developed in the middle colonies during this period.* (New York, New Jersey, Pennsylvania, Delaware; Alexander Hamilton represented John Peter Zenger in a jury trial that determined people can publish newspapers that criticize the government.)

Lesson Outcomes

What Am I Learning? Have students read the Lesson Question and Lesson Outcomes on page 114–115.

Why Am I Learning It? Make sure students understand the term *economy* as it relates to a state or a country. *Ask them if they remember learning about the economy of the earliest colonies? Say: Economy is the way a country manages its money and resources, such as workers and land. For example, the growth of shipyards contributed significantly to the economy of the New England colonies.*

How Will I Know That I Learned It? Ask students the following questions.

- What will you be able to describe? (the lives of people living in the Southern colonies)

- What is the purpose of this task? (to summarize how the way of life in the Southern colonies led to the rise of slavery)

- How will you support your summary? (with evidence from the text)

Talk About It COLLABORATE

Explain that when we look at illustrations, such as the stowage of a slave ship, we try to learn more about the conditions the slaves aboard endured. Have students look at the illustration, read the caption, and answer the questions to better understand what the illustration shows. Provide sentence frames as needed as students complete the activity.

- *The illustration shows _____.*

- *The enslaved persons were packed in crowded conditions in _____.*

- *I think the slave ship was designed and structured _____.*

Collaborative Conversations COLLABORATE

Add New Ideas As students engage in partner, small group, and whole-class discussions, encourage them to

- First read and view the material carefully.
- Be respectful of and listen to the opinions of others.
- Use evidence from the text or illustration to support their conclusions.

Lesson 5
How Did Economics Impact People in the Southern Colonies?

Lesson Outcomes

What Am I Learning?
In this lesson, you're going to use your investigative skills to explore how the economy of the Southern Colonies shaped people's lives.

Why Am I Learning It?
Reading and talking about the lives of people in the Southern Colonies will help you understand how the economy shaped their lives.

How Will I Know That I Learned It?
You will be able to summarize and describe the economy of the Southern Colonies, explain how this economy led to the rise of slavery, and support your explanation with facts and details from the text.

Talk About It
COLLABORATE

Look at the Details What does this cross-section of a British slave ship tell you about the conditions of the passage from Africa to the New World for African slaves?

REGULATED SLAVE TRADE

This drawing shows how African slaves were packed together below the deck of a British slave ship.

HSS.5.3.2, HSS.5.4.2, HSS.5.4.3, HSS.5.4.6, HAS.HR.2

114 Lesson 5 How Did Economics Impact People in the Southern Colonies?

Lesson 5 **115**

Inquiry Journal, pp. 114–115

ENGLISH LEARNERS SCAFFOLD

ELD.PI.5.2 Interacting with others in written English in various communicative forms (print, communicative technology, and multimedia).

Emerging	Expanding	Bridging
Identify Features Work with students to identify features of the British slave ship in the illustration. Provide them with vocabulary as needed.	**Describe Features** Have small groups create a list of words that describe the setup and structure of the British slave ship. Encourage them to share why they think the ship was set up as it was.	**Apply Language** Have students work together to explain why the slave ship was set up as it was. Guide them to describe the features of the slave ship that helped them come to those conclusions.

See the **Language Learner Teaching Guide** for more language support strategies.

Monitor and Differentiate

REACHING ALL LEARNERS

On Level

Have students look for more details in the illustration, such as an indication of how much space each enslaved person was allowed. Have them consider what the long journey must have been like for the slaves aboard the ship.

Beyond Level

Have students identify possible ways the people in charge of transporting slaves justified the inhumane living conditions aboard their ship.

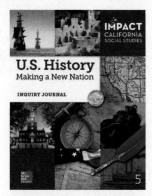

Inquiry Journal
pp. 116–117

 STANDARDS

Describe the introduction of slavery into America, the responses of slave families to their condition, the ongoing struggle between proponents and opponents of slavery, and the gradual institutionalization of slavery in the South.
HSS 5.4.6

CCSS Explain the relationships or interactions between two or more individuals, events, ideas, or concepts in a historical, scientific, or technical text based on specific information in the text.
CCSS.ELA.RI.5.3

Write informative/explanatory texts to examine a topic and convey ideas and information clearly. **CCSS.ELA.W.5.2**

Engage effectively in a range of collaborative discussions (one-on-one, in groups, and teacher-led) with diverse partners on *grade 5 topics and texts*, building on others' ideas and expressing their own clearly. **CCSS.ELA.SL.5.1**

Go *Digital!*

Model how to inspect and find evidence with online whole-class presentation tools.

Background Information

Olaudah Equiano Olaudah Equiano was born among the Igbo people in the kingdom of Benin, along the Niger River. As the youngest son of a village leader, he was expected to follow in his father's steps and become a village leader himself. Many African tribes engaged in slavery and the Igbo culture was no exception. Equiano's family owned slaves. This meant that there was always the threat of being kidnapped to become someone else's slave. This is exactly what happened to Equiano and his sister one day when they were home alone.

1 Inspect

Read Have students read the entire text, including the Primary Source, to focus on understanding overall meaning. Remind students to circle unknown words.

- What is an autobiography? (the story of a person's life written by that person)

- What important information does Equiano's autobiography provide? (details about slave trade and the experiences of enslaved Africans)

- What experience does the excerpt from Equiano's autobiography describe? (an experience on a Virginia plantation)

2 Find Evidence

Reread Have students reread the text.

Analyze the Primary Source Reread the excerpt from Equiano's autobiography aloud and then analyze the text as a class. Provide support for vocabulary as needed.

- Equiano indicates that he felt frightened as he fanned the slave owner. Why do you think this was? (Equiano is in an unfamiliar situation and has been taken away from his companions. The sight of the iron muzzle is particularly frightening for him.)

- Reread the statement "at last all my companions were distributed different ways, and only myself was left." What does the word *distributed* mean? Name a word that has the same meaning as *distributed*. (*Distributed* means to spread around. A word with a similar meaning is *scattered*.)

- What does the word *muzzle* mean? (a device that closes the mouth, preventing eating and speaking)

COLLABORATE
3 Make Connections

Write Think about the experiences Equiano describes. Then write a paragraph explaining why you think the colonists would force other human beings to live in the kinds of circumstances described by Equiano. (Responses will vary.)

Analyze the Source

1 Inspect

Read Look at the title. What will the text be about?

- **Circle** words you don't know.
- **Underline** clues that help answer the questions Who, What, Where, When, or Why.
- **Discuss** with a partner what you know about slavery in colonial America.

My Notes

_____
_____
_____
_____
_____
_____
_____
_____
_____
_____
_____
_____
_____
_____
_____

Olaudah Equiano's Account of Life as a Slave

One of the most detailed accounts of life as a slave was written by Olaudah Equiano in the 1700s. His autobiography provides important information about the slave trade and the experiences of African slaves. Equiano wrote that he was born in what is now the West African nation of Benin. When he was 11, slave traders kidnapped him. His account of traveling from Africa to the West Indies on a slave ship is a horrifying description of the brutal treatment of slaves. In the following excerpt, Equiano describes an experience on a Virginia plantation.

Olaudah Equiano

TEXT: Equiano, Olaudah. The Life of Olaudah Equiano or Gustavus Vassa, the African. Boston: Isaac Knapp, 1837. PHOTO: McGraw-Hill Education

PRIMARY SOURCE

In Their Words... Olaudah Equiano

I was a few weeks weeding grass, and gathering stones in a plantation; and at last all my companions were distributed different ways, and only myself was left. I was now exceedingly miserable, and thought myself worse off than any of the rest of my companions; for they could talk to each other, but I had no person to speak to that I could understand. In this state, I was constantly grieving and pining, and wishing for death rather than anything else. While I was in this plantation, the gentleman, to whom I suppose the estate belonged, being unwell, I was one day sent for to his dwelling-house to fan him; when I came into the room where he was I was very much affrighted at some things I saw, and the more so as I had seen a black woman slave as I came through the house, who was cooking the dinner, and the poor creature was cruelly loaded with various kinds of iron machines; she had one particularly on her head, which locked her mouth so fast that she could scarcely speak and could not eat nor drink. I was much astonished and shocked at this contrivance, which I afterwards learned was called the iron muzzle. Soon after I had a fan put in my hand, to fan the gentleman while he slept; and so I did indeed with great fear.

— from *The Interesting Narrative of the Life of Olaudah Equiano, or Gustavus Vassa, the African*

2 Find Evidence

Reread In the Primary Source quotation, Olaudah Equiano indicates he was frightened as he was fanning the slave owner. Why do you think this was?

Reread the statement "at last all my companions were distributed different ways, and only myself was left." What does the word *distributed* mean? Name a word that has the same meaning as *distributed*.

3 Make Connections

Write Think about what Olaudah Equiano describes in the Primary Source quotation. Then write a paragraph explaining why you think the colonists would force other human beings to live in the kinds of circumstances described.

COLLABORATE

116 Lesson 5 How Did Economics Impact People in the Southern Colonies?

Lesson 5 117

Inquiry Journal, pp. 116–117

EL ENGLISH LEARNERS SCAFFOLD

ELD.PI.5.1 Exchanging information and ideas with others through oral collaborative discussions on a range of social and academic topics

Emerging

Develop Language Read aloud the last part of the first sentence "...and at last all my companions were distributed in different ways, and only myself was left." Focus on the words *companions* and *distributed*. Students should understand that the word *companions* refers to the other slaves on the plantation. The word *distributed* means where the enslaved persons were working, or placed. The sentence means that Equiano was miserable because he was isolated.

Expanding and Bridging

Develop Language Guide students to describe what Equiano was feeling at the beginning of the excerpt and why he was feeling that way. Guide them to understand that Equiano was lonely because he was far away from the other enslaved persons and had no one to talk to.

See the **Language Learner Teaching Guide** for more language support strategies.

Monitor and Differentiate

REACHING ALL LEARNERS

Approaching Level

Have students discuss what they already know about the meaning of the word *muzzle*. Have them discuss when they have seen a muzzle used (on a dog or a horse, for example) and why the muzzle was used. Guide students to understand why Equiano was horrified to see a muzzle used on the enslaved woman.

Beyond Level

Have students speculate on why the muzzle was used on this woman. What might she have done to warrant such an extreme and cruel punishment?

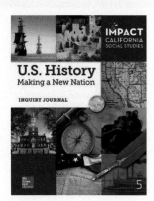

Inquiry Journal
pp. 118–119

 STANDARDS

Describe the introduction of slavery into America, the responses of slave families to their condition, the ongoing struggle between proponents and opponents of slavery, and the gradual institutionalization of slavery in the South. **HSS.5.4.6**

Students summarize the key events of the era they are studying and explain the historical contexts of those events. **HAS.HI.1**

CCSS Explain the relationships or interactions between two or more individuals, events, ideas, or concepts in a historical, scientific, or technical text based on specific information in the text. **CCSS.ELA.RI.5.3**

Write informative/explanatory texts to examine a topic and convey ideas and information clearly. **CCSS.ELA.W.5.2**

Go Digital!

- Model how to explore and investigate with online whole-class tools.

- Students can access the online graphic organizer to use the inquiry tools as they read.

Explore Cause and Effect

Explain Tell students that some of the events they will read about have cause-and-effect relationships. To better understand history, it is important to understand cause and effect. The causes of historical events explain why things happen, and the effects of an event show why it is important to people afterwards.

Read Have students read the step-by-step instructions about how to analyze cause-and-effect relationships. Remind students that many events have more than one cause and more than one effect.

Guide Practice Tell students that they often analyze information in their own lives. Give an example such as trying to figure out why they didn't get the grade in a test they wanted. In your example, include transitions related to cause-and-effect and a chronology of events.

Investigate!

Have students read pages 144–155 in the Research Companion. Tell them the information will help them answer the lesson question **How Did Economics Impact People in the Southern Colonies?**

Take Notes Tell students that they should take notes of the key events affecting the lives of people in the southern states on page 119 of the Inquiry Journal. Explain to students that they will take notes as they read each section. Remind them that taking notes will help them understand and remember what they read. Remind students that good note taking is about finding the most important information and writing key words or phrases about it. Explain to students the importance of paraphrasing, using their own words, when they take notes.

Inspect Guide students to read the text in each section to determine what the text says. Encourage them to make note of words they don't understand and look for answers to questions, such as *who? what? where? when? why?* and *how?*

Find Evidence Encourage students to reread the text to develop a deeper understanding of the content. Remind students that after they read and take notes, they should review and think about how the facts and details will help them answer the lesson question.

Collaborative Conversations

Text-Based Discussion Remind students of the goals of discussing the text with others.

- to discover a new points of view
- to find evidence from the text
- to build on each others' understanding of the text

Inquiry Tools

Explore Cause and Effect

Some of the events you will read about in this lesson have cause-and-effect relationships. To better understand history, it is important to know about cause and effect. The **causes** of historical events explain why things happened, and the **effects** of the events show why the events are important to people afterwards.

1. Look for transitional words related to causes and effects.

Because, therefore, as a result, in order to, and similar transitional words and phrases can indicate cause-and-effect relationships.

2. Take note of chronology.

Texts will often present cause-and-effect relationships in the order that they happen. This is not always true, though, so be careful.

3. Analyze the events.

Would an event have happened without this particular cause? Would the effect have been the same if the earlier event had never happened? Ask yourself questions like these to determine how strong the relationship between two events is.

4. Note that an event may have more than one cause or effect.

There are usually multiple causes for a historical event. Similarly, a historical event may impact many future events.

COLLABORATE Based on the text you just read, work with your class to complete the chart below.

Cause		Effect
Equiano saw an enslaved woman wearing an iron muzzle.	→	He was filled "with great fear" while attending to the plantation owner.

Investigate!

Read pages 144–155 in your Research Companion. Use your investigative skills to identify events and circumstances that led to the growth of slavery in the Southern Colonies.

Cause		Effect
Settlers plant tobacco, cotton, rice, and indigo in Southern Colonies.	→	These crops require large amounts of labor.
Southern plantations experience a shortage of laborers.	→	Plantation owners begin using slaves as labor.
The success of cotton and tobacco as crops in the South increases the demand for labor.	→	Slave traders provide more and more slaves to plantation owners.

Inquiry Journal, pp. 118–119

EL ENGLISH LEARNERS SCAFFOLD

ELD.PI.5.11 Supporting own opinions and evaluating others' opinions in speaking and writing

Emerging

Develop Language Encourage students to point out words in the text that describe the causes and effects of events.

Expanding

Cite Evidence Have students point out words in the text that describe the causes and effects of events. Then have them use two of those words in sentences of their own.

Bridging

Summarize Have students use descriptive words from the text in sentences of their own as they cite the causes and effects of events in the text. Have them compare their causes and effects in small groups.

See the **Language Learner Teaching Guide** for more language support strategies.

Monitor and Differentiate

REACHING ALL LEARNERS

On Level

Have students ask and answer more detailed questions to guide their reading, such as *What events struck you as being the most important or interesting? What were some of the causes and effects of these events? Why might I need to know this information to understand how economics impacted people living in the southern colonies?*

Beyond Level

Have a small group of students discuss why it is important to analyze cause-and-effect relationships when studying historical events. They should discuss why knowing what happened, why it happened (the cause), and what happened as a result (the effect) will help them have a better understanding of an event.

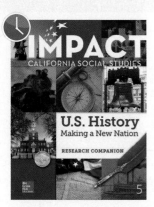

Research Companion
pp. 144–145

 STANDARDS

Understand the influence of location and physical setting on the founding of the original 13 colonies, and identify on a map the locations of the colonies and of the American Indian nations already inhabiting these areas. **HSS.5.4.1**

Students use map and globe skills to determine the absolute locations of places and interpret information available through a map's or globe's legend, scale, and symbolic representations. **HAS.CS.4**

(CCSS) Explain the relationships or interactions between two or more individuals, events, ideas, or concepts in a historical, scientific, or technical text based on specific information in the text. **CCSS.ELA.RI.5.3**

Go Digital!

Investigate the lesson content with online whole-class presentation tools.
- **Video:** Slavery In Charleston
- **iMap:** The Southern Colonies
- **iMap:** Triangular Trade Routes
- **iMap:** Northeast United States

Background Information

A Better Life Many of the first settlers emigrating from London to the southern colonies were lured by the promise of opportunity and a better life. For some the southern colonies did provide a better life. For others, the adjustment to hard and grueling work and new environment required proved impossible. Many succumbed to disease, starvation, and an inability to deal with Native Americans.

| TIMELINE | Invite students to look at the timeline at the top of page 145.

Analyze What happened after King Charles II granted proprietors land in the Carolinas in 1663? (In 1712 the Carolinas were split into two parts: North and South Carolina.) **HAS.CS.1**

Analyze the Source

Inspect Have students read about An Agricultural Economy on pages 144–145.

Find Evidence Use the questions below to check comprehension. Remind students to support their answers with text evidence.

Identify What crops could be easily grown in the southern colonies? (rice, cotton, tobacco, and indigo) **DOK 1**

Vocabulary What is a *natural resource*? (something like gold, that comes from Earth and is useful or valuable to people) **DOK 2**

Analyze How does the text help you understand why the economy of the South depended on crops like tobacco and cotton? (The climate of the South was different from the climate of the North, and it lacked natural resources. For this reason, the southern colonies depended on cash crops like tobacco and cotton.) **DOK 3**

Draw Conclusions Using what you know about the rural southern colonies, what conclusions can you draw about how the economies of specific regions depend on natural resources and climate? (The southern colonies provided rich soil and high humidity, which meant a long growing season. For this reason, the region was ideally suited for growing cotton and tobacco.) **DOK 3**

Make Connections

Consider Location Looking at the map of the Southern colonies on p. 145, what rivers and access to harbors did the southern colonies have? Why is access to rivers and harbors important? (rivers: Savannah and St. James; harbors: Charles Town and Savannah. Access to rivers and harbors aids in the transportation of goods.) **DOK 3**

Point of View If you were an immigrant longing for a better life, would you have chosen to move to North America, or would you have chosen to stay with the life you know? (Students may say they would prefer to stay rather than take on the risk and challenges of going to an unknown place.) **DOK 3**

Lesson 5

How Did Economics Impact People in the Southern Colonies?

Timeline

| 1634 | 1663 | 1732 | 1770 |
Lord Baltimore founds Maryland. — King Charles II grants proprietors land in Carolina. — James Oglethorpe founds Georgia. — About 500,000 African slaves are living in the Southern Colonies.

1600 | 1650 | 1700 | 1750 | 1800

1640 First recorded case of slavery in Virginia

1715 Yamasee War begins.

An Agricultural Economy

Life in the rural Southern Colonies differed sharply from life in the colonies to the north. The South provided the ideal **environment** for crops like rice, cotton, tobacco, and indigo. This was due to its rich soil, high humidity, and long growing season. However, the production of these crops required large areas of land and intense labor.

During the colonial period, the primary function of a colony was to produce raw goods for the mother country—England. The mother country would then, in turn, ship back to the colonies finished products. The original thirteen colonies lacked valuable resources like gold. What they could offer were agricultural goods. For New England and the Middle Colonies, this initially meant lumber and non-cash crops, such as wheat. For the Southern Colonies, it meant cash crops like tobacco and cotton.

As the colonies grew, the demand for domestic goods grew faster than Britain could keep up with. In response, the northern colonies began producing more valuable finished goods such as furniture, iron, and ships. Meanwhile, Southerners became more adept at producing cash crops. In time, finding the labor needed to produce crops like cotton and tobacco became a difficult problem for the Southern Colonies.

HSS.5.3.1, HSS.5.3.2, HSS.5.3.5, HSS.5.4.1, HSS.5.4.2, HSS.5.4.3, HSS.5.4.5, HSS.5.4.6, HAS.CS.5

144 Lesson 5 How Did Economics Impact People in the Southern Colonies?

(Map showing Southern Colonies)
MARYLAND (1634), Potomac River, Chesapeake Bay, NANTICOKE, St. Mary's City, POWHATAN, VIRGINIA (1607), Williamsburg, James River, FRENCH TERRITORY, TUTELO, TUSCARORA, SECOTAN, NORTH CAROLINA (1729), CHEROKEE, CATAWBA, WACCAMAW, Savannah River, SOUTH CAROLINA (1729), HITCHITI, GEORGIA (1732), Charles Town, ATLANTIC OCEAN, CREEK (MUSKOGEE), Savannah, YAMACRAW, YAMASEE, FLORIDA (SPAIN), APPALACHIAN MOUNTAINS

0   80   160 miles
0   80   160 kilometers

Lesson 5 **145**

Research Companion, pp. 144–145

ENGLISH LEARNERS SCAFFOLD

ELD.PI.5.1 Exchanging information and ideas with others through oral collaborative discussions on a range of social and academic topics.

Emerging

Organize Information As students look at the timeline, have them identify words, including proper nouns, with which they are unfamiliar. Have students keep a list of these words as a reference as they read the lesson. Have them write, draw on, or annotate the list as they learn about each term.

Expanding and Bridging

Collaborate Have students use information from the timeline to discuss what they think they will learn during Lesson 5. Have them write or share a few predictions that they can return to at the end of the lesson. Ask them to discuss what event or events they are most interested in learning about.

See the **Language Learner Teaching Guide** for more language support strategies.

Monitor and Differentiate

REACHING ALL LEARNERS

On Level

Encourage students to look at the timeline. Point out that in only took 60 years—from 1640 to 1700—an estimated 500,000 enslaved Africans were living in the southern colonies. Remind students to record as they make their notes what caused the rise in the enslaved African population in the southern colonies.

Beyond Level

Have students look at the timeline. Have them do additional research to predict what they will learn in this lesson. Explain that as students learn more in this lesson, they should add to the causes and effects of events their graphic organizer. Invite students to share what they have learned with the class.

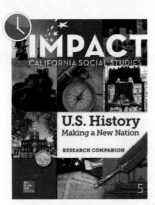

Research Companion
pp. 146–147

 STANDARDS

Understand the influence of location and physical setting on the founding of the original 13 colonies, and identify on a map the locations of the colonies and of the American Indian nations already inhabiting these areas. **HSS.5.4.1**

Identify the major individuals and groups responsible for the founding of the various colonies and the reasons for their founding (e.g., John Smith, Virginia; Roger Williams, Rhode Island; William Penn, Pennsylvania; Lord Baltimore, Maryland; William Bradford, Plymouth; John Winthrop, Massachusetts). **HSS.5.4.2**

(ccss) Draw on information from multiple print or digital sources, demonstrating the ability to locate an answer to a question quickly or to solve a problem efficiently.
CCSS.ELA.RI.5.7

Go Digital!

Investigate the lesson content with online whole-class presentation tools.

Background Information

The charter of **Maryland** stated that the people of the colony would have some say in government. It also said that people could not be taxed without their approval. By 1635 the colonists had created an assembly that made their own laws.

Analyze the Source

Inspect Have students read about Virginia and Maryland on pages 146–147.

Find Evidence Use the questions below to check comprehension. Remind students to support their answers with text evidence.

Identify What was the first colony in the American South? (Virginia) **DOK 1**

Explain Despite the fact that the tidewater area was often flooded, how were settlers in Virginia able to make money? (The flooding helped make the land fertile. For this reason, people were able to make money growing tobacco.) **DOK 2**

Compare and Contrast How did the colonies of Virginia and Maryland compare and contrast in regard to their attitudes concerning religion? (Virginia established the Church of England as the official church of the colony. Lord Baltimore of Maryland established a community for Roman Catholics, who were effectively shut out of Virginia.) **DOK 2**

Generate Based on the details you read about Virginia and Maryland, how would you define the word *persecution*? (hostility or anger based on someone's religious beliefs) **DOK 3**

Make Connections

Analyze When the Anglicans in Maryland outnumbered the Catholics, what prevented them from persecuting the Catholics In Maryland? (Maryland's charter—the Act Concerning Religion—protected the religious freedom of all Christians.) **DOK 3**

COLLABORATE

☑ Stop and Check

Talk Why did the people of Virginia and Maryland grow tobacco? (The soil of the Tidewater region was well suited to growing tobacco.)

Find Details Explain to students that after they read and take notes, they should review and think about how the facts and details will help them answer the Essential Question.

Virginia and Maryland

Starting with the Jamestown settlement, Virginia was the first colony in the American South. As Virginia's population grew, new settlements appeared west and north of the James River. This rich land was called the Tidewater. The Tidewater, a 75-mile-wide strip of Virginia's coast, often flooded. Despite the presence of salt water, the land is fertile. Settlers were able to make money growing tobacco. By 1700, the colony's population was 70,000.

In Virginia, the Church of England, also called the Anglican Church, was the established church of the colony. An established church is the official church of a nation or state. In Virginia, this meant that everyone had to pay a tax to the Anglican Church, even if they worshipped in another church.

In contrast to Virginia, Maryland was founded for religious reasons. In 1632, George Calvert, Lord Baltimore, of England decided to create a community especially for Roman Catholics. King Charles I granted Calvert land north of Virginia on which to start a colony. Calvert named the new colony "Maryland" in honor of the king's wife, Queen Henrietta Marie.

George Calvert died before he could visit the colony. As a result, his son Cecilius became the second Lord Baltimore. Cecilius decided to stay in England to make sure that the king continued to support a separate colony of Maryland. He sent his brother Leonard Calvert to Maryland in his place. Lord Leonard Calvert became the first governor of Maryland.

In 1634, Leonard Calvert, along with about 300 colonists, arrived at St. Clement's Island in Maryland. Calvert bought a village from the Yoacomoco, a group of American Indians. The village became known as St. Mary's City. Calvert promised to trade fairly with the Yoacomoco and to protect them from their enemies.

On the land that the Yoacomoco cleared, the Maryland colonists and slaves planted corn and tobacco. As the colony grew, Maryland colonists, like those in Virginia, discovered the profitability of selling tobacco to England. By the late 1600s, plantations—large farms that grow one crop—lined many of the creeks and rivers of Maryland. Chesapeake Bay had a harbor that was deep enough for large ships to use. This made it easy to transport goods to other colonies and to England.

Most of the settlers who came to Maryland from England were Catholic. Many of Maryland's other settlers, however, came from Virginia and were members of the Church of England. Soon, Anglicans in Maryland outnumbered the Catholics. This meant that Catholics might have faced persecution. Fortunately, Maryland's charter—the Maryland Toleration Act, passed in 1649—protected them. This protection did not extend to all Christians, but it was a significant stepping stone toward religious freedom in the colonies.

George Calvert, Lord Baltimore

✓ Stop and Check

COLLABORATE

Talk Why did the people of Virginia and Maryland grow tobacco?

Find Details As you read add additional information to the graphic organizer on page 119 in your Inquiry Journal.

A tobacco field

146 Lesson 5 How Did Economics Impact People in the Southern Colonies?

Lesson 5 **147**

Research Companion, pp. 146–147

(EL) ENGLISH LEARNERS SCAFFOLD

ELD.PI.5.1 Exchanging information and ideas with others through oral collaborative discussions on a range of social and academic topics

Emerging

Word Meaning Work with students individually to understand the word *persecution*. Encourage students to find information about numbers of Catholics and Anglicans in Maryland to understand the concept. Explain that when one group outnumbers the other, the larger group may persecute the smaller group. Tell students that *persecute* means to show hostility because of religion, race, or politics.

Expanding/Bridging

Develop Language Have students work in pairs to gather information about the number of Catholics and Anglicans in Maryland. Guide them to understand that when one group outnumbers the other, the larger group may *persecute,* or show hostility toward, the smaller group.

See the **Language Learner Teaching Guide** for more language support strategies.

Monitor and Differentiate

REACHING ALL LEARNERS

Approaching Level

Guide students to identify the causes that led to tobacco becoming a major crop in Virginia and Maryland. Have a small group of students work together to create a graphic organizer that identifies causes such as climate, soil, profitability, and ease of transportation.

Beyond Level

Encourage students to do more research into the colonies of Virginia and Maryland, focusing on each state's attitude toward religious freedom. Have students present their findings.

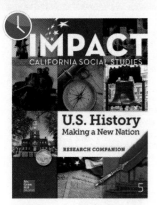

Research Companion
pp. 148–149

HSS **STANDARDS**

Describe the cooperation that existed between the colonists and Indians during the1600s and 1700s (e.g., in agriculture, the fur trade, military alliances, treaties, cultural interchanges). **HSS.5.3.2**

Identify the major individuals and groups responsible for the founding of the various colonies and the reasons for their founding (e.g., John Smith, Virginia; Roger Williams, Rhode Island; William Penn, Pennsylvania; Lord Baltimore, Maryland; William Bradford, Plymouth; John Winthrop, Massachusetts). **HSS.5.4.2**

CCSS Explain the relationships or interactions between two or more individuals, events, ideas, or concepts in a historical, scientific, or technical text based on specific information in the text. **CCSS.ELA.RI.5.3**

Go Digital!

Investigate the lesson content with online whole-class presentation tools.

Background Information

In 1732, James Oglethorpe and 114 settlers came to Savannah, Georgia. Oglethorpe worked to build the colony, even though its charter kept him from owning land or receiving a salary. He also banned slavery and treated Native Americans fairly, honoring treaties and protecting them from dishonest traders. As he tried to build a classless society, Oglethorpe lived up to the motto, "Not for self, but for others."

Analyze the Source

Inspect Have students read about The Carolinas and Georgia on pages 148–149.

Find Evidence Use the questions below to check comprehension. Remind students to support their answers with text evidence.

Recall What was it that made Charles Towne a center for agriculture and trade? (It had a natural harbor, warm climate, and natural resources.) **DOK 1**

Compare and Contrast What were the differences between the southern and the northern regions of the Carolinas? (The southern region had a good harbor, warm climate, and land ideal for growing tobacco, rice, and indigo. The northern region grew tobacco and sold forest products. It did not have good harbors, which made trade difficult.) **DOK 2**

Explain What caused tensions to erupt between the Tuscaroras and the colonists? (The colonists had a habit of cheating the Tuscaroras, who had lived in the northern Carolina's Coastal Plain for years. Tension erupted when a Tuscarora leader killed a local surveyor because the chief believed the surveyor was trying to cheat the Tuscarora of land.) **DOK 2**

Make Connections

Describe What was James Oglethorpe's plan for using Georgia as a home for debtors? Use text evidence in your response. (His plan was to use Georgia as a place where British debtors be relieved of the debt of they came to America as colonists. He believed they would want to start a new life as colonists.) **DOK 3**

COLLABORATE

✓ Stop and Check

Write How did land features impact the economies of North and South Carolina? (North Carolina lacked a good harbor and grew slowly. Charles Towne's harbor, as well as marshy land suitable for rice, helped South Carolina grow more rapidly.)

The Carolinas and Georgia

England kept adding to its North American colonies. The new king, Charles II, set his sights on land south of Virginia. In 1663, he gave a charter to eight **proprietors**. Seven years later, they founded their first settlement, the port city of Charles Towne.

From the beginning, Carolina had two regions. In the southern part, Charles Towne's natural harbor, warm climate, and natural resources made it a center for agriculture and trade. The southern part of Carolina also had large areas of low, marshy land—ideal for growing rice. Wealthy colonists built plantations outside the city. There they grew tobacco, rice, and indigo—a plant used to make blue dye.

Colonists who settled in northern Carolina grew tobacco and sold forest products, such as timber and tar. The economy in northern Carolina grew slowly due primarily to the lack of a good harbor, which made trade difficult. By 1729, the differences between colonial life in the north and in the south resulted in the colony splitting into North Carolina and South Carolina.

For years, the Tuscaroras had lived in northern Carolina's Coastal Plain. They were an agricultural tribe related to the Iroquois. The colonists had a habit of cheating the Tuscaroras in trade deals and moving in on their land. Tensions erupted in 1711 when Chief Hancock, a Tuscarora leader, killed a local surveyor. A surveyor is someone who determines land boundaries. The chief believed the surveyor had stolen Tuscarora land when he measured boundaries. The Tuscaroras then attacked settlements in the disputed area, named New Bern, killing more than 130 people. The colony's government sent troops to attack the Tuscaroras and forced them to surrender in 1713. Similarly, conflicts arose with the Yamasee, a tribe that had once been an ally to North Carolina. The Yamasee claimed the colonists owed them money. With a large army, the Yamasee attacked colonists in 1716. With help from the Cherokees, however, the colonists eventually defeated the Yamasee in 1717.

A rice field

Georgia, the last of the thirteen colonies created by the British, was founded in 1732. James Oglethorpe, a respected British general and member of the English Parliament, planned to use Georgia as a home for debtors. In England, debtors (people who owe money they can't repay) were sent to prison, often with their entire families. Oglethorpe thought that instead of wasting away in prison, debtors would be better off trying to make a fresh start for themselves as colonists.

But it was Oglethorpe's military experience, rather than his plan for dealing with debtors, that most interested King George II. The King worried about an invasion of South Carolina by the Spaniards from Florida or by the French from Louisiana. When Oglethorpe suggested that the new colony could help protect South Carolina, the King listened and granted Oglethorpe his charter. In November of 1732, a group of 114 men, women, and children left London bound for the newest English colony in America. It was called Georgia after King George II.

Oglethorpe understood that the colony's success depended on establishing peaceful relations with the American Indians in the area. A Creek group—the Yamacraw—lived near Yamacraw Bluff, where Oglethorpe planned to build his first settlement. Oglethorpe befriended the Yamacraw's leader, Chief Tomochichi. He agreed to sell Oglethorpe Yamacraw Bluff. It was here that Oglethorpe built his settlement and named it Savannah.

Initially, Georgia's growth was slow. Oglethorpe's plan to settle Georgia with English debtors failed because few debtors took up the offer. In the beginning, colonists grew corn and tobacco. Later, rice and indigo became important crops.

James Oglethorpe

✓ Stop and Check

COLLABORATE

Write How did land features affect the economies and population of North and South Carolina?

Find Details As you read, add additional information to the graphic organizer on page 119 in your Inquiry Journal.

148 Lesson 5 How Did Economics Impact People in the Southern Colonies?

Lesson 5 149

Research Companion, pp. 148–149

(EL) ENGLISH LEARNERS SCAFFOLD

ELD.PII.5.1 Exchanging information and ideas with others through oral collaborative discussions on a range of social and academic topics

Emerging

Understand Chronology Work with students to ensure they understand the chronological text structure used in this section. Begin by reviewing the meaning of the word *chronological*. Then have them identify and highlight signal words that show time order, such as "In 1663," "Seven years later," and "For years."

Expanding and Bridging

Analyze Structure Encourage students to make a list of the transitions and signal words that indicate the text structure used in this section. Have students discuss why the chronological text structure is useful to helping them understand what happened during the establishment of the colonies of the Carolinas and Georgia.

See the **Language Learner Teaching Guide** for more language support strategies.

Monitor and Differentiate

REACHING ALL LEARNERS

Special Needs

Pair students with an On-Level student to read the first paragraphs of pages 148 and 149. Have pairs work together to describe the founding of the colonies in the Carolinas and Georgia.

On Level

Work with students to create a timeline listing date and major events related to the colonies of North and South Carolina and Georgia. Have students make inferences about how major events are connected.

Beyond Level

Encourage students to research an aspect of the beginning of the colonies of North Carolina, South Carolina, or Georgia that interests them. Have them share their findings with the class

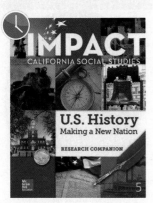

Research Companion
pp. 150–151

 STANDARDS

Describe the introduction of slavery into America, the responses of slave families to their condition, the ongoing struggle between proponents and opponents of slavery, and the gradual institutionalization of slavery in the South. **HSS.5.4.6**

Explain the relationships or interactions between two or more individuals, events, ideas, or concepts in a historical, scientific, or technical text based on specific information in the text. **CCSS.ELA.RI.5.3**

Engage effectively in a range of collaborative discussions (one-on-one, in groups, and teacher-led) with diverse partners on *grade 5 topics and texts*, building on others' ideas and expressing their own clearly. **CCSS.ELA.SL.5.1**

Go Digital!

Investigate the lesson content with online whole-class presentation tools.

Background Information

Few laws protected the five percent of free African Americans in the southern colonies. Even though they were free, they remained in danger of being forced back into slavery. Some formed organizations to help protect themselves, such as the Brown Fellowship of South Carolina founded in 1790. Churches also helped protect free African Americans. By 1787 there were African American Baptist, Methodist, and Episcopalian churches.

Analyze the Source

Inspect Have students read about Life in the Southern Colonies on pages 150–151.

Find Evidence Use the questions below to check comprehension. Remind students to support their answers with text evidence.

Describe In what ways were the lives of large plantation owners different from the lives of the owners of small farms? (Large plantation owners lived a wealthy lifestyle with slaves to help keep the plantation running. Large plantation owners also influenced the government and the way the southern economy worked. The owners of small farms had neither the wealth nor influence of large plantation owners.) **DOK 2**

Interpret Why might large plantation owners have found it necessary to hire an overseer? (Large plantation owners considered slaves property and wanted to get as much work out of them as possible. They knew that without someone watching them, enslaved people might not have worked as hard as they wanted them to.) **DOK 3**

Explain What kinds of things did enslaved Africans do to try to overcome the harshness of their lives? (Some visited their children. Others told stories and sang songs with families.) **DOK 2**

Explain How did free African Americans become free? (Some had been freed. Some escaped. Others bought their own freedom by working paid jobs.) **DOK 2**

Make Connections

Describe What was life on a small farm in the Southern Colonies like? (Every family member helped to keep the farm running. Often families combined work with play, as when they got together to help build houses, held plowing and corn husking competitions, or participated in quilting bees.) **DOK 3**

✓ Stop and Check

 COLLABORATE

Talk Have students discuss how the economy of the southern colonies impacted the lives of the various people living there. (Most white people lived on small farms. A small number of white people owned plantations, where they harvested such crops as tobacco. Plantation owners used enslaved Africans on their farms to harvest large amounts of crops. Enslaved Africans had difficult work and little opportunity to rest.)

Life in the Southern Colonies

Most Southern colonists lived on small farms with their families. Southern colonists who had once been indentured servants often ended up owning smaller farms. Every family member worked to keep the farm running. Religion was an important part of colonists' lives. Because colonists spent most of their time working, they often combined work with play. An entire community, for example, would get together to build houses for newly married people. Colonists held plowing and corn-husking competitions. At quilting bees, neighbors sewed together pieces of cloth to make a bedspread. When they were not helping their parents, children played with simple toys, such as balls, dolls, marbles, kites, and jump rope. In the evening, families often read books aloud, played music, or sang together.

Those who owned plantations, especially large plantations, lived a wealthy lifestyle. They hired workers or used slaves to keep the plantation running. Large plantation owners had great influence on government. Their view that the economy of the South would suffer without slaves was widely accepted in the region.

Large plantations were like small villages. Plantations often had a flourmill, a blacksmith, and a carpenter's shop. The planter's family lived in the center of the plantation, in a section called "the big house." Most plantations of the 1700s, however, were much smaller than the one shown in the diagram, with the average planter owning about 20 slaves. Male family members helped the planter manage the land and crops. The women worked to feed and care for everyone on the plantation. Most children on plantations were educated at home.

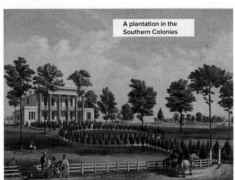

A plantation in the Southern Colonies

Library of Congress Prints and Photographs Division [LC-DIG-pga-01171]

By 1750, slaves had been living in the Southern Colonies for more than a hundred years. Although many slaves worked on small farms, most worked on large plantations.

In contrast to plantation owners, slaves lived in small, poorly made cabins near the crop fields. The work on plantations started at sunrise and ended at sundown. The overseer was the man hired by the plantation owner to oversee, or manage, work in the fields. The overseer told slaves what to do. The overseer also harshly punished people.

Slaves on Southern tobacco plantations did the backbreaking work of planting tobacco, caring for it, and then harvesting it. In South Carolina, slaves often had to move tons of dirt to build rice fields and irrigation canals. To help overcome the harshness of their lives, slaves often turned to family. On Sundays, usually the only day of the week they did not work, some slave parents could visit their children who had been sold away from them. However, this was only if the children lived on neighboring plantations. When families were together, they told stories and sang songs that mainly taught about values and beliefs. The stories about Africa gave children a sense of a different past. Sadly, these slave families were not officially recognized under the law.

A colonial-style cabin

(©McGraw-Hill Education; (b)Library of Congress Prints and Photographs Division [HABS TENN,19-NASH.V,19--35 (CT)]

Not all African Americans in the Southern Colonies were enslaved. About five percent were free. Some had been freed, while others had escaped. Some bought their freedom by working paid jobs. Free African Americans lived in cities and towns. They also lived in the backcountry—the eastern foothills of the Appalachian Mountains. There, many lived in friendship with local American Indians.

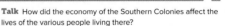

✓ Stop and Check

COLLABORATE

Talk How did the economy of the Southern Colonies affect the lives of the various people living there?

Find Details As you read, add additional information to the graphic organizer on page 119 in your Inquiry Journal.

Research Companion, pp. 150–151

(EL) ENGLISH LEARNERS SCAFFOLD

ELD.PI.5.8 Analyzing how writers and speakers use vocabulary and other language resources for specific purposes (to explain, persuade, entertain, etc.) depending on modality, text type, purpose, audience, topic, and content area

Emerging

Understand Vocabulary students to identify unfamiliar words that the author uses to describe life in the southern colonies. Words like community and cabins may have cognates in students' first languages. Have students make drawings to illustrate their understanding of each term.

Expanding/Bridging

Interpret Idioms Have students work together to make sure they understand idioms such as *from sunrise to sunset* and *backbreaking* that are used to describe the life and work of enslaved Africans. Have students work in groups to describe what the idioms mean. For example, students may choose to explain or act what backbreaking work is. Have students share their explanations with the class.

See the **Language Learner Teaching Guide** for more language support strategies.

Monitor and Differentiate

REACHING ALL LEARNERS

Approaching Level

Work with students to understand the differences between life on a small farm and life on a large plantation. Ask students to point to parts of the text that show those differences. Have students discuss as a group what daily life on a small farm was like.

Beyond Level

Have students conduct further research on large plantations in the southern colonies. Encourage students to investigate websites showing historic southern plantations. Guide students to share their findings with the class.

An Inhumane System

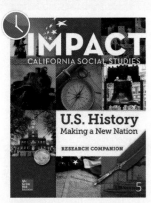

Research Companion
pp. 152–153

IMPACT
CALIFORNIA SOCIAL STUDIES
U.S. History
Making a New Nation
RESEARCH COMPANION
5

 STANDARDS

Describe the introduction of slavery into America, the responses of slave families to their condition, the ongoing struggle between proponents and opponents of slavery, and the gradual institutionalization of slavery in the South. **HSS.5.4.6**

CCSS Explain the relationships or interactions between two or more individuals, events, ideas, or concepts in a historical, scientific, or technical text based on specific information in the text. **CCSS.ELA.RI.5.3**

Engage effectively in a range of collaborative discussions (one-on-one, in groups, and teacher-led) with diverse partners on *grade 5 topics and texts*, building on others' ideas and expressing their own clearly. **CCSS.ELA.SL.5.1**

Go Digital!

Investigate the lesson content with online whole-class presentation tools.

Background Information

A revolt by enslaved Africans broke out in South Carolina in 1739. An enslaved African named Jemmy and about 20 of his followers stole guns and gunpowder from a warehouse in Stono, South Carolina, about 15 miles from Charles Town. The group killed several colonists and sent messages by drumbeats, spelling out the word *Liberty*. As many as 75 enslaved Africans joined the group. The group had hoped to escape to Florida. However, they were attacked by soldiers from South Carolina, and about 50 of the rebels were killed.

Analyze the Text

Inspect Have students read about an Inhumane System on pages 152–153

Find Evidence Use the questions below to check comprehension. Remind students to support their answers with text evidence.

Analyze How was slavery in the North different from slavery in the South? (Northern farms usually owned few slaves, while huge Southern plantations had many.) **DOK 3**

Cause and Effect Why did colonies, and later states, pass laws called slave codes? (Slave owners realized that they needed to have complete control over enslaved Africans. The slave codes were a way of legalizing that control.) **DOK 2**

Infer Why do you think the slave codes stipulated that enslaved Africans not be allowed to learn to read and write? (Answers may include: Allowing a slave to learn was probably considered dangerous because knowledge is power.) **DOK 2**

Infer Why do you think slave owners lived in constant fear of slave rebellions? (Answers may include: Even though they regarded slaves as property, deep down they also knew they were people. As people, slaves were almost certain to rebel against the life they were being forced to live.) **DOK 2**

Cite Evidence What does the fact that in spite of what they had endured, slaves managed to build a culture, tell you about their character and determination? (Answers may include: It shows that enslaved African Americans valued family, their traditions, and bettering the lives of their children. This shows a strong spirit and will to improve.) **DOK 3**

Analyze the Primary Source Read the text and the Primary Source.

Interpret What words in the songs focus on peace and relief in the afterlife? (*Just let me in the kingdom, Going to live with God forever, My Lord, I hope to meet my Jesus*) **DOK 2**

Make Connections How do you think music and song helped slaves survive? (Answers may include: Music and song helped slaves feel they were part of a group. It also helped to relieve the boredom and drudgery of their work.) **DOK 3**

✓ Stop and Check

Write Guide students to discuss the work of enslaved Africans. (In the North, few slave owners had more than one enslaved African. Many enslaved Africans in the North worked in shipyards or on small farms. In the South, large plantations with many enslaved Africans were common. Most slaves in the South planted and harvested cash crops.)

An Inhumane System

The type of work assigned to slaves depended on the economy of the colony in which they lived. In the North, many of the slaves worked in New England's busy shipyards. In Rhode Island and New York, slaves did farm work. It was rare for a Northerner to own more than one slave. Northern farms were small, and it was not profitable to use large numbers of slaves there.

Southern farms, on the other hand, were often huge and grew cash crops. The major cash crop of the Southern Colonies in the 1600s was tobacco. Both rice and tobacco required many workers to plant, tend, and harvest the crop. Most Southern plantations had about 20 slaves. South Carolina was unusual. By 1720, slaves made up more than half of the population of the colony.

The possibility of slave rebellions was a constant fear for colonial leaders. Leaders in states with large enslaved populations were especially concerned. In part to ease those worries, colonies and later states wrote laws defining the status of slaves and the rights of their owners. These laws were called slave codes. The purpose of the slave codes was to place harsh restrictions on slaves and give owners absolute power over them. The slave codes varied from state to state. Most prevented the slaves from learning to read and write. Most states also prevented them from leaving the plantation without permission, testifying in court, or gathering together without a white person being present.

Slaves had been kidnapped, forced to work, separated from their families, and punished harshly. Slaves resisted their situation by slowing their work, running away, and on occasion rebelling violently.

Despite the hardships they suffered through, slaves managed to build a culture. They orally passed down African traditions, introduced African words into the English language, and told stories to their children to teach them about life. They also created many work songs and spirituals that are still sung to this day.

Slave auction block

PHOTO: McGraw-Hill Education. TEXT: Slave Songs of the United States, compiled by William Francis Allen, Charles Pickard Ware, and Lucy McKim Garrison, 59. New York: A. Simpson & Company, 1867.

Education Images/Universal Images Group/Getty Images

PRIMARY SOURCE

In Their Words... African Slaves

Slaves working in the fields often sang work songs to relieve their boredom and to take their minds off their exhaustion. These songs sometimes had a "call and response" structure, in which one person sang a verse and the others responded with a chorus. Many lyrics featured Christian themes and dialect, or language that is specific to a region or group of people. The songs often focused on the peace and relief that a person could find in the afterlife.

Here are lyrics for two songs sung by slaves in the South:

I Don't Feel Weary

Chorus
I don't feel weary and noways tired,
O glory hallelujah

Verses
Just let me in the kingdom
While the world is all on fire
O glory hallelujah

Going to live with God forever
While the world is all on fire
O glory hallelujah

And keep the ark a-moving
While the world is all on fire
O glory hallelujah

In the Mansions Above

Chorus
Good Lord, in the mansions above,
Good Lord, in the mansions above,
My Lord, I hope to meet my Jesus
In the mansions above.

Verses
If you get to heaven before I do,
tell my Jesus I'm a-comin' too,
To the mansions above.

My Lord, I've had many trials here below;
My Lord, I hope to meet you
In the mansions above.

Fight on, my brother, for the mansions above,
For I hope to meet my Jesus there
In the mansions above.

✓ Stop and Check

Write How did the colony where slaves lived affect the kind of work they had to do?

Find Details As you read, add additional information to the graphic organizer on page 119 in your Inquiry Journal.

Research Companion, pp. 152–153

ENGLISH LEARNERS SCAFFOLD

ELD.PI.5.11 Supporting own opinions and evaluating others' opinions in speaking and writing

Emerging	Expanding	Bridging
Make a Claim Encourage students to make a claim about why slave owners had laws passed called the slave codes. Guide them to refer to the text as they make their claim.	**Paraphrase** Guide students to paraphrase information from the text as they make a claim about why slave owners had laws passed called the slave codes. Remind students that when they paraphrase, they restate the text in their own words.	**Cite Text** Have students quote accurately from the text as they give their opinion about why slave owners had laws passed called the slave codes. Remind students that when they quote, they must use the exact language the author uses, and they must set off that text with quotation marks.

See the **Language Learner Teaching Guide** for more language support strategies.

Monitor and Differentiate

REACHING ALL LEARNERS

Approaching Level

Guide students to understand why the slave system was inhumane. Review examples from the text, such as forced labor, the slave codes, and family separation. Lead a discussion about how enslaved Africans survived their ordeal.

Beyond Level

Have students conduct additional research into the slave system and its basic inhumanity. Guide students to identify appropriate primary and secondary sources to study, and have students reflect on how slavery in the Americas compares to other crimes against humanity in world history. Have students share their findings with the whole class.

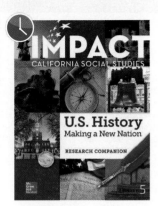

Research Companion
pp. 154–155

 STANDARDS

Describe the introduction of slavery into America, the responses of slave families to their condition, the ongoing struggle between proponents and opponents of slavery, and the gradual institutionalization of slavery in the South. **HSS.5.4.6**

Explain the relationships or interactions between two or more individuals, events, ideas, or concepts in a historical, scientific, or technical text based on specific information in the text. **CCSS.ELA.RI.5.3**

Engage effectively in a range of collaborative discussions (one-on-one, in groups, and teacher-led) with diverse partners on *grade 5 topics and texts*, building on others' ideas and expressing their own clearly. **CCSS.ELA.SL.5.1**

Go Digital!

Investigate the lesson content with online whole-class presentation tools.

Background Information

Triangle trade is a term used to describe trade that occurred between England, Africa, and the Americas. The trade fell into three categories: raw materials and natural resources from the colonies, manufactured products from England and Europe, and enslaved Africans from West Africa, many of whom would toil on plantations in the southern colonies.

Analyze the Text

Inspect Have students read about the Triangular Trade and Slavery on pages 154–155.

Find Evidence Use the questions below to check comprehension. Remind students to support their answers with text evidence.

Analyze What was the purpose of triangular trade? (It was designed for traders to make sure that they could sell products and pick up cargo at each stop.) **DOK 2**

Identify What good did ships carry in the first stage of the triangular trade? (guns, cloth, ironware and rum, all made in Britain) **DOK 1**

Infer What do you think was the motivation of the slave traders who kidnapped men, women, and children or bought them from African chiefs? (Answers may include: Their motivation was to make money.) **DOK 2**

Infer Why do you think the captains of slave ships took the time to make sure the ship was filled? (Answers may include: The more the ship was filled, the more money the captains would make.) **DOK 2**

Make Connections

Draw Conclusions In your opinion, why did some of the Africans aboard the slave ship choose to commit suicide? (Answers may include: They may have heard about the horrific journey and the subsequent life that awaited them and decided that death was a better alternative.) **DOK 3**

✓ Stop and Check

Talk Why do you think people called the journey from Africa to the Americas the "Middle Passage"? (It was called the Middle Passage because it was the middle stage of the triangular trade.)

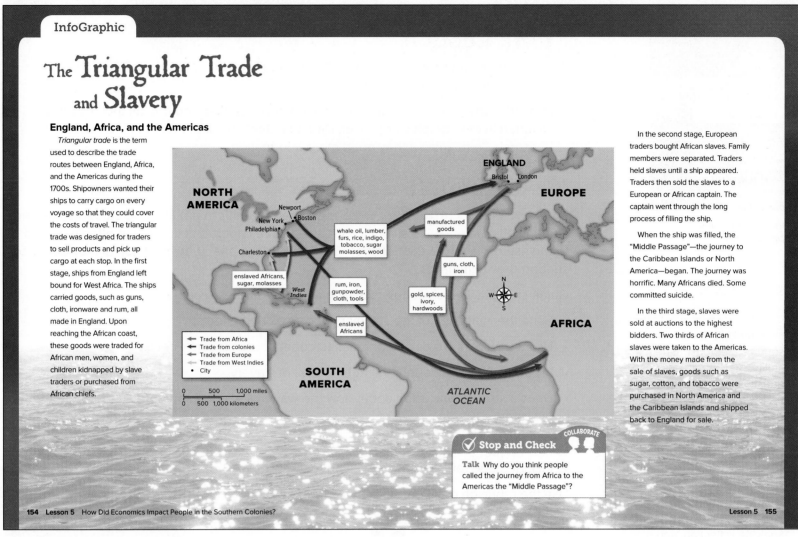

InfoGraphic

The Triangular Trade and Slavery

England, Africa, and the Americas

Triangular trade is the term used to describe the trade routes between England, Africa, and the Americas during the 1700s. Shipowners wanted their ships to carry cargo on every voyage so that they could cover the costs of travel. The triangular trade was designed for traders to sell products and pick up cargo at each stop. In the first stage, ships from England left bound for West Africa. The ships carried goods, such as guns, cloth, ironware and rum, all made in England. Upon reaching the African coast, these goods were traded for African men, women, and children kidnapped by slave traders or purchased from African chiefs.

In the second stage, European traders bought African slaves. Family members were separated. Traders held slaves until a ship appeared. Traders then sold the slaves to a European or African captain. The captain went through the long process of filling the ship.

When the ship was filled, the "Middle Passage"—the journey to the Caribbean Islands or North America—began. The journey was horrific. Many Africans died. Some committed suicide.

In the third stage, slaves were sold at auctions to the highest bidders. Two thirds of African slaves were taken to the Americas. With the money made from the sale of slaves, goods such as sugar, cotton, and tobacco were purchased in North America and the Caribbean Islands and shipped back to England for sale.

✓ Stop and Check

COLLABORATE

Talk Why do you think people called the journey from Africa to the Americas the "Middle Passage"?

154 Lesson 5 How Did Economics Impact People in the Southern Colonies?

Lesson 5 155

Research Companion, pp. 154–155

 ENGLISH LEARNERS SCAFFOLD

ELD.PI.56 Reading closely literary and informational texts and viewing multimedia to determine how meaning is conveyed explicitly and implicitly through language.

Emerging	Expanding	Bridging
Interpret Maps Guide students to follow on the map the route from England to Africa and back to the Americas. Help students with difficult vocabulary.	**Paraphrase** Guide students to paraphrase information shown on the map on Triangle Trade. Encourage them to name the products aboard ships on each leg of the journey. Remind students that when they paraphrase, they restate in their own words.	**Analyze Maps** Have students name the ports in England and America from which ships sailed and the goods that were likely traded at these stops.

See the **Language Learner Teaching Guide** for more language support strategies.

Monitor and Differentiate

REACHING ALL LEARNERS

Special Needs

Have students work with manipulatables to represent each point of the triangular trade. Guide students to match goods with each point.

Approaching Level

Work with students to understand that the primary purpose of triangular trade was to maximize profits. Review examples from the text that prove this point, such as kidnapping and making sure the ship was filled to capacity.

Beyond Level

Have students conduct additional research into triangular trade and its effect on the economies of Britain and the American colonies. Guide students to reflect on how the triangular trade compares with global commerce today.

Lesson 5 **The Triangular Trade and Slavery** T321

3 REPORT

Report Your Findings

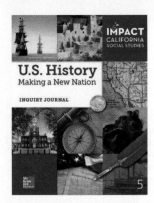

Inquiry Journal
pp. 120–121

STANDARDS

Draw on information from multiple print or digital sources, demonstrating the ability to locate an answer to a question quickly or to solve a problem efficiently. CCSS.ELA.RI.5.7

Write informative/explanatory texts to examine a topic and convey ideas and information clearly. **CCSS.ELA.W.5.2**

Draw evidence from literary or informational texts to support analysis, reflection, and research. **CCSS.ELA.W.5.9**

Engage effectively in a range of collaborative discussions (one-on-one, in groups, and teacher-led) with diverse partners on grade 5 topics and texts, building on others' ideas and expressing their own clearly. **CCSS.ELA.SL.5.1**

Go Digital!

- Students can go online to report their findings. Assess their responses online.

- Students can access the online graphic organizer to capture ideas from their investigation.

Think About It

Students will review their research and consider how the way of life in the southern colonies led to the rise of slavery.

- Remind students to review the information about causes and effects that they have included in their graphic organizer. Direct students back to pages 144–155 of their Research Companion if they need more information.

Write About It

Explain What Happened Read the Write About It prompt aloud to students. Remind students that an effective summary should include important causes and effects related to the rise of slavery in the colonies. Remind students that they must use text evidence to support their summaries.

Guide students to include the following elements in their response:

- State the main idea of the summary of causes and effects.

- Use transitional words and phrases to connect causes and effects.

- Include information about the human cost of slavery.

- Draw a strong conclusion about how the way of life in the southern states led to the rise of slavery.

- Use chapter vocabulary as appropriate.

- Include page references when citing text evidence.

Use the rubric on p. T324 to evaluate students' work.

Talk About It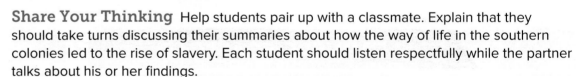

Share Your Thinking Help students pair up with a classmate. Explain that they should take turns discussing their summaries about how the way of life in the southern colonies led to the rise of slavery. Each student should listen respectfully while the partner talks about his or her findings.

 ## Connect to the
Essential Question

Read the prompt aloud to students. If necessary, ask them the following guiding questions:

- What was the economy of the southern colonies based on? (agriculture, especially cash crops that could provide wealth for the colonists as well as for England)

- What was the human cost of the slave system? (families were separated and freedoms were suppressed)

- How does the history of the slave system continue to affect the people of America? (Answers may include: Whites and blacks were not treated equally when the colonies were founded, and the goal of racial equality in American society has been an ongoing challenge since the founding of the colonies.)

Remind students to use the space provided in their journal to jot down notes.

Report Your Findings

Think About It

Review your research. Based on the information you have gathered, how did the way of life in the Southern Colonies lead to the rise of slavery?

Write About It

Explain What Happened

In your own words, write a summary of how the economy of the Southern Colonies led to the rise of slavery. Use facts and details from the text in your summary. What was the human cost of slavery? How could slavery have been avoided in the Southern economy?

Southerners chose to use slaves for labor on plantations raising cash crops. These plantations were successful, and so the plantation owners purchased more and more slaves. Cash crops became the foundation of the Southern economy, and so Southerners believed that slavery was a necessary part of their society. Slaves were treated cruelly, yet they managed to produce a culture of their own that helped them to try to endure this cruel treatment as best they could. Slavery could have been avoided if the Southern colonists had chosen to pay people to work the plantations.

Talk About It COLLABORATE

Share Your Thinking

Exchange summaries with a partner. Compare and contrast your explanations of how the economy of the Southern Colonies led to slavery. What did your partner include that you did not?

Connect to the EQ ESSENTIAL QUESTION

History

Pull It Together

What positive and negative effects did European settlements have on North America and the people living there?

Settlements sent raw materials to Europe and received finished goods in return. Demand for raw materials grew, and so the colonial economy did as well. A negative effect is that some of the raw materials were produced through slave labor.

Inquiry Project Notes

_____

_____

McGraw-Hill Education

120 Lesson 5 How Did Economics Impact People in the Southern Colonies?

Lesson 5 **121**

Inquiry Journal, pp. 120–121

EL ENGLISH LEARNERS SCAFFOLD

ELD.PI.5.10 Writing literary and informational texts to present, describe, and explain ideas and information, using appropriate technology

Emerging	Expanding	Bridging
Recap Guide students to summarize the economic reasons for slavery. *The economy of the southern colonies was based on_____.* *Large plantation owners used _____ to keep their plantations.* *Enslaved Africans were needed to harvest crops like _____.*	**Use Signal Words** Work with students to organize their writing. Have students consider using words that show time order or cause and effect. Provide signal words as needed, such as *First, second, third; because, as a result, then.*	**Use Vivid Details** Encourage students to use descriptive details. Remind them to consider language that is appropriate for their audience and purpose.

See the **Language Learner Teaching Guide** for more language support strategies.

Monitor and Differentiate

REACHING ALL LEARNERS

Approaching Level

Work with students to organize their writing based on the text structure that works best for the information they present. Review chronological order and cause-and-effect structure. If needed, provide a list of signal words for students to use.

Beyond Level

Have students use this writing project as a starting point for a larger project in which they explore the long-term effects of the slave system on the lives of all Americans.

Know what your students know!

Performance Task
Report Your Findings

Use this rubric to evaluate students' response.

Explain What Happened Students write a summary of how the Southern economy led to the rise of slavery. They discuss the human cost of slavery and give opinions about how slavery could have been avoided.

Share Your Thinking Students talk to classmates about their findings. They take turns discussing how the activity helped them understand causes and effects related to the rise of slavery.

Performance Task Evaluation Rubric

	4	3	2	1
Historical Understanding	Strong summary of causes and effects related to the rise of slavery	Adequate summary of causes and effects related to the rise of slavery	Uneven summary of causes and effects related to the rise of slavery	No understanding of causes and effects related to the rise of slavery
Explain What Happened	Clearly summarizes causes and effects	Adequately summarizes causes and effects	Somewhat clear or unclear summary of causes and effects	Summary of causes and effects, or student does not show understanding of the task
Support with Evidence	Summary contains thorough evidence	Summary contains adequate evidence	Summary contains uneven evidence	Summary contains no supporting evidence
Explain Your Thinking	Speaks clearly and at an understandable pace Speaks in complete sentences throughout the discussion	Speaks clearly during most of the discussion Speaks in complete sentences through most of the presentation	At times speaker is unclear Mixes complete and incomplete sentences	Speaks unclearly throughout the discussion. Does not use complete sentences

Lesson Assessment

Go *Digital!*

- Have students complete the Chapter 3 Lesson 5 Assessment online to monitor their understanding of the lesson content.

California Smarter Balanced Assessment Connections!

Standards Covered	Lesson Task	Lesson Assessment	Alignment with California Smarter Balanced Assessment
History Social Science Content 5.3.2; 5.4.1; 5.4.2; 5.4.3; 5.4.6	✔	✔	Claim 1 Targets 8, 9, 10, 11
History Social Science Analysis Skills Chronological and Spatial Thinking 5.4; 5.5 Research, Evidence, and Point of View 5.2 Historical Interpretation 5.3	✔	✔	Claim 1 Targets 11, 12
Writing W.5.2	✔	✔	Claim 2 Target 8, 9, 11
Research and Inquiry W.5.9	✔	✔	Claim 4 Targets 9, 11, 12
Reading RI.5.3	✔	✔	Claim 1 Targets 9, 10, 11
Speaking and Listening SL.5.1; SL.5.2	✔		Claim 3 Targets 9, 10, 11

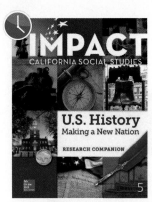

Research Companion,
pp. 156–157

 **STANDARDS**

Students know the location
of the current 50 states
and the names of their
capitals. **HSS.5.9**

DID YOU KNOW?

New York City was the capital of New York from the time of the American Revolution until 1797, when the legislature made the decision to relocate the state government to Albany. From 1785–90, New York City also served as the capital of the United States.

Analyze the Map

Inspect Have students read pp. 156–157.

Find Evidence Use the questions below to check comprehension. Remind students to support their answers with text evidence.

Identify How many colonies have different capitals now than they had in the 1780s? (all except Maryland and Massachusetts) **DOK 3**

Explain How did the overall populations of each colony change between 1790 and 2015? (Populations have mostly risen by several hundred thousand to several million people. Delaware has had the smallest increase over time.) **DOK 3**

Analyze Visuals How have the boundaries of the original 13 colonies changed over time? (All states except Rhode Island, Connecticut, New Jersey, Delaware, Maryland, and South Carolina have changed. Massachusetts owned what is now Maine. New York, Pennsylvania, North Carolina, and Georgia have expanded a little bit. Virginia has since expanded west and also split into Virginia and West Virginia.) **DOK 3**

Make Connections

Infer Why are most capitals on or near the ocean or major rivers? (because rivers allowed for easy and quick travel and trade, compared to riding on horseback) **DOK 3**

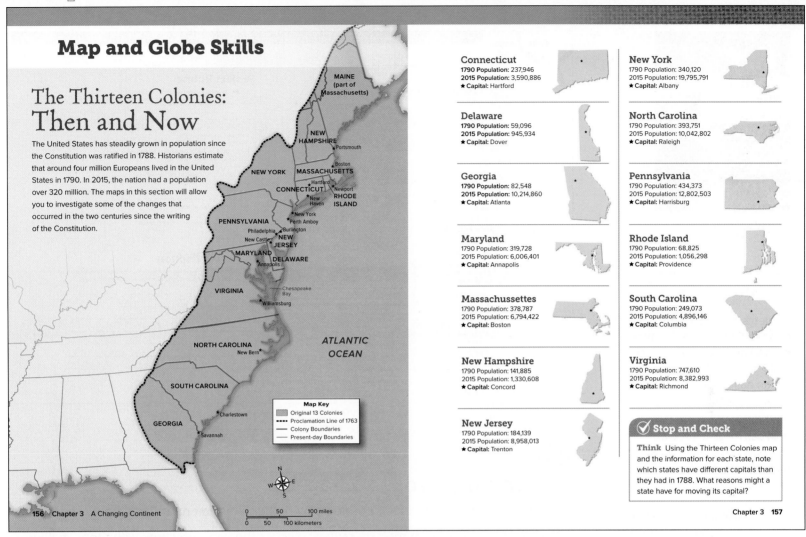

Research Companion, pp. 156–157

ENGLISH LEARNERS SCAFFOLD

ELD.PI.5.6 Reading closely literary and informational texts and viewing multimedia to determine how meaning is conveyed explicitly and implicitly through language

Emerging

Analyze Visuals Encourage students to compare the existing state boundaries with the colonies' boundaries in 1790. Guide them to describe the differences they see. Provide sentence frames as needed:

The boundaries of _____ were the same in 1790 and 2015.

The state of _____ is _____ now than it was in 1790.

Expanding/Bridging

Analyze Visuals Guide students to use the map's key to better understand what they see in the map. Have them find examples of each type of color and line. In small groups, have each student describe how he or she reads the map. Then have students collaborate to summarize the changes that occurred between 1790 and 2015.

See the **Language Learner Teaching Guide** for more language support strategies.

Monitor and Differentiate

REACHING ALL LEARNERS

Approaching Level

Guide students to use language pertaining to geography as they discuss the map. Have students first make a list of words, such as *ocean, river, mountain, trade route, population, capital,* and so on. Then have students refer to this list as they discuss how the colonies have changed since 1790.

Beyond Level

Have students conduct additional research into how the colonies changed over the course of the last 240 years. Students may choose to learn more about changes in population density or growth of cities. Invite students to share their findings with the whole class.

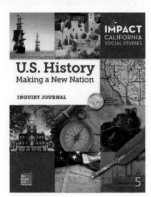

U.S. History
Making a New Nation

INQUIRY JOURNAL

Inquiry Journal
pp. 122–123

 STANDARDS

Students describe the cooperation and conflict that existed among the American Indians and between the Indian nations and the new settlers. **HSS.5.3**

Students understand the political, religious, social, and economic institutions that evolved in the colonial era. **HSS.5.4**

(CCSS) Explain the relationships or interactions between two or more individuals, events, ideas, or concepts in a historical, scientific, or technical text based on specific information in the text. **CCSS.ELA.RI.5.3**

Write narratives to develop real or imagined experiences or events using effective technique, descriptive details, and clear event sequences. **CCSS.ELA.W.5.3**

Go Digital!

Look online for the EQ Inquiry Project rubric.

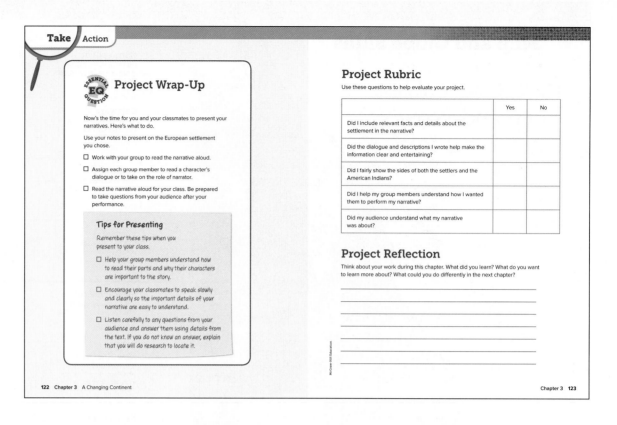

 Inquiry Project Wrap-Up

Have students share their inquiry projects by presenting their narratives.

- Before students present their narratives, discuss the wrap-up steps with them, making sure they know what's expected in their presentations.

- Allow time after each presentation for a Q-and-A session.

Tips for Presenting

Discuss the tips for presenting with students and the importance of communicating effectively with their audience. Remind students that it's also important to be a good listener.

Project Rubric

Discuss each question in the Project Rubric with students. If students have worked as part of a group to develop their projects, you might want to have them work as a group to address each question in the rubric.

Project Reflection

Student reflections can focus on the work they did as part of the group or their individual performance writing and presenting their narrative. Give groups time to discuss each phase of their projects and reflect on their work.

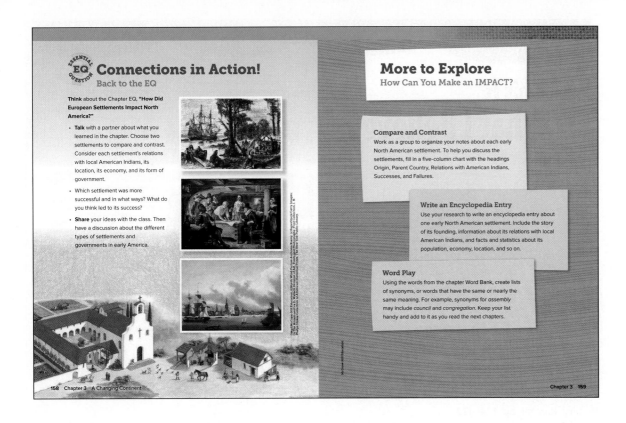

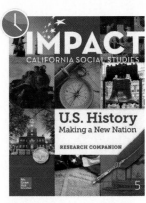

Research Companion
pp. 158–159

Connections in Action

To help focus students' conversations, you may want to discuss the EQ with the entire class before students discuss their ideas with a partner. Remind students to think about evidence they can provide that will support their ideas. After students present, allow time for others to ask questions.

More to Explore

Compare and Contrast Remind students to think about what they learned about each settlement. Encourage them to identify what sets each settlement or region apart from the others.

Write an Encyclopedia Entry Remind students of the importance of using facts when writing an encyclopedia entry. Guide students to look at real encyclopedia entries for good examples to emulate.

Word Play Have students compile their new words in an synonym Word Wall. Use the original words from the chapter word list as headings and organize the new synonyms or near synonyms under each one.

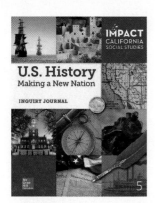

Inquiry Journal
pp. 124–127

Identify the major individuals and groups responsible for the founding of the various colonies and the reasons for their founding (e.g., John Smith, Virginia; Roger Williams, Rhode Island; William Penn, Pennsylvania; Lord Baltimore, Maryland; William Bradford, Plymouth; John Winthrop, Massachusetts). **HSS.5.4.2**

Describe the religious aspects of the earliest colonies (e.g., Puritanism in Massachusetts, Anglicanism in Virginia, Catholicism in Maryland, Quakerism in Pennsylvania). **HSS.5.4.3**

Explain the early democratic ideas and practices that emerged during the colonial period, including the significance of representative assemblies and town meetings. **HSS.5.4.7**

 Read grade-level prose and poetry orally with accuracy, appropriate rate, and expression on successive readings. **CCSS.ELA.RF.5.4.B**

Go *Digital!*

Investigate the Puritans with the online Reader's Theater. Use the printable script for whole-class or small-group presentations.

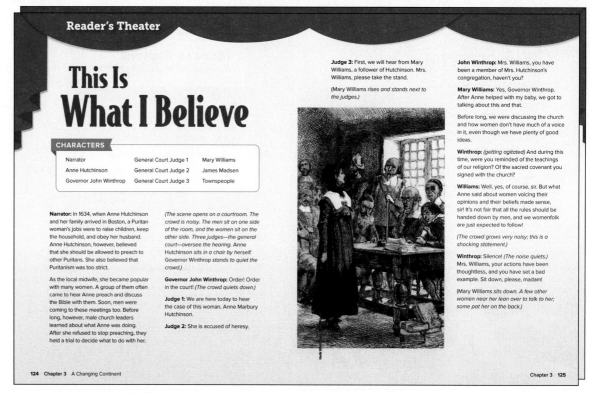

Inquiry Journal, pp. 124–127

Reader's Theater

Deepen students' understanding of the first European settlements in North America with the Reader's Theater selection, "This Is What I Believe."

Analyze the Source

GENRE Reader's Theater Reader's theater is a form of drama in which actors do not memorize their lines. They use their voices rather than sets or costumes to help listeners understand the text.

Inspect Have students read pp. 124–127 to determine the general meaning of the text.

1. Why was Anne Hutchinson on trial? (She was accused of heresy, or not following the teachings of the church. She preached to a group in the church, and women were not allowed to preach.)

Find Evidence Have students reread the selection and ask:

2. Why do you think there were people at the trial who supported Anne Hutchinson? Support your response with evidence from the text. (Answers will vary, but students might suggest that people's beliefs were changing and that they were more willing to consider that women might have a role in the church.)

Make Connections

3. Think about what Anne Hutchinson did to stand up for her beliefs. What other people do you know of in history who have stood up for their beliefs? What was the result? (Answers will vary, but students should mention both the person (or group of people) and what happened as a result.)

4. How does reading this story as a play help you understand the events? (Answers will vary, but students may say that reading the story as a play helps them better picture the events in their minds.)

Perform the Reader's Theater

Model the reading. Project the play with an interactive whiteboard or projector and read aloud as students follow along. Show how expression, pace, and word stress can communicate meaning.

- **Governor John Winthrop:** Order! Order in the court!
  How should the character read this line? Why do you think so? (The character should read this line loudly, in a commanding voice. People speak this way to get other people's attention.)

- **Anne Hutchinson:** (calmly) I understand. But to be untrue to myself would be heresy as well, for my ideas came from God.
  What does the word in parentheses tell you to do? How would you read these lines? (The word in parentheses is a stage direction that tells us how to read the line. I would read the words at a normal pace and with a voice that's not too soft or too loud.)

Practice the reading. Practice with techniques such as the following:

- Choral Read—Read together as a group to build fluency, practicing pacing and expression.

- Echo Read—Read a line and then have students repeat it.

Assign roles. Consider these strategies:

- Pair up students to read if some of your students are reluctant.

- Put students into performance groups so that every student has a chance to read a role.

- Have students highlight their dialogue and circle words they should emphasize.

Tips for Reader's Theater

- Students should have time to practice their lines before performing.
- Have students sit in a semi-circle so they can hear each other.

Remind students of strategies for reading aloud:

- Speak loudly so that your voice can be heard, and use expression.
- If you make a mistake, just keep going.

Write About It Have students complete the writing activity. Remind them to do additional research as they plan their play.

Connect to the Essential Question

Have students connect the reader's theater to the essential question. Ask: *How did Anne Hutchinson's experiences affect the futures of settlements in New England and North America?* (Her strong beliefs helped to pave the way for religious tolerance in North America. That principle still helps to define the United States today.)

Why Would a Nation Want to Become Independent?

In This Chapter ...

Students will investigate what caused the conflicts between France, Great Britain, and the American Indians in the French and Indian War (also known as the Seven Years' War). They will also analyze the differing points of view of colonists who were loyal to Great Britain, colonists who wanted independence, and the British. Finally, they will identify events that increased the tension between the colonies and Great Britain.

Lesson 1   The French and Indian War

Lesson 2   Patriots, Loyalists, and the British

Lesson 3   The Colonists Rebel

"Don't forget to use the Foldables."

 CHAPTER STANDARDS

✔ Students explain the causes of the American Revolution. **HSS.5.5**

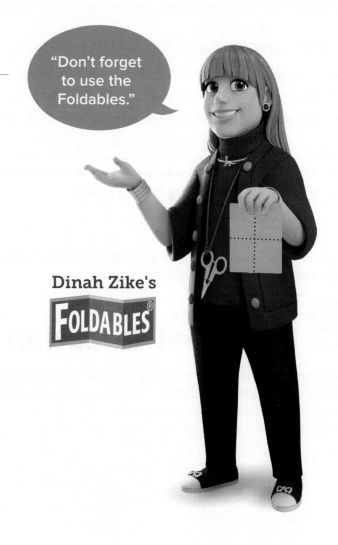

Dinah Zike's
FOLDABLES®

1 ENGAGE

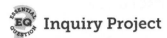

Inquiry Journal
pp. 128–131

 Inquiry Project

Which Side Will You Choose?

- **Explore Words**

- *Go Digital!*
  - IMPACT Chapter Video: The Road to War

2 INVESTIGATE

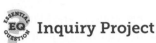

Research Companion
pp. 160–167

- **Step Into Time and Place**

- **Connect Through Literature**
  Johnny Tremain
  by Esther Forbes

- **People You Should Know**

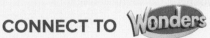

Weekly Explorer Magazine pp. 44–57

3 REPORT

Inquiry Journal
pp. 156–157

 Inquiry Project

Which Side Will You Choose?

 Short on Time? Look for the clock to teach core content in less time.

CULTIVATE MEANING AND SUPPORT LANGUAGE

Language Learner Teaching Guide,
pp. 86–87

Content Objectives

- Examine the different goals of the British, the French, and the American Indian groups in their conflict over North America.
- Explore events that led to the American Revolution

Language Objectives

- Demonstrate an understanding of suffixes.
- Compare and contrast viewpoints using transitional words.

CONNECT TO Wonders

Unit 2 Week 1
Reaching a Compromise

Read Aloud
"The Mayflower Compact"

Reading/Writing Workshop
"Creating a Nation"

Literature Anthology/Paired Selection
Who Wrote the Constitution?
"Parchment and Ink"

Leveled Readers
The Bill of Rights and "Having Your Say"

CONNECT TO SCIENCE

Explore how climate affected crops such as cotton, which was a major export from the American colonies.

Chapter 4
ASSESSMENT
Monitor Progress to
Know What Your Students Know

Choose the assessment options that work best for you and your students.

BEFORE
PRE-TEST

Measure students' content knowledge before you begin the chapter with the following questions.

 Quick Check

✔ Would the American Indians always present a united front against the white settlers?

✔ What would lead American colonists to get tired of British rule?

✔ Would reconciliation with Great Britain be possible after it had oppressed the colonies for so long?

1. Ask students to produce a response to each question by writing responses in their notebooks.

2. When all students have responded, ask them to rate how confident they are in their answers on a scale from 1 – not very confident to 5 – very confident.

3. Collect students' responses and review them for misconceptions, factual errors, and to inform instruction. You may wish to return to these questions as students investigate chapter 4.

4. **Don't Forget!** Revisit students' quick check responses with them. If students change their response, ask them to support the change with text evidence. You may wish to have students respond to a different prompt to measure students' content knowledge, such as *What specific events led the American colonists to rebel against British rule?*

EVERY LESSON
ONGOING ASSESSMENT

Use the lesson tools to monitor the IMPACT of your instruction.

 Stop and Check

Use the quick question prompts to monitor student comprehension of the content. The **Stop and Check** questions prompt students to make connections to their world today, engage in discussions to deepen their understanding of the content, and to look at different perspectives.

Report Your Findings

The lesson task, **Report Your Findings**, can be used to measure student understanding of the lesson content and ability to effectively express their understanding. See the Lesson Assessment pp. T364, T384, and T402 for task-specific evaluation rubrics.

(Go *Digital!*) Lesson Assessment

Use the **Lesson Assessment** to monitor student understanding of the lesson content. Have students complete the assessment online. See pp. T365, T385, and T403 for California Smarter Balanced Assessments Connections.

EVERY CHAPTER
POST TEST

Evaluate student understanding of core chapter content with one or more of the following assessment options.

Connections in Action

Use the **Connections in Actions** to evaluate student understanding of core chapter content through discussion.

Inquiry Project

Use the **EQ Inquiry Project** to measure student understanding of the chapter content and ability to effectively express their understanding. See the EQ Inquiry Project Wrap Up below for a task-specific evaluation rubric.

	4	3	2	1
Historical Understanding	Strong understanding of why different groups did or did not want to go to war with Great Britain	Adequate understanding of why different groups did or did not want to go to war with Great Britain	Uneven understanding of why different groups did or did not want to go to war with Great Britain	No understanding of why different groups did or did not want to go to war with Great Britain
Write an Essay	Carefully chooses and integrates facts and details from the text to support main ideas	Adequately uses facts and details from the text to support main ideas	Uses somewhat unclear facts and details from the text to support main ideas	No facts or details given or student does not show understanding of the task
Maintains a clear Perspective	Cleverly integrates the point of view of the character and/or group chosen	Adequately integrates character point of view	Includes little evidence of the character's point of view	Includes no clear point of view
Debate	Speaks clearly and does not interrupt during debate Debates from the point of view of the character	Speaks clearly during most of the debate Debates mainly from the character's point of view	Does not speak up or interrupts others during debate Does not always debate from the character's point of view	Does not participate in debate Does not remain in character during debate

(Go *Digital!*) **Chapter Benchmark Assessments**

Use the chapter tests to monitor student understanding of the chapter History-Social Science standards and content. Have students complete the assessment online.

pp. 44–57

⏱ Short on Time?
Use the Weekly Explorer Magazine during your reading block.

Go *Digital!*
Look online for the Weekly Explorer Magazine Teaching Guide.

Remind students to look for the Word Blasts as they read the Explorer Magazine.

FOLDABLES

Encourage students to use the Notetaking Foldables as they gather more information.

Weekly Explorer Magazine

The Weekly Explorer Magazine is designed to provide students with more information to use as they dig deeper into the **road to war**. The articles in a variety of formats explore the Essential Question and support the Inquiry Project.

Engage

Build background for students and share any information needed to provide a context for the chapter topic. Have students read the Essential Question and the Table of Contents.

Analyze the Visual Discuss the opening visual (photograph, photo essay, atwork) on the second page of the Magazine chapter. Help students connect the visual to the chapter topic and the Essential Question.

Analyze the Sources

Students will read and analyze the articles, graphic novel, poems, songs, literature excerpts, primary sources, and infographics.

Read and Analyze Before reading, provide any additional information you think students will need about the topics. Then guide students through the three-step process to read and analyze the articles.

1 Inspect Have students skim the article or articles on a page or multiple pages. Ask questions to help students recall and retell key ideas.

- What is this article mostly about?
- Who is _____?

2 Find Evidence Have students reread the articles and look for details they might have missed. Ask additional questions to help them read more closely.

- What details do you notice in the photographs?
- Why was _____ important?

3 Make Connections Have students work in pairs or small groups to discuss prompts that help them connect the article(s) to other texts, their own lives, current ideas and issues, and other topics.

- How is _____ similar to what we do today?
- How do you think _____ felt about what happened?
- What do you think about _____?

 **Bibliography**

The following suggested resources may help students' investigation of the chapter content.

EXPLORE PEOPLE, PLACES, AND EVENTS

▶ **Can't You Make Them Behave, King George?**
by Jean Fritz; Puffin Books, 1996.

▶ **Johnny Tremain**
by Esther Forbes; Houghton Mifflin, 1943.

▶ **Hannah's Winter of Hope**
by Jean Van Leeuwen; Dial Books, 2000.

Perspectives
▶ **Lafayette and the American Revolution**
by Russell Freedman; Holiday House, 2010.

▶ **The Last of the Mohicans**
by James Fenimore Cooper; Oxford University Press, 1998.

▶ **Notorious Benedict Arnold: A True Story of Adventure, Heroism, and Treachery**
by Steve Sheinkin; Flash Point/Roaring Book Press, 2010.

Perspectives
▶ **The Split History of the American Revolution**
by Michael Burgan; Compass Point Books, 2002.

▶ **Struggle for a Continent: The French and Indian Wars**
by Betsy Maestro; Harper Collins, 2000.

EXPLORE MUSIC

Did you know? A popular type of song in the mid-1700s was the ballad. Ballads usually told a sad tale about a lost love or a tragic death. **On Springfield Mountain** (ca. 1761) was one such ballad. The lyrics tell of a young man bitten by a rattlesnake while working in the fields. The song is actually based on a true story. Timothy Merrick died of snakebite on August 7, 1761.

Did you know? Considered to be the first real American art song, **My Days Have Been So Wondrous Free** was written in 1759 by Francis Hopkinson. Hopkinson was a signer of the Declaration of Independence and a designer of the first official American flag. An art song is a type of music composed for voice and piano and usually about love or nature. The first stanza of this song is:

My days have been so wondrous free,

The little Birds that fly,

With careless Ease from Tree to Tree

Were but as blest as I,

Were but as blest as I.

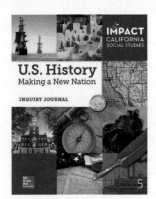

Inquiry Journal
pp. 128–131

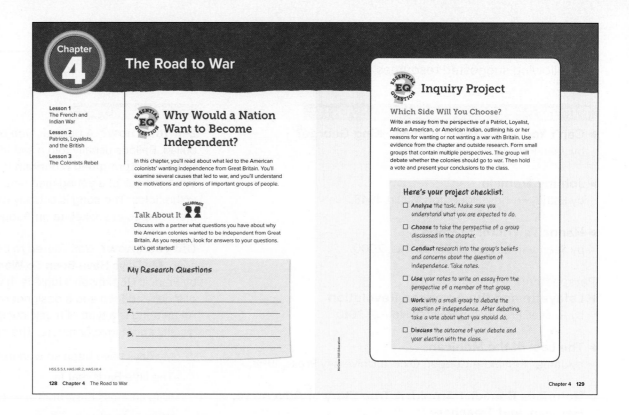

 STANDARDS

Students explain the causes of the American Revolution. **HSS.5.5**

 Write informative/ explanatory texts to examine a topic and convey ideas and information clearly. **CCSS.ELA.W.5.2**

Draw evidence from literary or informational texts to support analysis, reflection, and research. **CCSS.ELA.W.5.9**

Go Digital!

Explore Words: Interactive vocabulary activities support students as they explore the chapter words.

 See the **Language Learner Teaching Guide** pp. 86–87 for support strategies.

Why Would a Nation Want to Become Independent?

Have students read the Chapter Essential Question on p. 128.

Talk About It

- Prompt students to write what they would like to know about how tensions between Great Britain and the American colonies grew into a war.

- After jotting down their questions, have students discuss their questions with partners.

Inquiry Project

Which Side Will You Choose?

- Have students read aloud the EQ Inquiry Project.

- Tell students that they will use information gathered from the chapter and from independent research to complete the project.

- Make certain students understand the task by reviewing each step of the project.

Explore Words

Complete this chapter's Word Rater. Write notes as you learn more about each word.

boycott	My Notes
☐ Know It!	
☐ Heard It!	
☐ Don't Know It!	

outpost	My Notes
☐ Know It!	
☐ Heard It!	
☐ Don't Know It!	

habitat	My Notes
☐ Know It!	
☐ Heard It!	
☐ Don't Know It!	

recession	My Notes
☐ Know It!	
☐ Heard It!	
☐ Don't Know It!	

imposing	My Notes
☐ Know It!	
☐ Heard It!	
☐ Don't Know It!	

reconcile	My Notes
☐ Know It!	
☐ Heard It!	
☐ Don't Know It!	

monopoly	My Notes
☐ Know It!	
☐ Heard It!	
☐ Don't Know It!	

repeal	My Notes
☐ Know It!	
☐ Heard It!	
☐ Don't Know It!	

musket	My Notes
☐ Know It!	
☐ Heard It!	
☐ Don't Know It!	

vandalism	My Notes
☐ Know It!	
☐ Heard It!	
☐ Don't Know It!	

McGraw-Hill Education

Explore Words

- **Academic/Domain-Specific Vocabulary** Read the words aloud to students. Explain to students that these are words they will learn more about in the chapter.

- **Word Rater** Have students place a checkmark in one of the three boxes below each word, indicating that they "Know It," "Heard It," or "Don't Know It."

  ✓ **Know It** Tell students that if they know the word, they should write its meaning on the lines provided.

  ✓ **Heard It** Tell students that if they have heard, or are familiar with the word, they should write what they know about it on the lines provided. Remind them to take notes about the word as they encounter it.

  ✓ **Don't Know It** If they do not know the word's meaning, tell them to write down its meaning when they encounter the word in the chapter.

🔍 Explore Words Routine

Remind students that when they come to an unfamiliar word or phrase in their research, they should follow these steps to determine its meaning.

1. Look around the word or phrase for clues to unlock its meaning.

2. Look inside the word or phrase for word part clues.

3. Look up the word in other resources.

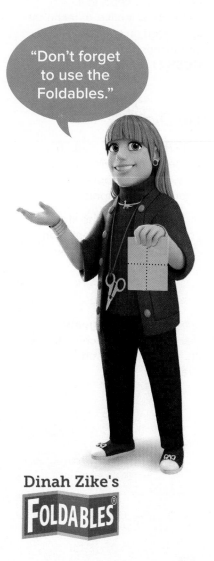

"Don't forget to use the Foldables."

Dinah Zike's

FOLDABLES®

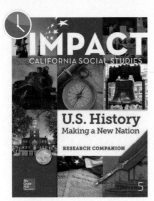

Research Companion
pp. 160–165

 STANDARDS

Students explain the causes of the American Revolution. **HSS.5.5**

CCSS Explain the relationships or interactions between two or more individuals, events, ideas, or concepts in a historical, scientific, or technical text based on specific information in the text. **CCSS.ELA.RI.5.3**

Go *Digital!*

- Investigate the lead up to the American Revolution with online whole-class presentation tools.

- Analyze the online literature selection so students can find evidence and make connections.

See the **Language Learner Teaching Guide** pp. 86–87 for support strategies.

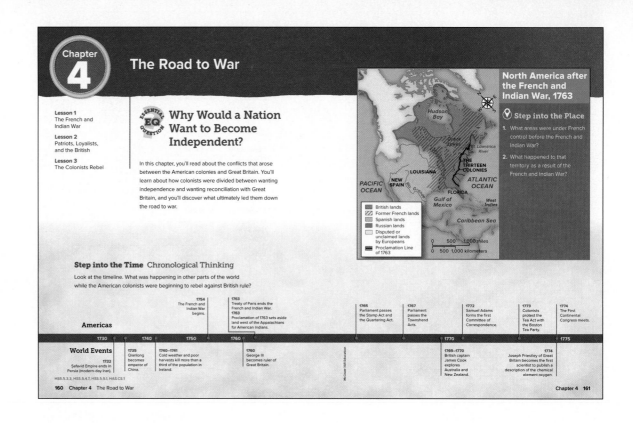

Step Into Time

Have students read over the events on the timeline, first examining the events from the Americas and then the events from around the world.

- What was happening in the Americas when King George III became ruler of Great Britain? (the French and Indian War [Seven Years' War])

- How many years passed between the Stamp Act and the Boston Tea Party? (about 8 years)

Step Into Place

In partners or in small groups, have students examine the map on p. 161 and answer the questions beneath it.

1. What areas were under French control before the French and Indian War? (much of the land between the East Coast and the Mississippi River.)

2. What happened to that territory as a result of the French and Indian War? (England and Spain divided up France's territory between themselves.)

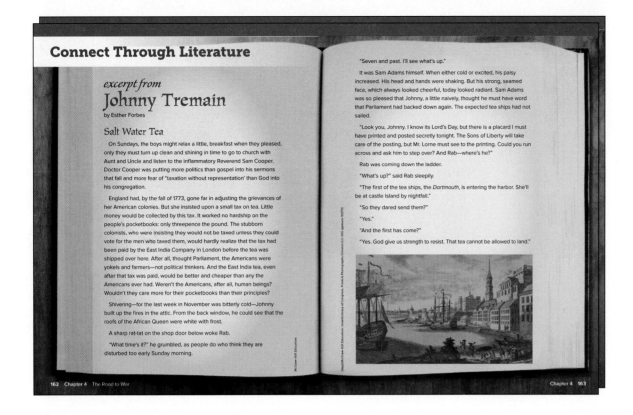

Connect Through Literature

excerpt from

Johnny Tremain

by Esther Forbes

Salt Water Tea

On Sundays, the boys might relax a little, breakfast when they pleased, only they must turn up clean and shining in time to go to church with Aunt and Uncle and listen to the inflammatory Reverend Sam Cooper. Doctor Cooper was putting more politics than gospel into his sermons that fall and more fear of "taxation without representation" than God into his congregation.

England had, by the fall of 1773, gone far in adjusting the grievances of her American colonies. But she insisted upon a small tax on tea. Little money would be collected by this tax. It worked no hardship on the people's pocketbooks: only threepence the pound. The stubborn colonists, who were insisting they would not be taxed unless they could vote for the men who taxed them, would hardly realize that the tax had been paid by the East India Company in London before the tea was shipped over here. After all, thought Parliament, the Americans were yokels and farmers—not political thinkers. And the East India tea, even after that tax was paid, would be better and cheaper than any the Americans ever had. Weren't the Americans, after all, human beings? Wouldn't they care more for their pocketbooks than their principles?

Shivering—for the last week in November was bitterly cold—Johnny built up the fires in the attic. From the back window, he could see that the roofs of the African Queen were white with frost.

A sharp rat-tat on the shop door below woke Rab.

"What time's it?" he grumbled, as people do who think they are disturbed too early Sunday morning.

"Seven and past. I'll see what's up."

It was Sam Adams himself. When either cold or excited, his palsy increased. His head and hands were shaking. But his strong, seamed face, which always looked cheerful, today looked radiant. Sam Adams was so pleased that Johnny, a little naively, thought he must have word that Parliament had backed down again. The expected tea ships had not sailed.

"Look you, Johnny. I know its Lord's Day, but there is a placard I must have printed and posted secretly tonight. The Sons of Liberty will take care of the posting, but Mr. Lorne must see to the printing. Could you run across and ask him to step over? And Rab—where's he?"

Rab was coming down the ladder.

"What's up?" said Rab sleepily.

"The first of the tea ships, the *Dartmouth*, is entering the harbor. She'll be at castle Island by nightfall."

"So they dared send them?"

"Yes."

"And the first has come?"

"Yes. God give us strength to resist. That tea cannot be allowed to land."

Background Information

Johnny Tremain, by Esther Forbes, is the story of a boy who lives in Boston during the events that occurred before the start of the American Revolution. He participates in the Boston Tea Party, which is where this excerpt begins.

GENRE Fiction *Johnny Tremain is a work of fiction. It tells a story using characters, setting, and plot.*

Analyze the Source

Inspect Have students read the selection on pp. 162–165 together to determine the general meaning of the text.

1. How would you describe Johnny's role in the resistance? (He passages messages, knows the identity of key members, keeps secrets, and knows secret codes.)

Find Evidence Have students reread the selection and ask:

2. Why do you think the Sons of Liberty used Johnny in this role? (As a young boy, he might arouse less suspicion than a grown man.)

Make Connections

3. Why is Sam Adams so determined to stop the arrival of the tea? (The tea had been taxed by the British government and if it was sold in the colonies, the colonists would be forced to pay a tax without representation.)

Perspectives How is reading about the lead up to the war through Johnny's eyes different than reading about it in a history book? (Answers will vary.)

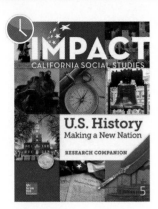

Research Companion
pp. 166–167

 STANDARDS

Students explain the causes of the American Revolution. **HSS.5.5**

Explain the relationships or interactions between two or more individuals, events, ideas, or concepts in a historical, scientific, or technical text based on specific information in the text. **CCSS.ELA.RI.5.3**

Go Digital!

investigate chapter content with the online teaching plan.

See the **Language Learner Teacher Guide** pp. 86–87 for support strategies.

People You Should Know

James Logan

The son of Chief Shikellamy of the Oneida people, James Logan was a respected figure in the Pennsylvania colony. His good relationship with the white settlers in the area of the Ohio River Valley lasted until 1774. At that time, a trader murdered Logan's family during the Yellow Creek Massacre. This treachery sparked the conflict that came to be called Lord Dunmore's War between the American Indians and European settlers. Later, he helped the British army during the American Revolution.

Sarah Bradlee Fulton

Called "Mother of the Boston Tea Party," Sarah Bradlee Fulton used her own kitchen as a meeting place for the men who dumped tea into Boston Harbor on December 16, 1773. She and other "Daughters of Liberty" showed similar resistance to the British throughout the revolution that was to come. She organized women to nurse wounded soldier after the Battle of Bunker Hill and acted as a courier, crossing enemy lines and risking her own life during the Revolutionary War.

William Pitt, the Elder

A British leader, William Pitt was a mastermind of Great Britain's strategy in the Seven Years' War, which included the French and Indian War. Pitt convinced Parliament to put him in charge, to give him almost unlimited resources, and to let him completely restructure the British military in order to win the conflict. His strategies worked, and Great Britain won the war. They also left Britain with tremendous debt that Britain wanted the colonists to help pay for. Later, Pitt spoke out against Britain's taxing the colonists without allowing them to be represented in Parliament.

Chief Pontiac

A chief of the Ottawa people of the Great Lakes region, Pontiac forged an alliance to beat back the British in the conflict known as Pontiac's War (1763–1766). His alliance included almost all of the American Indian tribes between Lake Superior and the lower Mississippi. His strategy was fairly successful at first, but years of fighting took their toll. Pontiac signed a peace treaty with the British in 1766.

166   Chapter 4   The Road to War

Chapter 4   167

People You Should Know

How do personal stories IMPACT our understanding of how the American colonies edged toward war with Great Britain?

- Have students read aloud the biographies.

- Tell them that they will learn about these people and others throughout the chapter.

- Prompt students to create portraits of five people associated with the events and tensions just before the outbreak of the Revolutionary War. Encourage students to use information from the People You Should Know feature, or they can use information from the text or their own research. Guide students to annotate each portrait with facts, details, quotes, or anecdotes about the person's life or legacy. Students may also consider the following people:

  ▷ Samuel Adams   ▷ Charles Townshend

  ▷ John Dickinson   ▷ John Hancock

  ▷ Edmund Burke   ▷ Patrick Henry

  ▷ George Mason   ▷ Thomas Clifford

- Students may draw, download, or photocopy portraits for the display. Hang the portraits in the classroom, and have students refer to the portraits throughout the chapter.

Teacher Notes

What Caused the Conflict between Great Britain, France, and the American Indians?

Background Information

In this lesson, students will learn about the 18th-century struggle for control of North America that led Britain, France, and Indian nations to warfare, including the French and Indian War.

Community Connections

To enrich their understanding, have students visit the museum or the website of a fort or battlefield associated with the French and Indian War, such as Old Fort Niagara in New York, the Fort Pitt Block House in Pennsylvania, Colonial Fort Michilimackinac in Michigan, or the Plains of Abraham in Quebec, Canada.

LESSON STANDARDS

✓ Describe the competition among the English, French, Spanish, Dutch, and Indian nations for control of North America. **HSS.5.3.1**

✓ Describe the cooperation that existed between the colonists and Indians during the 1600s and 1700s (e.g., in agriculture, the fur trade, military alliances, treaties, cultural interchanges). **HSS.5.3.2**

✓ Examine the conflicts before the Revolutionary War (e.g., the Pequot and King Philip's Wars in New England, the Powhatan Wars in Virginia, the French and Indian War). **HSS.5.3.3**

✓ Describe the internecine Indian conflicts, including the competing claims for control of lands (e.g., actions of the Iroquois, Huron, Lakota [Sioux]). **HSS.5.3.5**

✓ Students place key events and people of the historical era they are studying in a chronological sequence and spatial context; they interpret time lines. **HAS.CS.1**

✓ Students use map and globe skills to determine the absolute locations of places and interpret information available through a map's or globe's legend, scale, and symbolic representations. **HAS.CS.4**

✓ Students differentiate between primary and secondary sources. **HAS.HR.1**

✓ Students summarize the key events of the era they are studying and explain the historical context of those events. **HAS.HI.1**

✓ Identify and interpret the multiple causes and effects of historical events. **HAS.HI.3**

Connect to the **Essential Question**

The **Weekly Explorer Magazine** supports students' exploration of the Essential Question and provides additional resources for the EQ Inquiry Project.

Chapter 4, pp. 44–57

Inquiry Project

Which Side Will You Choose?

Remind students to use the information they learn in this lesson and other resources to complete their EQ Inquiry Project!

Dinah Zike's

FOLDABLES®   In this lesson you will use Foldables.

When Minutes Count!
Suggested Lesson Pacing

1 ENGAGE
One Day

- Lesson Opener
- Analyze the Source
- Inquiry Tools

Go Digital
- **iMap:** Map of New France and New England in 1750

2 INVESTIGATE
Two to Three Days

🕐 **Short on Time?** Look for the clock to teach core content in less time.

- Conflict in the Ohio River Valley
- The Battle at Fort Duquesne
- The French Gain the Upper Hand
- The Turning Point
- Outcome and Aftermath

3 REPORT
One Day

- Take a Stand
- Write and Cite Evidence
- Defend Your Claim

Make Connections!

(ccss) CONNECT TO ELA

Reading
Quote accurately from a text when explaining what the text says explicitly and when drawing inferences from the text. **RI.5.1**

Research
Recall relevant information from experiences or gather relevant information from print and digital sources; summarize or paraphrase information in notes and finished work, and provide a list of sources. **W.5.8**

Draw evidence from literary or informational texts to support analysis, reflection, and research. **W.5.9**

Writing
Write opinion pieces on topics or texts, supporting a point of view with reasons and information. **W.5.1**

Speaking and Listening
Engage effectively in a range of collaborative discussions (one-on-one, in groups, and teacher-led) with diverse partners on grade 5 topics and texts, building on others' ideas and expressing their own clearly. **SL.5.1**

Summarize a written text read aloud or information presented in diverse media and formats, including visually, quantitatively, and orally. **SL.5.2**

Classroom Resources

 Search for additional resources using the following key words.

Fort Pitt

French and Indian War

Iroquois

Sir William Johnson

Louis-Joseph de Montcalm

Pontiac

Seven Years' War

George Washington

James Wolfe

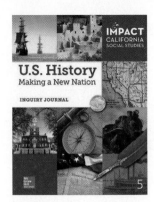

Inquiry Journal
pp. 132–133

 STANDARDS

STANDARDS

Describe the competition among the English, French, Spanish, Dutch, and Indian nations for control of North America. **HSS.5.3.1**

Examine the conflicts before the Revolutionary War (e.g., the Pequot and King Philip's Wars in New England, the Powhatan Wars in Virginia, the French and Indian War). **HSS.5.3.3**

CCSS Summarize information presented in diverse media and formats, including visually, quantitatively, and orally. **CCSS.ELA.SL.5.2**

Go Digital!

Explore the lesson content with online whole-class presentation tools.

- **iMap:** Map of New France and New England in 1750

What Caused the Conflict between Great Britain, France, and the American Indians?

Bellringer

Prompt students to retrieve information from the previous lessons. Say: *What European nation claimed land north and west of the Thirteen Colonies? Where was the Iroquois Confederacy in relation to the two groups of European colonies?* (France; between them)

Lesson Outcomes

What Am I Learning? Have students read the Lesson Question and Lesson Outcomes on page 132.

Why Am I Learning It? Discuss the term *Great Britain* in the lesson question. Explain that while England and Scotland had had the same monarch since 1603, they were still separate kingdoms until 1707, when they officially united as the kingdom of Great Britain. Clarify that after 1707, it is technically correct to call the Thirteen Colonies *British colonies*, rather than *English colonies*.

How Will I Know That I Learned It? Ask students the following questions:

- What will you be able to identify about the British, French, and American Indians in North America? (the differences between their goals)
- What major historical event will you study? (the French and Indian War)

Talk About It

Explain that when we talk about artwork, we describe, analyze, and interpret it and present our ideas in our own words. Provide sentence frames to help students form sentences as they talk about the artwork.

- ***The details in the painting show George Washington was a _____ during the French and Indian War.*** (colonel; soldier)
- ***He seems ready to go into _____ at a moment's notice.*** (battle)

Collaborative Conversations

Add New Ideas As students engage in partner, small group, and whole-class discussions, encourage them to

- Stay on topic.
- Connect their own ideas to things their peers have said.
- Look for ways to connect their personal experiences or prior knowledge to the conversation.

Lesson **1**

What Caused the Conflict between Great Britain, France, and the American Indians?

Lesson Outcomes

What Am I Learning?
In this lesson, you're going to use your investigative skills to examine the different goals of the British, the French, and the American Indian groups in their conflict over North America.

Why Am I Learning It?
Reading and talking about these goals will help you understand how they contributed to the development and outcome of the French and Indian War.

How Will I Know That I Learned It?
You will be able to identify the differences between these goals, make a claim about how these differences influenced the development and outcome of the French and Indian War, and support your opinion with evidence.

Talk About It COLLABORATE

Look at the Details This is a portrait of George Washington. What details do you see in this painting and what do you think they say about Washington and his life?

George Washington (circa 1779-1781) by Charles Willson Peale

HSS.5.3.1, HSS.5.3.3, HSS.5.3.5, HAS.CS.4

132 Lesson 1 What Caused the Conflict between Great Britain, France, and the American Indians?

Lesson 1 **133**

Inquiry Journal, pp. 132–133

 ENGLISH LEARNERS SCAFFOLD

ELD.PI.5.8 Analyzing how writers and speakers use vocabulary and other language resources for specific purposes

Emerging	Expanding	Bridging
Understand Academic Vocabulary Be sure students understand the meaning of *goals*, used in the discussion of the Lesson Outcomes. Distinguish between an *outcome* and a *goal*: an outcome is simply any ending; a goal is the ending someone wants or aims for.	**Understand Domain-Specific Terms** Help students with possibly unfamiliar terms in the Talk About It feature, such as *portrait, military orders,* and *musket*. Note that graphics may be part of the context that can clarify word meanings. Ask what the portrait of Washington makes clear a *musket* is. (a type of gun)	**Pronounce Terms** Discuss the word *colonel*, which as the caption on page 133 indicates was George Washington's rank in the British colonial army at the time of the portrait. Note the word's pronunciation owes to its origins in the French word *colonel*: despite its spelling, *colonel* sounds like *kernel*, meaning "a piece of corn."

See the **Language Learner Teaching Guide** for more language support strategies.

Monitor and Differentiate

REACHING ALL LEARNERS

Approaching Level

Encourage students to discuss the kind of military officer George Washington appears to be based on his portrait. Offer additional sentence frames to help in the discussion, such as *Washington seems very _____. He looks like he would be _____.*

On Level

Remind students that when something has more than one common term, such as *Thirteen Colonies, English colonies,* and *British colonies,* they should try all the terms when they do a database search in their research.

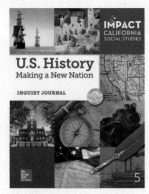

Inquiry Journal
pp. 134–135

 STANDARDS

Describe the competition among the English, French, Spanish, Dutch, and Indian nations for control of North America. **HSS.5.3.1**

Describe the cooperation that existed between the colonists and Indians during the 1600s and 1700s (e.g., in agriculture, the fur trade, military alliances, treaties, cultural interchanges). **HSS.5.3.2**

Examine the conflicts before the Revolutionary War (e.g., the Pequot and King Philip's Wars in New England, the Powhatan Wars in Virginia, the French and Indian War). **HSS.5.3.3**

Describe the internecine Indian conflicts, including the competing claims for control of lands (e.g., actions of the Iroquois, Huron, Lakota [Sioux]). **HSS.5.3.5**

Students differentiate between primary and secondary sources. **HAS.HR.1**

Go Digital!

Model how to inspect and find evidence with online whole-class presentation tools.

Background Information

The Iroquois Confederacy or Five Nations—Mohawk, Oneida, Onondaga, Cayuga, and Seneca—were united between 1570 and 1600, tradition has it by the Great Peacemaker Dekanawida. The confederacy became the Six Nations when the Tuscarora joined in 1722. All six groups spoke Iroquoian languages—as did their great enemy, the Huron. The Iroquois controlled a large area centered in upstate New York. Their alliance with the British, successful in the French and Indian War, contributed to their dispersal after the Revolution.

1 Inspect

Read Have students read the entire text, including the primary source. Note that the title asks a question. Ask:

- Which word in the title signals that the text will describe cause and effect? (*why*)

- Which Indian group is the text mainly about? (the Iroquois)

- With which European group did that Indian group ally itself? (the British)

- Which groups did it fight against? (the Huron, the Algonquin, and the French)

Collaborate Have partners discuss the reasons the Iroquois were important to the British. (They were a powerful group and an enemy of Britain's enemy, the French.)

2 Find Evidence

Reread Have students reread the text.

Analyze the Primary Source Read aloud the excerpt from Johnson's letter. Be sure students understand that the term *Five Nations* refers to the five groups united as the Iroquois—Mohawk, Oneida, Onondaga, Cayuga, and Seneca—and actually became *Six Nations* when the Tuscarora joined the confederacy.

- Ask what main point Johnson makes about the Iroquois. (They are a powerful group who will be useful to help the British fight the French in Canada.)

- Have students cite details to support their answer. (Details include the Iroquois' prowess, their likely success with proper support, and their recent expansion.)

3 Make Connections COLLABORATE

Talk Have partners discuss how French policy toward the Indians both helped and harmed the French. (Helping the Algonquin and Huron strengthened the French fur trade but also made enemies of the Iroquois, who then helped France's enemy, the British.)

Analyze the Source

1 Inspect

Read Look at the title "Why Were the Iroquois Important to the British?" Which word in the title signals that the text will describe cause and effect?

- **Circle** words that you don't know.
- **Underline** words that give reasons.
- **Discuss** with a partner the reasons why the Iroquois were important to the British.

My Notes

_____
_____
_____
_____
_____
_____
_____
_____
_____
_____
_____

Why Were the Iroquois Important to the British?

The Iroquois were a powerful confederacy of five (later six) American Indian groups whose homeland was in what is now the state of New York. During the 1600s and early 1700s, the Iroquois dominated the Northeast and Great Lakes regions. Because of this strength, the Iroquois were very important to the British in the French and Indian War. As a result, the British government gave a colonial official, Sir William Johnson, the job of keeping friendly relations between the Iroquois and British settlers.

The Iroquois became British allies because of French policy. When French settlers arrived in North America, they decided to aid the Algonquin and Huron in their struggles with their traditional enemy, the Iroquois. One effect of this policy was that the French strengthened their control over the fur trade. Another effect was that the Iroquois sided with the British against Britain's enemies, the French.

PRIMARY SOURCE

In Their Words...
Sir William Johnson

Such was the prowess of the Five Nations' Confederacy, that had they been properly supported by us, they would have long since put a period to the Colony of Canada, which alone they were near effecting in the year 1688. Since that time, they have admitted the Tuscaroras from the Southward, beyond Oneida, and they have ever since formed part of the Confederacy.

—from a letter to the British Board of Trade, November 13, 1763

Johnson, William. Sir W. Johnson to the Board of Trade, 13 November 1768. In: The Conspiracy of Pontiac and the Indian War After the Conquest of Canada, vol. 2, by Francis Parkman, app. A. Boston: Little, Brown, and Co., 1898.

Onondaga warriors and British soldiers around a council fire in the 1700s

(B)McGraw-Hill Education; (b)North Wind Picture Archives/Alamy

2 Find Evidence

Reread What did Sir William Johnson mean by the "prowess" of the Iroquois? Why did this quality make them important to the British?

What policy did Johnson want the British government to adopt toward the Iroquois? What effect did he expect from this policy?

3 Make Connections

Talk Discuss with a partner why France's policy toward the American Indians both helped and hurt the French.

134 Lesson 1 What Caused the Conflict between Great Britain, France, and the American Indians?

Lesson 1 **135**

Inquiry Journal, pp. 134–135

(EL) ENGLISH LEARNERS SCAFFOLD

ELD.PI.5.6 Reading closely literary and informational texts

Emerging	Expanding	Bridging
Clarify Vocabulary Help students with domain-specific vocabulary in the text about the primary source, such as *confederacy* ("a group that unites for a common goal"), *allies* ("groups or countries working together"), and *policy* ("a plan or principle made by a government or organization").	**Clarify Vocabulary** Help students with difficult vocabulary in the primary source, such as *prowess* ("skill") and *effecting* ("achieving"). Discuss the meaning of the idiomatic phrase *put a period to*, noting that when you put a period on a sentence, you end it. Then ask what students think *put a period to* means. ("put an end to")	**Distinguish Homophones** Mention the common words *affect*, a verb meaning "to change," and *effect*, a noun meaning "a change; a result." Explain that *effect* is much less often used as a verb meaning "to achieve." Note that this less common verb occurs in the primary source as *effecting*, or "achieving."

See the **Language Learner Teaching Guide** for more language support strategies.

Monitor and Differentiate

REACHING ALL LEARNERS

Approaching Level

Be sure students understand that the "Colony of Canada" in the primary source was a French colony before the French and Indian War.

On Level

Clarify the meaning of *negotiates*. Then ask how the picture of the British officer relates to the text. (It shows the British meeting with one of the members of the Iroquois confederacy, the Onondaga.)

Beyond Level

Have students discuss what the letter shows about Johnson's overall attitude toward the Iroquois. (respectful; thinks they can be useful)

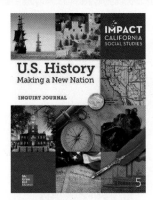

Inquiry Journal
pp. 136–137

 STANDARDS

Describe the competition among the English, French, Spanish, Dutch, and Indian nations for control of North America. **HSS.5.3.1**

Describe the cooperation that existed between the colonists and Indians during the 1600s and 1700s (e.g., in agriculture, the fur trade, military alliances, treaties, cultural interchanges). **HSS.5.3.2**

Examine the conflicts before the Revolutionary War (e.g., the Pequot and King Philip's Wars in New England, the Powhatan Wars in Virginia, the French and Indian War). **HSS.5.3.3**

Describe the internecine Indian conflicts, including the competing claims for control of lands (e.g., actions of the Iroquois, Huron, Lakota [Sioux]). **HSS.5.3.5**

Identify and interpret the multiple causes and effects of historical events. **HAS.HI.3**

Go Digital!

• Model how to explore and investigate with online whole-class tools.

• Students can access the online graphic organizer to use the inquiry tools as they read.

Explore Cause and Effect

Explain Tell students that cause and effect is one kind of structure that authors use to organize information in historical texts. Remind students that a cause is the reason something has happened; an effect is the outcome or result of the cause.

Read Have students read aloud the step-by-step instructions about how to identify cause and effect. Mention additional clue words that signal cause and effect, such as *since* and *for that reason.*

Guide Practice Have students work as a class to identify a cause and effect in the text and primary source that they read on page 134. Be sure they understand that the cause goes in the left box; the arrow means that it leads to the effect in the right box.

Investigate!

Have students read pages 168–177 in the Research Companion. Tell them the information will help them answer the lesson question **What Caused the Conflict between Great Britain, France, and the American Indians?**

Take Notes Tell students that as they read each section they will take notes on cause-and-effect relationships in the French and Indian War. They will record these notes in the graphic organizer on page 137 of their Inquiry Journal. Remind them that taking notes will help them understand and remember the information they learn. Stress the importance of paraphrasing, or using their own words, when they take notes.

Inspect Guide students to read the text in each section to determine what it says. Suggest that they ask *What happened?* to determine effects and *Why did it happen?* to determine causes. Remind them to look for words that signal cause and effect.

Find Evidence Encourage students to reread the text to develop a deeper understanding of the content. Remind them that after they read and take notes, they should review and think about how the facts and details will help them answer the lesson question.

Collaborative Conversations

Text-Based Discussion Remind students of the goals of discussing the text with others.

• to listen and respond to their partners' points
• to ask for evidence from the text
• to build on each other's ideas
• to see the text from a different point of view

Inquiry Tools

Explore Cause and Effect

A *cause* is a reason why something happens. An outcome or result is called an *effect*. Identifying cause-and-effect relationships will help you understand historical events.

1. **Read the text once, all the way through.**
   This will help you understand what the text is about.

2. **Look for words and phrases that signal cause-and-effect relationships.**
   Such signal words and phrases include *cause, effect, because, so, caused, resulted, as a result,* and *due to.*

3. **Identify the events that are linked by such signal words.**
   Be sure you have correctly identified which event is the cause and which is the effect.

4. **Be aware that a cause can have more than one effect, and an effect can have more than one cause.**
   Notice any cases in which more than one cause or effect is indicated.

 Based on the text you just read, work with your class to complete the chart below. Use the text you just read.

Cause		Effect
Sir William Johnson stays on friendly terms with Iroquois.	→	Iroquois become important to Britain's struggle against the French.

136   Lesson 1   What Caused the Conflict between Great Britain, France, and the American Indians?

Investigate!

Read pages 168–177 in your Research Companion. Use your investigative skills to identify cause-and-effect relationships among the events of the French and Indian War. Use the chart to organize the information.

Cause		Effect
British settlers want more land for farming.	→	French settlers fear that British will cut down trees and ruin the habitat for fur-bearing animals.
The French form alliances with the Algonquin and Huron, enemies of the Iroquois.	→	Iroquois form an alliance with the British.
The French build a line of forts in Ohio River Valley to halt expansion of British settlements.	→	British attack French forts but suffer defeats.
The British government pours more money and troops into the war.	→	The tide turns in favor of the British, who go on to win the war.

McGraw-Hill Education

Lesson 1   137

Inquiry Journal, pp. 136–137

EL ENGLISH LEARNERS SCAFFOLD

ELD.PII.5.1 Understanding text structure

Emerging

Identify Cause and Effect Give students practice with identifying everyday examples of cause and effect. For instance, say: *School let out early because of the bad storm.* Then ask: *What was the cause?* (the bad storm) *What was the effect?* (School let out early.)

Expanding

Understand Cause and Effect Illustrate the use of clue words to signal cause and effect. For example, say: *Because there was a bad storm, school let out early.* Elicit that *because* signals the cause. Then say: *There was a bad storm; as a result, school let out early.* Elicit that *as a result* signals the effect.

Bridging

Use Cause and Effect Have students give their own examples of cause and effect from everyday life. Ask them to include signal words.

See the **Language Learner Teaching Guide** for more language support strategies.

Monitor and Differentiate

REACHING ALL LEARNERS

Special Needs

Be sure students understand that the event that is the cause is always going to happen before the event that is the effect. They can remember "c comes before e," so cause is before effect.

On Level

Discuss why history books often use cause-and-effect organization. Elicit that in studying history, we learn what happened (the effect) and why it happened (the cause).

Beyond Level

Have students consider some of the general causes of war: Different groups want the same land or resources. One group mistreats another, and that group fights for its rights.

2 INVESTIGATE / Conflict in the Ohio River Valley

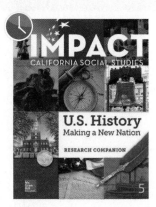

Research Companion
pp. 168–169

HSS STANDARDS

Describe the competition among the English, French, Spanish, Dutch, and Indian nations for control of North America. **HSS.5.3.1**

Describe the cooperation that existed between the colonists and Indians during the 1600s and 1700s (e.g., in agriculture, the fur trade, military alliances, treaties, cultural interchanges). **HSS.5.3.2**

Examine the conflicts before the Revolutionary War (e.g., the Pequot and King Philip's Wars in New England, the Powhatan Wars in Virginia, the French and Indian War). **HSS.5.3.3**

Describe the internecine Indian conflicts, including the competing claims for control of lands (e.g., actions of the Iroquois, Huron, Lakota [Sioux]). **HSS.5.3.5**

Go Digital!

Investigate the lesson content with online whole-class presentation tools.

- **iMap:** Map of New France and New England in 1750

Background Information

The Algonquin, a Canadian people, had friendly relations with Samuel de Champlain and became active in the fur trade. They are closely related to the Ojibwa (Chippewa) and Ottawa (Odawa), the three together forming the Anishinaabe cultural group. Their language, also called Algonquin, is so similar to Ojibwa and Ottawa that the three are sometimes considered dialects. All belong to the large Algonquian language family, which also includes Mohican, Delaware (Lenape), Micmac, Cree, Cheyenne, Shawnee, Yurok, and many others.

| TIMELINE | Invite students to look at the timeline at the top on page 169.

> **Analyze** Ask: How long did the French and Indian War last? (9 years) For how long after that did Pontiac struggle against the British? (3 years) **HAS.CS.1 DOK 2**

Analyze the Source

Inspect Have students read about conflict in the Ohio River Valley on pages 168–169.

Find Evidence Use the questions below to check comprehension. Remind students to support their answers with text evidence.

> **Categorize** In what different kinds of activities did the British and French colonial economies focus in the early 1700s? (The British focused on farming and trade; the French focused on the fur trade.) **DOK 1**

> **Explain** In what main way did British colonial activity come in conflict with French colonial activity? (Clearing forests for farmland ruined the habitat of the fur-bearing animals that trappers hunted for the fur trade.) **DOK 3**

> **Synthesize** For what reasons did the Algonquin and Huron side with the French? (They wanted to continue their traditional way of life, trapping animals in the forests, and did not want the forests turned to farmland. They also had received help from the French in fighting their enemies, the Iroquois.) **DOK 2**

> **Explain** Why did the Iroquois side with the British? (They were angry with the French for helping the Algonquin and Huron, their enemies.) **DOK 2**

Make Connections

> **Evaluate** Why do you think the French colonies had a population smaller than that of the British colonies? (Engaging in the fur trade does not encourage settlement the way farming does. Students may also mention Canada's cold climate.) **DOK 4**

Analyze the Illustration Direct students' attention to the illustration of a French officer meeting with the Huron people. Ask:

- What sort of relationship does the image suggest between the two? (friendly)

- Where does their meeting seem to be taking place? (wilderness or woodland area, which makes it more likely to be Huron territory than a French settlement)

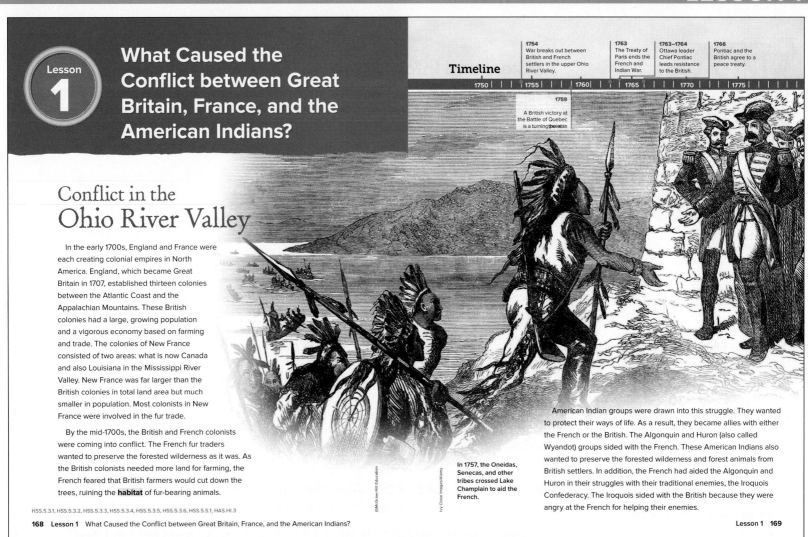

What Caused the Conflict between Great Britain, France, and the American Indians?

Timeline

1754 War breaks out between British and French settlers in the upper Ohio River Valley.

1759 A British victory at the Battle of Quebec is a turning point in the war.

1763 The Treaty of Paris ends the French and Indian War.

1763–1764 Ottawa leader Chief Pontiac leads resistance to the British.

1766 Pontiac and the British agree to a peace treaty.

| 1750 | 1755 | 1760 | 1765 | 1770 | 1775 |

Conflict in the Ohio River Valley

In the early 1700s, England and France were each creating colonial empires in North America. England, which became Great Britain in 1707, established thirteen colonies between the Atlantic Coast and the Appalachian Mountains. These British colonies had a large, growing population and a vigorous economy based on farming and trade. The colonies of New France consisted of two areas: what is now Canada and also Louisiana in the Mississippi River Valley. New France was far larger than the British colonies in total land area but much smaller in population. Most colonists in New France were involved in the fur trade.

By the mid-1700s, the British and French colonists were coming into conflict. The French fur traders wanted to preserve the forested wilderness as it was. As the British colonists needed more land for farming, the French feared that British farmers would cut down the trees, ruining the **habitat** of fur-bearing animals.

In 1757, the Oneidas, Senecas, and other tribes crossed Lake Champlain to aid the French.

American Indian groups were drawn into this struggle. They wanted to protect their ways of life. As a result, they became allies with either the French or the British. The Algonquin and Huron (also called Wyandot) groups sided with the French. These American Indians also wanted to preserve the forested wilderness and forest animals from British settlers. In addition, the French had aided the Algonquin and Huron in their struggles with their traditional enemies, the Iroquois Confederacy. The Iroquois sided with the British because they were angry at the French for helping their enemies.

HSS.5.3.1, HSS.5.3.2, HSS.5.3.3, HSS.5.3.4, HSS.5.3.5, HSS.5.3.6, HSS.5.5.1, HAS.HI.3

168 Lesson 1 What Caused the Conflict between Great Britain, France, and the American Indians?

Lesson 1 169

Research Companion, pp. 168–169

 ENGLISH LEARNERS SCAFFOLD

ELD.PI.5.8 Analyzing how writers and speakers use vocabulary and other language resources for specific purposes

Emerging	Expanding	Bridging
Understand Suffixes Discuss the term *vigorous economy*, explaining that *economy* refers to the way wealth is gotten and spent. Define *vigor* as "strength," and note that the suffix *-ous* usually means "having." Then ask what a *vigorous economy* is. (a strong economy)	**Understand Related Terms** Point out the word *wild* in *wilderness*, and explain that a *wilderness* is a wild, unsettled place. Then ask students what a *forest* is. (an area covered with trees) Finally, ask them what a *forested wilderness* most likely is. (a wild area covered with trees.)	**Understand Geographic Terms** Use a map to help students identify geographic areas mentioned in the text, such as the *Appalachian Mountains* and *Mississippi River Valley*. Clarify that *Louisiana* at the time referred to land along virtually the entire Mississippi River.

See the **Language Learner Teaching Guide** for more language support strategies.

Monitor and Differentiate

REACHING ALL LEARNERS

On Level

Distinguish between *Algonquin*, the tribe and its language, and *Algonquian*, the large language family to which Algonquin belongs. Note that Indian groups across the United States speak languages in the *Algonquian* family.

Beyond Level

Explain that Indian groups often have different names or spellings for their names: the *Huron*, for example, are also called the *Wyondot*; *Algonquin* may be spelled *Algonkin*. Suggest that students researching a group check an encyclopedia first for different spellings or names and then try each in database searches.

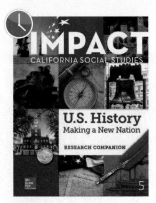

Research Companion
pp. 170–171

**STANDARDS**

Describe the competition among the English, French, Spanish, Dutch, and Indian nations for control of North America. **HSS.5.3.1**

Examine the conflicts before the Revolutionary War (e.g., the Pequot and King Philip's Wars in New England, the Powhatan Wars in Virginia, the French and Indian War). **HSS.5.3.3**

Students use map and globe skills to determine the absolute locations of places and interpret information available through a map's or globe's legend, scale, and symbolic representations. **HAS.CS.4**

Identify and interpret the multiple causes and effects of historical events. **HAS.HI.3**

CCSS Quote accurately from a text when explaining what the text says explicitly and when drawing inferences from the text. **CCSS.ELA.RI.5.1**

Engage effectively in discussions, building on others' ideas and expressing their own clearly. **CCSS.ELA.SL.5.1**

Go Digital!

Investigate the lesson content with online whole-class presentation tools.

Background Information

The Ohio River forms where the Allegheny and Monongahela rivers meet in what is now Pittsburgh in western Pennsylvania. It then flows west to the Mississippi River. The upper river valley, as well as portions of Pennsylvania to the east, was all in contention in the 1700s, when the British and French both tried to claim the area.

Analyze the Source

Inspect Have students read pp. 170–171.

Find Evidence Use the questions below to check comprehension.

Describe From where did most British settlers come to the area west of the Appalachian Mountains? (from the Pennsylvania and Virginia colonies) **DOK 2**

Infer Why did the French build forts from Lake Erie to western Pennsylvania? (to stop the incoming British settlers) **DOK 3**

Explain How did the British react to the French forts? (They saw the forts as a threat.) **DOK 2**

Interpret What reason did Robert Dinwiddie give for sending George Washington to the Ohio Valley? What was his real reason? (to strengthen a British outpost; to show the British government the threat the French posed) **DOK 3**

Identify Where was Fort Duquesne? Who named and controlled it? (in the Ohio Valley in present-day Pittsburgh; the French) **DOK 2**

Speculate Why do you think Washington's defeat did not harm his reputation? (He was not sent to fight the French but rather to prove a point.) **DOK 3**

📍 Map Skills

Project a large version of the map on p. 170. Tell students to use the map as they answer these questions:

- From where did the French come down to Detroit? (Canada)

- Which two countries were in a dispute over land in North America in 1750? (France and Great Britain)

Make Connections

Compare and Contrast How was Washington's mission both successful and unsuccessful? (He was forced to surrender and return to Virginia, but he did prove what Dinwiddie wanted proved.) **DOK 3**

✓ Stop and Check

Think How did France's choice of allies among American Indians cause the Iroquois to become allies of the British? (France allied itself with the Iroquois' traditional enemies.)

Talk Have students discuss with a partner how Washington's expedition into the Ohio Valley supported Robert Dinwiddie's views about the French. (The French response proved Dinwiddie's view that they posed a threat in the area.)

Find Details Explain to students that after they read and take notes, they should review and think about how the facts and details will help them answer the Essential Question.

The focus of the struggle between the French and the British, and their American Indian allies, was the upper Ohio River Valley. In firm control of the territories of New France, French settlers had spread southward into the Great Lakes region. They established a major outpost there at Detroit in 1701. By the 1750s, farmers and traders from the British colonies of Virginia and Pennsylvania had begun to cross the Appalachian Mountains, moving into the lands beyond. To halt this advance, the French built a line of forts from Lake Erie to western Pennsylvania. The British saw the forts as a threat and decided to try to drive the French out.

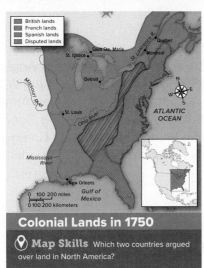

Colonial Lands in 1750

◉ Map Skills Which two countries argued over land in North America?

✓ Stop and Check

Think How did France's choice of allies among American Indians cause the Iroquois to become allies of the British?

Find Details As you read, add additional information to the graphic organizer on page 137 in your Inquiry Journal.

The Battle at Fort Duquesne

Robert Dinwiddie was the lieutenant governor of the British colony of Virginia. He wanted to convince the British government in London of the seriousness of the French threat in the Ohio Valley. So, in early 1754, Dinwiddie sent 22-year-old George Washington with a small force to strengthen a British **outpost** at the site of what is now the city of Pittsburgh. As Washington neared the fort, he discovered that French troops had already seized it and renamed it Fort Duquesne (doo KAIN).

Washington quickly built a temporary post in the area and named it Fort Necessity. From this base, Washington's troops launched a successful attack against the French on May 28, 1754. But the French counterattacked on July 3, forcing Washington to surrender. He and his men were allowed to return to Virginia, and the French destroyed Fort Necessity. The French and Indian War had begun.

Back in Virginia, Washington found his defeat had not harmed his reputation. The colonial government thanked him for his efforts, and he was named head of Virginia's militia on the frontier. Washington remarked in a letter to his brother, "I have heard the bullets whistle; and believe me, there is something charming in the sound."

An early map of Fort Duquesne, later renamed For Pitt

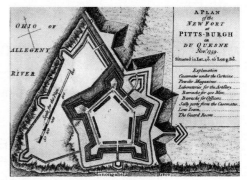

✓ Stop and Check

COLLABORATE

Talk How did Washington's expedition into the Ohio Valley support Robert Dinwiddie's views about the French? Discuss your opinion with a partner.

Research Companion, pp. 170–171

(EL) ENGLISH LEARNERS SCAFFOLD

ELD.PI.5.8 Analyzing how writers and speakers use vocabulary and other language resources for specific purposes

Emerging	Expanding	Bridging
Pronounce Place Names Explain that the French called their fort *Fort Duquesne* in honor of the governor-general of New France. Point out the pronunciation of *Duquesne* given in parentheses in the text. Explain that French often has silent letters, like the *s* in *Duquesne*.	**Explain Place Names** Explain that when the British later recaptured Fort Duquesne, they renamed it Fort Pitt after British Prime Minister William Pitt. Ask why students think the fort was named for Governor-General Duquesne and Prime Minister Pitt. (to honor them)	**Examine Place Names** Have students discuss why they think George Washington named his temporary outpost Fort Necessity. (Responses will vary but should show understanding that *necessity* means "something needed, often for survival.")

See the **Language Learner Teaching Guide** for more language support strategies.

Monitor and Differentiate

REACHING ALL LEARNERS

Approaching Level

Offer students sentence frames to describe what happened in the Battle of Fort Duquesne: ___ *sent Washington to* ___. *Washington launched* ___. *The French then* ___.

On Level

Have students summarize the battle of Fort Duquesne in a few sentences, focusing on George Washington's actions and experiences.

Beyond Level

Ask students what the remark in the letter to his brother seems to show about how Washington viewed war. (as noble, exciting, or fulfilling)

2 INVESTIGATE

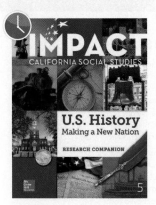

IMPACT
CALIFORNIA SOCIAL STUDIES

U.S. History
Making a New Nation

RESEARCH COMPANION

5

Research Companion
pp. 172–173

HSS STANDARDS

Describe the competition among the English, French, Spanish, Dutch, and Indian nations for control of North America. **HSS.5.3.1**

Describe the cooperation that existed between the colonists and Indians during the 1600s and 1700s (e.g., in agriculture, the fur trade, military alliances, treaties, cultural interchanges). **HSS.5.3.2**

Examine the conflicts before the Revolutionary War (e.g., the Pequot and King Philip's Wars in New England, the Powhatan Wars in Virginia, the French and Indian War). **HSS.5.3.3**

Students correctly apply terms related to time, including past, present, future, decade, century, and generation. **HAS.CS.2**

Identify and interpret the multiple causes and effects of historical events. **HAS.HI.3**

Go Digital!

Investigate the lesson content with online whole-class presentation tools.

Background Information

Clarifying Terms The French and Indian War is the American term for the colonial front of the Seven Years' War (1756–63), part of a series of Anglo-French conflicts including the Nine Years' War (1689–97), known here as King Williams' War; the War of the Spanish Succession (1701–14), known here as Queen Anne's War; and the War of the Austrian Succession (1740–48), known here as King George's War. The prime minister during the war was William Pitt the Elder, Earl of Chatham after 1766, as distinguished from his son William Pitt the Younger, a later prime minister.

Analyze the Source

Inspect Have students read The French Gain the Upper Hand on page 172 and The Turning Point on page 173.

Find Evidence Use the questions below to check comprehension.

Explain How did George Washington again come to command British troops attacking Fort Duquesne? (General Braddock and nearly all the other officers were killed in a French ambush.) **DOK 3**

Synthesize What happened when the fighting moved from the Ohio Valley to New York during 1756 and 1757? (The French continued to defeat the British.) **DOK 3**

Explain What was British Prime Minister William Pitt's view of the American war? (It was important to Britain's overall struggle with France.) **DOK 2**

Evaluate What three factors led to a shift to British victories? (more British money spent on the war, a naval blockade keeping shipments out of New France, and British soldiers and colonists learning Indian tactics in fighting) **DOK 3**

Make Connections

Evaluate Why do you think Indian tactics helped the French win victories at first? (Indians knew how to fight in the wilderness.) **DOK 4**

Then and Now

Although Fort Pitt no longer stands, one of its blockhouses does. A blockhouse is a small reinforced structure from which soldiers can fire in many directions. The Fort Pitt Block House was one of five built in 1764 to help protect the fort. More than 250 years old, it is today carefully preserved and a popular tourist attraction.

Stop and Check

Think What was the major cause of French success in the early part of the French and Indian War? (adopting the Indian style of wilderness warfare)

The French Gain the Upper Hand

The early phase of the war was marked by French victories. Their American Indian allies taught the French how to make surprise attacks from behind trees and rocks. By contrast, British troops, who marched into battle in formation, were easy targets. Such British tactics resulted in disaster in 1755 when General Edward Braddock led another group of British troops against Fort Duquesne. Colonel George Washington rode alongside Braddock. On July 9, the French and their allies ambushed the British force in the wilderness. British losses were severe. Some 900 of their 1,400 troops were killed or wounded, including nearly all the officers. Braddock himself was fatally wounded. Now in command, Washington was able to lead the remaining British forces to safety.

The French continued to be victorious. In 1756, their commander Louis-Joseph de Montcalm led a force of French soldiers and American Indians in the capture of an important British post, Fort Oswego, in the Great Lakes region. Montcalm reported that he had taken 1,600 prisoners and seized 100 cannon, six armed vessels, and a two-year supply of food. "All this cost us only 30 men killed and wounded," he said. Montcalm's victory gave the French full control of Lake Ontario. The following year, he captured another British post, Fort William Henry, which was near present-day Lake George, New York.

An engraving depicting the evacuation of Fort Duquesne, 1758

✓ Stop and Check

Think What was the major cause of French success in the early part of the French and Indian War?

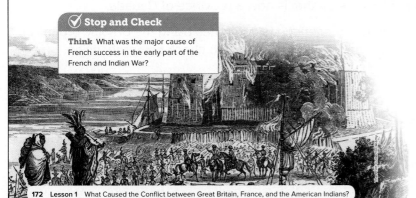

The Turning Point

News of French victories shocked the British colonies. The colonists begged the British Prime Minister, William Pitt, for more help. Pitt believed that the war in North America was critical to the overall struggle between Great Britain and France. The two nations were also at war in Europe. Pitt convinced the British government to pour more money, troops, and other supplies into the conflict. In addition, the British navy blockaded ports in New France, cutting off shipments of food and other supplies to French colonists. Finally, both British soldiers and American colonial militias became skilled in fighting the way American Indians did in the wilderness. All of these factors changed the course of the war.

In 1758, British troops defeated the French at Louisburg, Nova Scotia. Several months later, Colonel John Bradstreet led the British to victory over the French in a battle at Fort Frontenac on Lake Ontario. In November, the British finally retook Fort Duquesne. They renamed it Fort Pitt in honor of the British prime minister. In 1759, Sir William Johnson forced the French to surrender Fort Niagara. British General Jeffery Amherst then defeated the French at Fort Ticonderoga near Lake Champlain in upstate New York.

Then and Now

The city of Pittsburgh, Pennsylvania, was built around Fort Pitt. The land where Fort Pitt used to be is now a public park, though the brick outline of the old fort is still intact. The site is also home to the Fort Pitt Museum, which presents the story of western Pennsylvania's essential role in the French and Indian War as well as the American Revolution.

Fort Pitt in 1758 (background) and Fort Pitt Block House today (top-right)

Research Companion, pp. 172–173

ⒺⓁ ENGLISH LEARNERS SCAFFOLD

ELD.PI.5.8 Analyzing how writers and speakers use vocabulary and other language resources for specific purposes

Emerging	Expanding	Bridging
Understand Idioms Help students with the idiomatic headings on these pages, explaining that to *gain the upper hand* means "to get into a stronger position" and a *turning point* is "a point at which a change takes place that will decide the outcome."	**Understand Military Terms** Clarify the meaning of *victory* and *defeat*, which appear in the text in various forms. Clarify other military terms, such as *in formation* ("in lines of soldiers"), *tactics* ("ways of using military forces"), and *ambushed* ("attacked from a hidden position").	**Define Military Terms** Point out the word *blockaded* on page 173, and note that context clues help clarify its meaning. Have students use those clues to figure out the meaning of *blockade* and then offer a definition of the word. ("to prevent ships from entering")

See the **Language Learner Teaching Guide** for more language support strategies.

Monitor and Differentiate

REACHING ALL LEARNERS

Special Needs

Have small groups map the locations of all the forts mentioned on pp. 172–173. Note that Louisbourg, a fortified town, should be included. If groups struggle, model how to map Fort Oswego.

On Level

In conjunction with Then and Now, have students check online to find a Pittsburgh site still bearing the name *Duquesne*, such as the Duquesne Incline or Duquesne University.

Beyond Level

Have small groups research Fortress Louisbourg, a living museum of 18th-century life in a fortified town, and present their findings in a multimedia report.

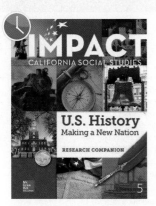

Research Companion
pp. 174–175

HSS STANDARDS

Describe the competition among the English, French, Spanish, Dutch, and Indian nations for control of North America. **HSS.5.3.1**

Describe the cooperation that existed between the colonists and Indians during the 1600s and 1700s (e.g., in agriculture, the fur trade, military alliances, treaties, cultural interchanges). **HSS.5.3.2**

Examine the conflicts before the Revolutionary War (e.g., the Pequot and King Philip's Wars in New England, the Powhatan Wars in Virginia, the French and Indian War). **HSS.5.3.3**

Students use map and globe skills to determine the absolute locations of places and interpret information available through a map's or globe's legend, scale, and symbolic representations. **HAS.CS.4**

Identify and interpret the multiple causes and effects of historical events. **HAS.HI.3**

Go Digital!

Investigate the lesson content with online whole-class presentation tools.

Background Information

Acadians In 1713 Britain officially acquired the French colony of Acadie, much of which it had been claiming as Nova Scotia. France, however, still pursued interests there—peopling the fortress at Louisbourg, for example. During the French and Indian War, when some of the area's French population, called Acadians, refused to swear loyalty to Britain, the British governor expelled them all. Many died, some went to the Thirteen Colonies or France, but others resettled in Louisiana, then still in French hands. They became known as *Cajuns*, a corruption of the term *Acadians*.

Analyze the Source

Inspect Have students continue reading about the turning point of the war on page 174 and begin reading about the outcome and aftermath on page 175. Clarify that *Quebec* here refers to the city, not the larger area that is now a province of Canada.

Find Evidence Remind students to continue taking notes using the graphic organizer in their Inquiry Journal. Then use these questions below to check comprehension.

> **Identify** Where did the battle that decided the war take place? (on the Plains of Abraham just outside the city of Quebec) **DOK 1**
>
> **Evaluate** How was the war both a triumph and a tragedy for British commander James Wolfe? (Britain won the war but Wolfe died in the decisive battle.) **DOK 2**
>
> **Explain** Why did Britain reserve all land west of the Appalachian Mountains for Indians? (to prevent colonial expansion that would make British colonies harder to protect) **DOK 3**

Make Connections

> **Evaluate** In what way does the Proclamation of 1863 seem inconsistent with the aims of Britain's war with France and its outcome? (The war gave Britain all of Canada, but now Britain was worried about too much land to protect; also, the war seemed to be fought to aid British colonial settlement in the Ohio Valley but now Britain did not want settlers there.) **DOK 4**

⊙ Map Skills

Project a large version of the two maps on page 175. Point out that 1750 was before the French and Indian War and 1763 was when it ended. Ask these questions:

- What land that was French or contested in 1750 became British in 1763? (land west of the Appalachian Mountains and Canada)

- Which European power lost the most land in North America between 1750 and 1763? (France)

- Which two European powers gained the most land? (Great Britain and Spain)

COLLABORATE

☑ Stop and Check

Talk Have students discuss the advantages that the land around Quebec provided to both the French and the British in their final battle. (The steep cliffs and strong currents gave the French protection, but fighting in open country helped the professionally trained British troops do what they did best.)

The climax of the war came in June 1759 when the British moved against the French stronghold at Quebec. The city of Quebec is located on steep cliffs above the St. Lawrence River. Both the river's strong currents and the fortress's cannon protected it. A British assault at the end of July failed. British commander James Wolfe decided on a daring plan—a surprise attack.

During the early hours of September 13, 1759, Wolfe landed an advance force in darkness. These soldiers climbed the steep cliffs and captured a French outpost. By morning, Wolfe's entire force was assembled on the Plains of Abraham outside the city. Like Wolfe, French commander Montcalm also decided to take a risk. He attacked immediately instead of waiting for reinforcements. The two armies both numbered about 4,500 men. However, Wolfe's troops were professional soldiers, while Montcalm's were volunteers. The battlefield was not forested wilderness, but open country. The careful musket fire of Wolfe's troops halted the advance of the French and then caused them to retreat. Both Montcalm and Wolfe were fatally wounded in the battle.

On September 18, the French surrendered Quebec City. A year later, the French surrendered their last stronghold, Montreal. The British now controlled New France.

British troops attack Quebec.

✓ Stop and Check

Talk What kinds of advantages did the land around Quebec provide to both the French and the British?

COLLABORATE

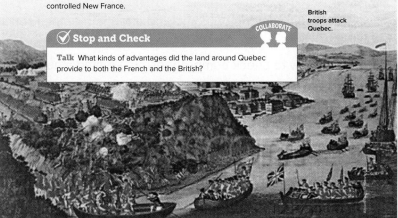

Outcomes and Aftermath

The French tried to retake Quebec in 1762 but failed. In Europe, meanwhile, Great Britain and France continued their war. Spain aided the French and, in return, France agreed to give Spain much of the Louisiana Territory. By 1763, the French were ready to negotiate a peace treaty with Great Britain. The Treaty of Paris was signed on February 10, 1763.

In October 1763, news of the Treaty of Paris reached North America. The defeated French could no longer aid American Indians in their resistance to British settlers. However, Great Britain wanted to keep down the cost of defending its American colonies. To stop British settlements in the Ohio River Valley, British King George III issued the Proclamation of 1763. This official order set aside all British land west of the Appalachian Mountains for American Indians. This decision satisfied the native peoples but angered American colonists hungry for land.

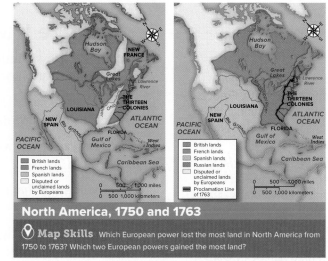

North America, 1750 and 1763

Map Skills Which European power lost the most land in North America from 1750 to 1763? Which two European powers gained the most land?

Research Companion, pp. 174–175

ⓔⓛ ENGLISH LEARNERS SCAFFOLD

ELD.PI.5.3 Offering and supporting opinions

Emerging	Expanding	Bridging
Discuss Opinions Help students explain the controversy surrounding the Proclamation of 1763: *Britain's Proclamation of 1763 set aside the land _____ for _____. The colonists were _____ with the proclamation, but the Indians were _____.* (west of the Appalachian Mountains; Indians; angry; satisfied)	**State and Support Opinions** Ask students to explain the controversy surrounding the Proclamation of 1763, summarizing the opinions or attitudes of the British, the Indians, and the American colonists' and the reasons for those opinions or attitudes.	**State and Support Opinions** Have students discuss the Proclamation of 1763, giving their opinions of the proclamation and the colonists' attitude toward it. Ask students to support their opinions with reasons and examples.

See the **Language Learner Teaching Guide** for more language support strategies.

Monitor and Differentiate

REACHING ALL LEARNERS

Approaching Level

Be sure students understand that *climax of the war* refers to the war's most decisive and *aftermath* to events that came after it ended.

On Level

Use the maps to illustrate geographic points made in the text—Quebec's location on the St. Lawrence River, for example.

Beyond Level

Note that *Plains of Abraham* sounds biblical but in fact the plains are probably named for Abraham Martin, an early settler who used the land as a pasture. Elicit that plains are flat, and discuss how flat terrain would affect the fighting.

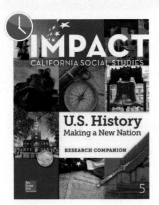

IMPACT
CALIFORNIA SOCIAL STUDIES

U.S. History
Making a New Nation

RESEARCH COMPANION

5

Research Companion
pp. 176–177

 STANDARDS

Describe the competition among the English, French, Spanish, Dutch, and Indian nations for control of North America. **HSS.5.3.1**

Describe the cooperation that existed between the colonists and Indians during the 1600s and 1700s (e.g., in agriculture, the fur trade, military alliances, treaties, cultural interchanges). **HSS.5.3.2**

Examine the conflicts before the Revolutionary War (e.g., the Pequot and King Philip's Wars in New England, the Powhatan Wars in Virginia, the French and Indian War). **HSS.5.3.3**

Students differentiate between primary and secondary sources. **HAS.HR.1**

Identify and interpret the multiple causes and effects of historical events. **HAS.HI.3**

CCSS Quote accurately from a text when explaining what the text says explicitly and when drawing inferences from the text. **CCSS.ELA.RI.5.1**

Go Digital!

Investigate the lesson content with online whole-class presentation tools.

Background Information

Pontiac's War or Pontiac's Rebellion, is the name generally given to the resistance Pontiac led by uniting against the British those Indians who had mostly fought or traded with the French. The conflict included the early use, by the British, of what today would be called biological or germ warfare: In a letter to Colonel Henry Bouquet, General Jeffery Amherst, commander of British forces, advised wiping out enemy Indians by supplying smallpox-infected blankets. A smallpox epidemic did take place, although history is unclear if Bouquet or someone else carried out the plan.

Analyze the Source

Inspect Have students continue reading about the outcome and aftermath of the French and Indian War on pages 176–177.

Find Evidence Use the questions below to check comprehension. Remind students to support their answers with text evidence.

Analyze What was the purpose of Pontiac's rebellion? (to prevent British takeover of Indian lands that would turn natives' hunting grounds into colonists' farms) **DOK 3**

Evaluate What skills did Pontiac show as a leader? (strong organizational skills; wisdom to foresee future threats) **DOK 4**

Summarize Why were many people in the Thirteen Colonies angry with Britain after the war? (The Proclamation of 1863 banned them from settling west of the Appalachian Mountains, which many of them wanted to do.) **DOK 2**

Make Connections

Evaluate What unexpected outcome did Britain's victory in the French and Indian War have for the British? (It united many American colonists against them.) **DOK 4**

Analyze the Primary Sources Note that a primary source can support, make clearer, or add information to the information in a secondary source. Ask:

Synthesize What information in the text on page 176 does the primary source on that page support? (Pontiac's view that the Indians should unite against the British) What information does it add? (Pontiac saw the French as sympathetic and the British as interested only in destroying the Indian way of life) **DOK 4**

Synthesize What sentence on page 176 does the primary source on page 177 make clearer? ("They also proved that they had strong leaders, such as George Washington.") **DOK 3**

COLLABORATE

☑ Stop and Check

Talk Ask students to discuss the reasons colonists disobeyed the Proclamation of 1863 and to offer opinions of whether they were right or wrong to disobey it. (Responses will vary, but students should recognize that the war seemed to have begun as a result of the issue of whether British colonists' had the right to settle in the Ohio Valley and that now Britain was demanding they not settle there.)

By 1760, although the British were defeating the French in North America, their control over the lands was not firm. Some of the American Indian allies of the French decided to resist British rule. The most important leader of this resistance was Pontiac. He was a member of the Ottawa, an Algonquin-speaking group whose homeland was in what is now northern Michigan and parts of Canada. As French outposts in Ottawa territory were surrendered to the British, Pontiac agreed not to attack British troops if they treated him with respect. His experience with the British convinced Pontiac, however, that they were a threat. Soon, settlers would follow these troops, Pontiac correctly believed. The settlers would want to turn Ottawa hunting grounds into farms.

In 1762, Pontiac organized almost every American Indian group from Lake Superior to the lower Mississippi River Valley. The plan, which Pontiac announced in early 1763, was for each group to attack the nearest British outpost. Then, all the American Indians would combine in a general attack on the British settlements. Pontiac himself was to attack Detroit. Although his attack on Detroit failed, the American Indians were successful in seizing many other British outposts and destroying frontier settlements. British troops struck back, though, and by 1764 American Indian resistance to the British in the Great Lakes region had ended.

As a result of the French and Indian War, British colonists saw themselves in a new way. They had helped fight a powerful enemy and had won. They also proved that they had strong leaders, such as George Washington. They had learned that the British colonies could unite in a common effort. This gave them a feeling of strength.

George Washington leads an attack on a French encampment.

The colonists also saw their relationship with Great Britain in a new light. They were angry with the British government for the Proclamation of 1763. Many colonists ignored the order and continued to cross the Appalachians to settle in the lands reserved for American Indians. The colonists knew that they could rely very little on British protection from American Indian attacks. In the end, the effect of the French and Indian War would be to unite the colonists in opposition to British government policy. Soon, this would lead them to fight for their own independence.

PRIMARY SOURCE

In Their Words... Pontiac

It is important for us, my brothers, that we exterminate from our lands this nation which seeks only to destroy us. You see as well as I that we can no longer supply our needs, as we have done from our brothers, the French.

—from a speech by Pontiac to the Ottawa people in May 1763

PRIMARY SOURCE

In Their Words... George Washington

The Virginia troops showed a good deal of bravery, and were nearly all killed; for I believe, out of three companies that were there, scarcely thirty men are left alive. ... I luckily escaped without a wound, though I had four bullets through my coat, and two horses shot under me.

—from George Washington's letter to his mother about Braddock's defeat, July 18, 1755

✓ Stop and Check

COLLABORATE

Talk Why didn't the British colonists obey the Proclamation of 1763? Were they right or wrong to disobey it?

176 Lesson 1 What Caused the Conflict between Great Britain, France, and the American Indians?

Lesson 1 **177**

Research Companion, pp. 176–177

(EL) ENGLISH LEARNERS SCAFFOLD

ELD.PI.5.6 Reading closely literary and informational texts

Emerging	Expanding	Bridging
Understand Primary Sources Read Pontiac's speech aloud with students. Clarify that *exterminate* means "destroy completely" and that "this nation" refers to Britain and its colonies. Help students identify the different views that Pontiac expresses toward the British and the French in his speech.	**Interpret Primary Sources** Have students take turns reading George Washington's letter aloud. Ask them to imagine he is reading it aloud and to use an appropriate tone for what he is saying. Clarify, if necessary, that the multiple-meaning word *companies* here means "groups of soldiers."	**Interpret Primary Sources** Have students reread Pontiac's speech. Point out that it is addressed to the Ottawa people. Then discuss what it shows about the relationship between the Ottawa people and the French. (The Ottawa obtained things of value trading with the French and considered them brothers.)

See the **Language Learner Teaching Guide** for more language support strategies.

Monitor and Differentiate

REACHING ALL LEARNERS

Approaching Level

Clarify that Lake Superior, mentioned in the text, is one of the Great Lakes and that the area in which Pontiac organized Indians had been mostly French before the Treaty of Paris.

On Level

Discuss with students how they think George Washington's mother felt when she read his letter. (Most students will probably feel she was concerned for her son's safety.)

Beyond Level

Encourage discussion of how and why the French and Indian War would help lead the American colonists to fight for their independence.

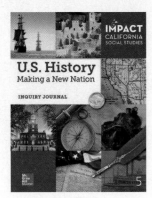

Inquiry Journal
pp. 138–139

 STANDARDS

Describe the competition among the English, French, Spanish, Dutch, and Indian nations for control of North America. **HSS.5.3.1**

Describe the cooperation that existed between the colonists and Indians during the 1600s and 1700s (e.g., in agriculture, the fur trade, military alliances, treaties, cultural interchanges). **HSS.5.3.2**

Examine the conflicts before the Revolutionary War (e.g., the Pequot and King Philip's Wars in New England, the Powhatan Wars in Virginia, the French and Indian War). **HSS.5.3.3**

Describe the internecine Indian conflicts, including the competing claims for control of lands (e.g., actions of the Iroquois, Huron, Lakota [Sioux]). **HSS.5.3.5**

Go Digital!

- Students can go online to report their findings. Assess their responses online.

- Students can access the online graphic organizer to capture ideas from their investigation.

Think About It

Take a Stand Students should review their research and consider causes and effects of the conflict between the British, the French, and Indian nations in North America. Remind students to review the details they gathered on their cause-and-effect graphic organizer. Direct them to pages 168–177 of their Research Companion if they need more information.

Write About It

Write and Cite Evidence Have students read the prompt. Stress that they will be making a claim and then listing reasons that support it. Remind students to include the following elements in their response:

- a statement that introduces the topic

- logical reasons supported by facts and details

- words that clearly signal cause and effect, such as *cause, effect, because, so, as a result*, and *due to.*

Use the rubric on page T364 to evaluate students' work.

Talk About It

Defend Your Claim Help students pair up with classmates who chose a different event.

- Tell students to take turns discussing their opinions and the evidence that supports those opinions.

- Ask students to discuss whether they agree or disagree with their partners' assessments and to explain why.

- Remind students to follow the rules of appropriate classroom conversation.

Connect to the Essential Question

Read the prompt aloud to students. Ask them the following guiding questions:

- As a result of the French and Indian War, how did the American colonists change their view of themselves? (They learned that they could join together and fight strongly against a powerful enemy.)

- As a result of the French and Indian War and the Proclamation of 1763, how did the American colonists change their view of Britain? (They realized that Britain would not protect their western settlements from attacks by American Indians.)

Remind students to use the space provided in their journal to jot down notes.

Report Your Findings

Think About It

Review your research. Based on the information you have gathered, which event do you think was the most important cause of the conflict between the British, the French, and the American Indians?

Write About It

Take a Stand

Write and Cite Evidence In your opinion, what was the most important event in the French and Indian War? What were its causes and effects? List three reasons that support your opinion. Include page references.

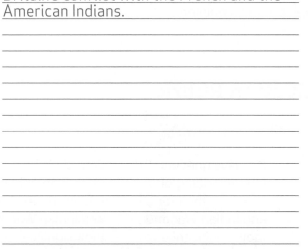

<u>Students should use evidence from the text to support their opinion as to which event was the most important cause of Great Britain's conflict with the French and the American Indians.</u>

Talk About It

Defend Your Claim

Talk to a classmate who chose a different event. Take turns discussing your opinions and supporting evidence. Do you agree or disagree with your partner's opinion?

Connect to the EQ

Citizenship

Pull It Together

Think about what you have learned about the experiences of the American colonists before, during, and after the French and Indian War. How might these experiences have begun to change how they viewed themselves as citizens?

<u>Students should be able to understand that before the French and Indian War, the American colonists viewed themselves as British subjects. The colonists' experience of fighting together and defeating a powerful enemy, along with their anger at the Proclamation of 1763, helped to start many of them thinking of themselves as separate from Great Britain.</u>

Inquiry Project Notes

138 Lesson 1 What Caused the Conflict between Great Britain, France, and the American Indians?

Lesson 1 **139**

Inquiry Journal, pp. 138–139

EL ENGLISH LEARNERS SCAFFOLD

ELD.PI.5.11 Supporting own opinions and evaluating others' opinions in speaking and writing

Emerging	Expanding	Bridging
State and Support Opinions Point out that in the Write About It assignment, students need to give three reasons for their opinions. Provide this sentence frame to help them: *In my opinion, the most important event of the French and Indian War was ___ because (1)_____, (2) ___, and (3) ____.*	**Ask and Answer Questions** Pair students for the Talk About It assignment. Then prompt their discussion by suggesting they ask and answer these questions: *What do you think was the most important event of the French and Indian War? Why do you think it was so important?*	**Develop Ideas** Have students review the text in the Reader's Companion and then discuss their ideas for Connect to the Essential Question. They should compare and contrast the American colonists' attitudes before, during, and after the French and Indian War and consider changes in attitude.

See the **Language Learner Teaching Guide** for more language support strategies.

Monitor and Differentiate

REACHING ALL LEARNERS

Approaching Level

Note that the Write About It assignment asks students to include *page references*—that is, to give the pages in their texts on which the evidence they cite appears. Tell them to put the page references in parentheses.

On Level

Help students use the causes and effects on which they took notes in order to determine the event they think most important in the war. Tell them to ask themselves: *What caused the event, and why was that important? What resulted from the event, and why was that important?*

Know what your students know!

Lesson Task
Report Your Findings

Use this rubric to evaluate students' responses.

Write and Cite Evidence Students make a claim about which event in the French and Indian War was the most important, explain the causes and effects of the event, and use reasons to support their opinion.

Defend Your Claim Students discuss with a partner who chose a different event the reasons for their own preference and consider whether they agree or disagree with their partner's opinion.

Performance Task Evaluation Rubric

	4	3	2	1
Historical Understanding	Displays strong understanding of events in the French and Indian War and their significance to the war	Displays adequate understanding of events in the French and Indian War and their significance to the war	Displays uneven understanding of events in the French and Indian War and their significance to the war	Displays no understanding of events in the French and Indian War and their significance to the war
Write and Cite Evidence	Provides a clear explanation of the student's preference	Provides an adequate explanation of the student's preference	Provides a somewhat clear or unclear explanation of the student's preference	Provides no statement or no explanation of the student's preference
Support with Evidence	Supports claims and reasons with thorough and convincing evidence	Supports claims and reasons with adequate evidence	Supports claims and reasons with too little or only somewhat convincing evidence	Supplies no claims or reasons or no supporting evidence
Defend Your Claim	Speaks clearly and at an understandable pace Speaks in complete sentences throughout the discussion	Speaks clearly during most of the discussion Speaks in complete sentences through most of the discussion	Speaks unclearly at times Mixes complete and incomplete sentences during the discussion	Speaks unclearly throughout the discussion Does not use complete sentences in the discussion

Lesson Assessment

Go Digital!

- Have students complete the Chapter 4 Lesson 1 Assessment online to monitor their understanding of the lesson content.

ONLINE ASSESSMENT

California Smarter Balanced Assessment Connections!

Standards Covered	Performance Assessment	Lesson Assessment	Alignment with California Smarter Balanced Assessment
History and Social Science Content 5.3.1; 5.3.2; 5.3.3; 5.3.5	✔	✔	Claim 1 Targets 8, 9, 11
History and Social Science Analysis Skills Chronological and Spatial Thinking 5.1; 5.3; 5.4 Research, Evidence, and Point of View 5.1; 5.2 Historical Interpretation 5.1; 5.3	✔	✔	Claim 1 Targets 11, 12 Claim 2 Target 6
Writing W.5.1; W.5.4	✔	✔	Claim 2 Target 6
Research and Inquiry W.5.8; W.5.9	✔	✔	Claim 4 Targets 1, 2
Reading RI.5.1	✔	✔	Claim 1 Target 11
Speaking and Listening SL.5.1; SL.5.1.a; SL.5.2	✔		Claim 3 Target 3

What Were the Views of the Patriots, the Loyalists, and the British?

Background Information

In this lesson, students will learn about issues that led many American colonists to favor independence, about the views of colonists staying loyal to Britain, and about the views of the British themselves.

Community Connections

To enrich their understanding, have students visit the sites or the websites of historical homes associated with a Patriot or a Loyalist, such as Gunston Hall, Virginia home of George Mason, or the John Dickinson Plantation in Delaware.

 LESSON STANDARDS

- ✓ Understand how political, religious, and economic ideas and interests brought about the Revolution (e.g., resistance to imperial policy, the Stamp Act, the Townshend Acts, taxes on tea, Coercive Acts). **HSS.5.5.1**

- ✓ Describe the views, lives, and impact of key individuals during this period (e.g., King George III, Patrick Henry, Thomas Jefferson, George Washington, Benjamin Franklin, John Adams). **HSS.5.5.4**

- ✓ Students place key events and people of the historical era they are studying in a chronological sequence and spatial context; they interpret time lines. **HAS.CS.1**

- ✓ Students differentiate between primary and secondary sources. **HAS.HR.1**

- ✓ Students pose relevant questions about events they encounter in historical documents, eyewitness accounts, oral histories, letters, diaries, artifacts, photographs, maps, artworks, and architecture. **HAS.HR.2**

Connect to the Essential Question

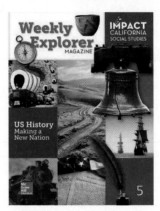

Chapter 4, pp. 44–57

The **Weekly Explorer Magazine** supports students' exploration of the Essential Question and provides additional resources for the EQ Inquiry Project.

Inquiry Project

Which Side Will You Choose?

Remind students to use the information they learn in this lesson and other resources to complete their EQ Inquiry Project!

 **Dinah Zike's** **FOLDABLES®** In this lesson you will use Foldables.

When Minutes Count!

Suggested Lesson Pacing

1 ENGAGE
One Day

- Lesson Opener
- Analyze the Source
- Inquiry Tools

2 INVESTIGATE
Two to Three Days

🕐 **Short on Time?** Look for the clock to teach core content in less time.

- New Taxes
- The Colonies Respond
- The Townshend Acts

3 REPORT
One Day

- Think About It
- Write and Cite Evidence
- Defend Your Claim

Make Connections!

(ccss) CONNECT TO ELA

Reading
Quote accurately from a text when explaining what the text says explicitly and when drawing inferences from the text. **RI.5.1**

Research
Recall relevant information from experiences or gather relevant information from print and digital sources; summarize or paraphrase information in notes and finished work, and provide a list of sources. **W.5.8**

Draw evidence from literary or informational texts to support analysis, reflection, and research. **W.5.9**

Writing
Write opinion pieces on topics or texts, supporting a point of view with reasons and information. **W.5.1**

Speaking and Listening
Engage effectively in a range of collaborative discussions (one-on-one, in groups, and teacher-led) with diverse partners on grade 5 topics and texts, building on others' ideas and expressing their own clearly. **SL.5.1**

Summarize a written text read aloud or information presented in diverse media and formats, including visually, quantitatively, and orally. **SL.5.2**

Classroom Resources

🔍 Search for additional resources using the following key words

Samuel Adams

Edmund Burke

John Dickinson

Joseph Galloway

King George III

Loyalists

George Mason

Patriots

Sons of Liberty

Stamp Act

Sugar Act

Townshend Acts

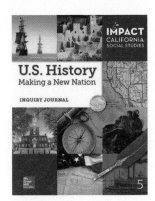

Inquiry Journal
pp. 140–141

 STANDARDS

Understand how political, religious, and economic ideas and interests brought about the Revolution (e.g., resistance to imperial policy, the Stamp Act, the Townshend Acts, taxes on tea, Coercive Acts). **HSS.5.5.1**

Describe the views, lives, and impact of key individuals during this period (e.g., King George III, Patrick Henry, Thomas Jefferson, George Washington, Benjamin Franklin, John Adams). **HSS.5.5.4**

CCSS Summarize information presented in diverse media and formats, including visually, quantitatively, and orally. **CCSS.ELA.SL.5.2**

Go Digital!

Explore the lesson content with online whole-class presentation tools.

What Were the Views of the Patriots, the Loyalists, and the British?

Bellringer

Prompt students to retrieve information from the previous lessons. Say: *The French and Indian War helped protect the Thirteen Colonies, and it made Canada a British colony. Still, it was a long and costly war, part of Britain's broader warfare with the French. Do you think the British government had the right to make the colonists pay for the French and Indian War? Why or why not?*

Lesson Outcomes

What Am I Learning? Have students read the Lesson Question and Lesson Outcomes.

Why Am I Learning It? Discuss the terms *Patriots* and *Loyalists* in the lesson question, explaining that the American colonists who wanted to stay part of Great Britain have come to be called *Loyalists*; those who supported the struggle for independence from Britain have come to be called *Patriots*.

How Will I Know That I Learned It? Ask students the following questions:

- Whose views will you be able to identify after reading the chapter? (Patriots, Loyalists, and the British)

- What kind of British policies toward the colonies will you explore? (British tax policies)

COLLABORATE
Talk About It

Explain that when we talk about artwork, we describe, analyze, and interpret it and present our ideas in our own words. Provide sentence frames to help students form sentences as they talk about the portraits on page 141.

- You can tell that the portrait ___ is of a British person because ___. (at the bottom left; the person is wearing a red coat and has a white wig)

- You can infer that the portrait ___ is of a Patriot or Loyalist because ___. (at the top right; the person is more plainly dressed and is not wearing a wig)

Collaborative Conversations

Add New Ideas As students engage in partner, small group, and whole-class discussions, encourage them to

- Stay on topic.

- Connect their own ideas to things their peers have said.

- Look for ways to connect their personal experiences or prior knowledge to the conversation.

Lesson 2

What Were the Views of the Patriots, Loyalists, and the British?

Lesson Outcomes

What Am I Learning?
In this lesson, you're going to use your investigative skills to explore British tax policies and the views of Patriots, Loyalists, and the British.

Why Am I Learning It?
Reading and talking about these events will help you understand economic and political issues that led to the American Revolution.

How Will I Know That I Learned It?
You will be able to identify the arguments and reasoning of Patriots, Loyalists, and the British, choose one side to defend, and support your argument with evidence from the text.

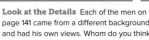

Talk About It COLLABORATE

Look at the Details Each of the men on page 141 came from a different background and had his own views. Whom do you think was in favor of independence?

Thomas Paine (top left), George Mason (top right), Joseph Galloway (bottom left), and John Dickinson (bottom right)

HSS.5.4.5, HSS.5.4.7, HSS.5.5.1, HSS.5.5.4, HAS.HI.4

140 Lesson 2 What Were the Views of the Patriots, Loyalists, and the British?

Lesson 2 **141**

Inquiry Journal, pp. 140–141

EL ENGLISH LEARNERS SCAFFOLD

ELD.PI.5.8 Analyzing how writers and speakers use vocabulary and other language resources for specific purposes (to explain, persuade, entertain, etc.) depending on modality, text type, purpose, audience, topic, and content area

Emerging	Expanding	Bridging
Understand Domain-Specific Vocabulary Explain *economic* and *political* issues in the discussion of the Lesson Outcomes. Note the term *British tax policies*, and clarify that it refers to the British government's plans for charging colonists a *tax*, or required payment.	**Understand Domain-Specific Vocabulary** Help students with possibly unfamiliar terms in the Talk About It feature, such as *Patriot* and *Loyalist*. Focus on word families by discussing the words *patriotic* and *loyal*. Elicit what these words mean.	**Use Domain-Specific Vocabulary** Note that the Lessons Outcomes say the lesson is about economic and political issues and tax policies. Ask how tax policies are both economic and political.

See the **Language Learner Teaching Guide** for more language support strategies.

Monitor and Differentiate

REACHING ALL LEARNERS

On Level

Have students examine the additional portraits on page 141 and speculate about whether each person portrayed is a Patriot or a Loyalist. Ask students to give reasons for their answers.

Beyond Level

Have small groups of students each choose a different person pictured on page 141, do online research to learn more about that person, and share their findings in oral or online reports.

Analyze the Source

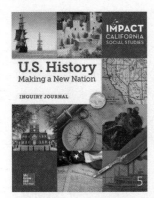

Inquiry Journal
pp. 142–143

 STANDARDS

Understand how political, religious, and economic ideas and interests brought about the Revolution (e.g., resistance to imperial policy, the Stamp Act, the Townshend Acts, taxes on tea, Coercive Acts). **HSS.5.5.1**

Describe the views, lives, and impact of key individuals during this period (e.g., King George III, Patrick Henry, Thomas Jefferson, George Washington, Benjamin Franklin, John Adams). **HSS.5.5.4**

Students differentiate between primary and secondary sources. **HAS.HR1**

Students pose relevant questions about events they encounter in historical documents, eyewitness accounts, oral histories, letters, diaries, artifacts, photographs, maps, artworks, and architecture. **HAS.HR.2**

Come to discussions prepared, having read or studied required material, to explore ideas under discussion. **CCSS.ELA.SL.5.1a**

Go Digital!

Model how to inspect and find evidence with online whole-class presentation tools.

Background Information

Edmund Burke was sympathetic to colonists' grievances and considered the British government's lack of response partly to blame for the American Revolution. When the French Revolution broke out in 1789, however, he argued it was completely against that nation's traditions and would lead to dangerous mob rule. For this reason, he is often called the Father of Modern Conservatism.

1 Inspect

Read Have students read the entire text, including the Primary Source. Clarify that *Parliament* is Britain's lawmaking body and *ministers* are members of Parliament. Ask:

- What does the title suggest the passage is about? (Burke's criticism of Parliament)

- Why did Parliament want the colonists to pay new taxes? (to pay the debt from the French and Indian War)

- How did the colonists feel about the taxes? (angry; considered the taxes to be unlawful)

Collaborate Have partners discuss Burke's opinion of Parliament's decisions. (Students should recognize Burke was critical of Parliament.)

2 Find Evidence

Reread Have students reread the text, focusing on Burke's views and attitude.

Analyze the Primary Source Read the text aloud and analyze it together. Ask:

- What attitude toward Parliament does Burke convey with words like *never, so little,* and *abandoned?* (a very negative opinion)

- What do Burke's images of a gaping gulf and a festering wound coming to a head show about how he sees the situation? (He sees it as dangerous and unhealthy.)

- What main point does Burke make about Parliament's treatment of the colonies? (It has been foolish and impractical.)

3 Make Connections

COLLABORATE

Write Have students summarize Burke's reasons for blaming Parliament for colonial unrest. (He thinks Parliament passed overly strict laws, did not consider their consequences, announced the Stamp Act too early, and refused to work with the colonists.)

Analyze the Source

1 Inspect

Read Look at the title. What does the title suggest the passage will be about?

- **Circle** any unfamiliar words.
- **Underline** clues about what led to the Stamp Act and what happened after the act was passed.
- **Discuss** with a partner why Edmund Burke criticized the way Parliament ruled the colonies.

My Notes

_____
_____
_____
_____
_____
_____
_____
_____
_____
_____
_____
_____
_____

Edmund Burke Blames Parliament

After the French and Indian War, Great Britain struggled with debt. To help pay for it, King George III and British leaders decided to raise taxes on the colonies. They argued that the colonists should help pay for the troops sent to protect them during the war. In 1765, the British government passed the Stamp Act. It was one of several laws that caused outrage in the colonies.

The Stamp Act required colonists to buy stamps and place them on all printed documents, from newspapers to playing cards. Colonists immediately protested. They called the act unlawful and argued that only elected colonial officials had the power to tax goods.

Colonists were not the only critics of the Stamp Act. A respected member of Parliament, Edmund Burke, spoke on the issue several times before Parliament. He argued that the act was passed in poor judgment. He criticized the British government's strict colonial laws and its refusal to work cooperatively with the colonies. Britain could not just ignore the colonists' complaints, Burke argued. Although he believed that Parliament had the right to tax the colonists, Burke felt that this authority should be used only as a last resort.

PRIMARY SOURCE

In Their Words... Edmund Burke

Never was so critical a measure pursued with so little provision against its necessary consequences. As if all common prudence had abandoned the ministers, and as if they meant to plunge themselves and us headlong into that gulf which stood gaping before them, by giving a year's notice of the project of their stamp act, they allowed time for all the discontents of that country to fester and come to a head, and for all the arrangements which factious men could make towards an opposition to the law.

—from "Observations on a Late State of the Nation," 1769

Edmund Burke speaking before the British Parliament

TEXT: Burke, Edmund. Observations on a Late State of the Nation. Dublin: Printed for A. Leathly, J. Exshaw, B. Grierson, and J. Williams, 1769.
PHOTO: (IM)/McGraw-Hill Education, (b)Historical Images Archive/Alamy

2 Find Evidence

Reread Note the words "never," "so little," and "abandoned." What do they reveal about Edmund Burke's attitude toward Parliament?

Reread this part of the second sentence: "as if they meant to plunge themselves and us headlong into that gulf which stood gaping before them." What image does Burke create by referring to a gaping gulf and using the word *fester*?

3 Make Connections

Write Summarize Edmund Burke's key reasons for blaming Parliament for unrest in the colonies. **COLLABORATE**

142 Lesson 2 What Were the Views of the Patriots, Loyalists, and the British?

Lesson 2 **143**

Inquiry Journal, pp. 142–143

(EL) ENGLISH LEARNERS SCAFFOLD

ELD.PI.5.6 Reading closely literary and informational texts and viewing multimedia to determine how meaning is conveyed explicitly and implicitly through language

Emerging	Expanding	Bridging
Clarify Text Help students with the text introducing the Primary Source, clarifying terms such as *debt* ("money owed"), *outrage* ("great anger"), *protested* ("showed disapproval"), *unlawful* ("against the law"), *critics* ("those who find fault"), *cooperatively* ("together"), and *as a last resort* ("as the last possible way").	**Clarify Vocabulary** Go over difficult words in the Primary Source, such as *provision* ("preparation"), *consequences* ("results"), *prudence* ("wisdom"), *headlong* ("recklessly"), *gulf* ("wide gap"), *gaping* ("wide open"), *discontents* ("those never satisfied"), *fester* ("swell below the surface"), and *factious* ("creating conflict").	**Paraphrase Text** Have students paraphrase the Primary Source, using a dictionary to help them with difficult words (see examples in the previous Expanding column). Then have students form small groups, share their paraphrases, and discuss which words and phrases best express Burke's meaning.

See the **Language Learner Teaching Guide** for more language support strategies.

Monitor and Differentiate

REACHING ALL LEARNERS

Approaching Level

Clarify that the Stamp Act fees were like taxes because they went to the British government and colonists were angry because they had no say in the government that charged the fees.

On Level

Discuss students' opinions of the situation. Was Britain right to expect colonists to pay for a war that had protected them? Were colonists right to feel Parliament had no right to tax them?

Beyond Level

Ask students to research Edmund Burke and to then consider whether his criticisms of Parliament may have been politically motivated.

1 ENGAGE

Inquiry Tools

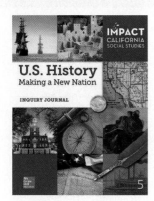

Inquiry Journal
pp. 144–145

 STANDARDS

Understand how political, religious, and economic ideas and interests brought about the Revolution (e.g., resistance to imperial policy, the Stamp Act, the Townshend Acts, taxes on tea, Coercive Acts). **HSS.5.5.1**

Describe the views, lives, and impact of key individuals during this period (e.g., King George III, Patrick Henry, Thomas Jefferson, George Washington, Benjamin Franklin, John Adams). **HSS.5.5.4**

 Recall or gather relevant information from sources; summarize or paraphrase information in notes and finished work.
CCSS.ELA.W.5.8

Draw evidence from literary or informational texts to support analysis, reflection, and research. **CCSS.ELA.W.5.9**

Go Digital!

- Model how to explore and investigate with online whole-class tools.

- Students can access the online graphic organizer to use the inquiry tools as they read.

Explore Compare and Contrast

Explain that compare and contrast is a text structure authors often use to organize information in historical texts. Showing how events, places, people, and ideas are alike or different puts them in perspective and makes them easier to understand.

Read Have students read aloud the step-by-step instructions about how to identify comparisons and contrasts. Offer additional signals for similarities, such as *similarly* and *in the same way,* and for contrasts, such as *although, however,* and *in contrast.*

Guide Practice Clarify how a Venn diagram works—differences go in non-overlapping parts; similarities go in the overlap. Then have students work together to complete the Venn diagram about what they just read in the section Edmund Burke Blames Parliament.

Investigate!

Have students read pages 178–185 in the Research Companion. Tell them the information will help them answer the lesson question *What Were the Views of the Patriots, the Loyalist, and the British?*

Take Notes Tell students that they should take notes in the Venn diagrams on pages 144–145 of the Inquiry Journal.

Inspect Guide students to read the text in each section to determine what it says about Patriot, Loyalist, and British views.

Find Evidence Encourage students to reread the text to develop a deeper understanding of the content and determine if they should add more information to their notes. Remind them that after they read and take notes, they should review and think about how the facts and details will help them answer the lesson question.

Collaborative Conversations

Text-Based Discussion Remind students of the goals of discussing the text with others:

- to listen and respond to their partner's points
- to ask for evidence from the text
- to build on each other's ideas
- to see the text from a different point of view

Inquiry Tools

Explore Compare and Contrast

To compare, look for similarities—things that are alike. To contrast, look for differences—things that are not alike. Comparing and contrasting the points of view of Patriots and Loyalists will help you better understand both sides of the issue.

1. Read the entire text once.
This will help you understand the topic and main idea.

2. Look at the title and section headings.
What clues do they give about the two ideas being compared in the passage?

3. Identify signal words and phrases.
Words like *both*, *likewise*, and *also* signal similarities. Words and phrases like *but*, *yet*, and *on the other hand* signal differences.

4. Analyze the details.
Take a close look at the details signaled by the clue words. How does each detail help you better understand the causes of the American Revolution?

 Based on the text you just read, work with your class to fill in the graphic organizer with Edmund Burke's own views and the views he shared with Parliament.

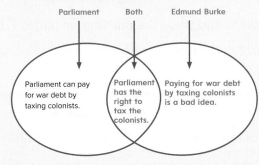

Parliament   Both   Edmund Burke

Parliament can pay for war debt by taxing colonists.

Parliament has the right to tax the colonists.

Paying for war debt by taxing colonists is a bad idea.

144 Lesson 2 What Were the Views of the Patriots, Loyalists, and the British?

Investigate!

Read pages 178–185 in your Research Companion. Use your investigative skills to compare and contrast the points of view of the Patriots, the Loyalists, and the British.

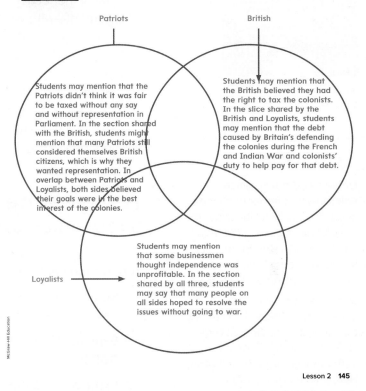

Patriots

Students may mention that the Patriots didn't think it was fair to be taxed without any say and without representation in Parliament. In the section shared with the British, students might mention that many Patriots still considered themselves British citizens, which is why they wanted representation. In overlap between Patriots and Loyalists, both sides believed their goals were in the best interest of the colonies.

British

Students may mention that the British believed they had the right to tax the colonists. In the slice shared by the British and Loyalists, students may mention that the debt caused by Britain's defending the colonies during the French and Indian War and colonists' duty to help pay for that debt.

Loyalists

Students may mention that some businessmen thought independence was unprofitable. In the section shared by all three, students may say that many people on all sides hoped to resolve the issues without going to war.

McGraw-Hill Education

Lesson 2 145

Inquiry Journal, pp. 144–145

EL ENGLISH LEARNERS SCAFFOLD

ELD.PII.5.7 Condensing ideas

Emerging	Expanding	Bridging
Organize Information Work with students individually to identify details to go in each section of the Venn diagram. Be sure students understand the way in which a Venn diagram shows comparisons and contrasts, with shared characteristics going in the middle.	**State Comparisons and Contrasts** To help students make comparisons and contrasts, offer sentence frames such as: *Both the Loyalists and the Patriots were __* or *The Patriots believed ____, while the British believed ____.*	**Generalize** Have students use the details they listed about Patriots and Loyalists to make general statements about the situation in the American colonies at the time. (Students should recognize the tense situation and disagreements between Patriots and Loyalists.)

See the **Language Learner Teaching Guide** for more language support strategies.

Monitor and Differentiate

REACHING ALL LEARNERS

Approaching Level

Have students work in pairs, identifying similarities and differences between the different groups by taking turns posing and answering questions, such as *How did Patriots feel about the Stamp Act? What views about the colonies did Loyalists and the British share?*

Beyond Level

Have students do additional research into the views and actions of Patriots, Loyalists, and members of the British government at this time and then add details to their diagrams.

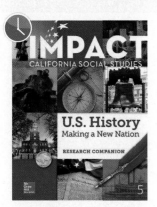

Research Companion
pp. 178–179

 STANDARDS

Understand how political, religious, and economic ideas and interests brought about the Revolution (e.g., resistance to imperial policy, the Stamp Act, the Townshend Acts, taxes on tea, Coercive Acts). **HSS.5.5.1**

Describe the views, lives, and impact of key individuals during this period (e.g., King George III, Patrick Henry, Thomas Jefferson, George Washington, Benjamin Franklin, John Adams). **HSS.5.5.4**

Students place key events and people of the historical era they are studying in a chronological sequence and spatial context; they interpret time lines. **HAS.CS.1**

(ccss) Quote accurately from a text when explaining what the text says explicitly and when drawing inferences from the text. **CCSS.ELA.RI.5.1**

Summarize information presented in diverse media and formats, including visually, quantitatively, and orally. **CCSS.ELA.SL.5.2**

Go Digital!

Investigate the lesson content with online whole-class presentation tools.

Background Information

George III became king in 1760, when his grandfather, George II, died. He was against the colonial expansion favored by William Pitt the Elder, who resigned soon after George took the throne. The king then appointed as his prime ministers a series of fairly ineffective politicians. It was Prime Minister George Grenville who made the argument—with which the king agreed—for the Sugar and Stamp Acts.

| TIMELINE | Invite students to look at the timeline at the top on page 179.

Analyze Ask: Which came first, the Stamp Act or the Sugar Act? (Sugar Act) How soon after the French and Indian War ended did Parliament pass the Stamp Act? (two years) **HAS.CS.1 DOK 2**

Analyze the Source

Inspect Have students read about new taxes and study the painting on pages 178–179.

Find Evidence Use the questions below to check comprehension. Remind students to support their answers with text evidence.

Summarize For what two things did the king and Parliament expect the colonies to pay? (the recent war and the troops still needed to protect them) **DOK 2**

Explain What did the Sugar Act make colonists do? (pay a tax on sugar products) **DOK 2**

Explain From the British government's point of view, what was the problem with the Sugar Act? (It did not bring in enough money.) **DOK 2**

Make Connections

Evaluate How might the king's desire to make his mark as a strong ruler wind up hurting him? (He could cause the colonists to rebel against him.) **DOK 4**

Analyze the Painting Direct students' attention to the painting of the House of Commons, explaining it is one of two houses that make up the British Parliament. Encourage students to use the image to help them understand details in the text. Remind them of what they read about Edmund Burke, a member of Parliament. Then discuss the painting, asking:

- Why do you think the members of Parliament are seated in two sections? (They probably belong to two different political parties or factions.)

- Do you think Edmund Burke would sit with those who supported the Stamp Act? Why or why not? (probably not, as he did not support it and criticized those who did)

Lesson 2

What Were the Views of the Patriots, Loyalists, and the British?

Timeline

| 1763 February Treaty of Paris ends the French and Indian War. | 1763 October Proclamation of 1763 sets aside land west of the Appalachians for American Indians. | 1764 Parliament passes the Sugar Act. | 1765 Parliament passes the Stamp Act. |

1762 | 1763 | 1764 | 1765

In the 1760s and 1770s, the British Parliament passed tax laws that made many colonists unhappy.

New Taxes

Great Britain's 1763 victory in the French and Indian War came at a great cost. The war doubled Britain's debt, which reached 122 million pounds in 1763. Adding to the cost were the British troops left behind to protect the colonies from further conflict. King George III, who had been on the throne for only three years, struggled to find ways to pay the massive debt.

George III was a young king determined to make his mark as a strong ruler. He surrounded himself with advisors who agreed he should rule the colonies with a firm hand. British citizens already paid high taxes. The advisors argued that it was only fair to tax colonists to help pay for Britain's protection during and after the war.

Parliament, the British legislature, passed the Sugar Act in 1764. It forced the colonists to pay a tax on all sugar products. An older British tax on sugar products already existed, but the British government had never enforced it. With the new Sugar Act, any colonist who refused to pay was arrested and fined. However, the Sugar Act did not bring in enough money to make a significant impact on Britain's debt.

HSS.5.5.1, HSS.5.5.4, HAS.HI.1, HAS.HI.4

178 Lesson 2 What Were the Views of the Patriots, Loyalists, and the British?

Lesson 2 **179**

Research Companion, pp. 178–179

 ENGLISH LEARNERS SCAFFOLD

ELD.PI.5.8 Analyzing how writers and speakers use vocabulary and other language resources for specific purposes (to explain, persuade, entertain, etc.) depending on modality, text type, purpose, audience, topic, and content area

Emerging	Expanding	Bridging
Clarify Terms Explan that *pounds* are British money and *debt* is the amount of money owed. Note that the word *massive* contains the word *mass*, which means "a very large body or amount of something," and elicit that the *massive debt* is a very large one.	**Clarify Terms** Point to the fourth sentence in the section, which mentions George III as "on the throne." Explain that *throne* and *crown* are often used to show that someone is king or queen. Ask what phrase with *crown* could be used to mean the same thing.	**Use Context Clues** Point out the context definition of *Parliament* in commas in the third paragraph of the section. Clarify that a *legislature* is a lawmaking group. Remind students to look for definitions or explanations that appear set off from the terms.

See the **Language Learner Teaching Guide** for more language support strategies.

Monitor and Differentiate

REACHING ALL LEARNERS

Special Needs

If students struggle to understand the meaning of the various taxes, point out that they all were passed to try to pay for the French and Indian War.

On Level

Refer students to the timeline. Remind them that the Proclamation of 1763 was another issue that angered colonists. The French and Indian War broke out west of the Appalachian Mountains. After the war, Britain said colonists could not settle there.

Beyond Level

Note that George III took the throne in 1760, when his grandfather, George II, died. Have students investigate how the change in kings led to policy changes that angered colonists.

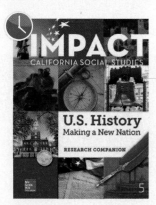

Research Companion
pp. 180–181

 STANDARDS

Understand how political, religious, and economic ideas and interests brought about the Revolution (e.g., resistance to imperial policy, the Stamp Act, the Townshend Acts, taxes on tea, Coercive Acts). **HSS.5.5.1**

Describe the views, lives, and impact of key individuals during this period (e.g., King George III, Patrick Henry, Thomas Jefferson, George Washington, Benjamin Franklin, John Adams). **HSS.5.5.4**

CCSS Quote accurately from a text when explaining what the text says explicitly and when drawing inferences from the text. **CCSS.ELA.RI.5.1**

Summarize information presented in diverse media and formats, including visually, quantitatively, and orally. **CCSS.ELA.SL.5.2**

Go Digital!

Investigate the lesson content with online whole-class presentation tools.

Background Information

Benjamin Franklin, then serving in London as a colonial agent for Pennsylvania, was invited to speak about the Stamp Act in Parliament's House of Commons. He spoke against it, explaining why it so upset colonists. His testimony, along with colonial actions, helped lead to the act's repeal—but it may also have led to the Townshend Acts, since he said colonists might accept a tax on imported goods.

Analyze the Source

Inspect Have students read pages 180–181 in the Research Companion.

Find Evidence Use the questions below to check comprehension.

Identify What did the Stamp Act tax? (all printed documents) **DOK 1**

Synthesize In what two ways did the colonists find the Stamp Act unlawful? (It was passed by a legislature in which the colonists had no say, and the money it raised went to Britain instead of colonial governments.) **DOK 3**

Explain For what purpose did Samuel Adams and others first form the Sons of Liberty? (to protest the Stamp Act) **DOK 2**

Analyze the Chart Have students read the information in Chart Skills and study the chart. Ask:

- In which year did Britain start owing more in debt than it produced? (1750)
- Did the debt go down or up from 1750 to 1760? (up)
- Why do you think the debt went down from 1760 to 1770? (Possibilities include end of the war with France, king's focus on lowering the debt, and new taxes.)

Make Connections

Synthesize What are three reasons Loyalists did not want independence? (They wanted to stay British citizens, feared independence would lead to chaos, and/or thought it would be bad for the economy.) **DOK 4**

Stop and Check

Think How did Britain plan on paying the war debt? (by taxing the colonists)

Find Details Explain to students that after they read and take notes, they should review and think about how the facts and details will help them answer the Essential Question.

One year later, Parliament passed the Stamp Act. It forced colonists to buy stamps for all printed documents. This included everyday paper products such as letters, newspapers, pamphlets, and even playing cards.

Many colonists were furious. They disagreed with Britain's **imposing** the tax on them. Colonists complained that Parliament passed the new tax laws without colonists' consent, or agreement. One strong opponent of the tax laws was Samuel Adams of Massachusetts. Adams sent protest letters to newspapers and addressed delegates from the colony's assembly. In one letter, he stated, "If our trade may be taxed, why not our lands? Why not . . . everything we possess or use?"

A British stamp used on printed documents

Chart Skills

GDP is the Gross Domestic Product, the total value of all goods and services a country produces in a year. When a country owes more in debt than it produces in a year, it can take a long time for the country to pay down its debt.

The Growth of Britain's Debt

Year	British Debt as a Percentage of GDP
1700	23
1710	34
1720	83
1730	76
1740	68
1750	107
1760	132
1770	126

Source: ukpublicspending.co.uk

✓ Stop and Check

Talk How did Britain plan on paying the war debt?

Find Details As you read, add additional information to the graphic organizer on page 145 in your Inquiry Journal.

180   Lesson 2   What Were the Views of the Patriots, Loyalists, and the British?

The Colonies Respond

Colonists were still British citizens. Since the British government had spent money to protect these citizens, Parliament believed that the colonists should pay for the French and Indian War in the form of taxes. Many colonists saw the Stamp Act as taxation without representation. That meant they were forced to pay taxes approved by officials they had not elected. Colonists who demanded that Americans have more control of their government were known as Patriots.

Before these tax laws, only colonial legislatures had taxed colonists. Colonists had accepted those taxes because they had elected the officials. These officials, they argued, were the only ones who should be allowed to tax goods. To make matters worse, the tax money collected from the colonists went to Britain instead of the colonial governments.

Every colony protested the new tax law. In Boston, some colonists formed a group to protest the Stamp Act. They called themselves the Sons of Liberty. Samuel Adams actively participated in this group. The Sons of Liberty met under an elm tree that Adams called "The Liberty Tree." As tensions continued between the colonies and Great Britain, many Patriots began talking about breaking away from Great Britain and becoming independent.

Colonists protesting in the streets

Lesson 2   181

Research Companion, pp. 180–181

(EL) ENGLISH LEARNERS SCAFFOLD

ELD.PI.5.12 Selecting and applying varied and precise vocabulary and language structures to effectively convey ideas

Emerging

Clarify Vocabulary Help students with domain-specific and other possibly unfamiliar terms, such as *opponent* ("someone who is against something"), *protest letters* ("letters of complaint"), *delegates* ("representatives"), *assuredly* ("definitely"), and *chaos* ("total confusion").

Expanding

Understand Related Words Point out the word *address* on page 180, and explain that here it is a noun meaning "a formal speech." Then explain that, like many nouns, *address* can also be used as a verb. Have students define the verb *addressed* in the sentence before it. ("spoke to an audience")

Bridging

Explain Historic Terms Have students explain the term "taxation without representation" and how it applied to the colonists. (It means being taxed by a government in which you have no one elected or appointed to speak or vote for your needs.)

See the **Language Learner Teaching Guide** for more language support strategies.

Monitor and Differentiate

REACHING ALL LEARNERS

Approaching Level

Help students understand the numbers on the graph by stating the information in sentences: In 1700, Britain's debt was 23 percent of the total value of the goods and services it produced; but in 1750, it was 107 percent, meaning Britain owed more than it produced.

On Level

Have students state in their own words the point Samuel Adams makes in the quotation from his letter on page 180. (Taxing some things can lead to taxes on everything colonists own or use.)

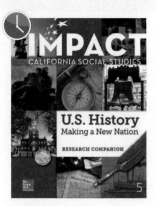

Research Companion
pp. 182–183

 STANDARDS

Understand how political, religious, and economic ideas and interests brought about the Revolution (e.g., resistance to imperial policy, the Stamp Act, the Townshend Acts, taxes on tea, Coercive Acts). **HSS.5.5.1**

Describe the views, lives, and impact of key individuals during this period (e.g., King George III, Patrick Henry, Thomas Jefferson, George Washington, Benjamin Franklin, John Adams). **HSS.5.5.4**

Students differentiate between primary and secondary sources. **HAS.HR.1**

Students pose relevant questions about events they encounter in historical documents, eyewitness accounts, oral histories, letters, diaries, artifacts, photographs, maps, artworks, and architecture. **HAS.HR.2**

Quote accurately from a text when explaining what the text says explicitly and when drawing inferences from the text. **CCSS.ELA.RI.5.1**

Go Digital!

Investigate the lesson content with online whole-class presentation tools.

Background Information

Boycott was not a term colonists used: they called for "non-consumption and non-importation" of British goods. The word *boycott* did not come into existence until the 1870s. It is named for Captain Charles C. Boycott, a British land agent in Ireland whose efforts to collect high rents in hard times were so unreasonable that tenants began what we now call a boycott against him.

Analyze the Source

Inspect Have students continue reading about the colonists' response on pp. 182–183.

Find Evidence Use the questions below to check comprehension. Remind students to support their answers with text evidence.

> **Explain** Why did colonists decided to form the Stamp Act Congress? (to discuss their opposition to the Stamp Act) **DOK 2**
>
> **Define** What is a boycott? (refusal to buy from or do business with a person, group, or country) **DOK 1**
>
> **Explain** Why did the Daughters of Liberty make a kind of cloth known as homespun? (to avoid buying British products) **DOK 2**

Make Connections

> **Draw Conclusion** How do you think British merchants viewed the Stamp Act? (They probably thought it was bad for business.) **DOK 4**

COLLABORATE

☑ Stop and Check

Talk Have students discuss the reasons that colonists' different types of protests were effective. (Students should recognize that the protests made colonists less reliant on British goods and had a negative impact on Britain's economy.)

Perspectives

Have students read Views from a Patriot and a Loyalist on page 183. Explain that George Mason was a rich farmer and member of Virginia's legislature, the House of Burgesses. Joseph Galloway was a prominent Philadelphia lawyer. Ask:

- What main point does Mason make about the Stamp Act? (It violates colonists' rights as Englishmen.)

- Why do you think Mason is writing to London merchants? (to get them to campaign against the Stamp Act, either because it is unfair or because it is bad for business)

- What is Galloway's main point about Parliament's taxes? (They pay for British military protection and are the price of protecting the colonists' freedom.)

Not all colonists were Patriots, however. A third of all colonists remained loyal to King George III. These people were called Loyalists. Many of them were wealthy, but others were ordinary people. Some business leaders were Loyalists. Philadelphia merchant Thomas Clifford complained that independence would "assuredly prove unprofitable." Many Loyalists wished to remain British citizens or were fearful that independence would lead to chaos.

In October 1765, representatives from nine colonies met in New York City and formed the Stamp Act Congress. The representatives declared that Parliament had no right to tax the colonists, since colonists were not allowed to vote for members of Parliament. These laws, they argued, were against British legal traditions.

Parliament created more conflict by ignoring colonists' concerns. On November 1, the Stamp Act took effect. In turn, angry colonists staged a **boycott**. Boycotting means refusing to do business with—or to buy goods from—a person, group, or country. Colonists refused to use the new stamps.

Colonial women joined the protest. They formed a group called the "Daughters of Liberty." They made a kind of cloth known as "homespun" and found other ways to replace British goods with homemade items.

Colonists refused to purchase British goods, such as tea. The boycott began to hurt British merchants. Because of the boycott, Parliament in 1766 voted to cancel the Stamp Act.

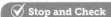

This teapot was made for sale in the colonies to celebrate the cancellation of the Stamp Act.

Smithsonian National Museum of American History, Kenneth E. Behring Center

✓ Stop and Check

Talk Why were colonists' different types of protests effective?

COLLABORATE

182 Lesson 2 What Were the Views of the Patriots, Loyalists, and the British?

Citizenship 👥

Perspectives
Views from a Patriot and a Loyalist

Colonists who demanded that Americans have more control of their government were known as Patriots. Colonists who wanted to remain loyal to the British government were called Loyalists. The following quotations show the points of view of George Mason, a Patriot, and Joseph Galloway, a Loyalist.

George Mason

"We claim nothing but the liberty and privileges of Englishmen, in the same degree, as if we had still continued among our brethren in Great Britain: these rights have not been forfeited by any act of ours, we can not be deprived of them without our consent, but by violence and injustice."

—George Mason, to the Committee of Merchants in London, June 6, 1766

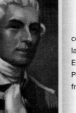

Joseph Galloway

"The protection of America has, in no small degree, contributed to this burden of the mother country. To the large sums of money that have been expended from the English treasury and the parental care of a British Parliament, we in a great measure owe our present freedom...."

—Americanus (pseudonym for Joseph Galloway), letter to the New York Gazette, 15 August 1765, reprinted two weeks later in the Pennsylvania Journal (29 August 1765)

What Do You Think? Whose argument do you think is more convincing? Why?

TEXT: (1)Mason, George. George Mason to the Committee of Merchants in London, 6 June 1766. In The Life of George Mason, 1725-1792, Volume 1, ed. Kate Mason Rowland, no. 3, New York: G.P. Putnam's Sons, 1892; (b)Galloway, Joseph. "Americanus." Letter to The New-York Gazette, 15 August 1765. PHOTO: (t)McGraw-Hill Education, (r)Bettmann/Getty Images

Lesson 2 183

Research Companion, pp. 182–183

(EL) ENGLISH LEARNERS SCAFFOLD

ELD.PI.5.8 Analyzing how writers and speakers use vocabulary and other language resources for specific purposes (to explain, persuade, entertain, etc.) depending on modality, text type, purpose, audience, topic, and content area

Emerging	Expanding	Bridging
Understand Vocabulary Help students with difficult terms in the text from Mason's letter: *brethren* ("brothers"), *forfeited* ("given up"), *be deprived of* ("stopped from having"). Clarify in Galloway's letter that the *mother country* is Britain.	**Paraphrase Text** Have students work in pairs, with one student paraphrasing the excerpt from Mason's letter and the other paraphrasing the excerpt from Galloway's letter. Then have them exchange paraphrases.	**Understand Sources** Note that Mason wrote Virginia's Declaration of Rights and is famous as a Founding Father; Galloway ultimately joined the British Army. Ask students what they think happened to him. (He was called a traitor and had to leave the colonies.)

See the **Language Learner Teaching Guide** for more language support strategies.

Monitor and Differentiate

REACHING ALL LEARNERS

Approaching Level

Clarify *legal traditions,* explaining it refers to things done in a certain way for a long time to follow a law, such as taxes collected only by a government in which taxpayers had a say.

On Level

Discuss why, in addition to making products to replace imports, women were an important group to involve in the boycott. (Women bought many things for their families' homes.)

Beyond Level

Have students discuss other boycotts and consider why they may not always be effective. (They may not create enough hardship for targets; some buyers might ignore boycotts).

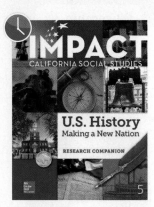

Research Companion
pp. 184–185

 STANDARDS

Understand how political, religious, and economic ideas and interests brought about the Revolution (e.g., resistance to imperial policy, the Stamp Act, the Townshend Acts, taxes on tea, Coercive Acts). **HSS.5.5.1**

Describe the views, lives, and impact of key individuals during this period (e.g., King George III, Patrick Henry, Thomas Jefferson, George Washington, Benjamin Franklin, John Adams). **HSS.5.5.4**

CCSS Quote accurately from a text when explaining what the text says explicitly and when drawing inferences from the text. **CCSS.ELA.RI.5.1**

Go Digital!

Investigate the lesson content with online whole-class presentation tools.

Background Information

John Dickinson straddled the line between Patriot and Loyalist. A leader in the peaceful protests against British tax policies, he nevertheless did not want a complete break with Britain. As a delegate to the Second Continental Congress, he refused to sign the Declaration of Independence; but he also believed in the will of the majority and so joined with the colonists to fight in the Revolution. His military service met with suspicion from many Patriots, while Loyalists looted his family estate and the British burned down his house in Philadelphia.

Analyze the Source

Inspect Have students read about the Townshend Acts on pp. 184—185.

Find Evidence Use the questions below to check comprehension.

Identify What did the Townshend Acts tax? (factory-made goods from Britain) **DOK 1**

Explain How did the boycott after the Townshend Acts extend to colonial businesses? (Businesses that did not participate in the boycott of British factory-made goods were themselves boycotted.) **DOK 3**

Synthesize What view toward Britain did many colonists, including John Dickinson, support at the time of the Townshend Acts? (They wanted to correct the problems, not seek independence.) **DOK 3**

Make Connections

Explain Was Parliament right about the effect of a tax on factory-made goods? Explain. (No, Parliament thought colonists would accept such a tax, but colonists were just as angry as they had been with the Stamp Act.) **DOK 3**

Stop and Check

Think Based on what you have read about colonists' protests, do you think Britain was justified in sending troops to Boston? (Students should state and support an opinion.)

Have students read about the effects of the boycott on Britain's economy. Ask:

- Why would pressure from British merchants have a greater effect than pressure from colonists? (Many would be people of influence who could affect Britain's government.)

- How does this reaction prove the colonists' complaint about taxation without representation? (It shows that those represented in government, whose support government officials need, are the ones likely to have their voices heard.)

What Do You Think?

Encourage students to use text evidence from the whole lesson as they respond to the prompt.

The Townshend Acts

Parliament gave in to colonial pressure when it **repealed** the Stamp Act in 1766, but the break from taxes did not last long. In 1767, Parliament found another way to raise taxes. It passed the Townshend Acts, which were named for the treasurer of the British government, Charles Townshend. Parliament believed colonists would be more accepting of a tax on factory-made goods imported from Great Britain. These included common imports such as tea, paper, glass, lead, and paint. Again, colonists were angry. They demanded Britain cancel the Townshend Acts. They also organized a boycott of the newly taxed items as well as any colonial businesses that continued to sell or use taxed goods.

Goods Taxed Under the Townshend Acts

tea
paper
glass
lead
paint

After the passage of the Townshend Acts, a Pennsylvania farmer named John Dickinson began writing a series of letters to the people of Great Britain. Although he was a Patriot, Dickinson was against independence and argued in favor of peaceful protest of Britain's taxes. Some other Patriots agreed with him. In fact, there were many among the British, Patriots, and Loyalists who did not wish to go to war. But in the coming years, relations between the colonists and Great Britain would become only more tense.

Britain feared the boycotts could lead to violence, and so they acted on these fears. Britain sent troops to Boston, which was the center of colonial protests. What happened next would push the two sides even closer to war.

✓ Stop and Check

Think Based on what you have read about colonists' protests, do you think Britain was justified in sending troops to Boston?

Colonial boycotts affected the economy in Britain as well as in the colonies.

Around the World

How Did the Boycott Hurt Britain's Economy?

The French and Indian War had left Britain not only with debt but also with an economic **recession**. Colonists' boycott of British goods weakened trade in a struggling British economy. British businesses and factories suffered losses from fewer products being exported to the colonies. So, like the colonists, British merchants began organizing to pressure Parliament to end the Stamp Act. Parliament took the merchants' concerns more seriously than the colonists' concerns. It canceled the Stamp Act.

What Do You Think? What was similar about colonists' and British merchants' organizing efforts? What was different about them?

Research Companion, pp. 184-185

ENGLISH LEARNERS SCAFFOLD

ELD.PI.5.3 Offering and supporting opinions and negotiating with others in communicative exchanges

Emerging	Expanding	Bridging
State and Support Opinions Clarify that *justified* in the Stop and Check feature means "right in doing" or "had good reason." Offer this sentence frame to help students state and support their opinion: *The British were justified/not justified in sending troops because___.*	**State and Support Opinions** To help with the Stop and Check question, ask students how the colonists are likely to react to the troops and whether it seems smart of Britain to send them. (Many students are likely to feel that the troops will antagonize the colonists and make the situation worse.)	**State and Support Opinions** Ask students what change has taken place between the troops Britain is now sending and those it sent earlier for which it has wanted colonists to pay. (Earlier troops were sent to protect colonists from French and Indian attack, but these will confront colonists to restore order.)

See the **Language Learner Teaching Guide** for more language support strategies.

Monitor and Differentiate

REACHING ALL LEARNERS

Approaching Level

Ask students how the chart on the page supports the text. (It highlights examples of items that the text describes as factory-made goods taxed under the Townshend Acts.)

On Level

Ask students why they think Parliament kept passing taxes in spite of colonial protests. (The British treasury needed the money, and complaints about taxes are not unusual.)

Beyond Level

Ask students how they think colonial businesses felt about the boycott. (Some probably supported it, but others probably disliked it as it was bad for business.)

3 REPORT

Report Your Findings

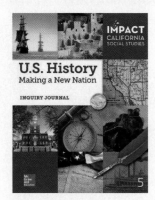

Inquiry Journal
pp. 146–147

 STANDARDS

Understand how political, religious, and economic ideas and interests brought about the Revolution (e.g., resistance to imperial policy, the Stamp Act, the Townshend Acts, taxes on tea, Coercive Acts). **HSS.5.5.1**

Describe the views, lives, and impact of key individuals during this period (e.g., King George III, Patrick Henry, Thomas Jefferson, George Washington, Benjamin Franklin, John Adams). **HSS.5.5.4**

Identify and interpret the multiple causes and effects of historical events. **HAS.HI.3**

CCSS Students write opinion pieces, supporting a point of view with reasons and information. **CCSS.ELA.W.5.1**

Draw evidence from literary or informational texts to support analysis, reflection, and research. **CCSS.ELA.W.5.9**

Go Digital!

- Students can go online to report their findings. Assess their responses online.

- Students can access the online graphic organizer to capture ideas from their investigation.

Think About It

Students should review their research and consider the reasons that some colonists wanted to stay unified with Britain and others wanted independence. Direct them to pages 178–185 of their Research Companion if they need more information.

Write About It

Write and Cite Evidence Have students read the prompt. Stress that an effective opinion essay includes a claim and evidence that supports it. Remind students to include the following elements in their response:

- a statement that introduces the topic

- logical reasons supported by facts and details

- words and phrases that clearly signal comparison and contrast, such as *both, similarly, but, in contrast,* and *on the other hand.*

Use the rubric on page T384 to evaluate students' work.

Talk About It

Defend Your Claim Help students pair up with classmates who took a different side.

- Tell students to take turns discussing their opinions and the evidence that supports those opinions.

- Ask students to discuss whether they agree or disagree with their partners' assessments and to explain why.

- Remind students to follow the rules of appropriate classroom conversation.

Connect to the Essential Question

Read the prompt aloud to students. Ask them the following guiding questions:

- What did the colonists do in reaction to the new taxes? (They protested.)

- What did the British plan to send in reaction to the colonists' reaction? (troops)

- What did the British government hope to get from the colonies? What did British merchants hope to get? (The government hoped to get tax money to pay for war debt; the merchants hoped to get colonial goods to sell.)

- Remind students to use the space provided in their journal to jot down notes.

Report Your Findings

Think About It

Review your research. Based on the information you have gathered, why did some colonists want to stay unified with Great Britain? Why did others want independence?

Write About It

Take a Stand

Write and Cite Evidence In your opinion, which side's views on taxation and independence make the most sense—the Patriots, the Loyalists, or the British? Take a side and defend it using information from the text.

Students should craft a clear opinion statement that chooses one side to defend. Students should support their opinion with several reasons and details from the text.

Talk About It

Defend Your Claim

Choose a partner who took a different side. Discuss your reasoning. Did your partner make any good points that changed your mind?

Connect to the EQ

Pull It Together

Why was it so dangerous for Patriots to act on their wishes to have self-government? Why did Great Britain feel the need to keep its hold on the colonies?

Students should mention that it was dangerous for Patriots to act because Great Britain viewed their protests as a threat of potential violence and responded to protests by sending troops to the colonies. Students should mention that Great Britain felt the need to keep its hold on the colonies because it benefited economically from the goods the colonies produced.

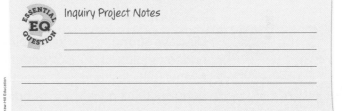

Inquiry Project Notes

146 Lesson 2   What Were the Views of the Patriots, Loyalists, and the British?

Lesson 2   **147**

Inquiry Journal, pp. 146–147

(EL) ENGLISH LEARNERS SCAFFOLD

ELD.PI.5.3 Offering and supporting opinions and negotiating with others in communicative exchanges

Emerging	Expanding	Bridging
State and Support Opinions Provide this framework to help students state and support their opinion: *The ___ believed that taxation was ____. I think this view makes the most sense because ___.*	**State and Support Opinions** Provide this frame to help students compare and contrast the different views and state and support opinions: *The ___ believed that taxation was ___, while the ___ believed it was ___, and the ___ believed it was ___. I think the ___ view makes the most sense because ___.*	**State and Support Opinions** Check students' understanding by asking these questions: *What were the reasons that the British decided to tax the colonists? What were the reasons Patriots objected to those taxes? How did Loyalists feel about the taxes?*

See the **Language Learner Teaching Guide** for more language support strategies.

Monitor and Differentiate

REACHING ALL LEARNERS

Special Needs

Ask students to talk about what the Patriots believed about taxes and independence. Help clarify their thoughts as a starting point for Write About It.

Approaching Level

Be sure students understand that the term *self-government* in the Connect to the Essential Question assignment refers to colonial independence from Great Britain.

On Level

For the Connect to the Essential Question assignment, ask students to consider what the Loyalists feared about independence and why they thought self-government might have been dangerous. Ask them also to consider the dangers faced during the French and Indian War.

Know what your students know!

Lesson Task
Report Your Findings

Use this rubric to evaluate students' response.

Write and Cite Evidence Students state which side's view of taxation and independence makes the most sense—the Patriots' the Loyalists', or Great Britain's.

Defend Your Claim Students discuss with a partner who chose the view of a different side the reasons for their preference and consider whether points their partner makes might change their mind.

Performance Task Evaluation Rubric

	4	3	2	1
Historical Understanding	Displays strong understanding of events, policies, and people's thinking in the years leading up to the Revolution	Displays adequate understanding of events, policies, and people's thinking in the years leading up to the Revolution	Displays uneven understanding of events, policies, and people's thinking in the years leading up to the Revolution	Displays no understanding of events, policies, and people's thinking in the years leading up to the Revolution
Take a Stand	Provides a clear explanation of the student's choice of side	Provides an adequate explanation of the student's choice of side	Provides a somewhat clear or unclear explanation of the student's choice of side	Provides no statement or no explanation of the student's choice of side
Support with Evidence	Supports claims and reasons with thorough and convincing evidence	Supports claims and reasons with adequate evidence	Supports claims and reasons with too little or only somewhat convincing evidence	Supplies no claims or reasons or no supporting evidence
Defend Your Claim	Speaks clearly and at an understandable pace Speaks in complete sentences throughout the discussion	Speaks clearly during most of the discussion Speaks in complete sentences through most of the discussion	Speaks unclearly at times Mixes complete and incomplete sentences during the discussion	Speaks unclearly throughout the discussion Does not use complete sentences in the discussion

Lesson Assessment

Go *Digital!*

- Have students complete the Chapter 4 Lesson 2 Assessment online to monitor their understanding of the lesson content.

California Smarter Balanced Assessment Connections!

Standards Covered	Performance Assessment	Lesson Assessment	Alignment with the California Smarter Balanced Assessment
History Social Science Content 5.5.1; 5.5.4	✔	✔	Claim 1 Targets 8, 9, 11
History and Social Science Analysis Skills Chronological and Spatial Thinking 5.1 Research, Evidence, and Point of View 5.1; 5.2	✔	✔	Claim 1 Targets 11, 12
Writing W.5.2; W.5.4	✔	✔	Claim 2 Targets 3, 4, 5
Research and Inquiry W.5.8; W.5.9	✔	✔	Claim 4 Targets 1, 2
Reading RI.5.1	✔	✔	Claim 1 Target 11
Speaking and Listening SL.5.1; SL.5.1.a; SL.5.2	✔		Claim 3 Target 3

What Increased Tensions Between Great Britain and the Colonists?

Background Information

In this lesson, students will learn about events that show the increase in tension between Britain and the American colonies, including the Boston Massacre, Boston Tea Party, and First Continental Congress.

Community Connections

To enrich what students have learned about events and figures in this lesson, have them visit the sit or the website of a related organization or historical location, such as the Samuel Adams Heritage Society or the Crispus Attucks Online Museum.

LESSON STANDARDS

- ✓ Understand how political, religious, and economic ideas and interests brought about the Revolution (e.g., resistance to imperial policy, the Stamp Act, the Townshend Acts, taxes on tea, Coercive Acts). **HSS.5.5.1**

- ✓ Know the significance of the first and second Continental Congresses and of the Committees of Correspondence. **HSS.5.5.2**

- ✓ Describe the views, lives, and impact of key individuals during this period (e.g., King George III, Patrick Henry, Thomas Jefferson, George Washington, Benjamin Franklin, John Adams). **HSS.5.5.4**

- ✓ Students place key events and people of the historical era they are studying in a chronological sequence and spatial context; they interpret time lines. **HAS.CS.1**

- ✓ Students differentiate between primary and secondary sources. **HAS.HR.1**

- ✓ Students pose relevant questions about events they encounter in historical documents, eyewitness accounts, oral histories, letters, diaries, artifacts, photographs, maps, artworks, and architecture. **HAS.HR.2**

- ✓ Students summarize the key events of the era they are studying and explain the historical context of those events. **HAS.HI.1**

- ✓ Students identify and interpret the multiple causes and effects of historical events. **HAS.HI.3**

 Connect to the
Essential Question

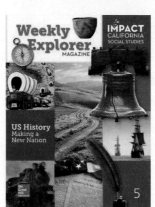

Chapter 4, pp. 44–57

The **Weekly Explorer Magazine** supports students' exploration of the Essential Question and provides additional resources for the EQ Inquiry Project.

 Inquiry Project

Which Side Will You Choose?

Remind students to use the information they learn in this lesson and other resources to complete their EQ Inquiry Project!

Dinah Zike's

 In this lesson you will use Foldables.

When Minutes Count!

Suggested Lesson Pacing

1 ENGAGE
One Day

- Analyze the Source
- Inquiry Tools

Go Digital
- **Video:** The Boston Tea Party
- **iMap:** Eastern United States map

2 INVESTIGATE
Two to Three Days

🕐 **Short on Time?** Look for the Clock to teach core content in less time.

- The Boston Massacre
- The Boston Tea Party
- The First Continental Congress

3 REPORT
One Day

- Think About It
- Take a Stand
- Defend Your Claim

Make Connections!

(ccss) CONNECT TO ELA

Reading
Quote accurately from a text when explaining what the text says explicitly and when drawing inferences from the text. **RI.5.1**

Research
Draw evidence from literary or informational texts to support analysis, reflection, and research. **W.5.9**

Writing
Write opinion pieces on topics or texts, supporting a point of view with reasons and information. **W.5.1**

Produce clear and coherent writing in which the development and organization are appropriate to task, purpose, and audience. **W.5.4**

Speaking and Listening
Engage effectively in a range of collaborative discussions (one-on-one, in groups, and teacher-led) with diverse partners on grade 5 topics and texts, building on others' ideas and expressing their own clearly. **SL.5.1**

Summarize a written text read aloud or information presented in diverse media and formats, including visually, quantitatively, and orally. **SL.5.2**

Classroom Resources

🔍 Search for additional resources using the following key words

Samuel Adams

Crispus Attucks

Boston Massacre

Boston Tea Party

Coercive (Intolerable) Acts

Committees of Correspondence

First Continental Congress

Quartering Act

Paul Revere

Stamp Act Congress

Townshend Acts

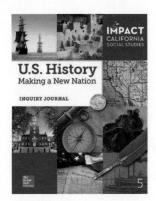

Inquiry Journal
pp. 148–149

 STANDARDS

Understand how political, religious, and economic ideas and interests brought about the Revolution (e.g., resistance to imperial policy, the Stamp Act, the Townshend Acts, taxes on tea, Coercive Acts). **HSS.5.5.1**

Know the significance of the first and second Continental Congresses and of the Committees of Correspondence. **HSS.5.5.2**

Describe the views, lives, and impact of key individuals during this period (e.g., King George III, Patrick Henry, Thomas Jefferson, George Washington, Benjamin Franklin, John Adams). **HSS.5.5.4**

CCSS Summarize a written text read aloud or information presented in diverse media and formats, including visually, quantitatively, and orally. **CCSS.ELA.SL.5.2**

Go Digital!

Explore the lesson content with online whole-class presentation tools.

- **Video:** The Boston Tea Party
- **iMap:** Eastern United States

What Increased Tensions Between Great Britain and the Colonists?

Bellringer

Prompt students to retrieve information from the previous lessons. Say: *Think about divisions in the colonies between Patriots, who wanted control of their own government, and Loyalists, who remained loyal to Britain and its king.* Ask: *Against which tax laws passed by Britain's Parliament did many colonists protest? What was their main objection?* (Sugar, Stamp, and Townshend Acts; taxation without representation)

Lesson Outcomes

What Am I Learning? Have students read the Lesson Question and Lesson Outcomes.

Why Am I Learning It? Remind students that England and Scotland officially united as Great Britain in 1707. After that date, the Thirteen Colonies should officially be called colonies of Great Britain.

How Will I Know That I Learned It? Clarify, if necessary, that a *sequence* of events is a series of events. Ask students the following questions:

- After learning the lesson, what sequence of events should you be able to identify? (the sequence of events that led to the American Revolution)

- How do you think colonists will feel as these events progress? (They will be more and more upset with British rule and more and more in favor of independence.)

Talk About It

Explain that in an incident in 1770 that became known as the Boston Massacre, British troops fired on a group of colonists protesting taxes, killing five. Have students analyze Paul Revere's engraving of the incident, providing these sentence frames to help them answer the questions in the text.

- The British soldiers are portrayed as _____, while the colonists are portrayed as _____. (armed and aggressive; unarmed victims)

- These differences show Revere's point of view was that of _____. (a Patriot)

Collaborative Conversations

Add New Ideas As students engage in partner, small group, and whole-class discussions, encourage them to

- Stay on topic.
- Connect their own ideas to things their peers have said.
- Look for ways to connect their personal experiences or prior knowledge to the conversation.

Lesson 3

What Increased Tensions Between Great Britain and the Colonists?

Lesson Outcomes

What Am I Learning?
In this lesson, you're going to use your investigative skills to explore events that led to the American Revolution.

Why Am I Learning It?
Reading and talking about these events will help you understand the reasons that many colonists wanted to break free from Great Britain.

How Will I Know That I Learned It?
You will be able to identify the sequence of events that led to the American Revolution, choose the most important event you believe led to the war, and support your analysis with evidence.

Talk About It COLLABORATE

Look at the Details What are the differences between the way the British soldiers are portrayed and the way the colonists are portrayed? How do those differences show Revere's point of view of the event?

The Bloody Massacre in King-Street by Paul Revere shows the Boston Massacre from the colonists' point of view.

HSS.5.5.1, HSS.5.5.2, HSS.5.5.4, HAS.CS.1, HAS.HI.3

148 Lesson 3 What Increased Tensions Between Great Britain and the Colonists?

Inquiry Journal, pp. 148–149

ENGLISH LEARNERS SCAFFOLD

ELD.PI.5.8 Analyzing how writers and speakers use vocabulary and other language resources for specific purposes (to explain, persuade, entertain, etc.) depending on modality, text type, purpose, audience, topic, and content area

Emerging	Expanding	Bridging
Understand Language Note the phrase *break free of Great Britain* in the Lesson Outcomes, and clarify that it refers to not wanting to be controlled by Great Britain. Have students supply another word or phrase that means the same as *break free of*.	**Understand Propaganda** Explain that *propaganda* refers to biased or misleading information used to promote or harm a particular cause, individual, or point of view. Have students discuss why the engraving might qualify as propaganda.	**Understand Connotations** Clarify that *massacre* is a synonym for *slaughter* but also suggests a large number killed with little concern. Discuss how calling the event a *massacre* promotes one point of view—the Americans'.

See the **Language Learner Teaching Guide** for more language support strategies.

Monitor and Differentiate

REACHING ALL LEARNERS

Approaching Level

Clarify that an *engraving* is a picture or text cut in metal that can then be used to make many prints. Paul Revere was by trade a silversmith, someone who made objects from silver, and he was also a copper engraver.

Beyond Level

Have small groups list details in Revere's engraving, such as the weather conditions, the time on the clock, and the way the British troops are standing. Then have students research the details of the actual event and compare and contrast them to those of the engraving.

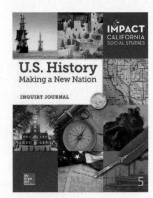

Inquiry Journal
pp. 150–151

 STANDARDS

Understand how political, religious, and economic ideas and interests brought about the Revolution (e.g., resistance to imperial policy, the Stamp Act, the Townshend Acts, taxes on tea, Coercive Acts). **HSS.5.5.1**

Know the significance of the first and second Continental Congresses and of the Committees of Correspondence. **HSS.5.5.2**

Describe the views, lives, and impact of key individuals during this period (e.g., King George III, Patrick Henry, Thomas Jefferson, George Washington, Benjamin Franklin, John Adams). **HSS.5.5.4**

Students place key events and people of the historical era they are studying in a chronological sequence and spatial context; they interpret time lines. **HAS.CS.1**

Students summarize the key events of the era they are studying and explain the historical context of those events. **HAS.HI.1**

Go Digital!

Model how to inspect and find evidence with online whole-class presentation tools.

Background Information

The Quartering Act of 1765 said colonists had to provide British troops with barracks or put them in alehouses, inns, barns, and other buildings. British officers had the additional privilege of living in colonists' homes. Colonists felt the act violated their rights; they also suspected the troops were being sent to quell protests.

1 Inspect

Read Have students read the timeline of events, circle Parliament's actions, and underline colonists' actions. Ask:

- To what does the title indicate events in the timeline lead? (the Boston Massacre)

- With what event does the time line start? (Sugar Act of 1764)

- How did colonists respond to that event? (They staged protests.)

Collaborate Have partners discuss the cause-and-effect relationship between Parliament's actions and the colonists' actions. (For example, the Stamp Act Congress was a direct result of passage of the Stamp Act; the Non-Importation Agreement was a result of the Townshend Acts.)

2 Find Evidence

Reread Have students reread the text.

Analyze the Source Go over the timeline events with students. Ask:

- In what year does the first event take place? (1764)

- How many years do the events of the timeline span? (six)

- Why is it significant that so much happened in a short time? (It means colonists' anger did not have time to die down but instead grew into a movement.)

- What does the timeline show about the relationship between colonists and Britain during these years? (It was bad and got worse.)

3 Make Connections
COLLABORATE

Talk Have partners discuss the behavior patterns in the time line. (Students should recognize that colonists responded with peaceful protests until the Boston Massacre, which turned violent. They may note the presence of troops as a cause for the change.)

Analyze the Source

1 Inspect

Read Look at the title of the timeline. What does it tell you about what happens next in American history?

- **Circle** Parliament's actions.
- **Underline** the colonists' actions.
- **Discuss** with a partner the cause-and-effect relationship between Parliament's actions and the colonists' actions.

My Notes

_____
_____
_____
_____
_____
_____
_____
_____
_____
_____
_____
_____
_____
_____

The Events That Led to the Boston Massacre

April 5, 1764 – The Sugar Act
To pay Britain's war debt, Parliament passes the Sugar Act. The act places a colonial tax on imported sugar and molasses. Previous sugar taxes were not enforced. Starting in 1764, colonists who do not pay the tax on sugar products are to be fined and arrested. The colonists stage protests.

March 22, 1765 – The Stamp Act
Parliament passes the Stamp Act, requiring colonists to purchase a stamp for all paper documents, such as newspaper and letters. The money collected from the sale of stamps goes directly to Great Britain, not the colonial government. Colonial protests increase.

May 15, 1765 – The Quartering Act
The Quartering Act is also passed. This requires colonial governments to pay for the housing of British troops and allows the British government to force colonists to let soldiers live on their property, if necessary. No similar law existed in Britain. Colonists call the act unfair.

October 7–25, 1765 – The Stamp Act Congress
Representatives from nine colonies form the Stamp Act Congress. They determine that, since colonists cannot vote in Parliamentary elections, Parliament has no right to tax them. They call for a boycott of British goods.

March 18, 1766 – The Declaratory Act
Parliament declares that it has the right to tax the colonies, but it also repeals the Stamp Act.

June 29, 1767 – The Townshend Acts
Parliament passes The Townshend Acts, adding a tax on goods that are imported from Great Britain. These goods include tea, glass, paper, lead, and paint. Colonists organize another boycott.

August 1, 1768 – The Non-Importation Agreement
Boston merchants declare an official boycott of British goods. They formally refuse to purchase or sell imported tea, paper, glass, or paint until the Townshend Acts are repealed.

October 1, 1768 – The Arrival of British Troops
Parliament sends more British soldiers to Boston to deal with the growing political unrest in the city.

March 5, 1770 – The Boston Massacre
A group of colonists begins to insult a squad of British soldiers and throws snowballs at them. The soldiers fire into the crowd. Five colonists are killed.

2 Find Evidence

Reread Note the year of the first event in the timeline. Then look at the year of the last event in the timeline. How many years do these events span?

Then reread the events in the timeline. Why is it important that so much happened within a short span of time? What does that tell you about the relationship between the colonists and Great Britain at this time in history?

3 Make Connections

Talk Discuss with a partner the patterns of behavior in the timeline. What did the colonists usually do in response to Parliament? When did they change their behavior? Why?

COLLABORATE

McGraw-Hill Education

Inquiry Journal, pp. 150–151

EL ENGLISH LEARNERS SCAFFOLD

ELD.PI.5.8 Analyzing how writers and speakers use vocabulary and other language resources for specific purposes (to explain, persuade, entertain, etc.) depending on modality, text type, purpose, audience, topic, and content area

Emerging

Understand Domain-Specific Vocabulary Explain terms *imported* ("shipped in"), *repeals* ("takes back a law"), and *merchants* ("traders or shop owners"). Remind students that a *boycott* is an action in which a group refuses to buy from another group.

Expanding

Clarify Prefixes Explain that the prefix *in-* or *im-* can mean "in" or "not"; it means "in" in *import,* "to take into port," or "something taken into port." Note that *export* is the opposite, and ask students what they think the prefix *ex-* means. ("out")

Bridging

Understand Origins Explain that *quarters* originally meant "a military dwelling place," from the idea that a quarter or portion of a district was used for that purpose; to *quarter* was "to house in a military dwelling place."

See the **Language Learner Teaching Guide** for more language support strategies.

Monitor and Differentiate

REACHING ALL LEARNERS

Special Needs

Help students identify patterns in the events on the timeline. Point out that some of the timeline entries can be paired: an action by Parliament can be connected with colonists' reaction to it.

On Level

Discuss some of the taxed items with students, explaining that sugar and tea were imported luxuries at the time. Clarify that molasses is a syrup produced when sugar is made.

Beyond Level

Have students consider why Boston merchants needed to join together for the Non-Importation Agreement. Elicit that they would not want others selling what they had agreed not to sell.

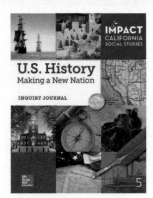

Inquiry Journal
pp. 152–153

 STANDARDS

Understand how political, religious, and economic ideas and interests brought about the Revolution (e.g., resistance to imperial policy, the Stamp Act, the Townshend Acts, taxes on tea, Coercive Acts). **HSS.5.5.1**

Know the significance of the first and second Continental Congresses and of the Committees of Correspondence. **HSS.5.5.2**

Describe the views, lives, and impact of key individuals during this period (e.g., King George III, Patrick Henry, Thomas Jefferson, George Washington, Benjamin Franklin, John Adams). **HSS.5.5.4**

Students identify and interpret the multiple causes and effects of historical events. **HAS.HI.3**

CCSS Draw evidence from literary or informational texts to support analysis, reflection, and research. **CCSS.ELA.W.5.9**

Go Digital!

Model how to explore and investigate with online whole-class tools.

Explore Chronology

Explain Remind students that *chronology* refers to the order of time. Note that history texts, like timelines, often present information in chronological order.

Read Have students read aloud the step-by-step instructions about how to identify chronology. Discuss other signal words and phrases, including those related to time measurements—*in May* or *later that year,* for example—or those that simply show time relationships—*next, after, before, during,* and *at the same time,* for example.

Guide Practice Write out a familiar process to students—such as how to make a sandwich—to model the strategy. In your example, include signal words and time expressions to help students identify the chronology of events. Ask students if you left any steps out and have them put any missing steps at the correct points in the sequence.

Investigate!

Have students read pages 186–191 in the Research Companion. Tell them the information will help them answer the lesson question **What Increased Tensions Between Great Britain and the Colonists?**

Take Notes Tell students that they will take notes as they read each section. Remind them that taking notes will help them understand and remember the information they learn. Stress the importance of paraphrasing, or using their own words, when they take notes.

Inspect Guide students to read the text in each section to determine what it says. Encourage them to make note of words they do not understand and to look for details that tell *who, what, where, how, why,* and, particularly for chronological order, *when.*

Find Evidence Encourage students to reread the text to confirm chronology and develop a deeper understanding of the content chronology. Remind them that after they read and take notes, they should review and think about how the facts and details will help them answer the lesson question.

Collaborative Conversations

Text-Based Discussion Remind students of the goals of discussing the text with others.

- to listen and respond to their partners' points
- to ask for evidence from the text
- to build on each other's ideas
- to see the text from a different point of view

Inquiry Tools

Explore Chronology

Thinking about chronology, or the order in which things happen, will help you make connections between related events.

1. Read the text all the way through.
This will help you understand how the text is organized.

2. Look at section titles.
This will give you clues about which events are significant.

3. Watch for specific dates and signal words.
Pay attention to dates and signal words as you read. Words and phrases such as *first, then, within a few months,* and a *few years later* signal the order in which events happen.

4. Find key facts about each event.
As you read about each event, think about what the key facts and details suggest about the growing tensions between the colonists and Great Britain.

 COLLABORATE Based on the text you just read, work with your class to complete the chart below.

Event	Date	Key Facts
The Sugar Act	April 5, 1764	Parliament passes and enforces a tax on sugar and molasses; colonists refusing to pay are fined or arrested; colonists protest.

Investigate!

Read pages 186–191 in your Research Companion. Use your investigative skills to identify the sequence of events that led to the American Revolution. Consider how each event is a reaction to another event.

Event	Date	Key Fact
Possible response: The Boston Massacre	March 5, 1770	The Boston Massacre happened because of unwanted taxes.

Event	Date	Key Fact
Possible response: The Boston Tea Party	December 16, 1773	The Boston Tea Party was a reaction to the Tea Act.

Event	Date	Key Fact
Possible response: The First Continental Congress	September 5, 1774	The First Continental Congress formed in response to the Coercive Acts.

Inquiry Journal, pp. 152–153

ENGLISH LEARNERS SCAFFOLD

ELD.PII.5.1 Understanding text structure

Emerging

Identify Chronology Give students practice with identifying everyday examples of chronological order. For instance, provide this sentence: *We went to the mall after we ate dinner.* Then ask: *What happened first?* (We ate dinner.) *What occurred next?* (We went to the mall.) Ask which word signals the order. (*after*)

Expanding

Understand Chronology Have students list chronologically four key details about Samuel Adams based on the biography on page 188. (organized Sons of Liberty; formed Committees of Correspondence; signed Declaration of Independence; became governor of Massachusetts)

Bridging

Use Chronology Have students relate in chronological order the story of the Boston Tea Party (pages 189–190), including events that led up to it and resulted from it. Ask them to make the sequence clear with signal terms such as *In 1773, in late November of that year, a few weeks later,* and *after the incident.*

See the **Language Learner Teaching Guide** for more language support strategies.

Monitor and Differentiate

REACHING ALL LEARNERS

Approaching Level

Remind students to look at the section titles to help them determine the events to include in their notes and the order of those events.

On Level

To help students take notes, tell then to ask *What happened?* to determine each event and its key facts and *When did it happen?* to determine its date and its place in sequence.

Beyond Level

Ask students why they think history books often use chronological organization. (The events take place in chronological order, and using it also helps make causes and effects clear.)

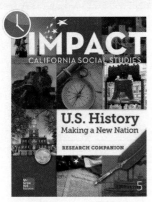

IMPACT
CALIFORNIA SOCIAL STUDIES

U.S. History
Making a New Nation

RESEARCH COMPANION

5

Research Companion
pp. 186–187

 STANDARDS

Understand how political, religious, and economic ideas and interests brought about the Revolution (e.g., resistance to imperial policy, the Stamp Act, the Townshend Acts, taxes on tea, Coercive Acts). **HSS.5.5.1**

Know the significance of the first and second Continental Congresses and of the Committees of Correspondence. **HSS.5.5.2**

Students place key events and people of the historical era they are studying in a chronological sequence and spatial context; they interpret time lines. **HAS.CST.1**

CCSS Quote accurately from a text when explaining what the text says explicitly and when drawing inferences from the text. **CCSS.ELA.RI.5.1**

Go *Digital!*

Investigate the lesson content with online whole-class presentation tools.

- **Video:** The Boston Tea Party
- **iMap:** Eastern United States

Background Information

Crispus Attucks, the first to be killed in the Boston Massacre, was thus the first casualty of the American Revolution. Details of his life are sketchy, but he is believed to have been the son of Prince Yongor, a slave from Africa, and Nancy Attucks, a Nantick Indian. After running away from a Massachusetts master, he apparently worked mostly on ships for twenty years and was also a rope maker.

| TIMELINE | Invite students to look at the timeline at the top on page 187.

Analyze Ask: How long after the Boston Massacre did Samuel Adams form the first Committee of Correspondence? (two years) In what year did the First Continental Congress meet? (1774) **HAS.CS.1 DOK 2**

Analyze the Source

Inspect Have students read about the Boston Massacre on page 186 and study the timeline on page 187 and the image on both pages.

Find Evidence Use the questions below to check comprehension. Remind students to support their answers with text evidence.

Explain Why were the people of Boston unhappy with the presence of British soldiers in the city? (The Quartering Act required that the colonists allow British officers to stay at their homes.) **DOK 2**

Summarize What apparently happened at the Boston Massacre? (After British troops were called to a colonial tax protest, angry words between the colonists and troops soon became physical. Colonists threw snowballs and ice, and some of the troops fired, killing five colonists.) **DOK 3**

Explain For what purpose did Samuel Adams and the Sons of Liberty use the incident? (to gain support for the movement for independence.) **DOK 2**

Make Connections

Evaluate Why do you think historians are uncertain of exactly what happened at the Boston Massacre? (The situation was confusing and upsetting, and people on both sides probably distorted facts to suit their purposes.) **DOK 4**

Analyze the Image Direct students' attention to the image of the Boston Massacre on pages 186–187. Ask:

- What does the image suggest about the British troops? (The angry expressions on the troops' faces suggest that they were not acting in self-defense.)

- What does the image suggest about the colonists? (The colonists were the helpless victims of a brutal attack.)

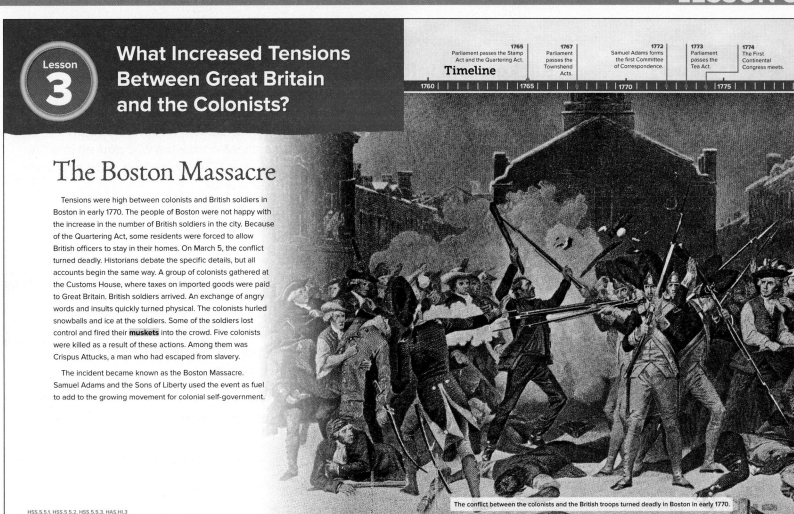

Lesson 3

What Increased Tensions Between Great Britain and the Colonists?

Timeline

1765	1767	1772	1773	1774
Parliament passes the Stamp Act and the Quartering Act.	Parliament passes the Townshend Acts.	Samuel Adams forms the first Committee of Correspondence.	Parliament passes the Tea Act.	The First Continental Congress meets.

1760 | 1765 | 1770 | 1775

The Boston Massacre

Tensions were high between colonists and British soldiers in Boston in early 1770. The people of Boston were not happy with the increase in the number of British soldiers in the city. Because of the Quartering Act, some residents were forced to allow British officers to stay in their homes. On March 5, the conflict turned deadly. Historians debate the specific details, but all accounts begin the same way. A group of colonists gathered at the Customs House, where taxes on imported goods were paid to Great Britain. British soldiers arrived. An exchange of angry words and insults quickly turned physical. The colonists hurled snowballs and ice at the soldiers. Some of the soldiers lost control and fired their **muskets** into the crowd. Five colonists were killed as a result of these actions. Among them was Crispus Attucks, a man who had escaped from slavery.

The incident became known as the Boston Massacre. Samuel Adams and the Sons of Liberty used the event as fuel to add to the growing movement for colonial self-government.

The conflict between the colonists and the British troops turned deadly in Boston in early 1770.

HSS.5.5.1, HSS.5.5.2, HSS.5.5.3, HAS.HI.3

186 Lesson 3 What Increased Tensions Between Great Britain and the Colonists?

Lesson 3 **187**

Research Companion, pp. 186–187

ENGLISH LEARNERS SCAFFOLD

ELD.PI.5.8 Analyzing how writers and speakers use vocabulary and other language resources for specific purposes (to explain, persuade, entertain, etc.) depending on modality, text type, purpose, audience, topic, and content area.

Emerging	Expanding	Bridging
Understand Prefixes Explain that the prefix *self-* means "yourself" or "oneself" and that *self-governance,* used in the text, means "the act of governing yourself," or "political independence." Then ask students what *self-confidence* and *self-respect* mean.	**Understand Idioms** Discuss what the text means when it says that angry words and insults *turned physical* and speaks of using the Boston Massacre as *fuel* for the independence movement.	**Understand Propaganda** Have students express opinions on whether the incident in Boston was a massacre. Then discuss why it was called one, eliciting that the term was good for rousing anger and fueling the movement for independence.

See the **Language Learner Teaching Guide** for more language support strategies.

Monitor and Differentiate

REACHING ALL LEARNERS

Approaching Level

Review the timeline with students. Encourage them to discuss what they already know about some of these events mentioned in the entries.

On Level

Have small groups of students work together to produce a news article about the Boston Massacre that might have appeared in a newspaper of the day.

Beyond Level

Have students research Crispus Attucks or one of the other four colonists killed in the Boston Massacre and then discuss their findings with students who investigated the other colonists.

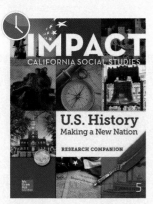

Research Companion
pp. 188–189

Understand how political, religious, and economic ideas and interests brought about the Revolution (e.g., resistance to imperial policy, the Stamp Act, the Townshend Acts, taxes on tea, Coercive Acts). **HSS.5.5.1**

Know the significance of the first and second Continental Congresses and of the Committees of Correspondence. **HSS.5.5.2**

Describe the views, lives, and impact of key individuals during this period (e.g., King George III, Patrick Henry, Thomas Jefferson, George Washington, Benjamin Franklin, John Adams). **HSS.5.5.4**

 Engage effectively in a range of collaborative discussions (one-on-one, in groups, and teacher-led) with diverse partners on grade 5 topics and texts, building on others' ideas and expressing their own clearly. **CCSS.ELA.SL.5.1**

Go *Digital!*

Investigate the lesson content with online whole-class presentation tools.

Background Information

Thomas Hutchinson, a descendent of religious reformer Anne Hutchison, was appointed governor of Massachusetts in 1771. **John Singleton Copley** (kō'plē), the celebrated colonial artist who painted the portrait of Samuel Adams shown on page 188, was the son-in-law of the Boston merchant whose tea was poured into the harbor at the Tea Party. Both men left the colonies in 1774 and settled in Britain, never to return. Boston's Copley Square is named for the artist.

Analyze the Source

Inspect Have students read about Samuel Adams on page 188 and the Boston Tea Party on page 189.

Find Evidence Use the questions below to check comprehension.

Define What was the purpose of the Committees of Correspondence? (to keep the Sons of Liberty informed about current events) **DOK 2**

Infer The text says that Paul Revere was a volunteer rider with the Boston Committee of Correspondence. Why would the Committees of Correspondence need riders? (to carry the letters) **DOK 3**

Synthesize What were two reasons that Samuel Adams and the Sons of Liberty were upset with the Tea Act? (It was taxation without representation and it favored a British company over colonial traders.) **DOK 3**

Sequence What was the *first* thing some Boston residents did to protest the Tea Act when the East India Company ships of tea arrived? (prevented them from unloading) **DOK 2**

Make Connections

Speculate How do you think Samuel Adams would communicate in a Committee of Correspondence today? (Students will probably suggest texting, e-mails, and other forms of electronic communication.) **DOK 3**

COLLABORATE

☑ Stop and Check

Talk Have students discuss what Samuel Adams did to show his opposition to British rule and how his actions helped the colonists. (Students should note his contributions in fighting the Stamp Act and founding the Sons of Liberty and Committees of Correspondence. They may also mention his signing the Declaration of Independence.)

Find Details Explain to students that after they read and take notes they should review and think about how the facts and details will help them answer the Essential Question.

Biography

Samuel Adams
AND THE COMMITTEES OF CORRESPONDENCE

Samuel Adams was a key figure in the colonists' quest for freedom. He was among the founders of the Sons of Liberty, a group that was organized to protest the Stamp Act. It continued to speak out against British rule. Anti-British feeling spread slowly throughout the colonies. Adams realized that the colonists needed a way to communicate. Having previously written letters to newspapers to protest the Stamp Act, Adams knew that the fastest and most reliable way to communicate was through letters. In 1772, he formed a 21-person committee to communicate the Patriots' plans and progress. He adapted this idea from a committee that was formed in 1764 to protest new British rules about currency and customs.

A portrait of Samuel Adams

By forming the committee, Adams—and other Sons of Liberty—could stay up-to-date with the events in the colonies. Thus, the Committee of Correspondence was born. Within a few months, more than 80 similar Committees of Correspondence formed throughout the colonies. A few years later, a volunteer rider for the Boston Committee of Correspondence would also make history. His name was Paul Revere.

Samuel Adams continued to be an influential figure during the Revolutionary War and in the early republic. In 1776, he signed the Declaration of Independence. Later, he was elected governor of Massachusetts. During his time in government, he fought for the rights of boys and girls to receive free and equal education.

✓ Stop and Check

COLLABORATE

Talk What did Samuel Adams do to show his opposition to the way Britain was ruling the colonies? How did his actions help the colonists?

Find Details As you read, add new information to the graphic organizer on page 153 in your Inquiry Journal.

188 Lesson 3 What Increased Tensions Between Great Britain and the Colonists?

The Boston Tea Party

Some of the colonists' protests worked. Parliament repealed the Townshend Acts. However, it also passed the Tea Act in 1773. The Tea Act gave the British East India Company the exclusive right to sell tea in the colonies without paying export taxes. This allowed the company to sell its tea at a price cheaper than that of other merchants' tea. Colonial tea merchants could no longer compete. Further, colonists still had to pay taxes when they bought the tea. This upset Samuel Adams, the Sons of Liberty, and other colonists for two reasons. First, it was another tax that they had not voted to approve. Second, it hurt local businesses because it gave a British company a **monopoly** on tea.

In late November 1773, three ships from the East India Company landed in Boston Harbor. Some Boston residents decided to protest the Tea Act by refusing to let the ships unload their cargo. Governor Thomas Hutchinson wanted to honor the new law and decided that the ships were to remain in the harbor until the tea was sold.

The angry colonists threw British tea into Boston Harbor.

Lesson 3 189

Research Companion, pp. 188–189

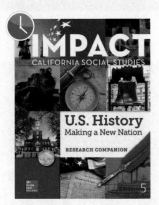

Research Companion
pp. 190–191

 STANDARDS

Understand how political, religious, and economic ideas and interests brought about the Revolution (e.g., resistance to imperial policy, the Stamp Act, the Townshend Acts, taxes on tea, Coercive Acts). **HSS.5.5.1**

Know the significance of the first and second Continental Congresses and of the Committees of Correspondence. **HSS.5.5.2**

Describe the views, lives, and impact of key individuals during this period (e.g., King George III, Patrick Henry, Thomas Jefferson, George Washington, Benjamin Franklin, John Adams). **HSS.5.5.4**

Students differentiate between primary and secondary sources. **HAS.HR.1**

Students pose relevant questions about events they encounter in historical documents, eyewitness accounts, oral histories, letters, diaries, artifacts, photographs, maps, artworks, and architecture. **HAS.HR.2**

Go Digital!

Investigate the lesson content with online whole-class presentation tools.

Background Information

The **Tea Act** was an effort by Lord North, British Prime Minister since 1770, to aid the failing British East India Company, which had warehouses of tea. Protest was widespread: in New York and Philadelphia, ships were not allowed to dock; in Charleston, South Carolina, the tea was stored, not sold; in Annapolis, Maryland, one ship was burned.

Analyze the Source

Inspect Have students read pp. 190–191. Use the questions below to check comprehension.

Summarize What happened at the Boston Tea Party? (The Sons of Liberty boarded a ship and dumped British East India Company tea into the harbor.) **DOK 2**

Identify What laws did Parliament pass to punish Boston for the Tea Party? (the Coercive Acts) **DOK 2**

Sequence When did Parliament close Boston Harbor? (after the Boston Tea Party) **DOK 3**

Classify In addition to petitioning the king, what did the First Continental Congress decide to do? (end trade with Britain until colonial demands were met) **DOK 3**

Analyze the Primary Source Note that a primary source can support, make clearer, or add information to the information in a secondary source. Ask:

Synthesize *What information in the text does the Primary Source support?* (what the First Continental Congress petitioned the king to do) **DOK 4**

Make Connections

Draw Conclusions Why do you think Boston was the only city to face immediate consequences from its Tea Act protests? (probably because there had been so much other trouble there before) **DOK 4**

✓ Stop and Check

Talk Have students discuss how the passage of laws motivated colonists to take action. (Students should note that the Tea Act resulted in the Boston Tea Party; the Coercive Acts resulted in the First Continental Congress)

Think How does having a common goal unite a large group of people? (Among other things, it makes them put aside differences to work for a common goal.)

The Sons of Liberty broke open 342 tea chests.

A few weeks later, on the night of December 16, 1773, the Sons of Liberty took action. About 50 members, some dressed as Mohawk Indians, boarded the ships. They broke open the tea chests and dumped the contents of the chests into the harbor. This act of **vandalism** became known as the Boston Tea Party. Similar protests happened in New York and in Annapolis, Maryland, but only the city of Boston would face immediate consequences.

Parliament wanted to punish the colonists for their actions. It closed Boston Harbor until the colonists paid for the tea they had destroyed. It also banned town meetings and sent more soldiers to live in the city. This series of acts was known as the Coercive Acts. The Patriots called them the Intolerable Acts, because they found the actions hard to tolerate, or live with. Instead of breaking the protestors' spirits, these acts unified the anti-British colonists in their struggle. Representatives from the colonies decided to meet to discuss what to do next. Their meeting would be called the First Continental Congress.

 Stop and Check

Talk How did the passage of laws after the Boston Tea Party motivate the colonists to take action?

190 Lesson 3 What Increased Tensions Between Great Britain and the Colonists?

The First Continental Congress

On September 5, 1774, representatives from the colonies met in Philadelphia to discuss the Coercive Acts. Their goal was to plan a response to these laws. Fifty-six men represented 12 of the 13 colonies. Each colony was granted one vote. After rejecting a plan to **reconcile** with the British government, the First Continental Congress decided to write a petition, or written request, to King George III. In the document, members of the congress outlined complaints about the way the British government had been treating them. They reminded the king of their status as British citizens. They demanded that they be given the same rights—including the right to representation—that were granted to other British citizens. Then they asked the king to repeal the Coercive Acts and other laws they felt were unfair to the colonists. Lastly, they proposed an end to trade with Britain until their demands were met.

Attendees of the First Continental Congress met at Carpenters' Hall in Philadelphia.

PRIMARY SOURCE

In Their Words... The First Continental Congress

The foundation of English liberty, and of all free government, is a right in the people to participate in their legislative council: and as the English colonists are not represented, and from their local and other circumstances, cannot properly be represented in the British parliament, they are entitled to a free and exclusive power of legislation in their several provincial legislatures, where their right of representation can alone be preserved, in all cases of taxation and internal polity, subject only to the negative of their sovereign, in such manner as has been heretofore used and accustomed.

—from the *Declaration of Rights and Grievances*, October 14, 1774

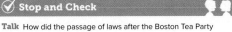 **Stop and Check**

Think How does having a common goal unite a large group of people?

Lesson 3 191

Research Companion, pp. 190–191

ENGLISH LEARNERS SCAFFOLD

ELD.PI.5.8 Analyzing how writers and speakers use vocabulary and other language resources for specific purposes (to explain, persuade, entertain, etc.) depending on modality, text type, purpose, audience, topic, and content area

Emerging	Expanding	Bridging
Understand Academic Vocabulary Clarify that *motivate* means "inspire" or "cause." Note that it is a verb formed from the word *motive,* meaning "goal" or "reason." Also explain that a *common goal,* in the Stop and Check question on page 191, is a shared goal.	**Understand Primary Sources** Clarify difficult language, such as *foundation* ("basis"), *legislative council* ("lawmaking group"), *provincial* ("colonial"), *internal polity* ("political decision-making within the colony").	**Paraphrase Primary Sources** Have students paraphrase the Primary Source in simpler language. Then ask students to exchange papers and discuss the effectiveness of each other's paraphrase.

See the **Language Learner Teaching Guide** for more language support strategies.

Monitor and Differentiate

REACHING ALL LEARNERS

On Level

Have students form groups to debate the decisions made on both sides at the time of the Boston Tea Party, addressing these questions: *Was the Tea Act fair? Was the protest justified? Was the punishment justified?* Remind students to cite facts and reasons to support opinions.

Beyond Level

Have students do additional research to find out who exactly participated in the Boston Tea Party and whether any of the Sons of Liberty had a financial stake in ending the British East India Company's new monopoly on tea.

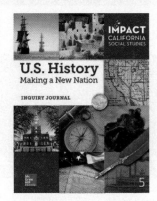

Inquiry Journal
pp. 154–155

IMPACT
CALIFORNIA
SOCIAL STUDIES

U.S. History
Making a New Nation

INQUIRY JOURNAL

5

 STANDARDS

Understand how political, religious, and economic ideas and interests brought about the Revolution (e.g., resistance to imperial policy, the Stamp Act, the Townshend Acts, taxes on tea, Coercive Acts). **HSS.5.5.1**

Know the significance of the first and second Continental Congresses and of the Committees of Correspondence. **HSS.5.5.2**

Students summarize the key events of the era they are studying and explain the historical context of those events. **HAS.HI.1**

CCSS Write opinion pieces on topics or texts, supporting a point of view with reasons and information. **CCSS.ELA.W.5.1**

Go Digital!

- Students can go online to report their findings. Assess their responses online.

- Students can access the online graphic organizer to capture ideas from their investigation.

Think About It

Students will review their research and decide which was the most important event on the road to war with Great Britain.

- Remind students to review the notes they took in the graphic organizer and the key details associated with each event. Direct them to pages 186–191 of their Research Companion if they need more information.

Write About It

Take a Stand Have students read the prompt. Stress that they will be stating an opinion and then listing reasons that support it. Remind students to include the following elements in their response:

- a statement that introduces the topic

- logical reasons supported by facts and details

- an understand of the chronology of events, and words and phrases that clearly signal the chronology, such as *first, then,* and *within a few months.*

Use the rubric on page T402 to evaluate students' work.

Talk About It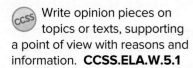

Defend Your Claim Help students pair up with classmates who chose a different event.

- Tell students to take turns discussing their opinions and the evidence that supports those opinions.

- Ask students to discuss whether they agree or disagree with their partners' assessments and to explain why.

- Remind students to follow the rules of appropriate classroom conversation.

 Connect to the
Essential Question

Read the prompt aloud to students. Ask them the following guiding questions:

- How does the growing tension in the colonies show a road leading to war? (The colonists are becoming more and more angry against the British government; they want self-government.)

- Why would the short amount of time between events contribute to the coming of war? (It shows that leaders are losing their patience and are quickly responding to the other side's actions.)

- What effect is uniting leaders in the First Continental Congress likely to have on the colonies? (They will be able to stand together and strongly oppose the actions of the British government.)

Remind students to use the space provided in their journal to jot down notes.

Report Your Findings

Think About It

Review your research. Based on the information you gathered, what was the most important event that led to war with Great Britain?

Write About It

Take a Stand

Write and Cite Evidence Write an opinion essay about the most important event that led to war with Great Britain. What events led up to this moment? What happened as a result of it? Use facts and details from the text to support your opinion.

Students should choose one event and use details from the text that show how that event led to war with Great Britain. They should describe the events that preceded their chosen event and the events that happened as a result.

Talk About It

Defend Your Claim

Choose a partner who wrote about a different event. Discuss the different impacts your events had. Do you agree or disagree with your partner? Why?

 **Connect to the EQ**
History

Pull It Together

How did the growing tension between the colonies and Great Britain eventually lead to war?

Students should note that the colonists first tried to fight back with several strategies, including boycotts and other protests. Students should also note that, although the British government did repeal some acts, Parliament continued to add more taxes until many colonists felt their best option was to break free from British rule.

Inquiry Project Notes

McGraw-Hill Education

154   Lesson 3   What Increased Tensions Between Great Britain and the Colonists?

Lesson 3   155

Inquiry Journal, pp. 154–155

ENGLISH LEARNERS SCAFFOLD

ELD.PI.5.3 Offering and supporting opinions and negotiating with others in communicative exchanges

Emerging

State and Support Opinions Review with students that a claim, or opinion, should be supported by evidence from the text. Remind them that a good opinion essay contains evidence that is strong enough to convince others of their point of view.

Expanding

Develop Ideas Offer students these sentence frames to help them develop their ideas: *In my opinion, the most important event in the growing tensions was _____. I think it was the most important event because _____.*

Bridging

Ask and Answer Questions Pair students for the Talk About It assignment. Then prompt their discussion by suggesting they ask and answer these questions: *What do you think was the most important event? Why do you think it was so important?*

See the **Language Learner Teaching Guide** for more language support strategies.

Monitor and Differentiate

REACHING ALL LEARNERS

Special Needs

Have students choose just two of the events from the lesson and write each event on two index cards or pieces of scrap paper. Then ask them to write, below the name of the event, why the event was important. Conclude by having students talk about which event they think is more imporant.

On Level

Point out that in the Write About It assignment, students need to respond to two questions about the event they choose, one in which they explain what led up to the event and another in which they tell its results. Remind them to discuss the sequence of events using correct chronological order and clear words and phrases to signal that order.

Know what your students know!

Lesson Task
Report Your Findings

Use this rubric to evaluate students' response.

Take a Stand Students make a claim about which event was the most important on the road to war with Great Britain, and they explain what led up to it and what it led to. They cite details to support their opinion.

Defend Your Claim Students discuss with a partner who chose a different event the reasons for their own preference and consider whether they agree or disagree with their partner's opinion.

Performance Task Evaluation Rubric

	4	3	2	1
Historical Understanding	Displays strong understanding of the events that increased tension between the colonies and Britain	Displays adequate understanding of the events that increased tension between the colonies and Britain	Displays uneven understanding of the events that increased tension between the colonies and Britain	Displays no understanding of the events that increased tension between the colonies and Britain
Take a Stand	Provides a clear explanation of the student's preference	Provides an adequate explanation of the student's preference	Provides a somewhat clear or unclear explanation of the student's preference	Provides no statement or no explanation of the student's preference
Support with Evidence	Supports claims and reasons with thorough and convincing evidence	Supports claims and reasons with adequate evidence	Supports claims and reasons with too little or only somewhat convincing evidence	Supplies no claims or reasons or no supporting evidence
Defend Your Claim	Speaks clearly and at an understandable pace Speaks in complete sentences throughout the discussion	Speaks clearly during most of the discussion Speaks in complete sentences through most of the discussion	Speaks unclearly at times Mixes complete and incomplete sentences during the discussion	Speaks unclearly throughout the discussion Does not use complete sentences in the discussion

Lesson Assessment

Go Digital!

- Have students complete the Chapter 4 Lesson 3 Assessment online to monitor their understanding of the lesson content.

California Smarter Balanced Assessment Connections!

Standards Covered	Performance Assessment	Lesson Assessment	Alignment with the California Smarter Balanced Assessment
History and Social Science Content 5.5.1; 5.5.2; 5.5.4	✔	✔	Claim 1 Targets 8, 9, 11
History and Social Science Analysis Skills Chronological and Spatial Thinking 5.1 Research, Evidence, and Point of View 5.1; 5.2 Historical Interpretation 5.1; 5.3	✔	✔	Claim 1 Targets 11, 12
Writing W.5.1; W.5.4	✔	✔	Claim 2 Target 6
Research and Inquiry W.5.9	✔	✔	Claim 4 Targets 1, 2
Reading RI.5.1	✔	✔	Claim 1 Target 11
Speaking and Listening SL.5.1; SL.5.2	✔		Claim 3 Target 3

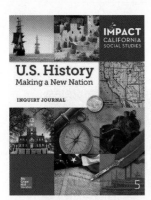

Inquiry Journal
pp. 156–157

 STANDARDS

Students explain the causes of the American Revolution. **HSS.5.5**

Explain the relationships or interactions between two or more individuals, events, ideas, or concepts in a historical, scientific, or technical text based on specific information in the text. **CCSS.ELA.RI.5.3**

Report on a topic or text or present an opinion, sequencing ideas logically and using appropriate facts and relevant, descriptive details to support main ideas or themes; speak clearly at an understandable pace. **CCSS.ELA.SL.5.4**

Go Digital!

Look online for the EQ Inquiry Project rubric.

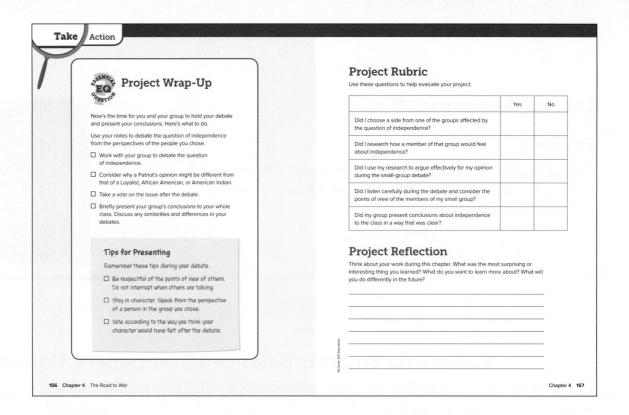

 Inquiry Project Wrap-Up

Have students share their inquiry projects by presenting their essays.

- Before students present their essays, discuss the wrap-up steps with them, making sure they know what's expected in their debates.

- Allow time after each presentation for a Q-and-A session.

Tips for Presenting

Discuss the tips for participating in a debate with students and the importance of communicating effectively with their audience. Remind students that it's also important to be a good listener.

Project Rubric

Discuss each question in the Project Rubric with students. If students have worked as part of a group to develop their projects, you might want to have them work as a group to address each question in the rubric. Remind them that their character's opinion might be swayed by the logical and effective arguments made by the opposing side.

Project Reflection

Student reflections can focus on the work they did as part of the group or their individual performance writing their essay and participating in the debate. Give groups time to discuss each phase of their projects and reflect on their work.

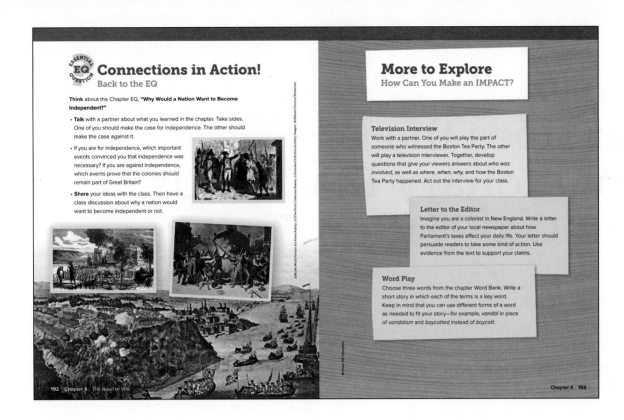

Think about the Chapter EQ, **"Why Would a Nation Want to Become Independent?"**

- **Talk** with a partner about what you learned in the chapter. Take sides. One of you should make the case for independence. The other should make the case against it.

- If you are for independence, which important events convinced you that independence was necessary? If you are against independence, which events prove that the colonies should remain part of Great Britain?

- **Share** your ideas with the class. Then have a class discussion about why a nation would want to become independent or not.

More to Explore
How Can You Make an IMPACT?

Television Interview
Work with a partner. One of you will play the part of someone who witnessed the Boston Tea Party. The other will play a television interviewer. Together, develop questions that give your viewers answers about *who was involved*, as well as *where, when, why,* and *how* the Boston Tea Party happened. Act out the interview for your class.

Letter to the Editor
Imagine you are a colonist in New England. Write a letter to the editor of your local newspaper about how Parliament's taxes affect your daily life. Your letter should persuade readers to take some kind of action. Use evidence from the text to support your claims.

Word Play
Choose three words from the chapter Word Bank. Write a short story in which each of the terms is a key word. Keep in mind that you can use different forms of a word as needed to fit your story—for example, *vandal* in place of *vandalism* and *boycotted* instead of *boycott*.

192 Chapter 4 The Road to War

Chapter 4 193

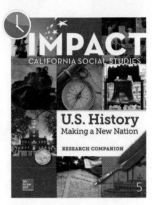

Research Companion
pp. 192–193

Connections in Action

To help focus students' conversations, you may want to discuss the EQ with the entire class before students discuss their ideas with a partner. Remind students to think about evidence they can provide that will support their ideas. After students present, allow time for others to ask questions.

More to Explore

Television Interview Remind students to think about what they learned about the events of and participants in the Boston Tea Party. Encourage them to think of questions that prompt their partner to provide important information.

Letter to the Editor Remind students of the importance of using facts to support a claim made in a persuasive letter to the editor. Encourage students to end with a call to action.

Word Play Have students write a short story using words from the chapter Word Bank. Encourage them to be creative as they choose words to feature prominently in the story.

What Does the Revolutionary Era Tell Us About Our Nation Today?

In This Chapter ...

Students will investigate the course and consequences of the American Revolution. They will learn about the ideals set forth in the Declaration of Independence and decide whether those ideals still matter today. Importantly, students will gain understanding of the period by exploring the personal stories of those who lived through it.

Lesson 1   The Revolution Begins

Lesson 2   The Declaration of Independence

Lesson 3   Defining Moments in the American Revolution

Lesson 4   Life During the Revolution

Lesson 5   Outcomes of the Revolution

CHAPTER STANDARDS

✔ Students explain the causes of the American Revolution. **HSS.5.5**

✔ Students understand the course and consequences of the American Revolution. **HSS.5.6**

Don't forget to use the Foldables.

Dinah Zike's FOLDABLES®

1 ENGAGE

Inquiry Journal
pp. 158–161

 Inquiry Project

How would our lives have been impacted if . . .?

- **Explore Words**

- *Go Digital!*
  - IMPACT Chapter Video: The American Revolution

2 INVESTIGATE

Research Companion
pp. 194–199

- **Step Into Time and Place**

- **Connect Through Literature**
  Paul Revere's Ride
  by Henry Wadsworth Longfellow

- **People You Should Know**

Weekly Explorer Magazine pp. 58–71

3 REPORT

Inquiry Journal
pp. 202–203

Inquiry Project

How would our life have been impacted if . . .?

 Short on Time? Look for the clock to teach core content in less time.

CULTIVATE MEANING AND SUPPORT LANGUAGE

Language Learner Teaching Guide,
pp. 106–107

Content Objectives

- Demonstrate understanding of the Declaration of Independence.
- Identify the defining moments of the Revolutionary War.
- Demonstrate understanding of what colonists gained by winning the American Revolution.

Language Objectives

- Discuss making inferences.
- Discuss character motivations.

CONNECT TO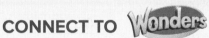

Unit 2 Week 1
Reaching a Compromise

Read Aloud
"The Mayflower Compact"

Reading/Writing Workshop
"Creating a Nation"

Literature Anthology/Paired Selection
Who Wrote the Constitution?
"Parchment and Ink"

Leveled Readers
The Bill of Rights and "Having Your Say"

Leveled Reader
The Bill of Rights and Having Your Say

CONNECT TO SCIENCE

Explore the connection between the goods and services in this lesson and the weather. How would a major storm, for example, affect the availability of goods for sale?

Soldiers in the Revolutionary War fired muskets and cannons. Have students explore the science related to the firing of muskets and cannons, such as projectile force and trajectory.

CONNECT TO MATH

Have students use the map scale on p. 203 to calculate the distance from Lexington to Concord. Discuss how to use map scale on other maps in the classroom, and be sure that students use scale as they create maps.

ASSESSMENT

Monitor Progress to
Know What Your Students Know

Choose the assessment options that work best for you and your students.

BEFORE
PRE-TEST

Measure students' content knowledge before you begin the chapter with the following questions.

 Quick Check

✔ Was war between the colonists and Great Britain inevitable? Why or why not?

✔ Why might some colonists want to stay part of Great Britain? Why might some colonists want to be independent?

✔ What do you think the biggest challenges would be for the colonies as they fought for independence?

1. Distribute one large index card to each student. Read aloud one of the questions. Ask students to write their response to the questions on the front of the index card.

2. When all students have responded, ask them to rate how confident they are in their answers on a scale from 1 – not very confident to 5 – very confident.

3. Collect the cards and review them for misconceptions, factual errors, and to inform instruction. You may wish to hang the cards in a two-column wall chart to review as students Investigate chapter 5.

4. **Don't Forget!** Revisit students' quick check responses with them. If students change their response, ask them to support the change with text evidence. You may wish to have students respond to a different prompt to measure their content knowledge, such as *Who were the most important figures in the American Revolution and why?*

EVERY LESSON
ONGOING ASSESSMENT

Use the lesson tools to monitor the IMPACT of your instruction.

 Stop and Check

Use the quick question prompts to monitor student comprehension of the content. The **Stop and Check** questions prompt students to make connections to their world today, engage in discussions to deepen their understanding of the content, and to look at different perspectives.

 Report Your Findings

The lesson task, **Report Your Findings**, can be used to measure student understanding of the lesson content and ability to effectively express their understanding. See the Lesson Assessment pp. T438, T460, T482, T502, and T524 for task-specific evaluation rubrics.

(*Go Digital!*) **Lesson Assessment**

Use the **Lesson Assessment** to monitor student understanding of the lesson content. Have students complete the assessment online. See pp. T439, T461, T483, T503, and T525 for California Smarter Balanced Assessments Connections.

EVERY CHAPTER
POST TEST

Evaluate student understanding of core chapter content with one or more of the following assessment options.

 Connections in Action

Use the **Connections in Action** to evaluate student understanding of core chapter content through discussion.

 Inquiry Project

Use the **EQ Inquiry Project** to measure student understanding of the chapter content and ability to effectively express their understanding. See the EQ Inquiry Project Wrap Up below for a task-specific evaluation rubric.

	4	3	2	1
Historical Understanding	Strong understanding of the events of the American Revolution	Adequate understanding of the events of the American Revolution	Uneven understanding of the events of the American Revolution	No understanding of the events of the American Revolution
Take a Stand	Clearly states opinion about most important events	Adequately states opinion about most important events	Somewhat clear or unclear opinion about most important events	No opinion or student does not show understanding of the task
Support with Evidence	Reasons contain thorough and convincing evidence	Reasons contain adequate evidence	Reasons contain uneven or only somewhat convincing evidence	Reasons are missing or contain no supporting evidence
Discuss the Results	Speaks clearly and at an understandable pace Provides a plausible explanation of how history would be different without an important event	Speaks clearly during most of the presentation Provides a reasonable explanation for how history would be different without an important event	At times speaker is unclear Loosely implies reasons history would be different without an important event	Does not use complete sentences Does not provide reasons history would be different without an important event

Go Digital! **Chapter Benchmark Assessments**

Use the chapter tests to monitor student understanding of the chapter History-Social Science standards and content. Have students complete the assessment online.

ONLINE ASSESSMENT

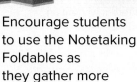

Weekly Explorer
MAGAZINE

IMPACT
CALIFORNIA
SOCIAL STUDIES

US History
Making a
New Nation

5

pp. 58–71

🕐 **Short on Time?**

Use the Weekly Explorer Magazine during your reading block.

___

Go Digital!

Look online for the Weekly Explorer Magazine Teaching Guide.

WordBlast

Remind students to look for the Word Blasts as they read the Explorer Magazine.

FOLDABLES

Encourage students to use the Notetaking Foldables as they gather more information.

Weekly Explorer Magazine

The Weekly Explorer Magazine is designed to provide students with more information to use as they dig deeper into the **American Revolution.** The articles in a variety of formats explore the Essential Question and support the Inquiry Project.

Engage

Build background for students and share any information needed to provide a context for the chapter topic. Have students read the Essential Question and the Table of Contents.

Analyze the Visual Discuss the opening visual (photograph, photo essay, artwork) on the second page of the Magazine chapter. Help students connect the visula to the chapter topic and the Essential Question.

Analyze the Sources

Students will read and analyze the articles, graphic novel, poems, songs, literature excerpts, primary sources, and infographics.

Read and Analyze Before reading, provide any additional information you think students will need about the topics. Then guide students through the three-step process to read and analyze the articles.

1 Inspect Have students skim the article or articles on a page or multiple pages. Ask questions to help students recall and retell key ideas.

- What is this article mostly about?
- Who is _____?

2 Find Evidence Have students reread the articles and look for details they might have missed. Ask additional questions to help them read more closely.

- What details do you notice in the photographs?
- Why was _____ important?

3 Make Connections Have students work in pairs or small groups to discuss prompts that help them connect the article(s) to other texts, their own lives, current ideas and issues, and other topics.

- How is _____ similar to what we do today?
- How do you think _____ felt about what happened?
- What do you think about _____?

Bibliography

The following suggested resources may help students' investigation of the chapter content.

EXPLORE PEOPLE, PLACES, AND EVENTS

▶ **African Americans in the Thirteen Colonies**
[Cornerstones of Freedom]
by Burgan Michael Scholastic January 2013

▶ **Soldier's Secret: The Story of Deborah Sampson**
by Sheila Solomon Klass
Henry Holt and Co., March 2009

▶ **The Horse-Riding Adventures of Sybil Ludington, Revolutionary War Messenger**
by Marsha Amstel
Illustrated by: Ted Hammond, Richard Pimentel Carbajal

▶ **The Top-Secret Adventure of John Darragh, Revolutionary War Spy**
by Connie Roop, Peter Roop
Illustrated by Zachary Trover

▶ **The Prison-Ship Adventure of James Forten, Revolutionary War Captive**
by Marty Rhodes Figley
Illustrated by Ted Hammand, Richard Pimental Carbajal
Graphic Universe January 2011

▶ **George vs. George: The American Revolution as Seen from Both Sides**
by Rosalyn Schanzer
National Geographic Children's Books; Reprint edition
September 2007

▶ **Revolutionary Poet: A Story About Phillis Wheatley**
by Maryann N. Weldt
Illustrated by Mary O'Keefe Young
Lerner Classroom 1997

▶ **Washington at Valley Forge**
by Russell Freedman
Holiday House; First Edition December 2008

▶ **The Scarlet Stocking Spy**
by Trinka Hakes Noble
Sleeping Bear Press, 2004

▶ **"A Spectacular Ride"**
by Drollene P. Brownfrom
Cobblestone, March 2016

▶ **Paul Revere's Midnight Ride**
by Stephen Krensky
HarperCollins, August 2002

EXPLORE MUSIC

▶ **Chester**   by William Billings (America's first great composer).
Did you know? "Chester" was the anthem of the Revolution.
Some of the lyrics: *Let tyrants shake their iron rod, And Slav'ry clank her galling chains, We fear them not, we trust in God, New England's God forever reigns.*

▶ **St. Clair's Defeat**   (also known as Sinclair's Defeat)
Did you know? It's about The Battle of Wabash River (also known as 'St. Clair's Defeat), fought on November 4, 1791 between the United States and an American Indian confederacy, as part of the Northwest Indian War (also known as "Little Turtle's War"). The American Indians were led by Michikinikwa ("Little Turtle") of the Miamis and Blue Jacket of the Shawnees. The Americans were led by General Arthur St. Clair. The American Indian confederacy was victorious. The battle was the most severe defeat ever suffered by the United States at the hands of American Indians; indeed, in proportional terms it was the worst defeat that United States forces have ever suffered in battle. As a result, President George Washington forced St. Clair to resign his post, and Congress initiated its first investigation of the executive branch.

▶ **The World Turned Upside Down**
Did you know? This British tune of the period was thought to have been played by the British at the surrender at Yorktown, but there's no actual proof of that.

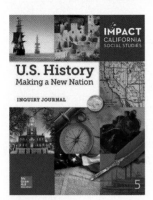

Inquiry Journal
pp. 158–161

 STANDARDS

Students explain the causes of the American Revolution. **HSS.5.5**

Students understand the course and consequences of the American Revolution. **HSS.5.6**

 Write informative/explanatory texts to examine a topic and convey ideas and information clearly. **CCSS.ELA.W.5.2**

Draw evidence from literary or informational texts to support analysis, reflection, and research. **CCSS.ELA.W.5.9**

Go Digital!

Explore Words: Interactive vocabulary activities support students as they explore the chapte words.

See the **Language Learner Teaching Guide** pp. 106–107 for support strategies.

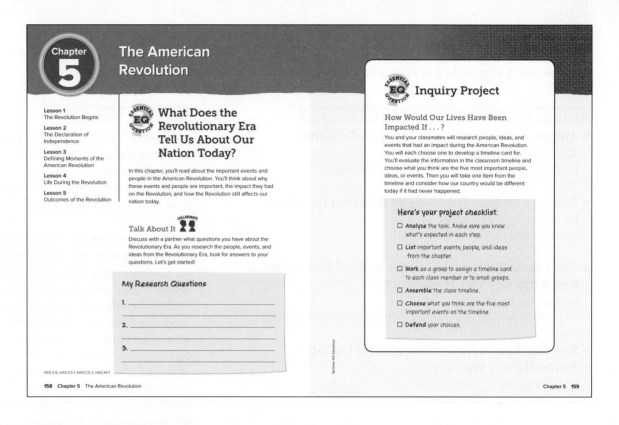

Chapter 5 — The American Revolution

Lesson 1
The Revolution Begins

Lesson 2
The Declaration of Independence

Lesson 3
Defining Moments of the American Revolution

Lesson 4
Life During the Revolution

Lesson 5
Outcomes of the Revolution

What Does the Revolutionary Era Tell Us About Our Nation Today?

In this chapter, you'll read about the important events and people in the American Revolution. You'll think about why these events and people are important, the impact they had on the Revolution, and how the Revolution still affects our nation today.

Talk About It

Discuss with a partner what questions you have about the Revolutionary Era. As you research the people, events, and ideas from the Revolutionary Era, look for answers to your questions. Let's get started!

My Research Questions

1. _____
2. _____
3. _____

HSS.5.6, HAS.CS.1, HAS.CS.3, HAS.HI.1

158 Chapter 5 The American Revolution

Inquiry Project

How Would Our Lives Have Been Impacted If . . . ?

You and your classmates will research people, ideas, and events that had an impact during the American Revolution. You will each choose one to develop a timeline card for. You'll evaluate the information in the classroom timeline and choose what you think are the five most important people, ideas, or events. Then you will take one item from the timeline and consider how our country would be different today if it had never happened.

Here's your project checklist.

☐ **Analyze** the task. Make sure you know what's expected in each step.

☐ **List** important events, people, and ideas from the chapter.

☐ **Work** as a group to assign a timeline card to each class member or to small groups.

☐ **Assemble** the class timeline.

☐ **Choose** what you think are the five most important events on the timeline.

☐ **Defend** your choices.

Chapter 5 159

 # What Does the Revolutionary Era Tell Us About Our Nation Today?

Have students read the Chapter Essential Question on p. 158.

Talk About It

- Prompt students to write three questions they would like to know the answers to after reading about the American Revolution.

- After jotting down their questions, have students discuss their questions with partners.

Inquiry Project

How would our life have been impacted if . . . ?

- Have students read aloud the EQ Inquiry Project.

- Tell students that they will use information gathered from the chapter and from independent research to complete the project.

- Make certain students understand the task by reviewing each step of the project.

Explore / Words

Complete this chapter's Word Rater. Write notes
as you learn more about each word.

blockade	My Notes
☐ Know It!	
☐ Heard It!	
☐ Don't Know It!	

inflation	My Notes
☐ Know It!	
☐ Heard It!	
☐ Don't Know It!	

mercenary	My Notes
☐ Know It!	
☐ Heard It!	
☐ Don't Know It!	

militia	My Notes
☐ Know It!	
☐ Heard It!	
☐ Don't Know It!	

monarch	My Notes
☐ Know It!	
☐ Heard It!	
☐ Don't Know It!	

negotiate	My Notes
☐ Know It!	
☐ Heard It!	
☐ Don't Know It!	

profiteer	My Notes
☐ Know It!	
☐ Heard It!	
☐ Don't Know It!	

rebel	My Notes
☐ Know It!	
☐ Heard It!	
☐ Don't Know It!	

reconciliation	My Notes
☐ Know It!	
☐ Heard It!	
☐ Don't Know It!	

traitor	My Notes
☐ Know It!	
☐ Heard It!	
☐ Don't Know It!	

McGraw-Hill Education

160 Chapter 5 The American Revolution

Chapter 5 161

Explore Words

- **Academic/Domain-Specific Vocabulary** Read the words aloud to students. Explain to students that these are words they will learn more about in the chapter.

- **Word Rater** Have students place a checkmark in one of the three boxes below each word, indicating that they "Know It," "Heard It," or "Don't Know It."

  ✓ **Know It** Tell students that if they know the word, they should write its meaning on the lines provided.

  ✓ **Heard It** Tell students that if they have heard, or are familiar with the word, they should write what they know about it on the lines provided. Remind them to take notes about the word as they encounter it.

  ✓ **Don't Know It** If they do not know the word's meaning, tell them to write down its meaning when they encounter the word in the chapter.

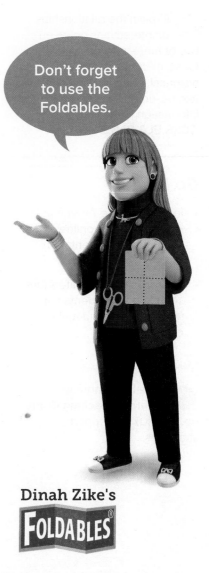

Don't forget to use the Foldables.

Dinah Zike's
FOLDABLES®

🔍 Explore Words Routine

Remind students that when they come to an unfamiliar word or phrase in their research, they should follow these steps to determine its meaning.

1. Look around the word or phrase for clues to unlock its meaning.

2. Look inside the word or phrase for word part clues.

3. Look up the word in other resources.

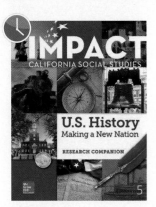

Research Companion
pp. 194–197

  STANDARDS

Students explain the causes of the American Revolution. **HSS.5.5**

Students understand the course and consequences of the American Revolution. **HSS.5.6**

Explain the relationships or interactions between two or more individuals, events, ideas, or concepts in a historical, scientific, or technical text based on specific information in the text. **CCSS.ELA.RI.5.3**

Go *Digital!*

- Investigate the American Revolution with online whole-class presentation tools.

- Analyze the online literature selection so students can find evidence and make connections.

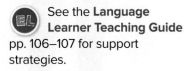

See the **Language Learner Teaching Guide** pp. 106–107 for support strategies.

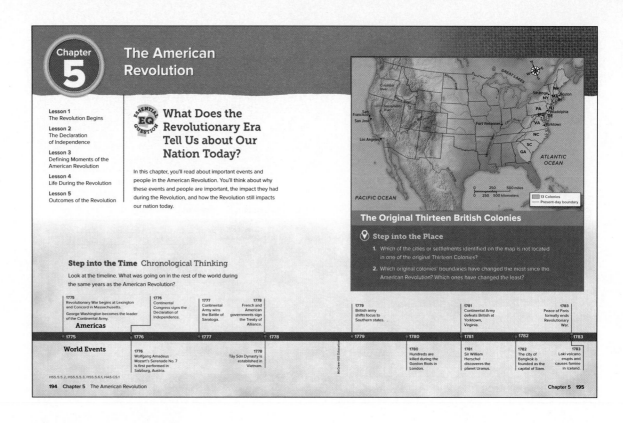

Step Into Time

Have students read over the events on the timeline, first examining the events from the Americas and then the events from around the world.

- What did Sir William Herschel discover the same year the Continental Army defeated the British at Yorktown? (the planet Uranus)

- What happened in the Americas during the same year as a natural disaster in Iceland? (The Continental Congress accepted the Peace of Paris.)

Step Into Place

In partners or small groups, have students examine the map on p. 195 and answer the questions beneath it.

1. Which of the cities or settlements identified on the map is not located in one of the original Thirteen Colonies? (Fort Vincennes, San Francisco, San Jose, Los Angeles)

2. Which original colonies' boundaries have changed the most since the American Revolution? (New York, Georgia, Pennsylvania, Virginia) Which ones have changed the least? (Massachusetts, Connecticut, Rhode Island, New Jersey, Delaware)

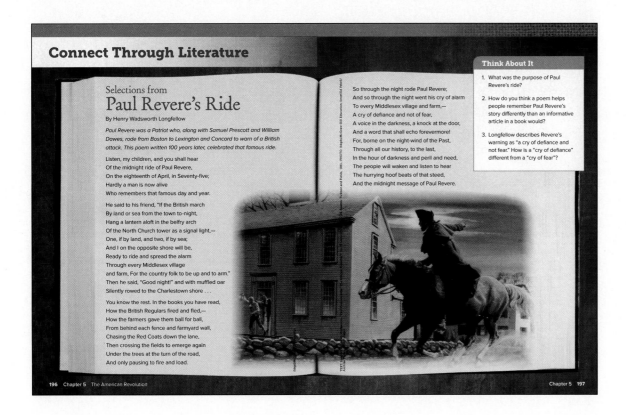

Selections from
Paul Revere's Ride
By Henry Wadsworth Longfellow

Paul Revere was a Patriot who, along with Samuel Prescott and William Dawes, rode from Boston to Lexington and Concord to warn of a British attack. This poem written 100 years later, celebrated that famous ride.

Listen, my children, and you shall hear
Of the midnight ride of Paul Revere,
On the eighteenth of April, in Seventy-five;
Hardly a man is now alive
Who remembers that famous day and year.

He said to his friend, "If the British march
By land or sea from the town to-night,
Hang a lantern aloft in the belfry arch
Of the North Church tower as a signal light,—
One, if by land, and two, if by sea;
And I on the opposite shore will be,
Ready to ride and spread the alarm
Through every Middlesex village
and farm, For the country folk to be up and to arm."
Then he said, "Good night!" and with muffled oar
Silently rowed to the Charlestown shore . . .

You know the rest. In the books you have read,
How the British Regulars fired and fled,—
How the farmers gave them ball for ball,
From behind each fence and farmyard wall,
Chasing the Red Coats down the lane,
Then crossing the fields to emerge again
Under the trees at the turn of the road,
And only pausing to fire and load.

So through the night rode Paul Revere;
And so through the night went his cry of alarm
To every Middlesex village and farm,—
A cry of defiance and not of fear,
A voice in the darkness, a knock at the door,
And a word that shall echo forevermore!
For, borne on the night-wind of the Past,
Through all our history, to the last,
In the hour of darkness and peril and need,
The people will waken and listen to hear
The hurrying hoof beats of that steed,
And the midnight message of Paul Revere.

Think About It

1. What was the purpose of Paul Revere's ride?

2. How do you think a poem helps people remember Paul Revere's story differently than an informative article in a book would?

3. Longfellow describes Revere's warning as "a cry of defiance and not of fear." How is a "cry of defiance" different from a "cry of fear"?

196   Chapter 5   The American Revolution

Chapter 5   197

Background Information

Henry Wadsworth Longfellow's poem "Paul Revere's Ride" was first published in 1861, nearly 100 years after the event. It is said that Longfellow wrote the poem during a time of political unrest to raise awareness of the country's noble past. He wasn't trying to rewrite history. He simply wanted to create a national hero.

GENRE Narrative Poem *"Paul Revere's Ride" is a narrative poem. A narrative poem tells a story, using characters, setting, and plot.*

Analyze the Source

Inspect Have students read the selection on pp. 196–197 together to determine the general meaning of the text.

1. What was the purpose of Paul Revere's Ride? (to warn colonists that the British were approaching)

Find Evidence Have students reread the selection and ask:

2. How do you think the poem helps people remember Paul Revere's story differently than an informative article in a book would? (Answers will vary but should include that poems are easy to remember. They help people tell information to new generations.)

Make Connections

3. Longfellow describes Revere's warning as "a cry of defiance and not of fear." How is a "cry of defiance" different from a "cry of fear"? (People want to fight, not give up.)

Perspectives How could Longfellow know about Paul Revere's ride if he wasn't there? (Answers will vary.)

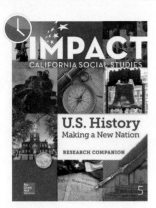

Research Companion
pp. 198–199

U.S. History
Making a New Nation
RESEARCH COMPANION
CALIFORNIA SOCIAL STUDIES

 STANDARDS

Students explain the causes of the American Revolution. **HSS.5.5**

Students understand the course and consequences of the American Revolution. **HSS.5.6**

CCSS Explain the relationships or interactions between two or more individuals, events, ideas, or concepts in a historical, scientific, or technical text based on specific information in the text. **CCSS.ELA.RI.5.3**

Go Digital!

Investigate chapter content with the onilne teaching plan.

EL See the **Language Learner Teacher Guide** pp. 106–107 for support strategies.

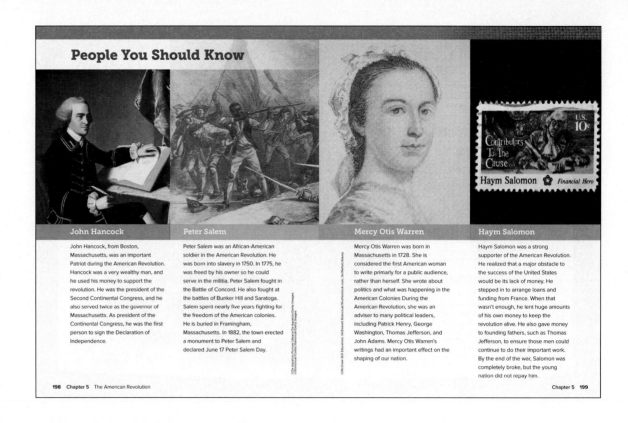

People You Should Know

John Hancock

John Hancock, from Boston, Massachusetts, was an important Patriot during the American Revolution. Hancock was a very wealthy man, and he used his money to support the revolution. He was the president of the Second Continental Congress, and he also served twice as the governor of Massachusetts. As president of the Continental Congress, he was the first person to sign the Declaration of Independence.

Peter Salem

Peter Salem was an African-American soldier in the American Revolution. He was born into slavery in 1750. In 1775, he was freed by his owner so he could serve in the militia. Peter Salem fought in the Battle of Concord. He also fought at the battles of Bunker Hill and Saratoga. Salem spent nearly five years fighting for the freedom of the American colonies. He is buried in Framingham, Massachusetts. In 1882, the town erected a monument to Peter Salem and declared June 17 Peter Salem Day.

Mercy Otis Warren

Mercy Otis Warren was born in Massachusetts in 1728. She is considered the first American woman to write primarily for a public audience, rather than herself. She wrote about politics and what was happening in the American Colonies During the American Revolution, she was an adviser to many political leaders, including Patrick Henry, George Washington, Thomas Jefferson, and John Adams. Mercy Otis Warren's writings had an important effect on the shaping of our nation.

Haym Salomon

Haym Salomon was a strong supporter of the American Revolution. He realized that a major obstacle to the success of the United States would be its lack of money. He stepped in to arrange loans and funding from France. When that wasn't enough, he lent huge amounts of his own money to keep the revolution alive. He also gave money to founding fathers, such as Thomas Jefferson, to ensure those men could continue to do their important work. By the end of the war, Salomon was completely broke, but the young nation did not repay him.

198   Chapter 5   The American Revolution

Chapter 5   199

People You Should Know

How do personal stories IMPACT our understanding of the American Revolution?

- Have students read aloud the biographies.

- Tell them that they will learn about these people and others throughout the chapter.

- Prompt student to create a class Infographic display board of important people during the Revolutionary War. Students can choose from one of the following individuals who played a significant role in the course of the American Revolution or they can do their own research:

▷ George Rogers Clark	▷ Nathan Hale
▷ Deborah Sampson	▷ Thomas Paine
▷ Casimir Pulaski	▷ Phillis Wheatley
▷ Haym Salomon	▷ Martha Washington
▷ Abigail Adams	

- Ask students to try to gather facts about the person as well as a memorable story that helps reveal what the person was like. Students can also draw, download, or photocopy portraits for the display. Have students assemble the class Infographic display board and encourage students to refer to it throughout the chapter.

✎ Teacher Notes

LESSON QUESTION

How Did the American Revolution Start?

Background Information

In this lesson, students will learn that a complex series of events caused the American Revolution. While the British had a larger and better-trained army, the Americans had strong leaders and were motivated by the hope of their own freedom.

Community Connections

To enrich what students have learned about the American Revolution, plan a field trip to a local history museum.

LESSON STANDARDS

✓ Know the significance of the first and second Continental Congresses and of the Committees of Correspondence. **HSS.5.5.2**

✓ Describe the views, lives, and impact of key individuals during this period (e.g., King George III, Patrick Henry, Thomas Jefferson, George Washington, Benjamin Franklin, John Adams). **HSS.5.5.4**

✓ Students understand the course and consequences of the American Revolution. **HSS.5.5.6**

✓ Identify and map the major military battles, campaigns, and turning points of the Revolutionary War, the roles of the American and British leaders, and the Indian leaders' alliances on both sides **HSS.5.6.1**

✓ Students place key events and people of the historical era they are studying in a chronological sequence and within a spatial context; they interpret time lines. **HAS.CS.1**

✓ Students explain how the present is connected to the past, identifying both similarities and differences between the two. **HAS.CS.3**

✓ Students use map and globe skills to determine the absolute locations of places and interpret information available through a map's or globe's legend, scale, and symbolic representations. **HAS.CS.4**

✓ Students summarize the key events of the era they are studying. **HAS.HI.1**

✓ Students identify and interpret the multiple causes and effects of historical events. **HAS.HI.3**

Connect to the Essential Question

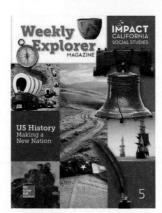

Chapter 5, pp. 58–71

The **Weekly Explorer Magazine** supports the students' exploration of the Essential Question and provides additional resources for the EQ Inquiry Project.

Inquiry Project

How would our lives have been impacted if . . .?

Remind students to use the information they learn in this lesson and other resources to complete the EQ Inquiry Project.

Dinah Zike's

In this lesson you will use Foldables.

When Minutes Count!

Suggested Lesson Pacing

1 ENGAGE
One Day

- Lesson Opener
- Analyze the Source
- Inquiry Tools

Go Digital
- **Video:** The American Revolution
- **iMap:** Map of Routes to Lexington and Concord

2 INVESTIGATE
Two to Three Days

🕐 **Short on Time?** Look for the clock to teach core content in less time.

- The Battles of Lexington and Concord
- The Second Continental Congress
- **InfoGraphic** Soldiers of the American Revolution
- The Battle of (Not) Bunker Hill

3 REPORT
One Day

- Take a Stand
- State Your Opinion
- Defend Your Claim

Make Connections!

(CCSS) CONNECT TO ELA

Reading
Compare and contrast the overall structure (e.g., chronology, comparison, cause/effect, problem/solution) of events, ideas, concepts, or information in two or more texts. **RI.5.5**

Integrate information from several texts on the same topic in order to write or speak about the subject knowledgeably. **RI.5.9**

Research
Conduct short research projects that use several sources to build knowledge through investigation of different aspects of a topic. **W.5.7**

Writing
Write opinion pieces on topics or texts, supporting a point of view with reasons and information. **W.5.1**

Draw evidence from literary or informational texts to support analysis, reflection, and research. **W.5.9**

Speaking and Listening
Report on a topic or text or present an opinion, sequencing ideas logically and using appropriate facts and relevant, descriptive details to support main ideas or themes; speak clearly at an understandable pace. **SL.5.4**

Classroom Resources

 Search for additional resources using the following key words.

Bunker Hill

Concord

Patrick Henry

Lexington

Paul Revere

Peter Salem

Deborah Sampson

Second Continental Congress

George Washington

Lesson 1   **Lesson Overview**   T419

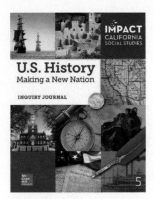

Inquiry Journal
pp. 162–163

IMPACT CALIFORNIA SOCIAL STUDIES

U.S. History
Making a New Nation

INQUIRY JOURNAL

 STANDARDS

Students understand the course and consequences of the American Revolution.
HSS.5.5.6

CCSS Engage effectively in a range of collaborative discussions (one-on-one, in groups, and teacher-led) with diverse partners on grade 5 topics and texts, building on others' ideas and expressing their own clearly.
CCSS.ELA.SL.5.1

Go Digital!

Explore the lesson content with online whole-class presentation tools.

- **Video:** The American Revolution
- **iMap:** Map of Routes to Lexington and Concord

How Did the American Revolution Start?

Bellringer

Prompt students to retrieve information from the previous lessons. Say: *The colonists believed that many of Great Britain's taxes were too harsh. They resented that the colonies had to pay taxes but could not vote in Parliament. Why did the colonists want to vote in parliament? How would this have benefited the colonists?* (Voting in parliament would give the colonists a voice in government this would allow them to have a say in how English rules affected life in the colonies.)

Lesson Outcomes

What Am I Learning? Have students read the Lesson Outcomes on p. 162.

Why Am I Learning It? Check that students understand the word *impact*. Ask them if they remember learning about causes and effects. Call on volunteers to define each term. Say, *Impact is an academic word that means an effect. For example: Wildfires can have a huge impact on people's lives. Many people can lose their homes in a fire.*

How Will I Know That I Learned It? Ask students the following questions.

- What will you identify? (chronology of events at the start of the American Revolution)
- What is the purpose of the task? (to state an opinion)
- How will you support your opinion? (with text evidence)

Talk About It COLLABORATE

Explain that when we talk about a work of art, we describe, analyze, and interpret it and present our ideas in our own words. Provide sentence frames to help students form sentences as they talk about the painting.

- The painting shows ___ and ___.
- I can tell it happened a long time ago because ___.

Collaborative Conversations COLLABORATE

Add New Ideas As students engage in partner, small group, and whole-class discussions, encourage them to

- Stay on topic.
- Connect their own ideas to things their peers have said.
- Look for ways to connect their personal experiences or prior knowledge to the conversation.

Lesson 1

How Did the American Revolution Start?

Lesson Outcomes

What Am I Learning?
In this lesson, you're going to use your investigative skills to explore events that happened at the beginning of the American Revolution.

Why Am I Learning It?
Reading and talking about these events will help you understand their impact on the American Revolution and our nation today.

How Will I Know That I Learned It?
You will be able to identify the chronology of events at the start of the American Revolution, state an opinion about which event was most important, and support your opinion with evidence.

Talk About It COLLABORATE

Look at the Details What do you think is happening? How do you know this happened long ago? What do their dress and appearance tell you about these men?

The Battle at Bunker's Hill drawn by Henry A. Thomas

HSS.5.5.2, HSS.5.5.4, HSS.5.6.1, HAS.CS.4

162 Lesson 1 How Did the American Revolution Start?

Lesson 1 **163**

Inquiry Journal, pp. 162–163

 ENGLISH LEARNERS SCAFFOLD

ELD.PI.5.6 Reading closely literary and informational texts and viewing multimedia to determine how meaning is conveyed explicitly and implicitly through language

Emerging	**Expanding**	**Bridging**
Identify Details Work with students individually to identify and name details in the painting. Provide specific words as needed.	**Describe Details** Guide students to work with partners to describe details in the painting. Encourage them to name the historical figures and use specific words to describe them.	**Use Language** Encourage students to describe what they find historically important about the events and people shown.

See the **Language Learner Teaching Guide** for more language support strategies.

Monitor and Differentiate

REACHING ALL LEARNERS

Approaching Level

Work with students to understand the art terms. Have them complete sentence frames, such as **The figures, or people, in the painting are _____.**

On Level

Have students identify more details in the painting. Encourage them to share with the whole class details they have noticed.

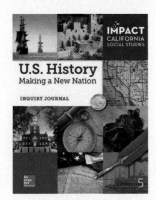

Inquiry Journal
pp. 164–165

 STANDARDS

Describe the views, lives, and impact of key individuals during this period (e.g., King George III, Patrick Henry, Thomas Jefferson, George Washington, Benjamin Franklin, John Adams). **HSS.5.5.4.**

Students differentiate between primary and secondary sources. **HAS.HR.1**

Students pose relevant questions about events they encounter in historical documents, eyewitness accounts, oral histories, letters, diaries, artifacts, photographs, maps, artworks, and architecture. **HAS.HR.2**

CCSS Engage effectively in a range of collaborative discussions (one-on-one, in groups, and teacher-led) with diverse partners on grade 5 topics and texts, building on others' ideas and expressing their own clearly. **CCSS.ELA.SL.5.1**

Go Digital!

Model how to inspect and find evidence with online whole-class presentation tools.

Background Information

Patrick Henry Many people know the end of Patrick Henry's famous speech to the Virginia House of Burgesses in 1775. What many people do not know is Henry was strongly opposed to the U.S. Constitution when it was being drafted in 1787. He believed the document needed a bill of rights to protect citizens' freedoms. His criticisms resulted in the creation of the Bill of Rights.

1 Inspect

Read Have students read the entire text, including the Primary Source, to focus on understanding the overall meaning. Remind them to circle unknown words.

- What was the House of Burgesses? (an assembly of elected members who represented the citizens of Virginia)

- When and where did the event take place? (March 1775; Richmond, Virginia)

- Why did the House of Burgesses meet? (to discuss a solution to painful taxes imposed by the British government)

Collaborate Have partners discuss what Patrick Henry believes the people of Virginia should do. What was Patrick Henry trying to tell the people? (take up arms and fight)

2 Find Evidence

Reread Have students reread the text.

Analyze the Primary Source Reread the excerpt from Patrick Henry's speech to the Virginia House of Burgesses aloud then analyze the excerpt together as a class.

- Ask partners to take turns explaining to each other what Patrick Henry means when he says, "give me liberty or give me death!" (give me freedom or give me death)

- What is the purpose of Patrick Henry's speech? (to point out the even though no shots had been fired, there was already a conflict between Britain and the colonies)

Examine **Context Clues** What does the word *idle* mean? (not active)

Analyze the Painting Guide students to discuss how history paintings serve as historical records. Students may note that, even though the details are up to the artist's interpretation, the paintings still tell audiences about events and people in the past.

3 Make Connections

Talk Have students discuss the reasons that Patrick Henry gives for fighting the British. (He felt the war was unavoidable, so the colonists of Virginia had to be ready.) How does the picture help you understand Patrick Henry?

Connect to Now Have partners discuss how Patrick Henry's speech has an effect on our country today.

Analyze the Source

Patrick Henry Speaks Out

1 Inspect

Read Look at the title. What does "Patrick Henry Speaks Out" suggest about the tone of the text?

- **Circle** words you don't know.
- **Underline** clues that help you answer the questions Who, What, Where, When, or Why.
- **Discuss** with a partner what Patrick Henry thinks the people of Virginia should do and why.

My Notes

_____

_____

_____

_____

_____

_____

_____

_____

_____

_____

_____

In March of 1775, the House of Burgesses met in Richmond, Virginia, to discuss a solution to painful taxes imposed by the British government. The House of Burgesses was an assembly of elected members who represented the settlements and plantations of Virginia.

Several members pleaded for more time to persuade the British government to repeal, or end, the taxes. Finally, a member named Patrick Henry rose to speak. He mentioned the city of Boston, where there had been conflicts between the colonists and the British. He asked what Virginia could do. He went on to say, "We have done everything that could be done to avert the storm which is now coming."

The only possible action left, Henry said, was to take up arms and fight. The House of Burgesses then voted to organize a **militia** for Virginia.

> **PRIMARY SOURCE**

In Their Words... Patrick Henry

Our brethren are already in the field! Why stand we here idle? What is it that gentlemen wish? What would they have? Is life so dear, or peace so sweet, as to be purchased at the price of chains and slavery? Forbid it, Almighty God! I know not what course others may take; but as for me, give me liberty or give me death!

—from "Speech to the Virginia House of Burgesses," March 23, 1775, Richmond, Virginia

Patrick Henry Addressing the Virginia Assembly

2 Find Evidence

Reread What do you think is the purpose of Patrick Henry's speech? What words does he use that will help accomplish his purpose?

Examine the statement "Our brethren are already in the field! Why stand we here *idle*?" What does the word *idle* mean? Name a word that has the same meaning as *idle*.

3 Make Connections

Talk Discuss with a partner the reasons that Patrick Henry gives for fighting the British.

Connect to Now How did Patrick Henry's speech have an effect on our country today?

Inquiry Journal, pp. 164–165

 ENGLISH LEARNERS SCAFFOLD

ELD.PI.5.7 Evaluating how well writers and speakers use language to support ideas and opinions with details or reasons depending on modality, text type, purpose, audience, topic, and content area

Emerging

Build Meaning Point out that Henry repeats the words *give me*. Guide students to describe how this repeated phrase helps to emphasize Henry's point.

Expanding/Bridging

Develop Language Point out that Henry's speech uses commands. Ask students to use their own words and use commands to explain what Henry was saying.

See the **Language Learner Teaching Guide** for more language support strategies.

Monitor and Differentiate

REACHING ALL LEARNERS

Special Needs

Encourage students to chorally read the primary source in small groups. Guide students to add emphasis and emotion to the words. Then have them discuss whether the speech would have inspired them to do what Patrick Henry asks.

Approaching Level

If students are unable to explain the meaning of the phrase "give me liberty or give me death," then remind them to look up unfamiliar words, such as *liberty*, and reread the excerpt.

Beyond Level

Encourage students to read the full text of Henry's speech and to identify the claims he makes and the reasons he gives. Have students present this information briefly to the group.

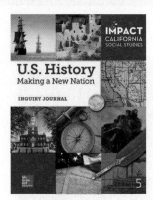

Inquiry Journal
pp. 166–167

Go Digital!

- Model how to explore and investigate with online whole-class tools.

- Students can access the online graphic organizer to use the inquiry tools as they read.

Explore Chronology

Explain Tell to students that chronology, or sequence, is one kind of text structure that authors use to organize information in an historical text. The information is presented in chronological order.

Read Have students read aloud the step-by-step instructions about how to identify chronology. Tell students that in addition to dates, they can use signal words and time expressions to identify the order of events.

Guide Practice Provide a model to students from the information about Patrick Henry: *When Patrick Henry addressed the Virginia House of Burgesses, he gave the speech on May 23, 1775. The group was discussing what to do about the taxes that King George kept putting upon the colonists. The other delegates wanted to wait to see what would happen; Patrick Henry said the time had come to act.*

Investigate!

Have students read pages 200–209 in the Research Companion. Tell them the information that will help them answer the lesson question **How Did the American Revolution Start?**

Take Notes Tell students that they should take notes of major events and battles in the graphic organizer on page 167 of the Inquiry Journal. Remind them that taking notes will help them understand and remember the information they learn. Explain to students the importance of paraphrasing, using their own words, when they take notes.

Inspect Guide students to read the text in each section to determine what it says. Encourage them to make note of words they don't understand and to look for answers to questions, such as *who? what? when? where? why?* and *how?*

Find Evidence Encourage students to reread the text to develop a deeper understanding of the content. Remind students that after they read and take notes, they should review and think about how the facts and details will help them answer the lesson question.

Collaborative Conversations

Text-Based Discussion Remind students of the goals of discussing the text with others.

- to listen and respond to their partners' points
- to ask for evidence from the text
- to build on each other's ideas
- to see the text from a different point of view

Inquiry Tools

Explore Chronology

Identifying the **chronology**, or order in which things happen, in what you read will help you understand how events in history are related.

1. **Read the text once all the way through.**
   This will help you understand what the text is about.

2. **Look at the section titles to see how the text is organized.**
   Do the titles offer any clues as to which important events are discussed in the text?

3. **Watch for specific dates.**
   Are the events described in the text presented in chronological order? It may help to look for sentences that begin with a date—for instance, "On May 10, 1775 . . ."

4. **Find key facts about the events.**
   While reading, ask yourself what key facts about each event show that it was important to the start of the American Revolution.

COLLABORATE Based on the text you just read, work with your class to complete the chart below.

Event	Date	Key Facts
Patrick Henry's speech to the House of Burgesses	March 23, 1775	Virginia assembly is discussing British taxes; some members want to give Britain more time to repeal taxes; Henry says only possible action is to take up arms against Britain

 ## Investigate!

Read pages 200–209 in your Research Companion. Use your investigative skills to identify the chronology of events at the start of the American Revolution. Use the chart to organize information.

Event	Date	Key Facts
Battles of Lexington and Concord	April 19, 1775	British troops attempt to seize colonial war supplies; Paul Revere and others warn colonists of planned attack; colonial militia is defeated at Lexington but rallies at Concord to drive back British
First meeting of Second Continental Congress	May 10, 1775	Representatives of colonies decide how to respond to start of war; they create an American army and persuade George Washington to lead the army; John Hancock elected president of the congress; Olive Branch Petition drafted
Battle of Bunker Hill	June 17, 1775	British troops attempt to occupy hills outside Boston; colonial militia build a fort at Breeds Hill; British troops take over the fort but at the cost of heavy casualties

McGraw-Hill Education

Inquiry Journal, pp. 166–167

(EL) ENGLISH LEARNERS SCAFFOLD

ELD.PI.5.1 Exchanging information and ideas with others through oral collaborative discussions on a range of social and academic topics

Emerging

Organize Information
Point to the arrows in the chart on p. 167. Explain to students that each arrow points to the next event in a sequence. Say: *Look at the chart. Where does information about the first event go?* (first row) *About the second event?* (second row) *About the third event?* (third row)

Expanding

Develop Language
Guide students to refer to information from the text as they discuss with a partner.

Bridging

Cite Evidence Guide students to cite text evidence as they discuss the text with a partner.

See the **Language Learner Teaching Guide** for more language support strategies.

Monitor and Differentiate

REACHING ALL LEARNERS

Approaching Level

Encourage students to work with a partner to organize their notes. Have them complete a graphic organizer such as the one below as they talk.

Who	What	Where	When	Why	How

On Level

Guide students to explain why understanding a sequence of events in history is important. As they read and take notes, have them discuss in small groups how some events have a cause-and-effect relationship with others.

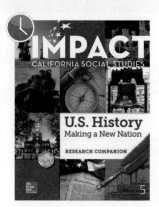

Research Companion
pp. 200–201

 STANDARDS

Identify and map the major military battles and turning points of the Revolutionary War, the roles of the American and British leaders, and the Indian leaders' alliances on both sides. **HSS.5.6.1**

Students place key events and people of the historical era they are studying in a chronological sequence and within a spatial context; they interpret time lines. **HAS.CS.1**

(ccss) Draw on information from multiple print or digital sources, demonstrating the ability to locate an answer to a question quickly or to solve a problem efficiently. **CCSS.ELA.RI.5.7**

Go Digital!

Investigate the lesson content with online whole-class presentation tools.

- **Video:** The American Revolution

- **iMap:** Map of Routes to Lexington and Concord

Background Information

Samuel Adams was outspoken against British taxes like the Sugar Act, the Stamp Act, the Townsend Act, and the Tea Act. **John Hancock** served with Adams in the Massachusetts general court. Warning Hancock and Adams was one of the objectives of Paul Revere's plan to ride to Concord on the night of April 18, 1775.

DID YOU KNOW?

Common Misconception Tell students that according to some sources, Paul Revere shouted "The British are coming" on his midnight ride. Many historians doubt that Revere would have made that cry because at that time, most colonists considered themselves British.

| TIMELINE | Invite students to look at the timeline at the top on p. 201.

Analyze What are the four events that happened between March and June of 1775? (Battle of Lexington and Concord, the Second Continental Congress began meeting, Battle of Bunker Hill)

Analyze the Source

Inspect Have students read pp. 200–201.

Find Evidence Use the questions below to check comprehension. Remind students to support their answers with text evidence.

Identify Who was General Thomas Gage? (a British general) **DOK 1**

Infer Why was Paul Revere ordered to "warn the men"? (because the British were planning a surprise attack) **DOK 2**

Cite Evidence Why did Revere say, "You'll have noise enough before long. The regulars (British troop) are coming!"? Ask students to cite evidence from the text in their answer. (a guard asked him not to make so much noise) **DOK 3**

Make Connections

Point of View Based on what you read, why did the British troops want their plans to remain secret? (to seize supplies and arrest Samuel Adams and John Hancock) **DOK 3**

Analyze the Painting Direct students' attention to the engraving. Encourage students to use images in the text to help them understand events.

- What does the setting look like? (a field)

- Where are the British? (in the distance)

- What does this picture tell you about the battle? (Students may include that the colonists look disorganized and weak compared to the nicely lined-up British soldiers.)

Lesson 1

How Did the American Revolution Start?

The Battles of Lexington and Concord

By 1775, the colonists were tired of British taxes and oppression. After some violent encounters with British troops, the colonists began stockpiling arms and gunpowder in Lexington and Concord, two towns near Boston, Massachusetts.

Paul Revere Rides

On April 18, 1775, British General Thomas Gage ordered 700 soldiers from Boston to seize and destroy colonial war supplies and to arrest patriot leaders Samuel Adams and John Hancock. Gage's plan was to make a surprise attack on Lexington and Concord, so he gave his troops orders not to allow any colonists to leave Boston that night.

Little did General Gage know that a small group of patriots had learned of his plan to attack the two towns. Under cover of night, Paul Revere, William Dawes, and Samuel Prescott set out to warn the people in the area. Revere arrived at Lexington around midnight. When a guard for Adams and Hancock asked him not to make so much noise, Revere told him, "You'll have noise enough before long. The regulars [British troops] are coming!"

HSS.5.5.4, HSS.5.6.1, HAS.CS.4

Paul Revere set out at night to warn of Britain's plan to attack Lexington and Concord.

Timeline

December 1773
Boston Tea Party dumps tea into Boston Harbor.

May 1775
Continental Congress meets in Philadelphia.

June 1775
Battle of Bunker Hill

1773 | 1774 | 1775

April 1775
Fighting begins at Lexington.

An engraving of the Battle of Lexington

Battle at Lexington

When the British troops reached Lexington, Captain John Parker was waiting with the local **militia**. The militia was a group of volunteer soldiers, like the minutemen, who fought only in an emergency. John Robbins, one of the colonial militiamen, described the sight of the British advancing: "There appeared a number of the King's troops . . . at the distance of about sixty or seventy yards from us . . . and on a quick pace toward us. . . ."

Library of Congress Prints & Photographs Division [LC-DIG-ppa-00995]

Research Companion, pp. 200–201

ENGLISH LEARNERS SCAFFOLD

ELD.PI.5.1 Exchanging information and ideas with others through oral collaborative discussions on a range of social and academic topics

Emerging

Establish Purpose Say: *This is a timeline. A time line shows readers events in chronological order from first to last.* Point to and read each event and date to reinforce the chronology. Share with students that the events listed on the timeline are the focus of this lesson.

Expanding/Bridging

Understand Point to the timeline. Explain that a timeline is a text feature often used in history texts to help establish chronology. Review the timeline with students. Ask: *What does the timeline show? In what order does it present the events?*

See the **Language Learner Teaching Guide** for more language support strategies.

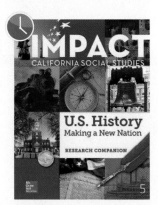

Research Companion
pp. 202–203

 STANDARDS

Identify and map the major military battles and turning points of the Revolutionary War, the roles of the American and British leaders, and the Indian leaders' alliances on both sides. **HSS.5.6.1**

CCSS Students use map and globe skills to determine the absolute locations of places and interpret information available through a map's or globe's legend, scale, and symbolic representations. **HAS.CS.4**

Go Digital!

Investigate the lesson content with online whole-class presentation tools.

Background Information

Battle of Lexington When British troops reached Lexington, the colonists were ready. The short battle left eight colonists dead, ten wounded, and the British marching toward Concord.

Analyze the Source

Inspect Have students continue reading about the Battle of Lexington and Concord on pp. 202–203.

Find Evidence Use the questions below to check comprehension. Remind students to support their answers with text evidence.

Identify Who was leading the militia? (Captain Jonas Parker) **DOK 1**

Cite Evidence Why did Captain Parker tell his troops, "Don't fire unless fired upon"? (because the colonists didn't have enough ammunition) **DOK 3**

Infer Based on what you read, why is the first shot fired in the Battle of Lexington called "the shot heard 'round the world"? (because it marked the beginning of the war between the colonies and England, which was over a thousand miles away) **DOK 2**

Make Connections

Compare and Contrast How were the battles of Lexington and Concord alike? How were they different? (The Battle of Lexington was over very quickly, the British killed 8 Americans, and the British did not suffer any losses. The Americans lost. At Concord, the Americans won, killing 90 British soldiers and wounding many more. The Americans knew the British were coming and were more prepared.) **DOK 3**

Map Skills

Project a large version of the map on page 203. Guide students to answer the Map Skills question in their books: Who traveled farthest, Dawes, Revere, or the British, and how far did each travel? If students have difficulty, point out that Revere's route is shown in purple and Dawes's is shown in blue. They should not include the portion of Revere's route continued by Prescott. Also point out the scale of the map. (British—about 15 miles, Dawes—about 14 miles, Revere—about 14 miles)

Find a landmark that is approximately 14 miles from your school. Point out that putting distances in context using maps can help students better understand the situations they read about in history texts.

✓ Stop and Check

Perspectives Have students defend their perspectives as they share their responses. (Students should identify that the colonists had time to react.)

Find Details Explain to students that after they read and take notes, they should review and think about how the facts and details will help them answer the Essential Question.

The First Shots

Captain Parker's orders to the militia were very simple, "Don't fire unless fired upon, but if they mean to have a war, let it begin here."

As the distance between the two groups grew smaller, someone in one of the groups fired a shot. To this day, no one knows which side fired first, but other shots quickly followed. Even though the battle lasted only a few minutes, eight militiamen were killed. The British succeeded in taking Lexington and marched on to Concord.

Arriving in Concord

Doctor Samuel Prescott, one of the men working with Paul Revere, had warned Concord of the impending attack. The townspeople moved most of the arms and gunpowder to nearby towns. When the British arrived, they found only the few supplies the townspeople of Concord had not had time to hide.

By now the church bells were ringing loudly to alert the local farmers of the British attack. The Concord **rebels** turned on the British troops. Minutemen, local farmers, and townspeople fired at the British troops from behind fences, houses, and trees.

The British troops were forced to retreat back to Boston, 18 miles away. By the time they reached safety, more than 90 British soldiers had been killed and 174 were wounded. With these two battles, the war for American independence had begun!

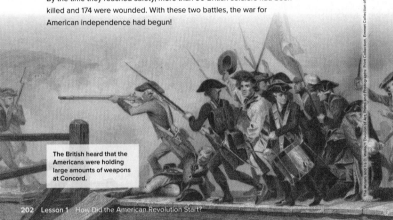

The British heard that the Americans were holding large amounts of weapons at Concord.

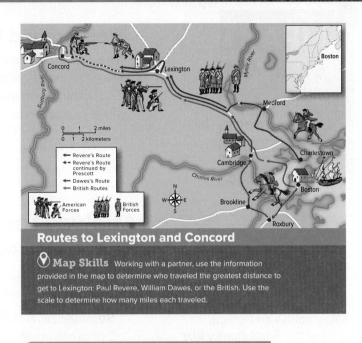

Routes to Lexington and Concord

🔍 **Map Skills** Working with a partner, use the information provided in the map to determine who traveled the greatest distance to get to Lexington: Paul Revere, William Dawes, or the British. Use the scale to determine how many miles each traveled.

☑ **Stop and Check**

Perspectives Why is it important that some colonists found out about the British plans ahead of time?

Find Details As you read, add additional information to the graphic organizer on page 167 in your Inquiry Journal.

Research Companion, pp. 202–203

ENGLISH LEARNERS SCAFFOLD

ELD.PI.5.1 Exchanging information and ideas with others through oral collaborative discussions on a range of social and academic topics

Emerging

Use Visuals Draw a chart with *seize* on the left. Explain that the word is a very strong way of saying "take," meaning specifically "use legal power to take." Have students discuss why it is important that the British seized the colonists' weapons.

Expanding/Bridging

Analyze Meaning Have students identify different words that mean "take" and compare them to *seize*. Have students chart them from weaker to stronger in meaning. Have students write a sentence that uses *seize*. Then have them rewrite the sentence three times using different synonyms. Have them discuss how the meaning of the sentence changed.

See the **Language Learner Teaching Guide** for more language support strategies.

Monitor and Differentiate

REACHING ALL LEARNERS

Approaching Level

Have students identify the main events of the Battles of Lexington and Concord. Have them list the events in chronological order.

On Level

Guide students to create a short timeline of the events of April 18, 1775. Then have students summarize the main events with a partner.

Beyond Level

Encourage students to choose an American or British leader referenced on these pages. Guide students to research the individual in more depth.

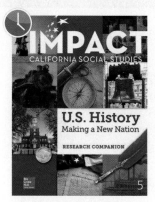

Research Companion
pp. 204–205

 STANDARDS

Identify and map the major military battles and turning points of the Revolutionary War, the roles of the American and British leaders, and the Indian leaders' alliances on both sides. **HSS.5.6.1**

Students differentiate between primary and secondary sources. **HAS.HR.1**

Go Digital!

Investigate the lesson content with online whole-class presentation tools.

Background Information

The Second Continental Congress The Continental Congress began 1772, in Massachusetts, when groups of citizens came together to discuss what to do about their problems with Great Britain. These Committees of Correspondence slowly appeared in other colonies. By 1774, the Committees transformed into the First Continental Congress, which was made up of many of the men who had been Committee delegates.

Analyze the Source

Inspect Have students read pp. 204–205, The Second Continental Congress.

Find Evidence Use the questions below to check comprehension. Remind students to support their answers with text evidence.

> **Summarize** Name the events that had occurred prior to the Second Continental Congress meeting. (the Stamp Act, the Boston Tea Party, the Battles of Lexington and Concord) **DOK 3**
>
> **Infer** What was the primary question that the Second Continental Congress was called together to answer? (to decide whether or not to go to war with Great Britain) **DOK 2**
>
> **Analyze** What did the Congress decide to do? (to form an American Army and name George Washington to lead it.) **DOK 4**

Analyze the Primary Source Point out the words *Trust* and *Cause* in the primary source. Ask students to discuss in a group what these words mean to Washington.

> **Draw Conclusions** Why did Washington decide to become commander of the army if he didn't think he was right for the job? (He believed in the cause (independence), and was willing to do what Congress asked him to do.) **DOK 3**

Make Connections Ask students to share their opinions. Say: *Based on what you read, why was the Second Continental Congress important? What evidence can you use to support your opinion?* (Responses will vary, but students should support their opinions with evidence from the text.) **DOK 4**

☑ Stop and Check

COLLABORATE

Connect to Now Encourage students to use text evidence as they respond to the prompt. Remind students that to be valid, their opinion must be supported by reasons based on evidence. (Responses will vary, but students may identify that the Second Continental Congress is somewhat similar to the U.S. Congress today, but Congress today has less power.)

The Second Continental Congress

The leaders of the thirteen colonies had known a war with Great Britain was possible. They had already met in 1774, in the First Continental Congress, to decide what to do about the recent taxes set by the British government. Great speakers such as Patrick Henry had given fiery speeches to urge the leaders to prepare to separate from Great Britain. The Second Continental Congress met in Philadelphia on May 10, 1775, just days after the battles of Lexington and Concord. Participants sent from each of the thirteen colonies had to decide how to respond to what had happened.

They decided that they had to prepare for war. First, they made the militia that had stood up to the British in Massachusetts part of an official American army. To lead that army, they nominated a veteran of the French and Indian War and a member of the Congress: George Washington. Washington did not think he was up to the task of commanding the entire army, but he agreed to do his best.

The Second Continental Congress Voting for Independence by Robert Pine and Edward Savage

©Stevphoto/iStockphoto/Getty Images; (inset)ClassicStock.com/SuperStock

TEXT: "Washington Accepts his Appointment as Commander of Continental Army." Journals of the Continental Congress, vol. 2, June 16, 1775. PHOTO: ©McGraw-Hill Education; ©Yale University Art Gallery

PRIMARY SOURCE

In Their Words... George Washington

Though I am truly sensible of the high Honor done me in this Appointment, yet I feel great distress, from a consciousness that my abilities and Military experience may not be equal to the extensive and important Trust: However, as the Congress desire it I will enter upon the momentous duty, and exert every power I Possess In their service and for the Support of the glorious Cause.

—address to the Continental Congress, June 16, 1775

The Second Continental Congress was not just a single meeting. It began as a series of meetings during the spring and summer of 1775. Besides establishing a Continental Army, the delegates also elected a president—John Hancock—and drafted the Olive Branch Petition. This was an attempt to resolve the conflicts between the colonies and Great Britain. However, King George refused to receive the Congress's peace offering.

As Great Britain's grip on the colonies weakened, the Continental Congress became the unofficial government. The war was far from over, but the colonists were learning how to govern themselves. The delegates would continue to meet throughout the war and even afterwards to make important decisions for the thirteen colonies.

✓ Stop and Check

Connect to Now Is the Second Continental Congress anything like our government today? Using what you know, discuss with a partner how the Second Continental Congress is similar or different.

Research Companion, pp. 204–205

EL ENGLISH LEARNERS SCAFFOLD

ELD.PI.5.11 Supporting own opinions and evaluating others' opinions in speaking and writing

Emerging

Understand Primary Sources Guide students in identifying the main idea by translating the quote into modern English.

"Though I am truly sensible of the high Honor done me in this Appointment, yet I feel great distress,"

"I know this is a big honor, but I'm concerned."

"My abilities and Military experience may not be equal to the extensive and important Trust:"

"My skills and experience as a soldier may not be enough for this important task."

See the **Language Learner Teaching Guide** for more language support strategies.

Monitor and Differentiate

REACHING ALL LEARNERS

Special Needs

Encourage students to act out how the Congress made the important decision of creating a national army. Have each student play the role of a delegate to the Congress and debate the pros and cons of arming the colonies.

Approaching Level

Students should note unfamiliar words in the primary source. In pairs, ask students to look up each word, then replace the unfamiliar words with synonyms. Then ask students to reread to identify Washington's point.

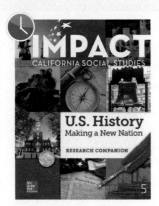

Research Companion
pp. 206–207

 STANDARDS

Identify and map the major military battles and turning points of the Revolutionary War, the roles of the American and British leaders, and the Indian leaders' alliances on both sides. **HSS.5.6.1**

Students correctly apply terms related to time, including past, present, future, decade, century, and generation. **HAS.CS.2**

CCSS Draw evidence from literary or informational texts to support analysis, reflection, and research. **CCSS.ELA.W.5.9**

Go Digital!

Investigate the lesson content with online whole-class presentation tools.

Background Information

Minutemen The Massachusetts colonists had endured so much oppression from British troops that they had organized a militia months ahead of the Battles of Lexington and Concord. One-third of the men in each regiment, or group of militia, were named "minutemen." They were expected to be ready to fight with very little notice.

Did You Know?

Minutemen earned about a shilling for each drill they practiced. In today's dollars, minutemen could earn about $13.64 per week. That doesn't sound like much, but that's what some craftsmen could earn in a single day. The minutemen got this money on top of what they earned doing their regular jobs. This extra pay was one of the incentives for the minutemen to be the first ones into danger.

Analyze the Source

Inspect Have students look closely at the images and read all of the captions.

Find Evidence Use the questions below to check comprehension. Remind students to support their answers with text evidence.

> **Describe** What are the major differences between the redcoats and the minutemen? (The minutemen didn't have uniforms. The redcoats had red uniforms to help them identify each other during battle) **DOK 3**

> **Compare** What advantage did the minutemen have over the Red Coats? (They were familiar with frontier hunting and the knew what the local land was like.) **DOK 3**

Make Connections Prompt students to make connections with the following questions.

> **Justify** The text states that "a good soldier could load and fire his musket three times per minute." Do you think that was significant? Why? (Responses will vary.) **DOK 4**

> **Connect to Now** How are the Soldiers of the American Revolution like soldiers today? How are they different? Are their goals the same? (Responses will vary.)

Stop and Check

Perspectives Encourage students to use text evidence as they respond to the prompt. Remind students that to be valid, their opinion must be supported by reasons based on evidence. (Responses will vary, but students may say that the British had the advantage because they had better equipment.)

The infographic above contains the following text:

InfoGraphic

Soldiers of the American Revolution

The Minutemen

The citizen soldiers in the local militia didn't have uniforms. Instead, they wore their own clothes. Because the minutemen were the first ones to arrive for battle, many of the colonies made an effort to arm them with muskets and other supplies. Minutemen had the advantage over British troops of being familiar with frontier hunting and knowing what the local land was like.

Hat
Since Minutemen provided their own clothing, they wore whatever hat they owned. Styles varied greatly among the Minutemen.

Waistcoat and Coat
A sleeveless and collarless waistcoat was worn over a man's shirt. Waistcoats were usually made of linen or wool. Men wore a coat over the waistcoat. These overcoats were usually made of heavy linen or wool.

Breeches
Knee breeches were common in the 18th century. These came just below the knee and were closed with ties or buttons. Breeches were made of leather, wool, or linen.

Musket
A good soldier could load and fire his musket three times per minute. Muskets weren't very accurate and didn't work well in wet weather.

The Redcoats

The British redcoats were all issued uniforms and muskets. Because battlefields of the 18th century could be smoky and confusing, the soldiers wore red. This way, British soldiers wouldn't have trouble separating friend from foe. The redcoats had the advantages of military training and better equipment over the colonial minutemen.

Hat
Hats identified which regiment a soldier belonged to.

Buttons
There could be as many as three dozen buttons on a soldier's uniform. Buttons often had the name of the soldier's regiment inscribed on them. Buttons had to be polished regularly.

Facings
These visible linings along the edges of the soldier's coat were colored to show the regiment he belonged to.

Musket
The British Short Land Pattern musket was standard issue. Soldiers would affix a bayonet, or attachable blade, to the musket's muzzle for close combat.

✓ Stop and Check

Perspectives Based on what you've just read about British and colonial fighters, who do you think had the advantage in battle? Discuss your opinion with a partner.

206 Lesson 1 How Did the American Revolution Start?

Lesson 1 207

 ENGLISH LEARNERS SCAFFOLD

ELD.PII.5.4 Using nouns and noun phrases

Emerging

Describe Guide students to find words that describe the minutemen, based on evidence in the text. Ask students to provide reasons that are based on text evidence, then guide them to follow their opinion with "because" and an important reason they found in the text. Once students understand how to form an opinion, make sure they restate the quote in their own words.

Bridging

Support Opinions Help students model building on their response using connecting words like *because* and *for example* to add information.

Student 1: Why did the British soldiers wear red uniforms?

Student 2: They wore red uniforms because _____.

Student 1: Did the colonists and the British soldiers use the same weapons?

Student 2: No, they didn't. They used different weapons. For example _____.

See the **Language Learner Teaching Guide** for more language support strategies.

Monitor and Differentiate

REACHING ALL LEARNERS

Approaching Level

Encourage students to use a graphic organizer to help them identify similarities and differences between the minutemen and the Redcoats.

Beyond Level

Have students conduct research about the supplies and gear the minutemen had. Ask students to share their findings with the group.

Lesson 1 **Soldiers of the American Revolution** T433

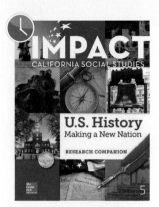

 Research Companion
pp. 208–209

(HSS) STANDARDS

Identify and map the major military battles and turning points of the Revolutionary War, the roles of the American and British leaders, and the Indian leaders' alliances on both sides. **HSS.5.6.1**

Students use map and globe skills to determine the absolute locations of places and interpret information available through a map's or globe's legend, scale, and symbolic representations. **HAS.CS.4**

Go Digital!

Investigate the lesson content with online whole-class presentation tools.

Background Information

Why Boston? Settled by Puritans in 1630, Boston governed itself for 50 years. However, it became such a wealthy trading port that the king took over the city in the 1680s. The colonists never quite forgot their early independence, becoming angrier as the king created even more taxes. This discontent eventually led to the area immediately around Boston becoming the site of the first battles.

Analyze the Source

Inspect Have students read The Battle of (Not) Bunker Hill on pp. 208–209.

Find Evidence Use the questions below to check comprehension. Remind students to support their answers with text evidence.

Summarize What did William Prescott want to do? (drive out British troops from Boston) What did he want to do first? (fortify Bunker Hill) What did the colonists end up doing? (fortify Breed's Hill) **DOK 1**

Interpret What does "don't shoot until you see the whites of their eyes" mean? Why did Prescott or Putnam say this? (don't shoot until the enemy is close; the colonists were running out of ammunition) **DOK 2**

Explain Why did both sides want to control the hills around Boston? Use text evidence to support response. (Responses will vary, but students may say that they wanted to take back the city or prevent the British from expanding their territory.) **DOK 3**

Make Connections

Critique Why is this section titled, The Battle of (Not) Bunker Hill? (The battle was actually fought at Breed's Hill not Bunker Hill.) **DOK 3**

Map Skills

Project the map on p. 209 and ask the following questions.

• What is the distance between Bunker Hill and Breed's Hill? (approximately 0.25 miles)

• How far is each hill from Boston? (Bunker Hill: approximately 1 mile; Breed's Hill: 0.75 miles)

Find a landmark that is approximately 1 mile from your school. Putting distances in context using maps can help students better understand the situations they read about in history texts.

☑ Stop and Check

Perspectives Guide students to think about how the Battle of Bunker Hill changed the way the British viewed the colonists. (Answers will vary but may include that they viewed each other as hostile opponents rather than as opposing sides.)

What Do You Think?

How did the events you've read about lead to the start of the American Revolution? Encourage students to use text evidence from the whole lesson as they respond to the prompt.

The Battle of (Not) Bunker Hill

On June 18, 1775, James Warren, a Boston colonist, explained the conflict in Boston to his wife, Mary Otis Warren, "It is impossible to describe the confusion in this place, women and children are flying into the country, armed men going to the field, and wounded men . . . fill the streets."

British general Thomas Gage decided to occupy the hills around Boston. Word about the British plan spread quickly. Colonel William Prescott and General Israel Putnam led one thousand colonial troops to hills north of Boston, across the Charles River. The original plan was to fortify Bunker Hill, which means to build earthen walls around it. This way, the colonists could fire cannons at the British troops stationed across the Charles River in Boston. Instead, the colonists decided to protect Breed's Hill, which was closer to the river. The colonists worked all night to build a fort for protection.

The Battle Begins

British troops crossed the Charles River by boat and marched up Breed's Hill. The militia and civilians, or ordinary citizens, waited, hidden behind the walls they had built. The colonists did not have much ammunition, or musket balls and gunpowder. Officers told them not to waste ammunition by firing at British soldiers who were too far away. Historians say that either Colonel Prescott or General Israel Putnam said, "Don't shoot until you see the whites of their eyes."

Then and Now

A 225-foot granite obelisk in Charlestown, Massachusetts, commemorates the Battle of Bunker Hill. The cornerstone was placed in 1825 on the fiftieth anniversary of the battle by the Marquis de Lafayette, a hero of the American Revolution. The monument was completed in 1842.

NPS Photo

A British Victory

Twice, the British charged up the hill only to be stopped by the militia. Both times they were forced down by American fire. After a third try, the British overwhelmed the colonists. The British won what became known as the Battle of Bunker Hill, but the victory was costly. More than a thousand soldiers were killed or wounded in the battle. Great Britain was one of the most powerful nations on Earth, but winning a war against the American colonists wasn't going to be easy.

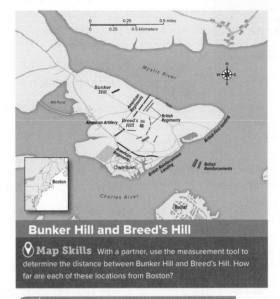

McGraw-Hill Education

Bunker Hill and Breed's Hill

Map Skills With a partner, use the measurement tool to determine the distance between Bunker Hill and Breed's Hill. How far are each of these locations from Boston?

Stop and Check

Perspectives How might the large number of casualties have changed the way the British viewed the colonists?

Research Companion, pp. 208–209

 ENGLISH LEARNERS SCAFFOLD

ELD.PII.5.1 Understanding text structure

Emerging	Expanding	Bridging
Order Nouns Guide practice using words that express time order: *On June 18, later, next, after that, finally,* and *first.*	**Use Transitions** Ask students to identify transitions that show when events happen. Explain the purpose of time order structure in history texts.	**Write a List** Have students retell the events of the Battle of Bunker Hill. Students may choose to create a bulleted list or to write a short paragraph that uses appropriate transitions.

See the **Language Learner Teaching Guide** for more language support strategies.

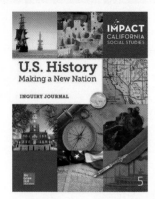

Inquiry Journal
pp. 168–169

 STANDARDS

Students understand the course and consequences of the American Revolution. **HSS.5.5.6**

Write opinion pieces on topics or texts, supporting a point of view with reasons and information. **CCSS.ELA.W.5.1**

Engage effectively in a range of collaborative discussions (one-on-one, in groups, and teacher-led) with diverse partners on grade 5 topics and texts, building on others' ideas and expressing their own clearly. **CCSS.ELA.SL.5.1**

Go Digital!

• Students can go online to report their findings. Assess their responses online.

• Students can access the online graphic organizer to capture ideas from their investigation.

Think About It

Take a Stand Students will review their research and consider which event discussed in the lesson was the most significant event at the start of the American Revolution.

• Remind students to review the events they have listed in their graphic organizer and the key details associated with each event. Direct students back to pages 200–209 of their Research Companion if they need more information.

Write About It

Write and Cite Evidence Have students read the prompt. Explain to students that an effective opinion essay includes a claim and evidence that supports it.

Remind students to include the following elements in their response.

• Introduce a Topic.

• Provide logical reasons supported by facts and details.

• Use transition words to link opinions and evidence.

Use the rubric on p. T438 to evaluate students' work.

COLLABORATE
Talk About It

Defend Your Claim Help students pair up with a classmate who chose a different event from theirs.

• Explain that they should take turns discussing their opinions and the reasons that helped them form that opinion.

• Students should discuss whether they agree or disagree with their partner's opinion and explain why.

• Remind students to follow the rules of appropriate classroom conversation.

Connect to the
Essential Question

Read the prompt aloud to students. Ask them the following guiding questions:

• Which events from this lesson have had the biggest impact on our nation today? (Responses will vary, but students should use evidence from the text in their response.)

• Whose actions or ideas are still important to our nation today? (Responses will vary, but students should use evidence from the text in their response.)

Remind students to use the space provided in their journal to jot down notes.

Report / Your Findings

Think About It

Take a Stand
Review your research. Based on the information you have gathered, what do you think was the most significant event at the start of the American Revolution?

Write About It

Write and Cite Evidence
In your opinion, what was the most significant event at the start of the American Revolution? List three reasons that support your opinion. Include page references.

Event *Students should choose an event from the text and use support that appears in the text, including page numbers.*

Reasons

1. _____

_____

_____

2. _____

_____

_____

3. _____

_____

_____

Talk About It

Defend Your Claim
Talk to a classmate who chose a different event. Take turns discussing your opinions and supporting evidence. Do you agree or disagree with your partner's opinion? Why?

History Connect to the EQ

Pull It Together
Think about the people and events that you read and talked about in this lesson. How did these help shape our nation today?

Students should mention at least one person and event discussed in the text and provide a connection to the nation today.

_____

_____

EQ Inquiry Project Notes

_____

_____

_____

_____

_____

_____

McGraw-Hill Education

168 Lesson 1 How Did the American Revolution Start?

Lesson 1 **169**

Inquiry Journal, pp. 168–169

(EL) ENGLISH LEARNERS SCAFFOLD

ELD.PI.5.7 Evaluating how well writers and speakers use language to support ideas and opinions with details or reasons depending on modality, text type, purpose, audience, topic, and content area

Emerging	Expanding	Bridging
State an Opinion Help students complete the following sentence frames:	**Support an Opinion** Ask students to complete the sentence frames. Encourage students to provide details.	**Defend an Opinion** Check for understanding. Ask: *What was the most significant event at the start of the American Revolution? What information did you use from the text to support your opinion?*
In my opinion, the most significant event at the start of the American Revolution was _____.	*In my opinion, the most significant event at the start of the American Revolution was _____.*	
I think _____ was the most significant event because _____.	*I think _____ was the most significant event because _____.*	

See the **Language Learner Teaching Guide** for more language support strategies.

Monitor and Differentiate

REACHING ALL LEARNERS

Approaching Level

Review with students that a claim, or opinion, should be supported by evidence from the text. Remind them that a good opinion essay contains evidence that is strong enough to convince others of your point of view.

On Level

Have students list the reasons that support their opinion and rank them from most to least convincing. Have students decide whether each reason they have listed is persuasive or if it needs to be replaced with a reason that is more convincing.

Know what your students know!

Lesson Task
Report Your Findings

Use the rubric to evaluate students' responses.

Take a Stand Students state an opinon and reasons about the most significant event at the start of the American Revolution.

Defend Your Claim Students take turns discussing their opinions and supporting evidence with another student who chose a different event.

Lesson Task Evaluation Rubric

	4	3	2	1
Historical Understanding	Strong understanding of the events at the start of the American Revolution	Adequate understanding of the events at the start of the American Revolution	Uneven understanding of the events at the start of the American Revolution	No understanding of the events at the start of the American Revolution
Take a Stand	Clearly states opinion	Adequately states opinion	Somewhat clear or unclear opinion	No opinion or student does not show understanding of the task
Support with Evidence	Reasons contain thorough and convincing evidence	Reasons contain adequate evidence	Reasons contain uneven or only somewhat convincing evidence	Reasons are missing or contain no supporting evidence
Defend Your Claim	Speaks clearly and at an understandable pace	Speaks clearly during most of the presentation	At times speaker is unclear	Does not use complete sentences
	Provides a concluding statement that relates to the speaker's position	Provides a concluding statement that mostly relates to the speaker's position	Loosely links reasons to the speaker's opinion	Does not link reasons to the speaker's opinion

Lesson Assessment

Go Digital!

- Have students complete the Chapter 5 Lesson 1 Assessment online to monitor their understanding of the lesson content.

California Smarter Balanced Assessment Connections!

Standards Covered	Lesson Task	Lesson Assessment	Alignment with California Smarter Balanced Assessment
History Social Science Content 5.5.2; 5.5.4; 5.5.6; 5.6.1	✔	✔	Claim 1 Targets 8, 9, 10
History Social Science Analysis Skills Chronological and Spatial Thinking 5.1; 5.3 Historical Interpretation 5.1; 5.3	✔	✔	Claim 1 Targets 11, 12
Writing W.5.1	✔	✔	Claim 2 Target 6a
Research and Inquiry W.5.7; W.5.8		✔	Claim 4 Targets 1, 2, 3, 4
Reading RI.5.1; RI.5.3; RI.5.9	✔	✔	Claim 1 Targets 8, 9, 10, 11, 12, 13
Speaking and Listening SL.5.1a; SL.5.1c	✔		Claim 3 Target 3

Why Is the Declaration of Independence Still Important Today?

Background Information

In this lesson, students learn about how the Declaration of Independence was developed. They will also discuss how the Declaration affected the budding American Revolution and why the document is important today.

Community Connections

To enrich what students have learned about the Declaration of Independence, plan a day with a special guest, such as a local lawyer or judge who can talk about why the Declaration was such an important influence on the laws we still use today.

LESSON STANDARDS

✔ Know the significance of the first and second Continental Congresses and of the Committees of Correspondence. **HSS.5.5.2**

✔ Understand the people and events associated with the drafting and signing of the Declaration of Independence and the document's significance, including the key political concepts it embodies, the origins of those concepts, and its role in severing ties with Great Britain. **HSS.5.5.3**

✔ Describe the views, lives, and impact of key individuals during this period (e.g., King George III, Patrick Henry, Thomas Jefferson, George Washington, Benjamin Franklin, John Adams. **HSS.5.5.4**

✔ Understand how the ideals set forth in the Declaration of Independence changed the way people viewed slavery. **HSS.5.6.7**

✔ Students place key events and people of the historical era they are studying in a chronological sequence and within a spatial context; they interpret time lines. **HAS.CS.1**

✔ Students judge the significance of the relative location of a place (e.g., proximity to a harbor, on trade routes) and analyze how relative advantages or disadvantages can change over time. **HAS CS.5**

✔ Students differentiate between primary and secondary sources. **HAS HR.1**

✔ Students pose relevant questions about events they encounter in historical documents, eyewitness accounts, oral histories, letters, diaries, artifacts, photographs, maps, artworks, and architecture. **HAS HR.2**

Connect to the Essential Question

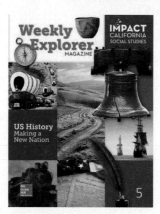

Chapter 5, pp. 58–71

The **Weekly Explorer Magazine** supports the students' exploration of the Essential Question and provides additional resources for the EQ Inquiry Project.

Inquiry Project

How Would Our Life Have Been Impacted If . . . ?

Remind students to use the information they learn in this lesson and other resources to complete the EQ Inquiry Project.

Dinah Zike's

In this lesson you will use Foldables.

When Minutes Count!

Suggested Lesson Pacing

1 ENGAGE
One Day

- Lesson Opener
- Analyze the Source
- Inquiry Tools

Go Digital
- **Video:** The Declaration of Independence

2 INVESTIGATE
Two to Three Days

 Short on Time? Look for the clock to teach core content in less time.

- Enlightened Thinking
- *Common Sense*
- Writing the Declaration
- Signing the Declaration
- **Infographic** Structure of the Declaration
- Does the Declaration Still Matter?
- Field Trip to Philadelphia

3 REPORT
One Day

- Think About It
- Write and Cite Evidence
- Support Your Thesis

Make Connections!

ⓒ CONNECT TO ELA

Reading
Explain how an author uses reasons and evidence to support particular points in a text, identifying which reasons and evidence support which point(s). **RI.5.8**

Research
Conduct short research projects that use several sources to build knowledge through investigation of different aspects of a topic. **W.5.7**

Recall relevant information from experiences or gather relevant information from print and digital sources; summarize or paraphrase information in notes and finished work, and provide a list of sources. **W.5.8**

Writing
Write opinion pieces on topics or texts, supporting a point of view with reasons and information. **W.5.1**

Speaking and Listening
Engage effectively in a range of collaborative discussions (one-on-one, in groups, and teacher-led) with diverse partners on *grade 5 topics and texts*, building on others' ideas and expressing their own clearly. **SL.5.1**

Classroom Resources

🔍 Search for additional resources using the following key words.

John Adams

Common Sense

Declaration of Independence

John Dickinson

Benjamin Franklin

Thomas Jefferson

John Locke

Thomas Paine

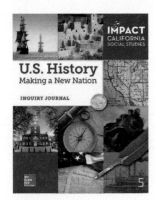

Inquiry Journal
pp. 170–171

Why Is the Declaration of Independence Still Important Today?

Bellringer

Prompt students to retrieve information from the previous lessons. Say: *What was the significance of the Battles of Lexington and Concord?* (These were the first battles of the American Revolution because most colonists saw them as an act of war.)

Lesson Outcomes

What Am I Learning? Have students read the Lesson Outcomes on p. 170.

Why Am I Learning It? Check that students understand the word *declaration*. Guide them to break apart the word into *declare* with the suffix *–tion*. Discuss with them that a declaration is something that is stated formally. Encourage students to create a declaration about classroom rules or a routine. Post the declaration in the classroom.

How Will I Know That I Learned It? Ask students the following questions.

 STANDARDS

Understand the people and events associated with the drafting and signing of the Declaration of Independence and the document's significance, including the key political concepts it embodies, the origins of those concepts, and its role in severing ties with Great Britain. **HSS.5.5.3**

Describe the views, lives, and impact of key individuals during this period (e.g., King George III, Patrick Henry, Thomas Jefferson, George Washington, Benjamin Franklin, John Adams. **HSS.5.5.4**

- What will you explain? (the reasons for parts of the Declaration of Independence)
- What is the purpose of the task? (to explain how the Declaration affects our lives today)
- How will you support your explanation? (with text evidence)

Go *Digital!*

Explore the lesson content with online whole-class presentation tools.

- **Video:** The Declaration of Independence

Talk About It COLLABORATE

Provide some scaffolding for students to use as they discuss the picture. Provide background information as needed.

- The painting shows _____.
- The mood of the scene is _____.
- The people in the painting seem _____ about what they are doing.
- I think the painting's title calls the people *Rebels* because _____.

Collaborative Conversations COLLABORATE

Add New Ideas As students engage in partner, small group, and whole-class discussions, encourage them to

- Think carefully about what the people's reactions are.
- Ask and answer questions that are about the painting or the Declaration of Independence.
- Draw or modify conclusions that are based on the discussion.

Lesson 2

Why Is the Declaration of Independence Still Important Today?

The Rebels of '76, or the First Announcement of the Great Declaration

Lesson Outcomes

What Am I Learning?
In this lesson, you're going to use your investigative skills to learn about the Declaration of Independence and explore why it is still important today.

Why Am I Learning It?
Reading and talking about the Declaration of Independence will help you learn more about what it means and how it affects your life today.

How Will I Know That I Learned It?
You will be able to explain the reasons for important parts of the Declaration of Independence and recognize the ways they still affect the country today.

Talk About It COLLABORATE

Look at the Details How do you think the members of the Second Continental Congress felt after declaring independence from Great Britain? How do the details in this picture support your answer?

HSS.5.5.2, HSS.5.5.3, HSS.5.5.4, HAS.CS.3

170 Lesson 2 Why Is the Declaration of Independence Still Important Today?

Lesson 2 171

Inquiry Journal, pp. 170–171

EL ENGLISH LEARNERS SCAFFOLD

ELD.PI.5.6 Reading closely literary and informational texts and viewing multimedia to determine how meaning is conveyed explicitly and implicitly through language

Emerging

Identify Details
Guide students to identify the people shown in the painting. Encourage them to examine details about the scene and the event. Help them understand the title by defining *rebel*, *'76,* and *declaration*.

Expanding

Describe Details Work with students to describe what they see in the painting using words that they have learned to use when describing art. Encourage them to describe the *scene*, the *figures*, and the *action* in the painting.

Bridging

Use Language
Encourage students to identify and discuss what the picture says about the feelings surrounding the issuing of the Declaration of Independence. Remind them to use language that describes the setting of the event shown in the picture.

See the **Language Learner Teaching Guide** for more language support strategies.

Monitor and Differentiate

REACHING ALL LEARNERS

Approaching Level

Work with students to identify what is happening in the painting. Have them compare how big news was broadcast then with how it happens now.

On Level

Encourage students to describe the events in the painting. Encourage them to discuss their ideas with a partner. Guide them to share how the painting is similar or different to their expectations about how people received the important event.

Beyond Level

Guide students to conduct research to find other depictions of this event or another event pertaining to the Declaration. Guide them to share their comparisons to this painting with the whole class.

Lesson 2 **Lesson Outcomes** T443

Analyze the Source

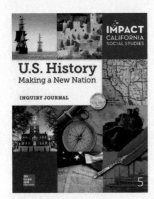

Inquiry Journal
pp. 172–173

 STANDARDS

Understand the people and events associated with the drafting and signing of the Declaration of Independence and the document's significance, including the key political concepts it embodies, the origins of those concepts, and its role in severing ties with Great Britain. **HSS.5.5.3**

Describe the views, lives, and impact of key individuals during this period (e.g., King George III, Patrick Henry, Thomas Jefferson, George Washington, Benjamin Franklin, John Adams). **HSS.5.5.4**

Students differentiate between primary and secondary sources. **HAS.HR.1**

CCSS Engage effectively in a range of collaborative discussions (one-on-one, in groups, and teacher-led) with diverse partners on *grade 5 topics and texts*, building on others' ideas and expressing their own clearly.
CCSS.ELA.SL.5.1

Go Digital!

Model how to inspect and find evidence with online whole-class presentation tools.

Build Background

Paintings as Secondary Sources In 1824, Congress commissioned John Trumbull to paint a series of four murals about the Revolution for the new Capitol in Washington, D.C. Explain that this painting shows a specific moment in history, but that Trumbull was not there on the day the Declaration was signed. Instead, the painting is a valuable secondary source, a source that was created after that event it references.

1 Inspect

Read Ask students to skim the text, including the excerpt from the Declaration of Independence, to focus on understanding the overall meaning. Remind them to circle words that are unfamiliar.

- What part of the Declaration of Independence is excerpted here? (the final paragraph)
- From whose point of view is the excerpt written? (the representatives of the United States of America in Congress)
- What does the paragraph doing to the relationship between America and Great Britain? (It dissolves or ends the colonial relationship.)

Collaborate Have partners take turns explaining what they think the writers want the reader to understand and agree with. (Responses should be based on the text.)

2 Find Evidence

Reread Have students reread the text.

Analyze the Primary Source Reread the excerpt aloud then analyze it as a class.

- What does *absolved* mean? (freed from)
- What does *allegiance* mean? *(loyalty)*
- Guide students to take turns explaining the phrase "Absolved from Allegiance to the British Crown." (We no longer have to be loyal to Great Britain.)

Analyze the Painting

- What is happening in the picture? (The delegates are signing the Declaration of Independence.)
- Why did the artist show this event the way he did? (He shows it as an important moment. Everyone is looking toward the Declaration as it is being signed.)

3 Make Connections

Talk Encourage students to think of what happens when members of a group want different things. (Possible response: They have to compromise because most people do not agree on how to solve important problems.)

Connect to Now Have students imagine that parts of the United States have decided to become an independent nation. How would that be different from what the Congress did in 1776 when it broke away from Great Britain?

Analyze the Source

1 Inspect

Read Look at the text. What point is the author making?

- **Circle** words you don't know.
- **Underline** clues that help you understand unfamiliar words and concepts.
- **Discuss** with a partner what point the author wants the reader to understand and agree with in this final paragraph.

My Notes

_____
_____
_____
_____
_____
_____
_____
_____
_____
_____
_____
_____
_____
_____

Jefferson's Bold Declaration

In the final paragraph of the Declaration of Independence, Thomas Jefferson made the most important statements in the entire document. These statements represented the creation of a new nation, the United States of America. The colonists were now on a dangerous path from which it would be difficult to turn back.

PRIMARY SOURCE

In Their Words... the Second Continental Congress

We, therefore, the Representatives of the united States of America, in General Congress, Assembled, appealing to the Supreme Judge of the world for the rectitude of our intentions, do, in the Name, and by Authority of the good People of these Colonies, solemnly publish and declare, That these United Colonies are, and of Right ought to be Free and Independent States; that they are Absolved from all Allegiance to the British Crown, and that all political connection between them and the State of Great Britain, is and ought to be totally dissolved; and that as Free and Independent States, they have full Power to levy War, conclude Peace, contract Alliances, establish Commerce, and to do all other Acts and Things which Independent States may of right do.

—from the Declaration of Independence

John Trumbull's painting of the writers of the Declaration of Independence presenting their draft to the Second Continental Congress hangs in the United States Capitol Rotunda.

2 Find Evidence

Reread the statement "Absolved from all Allegiance to the British Crown."

Give an example of a word that means the same thing as *absolved*. Then give a word that means the same as *allegiance*. Then explain what the phrase means.

3 Make Connections

Talk Did the 56 men who signed the Declaration of Independence have the authority to separate the colonies from Great Britain? Why or why not?

The Declaration of Independence, Preamble, July 4, 1776. The U.S. National Archives and Records Administration.

(t)McGraw-Hill Education; (b)John Parrot/Stocktrek Images/Getty Images

Inquiry Journal, pp. 172–173

ENGLISH LEARNERS SCAFFOLD

ELD.PI.5.7 Evaluating how well writers and speakers use language to support ideas and opinions with details or reasons depending on modality, text type, purpose, audience, topic, and content area

Emerging

Get the Gist Provide students with a translation of the Declaration into modern English. Encourage them to work together to understand the gist of the final paragraph excerpted here.

Expanding/Bridging

Analyze Point of View Encourage students to discuss each part of the excerpt. Guide them to identify who is speaking, who the document is directed toward, and what the most important parts of the excerpt are. Have them discuss the excerpt with a partner and come up with an explanation of how the author makes his point.

See the **Language Learner Teaching Guide** for more language support strategies.

Monitor and Differentiate

REACHING ALL LEARNERS

Approaching Level

Provide sentences that help students grasp some of the archaic language in the excerpt.

*The speaker gave a **solemn** speech at the memorial service.*

*The agreement between the companies was **dissolved** after one company started stealing the other's ideas.*

*The child became an **independent** adult when he left home after graduating from high school and went to college.*

Beyond Level

Have students read more of the Declaration of Independence. Ask them to summarize what they read and present it to the whole class.

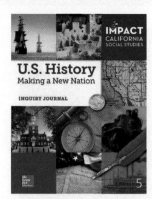

Inquiry Journal
pp. 174–175

 STANDARDS

Understand the people and events associated with the drafting and signing of the Declaration of Independence and the document's significance, including the key political concepts it embodies, the origins of those concepts, and its role in severing ties with Great Britain. **HSS.5.5.3**

(CCSS) Explain how an author uses reasons and evidence to support particular points in a text, identifying which reasons and evidence support which point(s). **CCSS.ELA.RI.5.8**

Go *Digital!*

- Model how to explore and investigate with online whole-class tools.

- Students can access the online graphic organizer to use the inquiry tools as they read.

Explore Cause and Effect

Explain Tell students that a cause is an event that makes something happen, and an effect is what happens because of that event. Some effects are the result of several causes, and some causes have multiple effects.

Read Have students read aloud the step-by-step instructions about how to identify cause and effect from a text's main ideas and details. Tell students that they should ask themselves questions such as *what happened?* and *why did it happen?* They can also look for signal words such as *because* or *so* that indicate a cause-and-effect relationship.

Guide Practice Present a brief model of a cause-and-effect relationship, such as *The colonies declared themselves to be independent from Great Britain. The effect of this declaration was that the colonies had the right to wage war, form alliances, and do anything else a free state could do.*

Investigate!

Have students read pages 210–219 in the Research Companion. Tell them the information that will help them answer the lesson question **Why is the Declaration of Independence still important today?**

Take Notes Tell students that they will take notes as they read each section. Explain that they will understand and better remember what they read when they take notes. Remind students that they should look for reasons and evidence in the text that show causes and effects.

Inspect Guide students to read the text in each section to determine what the text says. Encourage them to work to find ways to connect the information in the Declaration of Independence with something they know about the United States today.

Find Evidence Encourage students to reread the text to develop a deeper understanding. Remind students that they should think about how the facts and details will help them answer the lesson question.

Collaborative Conversations

Text-Based Discussion Remind students that discussing the text with others can help them

- Understand an author's reasons and evidence
- Practice presenting their own reasoning in a clear and effective way
- Understand someone else's perspective

Inquiry Tools

Explore Cause and Effect

A **cause** is an event that makes something else happen. An **effect** is an event that happens as a result of a cause. Looking for cause-and-effect relationships can help you better understand what you read.

To find the main idea and key details:

1. Read the text all the way through.
This will help you understand what the text is about.

2. Watch for specific changes.
Ask yourself, "What happened?" The answer to this question helps you identify an effect.

3. Look for explanations.
When you have identified an effect, ask yourself, "Why did this happen?" Knowing why something happened will help you explain its cause.

4. Look for clue words.
Words such as *because, therefore, so,* and *as a result* are clues that signal a cause-and-effect relationship. Recognizing these words will help you answer the question "Why did this happen?"

 COLLABORATE Based on the text you just read, work with your class to complete the chart below.

Cause	Effect
The colonies declare that all political connection between the United States and Great Britain is null and void.	The colonies have the right to wage war, make peace, form alliances, establish commerce, and act as free and independent states.

Investigate!

Read pages 210–219 in your Research Companion. Use your investigative skills to look for text evidence that tells you how important parts of the Declaration of Independence are still important today.

Possible responses:

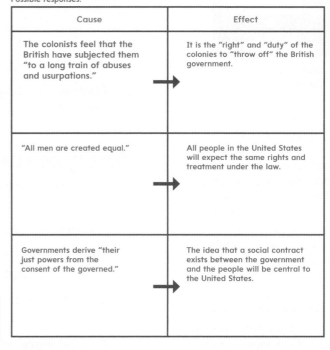

Cause	Effect
The colonists feel that the British have subjected them "to a long train of abuses and usurpations."	It is the "right" and "duty" of the colonies to "throw off" the British government.
"All men are created equal."	All people in the United States will expect the same rights and treatment under the law.
Governments derive "their just powers from the consent of the governed."	The idea that a social contract exists between the government and the people will be central to the United States.

Inquiry Journal, pp. 174–175

(EL) ENGLISH LEARNERS SCAFFOLD

ELD.PI.5.1 Exchanging information and ideas with others through oral collaborative discussions on a range of social and academic topics

Emerging

Identify Cause and Effect Encourage students to discuss with a partner the causes and effects of specific events in the text. Have them work together to distill their notes into the graphic organizer.

Expanding/Bridging

Use Signal Words Have students talk with a partner about specific sections of the text. Have them identify the causes and effects and then work together to discuss how the author presented that information. Guide them to identify signal words or other clues in the text.

See the **Language Learner Teaching Guide** for more language support strategies.

Monitor and Differentiate

REACHING ALL LEARNERS

Special Needs

Encourage students to make a version of the graphic organizer that uses large cards that can be moved around to create a mosaic on the floor. Have them write causes and effects on the cards and move them to the proper location to show their understanding of cause-and-effect relationships.

Approaching Level

Encourage students to identify at least two events to include in their graphic organizers that have multiple effects or multiple causes. Guide them to work together to discuss the relationship between those events.

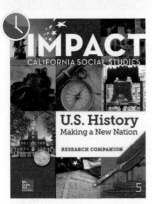

Research Companion
pp. 210–211

 STANDARDS

Understand the people and events associated with the drafting and signing of the Declaration of Independence and the document's significance, including the key political concepts it embodies, the origins of those concepts, and its role in severing ties with Great Britain. **HSS.5.5.3**

Describe the views, lives, and impact of key individuals during this period (e.g., King George III, Patrick Henry, Thomas Jefferson, George Washington, Benjamin Franklin, John Adams. **HSS.5.5.4**

Students place key events and people of the historical era they are studying in a chronological sequence and within a spatial context; they interpret time lines. **HAS.CS.1**

Go Digital!

Investigate the lesson content with online whole-class presentation tools.

- **Video:** The Declaration of Independence

Background Information

John Locke The English philosopher John Locke is the force behind two major ideas that influenced the new United States of America. The first is the social contract, which argues that a government derives its power from those who consent to be governed by it. Closely connected to this idea is his refutation of the divine right of kings to rule over their subjects absolutely.

| TIMELINE | Invite students to look at the timeline at the top on p. 211.

> **Analyze** What major battles happened before the Declaration of Independence was signed? (the Battles of Lexington and Concord) **HAS.CS.1**

Analyze the Source

Inspect Have students read pp. 210–211.

Find Evidence Use the questions below to check comprehension. Remind students to support their answers with text evidence.

> **Identify** When did the Enlightenment happen? (the seventeenth and eighteenth centuries) **DOK 1**

> **Infer** What does *divine right* mean? (*Divine* indicates that the monarch's right to rule comes from God.) **DOK 3**

> **Cite Evidence** What is the social contract, and why it is important to the Declaration of Independence? (It is the principle that a monarch only gets his or her power from the people he or she rules. The colonists felt that because of this principle, they had the right to declare their independence.) **DOK 2**

Make Connections

> **Justify** Why was the idea of a social contract so revolutionary? Use details from the text to justify your answer. (The texts states that before the Enlightenment, people believed that kings had the right to absolute power over their subjects. Replacing this belief with the idea that the ruler's power comes from the people instead of from God might have angered the monarchs and changed a lot about society.) **DOK 3**

Analyze the Painting Direct students' attention to the painting of the authors of the Declaration of Independence. Encourage them to look at details in the painting.

- Which man in the painting wrote the Declaration of Independence? Use details in the painting to find him. (The man on the left has a quill in his hand. That is what people used to write before there were pens.)

- Do you recognize any of the men in the painting? If so, who? Where have you seen his picture before? (Possible response: Benjamin Franklin; books about the American Revolution or about great inventors)

- What is the group doing? How do you know? (They are reviewing the Declaration of Independence. They are gathered around the document and some are pointing to it.)

Lesson 2

Why Is the Declaration of Independence Still Important Today?

Timeline

April 1775 Battles of Lexington and Concord

January 1776 Thomas Paine publishes *Common Sense*.

July 1776 Congress agrees on Declaration of Independence.

1775 | 1776 | 1777

May 1776 Second Continental Congress begins meeting.

August 1776 Members of Congress begin to sign Declaration of Independence.

Enlightened Thinking

Many European philosophers in the seventeenth and eighteenth centuries wanted to understand how reason and knowledge could improve people's lives. This movement was known as the Enlightenment. Thinkers such as John Locke and Thomas Hobbes in England and Jean-Jacques Rousseau (roo-SOH) in France also used these ideas to change the way people thought about government.

Before this time, most people in Europe believed that kings and queens had a divine right to rule. This right allowed the **monarchs** to rule with absolute power over their subjects. As Enlightenment ideas spread, however, people began to believe that the main duty of government was to protect its citizens. In return, the people would give their consent to be governed by a ruler. This idea is called the *social contract*.

The Enlightenment greatly influenced the American men who wrote the Declaration of Independence. The idea of the social contract is particularly important in the Declaration of Indpendence.

THE DECLARATION COMMITTEE.

The Committee of Five was appointed to draft the Declaration of Independence.

HSS.5.5.2, HSS.5.5.3, HSS.5.5.4, HAS.HR.2

210 Lesson 2 Why Is the Declaration of Independence Still Important Today?

Lesson 2 **211**

Research Companion, pp. 210–211

ENGLISH LEARNERS SCAFFOLD

ELD.PI.5.6 Reading closely literary and informational texts and viewing multimedia to determine how meaning is conveyed explicitly and implicitly through language

Emerging

Analyze Visuals
Encourage small groups of students to discuss the painting to help them understand the terms *declaration* and *committee*. Invite them to share their observations with other small groups.

Expanding/Bridging

Describe Visuals Have students use descriptive language to discuss the painting in small groups. Encourage them to use terms that relate to art that they have learned in previous lessons. Then have students draw conclusions based on their observations about the figures in the painting and the historical event it shows.

See the **Language Learner Teaching Guide** for more language support strategies.

Monitor and Differentiate

REACHING ALL LEARNERS

Approaching Level

Explain to students that they should use the information in the picture to help them understand how the Declaration of Independence was created. Point out that the committee had to work as a group to create the document. Guide them to make connections to work they do in groups at school.

Beyond Level

Have students conduct further research into the Declaration Committee. Students may choose to research one particular member of the committee, or they may choose to learn more about how the committee presented the document to the Congress. Have students share their findings with the whole class.

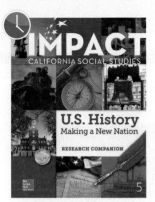

Research Companion
pp. 212–213

HSS STANDARDS

Understand the people and events associated with the drafting and signing of the Declaration of Independence and the document's significance, including the key political concepts it embodies, the origins of those concepts, and its role in severing ties with Great Britain. **HSS.5.5.3**

Describe the views, lives, and impact of key individuals during this period (e.g., King George III, Patrick Henry, Thomas Jefferson, George Washington, Benjamin Franklin, John Adams. **HSS.5.5.4**

Understand how the ideals set forth in the Declaration of Independence changed the way people viewed slavery. **HSS.5.6.7**

Students pose relevant questions about events they encounter in historical documents, eyewitness accounts, oral histories, letters, diaries, artifacts, photographs, maps, artworks, and architecture. **HAS.HR.2**

Go Digital!

Investigate the lesson content with online whole-class presentation tools.

Background Information

Adams and Jefferson John Adams had great respect for Thomas Jefferson's writing. He later said that Jefferson had a "peculiar felicity of expression," and cited that as a reason for Jefferson to write the Declaration of Independence. While they agreed on many issues, they later became political enemies. Later in their lives, however, they began a correspondence that totaled 158 letters and redeemed their friendship. They died on the same day—July 4, 1826—hundreds of miles away from each other.

Analyze the Source

Inspect Have students read Writing the Declaration on pp. 212–213.

Find Evidence Use the questions below to check comprehension. Remind students to support their answers with text evidence.

Identify What did Thomas Paine believe about America's future with Great Britain? (The relationship was ruined, and reconciliation was not possible.) **DOK 1**

Explain What events led the Second Continental Congress to debate the Declaration on Independence? (Henry Lee told Congress to consider independence. Congress created the Declaration Committee. Jefferson drafted the document. The committee reviewed it. They presented it to Congress.) **DOK 2**

Summarize What did Thomas Jefferson put into the original Declaration about slavery? (He talked about its evils.) What happened to the language? (Jefferson removed it to ensure the Southern delegates would sign the Declaration.) **DOK 3**

Analyze the Primary Source

Vocabulary Who are the *elected* and who are the *electors?* (The elected are elected representatives or rulers. The electors are the people who vote for them.) **DOK 2**

Make Inferences Why does Paine advocate for having elections often? (If they know their jobs are dependent on making the electors happy, elected officials will do a better job representing the people.) **DOK 3**

Make Connections

Draw Conclusions How does Richard Henry Lee's statement that "These United colonies are, and of a right, ought to be, free and independent states" connect to what John Locke thought about the social contract? (Locke believed that people and rulers should depend upon each other for power. Lee's statement shows that he believes the king has lost the Americans' consent to be ruled by him.) **DOK 3**

COLLABORATE
✓ Stop and Check

Talk Have students consider Jefferson's compromise on the paragraph about slavery in the Declaration. Encourage them to consider the long-term consequences of this decision. (Responses will vary, but students should acknowledge that these actions allowed slavery to continue and set the stage for the Civil War.)

Find Details Explain to students that after they read and take notes, they should think about how the information can help them answer the Essential Question.

Common Sense

Thomas Paine was living in London when he met Benjamin Franklin. Franklin advised Paine to emigrate to North America to build a new life there. When Paine arrived in Philadelphia in November 1774, the colonies were edging toward revolution. He got a job as the editor of *Pennsylvania Magazine*.

After fighting broke out in Lexington and Concord, Paine wrote a 50-page pamphlet titled *Common Sense*. He published it in January 1776. He argued that government should be a social contract, as other Enlightenment thinkers had suggested. Paine also believed that the colonies had lived through so much tyranny that there could be no **reconciliation** with Great Britain. Paine put his argument into such simple language that ordinary people easily understood his ideas. His powerful pamphlet got many colonists talking about independence.

PRIMARY SOURCE

In Their Words... Thomas Paine

. . . and that the *elected* might never form to themselves an interest separate from the *electors*, prudence will point out the propriety of having elections often; because as the *elected* might by that means return and mix again with the general body of the *electors* in a few months, their fidelity to the public will be secured by the prudent reflection of not making a rod for themselves. And as this frequent interchange will establish a common interest with every part of the community, they will mutually and naturally support each other, and on this, (not on the unmeaning name of king,) depends the *strength of government, and the happiness of the governed.*

—from *Common Sense*, published in January 1776

Writing the Declaration

In June 1776, Richard Henry Lee of Virginia told the Second Continental Congress, "These United colonies are, and of a right, ought to be, free and independent States." The Congress nominated five members to outline the colonies' reasons for wanting independence from Great Britain. The members of the committee were John Adams of Massachusetts, Benjamin Franklin of Pennsylvania, Robert Livingston of New York, Roger Sherman of Connecticut, and Thomas Jefferson of Virginia.

The committee chose Jefferson to write the first draft. He wrote for two weeks. Then Franklin and Adams made minor changes before presenting the declaration to the full Congress on June 28, 1776. The other members of the Congress argued about the wording of the document. One of the most controversial issues was language Jefferson had included about the evils of slavery. Representatives from the Southern Colonies, whose economies depended on slavery, wanted that language removed. John Adams later said, "I knew his southern brethren would never . . . [allow the section] to pass in Congress." Jefferson ultimately agreed to take out the section, and the Southern members gave their approval, leading to Congress's voting in favor of the Declaration.

Thomas Jefferson was born in Virginia.

✓ Stop and Check

Talk What prompted Congress to remove the language about slavery from the Declaration of Independence?

Find Details As you read, add new information to the graphic organizer on page 175 in your Inquiry Journal.

212 Lesson 2 Why Is the Declaration of Independence Still Important Today?

Lesson 2 213

Research Companion, pp. 212–213

 ENGLISH LEARNERS SCAFFOLD

ELD.PI.5.8 Analyzing how writers and speakers use vocabulary and other language resources for specific purposes (to explain, persuade, entertain, etc.) depending on modality, text type, purpose, audience, topic, and content area

Emerging

Provide Scaffolding Provide a translation of the primary source.

So that the officials never forget that they serve the people, you should hold elections often. This will remind the representatives that they work for the people and might lose their positions if they don't do a good job. This good relationship will make a strong nation full of happy people.

Expanding/Bridging

Unpack Language Encourage students to discuss what Paine meant by "And as this frequent interchange will establish a common interest with every part of the community, they will mutually and naturally support each other, and on this, (not on the unmeaning name of king,) depends the strength of government, and the happiness of the governed." Guide students to break the sentence into short phrases and translate each phrase into modern English.

See the **Language Learner Teaching Guide** for more language support strategies.

Monitor and Differentiate

REACHING ALL LEARNERS

Special Needs

Read aloud or have a student read aloud the excerpt from *Common Sense*. Encourage students to listen carefully and to read the text aloud to themselves before answering the questions.

Approaching Level

Encourage students to work together to identify what Thomas Paine means in the excerpt. Have them use a dictionary to identify the meanings of unfamiliar words. Supply translations into modern English as needed. Then have students make connections to the modern election process in the United States.

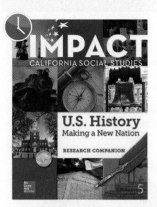

Research Companion
pp. 214–215

(HSS) STANDARDS

Know the significance of the first and second Continental Congresses and of the Committees of Correspondence. **HSS.5.5.2**

Understand the people and events associated with the drafting and signing of the Declaration of Independence and the document's significance, including the key political concepts it embodies, the origins of those concepts, and its role in severing ties with Great Britain. **HSS.5.5.3**

Describe the views, lives, and impact of key individuals during this period (e.g., King George III, Patrick Henry, Thomas Jefferson, George Washington, Benjamin Franklin, John Adams. **HSS.5.5.4**

Understand how the ideals set forth in the Declaration of Independence changed the way people viewed slavery. **HSS.5.6.7**

Go Digital!

Investigate the lesson content with online whole-class presentation tools.

Background Information

Triangle Trade Delegates from the Southern Colonies wanted to protect the practice of slavery because the economy of the South had relied upon free labor for more than a century. In the Triangle Trade, textiles and wine were shipped from Europe to Africa; Africans were kidnapped, enslaved, and taken to the Americas; and goods like cotton, sugar, and coffee were shipped from the Americas back to Europe. This reprehensible practice would continue well into the nineteenth century.

Analyze the Source

Inspect Have students read Signing the Declaration on pp. 214–215.

Find Evidence Use the questions below to check comprehension. Remind students to support their answers with text evidence.

Identify When did the members of Congress sign the Declaration of Independence? (on August 2, 1776) **DOK 1**

Infer Why was each man risking his life when he signed the Declaration? (If the United States lost the war, the king could punish each of the signers of the Declaration by taking away their property or even sentencing them to death.) **DOK 3**

Citizenship Why did John Dickinson disagree with those members of Congress who wanted independence from Great Britain? (He believed that America should reconcile with Great Britain.) **DOK 2**

Analyze the Infographic

Summarize What are the parts of the Declaration of Independence? (the preamble, an introduction to the document; a list of grievances with Great Britain; and a formal declaration that America is independent from Great Britain) **DOK 2**

Explain What is the purpose of the first paragraph, or preamble, of the Declaration of Independence? (It introduces the document and gives an overview of why the colonies are seeking their independence.) **DOK 2**

Make Connections

Draw Conclusions How did the structure of the Declaration make the representatives' argument effective? Guide students to make connections to how they structure their own written arguments. (The structure of an introduction, claims supported by evidence, and an inspiring conclusion makes any argument clear and effective.)

✓ Stop and Check

Think Have students carefully consider how King George III would have viewed the Declaration when he first read it. Remind students that at the time, many monarchs still believed they had a God-given right to rule their subjects. (Responses will vary, but students should use evidence from the text to support their response.)

Signing the Declaration

After two days of debating the details of the Declaration, the members passed the final version on July 4, 1776. Word spread. The document was reprinted in newspapers and posted in meetinghouses and churches. On August 2, the members began to sign the Declaration. John Hancock, the president of the Congress, signed first. The rest of the 56 members signed beneath his signature. Each man knew he was risking his life and his property by putting his name on the Declaration. But the signers believed so strongly in independence that they took the risk. They could only hope that the colonists' Continental Army would be strong enough to beat the British.

John Hancock was the first delegate to sign the Declaration of Independence.

Citizenship

A Call for Unity

The members knew that signing the Declaration of Independence would be viewed by the British government as an act of treason. This meant each man who signed put his life at risk. The members needed to be unified as they bravely met this danger. After signing, Ben Franklin is believed to have remarked, "We must all hang together, or assuredly we shall all hang separately."

Even though not every member of the Second Continental Congress wanted the colonies to gain independence from Great Britain, they did indeed "all hang together." John Dickinson argued that the colonies should reconcile with Great Britain. He refused to sign. After Congress passed the Declaration, however, Dickinson showed his support for the new nation by joining the Pennsylvania militia. He did this even though he had disagreed with the other delegates on the question of independence.

214　Lesson 2　Why Is the Declaration of Independence Still Important Today?

Library of Congress Prints and Photographs Division [LC-USZC2-2711]

Structure of the Declaration

Preamble

The first paragraph is the inspirational introduction to the document.

List of Grievances

This list of 27 complaints against King George outlines why the colonists want their independence from Great Britain.

Declaration of Independence

The concluding paragraph states in firm terms that the colonies are declaring themselves free and independent from Great Britain.

In CONGRESS, JULY 4, 1776.

(bkgd)McGraw-Hill Education; (c)DNY59/E+/Getty Images

✓ Stop and Check

Think Why was it important to list 27 reasons the colonists wanted to be free from King George and Great Britain?

Lesson 2　215

Research Companion, pp. 214–215

 ## ENGLISH LEARNERS SCAFFOLD

ELD.PI.5.11 Supporting own opinions and evaluating others' opinions in speaking and writing

Emerging	Expanding	Bridging
State an Opinion Work with students to understand why signing the Declaration was a major risk for the members of Congress. Encourage students to discuss what they would have done in the same situation. Remind them to refer to the text as they support their opinions.	**Support an Opinion** Have students use details from the text to support an opinion about whether or not they would have signed the Declaration, if they had been members of the Second Continental Congress. Remind them to state an opinion and support it with reasons.	**Defend an Opinion** Encourage students to quote from the text when they discuss whether or not they would have signed the Declaration of Independence. Remind them of the dangers the delegates could have faced if the United States lost the war. Have students state their views in small groups.

See the **Language Learner Teaching Guide** for more language support strategies.

Monitor and Differentiate

REACHING ALL LEARNERS

Approaching Level

Point out the structure of the Declaration of Independence. Guide small groups of students to think about why the declaration is stated at the end, referring students back to the excerpt on pp. 172 of the Inquiry Journal if needed.

Beyond Level

Divide up the 27 grievances among student pairs. Have students read their assigned grievance and report on it for the rest of the class. Have the whole group discuss why the colonists were upset about each problem and whether they think a war with Great Britain would be a good solution to that problem.

2 INVESTIGATE

Does the Declaration Still Matter?

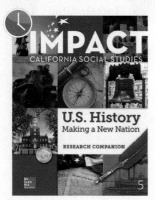

Research Companion
pp. 216–217

 STANDARDS

Understand the people and events associated with the drafting and signing of the Declaration of Independence and the document's significance, including the key political concepts it embodies, the origins of those concepts, and its role in severing ties with Great Britain. **HSS.5.5.3**

Students pose relevant questions about events they encounter in historical documents, eyewitness accounts, oral histories, letters, diaries, artifacts, photographs, maps, artworks, and architecture. **HAS.HR.2**

Go Digital!

Investigate the lesson content with online whole-class presentation tools.

Background Information

The Legacy of the Declaration of Independence Other nations around the world looked to the Declaration of Independence as a guiding principle for declaring or demanding their own right to self-government. The document was used in the French Revolution (1789) and in the ouster of the Spanish from South America (1811.)

Analyze the Source

Inspect Have students read Does the Declaration Still Matter on pp. 216–217.

Find Evidence Use the questions below to check comprehension. Remind students to support their answers with text evidence.

Identify What did the phrase "all men are created equal" mean when the Declaration was written? What does it mean today? (In 1776, it meant that all white men who owned property were created equal. Today it means that all people are created equal.) **DOK 1**

Explain What does the phrase "it is their right, it is their duty, to throw off such government" mean? (The people have an obligation to get rid of a bad government or ruler.) **DOK 1**

Infer How does the Declaration imply that war could be avoided? (It states that Great Britain and America could be friends in peace unless they wanted to be enemies in war.) **DOK 3**

Analyze the Primary Source

Vocabulary What does the phrase "We hold these truths to be self-evident" mean? (*Evident* means "clear." *Self-evident* means "clear without proof." So if a truth is "self-evident," it is so obvious that it shouldn't even need to be proven.) **DOK 3**

Context What does it mean that the rights to life, liberty, and the pursuit of happiness are "endowed by their Creator"? (It means that these rights come from God, or from simply being alive. They are natural rights.) **DOK 2**

Make Connections

Cause and Effect What events likely led Thomas Jefferson to write the phrase "Governments are instituted among Men, deriving their just powers from the consent of the governed"? (Jefferson likely read John Locke's writing about the social contract, as well as the writing of other Enlightenment thinkers who advocated for natural rights and reason.) **DOK 3**

COLLABORATE

✓ Stop and Check

Talk Encourage students to consider how America has changed since the Declaration of Independence was written. (Students should acknowledge that the meaning of the phrase has changed to include all people.)

Does the Declaration Still Matter?

More than 240 years after the Declaration of Independence was signed, it still inspires people in the United States and around the world to believe in the ideal of self-government. Part of the document's success is a result of how well Jefferson made his case. The document argues that freedom belongs to everyone and no tyrant deserves the right to rule.

Though the words are still powerful today, some of their meanings have changed. For example, our understanding of the important phrase "all men are created equal" has grown to include women, African Americans, American Indians, and people of all other backgrounds.

The phrase "Life, Liberty, and the Pursuit of Happiness" is often used today, too. It means that all people have natural rights, or rights they are born with. No government can take these rights away.

Another key phrase from the Preamble argues that a government derives its power from the "consent of the governed." This idea, taken from John Locke, describes the social contract that continues to exist between a ruler and the people: Each gains power from the other.

Independence Hall in Philadelphia, Pennsylvania, site of the Second Continental Congress

Library of Congress Prints and Photographs Division [HABS PA,51-PHILA,6--132 (CT)]

The statement "It is their right, it is their duty, to throw off such government" argues that the colonies are justified in their revolution. Because King George III was considered a tyrant, the Declaration states that it is the right and, more importantly, the duty of the colonists to "throw off" his rule over them.

What about the rest of the British people? The Declaration states that they will be considered "Enemies in War, in Peace Friends." This means that if the British continue to fight, the Americans will fight back. If they make peace, the Americans will be their friends.

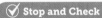
PRIMARY SOURCE

In Their Words... Thomas Jefferson

We hold these truths to be self-evident, that all men are created equal, that they are endowed by their Creator with certain unalienable Rights, that among these are Life, Liberty and the pursuit of Happiness.—That to secure these rights, Governments are instituted among Men, deriving their just powers from the consent of the governed, . . .

—from the Preamble to the Declaration of Independence

 Stop and Check

COLLABORATE

Talk Why has the meaning of the phrase "all men are created equal" changed over the years?

McGraw-Hill Education

216 Lesson 2 Why Is the Declaration of Independence Still Important Today?

Lesson 2 217

Research Companion, pp. 216–217

 ENGLISH LEARNERS SCAFFOLD

ELD.PI.5.6 Reading closely literary and informational texts and viewing multimedia to determine how meaning is conveyed explicitly and implicitly through language

Emerging

Understand an Argument Encourage students to identify the argument Jefferson makes. Provide a translation of the text into modern English.

It should be obvious, but all people are equal. Everyone has certain rights, such as the right to live, the right to be free, and the right to try to be happy. To protect these rights, people made governments. A government only has power because the people give it power.

Expanding and Bridging

Unpack Language Encourage students to consider what Jefferson meant by the phrase "that to secure these rights, Governments are instituted among Men, deriving their just powers from the consent of the governed." Have students break apart the sentence into phrases, using a dictionary to help with unfamiliar words as needed. Then have them rewrite the phrase in modern English and support a claim about why it is one of the most important phrases in the document.

See the **Language Learner Teaching Guide** for more language support strategies.

Monitor and Differentiate

REACHING ALL LEARNERS

Approaching Level

Encourage students to consider what self-government is. Then have them discuss in small groups why the principle is important in the United States. Have them share their opinions with other groups.

Beyond Level

Guide students to read the rest of the Preamble to the Declaration of Independence. Have them read the text carefully, using context clues or a dictionary to help them understand any unfamiliar words. Ask them to underline phrases that state or support the representatives' reasons for wanting independence from Great Britain. Have them share their findings with the entire class.

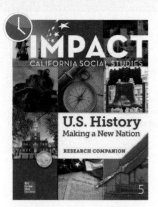

Research Companion
pp. 218–219

Students explain how the present is connected to the past, identifying both similarities and differences between the two, and how some things change over time and some things stay the same.
HAS.CS.3

Go Digital!

Investigate the lesson content with online whole-class presentation tools.

Background Information

Philadelphia Founded in 1681 by William Penn, Philadelphia sits at the junction of the Delaware and Schuylkill Rivers. By the 1770s, more than 30,000 people lived in the city. The city thrived on trade and shipping, and it became a center of culture and art during the same period in which the Founding Fathers were meeting at its State House (later renamed Independence Hall) to draft the Declaration of Independence.

Analyze the Source

Inspect Have students read Field Trip to Philadelphia on pp. 218–219.

Find Evidence Use the questions below to check comprehension. Remind students to support their answers with text evidence.

Identify Why was Philadelphia an important city in 1776? (It was centrally located among the states, and it was the largest city in the country.) **DOK 1**

Identify Where was the Liberty Bell in 1776? Where is it today? (It was in the belfry of Independence Hall. Today it is in its own building on the grounds of the Hall.) **DOK 1**

Infer Why are Benjamin Franklin's possessions still on display at Franklin Court in Philadelphia? (He was an important historical figure and an interesting person, having been an inventor, a statesman, a scientist, the post master, and a publisher. People want to know more about what he was like.) **DOK 2**

Explain Why is it important to visit or learn about historical places? (Responses will vary, but students should explain that historical sites give information about history that reading a text or a primary source cannot. They help people imagine what it was like to live during an important event of the past.) **DOK 3**

Make Connections

Draw Conclusions What does it say about the sites on this Field Trip that they are still around for us to visit today, more than 240 years later? (Students' responses will vary, but they should indicate that the sites are important to our history as a nation, so they have been preserved for future generations to visit.) **DOK 3**

 COLLABORATE

✓ Stop and Check

Talk Encourage students to share thoughts about how people traveled in 1776. Have them use their background knowledge as they explain why it was important to have a centrally located city as the meeting place for the Congress. (Students should include that Philadelphia was centrally located, making it easier for everyone to travel to.)

What Do You Think?

Encourage students to use text evidence from the whole lesson as they respond to the prompt.

Field Trip

Field Trip to Philadelphia

In 1777, Philadelphia, Pennsylvania, was the largest city in North America. It was centrally located among the new American states. This location made it a good place to hold meetings that included leaders from each state. In the city today, you can still tour Philadelphia's past.

Franklin Court

Visitors can view many objects that once belonged to Benjamin Franklin in Franklin Court. The area includes a working print shop as well as a post office once run by Franklin, who was America's first Postmaster General.

Liberty Bell

The Liberty Bell originally hung in the belfry of Independence Hall. It now resides in its own building nearby. The bell was rung for the First Continental Congress and the battles of Lexington and Concord. On July 8, 1776, the bell was rung before the public reading of the Declaration of Independence.

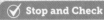

Betsy Ross House

According to legend, Betsy Ross made the first United States flag after a visit from George Washington in June 1776. During this visit, Ross showed Washington a 5-pointed star made from a folded square of cloth with a single cut of the scissors.

Elfreth's Alley

Near Independence Hall is Elfreth's Alley, the oldest street in the country. People have lived and worked in Elfreth's Alley since 1702.

✓ Stop and Check

Talk Why was Philadelphia an ideal place for the Second Continental Congress to meet?

What Do You Think? Why is the Declaration of Independence still important today?

218 Lesson 2 Why Is the Declaration of Independence Still Important Today?

Lesson 2 219

Research Companion, pp. 218–219

(EL) ENGLISH LEARNERS SCAFFOLD

ELD.PI.5.1 Exchanging information and ideas with others through oral collaborative discussions on a range of social and academic topics

Emerging

Find Context Have students work together to "walk" though the Field Trip to Philadelphia. Provide them with a map of Philadelphia and ask them to find and pinpoint the locations, if possible, to provide a sense of scale of the old part of the city.

Expanding/Bridging

Describe Encourage small groups of students to read and present on each location in the Field Trip to Philadelphia feature. Ask them to use descriptive language to tell about each place. Guide them to research terms that are unfamiliar, such as *belfry, print shop, post office,* or *5-pointed star,* using photographs to support understanding as needed.

See the **Language Learner Teaching Guide** for more language support strategies.

Monitor and Differentiate

REACHING ALL LEARNERS

Approaching Level

Have students consider what they would most like to see on a trip to historic Philadelphia. Encourage students to describe the historic site of their choice to a partner, using descriptive and spatial terms.

Beyond Level

Encourage students to identify other sites in Philadelphia that were important to the events of 1776. Have them present their findings to the whole class. Then have them plot the new sites on a map of the city to show them in relation to those listed in the Field Trip to Philadelphia.

Report Your Findings

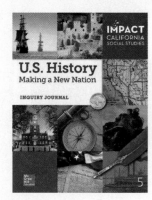

Inquiry Journal
pp. 176–177

 STANDARDS

Understand the people and events associated with the drafting and signing of the Declaration of Independence and the document's significance, including the key political concepts it embodies, the origins of those concepts, and its role in severing ties with Great Britain. **HSS.5.5.3**

Students identify and interpret the multiple causes and effects of historical events. **HAS.HI.3**

Write opinion pieces on topics or texts, supporting a point of view with reasons and information. **CCSS.ELA.W.5.1**

Engage effectively in a range of collaborative discussions (one-on-one, in groups, and teacher-led) with diverse partners on grade 5 topics and texts, building on others' ideas and expressing their own clearly. **CCSS.ELA.SL.5.1**

Go Digital!

- Students can go online to report their findings. Assess their responses online.

- Students can access the online graphic organizer to capture ideas from their investigation.

Think About It

Students will review their research and consider why the Declaration of Independence is still important today.

- Remind students to review the details about causes and effects of the language of the Declaration of Independence they have listed in their graphic organizer. Direct students back to pages 210–219 of their Research Companion if they need more information.

Write About It

Write and Cite Evidence Have students read the prompt. Explain to students that an opinion essay includes reasons that are supported by evidence from the text or from research.

Remind students to include the following elements in their response.

- State your opinion.

- Include facts and details that support your reasons.

- Use transition words to link your opinion to your reasons.

Use the rubric on p. T460 to evaluate students' work.

Talk About It

Support Your Thesis Help students pair up with a classmate and determine whether they wrote about the same or different causes and effects.

- Explain that they should take turns discussing their opinions about the Declaration of Independence and the evidence that supports their opinions.

- Students should discuss whether they agree or disagree with their partner's opinion and explain why.

- Remind students to be respectful and to follow the rules of appropriate classroom conversation.

Connect to the Essential Question

Read the prompt aloud to students. Ask them the following guiding questions:

- What are the key ideas of the Declaration of Independence? (Students should identify ideas such as the belief that all men are created equal.)

- Which of those ideas do you experience most often as someone who lives in the United States today? (Responses will vary.)

- How do you think living here might be different if the Declaration of Independence weren't remembered as an important document today, or if it hadn't been written at all? (Responses will vary.)

Remind students to use the space provided in their journal to jot down notes.

Report Your Findings

Think About It

Review your research. Based on the information you have gathered, what are the important ideas in the Declaration of Independence?

Write About It

Write and Cite Evidence
What was the most important effect of the Declaration of Independence? List reasons that support your opinion.

Sample response: "We hold these truths to be self-evident, that all men are created equal." This statement is the most important part of the Declaration of Independence because it opened the door to freedom and equality for all Americans. At the time, the idea of equality applied only to white men who owned property, but it gradually expanded to include all people.

Talk About It

Support Your Thesis
Talk to a classmate who chose a different effect. Take turns discussing your theses and supporting evidence. Do you agree or disagree with your partner's thesis? Why?

Connect to the
Civics

Make Connections
Which key ideas of the Declaration of Independence remain important today?

Sample response: The Declaration of Independence set the stage for many of the rights and protections in the United States today, such as the idea that all people are created equal, and that a social contract exists between the government and the people.

Inquiry Project Notes

McGraw-Hill Education

Inquiry Journal, pp. 176–177

EL ENGLISH LEARNERS SCAFFOLD

ELD.PII.5.2 Understanding cohesion

Emerging	Expanding	Bridging
Use Signal Words Encourage students to use signal words, such as *first, then, next,* to show how causes, effects, and other events are linked.	**Organize Your Writing** Guide students to show causal relationships by using increasingly complex signal words and phrases, such as *for example, because, as a result.*	**Organize with Style** Have students use words such as *consequently, however,* and *specifically* to show their understanding of the relationships between causes, effects, and other events.

See the **Language Learner Teaching Guide** for more language support strategies.

Monitor and Differentiate

REACHING ALL LEARNERS

Approaching Level

Have student pairs consider what makes a reason the *most important* reason. Encourage them to use these discussions as they choose one event to write about. Remind students that they should support their opinions with reasons and evidence from the text.

Beyond Level

Encourage students to write longer and more detailed explanations of why the Declaration of Independence is still important today. Have them use details from the text as well as their additional research into the document and its historical context. Remind students to use transitional words and phrases to organize their thoughts and guide their readers.

Know what your students know!

Lesson Task
Report Your Findings

Use the rubric to evaluate students' responses.

Write and Cite Evidence Students analyze what was the most important effect of the Declaration of Independence and list three reasons that support their opinion.

Support Your Thesis Students talk to a classmate who chose a different effect and take turns discussing their theses and supporting evidence.

Lesson Task Evaluation Rubric

	4	3	2	1
Historical Understanding	Strong understanding of the effects of the Declaration of Independence	Adequate understanding of the effects of the Declaration of Independence	Uneven understanding of the effects of the Declaration of Independence	No understanding the effects of the Declaration of Independence
Opinion Writing	Clearly states opinion	Adequately states opinion	Somewhat clear or unclear opinion	No opinion stated or student does not show understanding of the task
Support with Evidence	Opinion supported with relevant and adequate reasons	Opinion developed with adequate reasons	Opinion developed with uneven or few reasons	Reasons are missing or irrelevant
Support Your Thesis	Sequences ideas logically throughout discussion Includes important reasons to support opinion	Mostly sequences ideas logically Includes some reasons to support opinion	At times does not sequence ideas logically Includes few reasons to support opinion	Ideas do not follow a logical order Does not include enough reasons to support opinion

Lesson Assessment

Go *Digital!*

- Have students complete the Chapter 5 Lesson 2 Assessment online to monitor their understanding of the lesson content.

California Smarter Balanced Assessment Connections!

Standards Covered	Lesson Task	Lesson Assessment	Alignment with California Smarter Balanced Assessment
History Social Science Content 5.5.2; 5.5.3; 5.5.4; 5.6.7	✔	✔	Claim 1 Targets 8, 9, 11
History Social Science Analysis Skills Chronological and Spatial Thinking 5.1; 5.5 Research, Evidence, and Point of View 5.1; 5.2 Historical Interpretation 5.1; 5.3	✔	✔	Claim 1 Targets 8, 9, 11
Writing W.5.1	✔	✔	Claim 2 Target 6a
Research and Inquiry W.5.7		✔	Claim 4 Targets 1, 2
Reading RI.5.8	✔	✔	Claim 1 Target 11
Speaking and Listening SL.5.1	✔		Claim 3 Target 3 Claim 4 Target 1

What Were the Defining Moments of the War?

Background Information

In this lesson, students learn about the defining moments of the war, including the Battle of Saratoga and the winter at Valley Forge. They analyze why the Battle of Saratoga led to an alliance with France, which was a turning point in the war.

Community Connections

To enrich what students have learned about the defining moments of the war, plan a field trip to your local library so students can research the American Revolution.

LESSON STANDARDS

✓ Identify and map the major military battles, campaigns, and turning points of the Revolutionary War, the roles of the American and British leaders, and the Indian leaders' alliances on both sides. **HSS.5.6.1**

✓ Describe the contributions of France and other nations and of individuals to the outcome of the Revolution (e.g., Benjamin Franklin's negotiations with the French, the French navy, the Treaty of Paris, The Netherlands, Russia, the Marquis Marie Joseph de Lafayette, Tadeusz Kosciuszko, Baron Friedrich Wilhelm von Steuben). **HSS.5.6.2**

✓ Understand the personal impact and economic hardship of the war on families, problems of financing the war, wartime inflation, and laws against hoarding goods and materials and profiteering. **HSS.5.6.4**

✓ Students correctly apply terms related to time, including past, present, future, decade, century, and generation. **HAS.CS.2**

✓ Students use map and globe skills to determine the absolute locations of places and interpret information available through a map's or globe's legend, scale, and symbolic representations. **HAS.CS.4**

✓ Students pose relevant questions about events they encounter in historical documents, eyewitness accounts, oral histories, letters, diaries, artifacts, photographs, maps, artworks, and architecture. **HAS.HR.2**

✓ Students identify and interpret the multiple causes and effects of historical events. **HAS.HI.3**

Connect to the Essential Question

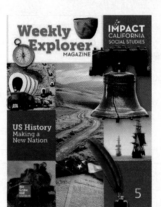

Chapter 5, pp. 58–71

The **Weekly Explorer Magazine** supports the students' exploration of the Essential Question and provides additional resources for the EQ Inquiry Project.

Inquiry Project

How Can You Make an Impact?

Remind students to use the information they learn in this lesson and other resources to complete the EQ Inquiry Project.

Dinah Zike's

In this lesson you will use Foldables.

When Minutes Count!

Suggested Lesson Pacing

1 ENGAGE
One Day

- Lesson Opener
- Analyze the Source
- Inquiry Tools

2 INVESTIGATE
Two to Three Days

 Short on Time? Look for the clock to teach core content in less time.

- Strengths and Weaknesses of the Two Sides
- Washington on the Offensive
- The Battle of Saratoga
- A Turning Point
- Winter at Valley Forge

3 REPORT
One Day

- Think About It
- Small-Group Discussions
- News Report

Make Connections!

Reading
Explain the relationships or interactions between two or more individuals, events, ideas, or concepts in a historical, scientific, or technical text based on specific information in the text. **RI.5.3**

Research
Conduct short research projects that use several sources to build knowledge through investigation of different aspects of a topic. **W.5.7**

Recall relevant information from experiences or gather relevant information from print and digital sources; summarize or paraphrase information in notes and finished work, and provide a list of sources. **W.5.8**

Writing
Write informative/explanatory texts to examine a topic and convey ideas and information clearly. **W.5.2**

Draw evidence from literary or informational texts to support analysis, reflection, and research. **W.5.9**

Speaking and Listening
Engage effectively in a range of collaborative discussions (one-on-one, in groups, and teacher-led) with diverse partners on *grade 5 topics and texts*, building on others' ideas and expressing their own clearly. **SL.5.1**

Classroom Resources

Search for additional resources using the following key words.

Benedict Arnold

General John Burgoyne

Tadeusz Kościuszko

Battle of Princeton

Casimir Pulaski

Battles of Saratoga

Baron Friedrich von Steuben

Battle of Trenton

George Washington

Valley Forge

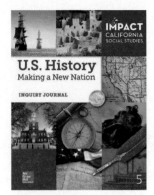

Inquiry Journal
pp. 178–179

 STANDARDS

Identify and map the major military battles, campaigns, and turning points of the Revolutionary War, the roles of the American and British leaders, and the Indian leaders' alliances on both sides. **HSS.5.6.1**

Students pose relevant questions about events they encounter in historical documents, eyewitness accounts, oral histories, letters, diaries, artifacts, photographs, maps, artworks, and architecture. **HAS.HR.2**

Go Digital!

Explore the lesson content with online whole-class presentation tools.

What Were the Defining Moments of the War?

Bellringer

Prompt students to retrieve information from the previous lessons. Say: *What events led to the writing of the Declaration of Independence?* (Congress wanted to consider the question of independence from Great Britain, so they appointed a committee of five delegates to draft a declaration listing all of their problems with the king.)

Lesson Outcomes

What Am I Learning? Have students read the Lesson Outcomes on p. 178.

Why Am I Learning It? Help students understand this meaning of the word *defining*. Guide students to consider the word in other contexts, such as the act of *defining* a word. Elicit the meaning of *definition* as it relates to an image (i.e., *high-definition*), "to show very clearly." Explain that a *defining* moment is one that shows what something is really about.

How Will I Know That I Learned It? Ask students the following questions.

- What will you learn about? (the defining moments of the war)

- What is the purpose of the task? (to write a news report that explains how the colonists ultimately won the war)

- How will you support your explanation? (with text evidence)

Talk About It

Provide some scaffolding for students to use as they discuss the picture. Provide background information as needed.

- *The painting shows _____.*
- *It looks like the main figure in the painting is _____.*
- *The other figures seem to be feeling _____ about what they are doing.*

Collaborative Conversations

Look at the Details As students engage in partner, small group, and whole-class discussions, encourage them to

- Think about how artists often show important events, and apply that knowledge to this painting.
- Ask and answer questions to identify details about the painting, the figures, and the event the painting shows.
- Draw or modify conclusions that are based on the discussion.

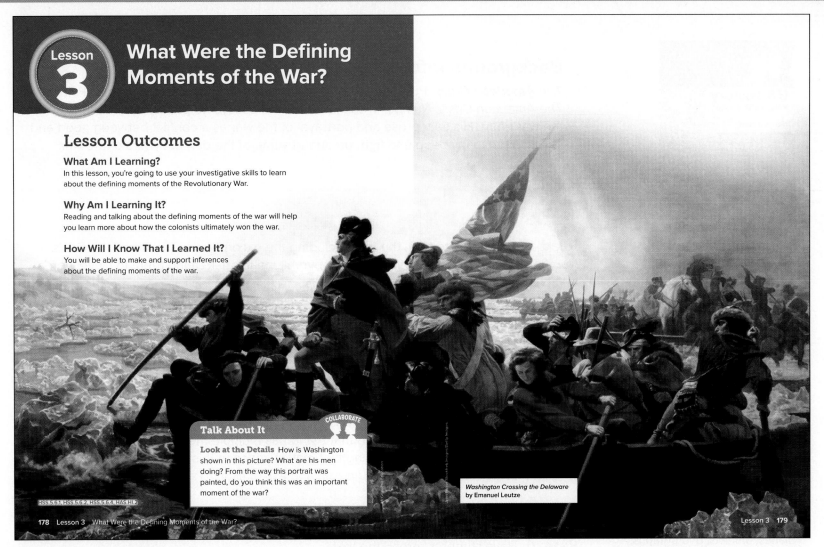

Lesson 3

What Were the Defining Moments of the War?

Lesson Outcomes

What Am I Learning?
In this lesson, you're going to use your investigative skills to learn about the defining moments of the Revolutionary War.

Why Am I Learning It?
Reading and talking about the defining moments of the war will help you learn more about how the colonists ultimately won the war.

How Will I Know That I Learned It?
You will be able to make and support inferences about the defining moments of the war.

Talk About It COLLABORATE

Look at the Details How is Washington shown in this picture? What are his men doing? From the way this portrait was painted, do you think this was an important moment of the war?

Washington Crossing the Delaware by Emanuel Leutze

178 Lesson 3 What Were the Defining Moments of the War?

Lesson 3 179

Inquiry Journal, pp. 178–179

ⒺⓁ ENGLISH LEARNERS SCAFFOLD

ELD.PI.5.6 Reading closely literary and informational texts and viewing multimedia to determine how meaning is conveyed explicitly and implicitly through language

Emerging	Expanding	Bridging
Identify Details Guide students to use the title and details in the painting to identify the people and the event shown. Encourage them to examine details closely. Explain that "Delaware" here refers to the river, and not to the state.	**Describe Details** Encourage students to use descriptive language to tell what they see in the painting. Invite students to share their descriptions with the whole class to start a discussion.	**Use Language** Have students share or write what they think about the painting, supporting their opinions with details in the image. Remind them to use appropriate language to describe an artwork.

See the **Language Learner Teaching Guide** for more language support strategies.

Monitor and Differentiate

REACHING ALL LEARNERS

Approaching Level

Work with students to identify the main figure in the painting. Guide them to ask and answer questions about the painting in small groups. Explain that in this lesson they will learn more about the event the painting shows.

On Level

Encourage students to discuss the painting with a partner. Guide them to share how they think learning about the events and people in the painting can help them to understand the defining moments of the war.

Beyond Level

Guide students to conduct research into the historical context of the painting or the artist who painted it. Invite students to share their thoughts with the whole class.

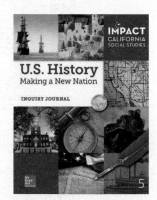

Inquiry Journal
pp. 180–181

Go Digital!

Model how to inspect and find evidence with online whole-class presentation tools.

Background Information

The American Crisis Published about a year after *Common Sense*, Thomas Paine's *The American Crisis, Number 1* was the first of 16 essays he published in defense of the war effort. His fiery prose and portrayal of the war as a conflict between good and evil inspired many people to fight on during some of the darkest years of the war.

1 Inspect

Read Ask students to skim the text, including the excerpt from *The American Crisis, Number 1*, to focus on understanding the overall meaning. Remind them to circle words that are unfamiliar.

- What is a crisis? (a major problem)

- What does it mean to "shrink from" something? (to back away from it, to decide against doing something)

- Who does Paine think "deserves the love and thanks of man and woman"? ("he that stands it now," or someone who decides to fight in the revolution)

Collaborate Have partners take turns explaining what they think "These are the times that try men's souls" means. Explain that *trying* has multiple meanings. Encourage students to look up the word to find a meaning that makes sense in this context. (Answers may include that the Revolution is very difficult, and it is difficult to stay positive.)

2 Find Evidence

Reread Have students reread the text.

Analyze the Primary Source Reread the excerpt aloud then analyze it as a class.

- Ask: What feelings do the phrases "summer soldier" and "sunshine patriot" create? (The words "summer" and "sunshine" make us think of things that are pleasant or easy.)

- Why does Paine think these types of people would "shrink from the service of their country"? (These people are only interested in taking the easy route, and the Revolution is difficult.)

- What does *esteem* mean? Encourage students to use *self-esteem* to help them define the word in context. (to think well of something)

Analyze the Painting Explain to students that they will learn in this lesson more about the hardships the American troops faced during the winter of 1777–1778 at Valley Forge. Ask them to identify elements of the painting that give them some information about what being a soldier in the American Revolution could be like.

3 Make Connections
COLLABORATE

Talk Guide students to consider what Paine thinks the Americans should do as a result of reading his essay. (Paine wants Americans to keep fighting the Revolution.)

Connect to Now Have partners discuss how Paine's words could apply to a challenge that the United States or the world is currently facing.

1 Inspect

Read Look at the text. What point is the author making?

- **Circle** words you don't know.
- **Underline** clues that help you understand unfamiliar words and concepts.
- **Discuss** with a partner what the first sentence means: "These are the times that try men's souls." How does that phrase describe what the Revolutionary War was like?

My Notes

_____
_____
_____
_____
_____
_____
_____
_____
_____
_____
_____

Trying Times

From 1776 to 1783, Thomas Paine published a series of sixteen papers called *The American Crisis*. The essays described the conflict with Great Britain as a fight between good and evil.

Paine wrote the first essay in December 1776. During the brutal winter of 1777–1778 at Valley Forge, George Washington ordered that the paper be read aloud to the troops. He hoped that it would inspire them to continue fighting despite the cold, disease, and starvation they faced.

PRIMARY SOURCE

In Their Words... Thomas Paine

These are the times that try men's souls. The summer soldier and the sunshine patriot will, in this crisis, shrink from the service of their country; but he that stands it now, deserves the love and thanks of man and woman. Tyranny, like hell, is not easily conquered; yet we have this consolation with us, that the harder the conflict, the more glorious the triumph. What we obtain too cheap, we esteem too lightly: it is dearness only that gives every thing its value.

—from *The American Crisis*, Number 1.

American soldiers endured brutal winters during the war.

Paine, Thomas. *The American Crisis*. London: Carlile, 1819.

(t)McGraw-Hill Education; (b)National Archives/Record Group 111/Photographs of American Military Activities

2 Find Evidence

Reread Examine the statement "the summer soldier and the sunshine patriot will, in the crisis, shrink from the service of their country." What type of people is Paine describing? What other types of people does Paine mention?

Put the phrase "What we obtain too cheap, we esteem too lightly" into your own words. What is Paine saying about the American Revolution with this phrase?

3 Make Connections

Talk What did Paine want to convince the readers of *The American Crisis* to do?

Inquiry Journal, pp. 180–181

(EL) ENGLISH LEARNERS SCAFFOLD

ELD.PI.5.7 Evaluating how well writers and speakers use language to support ideas and opinions with details or reasons depending on modality, text type, purpose, audience, topic, and content area

Emerging

Identify Nuances Provide students with a translation of the excerpt into modern English. Encourage them to work together to understand the gist of Paine's argument. Point out words that have surprising negative connotations in this context, such as "summer" and "sunshine."

Expanding/Bridging

Explain the Argument Encourage students to explain Paine's argument. Provide assistance with difficult language and syntax as needed. Have students share their thoughts about why Paine's attempt to persuade his readers is or is not effective.

See the **Language Learner Teaching Guide** for more language support strategies.

Monitor and Differentiate

REACHING ALL LEARNERS

Approaching Level

Have students break the text into phrases. Then have them work together to identify key words that signal important details as well as words they do not know. As a group, have students paraphrase the excerpt. Then have them chorally read the excerpt.

Beyond Level

Encourage students to read more of *The American Crisis, Number 1*. Have them look for common themes in the text that signal how Paine presents his argument. Explain that one of the reasons Paine's work was so popular is that his argument was easy to understand. Have students present their evaluations of whether this is still the case today.

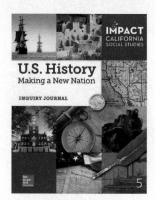

Inquiry Journal
pp. 182–183

 STANDARDS

Identify and map the major military battles, campaigns, and turning points of the Revolutionary War, the roles of the American and British leaders, and the Indian leaders' alliances on both sides. **HSS.5.6.1**

Describe the contributions of France and other nations and of individuals to the outcome of the Revolution (e.g., Benjamin Franklin's negotiations with the French, the French navy, the Treaty of Paris, The Netherlands, Russia, the Marquis Marie Joseph de Lafayette, Tadeusz Kosciuszko, Baron Friedrich Wilhelm von Steuben). **HSS.5.6.2**

(CCSS) Explain the relationships or interactions between two or more individuals, events, ideas, or concepts in a historical, scientific, or technical text based on specific information in the text. **CCSS.ELA.RI.5.3**

Go Digital!

- Model how to explore and investigate with online whole-class tools.

- Students can access the online graphic organizer to use the inquiry tools as they read.

Explore Making Inferences

Explain Tell students that when they make an inference, they combine what they already know with evidence from the text. Grounding an inference in text evidence is what distinguishes an inference from a guess.

Read Have students read aloud the step-by-step instructions about how to make a valid inference about a text. Tell students that they should ask themselves questions such as *What does the text say?* and *What do I already know?* They should also look for key details that signal important information.

Guide Practice Present a brief model of making an inference about a text, such as *George Washington must have believed that Thomas Paine's words were inspiring. I think this is true because I have read the excerpt, and I found it to be inspiring. If Washington thought it was important enough to read aloud to the troops, he must have thought so too.* Model filling out the graphic organizer with details from the text using a similar thought process.

Investigate!

Have students read pages 220–229 in the Research Companion. Tell them the information that will help them answer the lesson question **What Were the Defining Moments of the War?**

✏️ **Take Notes** Tell students that they will take notes as they read each section. Explain that taking notes will help them understand and make inferences about what they read. Remind students that they should look for key details and important information in the text.

Inspect Guide students to read the text in each section to determine what the it says. Encourage them to work to find evidence about defining moments in the Revolutionary War that helps them to make inferences about the events.

Find Evidence Encourage students to reread the text to develop a deeper understanding. Remind students that they should think about how the facts and details will help them answer the lesson question.

Collaborative Conversations

Text-Based Discussion Remind students that discussing the text with others can help them

- Understand how others make and support inferences
- Apply knowledge that they have already gained
- Understand someone else's perspective

Inquiry Tools

Explore Making Inferences

When you read, you make inferences about the text when the author does not directly state his or her purpose or point. To make a valid inference, you combine **evidence** from the text with what you know from your own experience.

To make an inference:

1. **Read the text all the way through.**
   This will tell you what the text is about.

2. **Reread the text looking for important information - key details, facts, and evidence.**
   Keep track of these clues. They will help you infer.

3. **Ask yourself, *What does the text say?***
   Consider the key ideas the author is telling you.

4. **Then ask yourself, *What do I already know?***
   Connect something you already know with key ideas you have learned from the text to make an observation.

COLLABORATE Based on the text you just read, work with your class to complete the chart below.

Text Evidence	What I Know	Inference
Washington had *The American Crisis* read to soldiers during their most challenging time.	People need inspiration during difficult times.	*The American Crisis* helped inspire the Continental Army when it needed it most.

IMPACT
U.S. History
Making a New Nation
RESEARCH COMPANION

Investigate!

Read pages 220–229 in your Research Companion. Use your investigative skills to look for text evidence that tells you about the defining moments of the Revolutionary War and helps you make inferences about those events.

Text Evidence	What I Know	Inference
Washington attacked the enemy in New Jersey just before his soldiers' term of service ran out.	Washington had lost battles in New York.	Washington needed to win battles to gain the confidence of his soldiers so that they would stay in the army.
After the British were defeated at the Battle of Saratoga, other European powers provided funding and supplies to the United States.	Funding and supplies are important to any war effort, and they were badly needed by the Continental Army.	The Americans might not have won the war without the support of European nations. Saratoga was an important turning point.
During a brutal winter at Valley Forge, 1777–1778, Washington made sure his army received military training.	In times of great hardship, people need strength, sacrifice, and leadership.	Washington's leadership kept his army together. While the men suffered, they also persevered and came out of the winter better trained.

Inquiry Journal, pp. 182–183

(EL) ENGLISH LEARNERS SCAFFOLD

ELD.PI.5.1 Exchanging information and ideas with others through oral collaborative discussions on a range of social and academic topics

Emerging

Identify Key Details Encourage students to answer questions about the text that help them find details. Have students ask and answer *who, what, where, when, why,* and *how* questions to understand the text.

Expanding/Bridging

Discuss Details Have students discuss specific sections of the text as they make and support inferences about it. Guide them to follow rules for classroom conversations by asking relevant questions, affirming or respectfully disagreeing with others, or providing feedback to group members about the validity of their inferences.

See the **Language Learner Teaching Guide** for more language support strategies.

Monitor and Differentiate

REACHING ALL LEARNERS

Special Needs

Encourage students to draw to show their understanding of how to make and support inferences. Students may create illustrated graphic organizers, or they may annotate the text or make notecards.

Approaching Level

Encourage students to work with a partner to confirm the validity of their inferences. Have students review each other's graphic organizers to confirm the truth of their background knowledge and their use of evidence. Have students answer the question *Does this make sense?*

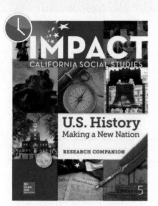

Research Companion
pp. 220–221

 STANDARDS

Identify and map the major military battles, campaigns, and turning points of the Revolutionary War, the roles of the American and British leaders, and the Indian leaders' alliances on both sides. **HSS.5.6.1**

Understand the personal impact and economic hardship of the war on families, problems of financing the war, wartime inflation, and laws against hoarding goods and materials and profiteering. **HSS.5.6.4**

Students place key events and people of the historical era they are studying in a chronological sequence and within a spatial context; they interpret time lines. **HAS.CS.1**

Go Digital!

Investigate the lesson content with online whole-class presentation tools.

Background Information

British Taxes Great Britain funded the war in part by taxing its citizens, who were taxed even more heavily before the war than the rebellious Americans. An average British citizen paid about 26 shillings per year in taxes, compared to about 1 shilling per year paid by every American colonist.

| TIMELINE | Invite students to look at the timeline at the top on p. 221.

Analyze What major battles occurred in 1777? (Battles in New Jersey and Saratoga) **HAS.CS.1**

Analyze the Source

Inspect Have students read pp. 220–221.

Find Evidence Use the questions below to check comprehension. Remind students to support their answers with text evidence.

Identify What resources gave Great Britain an advantage? (wealth, equipment, and soldiers) **DOK 1**

Infer Why would resources like money and equipment provide an advantage to Great Britain? (Wars are expensive because soldiers must be paid, fed, and given weapons.) **DOK 3**

Cite Evidence How did American colonists support the war effort? (They made musket balls and blankets for the soldiers.) **DOK 2**

Explain Why did many American soldiers desert the army? (Congress often did not have enough money to pay the troops or to keep them clothed, fed, or armed. As a result, many quit fighting.) **DOK 3**

Make Connections

Justify Was King George III right to raise taxes on British citizens to help pay for the war effort? Justify your response with evidence. (Responses will vary, but students should support their answers with evidence from the this lesson or a previous lesson in the text.) **DOK 3**

Analyze the Painting Direct students' attention to the painting of the Battle of Virginia Capes. Encourage them to look at details in the painting to learn more about it.

- What is happening in the scene, and how do you know? (Two groups of ships are fighting. One group is French, and the other is British. The caption explains the event, and you can tell the sides apart because of the flags at the top of each ship.)

- What do you notice about these participants in the American Revolution? (Possible response: None of the ships belong to the United States. France is fighting on behalf of the United States.)

Lesson 3

What Were the Defining Moments of the War?

Timeline

April 1775 Battles of Lexington and Concord

July 1776 Congress agrees on Declaration of Independence.

January 1777 After a series of losses in New York, George Washington's Continental Army triumphs over British twice in New Jersey.

| | 1775 | | | 1776 | | | 1777 | | | 1778 | | | 1779 | | |

1777–1778 Washington's Continental Army endures a brutal winter at Valley Forge in Pennsylvania.

February 1778 Americans and French sign Treaty of Alliance.

September 1777 British suffer a major defeat at the Battle of Saratoga.

Strengths and Weaknesses of the Two Sides

The American Revolution presented challenges for both the British and the Americans. Neither side was prepared to fight a war that would last eight years. They would often have shortages of equipment, soldiers, and the money to pay for both. While a wealthy and powerful nation like Britain would seem to have a great advantage, both sides had their strengths and weaknesses.

The war was very expensive for Britain. All soldiers and supplies had to be sent by ship across the Atlantic Ocean. Britain financed the war by raising taxes on citizens living in Britain. Many British people disagreed with the war because they did not want higher taxes.

The American army received its funding from the Second Continental Congress. Congress, however, often did not have enough money to pay soldiers or buy supplies or food for them. As a result, it was difficult to keep men from deserting, or leaving the army. Some people, known as **profiteers**, took advantage of the poor wartime economy to hoard goods and sell them at high prices. However, the war had tremendous support from civilians in the colonies. To help with the war effort, civilians made musket balls and blankets. They gathered food and supplies to send to the front.

French ships (on the left) battle the British Navy during the Revolutionary War. France's entry into the war on the American side was a defining moment of the war.

HSS.5.6.1, HSS.5.6.2, HSS.5.6.4

220 Lesson 3 What Were the Defining Moments of the War?

Lesson 3 **221**

Research Companion, pp. 220–221

ENGLISH LEARNERS SCAFFOLD

ELD.PII.5.1 Understanding text structure

Emerging	Expanding/Bridging
Organize Information Work with students to take notes about what they read. Invite them to write information about the painting and the text. Have them write how the painting helps them understand more about the text and how the text helps them understand more about the painting.	**Describe Visuals** Have students use descriptive language to discuss the painting in small groups. Encourage them to use terms that relate to art that they have learned in previous lessons. Then have students draw conclusions based on their observations about the painting and the historical event it shows.

See the **Language Learner Teaching Guide** for more language support strategies.

Research Companion
pp. 222–223

 STANDARDS

Identify and map the major military battles, campaigns, and turning points of the Revolutionary War, the roles of the American and British leaders, and the Indian leaders' alliances on both sides. **HSS.5.6.1**

Students pose relevant questions about events they encounter in historical documents, eyewitness accounts, oral histories, letters, diaries, artifacts, photographs, maps, artworks, and architecture. **HAS.HR.2**

Go Digital!

Investigate the lesson content with online whole-class presentation tools.

Background Information

German Mercenaries It was tradition for the British government to use foreign soldiers to supplement their own troops. At one point, the British employed about 30,000 mercenaries. These soldiers-for-hire came from several German kingdoms.

Analyze the Source

Inspect Have students read Washington on the Offensive on pp. 222–223.

Find Evidence Use the questions below to check comprehension. Remind students to support their answers with text evidence.

Identify What advantages did the British have over the Americans? (The British had more soldiers who were better trained and armed.) **DOK 1**

Identify What advantages did the Americans have over the British? (The Americans were more familiar with the landscape.) **DOK 1**

Infer Why would underestimating American perseverance become a downfall for the British? (Students may identify that a power who thinks they will win might miss opportunities, which could give their opponent an advantage.) **DOK 2**

Explain What happened to the Americans after the start of the war? (The Americans suffered defeats and some lost morale.) **DOK 2**

Summarize How did George Washington outsmart the British at Trenton and Princeton? (He crossed the Delaware River at night to surprise and defeat the British at Trenton. Then he left his campfires burning so the British would not know his men had slipped away to Princeton.) **DOK 3**

Make Connections

Draw Conclusions Review the painting *Washington Crossing the Delaware* that you analyzed on p. 179 of the Inquiry Journal. Reread the section about the event. How does the painting show what happened? Based on the time of year that Washington's men had to make this journey, do you think the painting accurately depicts what they experienced? Why is the painting a useful artifact for understanding the events? (Responses will vary, but students should provide a comparison and contrast between the actual events and how they are shown in the painting.) **DOK 3**

Stop and Check

Talk Have students consider why Washington needed to prove that he could win. Then have them discuss how he did it. (Responses may include that he used the advantages he had available to him, or he risked losing his men's trust and the war itself.)

Find Details Explain to students that after they read and take notes, they should think about how the information can help them answer the Essential Question.

The British had more soldiers, including American Indians and paid German **mercenaries**, or people who fight for money. The British soldiers were also better trained and armed than the American soldiers. However, the British soldiers were trained to fight only in open battlefields. Americans were more familiar with the land where they lived. The Americans took advantage of this British weakness to surprise the British in different kinds of terrain such as the swamps of the south and the forests of the north. The Americans' more plain-looking clothes helped them blend into the landscape, while the British soldiers' red coats made them easy targets.

Ultimately, the British failed to recognize both their own weaknesses and the Americans' strengths. One of their biggest mistakes was underestimating the Americans' willingness to risk everything to win their independence.

British soldiers were trained to fight only in open battlefields. Their red coats made them easy targets.

Michael Melford/National Geographic/Getty Images

222 Lesson 3 What Were the Defining Moments of the War?

Washington on the Offensive

After the Battles of Lexington and Concord and the signing of the Declaration of Independence, the Americans suffered some major setbacks. The Continental Army lost important battles in New York state. By the middle of 1776, George Washington's soldiers had been driven into Pennsylvania.

Washington needed victories to boost his soldiers' morale. He was concerned that many would leave his army and go home when their term of service ran out. On Christmas night, 1776, he led 2,400 soldiers across the Delaware River from Pennsylvania into New Jersey.

The army reached Trenton at dawn and attacked at once, surprising and defeating German mercenaries who were fighting for the British. A few days later, Washington won another victory when his soldiers left their campfires burning near Trenton so the British would not be aware that they had snuck away to attack Princeton successfully. It became clear that the Americans had a chance of winning the war after all.

✓ Stop and Check

Talk How did Washington prove in 1776 and 1777 that he was capable of defeating the British troops?

Find Details As you read, add new information to the graphic organizer on page 183 in your Inquiry Journal.

Library of Congress, Prints and Photographs Division (LC-USZC4-2737)

Commander-in-Chief George Washington led the Continental Army.

Lesson 3 **223**

Research Companion, pp. 222–223

(EL) ENGLISH LEARNERS SCAFFOLD

ELD.PI.5.3 Offering and supporting opinions and negotiating with others in communicative exchanges

Emerging

State an Opinion Encourage students to state an opinion about whether George Washington succeeded in proving he could lead the Americans to victory. Guide them to support their thinking during discussion.

Expanding/Bridging

Support an Opinion Guide students to support their opinion about whether Washington proved he was capable of leading the Americans to victory. During discussion, prompt students to be assertive in stating their thoughts, while providing counterarguments to their partners' statements when needed. Provide sentence frames:

I think _____.

That's interesting, but have you thought of _____?

I disagree because _____.

See the **Language Learner Teaching Guide** for more language support strategies.

Monitor and Differentiate

REACHING ALL LEARNERS

Special Needs

Encourage students to use images to help them understand what happened during this period of the war. Ask them to explain what is happening in the painting on p. 223, including how the soldiers seem to react to George Washington. Guide students to apply their knowledge when rereading the text.

Beyond Level

Encourage students to conduct additional research into how the British fought the war. Students may choose to research topics such as British use of German mercenaries, how the British funded the war by raising taxes on citizens, or how they transported supplies across the Atlantic Ocean. Have students share their findings with the whole class.

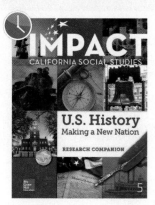

Research Companion
pp. 224–225

 STANDARDS

Identify and map the major military battles, campaigns, and turning points of the Revolutionary War, the roles of the American and British leaders, and the Indian leaders' alliances on both sides. **HSS.5.6.1**

Describe the contributions of France and other nations and of individuals to the outcome of the Revolution (e.g., Benjamin Franklin's negotiations with the French, the French navy, the Treaty of Paris, The Netherlands, Russia, the Marquis Marie Joseph de Lafayette, Tadeusz Kosciuszko, Baron Friedrich Wilhelm von Steuben). **HSS.5.6.2**

Go Digital!

Investigate the lesson content with online whole-class presentation tools.

Background Information

Iroquois League Dating from about 1600, the Iroquois League consisted of northeastern American Indians who worked together in government and in warfare. The group stayed more or less united until the American Revolution, when the Tuscarora and Oneida defected to support the Americans, while the remainder of the Confederacy fought for the British.

Analyze the Source

Inspect Have students read The Battle of Saratoga on pp. 224–225.

Find Evidence Use the questions below to check comprehension. Remind students to support their answers with text evidence.

Identify How did General Burgoyne plan to defeat the Americans in the Hudson River Valley? (by cutting off New York and New Jersey from the rest of the nation) **DOK 1**

Infer Why might Burgoyne have thought it was a good idea to work with Mohawk and Iroquois scouts? (He may have realized that the Americans often had the advantage of knowing the landscape better than the British. By using the help of American Indian scouts, he could try to improve his chances against the Americans.) **DOK 3**

Summarize Why did the Iroquois and Mohawk eventually desert the British? (They began to doubt promises the British had made about protecting the American Indians' lands from further settlement.) **DOK 2**

Explain What did Tadeusz Kościuszko do to help the Americans at the Battle of Saratoga? (He helped them fortify walls and roads so they could defend themselves and easily get more supplies.) **DOK 2**

Then and Now

Provide an Opinion What do you think you might learn from a visit to the site of the Battles of Saratoga? (Responses will vary, but students may identify that visiting a historic place might give them a sense of what it was like to be there during one of the battles.) **DOK 2**

Make Connections

Draw Conclusions Why do you think General Burgoyne did not want to give up on his plans to defeat the Americans at Saratoga? Use evidence from the text to support your response. (Responses will vary, but students should use evidence from the text to try to understand Burgoyne's point of view.)

The Battle of Saratoga

In 1777, the British decided to try to capture the Hudson River Valley, cutting off New York and New Jersey from the states in New England. British General John Burgoyne believed this would fatally weaken the American army. His army invaded the valley from its base in Canada.

British General Burgoyne surrenders at Saratoga, New York.

Part of Burgoyne's plan depended on help from Mohawk and Iroquois scouts. Burgoyne's army became bogged down in terrain made difficult by forests and swamps. The Mohawk and Iroquois began to lose confidence in British promises that they could prevent more colonists from taking their lands. As the scouts drifted away, Burgoyne had no information about where the Americans were or what they were doing.

The Americans, on the other hand, were prepared. General Thomas Gates planned an attack on British forces near Saratoga, New York. The American fighting force was three times the size of that of the British. Gates also sent expert riflemen to attack British troops as they moved through New York. By the time the British forces reached Saratoga, they had been badly weakened.

Even though his troops were weakened and outnumbered, Burgoyne was sure he could still defeat the Americans. He chose to attack at Freeman's Farm near Saratoga. Before the British could attack, however, a Polish engineer named Tadeusz Kościuszko (tah-DEH-oosh kohsh-CHOOSH-koh) helped the Americans fortify the walls around Freeman's Farm and the surrounding roads. Kościuszko helped protect the Americans and their supply lines from the British attack in this first Battle of Saratoga. General Gates was also able to obtain fresh troops to strengthen his lines of defense against the British.

Then and Now

The battlefields of Saratoga are now part of a National Park. When you visit, you can go on a self-guided tour. You can see a monument, a 155-foot tall obelisk to the American victory. You can also take a walk through Victory Woods, the site of General Burgoyne's last encampment before surrendering.

Research Companion, pp. 224–225

ENGLISH LEARNERS SCAFFOLD

ELD.PI.5.1 Exchanging information and ideas with others through oral collaborative discussions on a range of social and academic topics

Emerging

Outline Events Have students work together to create an outline of the events of the Battle of Saratoga. Students may choose to write on large note cards and place them to form a timeline.

Expanding/Bridging

Retell Events Encourage students to reread the pages about the Battle of Saratoga and take notes or make a timeline. Then have them work with partners or in small groups to retell or act out the events, using their notes as a guide. Remind students to use language that is specific to wartime or battles as they discuss the events.

See the **Language Learner Teaching Guide** for more language support strategies.

Monitor and Differentiate

REACHING ALL LEARNERS

Approaching Level

Have students consider the events that weakened Burgoyne's army. For instance, have them create a list of hardships or attacks. Work with students to understand language such as *bogged down* and *riflemen*. Then have them discuss how these setbacks affected the outcome of the battle.

Beyond Level

Guide students to conduct further research into the Mohawk and Iroquois involvement in the war. Students may research the history of the Iroquois Confederacy, or they may choose to focus on events specific to the American Revolution. Guide them to identify why some groups sided with the British while others sided with the Americans.

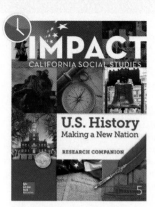

Research Companion
pp. 226–227

 STANDARDS

Identify and map the major military battles, campaigns, and turning points of the Revolutionary War, the roles of the American and British leaders, and the Indian leaders' alliances on both sides. **HSS.5.6.1**

Describe the contributions of France and other nations and of individuals to the outcome of the Revolution (e.g., Benjamin Franklin's negotiations with the French, the French navy, the Treaty of Paris, The Netherlands, Russia, the Marquis Marie Joseph de Lafayette, Tadeusz Kosciuszko, Baron Friedrich Wilhelm von Steuben). **HSS.5.6.2**

Students identify and interpret the multiple causes and effects of historical events. **HAS.HI.3**

CCSS Explain the relationships or interactions between two or more individuals, events, ideas, or concepts in a historical, scientific, or technical text based on specific information in the text. **CCSS.ELA.RI.5.3**

Go *Digital!*

Investigate the lesson content with online whole-class presentation tools.

Background Information

Alliance with France Although France did not formally declare its support for the United States prior to the Treaty of Alliance in 1778, it had been secretly providing resources since the revolution began. France was eager to see Britain lose what it had gained by defeating France in the Seven Years' War in the previous decade, but France did not want to risk provoking Great Britain until it was sure the United States could win the conflict.

Analyze the Source

Inspect Have students read A Turning Point on pp. 226–227.

Find Evidence Use the questions below to check comprehension. Remind students to support their answers with text evidence.

Identify What happened in the Second Battle of Saratoga? (American General Benedict Arnold beat a group of soldiers who had been trying to scout for more information.) **DOK 1**

Explain How are the two battles at Saratoga alike and different? (The first battle was at Freeman's Farm. The British attacked. The second battle happened when American soldiers engaged British scouts. The Americans won both battles.) **DOK 3**

Vocabulary What does an *ambassador* do? Use context clues. (As an ambassador, Franklin created a deal with the French government. Franklin was an American who must have spent a lot of time in France to make those arrangements. An ambassador must be an official who represents his or her country in another country.) **DOK 3**

Biography

Summarize How did Tadeusz Kościuszko prove his worth to the American Army? (Over time he showed that he had skills to provide as an engineer, first for Congress and then at Saratoga and at other battles later in the war.) **DOK 2**

Make Connections

Identify Cause and Effect What was the Treaty of Alliance? Why was it important? (The Treaty of Alliance was an agreement between the United States and France. France sent troops, ships, and supplies to the Americans to help them win the war. Because France and Spain were allies, Spain began to help the United States too.) **DOK 3**

☑ Stop and Check

Think Encourage students to consider why an army needs to have easy access to roads and why those roads need to be protected. (An army needs to be able to get more soldiers and supplies.)

Talk Encourage students to consider what happened as a result of the victory at Saratoga. (France made an alliance with the United States, giving them access to supplies and weapons.)

Throughout September 1777, American riflemen who were hidden in the hillsides shot at any British soldier who tried to fetch water from the Hudson River. This further weakened the British troops. On October 7, American General Benedict Arnold's forces drove back a portion of Burgoyne's soldiers who had been scouting the area to gain information. This battle became known as the Second Battle of Saratoga.

By mid-October, Burgoyne's troops were greatly reduced in number. As a result of the Americans' preparedness, the British were cut off from receiving more supplies. They were running out of food. Finally, after two more months of fighting, Burgoyne decided to surrender to Gates on October 17. The victory at Saratoga changed the direction of the war.

Biography

Tadeusz Kościuszko

Born in Poland, Tadeusz Kościuszko emigrated to the United States in 1776. He immediately joined the American fight for independence. Because he was a skilled engineer, Kościuszko was asked to help fortify the meeting place of the Continental Congress. In 1777, he joined General Gates in upstate New York. There, he helped fortify Freeman's Farm and the American supply lines. He went on to prove his bravery and cleverness at several more battles during the war before being promoted to the rank of brigadier general. After the Revolution, he was granted American citizenship.

✓ Stop and Check

Think Why did it matter that the American forces were able to fortify Freeman's Farm and the surrounding roads before the British attacked?

The Miriam and Ira D. Wallach Division of Art, Prints and Photographs, Print Collection, Emmet Collection of Manuscripts Etc. Reading to American History, The New York Public Library

A Turning Point

The Americans' victory at the two Battles of Saratoga proved to the rest of the world that the Americans were capable of defeating the British. In 1777 and 1778, Benjamin Franklin, who was then the American Ambassador to France, worked with French officials to create the Treaty of Alliance. As a result of this treaty, France sent troops, warships, and supplies to the United States.

Individual Europeans agreed to come to the aid of the United States, too. Baron Friedrich von Steuben of Prussia helped to train American soldiers to fight together. Casimir Pulaski of Poland trained soldiers to fight on horseback and became a general. He gave his life in battle for American independence. The Marquis de Lafayette of France became a valuable member of Washington's staff. He would prove his worth at the Battle of Yorktown.

Since it was allied with France, Spain also joined America's struggle with Great Britain. In 1779, the governor of the Spanish territory of Louisiana closed the port of New Orleans to British ships and opened it to American ships. Spain also made loans to support the American war effort. Spanish Colonel Bernárdo de Galvez led a force to fight the British in the South.

Casimir Pulaski

(I)McGraw-Hill Education; (b)Bettmann/Getty Images

✓ Stop and Check

Talk Why was the Battle of Saratoga a turning point in the Revolutionary War?

Research Companion, pp. 226–227

 ## ENGLISH LEARNERS SCAFFOLD

ELD.PI.5.6 Reading closely literary and informational texts and viewing multimedia to determine how meaning is conveyed explicitly and implicitly through language

Emerging

Use Context Clues Encourage students to use context clues to help them understand the following words from the first paragraph on p. 227. Remind them that a word's context is the words and sentences that surround it. Clues often come from other words that give a definition for the unfamiliar word or tell what it is *not*. Guide them to use their new understanding of these words as they reread the paragraph.

proved, capable, defeating, officials

Expanding/Bridging

Unpack Language Have students work together to unpack phrases such as *member of Washington's staff, prove his worth,* and *American war effort.* Guide them to reread the text and use context clues or a dictionary to understand the meaning of each phrase. Encourage students to use these phrases in new sentences during their discussions with a partner.

See the **Language Learner Teaching Guide** for more language support strategies.

Monitor and Differentiate

REACHING ALL LEARNERS

Approaching Level

Guide students to identify the reasons the Battle of Saratoga was a turning point in the war. Encourage students to reread the sections on the battle and make a graphic organizer to collect their notes. Then have students discuss why the Treaty of Alliance was so important. Remind students to use what they may already know about the outcome of the American Revolution in their discussion.

Beyond Level

Guide students to conduct further research into one of the Europeans who came to help the United States win the war. Students may choose to research one of the individuals listed in this section, or they may choose to write about someone else. Have students briefly present their findings to the whole class.

IMPACT
CALIFORNIA SOCIAL STUDIES

U.S. History
Making a New Nation

RESEARCH COMPANION

5

Research Companion
pp. 228–229

 STANDARDS

Identify and map the major military battles, campaigns, and turning points of the Revolutionary War, the roles of the American and British leaders, and the Indian leaders' alliances on both sides. **HSS.5.6.1**

Describe the contributions of France and other nations and of individuals to the outcome of the Revolution (e.g., Benjamin Franklin's negotiations with the French, the French navy, the Treaty of Paris, The Netherlands, Russia, the Marquis Marie Joseph de Lafayette, Tadeusz Kosciuszko, Baron Friedrich Wilhelm von Steuben). **HSS.5.6.2**

Go Digital!

Investigate the lesson content with online whole-class presentation tools.

Background Information

Baron von Steuben During his time with the American troops at Valley Forge, Steuben created a training manual, called *Regulations for the Order and Discipline of the Troops of the United States,* that would continue to help soldiers learn drills until 1812. It instructed troops on how they should dress, how soldiers and officers should behave, and how each officer should be positioned during a battle, among other things.

Analyze the Source

Inspect Have students read Winter at Valley Forge on pp. 228–229.

Find Evidence Use the questions below to check comprehension. Remind students to support their answers with text evidence.

Identify Why did Washington decide that his troops should spend the winter at Valley Forge? (They had suffered defeats nearby and needed somewhere to rest and wait for spring. They also needed to be able to defend the location if the British decided to attack, and Valley Forge seemed to be a good choice.) **DOK 1**

Summarize Why was the winter of 1777–1778 difficult for the American troops? (They suffered from cold, hunger, and loneliness. There wasn't enough food, supplies, or blankets. They caught diseases and many died.) **DOK 2**

Infer Why did many soldiers desert the army that winter? (Life was terrible at Valley Forge, and many men probably thought they would be better off at home.) **DOK 2**

Analyze Visuals How does the painting illustrate what life was like at Valley Forge? (Students should explain that the image shows the snow and wind. It also shows soldiers outside without proper coats or gear for the weather.) **DOK 3**

Analyze Events What did Washington do to make the time spent at Valley Forge useful for his men? (He asked Baron von Steuben to train the men and make them into a more professional fighting force. The time was used wisely, and that spring, the American Army was much better at fighting together.) **DOK 2**

Make Connections

Evaluate How did Baron von Steuben make such a difference in the American soldiers' habits if he only trained a few groups of 100 men each? Was this an effective way to train an army? (He turned each of those men into trainers as well. Then they could go out and teach others what Steuben had taught them. Students may recognize that in a huge army, no one man could hope to train everyone, so Steuben's tactics were effective.) **DOK 3**

☑ Stop and Check

Talk Encourage students to consider everything that happened to the troops at Valley Forge. (Students should list the hardships the soldiers faced.)

What Do You Think?

Encourage students to use text evidence from the whole lesson as they respond to the prompt.

Winter at Valley Forge

Despite the great victory at Saratoga, the Continental Army elsewhere suffered a number of defeats, including two near Philadelphia in late 1777. Washington's 11,000 men set up camp that winter at Valley Forge, Pennsylvania. The site seemed easy to defend, should the British attack. It was also close to good roads, which would allow the army to get supplies.

American soldiers suffered during the brutal winter at Valley Forge.

That winter, however, was a time of cold, hunger, and loneliness for the Patriot soldiers. Often the only food was "fire cakes," which were made of a paste of flour and water baked hard over a campfire. Many soldiers gave up and went home. At least 2,500 died of diseases that winter, including smallpox, typhoid, and influenza. Those who lived faced frostbite and starvation. The Marquis de Lafayette later wrote, "The unfortunate soldiers were in need of everything; they had neither coats, hats, shirts, nor shoes, their feet and legs froze."

Washington begged the Continental Congress and the state governors for supplies. He described the terrible sufferings of his army. His letters were answered with promises, but very little help arrived.

Washington held his army together with little but the force of his own leadership. He used the time at Valley Forge wisely, however. Groups of 100 soldiers took turns training with Baron von Steuben. Then each trainee taught another 100 men what he had learned. By the spring, more money became available due to the alliance with France. While Washington's troops came to Valley Forge a barefoot, ragged band, they marched away in 1778 as professional soldiers.

✓ Stop and Check

Talk What happened to the soldiers of the Continental Army at Valley Forge?

What Do You Think? How did the talents of individual Europeans like von Steuben, Pulaski, and Kościuszko strengthen the cause of American Independence?

Research Companion, pp. 228–229

ENGLISH LEARNERS SCAFFOLD

ELD.PII.5.6 Connecting ideas

Emerging

Unpack Language Have students work together to unpack sentences difficult structures. Model with the following example:

The site seemed easy to defend, should the British attack.

Explain to students that in this context, *should* **does not mean "must." Instead, it means "if." Restate the sentence so that the causal relationship is clearer:**

If the British attacked, the Americans could defend the site.

Encourage students to work through other complicated sentences in this section.

Expanding/Bridging

Use Language Guide students to unpack complicated sentences in order to better understand them. Then encourage them to have a discussion in which they use some of the constructions they found difficult. Provide sentence frames to support the discussions if needed, such as

We gathered candles, should the lights go out.

The snow got deeper, which would make it difficult to go to the store later.

During the storm, however, we stayed warm and dry inside.

See the **Language Learner Teaching Guide** for more language support strategies.

Monitor and Differentiate

REACHING ALL LEARNERS

Approaching Level

Have students discuss the hardships the American soldiers faced at Valley Forge. Then have them discuss why Washington chose the site and why he chose not to move them when the situation got worse. Remind students to use details from the text in their discussion.

Beyond Level

Encourage students to conduct further research into what the soldiers did to keep themselves alive and busy during the winter at Valley Forge. Students may try to find primary sources about the time, such as letters from soldiers to their families. They may also choose to read more about the hardships the men faced. Have students present their findings to the whole class.

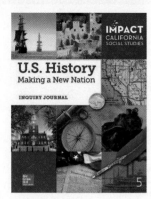

Inquiry Journal
pp. 184–185

 STANDARDS

Identify and map the major military battles, campaigns, and turning points of the Revolutionary War, the roles of the American and British leaders, and the Indian leaders' alliances on both sides. **HSS.5.6.1**

(CCSS) Write informative/ explanatory texts to examine a topic and convey ideas and information clearly. **CCSS.ELA.W.5.2**

Draw evidence from literary or informational texts to support analysis, reflection, and research. **CCSS.ELA.W.5.9**

Engage effectively in a range of collaborative discussions (one-on-one, in groups, and teacher-led) with diverse partners on *grade 5 topics and texts*, building on others' ideas and expressing their own clearly. **CCSS.ELA.SL.5.1**

Go Digital!

- Students can go online to report their findings. Assess their responses online.

- Students can access the online graphic organizer to capture ideas from their investigation.

Think About It

Students will review their research and consider why a nation as powerful as Great Britain was unable to win the war.

- Remind students to review the inferences they made and supported in their graphic organizer. Direct students back to pages 220–229 of their Research Companion if they need more information.

Talk About It COLLABORATE

Small-Group Discussions Ask students to work in small groups to decide two important reasons that allowed the colonists to turn the tide of the war.

- Explain that they should take turns discussing their reasons.

- Students should discuss whether they agree or disagree with the reasons their group members chose and explain why.

- Remind students to be respectful of their classmates.

Write About It

News Report Have students read the prompt. Explain to students that a news report gives facts and details about an event in such a way that the audience stays interested and is informed.

Remind students to include the following elements in their response.

- Include the most important information early in the report so your audience knows what the report is about.

- Include facts and details that support the information.

- Use informal language that seems like something a reporter would say.

Use the rubric on p. T482 to evaluate students' work.

Connect to the Essential Question

Read the prompt aloud to students. Ask them the following guiding questions:

- What qualities about Americans helped them turn the tide of the war? (Responses may include their desire for freedom and their perseverance.)

- Why were those qualities important? (Responses will vary.)

- Do you see those qualities at work in the nation today? Why or why not? (Responses will vary.)

Remind students to use the space provided in their journal to jot down notes.

Report / Your Findings

Think About It

Review your research. Based on the information you have gathered, why do you think a country as powerful as Great Britain was unable to stop the colonial forces?

Talk About It
COLLABORATE

Small-Group Discussions
Create a list of reasons that the colonists were able to turn the tide of the war. Read the completed list aloud and decide which two reasons are the most important.

Sample List:
1. Courage shown by the soldiers
2. Washington's boldness in the morale-boosting victory at Trenton
3. Intelligence to fortify the walls around Freeman's Farm
4. Money, supplies, and ships from France.
5. Determination to survive a harsh winter at Valley Forge

Write About It

News Report
Imagine you are a television reporter covering the Revolutionary War. You must write a report on why the colonies were able to turn the tide of the war.

Sample response: Anchor: In our investigative reports segment this evening, we look at how the colonies were able to turn the tide of the Revolutionary War. After suffering initial defeats in 1776, victory at Freeman's Farm near Saratoga, New York, has convinced France the United States can win the war. As a result, the French will probably provide the money, ships, and supplies that would help the Americans turn the tide of the war in their favor.

Connect to the
ESSENTIAL EQ QUESTION

Make Connections
Think about the qualities that helped the American army turn the tide of the war. How do you see those qualities at work in the United States today?

ESSENTIAL EQ QUESTION

Inquiry Project Notes

184   Lesson 3   What Were the Defining Moments of the War?

Lesson 3   185

Inquiry Journal, pp. 184–185

ENGLISH LEARNERS SCAFFOLD

ELD.PII.5.4 Using nouns and noun phrases

Emerging	Expanding	Bridging
Write a Conversation Explain that a news report is meant to be read aloud. It has to appeal to a variety of listeners. Encourage students to have fun and write as if they are having a conversation. Invite students to have a conversation with a partner before writing the news report.	**Think Like a Reporter** Remind students that a news report delivers facts, but it does so in a way that is engaging and interesting. Have students work in pairs to develop their reports. They should first identify the facts they want to deliver, then they should take turns giving the report aloud to see if it sounds like what they would hear on television.	**Write Like a Reporter** Have students carefully consider the tone of their news report. Encourage students to write conversationally. Model for them the difference between conversational and formal English, if needed.

See the **Language Learner Teaching Guide** for more language support strategies.

Monitor and Differentiate

REACHING ALL LEARNERS

Approaching Level

Work with students to understand the phrase *turn the tide.* Explain that it's an idiom that means "reverse events." Guide students to explain how the colonists were able to change the events of the war in their favor.

Beyond Level

Encourage students to expand on their news report by writing the script for an entire news show all about the events of the American Revolution between the Battles of Lexington and Saratoga. Have them perform their reports for the class.

Know what your students know!

Lesson Task
Report Your Findings

Use the rubric to evaluate students' responses.

Small-Group Discussions Students create a list of reasons that the colonists were able to turn the tide of the war. They read the completed list aloud and decide which two reasons are the most important.

News Report Students imagine they are television reporters covering the Revolutionary War. They must write a report on why the colonies were able to turn the tide of the war.

Lesson Task Evaluation Rubric

	4	3	2	1
Historical Understanding	Strong understanding of the defining moments of the war	Adequate understanding of the defining moments of the war	Uneven understanding of the defining moments of the war	No understanding of the defining moments of the war
News Report	Clearly provides information	Adequately provides information	Somewhat clear or unclear information	No relevant information stated or student does not show understanding of the task
Support with Evidence	Opinion supported with details and evidence	Opinion developed with details and evidence	Opinion developed with details and evidence	Details and evidence are missing or irrelevant
Small-Group Discussions	Lists ideas for reasons colonists turned the tide of war	Lists some ideas for reasons colonists turned the tide of war	Provides a few ideas for reasons colonists turned the tide of war	Provides no ideas for reasons colonists turned the tide of war
	Provides support for reasons for during discussion	Provides some support for reasons during discussion	At times does not provide support for reasons during discussion	Reasons are not present or supported

Lesson Assessment

Go Digital!

- Have students complete the Chapter 5 Lesson 3 Assessment online to monitor their understanding of the lesson content.

California Smarter Balanced Assessment Connections!

Standards Covered	Lesson Task	Lesson Assessment	Alignment with California Smarter Balanced Assessment
History Social Science Content 5.6.1; 5.6.2; 5.6.4	✔	✔	Claim 1 Targets 8, 9, 11
History Social Science Analysis Skills Chronological and Spatial Thinking 5.4 Research, Evidence, and Point of View 5.2 Historical Interpretation 5.3	✔	✔	Claim 1 Targets 8, 9, 11
Writing W.5.2	✔	✔	Claim 2 Target 3b, 5
Research and Inquiry W.5.7; W.5.9		✔	Claim 4 Targets 1, 2, 3, 4
Reading RI.5.3	✔	✔	Claim 1 Target 11, 12
Speaking and Listening SL.5.1	✔		Claim 3 Target 3 Claim 4 Target 1

LESSON QUESTION

What Was It Like to Live During the American Revolution?

Background Information

In this lesson, students learn about the women, African Americans, and American Indians who made an impact on the war effort.

Community Connections

To enrich what students have learned about the defining moments of the war, plan a field trip to a local American history museum.

 LESSON STANDARDS

- ✓ Identify and map the major military battles, campaigns, and turning points of the Revolutionary War, the roles of the American and British leaders, and the Indian leaders' alliances on both sides. **HSS.5.6.1**

- ✓ Describe the contributions of France and other nations and of individuals to the outcome of the Revolution (e.g., Benjamin Franklin's negotiations with the French, the French navy, the Treaty of Paris, The Netherlands, Russia, the Marquis Marie Joseph de Lafayette, Tadeusz Kosciuszko, Baron Friedrich Wilhelm von Steuben). **HSS.5.6.2**

- ✓ Identify the different roles women played during the Revolution (e.g., Abigail Adams, Martha Washington, Molly Pitcher, Phillis Wheatley, Mercy Otis Warren). **HSS.5.6.3**

- ✓ Understand the personal impact and economic hardship of the war on families, problems of financing the war, wartime inflation, and laws against hoarding goods and materials and profiteering. **HSS.5.6.4**

- ✓ Demonstrate knowledge of the significance of land policies developed under the Continental Congress (e.g., sale of western lands, the Northwest Ordinance of 1787) and those policies' impact on American Indians' land. **HSS.5.6.6**

 Connect to the
Essential Question

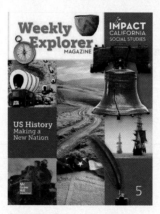

The **Weekly Explorer Magazine** supports the students' exploration of the Essential Question and provides additional resources for the EQ Inquiry Project.

Chapter 5, pp. 58–71

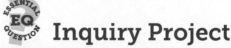 **Inquiry Project**

How Can You Make an Impact?

Remind students to use the information they learn in this lesson and other resources to complete the EQ Inquiry Project.

Dinah Zike's

 In this lesson you will use Foldables.

When Minutes Count!

Suggested Lesson Pacing

1 ENGAGE
One Day

- Lesson Opener
- Analyze the Source
- Inquiry Tools

2 INVESTIGATE
Two to Three Days

🕐 **Short on Time?** Look for the clock to teach core content in less time.

- Women of the Revolution
- The Secret War
- African Americans Join the Cause
- American Indians Choose Sides
- The Hardships of War
- **Citizenship** Were the contributions of women and African Americans to the Revolutionary War effort overlooked?

3 REPORT
One Day

- Think About It
- Write a Letter
- Interview

Make Connections!

(ccss) CONNECT TO ELA

Reading
Explain the relationships or interactions between two or more individuals, events, ideas, or concepts in a historical, scientific, or technical text based on specific information in the text. **RI.5.3**

Research
Conduct short research projects that use several sources to build knowledge through investigation of different aspects of a topic. **W.5.7**

Recall relevant information from experiences or gather relevant information from print and digital sources; summarize or paraphrase information in notes and finished work, and provide a list of sources. **W.5.8**

Writing
Write narratives to develop real or imagined experiences or events using effective technique, descriptive details, and clear event sequences. **W.5.3**

Speaking and Listening
Engage effectively in a range of collaborative discussions (one-on-one, in groups, and teacher-led) with diverse partners on *grade 5 topics and texts*, building on others' ideas and expressing their own clearly. **SL.5.1**

Classroom Resources

🔍 Search for additional resources using the following key words.

Abigail Adams

James Armistead

Benedict Arnold

Nathan Hale

Marquis de Lafayette

Molly Pitcher

Mercy Otis Warren

Hannah Winthrop

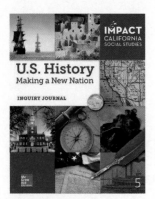

Inquiry Journal
pp. 186–187

(HSS) STANDARDS

Identify and map the major military battles, campaigns, and turning points of the Revolutionary War, the roles of the American and British leaders, and the Indian leaders' alliances on both sides. **HSS.5.6.1**

Students pose relevant questions about events they encounter in historical documents, eyewitness accounts, oral histories, letters, diaries, artifacts, photographs, maps, artworks, and architecture. **HAS.HR.2**

(CCSS) Engage effectively in a range of collaborative discussions (one-on-one, in groups, and teacher-led) with diverse partners on *grade 5 topics and texts*, building on others' ideas and expressing their own clearly. **CCSS.ELA.SL.5.1**

Go Digital!

Explore the lesson content with online whole-class presentation tools.

What Was It Like to Live During the American Revolution?

Bellringer

Prompt students to retrieve information from the previous lessons. Say: *Why was the Battle of Saratoga a turning point in the war?* (The French decided to support the United States by giving ships and other resources. The battle proved to them that the United States had a chance of winning the war.)

Lesson Outcomes

What Am I Learning? Have students read the Lesson Outcomes on p. 186.

Why Am I Learning It? Check that students understand the meaning of the word *hardships*. Explain that while it sounds like a compound word made up of *hard* and *ship*, *–ship* is actually a suffix that shows condition. In this case, it means that life was difficult. Encourage students to think of other words that end in *–ship* and show condition, such as *relationship, friendship,* and *membership.*

How Will I Know That I Learned It? Ask students the following questions.

- What will you learn about? (the motivations of people who lived during the American Revolution)

- What is the purpose of the task? (to understand different people's points of view)

- How will you support your explanation? (with descriptive details)

Talk About It

Provide some scaffolding for students to use as they discuss the primary source. Provide background information as needed.

- The primary source is written by _____.

- Based on his description, life during the American Revolution was _____.

Collaborative Conversations

Analyze Details As students engage in partner, small group, and whole-class discussions, encourage them to

- Think about why the Patriot soldiers were fighting the war.
- Ask and answer questions about how they would handle a similar situation.
- Draw or modify conclusions that are based on the discussion.

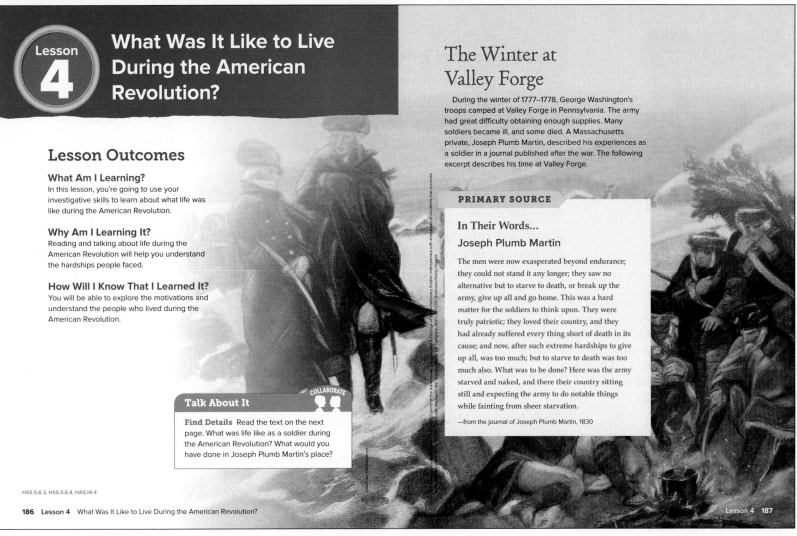

Lesson 4 — What Was It Like to Live During the American Revolution?

Lesson Outcomes

What Am I Learning?
In this lesson, you're going to use your investigative skills to learn about what life was like during the American Revolution.

Why Am I Learning It?
Reading and talking about life during the American Revolution will help you understand the hardships people faced.

How Will I Know That I Learned It?
You will be able to explore the motivations and understand the people who lived during the American Revolution.

Talk About It

COLLABORATE

Find Details Read the text on the next page. What was life like as a soldier during the American Revolution? What would you have done in Joseph Plumb Martin's place?

HSS.5.6.3, HSS.5.6.4, HAS.HI.4

186 Lesson 4 What Was It Like to Live During the American Revolution?

The Winter at Valley Forge

During the winter of 1777–1778, George Washington's troops camped at Valley Forge in Pennsylvania. The army had great difficulty obtaining enough supplies. Many soldiers became ill, and some died. A Massachusetts private, Joseph Plumb Martin, described his experiences as a soldier in a journal published after the war. The following excerpt describes his time at Valley Forge.

PRIMARY SOURCE

In Their Words...
Joseph Plumb Martin

The men were now exasperated beyond endurance; they could not stand it any longer; they saw no alternative but to starve to death, or break up the army, give up all and go home. This was a hard matter for the soldiers to think upon. They were truly patriotic; they loved their country, and they had already suffered every thing short of death in its cause; and now, after such extreme hardships to give up all, was too much; but to starve to death was too much also. What was to be done? Here was the army starved and naked, and there their country sitting still and expecting the army to do notable things while fainting from sheer starvation.

—from the journal of Joseph Plumb Martin, 1830

Lesson 4 187

Inquiry Journal, pp. 186–187

EL ENGLISH LEARNERS SCAFFOLD

ELD.PI.5.6 Reading closely literary and informational texts and viewing multimedia to determine how meaning is conveyed explicitly and implicitly through language

Emerging	Expanding	Bridging
Identify Details Provide scaffolding for difficult words and phrases, then read aloud the primary source again with students. Ask them what they would do in Plumb Martin's place.	**Use Details** Have students underline words that Plumb Martin uses to describe the situation at Valley Forge. Encourage students to use those words in sentences of their own to describe another event they've learned about.	**Apply Language** Have students share or write what they find more surprising or important about Plumb Martin's account. Ask them to identify what reading a primary source helps them to learn that a summary in a textbook does not.

See the **Language Learner Teaching Guide** for more language support strategies.

Monitor and Differentiate

REACHING ALL LEARNERS

Approaching Level
Work with students to identify the problem that Plumb Martin outlines. Guide them to discuss words that are unfamiliar to them. Then have them use those words to summarize the primary source verbally or in writing.

On Level
Have students create a drawing of a scene from Valley Forge. Encourage them to use any media that is available. Then have students present their work to the whole class.

Beyond Level
Guide students to conduct further research into what life was like as a soldier during the American Revolution. Have them share their findings with the class.

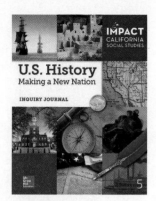

Inquiry Journal
pp. 188–189

 STANDARDS

Identify the different roles women played during the Revolution (e.g., Abigail Adams, Martha Washington, Molly Pitcher, Phillis Wheatley, Mercy Otis Warren). **HSS.5.6.3**

Students pose relevant questions about events they encounter in historical documents, eyewitness accounts, oral histories, letters, diaries, artifacts, photographs, maps, artworks, and architecture. **HAS.HR.2**

Go Digital!

Model how to inspect and find evidence with online whole-class presentation tools.

Background Information

Phillis Wheatley often wrote her poetry in honor or in memory of friends or prominent figures. Little of her overall work deals with the issue of slavery, but one of her poems, titled "On Being Brought from Africa to America," reminds white people that African Americans are capable of refinement.

1 Inspect

Read Ask students to skim the text, including the excerpt from "To His Excellency General Washington," to focus on understanding the overall meaning. Remind them to circle words and phrases that are unfamiliar.

- What happened after a century? (Great Britain and the United States got in an argument)
- Who is "heaven's defended race"? (the United States)
- Why is Britannia's head drooping? (in sadness because Great Britain is losing the war)
- Why should Washington receive a crown, a mansion, and a throne? (because he is leading America to victory)

Collaborate Have partners take turns explaining why they think Wheatley wrote the poem. (Students may say that she esteemed George Washington, and she supported what he did to help the United States win its freedom.)

2 Find Evidence

Reread Have students reread the text.

Analyze the Primary Source Reread the excerpt aloud then analyze it as a class.

- Ask: What is the tone of the poem? (The poem is almost triumphant in its praise of the United States and of Washington.)
- What does *virtue* mean? Encourage students to use a dictionary to find out. (a good quality)
- What do the symbols of a crown and a throne represent? (royalty or a monarch)
- Why might Washington think these are inappropriate gifts? (The American Revolution was fought to throw off a monarchy.)

3 Make Connections

Talk Guide students to identify the speaker's opinion of Great Britain. Then have them pinpoint the language that supports their thinking. (Students may say that the speaker says that Great Britain has "cruel blindness" and "thirst of boundless power.")

Connect to Now Have partners discuss how a poet or other artist might praise an American leader today.

Analyze the Source

A Hopeful Poet

Phillis Wheatley was born in Africa. In 1761, at a very young age, she was kidnapped from her family and brought on a slave ship to North America. In Boston, she was purchased by a tailor named John Wheatley. The Wheatleys taught Phillis to read and write, which was an uncommon practice for most slaveholders. She eventually learned Latin and Greek. As a teenager, she began writing poetry. Wheatley composed several of her poems in honor of the new United States. Many of her poems show Wheatley's excitement about the new nation's gaining its independence from Great Britain. That excitement also showed hopefulness for freedom for slaves.

Phillis Wheatley

Library of Congress Prints and Photographs Division [LC-USZC4-5316]

PRIMARY SOURCE

From "To His Excellency General Washington," by Phillis Wheatley

One century scarce perform'd its destined round,
When Gallic[1] powers Columbia's[2] fury found;
And so may you, whoever dares disgrace
The land of freedom's heaven-defended race!
Fix'd are the eyes of nations on the scales,[3]
For in their hopes Columbia's arm prevails.
Anon Britannia[4] droops the pensive head,
While round increase the rising hills of dead.
Ah! Cruel blindness to Columbia's state!
Lament thy thirst of boundless power too late.

Proceed, great chief, with virtue on thy side,
Thy ev'ry action let the Goddess guide.
A crown, a mansion, and a throne that shine,
With gold unfading, WASHINGTON! Be thine.

1 Gallic powers: Great Britain
2 Columbia: a female symbol of the United States
3 Fix'd are the eyes of nations on the scales: many nations are interested in the outcome of the war
4 Britannia: a female symbol of Great Britain

TEXT: Wheatley, Phillis. "To His Excellency General Washington." 1775. PHOTO: McGraw-Hill Education

188 Lesson 4 What Was It Like to Live During the American Revolution?

Lesson 4 189

Inquiry Journal, pp. 188–189

EL ENGLISH LEARNERS SCAFFOLD

ELD.PI.5.5 Listening actively to spoken English in a range of social and academic contexts

Emerging

Support Interpretation Read aloud the excerpt from the poem to students. Then read it again, stopping to provide explanations of its complex structure, unfamiliar words, and symbols. Guide students to ask and answer questions about the text to understand the general meaning.

Expanding/Bridging

Analyze Poetry Read the poem aloud to students. Reread it, stopping to answer questions about complicated ideas and language. Read it aloud again. Work with students to create a translation of the text into more modern English, maintaining the general theme and substance of the original. Guide them to analyze Wheatley's ideas and sentiments.

See the **Language Learner Teaching Guide** for more language support strategies.

Monitor and Differentiate

REACHING ALL LEARNERS

Approaching Level

Have students listen as you read aloud the poem. Guide them to think about the tone the speaker uses when discussing the United States and Great Britain. Work with students to compare and contrast to understand the overall feelings toward the two nations.

Beyond Level

Encourage students to read more of the poem "To His Excellency General Washington" or another of Wheatley's poems. Have them work to understand the language and structure of the poem, then present what they've learned to the rest of the class. Have them take turns reading aloud portions of the poem.

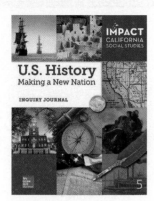

Inquiry Journal
pp. 190–191

 STANDARDS

Identify the different roles women played during the Revolution (e.g., Abigail Adams, Martha Washington, Molly Pitcher, Phillis Wheatley, Mercy Otis Warren). **HSS.5.6.3**

Students place key events and people of the historical era they are studying in a chronological sequence and within a spatial context; they interpret time lines. **HAS.CS.1**

Students summarize the key events of the era they are studying and explain the historical contexts of those events. **HAS.HI.1**

CCSS Explain the relationships or interactions between two or more individuals, events, ideas, or concepts in a historical, scientific, or technical text based on specific information in the text. **CCSS.ELA.RI.5.3**

Go Digital!

- Model how to explore and investigate with online whole-class tools.

- Students can access the online graphic organizer to use the inquiry tools as they read.

Explore Motivations

Explain Tell students that when they try to understand a person's motivations, they look for evidence about what they did and try to understand why they did it.

Read Have students read aloud the step-by-step instructions about how to identify a person's motivations. Tell students that they should ask themselves questions such as *Who is this person?* and *What made them act as they did?* They should also look for key details that signal important information.

Guide Practice Present a brief model of trying to understanding someone's motivations, such as *Phillis Wheatley was a slave. She wrote poems about the United States and important figures. She must have believed in American independence and wanted freedom for other enslaved people.* Model filling out the graphic organizer with details from the text.

Investigate!

Have students read pages 230–237 in the Research Companion. Tell them the information that will help them answer the lesson question **What Was It Like to Live During the American Revolution?**

Take Notes Tell students that they will take notes as they read each section. Explain that taking notes will help them understand the motivations of people from different groups. Remind students that they should look for key details and important information in the text.

Inspect Guide students to read the text in each section to determine what it says. Encourage them to work to find information about people from different groups to determine their motivations for fighting in the war or acting as they did.

Find Evidence Encourage students to reread the text to develop a deeper understanding. Remind students that they should think about how the facts and details will help them answer the lesson question.

Collaborative Conversations

Text-Based Discussion Remind students that discussing the text with others can help them

- Understand how others make inferences about people in history

- Better understand what they have read

- Appreciate the perspectives of other people

Inquiry Tools

Explore Motivations

Motivations are the reasons a person does something. When you understand people's motivations for acting a certain way, you learn more about them and the things they did.

1. **Read the text once all the way through.**
   This will help you understand what the text is about.

2. **Ask yourself, *Who is this person, and where did he or she come from?***
   Knowing a person's background will help you understand him or her.

3. **Consider how the person's background influenced what happened.**
   The circumstances of a person's life caused that person to make certain decisions or to act a certain way.

4. **Ask yourself, *How did this person's motivations influence the event?***
   Look for details about the person's motivations or life circumstances that caused him or her to make a decision or to perform some action.

 COLLABORATE Based on the text you just read, work with your class to complete the web below by filling out information about a person's background to discover his or her motivation.

- Phillis Wheatley was a slave.
- She began poems, many of which honored George Washington, American independence, and freedom.
- Motivation: She believed in American independence and hoped for freedom for slaves.

Investigate!

IMPACT U.S. History — Making a New Nation

Read pages 230–237 in your Research Companion. Use your investigative skills to look for text evidence that tells you about the motivations of a person from the lesson. Write the person's motivation in the center circle and details that help explain his or her motivation in the surrounding circles.

Possible responses:

- Abigail Adams asked her husband to remember women's rights.
- She asked her husband to be more generous and favorable to women than men who had come before.
- *(center)* In the newly independent nation, Abigail Adams wanted women to have the same rights as men.
- She threatened a rebellion if women weren't given representation.
- She wished for men to stop acting like "masters" of women and to begin acting as "friends."

McGraw-Hill Education

190 Lesson 4 What Was It Like to Live During the American Revolution?

Lesson 4 191

Inquiry Journal, pp. 190–191

(EL) ENGLISH LEARNERS SCAFFOLD

ELD.PI.5.1 Exchanging information and ideas with others through oral collaborative discussions on a range of social and academic topics

Emerging

Identify Key Details Encourage students to answer questions about the text that help them understand the people they read about. Have students ask and answer *who, what, where, when, why,* and *how* questions.

Expanding

Discuss Details Have students discuss specific people they read about in the text. Have them ask and answer questions about the lives and actions of those people. Then have them work together to identify language that effectively describes the people.

See the **Language Learner Teaching Guide** for more language support strategies.

Monitor and Differentiate

REACHING ALL LEARNERS

Special Needs

Encourage students to act out events that happened to the person they chose to research for the graphic organizer. Have them work alone or in small groups. For example, one student might read aloud from Abigail Adams' letters, pretending to be Abigail while she wrote to John.

Approaching Level

Encourage students to work with a partner to find information about a person they read about in the chapter. Have students pair up with someone who chose a different person. Guide students to think critically about what each person had to gain or lose by acting the way they did, and prompt students to place themselves in the same situation.

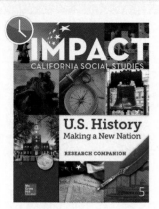

Research Companion
pp. 230–231

 STANDARDS

Identify and map the major military battles, campaigns, and turning points of the Revolutionary War, the roles of the American and British leaders, and the Indian leaders' alliances on both sides. **HSS.5.6.1**

Identify the different roles women played during the Revolution (e.g., Abigail Adams, Martha Washington, Molly Pitcher, Phillis Wheatley, Mercy Otis Warren). **HSS.5.6.3**

Students pose relevant questions about events they encounter in historical documents, eyewitness accounts, oral histories, letters, diaries, artifacts, photographs, maps, artworks, and architecture. **HAS.HR.2**

Students distinguish fact from fiction by comparing documentary sources on historical figures and events with fictionalized characters and events. Students distinguish fact from fiction by comparing documentary sources on historical figures and events with fictionalized characters and events. **HAS.HR.3**

Go Digital!

Investigate the lesson content with online whole-class presentation tools.

Background Information

"Molly Pitcher" Some scholars believe Molly Pitcher is only a legend, but others still attribute the story of "Molly Pitcher" or "Captain Molly" to Mary Ludwig Hays. Molly was a common nickname for women named Mary at the time. Many years after the war, Mary Hays received a special pension from the government in addition to the pension she received as a soldier's widow. Some scholars take this as evidence that she was being recognized for serving with the troops at the Battle of Monmouth.

Analyze the Source

Inspect Have students read pp. 230–231.

Find Evidence Use the questions below to check comprehension. Remind students to support their answers with text evidence.

Identify How did Mercy Otis Warren and Hannah Winthrop support the war effort? (by keeping journals and writing letters to record events for the future to learn about) **DOK 1**

Infer Why was it important that women managed farms and businesses during the war? (Women did not usually have many rights or responsibilities outside raising children, so when the men were away, women had to take over their jobs as well.) **DOK 3**

Cite Evidence Why were the actions of Mary Ludwig Hays extraordinary? (She actually took an active role in battles, which women did not do at the time.) **DOK 2**

Analyze Visuals What do you learn about the actions of Mary Ludwig Hays from the picture? (The picture of Hays shows that she has abandoned her bucket of water and taken over a fallen soldier's job at a cannon. She is actively engaged in the war.) **DOK 3**

Make Connections

Draw Conclusions Why did the war change women's lives? (Responses will vary, but students should support their answers with evidence from the this lesson.) **DOK 3**

Analyze the Painting Direct students' attention to the picture of Mary Ludwig Hays at the Battle of Monmouth. Encourage them to look at details in the painting to learn more about it.

• What is happening in the scene? (Hays is loading a cannon.)

• What are the other figures in the scene doing? (One man is down on the ground, possibly injured, and other is helping her with the cannon.)

• How does this picture help you understand what a battle during the American Revolution was like? (It shows details that managing the cannons was difficult work, the air is smoky, and the battle was dangerous.)

Lesson 4

What Was It Like to Live During the American Revolution?

Women of the Revolution

The Revolutionary War impacted the lives of more than just the soldiers and generals waging war. The Revolutionary War changed the lives of women, African Americans, American Indians, and every civilian in the colonies.

American women supported the war in many ways. Mercy Otis Warren and Hannah Winthrop recorded and wrote letters about the events of the Revolution so everyone knew what was happening. Phillis Wheatley, a freed African American, wrote poetry that inspired many people. Other women tended farms or minded shops while their husbands were away fighting in the army.

Some women followed their husbands to war and did whatever they could to help. Earning the nickname "Molly Pitcher," Mary Ludwig Hays carried pitchers of water to men on the battlefield. Legend has it that she took her husband's place at a cannon when he became too exhausted to fight during the Battle of Monmouth in 1778.

Molly Pitcher helps load a cannon at a battle in New Jersey.

HSS.5.6.3, HSS.5.6.4, HSS.5.6.7, HAS.HI.2

230 Lesson 4 What Was It Like to Live During the American Revolution?

Lesson 4 231

Research Companion, pp. 230–231

(EL) ENGLISH LEARNERS SCAFFOLD

ELD.PI.5.6 Reading closely literary and informational texts and viewing multimedia to determine how meaning is conveyed explicitly and implicitly through language

Emerging

Organize Information Work with students to take notes about what they read. Invite them to create a graphic organizer to collect their ideas, then guide them to ask and answer questions about the women the section describes.

Expanding/ Bridging

Describe Details Have students work together to think of adjectives that describe each of the women in this section. Guide them to create a list of terms and support their opinions for how each applies. Provide sentence starters.

Mary Ludwig Hays was _____ because she _____.

Phillis Wheatley's poems are _____ and help us to _____.

See the **Language Learner Teaching Guide** for more language support strategies.

Monitor and Differentiate

REACHING ALL LEARNERS

Approaching Level

Guide students to identify any unfamiliar words in this section. First, encourage them to use context clues to figure out what the word means. For example, students may understand *waging* because it pertains to how soldiers and generals participate in a war. If students cannot determine a meaning based on context, encourage them to use a dictionary.

Beyond Level

Have students conduct additional research into one of the women discussed in this section. Encourage them to try to distinguish between fact and legend when possible, and describe how those legends came to be. Have them present their findings to the whole class.

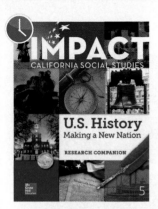

Research Companion
pp. 232–233

 STANDARDS

Identify and map the major military battles, campaigns, and turning points of the Revolutionary War, the roles of the American and British leaders, and the Indian leaders' alliances on both sides. **HSS.5.6.1**

Students identify and interpret the multiple causes and effects of historical events. **HAS.HI.3**

___

Go Digital!

Investigate the lesson content with online whole-class presentation tools.

Background Information

Abigail Adams was well educated, which was uncommon for a woman at the time. She gained her knowledge from her father's library rather than from formal schooling. Later in her life, she advocated for women's education, and scorned that fact that women's learning was laughed at by contemporary society.

Analyze the Source

Inspect Have students read pp. 232–233.

Find Evidence Use the questions below to check comprehension. Remind students to support their answers with text evidence.

> **Identify** Why did some people remain loyal to Great Britain? (for religious reasons or because their businesses depended on trade with Great Britain) **DOK 1**

> **Infer** What do John and Abigail Adams' letters tell us about their relationship? (They had a relationship of mutual respect, and Abigail felt comfortable sending her ideas to her powerful husband.) **DOK 3**

> **Explain** Why would someone be known today as a "Benedict Arnold"? (That person would be considered a traitor.) **DOK 2**

> **Summarize** How did James Armistead help the American cause? (He risked his own life to spy for the Americans against the British. He posed as a servant to Lord Cornwallis, but he was really passing information to General Lafayette. He helped the Americans to win the Battle of Yorktown.) **DOK 3**

Analyze the Primary Source

> **Analyze Language** Point out the words *foment* and *impunity*. Provide definitions (begin; freedom from punishment) or encourage students to look these terms up in the dictionary before rereading the primary source. **DOK 2**

> **Draw Conclusions** What did Abigail Adams want her husband to do as he helped to create new laws for the United States? (She wanted the laws to treat women fairly without subjecting them to tyranny and heartless control of men.) **DOK 3**

Make Connections

> **Draw Conclusions** Ask students to share their opinions about whether it was a good idea for the United States and Great Britain to use spies during the war. (Responses will vary, but students should provide reasons based on text evidence.) **DOK 3**

☑ Stop and Check

COLLABORATE

Talk Have students consider what Abigail Adams wants John Adams to do. (She wanted him to make laws that would give women more rights.)

Think Encourage students to think about why a traitor would be viewed as an enemy. (Responses should be based on text evidence.)

Find Details Explain to students that after they read and take notes, they should think about how the information can help them answer the Essential Question.

Still other women remained loyal to the British crown. Either for religious reasons, or because their families' businesses depended on British trade, Loyalist men and women wanted reconciliation with Great Britain. Some of them even worked actively against the revolution.

There were also women who worked actively to help create the new United States. Abigail Adams exchanged many letters with her husband, John, in which they discussed important issues facing the Continental Congress. Abigail asked her husband to remember women's rights as he helped to create the new government.

PRIMARY SOURCE

In Their Words... Abigail Adams

I long to hear that you have declared an independency—and by the way in the new Code of Laws which I suppose it will be necessary for you to make I desire you would Remember the Ladies, and be more generous and favorable to them than your ancestors. Do not put such unlimited power into the hands of the Husbands. Remember all Men would be tyrants if they could. If particular care and attention is not paid to the Ladies we are determined to foment a Rebellion, and will not hold ourselves bound by any Laws in which we have no voice, or Representation. That your Sex are Naturally Tyrannical is a Truth so thoroughly established as to admit of no dispute, but such of you as wish to be happy willingly give up the harsh title of Master for the more tender and endearing one of Friend. Why then, not put it out of the power of the vicious and the Lawless to use us with cruelty and indignity with impunity.

—from a letter to John Adams, March 31, 1776

TEXT: Adams, Abigail. Abigail Adams to John Adams, 31 March 1776. In Familiar Letters of John Adams and His Wife Abigail Adams, During the Revolution. With a Memoir of Mrs. Adams, ed. Charles Francis Adams, no. 91. New York: Hurd and Houghton, 1875. PHOTO: Courtesy National Gallery of Art, Washington

✓ Stop and Check

Talk Why did Abigail Adams ask John Adams to "remember the ladies"?

The Secret War

Life during the Revolutionary War was filled with divisions and intrigue. Many Loyalists spied on the Patriots for the British. Some who helped the British made it appear that they were instead helping the Patriot cause. Benedict Arnold was an American general who eventually turned **traitor**. He gave important information about a planned invasion of Canada to the British. He later fled to England, but people started calling any traitor a "Benedict Arnold" because of his treachery.

The Patriot side had its own spies. Nathan Hale was attempting to spy on the British in 1776 when he was captured. He was hanged without a trial. Reportedly, his famous last words were "I only regret that I have but one life to lose for my country."

One of the most successful American spies was James Armistead, a man born into slavery. He volunteered to spy for General Lafayette, managing to become a servant to the British general Cornwallis. Armistead smuggled important information to Lafayette, which helped the Continental Army win the Battle of Yorktown. After the war, Lafayette helped Armistead win his freedom.

Nathan Hale was put to death for being a Patriot spy.

✓ Stop and Check

Think With a partner, discuss why people call someone who betrays them a "Benedict Arnold."

Find Details As you read, add new information to the graphic organizer on page 191 in your Inquiry Journal.

Research Companion, pp. 232–233

EL ENGLISH LEARNERS SCAFFOLD

ELD.PI.5.3 Offering and supporting opinions and negotiating with others in communicative exchanges

Emerging

State an Opinion Encourage students to state an opinion about whether it was appropriate for both sides to use spies to gather information. Students should support their opinion by writing or speaking.

Expanding/Bridging

Support an Opinion Guide students to support an opinion about whether it was appropriate for both sides to use spies to gather information. Have students work with partners or in small groups. Encourage them to practice respectfully disagreeing with their partners by asserting what they think and questioning whether their partner has considered other evidence.

See the **Language Learner Teaching Guide** for more language support strategies.

Monitor and Differentiate

REACHING ALL LEARNERS

Special Needs

Have students illustrate the letter from Abigail Adams. Students may choose to depict Adams sitting at a desk writing the letter, or they may choose to create a cartoon strip that illustrates some of the fears Adams has about how women may be treated in the new nation. Have them post their drawings.

Beyond Level

Encourage students to research and read other letters between John and Abigail Adams. Point out that their letters often focused on life at home while John was away representing Massachusetts in Congress or the United States in Europe. They also discussed policy and politics. Ask students to summarize the letters they find for the class.

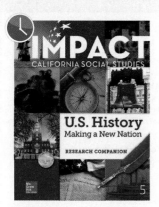

2 INVESTIGATE

African Americans Join the Cause

Research Companion
pp. 234–235

Go Digital!

Investigate the lesson content with online whole-class presentation tools.

Analyze the Source

Inspect Have students read pp. 234–235.

Find Evidence Use the questions below to check comprehension. Remind students to support their answers with text evidence.

Identify Why did the words "All men are created equal" give slaves hope? (They thought the war might free them.) **DOK 1**

Explain How did African Americans serve the United States during the war? (They fought in the army and the navy.) **DOK 2**

Summarize How did James Forten prove his loyalty to the United States? (He turned down an offer of freedom and spent months as a prisoner of war.) **DOK 2**

Context Clues Guns used during the Revolutionary War relied on gun powder to fire musket balls. What is a *powder boy*? (someone who supplies gun powder to soldiers) **DOK 2**

Summarize What was Chief Joseph Brant's role in the Revolutionary War? (He led the warriors of the Iroquois Confederacy to fight against the Americans.) **DOK 2**

Explain How did Brant help the British? (He helped by attacking American settlements in the Mohawk Valley, and he provided scouts.) **DOK 2**

Infer Why did Americans continue to treat American Indians poorly after the war? (They had been enemies during the war and felt no need to end their greed for land after the war.) **DOK 2**

Make Connections

Draw Conclusions Recall what you learned in Lesson 3 about the Battles of Saratoga. How did the choice of many American Indians to fight for the British affect the outcome of that battle? (The American Indians gave up on their hopes that the British could protect native lands from settlement, and they deserted General Burgoyne. The British lost the battle.) **DOK 3**

COLLABORATE

✓ Stop and Check

Think Encourage students to consider why British promises seemed appealing to American Indians and why many African Americans sided with the colonists. (The American Indians wanted any help they could get to stop white settlement of their lands. The African Americans looked forward to the promise of freedom as it was described in the Declaration of Independence.)

African Americans Join the Cause

This man is dressed as a soldier of the First Rhode Island Regiment.

The words "all men are created equal" in the Declaration of Independence gave hope to African slaves. Many supported the revolution because they believed those famous words might one day apply to them.

In all, about 5,000 African American soldiers served in the Continental Army. The First Rhode Island Regiment, formed in 1778, consisted mainly of African Americans. These included men freed from slavery in exchange for their service. Another African American freed from slavery in exchange for fighting was Peter Salem. He lived in Massachusetts and fought in the Battles of Concord and Bunker Hill.

African Americans also served in the Continental Navy. A 14-year old free African American named James Forten was captured in 1781 during his service as a powder boy. The British offered him his freedom, but he turned down the offer saying, "No, I'm a prisoner for my country and I'll never be a traitor to her." He was held for seven months as a prisoner of war.

234 Lesson 4 What Was It Like to Live During the American Revolution?

American Indians Choose Sides

During the Revolutionary War, American Indians had to decide whom to support. As the colonies grew bigger, they began to take more and more land from the American Indians. The British promised to protect American Indians' land from the Americans who wanted to settle there. Most of the Iroquois Confederacy, led by Chief Joseph Brant, sided with the British. The Oneida and Tuscarora supported the American cause.

Brant's Indian loyalists fighting for the British attacked American settlements in New York's Mohawk Valley. They also provided scouts to help the British troops. The Iroquois eventually lost faith in the British and stopped participating in the war.

However, Americans would continue to regard American Indians as enemies. As a result, many Americans felt no guilt about taking more lands from native peoples after the war.

Iroquois chief Joseph Brant supported the British army during the war.

> ### ✓ Stop and Check
> COLLABORATE
>
> **Think** Why did many American Indians at first side with the British during the Revolutionary War?
>
> Why did many African Americans choose to fight with the colonists?

Lesson 4 **235**

Research Companion, pp. 234–235

ⒺⓁ ENGLISH LEARNERS SCAFFOLD

ELD.PI.5.3 Offering and supporting opinions and negotiating with others in communicative exchanges

Emerging

Take Sides Have students work with a partner. Guide them to state opinions about what side they would have chosen to fight on, if they had been American Indians at the time of the Revolutionary War. Encourage them to use *I think* statements.

Expanding/Bridging

Defend Your Opinion Encourage students to discuss the Iroquois Confederacy with a partner. Students should state and defend an opinion about whether they would have chosen to side with the Americans or the British. Guide students to defend their choice and provide counterclaims for their partners' opinions when appropriate. Provide sentence frames when needed.

See the **Language Learner Teaching Guide** for more language support strategies.

Monitor and Differentiate

REACHING ALL LEARNERS

Approaching Level

Have students reread to identify words they do not understand. Guide them to make a list of the words and look them up before rereading. Then have students summarize the section about how African Americans participated in the war.

Beyond Level

Guide students to conduct further research into how African Americans participated in the war. Students may choose to research specific people, such as James Armistead or James Forten, or they may choose to research events, such as battles that the First Rhode Island Regiment fought in. Have students present their findings to the class.

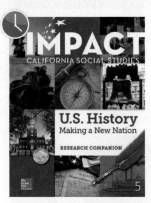

Research Companion
pp. 236–237

 STANDARDS

Identify and map the major military battles, campaigns, and turning points of the Revolutionary War, the roles of the American and British leaders, and the Indian leaders' alliances on both sides. **HSS.5.6.1**

Identify the different roles women played during the Revolution (e.g., Abigail Adams, Martha Washington, Molly Pitcher, Phillis Wheatley, Mercy Otis Warren). **HSS.5.6.3**

Understand the personal impact and economic hardship of the war on families, problems of financing the war, wartime inflation, and laws against hoarding goods and materials and profiteering. **HSS.5.6.4**

Students conduct cost-benefit analyses of historical and current events. **HAS.HI.4**

Go Digital!

Investigate the lesson content with online whole-class presentation tools.

Background Information

Continental Currency It is possible that Benjamin Franklin designed or suggested the first pattern for the Continental dollar coin. The original design included thirteen interlocking rings to symbolize the states' need for unity during a difficult time. It also featured the Latin phrase *fugio,* which means "I fly" and the English phrase "mind your business."

Analyze the Source

Inspect Have students read pp. 236–237.

Find Evidence Use the questions below to check comprehension. Remind students to support their answers with text evidence.

> **Identify** How did Congress try to pay for the war? (by printing more Continental dollars) **DOK 1**
>
> **Explain** Why did this turn out to be a bad idea? (The more money there was in circulation, the less it was worth. People couldn't use the money to buy anything after a while.) **DOK 3**
>
> **Vocabulary** What is the term for that economic process? (inflation) **DOK 2**
>
> **Explain** What did people do when it became difficult to find and buy goods? (Some people hoarded goods either for themselves or to sell for a profit. Selling scarce goods at a higher price during wartime is called *profiteering*.) **DOK 3**

Make Connections

> **Analyze a Graph** How many paper Continental dollars did it take to equal one dollar coin in 1777? How had that number changed by 1781? (10 paper dollars in 1777; more than 120 paper dollars to equal one coin in 1781.) **DOK 3**
>
> **Apply Data** If a loaf of bread cost a one-dollar coin, how many paper dollars did someone need to buy bread in 1777? How many paper dollars did he or she need to buy the bread in 1781? (10 paper dollars in 1777; 120 paper dollars in 1781) **DOK 3**

Citizenship Have students work with a partner. Provide materials for students to use as they design and model their monuments. Encourage students to use what they have learned in the lesson to complete the activity.

✓ Stop and Check

COLLABORATE

Talk Encourage students to think about how inflation affected everyday people who needed more and more money to buy the food and goods they needed. (Responses will vary, but students should identify that life got very hard for people who could not find or buy what they needed.)

What Do You Think?

Encourage students to use text evidence as they respond to the lesson question.

The Hardships of War

Wartime Shortages
Paper Dollars Equaling One-Dollar Coin, 1777–1781

The amount of paper Continental dollars needed to equal a one-dollar coin rose dramatically during the Revolutionary War.

Congress had trouble paying for the war. To afford expensive supplies, they began to print more and more dollars, called "Continentals." They printed so many Continentals, however, that the money began to lose value due to **inflation**. Soon the bills were nearly worthless. A pair of shoes that had cost a few Continental dollars at the start of the war cost 5,000 Continental dollars by the end.

Because their money lost almost all of its value, people had trouble buying the food and supplies they needed. Even for the wealthy, goods that had once been imported from Great Britain were now hard to find. These shortages led people to hoard food, clothes, and other goods. Some people hoarded to try to support their families. Others did it to make money by charging high prices to others. Laws were passed against this practice, called profiteering, but the laws were difficult to enforce.

 Stop and Check
COLLABORATE

Talk What problems did inflation cause?

What Do You Think? What would it have been like to live during the American Revolution?

236 **Lesson 4** What Was It Like to Live During the American Revolution?

Citizenship

Are Women and African Americans of the Revolution Overlooked?

Work with a partner. Design a monument that honors the contributions of women or African Americans during the war. Consider what your monument should look like.

- Make an outline of the ways women and African Americans contributed to the war.
- Who were some individuals you learned about, and how do they represent the larger groups?
- Think about other monuments you have seen, and think about how your monument could compare to them.

Draw or make a model of your monument.

Present your monument to the class. Explain what you have learned about how women and African Americans helped the war effort.

James Armistead, who was a slave, risked his life to spy for the colonists.

Deborah Sampson disguised herself as a man so she could join the Continental Army.

Lesson 4 **237**

Research Companion, pp. 236–237

(EL) ENGLISH LEARNERS SCAFFOLD

ELD.PI.5.9 Expressing information and ideas in formal oral presentations on academic topics

Emerging

Use Graphic Organizers Have students work together to create and complete a graphic organizer to identify ways that women, African Americans, and American Indians participated in the war. Then guide students to use their organizers as they present their citizenship probject.

Expanding/Bridging

Present a Project Have students work together to outline and present their citizenship project. Provide support as needed, such as guiding them to reread sections of the text, helping with language choices, or facilitating discussion.

See the **Language Learner Teaching Guide** for more language support strategies.

Monitor and Differentiate

REACHING ALL LEARNERS

Approaching Level

Guide students to reread the data in the graph. Explain that it took several paper dollars to equal one dollar's value in hard currency, such as gold or silver. As the war progressed, and Congress issued more and more paper dollars to cover the expenses, a buyer needed more and more paper money to equal one dollar of hard currency. Model this concept using classroom objects, substituting pencils for paper dollars and markers for hard currency.

Beyond Level

Guide students to conduct further research into the ways inflation affected people. Encourage students to provide concrete examples if possible. Have them present their findings to the whole class.

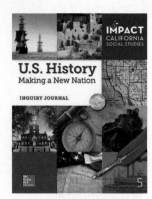

Inquiry Journal
pp. 192–193

 STANDARDS

Identify and map the major military battles, campaigns, and turning points of the Revolutionary War, the roles of the American and British leaders, and the Indian leaders' alliances on both sides. **HSS.5.6.1**

Write narratives to develop real or imagined experiences or events using effective technique, descriptive details, and clear event sequences. **CCSS.ELA.W.5.3**

Engage effectively in a range of collaborative discussions (one-on-one, in groups, and teacher-led) with diverse partners on *grade 5 topics and texts*, building on others' ideas and expressing their own clearly. **CCSS.ELA.SL.5.1**

Go Digital!

- Students can go online to report their findings. Assess their responses online.
- Students can access the online graphic organizer to capture ideas from their investigation.

Think About It

Students will review their research and consider the risks people took by fighting.

- Remind students to review the motivations they analyzed and included in their graphic organizer. Direct students back to pages 230–237 of their Research Companion if they need more information.

Write About It

Write a Letter Have students read the prompt. Explain that they will write a letter from the point of view of a made-up character. However, even though the character is made-up, he or she must represent one of the groups students read about in the lesson.

Remind students to include the following elements in their response.

- Include important information that makes the events of your letter factual and interesting.
- Use details to describe the events and people your character experiences and meets.
- Use informal language that seems like something your character would say.

Use the rubric on p. T496 to evaluate students' work.

Talk About It

Interview Ask students to work with a partner. Explain that one student will interview the other student, who will be playing the part of the character he or she created in the letter. Then partners will switch roles.

- Explain that they should develop relevant and interesting questions for each other to answer.
- The interviewee should remember to stay in character the whole time, responding as his or her character would respond.
- Remind students to be respectful of their classmates' opinions and work.

Connect to the
Essential Question

Read the prompt aloud to students. Ask them the following guiding questions:

- What were the defining qualities of the American Revolution, both the war and the people who fought in it? (Responses will vary, but should include perseverence and desire for freedom)
- Which of those qualities do you see at work in the nation today? (Responses will vary.)
- How are conflicts different today? (Responses will vary.)

Remind students to use the space provided in their journal to jot down notes.

Report Your Findings

Think About It

Review your research. Consider what you have learned about life during the American Revolution. What risks did people take by fighting?

Write About It

Write a Letter Create a character set in the Revolution. First, decide the character details: Which side is he or she on? Which group is he or she a part of? What motivates your character? Next, write a letter to a friend or family member from the perspective of your character. Discuss what he or she thinks of the war, how he or she is coping, and what he or she plans to do next.

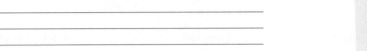

Responses will vary, but students should write about a realistic character who has believable motivations for participating in the American Revolution.

Talk About It

Interview

Work with a partner. Interview each other. One of you will take the role of a journalist, and the other will be the character you created. The journalist should ask questions such as "Why are you fighting / not fighting?" "What do you hope to accomplish?" "How has the war changed your life?" After the first interview, switch roles with your partner.

Connect to the

Make Connections

Think about what you have learned about the American Revolution. What does it have in common with modern conflicts? What is different?

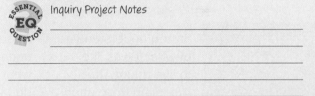

Sample response: The American Revolution was similar to modern conflicts because it caused turmoil among citizens in addition to being difficult and dangerous for soldiers. It is different from modern conflicts because of the weapons and because of slower means of transportation and communication.

> **Inquiry Project Notes**

192 Lesson 4 What Was It Like to Live During the American Revolution?

Lesson 4 **193**

Inquiry Journal, pp. 192–193

 ## ENGLISH LEARNERS SCAFFOLD

ELD.PII.5.4 Using nouns and noun phrases

Emerging	Expanding	Bridging
Write a Letter Explain that letters are usually written in a conversational tone. They usually include everyday details about the writer's life. In this case, the letter will also reference historical events. Remind students to write from the point of view of the character they make up.	**Use Descriptive Details** Remind students that a letter includes information about daily events. It will also reference the character's motivations for supporting or opposing the war. Students should use language that is specific to the character they make up and is consistent with his or her outlook on the war.	**Act Out the Letter** Have students imagine what their character sounds like, then have them read aloud the letter, staying in character. Encourage students to add emotion and emphasis when appropriate.

See the **Language Learner Teaching Guide** for more language support strategies.

Monitor and Differentiate

REACHING ALL LEARNERS

Approaching Level

Work with students as they write their letters. Encourage them to use language they have learned in the lesson as appropriate. Remind students that they are writing a character, and their wording should correspond to the character's actions and beliefs.

Beyond Level

Encourage students to work with a partner. Have them expand on their letters by writing a series of letters between their characters, similar to the letters of Abigail and John Adams. Have them develop the relationship between the two characters and identify the beliefs of both. Have them read aloud their letters to the class.

Know what your students know!

Lesson Task
Report Your Findings

Use the rubric to evaluate students' responses.

Write a Letter Students create a character and write a letter from the perspective of that character. The character discusses what he or she thinks of the war and what he or she plans to do next.

Interview Students work with a partner. They interview each other as character and journalist then switch roles.

Lesson Task Evaluation Rubric

	4	3	2	1
Historical Understanding	Strong understanding of what it was like to live during the American Revolution	Adequate understanding of what it was like to live during the American Revolution	Uneven understanding of what it was like to live during the American Revolution	No understanding of what it was like to live during the American Revolution
Letter	Clearly provides information and perspective	Adequately provides information and perspective	Somewhat clear or unclear information or perspective	No relevant information stated or student does not show understanding of the task
Develop Character with Details	Character and events developed with descriptive details	Character and events developed with adequate details	Character and events developed with few details	Character and events are missing or irrelevant
Small-Group Discussions	Asks relevant questions of partner	Asks thoughtful questions of partner	Asks few questions of partner	Asks no questions of partner
	Provides relevant and creative responses	Provides relevant responses	Provides few relevant responses	Provides no relevant responses

Lesson Assessment

Go Digital!

- Have students complete the Chapter 5 Lesson 4 Assessment online to monitor their understanding of the lesson content.

ONLINE ASSESSMENT

California Smarter Balanced Assessment Connections!

Standards Covered	Lesson Task	Lesson Assessment	Alignment with California Smarter Balanced Assessment
History Social Science Content 5.6.1; 5.6.2; 5.6.3; 5.6.4; 5.6.6	✔	✔	Claim 1 Targets 8, 9, 11
History Social Science Analysis Skills Chronological and Spatial Thinking 5.1; 5.2; 5.3 Research, Evidence, and Point of View 5.1; 5.2 Historical Interpretation 5.1; 5.3; 5.4	✔	✔	Claim 1 Targets 8, 9, 11
Writing W.5.3	✔	✔	Claim 2 Target 1
Research and Inquiry W.5.7		✔	Claim 4 Targets 1, 2
Reading RI.5.3	✔	✔	Claim 1 Target 11, 12
Speaking and Listening SL.5.1	✔		Claim 3 Target 3 Claim 4 Target 1

LESSON QUESTION

What Did the Colonists Gain by Winning the War?

Background Information

In this lesson, students learn about how the war ended and what the colonists gained by winning. Students will analyze the last major battles and understand how different groups were affected by the outcome of the war.

Community Connections

To enrich what students have learned about the end of the war, invite a guest speaker from a local college or university to talk to the class about the importance of the American victory.

LESSON STANDARDS

✔ Identify and map the major military battles, campaigns, and turning points of the Revolutionary War, the roles of the American and British leaders, and the Indian leaders' alliances on both sides. **HSS.5.6.1**

✔ Understand the personal impact and economic hardship of the war on families, problems of financing the war, wartime inflation, and laws against hoarding goods and materials and profiteering. **HSS.5.6.4**

✔ Explain how state constitutions that were established after 1776 embodied the ideals of the American Revolution and helped serve as models for the U.S. Constitution. **HSS.5.6.5**

✔ Demonstrate knowledge of the significance of land policies developed under the Continental Congress (e.g., sale of western lands, the Northwest Ordinance of 1787) and those policies' impact on American Indians' land. **HSS.5.6.6**

✔ Students place key events and people of the historical era they are studying in a chronological sequence and within a spatial context; they interpret time lines. **HAS.CS.1**

✔ Students use map and globe skills to determine the absolute locations of places and interpret information available through a map's or globe's legend, scale, and symbolic representations. **HAS.CS.4**

✔ Students differentiate between primary and secondary sources. **HAS.HR.1**

✔ Students conduct cost-benefit analyses of historical and current events. **HAS.HI.4**

Connect to the Essential Question

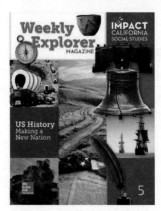

Chapter 5, pp. 58–71

The **Weekly Explorer Magazine** supports the students' exploration of the Essential Question and provides additional resources for the EQ Inquiry Project.

Inquiry Project

How Can You Make an Impact?

Remind students to use the information they learn in this lesson and other resources to complete the EQ Inquiry Project.

Dinah Zike's

You will be using Foldables in this lesson.

When Minutes Count!

Suggested Lesson Pacing

1 ENGAGE
One Day

- Lesson Opener
- Analyze the Source
- Inquiry Tools

Go Digital
- **iMap:** The Battle of Yorktown

2 INVESTIGATE
Two to Three Days

🕐 **Short on Time?** Look for the clock to teach core content in less time.

- The War Moves South
- The Battle of Yorktown
- Ending the War
- No Victory for Some

3 REPORT
One Day

- Think About It
- Write a Letter
- Defend Your Claims

Make Connections!

(CCSS) CONNECT TO ELA

Reading
Analyze multiple accounts of the same event or topic, noting important similarities and differences in the point of view they represent. **RI.5.6**

Research
Conduct short research projects that use several sources to build knowledge through investigation of different aspects of a topic. **W.5.7**

Recall relevant information from experiences or gather relevant information from print and digital sources; summarize or paraphrase information in notes and finished work, and provide a list of sources. **W.5.8**

Writing
Write opinion pieces on topics or texts, supporting a point of view with reasons and information. **W.5.1**

Speaking and Listening
Engage effectively in a range of collaborative discussions (one-on-one, in groups, and teacher-led) with diverse partners on *grade 5 topics and texts*, building on others' ideas and expressing their own clearly **SL.5.1**

Classroom Resources

🔍 Search for additional resources using the following key words.

Charles Cornwallis

Battle of Guilford Courthouse

Battle of Yorktown

Prince Hall

Marquis de Lafayette

Francis Marion

Peace of Paris

Comte de Rochambeau

George Washington

1 ENGAGE

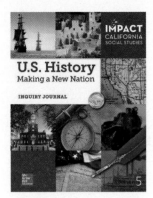

Inquiry Journal
pp. 194–195

 STANDARDS

Identify and map the major military battles, campaigns, and turning points of the Revolutionary War, the roles of the American and British leaders, and the Indian leaders' alliances on both sides. **HSS.5.6.1**

Students pose relevant questions about events they encounter in historical documents, eyewitness accounts, oral histories, letters, diaries, artifacts, photographs, maps, artworks, and architecture. **HAS.HR.2**

(ccss) Engage effectively in a range of collaborative discussions (one-on-one, in groups, and teacher-led) with diverse partners on *grade 5 topics and texts*, building on others' ideas and expressing their own clearly. **CCSS.ELA.SL.5.1**

Go Digital!

Explore the lesson content with online whole-class presentation tools.

• **iMap:** The Battle of Yorktown

What Did the Colonists Gain by Winning the War?

Bellringer

Prompt students to retrieve information from the previous lessons. Say: *How did women, African Americans, and American Indians participate in and contribute to the war?* (Women managed farms and businesses, and some even fought in the war; many African Americans fought in the war, hoping to gain their freedom; American Indians were divided between supporting the Americans and the British.)

Lesson Outcomes

What Am I Learning? Have students read the Lesson Outcomes on p. 194.

Why Am I Learning It? Check that students understand that they have been learning about the hardships that people faced during the war. In this lesson they will learn about the end of the war and what the former colonists gained by winning it.

How Will I Know That I Learned It? Ask students the following questions.

• What will you learn about? (the causes and effects of winning the war)

• What is the purpose of the task? (to understand what the colonists gained by winning)

• How will you support your explanation? (with text evidence)

Talk About It COLLABORATE

Provide some scaffolding for students to use as they discuss the picture. Provide background information as needed.

• *The picture shows _____.*

• *Some clues that tell me this are _____.*

• *The figure in the middle is _____.*

Collaborative Conversations COLLABORATE

Look at the Details As students engage in partner, small group, and whole-class discussions, encourage them to

• Think about the figures on the left and the right. Look at their positions, faces, flags, and even their horses for clues about who they are and why there are included in the picture.

• Ask and answer questions about the event shown in the picture, using the caption at the bottom for more clues.

• Draw or modify conclusions that are based on the discussion.

Lesson 5

What Did the Colonists Gain by Winning the War?

Lesson Outcomes

What Am I Learning?
In this lesson, you're going to use your investigative skills to learn about what Americans gained by winning the war.

Why Am I Learning It?
Reading and talking about what the American colonists gained will help you understand whether the war was worth fighting.

How Will I Know That I Learned It?
You will be able to understand the causes and effects of winning the war.

Talk About It COLLABORATE

Look at the Details How do you think the soldiers on each side of the drawing feel about what is happening?

General Cornwallis surrenders at Yorktown.

HSS.5.6.1, HSS.5.6.2, HAS.CS.4, HAS.HI.4

194 Lesson 5 What Did the Colonists Gain by Winning the War?

Lesson 5 **195**

Inquiry Journal, pp. 194–195

ENGLISH LEARNERS SCAFFOLD

ELD.PI.5.6 Reading closely literary and informational texts and viewing multimedia to determine how meaning is conveyed explicitly and implicitly through language

Emerging	Expanding	Bridging
Identify Details Encourage students to describe what they see in the picture. Guide students to explain why the figures are positioned as they are, and have them identify the main people in the painting.	**Analyze Details** Have students use descriptive words to tell about the scene in the picture. They may analyze facial expressions, placement of figures, or setting. Guide them to use these details to discuss the events of the painting with a partner.	**Analyze Words and Language** Point out the text at the bottom of the picture. Explain that this scene was printed, and the description below it tells what is happening. Describe the word *surrender* as a group. Then have students discuss how the caption tells more about the scene.

See the **Language Learner Teaching Guide** for more language support strategies.

Monitor and Differentiate

REACHING ALL LEARNERS

Approaching Level

Work with students to identify what is happening in the scene. Encourage them to look at the caption below the picture to understand what it is about. Have students take turns discussing the details they see in the picture.

On Level

Have students discuss the painting, stating opinions about how it might illustrate what the colonists gained by winning the war.

Beyond Level

Guide students to conduct further research into the scene shown in the painting. Encourage them to try to find out who Lord Cornwallis was and how he came to surrender to Washington.

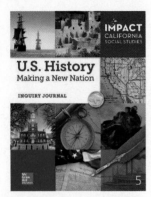

Inquiry Journal
pp. 196–197

 OBJECTIVES

Identify and map the major military battles, campaigns, and turning points of the Revolutionary War, the roles of the American and British leaders, and the Indian leaders' alliances on both sides. **HSS.5.6.1**

Students place key events and people of the historical era they are studying in a chronological sequence and within a spatial context; they interpret time lines. **HAS.CS.1**

Students differentiate between primary and secondary sources. **HAS.HR.1**

Go Digital!

Model how to inspect and find evidence with online whole-class presentation tools.

Build Background

Washington After the War Washington discharged his officers on December 4, 1783. After finalizing his own affairs, he traveled home to Mount Vernon on December 23. He genuinely believed he was finished with public life. His respite lasted until 1786 when he became increasingly concerned about the weakness of the Articles of Confederation as a means of governing the country. In 1787, he agreed to serve as a delegate to the Constitutional Convention in Philadelphia, over which he was asked to preside. Once the convention was over, he again believed he would be allowed to retire to Mount Vernon in peace, but in 1789, he accepted the nomination as the first president of the United States.

1 Inspect

Read Ask students to skim the text, including the excerpt from George Washington's Farewell Orders, to focus on understanding the overall meaning. Remind them to circle words and phrases that are unfamiliar.

- Who was George Washington addressing in his Farewell Orders? (his officers and soldiers)

- What did Washington want to praise? (the men's achievements)

- What is he suggesting that the men do once they get home to "civil life"? (to keep up the virtues, or good behaviors, they learned and practiced during the war)

Collaborate Have partners take turns finding terms in the primary source that show Washington's opinions. Encourage them to use those terms to describe an event they have experienced or a person they know. (Answers should include "beyond the reach of malevolence," "achievements and fame," "honorable actions," "private virtues," "amiable," "splendid qualities")

2 Find Evidence

Reread Have students reread the text.

Analyze the Primary Source Reread the excerpt aloud then analyze it as a class.

- Ask: What does the word *malevolence* mean? Use a dictionary if needed. (the cause of great harm or spite)

- What does Washington mean when he says that the army's reputation is "beyond the reach of malevolence"? (No one could think badly of them because they behaved so well and fought so bravely.)

- Do you think this was a good phrase to include in his farewell? (Answers will vary.)

COLLABORATE
3 Make Connections

Talk Guide students to identify the qualities Washington lists. Have students use context clues or a dictionary to determine the meaning of each. ("economy, prudence, industry, . . . valor, perseverance, and enterprise")

Connect to Now Have partners discuss what they think a general today might say to his or her men when a war ends.

Analyze the Source

Washington's Farewell Orders

1 Inspect

Read Look at the text. What is Washington saying about his men's service in the war?

• **Circle** words you don't know.

• **Underline** clues that help you understand unfamiliar words and concepts.

• **Discuss** the terms that show Washington's opinion.

My Notes

_____

_____

_____

_____

_____

_____

_____

_____

_____

_____

_____

_____

Washington gave these final orders to the troops believing that he was about to retire after a long career and return to his home, Mount Vernon, Virginia. He thanked the officers and men. He also reminded them of the good work they had done while fighting for independence. Washington wasn't aware at this time that he would later be asked to serve as the nation's first president.

PRIMARY SOURCE

In Their Words...
George Washington

... Let it be known and remembered, that the reputation of the Federal Armies is established beyond the reach of malevolence; and let a consciousness of their achievements and fame still unite the men, who composed them to honorable actions, under the persuasion that the private virtues of economy, prudence, and industry will not be less amiable in civil life than the more splendid qualities of valor, perseverance, and enterprise were in the field.

—from the Farewell Orders to Continental Army, November 2, 1783

Soldiers listen as General George Washington gives his final orders.

2 Find Evidence

Reread Examine the phrase "let it be known and remembered, that the reputation of the federal Armies is established beyond the reach of malevolence."

What does Washington mean when he says that the army's reputation is "beyond the reach of malevolence"? Use a dictionary to help you define any words that are unfamiliar.

Was this a good phrase to include in his farewell orders? Why or why not?

3 Make Connections

Talk What qualities does Washington say he hopes the men will continue to show in their everyday lives?

196 Lesson 5 What Did the Colonists Gain by Winning the War?

Lesson 5 **197**

Inquiry Journal, pp. 196–197

(EL) ENGLISH LEARNERS SCAFFOLD

ELD.PI.5.5 Listening actively to spoken English in a range of social and academic contexts

Emerging

Support Understanding Read the excerpt aloud and ask students to identify Washington's general tone. Choose several words that you can unpack using word parts, such as *honorable*, which also may have cognates in students' first languages. Break apart the words, then reread the section so students hear the word in context again.

Expanding/Bridging

Unpack Language Explain to students that writing from the past often uses different structure and punctuation than we use to today. Point out that this entire excerpt is actually part of a single sentence. Guide students to unpack each phrase to determine its meaning and how it fits into the whole of Washington's ideas.

See the **Language Learner Teaching Guide** for more language support strategies.

Monitor and Differentiate

REACHING ALL LEARNERS

Approaching Level

Have students identify unfamiliar words. Remind them to underline and annotate the primary source. Then have them practice using word parts to decipher unknown words before using a dictionary to confirm their meanings.

Beyond Level

Encourage students to conduct research to find other letters written by George Washington. Students may choose to find letters written during the war or letters written later that tell about his experiences during the war. Ask them to summarize for the class what they learn about Washington's personality and motivations.

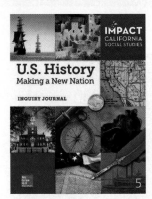

Inquiry Journal
pp. 198–199

 STANDARDS

Understand the personal impact and economic hardship of the war on families, problems of financing the war, wartime inflation, and laws against hoarding goods and materials and profiteering. **HSS.5.6.4**

Demonstrate knowledge of the significance of land policies developed under the Continental Congress (e.g., sale of western lands, the Northwest Ordinance of 1787) and those policies' impact on American Indians' land. **HSS.5.6.6**

Students identify and interpret the multiple causes and effects of historical events. **HAS.HI.3**

(CCSS) Analyze multiple accounts of the same event or topic, noting important similarities and differences in the point of view they represent. **CCSS.ELA.RI.5.6**

Go Digital!

- Model how to explore and investigate with online whole-class tools.

- Students can access the online graphic organizer to use the inquiry tools as they read.

Explore Cause and Effect

Explain Tell students that a cause is an event that makes something happen. An effect is something that happens as a result. Remind students that many causes have multiple effects and some effects stem from several causes. Complicated events like wars have many causes and many effects.

Read Have students read aloud the step-by-step instructions about how to identify cause and effect. Tell students that they should ask themselves questions such as *What happened?* and *Why did it happen?* They should also look for key details that signal important information.

Guide Practice Present a brief model of analyzing cause and effect. Say: *American soldiers wanted to fight for independence and defeat Great Britain. The Americans won the war, which means the United States is now an independent nation.* Remind students to look for signal words such as *because, so,* and *as a result* that indicate a cause-and-effect relationship.

Investigate!

Have students read pages 238–247 in the Research Companion. Tell them the information that will help them answer the lesson question *What Did the Colonists Gain by Winning the War?*

Take Notes Tell students that they will take notes as they read each section. Explain that taking notes will help them understand what different groups wanted, gained, or lost as a result of the war. Remind students that they should look for key details and important information in the text.

Inspect Guide students to read the text in each section to determine what it says. Encourage them to work to find information about what people in different groups gained or lost as a result of the war.

Find Evidence Encourage students to reread the text to develop a deeper understanding. Remind students that they should think about how the facts and details will help them answer the lesson question.

Collaborative Conversations

Text-Based Discussion Remind students that discussing the text with others can help them

- Better understand the importance of specific historical events
- Get more out of what they read
- Learn about the perspectives of other people

Inquiry Tools

Explore Cause and Effect

A **cause** is an event that makes something happen. An **effect** is an event that happens as a result of a cause. Looking for cause-and-effect relationships can help you better understand what you read.

To find the causes and effects:

1. **Look for transitions related to causes and effects.**
   Because, therefore, as a result, in order to, and similar transitional words and phrases can indicate cause-and-effect relationships.

2. **Take note of chronology.**
   Texts will often present cause-and-effect relationships in the order that they happen. This is not always true, though, so be careful.

3. **Analyze the events.**
   Ask yourself, would an event have happened without this particular cause? Would the effect have been the same if the earlier event had never happened?

4. **Note that an event may have more than one cause or effect.**
   There are usually multiple causes for a historical event. Similarly, a historical event may impact many future events.

COLLABORATE Based on the text you just read, work with your class to complete the chart below.

Group	Hoped to Gain	Gained or Lost	Results
American soldiers	Hoped for independence from Great Britain	Gained	These soldiers can now return to civil life as free and independent citizens.

Investigate!

Read pages 238–247 in your Research Companion. Use your investigative skills to look for text evidence that tells you about what people gained and lost because of their participation in the war.

Possible responses:

Group	Hoped to Gain	Gained or Lost	Results
Women	Hoped for more freedom and a bigger role in public life	Gained and Lost	Lost husbands and sons; some women made history by writing, leading, and fighting
African slaves	Hoped for freedom after the war	Lost	Slavery continued in the Southern Colonies for many years.
American Indian Loyalists	Hoped that Britain would win and prevent more American settlement of their lands	Lost	Britain could not deliver on its promise; Americans treated American Indians badly after the war.

McGraw-Hill Education

Inquiry Journal, pp. 198–199

ENGLISH LEARNERS SCAFFOLD

ELD.PI.5.1 Exchanging information and ideas with others through oral collaborative discussions on a range of social and academic topics

Emerging

Identify Cause and Effect Encourage students to identify key words as they read. These key words may indicate an important place, event, or person. Have students make a list of key words. When they fill out their graphic organizers, have them refer to this list when they narrow down the information to include.

Expanding/Bridging

Discuss Main Ideas Remind students that by identifying what a group wanted to gain they are identifying causes. By figuring out whether that group won or lost they are identifying effects. Encourage students to look for main ideas as they read. This will help them find out more information about what different groups wanted from the war. Then guide students to look for more details about what happened to that group.

See the **Language Learner Teaching Guide** for more language support strategies.

Monitor and Differentiate

REACHING ALL LEARNERS

Special Needs

Encourage students to chorally read sections of the text. Provide help with fluency as needed, guiding students to highlight main ideas and to call out important details.

Approaching Level

Encourage students to carefully reread each section looking for unfamiliar words. Guide them to use context to understand the word's meaning or use a dictionary to define the word. Have students use these words in their discussions and in their writing.

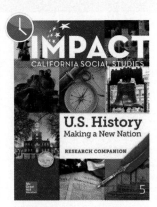

Research Companion
pp. 238–239

 STANDARDS

Identify and map the major military battles, campaigns, and turning points of the Revolutionary War, the roles of the American and British leaders, and the Indian leaders' alliances on both sides. **HSS.5.6.1**

Students place key events and people of the historical era they are studying in a chronological sequence and within a spatial context; they interpret time lines. **HAS.CS.1**

Students pose relevant questions about events they encounter in historical documents, eyewitness accounts, oral histories, letters, diaries, artifacts, photographs, maps, artworks, and architecture. **HAS.HR.2**

Go Digital!

Investigate the lesson content with online whole-class presentation tools.

• **iMap:** The Battle of Yorktown

Background Information

Charles Cornwallis Like Washington, Lord Cornwallis was a veteran of the Seven Years' War. At the beginning of the American Revolution, Cornwallis had defeated Washington in New Jersey. Later he was put in charge of the British forces in the South. When he met Washington again, it was at Yorktown, and Washington was laying siege to the city, trapping Cornwallis' men.

| TIMELINE | Invite students to look at the timeline on the top of p. 239.

> **Analyze** When did the American Revolution end? (1783 with the Peace of Paris) **HAS.CS.1**

Analyze the Source

Inspect Have students read pp. 238–239.

Find Evidence Use the questions below to check comprehension. Remind students to support their answers with text evidence.

> **Explain** Why did the British decide to move the war to the Southern Colonies after 1779? (They were losing in the North and West and hoped to have more success in the South, where more people were loyal to Great Britain.) **DOK 2**

> **Identify** Who became the leader of the British Army in 1780? (Cornwallis) **DOK 1**

> **Cite Evidence** Why did the Americans lose battles in the South? ("Congress had very little money and almost no supplies for forces in the Southern Colonies.") **DOK 2**

> **Analyze Signal Words** What does the signal word *however* indicate will happen to the British forces? (It indicates that while they are winning now, they will have trouble in the future.) **DOK 3**

Analyze the Primary Source

> **Analyze Cause and Effect** What led Washington to suspend hostilities for two hours? (He wanted to give their representatives a chance to discuss terms of surrender, so he ordered a ceasefire.) **DOK 2**

> **Context Clues** What does Washington mean when he said that "property taken in the country, will be reclaimed"? (He means that any American property the British soldiers stole or took during the course of the war must be returned.) **DOK 2**

Make Connections

> **Infer** The primary sources are Washington's responses to letters from General Cornwallis. How can we infer what Cornwallis wrote to Washington? (Washington says he received a letter earlier in the day, and he says that he is "readily [inclined] . . . to listen to . . . terms for the surrender." Cornwallis must have written to say he was ready to give up the fight.) **DOK 3**

Lesson 5

What Did the Colonists Gain by Winning the War?

The War Moves South

By 1779, the American Continental Army had turned back British attacks in the north and the west. British leaders decided to focus on the Southern Colonies. The Southern Colonies had higher proportions of Loyalists, and the British hoped to have their help in defeating the Americans once and for all. General Charles Cornwallis became the leader of British troops in the South in 1780.

Congress had very little money and almost no supplies for forces in the Southern Colonies. Between 1778 and 1781, the British won battles against American General Nathanael Greene at Savannah, Georgia, and at Charles Town and Camden in South Carolina. At first. it seemed as if Cornwallis's strategies were working. However, the colonists' greater knowledge of the land they were fighting for proved to be an advantage.

Soldiers listen as General George Washington gives his final orders.

HSS.5.6.1, HSS.5.6.2, HSS.5.6.7, HAS.CS.5

238 Lesson 5 What Did the Colonists Gain by Winning the War?

Timeline

June 1779 Spain declares war on Great Britain.

May 1780 General Charles Cornwallis becomes British commander in the South.

September 1783 Peace of Paris ends American Revolution.

1775 | 1780 | 1785

October 1781 British defeated at Yorktown, Virginia

PRIMARY SOURCE

In Their Words... George Washington

My Lord: I have had the Honor of receiving Your Lordship's Letter of this Date. An Ardent Desire to spare the further Effusion of Blood, will readily incline me to listen to such Terms for the Surrender of your Posts and Garrisons of York and Gloucester, as are admissible. I wish previously to the Meeting of Commissioners, that your Lordship's proposals in writing, may be sent to the American Lines: for which Purpose, a Suspension of Hostilities during two Hours from the Delivery of this Letter will be granted. I have the Honor etc.

The Officers will be indulged in retaining their Side Arms, and the Officers and Soldiers may preserve their Baggage and Effects, with this Reserve, that Property taken in the Country, will be reclaimed. With Regard to the Individuals in civil Capacities, whose Interests Your Lordship wishes may be attended to, until they are more particularly described, nothing definitive can be settled.

I have to add, that I expect the Sick and Wounded will be supplied with their own Hospital Stores, and be attended by British Surgeons, particularly charged with the Care of them. Your Lordship will be pleased to signify your Determination either to accept or reject the Proposals now offered, in the Course of Two Hours from the Delivery of this Letter, that Commissioners may be appointed to digest the Articles of Capitulation, or a Renewal of Hostilities may take place. I have the Honor etc.

— from Letters from George Washington to General Lord Cornwallis, October 17, 1781

Lesson 5 **239**

Research Companion, pp. 238–239

ENGLISH LEARNERS SCAFFOLD

ELD.PI.5.6 Reading closely literary and informational texts and viewing multimedia to determine how meaning is conveyed explicitly and implicitly through language

Emerging

Understand Syntax Help students understand the sentence structure used in the primary source. Encourage them to identify words that they want to define later. Have them unpack each phrase rather than trying to understand the lengthy sentences as a whole. Then work with them to create a translation of important passages of the primary source into modern English.

Expanding/Bridging

Summarize Main Ideas Have students work with a partner to summarize the main idea of each paragraph of the primary source. Then have them outline the key details, including names, places, and directions. Guide them to talk about why the events of the surrender are discussed in such formal terms.

See the **Language Learner Teaching Guide** for more language support strategies.

Monitor and Differentiate

REACHING ALL LEARNERS

Approaching Level

Have students work together to create a translation of the primary source into modern English. Remind them to identify the meaning of each part of the letters before trying to translate it.

Beyond Level

Have students conduct additional research into the events surrounding Cornwallis' surrender. Students may choose to research how the British soldiers were treated, how long it took for them to return to Great Britain, or what officers such as Cornwallis did after the war. Have them share their findings with the entire class.

Research Companion
pp. 240–241

 STANDARDS

Identify and map the major military battles, campaigns, and turning points of the Revolutionary War, the roles of the American and British leaders, and the Indian leaders' alliances on both sides. **HSS.5.6.1**

Students summarize the key events of the era they are studying and explain the historical contexts of those events. **HAS.HI.1**

Students identify and interpret the multiple causes and effects of historical events. **HAS.HI.3**

Go Digital!

Investigate the lesson content with online whole-class presentation tools.

Background Information

Marquis de Lafayette The Marquis de Lafayette was a French aristocrat who strongly believed in the ideals of the American Revolution. When he was 19, he traveled to America to fight in the Revolutionary War. He and General George Washington became close friends and remained so throughout Washington's life. Lafayette was a great general, and with his support, the Americans received help from France. This helped the Americans defeat the British.

Analyze the Source

Inspect Have students read pp. 240–241.

Find Evidence Use the questions below to check comprehension. Remind students to support their answers with text evidence.

Identify Who was Francis Marion? (an American captain called "The Swamp Fox" who led bands of raiders in small fights against the British in the swamps of South Carolina) **DOK 1**

Summarize Was the Battle of Guilford Court House a victory for the British? (Yes; they won, but they lost so many men that many thought it was really a defeat.) **DOK 2**

Context Clues What does the word *raiders* mean? (The text says that *raiders* are members of a small force of soldiers. This small force conducted surprise attacks on the British.) **DOK 2**

Identify Who was in charge of the American soldiers in the South before the Battle of Yorktown? (the Marquis de Lafayette) **DOK 1**

Analyze What did Lafayette plan to do to Cornwallis at Yorktown? (He planned to cut off Cornwallis from supply ships while giving Washington time to move his men to Virginia to surround the British.) **DOK 3**

Summarize How did James Armistead help Lafayette succeed? (He posed as a servant to Cornwallis and passed information about British plans to Lafayette. In turn, he fed incorrect information to the British, which led them believe the Americans were going to attack New York City rather than Yorktown.) **DOK 3**

Make Connections

Draw Conclusions How did the Americans work together to entrap the British at Yorktown? (Responses will vary, but students should identify that Lafayette made use of spies, and he and Washington hatched a plan to trap Cornwallis.) **DOK 3**

Stop and Check

Talk Encourage students to think about what a general needs in order to win a war. (Responses may include that Cornwallis won, but he lost too many men to really call it a victory.)

Find Details Explain to students that after they read and take notes, they should think about how the information can help them answer the Essential Question.

The Continental Army managed to surprise the British in several raids led by Captain Francis Marion. Marion was called "The Swamp Fox" because his small force of raiders attacked the British unexpectedly and then retreated into the swamps of South Carolina.

Cornwallis pursued the Continental Army through the Carolina backcountry. When the two armies met in March 1871 at Guilford Court House, in North Carolina, Cornwallis lost one-fourth of his men. He declared it a victory because Greene's troops had left the battlefield. The loss, however, crippled the British forces. When word of the battle reached England, Charles James Fox declared in Parliament that "Another such victory would destroy the British army."

Because of the heavy losses, Cornwallis knew his men needed to rest and resupply. He fled north to Virginia to await ships from British headquarters in New York City. This movement would present George Washington with an opportunity.

Key Battles in the Southern Colonies

Stop and Check

Talk Why was it important that Cornwallis lost so many men as a result of his victory at the Battle of Guilford Court House?

Find Details As you read, add new information to the graphic organizer on page 199 in your Inquiry Journal.

The Battle of Yorktown

George Washington had put the Marquis de Lafayette in charge of a troop of soldiers in Virginia. When Cornwallis marched north to Virginia, Lafayette wrote to Washington, "Were I to fight a battle, I should be cut to pieces. . . . I am not strong enough even to get beaten."

Lafayette did have an important secret weapon, however. James Armistead, who was enslaved in Virginia, volunteered to spy for Lafayette. From a position as Cornwallis's servant, he passed information about Cornwallis's plans and weaknesses.

From the intelligence Armistead provided, Lafayette formed a plan to **blockade** Chesapeake Bay. This prevented Cornwallis from resupplying his troops. Armistead told Cornwallis that the Americans planned to attack New York City, tricking Cornwallis into believing his army was safe at Yorktown.

Meanwhile, Washington's troops and a French army moved quickly and secretly to Yorktown to join Lafayette. By the time Cornwallis realized what had happened, he was surrounded by a force more than twice the size of his own.

French general Jean de Rochambeau, with George Washington, gives orders for the attack on Yorktown.

Lesson 5 241

Research Companion, pp. 240–241

ELD.PI.5.6 Reading closely literary and informational texts and viewing multimedia to determine how meaning is conveyed explicitly and implicitly through language

Emerging

Identify Details Work with students as they outline the problems or mistakes that caused Cornwallis to ultimately fail at Yorktown. Guide students to create a chart then use it in their discussions.

Expanding/Bridging

Use Details Have students create a list of events that led to Cornwallis' defeat at Yorktown. Encourage students to share their opinions about which event or mistake was the most important in securing the American victory. Students should use details from the text. They may make graphic organizers or lists if it helps their discussion.

See the **Language Learner Teaching Guide** for more language support strategies.

Monitor and Differentiate

REACHING ALL LEARNERS

Approaching Level

Work with students to understand that the word *intelligence* has multiple meanings. Encourage students to supply meanings of the word that are already familiar to them. Then have students look it up and choose the definition that most likely fits this context. Guide them to discuss how Armistead helped the war effort when he provided intelligence to Lafayette.

Beyond Level

Encourage students to conduct additional research into the events that preceded the Battle of Yorktown. Encourage them to research letters or first-hand accounts, maps, battle plans, or other documents that can give them insight into the American strategy.

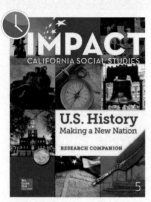

Research Companion
pp. 242–243

 STANDARDS

Identify and map the major military battles, campaigns, and turning points of the Revolutionary War, the roles of the American and British leaders, and the Indian leaders' alliances on both sides. **HSS.5.6.1**

Students place key events and people of the historical era they are studying in a chronological sequence and within a spatial context; they interpret time lines. **HAS.CS.1**

Students use map and globe skills to determine the absolute locations of places and interpret information available through a map's or globe's legend, scale, and symbolic representations. **HAS.CS.4**

Go *Digital!*

Investigate the lesson content with online whole-class presentation tools.

Analyze the Source

Inspect Have students continue reading about the Battle of Yorktown on pp. 242–243.

Find Evidence Use the questions below to check comprehension. Remind students to support their answers with text evidence.

Identify What happened during the Battle of Yorktown? (The Americans and French fired into the British camp at Yorktown and blockaded the port. They kept Cornwallis from receiving new troops and supplies.) **DOK 1**

Infer Why did Cornwallis finally surrender? (He couldn't receive food for his men. That meant that his men were beginning to go hungry. Cornwallis likely surrendered before his army started to starve to death.) **DOK 3**

Context Clues What is a *fleet*? (The text says that there was a "fleet of ships" so *fleet* must mean a group of ships.) **DOK 2**

Analyze the Infographic

Infer Why were French ships an important part of Washington and Lafayette's plan to defeat Cornwallis at Yorktown? (The French ships prevented British ships from getting through Chesapeake Bay to Cornwallis at Yorktown. If the British had been able to resupply, they might have been able to defend themselves better or even beat the Americans.) **DOK 3**

Use the Key How did French and American soldiers work together on land to defeat the British? (The French and Americans traveled together until it was time to surround the city. Then they split up to cover the most territory. There were enough soldiers to completely surround the area.) **DOK 3**

Make Connections

Explain Cause and Effect What events led Washington to join up with Lafayette in Virginia? Cite text evidence in your response. (Washington heard that Cornwallis was trapped at Yorktown. He wrote to Lafayette and formed a plan. He then marched quickly from New York to Maryland, where he boarded ships to Virginia.) **DOK 3**

COLLABORATE

✓ Stop and Check

Think Encourage students to think about the events that led up to this moment of the war. (Responses may include that the two sides had been fighting for more than five years at this point, and Washington likely saw a way to win a decisive—and hopefully final—victory over the British.)

The British battled the Americans and French at Yorktown for nearly three weeks. American cannons fired into the British camp. The French blockade of Chesapeake Bay continued to prevent Cornwallis from getting any fresh supplies or troops. Finally, on October 19, 1781, Cornwallis surrendered to Washington.

Did You Know?

George Washington and the Comte de Rochambeau, a French general, were in New York when word came that Cornwallis had fled to Virginia. Washington wrote to Lafayette, telling him to keep Cornwallis there. Washington left a few men in New York and began a rapid march south to join Lafayette. After marching his men to Maryland, Washington met up with a French fleet of ships at Chesapeake Bay. The ships carried the Americans and French troops south to Williamsburg, Virginia. From there, Washington's troops joined Lafayette's and surrounded Cornwallis at Yorktown.

Marquis de Lafayette

✓ Stop and Check   COLLABORATE

Talk Why did Washington move quickly from New York to Virginia?

242 Lesson 5   What Did the Colonists Gain by Winning the War?

InfoGraphic

Battle Map of Yorktown

Washington and Lafayette created a plan that trapped Cornwallis on the Yorktown peninsula. A combination of French ships and French and American soldiers kept Cornwallis from getting new supplies.

French ships carried French and American troops south to Williamsburg, Virginia.

Washington's troops met Lafayette's troops to surround the British.

A blockade of French ships prevented the British from getting supplies.

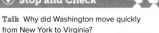

Chesapeake Bay

York River

Yorktown

Williamsburg

James River

ATLANTIC OCEAN

0   10   20 miles
0   10   20 kilometers

Yorktown

← American troops
← British troops
← French troops
⛵ British ships
⛵ French ships

Lesson 5   243

Research Companion, pp. 242–243

ENGLISH LEARNERS SCAFFOLD

ELD.PI.5.6 Reading closely literary and informational texts and viewing multimedia to determine how meaning is conveyed explicitly and implicitly through language

Emerging

Analyze a Map Guide students to use the key to identify what the participants in the Battle of Yorktown did. Explain that battle maps show troop movement and direction. The key uses color coding to highlight who did what. Guide them to ask and answer questions about the map.

Expanding/Bridging

Analyze the Infographic Encourage students to apply the callouts and the text from previous pages to the details on the map. Guide them to work together to make notes about the decisive moments of the battle and show how they are represented on the map. Ask them to discuss how a map provides information that text alone cannot, and how the text provides more details than the map can show.

See the **Language Learner Teaching Guide** for more language support strategies.

Monitor and Differentiate

REACHING ALL LEARNERS

Special Needs

Have students role-play how the Americans surrounded Cornwallis at Yorktown. Encourage groups of students to play Lafayette's Americans, Washington's Americans, French ships, and British forces. Have them act out how the different participants behaved during the siege and the surrender.

Approaching Level

Guide students to understand map-related terminology used in the infographic, such as *peninsula*. Encourage students to apply the context of the paragraph ("... the Yorktown peninsula") to the map to understand what the word means. Students should note that Yorktown is on a part of the land that extends far out into the bay.

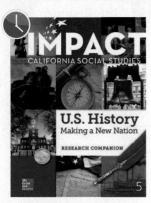

Research Companion
pp. 244–245

 STANDARDS

Identify and map the major military battles, campaigns, and turning points of the Revolutionary War, the roles of the American and British leaders, and the Indian leaders' alliances on both sides. **HSS.5.6.1**

Students pose relevant questions about events they encounter in historical documents, eyewitness accounts, oral histories, letters, diaries, artifacts, photographs, maps, artworks, and architecture. **HAS.HR.2**

Go Digital!

Investigate the lesson content with online whole-class presentation tools.

Background Information

John Jay served as president of the Continental Congress after John Hancock and Henry Laurens. He was sent in 1779 to serve as ambassador to the newly allied Spanish court, but met with little success there. He then transferred to Paris, where he joined Adams, Franklin, and Laurens in negotiating terms for the British surrender. After returning home, he helped to draft the new Constitution and then defended it in *The Federalist* with Alexander Hamilton and James Madison. He later served as the first chief justice of the Supreme Court of the United States and the governor of New York.

Analyze the Source

Inspect Have students read Ending the War on pp. 244–245.

Find Evidence Use the questions below to check comprehension. Remind students to support their answers with text evidence.

Identify What was the main result of the Battle of Yorktown? (The war was effectively over.) **DOK 1**

Explain What else had to happen before the war could officially end? (The remainder of the British troops had to leave the United States, and then the two sides had to negotiate a formal surrender.) **DOK 3**

Context Clues What is a *treaty*? (The text says that the British and the Americans had to agree to a treaty, which shows that a treaty is a formal agreement between nations that have fought a war.) **DOK 2**

Summarize What countries left the Peace of Paris with more land? (The United States: land to the Mississippi River; Spain: Florida. France: part of Africa.) **DOK 2**

Analyze the Primary Source

Identify Who was "His Brittanic Majesty"? (King George III of Great Britain) **DOK 1**

Context Clues What does the term *sovereign* mean? (The next words are "and independent," so *sovereign* must mean that the states are free to rule themselves.) **DOK 3**

Analyze Cause and Effect Why is this excerpt from the Peace of Paris important? (This paragraph states that Great Britain has to recognize the United States as an independent nation) **DOK 3**

Make Connections

Infer Why did the Continental Congress have to make the treaty official? (The representatives who negotiated the treaty could not speak for the entire country. Congress had to agree that the terms of the treaty were acceptable.) **DOK 3**

✓ Stop and Check

Talk Have students reread the paragraph that explains the terms of the treaty. (The British had to give up territory and recognize the independence of the United States, and France, Spain, and the United States all gained territory.)

Ending the War

The Battle of Yorktown marked the end of the main British resistance to American independence. There were still British troops in several cities and on the frontier, but the cost of the war had gotten so high that the British people were opposed to supporting the war with their taxes.

The slow process of ending the war began as Britain agreed to **negotiate** a treaty with the United States and its allies, France and Spain. The peace talks took place in Paris. John Adams, Benjamin Franklin, and John Jay were on hand to negotiate for the United States.

The Peace of Paris, as it came to be called, was the treaty that ended the American Revolution. As part of the agreement, Britain had to recognize American independence. The Mississippi River became the nation's new western boundary. Spain regained Florida, and France regained Senegal from the British in Africa. The Continental Congress made the treaty official in April 1783. After eight years of fighting, the 13 colonies were recognized as the United States of America.

John Adams (seated, left), Benjamin Franklin, and John Jay (standing, right) signed the Peace of Paris for the United States.

A modern reenactment of the battle at Yorktown, Virginia

PRIMARY SOURCE

Peace of Paris, Article I

His Brittanic Majesty acknowledges the said United States, viz., New Hampshire, Massachusetts Bay, Rhode Island and Providence Plantations, Connecticut, New York, New Jersey, Pennsylvania, Maryland, Virginia, North Carolina, South Carolina and Georgia, to be free sovereign and independent states, that he treats with them as such, and for himself, his heirs, and successors, relinquishes all claims to the government, propriety, and territorial rights of the same and every part thereof.

✓ **Stop and Check**   COLLABORATE

Talk What agreements were part of the Peace of Paris?

244   Lesson 5   What Did the Colonists Gain by Winning the War?

Lesson 5   245

Research Companion, pp. 244–245

 ENGLISH LEARNERS SCAFFOLD

ELD.PI.5.5 Listening actively to spoken English in a range of social and academic contexts

Emerging

Ask and Answer Questions Read aloud the primary source to students. Reread, stopping at place names. Encourage students to ask and answer questions to elicit that this list refers to the thirteen original states—the entire United States at the time. Then guide students to unpack the phrases that follow, understanding that this excerpt acknowledges that the United States is a free and independent nation. Provide scaffolding for the language in the primary source as needed.

Expanding/Bridging

Ask Detailed Questions Have students work together, reading the primary source aloud to each other. Encourage them to stop at words they do not understand and ask and answer questions to get the gist of the text. Ensure that in their discussions, students understand that the King of Great Britain has to acknowledge that the United States is a free nation.

See the **Language Learner Teaching Guide** for more language support strategies.

Monitor and Differentiate

REACHING ALL LEARNERS

Approaching Level

Guide students to work through the language used in the primary source. Explain that words such as *treats* have multiple meanings. Guide students to use a dictionary to confirm the word's meaning in this context, then help them to make a connection between *treats* and *treaty.* Also guide students to review word parts to understand terms such as *plantations* and *territorial,* finding *plant* and *territory,* then determining the meanings of the endings.

Beyond Level

Guide students to conduct further research into the Peace of Paris. Encourage them to research the dignitaries who were present from each nation, including John Adams, John Jay, and Benjamin Franklin.

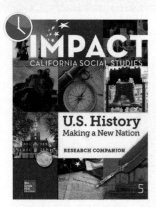

Research Companion
pp. 246–247

 STANDARDS

Understand the personal impact and economic hardship of the war on families, problems of financing the war, wartime inflation, and laws against hoarding goods and materials and profiteering. **HSS.5.6.4**

Demonstrate knowledge of the significance of land policies developed under the Continental Congress (e.g., sale of western lands, the Northwest Ordinance of 1787) and those policies' impact on American Indians' land. **HSS.5.6.6**

Students summarize the key events of the era they are studying and explain the historical contexts of those events. **HAS.HI.1**

Students identify and interpret the multiple causes and effects of historical events. **HAS.HI.3**

Go Digital!

Investigate the lesson content with online whole-class presentation tools.

Background Information

Loyalists Many Loyalists relocated to other countries after the end of the war. They experienced or feared reprisals for their actions despite a provision in the Treaty of Paris that stated they should be treated fairly and have any confiscated property restored.

Analyze the Source

Inspect Have students read No Victory for Some on pp. 246–247.

Find Evidence Use the questions below to check comprehension. Remind students to support their answers with text evidence.

Identify What happened after the war to the 40,000 Loyalists in the United States? (They moved to another country or stayed in the United States and tried to make the best of their lives.) **DOK 1**

Infer What were the results of the war for slaves in the United States? (Slavery continued despite opposition in Congress because Congress needed to secure Southern participation in government. Southern lawmakers would not agree to abolish slavery because they believed their economy depended on it.) **DOK 3**

Explain What happened to the American Indians who sided with the British? (After the war, Americans saw them as enemies, but the Mohawk and Iroquois eventually signed a peace agreement with the United States government.) **DOK 2**

Analyze the Primary Source

Analyze Point of View Why did Prince Hall write his petition to the Massachusetts state legislature? (He wanted to correct the unequal treatment that free African Americans living in Massachusetts faced. He wanted all children to have access to an education.) **DOK 2**

Analyze Language What does Hall mean when he says, "which we think is a great grievance"? (This is a big problem.) **DOK 2**

Make Connections

Draw Conclusions This petition happened in the 1780s. What leaders from the 1960s have you learned about who fought for equal education and rights for African Americans? (Students should recognize that Prince Hall is seeking equal rights for African Americans, and that his appeals sound similar to those from the civil rights movement of the 1960s, in which leaders such as Martin Luther King, Jr. called for equal rights. Students may highlight the fact that nearly 200 years later, people were still seeking the same rights.) **DOK 3**

☑ Stop and Check

Talk Guide students to think about how the Loyalists behaved after the war. (Many decided to leave the country, but many stayed and tried to make new lives.)

What Do You Think?

Encourage students to use text evidence as they respond to the lesson question.

No Victory for Some

After the war ended, the 40,000 Loyalists left in the country had to decide what to do. Some moved to Canada, which was still controlled by the British. Others remained in the United States. They tried to make the best of life there, but many were forced to give up their homes and property.

Slaves had hoped the end of the war would mean the end of slavery. To create a united government, however, the Congress agreed to allow slavery to continue in the Southern Colonies in return for Southern support.

American Indians—including the Mohawk and Iroquois—who had sided with the British found that more and more Americans settled on Indian lands. The Americans saw the native peoples as enemies because of the Iroquois alliance with the British. Eventually, the Mohawk and Iroquois signed a peace agreement with the United States.

It would still take many years before the phrase "all men are created equal" could truly include all people in the United States.

Those African Americans who were free at the end of the Revolutionary War also met with disappointments. They found themselves receiving unequal treatment in many forms. One free African American in Massachusetts, Prince Hall, collected signatures for a petition protesting one form of this discrimination.

PRIMARY SOURCE

In Their Words... Prince Hall

. . . we are of the humble opinion that we have the right to enjoy the privileges of free men. But that we do not will appear in many instances, and we beg leave to mention one out of many, and that is of the education of our children which now receive no benefit from the free schools in the town of Boston, which we think is a great grievance, as by woeful experience we now feel the want of a common education. We, therefore, must fear for our rising offspring to see them in ignorance in a land of gospel light when there is provision made for them as well as others and yet can't enjoy them, and for not other reason can be given this they are black.

—from a petition presented to the Massachusetts state legislature, October 1787

✓ Stop and Check

Talk What happened to Loyalists after the war?

What Do You Think? Did everyone in the United States gain his or her independence as a result of the war?

Research Companion, pp. 246–247

ENGLISH LEARNERS SCAFFOLD

ELD.PI.5.5 Listening actively to spoken English in a range of social and academic contexts

Emerging

Use Graphic Organizers Reread the primary source aloud. Have students make a graphic organizer that breaks up the primary source by phrase. Next to each phrase, have students write what they think the phrase means.

We are of the humble opinion that we have the right to enjoy the privileges of free men.

We believe that we should have all the rights that other free men have.

Expanding/Bridging

Ask and Answer Questions
Provide light or moderate support as students work together to unpack the language in the primary source. Guide students to go through each phrase, asking and answering questions to understand Hall's opinions and main ideas. Then have students discuss the excerpt as a group.

See the **Language Learner Teaching Guide** for more language support strategies.

Monitor and Differentiate

REACHING ALL LEARNERS

Approaching Level

Guide students to work together to understand Hall's language so they can get the gist of his argument. Provide assistance as needed, asking students to use context clues, word parts, and the dictionary to find the meanings of unfamiliar words. Work with students to break up Hall's long and complex sentences into shorter phrases. For example:

But that we do not [enjoy these privileges] will be clear in many instances. We want to mention one: education of our children. Right now, they don't get an education from the city of Boston. We think they should because they are falling behind. So, we fear for their futures in a land where other people are educated. It's clear they are only denied this right because they are black.

3 REPORT

Report Your Findings

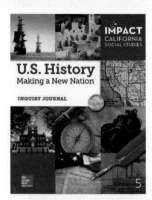

Inquiry Journal
pp. 200–201

 STANDARDS

Identify and map the major military battles, campaigns, and turning points of the Revolutionary War, the roles of the American and British leaders, and the Indian leaders' alliances on both sides.
HSS.5.6.1

(ccss) Analyze multiple accounts of the same event or topic, noting important similarities and differences in the point of view they represent.
CCSS.ELA.RI.5.6

Write opinion pieces on topics or texts, supporting a point of view with reasons and information. **CCSS.ELA.W.5.1**

Engage effectively in a range of collaborative discussions (one-on-one, in groups, and teacher-led) with diverse partners on *grade 5 topics and texts*, building on others' ideas and expressing their own clearly. **CCSS.ELA.SL.5.1**

Go Digital!

- Students can go online to report their findings. Assess their responses online.

- Students can access the online graphic organizer to capture ideas from their investigation.

Think About It

Students will review their research and what the colonists gained and lost by going to war.

- Remind students to review the causes and effects they outlined in their graphic organizer. Direct students back to pages 238–247 of their Research Companion if they need more information.

Write About It

Write a Letter Have students read the prompt. Explain that they will write a letter from the point of view of a representative of one of the groups they learned about in this chapter. The letter will explain what the group wants to be included in the treaty with Great Britain.

Remind students to include the following elements in their response.

- Include important information that is in keeping with the perspective of the group you chose.

- Use reasons and evidence to support your group's reasons for wanting what it does from the treaty.

- Use formal language that seems appropriate for writing a letter to an important official.

Use the rubric on p. T524 to evaluate students' work.

Talk About It

Defend Your Claims Engage your students in a class discussion. Guide them to identify what each side lost and won and whether there were real winners and losers in the war.

- Explain that they should support their responses and opinions with evidence from the text and their research.

- They should take turns speaking and avoid interrupting each other.

- Remind students to be respectful of their classmates' opinions and work.

Connect to the Essential Question

Read the prompt aloud to students. Ask them the following guiding questions:

- What happened as a result of the American Revolution? (The United States became an independent nation.)

- What would the United States be like today if the Revolutionary War had not been fought? What if the Americans had not won? (Responses will vary.)

- How is the American Revolution still important today? (Responses will vary.)

Remind students to use the space provided in their journal to jot down notes.

Report Your Findings

Think About It

Review your research. Recall what you have learned about the people involved in the Revolutionary War. What were their justifications for going to war? Did they succeed in their goals or not?

Write About It

Write a Letter Take the role of a representative of one of the groups involved in the American Revolution. This could be a Patriot, a Loyalist, an African American, an American Indian, a member of an ally nation, or even a British soldier. Write a letter to Benjamin Franklin, John Adams, and John Jay about the peace talks in Paris. What conditions would your group like to see included in the peace agreement? Persuade them with specific reasons why your group deserves these conditions.

Responses will vary, but students should write a letter that correctly outlines the position of their chosen group.

Talk About It

Defend Your Claims

Discuss as a class who were the real winners and losers of the war. Who got what they wanted? Who didn't? Who lost the most? What was fair and what was unfair?

Connect to the EQ

Make Connections

Think about how the American Revolution ended. What lasting effects did this have on our nation?

Sample response: The American Revolution ended with an American victory. In gaining its independence, the United States created a new place for itself in the world that has lasted to today.

Inquiry Project Notes

McGraw-Hill Education

Inquiry Journal, pp. 200–201

EL ENGLISH LEARNERS SCAFFOLD

ELD.PI.5.4 Adapting language choices to various contexts (based on task, purpose, audience, and text type)

Emerging	Expanding	Bridging
Understand Tone Explain that while some letters are written in a conversational tone, a letter to an important official would be written very formally. In a formal letter, a writer would quickly get to the point so the reader would take the argument seriously. Work with students to achieve a formal tone.	**Use Text Evidence** Remind students to refer to the text as they adapt their language choices. Explain that when writing a formal letter, they should include facts and details to support their claims. Have students reread the text to find details that strengthen their argument.	**Achieve a Specific Tone** Have students consider what they want their letter to sound like. Remind them that this letter needs a formal tone because it is addressed to an important person, and the writer needs to be taken seriously. Guide students to consider their word choice and syntax as they make their case.

See the **Language Learner Teaching Guide** for more language support strategies.

Monitor and Differentiate

REACHING ALL LEARNERS

Approaching Level

Encourage students to use language they have learned in the lesson if it is appropriate. Remind students that they are writing about real events and addressing their letter to a real person. Their wording and syntax should be formal so the reader will take their argument seriously. Their argument should be in keeping with the group they chose to represent.

Beyond Level

Encourage students to turn their letter into a short play that they can perform for the class. Guide them to portray the group writing the letter and the group that received it: Franklin, Adams, and Jay. The play should also show how the representatives decided to act on the arguments made in the letter.

Know what your students know!

Lesson Task
Report Your Findings

Use the rubric to evaluate students' responses.

Write a Letter Students take on the role of a colonist, a Loyalist, an African American, an American Indian, an ally nation, or even a British soldier. They write a persuasive letter to Benjamin Franklin, John Adams, and John Jay about the peace talks in Paris asking for inclusion in the terms of the Treaty of Paris.

Defend Your Claims The class discusses who the real winners and losers of the war were. They analyze who got what they wanted, who didn't, who lost the most, and what was fair and what was unfair.

Lesson Task Evaluation Rubric

	4	3	2	1
Historical Understanding	Strong understanding of what the colonists gained by winning the war	Adequate understanding of what the colonists gained by winning the war	Uneven understanding of what the colonists gained by winning the war	No understanding of what the colonists gained by winning the war
Persuasive Letter	Clearly provides an opinion and effective support	Adequately provides an opinion and support	Somewhat clear or unclear opinion or support	No relevant opinion stated or student does not show understanding of the task
Supported by Text Evidence	Reasons supported by evidence from the text	Reasons mostly supported by evidence from the text	Reasons not always supported by evidence from the text	Reasons are missing or irrelevant
Class Discussion	Carefully considers multiple perspectives about the war Provides relevant and creative responses	Considers some different perspectives about the war Provides relevant responses	Mentions a few perspectives, but thoughts are not developed Provides few relevant responses	Does not mention or develop details about different perspectives Provides no relevant responses

Lesson Assessment

Go Digital!

- Have students complete the Chapter 5 Lesson 5 Assessment online to monitor their understanding of the lesson content.

California Smarter Balanced Assessment Connections!

Standards Covered	Lesson Task	Lesson Assessment	Alignment with California Smarter Balanced Assessment
History Social Science Content 5.6.1; 5.6.4; 5.6.5; 5.6.6	✔	✔	Claim 1 Targets 8, 9, 11
History Social Science Analysis Skills Chronological and Spatial Thinking 5.1; 5.2; 5.4 Research, Evidence, and Point of View 5.1; 5.2 Historical Interpretation 5.1; 5.3; 5.4	✔	✔	Claim 1 Targets 8, 9, 11
Writing W.5.1	✔	✔	Claim 2 Target 6q
Research and Inquiry W.5.7		✔	Claim 4 Targets 1, 2
Reading RI.5.6	✔	✔	Claim 1 Target 11, 12
Speaking and Listening SL.5.1	✔		Claim 3 Target 3 Claim 4 Target 1

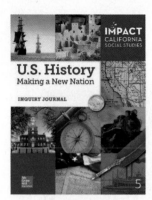

Inquiry Journal
pp. 202–203

 HSS **STANDARDS**

Students explain the causes of the American Revolution. **HSS.5.5**

Students understand the course and consequences of the American Revolution. **HSS.5.6**

CCSS Explain the relationships or interactions between two or more individuals, events, ideas, or concepts in a historical, scientific, or technical text based on specific information in the text. **CCSS.ELA.RI.5.3**

Report on a topic or text or present an opinion, sequencing ideas logically and using appropriate facts and relevant, descriptive details to support main ideas or themes; speak clearly at an understandable pace. **CCSS.ELA.SL.5.4**

Write informative/explanatory texts to examine a topic and convey ideas and information clearly. **CCSS.ELA.W.5.2**

Go Digital!

Look online for the EQ Inquiry Project rubric.

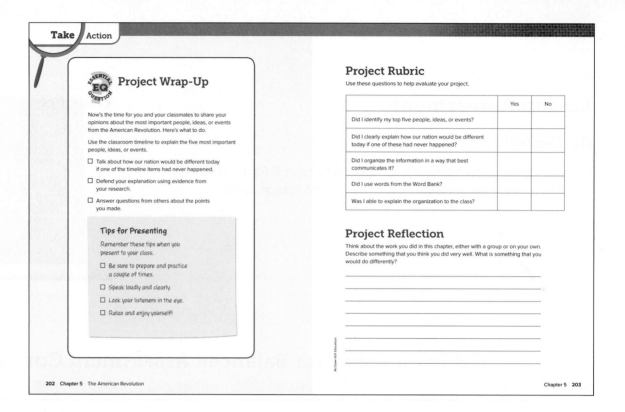

 # Inquiry Project Wrap-Up

Have students share their inquiry projects by debating.

- Before students debate, discuss the wrap-up steps with them, making sure they know what's expected in their presentations.

- Allow time after the debate for a Q-and-A session.

Tips for Presenting

Discuss the tips for presenting with students and the importance of communicating effectively with their audience. Remind students that it's also important to be a good listener.

Project Rubric

Discuss each question in the Project Rubric with students. If students have worked as part of a group to develop their projects, you might want to have them work as a group to address each question in the rubric.

Project Reflection

Student reflections can focus on the work they did as part of the group or their individual performance writing and presenting their information. Give groups time to discuss each phase of their projects and reflect on their work.

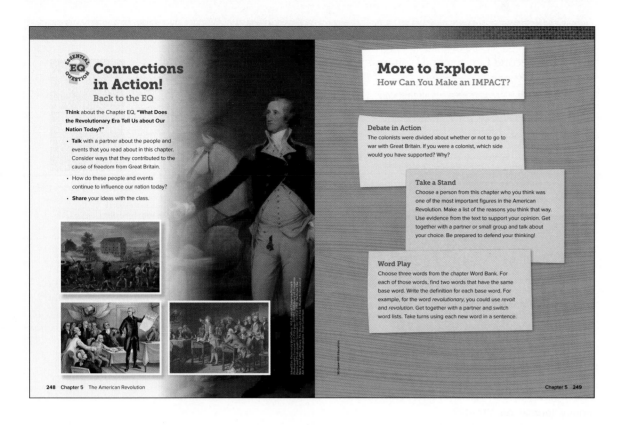

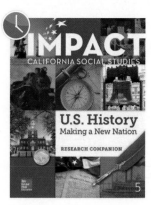

Research Companion
pp. 248–249

Connections in Action

To help focus students' conversations, you may want to discuss the EQ with the entire class before students discuss their ideas with a partner. Remind students to think about evidence they can provide that will support their ideas. After students present, allow time for others to ask questions.

More to Explore

Debate in Action Remind students to think about what they know about what life was like for the colonists before they consider which side they would have supported. You may want to have students who took different sides debate their decisions.

Take a Stand Remind students of the importance of evidence in supporting an opinion. After students meet with a partner or small group, invite volunteers to explain and defend their choice to the class.

Word Play Have students compile their new words in an American Revolution Word Wall. Use the original words from the chapter Word Bank as headings and organize the new words under each one. Encourage students to add other interesting words they found in the chapter and discuss what they know about them.

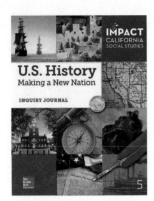

Inquiry Journal
pp. 204–207

STANDARDS

Students explain the causes of the American Revolution. **HSS.5.5**

Students understand the course and consequences of the American Revolution. **HSS.5.6**

Determine a theme of a story, drama, or poem from details in the text, including how characters in a story or drama respond to challenges or how the speaker in a poem reflects upon a topic; summarize the text. **CCSS.ELA.RL.5.2**

Read grade-level prose and poetry orally with accuracy, appropriate rate, and expression on successive readings. **CCSS.ELA.RF.5.4.B**

Adapt speech to a variety of contexts and tasks, using formal English when appropriate to task and specification. **CCSS.ELA.SL.5.6**

Go Digital!

Investigate the American Revolution with the online Reader's Theater. Use the printable script for whole-class or small-group presentations.

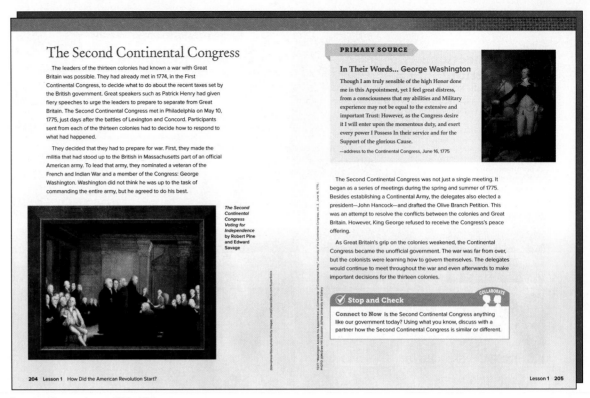

Inquiry Journal, pp. 124–127

Reader's Theater

Deepen students' understanding of how the American Revolution affected both soldiers and civilians with the Reader's Theater selection, "Surviving the Winter at Valley Forge."

Analyze the Source

GENRE Reader's Theater Reader's theater is a form of drama in which actors do not memorize their lines. They use their voices rather than sets or costumes to help listeners understand the text.

Inspect Have students read pages 204–207 to determine the general meaning of the text.

1. Why was Jonathan away from home? (He was fighting for the Americans in the Revolution. He was encamped at Valley Forge for the winter.)

Find Evidence Have students reread the selection and ask:

2. Why do you think Jonathan's family is supportive of him being away at war, even though they know he is having a tough time? Support your response with evidence from the text. (Answers will vary, but students might suggest that they are proud of the cause he is fighting for.)

Make Connections

3. Think about what Grandfather says about the Loyalists finding it difficult to change their ways. How does that perspective change your understanding of those who opposed independence? (Answers will vary, but students should mention that it might have been difficult for some people to imagine a world without being British subjects.)

4. How does the Narrator help you understand the story? (Answers will vary, but students may say the narrator helps to place the story in the context of historical events.)

Perform the Reader's Theater

Model the reading. Project the play with an interactive whiteboard or projector and read aloud as students follow along. Show how expression, pace, and word stress can communicate meaning.

- **Mother:** Come here, everyone! Gather around! I have a letter from Jonathan at Valley Forge!

  How should the character read this line? Why do you think so? (The character should read this line in a loud voice. People speak this way when they are excited.)

- **Jonathan** (appears, alone on the opposite side of the stage. He is seated as if writing a letter):

  What do the words in parentheses tell the character of Jonathan to do? (They tell the actor how to behave while he reads the line that follow.)

Practice the reading. Practice with techniques such as the following:

- Choral Read—Read together as a group to build fluency.
- Partner Read—Students take turns reading each line aloud to practice pacing.

Assign roles. Consider these strategies:

- Allow students time to practice aloud with a partner if they are nervous or shy.
- Have students highlight their dialogue and circle words they should emphasize.
- Encourage students to look up the meanings of unfamiliar words.

Tips for Reader's Theater

- Students should have time to practice their lines before performing.
- Have students sit in a circle so they can see and hear each other.

Remind students of strategies for reading aloud:

- Speak loudly so that your voice can be heard and use expression.
- Use expression. Pay attention to the punctuation.

Write About It Have students complete the writing activity. As they write their own play, have students consider what soldiers would have thought about fighting the war.

Connect to the
Essential Question

Have students connect the reader's theater to the essential question. Ask: *How did the Miller family's experiences help you understand what the Revolutionary Era tells about our nation today?* (Responses will vary, but students may identify that the Millers were a strong family who believed in the cause their son was fighting for, and that people today are also proud of military families and others who serve the nation.)

How Does the Constitution Help Us Understand What It Means to Be an American?

In This Chapter ...

Students will investigate how the United States Constitution was developed and ratified. They will learn about the people who created the government, their opinions about how it should be run, and the pressures that drove them to compromise on important issues. Students will examine how the Constitution has changed over the course of U.S. history to protect the rights of all people.

Lesson 1   The Articles of Confederation

Lesson 2   A New Framework for Governing

Lesson 3   Protecting the Rights of Citizens

 CHAPTER STANDARDS

✓ Students understand the course and consequences of the American Revolution. **HSS.5.6**

✓ Students describe the people and events associated with the development of the U.S. Constitution and analyze the Constitution's significance as the foundation of the American republic. **HSS.5.7**

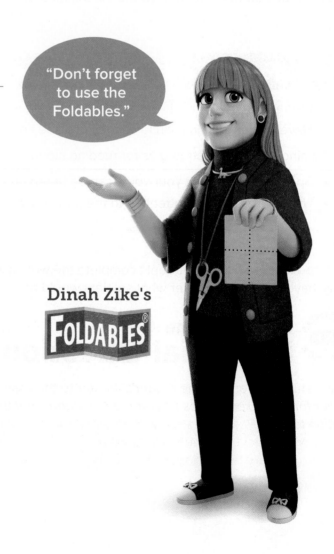

"Don't forget to use the Foldables."

Dinah Zike's

FOLDABLES®

1 ENGAGE

Inquiry Journal
pp. 208–211

 Inquiry Project

Which side wIll you choose?

- **Explore Words**

- *Go Digital!*
  - IMPACT Chapter Video: Forming a New Government

2 INVESTIGATE

Research Companion
pp. 250–257

- **Step Into Time and Place**

- **Connect Through Literature**
  A Ship Called the Hamilton
  by Virginia Calkins

- **People You Should Know**

Weekly Explorer Magazine pp. 72–83

3 REPORT

Inquiry Journal
pp. 236–237

Inquiry Project

Which side will you choose?

 Short on Time? Look for the clock to teach core content in less time.

CULTIVATE MEANING AND SUPPORT LANGUAGE

Language Learner Teaching Guide,
pp. 138–139

Content Objectives

- Explore the Articles of Confederation and the U.S. Constitution
- Explore how the Constitution and the Bill of Rights affect the people of the United States.

Language Objectives

- Determine pros and cons to think and write about the Articles of Confederation.
- Summarize a text.

CONNECT TO Wonders

Unit 2 Week 1
Reaching a Compromise

Read Aloud
"The Mayflower Compact"

Reading/Writing Workshop
"Creating a Nation"

Literature Anthology/Paired Selection
Who Wrote the Constitution?
"Parchment and Ink"

Leveled Readers
The Bill of Rights and "Having Your Say"

ASSESSMENT

Monitor Progress to
Know What Your Students Know

Choose the assessment options that work best for you and your students.

BEFORE
PRE-TEST

Measure students' content knowledge before you begin the chapter with the following questions.

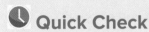 **Quick Check**

✔ What is the Constitution of the United States? How did it get written?

✔ Was it inevitable that the original thirteen colonies would become one united country? Why or Why not?

✔ What do you think the biggest challenges would be for forming a government for the new nation?

1. Distribute one large index card to each student. Read aloud one of the questions. Ask students to write their response to the following questions on the front of the index card.

2. When all students have responded, ask them to rate how confident they are in their answers on a scale from 1 – not very confident to 5 – very confident.

3. Collect the cards and review them for misconceptions, factual errors, and to inform instruction. You may wish to hang the cards in a two-column wall chart to review as students investigate chapter 6.

4. **Don't Forget!** Revisit students' quick check responses with them. If students change their response, ask them to support the change with text evidence. You may wish to have students respond to a different prompt to measure students' content knowledge, such as *Name some of the important figures who attended the Constitutional Convention in Philadelphia. What did they contribute to the Convention?*

EVERY LESSON
ONGOING ASSESSMENT

Use the lesson tools to monitor the IMPACT of your instruction.

✓ Stop and Check

Use the quick question prompts to monitor student comprehension of the content. The **Stop and Check** questions prompt students to make connections to their world today, engage in discussions to deepen their understanding of the content, and to look at different perspectives.

◯ Report Your Findings

The lesson task, **Report Your Findings**, can be used to measure student understanding of the lesson content and ability to effectively express their understanding. See the Lesson Assessment pp. T560, T584, and T606 for task-specific evaluation rubrics.

(Go *Digital!*) Lesson Assessment

Use the **Lesson Assessment** to monitor student understanding of the lesson content. Have students complete the assessment online. See pp. T561, T585, and T607 for California Smarter Balanced Assessments Connections.

EVERY CHAPTER
POST TEST

Evaluate student understanding of core chapter content with one or more of the following assessment options.

Connections in Action

Use the **Connections in Action** to evaluate student understanding of core chapter content through discussion.

Inquiry Project

Use the **EQ Inquiry Project** to measure student understanding of the chapter content and ability to effectively express their understanding. See the EQ Inquiry Project Wrap Up below for a task-specific evaluation rubric.

	4	3	2	1
Historical Understanding	Strong understanding of the process of forming a new government	Adequate understanding of the process of forming a new government	Uneven understanding of the process of forming a new government	No understanding of the process of forming a new government
Take a Stand	Clearly states opinion and addresses other group's claims	Adequately states opinion and addresses other group's claims	Somewhat clear or unclear opinion	No opinion or student does not show understanding of the task
Support with Evidence	Facts and details provide thorough evidence	Facts and details provide adequate evidence	Facts and details contain uneven or only somewhat convincing evidence	Facts and details are missing or contain no supporting evidence
Defend Your Claim	Speaks clearly and at an understandable pace Completely addresses group's claim, opposing side's claim, and opinions that changed as a result of collaboration	Speaks clearly during most of the presentation Adequately addresses group's claim, opposing side's claim, and opinions that changed as a result of collaboration	At times speaker is unclear Does not entirely address group's claim, opposing side's claim, or opinions changed as a result of collaboration	Speaks unclearly throughout the discussion Does not address group's claim, opposing side's claim, or opinions changed as a result of collaboration

(Go Digital!) Chapter Benchmark Assessments

Use the chapter tests to monitor student understanding of the chapter History-Social Science standards and content. Have students complete the assessment online.

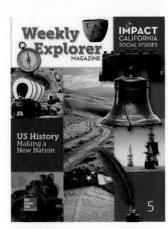

pp. 72–83

**Short on Time?**

Use the Weekly Explorer Magazine during your reading block.

Go Digital!

Look online for the Weekly Explorer Magazine Teaching Guide.

WordBlast

Remind students to look for the Word Blasts as they read the Explorer Magazine.

FOLDABLES

Encourage students to use the Notetaking Foldables as they gather more information.

Weekly Explorer Magazine

The Weekly Explorer Magazine is designed to provide students with more information to use as they dig deeper into **Forming a New Government.** The articles in a variety of formats explore the Essential Question and support the Inquiry Project.

Engage

Build background for students and share any information needed to provide a context for the chapter topic. Have students read the Essential Question and the Table of Contents.

Analyze the Visual Discuss the opening visual (photograph, photo essay, artwork) on the second page of the Magazine chapter. Help students connect the visual to the chapter topic and the Essential Question.

Analyze the Sources

Students will read and analyze the articles, graphic novel, poems, songs, literature excerpts, primary sources, and infographics.

Read and Analyze Before reading, provide any additional information you think students will need about the topics. Then guide students through the three-step process to read and analyze the articles.

1 Inspect Have students skim the article or articles on a page or multiple pages. Ask questions to help students recall and retell key ideas.

- What is the article mostly about?

- Who is _____?

2 Find Evidence Have students reread the articles and look for details they might have missed. Ask additional questions to help them read more closely.

- What details do you notice in the photographs?

- Why was _____ important?

3 Make Connections Have students work in pairs or small groups to discuss prompts that help them connect the article(s) to other texts, their own lives, current ideas and issues, and other topics.

- How is _____ similar to what we do today?

- How do you think _____ felt about what happened?

- What do you think about _____?

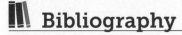

Bibliography

The following suggested resources may help students' investigation of the chapter content.

EXPLORE PEOPLE, PLACES, AND EVENTS

▶ **A Kid's Guide to America's Bill of Rights**
by Kathleen Krull; Avon, 2002.

Perspectives
▶ **Escape of Oney Judge: Martha Washington's Slave Finds Freedom**
by Emily Arnold McCully; Farrar, Straus and Giroux, 2007.

▶ **O Say, Can You see? America's Symbols, Landmarks, and Important Words**
by Sheila Keenan; Scholastic, 2007

▶ **Our Liberty Bell**
by Henry Jones Magaziner; Holiday House, 2007.

▶ **The Printer's Apprentice**
by Stephen Krensky; Yearling, 1996.

▶ **We the People: The Constitution of the United States of America**
by Peter Spier; Doubleday Books for Young People, 1991.

EXPLORE MUSIC

▶ **Liberty Song**   by John Dickenson
Did you know? The Liberty Song was thought to be the origin of the phrase "United we stand, divided we fall."

Some of the lyrics: *Then join hand in hand, brave Americans all, By united we stand, by dividing we fall; In so righteous a cause let us hope to succeed, For heaven approves of each generous deed.*

▶ **Free America(y) (to the tune of "The British Grenadiers")**   By Joseph Warren
Some of the lyrics: *That Seat of Science Athens, and Earth's great Mistress Rome, Where now are all their Glories, we scarce can find their Tomb; Then guard your Rights, Americans! Nor stoop to lawless Sway, Oppose, oppose, oppose, oppose, — my brave America.*

NOTE: "America" is pronounced "Americay" to rhyme with "sway".

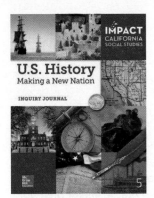

Inquiry Journal
pp. 208–211

 STANDARDS

Students describe the people and events associated with the development of the U.S. Constitution and analyze the Constitution's significance as the foundation of the American republic. **HSS.5.7**

Write opinion pieces on topics or texts, supporting a point of view with reasons and information. **CCSS.ELA.W.5.1**

Draw evidence from literary or informational texts to support analysis, reflection, and research. **CCSS.ELA.W.5.9**

Go *Digital!*

Explore Words: Interactive vocabulary activities support students as they explore the chapter words.

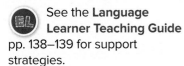 See the **Language Learner Teaching Guide** pp. 138–139 for support strategies.

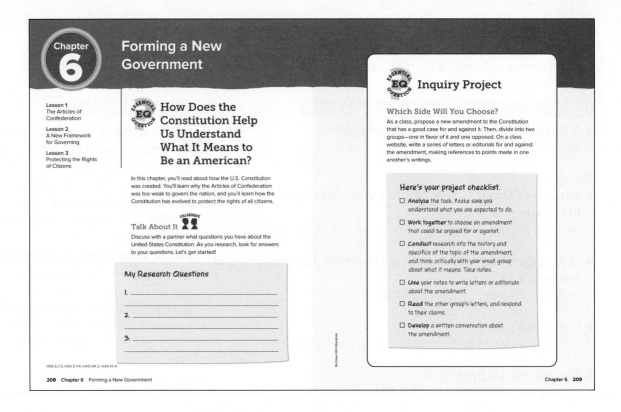

 # How Does the Constitution Help Us Understand What It Means to Be an American?

Have students read the Chapter Essential Question on p. 208.

Talk About It

- Prompt students to write three questions they would like to know the answers to after reading about the process of forming a new government.

- After jotting down their questions, have students discuss their questions with partners.

 ## Inquiry Project

Which side will you choose?

- Have students read aloud the EQ Inquiry Project.

- Tell students that they will use information gathered from the chapter and from independent research to complete the project.

- Make certain students understand the task by reviewing each step of the project.

Explore Words

Complete this chapter's Word Rater. Write notes as you learn more about each word.

amendment My Notes
☐ Know It!
☐ Heard It!
☐ Don't Know It!

issue My Notes
☐ Know It!
☐ Heard It!
☐ Don't Know It!

article My Notes
☐ Know It!
☐ Heard It!
☐ Don't Know It!

jury My Notes
☐ Know It!
☐ Heard It!
☐ Don't Know It!

bill My Notes
☐ Know It!
☐ Heard It!
☐ Don't Know It!

physical My Notes
☐ Know It!
☐ Heard It!
☐ Don't Know It!

currency My Notes
☐ Know It!
☐ Heard It!
☐ Don't Know It!

press My Notes
☐ Know It!
☐ Heard It!
☐ Don't Know It!

delegate My Notes
☐ Know It!
☐ Heard It!
☐ Don't Know It!

term My Notes
☐ Know It!
☐ Heard It!
☐ Don't Know It!

Explore Words

- **Academic/Domain-Specific Vocabulary** Read the words aloud to students. Explain to students that these are words they will learn more about in the chapter.

- **Word Rater** Have students place a checkmark in one of the three boxes below each word, indicating that they "Know It," "Heard It," or "Don't Know It."

  ✔ **Know It** Tell students that if they know the word, they should write its meaning on the lines provided.

  ✔ **Heard It** Tell students that if they have heard, or are familiar with the word, they should write what they know about it on the lines provided. Remind them to take notes about the word as they encounter it.

  ✔ **Don't Know It** If they do not know the word's meaning, tell them to write down its meaning when they encounter the word in the chapter.

🔍 Explore Words Routine

Remind students that when they come to an unfamiliar word or phrase in their research, they should follow these steps to determine its meaning.

1. Look around the word or phrase for clues to unlock its meaning.

2. Look inside the word or phrase for word part clues.

3. Look up the word in other resources.

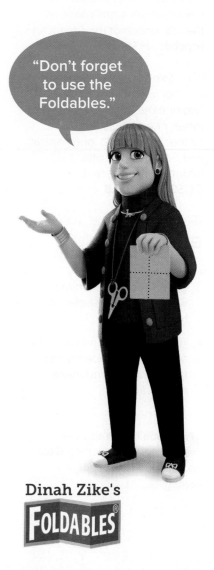

"Don't forget to use the Foldables."

Dinah Zike's

FOLDABLES®

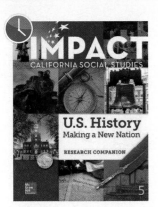

Research Companion
pp. 250–255

 STANDARDS

Students understand the course and consequences of the American Revolution. **HSS.5.6**

Students describe the people and events associated with the development of the U.S. Constitution and analyze the Constitution's significance as the foundation of the American republic. **HSS.5.7**

(CCSS) Explain the relationships or interactions between two or more individuals, events, ideas, or concepts in a historical, scientific, or technical text based on specific information in the text. **CCSS.ELA.RI.5.3**

Go *Digital!*

- Investigate the new government with online whole-class presentation tools.

- Analyze the online literature selection so students can find evidence and make connections.

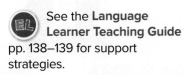 See the **Language Learner Teaching Guide** pp. 138–139 for support strategies.

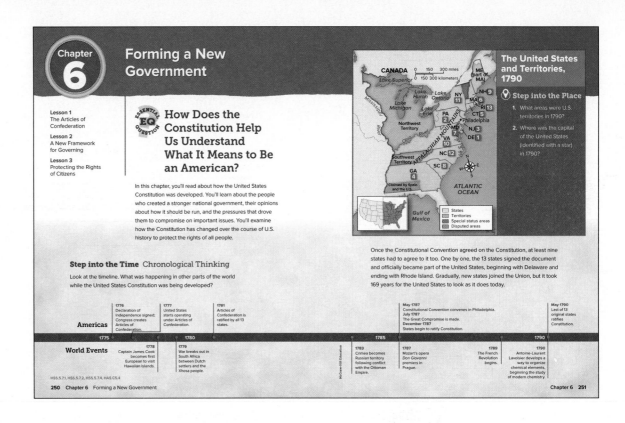

Step Into Time

Have students read over the events in the timeline, first examining events from the Americas and then events from around the world.

- How long did it take for the Articles of Confederation to be ratified by all thirteen states? (about three years)

- What was happening in other parts of the world while the United States Constitution was being developed? (Mozart was writing his opera *Don Giovanni*, and France was plunging into revolution of its own.)

Step Into Place

In partners or in small groups, have students examine the map on p. 251 and answer the questions beneath it.

1. What areas were U.S. territories in 1790? (Land that is currently Michigan, Indiana, and Wisconsin, and part of Tennessee)

2. What was the capital of the United States in 1790? (Philadelphia)

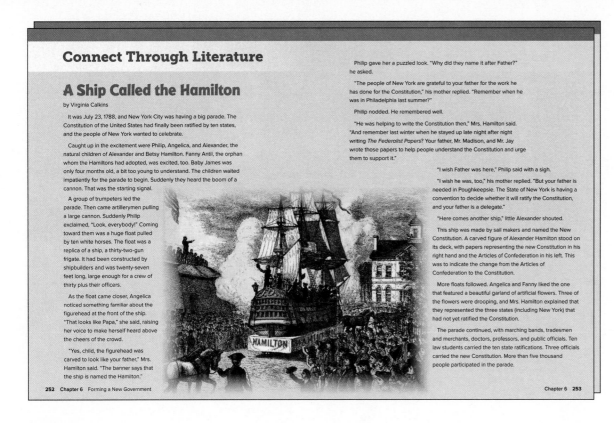
GENRE Historical Fiction   *"A Ship Called the* Hamilton*" is a fictional recounting of the parade and celebration in New York following the ratification of the Constitution of the United States.*

Analyze the Source

Inspect   Have students read the selection on pp. 252–255 together to determine the general meaning of the text.

1. Why was a parade held in New York City on July 23, 1788? (to celebrate the ratification of the U.S. Constitution)

Find Evidence   Have students reread the selection and ask:

2. What was Alexander Hamilton's tactic to get New York to ratify the constitution? (He tried to delay the convention while other states ratified the constitution, hoping New York would join once the new nation was born.)

Make Connections

3. What two pieces of evidence show that New York City was in favor of ratifying the Constitution even if the rest of the state was not? (New York City held a parade to celebrate ratification and considered seceding from the state if the state of New York did not ratify the Constitution.)

Perspectives   The children's perspective of things is very different from their father's. What did the children think was most important? What did Alexander Hamilton think was most important? (Answers will vary, but students should note that the children were most interested in the ship and that Alexander Hamilton was most interested in getting the Constitution ratified.)

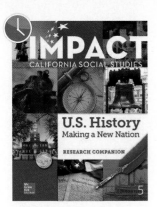

Research Companion
pp. 256–257

 STANDARDS

Students understand the course and consequences of the American Revolution. **HSS.5.6**

Students describe the people and events associated with the development of the U.S. Constitution and analyze the Constitution's significance as the foundation of the American republic. **HSS.5.7**

CCSS Explain the relationships or interactions between two or more individuals, events, ideas, or concepts in a historical, scientific, or technical text based on specific information in the text. **CCSS.ELA.RI.5.3**

Go *Digital!*

Investigate chapter content with the online teaching plan.

EL See the **Language Learner Teacher Guide** pp. 138–139 for support strategies.

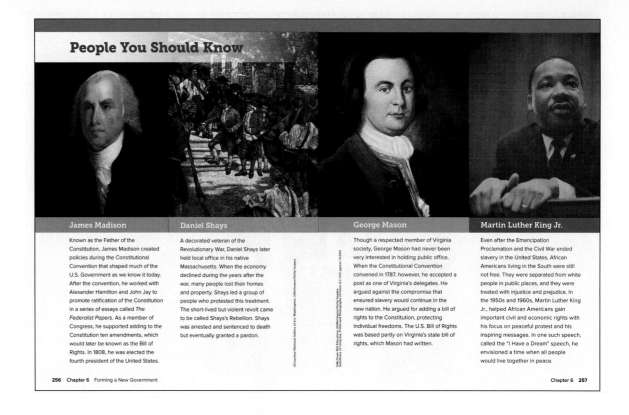

People You Should Know

James Madison

Known as the Father of the Constitution, James Madison created policies during the Constitutional Convention that shaped much of the U.S. Government as we know it today. After the convention, he worked with Alexander Hamilton and John Jay to promote ratification of the Constitution in a series of essays called *The Federalist Papers*. As a member of Congress, he supported adding to the Constitution ten amendments, which would later be known as the Bill of Rights. In 1808, he was elected the fourth president of the United States.

Daniel Shays

A decorated veteran of the Revolutionary War, Daniel Shays later held local office in his native Massachusetts. When the economy declined during the years after the war, many people lost their homes and property. Shays led a group of people who protested this treatment. The short-lived but violent revolt came to be called Shays's Rebellion. Shays was arrested and sentenced to death but eventually granted a pardon.

George Mason

Though a respected member of Virginia society, George Mason had never been very interested in holding public office. When the Constitutional Convention convened in 1787, however, he accepted a post as one of Virginia's delegates. He argued against the compromise that ensured slavery would continue in the new nation. He argued for adding a bill of rights to the Constitution, protecting individual freedoms. The U.S. Bill of Rights was based partly on Virginia's state bill of rights, which Mason had written.

Martin Luther King Jr.

Even after the Emancipation Proclamation and the Civil War ended slavery in the United States, African Americans living in the South were still not free. They were separated from white people in public places, and they were treated with injustice and prejudice. In the 1950s and 1960s, Martin Luther King Jr., helped African Americans gain important civil and economic rights with his focus on peaceful protest and his inspiring messages. In one such speech, called the "I Have a Dream" speech, he envisioned a time when all people would live together in peace.

256 Chapter 6 Forming a New Government

Chapter 6 257

People You Should Know

How do personal stories IMPACT our understanding of the Constitution of the United States?

- Have students read aloud the biographies.

- Tell them that they will learn about these people and others throughout the chapter.

- Prompt students to imagine a conversation they might have with one of the people who played an important role in the creation of the Constitution of the United States. Students can choose one of the individuals or do their own research and choose someone else, such as:

  ▷ Chief Little Turtle

  ▷ Edmund Randolph

  ▷ William Patterson

  ▷ Roger Sherman

  ▷ Patrick Henry

  ▷ Elbridge Gerry

- Ask students to use the information in the text and from their own research as they write questions and the answers of the historical character they have chosen. Suggest that students choose a partner and act out the questions and answers for the rest of the class.

Teacher Notes

What Was the Articles of Confederation and Why Did It fail?

Background Information

Explain to students that in this lesson they will learn about the laws passed in the Articles of Confederation and the process that led to the creation of the United States Constitution.

Community Connections

To enrich what students have learned about the process of creating the United States Constitution have students visit the local library to explore the many reputable sources and websites giving information on both the Constitution and the Founding Fathers.

LESSON STANDARDS

✔ Explain how state constitutions that were established after 1776 embodied the ideals of the American Revolution and helped serve as models for the U.S. Constitution. **HSS.5.6.5**

✔ Demonstrate knowledge of the significance of land policies developed under the Continental Congress (e.g., sale of western lands, the Northwest Ordinance of 1787) and those policies' impact on American Indians' land. **HSS.5.6.6**

✔ Students place key events and people of the historical era they are studying in a chronological sequence and within a spatial context; they interpret time lines. **HAS.CS.1**

✔ Students pose relevant questions about events they encounter in historical documents, eyewitness accounts, oral histories, letters, diaries, artifacts, photographs, maps, artworks, and architecture. **HAS.HR.2**

✔ Students summarize the key events of the era they are studying and explain the historical contexts of those events. **HAS.HI.1**

✔ Students identify and interpret the multiple causes and effects of historical events. **HAS.HI.3**

Connect to the Essential Question

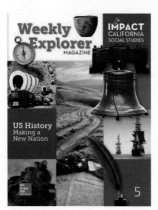

The **Weekly Explorer Magazine** supports students' exploration of the Essential Question and provides additional resources for the EQ Inquiry Project.

Chapter 6, pp. 72–83

Inquiry Project

Which Side Will You Choose?

Remind students to use the information they learn in this lesson and other resources to complete their EQ Inquiry Project!

Dinah Zike's

FOLDABLES®

In this lesson you will use Foldables.

When Minutes Count!

Suggested Lesson Pacing

1 ENGAGE
One Day

2 INVESTIGATE
Two to Three Days

 Short on Time? Look for the clock to teach core content in less time.

3 REPORT
One Day

- Lesson Opener
- Analyze the Source
- Inquiry Tools

Go Digital
- **Video:** The Articles of Confederation
- **iMap:** United States, 1787

- One Nation or Thirteen States?
- The Northwest Ordinance
- A Call for Stronger Government
- **Citizenship** Views on Rebellion

- Think About It
- Write and Cite Evidence
- Defend Your Claim

Make Connections!

(CCSS) CONNECT TO ELA

Reading

Explain the relationships or interactions between two or more individuals, events, ideas, or concepts in a historical, scientific, or technical text based on specific information in the text. **RI.5.3**

Determine two or more main ideas of a text and explain how they are supported by key details; summarize the text. **RI.5.2**

Research

Conduct short research projects that use several sources to build knowledge through investigation of different aspects of a topic. **W.5.7**

Recall relevant information from experiences or gather relevant information from print and digital sources; summarize or paraphrase information in notes and finished work, and provide a list of sources. **W.5.8**

Writing

Write informative/explanatory texts to examine a topic and convey ideas and information clearly. **W.5.2**

Draw evidence from literary or informational texts to support analysis, reflection, and research. **W.5.9**

Speaking and Listening

Engage effectively in a range of collaborative discussions (one-on-one, in groups, and teacher-led) with diverse partners on grade 5 topics and texts, building on others' ideas and expressing their own clearly. **SL.5.1**

Report on a topic or text or present an opinion, sequencing ideas logically and using appropriate facts and relevant, descriptive details to support main ideas or themes; speak clearly at an understandable pace. **SL.5.4**

Classroom Resources

Search for additional resources using the following key words.

Samuel Adams

Congress

United States Constitution

continental currency

Thomas Jefferson

Alexander Hamilton

Governor John Hancock

Henry Lee

national government

Northwest Ordinance

Second Continental Congress

Daniel Shays's Rebellion

Arthur St. Clair

Chief Little Turtle

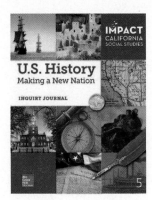

Inquiry Journal,
pp. 212–213

STANDARDS

Explain how state constitutions that were established after 1776 embodied the ideals of the American Revolution and helped serve as models for the U.S. Constitution. **HSS.5.6.5**

Students differentiate between primary and secondary sources. **HAS.HR.1**

Students pose relevant questions about events they encounter in historical documents, eyewitness accounts, oral histories, letters, diaries, artifacts, photographs, maps, artworks, and architecture. **HAS.HR.2**

Engage effectively in a range of collaborative discussions (one-on-one, in groups, and teacher-led) with diverse partners on *grade 5 topics and texts*, building on others' ideas and expressing their own clearly. **CCSS.ELA.SL.5.1**

Go Digital!

Explore the lesson content with online whole-class presentation tools.

- **Video:** The Articles of Confederation
- **iMap:** United States, 1787

What Was the Articles of Confederation and Why Did it Fail?

Bellringer

Prompt students to retrieve information from the previous lessons. Say: *The Battle of Yorktown was basically the end of the Revolutionary War. What is the name for an agreement that ends a war?* (peace treaty) *What was the name of the peace treaty that ended the Revolutionary War?* (Peace of Paris) *What was the western border of the new nation?* (the Mississippi River)

Lesson Outcomes

What Am I Learning? Have students read the Lesson Question and Lesson Outcomes on page 212.

Why Am I Learning It? Make sure students understand the noun *process*. Call on volunteers to define the term. Say: Process *is an academic word that means a series of actions or steps that produce something. For example, learning a new language can be a long* process*. The* process *often is much longer for adults than for children*

How Will I Know That I Learned It? Ask students the following questions.

- What will you be able to identify? (the Articles of Confederation)

- What is the purpose of this task? (to summarize the strengths and weaknesses of the Articles of Confederation)

- How will you support your writing? (with evidence from the text)

Talk About It

Analyze the Image Explain that when we talk about an image, we describe and interpret it and present our ideas in our own words. Provide sentence frames like these to help students form sentences as they talk about the image.

- *The image shows _____.*
- *The document is handwritten because _____.*

Collaborative Conversations

Add New Ideas As students engage in partner, small group, and whole-class discussions, encourage them to

- First and view read the material carefully.
- Be respectful of the opinions of others.
- Look for ways to connect their personal experiences or prior knowledge to the conversation.

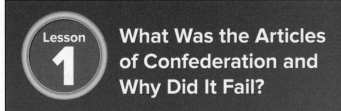

What Was the Articles of Confederation and Why Did It Fail?

Lesson Outcomes

What Am I Learning?
In this lesson, you're going to use your investigative skills to explore the Articles of Confederation.

Why Am I Learning It?
Reading and talking about the laws passed in the Articles will help you understand the process that led to the creation of the United States Constitution.

How Will I Know That I Learned It?
You will be able to evaluate the strengths and weaknesses of the first constitutional document of the United States.

Talk About It COLLABORATE

Look at the Details How is this image of the Articles of Confederation similar to other important documents from U.S. history? In what ways do you think this document differs from government documents written today?

HSS.5.6.6, HSS.5.7.1, HAS.HR.2, HAS.HI.1, HAS.HI.3

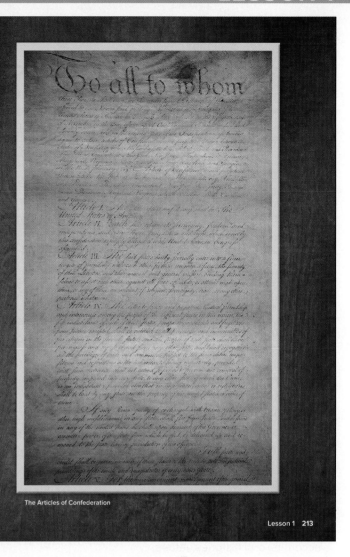

The Articles of Confederation

Inquiry Journal, pp. 212–213

EL ENGLISH LEARNERS SCAFFOLD

ELD.PI.5.2 Interacting with others in written English in various communicative forms (print, communicative technology, and multimedia

Emerging	Expanding	Bridging
Identify Details Work with students individually to identify what they see in the image of the Articles of Confederation. Supply vocabulary as needed.	**Describe Details** Have small groups create a list of words that describe what they see in the image of the Articles of Confederation. Encourage them to describe the paper and to note that the document is handwritten. Have groups share their list.	**Use Language** Have students work together to describe what they find historically important about the document shown in the image. Have them explain how they know the document is very old.

See the **Language Learner Teaching Guide** for more language support strategies.

Monitor and Differentiate

REACHING ALL LEARNERS

Approaching Level

Have students work together to describe what they see in the image. Have them discuss how they know the document is old and why it is handwritten. Encourage them to use words like *cursive* (handwriting in which all the letters in a word are joined) and *primary source* (direct, first-hand evidence of events, objects, and people) to describe what they see.

Beyond Level

Have students discuss the importance of studying primary source documents. Have them explain how these documents can enhance their understanding of history.

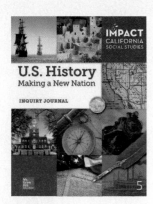

Inquiry Journal,
pp. 214–215

 STANDARDS

Explain how state constitutions that were established after 1776 embodied the ideals of the American Revolution and helped serve as models for the U.S. Constitution. **HSS.5.6.5**

Students differentiate between primary and secondary sources. **HAS.HR.1**

Students pose relevant questions about events they encounter in historical documents, eyewitness accounts, oral histories, letters, diaries, artifacts, photographs, maps, artworks, and architecture. **HAS.HR.2**

Engage effectively in a range of collaborative discussions (one-on-one, in groups, and teacher-led) with diverse partners on *grade 5 topics and texts*, building on others' ideas and expressing their own clearly. **CCSS.ELA.SL.5.1**

Go *Digital!*

Model how to inspect and find evidence with online whole-class presentation tools.

Background Information

Alexander Hamilton Alexander Hamilton (c. 1757–1804) came to America alone at the age of 15. When Alexander was still an infant, his father, James Hamilton, abandoned his family, and when Hamilton was 11 his mother died. Hamilton's intelligence and willingness to work hard allowed him to overcome these early, crushing disadvantages. Hamilton fought by Washington's side during the Revolutionary War. He was a member of the convention that drafted the U.S. Constitution and served as the new country's first Treasury secretary. The widely acclaimed musical *Hamilton* is based on Hamilton's life.

1 Inspect

Look Have students read the entire text, including the Primary Source, to focus on understanding the overall meaning. Remind them to circle unknown words.

- According to the document, what power do the states retain? (their sovereignty)
- What function does Congress or the federal government serve? (Congress oversees all bills of credit, monies borrowed, and debts contracted.)
- What problem related to the states and federal government is the Articles of Confederation trying to solve? (the power of states vs. the power of the federal government)

2 Find Evidence

Look Again Have students reread the text.

Analyze the Primary Source Reread the letter from Alexander Hamilton to James Duane aloud and then analyze the letter together as a class. Provide support for vocabulary as needed.

- What is Hamilton's assessment of the confederation? (He thinks it is defective and needs to be altered.)
- What is Hamilton's major objection? (He thinks it gives the states too much power.)
- What does the word *feeble* mean? (weak)

3 Make Connections

COLLABORATE

Talk Have students work with a partner to discuss how the Articles helped set up a central government. (The Articles give the central government power over bills, borrowed money, and debts contracted by Congress.) What aspect of government did the founders think was most important? (the sovereignty of the states)

Analyze the Source

1 Inspect

Read Look at the title. What can you infer about the author(s) of this text?

- **Circle** words you don't know. Look them up and rewrite each article in simpler language.
- **Underline** action words in the articles. What actions do the Articles of Confederation grant the states and Congress?
- **Discuss** with a partner why the writers of the Articles of Confederation might have decided to separate the document into different articles.

My Notes

_____

_____

_____

_____

_____

_____

_____

_____

_____

_____

_____

Excerpts from the Articles of Confederation

Article II.

Each state retains its sovereignty, freedom, and independence, and every power, jurisdiction, and right, which is not by this Confederation expressly delegated to the United States, in Congress assembled.

Article X.

The Committee of the States, or any nine of them, shall be authorized to execute, in the recess of Congress, such of the powers of Congress as the United States in Congress assembled, by the consent of the nine States, shall from time to time think expedient to vest them with; provided that no power be delegated to the said Committee, for the exercise of which, by the Articles of Confederation, the voice of nine States in the Congress of the United States assembled be requisite.

Article XIII.

All bills of credit emitted, monies borrowed, and debts contracted by, or under the authority of Congress, before the assembling of the United States, in pursuance of the present confederation, shall be deemed and considered as a charge against the United States, for payment and satisfaction whereof the said United States, and the public faith are hereby solemnly pledged.

Articles of Confederation, arts. 2, 10, 12. March 1, 1781. Documents Illustrative of the Formation of the Union of the American States. Government Printing Office, 1927. House Document No. 398.

PRIMARY SOURCE

In Their Words...

Alexander Hamilton

But the confederation itself is defective and requires to be altered. It is neither fit for war nor peace. The idea of an uncontrollable sovereignty in each state over its internal police will defeat the other powers given to Congress and make our union feeble and precarious. There are instances without number where acts necessary for the general good, and which rise out of the powers given to Congress, must interfere with the internal police of the states . . .

—from a letter to James Duane, September 2, 1780

TEXT: Hamilton, Alexander. Alexander Hamilton to James Duane, 3 September 1780. Founders Online, National Archives. PHOTO: (t)McGraw-Hill Education; (b)Library of Congress, Prints and Photographs Division [LC-USZC4-6423]

2 Find Evidence

Reread What weakness of the Articles of Confederation does Alexander Hamilton identify in this letter?

Examine Reread the statement "the idea of an uncontrollable sovereignty in each state over its internal police will defeat the other powers given to Congress and make our union feeble and precarious." Based on this context, what does the word *feeble* mean? Name a word that has the same meaning as *feeble*.

3 Make Connections

Talk Discuss with a partner how the Articles helped set up a central government. Which responsibilities of government did the founders think were most important?

COLLABORATE

214 Lesson 1 What Was the Articles of Confederation and Why Did It Fail?

Lesson 1 215

Inquiry Journal, pp. 214–215

EL ENGLISH LEARNERS SCAFFOLD

ELD.PI.5.6 Reading closely literary and informational texts and viewing multimedia to determine how meaning is conveyed explicitly and implicitly through language

Emerging	Expanding	Bridging
Develop Language Help students unpack the first sentence. Tell students that the Spanish cognate for *independence* is *independencia* and for *delegate* is *delegado*. Students should understand that this long sentence is naming what powers states have and what powers the central government has.	**Develop Language** Guide students to chunk the first sentence. Tell students that the Spanish cognate for *power* is *poder*. Guide students to understand that this long sentence is naming what powers states have and what powers the central government has. Supply vocabulary as needed.	**Use Language** Have students work in pairs, explaining to each other the meaning of small chunks of the first sentence. Help partners with difficult vocabulary, such as *sovereignty* (power) and *delegated* (assigned or given).

See the **Language Learner Teaching Guide** for more language support strategies.

Monitor and Differentiate

REACHING ALL LEARNERS

Special Needs

Tell students that Hamilton wanted a strong federal government. Have students read the primary source quote, pausing between each sentence to monitor comprehension. Allow students to explain what confusions arise from each sentence, and work with them to understand how the quote expresses Hamilton's ideas about federal government.

Beyond Level

Have students research how the rights of states versus the power of the federal government is still an issue today. Students might want to examine contemporary issues, such as the death penalty, assisted suicide, and gun control.

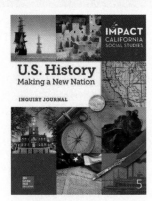

Inquiry Journal,
pp. 216–217

STANDARDS

CCSS Explain the relationships or interactions between two or more individuals, events, ideas, or concepts in a historical, scientific, or technical text based on specific information in the text. **CCSS.ELA.RI.5.3**

Draw evidence from literary or informational texts to support analysis, reflection, and research **CCSS.ELA.W.5.9**

Write informative/explanatory texts to examine a topic and convey ideas and information clearly. **CCSS.ELA.W.5.2**

Go *Digital!*

• Model how to explore and investigate with online whole-class tools.

• Students can access the online graphic organizer to use the inquiry tools as they read.

Determine Pros and Cons

Explain Tell students that determining the pros and cons of an issue is one way to organize information in a historical text. Examining the positive and negative outcomes of historical events will help you better understand historical events and their effects.

Read Have students read the step-by-step instructions about how to determine the pros and cons of an event. Remind students to begin by making inferences about how and why the event happened.

Guide Practice Tell students that they often determine pros and cons in their own lives. Give an example such as trying to decide whether or not to go to a concert. Students might ask and answer questions such as *How expensive is the concert? Do I have enough money? What important things could I be doing instead of going to the concert? How much do I like the group that will be playing?*

Investigate!

Have students read pages 258–265 in the Research Companion. Tell them the information will help them answer the lesson question **What was the Articles of Confederation and Why Did It Fail?**

Take Notes Tell students that they should take notes about pros and cons in the graphic organizer on page 217 of the Inquiry Journal. Explain to students that they will take notes as they read each section. Remind them that taking notes will help them understand and remember what they read. Remind students that good note taking is about finding the most important information and writing key words or phrases about it. Note takers do not rewrite every word from the text unless they plan to quote an author.

Inspect Guide students to read the text in each section to determine what the text says. Encourage them to make note of words they don't understand and look for answers to questions, such as *who? what? where? when? why?* and *how?*

Find Evidence Encourage students to reread the text to develop a deeper understanding of the content. Remind students that after they read and take notes, they should review and think about how the facts and details will help them answer the lesson question.

Collaborative Conversations

Text-Based Discussion Remind students of the goals of discussing the text with others.

• to listen and respond to another point of view

• to find additional evidence

• to see the text from a different point of view.

Inquiry Tools

Determine Pros and Cons

Asking questions about what you read will allow you to judge the positive and negative outcomes of historical events.

1. Read the text all the way through.
This will help you understand what the text is about.

2. Answer *who*, *what*, *where*, and *when*.
Write down the dates, places, events, and people mentioned in the text.

3. Make inferences about the historical reasons for an event.
Sometimes the author directly explains how and why something happened; other times, you will have to make inferences. Combine your prior knowledge with what you read in the text to understand the context of the events mentioned in the text.

4. Identify positive and negative effects.
Once you've answered questions about a text, you can use the information to list the pros and cons that resulted from the historical events you've read about.

 COLLABORATE Based on the text you just read, work with your class to complete the chart below.

Pros	Cons
The Articles give states much freedom to govern themselves.	Hamilton argues that the governing power given to the states weakens the United States as a whole.

 IMPACT U.S. History Making a New Nation RESEARCH COMPANION

Investigate!

Read pages 258–265 in your Research Companion. Use your investigative skills to identify the pros and cons of the Articles of the Confederation.

Pros	Cons
Established the first national government in the United States	Did not provide ways to help banks make sure loans were repaid
Created the Confederation Congress to govern the nation	Confederation Congress not given enough power to govern effectively
Allowed states to run their own governments independently	Some states created state constitutions that went against the Articles.
Did not allow for taxes by the national government	States have own currencies, making it hard for people to do business in more than one state
Enabled Congress to create the Northwest Ordinance	National government's money problems lead to violent conflicts, such as Shays's Rebellion.

McGraw-Hill Education

Inquiry Journal, pp. 216–217

EL ENGLISH LEARNERS SCAFFOLD

ELD.PI.5.11 Supporting own opinions and evaluating others' opinions in speaking and writing

Emerging

Develop Language Work with individual students to be sure that they understand the meaning of "pros" and "cons." Explain that "pros" are the favorable reasons for doing something and "cons" are the unfavorable reasons. Tell students that they can fill in the pros and cons in the chart by using a single word or drawing a picture.

Expanding

Cite Evidence Have students work with a partner to find words or phrases from the letter of Alexander Hamilton that suggest some of the cons of the Articles of Confederacy. Then have them use one of those words in a sentence of their own.

Bridging

Summarize Have students use descriptive words from the text in sentences of their own as they list important pros and cons of the Articles of the Confederacy. Have them share their list of descriptive words in small groups.

See the **Language Learner Teaching Guide** for more language support strategies.

Monitor and Differentiate

REACHING ALL LEARNERS

Approaching Level

Have students look closely at the third sentence from Alexander Hamilton's letter, which begins "The idea of an uncontrollable. . ." Ask and answer more detailed questions to help guide students' understanding, such as *What does Hamilton mean by "uncontrollable sovereignty in each state"? What does Hamilton foresee will be the problem with each state's internal police? Why, in Hamilton's opinion, would giving the states too much power make the union "feeble and precarious"?*

Beyond Level

Have a small group of students discuss why analyzing the pros and cons of historical events and of current events is a useful skill.

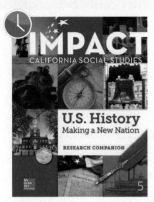

Research Companion,
pp. 258–259

HSS STANDARDS

Explain how state constitutions that were established after 1776 embodied the ideals of the American Revolution and helped serve as models for the U.S. Constitution. **HSS.5.6.5**

Students place key events and people of the historical era they are studying in a chronological sequence and within a spatial context; they interpret time lines. **HAS.CS.1**

Draw evidence from literary or informational texts to support analysis, reflection, and research **CCSS.ELA.W.5.9**

Go Digital!

Investigate the lesson content with online whole-class presentation tools.

- **Video:** The Articles of Confederation
- **iMap:** United States, 1787

Background Information

Continental Congress From 1774 until 1789 the Continental Congress served as the governing body for the American colonies. The First Continental Congress met in 1774, primarily as a reaction to steps taken by the British government in response to the colonies' resistance to taxation. The Second Continental Congress took the momentous step in 1776 of declaring America's independence from England. Five years later the Congress approved the country's first Constitution.

| TIMELINE | Invite students to look at the timeline at the top of page 259.

> **Analyze** What two significant events occurred between 1777 and 1787? (Congress creates the Articles of Confederation, and the Articles are ratified by all 13 states) **HAS.CS.1**

Analyze the Source

Inspect Have students read about One Nation or Thirteen States on pages 258–259.

Find Evidence Use the questions below to check comprehension. Remind students to support their answers with text evidence.

> **Identify** What was the first written document to establish a United States government? (The Articles of Confederation) **DOK 1**

> **Vocabulary** When the Second Continental Congress approved the Articles of Confederation, what did it do? (officially accept it) **DOK 2**

> **Infer** Why did the Articles of the Confederation assign Congress to oversee foreign affairs and war? (Answers may vary, but students should note that it wouldn't make much sense to have individual states making foreign policy or conducting war.) **DOK 2**

> **Summarize** Summarize the powers allocated to the states by the Articles of the Confederation. (States could run their own state government, print their own money, and could write their own constitutions. States did not have to pay taxes to the Confederation.) **DOK 2**

Make Connections Ask students to share their opinions. Say: *Based on what you have read, why were the Articles of the Confederation important?* (Answers will vary, but students should note that, while not perfect, the Articles of the Confederation provided an important first step in the process of writing the U.S. Constitution.) **DOK 4**

Analyze the Illustration Direct students' attention to the illustration of battle in Daniel Shays's rebellion on p. 259. Encourage students to use images in the text to help them understand events. Point out the farmers and the militia.

- What kinds of weapons do the soldiers have? (guns and cannons)

- What does the picture tell you about the battle? (Answers will vary, but students should note that it is violent and that people are getting hurt.)

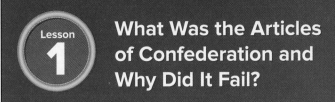

Lesson 1

What Was the Articles of Confederation and Why Did It Fail?

One Nation or Thirteen States?

The **Articles** of Confederation was the first written document to establish a United States government. The Second Continental Congress began writing the Articles of Confederation in 1776 and approved it in 1777. However, it was not ratified by all 13 states until 1781. Its writers imagined a nation unlike European countries. They promised a "firm league of friendship" in which each state was guaranteed its "freedom and independence."

The Articles granted new powers to the national government. It created a Confederation Congress to govern the country. The Congress created departments of finance, foreign affairs, war, and the post office. The Congress also signed a peace treaty with Great Britain, formally ending the Revolutionary War.

The Articles allowed the states to continue to run their own governments independently. States retained the right to print their own money. States also had the authority to tax while the Confederation Congress did not. By 1786, many of the thirteen states had written their own constitutions that challenged the authority of the Articles of Confederation. Meanwhile, the Confederation Congress passed laws controlling the growth of the new country.

HSS.5.6.5, HSS.5.6.6, HSS.5.7.1, HSS.5.9, HAS.HI.1, HAS.HI.3, HAS.CS.1, HAS.HR.1, HAS.HR.2

258 Lesson 1 What Was the Articles of Confederation and Why Did It Fail?

Timeline

1776 Declaration of Independence signed; Second Continental Congress creates Articles of Confederation.

1781 Articles ratified by all 13 states

1787 Northwest Ordinance passed; Constitutional Convention begins.

1770 | 1780 | 1790

1777 United States starts operating under the Articles.

1786–1787 Shays's Rebellion

Daniel Shays leads farmers in a rebellion against the government of Massachusetts.

Lesson 1 **259**

Research Companion, pp. 258–259

ENGLISH LEARNERS SCAFFOLD

ELD.PI.5.1 Exchanging information and ideas with others through oral collaborative discussions on a range of social and academic topics

Emerging

Build Vocabulary Have students look at the illustration of Daniel Shays and his supporters protesting high taxes on p. 259. Ask students to name what they see. Supply vocabulary as needed.

Expanding

Identify Have students look at the illustration of Daniel Shays and his supporters protesting high taxes on p. 259. Ask students to work with a partner to name what they see in the illustration. Have them keep a list of words naming what they see in the illustration.

Bridging

Use Vocabulary Have students look at the illustration of Daniel Shays and his supporters protesting high taxes on p. 259. Ask students to work with a partner to name what they see in the illustration. Have them keep a list of words naming what they see. Then have students choose two of their words and use them in sentences of their own.

See the **Language Learner Teaching Guide** for more language support strategies.

Monitor and Differentiate

REACHING ALL LEARNERS

Special Needs

Guide students to use maps and manipulatables to grasp what the text means when it describes the writers of the Articles of Confederation imagining "a nation not unlike European countries." Help students understand that European "states" like England and France are separate countries. The states that make up the United States are not separate countries, and all belong to the same union.

Approaching Level

Guide students to understand that the authors were trying to determine the rights and powers of the states versus the rights and powers of the central government. Have students work with a partner to identify the major problems that the writers of the Articles of Confederation were dealing with.

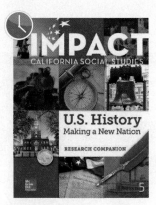

Research Companion,
pp. 260–261

 STANDARDS

Demonstrate knowledge of the significance of land policies developed under the Continental Congress (e.g., sale of western lands, the Northwest Ordinance of 1787) and those policies' impact on American Indians' land. **HSS.5.6.6**

CCSS Determine two or more main ideas of a text and explain how they are supported by key details; summarize the text. **CCSS.ELA.RI.5.2**

Go Digital!

Investigate the lesson content with online whole-class presentation tools.

Background Information

Little Turtle Little Turtle, also known by his American Indian name, Michikinikwa, was born around 1752, twenty miles northwest of what today is Fort Wayne Indiana. In the early 1790s, Little Turtle along with the Shawnee chief Tecumseh led the Miami and Shawnee people to resist white settlers in the western part of Ohio.

Analyze the Source

Inspect Have students read about the Northwest Ordinance on pages 260–261.

Find Evidence Use the questions below to check comprehension. Remind students to support their answers with text evidence.

> **Identify** What territory was included of the Northwest Ordinance? (land north of the Ohio River and east of the Mississippi River) **DOK 1**
>
> **Draw Conclusions** For what purpose did Congress issue the Northwest Ordinance? (to organize the settlement of the Northwest Territory) **DOK 2**
>
> **Analyze Cause and Effect** How did the treatment of Native Americans change when the government decided to treat American Indians as "conquered nations"? (The result was that Congress sent soldiers to the Northwest Territory to remove American Indians by force. Settlers also regularly attacked and killed groups of American Indians without government support.) **DOK 2**

Make Connections Prompt students to make connections with the following question.

> **Description** How did some American Indians respond to the encroachment on their land? (They defended themselves. The Miami, Shawnee, and Delaware people formed a military alliance. Miami chief Little Turtle attacked Author St. Claire's troops. Nine hundred men were killed or wounded in the attack.) **DOK 3**

Map Skills

Project the map on page 261, and ask the following questions.

- Have students use the map scale to estimate the distance between the northernmost and southernmost parts of the Northwest Territory. (about 1,500 miles)
- What does the yellow shading represent? (the Northwest Territory)
- What does the green shading represent? (the United States)

✓ Stop and Check

Talk Have students discuss the pros and cons of settling in the new territory. (Answers may vary, but students might discuss pros such as the appeal of new land, access to new resources in the Midwest, and fleeing slavery in other states. Cons include dangerous conflict with American Indians, land prices that were difficult to afford, and the Northwest Territory's lack of big cities such as Philadelphia and Boston.)

Find Details Explain to students that after they read and take notes, they should review and think about how the facts and details will help them answer the Essential Question.

The Northwest Ordinance

Congress organized the settlement of the Northwest Territory under the Articles of Confederation. This territory included land north of the Ohio River and east of the Mississippi River. The government would later divide the Northwest Territory into the states of Ohio, Indiana, Illinois, Michigan, and Wisconsin.

Congress **issued** the Northwest Ordinance to help organize the territory. The law defined a strict structure for the settlements. Areas with small populations could vote on legislators. Regions with at least 60,000 adults could register for statehood.

The Northwest Territory was divided into rectangular townships. Each township included 36 sections. Large companies bought much of the land in the townships. The companies sold smaller portions to settlers for a profit. Arthur St. Clair ran the Ohio Company. The company owned 1.5 million acres of the Northwest Territory. He became the first governor of the Northwest Territory.

In 1783, Congress ruled that, after the Revolutionary War, American Indians no longer held the right to land in the Northwest Territory. The U.S. government began to treat the native peoples as conquered nations. Congress sent soldiers to the territory to remove American Indians by force.

One army officer reported that settlers regularly attacked and killed groups of American Indians without government support. To defend themselves, the Miami, Shawnee, and Delaware peoples formed a military alliance. In 1791, Miami chief Little Turtle led an attack on Arthur St. Clair's troops. Nine hundred of the U.S. troops were killed. It was the worst defeat suffered by U.S. soldiers in the history of war against American Indians. Little Turtle died in one of the battles that followed, but the American Indians' resistance forced the U.S. government to negotiate peace agreements.

The Northwest Ordinance declared that "neither slavery nor involuntary servitude" was allowed in the Northwest Territory. In the mid-1780s, however, most states outside of the territory still permitted white men to own slaves. Even free African Americans had many fewer rights than whites.

Prohibited from worshipping in white churches, African Americans created their own churches. Richard Allen founded the first fully independent African-American church in Philadelphia in 1794, the African Methodist Episcopal (A.M.E.) Church. Communities of African-American worshippers would go on to build A.M.E. churches across the United States.

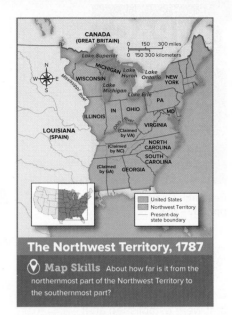

The Northwest Territory, 1787

🔍 **Map Skills** About how far is it from the northernmost part of the Northwest Territory to the southernmost part?

✅ **Stop and Check**

COLLABORATE

Talk If you were living in one of the original thirteen colonies, would you consider moving to the Northwest Territory? Working with a partner, discuss the pros and cons of settling in the territory.

Find Details As you read, add additional information to the graphic organizer on page 217 in your Inquiry Journal.

Research Companion, pp. 260–261

(EL) ENGLISH LEARNERS SCAFFOLD

ELD.PI.5.1 Exchanging information and ideas with others through oral collaborative discussions on a range of social and academic topics

Emerging

Build Vocabulary Direct students to look at the map on p. 261. Work with students individually to understand difficult vocabulary. Point out the states that make up the Northwest Territory. Say the names of the states aloud and have students pronounce the names after you.

Expanding

Collaborate Guide students to understand the words *territory, sections,* and *profit*. Use the map of the Northwest Ordinance for clues. Use concrete examples to explain that *territory* is an area of land, *sections* are parts into which something is divided, and *profits* are financial gains.

Bridging

Use Language Have students create a word list to describe the major features of the Northwest Ordinance. Have students work with a partner to write definitions for the words on their lists. Have students consult a dictionary as needed.

See the **Language Learner Teaching Guide** for more language support strategies.

Monitor and Differentiate

REACHING ALL LEARNERS

Approaching Level

Help students learn to identify main ideas and key details by asking and answering questions, such as "What is the text mostly about?"

On Level

Help students learn to identify main ideas and key details by asking and answering questions, such as "What is the text mostly about?" and "What important details are included?"

Beyond Level

Have students work with a partner to identify the main ideas and key details. Then have students write a brief summary of "The Northwest Ordinance" including main ideas and key details.

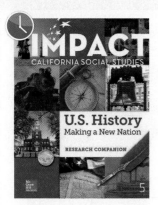

Research Companion,
pp. 262–263

Go *Digital!*

Investigate the lesson content
with online whole-class
presentation tools

Background Information

Continental Currency Continental currency was not backed by either gold or
silver. Instead, the government planned to pay them with anticipated tax revenues.
When the British started counterfeiting the currency, they quickly became
devalued. Hence, the phrase "not worth a continental" came about to describe
something of little value.

Analyze the Source

Inspect Have students read about A Call for a Stronger Government when issues arose
with the Articles of Confederation on pages 262–263.

Find Evidence Use the questions below to check comprehension. Remind students to
support their answers with text evidence.

Analyze Cause and Effect What was the effect of the national government not collecting
taxes during this period? (The United States owed 13.3 million dollars it debt.) **DOK 2**

Analyze Cause and Effect What effects did the weakness of the government called
for by the Articles of Confederation have on how effectively the nation functioned?
(Banks did not function well; merchants found it difficult to do business in more than
one state; because the government did not collect taxes, the country was in debt;
money owed to military officials and leaders could not be paid.) **DOK 2**

Make Connections Prompt students to make connections with the following question.

Draw Conclusions How were the government's money problems related to the violent
conflict of Shays's Rebellion? (Answers will vary, but students should note that because
of the government's money problems merchants in Boston required that their bills be
paid in gold and silver. When farmers could not produce the gold and silver, they were
jailed in large numbers. This led to Shays's Rebellion.) **DOK 3**

A Call for Stronger Government

The Articles of Confederation eventually proved to be weak in governing the United States as a single nation. Without the backing of a strong national government, American banks often found it difficult to make sure borrowers repaid their loans. In addition, each state maintained its own **currency**. Merchants and companies struggled to do business in more than one state. Doing so involved understanding highly complicated state laws as well as confusing differences in the value of states' money.

The national government, meanwhile, did not collect taxes. Instead, Congress asked for money from state governments. After the Revolutionary War, Congress needed $15.7 million to pay its debts. The states agreed to pay the national government only $2.4 million.

The United States could not afford to pay money owed to some of the military officials and leaders who had fought in the Revolutionary War. These people became increasingly frustrated with the government's lack of power over the states.

In the 1780s, the national government's money problems led to violent conflict. Merchants in Boston decided to require that their bills be paid in gold and silver. They thought that the Massachusetts currency was too unstable. When farmers in western Massachusetts could not produce the necessary gold and silver coins to pay off their debts, they were jailed in large numbers.

The imprisoned farmers appealed to the Massachusetts legislature to help them pay their debts. The members of the legislature, however, were mostly lawyers and merchants who paid little attention to the farmers' requests. The legislators voted to raise taxes. This decision further burdened poor farmers.

The angry farmers had just recently experienced the power of revolt in the Revolutionary War. In 1786, they blocked the entrances of several county courthouses to stop the legal processes required to take the indebted farmers' land. Rebels attacked jails and released farmers who had been imprisoned. Daniel Shays, a Revolutionary War captain who was now a struggling farmer, led the rebels.

Did You Know?

The U.S. government first issued print money during the Revolutionary War. These bills, called Continental Currency, helped pay for the war against the British. Realizing this, the British government printed counterfeit bills and passed them out in the United States. They succeeded in weakening the U.S. government by lowering the worth of the Continental Currency. This was the first example of paper-money counterfeiting as a form of economic warfare.

Paper money issued by the state of Massachusetts

Daniel Shays and his supporters protested high taxes.

A group of Shays's men attacked a state arsenal—a building where weapons are stored—in 1787. A local militia defeated Shays's forces as they attempted to seize the weapons. Four men died and 20 more were wounded. Shays's Rebellion persisted nonetheless.

As the rebels continued to cause havoc in the state, the governor of Massachusetts, John Hancock, sent more than 4,000 troops to stop the rebellion. Badly outnumbered, most of Shays's men fled. The Massachusetts government captured and sentenced fifteen rebels to death. Two of the accused were executed, while Hancock pardoned the rest. Daniel Shays left Massachusetts for New York, where he returned to farming.

262 Lesson 1 What Was the Articles of Confederation and Why Did It Fail?

Lesson 1 263

Research Companion, pp. 262–263

EL ENGLISH LEARNERS SCAFFOLD

ELD.PI.5.1 Exchanging information and ideas with others through oral collaborative discussions on a range of social and academic topics

Emerging

Monitor Comprehension Work with students individually to be sure they understand that the text shows reasons why the Articles of Confederation was not working. Work with them to understand important and difficult vocabulary, such as *borrower, merchants, debt, conflict, unstable, and rebellion*, giving as many concrete examples as possible.

Expanding/Bridging

Connect to Personal Experience Encourage students to use the word *rebellion* in a sentence. Have them describe a situation in which they or someone they know rebelled. Then have them explain what caused the rebellion. Encourage students to then compare that rebellion with Shays's Rebellion.

See the **Language Learner Teaching Guide** for more language support strategies.

Monitor and Differentiate

REACHING ALL LEARNERS

Approaching Level

Work with students to understand specific reasons why the Articles of the Confederation proved inadequate. As they discuss the concept, encourage them to use specific words from the text, such as *merchant, frustrated, counterfeit, and unstable*.

Beyond Level

Have students do additional research on examples of counterfeiting as a form of economic warfare in history. Suggest that they explore topics, such as trade, embargoes, boycotts, sanctions, freezing of capital assets, and suspension of aid.

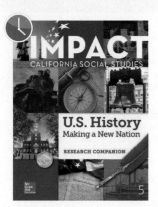

Research Companion,
pp. 264–265

 STANDARDS

Explain how state constitutions that were established after 1776 embodied the ideals of the American Revolution and helped serve as models for the U.S. Constitution. **HSS.5.6.5**

(ccss) Engage effectively in a range of collaborative discussions (one-on-one, in groups, and teacher-led) with diverse partners on *grade 5 topics and texts*, building on others' ideas and expressing their own clearly. **CCSS.ELA.SL.5.1**

Go Digital!

Investigate the lesson content with online whole-class presentation tools.

Background Information

Henry "Light-Horse Harry" Lee gained his nickname from his expert use of cavalry during the Revolutionary War. He rose in the ranks and became one of Washington's close friends. When Washington died, Lee delivered these words to Congress: "first in war, first in peace, and first in the hearts of his countrymen." Lee's son, Robert E. Lee, went on to become a general in his own right.

Analyze the Source

Inspect Have students read pages 264–265.

Find Evidence Use the questions below to check comprehension. Remind students to support their answers with text evidence.

> **Analyze Cause and Effect** How did Daniel Shays's rebellion affect American leaders' views about the need for a strong central government? (It convinced them of the need for a strong central government to manage money and to quell rebellions.) **DOK 2**

Analyze the Primary Source Point out the words "submit to the horrors of anarchy." Ask students to discuss what the words mean to Henry Lee.

> **Cite Evidence** Why does Henry Lee think that without a strong government the country will "submit to the horrors of anarchy"? (Lee believes that without a strong central government, business will suffer because of the instability of banks. This would leave many unemployed, confined to idleness, and intent on ruining society.) **DOK 3**

Citizenship

> **Infer** What can you infer about how Samuel Adams would have reacted to Shays's Rebellion? (Adams would have been totally against it.) **DOK 2**

> **Draw Conclusions** Based on the quotation, what conclusion can you draw about how Jefferson saw the role of government in people's lives? (Answers will vary, but students should note that Jefferson thinks the government exists to carry out the will of the people and should respect the people's wishes.) **DOK 3**

☑ Stop and Check

Think Have students discuss how the Articles of Confederation led to Shays's rebellion. (The lack of a strong central government led to issues in banking, which in turn led to creditors demanding that farmer pay their bills in gold and silver. Farmers could not pay, and this led to Shays's Rebellion.)

You Decide Encourage students to use text evidence as they respond to the prompt. (Answers will vary, but students should consider details that capture the anarchy of Shays's Rebellion.)

WHAT DO YOU THINK?

Why would Adams be opposed to rebellion? Encourage students to use text evidence from the whole lesson as they respond to the prompt.

In the end, the Massachusetts government easily stopped Shays's Rebellion. The event nonetheless cast doubt over the Articles of Confederation. Wealthy Americans wanted a government that could protect their property against rebellions. Farmers needed a government that could print money and make laws on trade. The writers of the Articles had tried to avoid creating another overbearing national government, such as the British Parliament, which had passed laws without consulting with the American colonies. As a result, the states did not always think of themselves as a united country.

The nation's early leaders began to make plans to change. They wanted to act fast to avoid more rebellions. Members of Congress met to discuss how best to strengthen the Articles of Confederation. Eventually, they decided to hold a conference to change the document by which the nation was governed. Henry Lee, Jr., a friend of George Washington, explained the need for a change.

PRIMARY SOURCE

In Their Words ... Henry Lee, Jr.

The period seems to be fast approaching when the people of these United States must determine to establish a permanent capable government or submit to the horrors of anarchy .... The decay of their commerce leaves the lower order unemployed, idleness in this body, and the intriguing exertions of another class whose desperate fortunes are remediable only by the ruin of society.

—from a letter to George Washington, September 8, 1786

 Stop and Check

Talk How did the weaknesses of the Articles of Confederation lead to Shays's Rebellion?

Citizenship

Views on Rebellion

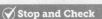

Thomas Jefferson and Samuel Adams—two of the signers of the Declaration of Independence—had widely different opinions regarding Shays's Rebellion. Read the following quotations from both men and consider their views in the context of what you have just read.

Thomas Jefferson

"I hold it that a little rebellion now and then is a good thing, and as necessary in the political world as storms in the **physical**. . . ."

Samuel Adams

"The man who dares to rebel against the laws of a republic ought to suffer death."

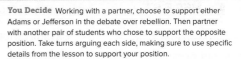 **Stop and Check**

You Decide Working with a partner, choose to support either Adams or Jefferson in the debate over rebellion. Then partner with another pair of students who chose to support the opposite position. Take turns arguing each side, making sure to use specific details from the lesson to support your position.

What Do You Think? Why would Adams, who rebelled against Britain, oppose a rebellion against the U.S. government?

Research Companion, pp. 264–265

(EL) ENGLISH LEARNERS SCAFFOLD

ELD.PI.5.8 Analyzing how writers and speakers use vocabulary and other language resources for specific purposes (to explain, persuade, entertain, etc.) depending on modality, text type, purpose, audience, topic, and content area

Emerging

Develop Language Provide support to help students understand the meaning of the word *rebellion*. Encourage them to look at the illustrations on pp. 259 and 263 of Shays and his men. Have students find details in the illustrations that show what the men were feeling and doing.

Expanding/Bridging

Understand Connotation Have students work together to make sure they understand the meaning of the word *rebellion*. Suggest that students make a list of words related to rebellion, such as *fight, anger, freedom*, etc. Then have students use the word *rebellion* in a sentence. Guide students to understand the word has different shades of meaning in the quotes from Jefferson and Adams.

See the **Language Learner Teaching Guide** for more language support strategies.

Monitor and Differentiate

REACHING ALL LEARNERS

Approaching Level

Work with students to help them understand the motivation of the men who participated in Shays's Rebellion. Why were the farmers so angry? Why did the rebellion alarm wealthy Americans?

Beyond Level

Have students conduct further research into the monetary debt crisis that occurred at the end of the Revolutionary War. What caused the crisis, and what steps were taken to address it?

3 REPORT

Report Your Findings

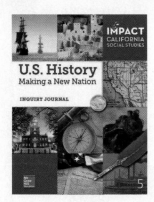

Inquiry Journal,
pp. 218–219

 STANDARDS

Explain how state constitutions that were established after 1776 embodied the ideals of the American Revolution and helped serve as models for the U.S. Constitution. **HSS.5.6.5**

Draw on information from multiple print or digital sources, demonstrating the ability to locate an answer to a question quickly or to solve a problem efficiently. **CCSS.ELA.RI.5.7**

Draw evidence from literary or informational texts to support analysis, reflection, and research **CCSS.ELA.W.5.9**

Write informative/explanatory texts to examine a topic and convey ideas and information clearly. **CCSS.ELA.W.5.2**

Go Digital!

- Students can go online to report their findings. Assess their responses online.

- Students can access the online graphic organizer to capture ideas from their investigation.

Think About It

Students will review their research and consider the pros and cons of the Articles of Confederation. Remind students to review the information they gathered and recorded on the graphic organizer. Direct students back to pages 258–265 of their Research Companion if they need more information.

Write About It

Write and Cite Evidence Have students read the prompt. Explain that an effective summary will give important information related to the pros and cons of the Articles of Confederation. Remind students to include the following elements in their response.

- A clear introduction that states the purpose of the summary

- Details from the text supporting the writer's analysis

- Transitional words and phrases that make clear the pros and cons

Use the rubric on p. T560 to evaluate students' work.

Talk About It

Defend Your Claim Have students exchange their summaries with a partner. Have partners discuss similarities and differences in their summaries.

- Explain that they should take turns discussing and explaining their summaries.

- Remind students to cite evidence from the text that supports their summaries.

- Remind students to follow the rules of appropriate classroom conversation.

Connect to the Essential Question

Read the prompt aloud to students. Ask them the following guiding questions:

- What events and/or groups of people from this lesson most transformed the nation and its people? (Answers will vary, but students may say Shays's Rebellion led to changes to the early government for the benefit of both wealthy and working-class people.)

- What actions and ideas are still important to our nation today? (Answers will vary, but students may say that the debate about the correct balance of power between the central, federal government and state governments continues today.)

Remind students to use the space provided in their journal to jot down notes.

Report Your Findings

Think About It

What were the pros and cons of the Articles of the Confederation?

Write About It

Take a Stand

Write and Cite Evidence Write a short summary of the pros and cons of the Articles of Confederation. How did using this document provide the new nation with lessons about governing?

Students' summaries should mention
the Northwest Ordinance as a pro and the
weakness of the national government
as a con.

Talk About It

Defend Your Claim

Discuss the Articles of Confederation with a partner. Why is it important to learn about the Founding Fathers' mistakes as well as their triumphs?

Connect to the

Civics

Pull It Together

What would it have meant to be an American citizen if the Articles of Confederation had lasted as the nation's government?

Students' responses should mention that the
United States would likely not be as powerful
because of the weakness of the national
government under the Articles.

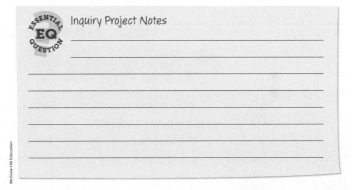

Inquiry Project Notes

Inquiry Journal, pp. 218–219

 ## ENGLISH LEARNERS SCAFFOLD

ELD.PI.5.4 Adapting language choices to various contexts (based on task, purpose, audience, and text type).

Emerging

Develop Language To help students understand new words, have them locate the word in the text, say the word aloud, and then complete sentence frames:

George Washington was the first president of our __(nation)__ .

The national government's money problems led to a __(violent)__ rebellion.

Expanding/Bridging

Use Language Working with a partner, have students locate three unknown words in the text. Together have partners define the words. Have partners use dictionaries to confirm their definitions. Then have partners use each word in a sentence.

See the **Language Learner Teaching Guide** for more language support strategies.

Monitor and Differentiate

REACHING ALL LEARNERS

Approaching Level

Have students use the section titles in the lesson as a way of organizing information in their summaries of the pros and cons of the Articles of Confederation. Say: *For example, one of the questions the Articles of Confederation raised was would the new country be one nation or thirteen colonies.*

Beyond Level

Encourage students to use challenging vocabulary from the lesson in their summaries. Examples of vocabulary students might use include *document, govern, territory, profit, conflict, legislators, rebels,* and *resistance.*

Know what your students know!

Lesson Task
Report Your Findings

Use this rubric to evaluate students' response.

Write and Cite Evidence Students write a summary of the pros and cons of the Articles of Confederation.

Defend Your Claim Students talk to classmates about their findings. They take turns discussing how the activity helped them understand the process of creating the Constitution of the United States.

Performance Task Evaluation Rubric

	4	3	2	1
Historical Understanding	Strong understanding of the pros and cons of the Articles of Confederation	Adequate understanding of the pros and cons of the Articles of Confederation	Uneven understanding of the pros and cons of the Articles of Confederation	No understanding of the pros and cons of the Articles of Confederation
Write a Summary	Clearly summarizes the pros and cons of the Articles of Confederation	Adequately summarizes the pros and cons of the Articles of Confederation	Somewhat clear or unclear summary of the pros and cons of the Articles of Confederation	No summary of the pros and cons of the Articles of Confederation
Support With Evidence	Facts and details provide thorough evidence	Facts and details provide adequate evidence	Facts and details provide uneven evidence	Facts and details are missing, or no supporting evidence is provided
Defend Your Claim	Speaks clearly and at an understandable pace Speaks in complete sentences throughout the discussion	Speaks clearly during most of the discussion. Speaks in complete sentences through most of the discussion	At times speaker is unclear. Mixes complete and incomplete sentences	Speaks unclearly throughout the discussion. Does not use complete sentences

Lesson Assessment

Go Digital!

- Have students complete the Chapter 6 Lesson 1 Assessment online to monitor their understanding of the lesson content.

ONLINE ASSESSMENT

California Smarter Balanced Assessment Connections!

Standards Covered	Lesson Task	Lesson Assessment	Alignment with California Smarter Balanced Assessment
History Social Science Content 5.6.5; 5.6.6	✔	✔	Claim 1 Targets 8, 9, 10
History Social Science Analysis Skills Chronological and Spatial Thinking 5.1; Research, Evidence, and Point of View 5.2 Historical Interpretation 5.3	✔	✔	Claim 1 Targets 11, 12
Writing W.5.2	✔	✔	Claim 2 Target 11
Research and Inquiry W.5.9	✔	✔	Claim 4 Targets 11, 12
Reading RI.5.3	✔	✔	Claim 1 Targets 11, 12
Speaking and Listening SL.5.1	✔		Claim 3 Targets 8, 9, 11

How Does the Constitution Set Up Our Government Framework?

Background Information

Explain to students that in this lesson they will learn about how the United States Constitution was written. They will also analyze the structure of government that delegates to the Constitutional Convention eventually agreed to.

Community Connections

To enrich what students have learned about the Constitution, have a local expert in Constitutional law talk with students about current constitutional issues.

 LESSON STANDARDS

✔ Explain how state constitutions that were established after 1776 embodied the ideals of the American Revolution and helped serve as models for the U.S. Constitution. **HSS.5.6.5**

✔ Understand the fundamental principles of American constitutional democracy, including how the government derives its power from the people and the primacy of individual liberty. **HSS.5.7.3**

✔ Understand how the Constitution is designed to secure our liberty by both empowering and limiting central government and compare the powers granted to citizens, Congress, the president, and the Supreme Court with those reserved to the states. **HSS.5.7.4**

✔ Students place key events and people of the historical era they are studying in a chronological sequence and within a spatial context; they interpret time lines. **HAS.CS.1**

✔ Students differentiate between primary and secondary sources. **HAS.HR.1**

✔ Students pose relevant questions about events they encounter in historical documents, eyewitness accounts, oral histories, letters, diaries, artifacts, photographs, maps, artworks, and architecture. **HAS.HR.2**

✔ Students summarize the key events of the era they are studying and explain the historical contexts of those events. **HAS.HI.1**

Connect to the
Essential Question

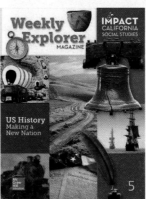

Chapter 6, pp. 72–83

The **Weekly Explorer Magazine** supports students' exploration of the Essential Question and provides additional resources for the EQ Inquiry Project.

Inquiry Project

Which Side Will You Choose?

Remind students to use the information they learn in this lesson and other resources to complete their EQ Inquiry Project!

Dinah Zike's

In this lesson you will use foldables.

When Minutes Count!

Suggested Lesson Pacing

1 ENGAGE
One Day

- Lesson Opener
- Analyze the Source
- Inquiry Tools

Go Digital
- **Video**: The American Constitution
- **iMap:** Ratification

2 INVESTIGATE
Two to Three Days

 Short on Time? Look for the clock to teach core content in less time.

- The Constitutional Convention
- Conflicts and Compromises
- The New Government
- **Infographic** Checks and Balances
- Economic Aspects of the Constitution

3 REPORT
One Day

- Think About It
- Take a Stand
- Act It Out

Make Connections!

(CCSS) CONNECT TO ELA

Reading

Determine two or more main ideas of a text and explain how they are supported by key details; summarize the text. **RI.5.2**

Explain how an author uses reasons and evidence to support particular points in a text, identifying which reasons and evidence support which point(s). **RI.5.8**

Research

Conduct short research projects that use several sources to build knowledge through investigation of different aspects of a topic. **W.5.7**

Recall relevant information from experiences or gather relevant information from print and digital sources; summarize or paraphrase information in notes and finished work, and provide a list of sources. **W.5.8**

Writing

Write narratives to develop real or imagined experiences or events using effective technique, descriptive details, and clear event sequences. **W.5.3**

Draw evidence from literary or informational texts to support analysis, reflection, and research. **W.5.9**

Speaking and Listening

Engage effectively in a range of collaborative discussions (one-on-one, in groups, and teacher-led) with diverse partners on grade 5 topics and texts, building on others' ideas and expressing their own clearly. **SL.5.1**

Report on a topic or text or present an opinion, sequencing ideas logically and using appropriate facts and relevant, descriptive details to support main ideas or themes; speak clearly at an understandable pace. **SL.5.4**

Classroom Resources

🔍 Search for additional resources using the following key words.

Congress

Constitutional Convention

Great Compromise

House of Representatives

James Madison

William Paterson

Edmund Randolph

Senate

Roger Sherman

Three-Fifths Compromise

United States Constitution

George Washington

U.S. History
Making a New Nation

INQUIRY JOURNAL

Inquiry Journal,
pp. 220–221

HSS STANDARDS

Understand the fundamental principles of American constitutional democracy, including how the government derives its power from the people and the primacy of individual liberty. **HSS.5.7.3**

Understand how the Constitution is designed to secure our liberty by both empowering and limiting central government and compare the powers granted to citizens, Congress, the president, and the Supreme Court with those reserved to the states. **HSS.5.7.4**

Students differentiate between primary and secondary sources. **HAS.HR.1**

Go Digital!

Explore the lesson content with online whole-class presentation tools.

- **Video:** The American Constitution

- **iMap:** Ratification

How Does the Constitution Set Up Our Government Framework?

Bellringer

Prompt students to retrieve information from the previous lessons. Say: *The Articles of Confederation was the first written document to establish a United States government. What powers does the document give to the states?* (States could run their own governments independently; states could print their own money; states did not have to pay taxes to the national government.) *What were some of the document's weaknesses?* (the national government needed more power than allocated by the Articles.)

Lesson Outcomes

What Am I Learning? Have students read the Lesson Question and Lesson Outcomes on page 220.

Why Am I Learning It? Make sure students understand the noun *draft* as it is used in the text. Encourage students to use context clues. Say: *In the text,* draft *is used to describe written versions of the U.S. Constitution. For example, if you are writing an essay, you most likely write several drafts before you write your final* <u>draft</u>.

How Will I Know That I Learned It? Ask students the following questions.

- What will you be able to identify? (how the Constitution establishes the U.S. government)

- What is the purpose of this task? (to explain the structure of our government and reasons for this structure)

- How will you support your explanation? (with evidence from the text)

Talk About It

PRODUCTIVE

Analyze the Image Explain that when we talk about an image, we describe and interpret it and present our ideas in our own words. Provide sentence frames to help students talk about the image.

- *The image shows _____.*

- *The document looks _____.*

COLLABORATE

Collaborative Conversations

Add New Ideas As students engage in partner, small group, and whole-class discussions, encourage them to

- First and view read the material carefully.

- Stay on topic.

- Be respectful of others' thoughts and opinions.

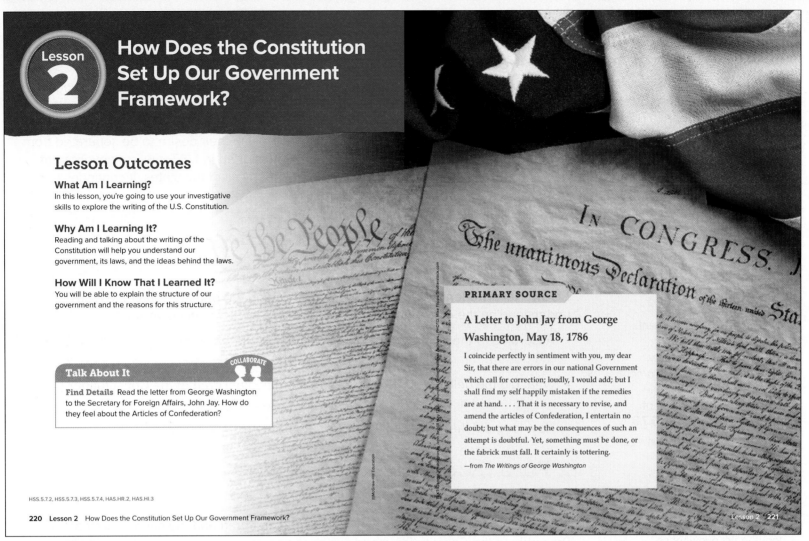

Lesson 2

How Does the Constitution Set Up Our Government Framework?

Lesson Outcomes

What Am I Learning?
In this lesson, you're going to use your investigative skills to explore the writing of the U.S. Constitution.

Why Am I Learning It?
Reading and talking about the writing of the Constitution will help you understand our government, its laws, and the ideas behind the laws.

How Will I Know That I Learned It?
You will be able to explain the structure of our government and the reasons for this structure.

Talk About It
COLLABORATE

Find Details Read the letter from George Washington to the Secretary for Foreign Affairs, John Jay. How do they feel about the Articles of Confederation?

PRIMARY SOURCE

A Letter to John Jay from George Washington, May 18, 1786

I coincide perfectly in sentiment with you, my dear Sir, that there are errors in our national Government which call for correction; loudly, I would add; but I shall find my self happily mistaken if the remedies are at hand. . . . That it is necessary to revise, and amend the articles of Confederation, I entertain no doubt; but what may be the consequences of such an attempt is doubtful. Yet, something must be done, or the fabrick must fall. It certainly is tottering.

—from *The Writings of George Washington*

HSS.5.7.2, HSS.5.7.3, HSS.5.7.4, HAS.HR.2, HAS.HI.3

220 Lesson 2 How Does the Constitution Set Up Our Government Framework?

Lesson 2 **221**

Inquiry Journal, pp. 220–221

EL ENGLISH LEARNERS SCAFFOLD

ELD.PI.5.6 Reading closely literary and informational texts and viewing multimedia to determine how meaning is conveyed explicitly and implicitly through language

Emerging	Expanding	Bridging
Identify Details Work with students individually to identify what they see in the image. Encourage students to name details. Supply vocabulary as needed.	**Describe Details** Have small groups create a list of words that describe what they see in the image. Encourage them to consider the associations people may have with the American flag and foundational documents. Have groups share their list with the rest of the class.	**Use Language** Have students work together to describe what they find historically important about the image. What important information does the image show?

See the **Language Learner Teaching Guide** for more language support strategies.

Monitor and Differentiate

REACHING ALL LEARNERS

Approaching Level

Help students to understand what George Washington is saying in his letter to John Jay. Make sure that students understand the meaning of the words *coincide, remedies, revise,* and *tottering.* Have students complete sentence frames as needed:

Washington ___(agrees)___ *with John Jay's thoughts about making corrections to the role of the national government.*

Washington believes that the Articles of Confederation need to be ___(revised)___.

Beyond Level

Have students research John Jay and his role in the drafting of the Constitution of the United States.

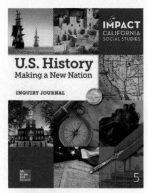

Inquiry Journal,
pp. 222–223

 STANDARDS

Understand the fundamental principles of American constitutional democracy, including how the government derives its power from the people and the primacy of individual liberty. **HSS.5.7.3**

Students differentiate between primary and secondary sources. **HAS.HR.1**

Students pose relevant questions about events they encounter in historical documents, eyewitness accounts, oral histories, letters, diaries, artifacts, photographs, maps, artworks, and architecture. **HAS.HR.2**

CCSS Engage effectively in a range of collaborative discussions (one-on-one, in groups, and teacher-led) with diverse partners on *grade 5 topics and texts*, building on others' ideas and expressing their own clearly. **CCSS.ELA.SL.5.1**

Go *Digital!*

Model how to inspect and find evidence with online whole-class presentation tools.

Background Information

The Declaration of Independence and the United States Constitution Although these two documents are connected in spirit, they were written for very different purposes. The Declaration of Independence was written in 1776. Its purpose was to list colonists' grievances against the king and justify their desire to be separated from Great Britain. The Constitution was written and signed in 1787. It was a government charter that needed to be ratified, or approved, by all of the states. It continues to be the supreme law of the land today.

1 Inspect

Look Have students read the entire text, including the primary source, to focus on understanding the overall meaning. Remind them to circle unknown words.

- According to the text, how was the Constitution written? (slowly and carefully; it went through two drafts)

- What did the delegates do before approving the final draft of the Constitution? (The delegates studied and added notes on the first draft.)

- How long did the entire process take? (four months)

2 Find Evidence

Look Again Have students reread the text.

Analyze the Primary Source Reread the first draft and the second draft of the Preamble to the Constitution aloud and then analyze them together as a class. Provide support for vocabulary as needed.

- Comparing the first draft of the Preamble with the final draft, what things were kept? What things were removed? (Things kept: We the People, declare and establish this Constitution. Things removed: the names of individual states.)

- What is the purpose of the Preamble? (to introduce the purpose of the Constitution)

- The final draft of the Preamble lists five things government must do. Think of an example of how government does each of these things. Compare your list of examples with those of other students. (Answers will vary, but students might list things like quelling riots, protecting civil rights, ensuring that federal laws are enforced.)

Analyze the Image Tell students that Howard Chandler Christy's painting was created in 1940. Guide students to discuss how historical paintings tell us not only about historical events but how historical events are remembered.

3 Make Connections

Write Imagine you are a delegate at the Constitutional Convention. Is there anything you think should be changed in the second version of the Preamble? Write a short speech explaining what you want added, changed, or removed, and why. (Responses will vary.)

Analyze the Source

Writing (and Rewriting) the Constitution

1 Inspect

Read Look at the two versions of the Preamble to the Constitution.

- **Circle** words you don't know.
- **Underline** phrases that are in both versions.
- **Discuss** in groups of three. Each group member should lead a short discussion for one of the following questions: Why were some things kept? Why were some things removed? Why were some things added?

My Notes

_____
_____
_____
_____
_____
_____
_____
_____
_____
_____

The Constitution was not written all at once. It had to be written carefully so that it could cover all of the important laws needed by a national government. On May 25, 1787, fifty-five members of the Constitutional Convention began meeting at Philadelphia's State House to discuss, plan, and write the Constitution.

A first draft was copied and given to the delegates on August 6. They studied and made notes on their copies before making a final draft, signed on September 17, 1787. The Preamble, or introduction, to the Constitution, changed significantly between the two versions. The entire process had taken four months, with only an eleven-day break.

The Constitutional Convention delegates taking turns signing the Constitution

PRIMARY SOURCE

In Their Words...

The Preamble, First Draft

We the People of the States of New-Hampshire, Massachusetts, Rhode-Island and Providence Plantations, Connecticut, New-York, New-Jersey, Pennsylvania, Delaware, Maryland, Virginia, North-Carolina, South-Carolina, and Georgia, do ordain, declare and establish the following Constitution for the Government of Ourselves and our Posterity.

—from the First Draft of the United States Constitution, August 6, 1787

PRIMARY SOURCE

In Their Words...

The Preamble, Final Draft

We, the People of the United States, in order to form a more perfect union, establish justice, insure domestic tranquility, provide for the common defence, promote the general welfare, and secure the blessings of liberty to ourselves and our posterity, do ordain and establish this Constitution for the United States of America.

—from the official United States Constitution, September 17, 1787

2 Find Evidence

Reread The Preamble lists five things the government must do: "establish justice, insure domestic tranquility, provide for the common defense, promote the general welfare, and secure the blessings of liberty to ourselves and our posterity, . . ."

Think of an example of how the government does each of these things. Compare your list of examples with lists from other students.

3 Make Connections

Write Imagine you are a delegate at the Constitutional Convention. Is there anything you think should be changed in the second version of the Preamble? Write a short speech explaining what you want added, changed, or removed, and why it is important.

COLLABORATE

Constitution [printing of first draft] (Committee of Detail), 6 August 1787, Philadelphia: Gilder Lehrman Collection # GLC00819.01 Gilder Lehrman Institute of American History.

TEXT: U.S. Constitution, preamble, 17 September 1787, www.whitehouse.gov;
PHOTO: (t)McGraw-Hill Education; (b)GraphicaArtis/Archive Photos/Getty Images

222 Lesson 2 How Does the Constitution Set Up Our Government Framework?

Lesson 2 223

Inquiry Journal, pp. 222–223

(EL) ENGLISH LEARNERS SCAFFOLD

ELD.PI.5.6 Reading closely literary and informational texts and viewing multimedia to determine how meaning is conveyed explicitly and implicitly through languages

Emerging	Expanding	Bridging
Identify Work with students to use domain-specific words and phrases to talk about the painting. Ask students to point out what they notice in the painting. Then help them find words to describe these things. Guide students to explain why George Washington is the most prominent person in the painting.	**Develop Language** Have students discuss the painting with a partner. Ask students to point out what they notice. Then, have students help each other find words to describe these things.	**Use Language** Have students work in pairs, explaining to each other what they see in the painting. Suggest the students make a list of the words they are using to describe the painting. Have students share their lists with the rest of the class.

See the **Language Learner Teaching Guide** for more language support strategies.

Monitor and Differentiate

REACHING ALL LEARNERS

Special Needs

Howard Chandler Christy's painting of the signing of the United States Constitution was completed in 1940. This was almost 200 years after the Constitution was signed. Have students make inferences about Christy's attitude toward the signers of the Constitution based on how he portrays them.

Beyond Level

Have students research the lengths to which Howard Chandler Christy went to make his painting as accurate as possible. The 29-by-30-foot framed oil-on-canvas scene is displayed in the east grand stairway in the House wing of the U.S. Capitol.

1 ENGAGE

Inquiry Tools

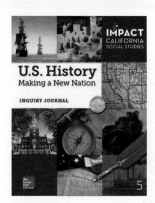

Inquiry Journal,
pp. 224–225

 STANDARDS

Understand the fundamental principles of American constitutional democracy, including how the government derives its power from the people and the primacy of individual liberty. **HSS.5.7.3**

Draw evidence from literary or informational texts to support analysis, reflection, and research **CCSS.ELA.W.5.9**

Write narratives to develop real or imagined experiences or events using effective technique, descriptive details, and clear event sequences. **CCSS.ELA.W.5.3**

Go Digital!

- Model how to explore and investigate with online whole-class tools.

- Students can access the online graphic organizer to use the inquiry tools as they read.

Explore Making Inferences

Explain Tell students that to infer is to find a meaning that is not directly written or spoken. When studying history, we often have to infer the reasons behind historical figures' decisions, especially if they have not left behind diaries, letters, or other writing that explains their decisions.

Read Have students read the step-by-step instructions about how to make inferences. Remind students to begin by making inferences about how and why the event happened.

Guide Practice Model making inferences for students. Say: *I read in the text that the Preamble to the U.S. Constitution highlights the goals of the document. I know that the Articles of Confederation was not successful, so I can infer that it did not meet the goals stated in the Preamble, so the new document, the U.S. Constitution, is taking its place.*

Investigate!

Have students read pages 266–277 in the Research Companion. Tell them the information will help them answer the lesson question. **How Does the Constitution Set up Our Government Framework?**

Take Notes Tell students that they should take notes about inferences they make and record their inferences in the graphic organizer. Explain to students that they will take notes as they read each section. Remind them that taking notes will help them understand and remember what they read.

Remind students that good note taking is about finding the most important information and writing key words or phrases about it. Note takers do not rewrite every word from the text unless they plan to quote an author later on.

Inspect Guide students to read the text in each section to determine what the text says and what they can infer from what the text says. Encourage them to recall what they know about the topic.

Find Evidence Encourage students to reread the text to develop a deeper understanding of the content. Remind students that after they read and take notes, they should review and think about how the facts and details will help them answer the lesson question.

Collaborative Conversations

Text-Based Discussion Remind students that discussing the text with partners can help them

- listen and respond to another point of view.
- find additional evidence.
- build on each others' ideas.

Inquiry Tools

Explore Making Inferences

To infer is to find a meaning that is not directly written or spoken. If a bill has trouble getting through Congress, you can infer that many people disagree with it. If a bill gets passed very quickly, on the other hand, then you can infer it was popular among members of Congress. These meanings that we find are called inferences.

When studying history, we often have to infer the reasons for historical persons' decisions, especially if they have not left behind diaries, letters, or other writing explaining their decisions. To make an inference:

1. **Read the text closely.**
   Make sure you understand what is being said.

2. **Recall what you know about the topic.**
   What do you know about the event being described? About the people involved? About what happened before and what came next?

3. **Combine what you know with what you have read.**
   Put the information together to form a more complete picture of what has happened.

What I Know	What I Read	My Inference
The Articles of Confederation was unsuccessful as a government framework.	The Preamble highlights several goals for drafting the U.S. Constitution.	The Articles of Confederation did not achieve the goals mentioned in the Preamble, so this new government document will take its place.

Investigate!

Read pages 266–277 in your Research Companion. Use your investigative skills to infer why some framers of the Constitution were concerned about either the Virginia Plan's or the New Jersey Plan's structure for a central government.

What I Know	What I Read	My Inference
Some states had many people and others didn't.	Virginia plan: too much power for states with the most people	framers opposed to the plan came from states with fewer people
Some people feared strong government.	Virginia plan: Congress can take over governments of smaller states	This power reminded people of the problems with British government.
Democracy means "rule by the majority of the people."	New Jersey plan: too much power for states with fewer people	framers opposed to the New Jersey plan came from larger states

McGraw-Hill Education

Inquiry Journal, pp. 224–225

ENGLISH LEARNERS SCAFFOLD

ELD.PI.5.6 Reading closely literary and informational texts and viewing multimedia to determine how meaning is conveyed explicitly and implicitly through language

Emerging

Develop Language Work with individual students to be sure that they understand the meaning of *inference* and how to make inferences. Then, practice filling in the graphic organizer with students. If students have difficulty writing sentences, suggest that they write single words or draw a picture.

Expanding

Cite Evidence Have students work with a partner to compare the first and final versions of the Preamble. What can they infer from the changes that were made?

Bridging

Summarize Have students use descriptive words and phrases in sentences of their own as they make inferences based on the first and second versions of the Preamble.

See the **Language Learner Teaching Guide** for more language support strategies.

Monitor and Differentiate

REACHING ALL LEARNERS

Approaching Level

Have students compare the first and second versions of the Preamble. Work with a partner to make inferences about the changes made. Then, write a sentence summarizing why the authors made the changes they did.

Beyond Level

Have a small group of students discuss why making inferences is an important skill when analyzing historical events and figures. Have students cite specific examples to support their point of view.

U.S. History
Making a New Nation
RESEARCH COMPANION
5

Research Companion
pp. 266–267

 STANDARDS

Understand the fundamental principles of American constitutional democracy, including how the government derives its power from the people and the primacy of individual liberty. **HSS.5.7.3**

Students place key events and people of the historical era they are studying in a chronological sequence and within a spatial context; they interpret time lines. **HAS.CS.1**

CCSS Draw evidence from literary or informational texts to support analysis, reflection, and research **CCSS.ELA.W.5.9**

Go Digital!

Investigate the lesson content with online whole-class presentation tools.

• **Video:** The American Constitution

• **iMap:** Ratification

Background Information

George Washington Washington arrived in Philadelphia for the Constitutional Convention a day early. In short order he was declared the Convention's president. During the four months he presided over the convention, he seldom said anything. Although Washington did not formally participate in the debate, outside of the hall, Washington did everything he could to convince people of the need to fix the defects of the Articles of Confederacy. Washington enjoyed almost universal respect, which helped him to convince even reluctant delegates to vote for the new Constitution.

| TIMELINE | Invite students to look at the timeline at the top of page 267.

Analyze What three significant events occurred between May and December 1787? (the Constitutional Convention begins, the Great Compromise is made, and Delaware is the first state to ratify the Constitution) **HAS.CS.1**

Analyze the Source

Inspect Have students read pages 266–267.

Find Evidence Use the questions below to check comprehension. Remind students to support their answers with text evidence.

Analyze Cause and Effect What was the effect of Shays's Rebellion? (It revealed the weaknesses and flaws in the Articles of Confederation.) **DOK 3**

Identify What was the only state that did not send delegates to the Constitutional Convention? (Rhode Island) **DOK 1**

Infer Why did the delegates meet in secret? (Answers will vary, but students should note that the delegates may have felt that they could have faced repercussions if their views were known publicly.) **DOK 2**

Make Connections

State an Opinion Based on what you have read, do you think the delegates were right to keep the meetings and what they said there a secret? (Answers will vary. Students may say that the delegates should have had all their discussions out in the open. Others may understand that the delegates wanted to be able to talk freely.) **DOK 3**

Analyze the Image Direct students' attention to the image of the Constitution on display in the National Archives. Explain that when we talk about an image, we describe and interpret it and present our ideas in our own words. Provide sentence frames like these to help students form sentences as they talk about the image.

• *The image shows _____.*

• *I know the important document is old because _____.*

• *I think the document is protected beneath glass because _____.*

Lesson 2

How Does the Constitution Set Up Our Government Framework?

Timeline

February 1787 Confederation Congress calls for the rewriting of the Articles of Confederation.	**July 1787** The Great Compromise is made.
	June 1788 New Hampshire ratifies the Constitution, making it the law of the land.

1787 — 1788 — 1789 — 1790

May 1787 Constitutional Convention begins.

December 1787 Delaware is the first state to ratify the Constitution.

May 1790 Rhode Island becomes the last of the original 13 colonies to ratify the Constitution.

The Constitutional Convention

Shays's Rebellion showed that there was much dissatisfaction with the Articles of Confederation. On February 21, 1787, the Confederation Congress decided to gather **delegates** to discuss changing the Articles. This convention of delegates would take place at the Pennsylvania State House in Philadelphia. Invitations were sent to the states. All but Rhode Island sent delegates to the Constitutional Convention. Members of the Continental Congress were not the only delegates at the convention. The delegates also included Revolutionary War veterans, governors, lawyers, plantation owners, merchants, and other influential people. In total, fifty-five men took part in the convention, which began on May 25, 1787. They met in secret so that the delegates could speak freely and suggest ideas that might have hurt their reputations if the ideas became known. The doors were locked and the windows were covered. Although the convention's purpose was to fix the Articles of Confederation, the delegates soon began to write a new constitution for a new government.

The U.S. Constitution on display at the National Archives

HSS 5.4.6, HSS 5.7.2, HSS 5.7.3, HSS.5.7.4, HAS.HI.3

Research Companion, pp. 266–267

ENGLISH LEARNERS SCAFFOLD

ELD.PI.5.1 Exchanging information and ideas with others through oral collaborative discussions on a range of social and academic topics

Emerging	Expanding	Bridging
Describe Chronology Guide students to describe the timeline using ordinal words, such as *first, then, next, after, last*, or *finally*. Help students with difficult vocabulary as needed.	**Provide Details** Guide students to describe events on the timeline using ordinal words, such as *first, then, next, after, last*, or *finally*. Encourage students to choose an event from the timeline and share what they know about it from their reading of text.	**Use Vocabulary** Have students work with a partner or with a small group to discuss how events in the timeline are related to each other. Have them keep a list of words describing events and how they are related.

See the **Language Learner Teaching Guide** for more language support strategies.

Monitor and Differentiate

REACHING ALL LEARNERS

Approaching Level

Guide students to understand how the purpose of the Constitutional Convention changed. Explain that initially it was to revise the Articles of Confederation. But eventually most delegates agreed that they needed to write a new constitution.

On Level

Based on what they have read, have students work with a partner to identify the type of people who attended the Constitutional Convention. Have students discuss why a lack of diversity in creating the government might cause problems for the United States later on.

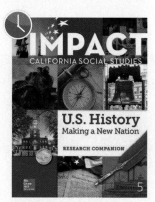

Research Companion
pp. 268–269

HSS STANDARDS

Explain how state constitutions that were established after 1776 embodied the ideals of the American Revolution and helped serve as models for the U.S. Constitution. **HSS.5.6.5**

Understand the fundamental principles of American constitutional democracy, including how the government derives its power from the people and the primacy of individual liberty. **HSS.5.7.3**

Understand how the Constitution is designed to secure our liberty by both empowering and limiting central government and compare the powers granted to citizens, Congress, the president, and the Supreme Court with those reserved to the states. **HSS.5.7.4**

CCSS Explain how an author uses reasons and evidence to support particular points in a text, identifying which reasons and evidence support which point(s). **CCSS.ELA.RI.5.8**

Go Digital!

Investigate the lesson content with online whole-class presentation tools.

Background Information

The Federalist Papers In the late 1780s, Alexander Hamilton, James Madison, and John Jay wrote a series of 85 letters that they sent to newspapers. The letters, since published as "The Federalist Papers," urged ratification of the U.S. Constitution. Although the essays did little to change people's opinions at the time, today they are widely regarded as an outstanding contribution to the literature on constitutional democracy.

Analyze the Source

Inspect Have students read pages 268–269.

Find Evidence Use the questions below to check comprehension. Remind students to support their answers with text evidence.

Summarize Summarize Madison's role in the Constitutional Convention. (He did most of the writing work, convinced the other delegates to abandon the idea of fixing the Articles, and urged the creation of a strong, national government.) **DOK 2**

Explain What was the Virginia Plan? (It called for a two-part legislature. The lower house would be elected by the people. The lower house selected the upper house, the president, and the judges.) **DOK 2**

Cite Evidence Explain why some delegates object to the Virginia plan. (Congress would consist mainly of delegates from states with the most people. States with more people could take control of the government of other states.) **DOK 2**

Compare/Contrast How did the New Jersey Plan differ from the Virginia Plan? (In the New Jersey Plan each state had only one delegate, regardless of the population of the state. It also gave the national government some control over trade and the ability to raise money through import and stamp duties.) **DOK 3**

Describe Why did many delegates feel the New Jersey plan would fail? (They thought it would have many of the same problems of the Articles of Confederation.) **DOK 2**

Make Connections

Draw Conclusions Why were some delegates fearful of a strong national government? (Students may say that the delegates were concerned that a strong national government might begin to behave more like a monarchy.) **DOK 2**

Washington Addressing the Constitutional Convention by Junius B. Stearns

Conflicts and Compromises

George Washington was elected to lead the convention, but James Madison of Virginia did most of the work on the actual writing of the Constitution. Madison was largely responsible for convincing the other delegates to abandon the idea of fixing the Articles of Confederation. Madison wanted to start over and create a stronger national government. He gave strong support to the Virginia Plan, a plan conceived by Virginia governor Edmund Randolph.

The Virginia Plan called for a two-part legislature to make the laws. The members of the first part, or lower house, were to be elected by voters. The members of the second part, or upper house, were to be chosen by the members of the lower house. The lower house would also select a president as well as judges for a national court. In the Virginia Plan, Congress had the ability to veto state laws and even take over a state's government. The number of legislators in the houses would be calculated based on the number of people in each state.

James Madison championed the Virginia Plan.

Some delegates had problems with the Virginia Plan. Under it, Congress would consist mainly of delegates from the states with the most people. These states would have more say in making laws and choosing officials. They could even take control of the governments of the smaller states. New Jersey delegate William Paterson offered an alternative. His New Jersey Plan also had a legislature to write laws. Its legislature would have only one house, and each state would have only one delegate. This way, every state would have an equal say.

This plan was opposed by the larger states. They asked why a small state should have the same power as a large state. If the government of a nation was not controlled by the majority of its people, then how could the government be a democracy? Furthermore, these delegates saw the plan as being too similar to the Articles of Confederation.

The New Jersey Plan did answer some of the problems in the Articles, however. The national government would have some control over trade and would be able to raise money through import and stamp duties. There would also be an executive position created to control the military. Nonetheless, these measures weren't enough to convince the other delegates. They believed the New Jersey Plan would fail just as the Articles of Confederation had.

William Paterson created the New Jersey Plan.

Research Companion, pp. 268–269

(EL) ENGLISH LEARNERS SCAFFOLD

ELD.PI.5.1 Exchanging information and ideas with others through oral collaborative discussions on a range of social and academic topics

Emerging

Build Vocabulary Make sure that students understand the words *conflict* and *compromise*. Have students say the words aloud. Identify cognates as applicable. Ask students to give an example of a time when they had conflict with someone else. They can also draw a picture that shows a conflict. Tell students that a compromise happens when both sides of an argument agree to give in a little. Suggest that students draw a picture of two people reaching a compromise.

Expanding/Bridging

Use Language Have students create a word list to describe the conflicts and compromises that occurred among delegates at the Constitutional Convention.

See the **Language Learner Teaching Guide** for more language support strategies.

Monitor and Differentiate

REACHING ALL LEARNERS

Approaching Level

Help students identify main ideas and key details by asking and answering questions, such as *What is the text mostly about?*

Beyond Level

Have students work with a partner to identify the main ideas and key details. Then have students write a brief summary of "Conflicts and Compromises" including main ideas and key details.

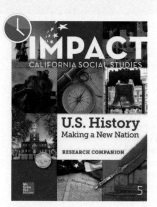

Research Companion
pp. 270–271

 STANDARDS

Explain how state constitutions that were established after 1776 embodied the ideals of the American Revolution and helped serve as models for the U.S. Constitution. **HSS.5.6.5**

Understand the fundamental principles of American constitutional democracy, including how the government derives its power from the people and the primacy of individual liberty. **HSS.5.7.3**

Understand how the Constitution is designed to secure our liberty by both empowering and limiting central government and compare the powers granted to citizens, Congress, the president, and the Supreme Court with those reserved to the states. **HSS.5.7.4**

(CCSS) Explain how an author uses reasons and evidence to support particular points in a text, identifying which reasons and evidence support which point(s). **CCSS.ELA.RI.5.8**

Go Digital!

Investigate the lesson content with online whole-class presentation tools.

Background Information

Constitutional Convention Delegates Two delegates, Roger Sherman and Robert Morris, were the only two Founding Fathers to have signed all four of the "great papers" of the United States—the Declaration of Independence, the Constitution, the Articles of Confederation, and the Articles of Association.

Analyze the Source

Inspect Have students read pages 270–271.

Find Evidence Use the questions below to check comprehension. Remind students to support their answers with text evidence.

Identify What does *democracy* mean? (laws should be agreed on by the majority of people, not just a small group of rulers) **DOK 1**

Explain How did Roger Sherman's plan combine the Virginia and New Jersey Plans? (It called for a legislature with two houses. In the House of Representatives the population of the state would determine delegates. In the Senate, each state would have two delegates.) **DOK 2**

Summarize Why was this called the Great Compromise? (It combined the best features of the Virginia and New Jersey plans.) **DOK 2**

Analyze the Infographic

Cite Evidence How did Sherman's compromise please both the people who wanted the vote based on population and people who wanted the vote based on state? (The House of Representatives based the number of representatives on population; in the Senate each state gets the same number of representatives: two.) **DOK 2**

Make Connections

Critique Give your opinion about the Three-Fifths Compromise. Do you think it was necessary in order to get the Constitution passed? Or, do you think people opposed to slavery should have stood fast and not voted for the compromise? (Answers will vary, but students should support their opinion with evidence from the text.) **DOK 3**

Draw Conclusions Why did the Southern states agree they would stop trading with other countries for enslaved Africans in 1808? (It was a compromise. The Southern states were afraid Congress would end slavery.) **DOK 3**

Stop and Check

Think Encourage students to analyze which parts of the Great Compromise came from the Virginia Plan and which came from the New Jersey Plan. (The Virginia Plan included the two-part legislature, but representation depended on the population of the state. The New Jersey Plan had only one house in which each state had two votes.)

WHAT DO YOU THINK?

Encourage students to use text evidence from the whole lesson as they respond to the prompt.

InfoGraphic

A Comparison of the Three Plans

New Jersey Plan

- Appealed to smaller states
- Had a one-part legislature
- Each state would get one representative in the legislature.

Virginia Plan

- Appealed to larger states
- Had a two-part legislature – a lower house would be elected by voters; an upper house would be elected by the lower house
- The number of representatives in the houses would be based on the number of people in each state.

Great Compromise

- Has a two-part legislature
- The House of Representatives' number of representatives would be determined by the population of each state.
- The Senate would have two delegates from each state.
- A law would not be approved until it passed through both the House of Representatives and the Senate.

So who was right? Both sides had fair points. *Democracy* means that laws should be agreed on by the majority of people, not by a small group of rulers. But states with small populations shouldn't be powerless against larger states. The argument continued for a month before Connecticut delegate Roger Sherman proposed the Great Compromise.

The Great Compromise combined the two plans. It called for a legislature with two houses. In one house, the House of Representatives, the population of a state would determine how many delegates the state would get. Here, the larger states had more power. In the other house, the Senate, each state would have two delegates. This would give the smaller states protection from the larger states. In order for a law to be approved, it would have to pass through both the House of Representatives and the Senate. In other words, a law would have to be supported by both a majority of the people and a majority of the states. The Great Compromise was adopted on July 16, 1787.

In addition to the Great Compromise, there was the Three-Fifths Compromise. Many of the delegates at the Constitutional Convention owned plantations with slaves. Should these people be counted as part of the population? Counting them would give states with slavery more representatives. Since the slaves didn't have any political power of their own, those extra votes would go to their masters. Without those extra votes, there was a good chance that Congress would outlaw slavery. The Southern states refused to join the new government unless they could be sure that Congress couldn't end slavery. Thus, the delegates decided that slaves would be counted, but for less than free persons. For every five slaves counted, three people would be added to the population count when determining representatives. The Southern states also agreed to stop future trading with other countries for slaves in 1808. However, people already enslaved, and their children, were to remain enslaved.

> ✓ **Stop and Check**
>
> **Think** Which parts of the Great Compromise came from the Virginia Plan? Which part came from the New Jersey Plan?
>
> **Find Details** As you read, add additional information to the graphic organizer on page 225 in your Inquiry Journal.

What Do You Think? Do you think the plan outlined in the Great Compromise was the best choice? Why or why not?

McGraw-Hill Education

270   Lesson 2   How Does the Constitution Set Up Our Government Framework?

Lesson 2   271

Research Companion, pp. 270–271

ENGLISH LEARNERS SCAFFOLD

ELD.PI.5.4 Adapting language choices to various contexts (based on task, purpose, audience, and text type)

Emerging	Expanding	Bridging
Develop Vocabulary Work individually with students to help them understand the word *argument*. Say the word aloud and have students repeat it. Suggest that students draw or act out a time when an argument occurred. Explain that an academic argument is based on text evidence rather than emotions.	**Use Vocabulary** Have students work in small groups to discuss the meanings of *argument* and *determining*. Say the words aloud and have students repeat them. Point out where in the text the words occur. Explain the meanings, then have students use both words in a sentence.	**Use Vocabulary** Have students work in pairs to figure out the meaning of the words *argument*, *determining*, and *supported*. Say the words aloud and have students repeat them. Point out where in the text the words occur. Have students use the three words in a sentence describing the process of agreeing to the Great Compromise.

See the **Language Learner Teaching Guide** for more language support strategies.

Monitor and Differentiate

REACHING ALL LEARNERS

Approaching Level

Work with students to understand the Great Compromise and why it was necessary to get the Northern and Southern states to agree to and sign the Constitution.

On Level

Work with students to understand the difference between the Great Compromise and the Three-Fifths Compromise. Have them discuss why both were necessary in order to get the Northern and Southern states to agree to and sign the Constitution.

Beyond Level

Have students research other examples of compromises in U.S. Legislative history, such as the Missouri Compromise, the Compromise of 1850, and the Compromise of 1877.

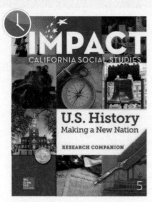

Research Companion
pp. 272–273

 STANDARDS

Understand how the Constitution is designed to secure our liberty by both empowering and limiting central government and compare the powers granted to citizens, Congress, the president, and the Supreme Court with those reserved to the states. **HSS.5.7.4**

Engage effectively in a range of collaborative discussions (one-on-one, in groups, and teacher-led) with diverse partners on grade 5 *topics and texts*, building on others' ideas and expressing their own clearly. **CCSS.ELA.SL.5.1**

Go *Digital!*

Investigate the lesson content with online whole-class presentation tools.

Background Information

John Locke One of the most important influences on the founding documents of the United States was John Locke, a 17th century English philosopher. According to Locke, government rulers gain legitimate authority only through the consent of those governed. Locke believed that it was the duty of government to protect people's natural rights—life, liberty, and property. If the government failed to protect these rights, citizens had every right to overthrow the government. Locke's ideas deeply influenced Thomas Jefferson, one of the major architects of the U.S. Constitution.

Analyze the Source

Inspect Have students read pages 272–273.

Find Evidence Use the questions below to check comprehension. Remind students to support their answers with text evidence.

Identify What was the primary belief of the founders of the United States? (A government is meant to serve its people.) **DOK 1**

Analyze How did the Founding Fathers try to ensure that the government would serve its people? (They wanted the government to be strong enough to help but weak enough so that it could not oppress people.) **DOK 3**

Infer Why was the fear of an oppressive government so real to the colonists? (They had all experienced the oppressive British government.) **DOK 2**

Summarize Summarize the responsibilities of the states under this new government. (determining marriage age, driving age, what is taught in public schools, running police and fire departments, running public libraries, establishing public transportation) **DOK 2**

Identify What are the three branches of government into which the national government is divided? (legislative branch, executive branch, and judicial branch) **DOK 2**

Make Connections

Draw Conclusions Why did the Founding Fathers decide to divide the government into three bodies? (They wanted to make sure that the government could check itself and always serve the people.) **DOK 3**

The New Government

After nearly four months of work, the delegates of the Constitutional Convention completed and signed the new U.S. Constitution. The document begins with a one-sentence Preamble, or introduction, that explains the purpose of the Constitution. The Preamble reflects the primary belief of the founders of this country: A government is meant to serve its people. The government has to be effective enough to help people but organized in a way to prevent it from oppressing them. The delegates believed that a national government should have only as much power as the people allow it to have. To prevent the government from becoming too strong, the Constitution created a federal system in which the powers of government are divided. There is division of powers between state and national government, and there is also division of powers among the three branches of the national government.

The thirteen colonies rebelled against Great Britain because the British government had too much power and the colonies had too little. The Articles of Confederation failed because the states had too much power and the national government had too little. This time, the framers of the Constitution wanted to get the balance of power just right.

The Pennsylvania State House, now known as Independence Hall, where the U.S. Constitution was signed on September 17, 1787

Both the state and the national governments can make laws and collect taxes. State governments, however, determine matters such as marriage age, driving age, and much of what is taught in public schools. State and local governments are also in charge of services like most police and fire protection, public libraries, and public transportation. What people need or want from a government can vary from person to person, city to city, and state to state. The founders thought it best to have many everyday duties handled by state and local governments. The average person can access these government bodies more easily. They also can shift more easily to suit the unique needs of their area.

Meanwhile, the national government is divided into three branches: the legislative branch, the executive branch, and the judicial branch. Each branch has its own set of powers and duties, and no branch can do the job of another. Not only that, each branch has powers and weaknesses compared with the other branches. This system of checks and balances ensures that no individual or group becomes too powerful.

A U.S. postal worker is a federal employee.

Law enforcement officers can be state, local, or federal.

A public school is run by the state government.

272   Lesson 2   How Does the Constitution Set Up Our Government Framework?

Lesson 2   273

Research Companion, pp. 272–273

ENGLISH LEARNERS SCAFFOLD

ELD.PI.5.6 Reading closely literary and informational texts and viewing multimedia to determine how meaning is conveyed explicitly and implicitly through language

Emerging	Expanding	Bridging
Develop Language Have students describe what they see in the photos. Make sure that students understand that *federal* means the government in Washington D.C.; *state* refers to the local government of your state; and *shared* means powers and responsibilities the federal and state governments share.	**Use Language** Have students work with a partner to describe what they see in the photos. Make sure that students understand the types of government. Suggest that students make a list of words describing federal, state, and shared powers.	**Use Language** Have students look at the photos showing federal, state, and shared powers. Have students add one more example to each of the federal, state, and shared powers.

See the **Language Learner Teaching Guide** for more language support strategies.

Monitor and Differentiate

REACHING ALL LEARNERS

Approaching Level

Work with students to understand how the writers of the Constitution anticipated the need for a strong national government but were wary of giving that government too much power.

On Level

Work with students to understand how the colonists' experience with the British led them to create the Articles of Confederation, which gave too much power to the states.

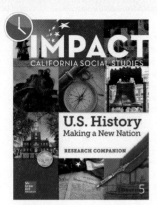

Research Companion
pp. 274–275

 STANDARDS

Understand how the Constitution is designed to secure our liberty by both empowering and limiting central government and compare the powers granted to citizens, Congress, the president, and the Supreme Court with those reserved to the states. **HSS.5.7.4**

Engage effectively in a range of collaborative discussions (one-on-one, in groups, and teacher-led) with diverse partners on *grade 5 topics and texts*, building on others' ideas and expressing their own clearly. **CCSS.ELA.SL.5.1**

Go Digital!

Investigate the lesson content with online whole-class presentation tools.

Background Information

Franklin D. Roosevelt and the Supreme Court One of the greatest struggles among the three branches of government occurred in 1937 when President Franklin D. Roosevelt, frustrated with the Court's rulings on many of his programs, asked Congress to empower him to appoint additional justices for anyone on the Court over the age of 70. Many people vehemently opposed the move and warned that if Roosevelt won, he would destroy the independence of the judiciary branch of government, thus threatening checks and balances. Roosevelt's plan did not succeed, and the Court remained as it had always been—comprised of nine justices who served for life or until they retired.

Analyze the Source

Inspect Have students read pages 274–275.

Find Evidence Use the questions below to check comprehension. Remind students to support their answers with text evidence.

Identify How long do members of the House of Representatives serve? (two years) How long do representatives in the Senate serve? (six years) **DOK 1**

Use Context Clues What is the president's *cabinet*? (senior officials, appointed by the president to oversee various departments) **DOK 2**

Summarize What are the main responsibilities of the executive, legislative, and judicial branches of government? (The legislative branch writes bills, or laws. The judicial branch interprets the law. The executive branch enforces out the law.) **DOK 2**

Analyze the Infographic Direct students' attention to the infographic on page 275. Say: *The infographic outlines the duties and responsibilities of each branch of government.*

Analyze Visuals Name one check that the executive branch of government has on the legislative branch. (The President can veto legislation passed by Congress.) **DOK 2**

Analyze Visuals Name one check that the judicial branch has on the executive branch. (The Supreme Court can determine whether or not the president's actions are constitutional.) **DOK 2**

Make Connections

Draw Conclusions What checks do the legislative and judicial branches of government have if the president fails to do his or her job properly? (The legislative branch can impeach the president; the judicial branch can declare the president's actions unconstitutional.) **DOK 2**

Stop and Check

Think Encourage students to think about why the founders wanted the government's powers and duties separated? (They wanted to limit the national government's powers.)

Think Give two examples of checks by the legislative branch. (It approves spending and taxes; it can charge judges with wrongdoing.)

The legislative branch is in charge of making laws. It consists of Congress, which has two houses. In the House of Representatives, each state has a number of representatives depending on how many people live in the state. The representatives serve for two-year **terms**, and then they have to be re-elected if they want to stay. The other house, the Senate, has two senators for every state. Senators serve six-year terms, and they also can be re-elected. The members of Congress write **bills**, and a bill must be approved by both houses to be passed. The bills passed by Congress must be approved by the executive branch to become laws. If a bill is not approved by the executive branch, it can still become a law if a large majority of Congress approves it. Laws can be ruled unconstitutional by the judicial branch.

The executive branch carries out the law. The highest position is the President of the United States, but the executive branch also includes the vice president and the cabinet, which is composed of the leaders of various government departments. These departments include the Department of State, the Department of Defense, and the Department of Justice. The department heads are chosen by the president. Through these departments, the executive branch enforces the law. The president also commands the military and has the ability to sign treaties. The president also chooses justices for the Supreme Court. If the president fails to do the job properly, the legislative branch can impeach him or her. The judicial branch can rule presidential actions as unconstitutional.

The judicial branch makes decisions on how laws are interpreted. It consists of the Supreme Court, a group of nine justices who make decisions about whether laws are fair and how they should be applied. Unlike the legislative and executive branches, most justices of the judicial branch serve for life. Each federal justice is selected by the president and must be approved by the Senate.

> ### ✓ Stop and Check
>
> **Think** Why did the founders want the government's powers and duties separated?

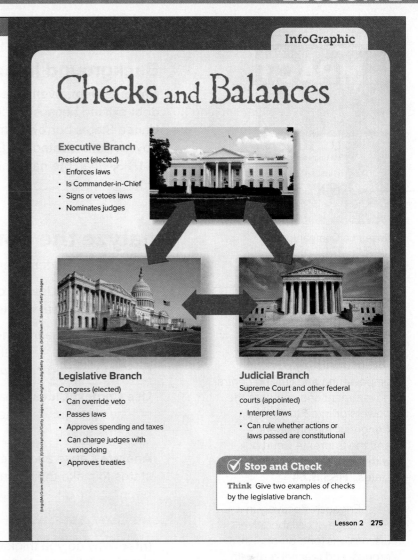

InfoGraphic

Checks and Balances

Executive Branch
President (elected)
- Enforces laws
- Is Commander-in-Chief
- Signs or vetoes laws
- Nominates judges

Legislative Branch
Congress (elected)
- Can override veto
- Passes laws
- Approves spending and taxes
- Can charge judges with wrongdoing
- Approves treaties

Judicial Branch
Supreme Court and other federal courts (appointed)
- Interpret laws
- Can rule whether actions or laws passed are constitutional

> ### ✓ Stop and Check
>
> **Think** Give two examples of checks by the legislative branch.

Research Companion, pp. 274–275

 ## ENGLISH LEARNERS SCAFFOLD

ELD.PI.5.6 Reading closely literary and informational texts and viewing multimedia to determine how meaning is conveyed explicitly and implicitly through language

Emerging	Expanding	Bridging
Develop Language Work with students individually to help them understand the basics of the three branches of government. Point to the picture of the White House and say "executive branch." Repeat with the other pictures. Have students say the words after you.	**Use Language** Have students work with a partner to understand the basics of the branches of government. Point to the three photos and have students say what branch of government each photo represents. Suggest that students make a list of words describing each branch.	**Use Language** Have students work with a partner to discuss the infographic. Help students with difficult vocabulary as needed. Then have students write a paragraph summarizing the duties and responsibilities of the executive branch.

See the **Language Learner Teaching Guide** for more language support strategies.

Monitor and Differentiate

REACHING ALL LEARNERS

Special Needs

Work with students to be sure they understand the basic duties and responsibilities of the three branches of government. Use the pictures and text in the infographic to help students understand that executive refers to the president, legislative refers to Congress, and judicial refers to the Supreme Court and other courts.

On Level

Work with students to be sure they understand academic vocabulary, such as *consists, approved, composed,* and *interpreted*. Have students find the words in the text to see if they can use context clues to define the words. If necessary use a dictionary to check meaning.

2 INVESTIGATE

Economic Aspects of the Constitution

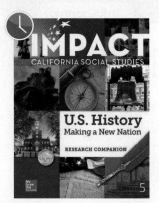

Research Companion
pp. 276–277

HSS STANDARDS

Understand how the
Constitution is designed to
secure our liberty by both
empowering and limiting central
government and compare the
powers granted to citizens,
Congress, the president,
and the Supreme Court
with those reserved to the
states. **HSS.5.7.4**

CCSS Engage effectively in a
range of collaborative
discussions (one-on-one, in
groups, and teacher-led) with
diverse partners on *grade 5
topics and texts*, building on
others' ideas and expressing
their own clearly.
CCSS.ELA.SL.5.1

Go Digital!

Investigate the lesson content
with online whole-class
presentation tools.

Background Information

National Debt Even before the United States was officially founded in 1776,
debt existed because of the need to fund the Revolutionary War (1775–1783). The
United States borrowed money from France and the Netherlands. In 1781, the
government created the Department of Finance to manage the new country's money.
In 1783, when the national debt was first reported, it was $43 million.

Analyze the Source

Inspect Have students read pages 276–277.

Find Evidence Use the questions below to check comprehension. Remind students to
support their answers with text evidence.

Summarize What did the Constitution do to exercise some control over the U.S.
economy? (It gave additional powers to Congress, including the ability to create and
collect taxes and borrow money.) **DOK 2**

Use Context Clues What is the meaning of the word *economics*? (Answers will vary,
but students should note that the term refers to how goods and services are produced,
distributed, and consumed.) **DOK 2**

Analyze Cause and Effect What were the effects of Constitution forbidding individual
states to make their own currency? (The whole nation would use a single currency and
people from different states could more easily do business with other states.) **DOK 2**

Make Connections

Infer Why do you think the framers of the Constitution made certain that Congress did
not have full control of the economy? (They wanted to limit the power of the federal
government and to make sure that the U.S. economy would be fair to everyone.) **DOK 2**

Analyze the Primary Source Have students reread the excerpt from the
Constitution and discuss the purpose of this section. (to explain how laws are made.)

Draw Conclusions What evidence of checks and balances can you see in this
excerpt from the Constitution? (Laws passed by Congress have to be presented to the
President; the President can veto the law; if the two thirds of the House approves the
bill, the House can override the veto.) **DOK 3**

Use Context Clues What is the meaning of the phrase, "…it shall be sent, together
with the president's objections, to the other House." (the bill will be sent to the House
of Representatives, with the President's objections noted) **DOK 2**

✓ Stop and Check

Talk Have students debate the most important improvement the Constitution made
to the Articles of Confederation. (Answers will vary, but students should support their
opinions with evidence from the text.)

WHAT DO YOU THINK?

Encourage students to use text evidence from the whole lesson as they respond to
the prompt.

Economic Aspects of the Constitution

One of the weaknesses of the national government under the Articles of Confederation was its lack of power in economic matters. An important part of the new constitution was granting additional powers to Congress so that it could have some control of the U.S. economy. Under the Constitution, Congress could create and collect taxes and similar fees and borrow money if needed. This way, the government was finally able to pay some of its outstanding debts from the Revolutionary War.

On another economic matter, states would no longer be able to make their own currency. Congress now had the power to coin, or create, money. The whole nation would now use a single currency. This made it much easier for people from different states to do business across state lines. Congress also became responsible for overseeing trade with other nations, including American Indian groups.

Congress did not have total control of the economy, though. It wasn't allowed to pass certain types of taxes. Nor could it tax trade between states or do anything else that would favor one state over another. Any money that Congress received had to be appropriated, or set aside for a specific purpose. That money could not be spent on anything else. These rules were intended to ensure the fairness of the U.S. economy so that many people had a chance to prosper.

McGraw-Hill Education

PRIMARY SOURCE

In Their Words... The Constitution

Article I Section 8. Powers Granted to Congress

1. The Congress shall have power to lay and collect taxes, duties, imposts and excises, to pay the debts and provide for the common defense and general welfare of the United States; but all duties, imposts, and excises shall be uniform throughout the United States;

2. To borrow money on the credit of the United States;

3. To regulate commerce with foreign nations, and among the several states, and with the Indian tribes;

4. To establish a uniform rule of naturalization, and uniform laws on the subject of bankruptcies throughout the United States;

5. To coin money, regulate the value thereof, and of foreign coin, and fix the standard of weights and measures;

6. To provide for the punishment of counterfeiting the securities and current coin of the United States;

7. To establish post offices and post roads . . .

What Do You Think? Reread the excerpt of the Constitution above. Why is it important that these duties are performed at the national level rather than at the state level?

✓ Stop and Check

COLLABORATE

Talk What was the most important improvement the Constitution had over the Articles of Confederation? Debate your opinion with a partner.

Find Details Complete the graphic organizer on page 225 in your Inquiry Journal using information you have gathered.

276 Lesson 2 How Does the Constitution Set Up Our Government Framework?

Lesson 2 277

Research Companion, pp. 276–277

ENGLISH LEARNERS SCAFFOLD

ELD.PI.5.1 Exchanging information and ideas with others through oral collaborative discussions on a range of social and academic topics

Emerging	Expanding	Bridging
Develop Language Make sure students understand the academic vocabulary, such as the word *aspects*. Have students locate the word in the text. Say the word aloud and have students repeat it. Explain that the word means "a part of something." Provide sentence frames, such as: ***We decided to begin by researching all _____ of the problem.***	**Use Language** Have students work with a partner to be sure they understand the meaning of academic vocabulary, such as *aspects* and *originated*. Have students locate the words in the text. Say each word aloud and have students repeat it. Have students work together to use the words in sentences of their own.	**Use Language** Have students locate academic vocabulary, such as *aspects, originated*, and *proceed*. Help with pronunciation as needed Have volunteers define the words. If necessary, have students check the meaning of the words in a dictionary. Have students use the words in sentences of their own.

See the **Language Learner Teaching Guide** for more language support strategies.

Monitor and Differentiate

REACHING ALL LEARNERS

Approaching Level

Work with students to be sure they understand some of the long sentences in the excerpt from the Constitution. Help students to break the sentence into manageable chunks and discuss the meaning of each chunk separately. Help students with difficult vocabulary as needed.

On Level

Have students list the steps involved in the process of making a law. Have students share their list with their classmates.

3 REPORT

Report Your Findings

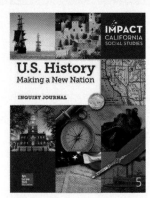

Inquiry Journal
pp. 226–227

 STANDARDS

Understand the fundamental principles of American constitutional democracy, including how the government derives its power from the people and the primacy of individual liberty. **HSS.5.7.3**

Understand how the Constitution is designed to secure our liberty by both empowering and limiting central government and compare the powers granted to citizens, Congress, the president, and the Supreme Court with those reserved to the states. **HSS.5.7.4**

CCSS Write narratives to develop real or imagined experiences or events using effective technique, descriptive details, and clear event sequences. **CCSS.ELA.W.5.3**

Go Digital!

- Students can go online to report their findings. Assess their responses online.

- Students can access the online graphic organizer to capture ideas from their investigation.

Think About It

Students will review their research about the difficulties in writing the Constitution and think about how the structure of the legislature illustrates the way the Constitution came to be written. Remind students to review the information they gathered and recorded on the graphic organizer. Direct students back to pages 266–277 of their Research Companion if they need more information.

Write About It

Take a Stand Have students read the prompt. Explain to students that an effective dialogue will show the opposing viewpoints in the dispute over the structure of the legislature, which eventually ended in the Great Compromise. An effective dialogue will also show clearly each delegate's point of view and arguments and counterarguments for each side. Remind students to include the following elements in their response:

- two characters with opposing viewpoints about the structure of the legislature.

- details from the text that support each character's point of view.

- arguments and counterarguments for each character.

Use the rubric on p. T584 to evaluate students' work.

Talk About It

Act It Out Have students exchange their dialogue with a partner. Have partners discuss the similarities and differences in their dialogues before acting out each other's dialogues.

- Explain that they should take turns discussing and explaining their dialogues.

- Remind students to cite evidence from the text that supports their dialogues.

- Remind students to follow the rules of appropriate classroom conversation.

Connect to the
Essential Question

Read the prompt aloud to students. Ask them the following guiding questions:

- What events from this lesson most transformed the nation and its people? (Responses will vary.)

- What actions and ideas from the debate over the Constitution are still important to our nation today? (Responses will vary, but students may say that the idea of compromise and checks and balances are important.)

Remind students to use the space provided in their journal to jot down notes.

Report Your Findings

Think About It

Look back on your research about the difficulties in writing the Constitution. How does the argument over the structure of the legislature illustrate the way the Constitution came to be written?

Write About It

Take a Stand

Write and Cite Evidence Write a dialogue between two delegates at the Constitutional Convention. The dialogue should show the opposing viewpoints in the dispute over the structure of the legislature, which eventually ended in the Great Compromise. In the dialogue, show each delegate's point of view and his reason for thinking that way.

Students should be able to write dialogue from opposing viewpoints and provide arguments and counterarguments for each side.

Talk About It

Act It Out

Work with a partner to read aloud or act out each other's dialogues. Afterwards, give your partner feedback. How did your partner illustrate the dispute and compromise?

Connect to the

Civics

Pull It Together

What does the process of writing the Constitution reveal about our system of government?

Students may say that the compromises made reflect the system of checks and balances and that decisions should be approved by the majority.

Inquiry Project Notes

226 Lesson 2 How Does the Constitution Set Up Our Government Framework?

Lesson 2 227

Inquiry Journal, pp. 226–227

ENGLISH LEARNERS SCAFFOLD

ELD.PI.5.3 Offering and supporting opinions and negotiating with others in communicative exchanges

Emerging

Develop Language Make sure students understand the terms *dialogue* and *point of view*. Have students draw two delegates arguing. Use sentence frames to describe the argument:

They are having a (dialogue) ***about the legislature.***

They have different (points of view).

Expanding

Use Language Have students make sure they understand the terms *dialogue* and *point of view*. Suggest that students draw two delegates arguing. Then have them write two sentences that sum up each delegate's point of view.

Bridging

Develop Point of View Have students work with a partner and choose two delegates with opposing points of view on the subject of how many votes each state should get. Then have partners write a sentence that sums up each delegate's point of view.

See the **Language Learner Teaching Guide** for more language support strategies.

Monitor and Differentiate

REACHING ALL LEARNERS

Approaching Level

Make sure that students understand the terms *dialogue* (conversation between two people) and *point of view* (opinion). To help students with the assignment, remind them that the argument was essentially about how many votes each state would get in the legislature.

On Level

Encourage students to use in their dialogues two actual delegates with different points of view, such as Edmund Randolph and William Paterson.

Beyond Level

Encourage students to use in their dialogues precise words from the text, such as *upper house, lower house, veto, calculated, alternative, majority, determine,* and *political power.*

Know what your students know!

Lesson Task
Report Your Findings

Use this rubric to evaluate students' response.

Take a Stand Students write a dialogue between two delegates to the Constitutional Convention who have opposing viewpoints about the structure of the legislature.

Act It Out Students act out each other's dialogues. They take turns discussing how the dialogues helped them understand the dispute and compromise.

Performance Task Evaluation Rubric

	4	3	2	1
Historical Understanding	Strong understanding of opposing viewpoints regarding the structure of the legislature	Adequate understanding of opposing viewpoints regarding the structure of the legislature	Uneven understanding of opposing viewpoints regarding the structure of the legislature	No understanding of opposing viewpoints regarding the structure of the legislature
Write a Dialogue	Dialogue clearly shows differing points of view	Dialogue adequately shows differing points of view	Dialogue shows uneven points of view	Dialogue does not show differing points of view
Support with Evidence	Facts and details provide thorough evidence	Facts and details provide adequate evidence	Facts and details provide uneven evidence	Facts and details are missing, or no supporting evidence is provided
Act It Out	Speaks clearly and at an understandable pace Actively participates in acting out dialogues	Speaks clearly during most of the dialogue Participates in acting out dialogues	At times speaker is unclear Loses focus when participating in dialogues	Speaks unclearly or does not participate in acting out the dialogues

Lesson Assessment

Go Digital!

- Have students complete the Chapter 6 Lesson 2 Assessment online to monitor their understanding of the lesson content.

California Smarter Balanced Assessment Connections!

Standards Covered	Lesson Task	Lesson Assessment	Alignment with California Smarter Balanced Assessment
History Social Science Content 5.6.5; 5.7.3; 5.7.4	✔	✔	Claim 1 Targets 8, 9, 10, 11
History Social Science Analysis Skills Chronological and Spatial Thinking 5.1 Research, Evidence, and Point of View 5.1; 5.2 Historical Interpretation 5.1	✔	✔	Claim 1 Targets 11, 12
Writing W.5.3	✔	✔	Claim 2 Target 1
Research and Inquiry W.5.9	✔	✔	Claim 4 Targets 2, 3, 4
Reading RI.5.8	✔	✔	Claim 1 Targets 11, 12
Speaking and Listening SL.5.1	✔		Claim 3 Target 4

How Do the Constitution and Bill of Rights Impact Citizens?

Background Information

Explain to students that in this lesson they will learn how the Constitution and the Bill of Rights affect the lives of people of the United States.

Community Connections

To enrich what students have learned about the Constitution and the Bill of Rights, ask a local person involved with town or city meetings to talk with students about the importance of exercising their right of free speech by participating in local government.

 LESSON STANDARDS

✓ Explain the significance of the new Constitution of 1787, including the struggles over its ratification and the reasons for the addition of the Bill of Rights. **HSS.5.7.2**

✓ Understand the fundamental principles of American constitutional democracy, including how the government derives its power from the people and the primacy of individual liberty. **HSS.5.7.3**

✓ Understand how the Constitution is designed to secure our liberty by both empowering and limiting central government and compare the powers granted to citizens, Congress, the president, and the Supreme Court with those reserved to the states. **HSS.5.7.4**

✓ Discuss the meaning of the American creed that calls on citizens to safeguard the liberty of individual Americans within a unified nation, to respect the rule of law, and to preserve the Constitution. **HSS.5.7.5**

✓ Students place key events and people of the historical era they are studying in a chronological sequence and within a spatial context; they interpret time lines. **HAS.CS.1**

✓ Students explain how the present is connected to the past, identifying both similarities and differences between the two, and how some things change over time and some things stay the same. **HAS.CS.3**

✓ Students pose relevant questions about events they encounter in historical documents, eyewitness accounts, oral histories, letters, diaries, artifacts, photographs, maps, artworks, and architecture. **HAS.HR.2**

Connect to the Essential Question

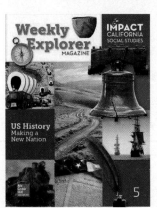

The **Weekly Explorer Magazine** supports students' exploration of the Essential Question and provides additional resources for the EQ Inquiry Project.

Chapter 6, pp. 72–83

Inquiry Project

Which Side Will You Choose?

Remind students to use the information they learn in this lesson and other resources to complete their EQ Inquiry Project!

Dinah Zike's

In this lesson you will use Foldables.

When Minutes Count!

Suggested Lesson Pacing

1 ENGAGE
One Day

- Lesson Opener
- Analyze the Source
- Inquiry Tools

Go Digital
- **Video:** The Bill of Rights

2 INVESTIGATE
Two to Three Days

 Short on Time? Look for the clock to teach core content in less time.

- The Debate over Ratification
- The Bill of Rights
- Amendments and Expanding Rights
- **Citizenship** Civic Responsibilities

3 REPORT
One Day

- Think About It
- Give an Example
- Explain

Make Connections!

(ccss) CONNECT TO ELA

Reading

Determine two or more main ideas of a text and explain how they are supported by key details; summarize the text. **RI.5.2**

Integrate information from several texts on the same topic in order to write or speak about the subject knowledgeably. **RI.5.9**

Research

Conduct short research projects that use several sources to build knowledge through investigation of different aspects of a topic. **W.5.7**

Recall relevant information from experiences or gather relevant information from print and digital sources; summarize or paraphrase information in notes and finished work, and provide a list of sources. **W.5.8**

Writing

Write informative/explanatory texts to examine a topic and convey ideas and information clearly. **W.5.2**

Draw evidence from literary or informational texts to support analysis, reflection, and research. **W.5.9**

Speaking and Listening

Engage effectively in a range of collaborative discussions (one-on-one, in groups, and teacher-led) with diverse partners on grade 5 topics and texts, building on others' ideas and expressing their own clearly. **SL.5.1**

Report on a topic or text or present an opinion, sequencing ideas logically and using appropriate facts and relevant, descriptive details to support main ideas or themes; speak clearly at an understandable pace. **SL.5.4**

Classroom Resources

Search for additional resources using the following key words.

Samuel Adams

Antifederalists

Bill of Rights

Freedom to Assemble

Freedom to Petition

Freedom of the Press

Freedom of Religion

Freedom of Speech

Federalists

Alexander Hamilton

Patrick Henry

John Jay

James Madison

George Mason

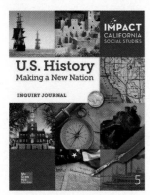

Inquiry Journal
pp. 228–229

Explain the significance of
the new Constitution of 1787,
including the struggles over
its ratification and the reasons
for the addition of the Bill of
Rights. **HSS.5.7.2**

Understand the fundamental
principles of American
constitutional democracy,
including how the government
derives its power from the
people and the primacy of
individual liberty. **HSS.5.7.3**

Understand how the
Constitution is designed to
secure our liberty by both
empowering and limiting central
government and compare the
powers granted to citizens,
Congress, the president,
and the Supreme Court
with those reserved to the
states. **HSS.5.7.4**

Go *Digital!*

Explore the lesson content
with online whole-class
presentation tools.

- **Video:** The Bill of Rights

How Do the Constitution and Bill of Rights Impact Citizens?

Bellringer

Prompt students to retrieve information from the previous lessons. Say: *The Constitutional Convention was characterized by conflicts and compromises. Name one of the conflicts and the compromise that solved it.* (The major conflict centered on how many votes individual states would get. The compromises that resolved that conflict were the Great Compromise and the Three-Fifths Compromise.)

Lesson Outcomes

What Am I Learning? Have students read the Lesson Question and Lesson Outcomes on page 228.

Why Am I Learning It? Make sure students understand the noun *rights* as it is used in the text. Encourage students to use context clues to understand the meaning of *rights*. Call on volunteers to define the term. Say: *In the text,* rights *refers things that are due to a person. For example, when women and African Americans fought for the <u>right</u> to vote, they were fighting for something that was due to them.*

How Will I Know That I Learned It? Ask students the following questions.

- What will you be able to identify? (the rights of U.S. citizens as spelled out in the Constitution and the Bill of Rights)

- What is the purpose of this task? (to write and illustrate a comic strip that shows a particular amendment to the Constitution in action)

- How will you support your writing? (with evidence from the text)

Talk About It

Read the quotation from Benjamin Franklin. How did Franklin feel about the Constitution? (He felt it was imperfect, but he thought it was the best delegates could do.) What "faults" might he be referring to? (Answers will vary, but students should note that in any compromise neither side will be completely satisfied. Franklin probably thought that the Constitution did not give the national government enough power.)

Collaborative Conversations

Add New Ideas As students engage in partner, small-group, and whole-class discussions, encourage them to

- Read and view the material carefully.
- Connect their own ideas to things their peers have said.
- Look for ways to connect their personal experiences and prior knowledge to the conversation.

Lesson 3

How Do the Constitution and Bill of Rights Impact Citizens?

Lesson Outcomes

What Am I Learning?
In this lesson, you're going to use your investigative skills to explore how the Constitution and the Bill of Rights affect the people of the United States.

Why Am I Learning It?
Reading and talking about the liberties protected by the Constitution and the Bill of Rights will help you understand the rights of U.S. citizens.

How Will I Know That I Learned It?
You will be able to summarize how the lives of U.S. citizens are influenced by the country's founding documents.

Talk About It COLLABORATE

Find Details Read the quotation from Benjamin Franklin. How did Franklin feel about the Constitution? What "faults" might he be referring to?

228 Lesson 3 How Do the Constitution and Bill of Rights Impact Citizens?

PRIMARY SOURCE

In Their Words...

Benjamin Franklin

I agree to this Constitution, with all its faults ... because I think a general Government necessary for us.... I doubt too, whether any other Convention we can obtain, may be able to make a better Constitution....

—Benjamin Franklin at the conclusion of the Constitutional Convention in 1787

Did You Know?

At the time of the Constitutional Convention, Ben Franklin was in his 80s and in poor health. Much of the convention occurred during summer months, and the hot room made Franklin even more uncomfortable. Yet, he played an important role at the convention, helping to calm things down when tempers flared. Franklin had many of his ideas shot down by other delegates. Among these was a belief that the executive branch should be led by a committee and that Congress should consist of only one house, not two. Nonetheless, Franklin supported the final version of the Constitution.

At the conclusion of the convention, Franklin noted to some of his fellow delegates that George Washington's chair had a half-sun on the back. For months, he had thought about the sun as a possible metaphor for the convention, and he told his colleagues he had wondered "whether it was rising or setting. But now at length I have the happiness to know that it is a rising and not a setting sun."

Lesson 3 229

Inquiry Journal, pp. 228–229

ENGLISH LEARNERS SCAFFOLD

ELD.PI.5.1 Exchanging information and ideas with others through oral collaborative discussions on a range of social and academic topics.

Emerging	Expanding	Bridging
Identify Details Work with students individually to identify what they see in the image of Ben Franklin. Encourage students to notice and name details. Supply vocabulary as needed.	**Describe Details** Have small groups create a list of words that describe what they see in the image of Ben Franklin. Encourage them to consider what the placement of Ben Franklin's hand and the expression on his face suggests. What do students think he is doing and thinking? Have groups share their list with the rest of the class.	**Use Language** Have students work together to describe what they find historically important about this image of Ben Franklin. What significant information about Ben Franklin and the other delegates to the Convention does the image show?

See the **Language Learner Teaching Guide** for more language support strategies.

Monitor and Differentiate

REACHING ALL LEARNERS

Approaching Level

Guide students to break down the quote from Ben Franklin into manageable chunks. Then discuss each chunk with students. Have students fill in sentence frames to explain what Franklin is saying.

Ben Franklin is not totally pleased with the __(Constitution)__ .

Franklin believes that further talk about the Constitution will not __(help)__ .

On Level

Have students work in pairs to discuss the three parts of the quotation. Then, have students write two sentences summarizing Franklin's thoughts.

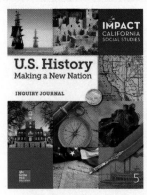

Inquiry Journal
pp. 230–231

Background Information

Amendments to the Constitution Five of the states that ratified the Constitution did so with the understanding the Congress would add a Bill of Rights, or amendments. In 1789, James Madison, who represented Virginia, recommended that 12 amendments be added to the Constitution. During the next two years, state legislatures ratified ten of those 12 amendments. In December of 1791, these amendments, known as the Bill of Rights, were added to the Constitution.

1 Inspect

Look Have students read the entire text, including the Primary Source, to focus on understanding the overall meaning. Remind them to circle unknown words.

- How are the titles "The Freedoms of Religion and Expression" and "The First Amendment" related? (The First Amendment of the Constitution specifically protects Americans' freedoms of religion and of expression.)

- What four basic rights of expression does the First Amendment protect? (freedom of religion, freedom of speech, freedom of the press, freedom of assembly, and the freedom to sign petitions)

- What protest campaigns did the First Amendment support? (women's suffrage movement and the civil rights movement)

2 Find Evidence

Look Again Have students reread the text.

Analyze the Primary Source Read the text of the First Amendment aloud and then analyze it together as a class. Provide support for vocabulary as needed.

- How does the author present the details of the First Amendment? (The author presents the details by listing the kinds of laws that Congress may not make.)

- What is the purpose if the First Amendment? (to list areas of life that the national government may not interfere with)

Analyze the Photograph Tell students that the First Amendment gives U.S. citizens the right to express their opinions publicly without fear of punishment. Guide students to note details in the photographs and discuss how it illustrates the First Amendment.

3 Make Connections COLLABORATE

Draw Work with a partner to draw a chart of the five basic freedoms protected by the First Amendment. In one column, list the name of the freedom. (freedom of religion, freedom of speech, freedom of the press, freedom to assemble, freedom to petition the government) In the next, list the right that it grants U.S. citizens. (The right to choose and practice a religion, the freedom to state an opinion, the right of the press to report honestly, the right to assemble, and the right to sign a petition.) In the final column, list any exceptions that are not protected by the First Amendment.

Connect to Now Have student discuss how the First Amendment impacts their lives (Students may say that people have to listen peacefully to ideas they disagree with so that all citizens have a right to express themselves freely.)

Analyze the Source

1 Inspect

Read Look at the titles "The Freedoms of Religion and Expression" and "The First Amendment." What connections are there between the two?

- **Circle** words you don't know.
- **Underline** words related to the concept of "The Freedoms of Religion and Expression."
- **Discuss** with a partner why the writers of the Bill of Rights chose the rights of expression and religious freedom to include as the first addition to the Constitution.

My Notes

_____
_____
_____
_____
_____
_____
_____
_____
_____
_____

The Freedoms of Religion and Expression

The First Amendment of the Constitution protects Americans' freedoms of religion and expression. The amendment is intended to prevent the federal government from punishing citizens for what they say or what they believe. Since the writing of the Constitution, the Supreme Court has ruled on many cases concerning the First Amendment.

The Supreme Court has interpreted the First Amendment to grant four basic rights of expression. Freedom of speech gives people the right to share their ideas openly. Freedom of the press guarantees the right of the media to publish news freely. Freedom of assembly allows U.S. citizens to gather and hold meetings. Freedom of petition grants the right to sign petitions and to protest government policies. The broad freedoms of expression granted by the First Amendment made possible major U.S. protest campaigns such as the women's suffrage movement and the civil rights movement.

PRIMARY SOURCE

The First Amendment

Congress shall make no law respecting an establishment of religion, or prohibiting the free exercise thereof; or abridging the freedom of speech, or of the press; or the right of the people peaceably to assemble, and to petition the Government for a redress of grievances.

U.S. Constitution, amend.1, (1791), www.senate.gov

The First Amendment gives U.S. citizens the right to express their opinions publicly.

2 Find Evidence

Reread How does the author present the details of the First Amendment?

Examine Underline the transitional words and phrases that the author uses.

3 Make Connections

Draw Work with a partner to draw a chart of the five basic freedoms protected by the First Amendment. In one column, list the name of the freedom. In the next, list the right that it grants U.S. citizens. In the final column, list any exceptions that are not protected by the First Amendment.

Connect to Now How does the First Amendment affect the freedoms you enjoy today?

230 Lesson 3 How Do the Constitution and Bill of Rights Impact Citizens?

Lesson 3 231

Inquiry Journal, pp. 230–231

ENGLISH LEARNERS SCAFFOLD

ELD.PI.5.3 Offering and supporting opinions and negotiating with others in communicative exchanges

Emerging

Interpret Images Work with students individually to closely examine the photograph. Start by asking students to point out what they notice in it and then help them to find words to describe these things. Help students understand the words on the posters ("Dr. King" and "Peace") as needed. Guide students to understand that the young people in the photograph are expressing their opinion and that this is a right guaranteed by the First Amendment.

Expanding/Bridging

Develop Language Have students work with a partner to find words and phrases to talk about the photograph. Start by asking students to point out to their partner what they notice. Then, have students help each other to find words to describe these things. Guide students to understand that the young people in the photograph are expressing their opinion and that this is a right guaranteed by the First Amendment.

See the **Language Learner Teaching Guide** for more language support strategies.

Monitor and Differentiate

REACHING ALL LEARNERS

Approaching/on Level

Define and explain the following words as needed: *respecting* (about), *prohibiting* (forbidding), *abridging* (limiting), *assemble* (gather together), *redress* (correct or make right) and *grievances* (real or imagined wrongs). Once students understand the difficult vocabulary in the First Amendment, have them work in pairs to paraphrase it.

Beyond Level

On many occasions the Supreme Court has had to decide how free speech can and cannot be restricted by the government. Have students research some of these cases. The might start with *Tinker v. Des Moines Independent Community School District, 1969* or *Hazelwood School v. Kuhlmeir, 1989*.

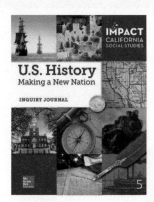

Inquiry Journal
pp. 232–233

STANDARDS

CCSS Write informative/explanatory texts to examine a topic and convey ideas and information clearly. **CCSS.ELA.W.5.2**

Draw evidence from literary or informational text to support analysis, reflection, and research. **CCSS.ELA.W.5.9**

Go *Digital!*

- Model how to explore and investigate with online whole-class tools.

- Students can access the online graphic organizer to use the inquiry tools as they read.

Summarize

Explain Tell students that when you write a summary, you list the most important details on a text. Your summary will help you to remember and think about the structure of a text.

Read Have students read the step-by-step instructions about how to write a summary. Remind students that their summaries will not list everything—only the main ideas and key details. Summaries should be brief.

Guide Practice Tell students that they often summarize events in their own lives. Give an example, such as telling someone what you did over the weekend. You would not include every detail of everything that happened, but instead choose one or two events and give key details about those events. Students might ask and answer questions such as *What is the main thing or things that happened? What are important details about the events? How can I convey this information briefly?*

Investigate!

Have students read pages 278–287 in the Research Companion. Tell them the information will help them answer the lesson question ***How Do the Constitution and Bill of Rights Impact Citizens?***

Take Notes Tell students that they should take notes about main events and key details and record their inferences in the graphic organizer on page 233 of the Inquiry Journal. Explain to students that they will take notes as they read each section. Remind them that taking notes will help them understand and remember what they read.

Remind students that good note taking is about finding the most important information and writing key words or phrases about it. Note takers do not rewrite every word from the text unless they plan to quote an author later on.

Inspect Guide students to read the text in each section to determine what the text says and what the main idea and key details are. Encourage them also to recall what they know about the topic.

Find Evidence Encourage students to reread the text to develop a deeper understanding of the content. Remind students that after they read and take notes, they should review and think about how the facts and details will help them answer the lesson question.

Collaborative Conversations

Text-Based Discussion Remind students of the goals of discussing the text with others.

- to listen and respond to another point of view
- to find additional evidence
- to respond respectfully to their partner's ideas

Inquiry Tools

Summarize

When you write a summary, you list the most important details in a text. Your summary will help you remember and think about the structure of a text.

To write a summary:

1. Read through the text.
This will help you determine the main idea of the text.

2. Reread and jot down notes.
Make notes about the people, places, events, and ideas discussed. Make sure to include only details directly from the text, and not your opinions.

3. List the most important details.
Write down the main details in the order that they appear in the text.

4. Keep your summary brief.
Your summary should be shorter than the original text.

COLLABORATE Based on the text you just read, work with your class to complete the chart below.

Possible answers:

Details	The First Amendment to the Constitution protects Americans' freedoms of religion and expression.	The Supreme Court has interpreted the First Amendment to grant four basic freedoms of expression.	These broad freedoms of expression helped foster some of the country's most important protest movements.
Summary	The First Amendment, which was written into the Constitution and interpreted to grant four basic freedoms of expression, helped foster some of the country's most important protest movements.		

Investigate!

Read pages 278–287 in your Research Companion. Use your investigative skills to list important details and to write a summary of one section of the text you read.

Details				
Summary	Students should identify four details from one section of the text and write a summary that includes information from all four details without introducing any bias or other form of opinion.			

Inquiry Journal, pp. 232–233

EL ENGLISH LEARNERS SCAFFOLD

ELD.PI.5.10 Writing literary and informational texts to present, describe, and explain ideas and information, using appropriate technology

Emerging

Develop Language Work with individual students to be sure that they understand what it means to summarize. Then, practice filling in the graphic organizer with students. If students have difficulty writing sentences, suggest that they write single words or draw a picture.

Expanding

Cite Evidence Have students work with a partner to summarize the text they have read thus far. If students have difficulty writing whole sentences, suggest that they write single words or phrases. Remind students that summaries should be short and contain only main ideas and key details.

Bridging

Use Language Have students use precise words from the text as they summarize what they have read. Suggest these words: *document, citizens, expression, petitions,* and *interpret.*

See the **Language Learner Teaching Guide** for more language support strategies.

Monitor and Differentiate

REACHING ALL LEARNERS

Approaching Level

Be sure that students understand that the First Amendment protects citizens' rights by limiting the power of the federal government. Have them discuss why colonists might have been particularly eager to have this safeguard. Then, have students write a sentence summarizing why limiting the power of the federal government was important to colonists.

Beyond Level

Have a small group of students discuss why summarizing is an important skill when analyzing historical events and important historical figures. Have students cite specific examples to support their point of view.

2 INVESTIGATE
The Debate over Ratification

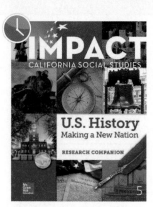

Research Companion
pp. 278–279

 STANDARDS

Explain the significance of the new Constitution of 1787, including the struggles over its ratification and the reasons for the addition of the Bill of Rights. **HSS.5.7.2**

Understand how the Constitution is designed to secure our liberty by both empowering and limiting central government and compare the powers granted to citizens, Congress, the president, and the Supreme Court with those reserved to the states. **HSS.5.7.4**

Students place key events and people of the historical era they are studying in a chronological sequence and within a spatial context; they interpret time lines. **HAS.CS.1**

(ccss) Draw evidence from literary or informational texts to support analysis, reflection, and research. **CCSS.ELA.W.5.9**

Go *Digital!*

Investigate the lesson content with online whole-class presentation tools.

• **Video:** The Bill of Rights

Background Information

The Nineteenth Amendment On August 18, 1920 the Nineteenth Amendment to the Constitution granted women the right to vote. When the United States was founded, women did not share the same rights as men—including the right to vote. It took a 70-year battle for women to finally secure the right to vote.

| TIMELINE | Invite students to look at the timeline at the top of page 279.

Analyze What does the fact that six amendments were added to the Constitution between 1865 and 1964 tell you about it as a document? (The Constitution is a living document and can be amended as times and attitudes change.) **HAS.CS.1**

Analyze the Source

Inspect Have students read The Debate over Ratification on pages 278–279.

Find Evidence Use the questions below to check comprehension. Remind students to support their answers with text evidence.

Identify What group of people defended the Constitution? (The Federalists) What group of people opposed it? (the Antifederalists) **DOK 1**

Infer What did Madison mean when he said, "If men were angels no government would be necessary"? (because men and women do bad things government is needed to preserve and maintain order) **DOK 2**

Summarize Summarize the Federalists' argument for ratifying the Constitution. (Federalists believed that the Constitution would unite the states and maintain order in the nation.) **DOK 2**

Make Connections

State an Opinion Based on what you have read, why do you think they delegates argued so much about the best way to form the new government? (Answers will vary, but students should note that delegates on both sides of the argument cared very much about the future of the new nation and how laws and safeguards were set up.) **DOK 3**

Analyze the Image Direct students' attention to the image of a woman casting a ballot on p. 279. Explain that when we talk about an image, we describe and interpret it and present our ideas in our own words. Provide sentence frames like these to help students form their ideas as they discuss the image.

The image shows _(a woman voting)_ .

The Nineteenth Amendment gave _(women the right to vote)_ .

Lesson 3

How Do the Constitution and Bill of Rights Impact Citizens?

Timeline

| 1791 Bill of Rights ratified | 1865 Thirteenth Amendment ratified | 1870 Fifteenth Amendment ratified | 1961 Twenty-Third Amendment ratified | 1971 Twenty-Sixth Amendment ratified |

1750 | | | 1800 | | | 1850 | | | 1900 | | | 1950 | | | 2000

| 1868 Fourteenth Amendment ratified | 1920 Nineteenth Amendment ratified | 1964 Twenty-Fourth Amendment ratified |

The Debate over Ratification

The states had to ratify, or officially approve, the Constitution for it to become law. The two sides of the constitutional debate went to work to earn the support of the people of the United States. The Federalists defended the Constitution. Their ranks included George Washington, James Madison, and Alexander Hamilton. The Antifederalists opposed the Constitution. Antifederalists such as Samuel Adams, George Mason, and Patrick Henry preferred the Articles of Confederation. Both the Federalists and Antifederalists wrote papers in defense of their positions.

The Federalists insisted that the Constitution would unify the states. They wanted to divide power between different parts of the federal government. They hoped to avoid giving too much power to any one person. James Madison, Alexander Hamilton, and John Jay made the case for Federalism in a series of 85 essays called *The Federalist Papers.* They wrote anonymously under the pen name "Publius." From 1787 to 1788, the essays appeared in several New York newspapers. Their authors reasoned that the Constitution would maintain order in the nation. "If men were angels," Madison wrote, "no government would be necessary."

Women did not receive the constitutional right to vote in national elections until 1920.

HSS.5.7.2, HSS.5.7.3, HSS.5.7.4, HSS.5.7.5, HAS.CS.1, HAS.CS.3, HAS.HR.1, HAS.HR.2, HAS.HI.1, HAS.HI.3

278 **Lesson 3** How Do the Constitution and Bill of Rights Impact Citizens?

Lesson 3 **279**

Research Companion, pp. 278–279

ENGLISH LEARNERS SCAFFOLD

ELD.PI.5.6 Reading closely literary and informational texts and viewing multimedia to determine how meaning is conveyed explicitly and implicitly through language

Emerging	**Expanding**	**Bridging**
Describe Chronology Guide students to describe the timeline using time-signal words, such as *first, then, next, after, last,* or *finally.* Help students with difficult vocabulary as needed.	**Provide Details** Guide students to describe events on the timeline using time-signal words, such as *first, then, next, after, last,* or *finally.* Encourage students to choose one of the beginning events from the timeline and share what they know about it based on the text.	**Use Vocabulary** Have students work with a partner or with a small group to discuss how events in the timeline are related to each other. Have them keep a list of words describing events and how they are related.

See the **Language Learner Teaching Guide** for more language support strategies.

Monitor and Differentiate

REACHING ALL LEARNERS

Special Needs

Have students slide their finger across the timeline along to track each entry. Guide them to focus on the entry at hand without being distracted by the previous or following entry. Have students copy the timeline into a list and then report the order of events by year.

On Level

Have students write sentences summarizing the point of view of the Federalists and the Antifederalists. Remind students to base their summaries on evidence from the text.

2 INVESTIGATE

The Debate over Ratification

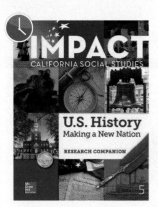

Research Companion
pp. 280–281

Explain the significance of the new Constitution of 1787, including the struggles over its ratification and the reasons for the addition of the Bill of Rights. **HSS.5.7.2**

Understand how the Constitution is designed to secure our liberty by both empowering and limiting central government and compare the powers granted to citizens, Congress, the president, and the Supreme Court with those reserved to the states. **HSS.5.7.4**

Students differentiate between primary and secondary sources. **HAS.HR.1**

CCSS Draw evidence from literary or informational texts to support analysis, reflection, and research. **CCSS.ELA.W.5.9**

Go *Digital!*

Investigate the lesson content with online whole-class presentation tools.

Background Information

Patrick Henry Patrick Henry, one of the great figures of the revolutionary generation, was a talented and effective orator, passionately devoted to the idea of individual liberty. Patrick Henry believed that the Constitution gave too much power to the federal government and demanded that the Constitution be amended to protect the liberties of individual Americans. In speech after speech, he denounced the absence of a bill of rights in the document. In the end, his arguments were persuasive, and James Madison introduced the amendments that became the Bill of Rights.

Analyze the Source

Inspect Have students read pages 280–281.

Find Evidence Use the questions below to check comprehension. Remind students to support their answers with text evidence.

Summarize What was the Antifederalists' objection to the Constitution? (The Antifederalists believed that the Constitution had a limited ability to protect Americans' liberties; they felt that the Constitution did not protect the press, did not affirm the need for trials by jury, and did not address the danger of standing armies in times of peace.) **DOK 2**

Identify What state gave the decisive ninth vote to ratify the Constitution? (New Hampshire) **DOK 1**

Make Connections Prompt students to make connections with the following question.

Draw Conclusions How was the fear of an autocratic federal government related to the Antifederalists' stand on the Constitution? (The colonists recently experienced Britain's autocratic government, and many of them wanted to avoid a repeat of that experience at all costs.) **DOK 3**

Analyze the Primary Source Point out the words "the liberties of people were placed on the sole chance of their rulers being good men." Ask students in a group to discuss what these words meant to Patrick Henry.

Draw Conclusions Why did Patrick Henry fear not having significant checks on the power of government leaders? (Patrick Henry believed that it was foolish to hope that rulers would be "good men." Other checks had to be put into place.)

Stop and Check

Perspectives Why did the Federalists continue to seek approval from all remaining states after the Constitution was ratified? (They worried that the remaining states, particularly New York and Virginia, would prevent the Constitution from being enforced.)

Find Details Explain to students that after they read and take notes, they should review and think about how the facts and details will help them answer the Essential Question.

Antifederalists objected to the Constitution by pointing to its limited ability to protect Americans' liberties. In his essay "Objections to This Constitution of Government," George Mason attacked the document. He argued, "There is no declaration of any kind, for preserving the liberty of the **press**, or the trial by **jury** in civil cases; nor against the danger of standing armies in time of peace."

Nine out of thirteen states' votes were required to pass the Constitution. Delaware, New Jersey, and Pennsylvania first ratified the Constitution in December of 1787. New Hampshire gave the decisive ninth vote to accept the Constitution in 1788.

Some worried that the remaining states would prevent the Constitution from being enforced. New York and Virginia were the two largest states in the country. Many of their leaders refused to support the Constitution as written. In Massachusetts, Elbridge Gerry had argued against the Constitution. He felt that "a free people," not the government, "are the proper guardians of their rights and liberties." Massachusetts Antifederalists demanded that the Constitution be revised to clearly indicate the rights of citizens.

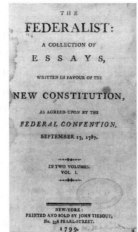

The Federalist Papers appeared in New York newspapers from 1787 to 1788.

PRIMARY SOURCE

In Their Words... Patrick Henry

Show me that age and country where the rights and liberties of the people were placed on the sole chance of their rulers being good men without a consequent loss of liberty! I say that the loss of that dearest privilege has ever followed, with absolute certainty, every such mad attempt.

—from a speech at the Virginia Constitution Ratifying Convention, 1788

James Madison, a Federalist, agreed to propose a Bill of Rights to Congress. The Bill of Rights included liberties that the Antifederalists believed the Constitution would not guarantee Americans. Madison promised to argue on behalf of the bill if the Antifederalists ratified the Constitution.

The agreement worked. Virginia and New York ratified the Constitution in 1788. The House of Representatives received the Bill of Rights in June 1789. North Carolina and Rhode Island then became the final states to ratify the Constitution.

Many Antifederalists would not support the Constitution without a Bill of Rights.

✓ Stop and Check

Perspectives Why did the Federalists continue to seek approval from all remaining states after the Constitution was ratified?

Find Details As you read, add additional information to the graphic organizer on page 233 in your Inquiry Journal.

TEXT: Patrick Henry, speaking before the Virginia Ratifying Convention, June 1788. PHOTO: Library of Congress, Prints & Photographs Division, LC-USZ62-70508

(t)McGraw-Hill Education; (b)iStockphoto.com/eezaznow

Research Companion, pp. 280–281

(EL) ENGLISH LEARNERS SCAFFOLD

ELD.PI.5.1 Exchanging information and ideas with others through oral collaborative discussions on a range of social and academic topics

Emerging

Build Vocabulary Guide students to understand the words *debate* and *ratification*. Have students say the words aloud. Tell students that the Spanish cognate for *debate* is *debate*. Ask students to give an example of a time when they debated or argued with someone else, or suggest that they draw a picture showing people debating. Tell students that a *debate* happens when people argue about a subject, and that *ratification* means giving consent or approval.

Expanding/Bridging

Collaborate Have students create a word list to describe the debates that occurred among delegates at the Constitutional Convention. Guide students to look for words from the text and to brainstorm words they know from their knowledge and experience. Remind students to use appropriate, academic vocabulary in their lists.

See the **Language Learner Teaching Guide** for more language support strategies.

Monitor and Differentiate

REACHING ALL LEARNERS

Approaching Level

Help students learn to identify main ideas and key details by asking and answering questions, such as "What is the text mostly about?"

On Level

Help students learn to identify main ideas and key details by asking and answering questions, such as "What is the text mostly about?" and "What important details are included?"

Beyond Level

Guide students to write a brief news story about the Debate Over Ratification. Have students imagine they are a reporter at the time of the debate writing a news story for an audience of colonists. Guide them to include main ideas and key details in their story.

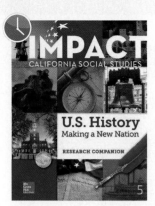

Research Companion
pp. 282–283

 STANDARDS

Explain how state constitutions that were established after 1776 embodied the ideals of the American Revolution and helped serve as models for the U.S. Constitution. **HSS.5.7.2**

Understand the fundamental principles of American constitutional democracy, including how the government derives its power from the people and the primacy of individual liberty. **HSS.5.7.3**

Understand how the Constitution is designed to secure our liberty by both empowering and limiting central government and compare the powers granted to citizens, Congress, the president, and the Supreme Court with those reserved to the states. **HSS.5.7.4**

CCSS Explain how an author uses reasons and evidence to support particular points in a text, identifying which reasons and evidence support which point(s). **CCSS.ELA.RI.5.8**

Go Digital!

Investigate the lesson content with online whole-class presentation tools.

Background Information

Supreme Court Rulings on the Bill of Rights One of the duties of the Supreme Court is to interpret the law. A famous example of this is the 1966 Supreme Court ruling that the Constitution's Fifth Amendment prohibition against self-incrimination applied when an individual was in police custody. In *Miranda v. Arizona,* the Court ruled that detained criminal suspects, prior to police questioning, must be informed of their constitutional rights to an attorney and against self-incrimination.

Inspect Have students read about the Bill of Rights on pages 282–283.

Find Evidence Use the questions below to check comprehension. Remind students to support their answers with text evidence.

> **Identify** What is the Bill of Rights? (The 10 Amendments added to the Constitution in 1791.) **DOK 1**

> **Cite Evidence** Although the Second Amendment protects the right of U.S. citizens to bear arms, the Supreme Court's Interpretation of that amendment sets two additional constitutional rules. What are these? (States can maintain militias, and the government may pass laws to control, but not prevent, the use of firearms by citizens.) **DOK 2**

> **Critique** Give your opinion about the importance to all citizens of Amendments Four through Eight. (Answers will vary, but students should note the importance of citizens having protection against unfair or arbitrary legal actions.) **DOK 3**

Make Connections Prompt students to make connections with the following question.

> **Draw Conclusions** Why do you think the founders added the Third Amendment to the Constitution? (They added it because during the Revolutionary War the British had forced colonists to house British soldiers.) **DOK 2**

Analyze the Images Direct students' attention to the images on pages 282 and 283. Say: *These images show examples of the Bill of Rights in action.* Encourage students to use the images in the text to help them understand the Bill of Rights.

- What parts of the Bill of Rights does the image of the protest illustrate? (the First Amendment right to free speech and the right to assemble peacefully)

- What parts of the Bill of Rights does the image of a courtroom scene illustrate? (the Fifth Amendment rights of accused persons and the Sixth Amendment right to a fair trial)

☑ Stop and Check

Connect to Now Work with a partner to reread the paragraph about the First Amendment at the top of the page. Discuss why you think many people consider the First Amendment "the most important for a functioning democracy." (Answers will vary, but students should note concrete examples of the real-life protections the First Amendment gives all American citizens.)

The Bill of Rights

In 1789, James Madison approached Congress with the first draft of a list of constitutional **amendments**. Congress chose 12 of these amendments to send to the states for approval. State leaders picked 10 of the amendments to ratify. Congress added the amendments, called the Bill of Rights, to the Constitution in December 1791.

Previously, government leaders had written documents defining the rights of their citizens. The British government signed a bill of rights in 1689. Several American states already had their own bills of rights by 1790. James Madison based his amendments partly on Virginia's bill of rights. Madison's Antifederalist rival, George Mason, had written this document in 1776.

The Bill of Rights was ratified after the main text of the Constitution, but that does not make the section any less important. The rights outlined in the Bill of Rights define many aspects of life in the United States. The Bill of Rights sets limits on the U.S. government and protects the basic rights of all U.S. citizens.

The first part of the Bill of Rights secures the individual rights of the citizens of the United States. The First Amendment protects five freedoms: freedom of religion, freedom of speech, freedom of the press, freedom of assembly, and freedom to petition.

The Second Amendment protects the right of U.S. citizens "to keep and bear arms." The Supreme Court's interpretation of the amendment sets two constitutional rules. First, states can maintain militias. And second, the government may pass laws to control, but not prevent, the use of firearms by citizens. The Third Amendment makes it unconstitutional for the government to force people to house soldiers.

The Fourth through Eighth Amendments guarantee the right to "due process." Due process of the law requires the government to follow a set of procedures when taking legal action against citizens. Due process is important in limiting the power of government. The amendments name specific actions that the government cannot take against its people.

The Ninth Amendment states that the rights of Americans extend beyond what is recorded in the Constitution. In the Tenth Amendment, the Constitution reserves all rights not provided to the federal government to be left for the states and the people.

Included in the Bill of Rights is freedom of speech, which includes the right to protest.

National Archives and Records Administration (NWDNS-306-SSM-4A-35-6)

Due process includes the right to trial by jury.

©McGraw-Hill Education, (bottom) Gary/Getty Images

✓ Stop and Check

Connect to Now Work with a partner to reread the paragraph about the First Amendment at the top of this page. Discuss why you think many people consider the First Amendment the most important for a functioning democracy in the United States.

COLLABORATE

Research Companion, pp. 282–283

ENGLISH LEARNERS SCAFFOLD

ELD.PI.5.1 Exchanging information and ideas with others through oral collaborative discussions on a range of social and academic topics

Emerging

Develop Vocabulary Work individually with students to understand the word *procedures*. Say the word aloud and have students repeat it. Explain that *procedures* are particular ways of doing things. Give examples, such as how your teacher expects you to behave once class begins. Suggest that students draw or act out a time when they followed a procedure.

Expanding/Bridging

Use Vocabulary Have students work in pairs to figure out the meaning of the words *procedures*, *outlined*, and *defined*. Say the words aloud and have students repeat them. Have volunteers suggest what the words mean. If needed, explain to students that *procedures* means particular ways of doing things, *outlined* means listed or described the most important features of something, and *defined* means explained or identified. Have students use the three words in sentences describing the Bill of Rights.

See the **Language Learner Teaching Guide** for more language support strategies.

Monitor and Differentiate

REACHING ALL LEARNERS

Approaching Level

Work with students to understand the importance of the First Amendment. Have small groups discuss specific examples of freedom of religion, freedom of speech, freedom of the press, freedom of assembly, and freedom to petition. Be sure that students understand that *petition* means to make a formal request to a government official.

Beyond Level

Have students do research on other examples of Supreme Court interpretations of the Bill of Rights. Suggest that they investigate *Texas v. Johnson* (1989) or *Bethel School District #43 v. Fraser* (1987). Students may also research background information on *Miranda v. Arizona* (1966). Have students share what they learned with the rest of the class.

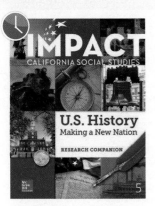

Research Companion
pp. 284–285

 STANDARDS

Understand the fundamental principles of American constitutional democracy, including how the government derives its power from the people and the primacy of individual liberty. **HSS.5.7.3**

Engage effectively in a range of collaborative discussions (one-on-one, in groups, and teacher-led) with diverse partners on *grade 5 topics and texts*, building on others' ideas and expressing their own clearly.
CCSS.ELA.SL.5.1

Go Digital!

Investigate the lesson content with online whole-class presentation tools.

Background Information

Failed Constitutional Amendments It is very difficult for an amendment to make it through the entire ratification process. More than 11,000 amendments have been proposed in congressional history. Yet, since the Bill of Rights was passed in 1791, only 17 amendments have been added to the Constitution (making 27 total amendments). Among the proposed amendments, some of the most unusual were an 1893 proposal to rename the United States "the United States of the Earth" and a 1933 proposal to outlaw multi-millionaires by having incomes over one million dollars applied to the national debt.

Analyze the Source

Inspect Have students read pages 284–285.

Find Evidence Use the questions below to check comprehension.

Summarize What are the two ways to propose an amendment to the Constitution? (Amendments can be proposed with the support of two-thirds of Congress or if two-thirds of state legislators call for a national convention.) **DOK 2**

Analyze Why was it necessary to ratify the Thirteenth and Fourteenth Amendments before the Fifteenth Amendment could be ratified? (The Thirteenth Amendment called for the abolition of slavery, and the Fourteenth Amendment gave citizenship to former slaves. Without these two amendments, the Fifteenth Amendment, which allowed formerly enslaved black men the right to vote, could not have been passed.) **DOK 3**

Then and Now Have students reread the text and review the images on p. 285.

Identify Who had voting rights up until 1870? (only white males)

Explain What was the impact of the Voting Rights Act of 1965? (The law put in place rules to help enforce the Fifteenth Amendment and voting rights for all Americans.)

Analyze Visuals What do the two images show? (women demanding the right to vote; volunteers registering voters)

Make Connections

Draw Conclusions Why are the Thirteenth, Fourteenth, and Fifteenth Amendments called the Civil War Amendments? (These amendment were all passed in the aftermath of the Civil War. They were designed to protect the rights of freed slaves.) **DOK 2**

Analyze the Image Direct students' attention to the image on p. 284.

- What does the image show? (white males in colonial government)

- What does the image tell you about who had voting rights in colonial America? (Only white males had a voice in colonial governments.)

✓ Stop and Check

Connect to Now Have students discuss how their law guarantees liberties protected by the amendment. (Answers will vary, but students should choose an amendment mentioned in the section that they think needs stronger enforcement and create a law that would provide it.)

Amendments and Expanding Rights

The Bill of Rights introduced the first ten amendments to the Constitution. Seventeen more amendments have since been added. The Constitution's writers knew that the constitutional system needed flexibility. They wrote Article Five of the Constitution to define a process for amending the Constitution.

To become a part of the Constitution, an amendment must go through proposal and ratification. There are two ways to propose an amendment and two ways to ratify it.

Amendments may be proposed with the support of two-thirds of Congress. Alternatively, an amendment can be proposed if two-thirds of state legislatures call for a national convention. The amendment can then be ratified through approval by three-fourths of state legislatures.

Many of the seventeen amendments outside of the Bill of Rights expanded voting rights. In 1870, ratification of the Fifteenth Amendment allowed formerly enslaved African American men to vote. The Fifteenth Amendment would not be possible without the Thirteenth and Fourteenth Amendments. These amendments are sometimes called the Civil War amendments. The Thirteenth Amendment made slavery illegal. The Fourteenth Amendment guaranteed African Americans U.S. citizenship and the same legal rights as whites.

Only white males had a voice in colonial governments.

Then and Now

Voting Then

Until 1870, only white men could vote. Even after several amendments guaranteed voting rights for other groups such as women, nonwhite citizens were often discriminated against. In many cases, the government has tried to enforce the amendments by passing voter protection laws. For example, the Voting Rights Act of 1965 put into place specific rules that helped enforce the Fifteenth Amendment.

Voting Now

Today, most United States citizens who are 18 years or older can vote. U.S. citizens living in other countries can submit their ballots by mail. Different states have different laws about whether people who have been convicted of certain crimes can vote. States also require varying types of registration and identification to vote on Election Day.

Protests for voting rights for women led to the ratification of the Nineteenth Amendment in 1920. The Twenty-Third Amendment gave residents of Washington, D.C., voting rights in 1961. Three years later, the practice of poll taxes was made illegal in the Twenty-Fourth Amendment. Poll taxes, or fees citizens had to pay to vote, had prevented many people from voting, especially African Americans in the South.

Until 1971, only citizens 21 and older could vote. Some Americans argued that if 18-year-olds could fight in wars, they should be allowed to vote. The Twenty-Sixth Amendment set the new voting age at 18.

✓ Stop and Check

Connect to Now Choose one of the amendments mentioned in the section. Write a law that would help enforce the amendment. How does your law help guarantee the liberties protected by the amendment?

284 Lesson 3 How Do the Constitution and Bill of Rights Impact Citizens?

Lesson 3 285

Research Companion, pp. 284–285

ENGLISH LEARNERS SCAFFOLD

ELD.PI.5.6 Reading closely literary and informational texts and viewing multimedia to determine how meaning is conveyed explicitly and implicitly through language

Emerging

Develop Language Have students look at the image on p. 284 of white males in colonial government. Have them point to and/or describe what they see and what they think is important in the image. Ask students say the words *voice, colonial,* and *government* aloud with you. Tell students that here the word *voice* means the right to express an opinion. Use the image to make sure that students understand that in colonial government only white males had a voice.

Expanding/Bridging

Use Language Have students look at the image on p. 284 of white males in colonial government. Have them describe what they see and what they think is important in the image. Tell students that here the word *voice* means the right to express an opinion. Have students use the words *voice, colonial,* and *government* in sentences describing who had rights in colonial America.

See the **Language Learner Teaching Guide** for more language support strategies.

Monitor and Differentiate

REACHING ALL LEARNERS

Approaching Level

Work with students to understand the process of proposing and ratifying amendments. Make sure that students understand the words *flexibility* (the ability to be easily changed or modified), *propose* (to put an idea forward) and *ratification* (the act of giving formal consent or approval). Have students use the words *flexibility, propose,* and *ratification* in sentences describing how the Constitution allows for adding amendments.

Beyond Level

Have students do research on either past or current proposed amendments that have failed to become ratified.

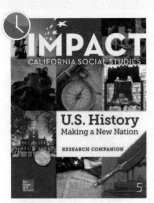

Research Companion
pp. 286–287

Discuss the meaning of the American creed that calls on citizens to safeguard the liberty of individual Americans within a unified nation, to respect the rule of law, and to preserve the Constitution. **HSS.5.7.5**

CCSS Engage effectively in a range of collaborative discussions (one-on-one, in groups, and teacher-led) with diverse partners on *grade 5 topics and texts*, building on others' ideas and expressing their own clearly. **CCSS.ELA.SL.5.1**

Go *Digital!*

Investigate the lesson content with online whole-class presentation tools.

Background Information

The American's Creed In 1916, on the eve of America's entry into World War I, Henry Sterling Chaplain, Commissioner of Education of New York State, devised a national writing competition intended to foster patriotism and civic responsibility. More than three thousand people entered the contest, and William Tyler Page was the winner. William Tyler Page had come to Washington at the age of thirteen to serve as a Capitol page and later as an employee of the Capitol Building. Page, who received $1,000 for his winning entry, recited "The American's Creed" on the Capitol steps.

Analyze the Source

Inspect Have students read pages 286–287.

Find Evidence Use the questions below to check comprehension. Remind students to support their answers with text evidence.

> **Identify** What citizenship duties does William Tyler Page list in "The American's Creed"? (to love the country, to support its Constitution, to obey laws, to respect the flag, and to defend the country against all enemies) **DOK 1**

> **Use Context Clues** What is the meaning of the word *responsibilities*? (duties; things you are obligated to do) **DOK 2**

> **Draw Conclusions** Why is citizens' participation in juries an essential part of ensuring due process? (In many cases, juries make the final decision about whether someone is guilty or innocent. A trial by jury is part of the due process promised to American citizens. Without citizens' participation in the jury system there would by no trials by juries.) **DOK 2**

Make Connections

> **Summarize** In addition to voting, how can citizens participate in politics? (Citizens can convey important information to government leaders, sign petitions to argue for change, or protest or march for causes they think need attention.) **DOK 2**

Analyze the Images Direct students' attention to the images on pages 286 and 287.

• Examine the image of people at voting booths. What does it tell you about the voting process? (that people's votes are private)

• Look at the image of citizens expressing opinions at a town meeting. What does it tell you about the First Amendment right to free speech? (Because of free speech, people have the right to express themselves even if others don't agree with their opinions.)

PRODUCTIVE
✓ Stop and Check

Perspectives Have students discuss the Creed as well as other responsibilities they believe are important for citizens. (Answers will vary, but students should address specific responsibilities not mentioned in the Creed and give reasons for why they think these responsibilities are important.)

Citizenship 👥

Civic Responsibilities

Citizens of the United States are responsible for participating in certain aspects of the government. William Tyler Page expressed these responsibilities in his 1917 patriotic statement "The American's Creed." He wrote that Americans had a duty "to love it, to support its Constitution, to obey its laws, to respect its flag, and to defend it against all enemies."

Obeying the law is a civic responsibility because it contributes to the safety of U.S. citizens. The government can also call on citizens to defend the nation. People can sometimes be required to join the military if the country is at war. U.S. citizens have a civic responsibility to pay taxes. State and federal governments use taxes for programs and projects that better the country. Roads, government buildings, and public schools rely on tax money for maintenance and improvements.

As a part of due process, the Sixth Amendment guarantees the right to a trial by jury. Americans must judge court cases as part of a jury. In many cases, the jury makes the final decision about whether someone is guilty or innocent. Without citizens' participation in juries, Americans could not be guaranteed their right to due process.

One important way citizens can participate in politics is by expressing their opinions at local-government meetings.

Citizens can help their government by exercising their voting rights.

Participating in Politics

U.S. citizens have the right to vote. Participating in elections is not required, though. Our government depends on people exercising their right to vote. Citizens of the United States are responsible for guiding the direction of the country. Responsible citizens stay informed about the issues and candidates. Each person's vote influences the direction of government. Voting is one of the ways citizens make their voices heard.

Citizens participate in United States politics in other ways. Government leaders use information from citizens to act in the public interest. People can write, email, or call their elected officials. They can sign petitions to argue for change in government. Protesting and marching are other direct ways for citizens to express their support or opposition to a political position.

Citizens can also contribute to the nation by volunteering. Volunteers often respond to civic issues that affect the health, safety, and liberties of people in the United States. Political campaigns also depend on volunteers to reach voters.

Finally, citizens may serve as public officials. Any citizen who fulfills basic requirements is eligible to run for office. Public officials help determine the course of the country.

✓ Stop and Check
COLLABORATE

Perspectives Work with a partner to reread the section on civic responsibilities. Talk about the quotation from "The American's Creed." What do you think about the duties mentioned in the Creed? What other responsibilities do you think are important for citizens in a country?

What Do You Think? Should Americans be required to vote?

286 Lesson 3 How Do the Constitution and Bill of Rights Impact Citizens?

Lesson 3 287

Research Companion, pp. 286–287

EL ENGLISH LEARNERS SCAFFOLD

ELD.PI.5.6 Reading closely literary and informational texts and viewing multimedia to determine how meaning is conveyed explicitly and implicitly through language

Emerging

Develop Language
Use the images in the lesson to help students understand civic responsibilities. Have students examine the image of people in voting booths on p. 286. Ask students to name or point to parts of the image they think are important. Supply vocabulary as needed. Have students draw pictures or write a word describing *voting booth* and *citizen*.

Expanding/Bridging

Use Language Working in pairs, have students discuss the information presented in the images. Suggest that partners compile a list of words describing both images. Help students with difficult vocabulary as needed. Then have students write a paragraph summarizing how citizens fulfill their civic responsibilities by voting and participating in town meetings.

See the **Language Learner Teaching Guide** for more language support strategies.

Monitor and Differentiate

REACHING ALL LEARNERS

Approaching Level

Work with students to be sure they understand the civic responsibilities of American citizens. Use the images and text to help students understand that voting and participating in town meetings is a part of exercising civic responsibility.

On Level

Work with students to be sure they understand the civic responsibilities of American citizens. Use the images and the text to be sure students understand that obeying laws, defending the nation, paying taxes, serving on juries, voting, and participating in politics are all civic responsibilities.

3 REPORT

Report Your Findings

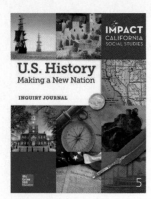

Inquiry Journal
pp. 234–235

STANDARDS

CCSS Integrate information from several texts on the same topic in order to write or speak about the subject knowledgeably. **CCSS.ELA.RI.5.9**

Write informative/explanatory texts to examine a topic and convey ideas and information clearly. **CCSS.ELA.W.5.2**

Draw evidence from literary or informational texts to support analysis, reflection, and research. **CCSS.ELA.W.5.9**

Engage effectively in a range of collaborative discussions (one-on-one, in groups, and teacher-led) with diverse partners on *grade 5 topics and texts*, building on others' ideas and expressing their own clearly. **CCSS.ELA.SL.5.**

Go Digital!

- Students can go online to report their findings. Assess their responses online.

- Students can access the online graphic organizer to capture ideas from their investigation.

Think About It

Students will review their research about the purpose of the Bill of Rights. Remind students to review the information they gathered and recorded on the graphic organizer. Direct students back to pages 278–287 of their Research Companion if they need more information.

Write About It

Give an Example Have students read the prompt. Explain to students that an effective comic strip showing a particular amendment in action will show figures and dialogue that demonstrate how the amendment affects real people's lives. Remind students to include the following elements in their response:

- at least two comic strip characters who will show the amendment in action

- dialogue from the characters that demonstrates the amendment in action

Use the rubric on p. T606 to evaluate students' work.

Talk About It

Explain Have students exchange their comic strips with a partner who chose a different amendment to illustrate. Have partners discuss likenesses and differences in their comic strips.

- Explain that students should take turns discussing and explaining their comic strips.

- Remind students to be ready to cite evidence from the text that supports their comic strips.

- Remind students to follow the rules of appropriate classroom conversation.

Connect to the Essential Question

Read the prompt aloud to students. Ask them the following guiding questions:

- What concepts from this lesson most transformed the nation and its people? (Answers will vary, but students may say that the push for civil liberties led by such Antifederalists as Patrick Henry and George Mason led to the Bill of Rights and greatly transformed the nation and the freedoms enjoyed by individual citizens.)

- What concepts and ideas are still important to our nation today? (Answers will vary, but students may say that the Constitution and the Bill of Rights have enduring importance, while some parts of them are subject to change through amendments.)

Remind students to use the space provided in their journal to jot down notes.

Report Your Findings

Think About It

What is the purpose of the Bill of Rights?

Write About It

Give an Example
Illustrate Choose one right protected by the Bill of Rights. Write and illustrate a comic strip that shows that particular amendment in action.

Talk About It

Explain
Work with a partner who chose a different amendment in the Bill of Rights. Read each other's comic strip, and discuss situations from your own lives in which the amendments would provide you with freedoms.

 Connect to the EQ
Citizenship

Pull It Together
How does the Bill of Rights help define what it means to be a citizen of the United States?

Responses will vary, but students should provide specific ways the Bill of Rights defines the limits of government and protects basic rights of citizens.

Inquiry Project Notes

McGraw-Hill Education

234 Lesson 3 How Do the Constitution and Bill of Rights Impact Citizens?

Lesson 3 235

Inquiry Journal, pp. 234–235

 ENGLISH LEARNERS SCAFFOLD

ELD.PI.5.10 Writing literary and informational texts to present, describe, and explain ideas and information, using appropriate technology

Emerging	Expanding/Bridging
Develop Language Display examples of comic strips. Explain the use of characters and dialogue (in speech bubbles). Have students choose an amendment that interests them. Students may have an easier time drawing characters than writing dialogue. Help them create words or short phrases to go in the speech bubbles.	**Refine Language** Working with a partner, have students work with a partner to refine the dialogue in their speech bubbles. Supply vocabulary to students struggling to fill in the speech bubbles in their comic strips. Urge partners to try to make the words in the speech bubbles as precise as possible.

See the **Language Learner Teaching Guide** for more language support strategies.

Monitor and Differentiate

REACHING ALL LEARNERS

Special Needs

Provide students with an amendment to focus on. Then guide students to create their comic strip step-by-step. First have them draw the background scene, and then have them draw a person who is the subject of the scene. Then have them write dialogue in a speech bubble for that person.

Beyond Level

Have students review some recent graphic novels and discuss how their comic strips could be adapted into a full graphic novel. Guide students to create a proposal and a table of contents for such a graphic novel, and have them explain how their comic strip would fit into the larger work.

Know what your students know!

Lesson Task
Report Your Findings

Use this rubric to evaluate students' response.

Give an Example Students choose one right protected by the Bill of Rights and then create a comic strip that shows that amendment in action.

Explain Students talk to classmates about their findings. They take turns discussing how the activity helped them understand how the Bill of Rights protects the rights of American citizens.

Performance Task Evaluation Rubric

	4	3	2	1
Historical Understanding	Strong understanding of the Bill of Rights and how it protects the rights of American citizens	Adequate understanding of the Bill of Rights and how it protects the rights of American citizens	Uneven understanding of the Bill of Rights and how it protects the rights of American citizens	No understanding of the Bill of Rights and how it protects the rights of American citizens
Illustrate and Write Dialogue	Illustrates and writes dialogue that clearly shows an understanding of the rights protected by one of the amendments in the Bill of Rights	Illustrates and writes dialogue that adequately shows an understanding of the rights protected by one of the amendments in the Bill of Rights	Illustrates and writes dialogue that somewhat shows an understanding of the rights protected by one of the amendments in the Bill of Rights	No illustrations or dialogue showing an understanding of the rights protected by one of the amendments in the Bill of Rights
Support with Evidence	Facts and details communicated through illustrations and dialogue provide thorough evidence	Facts and details communicated through illustrations and dialogue provide adequate evidence	Facts and details communicated through illustrations and dialogue provide uneven evidence	Facts and details communicated through illustrations and dialogue are missing, or no supporting evidence is provided
Explain	Speaks clearly and at an understandable pace Speaks in complete sentences throughout the discussion	Speaks clearly during most of the discussion Speaks in complete sentences through most of the discussion	At times speaker is unclear Mixes complete and incomplete sentences	Speaks unclearly throughout the discussion. Does not use complete sentences

Lesson Assessment

Go Digital!

- Have students complete the Chapter 6 Lesson 3 Assessment online to monitor their understanding of the lesson content.

California Smarter Balanced Assessment Connections!

Standards Covered	Lesson Task	Lesson Assessment	Alignment with California Smarter Balanced Assessment
History Social Science Content 5.7.2; 5.7.3; 5.7.4; 5.7.5	✔	✔	Claim 1 Targets 8, 9, 10, 11
History Social Science Analysis Skills Chronological and Spatial Thinking 5.1; 5.3 Research, Evidence, and Point of View 5.1; 5.2 Historical Interpretation 5.1; 5.3	✔	✔	Claim 1 Targets 11, 12
Writing W.5.2	✔	✔	Claim 2 Target 11, 12
Research and Inquiry W.5.9	✔	✔	Claim 4 Targets 11, 12
Reading RI.5.9	✔	✔	Claim 1 Targets 11, 12
Speaking and Listening SL.5.1	✔		Claim 3 Targets 8, 9, 11

Inquiry Journal
pp. 236–237

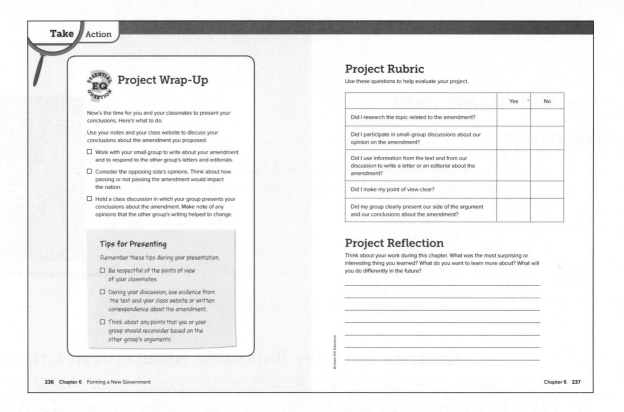

Go Digital!

Look online for the EQ Inquiry Project rubric.

 Inquiry Project Wrap-Up

Have students share their inquiry projects by presenting the pros and cons of their amendment.

- Before students present the pros and cons of their amendment, discuss the wrap-up steps with them, making sure they know what's expected in their presentations.

- Allow time after each presentation for a Q-and-A session.

Tips for Presenting

Discuss the tips for presenting with students and the importance of communicating effectively with their audience. Remind students that it's also important to be a good listener.

Project Rubric

Discuss each question in the Project Rubric with students. If students have worked as part of a group to develop their projects, you might want to have them work as a group to address each question in the rubric.

Project Reflection

Student reflections can focus on the work they did as part of the group or their individual performance on the project. Give groups time to discuss each phase of their projects and reflect on their work.

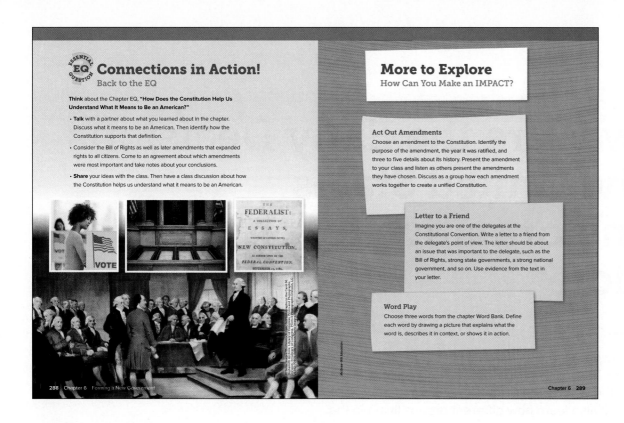

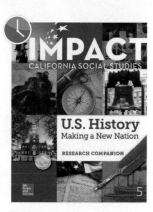

Research Companion
pp. 288–289

Connections in Action

To help focus students' conversations, you may want to discuss the EQ with the entire class before students discuss their ideas with a partner. Remind students to think about evidence they can provide that will support their ideas. After students present, allow time for others to ask questions.

More to Explore

Act Out Amendments Remind students to choose an amendment that interests or surprises them. Guide students to choose the most important details about the amendment to present to the class.

Letter to a Friend If students find it easier to write to a real person, have student pairs work together, each pretending to be a different delegate to the Constitutional Convention. Encourage students to write to each other from the perspective of the Founding Fathers.

Word Play Encourage students to consider the part of speech of each word. Encourage students to act out the applicable words for a small group, and have the group guess what the words are.

How Were the Early Decisions of the United States Transformative for the Nation?

In This Chapter ...

Students will investigate the early decisions that lawmakers made and how those decisions shaped the new nation. They will analyze how inventions and innovations launched the United States into the nineteenth century and created new possibilities for travel and expansion. They will also learn how different groups living in the United States interacted.

Lesson 1　Early Leaders and Decisions

Lesson 2　Advancements in Technology and Transportation

Lesson 3　People of the Young Republic

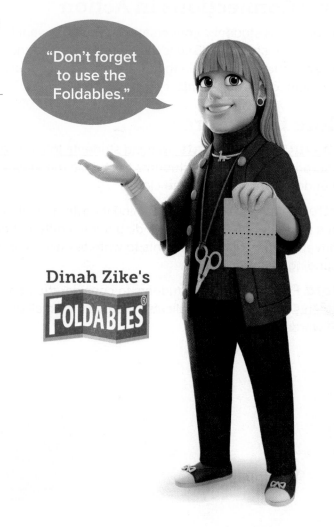

"Don't forget to use the Foldables."

Dinah Zike's

FOLDABLES®

CHAPTER STANDARDS

✔ Students trace the colonization, immigration, and settlement patterns of the American people from 1789 to the mid-1800s, with emphasis on the role of economic incentives, effects of the physical and political geography, and transportation systems. **HSS.5.8**

1 ENGAGE

Inquiry Journal
pp. 238–241

 **Inquiry Project**

Which change will you choose?

- **Explore Words**

- *Go Digital!*
  - IMPACT Chapter Video: Life in the Young Republic

2 INVESTIGATE

Research Companion
pp. 290–297

- **Step Into Time and Place**

- **Connect Through Literature**
  The Petticoat Skipper
  by Josephine Rascoe Keenan

- **People You Should Know**

Weekly Explorer Magazine pp. 84–99

3 REPORT

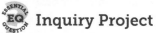

Inquiry Journal
pp. 266–267

Inquiry Project

Which change will you choose?

 Short on Time? Look for the clock to teach core content in less time.

CULTIVATE MEANING AND SUPPORT LANGUAGE

Language Learner Teaching Guide,
pp. 158–159

Content Objectives

- Demonstrate understanding about transformative changes in government, communication, and transportation in the early years of the United States.

Language Objectives

- Explore cause and effect.
- Use and identify past perfect tense verbs.
- Ask and answer questions.

CONNECT TO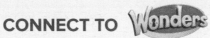

Unit 1, Week 4
Inventions

Read Aloud
"A Pioneer of Photography"

Reading/Writing Workshop
"Fantasy Becomes Fact"

Literature Anthology/Paired Selection
The Boy Who Invented TV
"Time to Invent"

Leveled Readers
Snapshot! The Story of George Eastman
and "The Ultimate Birthday"

CONNECT TO SCIENCE

Explore how inventions, such as the cotton gin, led to agricultural and environmental changes across specific regions.

CONNECT TO MATH

Compare and contrast populations through time.

ASSESSMENT

Monitor Progress to
Know What Your Students Know

Choose the assessment options that work best for you and your students.

BEFORE
PRE-TEST

Measure students' content knowledge before you begin the chapter with the following questions.

🕐 Quick Check

✓ What was the Louisiana Purchase, and how did it transform the United States?

✓ How could easy means of communication change the nation?

✓ Why did some groups in the young republic struggle for rights and freedom?

1. Ask students to produce a response to each question.

2. When all students have responded, ask them to rate how confident they are in their answers on a scale from 1 – not very confident to 5 – very confident.

3. Collect students' responses and review them for misconceptions, factual errors, and to inform instruction. You may wish to return to these questions as students investigate chapter 7.

4. **Don't Forget!** Revisit students' quick check responses with them. If students change their response, ask them to support the change with text evidence. You may wish to have students respond to a different prompt to measure their content knowledge, such as *How did the steamboat change American travel?*

EVERY LESSON
ONGOING ASSESSMENT

Use the lesson tools to monitor the IMPACT of your instruction.

☑ Stop and Check

Use the quick question prompts to monitor student comprehension of the content. The **Stop and Check** questions prompt students to make connections to their world today, engage in discussions to deepen their understanding of the content, and to look at different perspectives.

🔎 Report Your Findings

The lesson task, **Report Your Findings**, can be used to measure student understanding of the lesson content and ability to effectively express their understanding. See the Lesson Assessment pp. T644, T664, and T686 for task-specific evaluation rubrics.

(Go *Digital!*) Lesson Assessment

Use the **Lesson Assessment** to monitor student understanding of the lesson content. Have students complete the assessment online. See pp. T645, T665, and T687 for California Smarter Balanced Assessments Connections.

EVERY CHAPTER
POST TEST

Evaluate student understanding of core chapter content with one or more of the following assessment options.

 Connections in Action

Use the **Connections in Action** to evaluate student understanding of core chapter content through discussion.

 Inquiry Project

Use the **EQ Inquiry Project** to measure student understanding of the chapter content and ability to effectively express their understanding. See the EQ Inquiry Project Wrap Up below for a task-specific evaluation rubric.

	4	3	2	1
Historical Understanding	Strong understanding of how early changes transformed the young United States	Adequate understanding of how early changes transformed the young United States	Uneven understanding of how early changes transformed the young United States	No understanding of how early changes transformed the young United States
State an Opinion	Clearly states which change was most transformative	Adequately states which change was most transformative	Somewhat clearly states which change was most transformative	Does not state an opinion or student does not show understanding of the task
Support Opinion with Multimedia	Incorporates relevant and adequate visuals into presentation to support opinion	Incorporates visuals into presentation to support opinion	Incorporates few or irrelevant visuals into presentation	Incorporates no visuals into presentation to support opinion
Presentation	Speaks slowly and clearly, staying on topic Addresses how each piece of visual evidence supports opinion	Speaks clearly and stays on topic Addresses how evidence supports opinion	Sometimes speaks unclearly or is disorganized Does not explain each piece of evidence or show how it supports opinion	Does not speak clearly and is difficult to follow Does not explain or include any evidence

(Go *Digital!*) Chapter Benchmark Assessments

Use the chapter tests to monitor student understanding of the chapter History-Social Science standards and content. Have students complete the assessment online.

pp. 84–99

⏱ Short on Time?
Use the Weekly Explorer Magazine during your reading block.

Go Digital!
Look online for the Weekly Explorer Magazine Teaching Guide.

WordBlast
Remind students to look for the Word Blasts as they read the Explorer Magazine.

FOLDABLES
Encourage students to use the Notetaking Foldables as they gather more information.

Weekly Explorer Magazine

The Weekly Explorer Magazine is designed to provide students with more information to use as they dig deeper into the **changes that transformed the young United States.** The articles in a variety of formats explore the Essential Question and support the Inquiry Project.

Engage

Build background for students and share any information needed to provide a context for the chapter topic. Have students read the Essential Question and the Table of Contents.

Analyze the Visual Discuss the opening visual (photograph, photo essay, artwork) on the second page of the Magazine chapter. Help students connect the visual to the chapter topic and the Essential Question.

Analyze the Sources

Students will read and analyze the articles, graphic novel, poems, songs, literature excerpts, primary sources, and infographics.

Read and Analyze Before reading, provide any additional information you think students will need about the topics. Then guide students through the three-step process to read and analyze the articles.

1 Inspect Have students skim the article or articles on a page or multiple pages. Ask questions to help students recall and retell key ideas.

- What is this article mostly about?
- Who is _____?

2 Find Evidence Have students reread the articles and look for details they might have missed. Ask additional questions to help them read more closely.

- What details do you notice in the photographs?
- Why was _____ important?

3 Make Connections Have students work in pairs or small groups to discuss prompts that help them connect the article(s) to other texts, their own lives, current ideas and issues, and other topics.

- How is _____similar to what we do today?
- How do you think _____ felt about what happened?
- What do you think about _____?

 Bibliography

The following suggested resources may help students' investigation of the chapter content.

EXPLORE PEOPLE, PLACES, AND EVENTS

▶ **The Amazing Impossible Erie Canal**
by Cheryle Harness; Aladdin Picture Books, 1999.

▶ **Chains**
by Laurie Halse Anderson; Atheneum Books for Young Readers, 2008.

▶ **Children of the Wild West**
By Russell Fredeman; Houghton Mifflin, 1992.

Perspectives

▶ **The Dreadful, Smelly Colonies: The Disgusting Details About Life in Colonial America**
by Elizabeth Raum; Capstone Press, 2011.

▶ **Duel! Burr and Hamilton's Deadly War of Words**
by Dennis Brindell Fradin; Walker & Company, 2008.

▶ **Fever 1793**
by Laure Halse Andreson; Simon & Schuster Books for Young Readers, 2002.

▶ **The Ingenious Mr. Peale: Painter, Patriot, and Man of Science**
by Janet Wilson; Atheneum, 1996.

Perspectives

▶ **The Journal of Jesse Smoke: A Cherokee Boy**
by Joseph Bruchac; Scholastic, 2001.

▶ **Path of the Pale Horse**
by Paul Fleischman; Harper & Rowe, 1983.

▶ **Return to the Island**
by Gloria Whelan; Harper Collins, 2002.

▶ **Science in Colonial America**
by Brendan January; Franklin Watts, 1999.

EXPLORE MUSIC

Did you know? As the newly-born United States of America began to make its way in the world of nations, the music of the new nation reflected a new feeling of patriotism. Songs like **Hail, Columbia (The President's March)** were written to glorify the new democracy. In fact, the words of the song were written by Joseph Hopkinson, son of Francis Hopkinson. Francis Hopkinson was a signer of the Declaration of Independence and a designer of the first official American flag.

Did you know? Perhaps the most famous song of the new republic is our National Anthem **The Star-Spangled Banner**. Written by Francis Scott Key in 1814 during the War of 1812, the lyrics tell of how during the Battle of Fort McHenry, the American flag (the "star-spangled banner" of the title) remained in full view during the battle and was not lowered in defeat.

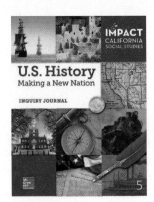

Inquiry Journal
pp. 238–241

 STANDARDS

Students trace the colonization, immigration, and settlement patterns of the American people from 1789 to the mid-1800s, with emphasis on the role of economic incentives, effects of the physical and political geography, and transportation systems. **HSS.5.8**

Write opinion pieces on topics or texts, supporting a point of view with reasons and information. **CCSS.ELA.W.5.1**

Draw evidence from literary or informational texts to support analysis, reflection, and research. **CCSS.ELA.W.5.9**

Go Digital!

Explore Words: Interactive vocabulary activities support students as they explore the chapter words.

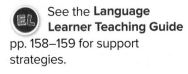
See the **Language Learner Teaching Guide** pp. 158–159 for support strategies.

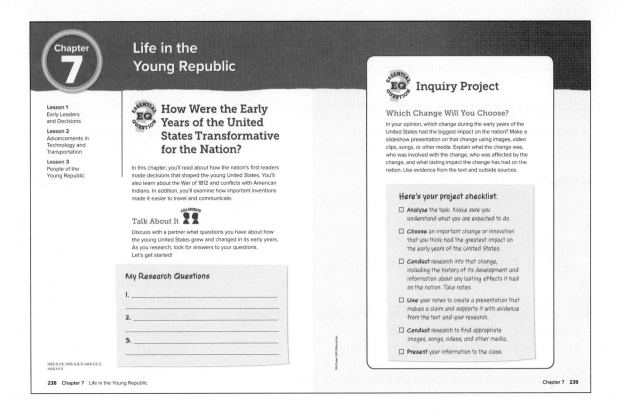

 # How Were the Early of the United States Transformative for the Nation?

Have students read the Chapter Essential Question on p. 238.

Talk About It

- Prompt students to write what they would like to know about life in the young republic after reading the chapter.

- After jotting down their questions, have students discuss their questions with partners.

 # Inquiry Project

Which change will you choose?

- Have students read aloud the EQ Inquiry Project.

- Tell students that they will use information gathered from the chapter and from independent research to complete the project.

- Make certain students understand the task by reviewing each step of the project.

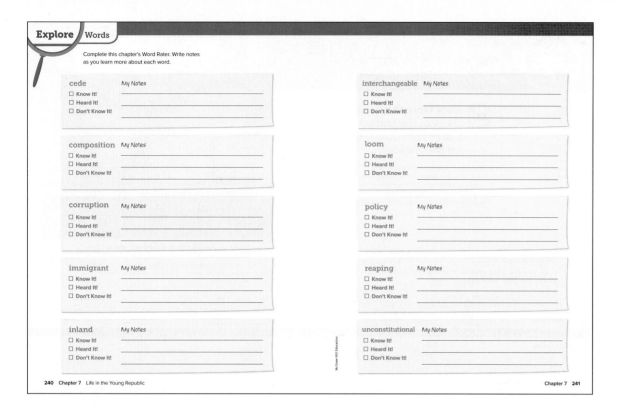

Explore Words

- **Academic/Domain-Specific Vocabulary** Read the words aloud to students. Explain to students that these are words they will learn more about in the chapter.

- **Word Rater** Have students place a checkmark in one of the three boxes below each word, indicating that they "Know It," "Heard It," or "Don't Know It."

  - ✔ **Know It** Tell students that if they know the word, they should write its meaning on the lines provided.

  - ✔ **Heard It** Tell students that if they have heard, or are familiar with the word, they should write what they know about it on the lines provided. Remind them to take notes about the word as they encounter it.

  - ✔ **Don't Know It** If they do not know the word's meaning, tell them to write down its meaning when they encounter the word in the chapter.

🔍 Explore Words Routine

Remind students that when they come to an unfamiliar word or phrase in their research, they should follow these steps to determine its meaning.

1. Look around the word or phrase for clues to unlock its meaning.

2. Look inside the word or phrase for word part clues.

3. Look up the word in other resources.

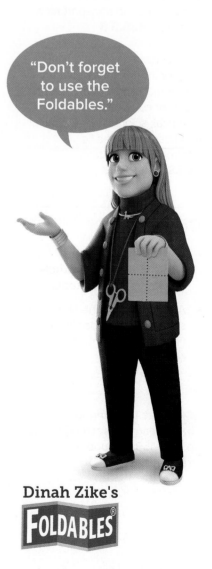

"Don't forget to use the Foldables."

Dinah Zike's
FOLDABLES®

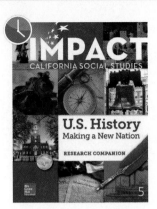

Research Companion
pp. 290–295

Life in the Young Republic

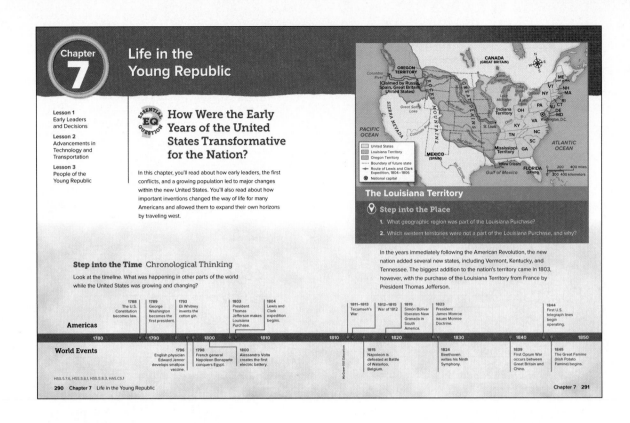

 ## STANDARDS

Students trace the colonization, immigration, and settlement patterns of the American people from 1789 to the mid-1800s, with emphasis on the role of economic incentives, effects of the physical and political geography, and transportation systems. **HSS.5.8**

(ccss) Explain the relationships or interactions between two or more individuals, events, ideas, or concepts in a historical, scientific, or technical text based on specific information in the text. **CCSS.ELA.RI.5.3**

Go *Digital!*

- Investigate the young republic with online whole-class presentation tools.
- Analyze the online literature selection so students can find evidence and make connections.

See the **Language Learner Teaching Guide** pp. 158–159 for support strategies.

Step Into the Time

Have students read over the events on the timeline, first examining the events from the Americas and then the events from around the world.

- What was happening to American agriculture while Napoleon was fighting wars in Egypt and Belgium? (The cotton gin was transforming American agriculture.)

- Would people have been able to listen to Beethoven's *Ninth Symphony* during the War of 1812? (No, because Beethoven wrote it in 1824, and the war ended in 1815.)

Step Into the Place

In partners or in small groups, have students examine the map on p. 291 and answer the questions beneath it.

1. Which geographic region was part of the Louisiana Purchase?
   (the Midwest and the West, including modern states of Iowa, Missouri, Arkansas, Oklahoma, Kansas, Nebraska, South Dakota, and parts of Montana, Wyoming, Colorado, Texas, North Dakota, Minnesota, and Louisiana.)

2. What western territories were not a part of the Louisiana Purchase, and why? (Possible response: Spanish Territory, Oregon Territory, and British Territory were controlled by powers other than France. Spanish Territory included most of the Southwest, California, and Mexico. Great Britain controlled most of Canada, and the Oregon Territory in the northwest was claimed by all three nations.)

Connect Through Literature

The
Petticoat Skipper
by Josephine Rascoe Keenan

Illustrated by Sue Todd

Mary grew up working in a store, but always dreamed of captaining a steamboat. However, Mary was discouraged from her dream when her mother told her, "Steamboat captains don't wear petticoats." Mary got her chance to live on a steamboat after marrying a steamboat captain, but would she ever be captain of her own ship?

On November 18, 1890, when I was twenty-two and he was twenty-eight, I married Captain Gordon Greene. I loved the dusky smells of river warehouses and the sight of goods on the wharves ready to be loaded. My blood ran faster when the showboat steamed by with its calliope piping bright tunes. A nip of excitement filled the air when the steamboat whistle blew. Folks rushed to the riverbanks to see her tall stacks puffing smoke billows and the paddle wheel splashing through the water.

Serving as a lifeline to folks living on the river, we transported all kinds of supplies on the steamboat. The big pine packing boxes held yard goods. (That's fabrics sold by the yard, not flower seeds!) We hauled all kinds of things—shoes, dresses, and overalls for dry-goods merchants like my father. We brought machinery and sugar, salt and flour. Folks came into town from their farms to trade eggs, butter, apples, and meat for "store-boughten" goods from the steamboat.

Hard as we tried to stick to a schedule, the river current dictated how fast we moved. If the river was high, boats could go fifteen miles an hour in midstream! But in the hot summer the current slowed, and so did we. We completely stopped whenever we saw produce or livestock waiting on the riverbank to be picked up. Once we stopped to let a woman get off the boat for a minute to gossip with another on the riverbank.

The passengers slept in staterooms, so called because the suites were named after states. A whole deck was named for our biggest state in those days, Texas, and that's where Gordon's and my stateroom was. I loved steamboat life, except for one thing— I still wanted to be a riverboat captain.

One day Gordon said, "I dream about steamboats. Someday I want to own a whole fleet of 'em. But right now, I want to buy just one, and I don't have the money to pay another captain."

"I know someone you wouldn't have to pay."

"I can tell by your conniving look that you're up to something, Mary."

"Let me be the captain of the new boat! I can do it, Gordon! Give me a chance."

"All right, see that sand bar in the river? You have to memorize where it is, so you don't run the boat aground."

That night in the pilothouse, after we'd unloaded and turned around to head back the way we came, Gordon said, "Mary, remember that sand bar I pointed out this afternoon? I'm relying on you to tell me where it is."

"But, Gordon, it's dark!"

292 Chapter 7 Life in the Young Republic

Chapter 7 293

Background Information

This memoir is a piece of historical fiction. It tells about events from the point of view of Mary Greene, a woman who wants to captain a steamboat.

GENRE Historical Fiction *"The Petticoat Skipper" is a work of historical fiction, using character, plot, and setting to tell the story of a woman skippering a steamboat.*

Analyze the Source

Inspect Have students read the selection on pp. 292–295 together to determine the general meaning of the text.

1. What does Mary's mother mean when she tells her "Steamboat captains don't wear petticoats"? (At that time, women did not often take jobs such as captaining a steamboat.)

Find Evidence Have students reread the selection and ask:

2. Why does Mary have to put both feet on the steering wheel to hold the ship steady? (Students should infer that it takes a lot of physical strength to steer a steamboat.)

Make Connections

3. What are three things Mary does to prove she is a good captain? (She earned her pilot's license and master's credential, beat the time of her biggest competitor, and comforted passengers during a storm.)

Perspectives How did Mary overcome challenges to achieve her goals? (Answers will vary.)

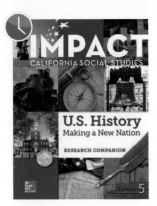

IMPACT
CALIFORNIA SOCIAL STUDIES

U.S. History
Making a New Nation

RESEARCH COMPANION

5

Research Companion
pp. 296–297

HSS STANDARDS

Students trace the colonization, immigration, and settlement patterns of the American people from 1789 to the mid-1800s, with emphasis on the role of economic incentives, effects of the physical and political geography, and transportation systems. **HSS.5.8**

CCSS Explain the relationships or interactions between two or more individuals, events, ideas, or concepts in a historical, scientific, or technical text based on specific information in the text. **CCSS.ELA.RI.5.3**

Go *Digital!*

Investigate chapter content with the online teaching plan.

See the **Language Learner Teacher Guide** pp. 158–159 for support strategies.

People You Should Know

Alexander Hamilton

After serving as George Washington's aide during the Revolutionary War, Alexander Hamilton was chosen as a delegate to the Constitutional Convention. He argued for a strong central government, which put him at odds with some other founders. The essays he wrote in *The Federalist Papers* argued for specific elements of the Constitution in an effort to convince the states to ratify the document. He served as Washington's Secretary of the Treasury and developed much of the plan for the United States financial system. Hamilton died in a duel with Vice President Aaron Burr in 1804.

Dolley Madison

First Lady Dolley Madison is best remembered for her actions during the War of 1812. As the British neared Washington D.C., Madison realized that the brand new White House would be a tempting target. She managed to find a wagon, had it loaded with fine china and other valuable objects, and sent it off for safekeeping at the Bank of Maryland. Just before she was forced to leave, she convinced her staff to break the frame on the famous portrait of George Washington by Gilbert Stuart so that the painting could be removed. Her quick thinking saved important pieces of U.S. history and culture from the fire that later burned down the mansion.

Sacagawea

When she was about 12 years old, Sacagawea (also spelled Sacajawea and Sakakawea) was kidnapped by the Hidatsa people from her Shoshone family. A few years later, a French Canadian fur trader named Toussaint Charbonneau purchased her. She later became his wife. Soon after, Lewis and Clark hired Charbonneau as a guide and interpreter for their expedition to explore the Louisiana Purchase. However, when they realized they would need someone who also spoke Shoshone, they agreed to bring Sacagawea along. She was pregnant at the time, and she gave birth on the trail to a son, Jean Baptiste. She lent her knowledge of languages and landmarks to the expedition, helping to make it a success.

Tecumseh

Shawnee chief Tecumseh was a respected leader in the Ohio River Valley. A gifted and inspiring orator, he crafted an alliance between several groups of American Indians to try to stop white expansion. He used this alliance to help the British fight the Americans during the War of 1812. Tecumseh helped the British win several important battles before the Americans defeated him in Canada. Tecumseh's death at the Battle of the Thames in 1813 signaled the end of American Indian resistance to U.S. settlement of the Ohio River Valley.

296 Chapter 7 Life in the Young Republic

Chapter 7 297

People You Should Know

How do personal stories IMPACT our understanding of the changes that transformed the young republic?

- Have students read aloud the biographies.

- Tell them that they will learn about these people and others throughout the chapter.

- Prompt students to write a short script for a play about one of the people in the People You Should Know feature or another key figure in the chapter. Other people they encounter will include:

  ▷ Henry Knox
  ▷ Benjamin Banneker
  ▷ Pierre L'Enfant
  ▷ James Madison
  ▷ Thomas Jefferson
  ▷ Meriweather Lewis
  ▷ William Clark
  ▷ Francis Scott Key

  ▷ James Monroe
  ▷ Frances Cabot Lowell
  ▷ Eli Whitney
  ▷ Robert Fulton
  ▷ Samuel F. B. Morse
  ▷ Daniel Boone
  ▷ Benjamin Rush

- Ask students to try to incorporate facts about the person into the script while also making it entertaining. Have students perform their plays in small groups. Refer to the plays throughout the chapter.

Teacher Notes

How Did Early Decisions Shape the Nation?

Background Information

In this lesson, students will learn about the groundbreaking precedents and important events of the first five presidential administrations, including the Louisiana Purchase, the Lewis and Clark Expedition, the War of 1812, and the Monroe Doctrine.

Community Connections

To enrich what students have learned about events and figures in this lesson, have them visit websites for George Washington's Mount Vernon, Thomas Jefferson's Monticello, James Monroe's Highland, the Lewis & Clark National Historical Trail, or the Fort McHenry National Monument.

 LESSON STANDARDS

✓ Demonstrate knowledge of the significance of land policies developed under the Continental Congress (e.g., sale of western lands, the Northwest Ordinance of 1787) and those policies' impact on American Indians' land. **HSS.5.6.6**

✓ Students describe the people and events associated with the development of the U.S. Constitution and analyze the Constitution's significance as the foundation of the American republic. **HSS.5.7**

✓ Know the songs that express American ideals (e.g., "America the Beautiful," "The Star Spangled Banner"). **HSS.5.7.6**

✓ Demonstrate knowledge of the explorations of the trans-Mississippi West following the Louisiana Purchase (e.g., Meriwether Lewis and William Clark, Zebulon Pike, John Fremont). **HSS.5.8.3**

✓ Students place key events and people of the historical era they are studying in a chronological sequence and spatial context; they interpret time lines. **HAS.CS.1**

✓ Students use map and globe skills to determine the absolute locations of places and interpret information available through a map's or globe's legend, scale, and symbolic representations. **HAS.CS.4**

✓ Students pose relevant questions about events they encounter in historical documents, eyewitness accounts, oral histories, letters, diaries, artifacts, photographs, maps, artworks, and architecture. **HAS.HR.2**

✓ Students identify and interpret the multiple causes and effects of historical events. **HAS.HI.3**

 Connect to the
Essential Question

Chapter 7, pp. 84–99

The **Weekly Explorer Magazine** supports students' exploration of the Essential Question and provides additional resources for the EQ Inquiry Project.

 ## Inquiry Project

Which Change Will You Choose?

Remind students to use the information they learn in this lesson and other resources to complete their EQ Inquiry Project!

Dinah Zike's

 In this lesson you will use Foldables.

When Minutes Count!

Suggested Lesson Pacing

1 ENGAGE
One Day

- Analyze the Source
- Inquiry Tools

Go Digital

- **Video**: The Louisiana Purchase
- **iMap:** The Corps of Discovery, 1804–1806

2 INVESTIGATE
Two to Three Days

🕐 **Short on Time?** Look for the clock to teach core content in less time.

- A New Government Is Launched
- A Nation Expands
- The Louisiana Purchase
- The War of 1812
- The Monroe Doctrine

3 REPORT
One Day

- Think About It
- Write a Diary Entry
- Defend Your Claim

Make Connections!

(CCSS) CONNECT TO ELA

Reading
Quote accurately from a text when explaining what the text says explicitly and when drawing inferences from the text. **RI.5.1**

Research
Conduct short research projects that use several sources to build knowledge through investigation of different aspects of a topic. **W.5.7**

Draw evidence from literary or informational texts to support analysis, reflection, and research. **W.5.9**

Writing
Write narratives to develop real or imagined experiences or events using effective technique, descriptive details, and clear event sequences. **W.5.3**

Speaking and Listening
Engage effectively in a range of collaborative discussions (one-on-one, in groups, and teacher-led) with diverse partners on *grade 5 topics and texts*, building on others' ideas and expressing their own clearly. **SL.5.1**

Summarize a written text read aloud or information presented in diverse media and formats, including visually, quantitatively, and orally. **SL.5.2**

Classroom Resources

🔍 Search for additional resources using the following key words.

John Adams

District of Columbia

Alexander Hamilton

Thomas Jefferson

Lewis & Clark

Louisiana Purchase

James Madison

Monroe Doctrine

Sacajawea

War of 1812

George Washington

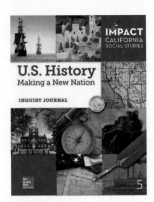

Inquiry Journal
pp. 242–243

HSS STANDARDS

Demonstrate knowledge of the significance of land policies developed under the Continental Congress (e.g., sale of western lands, the Northwest Ordinance of 1787)and those policies' impact on American Indians' land. **HSS.5.6.6**

CCSS Summarize a written text read aloud or information presented in diverse media and formats, including visually, quantitatively, and orally. **CCSS.ELA.SL.5.2**

Go Digital!

Explore the lesson content with online whole-class presentation tools.

- **Video:** The Louisiana Purchase
- **iMap:** The Corps of Discovery, 1804–1806

How Did Early Decisions Shape the Nation?

Bellringer

Prompt students to retrieve information from the previous lessons. Say: *The Constitution, which became law in 1788, presented an outline of how the nation's new government would operate. How did the Constitution establish checks and balances on the power of the federal government?* *(by establishing the separation of powers between the executive, legislative, and judicial branches)*

Lesson Outcomes

What Am I Learning? Have students read the Lesson Outcomes on p. 242.

Why Am I Learning It? Stress that the decisions made in the early years of our nation continue to impact the way the nation is run today.

How Will I Know That I Learned It? Ask students the following questions:

- What causes and effects will you be able to describe? (the causes and effects of important events and decisions in the nation's early years)

- On whose decisions and policies will you focus? (those of the nation's early leaders)

- How will you support your analysis? (with text evidence)

Talk About It

Explain that the War of 1812 was fought between Great Britain and the United States. Have students look at the painting of an episode from that war and read the caption. Provide sentence frames to help students talk about the painting.

- *The American fort is in the* __(center)__ *of the scene.*

- *It is being bombarded, or hit with* __bombs__ *from the ships in the harbor.*

Collaborative Conversations

Add New Ideas As students engage in partner, small group, and whole-class discussions, encourage them to

- Stay on topic.
- Connect their own ideas to things their peers have said.
- Look for ways to connect their personal experiences or prior knowledge to the conversation.

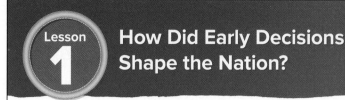

Lesson 1: How Did Early Decisions Shape the Nation?

Lesson Outcomes

What Am I Learning?
In this lesson, you're going to use your investigative skills to learn about important events and government decisions in the early years of the United States.

Why Am I Learning It?
Reading and talking about those early events and decisions will help you understand the direction the nation took and what effects it had on the future.

How Will I Know That I Learned It?
You will be able to describe the causes and effects of important events in the nation's early years as well as the decisions and policies that the nation's early leaders made.

Talk About It COLLABORATE

Look at the Details What object near the center of this image stands out among all the cannon fire? What is the artist suggesting with this image?

HSS.5.6.6, HSS.5.7.6, HSS.5.8.3, HAS.HR.1, HAS.HR.2, HAS.HI.1, HAS.HI.3

242 Lesson 1 How Did Early Decisions Shape the Nation?

During the War of 1812, the British tried to capture Fort McHenry, just outside of Baltimore, Maryland.

Lesson 1 **243**

Inquiry Journal, pp. 242–243

 ## ENGLISH LEARNERS SCAFFOLD

ELD.PI.5.6 Reading closely literary and informational texts and viewing multimedia to determine how meaning is conveyed explicitly and implicitly through language

Emerging

Describe an Image Provide sentence frames to help students describe what the painting shows.

Ships **in the harbor are** _firing on a fort_ .

A(n) _America flag_ **is flying over the** _fort_ .

Expanding/Bridging

Understand Images Have students describe the feelings that the painting captures. Have students indicate the details that help it to inspire those feelings. (Students may recognize that the gunfire makes the painting tense and exciting and that the incident depicted and waving flag make the painting patriotic to viewers from the United States.)

See the **Language Learner Teaching Guide** for more language support strategies.

Monitor and Differentiate

REACHING ALL LEARNERS

On Level

Have students discuss what they already know about George Washington, John Adams, Thomas Jefferson, James Madison, and James Monroe. Tell them that the lesson is about what happened when these founders served as the earliest presidents of the United States.

Beyond Level

Remind students that the American Revolution, in which the colonists fought the British, ended in 1783. Have them speculate about why the young nation might be fighting Britain again less than thirty years later.

1 ENGAGE

Analyze the Source

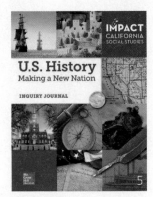

Inquiry Journal
pp. 244–245

 STANDARDS

Know the songs that express American ideals (e.g., "America the Beautiful," "The Star Spangled Banner"). **HSS.5.7.6**

Students differentiate between primary and secondary sources. **HAS.HR.1**

Students pose relevant questions about events they encounter in historical documents, eyewitness accounts, oral histories, letters, diaries, artifacts, photographs, maps, artworks, and architecture. **HAS.HR.2**

CCSS Engage effectively in a range of collaborative discussions (one-on-one, in groups, and teacher-led) with diverse partners on grade 5 topics and texts, building on others' ideas and expressing their own clearly. **CCSS.ELA.SL.5.1**

Go Digital!

Model how to inspect and find evidence with online whole-class presentation tools.

Background Information

Francis Scott Key's poem, which he called "The Defense (or *Defence*) of Fort McHenry," actually has three more stanzas. Set to an older tune, it came to be called "The Star-Spangled Banner" from its description of the U.S. flag. It did not officially become the national anthem until 1931.

1 Inspect

Read Have students read the Primary Source and text introducing it, circling unfamiliar words and underlining clues that tell *who, what, where, when, why,* and *how.* Ask:

- What do the introduction and title suggest the song is about? (the U.S. flag)

- Where do the song's events take place? (at Baltimore Harbor near Fort McHenry)

- When do the events of the song take place? What times of day are mentioned? (during the War of 1812; dawn, twilight, and night)

Collaborate Have partners discuss the event Francis Scott Key witnessed. (Discussions should identify the British bombardment of Fort McHenry.)

2 Find Evidence

Reread Have students reread the text, focusing on unraveling the long sentences.

Analyze the Primary Source Read the text aloud and analyze it together. Ask:

- What item or thing is the opening question about? (the U.S. flag waving over the fort at dawn)

- Which details in the first four lines make this clear? (It has "broad stripes and bright stars," was "proudly hailed" at twilight, and is "gallantly streaming" over the fort.)

- What is the significance of this item's still being there "by the dawn's early light"? (It means the British bombardment did not succeed in capturing the fort.)

3 Make Connections

Talk Have students discuss why the song is called "The Star-Spangled Banner." (Students should recognize that the title is from the lyrics' memorable description of the flag, spangled with stars. They may note that the stars suggest something glorious and enduring and that the title stresses that the flag and the nation it represents are also glorious and enduring.)

Analyze the Source

1 Inspect

Read Look at the lyrics of this primary source and the sentences that introduce them.

- **Circle** words you don't know.
- **Underline** clues that tell you *what* event the text is about, *where* and *when* it takes place, and *how* and *why* it is happening.
- **Discuss** with a partner the event that Francis Scott Key witnessed.

My Notes

_____
_____
_____
_____
_____
_____
_____
_____
_____
_____
_____
_____
_____
_____

The Star-Spangled Banner

During the War of 1812, American Francis Scott Key was detained by the British on a ship in Baltimore Harbor. From the ship, he witnessed the British bombardment of Fort McHenry on September 13, 1814. The next morning, he saw the American flag still flying over the fort. He expressed his feelings in a poem that was later set to music. Known as "The Star-Spangled Banner," it eventually became the national anthem of the United States on March 3, 1931.

PRIMARY SOURCE

O say can you see, by the dawn's early light,

What so proudly we hail'd at the twilight's last gleaming,

Whose broad stripes and bright stars through the perilous fight

O'er the ramparts we watch'd were so gallantly streaming?

And the rocket's red glare, the bombs bursting in air,

Gave proof through the night that our flag was still there,

O say does that star-spangled banner yet wave

O'er the land of the free and the home of the brave?

– from "The Star-Spangled Banner" by Francis Scott Key

2 Find Evidence

Reread Look at the lyrics. What item or thing is the opening question about? Which details in the first two sentences make this clear? What is the significance of this item still being there "by the dawn's early light"?

3 Make Connections

Talk Discuss with a partner why the song is called "The Star-Spangled Banner."

Inquiry Journal, pp. 244–245

ENGLISH LEARNERS SCAFFOLD

ELD.PI.5.6 Reading closely literary and informational texts and viewing multimedia to determine how meaning is conveyed explicitly and implicitly through language

Emerging

Clarify Text Clarify difficult terms in the introductory text, such as *detained* ("forced to stay") and *bombardment* ("bombing"), and in the lyrics, such as *hailed* ("saluted"), *perilous* ("dangerous"), *ramparts* ("protective walls [of the fort]"), *gallantly* ("bravely; nobly"), and *o'er* ("over").

Expanding

Paraphrase Text Ask what a more modern equivalent of *Oh, say,* would be. (Hey; Yo) Help clarify confusing clauses in the lyrics by telling students to substitute *the thing that* for *what* in the second line and add *the thing* before *whose* in the third line.

Bridging

Perform Text Ask students to read the lyrics as a poem, expressing it with appropriate tone, pacing, and feeling to try to convey the meaning. Students might also work in groups to perform the lyrics as a song or do a choral reading of it. Encourage students to include live or recorded musical accompaniment.

See the **Language Learner Teaching Guide** for more language support strategies.

Monitor and Differentiate

REACHING ALL LEARNERS

Special Needs

Have students visit the Smithsonian's website for the National Museum of American History to view photographs of the original "Star-Spangled Banner" that Key saw and read the information about it. Ask them to report their experiences in a multimedia presentation about their virtual field trip.

Beyond Level

Have small groups of students find online the other three stanzas of Key's original poem, work together to decipher difficult language, and then discuss the ideas and emotions those stanzas convey about the flag and the nation.

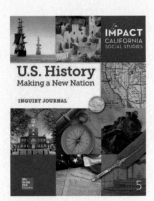

Inquiry Journal
pp. 246–247

Demonstrate knowledge of the significance of land policies developed under the Continental Congress (e.g., sale of western lands, the Northwest Ordinance of 1787) and those policies' impact on American Indians' land. **HSS.5.6.6**

Students describe the people and events associated with the development of the U.S. Constitution and analyze the Constitution's significance as the foundation of the American republic. **HSS.5.7**

Know the songs that express American ideals (e.g., "America the Beautiful," "The Star Spangled Banner"). **HSS.5.7.6**

Demonstrate knowledge of the explorations of the trans-Mississippi West following the Louisiana Purchase (e.g., Meriwether Lewis and William Clark, Zebulon Pike, John Fremont). **HSS.5.8.3**

Go Digital!

- Model how to explore and investigate with online whole-class tools.

- Students can access the online graphic organizer to use the inquiry tools as they read.

Explore Cause and Effect

Explain Tell students that cause and effect is one kind of structure that authors use to organize information in historical texts. Remind students that a cause is the reason something has happened; an effect is the outcome or result of the cause.

Read Have students read aloud the step-by-step instructions about how to identify cause and effect. Tell students also to look for words and phrases that signal cause and effect, such as because, since, so, as a result, therefore, and for that reason.

Guide Practice Model identifying cause and effect. Say: *I know that Francis Scott Key wrote "the Star-Spangled Banner" because he witnessed the United States win the Battle of Fort McHenry against Great Britain during the War of 1812. Writing the song was an effect of watching the battle.*

Investigate!

Have students read pages 298–309 in the Research Companion. Tell them the information will help them answer the lesson question ***How Did Early Decisions Shape the Nation?***

Take Notes Tell students that they will take notes as they read each section. Remind them that taking notes will help them understand and remember the information they learn. Stress the importance of paraphrasing, or using their own words, when they take notes.

Inspect Guide students to read the text in each section to determine what it says. Suggest that they ask *What happened?* to determine effects and *Why did it happen?* to determine causes. Remind them to look for words that signal cause and effect.

Find Evidence Encourage students to reread the text to develop a deeper understanding of the content. Tell them that after they read and take notes, they should review and think about how the facts and details will help them answer the lesson question.

Collaborative Conversations

Text-Based Discussion Remind students of the goals of discussing the text with others:

- to listen and respond to their partners' points
- to ask for evidence from the text
- to build on each other's ideas
- to see the text from a different point of view

Inquiry Tools

Explore Cause and Effect

A **cause** is an event or action that is the reason something happens. An **effect** is the result of a cause. Often, a situation, event, or decision has more than one cause or more than one effect. Consider the causes and effects of government decisions and policies in the early years of the United States.

1. **Read the text once all the way through.**
   This will help you understand what the text is about.

2. **Look at the section titles to see how the text is organized.**
   This will help you find key events, decisions, and policies in the text.

3. **Find reasons or explanations.**
   While reading, ask yourself what specific reasons led to a particular decision or policy.

4. **Watch for specific changes.**
   While reading, also ask yourself what specific changes resulted from a particular decision or policy.

COLLABORATE Based on the text you just read, work with your class to complete the chart below.

Cause		Effect
Francis Scott Key witnesses Britain's unsuccessful assault on Fort McHenry.	→	Key writes "The Star-Spangled Banner."

Investigate!

Read pages 298–309 in your Research Companion. Use your investigative skills to determine the effects of important decisions made in the early years of the United States. In the "Cause" column, write the decision. In the "Effect" column, describe how the decision impacted the nation.

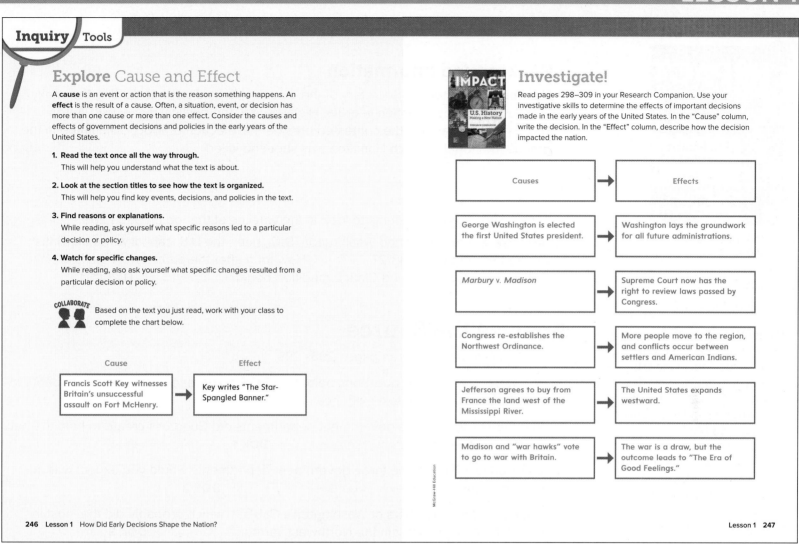

Causes		Effects
George Washington is elected the first United States president.	→	Washington lays the groundwork for all future administrations.
Marbury v. *Madison*	→	Supreme Court now has the right to review laws passed by Congress.
Congress re-establishes the Northwest Ordinance.	→	More people move to the region, and conflicts occur between settlers and American Indians.
Jefferson agrees to buy from France the land west of the Mississippi River.	→	The United States expands westward.
Madison and "war hawks" vote to go to war with Britain.	→	The war is a draw, but the outcome leads to "The Era of Good Feelings."

Inquiry Journal, pp. 246–247

(EL) ENGLISH LEARNERS SCAFFOLD

ELD.PII.5.1 Understanding text structure

Emerging	Expanding	Bridging
Identify Cause and Effect Give students practice with cause and effect by having them identify everyday examples. For instance, say: *I studied hard tonight for tomorrow's test.* Then ask: *What was the cause?* (tomorrow's test) *What was the effect?* (I studied hard tonight.)	**Understand Cause and Effect** Illustrate the use of clue words to signal cause and effect. For example, say: *Because I have a test tomorrow, I studied hard tonight.* Elicit that *because* signals the cause. Then say: *I have a test tomorrow; as a result, I studied hard tonight.* Elicit that *as a result* signals the effect.	**Use Cause and Effect** Have students give their own examples of cause and effect from everyday life. Ask them to include signal words and phrases.

See the **Language Learner Teaching Guide** for more language support strategies.

Monitor and Differentiate

REACHING ALL LEARNERS

Approaching Level

Explain that some effects can have more than one cause and that some causes can have more than one effect. Note that multiple causes and effects are common in history.

On Level

Discuss why history books often use cause-and-effect organization. Elicit that in studying history, you often learn what happened (the effect) and why it happened (the cause).

Beyond Level

Have students consider general causes or reasons that nations grow in size: People want more land on which to live, for example, or businesses are looking for more resources.

2 INVESTIGATE / A New Government Is Launched

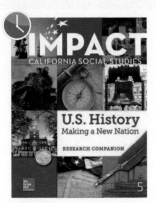

Research Companion
pp. 298–299

 HSS STANDARDS

Students describe the people and events associated with the development of the U.S. Constitution and analyze the Constitution's significance as the foundation of the American republic. **HSS.5.7**

CCSS Quote accurately from a text when explaining what the text says explicitly and when drawing inferences from the text. **CCSS.ELA.RI.5.1**

Summarize a written text read aloud or information presented in diverse media and formats, including visually, quantitatively, and orally. **CCSS.ELA.SL.5.2**

Go Digital!

Investigate the lesson content with online whole-class presentation tools.

- **Video:** The Louisiana Purchase
- **iMap:** The Corps of Discovery, 1804–1806

Background Information

Alexander Hamilton, as Secretary of the Treasury, is credited with putting the shaky finances of the young nation in order. His personal and political rivalry with Aaron Burr, which escalated in the contested presidential election of 1800, culminated in the famous 1804 duel in which Hamilton was shot and killed.

| **TIMELINE** | Invite students to look at the timeline at the top on page 299.

Analyze For how long had Washington, D.C., been the U.S. capital when the British burned it in the War of 1812? (14 years) How long after the purchase of the Louisiana Territory did the Lewis and Clark Expedition begin? (the next year) **HAS.CS.1**

Analyze the Source

Inspect Have students read pages 298–299.

Find Evidence Use the questions below to check comprehension. Remind students to support their answers with text evidence.

Summarize What three government departments did Congress create to help the new president govern? (Treasury, State, and War) **DOK 1**

Categorize Which of the three government departments would you expect was in charge of printing money? (Department of Treasury) **DOK 2**

Analyze Of the members of Washington's Cabinet, which probably did the most in handling growing unrest in the Northwest Territory? (Henry Knox) **DOK 3**

Make Connections

Speculate How do you think George Washington felt about being the first president? (He probably was honored, felt the weight of responsibility, and realized he was establishing precedents.) **DOK 4**

Analyze the Image Direct students' attention to the painting and caption on page 299. Ask:

- Where is Washington in the scene, and why did the artist place him there? (in the center; he is the most important figure of the painting)
- How would you describe the scene shown in the painting? (excited)
- What groups of people are represented in the painting? (soldiers, statesmen, women, city dwellers)

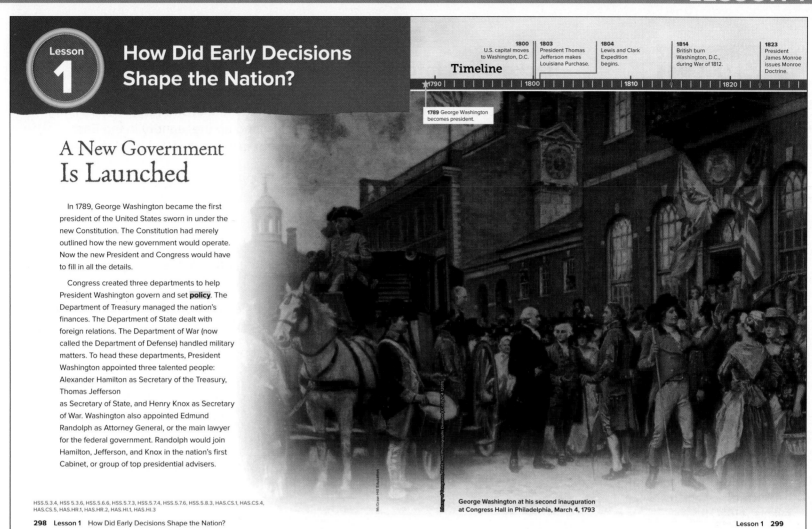

Lesson 1

How Did Early Decisions Shape the Nation?

Timeline

1800	1803	1804	1814	1823
U.S. capital moves to Washington, D.C.	President Thomas Jefferson makes Louisiana Purchase.	Lewis and Clark Expedition begins.	British burn Washington, D.C., during War of 1812.	President James Monroe issues Monroe Doctrine.

1790 | 1800 | 1810 | 1820

1789 George Washington becomes president.

A New Government Is Launched

In 1789, George Washington became the first president of the United States sworn in under the new Constitution. The Constitution had merely outlined how the new government would operate. Now the new President and Congress would have to fill in all the details.

Congress created three departments to help President Washington govern and set **policy**. The Department of Treasury managed the nation's finances. The Department of State dealt with foreign relations. The Department of War (now called the Department of Defense) handled military matters. To head these departments, President Washington appointed three talented people: Alexander Hamilton as Secretary of the Treasury, Thomas Jefferson as Secretary of State, and Henry Knox as Secretary of War. Washington also appointed Edmund Randolph as Attorney General, or the main lawyer for the federal government. Randolph would join Hamilton, Jefferson, and Knox in the nation's first Cabinet, or group of top presidential advisers.

HSS.5.3.4, HSS 5.3.6, HSS.5.6.6, HSS.5.7.3, HSS.5.7.4, HSS.5.7.6, HSS.5.8.3, HAS.CS.1, HAS.CS.4, HAS.CS.5, HAS.HR.1, HAS.HR.2, HAS.HI.1, HAS.HI.3

George Washington at his second inauguration at Congress Hall in Philadelphia, March 4, 1793

298 Lesson 1 How Did Early Decisions Shape the Nation?

Lesson 1 **299**

Research Companion, pp. 298–299

 ENGLISH LEARNERS SCAFFOLD

ELD.PI.5.8 Analyzing how writers and speakers use vocabulary and other language resources for specific purposes (to explain, persuade, entertain, etc.) depending on modality, text type, purpose, audience, topic, and content area

Emerging

Understand Domain-Specific Terms Have students explain in their own words the duties of the four members of the President's Cabinet.

Be sure students they understand that *Secretary* here means the head of a department. Clarify the terms *federal government* and *foreign relations,* if necessary.

Expanding

Understand Words in Context Point to the term *Cabinet* on page 298, and have students identify the words in the text that explain what it means. (group of top presidential advisers) Note that terms in textbooks are often explained after commas sometimes followed by the word *or.* Ask what other term in the same paragraph is explained in that way, and have students say what it means. (Attorney General; main lawyer for the federal government)

See the **Language Learner Teaching Guide** for more language support strategies.

Monitor and Differentiate

REACHING ALL LEARNERS

Approaching Level

Review the timeline with students. Encourage them to discuss what they already know about some of the events in the entries.

On Level

Have student groups produce news articles about Washington's inauguration, using details from the painting, the timeline, and the text.

Beyond Level

Have students do online research into Congress Hall in Philadelphia, the building shown in the painting, which still stands. What other important building is near Congress Hall? How did the building get its name? Why was Washington inaugurated there? Have students share their findings with the class.

2 INVESTIGATE / A New Government Is Launched

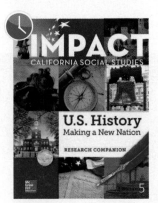

Research Companion
pp. 300–301

 STANDARDS

Students describe the people and events associated with the development of the U.S. Constitution and analyze the Constitution's significance as the foundation of the American republic. **HSS.5.7**

Students summarize the key events of the era they are studying and explain the historical context of those events. **HAS.HI.1**

CCSS Quote accurately from a text when explaining what the text says explicitly and when drawing inferences from the text. **CCSS.ELA.RI.5.1**

Engage effectively in a range of collaborative discussions (one-on-one, in groups, and teacher-led) with diverse partners on grade 5 topics and texts, building on others' ideas and expressing their own clearly. **CCSS.ELA.SL.5.1**

Go *Digital!*

Investigate the lesson content with online whole-class presentation tools.

Background Information

Abigail Adams, wife of President John Adams, was the first First Lady to live in the newly completed White House. Her letters indicate that she found the building cold and damp and that she sometimes had to hang up the laundry in the East Room to dry. She and her husband lived there for just five months, leaving after John Adams's defeat in the election of 1800.

Analyze the Source

Inspect Have students continue reading about the launch of the new government on pages 300–301.

Find Evidence Use the questions below to check comprehension. Remind students to support their answers with text evidence.

Explain Why did the capital of the new nation soon need to move? (Government was growing bigger.) **DOK 3**

Explain Why did Thomas Jefferson fear a strong central government? (He thought it would lead to corruption.) **DOK 2**

Identify Who won the election of 1800? (Thomas Jefferson) **DOK 1**

Summarize What was the main significance of *Marbury v. Madison?* (It established the idea that the Supreme Court could review laws and declare them unconstitutional.) **DOK 2**

Make Connections

Synthesize Sum up the differences in Federalist and Democratic-Republican views in the 1790s. (Federalists stressed strong central government, commerce, and industry. Democratic-Republicans preferred weaker central government and an economy based on agriculture.) **DOK 3**

PRODUCTIVE

✓ Stop and Check

Talk Have students discuss the government divisions, positions, and other "firsts" established in Washington's presidency. (Students should discuss the three departments and secretaries, the role of attorney general, and the Cabinet. They may also discuss Washington's retiring after two terms and moving the capital to a new location.)

Find Details Explain to students that after they read and take notes, they should review and think about how the facts and details will help them answer the Essential Question.

All of these changes to help the government work also made it bigger. So in 1790, President Washington signed a law to establish a new national capital called the District of Columbia. The President hired Pierre L'Enfant, a French engineer, to design the city and later replaced him with Andrew Ellicott, who kept much of L'Enfant's grand plan. Working with Ellicott was Benjamin Banneker, a free-born African American, who helped lay out the city. Banneker was one of the first African Americans appointed by a President to work for the federal government.

The years of George Washington's presidency saw a rise in political tension. Washington had chosen his Cabinet to provide a variety of opinions. Alexander Hamilton and Thomas Jefferson had very different views of what the new nation should be like. Hamilton thought the United States should have a strong central government and an economy that emphasized commerce and industry. Jefferson thought a strong central government would lead to **corruption**. He preferred a more agricultural nation with a weak federal government and more political power for the states. In general, President Washington agreed with Hamilton's economic proposals. He believed they were vital to the foundation of the new nation's economy.

Benjamin Banneker

MPVHistory/Alamy

After two terms in office, George Washington decided to leave the presidency. He wished to retire from public life and establish that the president was not a monarch. By then, the division in his Cabinet had led to the beginning of the nation's first political parties. John Adams, Washington's vice president, shared Hamilton's views, and they helped to form what became known as the Federalist Party. James Madison and many other Southern politicians shared Jefferson's views in what became known as the Democratic-Republican Party. In the election of 1796 to succeed Washington, John Adams ran against Thomas Jefferson and won. Four years later, Adams ran against Jefferson again and lost.

Just before leaving office, President Adams appointed a judge named William Marbury. Then James Madison, Secretary of State for President Jefferson, refused to give Marbury his official papers, even though a section of the Judiciary Act of 1789 passed by Congress said he should. At a famous hearing of the U.S. Supreme Court, Chief Justice John Marshall ruled that this section of the Judiciary Act was **unconstitutional**, or against the guidelines included in the U.S. Constitution. The case, *Marbury* v. *Madison*, is very important. It established the principle that the Supreme Court can review laws passed by Congress and, if necessary, declare them unconstitutional.

John Marshall

((t)McGraw-Hill Education; (b)Library of Congress Prints and Photographs Division [LC-USZ62-54940])

✓ Stop and Check

Talk What government divisions, positions, and other "firsts" were established during George Washington's presidency?

Find Details As you read, add additional information to the graphic organizer on page 247 in your Inquiry Journal.

COLLABORATE

Research Companion, pp. 300–301

🌐 ENGLISH LEARNERS SCAFFOLD

ELD.PI.5.6 Reading closely literary and informational texts and viewing multimedia to determine how meaning is conveyed explicitly and implicitly through language

Emerging	Expanding	Bridging
State Causes and Effects Help students state cause-and-effect relationships by providing sentence frames that contain signal words and phrases: ***Because the government was getting bigger, Washington decided to _____.*** **The government was getting bigger. As a result, _____.**	**Explain Causes** Note that the Constitution originally said nothing about how many terms a president could serve. Ask why Washington left the presidency after two terms. Be sure students know what a *monarch* is. (He wanted to retire from public life and show the president was not a monarch ruling for life.)	**Explain Causes and Effects** Have students write a paragraph explaining the cause-and-effect relationships between the different views of Hamilton and Jefferson and the growth of political parties. Students' explanations should mention other founders who shared those views.

See the **Language Learner Teaching Guide** for more language support strategies.

Monitor and Differentiate

REACHING ALL LEARNERS

Approaching Level

Note that the federal territory is the *District of Columbia* but the city (with the same land) is called *Washington*. Have students explain why. (to honor George Washington)

On Level

Discuss the term *District of Columbia*, explaining that *Columbia* comes from *Christopher Columbus*. Have them investigate the popularity of the term at the time of the nation's founding.

Beyond Level

Point out that the growing government could simply have moved into larger buildings in New York. Have students research and report on the reasons the capital was moved further south.

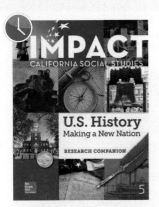

Research Companion
pp. 302–303

 STANDARDS

Demonstrate knowledge of the significance of land policies developed under the Continental Congress (e.g., sale of western lands, the Northwest Ordinance of 1787) and those policies' impact on American Indians' land. **HSS.5.6.6**

Demonstrate knowledge of the explorations of the trans-Mississippi West following the Louisiana Purchase (e.g., Meriwether Lewis and William Clark, Zebulon Pike, John Fremont). **HSS.5.8.3**

Students summarize the key events of the era they are studying and explain the historical context of those events. **HAS.HI.1**

CCSS Quote accurately from a text when explaining what the text says explicitly and when drawing inferences from the text. **CCSS.ELA.RI.5.1**

Go Digital!

Investigate the lesson content with online whole-class presentation tools.

Background Information

Napoleon Bonaparte took over the French government in 1799. Revolutionary France had been battling the monarchies of Europe, including Britain, since imprisoning and killings its own royal family; Napoleon was one of its most successful generals. At the time Livingston and Monroe began negotiating with the French, Napoleon had recently signed a peace treaty with Britain, but he planned to restart the fighting soon, and he needed money to pay for it.

Analyze the Source

Inspect Have students read pages 302–303.

Find Evidence Use the questions below to check comprehension. Remind students to support their answers with text evidence.

> **Explain** What difficulties did African Americans face in the Northwest? (Although slavery was banned north of the Ohio River, laws kept African Americans out or required them to show papers proving they were free.) **DOK 2**
>
> **Summarize** What was the outcome of fighting between U.S. citizens and American Indians in Ohio? (The American Indians had to give up most of their territory.) **DOK 3**
>
> **Explain** Why did Jefferson want to buy New Orleans? (France was taking it back from Spain and might close the Mississippi River and port of New Orleans to U.S. commerce.) **DOK 2**
>
> **Analyze Cause and Effect** What caused France to sell the entire Louisiana Territory? (France needed money to fight in Europe and could not protect the territory from British attack.) **DOK 3**

Make Connections

> **Explain** Why was purchasing Louisiana a hard decision for Jefferson, even though it was such a good deal? (Jefferson believed in keeping federal power limited, not in expanding it by buying land.) **DOK 3**

Analyze the Images Have students compare and contrast the images on both pages and read the captions that accompany them. Ask:

- What is similar about scenes in both paintings? (Americans are in the process of expanding their territory.)

- What is different about the two scenes? (While the Americans and French at New Orleans are peacefully transferring power, the Miami and Americans are battling over territory in Ohio.)

✓ Stop and Check

Talk Have students discuss why settlers were able to bring slaves to new territories. (Students may recognize that slavery was so ingrained in the economy and in society of the Southern states that many would have disregarded the rules about bringing slaves with them to a new home.)

A Nation Expands

In 1789, George Washington signed a new Northwest Ordinance. It made clear that the rules for settling territory, established in the previous ordinance, were still in effect under the new Constitution. One part of the ordinance banned slavery north of the Ohio River. However, settlers from the South brought slaves into Kentucky and Tennessee. Even in the northern territories, African Americans had a difficult time. Laws were passed to keep African Americans out of some states. These same states forced free African Americans already there to show papers proving they were free.

American Indians did not recognize the right of U.S. citizens to purchase land in the new territories. As newcomers poured in, tensions mounted. Violence between native peoples and new settlers led President Washington to send the army to Ohio three times during his presidency. The American Indians would eventually be forced to give up most of Ohio.

✓ Stop and Check

COLLABORATE

Talk Why do you think settlers were able to bring slaves into the new territory even though it was against the law?"

General Harmar defeated by Miamis, 1790

302 **Lesson 1** How Did Early Decisions Shape the Nation?

The Louisiana Purchase

During the 1790s, control of the port of New Orleans had passed from France to Spain, and back to France again. While the United States had a deal with Spain to use the river and port, Jefferson was worried that the French could close the river and port to U.S. commerce. So he sent Robert Livingston, U.S. Minister to France, and future President James Monroe, a special ambassador, to meet with the French and offer to buy New Orleans.

France and Great Britain were involved in a series of conflicts. France needed money for its military. The French also realized that they could not protect Louisiana if the British attacked from Canada. So the French government made a surprising offer: France would sell not just New Orleans but the entire Louisiana colony to the United States.

The deal was an excellent one for Jefferson—530 million acres of land for 15 million dollars. That's about 3.5 cents an acre. Still, making the purchase was a hard decision for the president. For years, he had argued for a federal government with limited power. Having the federal government buy new territory was not a power spelled out in the Constitution. Nevertheless, Jefferson decided that he could not pass up such a good opportunity for the nation.

The American flag is raised in New Orleans after the city became part of the United States as a result of the Louisiana Purchase.

(0)McGraw-Hill Education; (b)Nday Picture Library/Alamy

Lesson 1 **303**

Research Companion, pp. 302–303

(EL) **ENGLISH LEARNERS SCAFFOLD**

ELD.PI.5.8. Analyzing how writers and speakers use vocabulary and other language resources for specific purposes (to explain, persuade, entertain, etc.) depending on modality, text type, purpose, audience, topic, and content area

Emerging	Expanding	Bridging
Understand Geographic Terms Remind students that *Northwest* at the time referred to land between the Appalachian Mountains and Mississippi River north of the Ohio River—the present-day states of Ohio, Michigan, Indiana, Illinois, and Wisconsin, and part of Minnesota.	**Understand Geography** Use a map to show students why those who settled the land west of the Appalachian Mountains would need to be able to use the Mississippi River and port of New Orleans for shipping.	**Clarify Terms** Help students do the math to calculate how 530 million acres of land for 15 million dollars works out to about 3.5 cents an acre. Clarify that land is commonly measured in acres. Have students investigate how many acres the school building sits upon.

See the **Language Learner Teaching Guide** for more language support strategies.

Monitor and Differentiate

REACHING ALL LEARNERS

Special Needs

Help students understand events by numbering and listing the steps that led to the Louisiana Purchase.

On Level

Have students check online to learn the amount the U.S. paid per acre in other land purchases, such as the Gadsden or Alaska Purchases, and compare the price to the Louisiana Purchase.

Beyond Level

Have students research and report on events in Haiti at the time of the Louisiana Purchase and analyze how they contributed to Napoleon's decision to sell Louisiana.

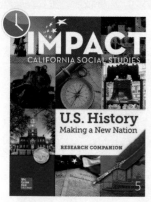

Research Companion
pp. 304–305

 STANDARDS

Demonstrate knowledge of the explorations of the trans-Mississippi West following the Louisiana Purchase (e.g., Meriwether Lewis and William Clark, Zebulon Pike, John Fremont). **HSS.5.8.3**

Students use map and globe skills to determine the absolute locations of places and interpret information available through a map's or globe's legend, scale, and symbolic representations. **HSS.CS.4**

Students differentiate between primary and secondary sources. **HAS.HR.1**

CCSS Quote accurately from a text when explaining what the text says explicitly and when drawing inferences from the text. **CCSS.ELA.RI.5.1**

Go Digital!

Investigate the lesson content with online whole-class presentation tools.

Background Information

Sacajawea, a Shoshone, was kidnapped by her people's enemy, the Hidatsa, during a buffalo hunt in 1800. Six months' pregnant when she and her husband left on the Lewis and Clark Expedition, she gave birth to her son, Jean-Baptiste Charbonneau (called Baptiste), on February 11, 1805. Continuing west with the expedition, she was reunited with her brother, a Shoshone leader, in a joyous meeting.

Analyze the Source

Inspect Have students read pages 304–305, including the two primary sources.

Find Evidence Use the questions below to check comprehension. Remind students to support their answers with text evidence.

Identify When did the expedition to explore the Louisiana Purchase begin? (May 14, 1804)

Speculate Why do you think Jefferson chose Meriwether Lewis to lead the expedition west? (He had army experience on the frontier, and Jefferson knew his work habits and probably trusted him to do the job.) **DOK 3**

Summarize What impact would the Louisiana Purchase have on native peoples? (more conflict and loss of land) **DOK 2**

Analyze the Primary Source Note that a primary source can support, make clearer, or add information to the information in a secondary source. Ask:

Synthesize What information in the text does the primary source from the Louisiana Purchase make clearer? (details about the United States obtaining the territory and American Indian claims being ignored) **DOK 3**

Make Connections

Evaluate What qualities would members of the Corps of Discovery probably need for a successful expedition? (good physical shape; knowledge of surviving in the wilderness; ability to work with others) **DOK 3**

📍 Map Skills

Project a large version of the map on page 305. Guide students to examine the map as they read about the Louisiana Purchase. Ask:

- What were the eastern and western borders of the Louisiana Territory? (Mississippi River and Rocky Mountains)

- About how much larger was the United States after buying the territory? (twice as large)

- What four rivers on the map go through the territory? (Missouri, Platte, Arkansas, Red)

- Which of these did the Lewis and Clark Expedition mainly use? (Missouri)

President Jefferson officially announced the Louisiana Purchase on July 4, 1803. The Louisiana Territory became part of the United States, doubling the size of the nation. As in the past, these land exchanges involved European nations, and the United States would mostly ignore the claims of American Indians already living on the land. This would bring conflict in future decades, when more and more settlers came west to mine and farm the land.

Meanwhile, to most U.S. citizens living east of the Mississippi River, the land that the nation had purchased was largely unknown territory. Jefferson himself had been fascinated by the West and its potential for some time. Even before the Louisiana Purchase, Jefferson had asked Congress for money to fund an expedition to explore the western part of the continent and seek a route to the Pacific Ocean. Those plans took on new significance after the Louisiana Purchase.

To lead the expedition, Jefferson chose his personal secretary, Meriwether Lewis, an army captain with experience on the frontier. Lewis then asked William Clark, an army friend, to share his command. Calling their group the Corps of Discovery, Lewis, Clark, and more than thirty others set out from a camp near St. Louis on May 14, 1804. Among them were John Ordway, a New Hampshire soldier who kept a daily log of the journey, and a slave named York.

PRIMARY SOURCE

In Their Words... The Louisiana Purchase

The inhabitants of the ceded territory shall be incorporated in the Union of the United States and admitted as soon as possible according to the principles of the federal Constitution to the enjoyment of all these rights, advantages and immunities of citizens of the United States, and in the mean time they shall be maintained and protected in the free enjoyment of their liberty, property and the Religion which they profess.

—from the Louisiana Purchase, Article III

Louisiana Purchase: Treaty between the United States of America and the French Republic, art. 3, April 30, 1803. National Archives and Records Administration.

McGraw-Hill Education.

The Louisiana Territory, 1806

Map Skills Identify four rivers that go through the Louisiana Territory. On which of these did Lewis and Clark mostly travel?

The Corps traveled west on the Missouri River, meeting with many native tribes, including the Oto, the Missouri, and the Teton and Yankton Sioux. In late October of 1804, near Mandan and Hidatsa villages in what is now North Dakota, the explorers established a winter camp that they called Fort Mandan. Not long afterward, Lewis and Clark hired a French-Canadian fur trapper named Toussaint Charbonneau and his American Indian wife, Sacajawea, to serve as interpreters and guides for the rest of the trip.

304 Lesson 1 How Did Early Decisions Shape the Nation?

Lesson 1 **305**

Research Companion, pp. 304–305

ENGLISH LEARNERS SCAFFOLD

ELD.PI.5.6 Reading closely literary and informational texts and viewing multimedia to determine how meaning is conveyed explicitly and implicitly through language

Emerging	Expanding	Bridging
Use Maps Help students use the map on page 305 to follow the route of the Louis and Clark expedition as they read about it in their texts. Have them use the key to identify the way in which the expedition's route is marked on the map, and ask them to identify the starting point, St Louis.	**Compare Maps** Have students compare the map on page 305 with a current one and identify present-day states formed all or mainly from the Louisiana Territory. (Arkansas, Colorado, Iowa, Kansas, Louisiana, Minnesota, Missouri, Montana Nebraska, North Dakota, Oklahoma, South Dakota, Wyoming)	**Interpret Maps** Ask students why they think Lewis and Clark chose to take the Missouri River west, even though it was farthest north and likely meant more severe winter weather. (to avoid Spanish territory and instead go toward the Oregon Territory, which the U.S.—among others—claimed)

See the **Language Learner Teaching Guide** for more language support strategies.

Monitor and Differentiate

REACHING ALL LEARNERS

Approaching Level

Provide students with sentence frames to help them talk about the Lewis and Clark Expedition. For examples: *The left from ____ with ____ members in the group. They then traveled ____.*

On Level

Have pairs of students create a timeline of the Lewis and Clark Expedition, starting with May 14, 1804, when the group set out. Invite them to do online research to supplement text details.

Beyond Level

Have students research and report on Sacajawea, focusing on the help she provided for the Lewis and Clark Expedition.

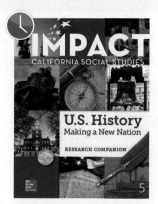

Research Companion
pp. 306–307

STANDARDS

Demonstrate knowledge of the explorations of the trans-Mississippi West following the Louisiana Purchase (e.g., Meriwether Lewis and William Clark, Zebulon Pike, John Fremont). **HSS.5.8.3**

Students differentiate between primary and secondary sources. **HAS.HR.1**

Students pose relevant questions about events they encounter in historical documents, eyewitness accounts, oral histories, letters, diaries, artifacts, photographs, maps, artworks, and architecture. **HAS.HR.2**

Students identify and interpret the multiple causes and effects of historical events. **HAS.HI.3**

Go Digital!

Investigate the lesson content with online whole-class presentation tools.

Background Information

Zebulon Pike, sent to explore the Arkansas and Red Rivers in the southwestern part of the Louisiana Purchase, strayed onto Spanish land in New Mexico and was taken captive. After his release, he served in the War of 1812, rising to the rank of general before being killed in the attack on York (now part of Toronto).

Analyze the Source

Inspect Have students read pages 306–307.

Find Evidence Use the questions below to check comprehension. Remind students to support their answers with text evidence.

Infer Why would the Corps of Discovery travel by water whenever possible? (It was faster and easier than lugging equipment over land.) **DOK 4**

Compare and Contrast How did Zebulon Pike's explorations compare and contrast to the Lewis and Clark Expedition? (They were less successful—he did not find the source of the Mississippi River, his objective.) **DOK 3**

Define What is *impressment*? (taking sailors against their will and forcing them to serve in your navy) **DOK 2**

Summarize What happened to Washington, D.C., during the War of 1812? (It was burned.) **DOK 2**

Analyze the Primary Source Read the Primary Source aloud. Ask:

Speculate How do you think Dolley Madison felt when she had to leave the White House? (anxious but determined) **DOK 3**

Make Connections

Analyze Why were war hawks angry with Great Britain? (for blocking trade, impressing U.S. sailors, and stirring American Indian unrest) **DOK 3**

☑ Stop and Check   PRODUCTIVE

Talk Have students explain why Jefferson bought the Louisiana Territory and the role Sacajawea played in helping explore it. (Students should recognize Jefferson's interest in westward expansion, desire for U.S. access to the Mississippi and New Orleans; and inability to pass up a bargain. They should mention Sacajawea's knowledge of the land and skills in communicating with other Indians.)

Sacajawea, traveling with a newborn baby, proved enormously helpful to the expedition. As a member of the Shoshone people from what is now Idaho, she was familiar with some of the area the Corps would cross. Her presence made other American Indians friendlier, and she could learn from them the best trails to use. In a famous incident, she even saved important supplies and papers when one of the expedition's boats overturned on the Missouri River.

Traveling on water when possible and land when necessary, the expedition crossed the Rocky Mountains, continued to the Columbia River, and then went down it to the Pacific Ocean. There the Corps camped for another winter before traveling back east, reaching St. Louis on September 23, 1806. Having completed a journey of about 8,000 miles, Lewis and Clark were treated as national heroes.

Lewis and Clark's Corps of Discovery was not the only group to explore the Louisiana Territory. In 1805, President Jefferson sent army lieutenant Zebulon Pike to search for the source of the Mississippi River. He did not find it. A year later, Pike was sent to explore the southwestern portion of the Louisiana Purchase. There he tried and failed to climb the mountain peak now named in his honor.

Sacajawea, shown in the statue with her newborn baby, is also honored on a one-dollar coin.

✓ Stop and Check

COLLABORATE

Talk Why did Jefferson purchase the Louisiana Territory? What role did Sacajawea play in helping to explore it?

306 Lesson 1 How Did Early Decisions Shape the Nation?

The War of 1812

Britain and France were at war when James Madison was elected president in 1808. The United States tried to stay neutral and trade with both sides. Neither side liked that policy. Each kept trying to block the United States from trading with its enemy. British actions, however, made that nation very unpopular with the United States.

The British stopped U.S. ships, claiming they were searching for British sailors who had deserted. Then they took American sailors off the ships, claiming they were British, and forced them to serve in the British navy. This policy, called impressment, made people in the United States furious. Many also thought the British in Canada were purposely causing American Indian unrest in the Northwest Territories with the hope of getting back land they had lost to the United States. In Congress, pro-war politicians, or "war hawks," demanded U.S. action. President Madison came to agree with them. And so, with Congress eager for war and the president in agreement, the War of 1812 began.

U.S. attacks on Canada were unsuccessful, although one attack resulted in the burning of legislative buildings in the town of York. A British attack from Canada was also repelled in the Battle of Lake Erie in 1813. The next year, British troops landed in Maryland and successfully attacked Washington, D.C. The entire government had to flee the capital. Evacuating the White House, First Lady Dolley Madison managed to save important government papers. White House employees saved a famous portrait of George Washington. The British destroyed the White House and badly damaged the Capitol, which had been under construction.

PRIMARY SOURCE

In Their Words... Dolley Madison

I have pressed as many Cabinet papers into trunks as to fill one carriage; our private property must be sacrificed, as it is impossible to procure [get] wagons for its transportation. I am determined not to go myself until I see Mr. Madison safe.

—from Dolley Madison's Letter to Her Sister, August 23, 1814

Lesson 1 307

Research Companion, pp. 306–307

(EL) ENGLISH LEARNERS SCAFFOLD

ELD.PI.5.8 Analyzing how writers and speakers use vocabulary and other language resources for specific purposes (to explain, persuade, entertain, etc.) depending on modality, text type, purpose, audience, topic, and content area

Emerging	Expanding	Bridging
Clarify Terms Clarify terms used for the group led by Lewis and Clark: An *expedition* is a group traveling for a specific purpose. A *corps* is a body of soldiers or others working together.	**Clarify Terms** Point to the term *neutral* in the text, clarifying that it means the United States did not want to favor either side in the conflict between Britain and France. Then point to *pro-war*, explaining that the prefix *pro-* means "in favor of."	**Distinguish Multiple-Meaning Words** Explain that *deserted* can mean (1) empty or (2) left a military post without permission. Ask which meaning applies to its use on page 307. (2) Explain that *repelled* can mean (1) pushed back or (2) disgusted. Ask which meaning applies. (1)

See the **Language Learner Teaching Guide** for more language support strategies.

Monitor and Differentiate

REACHING ALL LEARNERS

Approaching Level

Refer to the Stop and Check, showing students how they can sometimes turn questions into statements to help them answer: *Jefferson purchased the Louisiana Territory because ____.*

On Level

Have students conduct research to learn more about the term *war hawk*, or simply *hawk*, used to describe someone in favor of war. What bird is often to mean the opposite? (dove)

Beyond Level

Have students research Pike's Peak, named for Zebulon Pike. Ask them to find out its location, its altitude or height, and its role in the writing of "America, the Beautiful."

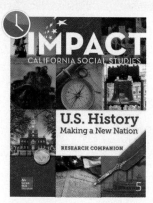

Research Companion
pp. 308–309

 STANDARDS

Students summarize the key events of the era they are studying and explain the historical context of those events. **HAS.HI.1**

Students identify and interpret the multiple causes and effects of historical events. **HAS.HI.3**

Quote accurately from a text when explaining what the text says explicitly and when drawing inferences from the text. **CCSS.ELA.RI.5.1**

Conduct short research projects that use several sources to build knowledge through investigation of different aspects of a topic. **CCSS.ELA.W.5.7**

Go Digital!

Investigate the lesson content with online whole-class presentation tools.

Background Information

Latin American independence was spurred by the activities of Napoleon Bonaparte, whose military efforts in Spain and Portugal so weakened those nations that many of their American colonies were emboldened to declare independence. After his defeat, restored European monarchies seemed likely to try to reacquire their colonies. The Monroe Doctrine was the U.S. response.

Analyze the Source

Inspect Have students read pages 308–309.

Find Evidence Use the questions below to check comprehension. Remind students to support their answers with text evidence.

> **Summarize** Sum up the outcome of the War of 1812. (Neither side won or lost, but Britain agreed to stop trying to create an American Indian state in the Northwest Territory.) **DOK 3**
>
> **Evaluate** What was the main effect of the War of 1812 on American Indians? (It extended and cemented their land losses.) **DOK 2**

Citizenship

> **Explain** Have students read about the Monroe Doctrine on page 309. Read aloud the two points of view about the doctrine, and respond to the Think About It questions. (Students' responses will vary, depending on the point of view with which they agree, but should show an understanding of historical events.) **DOK 3**

Make Connections

> **Analyze** Why did the Federalist Party all but vanish in the so-called Era of Good Feelings? (Its antiwar stand was not popular, and most Americans now supported the other party.) **DOK 4**

✓ Stop and Check

Talk Have students sum up the causes of the War of 1812. (interference with U.S. trade, impressment of sailors, and possible British efforts to stir American Indian unrest)

This print gives a British artist's impression of what the 1814 burning of Washington, D.C., might have looked like.

The British attempt to attack Baltimore was less successful. Francis Scott Key, an American lawyer and poet held captive on a British ship in Baltimore Harbor, watched the British attack Fort McHenry there. The next morning, the American flag was still flying over the fort. Key was so moved that he wrote a poem that later became the words to the U.S. national anthem, "The Star-Spangled Banner."

Finally, British and U.S. diplomats met in Europe and signed the Treaty of Ghent to end the war. Neither side won or lost, but Britain abandoned its efforts to establish an Indian state in the Northwest. American Indians in the Northwest Territory suffered the most losses in the War of 1812. The United States defeated them and forced them to sign away lands with no interference from the British.

The Federalist Party, which had opposed the war, now nearly vanished from the political scene. With just one effective political party and a strong sense of national unity and purpose, the period following the War of 1812 is often called the Era of Good Feeling. The president most associated with this era is James Monroe, who won the election of 1816 with the support of retiring President Madison and was reelected with little opposition four years later.

✓ Stop and Check

Think What were the causes of the War of 1812?

Citizenship 👥

The Monroe Doctrine

Starting in 1810, many colonies in Latin America began declaring their independence from the European countries that had colonized them. The United States generally supported these efforts and worried that European nations would try to reestablish colonial rule. In an 1823 speech to Congress, President Monroe laid out U.S. policy on such behavior. That policy came to be called the Monroe Doctrine. It would become the single most influential piece of foreign policy in U.S. history. The doctrine had these main points:

- The United States would not involve itself in European politics.
- The United States recognized current European colonies in the Americas.
- Except for the colonies existing at the time, the United States expected Europe to stay out of North and South America and would regard any interference there as a hostile act—an act that could lead to warfare.

James Monroe

Read the two different points of view about the Monroe Doctrine. Then answer the questions that follow.

Pro-Monroe Doctrine View	Anti-Monroe Doctrine View
The Monroe Doctrine shows that the United States wanted to protect its neighbors in the Americas and wanted them to be free and independent nations.	The Monroe Doctrine shows that the United States thought of itself as the main power in the Americas and wanted to control its neighbors without any competition.

Think About It

1. Think about the conflicts that led up to the Monroe Doctrine. What earlier events or conflicts might have caused the United States to be wary of European powers in North America?

2. Research times when the United States has used the Monroe Doctrine, such as the Spanish American War or the Cuban Missile Crisis. Was the United States justified in its actions?

3. Do you agree with either of the points of view above? Why or why not? Can you think of a point of view different from both of these?

Research Companion, pp. 308–309

📘 ENGLISH LEARNERS SCAFFOLD

ELD.PI.5.8 Analyzing how writers and speakers use vocabulary and other language resources for specific purposes (to explain, persuade, entertain, etc.) depending on modality, text type, purpose, audience, topic, and content area

Emerging

Clarify Vocabulary Be sure students understand that *preserved* in the statement "U.S. independence was preserved" means "kept safe" or "protected."

Expanding

Understand Prefixes Remind students that the prefix *pro-* means "in favor of." Note that its opposite is the prefix *anti-*, which means "against." Point out that these prefixes can be temporarily attached to just about any noun. Have students list examples.

Bridging

Understand Domain-Specific Terms Mention the term *Era of Good Feelings,* and note that the word *era* appears frequently in the study of history. Elicit that an *era* is a period of time associated with something. Discuss similar words—*epoch* or *period.*

See the **Language Learner Teaching Guide** for more language support strategies.

Monitor and Differentiate

REACHING ALL LEARNERS

On Level

In conjunction with the second Think About It question, have students work in groups to research times when the Monroe Doctrine has been used to justify U.S. military or other action in the hemisphere.

Beyond Level

Have students form groups to debate the Monroe Doctrine, with one side taking the Pro-Doctrine position and the other taking the Anti-Doctrine position. Encourage students to research times when the Monroe Doctrine was used and cite them in their debates.

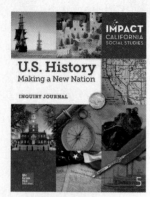

Inquiry Journal
pp. 248–249

 STANDARDS

Demonstrate knowledge of the significance of land policies developed under the Continental Congress (e.g., sale of western lands, the Northwest Ordinance of 1787) and those policies' impact on American Indians' land. **HSS.5.6.6**

Know the songs that express American ideals (e.g., "America the Beautiful," "The Star Spangled Banner"). **HSS.5.7.6**

Demonstrate knowledge of the explorations of the trans-Mississippi West following the Louisiana Purchase (e.g., Meriwether Lewis and William Clark, Zebulon Pike, John Fremont). **HSS.5.8.3**

CCSS Write narratives to develop real or imagined experiences or events using effective technique, descriptive details, and clear event sequences. **CCSS.ELA.W.5.3**

Go Digital!

- Students can go online to report their findings. Assess their responses online.

- Students can access the online graphic organizer to capture ideas from their investigation.

Think About It

Students should review their research, focusing especially on the Louisiana Territory and its exploration. Remind them to review the notes they took in their cause-and-effect graphic organizer. Direct them to pages 298–309 of their Research Companion if they need more information.

Write About It

Write a Diary Entry Have students read the prompt. Remind students that a diary is a work in which a person describes his or her experiences soon after they happened and expresses his or her thoughts and feelings about them. Tell them to include the following elements in their response:

- a statement that introduces the decision or policy

- a description of how the decision or policy affects the writer

- words that clearly signal cause and effect, such as *cause, effect, because, so, as a result,* and *due to*

- the writer's feelings or opinions about the decision or policy

- first-person pronouns, such as *I* and *me*

Use the rubric on page T644 to evaluate students' work.

Talk About It

Defend Your Claim Help students pair up with classmates to discuss their diary entries.

- Tell students to take turns asking and answering questions that explain who each diary writer is, what that person has been doing, and how one or more government policies or decisions has affected him or her.

- Ask students to discuss whether they agree or disagree with their partners' descriptions and reactions and to explain why.

- Remind students to follow the rules of appropriate classroom conversation.

Connect to the
Essential Question

Read the prompt aloud to students. Ask them the following guiding questions:

- How did the policy or decision you wrote about change the nation? (Responses will vary.)

- What group or groups of people were most affected by the policy or decision you wrote about? How was each group affected? (Responses will vary.)

Remind students to use the space provided in their journal to jot down notes.

Report Your Findings

Think About It

Review your research. Why was it important to explore the Louisiana Territory?

Write About It

Write a Diary Entry

Imagine you are someone living in the early United States who was affected by a decision or policy made by an early leader. Perhaps this person is an American Indian, a settler, or a member of the Corps of Discovery. Explain, in a diary entry from this person's perspective, how he or she was affected by the decision and why this decision was important. Remember to use evidence from the text.

Students should choose a decision or policy mentioned in this lesson and give a person's perspective on it, supported by text evidence.

Talk About It COLLABORATE

Defend Your Claim

Working with a partner, discuss your diary entries. Take turns asking and answering questions that explain who each diary writer is, what that person has been doing, and how one or more government policies or decisions have affected him or her.

Connect to the ESSENTIAL QUESTION

History

Consider Cause and Effect

Think about a policy or decision you wrote about in your diary entry. In general, how did it change the nation and its people?

Student responses should be based on information in the text and should mention a change that occurred in the United States.

EQ Inquiry Project Notes

Inquiry Journal, pp. 248–249

EL ENGLISH LEARNERS SCAFFOLD

ELD.PI.5.11 Supporting own opinions and evaluating others' opinions in speaking and writing

Emerging	Expanding	Bridging
State and Support Opinions Point out that in the Write About It assignment, students are asked to describe effects of events and give their feelings or opinions about them as if they were there. Provide sentence frames to help them: *My life changed when ___.* *In my experience, the change was good/bad because ___.*	**Ask and Answer Questions** Pair students for the Talk About It assignment. Then have them turn the prompts into questions for their partner to answer, such as *Who are you supposed to be? What have you been doing as that person? How has a government policy or decision affected you?*	**Develop Ideas** Have students review the text about the Louisiana Purchase and add details to the notes they took on the subject in their graphic organizer. Then have them discuss the importance of the Louisiana Purchase as a class or in small groups.

See the **Language Learner Teaching Guide** for more language support strategies.

Monitor and Differentiate

REACHING ALL LEARNERS

Approaching Level

Point out that students will be writing a diary entry in which they pretend to be someone who lived at the time of the decision or policy they will discuss. Remind them to use first-person pronouns like *I, me, my,* and *we.*

On Level

Help students use the causes and effects on which they took notes to complete the Connect to the Essential Question activity. Tell them to ask themselves: *What caused the event, and why was that important? What resulted from the event, and why was that important?*

Know what your students know!

Lesson Task
Report Your Findings

Use this rubric to evaluate students' response.

Write a Diary Entry Students pretend to be someone living in the United States, such as an American Indian, a settler, or a member of the Corps of Discovery, who was affected by a decision or policy made by an early leader. They write a diary entry from that person's perspective, explaining the effects of the decision or policy on that person and describing that person's feelings about it.

Defend Your Claim Students question a partner about who the diary writer is, what that person has been doing, and how one or more government policies or decisions have affected him or her.

Performance Task Evaluation Rubric

	4	3	2	1
Historical Understanding	Displays strong understanding of the decision or policy and its effects on members of a particular group	Displays adequate understanding of the decision or policy and its effects on members of a particular group	Displays uneven understanding of the decision or policy and its effects on members of a particular group	Displays no understanding of events of the decision or policy and its effects on members of a particular group
Write a Diary Entry	Provides a clear description of the effects of the decision or policy on the person the students is pretending to be	Provides an adequate explanation of the effects of the decision or policy on the person the students is pretending to be	Provides a somewhat clear or unclear explanation of the effects of the decision or policy on the person the students is pretending to be	Provides no statement or no explanation of the effects of the decision or policy on the person the students is pretending to be
Support with Evidence	Supports claims and reasons with thorough and convincing evidence	Supports claims and reasons with adequate evidence	Supports claims and reasons with too little or only somewhat convincing evidence	Supplies no claims or reasons or no supporting evidence
Defend Your Claim	Respectfully takes turns speaking during discussion Speaks in complete sentences throughout the discussion	Takes turns speaking during discussion Speaks in complete sentences through most of the discussion	At times does not take turns speaking during discussion Mixes complete and incomplete sentences during the discussion	Does not take turns speaking during discussion Does not use complete sentences in the discussion

Lesson Assessment

Go *Digital!*

- Have students complete the Chapter 7 Lesson 1 Assessment online to monitor their understanding of the lesson content.

ONLINE ASSESSMENT

California Smarter Balanced Assessment Connections!

Standards Covered	Lesson Task	Lesson Assessment	Alignment with California Smarter Balanced Assessment
History and Social Science Content 5.6.6; 5.7; 5.7.8; 5.8.3	✔	✔	Claim 1 Targets 8, 9, 11
History and Social Science Analysis Skills Chronological and Spatial Thinking 5.1; 5.4 Research, Evidence, and Point of View 5.1; 5.2 Historical Interpretation 5.1; 5.3	✔	✔	Claim 1 Targets 8, 9, 11
Writing W.5.3	✔	✔	Claim 2 Target 1
Research and Inquiry W.5.7; W.5.9	✔	✔	Claim 4 Targets 1, 2, 3, 4
Reading RI.5.1	✔	✔	Claim 1 Target 8, 11, 13
Speaking and Listening SL.5.1; SL.5.2	✔		Claim 3 Target 3 Claim 4 Target 1

LESSON QUESTION

How Did Advancements in Technology and Transportation Shape the Nation?

Background Information

In this lesson, students will learn about the early Industrial Revolution in the United States, the new technologies it produced, and its effects on transportation, communication, and urban growth.

Community Connections

To enrich what students have learned in this lesson, have them visit the website of the Lowell National Historical Park, the Eli Whitney Museum and Workshop, the B & O Railroad Museum, or another museum or historical site focusing on technology or urban life in the early nineteenth century.

LESSON STANDARDS

✓ Students trace the colonization, immigration, and settlement patterns of the American people from 1789 to the mid-1800s, with emphasis on the role of economic incentives, effects of the physical and political geography, and transportation systems. **HSS.5.8**

✓ Discuss the waves of immigrants from Europe between 1789 and 1850 and their modes of transportation into the Ohio and Mississippi Valleys and through the Cumberland Gap (e.g., overland wagons, canals, flatboats, steamboats). **HSS.5.8.1**

✓ Students place key events and people of the historical era they are studying in a chronological sequence and spatial context; they interpret time lines. **HAS.CS.1**

✓ Students judge the significance of the relative location of a place (e.g., proximity to a harbor, on trade routes) and analyze how relative advantages or disadvantages can change over time. **HAS.CS.5**

✓ Students differentiate between primary and secondary sources. **HAS.HR.1**

✓ Students pose relevant questions about events they encounter in historical documents, eyewitness accounts, oral histories, letters, diaries, artifacts, photographs, maps, artworks, and architecture. **HAS.HR.2**

 Connect to the
Essential Question

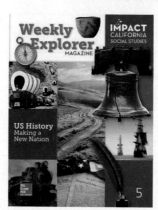

Chapter 7, pp. 84–99

The **Weekly Explorer Magazine** supports students' exploration of the Essential Question and provides additional resources for the EQ Inquiry Project.

 ## Inquiry Project

Which Change Will You Choose?

Remind students to use the information they learn in this lesson and other resources to complete their EQ Inquiry Project!

Dinah Zike's

In this lesson you will use Foldables.

When Minutes Count!

Suggested Lesson Pacing

1 ENGAGE
One Day

- Analyze the Source
- Inquiry Tools

Go Digital
- **iMap:** Cotton Production, 1820–1860
- **iMap:** Major Railroads, 1860

2 INVESTIGATE
Two to Three Days

🕐 **Short on Time?** Look for the clock to teach core content in less time.

- New Technology Paves the Way
- New Forms of Transportation
- Advancements in Communication
- The Growth of Cities

3 REPORT
One Day

- Think About It
- Write an Advertisement
- Compare Advertisements

Make Connections!

ⓒⓒⓢⓢ CONNECT TO ELA

Reading
Quote accurately from a text when explaining what the text says explicitly and when drawing inferences from the text. **RI.5.1**

Research
Conduct short research projects that use several sources to build knowledge through investigation of different aspects of a topic. **W. 5.7**

Draw evidence from literary or informational texts to support analysis, reflection, and research. **W.5.9**

Writing
Write opinion pieces on topics or texts, supporting a point of view with reasons and information. **W.5.1**

Produce clear and coherent writing in which the development and organization are appropriate to task, purpose, and audience. **W.5.4**

Speaking and Listening
Engage effectively in a range of collaborative discussions (one-on-one, in groups, and teacher-led) with diverse partners on grade 5 topics and texts, building on others' ideas and expressing their own clearly. **SL.5.1**

Classroom Resources

🔍 Search for additional resources using the following key words.

B & O Railroad

Erie Canal

Industrial Revolution

Lowell, Massachusetts

McCormick reaper

National Road

steamboat travel

telegraph

Eli Whitney

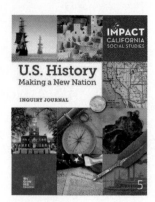

Inquiry Journal
pp. 250–251

HSS **STANDARDS**

Students trace the colonization, immigration, and settlement patterns of the American people from 1789 to the mid-1800s, with emphasis on the role of economic incentives, effects of the physical and political geography, and transportation systems. **HSS.5.8**

Discuss the waves of immigrants from Europe between 1789 and 1850 and their modes of transportation into the Ohio and Mississippi Valleys and through the Cumberland Gap (e.g., overland wagons, canals, flatboats, steamboats). **HSS.5.8.1**

CCSS Summarize a written text read aloud or information presented in diverse media and formats, including visually, quantitatively, and orally. **CCSS.ELA.SL.5.2**

Go Digital!

Explore the lesson content with online whole-class presentation tools.

- **iMap:** Cotton Production, 1820–1860
- **iMap:** Major Railroads, 1860

How Did Advancements in Technology and Transportation Shape the Nation?

Bellringer

Prompt students to retrieve information from the previous lessons. Say: *In the decades after the Revolution, many U.S. citizens moved west of the Appalachian Mountains. With the Louisiana Purchase, the nation spread even further west. Why do you think new forms of transportation and communication would be important?* (to keep the growing nation united)

Lesson Outcomes

What Am I Learning? Have students read the Lesson Question and Lesson Outcomes.

Why Am I Learning It? Stress that the new technology and transportation changed the way Americans lived.

How Will I Know That I Learned It? Ask students the following questions:

- What will you be able to describe? (important inventions and changes)
- What problems will the new inventions solve? (problems in travel and communication, among other things)

Talk About It

Explain that Currier & Ives was a printing company in 19th-century America, famous for creating engravings of artwork and using them to produce popular, inexpensive prints. Have students view the image of the Currier & Ives engraving and read the caption. Provide sentence frames to help them respond to the questions about it.

- ***The flatboat is powered by*** rowing . ***You can tell this from*** the oars .
- ***The boats in the background are powered by*** steam .
- ***You can tell this from*** the steam coming out of their smokestacks .

Collaborative Conversations

Add New Ideas As students engage in partner, small group, and whole-class discussions, encourage them to

- Stay on topic.
- Connect their own ideas to things their peers have said.
- Look for ways to connect their personal experiences or prior knowledge to the conversation.

Lesson 2

How Did Advancements in Technology and Transportation Shape the Nation?

Lesson Outcomes

What Am I Learning?
In this lesson, you will use your investigative skills to learn about new technology and transportation in the decades after the American Revolution and the way it affected the lives of U.S. citizens.

Why Am I Learning It?
Reading and talking about new technology and transportation will help you understand their importance in contributing to the growth of the U.S. economy and how they impacted people's lives.

How Will I Know That I Learned It?
You will be able to describe important inventions and other changes and how they addressed problems of travel and communication as well as how they affected the way people worked.

Talk About It COLLABORATE

Look at the Details How are the different types of boats being powered? How can you tell?

This painting of a river scene shows a flatboat used to transport goods and several passenger steamboats in the background.

(BeigeBC Squared Studios/Getty Images)
(InvettView University Art Gallery)

McGraw-Hill Education

HSS.5.8.1, HAS.HR.1, HAS.HR.2, HAS.HI.1, HAS.HI.2, HAS.HI.3

250 Lesson 2 How Did Advancements in Technology and Transportation Shape the Nation?

Lesson 2 **251**

Inquiry Journal, pp. 250–251

ENGLISH LEARNERS SCAFFOLD

ELD.PI.5.6 Reading closely literary and informational texts and viewing multimedia to determine how meaning is conveyed explicitly and implicitly through language

Emerging	Expanding	Bridging
Describe an Image Provide additional sentence frames to help students describe what the engraving shows. **There are** six **men on the flatboat, which is carrying** cargo, or freight or goods **underneath. There are** several or five **steamboats on the river, each with** two **smokestacks**.	**Recognize Visual Details** Ask students what the men on the flatboat seem to be doing. (rowing and entertaining themselves) Have students speculate about why the men are on the flatboat. (They are probably all workers, with some taking a break and entertaining themselves.)	**Understand Images** Discuss the contrast between the one flatboat and many steamboats in the print. Have students identify the U.S. flag waving from one of the steamboats. Ask what change the flag and the many steamboats suggest. (Steamboats are becoming the main form of river transportation.)

See the **Language Learner Teaching Guide** for more language support strategies.

Monitor and Differentiate

REACHING ALL LEARNERS

Approaching Level

Be sure students know that *transportation* refers to the ways people travel or move goods and *communication* refers to the ways they give and send messages.

On Level

Have students do simple online research to find out how fast steamboats usually traveled. (about 5 miles an hour)

Beyond Level

Have students research lithography, the method that Currier & Ives used to produce engravings for prints, and explain it in an illustrated report.

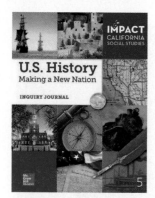

Inquiry Journal
pp. 252–253

 STANDARDS

Students trace the colonization, immigration, and settlement patterns of the American people from 1789 to the mid-1800s, with emphasis on the role of economic incentives, effects of the physical and political geography, and transportation systems. **HSS.5.8**

Discuss the waves of immigrants from Europe between 1789 and 1850 and their modes of transportation into the Ohio and Mississippi Valleys and through the Cumberland Gap (e.g., overland wagons, canals, flatboats, steamboats). **HSS.5.8.1**

Students differentiate between primary and secondary sources. **HAS.HR.1**

Go Digital!

Model how to inspect and find evidence with online whole-class presentation tools.

Background Information

Charles Dickens had already published *Oliver Twist* and other popular books when he arrived in the United States in 1842. He lost friends by complaining of the lack of U.S. copyright laws (making most of his books here pirated editions) and later by portraying Americans as somewhat boorish in *American Notes* and *Martin Chuzzlewit*. Still, he remained popular, and when he returned in 1867 for public readings of *A Christmas Carol,* his "quarrel with America" was declared over.

1 Inspect

Read Have students read the primary source and text introducing it, circling unfamiliar words and underlining clues that tell *what, where,* and *when.* Ask:

• What is Charles Dickens's steamboat cabin like? (small but peaceful)

• Where is he traveling? (from Pittsburgh to Cincinnati on the Ohio River)

• When does he expect to arrive? (in three days—Monday morning)

Collaborate Have partners discuss the opinions Dickens seems to have about the steamboat. (Students should recognize that he likes the boat but not the food.)

2 Find Evidence

Reread Have students reread the text, focusing on specific details.

Analyze the Primary Source Read the text aloud and analyze it together. Ask:

• What does the primary source show about the two kinds of passengers on steamboats? (Poorer passengers were on the lower deck; wealthier ones had staterooms with sleeping berths.)

• What kind of passenger is Charles Dickens? (wealthier)

Analyze the Image Explain that *caricatures* are exaggerated, usually humorous pictures. Why is this picture a caricature. (It exaggerates Dickens' importance or self-importance by giving him a big head and tiny feet and a long, scraggly beard.)

COLLABORATE
3 Make Connections

Talk Have students discuss what they learn about steamboat travel from the primary source. (Students should recognize that steamboats were popular, still slow by today's standards, and offered accommodations and full meals to those who paid for them.)

Analyze the Source

1 Inspect

Read Examine the text of this primary source and the sentences that introduce it.

- **Circle** words you don't know.
- **Underline** details that tell you *what* the steamboat cabin is like, *where* Charles Dickens is going, and *when* he expects to arrive there.
- **Discuss** with a partner the opinions that Dickens seems to have about the steamboat.

My Notes

_____

_____

_____

_____

_____

_____

_____

_____

_____

_____

_____

_____

Charles Dickens Takes an American Steamboat

Britain's Charles Dickens was already a famous writer when he and his wife visited the United States in 1842. After stops on the East Coast, they traveled by canal boat, railroad, and stagecoach to Pittsburgh, Pennsylvania. From there, they took a steamboat called the *Messenger* down the Ohio River to Cincinnati, Ohio. Before the invention of the steamboat, travel by waterway took a long time and relied on the water's current. The following text comes from Dickens's description of that trip.

A caricature of the British author, Charles Dickens

Library of Congress, Prints & Photographs Division [LC-USZ62-88778]

PRIMARY SOURCE

In Their Words... Charles Dickens

The *Messenger* was one among a crowd of high-pressure steamboats, clustered together by a wharf side, which, looked down upon from the rising ground that forms the landing place, and backed by the lofty bank on the opposite side of the river, appeared no larger than so many floating models. She had some forty passengers on board, exclusive of the poorer persons on the lower deck; and in half an hour, or less, proceeded on her way.

We had, for ourselves, a tiny stateroom with two berths in it. . . . It was an unspeakable relief to have any place, no matter how confined, where one could be alone. . . .

We are to be on board the *Messenger* three days: arriving at Cincinnati (barring accidents) on Monday morning. There are three meals a day. Breakfast at seven, dinner at half-past twelve, supper about six. At each, there are a great many small dishes and plates upon the table, with very little in them; so that although there is every appearance of a mighty "spread," there is seldom really more than a joint: except for those who fancy slices of beet-root, shreds of dried beef, complicated entanglements of yellow pickle; maize, Indian corn, apple-sauce, and pumpkin.

—from *American Notes*, Chapter XI

TEXT: Dickens, Charles. American Notes. New York: John W. Lovell Company, 1883. PHOTO: McGraw-Hill Education

2 Find Evidence

Reread What does the quotation show you about the two kinds of passengers on steamboats? Which kind of passenger is Charles Dickens?

3 Make Connections

Talk Discuss with a partner what you learn about steamboat travel from this primary source.

COLLABORATE

252 Lesson 2 How Did Advancements in Technology and Transportation Shape the Nation?

Lesson 2 **253**

Inquiry Journal, pp. 252–253

(EL) ENGLISH LEARNERS SCAFFOLD

ELD.PI.5.6 Reading closely literary and informational texts and viewing multimedia to determine how meaning is conveyed explicitly and implicitly through language

Emerging

Clarify Vocabulary
Clarify terms in the primary source, such as *clustered* ("grouped together"), *lofty* ("high"), *exclusive of* ("not counting"), *proceeded* ("went"), *confined* ("closed in"), *barring* ("unless there should be"), *joint* ("large cut of meat with the bone still in"), and *fancy* ("have a liking or desire for").

Expanding

Clarify Technical Terms
Clarify terms related to water travel, such as *current* ("strong flow of water"), *wharf* ("dock"), *bank* ("riverside"), *deck* ("floor or level on a boat"), *stateroom* ("private cabin"), and *berth* ("built-in or bunk bed"). Ask students to use the words in a paragraph about a boat trip.

Bridging

Understand Anglicisms
Explain that Dickens, a British author, uses terms specific to British English but rarely or never used in the U.S. Note that his use of *maize*, the original word for *corn*, is an Anglicism, used in Britain long after it fell from use in the U.S. (The British used *corn* to mean "any staple grain.")

See the **Language Learner Teaching Guide** for more language support strategies.

Monitor and Differentiate

REACHING ALL LEARNERS

On Level

Have students discuss the meal Dickens describes and sum up his complaints about it. (The spread looked big but actually had small portions; the side dishes were strange and not appealing.) Ask if students think the poorer passengers had such a meal. (It is unlikely.)

Beyond Level

Have students read more in Dickens' *American Notes*, available online, and report on one of his stops, such as the new factory town of Lowell, Massachusetts; Philadelphia; the Looking-Glass Prairie near St. Louis; or "the Falls of Niagara."

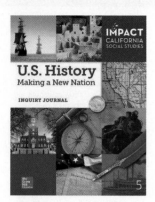

Inquiry Journal
pp. 254–255

 STANDARDS

Students trace the colonization, immigration, and settlement patterns of the American people from 1789 to the mid-1800s, with emphasis on the role of economic incentives, effects of the physical and political geography, and transportation systems. **HSS.5.8**

Discuss the waves of immigrants from Europe between 1789 and 1850 and their modes of transportation into the Ohio and Mississippi Valleys and through the Cumberland Gap (e.g., overland wagons, canals, flatboats, steamboats). **HSS.5.8.1**

Go Digital!

- Model how to explore and investigate with online whole-class tools.
- Students can access the online graphic organizer to use the inquiry tools as they read.

Explore Problem and Solution

Explain Tell students that problem and solution is one kind of structure that authors use to present information. Clarify, if necessary, that a solution is a way to fix a problem.

Read Have students read aloud the step-by-step instructions about how to identify problems and solutions.

Guide Practice Model how to complete the graphic organizer. Say: *One of the problems people faced was that travel by waterway took a long time and depended on the water's natural current. An inventor came up with a solution to this problem by creating an engine that ran on steam.*

Investigate!

Have students read pages 310–317 in the Research Companion. Tell them the information will help them answer the lesson question *How Did Advancements in Technology and Transportation Shape the Nation?*

Take Notes Tell students that they will take notes as they read each section. Remind them that taking notes will help them understand and remember the information they learn. Stress the importance of paraphrasing, or using their own words, when they take notes.

Inspect Guide students to read the text in each section to determine what it says. Suggest that they ask these questions after each paragraph: *What problem did people have? What invention or change solved the problem?* Point out that some problems can have more than one solution.

Find Evidence Encourage students to reread the text to develop a deeper understanding of the content. Tell them that after they read and take notes, they should review and think about how the facts and details will help them answer the lesson question.

Collaborative Conversations

Text-Based Discussion Remind students of the goals of discussing the text with others:

- to listen and respond to their partners' points
- to ask for evidence from the text
- to build on each other's ideas
- to see the text from a different point of view

Inquiry Tools

Explore Problem and Solution

Text is often organized by presenting problems and then showing how those problems have been or could be solved.

1. Read the text once all the way through.
This will help you understand what the text is about.

2. Look at the section titles to see how the text is organized.
This will help you find key events, decisions, and policies in the text.

3. Find specific problems.
While reading, ask yourself what problems people in the early United States had.

4. Watch for specific solutions.
While reading, also ask yourself which particular inventions or changes offered solutions to those problems.

 COLLABORATE Based on the text you just read, work with your class to complete the chart below.

Problem	Solution
Travel by waterway took a long time and was affected by the water's current.	The steamboat is invented.

Investigate!

Read pages 310–317 in your Research Companion. Use your investigative skills to determine how advancements in technology and transportation solved various problems in the early United States. Use the chart below to organize the information.

Problem	Solution
Farmers use slow, hand-held tool to cut down crops.	McCormick invents horse-drawn reaper.
Rubber does not withstand heat and cold.	Charles Goodyear develops vulcanized rubber.
bad dirt roads	National Road, including portions made of macadam
One end of Erie Canal is higher than the other.	Locks lift and lower boats in the water.
Messages over long distances must be transported and delivered by hand.	invention of telegraph

McGraw-Hill Education

Inquiry Journal, pp. 254–255

(EL) ENGLISH LEARNERS SCAFFOLD

ELD.PII.5.1 Understanding text structure

Emerging

Identify Problem and Solution Mention words that signal problems and solutions, such as *solve, improve, fix, problem, solution, improvement,* and *make better.*

Expanding

Understand Problem and Solution Give students practice with problems and solutions by having them identify everyday examples. For instance, say: *Those gloves were not warm enough, but Ali knitted me a warmer pair.* Then ask: *What was the problem?* (gloves not warm) *What was the solution?* (knit a warmer pair)

Bridging

Use Problem and Solution Have students give their own examples of problems and solutions from everyday life. Ask them to focus especially on new products or changes that have solved problems that people had before.

See the **Language Learner Teaching Guide** for more language support strategies.

Monitor and Differentiate

REACHING ALL LEARNERS

Approaching/On Level

Mention words that sometimes signal problems and solutions, such as *problem, fix, solve, solution, better, improve,* and *improvement.*

Beyond Level

Discuss the term *Yankee* or *American ingenuity.* Explain that *ingenuity* means "cleverness" and that in the 19th century, Americans—especially New Englanders—were becoming known for clever inventions or solutions to problems, often with whatever was at hand. Clarify that *Yankee* can mean "New Englander," "Northerner," or "any American."

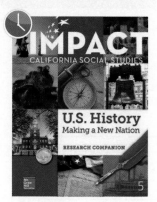

Research Companion
pp. 310–311

Go Digital!

Investigate the lesson content with online whole-class presentation tools.

- **iMap:** Cotton Production, 1820–1860

- **iMap:** Major Railroads, 1860

Background Information

The Industrial Revolution is sometimes said to begin in 1771 with James Hargreaves invention of the spinning jenny, which spun yarn from eight spindles instead of one. Then Richard Arkwright invented the water frame to run a spinning wheel with water power and set up mills where the spinning was done. In 1779, Samuel Crompton combined the water frame and spinning jenny to create the Crompton mule. A few years later, Edmund Cartwright created a simple water-powered loom to weave the yarn that was being produced. By the mid-1780s, Britain had all the basic equipment for its early textile factories.

| TIMELINE | Invite students to look at the timeline at the top on page 311.

Analyze How long after construction began on the National Road did the Erie Canal open? (14 years) How long after that did the B & O Railroad begin using the first steam locomotive? (5 years) **HAS.CS.1**

Analyze the Source

Inspect Have students read pages 310–311.

Find Evidence Use the questions below to check comprehension. Remind students to support their answers with text evidence.

Define How would you define the Industrial Revolution? (the shift from making and doing things by hand to making and doing things with machines) **DOK 3**

Identify What sort of factory was the first American factory? (a textile mill) **DOK 1**

Explain What is a textile mill? (a factory where cloth is made) **DOK 1**

Make Connections

Infer Why was Samuel Slater able to build the first American factory? (He had worked in a British factory and knew the secrets of its water-powered machinery.) **DOK 3**

Analyze the Image Direct students' attention to the photograph and caption. Ask:

- From the picture, what part of a train do you conclude a locomotive is? (the engine)

- What household item or equipment used today does the steam locomotive resemble? (Students are likely to say a hot water heater or a furnace.)

- What seems unusual to you about the locomotive's appearance? (Students may find its height unusual or the fact that it is not more enclosed.)

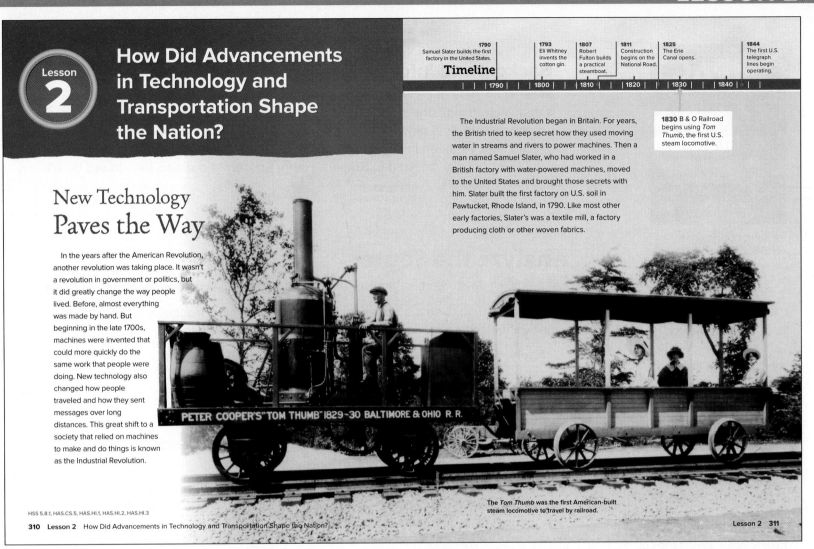

Lesson 2

How Did Advancements in Technology and Transportation Shape the Nation?

Timeline

1790	1793	1807	1811	1825	1844
Samuel Slater builds the first factory in the United States.	Eli Whitney invents the cotton gin.	Robert Fulton builds a practical steamboat.	Construction begins on the National Road.	The Erie Canal opens.	The first U.S. telegraph lines begin operating.

| | 1790 | | 1800 | | 1810 | | 1820 | | 1830 | | 1840 | |

The Industrial Revolution began in Britain. For years, the British tried to keep secret how they used moving water in streams and rivers to power machines. Then a man named Samuel Slater, who had worked in a British factory with water-powered machines, moved to the United States and brought those secrets with him. Slater built the first factory on U.S. soil in Pawtucket, Rhode Island, in 1790. Like most other early factories, Slater's was a textile mill, a factory producing cloth or other woven fabrics.

1830 B & O Railroad begins using *Tom Thumb*, the first U.S. steam locomotive.

New Technology Paves the Way

In the years after the American Revolution, another revolution was taking place. It wasn't a revolution in government or politics, but it did greatly change the way people lived. Before, almost everything was made by hand. But beginning in the late 1700s, machines were invented that could more quickly do the same work that people were doing. New technology also changed how people traveled and how they sent messages over long distances. This great shift to a society that relied on machines to make and do things is known as the Industrial Revolution.

PETER COOPER'S "TOM THUMB" 1829–30 BALTIMORE & OHIO R. R.

The *Tom Thumb* was the first American-built steam locomotive to travel by railroad.

HSS 5.8.1, HAS.CS.5, HAS.HI.1, HAS.HI.2, HAS.HI.3

310   Lesson 2   How Did Advancements in Technology and Transportation Shape the Nation?

Lesson 2   311

Research Companion, pp. 310–311

 ENGLISH LEARNERS SCAFFOLD

ELD.PI.5.8 Analyzing how writers and speakers use vocabulary and other language resources for specific purposes (to explain, persuade, entertain, etc.) depending on modality, text type, purpose, audience, topic, and content area

Emerging

Understand Multiple-Meaning Terms Discuss the two meanings of the word *revolution* used in the opening paragraph—"the overthrow of a government" and "a great change of any kind." Ask how the second meaning relates to the first. (Overthrowing a government is a great change.)

Expanding/Bridging

Understand Words in Context Point to the term *textile mill* on page 311, and have students identify the words in the text that explain what the term means. (a factory producing cloth or woven fabrics) Note that terms in textbooks are often explained after commas, as *textile mill* is here. Clarify, or have students clarify, which word in the term means "factory" *(mill)* and which refers to "cloth or woven fabrics" *(textile)*.

See the **Language Learner Teaching Guide** for more language support strategies.

Monitor and Differentiate

REACHING ALL LEARNERS

Special Needs

Have students discuss the steam locomotive shown in the photograph. Would they have wanted to ride it? Why or why not?

Approaching Level

Review the timeline with students, asking them which inventions and other changes are familiar and which are not.

Beyond Level

Explain that *Tom Thumb* was a thumb-sized hero of traditional children's stories. Ask why the locomotive might have been called *Tom Thumb*. (It was small but did a heroic job.)

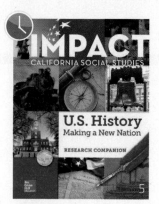

Research Companion
pp. 312–313

 STANDARDS

Students trace the colonization, immigration, and settlement patterns of the American people from 1789 to the mid-1800s, with emphasis on the role of economic incentives, effects of the physical and political geography, and transportation systems. **HSS.5.8**

Students judge the significance of the relative location of a place (e.g., proximity to a harbor, on trade routes) and analyze how relative advantages or disadvantages can change over time. **HAS.CS.5**

Students summarize the key events of the era they are studying and explain the historical context of those events. **HAS.HI.1**

Students identify and interpret the multiple causes and effects of historical events. **HAS.HI.3**

Go Digital!

Investigate the lesson content with online whole-class presentation tools.

Background Information

Steel is an alloy of iron and carbon. Stronger than iron, it came to be used extensively in industry, including for office buildings and railroads. When John Deere introduced his steel plow, however, the process of mass-producing steel for industrial use had not yet been invented. That came with the development of air-blown steel in the 1850s, usually credited to Britain's Henry Bessemer but also developed by William Kelly in Pittsburgh.

Analyze the Source

Inspect Have students continue reading about new technology on pages 312–313.

Find Evidence Use the questions below to check comprehension. Remind students to support their answers with text evidence.

Apply Why was Lowell, Massachusetts, built on a river? (Its textile mills needed fast-moving water to power the machinery). **DOK 3**

Infer With the cotton gin, what step in preparing cotton was no longer done by hand? (separating cotton seeds from the fiber) **DOK 3**

Explain What two farm activities became more productive with the Newbold and Deere plows and the McCormick reaper? (planting seeds and harvesting, or gathering, crops) **DOK 2**

Define What is vulcanization? (a method developed by Charles Goodyear to make rubber withstand heat and cold) **DOK 2**

Make Connections

Analyze In what way did New England's factory economy still rely on farming? (The factories needed wool from sheep and cotton from southern plantations.) **DOK 4**

☑ Stop and Check

Talk Have students describe the good and bad effects of the cotton gin on the southern economy and the importance of interchangeable parts in the Industrial Revolution. (The cotton gin made growing cotton very profitable but also increased the demand for slaves. Interchangeable parts allowed factories to make products much more quickly and cheaply.)

Find Details Explain to students that after they read and take notes, they should review and think about how the facts and details will help them answer the Essential Question.

Twenty years later, a Boston merchant named Frances Cabot Lowell went to Britain to learn about new developments in its factories. In 1813, he built his own factory on the Charles River in Waltham, Massachusetts. It had a large power **loom** for weaving and all the equipment for making cloth under one roof. Lowell died soon after starting the factory. But his partners decided to expand. They built several mills on the Merrimack River and a town for their workers, which they called Lowell. Many of those workers were **immigrants** from other nations. They also hired young women from farms all over New England; these women became known as the Lowell Mill Girls.

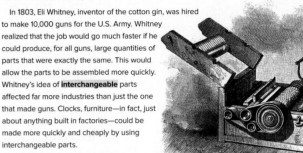

Cotton mill workers spun cotton into thread and wove thread into cloth.

Lowell, Massachusetts, was the first of many U.S. mill towns. These towns needed to be on rivers or streams with moving water to power the machinery. The towns were especially common in New England. The region had many rapidly flowing rivers. Its rocky soil and short growing season made it hard to earn a lot of money from farming. This is why farmers were glad to have their daughters working in the mills. The chief products of the mills were cotton cloth and woolen fabric. Wool came from sheep. Cotton came from plants that needed a warm climate to grow. In the United States, it was grown mainly in the South.

While visiting a cotton plantation, a New Englander named Eli Whitney saw that common green-seed cotton was very hard to clean because the seeds stuck to the fiber. He began working on a machine to separate the seeds from the fiber. That machine, the cotton gin, revolutionized Southern agriculture. It made growing cotton so profitable that most plantation owners made it their main crop. Growing cotton still required much labor, however. As cotton plantations grew larger, more and more slaves were put to work in the cotton fields. By 1850, there were five times as many slaves in the United States as there had been in 1790.

The use of the cotton gin was not the only big change in agriculture. For thousands of years, farmers had cut down their crops using a hand-held tool called a scythe. The slow process limited the number of crops farmers could harvest. Then, in 1831, a farmer's son named Cyrus McCormick invented a horse-drawn **reaping** machine that could harvest crops much faster. Farmers using the McCormick reaper could plant many more acres of crops. Planting itself was made easier by another invention, the mechanical plow. This device dug up the soil so seeds could be planted. Charles Newbold, a New Jersey blacksmith, invented the first cast iron plow in 1797. Another blacksmith, John Deere, improved the plow in 1837 by using steel blades. Steel was stronger than the iron previously used.

Many other inventions changed the way people made or did things. In 1845, Elias Howe, who had once worked in a machine shop in Lowell, created the first practical sewing machine. Also in the 1840s, Charles Goodyear developed a way to make rubber withstand heat and cold without cracking. The process, called vulcanization, made rubber the useful material it is today.

In 1803, Eli Whitney, inventor of the cotton gin, was hired to make 10,000 guns for the U.S. Army. Whitney realized that the job would go much faster if he could produce, for all guns, large quantities of parts that were exactly the same. This would allow the parts to be assembled more quickly. Whitney's idea of **interchangeable** parts affected far more industries than just the one that made guns. Clocks, furniture—in fact, just about anything built in factories—could be made more quickly and cheaply by using interchangeable parts.

The cotton gin, invented by Eli Whitney, separated seeds from cotton fiber much more quickly and easily than could be done by hand.

Stop and Check

Talk What effects, both good and bad, did the cotton gin have on the Southern economy? Why was Eli Whitney's development of interchangeable parts so important?

Find Details As you read, add additional information to the graphic organizer on page 255 in your Inquiry Journal.

Research Companion, pp. 312–313

ENGLISH LEARNERS SCAFFOLD

ELD.PII.5.6 Connecting ideas

Emerging	Expanding	Bridging
Understand Geography Help students understand how New England's geography led to its factories: Its fast-moving rivers could power the equipment; and its rocky soil and short growing season (being far north) made farming less productive, so people turned to factories for profits or employment.	**Explain Geography** Have students explain how geography encouraged more factories in New England than elsewhere in the nation. (Other areas had less rocky soil and longer growing seasons, making farming more profitable. New England had fast-moving rivers, needed for powering factory equipment.)	**Explain Geographic Relationships** Have students explain the role of geography and technology in making cotton the chief cash crop in the South. (The South's warm climate suited cotton growing. The invention of the cotton gin made growing cotton far more productive, and many plantations switched to growing it.)

See the **Language Learner Teaching Guide** for more language support strategies.

Monitor and Differentiate

REACHING ALL LEARNERS

Approaching Level

Be sure students understand the basic steps in farming: You *plow* or turn the soil to *sow* or plant seeds, then grow the crops, and then *reap* or cut them down to *harvest* or gather them.

On Level

Have small groups use their texts and online research to prepare charts of inventions of the period, listing inventor, country, date, and use.

Beyond Level

Have students describe the effects of an invention or change in an imaginary diary entry. For example, they might pretend to be a Lowell Mill Girl, a slave, or a farmer.

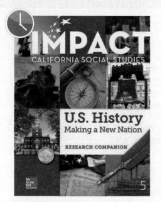

 IMPACT
CALIFORNIA SOCIAL STUDIES

U.S. History
Making a New Nation

RESEARCH COMPANION

Research Companion
pp. 314–315

HSS STANDARDS

Students trace the colonization, immigration, and settlement patterns of the American people from 1789 to the mid-1800s, with emphasis on the role of economic incentives, effects of the physical and political geography, and transportation systems. **HSS.5.8**

Discuss the waves of immigrants from Europe between 1789 and 1850 and their modes of transportation into the Ohio and Mississippi Valleys and through the Cumberland Gap (e.g., overland wagons, canals, flatboats, steamboats). **HSS.5.8.1**

Students summarize the key events of the era they are studying and explain the historical context of those events. **HAS.HI.1**

Go Digital!

Investigate the lesson content with online whole-class presentation tools.

Background Information

The steam engine is another invention often named as the starting point of the Industrial Revolution. Although steam engines had been around for decades, used to pump water from mines, in 1769 Scottish inventor James Watt patented an improved steam engine that would then be adapted for use in paper, flour, cotton, and iron mills. Steamboats and locomotives soon followed.

Analyze the Source

Inspect Have students read New Forms of Transportation on pages 314–315.

Find Evidence Use the questions below to check comprehension. Remind students to support their answers with text evidence.

Explain How did the National Road improve the nation's roads? (It was partly paved with crushed gravel so that it was less muddy and had fewer potholes. Students may also say that it created a longer, smoother connection over a distance.) **DOK 3**

Explain Why did people build canals instead of relying on natural waterways? (Natural waterways did not always connect. Students may also note natural difficulties such as such as rapids and shallows.) **DOK 3**

Synthesize What two new forms of transportation both relied on steam engines? (steamboats and trains) **DOK 2**

Compare and Contrast Of the new forms of transportation of the period, which was fastest? (trains) **DOK 2**

Make Connections

Analyze What reasons were there for criticizing the Erie Canal project? How was the criticism proved wrong? (It was expensive and complicated to build but proved to be a great success.) **DOK 3**

✓ Stop and Check PRODUCTIVE

Talk Have students explain why trains were particularly helpful in uniting the nation. (They allowed people and goods to go from one region to another in relatively little time.)

New Forms of Transportation

In 1800, there were four main ways to travel: on foot, on horseback, by water, or in horse-drawn vehicles such as stagecoaches. All were very slow. Private roads, which charged tolls, were better maintained than public roads. Both types of roads, however, grew muddy when it rained, and they developed potholes. Yet roads were needed to unify the expanding nation. In 1806, Congress voted to fund a road connecting the East and the Midwest. By the early 1830s, the National Road carried many carts and stagecoaches along a route that extended from Maryland to Illinois. Parts of the road were among the first U.S. roadways made of macadam, a newly developed paving material using crushed gravel.

In 1800, the easiest way to ship goods was by water, but waterways did not always connect. One way to solve this problem was to build artificial waterways called canals to make the connections. In 1817, New York Governor DeWitt Clinton began a project to build a canal connecting the Hudson River in the eastern part of the state with Lake Erie on New York's western border. Critics called the expensive project Clinton's Ditch. It was complicated because the land was higher at one end than the other. Engineers solved this problem by building locks, which worked like elevators to lift and lower boats in the water. When the Erie Canal finally opened in 1824, Clinton's critics were proved wrong. An instant success, the canal let people ship goods much more quickly and cheaply. Soon people in the United States began building other canals.

Steamboats on the Hudson River

The steam engine, one of the most important inventions of the Industrial Revolution, could be used to run many kinds of equipment. In 1807, Robert Fulton showed the world that a steam engine could be used to run a boat. His steamboat took about a day and a half to travel up the Hudson River from New York City to Albany, New York—a distance of about 150 miles. Before the steamboat, the same trip took much longer. Fulton's steamboat was not the first one ever invented, but it was the first to prove successful. Soon many different kinds of steamboats were traveling the nation's waterways. They were especially important for quickly moving goods against the direction of a river's current—for example, north on the Mississippi River.

Steam power was also the source of another form of transportation, the train. For centuries, people had recognized that running carts on rails instead of bumpy dirt roads made the ride smoother. However, early vehicles on rails were pulled by animals. Now engineers began experimenting with iron locomotives, engines that ran on rails and were powered by steam. The first locomotives were built in Britain. As the design improved, the locomotive was used to pull cars behind it in a new form of transportation—the train. It was nicknamed the Iron Horse. The rails on which trains ran were called railroads, and so were the companies that ran them. In 1828, the first U.S. railroad company, the Baltimore & Ohio (B & O) Railroad, was formed. Many more would follow.

Trains were much faster than other types of transportation at the time. Even the earliest trains cut down on travel time by about half. Trains made it possible to go from one region to another in a reasonable time. This meant that trains helped unite the large, spread-out nation that the United States was becoming.

Stop and Check

Talk Why were trains particularly helpful in uniting the nation?

314 Lesson 2 How Did Advancements in Technology and Transportation Shape the Nation?

Lesson 2 315

Research Companion, pp. 314–315

ENGLISH LEARNERS SCAFFOLD

ELD.PI.5.8 Analyzing how writers and speakers use vocabulary and other language resources for specific purposes (to explain, persuade, entertain, etc.) depending on modality, text type, purpose, audience, topic, and content area

Emerging	Expanding	Bridging
Understand Technical Processes Clarify how a canal lock works: A boat enters the lock. The gates close. Water slowly fills the lock, bringing the boat up to a higher level; or water slowly drains from the lock, taking the boat to a lower level. The lock gates open. The boat leaves the lock.	**Understand Technical Terms** Have students define *macadam* based on the details in the text. (a paving material using crushed gravel) Explain that it is named for John McAdam, the Scottish engineer who invented it. Have students guess what the verb *macadamize* means.	**Explain Technical Processes** Have students discuss how a steamboat solved the problem of traveling against a river's current. (Because it had an engine, it moved through the water with enough strength to overcome currents pushing in the other direction.)

See the **Language Learner Teaching Guide** for more language support strategies.

Monitor and Differentiate

REACHING ALL LEARNERS

Special Needs

Students may be familiar with the song about the Erie Canal that begins "I've got a mule, her name is Sal." Explain that mules often pulled barges of goods on canals from towpaths along the side. Have students find the lyrics to the song and sing it as a group.

Beyond Level

Have students research and report on an aspect of Robert Fulton's achievement, such as his design of the *Clermont*, his efforts to invent a submarine, or contributions to the success of his steamboat by builder Charles Brown or Fulton's father-in-law, diplomat Robert Livingston.

Research Companion
pp. 316–317

 STANDARDS

Students trace the colonization, immigration, and settlement patterns of the American people from 1789 to the mid-1800s, with emphasis on the role of economic incentives, effects of the physical and political geography, and transportation systems. **HSS.5.8**

Students judge the significance of the relative location of a place (e.g., proximity to a harbor, on trade routes) and analyze how relative advantages or disadvantages can change over time. **HAS.CS.5**

Students summarize the key events of the era they are studying and explain the historical context of those events. **HAS.HI.1**

Students identify and interpret the multiple causes and effects of historical events. **HAS.HI.3**

Go Digital!

Investigate the lesson content with online whole-class presentation tools.

Background Information

Samuel F. B. Morse, before working on the telegraph, won fame as an artist. He trained in London, where he learned to paint historical scenes, but on returning to the United States painted mostly portraits to earn a living. Among his best-known works is his portrait of the Marquis de Lafayette, a personal friend.

Analyze the Source

Inspect Have students read pages 316–317. Use the questions below to check comprehension.

Find Evidence Use the questions below to check comprehension. Remind students to support their answers with text evidence.

Explain How did Morse Code communicate messages? (It used short and long electrical signals to represent letters in words.) **DOK 2**

Synthesize From where did workers come to cities to work in factories? (rural areas and other nations, mostly Canada and Europe) **DOK 2**

Speculate Why do you think Chicago became the great railroad center? (Students should recognize that the city is centrally located.) **DOK 3**

Make Connections

Describe What changes to the American landscape were necessary for telegraphs to operate? (Telegraph poles and wires had to be put up. Students may also mention that telegraph offices were opened.) **DOK 3**

Explain Why would port cities grow because of steamboat traffic? (The steamboats brought people and goods and required workers and businesses to service them.) **DOK 3**

Analyze the Image Explain that the painting on page 317 shows a New York street. Ask students what the details in the painting tell them about the city. (It is a busy and bustling place with all kinds of people and activities.)

Stop and Check

PRODUCTIVE

Talk Have students explain how the telegraph was different from previous types of long-distance communication. (It did not rely on some form of transportation, since it did not require that messages be physically carried.)

Talk Have students identify two reasons for the growth of cities. (Factories brought workers and new forms of transportation made cities busier.)

Advancements in Communication

When George Washington became President in 1789, the United States had about 75 post offices. That number grew as the nation grew. Mail traveled by horse, stagecoach, boat, and eventually train. As transportation improved, so did communication, since messages could be carried more quickly. Nevertheless, the messages still had to be carried.

An important new invention changed the way Americans communicated. In the 1830s, a group of inventors including Samuel F. B. Morse developed a device called a telegraph that could send messages by using electrical signals over a wire. Morse and his fellow inventor Albert Vail also developed a code—called Morse Code—to give meaning to the electrical signals. The code used different sequences of short and long signals to represent letters. Workers used the coded letters to spell out the words of a message. Morse demonstrated the telegraph to members of Congress, who awarded him $30,000 to set up a telegraph line between Baltimore, Maryland, and Washington, D.C. On May 24, 1844, Morse tapped out his first long-distance message on the telegraph, "What hath God wrought?"

By pressing down on a key, the telegraph operator could send electrical messages in Morse code.

Over the next few years, telegraph poles went up across the United States, with telegraph wires strung between them. A person would go to a telegraph office and pay to send a message to another office in a distant location. The message would usually move across the wires and reach its destination in minutes. Like the new forms of transportation, this rapid new form of communication helped tie the nation together.

> ✓ **Stop and Check**
> COLLABORATE
>
> **Talk** How was the telegraph different from the type of long-distance communication people had used before?

316 Lesson 2 How Did Advancements in Technology and Transportation Shape the Nation?

The Growth of Cities

The Industrial Revolution turned towns into cities and made existing cities much larger. Factory jobs paid better than farm labor did. So factories lured people away from farms to cities and towns. They also drew immigrants to the United States, mostly from Canada and Europe. In 1820, only about 700,000 people lived in all the cities of the United States. By 1840, the population of cities was nearly 1.8 million.

New forms of transportation also led to the growth of cities. Steamboat traffic helped make river ports, like Cincinnati and St. Louis, much busier. The Erie Canal in upstate New York spurred the growth of Albany at its eastern end, Buffalo at its western end, and Syracuse and Rochester in between. It also made New York City an even greater center of shipping and trade.

Like boat traffic, the growth of railroads also led to the growth of cities. Atlanta, Georgia, began its existence as the junction, or meeting point, between the Georgia Railroad and the Western & Atlantic Railroad. Indianapolis, Indiana, had fewer than 8,000 residents in 1847. Then the Indianapolis & Madison Railroad came to town. The city's population quickly doubled. As the railroads moved farther west, Chicago, Illinois, emerged as the great railroad center of the nation. Chicago had fewer than 5,000 residents in 1840. Twenty years later, it had well over 100,000.

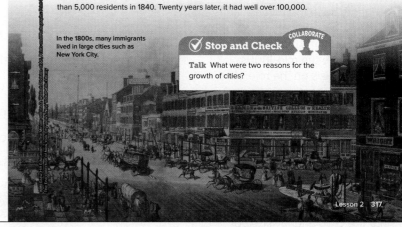

In the 1800s, many immigrants lived in large cities such as New York City.

> ✓ **Stop and Check**
> COLLABORATE
>
> **Talk** What were two reasons for the growth of cities?

Lesson 2 317

Research Companion, pp. 316–317

ELD.PI.5.8 Analyzing how writers and speakers use vocabulary and other language resources for specific purposes (to explain, persuade, entertain, etc.) depending on modality, text type, purpose, audience, topic, and content area

Emerging	Expanding	Bridging
Understand Domain-Specific Vocabulary Point to the term *long-distance communication*. Discuss how English often creates adjectives by combining (by hyphenating) words before the noun they modify.	**Understand Geographic Terms** Note the term *upstate New York* on page 317, and explain that *upstate* basically means "in the more northern part of the state, north of New York City and its suburbs."	**Understand Biblical Language** Explain that the telegraph message "What hath God wrought?" is from the Bible, noting that *hath* is an archaic or outdated form of the verb *has,* and that *wrought* means "formed."

See the **Language Learner Teaching Guide** for more language support strategies.

Monitor and Differentiate

REACHING ALL LEARNERS

Approaching Level

Provide students with a sentence frame to help them talk about the growth of cities: *The population of _____ became much greater after _____.*

On Level

Have students research U.S. Census statistics on the largest urban places in 1800, 1820, 1840, and 1860 and make charts of the 20 largest U.S. cities in each year.

Beyond Level

Have students research and report on the birth of photography in the early 1800s and how it affected our understanding of historical events that are recorded through photographs.

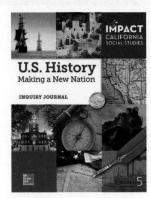

Inquiry Journal
pp. 256–257

 STANDARDS

Students trace the colonization, immigration, and settlement patterns of the American people from 1789 to the mid-1800s, with emphasis on the role of economic incentives, effects of the physical and political geography, and transportation systems. **HSS.5.8**

Discuss the waves of immigrants from Europe between 1789 and 1850 and their modes of transportation into the Ohio and Mississippi Valleys and through the Cumberland Gap (e.g., overland wagons, canals, flatboats, steamboats). **HSS.5.8.1**

Students summarize the key events of the era they are studying and explain the historical context of those events. **HAS.HI.1**

Write opinion pieces on topics or texts, supporting a point of view with reasons and information. **CCSS.ELA.W.5.1**

Go Digital!

- Students can go online to report their findings. Assess their responses online.

- Students can access the online graphic organizer to capture ideas from their investigation.

Think About It

Students will review their research and consider what it was like to communicate with someone living far away.

- Remind students to review each invention they have listed in their graphic organizer and identify one or more related to communication and the key details associated with it. Direct students back to pages 310–317 of their Research Companion if they need more information.

Write About It

Write an Advertisement Have students read the prompt. Explain that an effective advertisement attempts to persuade a particular audience to think or do something. Remind students to include the following in their response:

- Make a claim about the new item or service you are advertising and the problem it can help solve.

- Provide facts and details as evidence to support the claim.

- Include a sketch or describe a graphic to accompany the advertisement.

- Indicate what you want your audience to do with the item or service.

- Provide logical reasons to show why your audience should do or have it.

- Use language and emotional appeals designed to persuade your audience.

Use the rubric on page T664 to evaluate students' work.

Talk About It

Compare Advertisements Help students pair up with a classmate and compare and contrast the ads they wrote. Have them discuss which ad is more likely to persuade people to use the new technology it advertises.

- Tell students to take turns discussing their opinions and the reasons that helped them form those opinions.

- Ask students to discuss whether they agree or disagree with their partner's opinions and to explain why.

- Remind students to follow the rules of appropriate classroom conversation.

Connect to the
Essential Question

Read the prompt aloud to students. Ask them the following guiding questions:

- Which advances in transportation and communication helped shape the early United States? (Responses should include the steamboat, the steam engine, and the telegraph.)

- How did those advances help transform the nation? (Responses will vary, but students should include that these inventions made it easier to move west, which allowed the nation to expand and grow.)

Remind students to use the space provided in their journal to jot down notes.

Report Your Findings

Think About It

In the early 1800s, what was it like to communicate with someone living far away? Review your research to help you answer.

Write About It

Write an Advertisement

Develop an advertisement aimed at getting people to use one of the new technologies discussed in this lesson. Encourage those who are wary of the new technology to give it a try. Support your claims about the new technology with facts and details from the text. Sketch or describe a graphic to accompany your ad.

Advertisements should use persuasion and should focus on a technology in this lesson, including support from the text.

Talk About It

Compare Advertisements

Compare your advertisement with a partner's. Which is more likely to persuade people to use the new technology? Why?

✎ Connect to the EQ

History

Consider Cause and Effect

How did advances in transportation and communication shape the early United States?

Student response should include inventions mentioned in this chapter and explain their effects on the United States.

Inquiry Project Notes

EQ

256 Lesson 2 How Did Advancements in Technology and Transportation Shape the Nation?

Lesson 2 257

Inquiry Journal, pp. 256–257

ENGLISH LEARNERS SCAFFOLD

ELD.PI.5.11 Supporting own opinions and evaluating others' opinions in speaking and writing

Emerging	Expanding	Bridging
State and Support Opinions Provide this sentence frame to help students state and support opinions: *In my opinion, this ad for___ is more effective because it ____.*	**Make and Support Claims** Provide this sentence frame to help students Connect to the Essential Question: ___ *helped change the early United States because it improved ___ by ___.*	**State and Support Claims** Help students explore their ideas by asking these questions: *What did the technology do? How was it new or different? How did it change people's lives? What general effect did it have on the nation?* Remind students to use facts to support responses.

See the **Language Learner Teaching Guide** for more language support strategies.

Monitor and Differentiate

REACHING ALL LEARNERS

Approaching Level

Clarify that students are to write advertisements for a new product or service aimed at an audience of the period. For example, they might advertise a new McCormick reaper, a product made in part with the new vulcanized rubber, or a new steamboat, train, or telegraph service.

On Level

Explain that a good advertisement considers the audience it wants to reach. Point out that the writing assignment indicates the audience for the new technology is *wary*, or cautious, so the advertisement should address worries or fears in soothing and encouraging language.

Know what your students know!

Lesson Task
Report Your Findings

Use this rubric to evaluate students' response.

Write an Advertisement Students write an advertisement aimed at getting wary people to use one of the new technologies discussed in the lesson. They support claims about the new technology with facts and details from the lesson and sketch or describe a graphic to accompany the ad.

Compare Advertisements Students compare their ad with that of a partner. They discuss which ad is more likely to persuade people to use the new technology and explain why.

Performance Task Evaluation Rubric

	4	3	2	1
Historical Understanding	Displays strong understanding of the technology and its effects on nation	Displays adequate understanding of the technology and its effects on nation	Displays little understanding of the technology or its effects on nation	Displays no understanding of technology or its effects on nation
Write an Advertisement	Provides a clear explanation of how the technology works	Provides an adequate explanation of how the technology works	Provides a somewhat clear or unclear explanation of how the technology works	Provides no explanation or a very unclear or inaccurate explanation of how the technology works
Support with Evidence	Supports claims or reasons with thorough and convincing evidence Uses language that would appeal to a wary audience for the advertisement	Supports claims and reasons with adequate evidence Uses some language that would appeal to a wary audience for the advertisement	Supports claims and reasons with too little or only somewhat convincing evidence Uses little language that would appeal to a wary audience for the advertisement	Supplies no claims or reasons or no supporting evidence Uses no language that would appeal to a wary audience for the advertisement
Defend Your Claim	Thoroughly compares and contrasts advertisements Speaks in complete sentences throughout the discussion	Adequately compares and contrasts advertisements Speaks in complete sentences through most of the discussion	Unevenly compares and contrasts advertisements Mixes complete and incomplete sentences during the discussion	Does not compare and contrast advertisements Does not use complete sentences in the discussion

Lesson Assessment

Go *Digital!*

- Have students complete the Chapter 7 Lesson 2 Assessment online to monitor their understanding of the lesson content.

California Smarter Balanced Assessment Connections!

Standards Covered	Lesson Task	Lesson Assessment	Alignment with California Smarter Balanced Assessment
History and Social Science Content 5.8; 5.8.1	✔	✔	Claim 1 Targets 8, 9, 11
History and Social Science Analysis Skills Chronological and Spatial Thinking 5.1; 5.5; Research, Evidence, and Point of View 5.1; 5.2; Historical Interpretation 5.1; 5.3	✔	✔	Claim 1 Targets 8, 9, 11
Writing W.5.1; W.5.4	✔	✔	Claim 2 Target 6a
Research and Inquiry W.5.7; W.5.9	✔	✔	Claim 4 Targets 1, 2
Reading RI.5.1	✔	✔	Claim 1 Target 8, 11, 13
Speaking and Listening SL.5.1; SL.5.2	✔		Claim 3 Target 3 Claim 4 Target 1

Who Were the People of the Early United States?

Background Information

Explain to students that in this lesson they will learn about the people who lived in the early United States, including pioneers, American Indians, African Americans, and immigrants.

Community Connections

To enrich what students have learned about people in the early United States, plan a field trip to a local museum that features exhibits about the early inhabitants of your region.

 LESSON STANDARDS

- ✓ Explain the influence and achievements of significant leaders of the time (e.g., John Marshall, Andrew Jackson, Chief Tecumseh, Chief Logan, Chief John Ross, Sequoyah). **HSS.5.3.6**

- ✓ Demonstrate knowledge of the significance of land policies developed under the Continental Congress (e.g., sale of western lands, the Northwest Ordinance of 1787) and those policies' impact on American Indians' land. **HSS.5.6.6**

- ✓ Understand how the ideals set forth in the Declaration of Independence changed the way people viewed slavery. **HSS.5.6.7**

- ✓ Discuss the waves of immigrants from Europe between 1789 and 1850 and their modes of transportation into the Ohio and Mississippi Valleys and through the Cumberland Gap (e.g., overland wagons, canals, flatboats, steamboats). **HSS.5.8.1**

- ✓ Students place key events and people of the historical era they are studying in a chronological sequence and within a spatial context; they interpret time lines. **HAS.CS.1**

- ✓ Students use map and globe skills to determine the absolute locations of places and interpret information available through a map's or globe's legend, scale, and symbolic representations. **HAS.CS.4**

- ✓ Students differentiate between primary and secondary sources. **HAS.HR.1**

- ✓ Students pose relevant questions about events they encounter in historical documents, eyewitness accounts, oral histories, letters, diaries, artifacts, photographs, maps, artworks, and architecture. **HAS.HR.2**

 Connect to the
Essential Question

The **Weekly Explorer Magazine** supports students' exploration of the Essential Question and provides additional resources for the EQ Inquiry Project.

Chapter 7, pp. 84–99

 **Inquiry Project**

Which Change Will You Choose?

Remind students to use the information they learn in this lesson and other resources to complete their EQ Inquiry Project!

Dinah Zike's
FOLDABLES

In this lesson you will use Foldables.

When Minutes Count!
Suggested Lesson Pacing

1 ENGAGE
One Day

- Lesson Opener
- Analyze the Source
- Inquiry Tools

Go Digital

- **iMap:** The War of 1812
- **iMap:** The Wilderness Road
- **iMap:** Indian Removal Act, 1830–1840
- **iMap:** The Missouri Compromise, 1820

2 INVESTIGATE
Two to Three Days

🕐 **Short on Time?** Look for the clock to teach core content in less time.

- The First Pioneers
- American Indians in the Early Republic
- African Americans in the Early United States
- A Nation of Immigrants
- **Citizenship** Fighting for Women's Education

3 REPORT
One Day

- Think About It
- Write a Blog Post
- Share Your Thinking

Make Connections!

Reading

Determine two or more main ideas of a text and explain how they are supported by key details; summarize the text. **RI.5.2**

Draw on information from multiple print or digital sources, demonstrating the ability to locate an answer to a question quickly or to solve a problem efficiently. **RI.5.7**

Research

Conduct short research projects that use several sources to build knowledge through investigation of different aspects of a topic. **W.5.7**

Recall relevant information from experiences or gather relevant information from print and digital sources; summarize or paraphrase information in notes and finished work, and provide a list of sources. **W.5.8**

Writing

Write informative/explanatory texts to examine a topic and convey ideas and information clearly. **W.5.2**

Draw evidence from literary or informational texts to support analysis, reflection, and research. **W.5.9**

Speaking and Listening

Engage effectively in a range of collaborative discussions (one-on-one, in groups, and teacher-led) with diverse partners on grade 5 topics and texts, building on others' ideas and expressing their own clearly. **SL.5.1**

Report on a topic or text or present an opinion, sequencing ideas logically and using appropriate facts and relevant, descriptive details to support main ideas or themes; speak clearly at an understandable pace. **SL.5.4**

Classroom Resources

🔍 Search for additional resources using the following key words.

American canals

Battle of Fallen Timbers

Cumberland Gap

John Findley

The Great Famine

Northwest Ordinance

Benjamin Rush

War of 1812

The Young Ladies' Academy of Philadelphia

1 ENGAGE

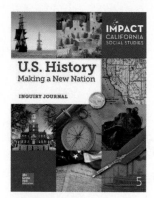

Inquiry Journal
pp. 258–259

 STANDARDS

Discuss the waves of immigrants from Europe between 1789 and 1850 and their modes of transportation into the Ohio and Mississippi Valleys and through the Cumberland Gap (e.g., overland wagons, canals, flatboats, steamboats). **HSS.5.8.1**

CCSS Determine two or more main ideas of a text and explain how they are supported by key details; summarize the text. **CCSS.ELA.RI.5.2**

Engage effectively in a range of collaborative discussions (one-on-one, in groups, and teacher-led) with diverse partners on *grade 5 topics and texts*, building on others' ideas and expressing their own clearly. **CCSS.ELA.SL.5.1**

Go *Digital!*

Explore the lesson content with online whole-class presentation tools.

- **iMap:** The War of 1812
- **iMap:** The Wilderness Road
- **iMap:** Indian Removal Act, 1830–1840
- **iMap:** The Missouri Compromise, 1820

Who Were the People of the Early United States?

Bellringer

Prompt students to retrieve information from the previous lessons. Say: *Inventions led to the growth of the textile industry. What are some of the inventions that spurred the growth of the textile industry?* (sewing machines, double-sided needles, spinning machines)

Lesson Outcomes

What Am I Learning? Have students read the Lesson Question and Lesson Outcomes on page 258.

Why Am I Learning It? Make sure students understand the word *famine*. Say: *A famine happens when there is a severe shortage of food. The shortage can be so serious that people die from starvation. For example: When crops fail, a famine and a severe shortage of food can result.*

How Will I Know That I Learned It? Ask students the following questions.

- What will you be able to identify? (the people who lived in the early United States)

- What is the purpose of this task? (to compare and contrast the experiences of people who lived in the early United States)

- How will you support your writing? (with evidence from the text)

Talk About It PRODUCTIVE

Explain that when we read words set to music (lyrics), we try to learn more about what the words in combination with the music mean. Tell students that "amber waves of grain" refers to the wheat field shown in the image. Guide students to read the title and lyrics and look at the image to better understand what the lyrics mean.

- *The image shows _____.*

- *The lyrics describe a _____ country.*

 COLLABORATE

Collaborative Conversations

Add New Ideas As students engage in partner, small-group, and whole-class discussions, encourage them to

- First read the material carefully.
- Be respectful of the opinions of others.
- Use evidence from the text to support their conclusions.

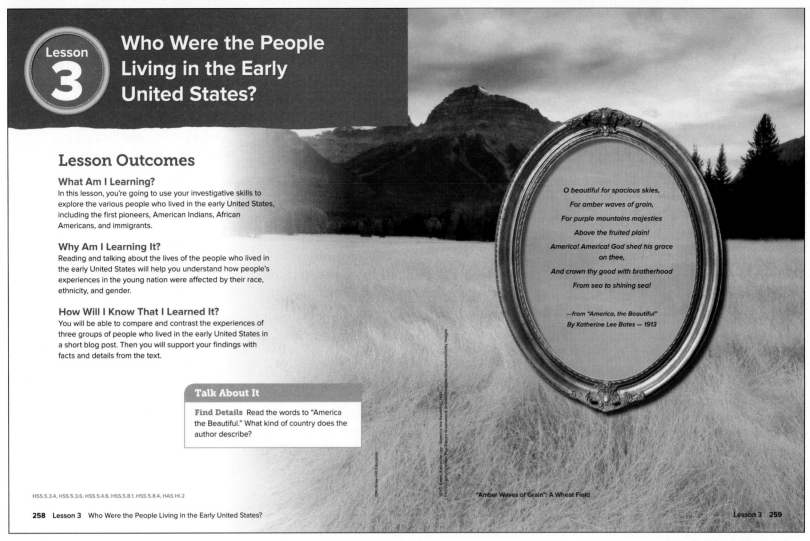

Lesson 3

Who Were the People Living in the Early United States?

Lesson Outcomes

What Am I Learning?
In this lesson, you're going to use your investigative skills to explore the various people who lived in the early United States, including the first pioneers, American Indians, African Americans, and immigrants.

Why Am I Learning It?
Reading and talking about the lives of the people who lived in the early United States will help you understand how people's experiences in the young nation were affected by their race, ethnicity, and gender.

How Will I Know That I Learned It?
You will be able to compare and contrast the experiences of three groups of people who lived in the early United States in a short blog post. Then you will support your findings with facts and details from the text.

> **Talk About It**
>
> **Find Details** Read the words to "America the Beautiful." What kind of country does the author describe?

O beautiful for spacious skies,

For amber waves of grain,

For purple mountains majesties

Above the fruited plain!

America! America! God shed his grace on thee,

And crown thy good with brotherhood

From sea to shining sea!

—from "America, the Beautiful"
By Katherine Lee Bates — 1913

HSS.5.3.4, HSS.5.3.6, HSS.5.4.6, HSS.5.8.1, HSS.5.8.4, HAS.HI.2

"Amber Waves of Grain": A Wheat Field

258 Lesson 3   Who Were the People Living in the Early United States?

Lesson 3   **259**

Inquiry Journal, pp. 258–259

ENGLISH LEARNERS SCAFFOLD

ELD.PI.5.2 Interacting with others in written English in various communicative forms (print, communicative technology, and multimedia)

Emerging	Expanding	Bridging
Identify Features Work with students to identify what they see in the image of a field of wheat. Supply vocabulary to students as needed.	**Describe Features** Have small groups create a list of words that describe what they see in the image of a field of wheat. Encourage them to express what they see.	**Apply Language** Have students work together to explain why the author of the lyrics compares wheat fields to "amber waves." How are wheat fields like waves?

See the **Language Learner Teaching Guide** for more language support strategies.

Monitor and Differentiate

REACHING ALL LEARNERS

Special Needs

Have students focus on one line from the lyrics. Ask: *What pictures does the author paint with her words?* Guide them to describe what they see when they visualize the image in the line. Then have students compare what they visualize with the image on the page.

Beyond Level

Have students identify ways in which the lyrics show the varied landscape, the vast expanse, and the beauty of America. Then guide student to analyze the imagery in the lyrics—both its literal meaning and what it symbolizes.

1 ENGAGE

Analyze the Source

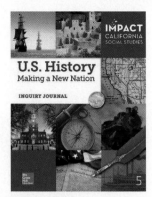

Inquiry Journal
pp. 260–261

 STANDARDS

Discuss the waves of immigrants from Europe between 1789 and 1850 and their modes of transportation into the Ohio and Mississippi Valleys and through the Cumberland Gap (e.g., overland wagons, canals, flatboats, steamboats). **HSS.5.8.1**

CCSS Draw evidence from literary or informational texts to support analysis, reflection, and research. **CCSS.ELA.W.5.9**

Go Digital!

Model how to inspect and find evidence with online whole-class presentation tools.

Background Information

Irish Potato Famine During the Great Famine of the 1840s in Ireland, thousands fled starvation and poverty by coming to the United States. Once they arrived, life was not easy. Cities like Boston, swamped with poor and desperate immigrants, did not take kindly to the sudden influx of these poorly educated, ill-clad, and unskilled people. Often, they were victims of unscrupulous landlords. When they could find work, the men worked as unskilled laborers and the women as servants.

1 Inspect

Look Have students read the entire text, including the Primary Source, to focus on understanding the overall meaning. Remind them to circle unknown words.

- Why did Irish immigrants of the period flee their country to come to the United States? (They were escaping famine in Ireland.)

- What were the practical needs of newly arrived immigrants? (a place to stay, a job)

- What emotional problems did many immigrants face? (intense loneliness)

Collaborate Have partners discuss the difficulties newly arrived immigrants faced. (Answers will vary, but students should note: a very different environment from the Irish countryside, finding a place to stay, finding work, and combating loneliness)

2 Find Evidence

Look Again Have students reread the text.

Analyze the Primary Source Reread the letter from Cathy Greene to her mother aloud and then analyze the letter together as a class. Provide support for vocabulary (especially the use of "ye" in place of "you") as needed.

- Notice the problems Cathy Greene has to deal with. How do you think these problems affect her anxiety over not hearing from her mother? (Answers will vary, but students should note that the author recently lost her job.)

- Reread the line "I would battle with the world and never feel dissatisfied if I would ever hear from ye." What is Cathy Greene trying to tell her mother in these lines? (Answers will vary, but students should note how alone and lost Cathy feels. She desperately needs to feel connected to someone.)

- What does the word *fretting* mean? (worrying)

3 Make Connections

Talk Encourage students to work with a partner to make inferences about other difficulties, in addition to those mentioned in the text, that immigrants may have faced.

Analyze the Source

1 Inspect

Read Look at the title. What do the words "letter to her mother" suggest about the kind of text this will be?

- **Circle** words you don't know.
- **Underline** clues that help you answer the questions *who, what, where, when,* or *why.*
- **Discuss** with a partner how Cathy Greene feels and what her experience as a recent immigrant has been like.

My Notes

_____
_____
_____
_____
_____
_____
_____
_____
_____
_____
_____
_____

Cathy Greene Writes a Letter to Her Mother

Irish immigrants escaping poverty and famine in their own country faced many difficulties once they arrived in the United States. New York City, for example, was very different from the Irish countryside. The environment for many was strange and frightening. In addition, within a very short time, immigrants had to make sure that practical needs were met. They needed to find a place to stay. They needed to find a job in order to support themselves. And then, many experienced the crushing weight of loneliness. They had to leave home; there was very little opportunity there. But they missed home and their families, often intensely.

Cathy Greene, a recent Irish immigrant living in Brooklyn, New York, wrote to her mother in County Kilkenny, Ireland, in 1884, begging her to write her back.

In the mid-1800s, many Irish immigrants came to the United States hoping to escape poverty and starvation.

PRIMARY SOURCE

In Their Words... Cathy Greene

My Dear Mama,

What on earth is the matter with ye all, that none of you would think of writing to me? The fact is I am heart-sick, fretting. I cannot sleep the night and if I chance to sleep I wake with the most frightful dreams.

To think that it's now going and gone into the third month since ye wrote to me. I feel as if I'm dead to the world. I've left the place I was employed. They failed in business. I was out of place all summer and the devil knows how long. This is a world of troubles.

I would battle with the world and would never feel dissatisfied if I would hear often for ye ... I know if I don't hear from ye prior to the arrival of this letter...I will be almost dead."

—from Cathy Greene's letter to her mother, August 1, 1884

2 Find Evidence

Reread Notice the problems Cathy Greene has to deal with. How do you think these problems affect her anxiety over not hearing from her mother?

Reread the line "I would battle with the world and never feel dissatisfied if I would hear often from ye." What is Cathy Greene trying to tell her mother in these lines?

3 Make Connections

Talk Discuss with a partner the many feelings an immigrant might feel when family members are far away.

COLLABORATE

TEXT: Cathy Greene, Brooklyn, NY, to her mother, Ballykelan, Callan, County Kilkenny, 1 August 1884, Greene/Norris Family Papers, Archives Department, University College, Dublin. PHOTO: McGraw-Hill Education

Axelle/Shutterstock.com

Inquiry Journal, pp. 260–261

(EL) ENGLISH LEARNERS SCAFFOLD

ELD.PI.5.1 Exchanging information and ideas with others through oral collaborative discussions on a range of social and academic topics

Emerging

Develop Language Work with students to understand the sentence. Tell students that the Spanish cognate for *immigrant* is *immigrante* and for *difficulty* is *difficutad*. Students should understand that immigrants are people coming into a country, and that the Irish immigrants were fleeing famine in their own country. Once they arrived, they faced a whole new set of difficulties.

Expanding/Bridging

Develop Language Guide students to describe why Irish immigrants came to the United States and the difficulties they encountered once they got here. Supply vocabulary as needed.

See the **Language Learner Teaching Guide** for more language support strategies.

Monitor and Differentiate

REACHING ALL LEARNERS

Approaching Level

Have students discuss why Irish immigrants might not have realized beforehand how much they would miss their country and their families. Guide them to analyze the reasons immigrants left Ireland and what their expectations of life in America might have been before they arrived.

Beyond Level

Have students research why Irish famine immigrants faced particular difficulties in Boston, Massachusetts. Have them examine such things as the population of Boston as compared with New York City, the attitudes of Bostonians, and where the new immigrants lived in the new country.

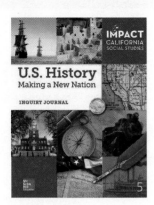

Inquiry Journal
pp. 262–263

HSS **STANDARDS**

Discuss the waves of immigrants from Europe between 1789 and 1850 and their modes of transportation into the Ohio and Mississippi Valleys and through the Cumberland Gap (e.g., overland wagons, canals, flatboats, steamboats). **HSS.5.8.1**

CCSS Draw evidence from literary or informational texts to support analysis, reflection, and research. **CCSS.ELA.W.5.9**

Write informative/explanatory texts to examine a topic and convey ideas and information clearly. **CCSS.ELA.W.5.2**

Go Digital!

- Model how to explore and investigate with online whole-class tools.

- Students can access the online graphic organizer to use the inquiry tools as they read.

Explore Comparison and Contrast

Explain Tell students that comparing and contrasting is one kind of text structure that authors use to organize information in a historical text. Comparing and contrasting groups of people in the early United States will help you understand the unique and common experiences of each group.

Read Have students read the step-by-step instructions about how to compare and contrast information. Tell students that comparing and contrasting the experiences of various groups will help them better understand the unique and similar experiences of people living in the early United States.

Guide Practice Tell students that they often analyze information in their own lives. Give an example such as comparing and contrasting books on a similar subject. Students might ask and answer questions such as *How interesting is each book? What new information does each book give me? Is each author reputable, that is, can I trust the information he or she gives me?*

Investigate!

Have students read pages 318–327 in the Research Companion. Tell them the information will help them answer the lesson question **Who Were the People Living in the Early United States?**

Take Notes Tell students that they should take notes of each group and their experiences in the graphic organizer on page 263 of the Inquiry Journal. Explain to students that they will take notes as they read each section. Remind them that taking notes will help them understand and remember what they read.

Remind students that good note taking is about finding the most important information and writing key words or phrases about it. Note takers do not rewrite every word from the text unless they plan to quote an author later on.

Inspect Guide students to read the text in each section to determine what the text says. Encourage them to make note of words they don't understand and look for answers to questions, such as *who? what? where? when? why?* and *how?*

Find Evidence Encourage students to reread the text to develop a deeper understanding of the content. Remind students that after they read and take notes, they should review and think about how the facts and details will help them answer the lesson question.

Collaborative Conversations

Text-Based Discussion Remind students of the goals of discussing the text with others.

- to listen and respond to another point of view
- to find additional evidence
- to build on each other's ideas

Inquiry Tools

Explore Compare and Contrast

Comparing and contrasting groups of people in the early United States will help you understand how the experiences of the groups are alike and different.

1. Read the text all the way through.
This will help you understand what the text is about.

2. Look for groups of people whose experiences are described.
This will help you help you decide which groups of people you will compare and contrast.

3. Choose three groups that you can easily compare and contrast.
This will help you analyze the experience of three groups of people.

4. List the main experiences of each group and how they are similar to or different from the experience of other groups.
This will help you find likenesses and differences among the groups.

 COLLABORATE Based on the text you just read, work with your class to describe the experiences of immigrants and to compare them to the experiences of another group you know of.

Group	Experiences	Likenesses/Differences
Immigrants	Travel to United States for better opportunities	Like pioneers, they are searching for a better life.

 Investigate!

Read pages 318–327 in your Research Companion. Use your investigative skills to identify different groups of people and their experiences. Then compare their experiences with those of a different group.

Group	Experiences	Likenesses/Differences
American Indians	Attacked by white settlers seeking land	Unlike the pioneers, native peoples wanted to stay where they were.
African Americans	Discrimination in North, slavery in South	Like Indians, they suffered mistreatment by white people.
Immigrants	Often had to take dangerous jobs	Like pioneers, they tried to avoid poverty.

McGraw-Hill Education

Inquiry Journal, pp. 262–263

(EL) ENGLISH LEARNERS SCAFFOLD

ELD.PI.5.11 Supporting own opinions and evaluating others' opinions in speaking and writing

Emerging	Expanding	Bridging
Develop Language Encourage students to point out words that describe similarities and differences among the groups that lived in the early United States.	**Cite Evidence** Have students point out words in the text that describe similarities and differences among the groups that lived in the early United States. Then have them use two of those words in sentences of their own.	**Summarize** Have students use descriptive words from the text in sentences of their own as they summarize important similarities and differences among the groups in the text. Have students share their summaries in groups.

See the **Language Learner Teaching Guide** for more language support strategies.

Monitor and Differentiate

REACHING ALL LEARNERS

Approaching Level

Have students ask and answer more detailed questions to guide their reading, such as *Where did the various groups live? What work did they do to support themselves? How hard and/or dangerous was this work? Why might I need to know this information to understand the contribution made by the people living in the early United States?*

Beyond Level

Have a small group of students discuss why it is important to analyze information when learning about historical events. Students should discuss why studying comparisons and contrasts among groups living in the same time period helps them to have a better understanding of a historical period.

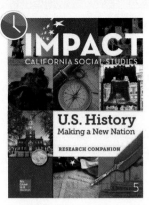

Research Companion
pp. 318–319

(HSS) STANDARDS

Discuss the waves of immigrants from Europe between 1789 and 1850 and their modes of transportation into the Ohio and Mississippi Valleys and through the Cumberland Gap (e.g., overland wagons, canals, flatboats, steamboats). **HSS.5.8.1**

(CCSS) Determine two or more main ideas of a text and explain how they are supported by key details; summarize the text. **CCSS.ELA.RI.5.2**

Draw evidence from literary or informational texts to support analysis, reflection, and research **CCSS.ELA.W.5.9**

Go Digital!

Investigate the lesson content with online whole-class presentation tools.

- **Map:** The War of 1812
- **iMap:** The Wilderness Road
- **iMap:** Indian Removal Act, 1830–1840
- **iMap:** The Missouri Compromise, 1820

Background Information

The Cumberland Gap In 1775 Daniel Boone blazed a trail through the Cumberland Gap, which is a natural passage through the Cumberland Mountains at the junction of what is now Virginia, Kentucky, and Tennessee. This trail would be the major route to the western United States for some 300,00 settlers for over the next 35 years.

| TIMELINE | Invite students to look at the timeline at the top of page 319.

Analyze What two significant events occurred between 1811 and 1815? (Tecumseh's War and the War of 1812) **HAS.CS.1**

Analyze the Source

Inspect Have students read pages 318–319.

Find Evidence Use the questions below to check comprehension. Remind students to support their answers with text evidence.

Infer Why did people need land in order to improve their lives? (Answers may vary, but students should note that without land farmers would not be able to grow crops and earn a living.) **DOK 2**

Vocabulary What did explorers do? (Answers may vary, but students should note that explorers helped find routes for people travelling west.) **DOK 2**

Assess Why did Daniel Boone and other pioneers work to improve the trails between the Carolinas and the West? (They wanted to make money from the new land.) **DOK 3**

Make Connections Prompt students to make connections with the following questions.

Draw Conclusions Why do you think that between 1790 and 1820 the population of the United States grew from about 4 million to nearly 10 million? (Answers will vary, but students should note that more and more people were becoming aware of America's rich farmlands and the opportunity they would have here to better their lives.) **DOK 3**

Point of View If you were a person in search of land and a better life, would trust your fortunes to a man like Daniel Boone? Explain why or why not. (Answers will vary, If students say that they would trust Boone they should note their willingness to take risks to secure a better life; if students say that they wouldn't trust Boone they should indicate why the level of risk would not be acceptable.) **DOK 3**

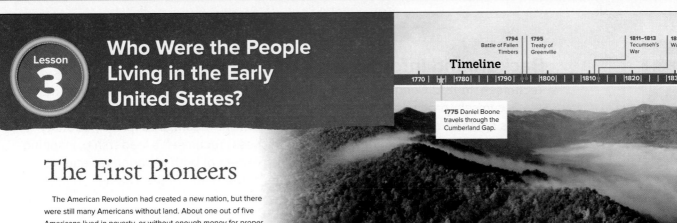

Lesson 3

Who Were the People Living in the Early United States?

Timeline

1794 Battle of Fallen Timbers	1795 Treaty of Greenville	1811–1813 Tecumseh's War	1812–1815 War of 1812	1845–1849 The Great Famine (Irish Potato Famine)

|1770| |1780| |1790| |1800| |1810| |1820| |1830| |1840| |1850| |

1775 Daniel Boone travels through the Cumberland Gap.

The First Pioneers

The American Revolution had created a new nation, but there were still many Americans without land. About one out of five Americans lived in poverty, or without enough money for proper food or supplies. Without land, people were unlikely to improve their lives.

Between 1790 and 1820, the population of the United States grew, from about 4 million to nearly 10 million. Most Americans were farmers. They needed large families to do the many chores a farm required. When farmers died, their land was divided among their children. Even a large farm might not provide enough land for all of the children. Some people moved to cities, but others looked to the lands in the West. For poor people, these lands offered a chance to build a new life.

After the British gave up its western lands in 1783, settlers rushed into western Georgia, Pennsylvania, New York, and beyond. Some of this area later became the states of Kentucky, Tennessee, and Ohio. A person who is the first to enter a new land or region is called a pioneer. Even though we call the white settlers who moved into the area west of the Appalachians "pioneers," they were not the first people in these lands. This area had been inhabited by American Indians for centuries.

In 1769, a trader named John Findley chose an experienced explorer, Daniel Boone, to help him find an **inland** trail from North Carolina to Kentucky. They found a natural passage through the Appalachian Mountains, which they called the Cumberland Gap. When they crossed the Cumberland Gap into Kentucky, they found a land of rich soil. Boone and his friends wanted to make money from this new land. In 1775, Boone and 30 other pioneers began to improve the trails between the Carolinas and the West.

Settlers often passed through the Cumberland Gap (above).

HSS.5.3.4, HSS.5.3.6, HSS.5.6.6, HSS.5.8.1, HAS.CS.5

318 Lesson 3 Who Were the People Living in the Early United States?

Lesson 3 **319**

Research Companion, pp. 318–319

ENGLISH LEARNERS SCAFFOLD

ELD.PI.5.1 Exchanging information and ideas with others through oral collaborative discussions on a range of social and academic topics

Emerging

Organize Information As students look at the timeline, have them identify words, including proper nouns, with which they are unfamiliar. Have students keep a list of these words as a reference as they read the lesson. Have them write, draw, or annotate the list as they learn about each term.

Expanding and Bridging

Collaborate Have students use information from the timeline to discuss what they think they will learn during Lesson 3. Have them write or share a few predictions that they can return to at the end of the lesson. Ask them to discuss what event or events they are most interested in learning about.

See the **Language Learner Teaching Guide** for more language support strategies.

Monitor and Differentiate

REACHING ALL LEARNERS

Approaching Level

Encourage students to discuss the vital role that explorers like Daniel Boone played in the settlement of the West. Why was it important that someone found routes for others to travel? What dangers did explorers like Daniel Boone take on?

Beyond Level

Have students do additional research on Daniel Boone. Suggest that they examine his early life, his participation in the French and Indian War, or the difficulties with the founding of Boonesborough.

2 INVESTIGATE

American Indians in the Early Republic

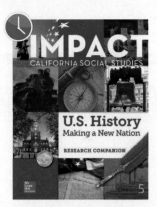

Research Companion
pp. 320–321

HSS STANDARDS

Demonstrate knowledge of the significance of land policies developed under the Continental Congress (e.g., sale of western lands, the Northwest Ordinance of 1787) and those policies' impact on American Indians' land. **HSS.5.6.6**

CCSS Determine two or more main ideas of a text and explain how they are supported by key details; summarize the text. **CCSS.ELA.RI.5.2**

Go Digital!

Investigate the lesson content with online whole-class presentation tools.

Background Information

Tecumseh In 1812 Congress declared war on Great Britain. This forced Indian leaders like Tecumseh to decide whether to side with the British or the Americans. Tecumseh and his confederacy decided to side with the British. Tecumseh's military strategy helped make the British siege of Detroit a success. Tecumseh's leadership, inspiring words, and personal bravery earned him the respect of both his enemies and his friends. He was killed by the American forces at the Battle of the Thames (in upper Canada) on October 5, 1813.

Analyze the Source

Inspect Have students read pages 320–321.

Find Evidence Use the questions below to check comprehension. Remind students to support their answers with text evidence.

> **Draw Conclusions** When Daniel Boone was captured by the Shawnee people, he gained their trust. What does this tell you about Daniel Boone? (Answers may vary, but students should note that Boone understood people and how to navigate between different cultures.) **DOK 3**

> **Identify** What promise did the Northwest Ordinance include that was not kept? (that American Indian lands and territories would never be taken away) **DOK 1**

Make Connections Prompt students to make connections with the following question.

> **Cause/Effect** Why did some American Indians continue, even after the Treaty of Greenville, to resist white settlers? (Answers may vary, but students should note that some American Indians were determined to preserve their way of life.) **DOK 2**

Analyze the Primary Source Point out the words "cede and relinquish forever" in the primary source. Have discuss exactly what American Indians were agreeing to do.

> **Explain** What land did American Indians agree to give up permanently in the treaty? (They gave up land to the east and to the south of the boundary line in Ohio.) **DOK 3**

☑ Stop and Check

Write Have students discuss why settlers moved west. (Land ownership was one of the few ways for people of the time to raise out of poverty. Since land in the eastern part of the United States was claimed by the first settlers, pioneers continued moving west to find open lands—often battling American Indians who had lived on the land for generations.)

Find Details Explain to students that after they read and take notes, they should review and think about how the facts and details will help them answer the Essential Question.

Daniel Boone was the most famous of the American pioneers of this era. His father had come from Great Britain and settled in Pennsylvania. Boone was born in 1734. Young Boone learned to survive on the unsettled lands around his home. When Boone was 16, his family moved to North Carolina. Boone married Rebecca Bryan in 1756 and tried farming, but he preferred life on the frontier.

Boone had a sense of humor. He is believed to have once said, "I have never been lost, but I will admit to being confused for several weeks."

In 1775, Boone founded Boonesborough, Kentucky. In 1776, during the Revolutionary War, he and his men were captured by Shawnee people and taken to a British military post. Boone gained the trust of the Shawnee and learned of a British plan to attack Boonesborough. He escaped in time to save the town. After exploring Tennessee and Kentucky in the early 1770s, Boone and his family moved to what is now Missouri in 1799. Daniel Boone died in 1820.

Daniel Boone leading settlers through the Cumberland Gap in 1775

 Stop and Check

COLLABORATE

Talk What were some of the reasons people in the early United States moved farther west?

American Indians in the Early Republic

The greatest threat to American Indians during this period was white settlers. For more than 150 years, American Indians had seen settlers stream west and into their territory. This threatened their land and their way of life.

In 1787, Congress passed the Northwest Ordinance. The law was intended to outline how the western territories should be governed and the rules for becoming a state. It did, however, include a promise that Indian lands and territories would never be taken away from them. But that promise was not kept.

In 1794, eight American Indian groups joined together to drive invading settlers out of their land in what is today Ohio. They were defeated by the United States Army at the Battle of Fallen Timbers in northwestern Ohio.

The next year, these American Indians had to accept the Treaty of Greenville. The treaty forced them to give up most of their land in the Ohio Territory. However, some American Indians would continue to resist the settlers.

PRIMARY SOURCE

In Their Words... The Treaty of Greenville

And in consideration of the peace now established . . . the said Indian tribes do hereby cede and relinquish forever, all their claims to the lands lying eastwardly and southwardly of the general boundary line now described: and these lands, or any part of them, shall never hereafter be made a cause or pretense, on the part of said tribes, or any of them, of war or injury to the United States, or any people thereof.

—from The Treaty of Greenville, August 3, 1795

Research Companion, pp. 320–321

(EL) ENGLISH LEARNERS SCAFFOLD

ELD.PI.5.1 Exchanging information and ideas with others through oral collaborative discussions on a range of social and academic topics

Emerging

Develop Language Point out the idiom *stream* in the first paragraph of the text. Tell students that in this case *stream* means to move quickly into something. Help students understand that the phrase "settlers stream west" means that settlers were quickly moving in to, or invading, western territories.

Expanding/Bridging

Collaborate Have students work together to understand the meaning of the words *ordinance* and *treaty*. If students need support, explain that an *ordinance* is a law passed by the government, and a *treaty* is an agreement made between two or more parties. Encourage students to use the words in sentences describing the relationship between American Indians and white settlers.

See the **Language Learner Teaching Guide** for more language support strategies.

Monitor and Differentiate

REACHING ALL LEARNERS

Special Needs

Have students focus on the quote from Daniel Boone on page 320, "I have never been lost, but I will admit to being confused for several weeks." Explain that Boone is using humor to mean that he didn't know where he was for a while, which is another way of saying he actually was lost. Guide students to discuss how understanding Boone's sense of humor helps them understand this historical figure.

Beyond Level

Encourage students to do more research into the Treaty of Greenville and other such treaties between the United States government and American Indian groups. Guide students to consider how these treaties can lead to both positive and negative outcomes.

2 INVESTIGATE

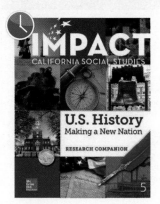

Research Companion
pp. 322–323

 STANDARDS

Understand how the ideals set forth in the Declaration of Independence changed the way people viewed slavery. **HSS.5.6.7**

ccss Determine two or more main ideas of a text and explain how they are supported by key details; summarize the text. **CCSS.ELA.RI.5.2**

Engage effectively in a range of collaborative discussions (one-on-one, in groups, and teacher-led) with diverse partners on *grade 5 topics and texts*, building on others' ideas and expressing their own clearly. **CCSS.ELA.SL.5.1**

Go Digital!

Investigate the lesson content with online whole-class presentation tools.

Background Information

Denmark Vesey African Americans, of course, opposed any expansion of slavery, and news of congressional opposition to the expansion of slavery circulated widely within slave communities. In 1822 in Charleston, South Carolina, Denmark Vesey organized what would have been the largest revolt of slaves in American history had it not been thwarted at the last minute by an informer. Charleston slave owners, fearing their own slaves and the possibility of other uprisings, had Vesey and his co-conspirators put to death.

Analyze the Source

Inspect Have students read pages 322–323.

Find Evidence Use the questions below to check comprehension. Remind students to support their answers with text evidence.

Draw Conclusions Why did American Indians like Tecumseh and his Confederacy side with the British during the War of 1812? (They hoped that a British victory would stop the invasion of American settlers into American Indian territories.) **DOK 2**

Recall What difficulties did free blacks in Ohio, Indiana, and Illinois face? (They had to show papers proving that they were free.) **DOK 1**

Draw Conclusions Why was it that the owners of large plantations were the wealthiest and most powerful people in the South? (Answers will vary, but students should note that the owners of large plantations were wealthy because of the enormous amount of work done by slaves. They had political power because of their wealth.) **DOK 2**

Analyze the Primary Source

Explain What did Tecumseh argue about why land could not be bought or sold? (He believed that the land belonged to everyone, so no one person or group had the right to buy and sell it to another.) **DOK 3**

Make Connections

Draw Conclusions Why was it important that the number of slave states and states with no slavery remain the same? (The number needed to remain the same in order to balance the interests of slave states and free states in Congress.) **DOK 2**

☑ Stop and Check

PRODUCTIVE

Write Have students discuss the relationship between Tecumseh and Henry Harrison. (Tecumseh united native peoples to fight settlers. Tecumseh also helped the British fight the Americans in the War of 1812. Henry Harrison was governor of the Indiana Territory. He was alarmed by the amount of people on Tecumseh's side, so Harrison organized an attacked on Tecumseh's people.)

One of the American Indians who remained in Ohio and had not signed the Treaty of Greenville was Tecumseh of the Shawnee people. Tecumseh spoke to his people of native pride and hoped that native peoples could reclaim some of their lost territory in what are now Ohio and Indiana. Tecumseh founded his own community in Indiana. Tecumseh tried to unite all western native peoples to fight against invading settlers. William Henry Harrison, who was the governor of the Indiana Territory, became alarmed at Tecumseh's growing power. In 1811, Harrison attacked and destroyed Tecumseh's community. Tecumseh and the Shawnees were among the American Indian groups who sided with the British in the War of 1812. Native peoples hoped that a British victory would stop the invasion of U.S. settlers into their territories. Tecumseh was eventually killed in 1813 while fighting for the British.

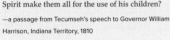

PRIMARY SOURCE

In Their Words... Tecumseh

You ought to know what you are doing to the Indians. . . . It is a very bad thing and we do not like it. . . . No groups among us have the right to sell, even to one another, and surely not to outsiders who want it all, and will not do with less. . . . Sell a country! Why not sell the air, the clouds, and the Great Sea, as well as the earth? Did not the Great Spirit make them all for the use of his children?

—a passage from Tecumseh's speech to Governor William Harrison, Indiana Territory, 1810

TECUMSEH.

TEXT: Tecumseh, In a speech to William Henry Harrison, Vincennes, Indiana Territory, 12 August 1810.; PHOTO: cbpaquette/iStock/Getty Images

✓ **Stop and Check**

COLLABORATE

Talk What about Tecumseh made William Henry Harrison alarmed?

Find Details As you read, add additional information to the graphic organizer on page 263 in your Inquiry Journal.

322 Lesson 3 Who Were the People Living in the Early United States?

African Americans in the Early United States

In the late 1700s, feelings about slavery began to change in the United States. The economies, cultures, and attitudes of the North and South grew increasingly different.

Large cities and new factories were growing quickly in the North. Immigrants flooded the United States to fill factory jobs. By 1804 all northern states had outlawed slavery. Slavery may have been illegal north of the Ohio River, but free African Americans faced prejudice there. Ohio, Indiana, and Illinois passed laws requiring African Americans to show papers proving they were free.

In the South, the economy had not changed much. The plantation was still the main way of life. On large farms, hundreds of slaves worked without pay. There were very few free African Americans in the region. Some white Southerners worked on small farms, and not all had slaves. However, the plantation owners were the wealthiest and had the most political power.

As the United States expanded west, many wondered if slavery would expand as well. In 1819 Missouri applied for statehood as a slave state, a state in which slavery is allowed. At the time, the nation had a balance of 11 slave states and 11 free states in which slavery was not allowed. Letting Missouri enter the Union as a slave state would give slave states more votes in the U.S. Senate.

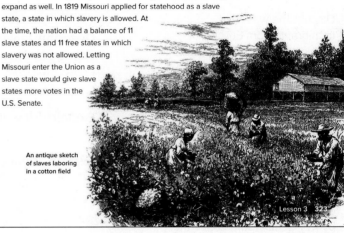

An antique sketch of slaves laboring in a cotton field

©McGraw-Hill Education; (B)ilbusca/iStock/Getty Images

Lesson 3 323

Research Companion, pp. 322–323

ENGLISH LEARNERS SCAFFOLD

ELD.PI.5.1 Exchanging information and ideas with others through oral collaborative discussions on a range of social and academic topics

Emerging

Develop Language Work with students to ensure they understand the meaning of the word *compromise*. Tell students that the Spanish cognate for *compromise* is *compromiso*. Have students tell about a time when they made a compromise, or reached an agreement with someone by giving in.

Expanding/Bridging

Apply Vocabulary Encourage students to use the word *compromise* in a sentence. Have them describe a disagreement they may have had with someone and how they resolved the disagreement by reaching a compromise.

See the **Language Learner Teaching Guide** for more language support strategies.

Monitor and Differentiate

REACHING ALL LEARNERS

Approaching Level

Work with students to understand why attitudes toward slavery in the North and in the South were so different. Have students look particularly at the economies of the North and the South.

Beyond Level

Have students conduct further research on the Missouri Compromise and how it provided only a temporary solution to a huge problem. Have students share their findings with the class.

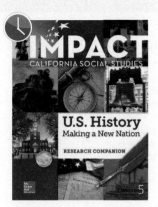

Research Companion
pp. 324–325

 STANDARDS

Discuss the waves of immigrants from Europe between 1789 and 1850 and their modes of transportation into the Ohio and Mississippi Valleys and through the Cumberland Gap (e.g., overland wagons, canals, flatboats, steamboats). **HSS.5.8.1**

Determine two or more main ideas of a text and explain how they are supported by key details; summarize the text. **CCSS.ELA.RI.5.2**

Engage effectively in a range of collaborative discussions (one-on-one, in groups, and teacher-led) with diverse partners on *grade 5 topics and texts*, building on others' ideas and expressing their own clearly. **CCSS.ELA.SL.5.1**

Go Digital!

Investigate the lesson content with online whole-class presentation tools.

Background Information

Erie Canal As early as 1790 George Washington had proposed the idea of building a canal connecting the east coast with the interior of North America. Washington's dream never materialized, and when New York's governor DeWitt Clinton proposed building such a canal many people thought he was foolish and mockingly called his project "Clinton's Big Ditch" or "Clinton's Folly." Despite the numerous obstacles, however, the Erie Canal—a marvel of modern engineering—was completed in October of 1825.

Analyze the Source

Inspect Have students read pages 324–325.

Find Evidence Use the questions below to check comprehension.

> **Describe** In what ways did the composition of the population of the United States change in the mid 1880s? (Between 1845 and 1860 more immigrants came to the United States than ever before. Europeans, Chinese, and Irish immigrants came to the United States seeking a better life.) **DOK 2**

> **Explain** Why did many Chinese people come to the United States? (to seek a fortune, and later to work on the railroad) **DOK 2**

> **Explain** What caused the Irish to be so dependent on the single crop of potatoes? (British property owners took most of the livestock and other food raised by the Irish. As a result, they had no choice other than to rely on the potato crop.) **DOK 2**

Make Connections

> **Draw Conclusions** What effects did the Missouri Compromise have on the United States? (The nation continued to be divided between slave states and free states.) **DOK 2**

Map Skills

Project the map on page 324.

- Working with a partner, use the information provided in the key to determine which states made up the larger area of the United States—slave states or free states. (slave states)

☑ Stop and Check

Write Have students compare life for African Americans in the North and the South. (African Americans faced racial prejudice in both the North and the South, but life was far worse in the South because most African Americans in the South were slaves.)

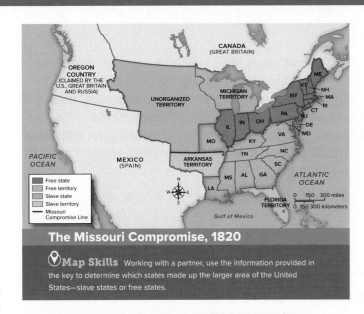

Free state
Free territory
Slave state
Slave territory
Missouri Compromise Line

The Missouri Compromise, 1820

 Map Skills Working with a partner, use the information provided in the key to determine which states made up the larger area of the United States—slave states or free states.

Congress argued over Missouri for a year. In 1820, Senator Henry Clay from Kentucky came up with the Missouri Compromise. Under this plan, Missouri was added as a slave state. Maine, which had been part of Massachusetts, became a free state. The compromise stated that, in the future, slavery would not be allowed in any states north of Missouri's southern border.

This compromise was only a temporary solution. As the United States continued to expand, new compromises and decisions had to be made.

> ### ✓ Stop and Check
>
> **Write** How was life for African Americans in the South different from those in the north?

324 Lesson 3 Who Were the People Living in the Early United States?

A Nation of Immigrants

In the mid-1800s, the **composition** of the U.S. population began to change dramatically. More immigrants came to the United States between 1845 and 1860 than ever before. Many Europeans came to find work. Some Chinese came in the 1840s to seek fortunes. Later, they worked on the railroads. The Irish, however, left their homeland for a very different reason.

In the mid-1800s, many people in Ireland were forced by British property owners to plant and eat potatoes, and little else. Most of the livestock and food the Irish raised went to England or was sold to pay high rents. Depending on only one crop proved disastrous. Starting in 1846, potatoes throughout Ireland did not grow because of a plant disease involving a fungus. The results were devastating. About 2.5 million people starved to death. Between 1846 and 1861, a million Irish people immigrated to the United States to escape starvation.

Immigrants often found work at docks along the East Coast.

Lesson 3 325

Research Companion, pp. 324–325

(EL) ENGLISH LEARNERS SCAFFOLD

ELD.PI.5.8 Analyzing how writers and speakers use vocabulary and other language resources for specific purposes (to explain, persuade, entertain, etc.) depending on modality, text type, purpose, audience, topic, and content area

Emerging

Build Vocabulary Work with students to identify and pronounce unfamiliar words in the cause-and-effect chart. Words like *exclusive, control, depend, ruin,* and *attack* have Spanish cognates. Have students make drawings to illustrate their understanding of each term.

Expanding/Bridging

Explain Vocabulary Have students work together to make sure they understand the language used in the cause-and-effect chart. Have students work in groups to explain the meaning of words like *exclusively, control, depend, ruined,* and *attacked.* Students may choose to act out the meaning of difficult words. Have students share their explanations with the class.

See the **Language Learner Teaching Guide** for more language support strategies.

Monitor and Differentiate

REACHING ALL LEARNERS

Approaching Level

Work with students to help them understand the motivation of immigrants coming to the United States in the 1880s. Were they fleeing hardship? How did they want to improve their lives? Why were they willing to take dangerous jobs to support themselves?

Beyond Level

Have students conduct further research into the people who immigrated to the United States in the 1880s. Have them investigate where they came from, where they settled in the United States, and what they hoped would happen once they came to the United States. Have students share their findings.

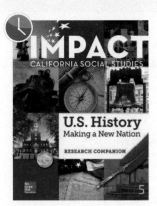

Research Companion
pp. 326–327

STANDARDS

Explain the influence and achievements of significant leaders of the time (e.g., John Marshall, Andrew Jackson, Chief Tecumseh, Chief Logan, Chief John Ross, Sequoyah). **HSS.5.3.6**

Determine two or more main ideas of a text and explain how they are supported by key details; summarize the text. **CCSS.ELA.RI.5.2**

Draw evidence from literary or informational texts to support analysis, reflection, and research **CCSS.ELA.W.5.9**

Engage effectively in a range of collaborative discussions (one-on-one, in groups, and teacher-led) with diverse partners on *grade 5 topics and texts,* building on others' ideas and expressing their own clearly. **CSS.ELA.SL.5.1**

Go Digital!

Investigate the lesson content with online whole-class presentation tools.

Background Information

Education for Women Prior to the Revolutionary War, most colonists believed that women did not need an education beyond the rudiments of reading and writing. Girls received more education only if their parents were willing to pay for it, usually in subjects like music, dancing, and needlework. But during the Revolutionary War, the absence of husbands forced many women to take responsibility for the families and households. The experience of war convinced many Americans that women needed to be better educated.

Analyze the Text

Inspect Have students read pages 326–327.

Find Evidence Use the questions below to check comprehension.

Explain Why do you think that it was newly arrived immigrants who did most of the work building canals? (Answers will vary, but students should not that those in charge of the building probably wanted to save money and that immigrants, in desperate need of jobs, were willing to do almost anything.) **DOK 3**

Cite Evidence How is the building of the Erie Canal related to the economic prosperity of New York? (The canal would allow for the transportation of goods to other parts of the country. This increased commerce would benefit New York's economy.) **DOK 3**

Analyze What motivated Benjamin Rush to lead the way in educational reform for women? (Rush believed that the education of women was good for the country.) **DOK 2**

Describe What educational opportunities were open to women in colonial America? (There were few opportunities open to women because most people believed that women only needed the basics of reading, writing, and math.) **DOK 1**

Make Inferences What does Rush mean when he describes people who didn't support the rigorous education of women as having "little minds"? ("Little minds" implies that people who don't favor women's education are not very intelligent.) **DOK 2**

Make Connections

Cite Evidence Benjamin Rush believed that a rigorous education for both men and women would create good citizens, national character, and a unified country. Do you agree or disagree with his assessment? Use evidence from the text and your own experience to support your opinion. (Answers will vary, but students should support their opinions with evidence from the text and from their own experience.) **DOK 3**

Think about It Have students discuss how they compare their cause to what Rush did for women's education. (Students should use text evidence to compare with their cause.)

✓ Stop and Check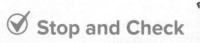

Talk What was difficult about working on the Erie Canal? (It was dangerous; many workers died from disease and accidents.)

The 1820s and 1830s is often called the Canal Age. It was during this period that the construction of several major canals filled the transportation needs of the young country. One of the largest such projects was the construction of the Erie Canal. Irish, German, and English immigrants did most of the backbreaking work required to build these canals. The work was difficult and often dangerous. Many of the workers died from accidents and disease. Later, when the canal work was done, some immigrants settled in towns and cities along the canal. Others decided to seek their fortunes by traveling west.

Around the World

Causes

- British control of Ireland results in poor Irish farmers' giving or selling to Britain most of their crops.
- As a result, most of Ireland's poor depended almost exclusively on the potato for food.
- In 1846, a blight—a destructive disease caused by a fungus—attacked Ireland's potatoes, and most of the crop was ruined.
- Ireland's poor lacked the money to purchase the food their farms produced.

A disease that destroyed potato crops in Ireland in 1846 would have a massive impact on the United States

Effects

- Famine occurred among Ireland's poor.
- About 2.5 million people starved to death.
- Between 1846 and 1861, a million Irish people immigrated to the United States.

✓ Stop and Check   COLLABORATE

Talk What was difficult about working on the Erie Canal?

326   Lesson 3   Who Were the People Living in the Early United States?

Citizenship 👥

Fighting for Women's Education

Benjamin Rush (1746–1813) is perhaps best known for his political activities during the American Revolution, which included signing the Declaration of Independence. He is also known for his career as a doctor, a professor of chemistry, and a political leader. Somewhat overlooked, however, are the various causes to which he devoted himself. One of these causes was the education of women.

Colonial America did not offer many educational opportunities to women. It was widely believed that there was no need to educate women beyond the very basics of reading, writing, and math. The Young Ladies' Academy of Philadelphia was founded in 1787 and sponsored and supervised by many of Philadelphia's male religious and political leaders, including Benjamin Rush. The academy offered its female students a wide variety of courses, including writing, English grammar, mathematics, geography, chemistry, and natural philosophy.

Benjamin Rush led the way in educational reform for women because he believed that such reform was good for the country. Rush gave many speeches on the importance of women's education. Rush believed that all children, including girls, should be rigorously educated. Rush believed that people who did not support the education of women had "little minds." His hope was that education would help students become good citizens, create national character, and unite the country.

Benjamin Rush

✓ Think About It

Imagine you are in a position to devote yourself to a cause, as Benjamin Rush did. What would the cause be? What would you do to benefit the cause?

Lesson 3   327

Research Companion, pp. 326–327

ELD.PI.5.1 Exchanging information and ideas with others through oral collaborative discussions on a range of social and academic topics

Emerging

Identify Important Vocabulary Help students locate and pronounce the words *cause*, *basics*, and *reform*. Tell students that there are Spanish cognates for each word. Encourage students to tell what they know about the meaning of each word or to draw a picture that expresses their understanding of the word.

Expanding

Use Important Vocabulary Guide students to use the words *cause*, *basics*, and *reform* in sentences describing the life and work of Benjamin Rush.

See the **Language Learner Teaching Guide** for more language support strategies.

Monitor and Differentiate

REACHING ALL LEARNERS

Approaching Level

Work with students to understand why Benjamin Rush believed so ardently that both boys and girls receive a rigorous education. Guide students to discuss what makes "good citizens" and what creates "national character."

Beyond Level

Have students conduct additional research into the education of women in colonial America. Ask them to consider what most people of the time considered the appropriate role for women and how these assumptions influenced people's opinions about the education of women. Have students share their findings.

Report Your Findings

Inquiry Journal
pp. 264–265

INQUIRY JOURNAL

(HSS) STANDARDS

Demonstrate knowledge of the significance of land policies developed under the Continental Congress (e.g., sale of western lands, the Northwest Ordinance of 1787) and those policies' impact on American Indians' land. **HSS.5.6.6**

Discuss the waves of immigrants from Europe between 1789 and 1850 and their modes of transportation into the Ohio and Mississippi Valleys and through the Cumberland Gap (e.g., overland wagons, canals, flatboats, steamboats). **HSS.5.8.1**

(CCSS) Write narratives to develop real or imagined experiences or events using effective technique, descriptive details, and clear event sequences. **CCSS.ELA.W.5.3**

Go Digital!

• Students can go online to report their findings. Assess their responses online.

• Students can access the online graphic organizer to capture ideas from their investigation.

Think About It

Students will review their research and consider how the experiences of people living in the early United States varied depending on their race, ethnicity or gender. Remind students to review the information they gathered about groups of people living in the early United States. Direct students back to pages 318–327 of their Research Companion if they need more information.

Write About It

Write a Blog Post Have students read the prompt. Explain to students that an effective blog post will give important information and use words and phrases that signal comparisons and contrasts. Remind students to include the following elements in their response:

• a clear introduction that states the groups the writer will compare and contrast

• details from the text supporting the writer's analysis

• transitional words and phrases that make clear the comparisons and contrasts

Use the rubric on p. T686 to evaluate students' work.

Talk About It

Share Your Thinking Help students exchange the text of their blog with a partner. Have partners discuss likenesses and similarities in their blogs.

• Explain that they should take turns discussing and explaining their blogs.

• Remind students to cite evidence from the text that supports their comparisons and contrasts.

• Remind students to follow the rules of appropriate classroom conversation.

Connect to the Essential Question

Read the prompt aloud to students. Ask them the following guiding questions:

• What events and/or groups of people from this lesson most transformed the nation and its people? (Answers will vary, but students may say that Benjamin Rush's work for women's education left the most enduring and positive impact on society.)

• What actions and ideas are still important to our nation today? (Answers will vary, but students may say that the food safety remains important today so that we avoid a large-scale contamination, such as the one that led to the Great Famine in Ireland.)

Remind students to use the space provided in their journal to jot down notes.

Report Your Findings

Think About It

How were people's experiences in the early United States different depending on their race, ethnicity, or gender?

Write About It

Write a Blog Post
Choose three groups of people who lived in the young United States. Compare and contrast their experiences in a short blog post. Use facts and details from the text in your comparison-contrast blog.

Pioneers traveled west sometimes for adventure but often in search of a better life. By contrast, American Indians wanted to stay where they were. They were under constant assault from pioneers who wanted to take their land from them. Like pioneers, immigrants came to the United States in search of a better life. In contrast to the pioneers, they often had to do dangerous work, like building canals, to support their families.

Talk About It **COLLABORATE**

Share Your Thinking
Exchange your blog post with that of a partner. What likenesses or similarities did your partner include that you did not?

History Connect to the **EQ ESSENTIAL QUESTION**

Pull It Together
What were the early years of the United States like for different groups of people?

Student responses should mention at least two of the groups discussed in this lesson.

EQ ESSENTIAL QUESTION Inquiry Project Notes

264 Lesson 3 Who Were the People Living in the Early United States?

Lesson 3 265

McGraw-Hill Education

Inquiry Journal, pp. 264–265

ENGLISH LEARNERS SCAFFOLD

ELD.PI.5.10 Writing literary and informational texts to present, describe, and explain ideas and information, using appropriate technology

Emerging

Use Transitional Words Encourage students to use transitional words and phrases that signal comparison and contrasts in their writing, such as *both*, *like*, *compared to*, *in contrast*, *however*, and *similarly*. Define the words and phrases as needed.

Expanding/Bridging

Use Structure Work with students to organize their writing. Have students consider using words that show comparisons and contrasts, such as *both*, *like*, *compared to*, *in contrast*, *however*, *similarly*, and *on the other hand*. Point out to students that the phrase *on the other hand* is an idiom that means "looked at from another point of view."

See the **Language Learner Teaching Guide** for more language support strategies.

Monitor and Differentiate

REACHING ALL LEARNERS

Approaching Level

Work with students to organize their writing based on a comparison and contrast text structure. Review transitional words and phrases that signal comparison-contrast structure, such as *both*, *like*, *compared to*, *however*, *similarly*, and *on the other hand*.

Beyond Level

Have students use this writing project as a starting point for a larger project on how gender, ethnicity, or race can affect the way various groups of people are treated in the United States. Have students share the results of their research with the class.

Know what your students know!

Lesson Task
Report Your Findings

Use the rubric to evaluate students' responses.

Write a Blog Post Students write a blog post comparing and contrasting groups of people who lived in the early United States.

Share Your Thinking Students talk to classmates about their findings. They take turns discussing how the activity helped them understand how race, ethnicity, and gender affected the experiences of people who lived in the early United States.

Performance Task Evaluation Rubric

	4	3	2	1
Historical Understanding	Strong understanding of the different experiences of people who lived in the early United States	Adequate understanding of the different experiences of people who lived in the early United States	Uneven understanding of the different experiences of people who lived in the early United States	No understanding of the different experiences of people who lived in the early United States
Compare and Contrast	Clearly compares and contrasts the experiences of people who lived in the Early United States	Adequately compares and contrasts the experiences of people who lived in the Early United States	Somewhat clear or unclear comparison and contrast of the experiences of people who lived in the Early United States	No comparison and contrast of the experiences of people who lived in the Early United States
Support with Evidence	Facts and details provide thorough evidence	Facts and details provide adequate evidence.	Facts and details provide uneven evidence	Facts and details are missing, or no supporting evidence is provided
Share Your Thinking	Speaks clearly and at an understandable pace Speaks in complete sentences throughout the discussion	Speaks clearly during most of the discussion Speaks in complete sentences through most of the discussion	At times speaker is unclear Mixes complete and incomplete sentences	Speaks unclearly throughout the discussion. Does not use complete sentences

Lesson Assessment

Go *Digital!*

- Have students complete the Chapter 7 Lesson 3 Assessment online to monitor their understanding of the lesson content.

California Smarter Balanced Assessment Connections!

Standards Covered	Lesson Task	Lesson Assessment	Alignment with California Smarter Balanced Assessment
History Social Science Content 5.3.6; 5.6.6; 5.6.7; 5.8.1	✔	✔	Claim 1 Targets 8, 9, 10
History Social Science Analysis Skills Chronological and Spatial Thinking 5.1; Research, Evidence, and Point of View 5.2 Historical Interpretation 5.1	✔	✔	Claim 1 Targets 11, 12
Writing W.5.8	✔	✔	Claim 2 Target 11
Research and Inquiry W.5.9	✔	✔	Claim 4 Targets 11, 12
Reading RI.5.2; RI.5.7	✔	✔	Claim 1 Targets 11, 12
Speaking and Listening SL.5.1	✔		Claim 3 Target 8, 9, 11

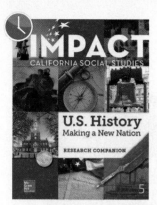

Research Companion,
pp. 328–329

 STANDARDS

Name the states and territories that existed in 1850 and identify their locations and major geographical features (e.g., mountain ranges, principal rivers, dominant plant regions). **HSS.5.8.2**

Students know the location of the current 50 states and the names of their capitals. **HSS.5.9**

DID YOU KNOW?

Vermont was the fourteenth state in the Union. Its territory was originally disputed by New York and New Hampshire. In 1777, the people of the territory created an independent state and wrote a constitution.

Analyze the Map

Inspect Have students read pp. 328–329.

Find Evidence Use the questions below to check comprehension. Remind students to support their answers with text evidence.

Identify What is the capital of Kentucky? (Frankfort) **DOK 1**

Analyze What information is on the map, but not on the table? (The map shows locations of the free and slave states.) What information is in the table but not in the map? (The table provides capitals and population data.) **DOK 2**

Summarize What are the strengths and weaknesses of maps? (Possible response: Maps are good for showing territory but cannot show large amounts of information, such as population, without getting cluttered.) **DOK 3**

Explain What differentiates slave states from free states on the map? (They are differentiated by color.) **DOK 3**

Make Connections

Analyze Visuals How does the map help you understand some of the major changes to the United States in the years after the Revolutionary War ended? (Responses will vary, but students should identify that the map helps them see the divisions between slave states and free states that would continue to cause problems for the new nation in the coming years.) **DOK 3**

Map and Globe Skills

Map and Globe Skills

The United States, 1821

By the time of the Missouri Compromise, the United States had changed significantly. A nation that had begun with thirteen states now had twenty-four. The United States had covered about 860,000 square miles in 1790. By the 1820 census, the area was roughly 1.7 million square miles, about double its original size. The population had grown from about 3.9 million people to about 9.6 million.

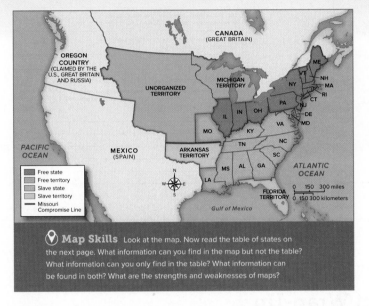

Free state
Free territory
Slave state
Slave territory
Missouri Compromise Line

PACIFIC OCEAN

CANADA (GREAT BRITAIN)

OREGON COUNTRY (CLAIMED BY THE U.S., GREAT BRITAIN AND RUSSIA)

UNORGANIZED TERRITORY

MICHIGAN TERRITORY

MEXICO (SPAIN)

ARKANSAS TERRITORY

FLORIDA TERRITORY

ATLANTIC OCEAN

Gulf of Mexico

0   150   300 miles
0 150 300 kilometers

Map Skills Look at the map. Now read the table of states on the next page. What information can you find in the map but not the table? What information can you only find in the table? What information can be found in both? What are the strengths and weaknesses of maps?

Alabama
1820 Population: 127,901
2015 Population: 4,858,979
★ Capital: Montgomery

Mississippi
1820 Population: 75,448
2015 Population: 2,992,333
★ Capital: Jackson

Illinois
1820 Population: 55,211
2015 Population: 12,859,995
★ Capital: Springfield

Missouri
1820 Population: 66,586
2015 Population: 6,083,672
★ Capital: Jefferson City

Indiana
1820 Population: 147,178
2015 Population: 6,619,680
★ Capital: Indianapolis

Ohio
1820 Population: 581,434
2015 Population: 11,613,423
★ Capital: Columbus

Kentucky
1820 Population: 564,317
2015 Population: 4,425,092
★ Capital: Frankfort

Tennessee
1820 Population: 422,813
2015 Population: 6,600,299
★ Capital: Nashville

Louisiana
1820 Population: 153,407
2015 Population: 4,670,724
★ Capital: Baton Rouge

Vermont
1820 Population: 235,764
2015 Population: 626,042
★ Capital: Montpelier

Maine
1820 Population: 298,335
2015 Population: 1,329,328
★ Capital: Augusta

Research Companion, pp. 328–329

ENGLISH LEARNERS SCAFFOLD

ELD.PI.5.6 Reading closely literary and informational texts and viewing multimedia to determine how meaning is conveyed explicitly and implicitly through language

Emerging

Analyze Visuals Encourage students to compare the existing state populations with the populations in 1820. Provide sentence frames as needed:

The population of _____ was _____ in 1820 and _____ in 2015.

The state of _____ once had more people than _____. Now, _____ has more people.

Expanding/Bridging

Analyze Visuals Guide students to compare and contrast the populations of each state in 1820 and 2015. Encourage them to describe what they see in the chart.

See the **Language Learner Teaching Guide** for more language support strategies.

Monitor and Differentiate

REACHING ALL LEARNERS

Approaching Level

Guide students to compare and contrast the data given for each state. Guide students to find on the map each state added to the Union between the American Revolution and 1821.

On Level

Encourage students to share what they know about each state that joined the United Stated between the Revolution and 1821.

Beyond Level

Have students conduct additional research into one of the states referenced in the chart. Students may research how and why the state joined the Union or another aspect of the state's history, industry, or economy.

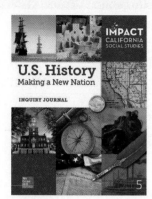

Inquiry Journal
pp. 266–267

 STANDARDS

Students trace the colonization, immigration, and settlement patterns of the American people from 1789 to the mid-1800s, with emphasis on the role of economic incentives, effects of the physical and political geography, and transportation systems. **HSS.5.8**

Explain the relationships or interactions between two or more individuals, events, ideas, or concepts in a historical, scientific, or technical text based on specific information in the text. **CCSS.ELA.RI.5.3**

Report on a topic or text or present an opinion, sequencing ideas logically and using appropriate facts and relevant, descriptive details to support main ideas or themes; speak clearly at an understandable pace. **CCSS.ELA.SL.5.4**

Write opinion pieces on topics or texts, supporting a point of view with reasons and information. **CCSS.ELA.W.5.1**

Go Digital!

Look online for the EQ Inquiry Project rubric.

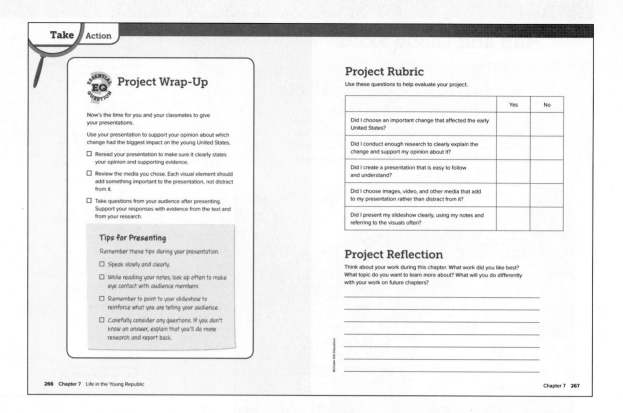

Take Action

Project Wrap-Up

Now's the time for you and your classmates to give your presentations.

Use your presentation to support your opinion about which change had the biggest impact on the young United States.

☐ Reread your presentation to make sure it clearly states your opinion and supporting evidence.

☐ Review the media you chose. Each visual element should add something important to the presentation, not distract from it.

☐ Take questions from your audience after presenting. Support your responses with evidence from the text and from your research.

Tips for Presenting

Remember these tips during your presentation.

☐ Speak slowly and clearly.

☐ While reading your notes, look up often to make eye contact with audience members.

☐ Remember to point to your slideshow to reinforce what you are telling your audience.

☐ Carefully consider any questions. If you don't know an answer, explain that you'll do more research and report back.

266   Chapter 7   Life in the Young Republic

Project Rubric

Use these questions to help evaluate your project.

	Yes	No
Did I choose an important change that affected the early United States?		
Did I conduct enough research to clearly explain the change and support my opinion about it?		
Did I create a presentation that is easy to follow and understand?		
Did I choose images, video, and other media that add to my presentation rather than distract from it?		
Did I present my slideshow clearly, using my notes and referring to the visuals often?		

Project Reflection

Think about your work during this chapter. What work did you like best? What topic do you want to learn more about? What will you do differently with your work on future chapters?

_____

_____

_____

_____

_____

_____

Chapter 7   267

 ## Inquiry Project Wrap-Up

Have students share their inquiry projects by presenting their multimedia presentations.

- Before students present their multimedia presentations, discuss the wrap-up steps with them, making sure they know what's expected in their presentations.

- Allow time after each presentation for a Q-and-A session.

Tips for Presenting

Discuss the tips for presenting with students and the importance of communicating effectively with their audience. Explain that they should practice clicking through the presentation before delivering it.

Project Rubric

Discuss each question in the Project Rubric with students. If students have worked as part of a group to develop their projects, you might want to have them work as a group to address each question in the rubric.

Project Reflection

Student reflections can focus on the work they did as part of the group or their individual performance presenting on the most important change in the young United States. Give groups time to discuss each phase of their projects and reflect on their work.

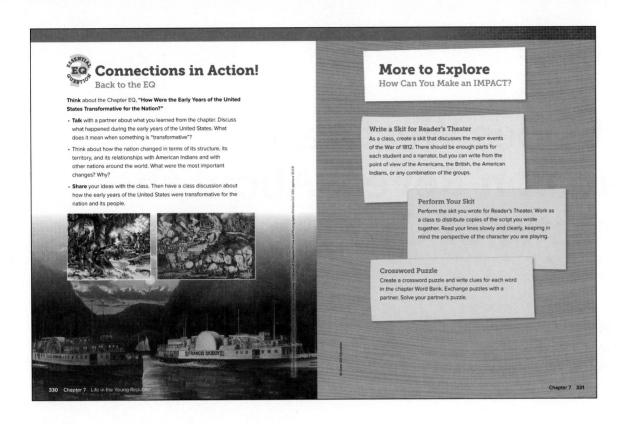

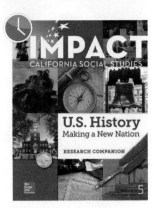

Research Companion
pp. 330–331

Connections in Action

To help focus students' conversations, you may want to discuss the EQ with the entire class before students discuss their ideas with a partner. Remind students to think about evidence they can provide that will support their ideas. After students present, allow time for others to ask questions.

More to Explore

Write a Skit for Reader's Theater Remind students to think about what they learned about the War of 1812. Encourage them to try to capture in the script what was so important about those events.

Perform Your Skit Encourage students to present the skits they created. Provide ways for them to record and present the skits, or have a live performance in class.

Crossword Puzzle Have students create crossword puzzles from the chapter Word Bank. Remind them that the clues should be challenging but clear.

What Does Westward Expansion Reveal About the Character of Our Nation?

In This Chapter ...

Students will investigate what settlers experienced in their move westward along trails in wagon trains. They will also analyze how westward expansion affected American Indians, including tragedies such as the Trail of Tears and conflicts such as the Seminole Wars. Finally, students will learn about the events and conflicts that led to Texas and California joining the United States.

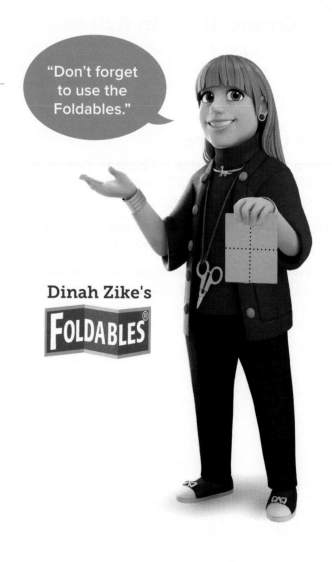

"Don't forget to use the Foldables."

Dinah Zike's
FOLDABLES®

 CHAPTER STANDARDS

✔ Students describe the cooperation and conflict that existed among the American Indians and between the Indian nations and the new settlers. **HSS.5.3**

✔ Students trace the colonization, immigration, and settlement patterns of the American people from 1789 to the mid-1800s, with emphasis on the role of economic incentives, effects of the physical and political geography, and transportation systems. **HSS.5.8**

✔ Students know the location of the current 50 states and the names of their capitals. **HSS.5.9**

1 ENGAGE

Inquiry Journal
pp. 268–271

 Inquiry Project

Create a Museum Gallery

- **Explore Words**

- *Go Digital!*
  - IMPACT Chapter Video: The Westward Expansion

2 INVESTIGATE

Research Companion
pp. 332–339

- **Step Into the Time and Place**

- **Connect Through Literature**
  A Time of Troubles
  by Ruth Spencer Johnson

- **People You Should Know**

Weekly Explorer Magazine pp. 100–111

3 REPORT

Inquiry Journal
pp. 296–297

Inquiry Project

Create a Museum Gallery

 Short on Time? Look for the clock to teach core content in less time.

CULTIVATE MEANING AND SUPPORT LANGUAGE

Language Learner Teaching Guide,
pp. 178–179

Content Objectives

- Demonstrate understanding of what U.S. settlers and American Indians experienced as the nation expanded.

- Explore the events that led to statehood for Texas and California.

Language Objectives

- Discuss point of view.
- Recognize personification.
- Identify cause and effect.
- Use linking verb be.

CONNECT TO

Unit 4, Week 1
Sharing Stories

Read Aloud
"The Legend of John Henry"

Reading/Writing Workshop
"How Mighty Kate Stopped the Train"

Literature Anthology/Paired Selection
Davy Crockett Saves the World
"How Grandmother Spider Stole the Sun"

Leveled Readers
Paul Bunyan, Pecos Bill, An Extraordinary Girl, "One Grain of Rice," "The Fountain of Youth," and "How Coqui Got Her Song"

CONNECT TO SCIENCE

Explore how westward expansion affected the ecosystem of the American West, including migration patterns, hunting and overhunting, and destruction of habitats.

CONNECT TO MATH

Using a map's scale, apply measurement and the formula for area to calculate distance and square miles.

Choose the assessment options that work best for you and your students.

BEFORE
PRE-TEST

Measure students' content knowledge before you begin the chapter with the following questions.

 Quick Check

✓ What was it like to move westward on wagon trains?

✓ Did American settlers in new areas of the United States coexist and work peacefully with American Indians who already lived there?

✓ What conflicts occurred over the territories that eventually became California and Texas?

1. Ask students to produce a response to each question.

2. When all students have responded, ask them to rate how confident they are in their answers on a scale from 1 – not very confident to 5 – very confident.

3. Collect students' responses and review them for misconceptions, factual errors, and to inform instruction. You may wish to return to these questions as students investigate chapter 8.

4. **Don't Forget!** Revisit students' quick check responses with them. If students change their response, ask them to support the change with text evidence. You may wish to have students respond to a different prompt to measure their content knowledge, such as *How did Americans treat the Cherokee after gold was discovered on Cherokee lands in Georgia?*

EVERY LESSON
ONGOING ASSESSMENT

Use the lesson tools to monitor the IMPACT of your instruction.

 Stop and Check

Use the quick question prompts to monitor student comprehension of the content. The **Stop and Check** questions prompt students to make connections to their world today, engage in discussions to deepen their understanding of the content, and to look at different perspectives.

🔍 **Report Your Findings**

The lesson task, **Report Your Findings**, can be used to measure student understanding of the lesson content and ability to effectively express their understanding. See the Lesson Assessment pp. T720, T740, and T762 for task-specific evaluation rubrics.

(*Go Digital!*) **Lesson Assessment**

Use the **Lesson Assessment** to monitor student understanding of the lesson content. Have students complete the assessment online. See pp. T721, T741, and T763 for California Smarter Balanced Assessments Connections.

EVERY CHAPTER
POST TEST

Evaluate student understanding of core chapter content with one or more of the following assessment options.

 Connections in Action

Use the **Connections in Action** to evaluate student understanding of core chapter content through discussion.

 Inquiry Project

Use the **EQ Inquiry Project** to measure student understanding of the chapter content and ability to effectively express their understanding. See the EQ Inquiry Project Wrap Up below for a task-specific evaluation rubric.

	4	3	2	1
Historical Understanding	Strong understanding of how artwork tells the story of westward expansion	Adequate understanding of how artwork tells the story of westward expansion	Uneven understanding of how artwork tells the story of westward expansion	No understanding of how artwork tells the story of westward expansion
Create a Gallery	Chooses paintings that describe multiple aspects of westward expansion	Chooses paintings that describe one aspect of westward expansion	Chooses paintings that are somewhat about westward expansion	No paintings chosen or students does not show understanding of the task
Include Relevant Information	Incorporates relevant and adequate research into museum card	Incorporates adequate research into museum card	Incorporates little research into museum card	Incorporates no research into museum card
Gallery Talk	Includes relevant reasons to support opinions Thoughtfully considers how paintings work together to tell the story of westward expansion	Includes some reasons to support opinions Considers how paintings work together	Gives opinions without supporting reasons Superficially discusses paintings	Does not provide opinions or reasons Does not participate in discussion or does not consider the story the paintings tell

(**Go** *Digital!*) **Chapter Benchmark Assessments**

Use the chapter tests to monitor student understanding of the chapter History-Social Science standards and content. Have students complete the assessment online.

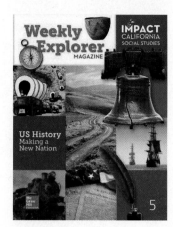

pp. 100–111

 **Short on Time?**

Use the Weekly Explorer Magazine during your reading block.

Go Digital!

Look online for the Weekly Explorer Magainze Teaching Guide.

WordBlast

Remind students to look for the Word Blasts as they read the Explorer Magazine.

FOLDABLES

Encourage students to use the Notetaking Foldables as they gather more information.

Weekly Explorer Magazine

The Weekly Explorer Magazine is designed to provide students with more information to use as they dig deeper into the **reasons Americans wanted to expand west.** The articles in a variety of formats explore the Essential Question and support the Inquiry Project.

Engage

Build background for students and share any information needed to provide a context for the chapter topic. Have students read the Essential Question and the Table of Contents.

Analyze the Visual Discuss the opening visual (photograph, photo essay, artwork) on the second page of the Magazine chapter. Help students connect the visual to the chapter topic and the Essential Question.

Analyze the Sources

Students will read and analyze the articles, graphic novel, poems, songs, literature excerpts, primary sources, and infographics.

Read and Analyze Before reading, provide any additional information you think students will need about the topics. Then guide students through the three-step process to read and analyze the articles.

1 Inspect Have students skim the article or articles on a page or multiple pages. Ask questions to help students recall and retell key ideas.

- What is this article mostly about?
- Who is _____?

2 Find Evidence Have students reread the articles and look for details they might have missed. Ask additional questions to help them read more closely.

- What details do you notice in the photographs?
- Why was _____ important?

3 Make Connections Have students work in pairs or small groups to discuss prompts that help them connect the article(s) to other texts, their own lives, current ideas and issues, and other topics.

- How is _____ similar to what we do today?
- How do you think _____ felt about what happened?
- What do you think about _____?

Bibliography

The following suggested resources may help students' investigation of the chapter content.

EXPLORE PEOPLE, PLACES, AND EVENTS

▶ **Daniel Boone and the Exploration of the Frontier**
by Richard Kozar; Chelsea House Publications, 2000.

Perspectives
▶ **Dear Levi: Letters from the Overland Trail**
by Elvira Woodruff: Yearling, 1998.

▶ **How We Crossed the West: The Adventures of Lewis and Clark**
by Rosalyn Schanzer; National Geographic Society, 1997.

▶ **Miranda's Last Stand**
by Gloria Whelan; HarperCollins, 1999.

▶ **Mr. Tuckett**
by Gary Paulsen; Yearling, 1994.

▶ **Prairie Songs**
by Pam Conrad; HarperCollins, 1985.

▶ **The Saga of Lewis and Clark in the Uncharted West**
by Thomas Schmidt and Jermy Schmidt; DK Publishing, 1999.

▶ **Seaman: The Dog Who Explored West with Lewis and Clark**
by Gail Langer Karwoski; Peachtree Publishing, 1999.

▶ **Ten-Mile Day: And the Building of the Transcontinental Railroad**
by Mary Ann Fraser; Square Fish, 1996.

EXPLORE MUSIC

Did you know? During the period of Westward Expansion, many popular songs reflected current events and the popular desire to move into the western territories of the American continent.

Songs like: **Oh Susanna**, **Ho! For California**, and **Paddy Works on the Railway** were about events like the California Gold Rush and the building of the transcontinental railroad.
[**Oh, Susanna** - Spotlight on Music, Gr. 4]
[**Paddy (Pat) Works on the Railway** - Spotlight on Music, Gr. 4]

A song like: **Shenandoah** is a haunting lament about fur traders who, after a season of trapping up north would take their canoes full of fur and travel down to the trading posts along the Missouri River.
[**Shenandoah** - Spotlight on Music, Gr. 4]

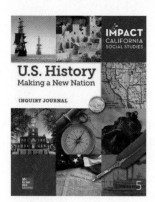

Inquiry Journal
pp. 268–271

 STANDARDS

Students describe the cooperation and conflict that existed among the American Indians and between the Indian nations and the new settlers. **HSS.5.3**

Students trace the colonization, immigration, and settlement patterns of the American people from 1789 to the mid-1800s, with emphasis on the role of economic incentives, effects of the physical and political geography, and transportation systems. **HSS.5.8**

 Write informative/ explanatory texts to examine a topic and convey ideas and information clearly. **CCSS.ELA.W.5.2**

Draw evidence from literary or informational texts to support analysis, reflection, and research. **CCSS.ELA.W.5.9**

Go Digital!

Explore Words: Interactive vocabulary activities support students as they explore the chapter words.

 See the **Language Learner Teaching Guide** pp. 178–179 for support strategies.

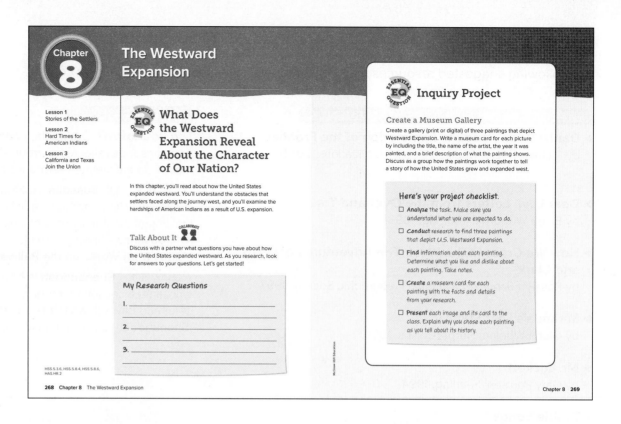

What Does the Westward Expansion Reveal about the Character of Our Nation?

Have students read the Chapter Essential Question on p. 268.

Talk About It

- Prompt students to write what they would like to know about westward expansion after reading the chapter.

- After jotting down their questions, have students discuss their questions with partners.

Inquiry Project
Create a Museum Gallery

- Have students read aloud the EQ Inquiry Project.

- Tell students that they will use information gathered from the chapter and from independent research to complete the project.

- Make certain students understand the task by reviewing each step of the project.

Complete this chapter's Word Rater. Write notes as you learn more about each word.

boundary   My Notes
☐ Know It!
☐ Heard It!
☐ Don't Know It!

hostility   My Notes
☐ Know It!
☐ Heard It!
☐ Don't Know It!

Manifest Destiny   My Notes
☐ Know It!
☐ Heard It!
☐ Don't Know It!

oxen   My Notes
☐ Know It!
☐ Heard It!
☐ Don't Know It!

republic   My Notes
☐ Know It!
☐ Heard It!
☐ Don't Know It!

sovereign   My Notes
☐ Know It!
☐ Heard It!
☐ Don't Know It!

surge   My Notes
☐ Know It!
☐ Heard It!
☐ Don't Know It!

survey   My Notes
☐ Know It!
☐ Heard It!
☐ Don't Know It!

territory   My Notes
☐ Know It!
☐ Heard It!
☐ Don't Know It!

veto   My Notes
☐ Know It!
☐ Heard It!
☐ Don't Know It!

Explore Words

- **Academic/Domain-Specific Vocabulary** Read the words aloud to students. Explain to students that these are words they will learn more about in the chapter.

- **Word Rater** Have students place a checkmark in one of the three boxes below each word, indicating that they "Know It," "Heard It," or "Don't Know It."

  ✔ **Know It** Tell students that if they know the word, they should write its meaning on the lines provided.

  ✔ **Heard It** Tell students that if they have heard, or are familiar with the word, they should write what they know about it on the lines provided. Remind them to take notes about the word as they encounter it.

  ✔ **Don't Know It** If they do not know the word's meaning, tell them to write down its meaning when they encounter the word in the chapter.

"Don't forget to use the Foldables."

🔍 Explore Words Routine

Remind students that when they come to an unfamiliar word or phrase in their research, they should follow these steps to determine its meaning.

1. Look around the word or phrase for clues to unlock its meaning.

2. Look inside the word or phrase for word part clues.

3. Look up the word in other resources.

Dinah Zike's
FOLDABLES®

The Westward Expansion

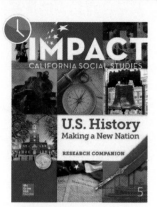

U.S. History
Making a New Nation

RESEARCH COMPANION

5

Research Companion
pp. 332–337

 STANDARDS

Students describe the cooperation and conflict that existed among the American Indians and between the Indian nations and the new settlers. **HSS.5.3**

Students trace the colonization, immigration, and settlement patterns of the American people from 1789 to the mid-1800s, with emphasis on the role of economic incentives, effects of the physical and political geography, and transportation systems. **HSS.5.8**

Go Digital!

- Investigate westward expansion with online whole-class presentation tools.

- Analyze the online literature selection so students can find evidence and make connections.

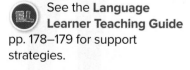 See the **Language Learner Teaching Guide** pp. 178–179 for support strategies.

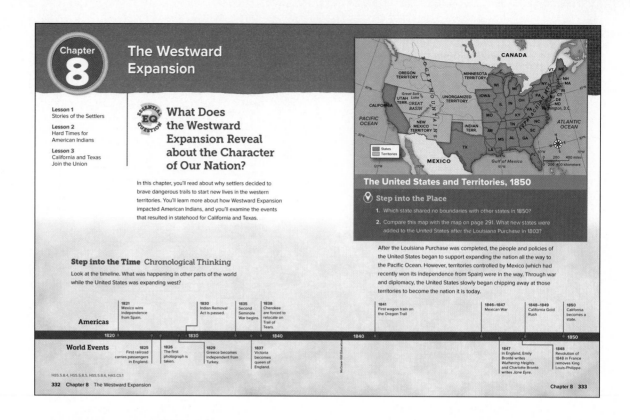

Step Into the Time

Have students read over the events on the timeline, first examining the events from the Americas and then the events from around the world.

- What was happening in the Americas when France had its Revolution of 1848? (The California Gold Rush)

- Would it have been technologically possible to take a photograph of someone on the first wagon train on the Oregon Trail? (Yes, because the first photograph was taken in 1826, and people began traveling on the Oregon Trail in 1841.)

Step Into the Place

In partners or in small groups, have students examine the map on p. 333 and answer the questions beneath it.

1. Which state shared no boundaries with other states in 1850? (California)

2. Compare this map with the map on p. 291. What new states were added to the United States since the Louisiana Purchase in 1803? (Possible response: California, Texas, Louisiana, Missouri, Arkansas, Ohio, Illinois, and Wisconsin to name a few)

GENRE Historical Fiction *"A Time of Troubles" is a piece of historical fiction. It tells about events as they happened, but it is from the point of view of a fictional character.*

Analyze the Source

Inspect Have students read the selection on pp. 334–337 together to determine the general meaning of the text.

1. What has changed for the Sioux girl and her family? (They once roamed free, but now they are forced to stay in reservations.)

Find Evidence Have students reread the selection and ask:

2. How does life on the reservation compare with the life the Sioux led before? (They must farm rather than hunt, they do not have a lot of food, they are forced to wear cloth clothing, and cannot use traditional medicine men.)

Make Connections

3. How do the Sioux maintain their way of life despite the hardships of the reservation? (The children still play warriors and hunters, many still follow traditions, and they will always love the earth and its creatures.)

Perspectives What would it have been like for the Sioux to have to adapt to new surroundings and customs? (Responses will vary.)

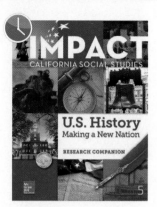

Research Companion
pp.338–339

 STANDARDS

Students describe the cooperation and conflict that existed among the American Indians and between the Indian nations and the new settlers. **HSS.5.3**

Students trace the colonization, immigration, and settlement patterns of the American people from 1789 to the mid-1800s, with emphasis on the role of economic incentives, effects of the physical and political geography, and transportation systems. **HSS.5.8**

CCSS Explain the relationships or interactions between two or more individuals, events, ideas, or concepts in a historical, scientific, or technical text based on specific information in the text. **CCSS.ELA.RI.5.3**

Go Digital!

Investigate chapter content with the online teaching plan.

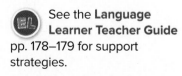 See the **Language Learner Teacher Guide** pp. 178–179 for support strategies.

People You Should Know

Antonio López de Santa Anna

In 1833, after assuming the presidency of the independent nation of Mexico, Antonio López de Santa Anna established a strong national government. In 1836, Texas declared its independence from Mexico and its desire to join the United States. Santa Anna tried to bring Texas back into Mexico. He had a small victory when he trapped Texas forces at the Alamo, but he lost to Sam Houston at the Battle of San Jacinto. Later, he overthrew the Mexican government to become president a second time. He fought the United States again from 1846–1848 in the Mexican War. After Mexico lost, he fled to Jamaica.

338 Chapter 8 The Westward Expansion

Osceola

As a leader during the Second Seminole War (1835), Osceola used guerilla warfare against U.S. troops. In guerilla warfare, one side uses the landscape to hide and attack the other side by surprise. Osceola and the Seminoles used the swamps of southern Florida to fight the Americans who wanted to move the Seminoles away from their ancestral lands. The Seminoles had success until they went to St. Augustine to try to come to an agreement with U.S. military leaders. The soldiers captured and imprisoned Osceola and his men. Osceola later died in prison, and the Second Seminole War came to an end.

Laura Ingalls Wilder

In 1932, Laura Ingalls Wilder published her first children's book, *Little House in the Big Woods*. The book told stories about her own childhood on the prairie in the late 1800s. Wilder's father had taken his family in a covered wagon across the northern plains states before settling in Missouri, where Laura also raised her own family. She worked as an editor and writer for many newspapers and magazines, but it is her books, often called the "Little House" series, that won her lasting fame as an American writer.

Cesar Chavez

Born into a family of migrant farm workers, Cesar Chavez devoted his life to making sure farm laborers in the United States were treated fairly. In 1962, he founded the NFWA, the National Farm Workers Association. This union of farm workers conducted strikes and boycotts of large farms that refused to provide good wages and benefits to their workers. This brought national attention to the issue and economic pressure on the farm owners. After about five years, the farms gave in and signed agreements with the NFWA.

Chapter 8 339

People You Should Know

How do personal stories IMPACT our understanding of what westward expansion reveals about the character of our nation?

- Have students read aloud the biographies.

- Tell them that they will learn about these people and others throughout the chapter.

- Prompt students to write a diary entry from the point of view of one of the people in the People You Should Know feature or another key figure in the chapter. Other people they encounter will include:

▷ Brigham Young

▷ Joseph Smith

▷ Andrew Jackson

▷ Chief John Ross

▷ Sequoyah

▷ David Crockett

▷ Sam Houston

▷ Stephen F. Austin

▷ John C. Frémont

▷ James K. Polk

- Ask students to try to incorporate facts about the person into the diary entry while making the entry seem like something he or she would have written. Students can also draw, download, or photocopy portraits for the display. Have students assemble their diary entries into a book. Refer to the book throughout the chapter.

Teacher Notes

What Did Settlers Experience in Their Movement Westward?

Background Information

In this lesson, students learn about what settlers experienced on the trails as they moved farther west. They will also learn about the differing motivations that led people to travel.

Community Connections

To enrich what students have learned about the move west, plan a visit to a local museum that houses American art that focuses on Westward Expansion.

LESSON STANDARDS

✓ Name the states and territories that existed in 1850 and identify their locations and major geographical features (e.g., mountain ranges, principal rivers, dominant plant regions). **HSS.5.8.2**

✓ Discuss the experiences of settlers on the overland trails to the West (e.g., location of the routes; purpose of the journeys; the influence of the terrain, rivers, vegetation, and climate; life in the territories at the end of these trails). **HSS.5.8.4**

✓ Relate how and when California, Texas, Oregon, and other western lands became part of the United States, including the significance of the Texas War for Independence and the Mexican-American War. **HSS.5.8.6**

✓ Students place key events and people of the historical era they are studying in a chronological sequence and within a spatial context; they interpret time lines. **HAS CS.1**

✓ Students correctly apply terms related to time, including *past, present, future, decade, century,* and *generation.* **HAS CS.2**

✓ Students explain how the present is connected to the past, identifying both similarities and differences between the two, and how some things change over time and some things stay the same. **HAS CS.3**

✓ Students pose relevant questions about events they encounter in historical documents, eyewitness accounts, oral histories, letters, diaries, artifacts, photographs, maps, artworks, and architecture. **HAS HR.2**

✓ Students identify and interpret the multiple causes and effects of historical events. **HAS HI.3**

Connect to the Essential Question

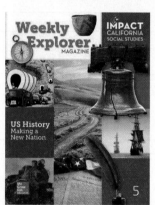

The **Weekly Explorer Magazine** supports the students' exploration of the Essential Question and provides additional resources for the EQ Inquiry Project.

Chapter 8, pp. 100–111

Inquiry Project

Create a Museum Gallery

Remind students to use the information they learn in this lesson and other resources to complete the EQ Inquiry Project.

Dinah Zike's
FOLDABLES®   Remind students to use their note taking Foldables.

When Minutes Count!

Suggested Lesson Pacing

1 ENGAGE
One Day

2 INVESTIGATE
Two to Three Days

 Short on Time? Look for the clock to teach core content in less time.

3 REPORT
One Day

- Lesson Opener
- Analyze the Source
- Inquiry Tools

Go Digital

- **Video:** Westward Expansion
- **iMap:** Trails to the West, 1840–1860

- Trails to the West
- Life on the Wagon Train
- Mormons Head West

- Think About It
- Write a Travel Guide
- Defend Your Claims

Make Connections!

(ccss) CONNECT TO ELA

Reading
Draw on information from multiple print or digital sources, demonstrating the ability to locate an answer to a question quickly or to solve a problem efficiently. **ELA.RI.5.7**

Research
Conduct short research projects that use several sources to build knowledge through investigation of different aspects of a topic. **W.5.7**

Recall relevant information from experiences or gather relevant information from print and digital sources; summarize or paraphrase information in notes and finished work, and provide a list of sources. **W.5.8**

Writing
Write opinion pieces on topics or texts, supporting a point of view with reasons and information. **ELA.W.5.1**

Speaking and Listening
Engage effectively in a range of collaborative discussions (one-on-one, in groups, and teacher-led) with diverse partners on *grade 5 topics and texts*, building on others' ideas and expressing their own clearly. **SL.5.1**

Classroom Resources

Search for additional resources using the following key words.

Manifest Destiny

Mormon Trail

Oregon Fever

Oregon Trail

James K. Polk

Prairie Schooner

Second Great Awakening

What Did Settlers Experience in Their Movement West?

Inquiry Journal
pp. 272–273

Go *Digital!*

Explore the lesson content with online whole-class presentation tools.

- **Video:** Westward Expansion
- **iMap:** Trails to the West, 1840–1860

Bellringer

Prompt students to retrieve information from the previous lessons. Say: *What was the Missouri Compromise, and why would it be important to future conflict in the United States?* (The Missouri Compromise was an agreement that kept the balance between slave and free states. In the future, any state north of Missouri's southern border that joined the Union would be admitted as a free state. This conflict between slave and free states would only get worse.)

Lesson Outcomes

What Am I Learning? Have students read the Lesson Outcomes.

Why Am I Learning It? Check that students understand that they will be learning about how and why people decided to move from the East Coast to the West. Encourage them to consider why some people feel the desire to start a new life in a new place with new opportunities.

How Will I Know That I Learned It? Ask students the following questions.

- What will you learn about? (settlers' experiences as they moved west)
- What is the purpose of the task? (to write a travel guide about these experiences)
- How will you support your description? (with text evidence)

Talk About It

Provide some scaffolding for students to use as they discuss the picture. Provide background information as needed.

- *The picture shows _____.*
- *Some clues that tell me this are _____.*
- *Life would have been _____ on the trail.*

Collaborative Conversations

Look at the Details As students engage in partner, small group, and whole-class discussions, encourage them to

- Think about what is happening in the picture. Where are they going?
- Ask and answer questions about the object shown in the picture.
- Draw or modify conclusions that are based on the discussion.

Lesson 1

What Did Settlers Experience in Their Movement Westward?

A covered wagon at Scotts Bluff National Monument

Lesson Outcomes

What Am I Learning?
In this lesson, you're going to use your investigative skills to learn about what U.S. settlers experienced as they moved farther west.

Why Am I Learning It?
Reading and talking about what the settlers experienced will help you understand why the move west was important.

How Will I Know That I Learned It?
You will be able to ask and answer questions about the settlers' experiences as they moved west, and you will write a travel guide.

Talk About It

Look at the Details What would it have been like to live in a wagon and travel a trail westward for six months?

HSS.5.8.2, HSS.5.8.4, HSS.5.8.6, HAS.CS.4

Inquiry Journal, pp. 272–273

 ENGLISH LEARNERS SCAFFOLD

ELD.PI.5.6 Reading closely literary and informational texts and viewing multimedia to determine how meaning is conveyed explicitly and implicitly through language

Emerging	Expanding	Bridging
Identify Details Encourage students to describe what they see in the picture. Work with them to explain what it shows.	**Analyze Details** Have students use descriptive words to tell about the picture. They may analyze the placement of objects or the setting. Guide them to use these details to discuss the painting with a partner.	**Analyze Words and Language** Encourage students to describe what they see and predict what they will learn in the lesson.

See the **Language Learner Teaching Guide** for more language support strategies.

Monitor and Differentiate

REACHING ALL LEARNERS

Approaching Level

Encourage students to think about what they will learn in the lesson. Guide them to access any prior knowledge they may have about how people moved west.

On Level

Have students discuss the painting, stating opinions about what it would be like to live in a wagon for an extended period of time.

Beyond Level

Guide students to conduct further research into the methods of transportation from the East Coast to the West. Guide students to share their findings with the whole class.

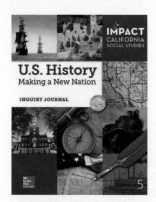

Inquiry Journal
pp. 274–275

Crofutt, George A. *Crofutt's New Overland Tourist and Pacific Coast Guide....* Chicago: The Overland Publishing Company, 1878.

HSS STANDARDS

Name the states and territories that existed in 1850 and identify their locations and major geographical features (e.g., mountain ranges, principal rivers, dominant plant regions). **HSS.5.8.2**

Discuss the experiences of settlers on the overland trails to the West (e.g., location of the routes; purpose of the journeys; the influence of the terrain, rivers, vegetation, and climate; life in the territories at the end of these trails). **HSS.5.8.4**

Students explain how the present is connected to the past, identifying both similarities and differences between the two, and how some things change over time and some things stay the same. **HAS.CS.3**

Go Digital!

Model how to inspect and find evidence with online whole-class presentation tools.

Build Background

John Gast's *American Progress* The painting that illustrates Manifest Destiny was originally a print published in *Crofutt's Western World*, a magazine run by George Crofutt. Crofutt asked Gast to create the picture. Crofutt described what the woman holds: *"In her right hand she carries a book . . . the emblem of education and . . . national enlightenment, while with the left hand she unfolds and stretches the slender wires of the telegraph, that are to flash intelligence throughout the land."*

1 Inspect

View Ask students to examine the image and read the text that explains Manifest Destiny to focus on understanding the overall meaning.

- Who do you see in the painting? (There are American Indians, settlers, farmers, and a large female figure in the center.)

- What does each part of the picture show? (The right side shows the East Coast, with a train, telegraph wires, and a busy harbor. The left side shows American Indians, mountains, and buffalo.)

- What does the text say that helps you understand what the painting is about? (It explains that the painting is meant to show major advances and the progress of civilization from the East to the West.)

Collaborate Have partners take turns discussing why they think the artist made the picture. (Students may say that he is showing the positive effects of westward migration.)

2 Find Evidence

Look Again Have students look again at the image.

Analyze the Picture Explain to students that analyzing an image involves looking closely at details, identifying choices that the artist made, and analyzing the overall structure and style of the image.

- Ask: What is the woman in the center holding? (She is holding a book, which the text says symbolizes knowledge.)

- Where is she coming from and where is she going? (She seems to be coming from the East and heading West.)

- Do you think this is a real woman? Why or why not? (Students should identify that because she is shown as much larger than the other figures, is in a different style of dress, and seems to be floating, she is probably not real.) What does she represent? (She symbolizes the progress of civilization.)

3 Make Connections COLLABORATE

Talk Guide students to decide whether they would have been inspired to move west as a result of the picture. (Students may say that it is inspiring, but it doesn't show the hardships settlers faced on their journey, only the progress they made.)

Connect to Now Have partners discuss what might make people move to a new location today and how that compares to what led people to move west in the 1800s.

Analyze the Source

What Is Manifest Destiny?

1 Inspect

View Look at the image. What is the picture showing?

- **Think** about the figures shown in the painting.
- **Examine** clues that help you understand what event each part of the picture shows.
- **Discuss** why you think the artist painted it.

My Notes

_____
_____
_____
_____
_____
_____
_____
_____
_____
_____
_____
_____
_____
_____
_____
_____
_____
_____

In the 1800s, people who struggled on the East Coast found the prospect of settling the open territory of the West appealing. They wanted to make the trip despite the obstacles they would face on the long, slow journey. This drive to settle the West was known as Manifest Destiny. It eventually led to the United States stretching from the Atlantic to the Pacific.

Many works of art explore the openness and natural beauty of the West. John Gast's painting *American Progress* shows major advances such as the telegraph, the stagecoach, and the steam engine. This progress is represented by the figure of a woman moving gracefully from the East to the West. The book she is carrying shows that she is bringing along a civilization's knowledge.

Opponents of Manifest Destiny pointed out that it ignored the rights of native peoples living in the West and disrespected their ways of life. Many settlers believed that it was God's will for the nation to expand westward. These settlers believed that their way of life and their religion ought to dominate the continent from East to West.

John Gast was a Prussian-born artist who lived in Brooklyn. He was known for allegorical, or symbolic, painting. George Crofutt, the publisher of the era's most popular travel guides, commissioned the painting *American Progress* in 1872 from Gast. This was more than twenty years after the concept of Manifest Destiny was born. Crofutt published the reproductions of the painting in his Western travel guides, where thousands saw the image.

American Progress by John Gast

[©McGraw-Hill Education, (b)Library of Congress Prints and Photographs Division (LC-DIG-ppmsca-09855]]

2 Find Evidence

Look Again Examine the woman at the center of the picture. What is she holding? From which direction does she seem to be coming? Where is she going? Is this a portrait of a real woman? What might she represent?

Examine Read the statement "John Gast's painting *American Progress* shows major advances such as the telegraph, the stagecoach, and the steam engine." Why do you think Gast included these in the painting?

3 Make Connections

Talk Do you think those who saw this painting reprinted in travel guides at the time of westward expansion would have been inspired to travel west? Do you think American Indians would have been offended by this painting? Why or why not?

Inquiry Journal, pp. 274–275

EL ENGLISH LEARNERS SCAFFOLD

ELD.PI.5.6 Reading closely literary and informational texts and viewing multimedia to determine how meaning is conveyed explicitly and implicitly through language

Emerging

Discuss Details Work with students to name the figures, animals, and other details they see in the painting. Encourage them to use these names as they discuss the concept of Manifest Destiny.

Expanding and Bridging

Use Details Guide students to identify the animals, people, activities, and places they see in the painting. Then guide them to use those details to discuss whether the painting accurately represents what it might have been like to move west.

See the **Language Learner Teaching Guide** for more language support strategies.

Monitor and Differentiate

REACHING ALL LEARNERS

Approaching Level

Have students reread the text to identify why people decided to move west. Encourage them to discuss whether this signaled progress, decline, or both—and for what groups.

Beyond Level

Encourage students to conduct additional research into how settling the West changed over the course of the 1800s. Guide them to identify how technological advances made the journey easier, then have them share their findings with the class.

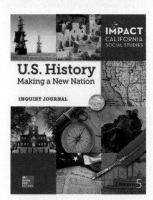

Inquiry Journal
pp. 276–277

 STANDARDS

Discuss the experiences of settlers on the overland trails to the West (e.g., location of the routes; purpose of the journeys; the influence of the terrain, rivers, vegetation, and climate; life in the territories at the end of these trails). **HSS.5.8.4**

Students pose relevant questions about events they encounter in historical documents, eyewitness accounts, oral histories, letters, diaries, artifacts, photographs, maps, artworks, and architecture. **HAS.HR.2**

Quote accurately from a text when explaining what the text says explicitly and when drawing inferences from the text. **CCSS.ELA.RI.5.1**

Go *Digital!*

- Model how to explore and investigate with online whole-class tools.

- Students can access the online graphic organizer to use the inquiry tools as they read.

Explore Asking and Answering Questions

Explain Tell students that by asking and answering questions, they learn more about what they are reading. Explain that they will ask and answer questions about important details, such as people, places, events, and conflicts.

Read Have students read aloud the step-by-step instructions about how to ask and answer questions. Tell students that they should ask themselves questions such as *who, what, where, when, why,* and *how.* They should also look for key details that signal important information.

Guide Practice Present a brief model of asking and answering questions that helps students understand the process. *Why did John Gast name his painting* American Progress? *I think he did it because the whole painting shows how the light of knowledge is moving from the populated and developed East Coast to the West Coast. The painting shows steamboats, a train, and the telegraph in the East, and the movement of people to the West shows how the country is physically growing too.*

Investigate!

Have students read pages 340–345 in the Research Companion. Tell them the information that will help them answer the lesson question *What Did Settlers Experience in Their Movement Westward?*

Take Notes Tell students that they will take notes as they read each section. Explain that taking notes will help them understand settlers' experiences. Remind students that they should look for key details and important information in the text.

Inspect Guide students to read the text in each section to determine what it says. Encourage them to work to find information about what settlers experienced in their move westward.

Find Evidence Encourage students to reread the text to develop a deeper understanding. Remind students that they should think about how the facts and details will help them answer the lesson question.

Collaborative Conversations

Text-Based Discussion Remind students that discussing the text with others can help them

- Develop new perspectives about historical events
- Better understand what they read
- Appreciate the points of view of other people

Inquiry Tools

Explore Asking and Answering Questions

You can better understand what you read if you ask and answer questions about it. Support your answers with evidence from the text.

1. **Read the text all the way through.**
   This will help you understand what the text is about.

2. **Reread the text, looking for key details.**
   Locate the important information, facts, or evidence in the text.

3. **Ask yourself about the important people and events in the text.**
   This will help you identify ideas or information you may have missed.

4. **Answer your questions using evidence from the text.**
   This will help you clarify your understanding of what you've read.

COLLABORATE Based on the source you just studied, work with your class to complete the chart below.

Question	Answer	Text Evidence
Why was Gast's painting titled *American Progress*?	The painting depicts the nation's progress, both technologically and geographically.	The railroad and telegraph lines show technological progress; the woman and settlers headed westward show geographic growth.

Investigate!

Read pages 340–345 in your Research Companion. Use your investigative skills to look for text evidence that tells you about important events and people.

Possible responses:

Question	Answer	Text Evidence
What was important about "Oregon Fever"?	It was the strong desire of settlers to get land in the Oregon Territory.	"It was said that these people had 'Oregon Fever' because of their desire to start new lives in the far West."
What event created the border between the United States and Canada in the West?	The 49th parallel became the U.S.-Canada border as a result of the signing of the Oregon Treaty.	The two nations agreed to extend the United States-Canada border at the 49th parallel of latitude all the way to the Pacific Ocean."
What was life like on the trail west?	Life was difficult and often dangerous.	"The settlers had to face dangerous thunderstorms, floods, snow and ice, rocky terrain, and deep rivers."

McGraw-Hill Education

Inquiry Journal, pp. 276–277

(EL) ENGLISH LEARNERS SCAFFOLD

ELD.PI.5.1 Exchanging information and ideas with others through oral collaborative discussions on a range of social and academic topics

Emerging

Choose Details Encourage students to first scan the text to find proper nouns, such as the names of people, places, and important events. They should also look for dates. Guide them to reread, looking specifically for information about these details. This will help them figure out what types of questions they should ask and answer.

Expanding and Bridging

Discuss Main Ideas Have students read each section in the text, looking for the main idea. It may help them to ask what the most important thing was that they learned from the section. Then guide them to form questions about that main idea for use in their graphic organizer.

See the **Language Learner Teaching Guide** for more language support strategies.

Monitor and Differentiate

REACHING ALL LEARNERS

Special Needs

Encourage students to annotate the text or otherwise take notes to identify the most important details to ask and answer questions about. Students may choose to dictate their ideas aloud to you or a partner, or they may choose to make a creative display of their notes for use in their writing later on.

Approaching Level

Encourage students to read each section looking for important details. Remind them to look for context clues that help them understand unfamiliar words and phrases. Explain that a context clue is usually a synonym, an antonym, or an example that helps to define a word.

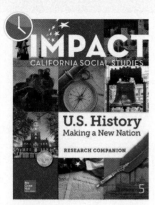

Research Companion
pp. 340–341

 STANDARDS

Discuss the experiences of settlers on the overland trails to the West (e.g., location of the routes; purpose of the journeys; the influence of the terrain, rivers, vegetation, and climate; life in the territories at the end of these trails). **HSS.5.8.4**

Relate how and when California, Texas, Oregon, and other western lands became part of the United States, including the significance of the Texas War for Independence and the Mexican-American War. **HSS.5.8.6**

Students place key events and people of the historical era they are studying in a chronological sequence and within a spatial context; they interpret time lines. **HAS.CS.1**

***

Go Digital!

Investigate the lesson content with online whole-class presentation tools.

• **Video:** Westward Expansion

• **iMap:** Trails to the West, 1840–1860

Background Information

European Fur Traders Because of the popularity in the 1880s of hats made with felted beaver fur, the demand for beaver pelts was high. Experienced trappers—mostly French, but some American and Spanish—could make good money as fur traders in the western and northern areas of the United States. As the demand for beaver fur hats dropped, the traders turned to other lines of work, often serving as guides for pioneers who wanted to settle in the West.

| TIMELINE | Invite students to look at the timeline on the top of p. 341.

Analyze How much time passed between when mountain men first traveled to the Rockies and when wagon trains first followed the Oregon Trail? (about 20 years) **HAS.CS.1**

Analyze the Source

Inspect Have students read pp. 340–341.

Find Evidence Use the questions below to check comprehension. Remind students to support their answers with text evidence.

Identify Who were the first European settlers to travel in the West? (fur traders, called "mountain men") **DOK 1**

Explain Who were the first settlers to travel in groups of wagons? (mostly families who traveled with experienced guides) **DOK 2**

Cite Evidence Where were these people headed? ("the rich farmland of Oregon Territory") **DOK 2**

Analyze Signal Words What do the dates in the second paragraph tell you about the events? (In 1818, there was a problem. In 1840, it got worse. The problem wasn't solved until the Oregon Treaty, which was an important effect.) **DOK 3**

Analyze the Photograph Explain to students that this photo is from the modern day, but it shows something from long ago.

Analyze Setting Where is the photograph set? What is it trying to recreate? (The photo shows a wagon train. It is meant to recreate a wagon train moving west in the 1800s.) **DOK 2**

Make Connections

Infer How was "Oregon Fever" related to the need for the Oregon Treaty? (Students should identify that the drive to move west got more and more people interested in staking claims in Oregon. That led to land disputes and the need to determine which nation owned the land.) **DOK 3**

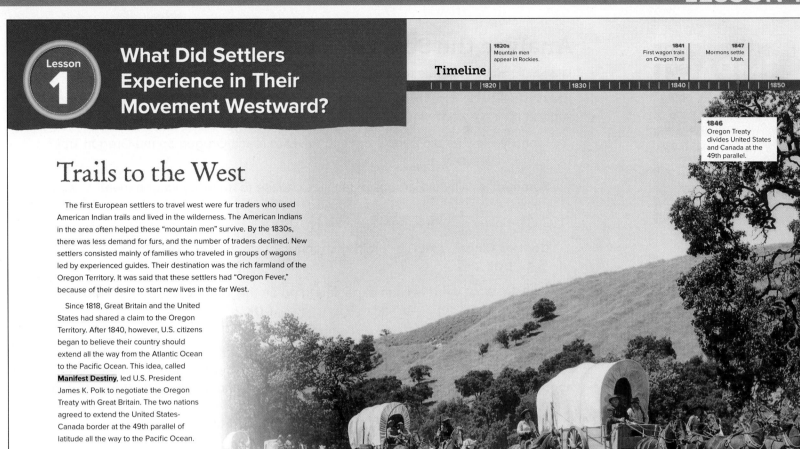

What Did Settlers Experience in Their Movement Westward?

Timeline

1820s Mountain men appear in Rockies.

1841 First wagon train on Oregon Trail

1847 Mormons settle Utah.

| | | | | | 1820 | | | | | | | | 1830 | | | | | | | 1840 | | | | | | | 1850

1846 Oregon Treaty divides United States and Canada at the 49th parallel.

Trails to the West

The first European settlers to travel west were fur traders who used American Indian trails and lived in the wilderness. The American Indians in the area often helped these "mountain men" survive. By the 1830s, there was less demand for furs, and the number of traders declined. New settlers consisted mainly of families who traveled in groups of wagons led by experienced guides. Their destination was the rich farmland of the Oregon Territory. It was said that these settlers had "Oregon Fever," because of their desire to start new lives in the far West.

Since 1818, Great Britain and the United States had shared a claim to the Oregon Territory. After 1840, however, U.S. citizens began to believe their country should extend all the way from the Atlantic Ocean to the Pacific Ocean. This idea, called **Manifest Destiny**, led U.S. President James K. Polk to negotiate the Oregon Treaty with Great Britain. The two nations agreed to extend the United States-Canada border at the 49th parallel of latitude all the way to the Pacific Ocean.

Settlers on a trail, traveling westward

HSS.5.8.2, HSS.5.8.4, HAS.CS.4, HAS.HR.2

340 Lesson 1 What Did Settlers Experience in Their Movement Westward?

Lesson 1 341

Research Companion, pp. 340–341

 ENGLISH LEARNERS SCAFFOLD

ELD.PI.5.8 Analyzing how writers and speakers use vocabulary and other language resources for specific purposes (to explain, persuade, entertain, etc.) depending on modality, text type, purpose, audience, topic, and content area

Emerging

Understand Nuance Work with students to identify the meaning of the word "Fever" in the context of this lesson. Guide students to recognize the difference in connotation between *fever* and *excitement*. Encourage them to find other examples of words with strong meanings in the lesson.

Expanding and Bridging

Use Nuance Have students work together to analyze phrases that paint vivid pictures for the audience. For example, point out the phrase "Oregon Fever." Guide them to acknowledge that someone with a fever is usually sick. Ask students to identify how the word has been modified in this context.

See the **Language Learner Teaching Guide** for more language support strategies.

Monitor and Differentiate

REACHING ALL LEARNERS

Approaching Level

Have students work together to understand the concept of Manifest Destiny. Encourage them to use clues from the images they have analyzed and what they know about people's desire to move west.

Beyond Level

Have students conduct additional research into the Oregon Treaty. Guide students to learn more about the need for it, the participants who negotiated it, and its results for Americans. Invite students to share their ideas with the entire class.

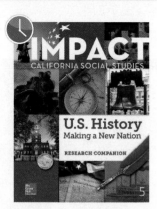

Research Companion
pp. 342–343

 STANDARDS

Name the states and territories that existed in 1850 and identify their locations and major geographical features (e.g., mountain ranges, principal rivers, dominant plant regions). **HSS.5.8.2**

Discuss the experiences of settlers on the overland trails to the West (e.g., location of the routes; purpose of the journeys; the influence of the terrain, rivers, vegetation, and climate; life in the territories at the end of these trails). **HSS.5.8.4**

Students pose relevant questions about events they encounter in historical documents, eyewitness accounts, oral histories, letters, diaries, artifacts, photographs, maps, artworks, and architecture. **HAS.HR.2**

Go Digital!

Investigate the lesson content with online whole-class presentation tools.

Analyze the Source

Inspect Have students read Life on the Wagon Train on pp. 342–343.

Find Evidence Use the questions below to check comprehension. Remind students to support their answers with text evidence.

Identify How far did people have to travel to reach Oregon on the Oregon Trail? (2,000 miles) **DOK 1**

Summarize Why did groups of families choose to travel by wagon train? (In a wagon train, many people could help to protect each other from raids by American Indians and help each other in times of trouble.) **DOK 2**

Context Clues What is a "prairie schooner"? (a type of wagon pulled by a team of oxen) **DOK 2**

Explain What were women expected to do on the journey west? (cook, clean, set up camp, manage supplies, and teach children) **DOK 2**

Map Skills

Project a large version of the map on p. 342. Guide students to identify the trails they read about. Encourage students to identify a starting point and to follow the trail until it forks. Then have them follow the forks until they fork off too. Have them discuss why people might have made the decision to break away from the existing route.

- What do the green lines show? (trails)

- What does a dotted line represent? (modern-day boundary of state or nation)

- Where did the trails begin? (Independence, Missouri, and Nauvoo, Illinois)

- Where did the California Trail end? (Sacramento)

Make Connections

Connect to Now What kind of planning did a trip across the country require in the early 1800s? How is that different to planning for a trip across the country today? (Students should note that people had to plan for a very long journey by bringing many supplies. Today, the journey can take as little as half a day by plane, so people do not need to plan to spend months traveling now unless they want to.) **DOK 3**

PRODUCTIVE
Stop and Check

Talk Encourage students to discuss why people decided to make the dangerous and difficult trek west. (Responses may include that people wanted a new life.)

Find Details Explain to students that after they read and take notes, they should think about how the information can help them answer the Essential Question.

WHAT DO YOU THINK?

Encourage students to use text evidence from the whole lesson as they respond to the prompt.

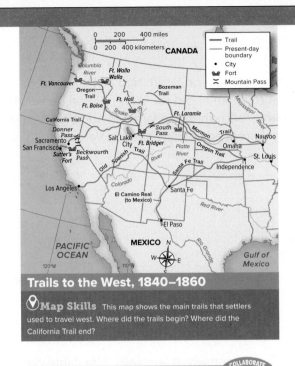

Trails to the West, 1840–1860

Map Skills This map shows the main trails that settlers used to travel west. Where did the trails begin? Where did the California Trail end?

✓ **Stop and Check** COLLABORATE

Talk Why did "Oregon Fever" cause settlers to move west?

Find Details As you read, add new information to the graphic organizer on page 277 in your Inquiry Journal.

What Do You Think? Would you have been willing to leave your livelihood in the East to stake your claim to land in the West? Why?

342 Lesson 1 What Did Settlers Experience in Their Movement Westward?

Life on the Wagon Train

Life on the trails was challenging but exciting. On the Oregon Trail, settlers had to travel for six months across about 2,000 miles of wilderness. Many families traveled in groups of wagons called wagon trains. These families were able to provide protection for one another.

Most wagon trains consisted of wagons called "prairie schooners" because their white covers looked like a ship's sails from a distance. This type of wagon was usually pulled by a team of **oxen**. The wagon had to carry everything the family would need for the journey and for its new home. The supplies included tools, weapons, food, seeds for planting, books, cooking utensils, spare wagon parts, medicine, and clothes.

Each member of the family had jobs to do on the journey. Men drove the wagon and were responsible for repairing it. They also hunted for food and protected their families. Women cooked and cleaned, set up camp, and were responsible for managing their families' supplies. They also cared for and taught their children. Children helped out where they could, and collected "buffalo chips," manure that was used as fuel for campfires.

A wagon train traveling west with the Rocky Mountains in the background

Lesson 1 343

Research Companion, pp. 342–343

ELD.PI.5.6 **ENGLISH LEARNERS SCAFFOLD**

ELD.PI.5.6 Reading closely literary and informational texts and viewing multimedia to determine how meaning is conveyed explicitly and implicitly through language

Emerging

Read a Key Work with students as they read the map key. Point out an example of each type of symbol on the map. Encourage students to find other examples of the same type of symbol.

Expanding/Bridging

Read a Map Have students consider how the map helps them to understand what it meant to travel west. Encourage students to point out where you live, using this map or a map of the entire country. Point to the location of a relatively nearby landmark with which students are familiar. Guide students to conceptualize the magnitude of the journey. Then have them use the map scale to determine approximately how long each trail was.

See the **Language Learner Teaching Guide** for more language support strategies.

Monitor and Differentiate

REACHING ALL LEARNERS

Approaching Level

Work with students to understand life on the wagon train. Encourage them to repeat words after you, such as *schooner, utensils, buffalo chips,* and so on. Then have students use these words as they discuss what people did on the trail as they journeyed west.

Beyond Level

Encourage students to conduct additional research into gender roles on the trails. Students may choose to find primary sources that tell about someone's experiences, or they may choose to find images or maps that show more details about the landmarks or other aspects of the journey. Encourage students to share their findings with the class.

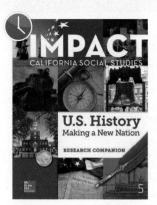

Research Companion
pp. 344–345

 STANDARDS

Name the states and territories that existed in 1850 and identify their locations and major geographical features (e.g., mountain ranges, principal rivers, dominant plant regions). **HSS.5.8.2**

Discuss the experiences of settlers on the overland trails to the West (e.g., location of the routes; purpose of the journeys; the influence of the terrain, rivers, vegetation, and climate; life in the territories at the end of these trails). **HSS.5.8.4**

Students correctly apply terms related to time, including *past, present, future, decade, century,* and *generation.* **HAS.CS.2**

Go Digital!

Investigate the lesson content with online whole-class presentation tools.

Background

Mormonism Mormonism began in 1823 when Joseph Smith had a vision of an angel. He later found several tablets that told him about the new religion he was to found. He soon gathered followers in New York, where he lived. In addition to new views about Christianity, Mormonism also stressed specific secular values, such as abstinence from alcohol or tobacco.

Analyze the Source

Inspect Have students read pp. 344–345.

Find Evidence Use the questions below to check comprehension. Remind students to support their answers with text evidence.

Analyze the Primary Source

Analyze Language What does Sarah Byrd mean when she says "We came out from I-O-WAY"? (She means that she lived in Iowa.) **DOK 2**

Analyze Cause and Effect Why did people camp inside a circle of wagons at night? (So they could have some protection and so the guards could watch over the livestock.) **DOK 3**

Summarize What dangers did people face on the trail? (bad weather, rough terrain, disease, and death) **DOK 3**

Identify How many people traveled west between 1841 and 1861? (approximately 300,000 people) **DOK 1**

Identify Why did the Mormons leave New York? (They wanted to escape religious persecution.) **DOK 1**

Infer Why did the Mormons need to learn how to build irrigation where they settled in Utah? (Because they settled in a very dry area, and they had to figure out how to feed their 2,000 people.) **DOK 3**

Context Clues What is a "camp meeting"? (A camp meeting is an informal kind of religious service that was part of the Second Great Awakening.) **DOK 2**

Make Connections

Compare and Contrast How were Mormons' reasons for leaving their original homes similar to and different from other pioneers' reasons? (They were searching for religious freedom, not only a new start or economic opportunities.) **DOK 2**

☑ Stop and Check

Talk Encourage students to consider why people traveled west and what they might have lost if the trip went badly. (Responses will vary.)

Talk Guide students to make connections to other instances of religious persecution they have read about in this text. (Responses will vary.)

PRIMARY SOURCE

In Their Words... Sarah Byrd

We came from I-O-WAY in 1848. That's a long time ago, ain't it? Joe Watt was captain of our train. Bein' so little, I don't remember how many was in the train, but I've heard 'em say it was a big one. Every night when we camped the wagons was pulled in a circle an' hooked together with chains an' oxen yokes. The folks camped inside that circle, an' close along-side was the [livestock], an' a guard was set up for the night.

Yes, it must have ban an awful job cookin'. I was too little to do anything. 'Course they had to cook on the open fire, an' on the plains, most o' the time there was nothin' to burn but buffalo chips. I guess they got use to it, but I wouldn't like to.

—from an interview of Byrd recalling her journey to Oregon, February 28, 1939

Along the trail, conditions could be difficult. The settlers had to face dangerous thunderstorms, floods, snow and ice, rocky terrain, and deep rivers. Disease was also a danger, as settlers lacked access to good medical care. Each obstacle put the people and their precious supplies in danger.

The dangers didn't stop people from using the trails, however. By 1861, about 300,000 people had traveled the Oregon Trail to the West.

> **✓ Stop and Check** COLLABORATE
>
> **Talk** What were the benefits and drawbacks of moving west?

An early engraving of Salt Lake City, Utah

Mormons Head West

While some people wanted to journey west to find land and a fresh start in life, others traveled to find religious freedom. The members of the Church of Jesus Christ of Latter-Day Saints, also known as Mormons, left New York when their beliefs caused difficulties with their neighbors. They moved to Illinois but again experienced **hostility** from neighbors. After their leader, Joseph Smith, was shot and killed by a mob in 1844, they decided to move farther west.

In 1845, led by Brigham Young, the Mormons set out on a route near the Oregon Trail. They turned southwest at Fort Bridger, in what is now Wyoming. They decided to settle in present-day Utah at the Great Salt Lake. Soon there were about 2,000 people in the settlement, which they named Salt Lake City. While the area around the lake was dry and difficult to farm, the Mormon settlers were able to use irrigation to grow crops.

Other religious movements also thrived on the trails to the West. One popular style of worship, called "camp meetings," was the result of the Second Great Awakening. At these meetings, pioneers attended services in tents.

> **✓ Stop and Check** COLLABORATE
>
> **Talk** Why did the Mormons leave New York and Illinois? Is their relocation similar to any earlier migrations of people you have read about?

344 Lesson 1 What Did Settlers Experience in Their Movement Westward?

Lesson 1 345

Research Companion, pp. 344–345

(EL) ENGLISH LEARNERS SCAFFOLD

ELD.PI.5.6 Reading closely literary and informational texts and viewing multimedia to determine how meaning is conveyed explicitly and implicitly through language

Emerging

Listen to Dialect Read aloud the primary source while students listen. Point out that the primary source is written exactly as the speaker said it, and it is not written in Standard English. Point out potentially confusing words and phrases, such as *I-O-WAY*, *ain't*, and *an'*.

Expanding and Bridging

Analyze the Primary Source Encourage students to read the primary source aloud. Provide support for dialect as needed. Then have students summarize what Sarah Byrd remembers about her experiences as a little girl on the trail. Prompt students to ask and answer questions about her memories.

See the **Language Learner Teaching Guide** for more language support strategies.

Monitor and Differentiate

REACHING ALL LEARNERS

Special Needs

Have students take turns reading aloud the excerpt from the interview with Sarah Byrd. Guide students to listen carefully to get the gist of the primary source. Then have students discuss the text in small groups.

Approaching Level

Guide students to make notes about the dangers and difficulties settlers might encounter on the trail. Provide time for them to look up any unfamiliar words. Ask students to discuss whether they would want to make the journey given these obstacles.

Report Your Findings

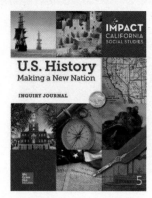

Inquiry Journal
pp. 278–279

 STANDARDS

Discuss the experiences of settlers on the overland trails to the West (e.g., location of the routes; purpose of the journeys; the influence of the terrain, rivers, vegetation, and climate; life in the territories at the end of these trails). **HSS.5.8.4**

Students judge the significance of the relative location of a place (e.g., proximity to a harbor, on trade routes) and analyze how relative advantages or disadvantages can change over time. **HAS.CS.5**

Write opinion pieces on topics or texts, supporting a point of view with reasons and information. **CCSS.ELA.W.5.1**

Go Digital!

- Students can go online to report their findings. Assess their responses online.

- Students can access the online graphic organizer to capture ideas from their investigation.

Think About It

Students will review their research and determine what it was like to move west in the early 1800s.

- Remind students to review the questions they asked and answered in their graphic organizer. Direct students back to pages 340–345 of their Research Companion if they need more information.

Write About It

Write a Travel Guide Have students read the prompt. Explain that they will write a travel guide that attempts to persuade people to travel west to Oregon Territory. Students will try to make their travel guide convincing by including details from the text.

Remind students to include the following elements in their response.

- Include clear, persuasive statements about why people should move to the Oregon Territory.

- Use details from the text to support their persuasive statements.

- Use language that attempts to grab the reader's attention.

Use the rubric on p. T720 to evaluate students' work.

Talk About It

Defend Your Claims Assist students in finding a partner who chose a different trail. Guide them to identify which travel guide seems more persuasive, and why. They should also analyze how the travel guides deal with (or omit) the hardships settlers will face on the journey.

- Explain that they should support their opinions with evidence from the text and their research.

- They should take turns speaking and avoid interrupting each other.

- Remind students to be respectful of their classmates' opinions and work.

Connect to the Essential Question

Make Connections Read the prompt aloud to students. Ask them the following guiding questions:

- What drove people to settle in the West? (Students may say that the urge to start a new life was strong for many who struggled on the East Coast.)

- What were the challenges and dangers they faced? (Students should identify dangers such as bad weather, American Indian attacks, and disease.)

- Why do you think they decided to make the journey despite those dangers? (Responses will vary.)

Remind students to use the space provided in their journal to jot down notes.

Report Your Findings

Think About It

Review your research. What was it like to move west in the early 1800s?

Write About It

Write a Travel Guide

Choose a trail and write a short travel guide for people living in the East who were considering moving west. Make your travel guide convincing by including details about landmarks, the comforts and companionship of trail life, and the opportunities available on arrival in the Oregon Territory.

Responses will vary, but students should write a trail travel guide that is persuasive and effective.

Talk About It COLLABORATE

Defend Your Claims

Work with a partner who chose a different trail. Which travel guide would you be more likely to believe? What are some of the hardships that both travel guides do not mention?

Connect to the EQ

Make Connections

What drove people to settle in the West despite challenges and dangers?

Sample response: People were eager to make a fresh start in a new and less developed part of the country. They wanted good farmland and freedom to follow their own beliefs.

EQ Inquiry Project Notes

278 Lesson 1 What Did Settlers Experience in Their Movement Westward?

Lesson 1 **279**

Inquiry Journal, pp. 278–279

(EL) ENGLISH LEARNERS SCAFFOLD

ELD.PI.5.4 Adapting language choices to various contexts (based on task, purpose, audience, and text type)

Emerging	Expanding	Bridging
Understand Tone Explain that their travel guide should have a persuasive tone. Remind students that they are trying to sell an idea, and their language should reflect that.	**Use Text Evidence** Explain that when trying to write a travel guide, they should include facts and details to support their claims and persuade their readers. Have students reread the text and use their notes to find details that strengthen the argument they want to make.	**Achieve a Specific Tone** Have students consider what they want their travel guide to sound like. Explain that a persuasive travel guide attempts to sell people on an idea. It is also selective in its choice of evidence, leaving out details about the more dangerous obstacles on the journey.

See the **Language Learner Teaching Guide** for more language support strategies.

Monitor and Differentiate

REACHING ALL LEARNERS

Approaching Level

Work with students as they write their travel guides. Encourage them to use language they have learned in the lesson if it is appropriate. Remind them to consider the tone and choice of details from the text that they use in their guides.

Beyond Level

Encourage students to work together to create a larger brochure about traveling west on all of the trails. Guide them to create a cohesive style for the brochure or booklet, to collaborate on the details they want to include, to find appropriate imagery to illustrate the booklet, and to agree on the language they want to use to describe the journey and destinations.

Know what your students know!

Lesson Task
Report Your Findings

Use the rubric to evaluate students' responses.

Write a Travel Guide Students choose a trail and write a short travel guide for people living in the East who were considering moving west. They include details about landmarks, the comforts and companionship of trail life, and the opportunities available on arrival in the Oregon Territory.

Defend Your Claims Students work with a partner who chose a different trail. They discuss which travel guide is more convincing.

Lesson Task Evaluation Rubric

	4	3	2	1
Historical Understanding	Strong understanding of what life was like moving west during the early 1800s	Adequate understanding of what life was like moving west during the early 1800s	Uneven understanding of what life was like moving west during the early 1800s	No understanding of what life was like moving west during the early 1800s
Write a Travel Guide	Clearly provides an opinion and effective support	Adequately provides an opinion and support	Somewhat clear or unclear opinion or support	No relevant opinion stated or student does not show understanding of the task
Support with Evidence	Opinion supported by information from the text	Opinion mostly supported by information from the text	Opinion not always supported by information from the text	Opinion missing or irrelevant
Defend Your Claims	Carefully considers what travel guides miss Provides relevant and creative points	Considers some issues that travel guides miss Provides relevant points	Considers briefly what travel guides miss Provides few relevant points	Does not consider what travel guides miss Provides no relevant points

Lesson Assessment

Go *Digital!*

- Have students complete the Chapter 8 Lesson 1 Assessment online to monitor their understanding of the lesson content.

California Smarter Balanced Assessment Connections!

Standards Covered	Lesson Task	Lesson Assessment	Alignment with California Smarter Balanced Assessment
History Social Science Content 5.8.2; 5.8.4; 5.8.6	✔	✔	Claim 1 Targets 8, 9, 11
History Social Science Analysis Skills Chronological and Spatial Thinking 5.1; 5.2; 5.3; 5.5 Research, Evidence, and Point of View 5.2 Historical Interpretation 5.3	✔	✔	Claim 1 Targets 8, 9, 11
Writing W.5.1	✔	✔	Claim 2 Target 6a
Research and Inquiry W.5.7	✔	✔	Claim 4 Targets 1, 2
Reading RI.5.7	✔	✔	Claim 1 Targets 8, 11, 13
Speaking and Listening SL.5.1	✔		Claim 3 Target 3 Claim 4 Target 1

How Did Westward Expansion Impact American Indians?

Background Information

In this lesson, students learn about how settlers and the American government treated the American Indians during the time of Westward Expansion. They will learn about the hardships American Indians faced as they were persecuted and relocated from their homes to designated territories in the West.

Community Connections

To enrich what students have learned about how Westward Expansion affected American Indians, plan a guest visit from an expert in American history or American Indian history.

LESSON STANDARDS

- ✓ Discuss the role of broken treaties and massacres and the factors that led to the Indians' defeat, including the resistance of Indian nations to encroachments and assimilation (e.g., the story of the Trail of Tears). **HSS.5.3.4**

- ✓ Describe the internecine Indian conflicts, including the competing claims for control of lands (e.g., actions of the Iroquois, Huron, Lakota [Sioux]). **HSS.5.3.5**

- ✓ Explain the influence and achievements of significant leaders of the time (e.g., John Marshall, Andrew Jackson, Chief Tecumseh, Chief Logan, Chief John Ross, Sequoyah). **HSS.5.3.6**

- ✓ Students place key events and people of the historical era they are studying in a chronological sequence and within a spatial context; they interpret time lines. **HAS.CS.1**

- ✓ Students explain how the present is connected to the past, identifying both similarities and differences between the two, and how some things change over time and some things stay the same. **HAS.CS.3**

- ✓ Students use map and globe skills to determine the absolute locations of places and interpret information available through a map's or globe's legend, scale, and symbolic representations. **HAS.CS.4**

- ✓ Students differentiate between primary and secondary sources. **HAS.HR.1**

- ✓ Students pose relevant questions about events they encounter in historical documents, eyewitness accounts, oral histories, letters, diaries, artifacts, photographs, maps, artworks, and architecture. **HAS.HR.2**

Connect to the Essential Question

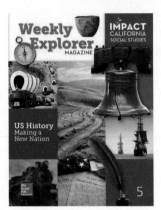

The **Weekly Explorer Magazine** supports the students' exploration of the Essential Question and provides additional resources for the EQ Inquiry Project.

Chapter 8, pp. 100–111

Inquiry Project

Create a Museum Gallery

Remind students to use the information they learn in this lesson and other resources to complete the EQ Inquiry Project.

Dinah Zike's

In this lesson you will use Foldables.

When Minutes Count!
Suggested Lesson Pacing

1 ENGAGE
One Day

- Lesson Opener
- Analyze the Source
- Inquiry Tools

Go Digital
- **Video:** Trail of Tears
- **iMap:** Seminole Lands

2 INVESTIGATE
Two to Three Days

 Short on Time? Look for the clock to teach core content in less time.

- The Age of Jackson
- The Indian Removal Act
- The Trail of Tears
- **Biography** Sequoyah
- The Seminole Wars

3 REPORT
One Day

- Think About It
- Take a Stand
- Defend Your Claim

Make Connections!

(CCSS) CONNECT TO ELA

Reading
Explain how an author uses reasons and evidence to support particular points in a text, identifying which reasons and evidence support which point(s). **RI.5.8**

Research
Conduct short research projects that use several sources to build knowledge through investigation of different aspects of a topic. **W.5.7**

Recall relevant information from experiences or gather relevant information from print and digital sources; summarize or paraphrase information in notes and finished work, and provide a list of sources. **W.5.8**

Writing
Write opinion pieces on topics or texts, supporting a point of view with reasons and information. **W.5.1**

Speaking and Listening
Engage effectively in a range of collaborative discussions (one-on-one, in groups, and teacher-led) with diverse partners on *grade 5 topics and texts*, building on others' ideas and expressing their own clearly. **SL.5.1**

Classroom Resources

Search for additional resources using the following key words.

Cherokee

Indian Removal Act

Indian Territory

Andrew Jackson

Osceola

Seminole

Sequoyah

Trail of Tears

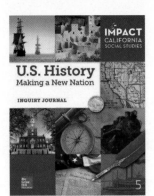

Inquiry Journal
pp. 280–281

 STANDARDS

Discuss the role of broken treaties and massacres and the factors that led to the Indians' defeat, including the resistance of Indian nations to encroachments and assimilation (e.g., the story of the Trail of Tears). **HSS.5.3.4**

Students pose relevant questions about events they encounter in historical documents, eyewitness accounts, oral histories, letters, diaries, artifacts, photographs, maps, artworks, and architecture. **HAS.HR.2**

CCSS Engage effectively in a range of collaborative discussions (one-on-one, in groups, and teacher-led) with diverse partners on *grade 5 topics and texts*, building on others' ideas and expressing their own clearly. **CCSS.ELA.SL.5.1**

Go Digital!

Explore the lesson content with online whole-class presentation tools.

- **Video:** Trail of Tears
- **iMap:** Seminole Lands

How Did Westward Expansion Impact American Indians?

Bellringer

Prompt students to retrieve information from the previous lessons. Say: *What led Americans to take the long journey west?* (Many people wanted to start new lives in the West, and others were seeking religious freedom.)

Lesson Outcomes

What Am I Learning? Have students read the Lesson Outcomes.

Why Am I Learning It? Check that students understand that they will be learning about how American Indians were treated in the 1800s. They will analyze legislation that American leaders put in place to restrict the American Indians' lands and open it to settlement by white people.

How Will I Know That I Learned It? Ask students the following questions.

- What will you identify? (Andrew Jackson's point of view about the Indian Removal Act)
- What is the purpose of the task? (to write a speech that opposes the act)
- How will you support your argument? (with text evidence and persuasive language)

Talk About It

Provide some scaffolding for students to use as they discuss the picture. Provide background information as needed.

- *The picture shows _____.*
- *The title suggests that the painting is about _____.*
- *The people I see in the painting include _____.*
- *The people in the painting look _____.*

Collaborative Conversations

Look at the Details As students engage in partner, small group, and whole-class discussions, encourage them to

- Think about what is happening in the picture. Why are they traveling?
- Ask and answer questions about how the events in the picture affect the lives of the American Indians.
- Draw or modify conclusions that are based on the discussion.

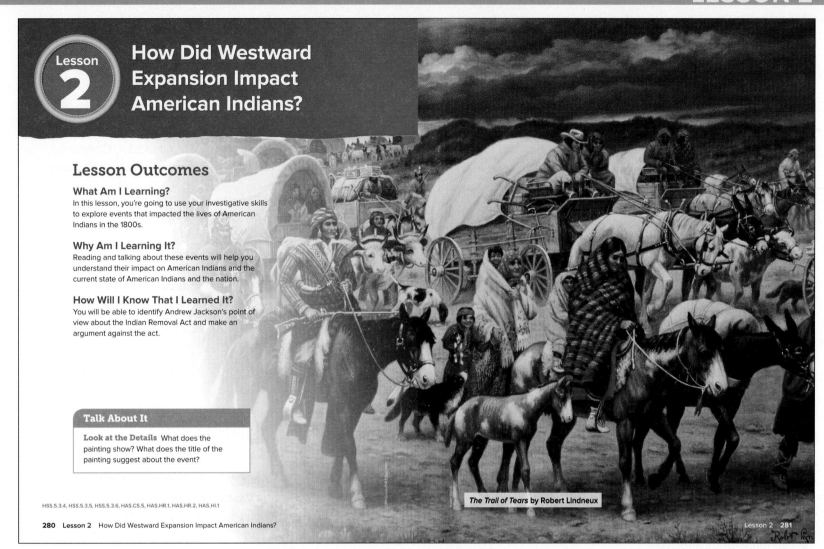

Lesson 2

How Did Westward Expansion Impact American Indians?

Lesson Outcomes

What Am I Learning?
In this lesson, you're going to use your investigative skills to explore events that impacted the lives of American Indians in the 1800s.

Why Am I Learning It?
Reading and talking about these events will help you understand their impact on American Indians and the current state of American Indians and the nation.

How Will I Know That I Learned It?
You will be able to identify Andrew Jackson's point of view about the Indian Removal Act and make an argument against the act.

Talk About It

Look at the Details What does the painting show? What does the title of the painting suggest about the event?

HSS.5.3.4, HSS.5.3.5, HSS.5.3.6, HAS.CS.5, HAS.HR.1, HAS.HR.2, HAS.HI.1

280 Lesson 2 How Did Westward Expansion Impact American Indians?

The Trail of Tears by Robert Lindneux

Lesson 2 281

Inquiry Journal, pp. 280–281

 ENGLISH LEARNERS SCAFFOLD

ELD.PI.5.6 Reading closely literary and informational texts and viewing multimedia to determine how meaning is conveyed explicitly and implicitly through language

Emerging	Expanding	Bridging
Identify Details Encourage students to describe what they see in the picture. Work with them to explain what is happening. Guide them to state opinions about the events they see.	**Analyze Details** Have students use descriptive language to tell about the picture. They should describe everything they see, from the people to the setting. Guide them to use these details to discuss the painting with a partner. Provide moderate support as needed.	**Analyze Words and Language** Encourage students to describe what they see in the painting. Guide them to use the expressions on the people in the painting to help them respond to the image.

See the **Language Learner Teaching Guide** for more language support strategies.

Monitor and Differentiate

REACHING ALL LEARNERS

Approaching Level

Encourage students to view the painting and to discuss it with a partner. Ask students to share what they see, focusing on the body language of the figures and their facial expressions.

On Level

Have students discuss the painting, stating opinions about what it might have been like for the people on the Trail of Tears.

Beyond Level

Guide students to conduct further research into the Trail of Tears. Students may choose to find other depictions of the events, or to research people involved or the territory where the American Indians were sent. Invite students to share what they learn with the class.

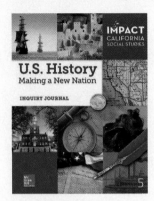

Inquiry Journal
pp. 282–283

 STANDARDS

Discuss the role of broken treaties and massacres and the factors that led to the Indians' defeat, including the resistance of Indian nations to encroachments and assimilation (e.g., the story of the Trail of Tears). **HSS.5.3.4**

Students differentiate between primary and secondary sources. **HAS.HR.1**

Engage effectively in a range of collaborative discussions (one-on-one, in groups, and teacher-led) with diverse partners on *grade 5 topics and texts*, building on others' ideas and expressing their own clearly. **CCSS.ELA.SL.5.1**

Go *Digital!*

Model how to inspect and find evidence with online whole-class presentation tools.

Build Background

Indian Territory The area known as Indian Territory was an officially an area "west of the Mississippi, and not within the States of Missouri and Louisiana, or the Territory of Arkansas." The area where American Indians were moved is now Oklahoma, but between 1830 and 1907, all or part of the land was set aside for Choctaw, Cherokee, Seminole, Chickasaw, and Creek who had been forcibly relocated from their homes.

1 Inspect

Read Ask students to read the text and analyze the primary source. Remind them to circle words and phrases that are unfamiliar.

- What words in the primary source evoke a strong emotion in you? (Responses will vary, but students may include "helpless," "dragged from their home," "loaded like cattle.")

- How do you know from reading the primary source that the Cherokee were forced to leave their homes? (The primary source says they were "dragged from their homes," and later says they were "driven from home.")

- What does Burnett say that the journey quickly became? (It became a "trail of death" because so many people died along the way from exposure and illness.)

Collaborate Have partners take turns discussing what John G. Burnett felt during the Trail of Tears. Encourage students to point to specific words and phrases that show his thinking. (Students should identify that Burnett is sickened by what he witnessed, using words such as "Somebody must explain the 4,000 silent graves that mark the trail of the Cherokees to their exile.")

2 Find Evidence

Reread Have students reread the primary source.

Analyze the Primary Source Reread the primary source with students, guiding them to read for vivid details that help them understand Burnett's point of view. Provide support for vocabulary as needed.

- Ask: What examples of vivid language do you notice? (Students may identify examples such as "I saw them loaded like cattle or sheep into six hundred and forty-five wagons.")

- Encourage students to explain what image "silent graves" evokes in the last paragraph of the primary source. (Responses will vary.)

- Why do you think Burnett wrote this memoir? (Responses will vary, but students may say that he wanted to share his anger about the events with a larger audience.)

3 Make Connections

Talk Guide students to discuss how Burnett shows his point of view about the events and how he portrays the hardships and events of the Trail of Tears. (Responses will vary; students may say that he uses language the appeals to his readers' emotions.)

Connect to Now Have partners discuss what people can do to help those whose rights are stripped away.

Analyze the Source

1 Inspect

Read Look at the first line of the quotation on the next page. Which words provoke strong emotions in you?

- **Circle** unfamiliar words.
- **Underline** clues that show that American Indians were forced to leave.
- **Discuss** with a partner how John G. Burnett feels about the event. What words does he use to describe what he saw?

My Notes

_____
_____
_____
_____
_____
_____
_____
_____
_____
_____
_____
_____
_____
_____

Witnessing the Trail of Tears

In the 1800s, the nation began expanding westward rapidly. By 1824, about 3 million people, or 30 percent of the U.S. population, lived on the frontier.

Treaties between American Indians and the U.S. government guaranteed native people's rights to their land in these regions. Initially, settlers respected the treaties and lived peacefully alongside American Indians. Settlers soon demanded more land, however, triggering conflict. President Andrew Jackson supported the seizure of American Indians' lands and used the office of the presidency to break the treaties.

In 1830, Congress passed the Indian Removal Act. This forced American Indians in the southeastern United States to leave their homes and march about 800 miles into present-day Oklahoma. Despite a Supreme Court ruling against the act, President Jackson defied the highest court in the land and ordered soldiers to round up Cherokee and burn their homes. Of the 15,000 Cherokee forced to relocate 800 miles west, 4,000 died.

John G. Burnett, a young U.S. soldier who spoke Cherokee, served as an interpreter on the Trail of Tears. The Cherokee called him "the soldier who was good to us." In an 1890 publication, Burnett reflected on what he saw during the 800-mile "Trail of Tears."

PRIMARY SOURCE

In Their Words... John G. Burnett

[In] May 1838 ... I saw helpless Cherokee arrested and dragged from their homes . ... I saw them loaded like cattle or sheep into six hundred and forty-five wagons and starting toward the west. . . . Many of the children rose to their feet and waved their little hands good-by to their mountain homes, knowing they were leaving them forever. Many of . . . them had been driven from home barefooted.

On the morning of November the 17th we encountered a terrific sleet and snow storm with freezing temperatures and from that day until we reached the end of the fateful journey on March the 26th, 1839, the sufferings of the Cherokees were awful. The trail of the exiles was a trail of death. They had to sleep in the wagons and on the ground without fire. And I have known as many as twenty-two of them to die in one night of pneumonia due to ill treatment, cold, and exposure. . . .

The long painful journey to the west ended March 26th, 1839, with four-thousand silent graves reaching from the foothills of the Smoky Mountains to what is known as Indian territory in the West...

Somebody must explain the streams of blood that flowed in the Indian country in the summer of 1838. Somebody must explain the 4000 silent graves that mark the trail of the Cherokees to their exile. I wish I could forget it all, but the picture of 645 wagons lumbering over the frozen ground with their Cargo of suffering humanity still lingers in my memory.

—from *Story of the Trail of Tears*, published in 1890

TEXT: Burnett, John G. 1838-39. Removal of the Cherokee 1838-1839. The King Research Collection: Trail of Tears. Museum of the Cherokee Indian (2009.003.0577).; PHOTO: McGraw-Hill Education

2 Find Evidence

Reread Notice how John Burnett gives vivid details to help readers picture what he saw and heard on the journey.

Examine Read the statement "Somebody must explain the 4000 silent graves that mark the trail of the Cherokees to their exile." What impact does this image of "silent graves" have on the reader emotionally? What do you think Burnett hoped to achieve by writing this?

3 Make Connections

Talk Discuss with a partner the details in Burnett's story that show the hardships of the Trail of Tears. How does Burnett's description reveal his own viewpoint about the event?

COLLABORATE

Inquiry Journal, pp. 282–283

ENGLISH LEARNERS SCAFFOLD

ELD.PI.5.6 Reading closely literary and informational texts and viewing multimedia to determine how meaning is conveyed explicitly and implicitly through language

Emerging

Discuss Details Encourage students to unpack Burnett's language to understand the events he describes. Provide support as needed, guiding students to break apart lengthy sentences into shorter phrases to access his meaning.

Expanding/Bridging

Use Details Guide students to consider each of the events that Burnett describes. Guide them to annotate the text, using an exclamation point to indicate details that shock or surprise them. Then have students discuss the text in small groups, quoting Burnett as often as possible.

See the **Language Learner Teaching Guide** for more language support strategies.

Monitor and Differentiate

REACHING ALL LEARNERS

Approaching Level

Have students read the text to identify what happened to the Cherokees. Then have them reread to determine what words Burnett uses to describe the events in a way that makes them vivid to the reader. Guide students to analyze how these words show what Burnett wants his readers to do.

Beyond Level

Encourage students to conduct additional research into firsthand accounts of the Trail of Tears. Guide students to compare and contrast those accounts with Burnett's. Invite them to share their findings with the class.

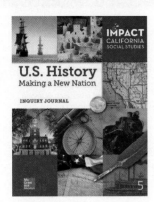

Inquiry Journal
pp. 284–285

Discuss the role of broken treaties and massacres and the factors that led to the Indians' defeat, including the resistance of Indian nations to encroachments and assimilation (e.g., the story of the Trail of Tears). **HSS.5.3.4**

Explain the influence and achievements of significant leaders of the time (e.g., John Marshall, Andrew Jackson, Chief Tecumseh, Chief Logan, Chief John Ross, Sequoyah). **HSS.5.3.6**

Students place key events and people of the historical era they are studying in a chronological sequence and within a spatial context; they interpret time lines. **HAS.CS.1**

(CCSS) Explain how an author uses reasons and evidence to support particular points in a text, identifying which reasons and evidence support which point(s). **CCSS.ELA.RI.5.8**

Go Digital!

- Model how to explore and investigate with online whole-class tools.

- Students can access the online graphic organizer to use the inquiry tools as they read.

Explore Point of View

Explain Tell students that a person's point of view is his or her opinion on a topic. Explain that finding out a person's point of view will help them better understand what they read.

Read Have students read aloud the step-by-step instructions about how to determine a person's point of view. Tell students that they should ask themselves questions such as *What words show opinions? What actions did the person take? How did his or her opinions affect those actions?* They should also look for key details that signal important information.

Guide Practice Present a brief model of determining point of view that helps students understand the process. *John Burnett's point of view seems to be that the Trail of Tears was an injustice against the Cherokee. In his memoir, he says that he wishes he "could forget it all," but that the "suffering humanity still lingers in [his] memory."*

Investigate!

Have students read pages 346–353 in the Research Companion. Tell them the information that will help them answer the lesson question *How Did Westward Expansion Impact American Indians?*

✏ **Take Notes** Tell students that they will take notes as they read each section. Explain that taking notes will help them understand what Andrew Jackson thought of the removal of American Indians from their native lands. Remind students that they should look for key details and important information in the text.

Inspect Guide students to read the text in each section to determine what it says. Encourage them to work to find information about hardships and injustices American Indians faced as a result of the American desire to expand west.

Find Evidence Encourage students to reread the text to develop a deeper understanding. Remind students that they should think about how the facts and details will help them answer the lesson question.

Collaborative Conversations

Text-Based Discussion Remind students that discussing the text with others can help them

- Better understand what they read
- Grasp differing points of view on a topic
- Appreciate the perspectives of other people

Inquiry Tools

Explore Point of View

A person's point of view is his or her opinion on a topic. Determining point of view can help you understand a person's choices and actions.

1. Identify opinion words.
Which words indicate that someone's opinion is being conveyed? Which words express positive or negative emotions?

2. Look for reasons and evidence.
What reasoning and supporting details can you find that support his or her point of view?

3. Identify actions and choices.
What important decisions or actions does the person make?

4. Evaluate actions for point of view.
Ask yourself, Did this person's point of view impact his or her actions?

 COLLABORATE Based on the text you just read, work with your class to fill in the details that support the point of view in the center oval.

- "I wish I could forget it all."
- "...suffering humanity still lingers in my memory."
- The Trail of Tears was an injustice against the Cherokee.
- "I saw them loaded like cattle or sheep. . . ."
- "The trail of the exiles was a trail of death."

284 Lesson 2 How Did Westward Expansion Impact American Indians?

Investigate!

 Read pages 346–353 in your Research Companion. Use your investigative skills to determine President Andrew Jackson's point of view about the removal of American Indians from their lands. Use the organizer to track key details that support this point of view.

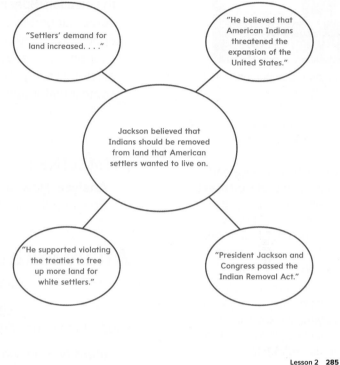

- "Settlers' demand for land increased. . . ."
- "He believed that American Indians threatened the expansion of the United States."
- Jackson believed that Indians should be removed from land that American settlers wanted to live on.
- "He supported violating the treaties to free up more land for white settlers."
- "President Jackson and Congress passed the Indian Removal Act."

Lesson 2 285

Inquiry Journal, pp. 284–285

(EL) ENGLISH LEARNERS SCAFFOLD

ELD.PI.5.1 Exchanging information and ideas with others through oral collaborative discussions on a range of social and academic topics

Emerging

Choose Details Work with students to carefully choose details from the text that support their understanding of Jackson's opinions on the removal of American Indians.

Expanding

Use Text Evidence Encourage students to refer to the text as they find details that support their understanding of Jackson's point of view. Remind students that they should find multiple pieces of evidence to create a more complete understanding.

Bridging

Discuss Main Ideas Guide students to discuss the main ideas of specific sections of the text as they try to identify Jackson's opinions about the removal of American Indians from their native lands. Encourage students to share their ideas with a partner.

See the **Language Learner Teaching Guide** for more language support strategies.

Monitor and Differentiate

REACHING ALL LEARNERS

Special Needs

Encourage students to take notes to identify the most important details that show Jackson's point of view. Students may choose to dictate their ideas aloud to you or a partner. They may also choose to make a drawing or other piece of visual art that shows Jackson's behavior while they consider his point of view.

Approaching Level

Encourage students to first skim sections of the text looking for names, places, and dates. Then guide them to reread the section looking for important details that show someone's point of view. Remind them to use a dictionary to define or confirm their understanding of unfamiliar words.

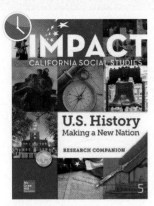

Research Companion
pp. 346–347

(HSS) STANDARDS

Explain the influence and achievements of significant leaders of the time (e.g., John Marshall, Andrew Jackson, Chief Tecumseh, Chief Logan, Chief John Ross, Sequoyah). **HSS.5.3.6**

Students summarize the key events of the era they are studying and explain the historical contexts of those events. **HAS.HI.1**

Go Digital!

Investigate the lesson content with online whole-class presentation tools.

• **Video:** Trail of Tears
• **iMap:** Seminole Lands

Background Information

Andrew Jackson became president in 1828 after defeating John Quincy Adams, but in 1824 he had lost his bid for election to the same opponent. In 1824, Jackson won more electoral votes than any other candidate. However because none of the four presidential candidates received a majority of electoral votes, the House of Representatives decided the election. Speaker of the House Henry Clay, who had finished fourth in electoral votes, supported John Quincy Adams, leading to his election. Clay was subsequently appointed Secretary of State by Adams, leading to charges of corruption from Jackson supporters. The 1828 election, in which Jackson won the popular vote and the electoral college by appealing to the "common man", was so bitterly contested contest that Adams boycotted Jackson's inauguration.

| TIMELINE | Invite students to look at the timeline on the top of p. 347.

> **Analyze** How many years were between the first and second Seminole wars? Between the second and third wars? (18 years; 20 years) **HAS.CS.1**

Analyze the Source

Inspect Have students read pp. 346–347.

Find Evidence Use the questions below to check comprehension. Remind students to support their answers with text evidence.

> **Identify** How was the election of 1824 different from the election of 1828? (approximately 1 million more people voted in the election of 1828) **DOK 1**

> **Explain** Why did so many more people vote in 1828? (New laws were passed that allowed all white men over 21 to vote. Before only landowners could vote.) **DOK 2**

> **Cite Evidence** How did this change pave the way for the election of Andrew Jackson as president? (Many of the new voters were "farmers, frontier settlers, and workers," who wanted for president someone like Jackson, who was a "common man.") **DOK 3**

> **Compare and Contrast** In what ways was Jackson different from the presidents who preceded him? (He was not a politician, nor was he educated.) **DOK 3**

> **Understand Cause and Effect** What caused the major conflict that Jackson faced in 1832? (He tried to use military force to get South Carolina to pay a new tax. People thought this was too similar to what Great Britain had forced the colonies to do before the American Revolution.) **DOK 3**

Analyze the Image Explain to students that analyzing a historical painting or print requires them to look at details such as the people shown, how they are shown, and the setting of the event.

> **Analyze Visuals** What is happening in the picture? (Andrew Jackson is taking the Oath of Office to become president.) Who is shown in the picture? (Jackson, Supreme Court Chief Justice John Marshall) **DOK 3**

Make Connections

> **Infer** How did electing a "common man" present challenges for the United States? (Responses will vary, but they may identify that Jackson's lack of experience in government led him to make decisions that divided the nation.) **DOK 3**

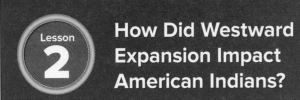

Lesson 2 — How Did Westward Expansion Impact American Indians?

Timeline

| 1817 First Seminole War | 1830 Indian Removal Act | 1835 Second Seminole War | 1838 Cherokee forced to relocate | 1855 Third Seminole War |

1820 · ★1830 · 1840 · 1850

1829 Andrew Jackson takes office as President.

The Age of Jackson

As the United States expanded westward, the government began to include members of Congress who gave a voice to the needs and opinions of western settlers. In 1824, only about 360,000 American citizens voted. Then new laws allowed all white men age 21 or older to vote. Before then, only wealthy male landowners could vote. Four years later, the number of voters increased more than 200 percent to about 1.2 million. This **surge** of new voters—farmers, frontier settlers, and city workers—helped elect a "common man," Andrew Jackson, as president in 1828. Born on the frontier, Jackson was a farmer-politician with no college education or public-speaking skills. He had fought in the Revolutionary War at the age of 13 and later became a popular general during the War of 1812. This "man of the people" went on to become one of the most powerful and controversial presidents in U.S. history.

Jackson's actions as president ignited much conflict. Opponents accused Jackson of trying to take away Congress's power. He **vetoed** much legislation, preventing Congress from passing the laws it wanted.

One major conflict arose in South Carolina. When Congress passed a new federal tax on imported goods in 1832, South Carolina politicians threatened to leave the Union. Because Southern states had few local industries, they relied on imported products. The new tax would make these products very expensive. Jackson responded to South Carolina's threat by sending troops and warships to force the state to pay the tax. The action enraged citizens, who compared the move to Britain's attempts to enforce new taxes on colonists in the 1700s.

Chief Justice John Marshall swears in Andrew Jackson as president.

HSS.5.3.4, HSS.5.3.5, HSS.5.3.6, HAS.CS.1, HAS.CS.3, HAS.CS.4, HAS.HR.1, HAS.HR.2, HAS.HI.1

346 Lesson 2 How Did Westward Expansion Impact American Indians?

Lesson 2 **347**

Research Companion, pp. 346–347

ENGLISH LEARNERS SCAFFOLD

ELD.PI.5.3 Offering and supporting opinions and negotiating with others in communicative exchanges

Emerging

State Opinions Work with students to state opinions about how Andrew Jackson came into office. Guide students to use *I think* statements. Provide sentence frames as needed:

People elected Andrew Jackson because _____.

I think this was a _____ idea because _____.

Expanding/Bridging

Support Opinions Have students refer to or cite evidence from the text to support their opinions about how Andrew Jackson was elected president. Encourage students to defend their opinions by evaluating their group members' use of evidence:

I agree with that, but have you thought of _____?

The text does not support your opinion because it says _____.

See the **Language Learner Teaching Guide** for more language support strategies.

Monitor and Differentiate

REACHING ALL LEARNERS

Approaching Level

Have students work together to understand the events that led to the conflict in South Carolina. Guide them to make a graphic organizer to help them keep track of their notes. Remind them that an event can have multiple causes.

Beyond Level

Have students conduct additional research into the conflict in South Carolina. Invite students to research how the tax would have affected the state and to try to understand why Jackson felt he needed to use the military to enforce the new rule. Have students share their findings with the class.

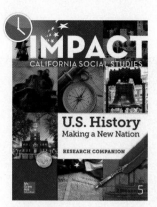

Research Companion
pp. 348–349

 STANDARDS

Discuss the role of broken treaties and massacres and the factors that led to the Indians' defeat, including the resistance of Indian nations to encroachments and assimilation (e.g., the story of the Trail of Tears). **HSS.5.3.4**

Describe the internecine Indian conflicts, including the competing claims for control of lands (e.g., actions of the Iroquois, Huron, Lakota [Sioux]). **HSS.5.3.5**

Explain the influence and achievements of significant leaders of the time (e.g., John Marshall, Andrew Jackson, Chief Tecumseh, Chief Logan, Chief John Ross, Sequoyah). **HSS.5.3.6**

Students summarize the key events of the era they are studying and explain the historical contexts of those events. **HAS.HI.1**

Go Digital!

Investigate the lesson content with online whole-class presentation tools.

Background Information

Peace of Paris and American Indians After losses during Pontiac's War (1763–1764), Great Britain granted American Indians legal protections for the land between the Appalachian Mountains and the Mississippi River. The agreement lost some of its validity, however, when Great Britain lost the rights to that territory in the Peace of Paris after the American Revolution. However, the U.S. government made treaties with American Indian groups to strengthen boundaries shared with Spain and France.

Analyze the Source

Inspect Have students read pages 348–349.

Find Evidence Use the questions below to check comprehension. Remind students to support their answers with text evidence.

Analyze the Infographic Encourage students to read the caption and analyze the political cartoon.

- What is the purpose of a political cartoon? (to show an opinion about a current event)
- How can you read a political cartoon to understand the artist's opinion? (Look at how the people are drawn; look for words that show positive or negative opinions.)
- What is the artist's opinion about Andrew Jackson? (Jackson is behaving like a king.)
- What details tell you that? (Jackson is standing on top of the ripped up Constitution. He holds a scroll that says "Veto." These show that Jackson is abusing his power.) **DOK 3**

> **Identify** What did Jackson believe about the Bank of the United States? (that it was unconstitutional) **DOK 1**
>
> **Summarize** What did Jackson do that upset the economic balance in the United States? (He removed all money from the U.S. Bank and put it in state and local banks. When those banks collapsed, the money was lost.) **DOK 2**

Make Connections

> **Analyze Cause and Effect** Why did the conflict between settlers and American Indians in Georgia grow worse? (More settlers arrived. Then gold was discovered on Cherokee lands, which made settlers want to claim the land and riches for themselves.) **DOK 3**
>
> **Understand Point of View** What events in Jackson's life contributed to his negative view of American Indians? (He had fought them during several wars.) **DOK 3**

✓ Stop and Check

PRODUCTIVE

Talk Guide students to compare and contrast Jackson's leadership and experience with the presidents who came before him. (Students should note that Jackson was not a politician or well educated.)

Discuss Why did Jackson want to relocate American Indians? (Jackson wanted to end what he saw as a threat to U.S. expansion by freeing up land for white settlers.)

Find Details Explain to students that after they read and take notes, they should think about how the information can help them answer the Essential Question.

InfoGraphic

Political Cartoons

Through political cartoons, artists express their opinions on current news, people, and events. Cartoons usually exaggerate details in a humorous or ridiculous way to make a statement. To identify the artist's opinion, look closely at the title, labels, and details of the cartoon. How do you think this artist felt about Jackson's actions as president?

King Andrew the First (artist unknown)

Subject
Andrew Jackson

Symbol
King's clothing stands for Jackson's power

Detail
Jackson holds the veto in his hand

Detail
Jackson tramples on the Constitution

Title

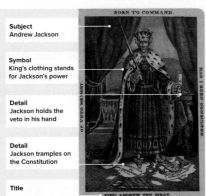

Library of Congress Prints and Photographs Division [LC-USZ62-1562]

Another controversial action by Jackson concerned the Second Bank of the United States, which helped to manage the nation's money supply. Convinced that the **charter** of the Bank of the United States was unconstitutional, Jackson removed all of the federal government's money from the bank in 1836. He ordered that the money be transferred to state and local banks. There were no regulations in place to monitor these banks, however. Many of them made unwise investments in land. When the economy weakened in 1837, the invested money could not be recovered.

The "man of the people" had caused a major economic crisis, putting many working people he claimed to represent in difficult times.

✓ Stop and Check

Think How was Jackson's leadership different from that of the presidents before him?

Find Details As you read, add additional information to the graphic organizer on page 285 in your Inquiry Journal.

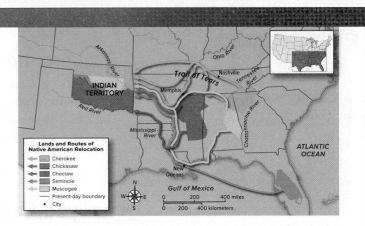

McGraw-Hill Education

The Indian Removal Act

In the early 1800s, American Indians in the Southeast were protected by the treaties signed with the U.S. government. The treaties guaranteed their right to their homeland and protection from settlers. American Indian communities flourished with their own schools and local governments. Life alongside settlers was peaceful until settlers began demanding more land. Settlers' demands for land increased when gold was discovered on Cherokee lands in Georgia. Conflict grew worse.

As a general, Andrew Jackson had fought several campaigns against American Indians. He believed that American Indians threatened the expansion of the United States. He supported violating the treaties to free up more land for white settlers. He believed that moving American Indians to land west of the Mississippi would end the threat.

In 1830, Congress passed the Indian Removal Act and Andrew Jackson signed it into law. This law forced American Indians to leave their homelands so settlers could live there. The act allowed the U.S. government to relocate American Indians to "Indian Territory," in parts of what is now Oklahoma.

✓ Stop and Check

Discuss Why did Andrew Jackson want to relocate American Indians?

348 Lesson 2 How Did Westward Expansion Impact American Indians?

Lesson 2 349

Research Companion, pp. 348–349

(EL) ENGLISH LEARNERS SCAFFOLD

ELD.PI.5.6 Reading closely literary and informational texts and viewing multimedia to determine how meaning is conveyed explicitly and implicitly through language

Emerging

Read a Political Cartoon Work with students as they read the infographic and the political cartoon. Encourage students to consider how the artist's opinion shows in the way he portrays Jackson. Remind them to look for clues in the details of the cartoon. Provide vocabulary support as needed.

Expanding/Bridging

Read an Infographic Have students consider how the artist shows Andrew Jackson. Invite them to discuss the infographic as a group. Provide sentence frames as needed:

In the picture, Andrew Jackson's expression is _____.

He is standing on _____.

He is holding _____.

I think this means that the artist believes Jackson is _____.

The title "King Andrew the First" is another clue that _____.

See the **Language Learner Teaching Guide** for more language support strategies.

Monitor and Differentiate

REACHING ALL LEARNERS

On Level

Have students take notes on their impressions of Jackson in the picture. Then, have them describe things the artist did to help give them those impressions.

Beyond Level

Have students draw their own political cartoon for a person or an event they have read about in a previous chapter.

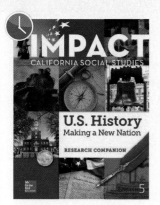

Research Companion
pp. 350–351

 STANDARDS

Discuss the role of broken treaties and massacres and the factors that led to the Indians' defeat, including the resistance of Indian nations to encroachments and assimilation (e.g., the story of the Trail of Tears). **HSS.5.3.4**

Explain the influence and achievements of significant leaders of the time (e.g., John Marshall, Andrew Jackson, Chief Tecumseh, Chief Logan, Chief John Ross, Sequoyah). **HSS.5.3.6**

Students pose relevant questions about events they encounter in historical documents, eyewitness accounts, oral histories, letters, diaries, artifacts, photographs, maps, artworks, and architecture. **HAS.HR.2**

Go *Digital!*

Investigate the lesson content with online whole-class presentation tools.

Background Information

Worcester v. Georgia The Supreme Court ruled in favor of the American Indians whom Jackson wanted relocated out of Georgia in the *Worcester v. Georgia* decision. The court stated that an individual state cannot impose regulation on lands reserved for American Indians. Only the federal government has this power.

Analyze the Source

Inspect Have students read The Trail of Tears on pp. 350–351.

Find Evidence Use the questions below to check comprehension. Remind students to support their answers with text evidence.

> **Identify** What did Chief John Ross do to try to prevent the Cherokee from being removed from their homes? (He fought the Indian Removal Act in the U.S. Supreme Court.) **DOK 1**

> **Explain** What was the outcome of the trial? (The Supreme Court agreed with the Cherokee.) **DOK 1**

> **Summarize** How did this decision help the Cherokee people? (It did not. Jackson went around the Court's decision to continue with his program of removal.) **DOK 2**

Analyze the Primary Sources

> **Unpack an Argument** What argument did John Ross make to Congress? (That the Cherokee were just like other Americans. They believed in freedom and justice, and they counted Washington and Jefferson among own heroes.) **DOK 3**

> **Find the Main Idea** What did John Marshall say about the political status of the Cherokee Nation? (That it was a "sovereign nation"; it was independent.) **DOK 2**

> **Supporting Details** From whom are the Cherokee free from "interference"? (They are free from interference from "states.") **DOK 2**

> **Summarize** In addition to being removed from their homes and forced to relocate, what made the Trail of Tears so terrible? (Approximately 4,000 people died during the period of relocation.) **DOK 3**

Make Connections

> **Compare and Contrast** What do you think would happen today if a president ignored a decision from the Supreme Court? How would people be able to stand up against such an action? (Responses will vary.) **DOK 2**

☑ Stop and Check

Talk Encourage students to consider the ways that Jackson and Congress broke the law. Guide them to recall what they learned about the separation of powers and checks and balances that make up the U.S. system of government. (Responses should be supported with text evidence.)

The Trail of Tears

The Cherokee fought against the Indian Removal Act. Led by Chief John Ross, they took their case to court and sued the state of Georgia. Eventually, the U.S. Supreme Court, the highest court in the land, ruled in favor of the Cherokee, determining that "the laws of Georgia can have no force" on American Indian lands. President Jackson ignored that ruling, however. He ordered soldiers to force the Cherokee off the lands they legally owned.

In 1838, General Winfield Scott led about 7,000 federal troops onto Cherokee lands in northwest Georgia and neighboring areas. He told the Cherokee that they were surrounded, escape was impossible, and force would be used if they did not comply. The soldiers then burned the Cherokee's homes and forced them to travel 800 miles into Indian Territory.

PRIMARY SOURCE

In Their Words... Chief John Ross
We are overwhelmed! Our hearts are sickened, our utterance is paralyzed, when we reflect on the condition in which we are placed, by the audacious practices of unprincipled men. . . . In truth, our cause is your own; it is the cause of liberty and of justice; it is based upon your own principles, which we have learned from yourselves; for we have gloried to count your Washington and your Jefferson our great teachers . . .

—from a letter to the U.S. Congress, 1836

TEXT: The Papers of Chief John Ross, vol 1, 1807-1839. Translated by Gary E. Moulton Norman OK: University of Oklahoma Press, 1985.; PHOTO: Library of Congress, Prints & Photographs Division [LC-DIG-pga-07818]

PRIMARY SOURCE

In Their Words... Chief Justice John Marshall
Treaties have been duly ratified by the Senate of the United States of America, and by which treaties the United States of America acknowledge the said Cherokee Nation to be a sovereign nation, authorized to govern themselves, and all persons who have settled within their territory, free from any right of legislative interference by the several states composing the United States of America in reference to acts done within their own territory, and by which treaties the whole of the territory now occupied by the Cherokee Nation on the east of the Mississippi has been solemnly guarantied to them, all of which treaties are existing treaties at this day, and in full force . . .

—from *Worcester v. Georgia* ruling, 1831

Of the approximately 15,000 Cherokee forced to leave their homes, about 2,000 died in camps waiting for the move to begin. During the one-year march, another 2,000 Cherokee died from disease, starvation, and severe weather conditions. The Cherokee called this forced march "the place where they cried." In English, it became known as the Trail of Tears.

✓ Stop and Check

Think What illegal actions did President Jackson and Congress take to force the removal of the Cherokee from their own land?

TEXT: Worcester v. Georgia, 31 U.S. 515 (1832).; PHOTO: McGraw-Hill Education

350   Lesson 2   How Did Westward Expansion Impact American Indians?

Lesson 2   351

Research Companion, pp. 350–351

 ## ENGLISH LEARNERS SCAFFOLD

ELD.PI.5.5 Listening actively to spoken English in a range of social and academic contexts

Emerging

Listen for Language Read aloud both primary sources. Pause to explain obscure references or to invite students to suggest word meanings. Encourage students to use context clues to understand unfamiliar words when possible; for example, "sovereign nation" is explained by the definition that follows it, "authorized to govern themselves." Guide students to find other examples.

Expanding/Bridging

Analyze the Primary Sources Encourage students to read the primary sources aloud. Provide support for unfamiliar words and references as needed. Then have students summarize both sources. Prompt students to share what they think about the point of view of each writer.

See the **Language Learner Teaching Guide** for more language support strategies.

Monitor and Differentiate

REACHING ALL LEARNERS

Special Needs

Read the primary sources aloud to students. Have them take notes as you read. Ask them to ask and answer questions to determine key details from each text, such as *Who wrote the primary source? Why is he writing? What is his opinion on the topic? What did he expect his readers to think or do?*

Approaching Level

Guide students to use the text to make a timeline of events that led up to the Trail of Tears. Encourage students to use this timeline as they think about the points of view of the writers of each primary source.

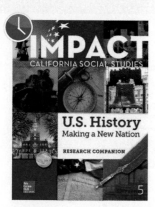

Research Companion
pp. 352–353

IMPACT
CALIFORNIA SOCIAL STUDIES

U.S. History
Making a New Nation

RESEARCH COMPANION

5

 STANDARDS

Discuss the role of broken treaties and massacres and the factors that led to the Indians' defeat, including the resistance of Indian nations to encroachments and assimilation (e.g., the story of the Trail of Tears). **HSS.5.3.4**

Explain the influence and achievements of significant leaders of the time (e.g., John Marshall, Andrew Jackson, Chief Tecumseh, Chief Logan, Chief John Ross, Sequoyah). **HSS.5.3.6**

Students summarize the key events of the era they are studying and explain the historical contexts of those events. **HAS.HI.1**

Go Digital!

Investigate the lesson content with online whole-class presentation tools.

Background Information

The *Cherokee Phoenix* The newspaper of the Cherokee people began publication in Georgia before the Trail of Tears. Chief John Ross used the newspaper as a way to rally people against the Indian Removal Act. After the Trail of Tears, a new newspaper, the *Cherokee Advocate* emerged in Tahlequah, Oklahoma. It has continued under several names since then. Today it is once again called the *Cherokee Phoenix*, and prints a newspaper in addition to maintaining Facebook and Twitter feeds.

Analyze the Source

Inspect Have students read The Seminole Wars on pp. 352–353.

Find Evidence Use the questions below to check comprehension. Remind students to support their answers with text evidence.

Analyze the Biography

Identify For what is Sequoyah best known? (inventing the Cherokee alphabet) **DOK 1**

Explain How did Sequoyah go about inventing a brand new alphabet? (He borrowed characters from other languages and matched them to the sounds of the Cherokee language.) **DOK 2**

Analyze Cause and Effect How did the Cherokee people receive the new alphabet? (They learned it quickly and used it to communicate with people who were far away. In a few months, almost everyone was literate. Some people even began a Cherokee newspaper.) **DOK 3**

Summarize What was Andrew Jackson's record for interfering with the rights of American Indians? (He led American troops to Seminole territory to track down runaway slaves in 1817. He tried to enforce the Indian Removal Act on the Seminole in the 1830s.) **DOK 3**

Explain What did the Seminole do when Jackson tried to enforce the Indian Removal Act? (Some Seminole leaders surrendered and agreed to relocate. Others, led by Osceola, tried to fight back to keep their lands.) **DOK 1**

Context Clues What does it mean to *cede* something? (The text says that Spain lost some land to Jackson in 1817. Then it *ceded* the remainder of its territory to the United States. *Cede* must mean to give up or give over.) **DOK 2**

Make Connections

Justify Did the United States succeed or fail in its fight to remove the Seminole? Use text evidence to support your response. (Responses will vary, but students should identify that the wars were long, they cost millions of dollars, and—in the end—some Seminole still remained in the swamps.) **DOK 3**

✓ Stop and Check

Talk Encourage students to consider how the experiences of the Cherokee and the Seminole differed. Guide them to provide examples of the different types of hardships as they look for commonalities. (The Cherokee suffered during the Trail of Tears. The Seminole suffered during wars and more gradual relocation.)

Biography

Sequoyah

A Cherokee silversmith named Sequoyah developed the first written American Indian alphabet. Borrowing letters from Greek, Hebrew, and English, Sequoyah created 85 symbols, each of which represented a Cherokee sound. It took him 12 years to create the alphabet. He compared the difficult task to "catching a wild animal and taming it."

In 1824, Sequoyah began using this new writing system to send printed messages from Arkansas to Cherokee people living farther east. Since the symbols were based on the way the spoken language sounded, Cherokee learned the alphabet quickly. Within a few months, thousands of Cherokee had learned the new alphabet. They called it "talking leaves," since it was printed on paper that resembled tree leaves and allowed them to talk with others over long distances.

In 1828, Sequoyah's alphabet was used in the first American Indian newspaper, the *Cherokee Phoenix*. The paper focused on issues affecting American Indian communities. A version of it still exists today.

Sequoyah became a respected leader for his contribution to American Indian culture. The California giant redwood tree is named *sequoia* in his honor.

Sequoyah with his Cherokee alphabet, called "talking leaves"

352 Lesson 2 How Did Westward Expansion Impact American Indians?

The Seminole Wars

Andrew Jackson had a long history of interfering with the rights of American Indians, starting when he was a general in the U.S. military. It was then that he first became involved in wars between the U.S. military and the Seminole people of Florida.

In the first Seminole War in 1817, General Jackson led forces in an invasion of Seminole land to recapture runaway slaves that the Seminole had welcomed. U.S. soldiers burned down the towns in this region.

When Jackson became president, he again attempted to relocate the Seminole in Florida and take over their land. Settlers and Jackson sought to enforce the Indian Removal Act in Florida. Some of the Seminole formed an army under the leadership of Chief Osceola and fought against U.S. troops. When the U.S. Army approached Osceola, claiming to come in peace, they took him prisoner. He later died in prison. Even so, the Seminole continued fighting to remain in Florida. By the end of the Seminole Wars, U.S. soldiers had removed 3,000 Seminole from their Florida homes and killed 1,500 more.

Chief Osceola

✓ Stop and Check

Talk What similarities were there between the Trail of Tears and the Seminole Wars?

Lesson 2 353

Research Companion, pp. 352–353

(EL) ENGLISH LEARNERS SCAFFOLD

ELD.PI.5.6 Reading closely literary and informational texts and viewing multimedia to determine how meaning is conveyed explicitly and implicitly through language

Emerging

Read for Understanding Read aloud the section on the Seminole Wars to students. Then have students chorally read the section in small groups. Guide students to identify words that are unfamiliar and make a note to look them up later. Encourage students to verbally summarize in one or two sentences the main idea of the section. Then guide students to reread the text, identify the meanings of unfamiliar words, and look for important details.

Expanding/Bridging

Read for Analysis Encourage students to reread the section on the Seminole Wars. Guide students to discuss the main idea in a small group, then have students reread to identify key details that support and expand on those main ideas. Have students add information to a graphic organizer, if needed.

See the **Language Learner Teaching Guide** for more language support strategies.

Monitor and Differentiate

REACHING ALL LEARNERS

Approaching Level

Guide students to review their notes about the Trail of Tears and the hardships the Cherokee faced before, during, and after relocation to Indian Territory. Then have students reread the section on the Seminole Wars, identifying similarities and differences between the struggles of both groups.

Beyond Level

Guide students to conduct further research into the Seminole Wars and the leadership and life of Osceola. Encourage students to share their findings with the class during discussion.

3 REPORT

Report Your Findings

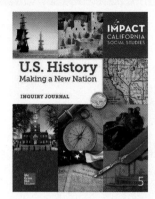

Inquiry Journal
pp. 286–287

 STANDARDS

Discuss the role of broken treaties and massacres and the factors that led to the Indians' defeat, including the resistance of Indian nations to encroachments and assimilation (e.g., the story of the Trail of Tears). **HSS.5.3.4**

Explain the influence and achievements of significant leaders of the time (e.g., John Marshall, Andrew Jackson, Chief Tecumseh, Chief Logan, Chief John Ross, Sequoyah). **HSS.5.3.6**

Students pose relevant questions about events they encounter in historical documents, eyewitness accounts, oral histories, letters, diaries, artifacts, photographs, maps, artworks, and architecture. **HAS.HR.2**

(CCSS) Write opinion pieces on topics or texts, supporting a point of view with reasons and information. **CCSS.ELA.W.5.1**

Go *Digital!*

- Students can go online to report their findings. Assess their responses online.

- Students can access the online graphic organizer to capture ideas from their investigation.

Think About It

Students will review their research and determine the effect of Andrew Jackson's opinions about American Indian removal.

- Remind students to review the information they discovered about point of view in their graphic organizer. Direct students back to pages 346–353 of their Research Companion if they need more information.

Write About It

Take a Stand Have students read the prompt. Explain that they will write a speech that opposes Jackson's stand on the Indian Removal Act. Students will write from the point of view of a senator who could vote against the law.

Remind students to include the following elements in their response.

- Include clear, persuasive statements about why the Indian Removal Act is a bad idea.

- Outline Jackson's opinions on the Indian Removal Act.

- Use details from the text to refute Jackson's views.

- Use language that attempts to persuade the reader.

Use the rubric on p. T740 to evaluate students' work.

Talk About It

Defend Your Claim Ask students to work with a partner to compare and contrast their speeches. Encourage students to identify how persuasive both speeches are, and why one may be more effective than the other.

- Explain that they should support their opinions after carefully considering how effective the writer was at persuading the audience.

- They should take turns speaking and avoid interrupting each other.

- Remind students to be respectful of their classmates' opinions and work.

Connect to the Essential Question

Pull It Together Read the prompt aloud to students. Ask them the following guiding questions:

- What was the Indian Removal Act? (The law that ordered the Cherokee and other groups removed from their lands.)

- Upon what principles was the United States founded? (Students may say freedom and justice for all.)

- How is the Indian Removal Act in conflict with those values? (Students may say that it denied freedom and justice for American Indians.)

- What does it say about the spirit of the nation at that time in history? (Responses will vary, but students should support their opinions with text evidence.)

Remind students to use the space provided in their journal to jot down notes.

Report / Your Findings

Think About It

What was the effect of Andrew Jackson's opinions about American Indian removal?

Write About It

Take a Stand

Write and Cite Evidence Imagine you are a senator in Congress in 1830, and you have the opportunity to argue against the Indian Removal Act. Write a speech that defends your opinions about the act and refutes Jackson's views.

Student responses should include a claim against the Indian Removal Act supported by text evidence.

Talk About It

Defend Your Claim

Work with a partner, and compare your speeches. Which of your speeches is the most convincing, and why?

 Connect to the EQ

History

Pull It Together

How is the Indian Removal Act in conflict with the spirit in which the United States was founded? What does the Indian Removal Act reveal about the character of the nation at that time?

Students should make clear connections between the lesson topic and the Essential Question. For example, students should state that the Indian Removal Act contradicts the spirit of equal treatment under the law, on which the United States was founded. It reveals that the government was willing to help one group of people at the expense of the rights of another group.

 Inquiry Project Notes

286 Lesson 2 How Did Westward Expansion Impact American Indians?

Lesson 2 287

Inquiry Journal, pp. 286–287

ENGLISH LEARNERS SCAFFOLD

ELD.PI.5.4 Adapting language choices to various contexts (based on task, purpose, audience, and text type)

Emerging	Expanding	Bridging
Understand Persuasion Explain that students will write a speech in which they try to persuade their audience of the problems with the Indian Removal Act. Encourage students to make persuasive statements orally before putting them in writing to identify what makes a persuasive statement more effective.	**Use Persuasive Language** Remind students that the character from which they are writing has a specific point of view. That point of view is to oppose the Indian Removal Act. Encourage them to think about why their character does not want the Indian Removal Act to pass, using details from the text to support their claims.	**Apply Persuasive Language** Have students write their speeches then say them aloud to a partner or a small group. Encourage students to use emphasis and emotion when appropriate.

See the **Language Learner Teaching Guide** for more language support strategies.

Monitor and Differentiate

REACHING ALL LEARNERS

Approaching Level

Work with students as they write their speeches. Remind them that an effective speech is organized. It presents the speaker's opinion clearly and then supports it with facts and evidence. It also includes emotional appeals when appropriate.

Beyond Level

Encourage students to deliver their speeches to the class, using appropriate pacing, tone of voice, volume, and emphasis. Invite students to ask questions of the speakers. The speakers should defend their responses with text evidence if possible.

Know what your students know!

Lesson Task
Report Your Findings

Use the rubric to evaluate students' responses.

Take a Stand Students imagine they are a senator in Congress in 1830, and they have the opportunity to argue against the Indian Removal Act. They write a speech that defends their opinions about the act and refutes Jackson's views.

Defend Your Claim Students work with a partner to compare speeches and determine which is the most convincing, and why.

Lesson Task Evaluation Rubric

	4	3	2	1
Historical Understanding	Strong understanding of the effect of Andrew Jackson's opinions about American Indian removal	Adequate understanding of the effect of Andrew Jackson's opinions about American Indian removal	Uneven understanding of the effect of Andrew Jackson's opinions about American Indian removal	No understanding of the effect of Andrew Jackson's opinions about American Indian removal
Write a Speech	Provides a strong opinion supported by reasons	Provides an opinion supported by reasons	Somewhat unclear opinion supported by few reasons	No relevant opinion stated or student does not show understanding of the task
Supported by Text Evidence	Reasons clearly supported by evidence	Reasons mostly supported by evidence	Reasons not always supported by evidence	Reasons missing or irrelevant
Defend Your Claim	Carefully and critically compares speeches	Adequately compares speeches	Comparison of speeches lacks thorough critique	Does not compare speeches
	Provides relevant reasons for choice of most convincing speech	Provides some reasons for choice of most convincing speech	Provides few reasons for choice of convincing speech	Provides no relevant reasons during discussion

Lesson Assessment

Go Digital!

- Have students complete the Chapter 8 Lesson 2 Assessment online to monitor their understanding of the lesson content.

California Smarter Balanced Assessment Connections!

Standards Covered	Lesson Task	Lesson Assessment	Alignment with California Smarter Balanced Assessment
History Social Science Content 5.3.4; 5.3.5; 5.3.6	✔	✔	Claim 1 Targets 8, 9, 11
History Social Science Analysis Skills Chronological and Spatial Thinking 5.1; 5.3; 5.4 Research, Evidence, and Point of View 5.1; 5.2 Historical Interpretation 5.1	✔	✔	Claim 1 Targets 8, 9, 11
Writing W.5.1	✔	✔	Claim 2 Target 6a
Research and Inquiry W.5.7		✔	Claim 4 Targets 1, 2
Reading RI.5.8	✔	✔	Claim 1 Target 11 Claim 4 Target 2
Speaking and Listening SL.5.1	✔		Claim 3 Target 3 Claim 4 Target 1

How Did California and Texas Become Part of the United States?

Background Information

In this lesson, students learn about how California and Texas entered the Union. They will also learn about the events of the Mexican-American War and the Gold Rush.

Community Connections

To enrich what students have learned about how California and Texas became states, plan a visit to a museum that focuses on American history.

LESSON STANDARDS

✔ Describe the continued migration of Mexican settlers into Mexican territories of the West and Southwest. **HSS.5.8.5**

✔ Relate how and when California, Texas, Oregon, and other western lands became part of the United States, including the significance of the Texas War for Independence and the Mexican-American War. **HSS.5.8.6**

✔ Students place key events and people of the historical era they are studying in a chronological sequence and within a spatial context; they interpret time lines. **HAS.CS.1**

✔ Students use map and globe skills to determine the absolute locations of places and interpret information available through a map's or globe's legend, scale, and symbolic representations. **HAS.CS.4**

✔ Students identify and interpret the multiple causes and effects of historical events. **HAS.HI.3**

 Connect to the
Essential Question

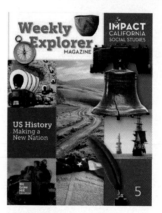

The **Weekly Explorer Magazine** supports the students' exploration of the Essential Question and provides additional resources for the EQ Inquiry Project.

Chapter 8, pp. 100–111

 ## Inquiry Project

Create a Museum Gallery

Remind students to use the information they learn in this lesson and other resources to complete the EQ Inquiry Project.

Dinah Zike's

In this lesson you will use Foldables.

When Minutes Count!

Suggested Lesson Pacing

1 ENGAGE
One Day

- Lesson Opener
- Analyze the Source
- Inquiry Tools

Go Digital
- **iMap:** Railways

2 INVESTIGATE
Two to Three Days

🕐 **Short on Time?** Look for the clock to teach core content in less time.

- Americans in Texas
- The Settlers Rebel
- The Mexican-American War
- **Biography** John C. Frémont
- The Gold Rush
- The Golden State

3 REPORT
One Day

- Take a Stand
- Write and Cite Evidence
- Defend Your Claim

Make Connections!

CCSS CONNECT TO ELA

Reading
Explain the relationships or interactions between two or more individuals, events, ideas, or concepts in a historical, scientific, or technical text based on specific information in the text. **RI.5.3**

Research
Conduct short research projects that use several sources to build knowledge through investigation of different aspects of a topic. **W.5.7**

Recall relevant information from experiences or gather relevant information from print and digital sources; summarize or paraphrase information in notes and finished work, and provide a list of sources. **W.5.8**

Writing
Write informative/explanatory texts to examine a topic and convey ideas and information clearly. **W.5.2**

Speaking and Listening
Engage effectively in a range of collaborative discussions (one-on-one, in groups, and teacher-led) with diverse partners on *grade 5 topics and texts*, building on others' ideas and expressing their own clearly. **SL.5.1**

Classroom Resources
🔍 Search for additional resources using the following key words.

The Alamo

Stephen Austin

John C. Frémont

Gold Rush

Sam Houston

Mexican-American War

Antonio López de Santa Anna

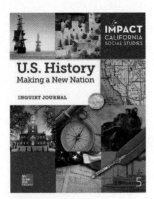

Inquiry Journal,
pp. 288–289

 STANDARDS

Describe the continued migration of Mexican settlers into Mexican territories of the West and Southwest. **HSS.5.8.5**

Relate how and when California, Texas, Oregon, and other western lands became part of the United States, including the significance of the Texas War for Independence and the Mexican-American War. **HSS.5.8.6**

CCSS Engage effectively in a range of collaborative discussions (one-on-one, in groups, and teacher-led) with diverse partners on *grade 5 topics and texts*, building on others' ideas and expressing their own clearly. **CCSS.ELA.SL.5.1**

Go Digital!

Explore the lesson content with online whole-class presentation tools.

- **iMap:** Railways

How Did California and Texas Become Part of the United States?

Bellringer

Prompt students to retrieve information from the previous lessons. Say: *What happened to American Indians as a result of Andrew Jackson's presidency and policies?* (Many American Indians, including the Cherokee and the Seminole, were forcibly removed from their homes and relocated to Indian Territory in present-day Oklahoma.)

Lesson Outcomes

What Am I Learning? Have students read the Lesson Outcomes on p. 288.

Why Am I Learning It? Check that students understand that they will be learning about the conflicts that led to California and Texas joining the United States.

How Will I Know That I Learned It? Ask students the following questions.

- What will you learn about? (the causes and effects of the Mexican War)

- What is the purpose of the task? (to explain how the war affected the United States)

- How will you support your information? (with text evidence)

Talk About It

Provide some scaffolding for students to use as they discuss the picture. Provide background information as needed.

- *The picture shows _____.*

- *The caption suggests that the picture is about _____.*

- *The people I see in the painting include _____.*

- *The people in the painting seem _____.*

Collaborative Conversations

Add New Ideas As students engage in partner, small group, and whole-class discussions, encourage them to

- Stay on topic.

- Connect their own ideas to things their classmates have said.

- Look for ways to add their personal experiences and prior knowledge to the conversation.

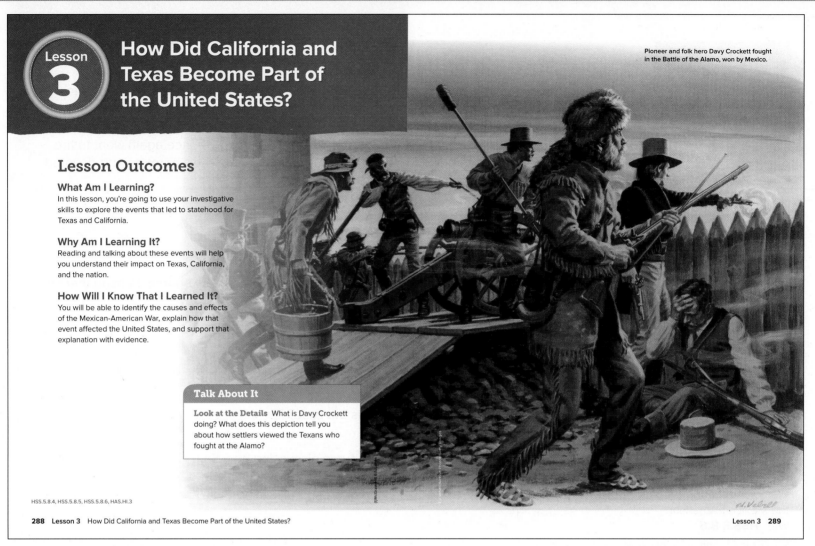

Pioneer and folk hero Davy Crockett fought in the Battle of the Alamo, won by Mexico.

Lesson 3

How Did California and Texas Become Part of the United States?

Lesson Outcomes

What Am I Learning?
In this lesson, you're going to use your investigative skills to explore the events that led to statehood for Texas and California.

Why Am I Learning It?
Reading and talking about these events will help you understand their impact on Texas, California, and the nation.

How Will I Know That I Learned It?
You will be able to identify the causes and effects of the Mexican-American War, explain how that event affected the United States, and support that explanation with evidence.

Talk About It

Look at the Details What is Davy Crockett doing? What does this depiction tell you about how settlers viewed the Texans who fought at the Alamo?

HSS.5.8.4, HSS.5.8.5, HSS.5.8.6, HAS.HI.3

288 Lesson 3 How Did California and Texas Become Part of the United States?

Lesson 3 **289**

Inquiry Journal, pp. 288–289

 ENGLISH LEARNERS SCAFFOLD

ELD.PI.5.6 Reading closely literary and informational texts and viewing multimedia to determine how meaning is conveyed explicitly and implicitly through language

Emerging	Expanding	Bridging
Identify Details Encourage students to identify what they see in the picture. Explain that the Battle of the Alamo was an important moment in the conflict between the United States and Mexico over the southwestern territories. Guide students to state opinions about the picture.	**Describe Details** Have students describe the picture. Guide them to discuss the details of the picture with a partner. Provide moderate support as needed.	**Analyze Details** Encourage students to analyze what they see in the picture. Have students work with a partner. Encourage them to describe how the artist decided to show the people and the event.

See the **Language Learner Teaching Guide** for more language support strategies.

Monitor and Differentiate

REACHING ALL LEARNERS

Approaching Level
Encourage students to view the picture and to discuss it with a partner. Ask students to share what they see, focusing on what the people are doing, and who they notice first.

On Level
Have students discuss the picture. Guide them to discuss what is happening in the scene and why it is important.

Beyond Level
Guide students to conduct further research into the Battle of the Alamo. Students may choose to research the people who participated in the battle, the events of the siege itself, or how the events went on to influence Mexican-American relations for the next few years. Have students share their findings with the whole class.

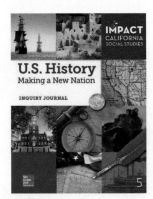

Inquiry Journal,
pp. 290–291

Describe the continued migration of Mexican settlers into Mexican territories of the West and Southwest. **HSS.5.8.5**

Relate how and when California, Texas, Oregon, and other western lands became part of the United States, including the significance of the Texas War for Independence and the Mexican-American War. **HSS.5.8.6**

Students identify and interpret the multiple causes and effects of historical events. **HAS.HI.3**

CCSS Explain the relationships or interactions between two or more individuals, events, ideas, or concepts in a historical, scientific, or technical text based on specific information in the text. **CCSS.ELA.RI.5.3**

Go *Digital!*

Model how to inspect and find evidence with online whole-class presentation tools.

Build Background

Sam Houston When he was a teenager living in Tennessee, Sam Houston decided to run away from home. He fled to a nearby Cherokee settlement. The group took him in, and he lived there for several years. Years later when his first marriage crumbled, Houston—already a former governor Tennessee by now—once again went to the Cherokee for refuge. He became an official member of the Cherokee and devoted his time to advocating for the group in Washington.

1 Inspect

Read Ask students to read the text and analyze the primary source. Remind them to circle words and phrases that are unfamiliar.

- What is Sam Houston writing to Andrew Jackson? (that Texas should become part of the United States)

- In Houston's opinion, which side would benefit more—Texas or the United States? (Houston says the United States would benefit more.)

- Why does Houston believe this is the case? (He believes that Texas will be instrumental in helping the United States win wars.)

Collaborate Have partners take turns discussing how Sam Houston makes his main ideas seem convincing or powerful. (Responses will vary. Students should identify language that asserts Houston's argument, such as "it is indispensably necessary to the United States.")

2 Find Evidence

Reread Have students reread the primary source.

Analyze the Primary Source Reread the primary source with students, guiding them to read for vivid details that help them understand Houston's argument. Provide support for vocabulary as needed.

- Ask: What examples do you see that Sam Houston strongly believes what he is saying? (Responses will vary, but students may identify examples such as "I am determined,""indispensably necessary to the United States,""the United States cannot exist without great hazard to the security of their institutions exist without Texas.")

- What do you know about the events of the history of Texas that support Houston's claims? (Responses will vary, but students may say that Texas achieved its own independence from Mexico, or that because of its geographical placement, it acts as a barrier between the U.S. and Mexico.)

3 Make Connections

Talk Guide students to discuss why Houston feels so strongly that Texas should join the Union. Encourage them to think of what the United States would gain if Texas were part of it. (Responses will vary; students may identify that the United States needs a strong border with a nation that had attempted to go to war before, and Texas might provide a good buffer.)

Connect to Now Have partners discuss what Texas adds to the United States.

Analyze the Source

1 Inspect

Read Scan the excerpt from Sam Houston's letter. What is Houston's main idea?

- **Circle** repeated phrases.
- **Underline** words that change within those phrases.
- **Discuss** with a partner how Houston's phrasing makes his ideas sound more convincing or powerful.

My Notes

_____

_____

_____

_____

_____

_____

_____

_____

_____

_____

_____

_____

Sam Houston's Letter to Andrew Jackson

General Sam Houston won the Battle at San Jacinto, and Houston was praised as a hero. His victory after the loss at the Alamo helped form Texas's identity as a unified state. With Texas's independence from Mexico secured, he was elected as president of the brand-new Republic of Texas.

Houston held the office from 1836 to 1838 and again from 1841 to 1844. During his second term, Houston also played a key role in finally securing statehood for Texas in 1845. He wrote to many U.S. leaders, including former president Andrew Jackson, arguing that Texas should be annexed, or added, to the United States. Once Texas became a state, he became one of the state's first United States senators.

Sam Houston

The Miriam and Ira D. Wallach Division of Art, Prints and Photographs: Print Collection, Emmet Collection of Manuscripts Etc. Relating to American History. The New York Public Library

PRIMARY SOURCE

In Their Words... Sam Houston

So far as I am concerned, or my hearty cooperation required, I am determined upon immediate annexation to the United States.

It is not the result of feeling, nor can I believe that the measure would be as advantageous to Texas, as it is indispensably necessary to the United States. Texas, with peace, could exist without the United States, but the United States cannot without great hazard to the security of their institutions exist without Texas. The United States are one of the rival powers of earth, and from their importance, as well as the peculiarity of their institutions and the extent of their commercial relations, they must expect, at no distant day, wars, the object of which will be to prevent their continuance, if possible, as a nation.

—from a letter to Andrew Jackson, February 16, 1844

TEXT: Sam Houston to Andrew Jackson, Washington, TX, 16 February 1844. In Life and Select Literary Remains of Sam Houston of Texas, by William Carey Crane. Philadelphia: J.B. Lippincott Company, 1884.; PHOTO: McGraw-Hill Education

2 Find Evidence

Reread Identify what Houston wants to do. Why does he feel so strongly about his goal? Reread the claim Houston makes in this letter. What events in history support the idea that Texas can exist without the United States?

3 Make Connections

Talk Discuss with a partner why Sam Houston felt so strongly about Texas. How might adding Texas to the Union strengthen the United States? **COLLABORATE**

Connect to Now How does the inclusion of Texas in the United States make the United States stronger today?

Inquiry Journal, pp. 290–291

EL ENGLISH LEARNERS SCAFFOLD

ELD.PI.5.6 Reading closely literary and informational texts and viewing multimedia to determine how meaning is conveyed explicitly and implicitly through language

Emerging

Discuss Details Encourage students to unpack Houston's language as you read the primary source aloud. After reading once, reread. Stop to clarify language and references as needed.

Expanding/Bridging

Use Details Guide students to consider Houston's argument. Encourage them to identify specific words and phrases that show his opinion. Remind students to use context clues to identify the meanings of unfamiliar words and phrases. Provide light to moderate support as needed.

See the **Language Learner Teaching Guide** for more language support strategies.

Monitor and Differentiate

REACHING ALL LEARNERS

Approaching Level

Have students read the text to identify Sam Houston's claim. Then have them look for the reasons and evidence he supplies to support that claim. Encourage students to identify how Houston's text structure could apply to a persuasive or opinion text that students write.

Beyond Level

Encourage students to conduct additional research into Sam Houston's life to better understand his point of view. Students may research his time living with the Cherokee, his time as governor of Tennessee, or the reasons that drove him to become involved with Texas politics. Have them share their findings with the whole class.

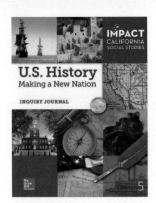

Inquiry Journal,
pp. 292–293

 STANDARDS

Relate how and when California, Texas, Oregon, and other western lands became part of the United States, including the significance of the Texas War for Independence and the Mexican-American War. **HSS.5.8.6**

Students identify and interpret the multiple causes and effects of historical events. **HAS.HI.3**

Go Digital!

- Model how to explore and investigate with online whole-class tools.

- Students can access the online graphic organizer to use the inquiry tools as they read.

Explore Cause and Effect

Explain Tell students that an effect is something that happens. Effects are results of causes. In history, causes usually have multiple effects. Effects can also have multiple causes.

Read Have students read aloud the step-by-step instructions about how to determine causes and effects. Tell students that they should ask themselves questions such as *What happened?* and *Why did it happen?* They should also look for key details that signal important information.

Guide Practice Present a brief model of analyzing cause and effect. Say: *Sam Houston wanted Texas to become part of the United States. Then Texas* did *become part of the United States. That happened in part because of Sam Houston's work, so his work was one of many causes for which statehood was the effect.*

Investigate!

Have students read pages 354–363 in the Research Companion. Tell them the information that will help them answer the lesson question ***How Did California and Texas Become Part of the United States?***

Take Notes Tell students that they will take notes as they read each section. Explain that taking notes will help them understand key events that led to California and Texas joining the United States. Remind students that they should look for key details and important information in the text.

Inspect Guide students to read the text in each section to determine what it says. Encourage them to work to find information how California and Texas became states.

Find Evidence Encourage students to reread the text to develop a deeper understanding. Remind students that they should think about how the facts and details will help them answer the lesson question.

Collaborative Conversations

Text-Based Discussion Remind students that discussing the text with others can help them

- Enjoy what they read
- Appreciate someone else's point of view
- Better understand cause-and-effect relationships.

Inquiry Tools

Examine Cause and Effect

As you read, identifying the relationship between historical events will help you understand how and why the events happened.

1. **Read the text once all the way through.**
   This will help you understand the main ideas.

2. **Identify key events.**
   As you read, think about which events seem to be related.

3. **Look for signal words and phrases.**
   Words and phrases such as *because, consequently, thus,* and *as a result* show a cause-and-effect relationship.

4. **Examine cause and effect.**
   Remember that a **cause** is an event or action that makes something happen. An **effect** is what happens as a result of that cause. Many events in history happen as a direct result of other events.

COLLABORATE Based on the text you have just read, work with your class to complete the chart below.

Cause	→	Effect
Texas President Sam Houston argued for Texas to be annexed to the United States.	→	Texas became a state.

Investigate!

Read pages 354–363 in your Research Companion. Use your investigative skills to identify key events that led to statehood for Texas and California. Use the chart to organize information.

Cause	→	Effect
The Mexican government offered land to U.S. citizens at low cost.	→	Many Americans moved to Texas.
The Americans won the Battle of San Jacinto.	→	The people of Texas voted to join the United States.
The U.S. and Mexican governments disagreed over the border between the two countries.	→	The two countries fought the Mexican War. When the United States won, the territory that became California joined the Union.

McGraw-Hill Education

Inquiry Journal, pp. 292–293

(EL) ENGLISH LEARNERS SCAFFOLD

ELD.PI.5.1 Exchanging information and ideas with others through oral collaborative discussions on a range of social and academic topics

Emerging

Choose Details Work with students to carefully choose details from the text that help them understand how California and Texas became states. Help them separate important and unimportant details.

Expanding/Bridging

Use Text Evidence Encourage students to quote directly from the text as they fill out the graphic organizer. They can use these notes and quotes later when they write their article about the Mexican-American War. Provide assistance in how to cite directly from the text, using quotation marks and page references.

See the **Language Learner Teaching Guide** for more language support strategies.

Monitor and Differentiate

REACHING ALL LEARNERS

Special Needs

Encourage students to work together to discuss the text. Have them read sections of the text aloud in small groups. Then have them discuss what they read and work as a group to identify the main ideas and key details. Then have students talk about the relationships between causes and effects. Remind them that important and complex events such as statehood will likely have more than one cause and more than one effect.

Approaching Level

Encourage students to first skim sections of the text to find key details, such as places, people's names, and dates. Then guide them to reread the section looking for important details.

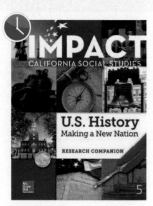

Research Companion,
pp. 354–355

Describe the continued migration of Mexican settlers into Mexican territories of the West and Southwest. **HSS.5.8.5**

Students place key events and people of the historical era they are studying in a chronological sequence and within a spatial context; they interpret time lines. **HAS.CS.1**

Go Digital!

Investigate the lesson content with online whole-class presentation tools.

• **iMap:** Railways

Background

Mexican Independence Antonio López de Santa Anna would become a staple of Mexican history over the next few decades, but in 1824, he was a young general in the newly independent Mexican Empire. Santa Anna and his compatriots decided that the empire should become a republic instead. They overthrew the new emperor, Agustín I, and declared that the republic was born.

| TIMELINE | Invite students to look at the timeline on the top of p. 355.

Analyze How long did it take between Mexican independence and Texas joining the Union? (24 years) **HAS.CS.1**

Analyze the Source

Inspect Have students read pp. 354–355.

Find Evidence Use the questions below to check comprehension. Remind students to support their answers with text evidence.

Identify How far north did Mexico reach in the 1820s? (all the way up through California) **DOK 1**

Explain Why did the Mexican government plan to offer land in Mexico to U.S. citizens? (to encourage more people to settle there) **DOK 2**

Cite Evidence What did settlers have to do in order to live in Mexico? (They had to become Mexican citizens, convert to Catholicism, and follow Mexican laws.) **DOK 3**

Understand Cause and Effect Why were there 2,000 slaves living in Mexico by 1835? (Settlers brought slaves with them, even though slavery was illegal in Mexico.) **DOK 3**

Analyze the Image Explain to students that analyzing a photograph of a historical site helps them to understand what people who lived during a historical event might have experienced.

Connect to Now What does the picture show? (The Alamo)

Analyze Cause and Effect Why is the Alamo important? (There was an important battle there, and today, it is the most visited historical landmark in Texas.) **DOK 3**

Make Connections

Justify If you were a settler, would you have wanted to move to Texas, despite the Mexican government's rules? Use details from the text to support your response. (Responses will vary, but students may say that moving to a new place that was basically uninhabited seems like a great adventure, even if it meant making some sacrifices.) **DOK 3**

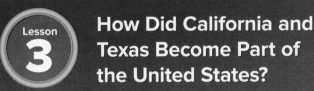

Lesson
3

How Did California and Texas Become Part of the United States?

Timeline

1821 Mexico wins independence from Spain.

1836 The Republic of Texas declares independence from Mexico.

1846–1847 Mexican-American War

1845 Texas joins the Union.

1848 The Treaty of Guadalupe Hidalgo is signed.

1850 California becomes a state.

| | | | | |
| 1820 | 1830 | 1840 | 1850 | |

1848–1849 The Gold Rush begins.

Americans in Texas

In 1821, Mexico won its independence from Spain. At that time, Mexico was a much larger country than it is today. Mexican **territories** also included land that stretches from present-day Texas to California. Despite covering a large land area, the northern provinces of Mexico had small populations. In the early 1820s, for example, there were only about 2,500 Mexicans living throughout Texas.

The Mexican government came up with a plan to draw new groups of settlers to the area. It offered land to U.S. citizens almost free of charge, but there were some conditions. The new residents had to become Mexican citizens, and they had to convert to Catholicism, which was the main religion of Mexico. They also had to follow laws that made slavery illegal in Mexico and its territories.

Because of this plan, Americans began to move to Texas. Among them were Moses Austin and his son Stephen. In 1821, Moses Austin received almost 18,000 acres of land from the Mexican government to sell to other Americans. By 1835, more than 25,000 Americans had moved to Texas, including about 2,000 people who were enslaved, despite Mexican law.

Today, the Alamo is the most visited historical landmark in the state of Texas.

HSS.5.8.5, HSS.5.8.6, HAS.CS.4, HAS.HI.3, EEI.PV

354 Lesson 3 How Did California and Texas Become Part of the United States?

Lesson 3 **355**

Research Companion, pp. 354–355

(EL) ENGLISH LEARNERS SCAFFOLD

ELD.PI.5.3 Offering and supporting opinions and negotiating with others in communicative exchanges ☐

Emerging

State Opinions Work with students to state opinions about whether they would want to travel to a new territory if the government gave them land there.

I would have moved to Mexico because _____.

I would not have moved to Mexico because _____.

I think it would be _____ to have my own ranch or farm because _____.

Expanding/Bridging

Support Opinions Have students refer to or cite evidence from the text to support their opinions about whether they would want to travel to a new territory if the government gave them land there. Encourage students to defend their opinions by evaluating their group members' use of evidence.

I agree with that because _____.

That's interesting, but have you thought about _____?

See the **Language Learner Teaching Guide** for more language support strategies.

Monitor and Differentiate

REACHING ALL LEARNERS

Approaching Level

Have students work together to understand the events that led more and more Americans to settle in Mexico in the 1820s and 1830s. Encourage them to identify and make note of key details in this process. Then have them discuss as a group why the effects of this mass migration might cause problems for the Mexican government in the future.

Beyond Level

Have students conduct additional research into the numbers of people who moved to Texas in the 1820s and 1830s. Encourage students to search for primary sources from American settlers or native Mexicans. Have students share their findings with the class.

Research Companion,
pp. 356–357

 STANDARDS

Describe the continued migration of Mexican settlers into Mexican territories of the West and Southwest. **HSS.5.8.5**

Relate how and when California, Texas, Oregon, and other western lands became part of the United States, including the significance of the Texas War for Independence and the Mexican-American War. **HSS.5.8.6**

___

Go Digital!

Investigate the lesson content with online whole-class presentation tools.

Background Information

The Alamo Built as the chapel of the Spanish Mission San Antonio de Valero, the Alamo was used off and on by Spanish troops for years before the famous battle there. Franciscan missionaries built the mission complex in the early 1700s, but the other buildings were abandoned and fell into disrepair.

Analyze the Source

Inspect Have students read pp. 356–357.

Find Evidence Use the questions below to check comprehension. Remind students to support their answers with text evidence.

Identify Why did settlers rebel against Mexico? (They didn't want to agree to convert to Catholicism, become Mexican citizens, or agree to not own slaves.) **DOK 1**

Summarize What happened when settlers took over the Alamo in San Antonio? (They held the fort for several months, through Texas' declaration of independence from Mexico. Four days after Texas declared independence, Santa Anna attacked, killing all the Americans.) **DOK 2**

Analyze Cause and Effect What events led to the Battle of San Jacinto? (It was a major consequence of Santa Anna's actions at the Alamo.)

Analyze Cause and Effect What happened as a result of the battle? (After the Americans won, Texas voted to join the United States.) **DOK 3**

Identify Sequence of Events When did Texas actually get to join the Union? (1845) **DOK 2**

Then and Now How is the modern Texas flag a result of the original flag of the Lone Star Republic? (It borrowed elements such as a star on a blue field.) **DOK 1**

Identify What caused more disputes between the United States and Mexico after Texas joined the Union? (The United States and Mexico didn't agree on where the border between the United States and Texas should be.) **DOK 1**

Explain What event started the Mexican-American War? (The United States marched through Texas to the Rio Grande River. This was 130 miles into what Mexico considered to be its territory.) **DOK 2**

Make Connections

Analyze Cause and Effect What caused the United States to claim California as part of the Union? (Citizens in California were loyal to the United States and declared it to be the known as the Bear Flag Republic. The United States supported this move, claiming California for its own.) **DOK 3**

The Settlers Rebel

Many Americans resisted Mexico's conditions. They did not want to become Mexican citizens or convert to Catholicism. They also complained about Mexican laws, especially those regarding slavery.

In December 1835, 500 Texans, including Stephen Austin, attacked San Antonio. They took control of the Alamo, a Spanish mission that the Mexican Army had turned into a fort. On March 2, 1836, Texas declared its independence. Four days later, Mexican General Antonio López de Santa Anna recaptured the Alamo, killing every American inside. Consequently, Texas General Sam Houston attacked a large Mexican force at San Jacinto a month later. The battle cry "Remember the Alamo!" inspired Texas troops, who defeated Santa Anna in less than 20 minutes.

Texans voted to join the United States. They adopted a constitution and legalized slavery. The U.S. government did not want to admit a slave state and feared war with Mexico, so it did not let Texas join the Union in 1835. Texas became an independent country, the Republic of Texas. Its flag had a single star, so it was also known as the Lone Star **Republic**.

Then and Now

The first official flag of the Republic of Texas

The current state flag of Texas

The current state flag of Texas was not always the official flag. In addition to the first official flag, shown above, another design was recognized by the Congress of Texas. That flag had a blue star along with thirteen red and white stripes. In time, the elements of these flags were combined to create the state flag that Texas flies today.

The Mexican-American War

The Lone Star Republic came to an end in 1845. American ideas about Texas had changed. U.S. President James K. Polk did not fear a war with Mexico. Congress voted to accept Texas into the Union. Along with statehood came a disagreement over Texas's **boundaries**. The United States believed the Rio Grande was the border between Texas and Mexico, but Mexico claimed it was the Nueces River, 130 miles to the north. President Polk's interest in California and other Mexican territories

The Battle of Resaca de la Palma in Texas during the Mexican-American War

also caused tension. He tried to buy the land for $30 million, but his offer was rejected. In 1846, Polk ordered General Zachary Taylor to march through Texas to the Rio Grande. As a result, fighting broke out between the U.S. and Mexican armies, and Congress declared war on Mexico.

Meanwhile, few Americans living in California were loyal to Mexico. In 1846, a group including John C. Frémont raised a flag with a bear on it and declared the area to be a free republic. The republic lasted only a month. When Polk heard about the Bear Flag Republic, he sent troops to claim California for the United States.

Research Companion, pp. 356–357

(EL) ENGLISH LEARNERS SCAFFOLD

ELD.PI.5.6 Reading closely literary and informational texts and viewing multimedia to determine how meaning is conveyed explicitly and implicitly through language

Emerging	Expanding/Bridging
Identify Details Work with students as they read the section about the Mexican-American War. Encourage them to underline key details that help them understand the major players, and the causes and effects of the war.	**Analyze Cause and Effect** Have students analyze the relationships between the causes and effects of the Mexican-American War. Encourage students to discuss these relationships with a partner. Provide sentence frames as needed:

In 1845, _____ happened.

Then, the United States _____, while Mexico _____.

Then, the United States _____.

I can infer that the Mexican-American War was mainly about _____.

See the **Language Learner Teaching Guide** for more language support strategies.

Monitor and Differentiate

REACHING ALL LEARNERS

Approaching Level

Work with students to understand reasons the settlers rebelled and the reasons the United States did not want to admit Texas into the Union. Clarify the meaning of terms such as "independence," "border," and "republic" as necessary.

Beyond Level

Encourage students to conduct additional research into the Lone Star Republic. What advantages would they have if they joined the United States? What advantages would they have if they maintained their independence?

Research Companion,
pp. 358–359

Relate how and when California, Texas, Oregon, and other western lands became part of the United States, including the significance of the Texas War for Independence and the Mexican-American War. **HSS.5.8.6**

Students use map and globe skills to determine the absolute locations of places and interpret information available through a map's or globe's legend, scale, and symbolic representations. **HAS.CS.4**

Go Digital!

Investigate the lesson content with online whole-class presentation tools.

Analyze the Source

Inspect Have students continue reading about the Mexican-American War on pp. 358–359.

Find Evidence Use the questions below to check comprehension. Remind students to support their answers with text evidence.

Identify What was the Treaty of Guadalupe Hidalgo? (The agreement that ended the Mexican-American War.) **DOK 1**

Describe What did each side agree to in the Treaty of Guadalupe Hidalgo? (Mexico would sell 320 million acres of land to the United States for $15 million, and the Rio Grande would become the border between the two countries.) **DOK 1**

Biography Encourage students to read and analyze the events outlined in the biography of John C. Frémont.

Identify What was John C. Frémont's original job with the U.S. government? (He was supposed to lead an expedition to map the Mississippi and Missouri Rivers.) **DOK 1**

Explain What did Frémont do once he got to California? (He joined the U.S. side in the Mexican-American War, and established the Bear Flag Republic of California.) **DOK 2**

Map Skills

Encourage students to analyze the map on p. 358. Guide them to analyze how the western United States grew as a result of war, purchases, and gifts.

Use a Map Scale Explain that students can use a straight object, such as a pencil, to help them compare the distance on the scale to distances on the map. Ask them to determine how many square miles or square kilometers of land the United States received in 1845, 1848, and 1853. Remind them that the formula to measure area is: length x width = square miles (mi²) or square kilometers (km²) (1845: approx. 300,000 mi² (480,000 km²); 1848: approx. 500,000 mi² (800,000 km²); 1853: approx. 50,000 mi² (80,000 km²)) **DOK 3**

Summarize What was the significance of the Treaty of Guadalupe Hidalgo? (The mainland United States as we know it today had taken shape.) **DOK 3**

Make Connections

Justify Do you think the Mexican-American War was worth fighting? Why or Why not? Use text evidence to justify your response. (Responses will vary.) **DOK 3**

Stop and Check

Think Encourage students to consider what led to the Mexican-American War. (Students should consider social, economic, political, and geographical reasons that the United States and Mexico fought.)

Talk Have students analyze Frémont's interests in western land throughout his life. (Responses will vary, but students may say that surveying rivers in the West gave him a deep appreciation for life there.)

WHAT DO YOU THINK?

Encourage students to use text evidence from the whole lesson as they respond to the prompt.

In 1847, U.S. troops attacked Mexico City, the Mexican capital. The Mexican government agreed to end the war. Both nations signed the Treaty of Guadalupe Hidalgo in 1848. According to the terms of the treaty, Mexico would sell a total of 320 million acres of land—55 percent of its territory—to the United States for $15 million. As a result, the Rio Grande was recognized as Texas's southern border. The future states of California, Nevada, and Utah, and parts of Arizona, New Mexico, Colorado, and Wyoming were also part of the deal.

Annexed in 1845

Mexican land awarded to the U.S. under the Treaty of Guadalupe Hidalgo, 1848

Gadsden Purchase, 1853

— Present-day boundary

0   150   300 miles
0   150   300 kilometers

Land Acquired from Mexico, 1845–1853

Map Skills Working with a partner, use the information in the map to determine how the United States changed from 1845 to 1853. Use the scale to determine how much land the United States took over in 1845, 1848, and 1853.

✓ Stop and Check

Talk What factors contributed to the Mexican-American War?

Find Details As you read, add additional information to the graphic organizer on page 293 in you Inquiry Journal.

What Do You Think? Of the many factors that led to the war, which do you think had the biggest impact? Why?

358   Lesson 3   How Did California and Texas Become Part of the United States?

John C. Frémont

Born in Savannah, Georgia, in 1813, John C. Frémont spent many years exploring the United States. In 1838, the U.S. Secretary of War chose Frémont to assist Joseph Nicolas Nicollet, a French scientist, on a three-year mission to **survey** and map the Mississippi and Missouri Rivers. From there, Frémont went on to explore much of the land between the Mississippi River and the Pacific Ocean.

In 1843, Frémont traveled through the least-known parts of the American West. His route covered the present-day states of Oregon, Idaho, Wyoming, Colorado, Utah, Nevada, and California. His reports on what he saw in these areas led many Americans to move westward.

When the Mexican-American War began, Frémont joined a group of Americans near Sonoma in Mexico's California Territory. The group created the Bear Flag Republic. Then Frémont was made a major in the U.S. Army and fought to seize California for the United States.

After the war, Frémont served as governor of California for two months before moving to Washington, D.C., but he returned to his home on the West Coast in time for the Gold Rush. Gold was found on his property, and he soon became a multimillionaire. He also was elected one of the state's first senators in 1850, and he was nominated as the first Republican candidate for the presidency in 1856. He lost to James Buchanan.

John C. Frémont in about 1850

✓ Stop and Check

Talk How do you think Frémont's early years surveying rivers influenced his later life?

Lesson 3   359

Research Companion, pp. 358-359

ENGLISH LEARNERS SCAFFOLD

ELD.PI.5.6 Reading closely literary and informational texts and viewing multimedia to determine how meaning is conveyed explicitly and implicitly through language

Emerging

Use the Map Guide students to understand the Map's key. Encourage them to identify the areas that the key indicates, such as the area that illustrates the land gained by the annexation of Texas in 1845, the land won in the Treaty of Guadalupe Hidalgo, and the remaining land bought by the Gadsden Purchase. Guide students to discuss how each addition changed the shape and makeup of the United States.

Expanding/Bridging

Analyze the Map Encourage students to consider the events that they read about that led to each addition to the territory of the United States. Guide students to use the map when discussing the events of the Mexican-American War in small groups. Provide support as needed.

See the **Language Learner Teaching Guide** for more language support strategies.

Monitor and Differentiate

REACHING ALL LEARNERS

Special Needs

Work with students to describe what they see in the map. Model using the key to analyze the map, then have students work together to share ideas about how a map can help them visualize what they read in a text. Guide them to participate in a discussion about the importance of the Mexican-American War, using the map to organize their thoughts.

Beyond Level

Guide students to conduct further research into the Treaty of Guadalupe Hidalgo or another significant event of the Mexican-American War. Have students share their findings with the entire class.

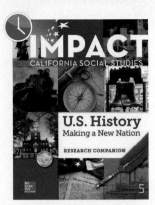

Research Companion,
pp. 360–361

 STANDARDS

Relate how and when California, Texas, Oregon, and other western lands became part of the United States, including the significance of the Texas War for Independence and the Mexican-American War. **HSS.5.8.6**

Go Digital!

Investigate the lesson content with online whole-class presentation tools.

Background

Sutter's Mill was a sawmill owned by John Sutter. It was his carpenter, James Marshall, who first found gold on Sutter's property. The two agreed to become partners. Sutter, however, did not benefit much from the Gold Rush. In fact, so many men wanted to search for gold that no one was left to help run his sawmill. The mill soon closed, as did his tannery and other business ventures. Sutter's career and life were left in ruins.

Analyze the Source

Inspect Have students read The Gold Rush on pp. 360–361.

Find Evidence Use the questions below to check comprehension. Remind students to support their answers with text evidence.

Identify What started the Gold Rush? (James Marshall found gold at Sutter's Mill in California.) **DOK 1**

Explain What happened quickly after the discovery of gold? (Thousands of miners arrived in California, hoping to strike it rich.) **DOK 2**

Infer How did women often benefit more from the Gold Rush than the men? (Women set up businesses and livelihoods that supported them better than the men who worked hard at trying to pan or mine for gold and often found nothing.) **DOK 3**

Summarize Who came to try to make a new life in California? (People from the United States, China, Australia, Latin America, and Europe.) **DOK 3**

Describe How was living in Gold Rush-Era California difficult for many groups of people? (African Americans and Chinese people were often discriminated against, sometimes in everyday life, and sometimes in public life.) **DOK 3**

Make Connections

Draw Conclusions How did the hope of making money outweigh the difficulties of camp life in Gold Rush-Era California? Use text evidence to support your conclusions. (Responses will vary, but students may identify that the American spirit, or trying to live life to the fullest, led people to venture to new places and overcome difficult obstacles.) **DOK 3**

The Gold Rush

The Mexican-American War was not the only major event that transformed California and the United States in the 1840s and 1850s. In January 1848, a worker named James Marshall saw something glittering in the water at Sutter's Mill, a sawmill near Sacramento in the California Territory. It was gold. As news of his find spread by the end of 1848, about 6,000 miners soon flooded the area. The Gold Rush had begun.

Prospecting, or searching for gold, was time-consuming, but all it required was a few tools and dedication. Thousands of people swarmed the West Coast in the following year. By May 1849, more than 10,000 wagons had crossed the Missouri River heading for California. That year, a total of 80,000 people came from all over the world to seek a fortune. They were known as forty-niners, a term that reflected the year of their journey to the American West. The majority of the fortune hunters were young, unmarried men. There were also some women among the forty-niners, however. Many sought to benefit from the Gold Rush in a different way. Instead of joining miners at the edges of rivers and streams, they made money by cooking, cleaning houses, running boardinghouses and taverns, and washing laundry.

Miners used flat, shallow dishes to pan for gold.

Americans were not the only ones who traveled to California seeking gold. A quarter of the forty-niners came from places outside of the United States, including China, Latin America, Australia, and Europe. Journeys to California could take between three and six months. Travelers coming from Europe or the East Coast of the United States could sail around South America. They could also dock in Panama, cross the thin strip of land, and sail to California from the other side. Forty-niners coming from Asia faced a lengthy sea voyage. Those who chose to make the trip on land made a difficult, dangerous, and emotionally challenging journey. One traveler wrote, "The trip is a sort of magic mirror and exposes every man's qualities of heart connected with it, vicious or amiable."

Despite the difficulty and length of the journey, about 100,000 people made their way to California. Among them there were about 2,000 African Americans and 20,000 Chinese. For these groups, getting to California was only part of the challenge. Discrimination was common against nonwhite people in California. California Indians, Chinese, Latin Americans, and African Americans were often prevented from staking claims on land. In 1850, the state of California passed a law that made it illegal for nonwhite people to speak under oath in court cases involving white people. The law remained in place until 1872.

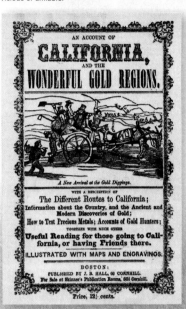

"Gold fever" drew people to California.

360 **Lesson 3** How Did California and Texas Become Part of the United States?

Lesson 3 **361**

Research Companion, pp. 360–361

ENGLISH LEARNERS SCAFFOLD

ELD.PI.5.3 Offering and supporting opinions and negotiating with others in communicative exchanges

Emerging	Expanding/Bridging
State an Opinion Encourage students to state an opinion about whether they would have liked to be a forty-niner. Guide them to refer to the text in their discussions. Provide substantial support as needed.	**Defend an Opinion** Encourage students to reread the section on the Gold Rush. Guide them to cite evidence from the text as they state an opinion about whether they would have wanted to be a forty-niner.

See the **Language Learner Teaching Guide** for more language support strategies.

Monitor and Differentiate

REACHING ALL LEARNERS

Approaching Level

Guide students to identify unfamiliar words and phrases in the section about the Gold Rush. Encourage them to use word parts to determine the meaning of each word. Have students use a dictionary to confirm their definitions.

Beyond Level

Guide students to conduct further research into the occupations people had during the Gold Rush. Invite students to share their findings with the entire class.

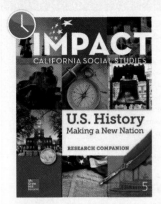

Research Companion,
pp. 362–363

 STANDARDS

Relate how and when California, Texas, Oregon, and other western lands became part of the United States, including the significance of the Texas War for Independence and the Mexican-American War. **HSS.5.8.6**

Go Digital!

Investigate the lesson content with online whole-class presentation tools.

Background

Californios were people of Spanish and Mexican descent who lived in the area that became California. When the Spanish missions were dissolved, much of the land was divided up between land-owning Californio families. Other Californios worked on those ranches.

Analyze the Source

Inspect Have students read pp. 362–363.

Find Evidence Use the questions below to check comprehension. Remind students to support their answers with text evidence.

Identify How did people find gold at the beginning of the Gold Rush? (by panning for it in rivers or streams) **DOK 1**

Explain What did a forty-niner have to do to pan for gold? (wash dirt through a strainer to find the gold nuggets) **DOK 2**

Analyze Cause and Effect Why did people soon have to resort to using mining equipment to find gold? (All the gold that was easy to find was found quickly. Then people had to mine into the earth to find more.) **DOK 3**

Explain How was California's constitution created? (A group of delegates was elected to draft it. The group included people who had moved to California during the Gold Rush as well as Spanish Mexicans who had lived in the area for years.) **DOK 2**

Analyze Cause and Effect Why was it important that California entered the Union as a free state? (It could have overthrown the balance between slave and free states. The Compromise of 1850 solved the problem by allowing California in as a free state, while giving Utah and New Mexico the choice of being slave or free.) **DOK 3**

Make Connections

Draw Conclusions If not the actual forty-niners, who benefited from the Gold Rush? Use text evidence in your response. (The city of San Francisco grew, and California's population got so big that it was able to apply to become a state. Women also benefited because they had a chance to own property and have professions.) **DOK 3**

✓ Stop and Check PRODUCTIVE

Think In their discussions, encourage students to consider how the West Coast would be different today if someone hadn't discovered gold and begun a mass migration to California. (Students may say that the population of the West Coast would not be as large as it is today.)

Perspectives Have students think back to what they have learned about the ways that white settlers treated American Indians. Then have them compare that to the details about the role Californios played in creating the government of the state of California. (Responses may include that white settlers initially involved the Californios in government, but eventually took their land just as they had taken the American Indians' land.)

At first, mining for gold was simple. All a miner had to do was pan for it. That meant uncovering gold nuggets by washing dirt in a flat, shallow strainer. By 1853, however, most of the easy-to-find gold had already been collected. Miners formed companies to pay for machinery that could be used to dig deeper. With hydraulic mining, companies used powerful streams of water to blast gold-bearing gravel directly from the sides of mountains. However, hydraulic mining was very hard on the land. It washed away millions of tons of soil, destroying thousands of acres of land in California.

Nonetheless, California thrived during the Gold Rush. In particular, the city of San Francisco benefited from the steady stream of travelers. Located along the Pacific Ocean, San Francisco's harbor helped the city become the center of trade for the region. The people of San Francisco made money by feeding, clothing, housing, supplying, and entertaining the miners who settled in the city.

Stop and Check

Talk How did the discovery of gold in California change the nation?

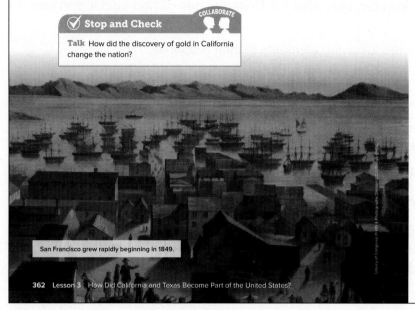
San Francisco grew rapidly beginning in 1849.

362 Lesson 3 How Did California and Texas Become Part of the United States?

The Golden State

Due to the Gold Rush, California's population boomed. By 1849, California had enough people to form a state. Californians wanted the benefits of government services, including a court system, land and water laws, and mail delivery. A group of delegates formed to draft a state constitution. It was made up of men who had moved to California during the Gold Rush as well as eight Californios, or people of Mexican or Spanish descent who had lived on the land since the time it had been a Mexican territory. The constitution they drafted gave the vote to white males only, whom it defined as including Latinos, but it allowed married women to hold property. It also outlawed slavery.

Congress was hesitant to admit California to the Union. The Senate was equally divided between slave states and free states. Senators from slave states did not want to give free states more power in Congress. The Compromise of 1850 solved this problem. California would enter the Union as a free state, and in return, the territories of Utah and New Mexico could decide whether or not to allow slavery.

When California became the thirty-first state, less than one percent of the population was made up of Californios. Even though Californios had lived in California for generations, most Americans treated them as if they had no right to the land. Settlers moved onto Californios' ranches without permission and used the courts to make unfair claims on their property.

Although the Bear Flag Republic did not last, a bear still appears on the California state flag.

Stop and Check

Perspectives What similarities are there between the way settlers treated the Californios and how settlers treated American Indians elsewhere?

Lesson 3 363

Research Companion, pp. 362–363

Monitor and Differentiate

REACHING ALL LEARNERS

Approaching Level

Guide students to think critically about the events that led to California's statehood. Encourage them to create a graphic organizer or a timeline for their notes and ideas.

Beyond Level

Guide students to conduct further research into the California constitution. Students should identify any other constitutions that helped to form the basis of California's laws. They may also analyze what sets California's laws apart from those of other states. Have students summarize their findings and share them with the whole class.

Report Your Findings

Inquiry Journal,
pp. 294–295

U.S. History
Making a New Nation

IMPACT
CALIFORNIA
SOCIAL STUDIES

INQUIRY JOURNAL

5

STANDARDS

Describe the continued migration of Mexican settlers into Mexican territories of the West and Southwest. **HSS.5.8.5**

Relate how and when California, Texas, Oregon, and other western lands became part of the United States, including the significance of the Texas War for Independence and the Mexican-American War. **HSS.5.8.6**

Students identify and interpret the multiple causes and effects of historical events. **HAS.HI.3**

Write informative/explanatory texts to examine a topic and convey ideas and information clearly. **CCSS.ELA.W.5.2**

Go Digital!

- Students can go online to report their findings. Assess their responses online.

- Students can access the online graphic organizer to capture ideas from their investigation.

Think About It

Students will review their research and determine what was so important about the southwest territories that caused disputes between Mexico and the United States.

- Remind students to review the information they discovered about cause and effect in their graphic organizer. Direct students back to pages 354–363 of their Research Companion if they need more information.

Write About It

Write and Cite Evidence Have students read the prompt. Explain that they will write an article that explains the Mexican War, what the United States gained from it, and how it changed the country.

Remind students to include the following elements in their response.

- Include a main idea that tells about the topic of the article.

- Use important details to support your main idea.

- Use language that makes clear the position of the United States after the war, defining terms for your readers as needed.

Use the rubric on p. T762 to evaluate students' work.

Talk About It

PRODUCTIVE

Defend Your Claim Ask students to work with a partner as they discuss the Treaty of Guadalupe Hidalgo and how it changed the makeup of the United States.

- Explain that they should outline what the treaty said and why it was important.

- They should cite evidence from the text to support their points.

- Remind students to be respectful of their classmates' opinions.

Connect to the Essential Question

EQ

Read the prompt aloud to students. Ask them the following guiding questions:

- Why did the United States fight with Mexico? (Responses should include disputes over land and settlers.)

- What do you know about the character of the United States up to this time? (Responses will vary, but should include that people were excited about expanding the nation through Manifest Destiny.)

- What does the fight with Mexico reveal about the changing nation? (Responses should be supported by text evidence.)

Remind students to use the space provided in their journal to jot down notes.

Report Your Findings

Think About It

Take a Stand

Review your research. Based on the information you have gathered, what do you think was so important about the southwest territories that caused disputes between Mexico and the United States?

Write About It

Write an Article

Write an article about the outcome of the Mexican-American War. Identify what the United States gained and how it changed the country. Cite evidence from the text.

Students should note that the Texans and Californians who wanted to go to war with Mexico had already developed a strong national identity, even before Texas and California were states. For instance, new settlers in Texas resisted the conditions of citizenship that the Mexican government tried to impose.

Talk About It

Defend Your Claim

Work with a partner. Discuss how the Treaty of Guadalupe Hildago changed the makeup of the United States.

 **Connect to the EQ**

Pull It Together

What did outcome of the war with Mexico reveal about the spirit and character of the young United States?

Responses will vary, but students should note some of the results of the victory in the Mexican War (for example, the expansion of the United States into Texas, California, and the southwest territories) and offer an opinion about what that reveals about the spirit and character of the young United States.

> **Inquiry Project Notes**

Inquiry Journal, pp. 294–295

EL ENGLISH LEARNERS SCAFFOLD

ELD.PI.5.10 Writing literary and informational texts to present, describe, and explain ideas and information, using appropriate technology

Emerging	Expanding	Bridging
Plan an Article Guide students to work with a partner to write the article. Guide them to use the graphic organizer they created to understand cause and effect. Provide support as needed.	**Write an Article** Encourage students to write the article independently, including a clear main idea and key details from the text. Then have students work with a partner. Have them read their articles aloud and make suggestions about each other's work.	**Organize Ideas** Have students work with a partner to organize ideas for the article. Encourage them to write the article independently after planning as a group. Then encourage students to reread each other's articles for sense and organization.

See the **Language Learner Teaching Guide** for more language support strategies.

Monitor and Differentiate

REACHING ALL LEARNERS

Approaching Level

Work with students as they write their articles. Remind them that an effective article is organized. It might present the main idea first and then support it with details and evidence, or it might supply the details first and build to the main idea at the end. Encourage students to outline their articles before beginning to write.

Beyond Level

Encourage students to expand the topic of the article to include the entire conflict with Mexico over the southwest territories, not to focus solely on the Mexican-American War. Encourage students to conduct additional research as needed to find more information.

Know what your students know!

Lesson Task

Report Your Findings

Use the rubric to evaluate students' responses.

Write and Cite Evidence Students write an article about the outcome of the Mexican-American War. They identify what the United States gained and how it changed the country.

Defend Your Claim Students work with a partner to discuss how the Treaty of Guadalupe Hidalgo changed the makeup of the United States.

Lesson Task Evaluation Rubric

	4	3	2	1
Historical Understanding	Strong understanding of the importance of the southwest territories	Adequate understanding of the importance of the southwest territories	Uneven understanding of the importance of the southwest territories	No understanding of the importance of the southwest territories
Write an Article	Provides a clear main idea about how the United States changed after the Mexican-American War	Provides adequate information about how the United States changed after the Mexican-American War	Somewhat unclear information about how the United States changed after the Mexican-American War	No relevant main idea or information stated about how the United States changed after the Mexican-American War
Supported by Text Evidence	Main Ideas clearly supported by evidence	Main ideas mostly supported by evidence	Main ideas not always supported by evidence	Main ideas missing or irrelevant
Defend Your Claim	Strongly supports reasons the Treaty of Guadalupe Hidalgo changed the United States Thoughtfully considers and responds to partner's comments	Supports reasons the Treaty of Guadalupe Hidalgo changed the United States Considers and responds to partner's comments	Lacks supports for reasons the Treaty of Guadalupe Hidalgo changed the United States Does not always thoughtfully consider partner's comments	Does not consider or support how the Treaty of Guadalupe Hidalgo changed the United States Provides no relevant contributions to discussion

Lesson Assessment

Go *Digital!*

- Have students complete the Chapter 8 Lesson 3 Assessment online to monitor their understanding of the lesson content.

California Smarter Balanced Assessment Connections!

Standards Covered	Lesson Task	Lesson Assessment	Alignment with California Smarter Balanced Assessment
History Social Science Content 5.8.5; 5.8.6	✔	✔	Claim 1 Targets 8, 9, 11
History Social Science Analysis Skills Chronological and Spatial Thinking 5.1; 5.4 Historical Interpretation 5.3	✔	✔	Claim 1 Targets 8, 9, 11
Writing W.5.2	✔	✔	Claim 2 Target 3b, 5
Research and Inquiry W.5.7		✔	Claim 4 Targets 1, 2
Reading RI.5.3	✔	✔	Claim 1 Targets 11, 12
Speaking and Listening SL.5.1	✔		Claim 3 Target 3 Claim 4 Target 1

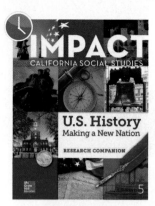

Research Companion,
pp. 364–367

 STANDARDS

Name the states and territories that existed in 1850 and identify their locations and major geographical features (e.g., mountain ranges, principal rivers, dominant plant regions). **HSS.5.8.2**

Students know the location of the current 50 states and the names of their capitals. **HSS.5.9**

DID YOU KNOW?

Puerto Rico The United States obtained Puerto Rico as part of the Treaty of Paris of 1898, following the Spanish-American War. The island is still a commonwealth of the United States. It's citizens are all U.S. citizens, but they cannot vote in presidential elections. However, Puerto Ricans do vote for a Congressional commissioner, an official who represents Puerto Rico in the U.S. House of Representatives, but who cannot vote on issues outside of small committees.

Analyze the Map

Inspect Have students read pp. 364–365.

Find Evidence Use the questions below to check comprehension. Remind students to support their answers with text evidence.

> **Summarize** How did the Treaty of Guadalupe Hidalgo affect the nation's boundaries? (It increased the territory of the United States.) **DOK 3**
>
> **Explain** How did the population of California change between 1850 and 2015? (The population exploded, increasing by more than 39 million.) **DOK 3**
>
> **Analyze Visuals** Based on the map, what were the major geographical challenges the settlers had to face as they moved from the East Coast toward California? (mountain ranges, such as the Rocky Mountains) **DOK 3**

Make Connections

> **Infer** Why would it have been dangerous and difficult to travel from the East Coast to the West Coast in the 1850s? (because people traveled by horse and wagon train, and the trip would have taken a long time and included many dangers along the way, including bad weather and disease) **DOK 3**

Analyze the Map

Inspect Have students read pp. 366–367.

Find Evidence Use the questions below to check comprehension. Remind students to support their answers with text evidence.

> **Identify** Which part of the country gained the most states after 1850? (the Great Plains or Midwest) **DOK 3**
>
> **Explain** Which two new states share no borders with the other 48? (Hawaii and Alaska) **DOK 3**
>
> **Analyze Data** Of the states that joined the Union after 1850, which state has added the most people? Which state has added the fewest people? (Arizona has added 6.7 million people; North Dakota has added just over 430,000 people) **DOK 3**

Make Connections

> **Infer** Why have people begun statehood movements in Washington, D.C.? (Possible response: The city of Washington, D.C., does not enjoy some of the benefits of being its own state.) **DOK 3**

Map and Globe Skills

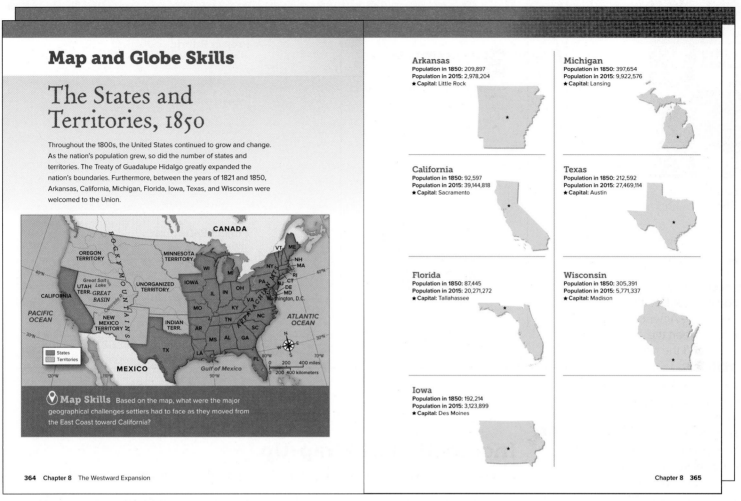

Map and Globe Skills

The States and Territories, 1850

Throughout the 1800s, the United States continued to grow and change. As the nation's population grew, so did the number of states and territories. The Treaty of Guadalupe Hidalgo greatly expanded the nation's boundaries. Furthermore, between the years of 1821 and 1850, Arkansas, California, Michigan, Florida, Iowa, Texas, and Wisconsin were welcomed to the Union.

 Map Skills Based on the map, what were the major geographical challenges settlers had to face as they moved from the East Coast toward California?

Arkansas
Population in 1850: 209,897
Population in 2015: 2,978,204
★ Capital: Little Rock

California
Population in 1850: 92,597
Population in 2015: 39,144,818
★ Capital: Sacramento

Florida
Population in 1850: 87,445
Population in 2015: 20,271,272
★ Capital: Tallahassee

Iowa
Population in 1850: 192,214
Population in 2015: 3,123,899
★ Capital: Des Moines

Michigan
Population in 1850: 397,654
Population in 2015: 9,922,576
★ Capital: Lansing

Texas
Population in 1850: 212,592
Population in 2015: 27,469,114
★ Capital: Austin

Wisconsin
Population in 1850: 305,391
Population in 2015: 5,771,337
★ Capital: Madison

Research Companion, pp. 364–367

ENGLISH LEARNERS SCAFFOLD

ELD.PI.5.6 Reading closely literary and informational texts and viewing multimedia to determine how meaning is conveyed explicitly and implicitly through language

Emerging

Analyze Visuals Encourage students to compare the existing state populations with the populations in 1850. Guide them to describe the differences they see. Provide sentence frames as needed:

The population of _____ was _____ in 1850 and _____ in 2015.

The state of _____ once had more people than _____. Now, _____ has more people.

Expanding/Bridging

Analyze Visuals Encourage students to consider how the United States has changed over the course of 240 years. Guide students to describe the growth of the United States, starting with what they recall about the thirteen original colonies. Students should identify that the process was a gradual one, full of hardships, war, oppression of American Indians, and obstacles.

See the **Language Learner Teaching Guide** for more language support strategies.

Monitor and Differentiate

REACHING ALL LEARNERS

Approaching Level

Guide students to use domain-specific language as they discuss the maps. Encourage them to use a reference text, such as an atlas, to learn more about the definitions of geographical terms.

On Level

Encourage students to share what they found most interesting about the changes to these states between 1850 and 2015. Encourage them to use details from the text in their discussion.

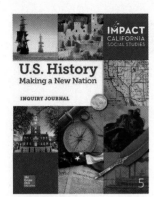

Inquiry Journal
pp. 296–297

 STANDARDS

Students describe the cooperation and conflict that existed among the American Indians and between the Indian nations and the new settlers. **HSS.5.3**

Students trace the colonization, immigration, and settlement patterns of the American people from 1789 to the mid-1800s, with emphasis on the role of economic incentives, effects of the physical and political geography, and transportation systems. **HSS.5.8**

CCSS Explain the relationships or interactions between two or more individuals, events, ideas, or concepts in a historical, scientific, or technical text based on specific information in the text. **CCSS.ELA.RI.5.3**

Write informative/explanatory texts to examine a topic and convey ideas and information clearly. **CCSS.ELA.W.5.2**

Go Digital!

Look online the EQ Inquiry Project rubric.

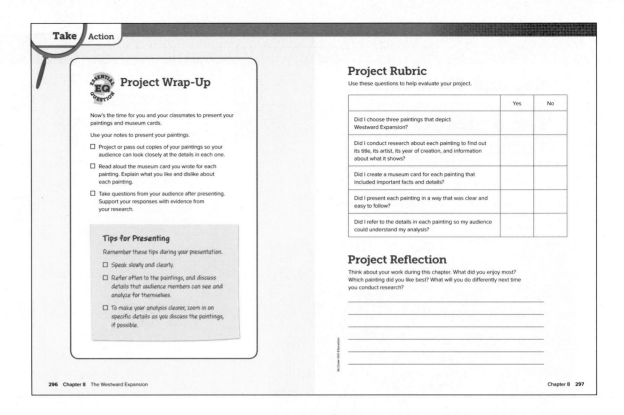

Inquiry Project Wrap-Up

Have students share their inquiry projects by presenting their collection of paintings.

- Before students present their paintings, discuss the wrap-up steps with them, making sure they know what's expected in their presentations.

- Allow time after each presentation for a Q-and-A session.

Tips for Presenting

Discuss the tips for presenting with students and the importance of communicating effectively with their audience. Explain that they should try to project the paintings on the whiteboard or projector so that the audience can better see details.

Project Rubric

Discuss each question in the Project Rubric with students. If students have worked as part of a group to develop their projects, you might want to have them work as a group to address each question in the rubric.

Project Reflection

Student reflections can focus on the work they did as part of the group or their individual performance curating and presenting their collection of paintings. Give groups time to discuss each phase of their projects and reflect on their work.

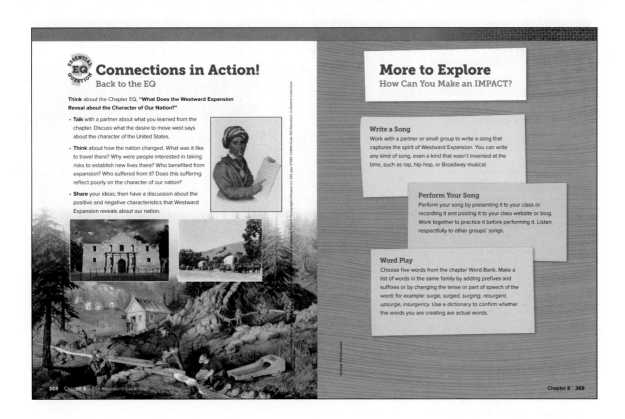

Connections in Action

To help focus students' conversations, you may want to discuss the EQ with the entire class before students discuss their ideas with a partner. Remind students to think about evidence they can provide that will support their ideas. After students present, allow time for others to ask questions.

More to Explore

Write a Song Remind students to think about what they learned about westward expansion. Encourage them to try to capture the spirit of the American West in a song.

Perform Your Song Encourage students to present the songs they created. Provide ways for them to record and present the song, or have a live concert in class.

Word Play Have students compile their new words on the classroom Word Wall. Use the original words as headings, and place the new words made with prefixes and suffixes below.

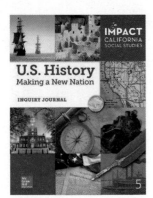

Inquiry Journal
pp. 298–301

Students describe the cooperation and conflict that existed among the American Indians and between the Indian nations and the new settlers. **HSS.5.3**

Students trace the colonization, immigration, and settlement patterns of the American people from 1789 to the mid-1800s, with emphasis on the role of economic incentives, effects of the physical and political geography, and transportation systems. **HSS.5.8**

Determine a theme of a story, drama, or poem from details in the text, including how characters in a story or drama respond to challenges or how the speaker in a poem reflects upon a topic; summarize the text. **CCSS.ELA.RL.5.2**

Read grade-level prose and poetry orally with accuracy, appropriate rate, and expression on successive readings. **CCSS.ELA.RF.5.4.B**

___

Go Digital!

Investigate the Gold Rush with the online Reader's Theater. Use the printable script for whole-class or small-group presentations.

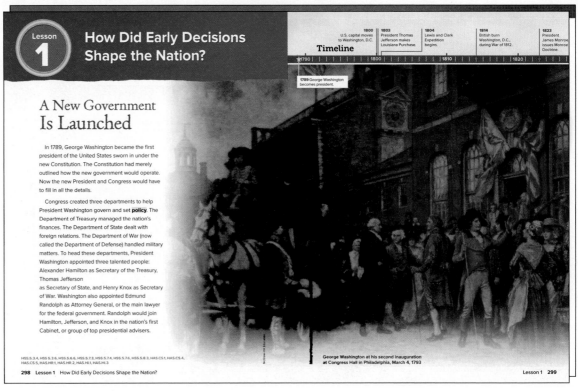

Inquiry Journal, pp. 298–301

Reader's Theater

Deepen students' understanding of westward expansion with the Reader's Theater selection, "The California Gold Rush."

Analyze the Source

GENRE Reader's Theater Reader's theater is a form of drama in which actors do not memorize their lines. They use their voices rather than sets or costumes to help listeners understand the text.

Inspect Have students read pp. 298–301 to determine the general meaning of the text.

1. Who are Louisa and Joe Lansdown? How do you know? (They are forty-niners hoping to strike gold in California. The Narrator introduces them.)

Find Evidence Have students reread the selection and ask:

2. What does Susanna want from Joe and Louisa? (Answers will vary, but students may recognize that Susanna needs to sell her wares, and she doesn't want anyone to discourage Joe and Louisa from buying from her store.)

Make Connections

3. What is problematic about the way Malcolm believes he can find gold? (Answers will vary, but students should identify that some forty-niners were so eager to make money that they fell for tricks and bad deals.)

4. What do you think Louisa will do now that she knows a little more about what it takes to strike gold? (Answers will vary, but students may predict that she will go into business doing laundry or cleaning houses, since Lily says she can make money.)

Perform the Reader's Theater

Model the reading. Project the play with an interactive whiteboard or projector and read aloud as students follow along. Show how expression, pace, and word stress can communicate meaning.

- **Joe:** Twenty dollars! That's half our savings!

  How should the character read this line? Why do you think so? (The character should read this line loudly, in disbelief. He can't believe that a pan costs so much money.)

- **Susanna:** (Susanna is starting to worry about making a sale. She tries to be positive.) So you'll need good tools! I have a shovel that will dig through just about anything. Take a look.

  What do the words in parentheses tell Susanna to do? How would you read these lines? (She is getting nervous. She might speak quickly to regain her customers' attention.)

Practice the reading. Before students read aloud on their own, give them time to practice reading. Use techniques such as the following:

- Silent Read—Have students read the text to themselves the first time they read it.
- Echo Read—Read a line and have students repeat it, echoing your expression and tone.

Assign roles. Consider these strategies:

- Put students into performance groups so that every student has a chance to read a role.
- Have students annotate the text to help them understand events or unfamiliar words.

Tips for Reader's Theater

- Students should have time to practice their lines before performing.
- Place students in a circle and have them step into the center "spotlight" to read.

Remind students of strategies for reading aloud:

- Look up. Don't bury your face in your script, or no one will be able to hear you.
- Use expression. Pay attention to the punctuation and stage directions in italics.

Write About It Have students complete the writing prompt. As students write their own play, have them predict what will happen to the characters in the future.

Connect to the
Essential Question

Have students connect the reader's theater to the essential question. Ask: *How did the characters' experiences in the general store help you understand the spirit of westward expansion?* (Responses will vary, but students may say that Joe and Louisa embody the optimism that led people to the West, and that women like Susanna and Lily show that practicality can still yield success.)

✎ Teacher Notes

_____

_____

_____

_____

_____

_____

_____

_____

_____

_____

_____

_____

_____

_____

_____

_____

_____

_____

References Sources

All page numbers shown here are from the student Research Companion.

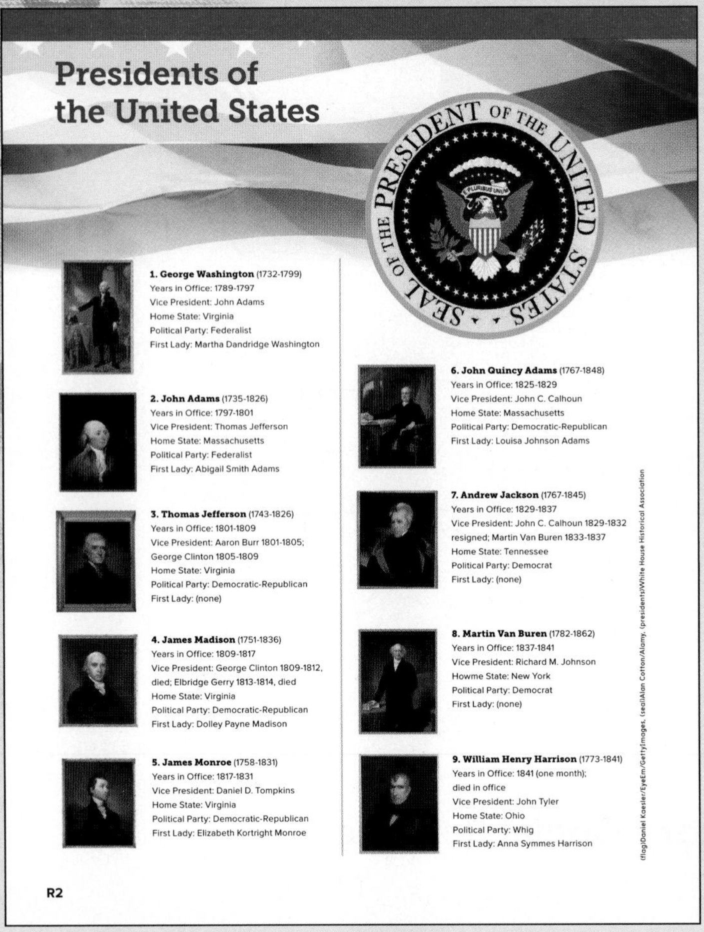

Presidents of the United States

SEAL OF THE PRESIDENT OF THE UNITED STATES

1. George Washington (1732-1799)
Years in Office: 1789-1797
Vice President: John Adams
Home State: Virginia
Political Party: Federalist
First Lady: Martha Dandridge Washington

2. John Adams (1735-1826)
Years in Office: 1797-1801
Vice President: Thomas Jefferson
Home State: Massachusetts
Political Party: Federalist
First Lady: Abigail Smith Adams

3. Thomas Jefferson (1743-1826)
Years in Office: 1801-1809
Vice President: Aaron Burr 1801-1805; George Clinton 1805-1809
Home State: Virginia
Political Party: Democratic-Republican
First Lady: (none)

4. James Madison (1751-1836)
Years in Office: 1809-1817
Vice President: George Clinton 1809-1812, died; Elbridge Gerry 1813-1814, died
Home State: Virginia
Political Party: Democratic-Republican
First Lady: Dolley Payne Madison

5. James Monroe (1758-1831)
Years in Office: 1817-1831
Vice President: Daniel D. Tompkins
Home State: Virginia
Political Party: Democratic-Republican
First Lady: Elizabeth Kortright Monroe

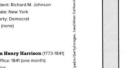

6. John Quincy Adams (1767-1848)
Years in Office: 1825-1829
Vice President: John C. Calhoun
Home State: Massachusetts
Political Party: Democratic-Republican
First Lady: Louisa Johnson Adams

7. Andrew Jackson (1767-1845)
Years in Office: 1829-1837
Vice President: John C. Calhoun 1829-1832 resigned; Martin Van Buren 1833-1837
Home State: Tennessee
Political Party: Democrat
First Lady: (none)

8. Martin Van Buren (1782-1862)
Years in Office: 1837-1841
Vice President: Richard M. Johnson
Howme State: New York
Political Party: Democrat
First Lady: (none)

9. William Henry Harrison (1773-1841)
Years in Office: 1841 (one month); died in office
Vice President: John Tyler
Home State: Ohio
Political Party: Whig
First Lady: Anna Symmes Harrison

(flag)Daniel Koesler/EyeEm/Getty Images, (seal)Alan Cotton/Alamy, (presidents)White House Historical Association

R2

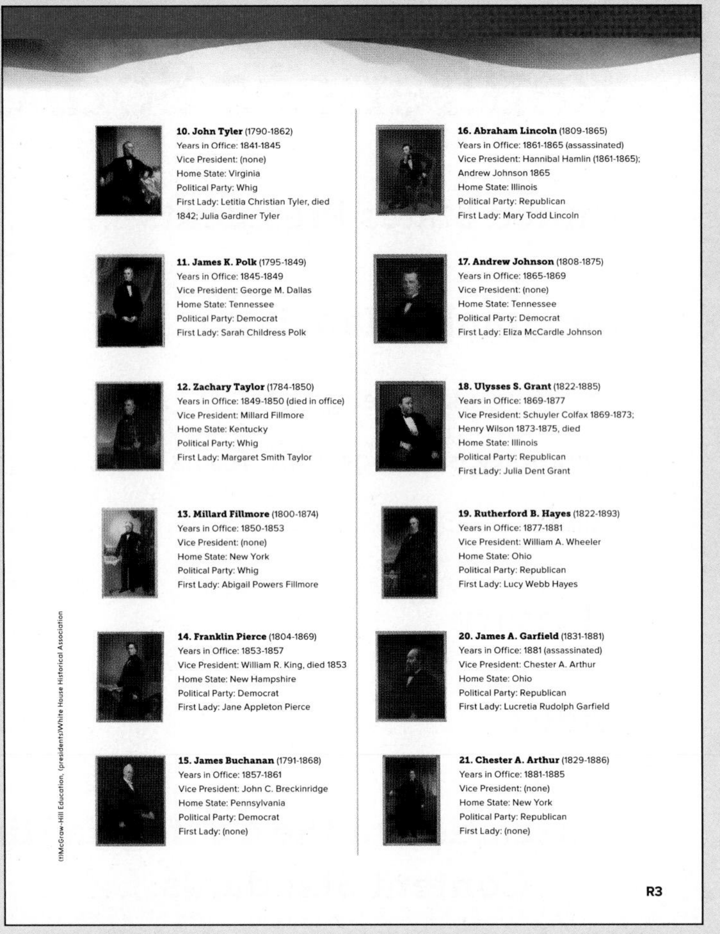

10. John Tyler (1790-1862)
Years in Office: 1841-1845
Vice President: (none)
Home State: Virginia
Political Party: Whig
First Lady: Letitia Christian Tyler, died 1842; Julia Gardiner Tyler

11. James K. Polk (1795-1849)
Years in Office: 1845-1849
Vice President: George M. Dallas
Home State: Tennessee
Political Party: Democrat
First Lady: Sarah Childress Polk

12. Zachary Taylor (1784-1850)
Years in Office: 1849-1850 (died in office)
Vice President: Millard Fillmore
Home State: Kentucky
Political Party: Whig
First Lady: Margaret Smith Taylor

13. Millard Fillmore (1800-1874)
Years in Office: 1850-1853
Vice President: (none)
Home State: New York
Political Party: Whig
First Lady: Abigail Powers Fillmore

14. Franklin Pierce (1804-1869)
Years in Office: 1853-1857
Vice President: William R. King, died 1853
Home State: New Hampshire
Political Party: Democrat
First Lady: Jane Appleton Pierce

15. James Buchanan (1791-1868)
Years in Office: 1857-1861
Vice President: John C. Breckinridge
Home State: Pennsylvania
Political Party: Democrat
First Lady: (none)

16. Abraham Lincoln (1809-1865)
Years in Office: 1861-1865 (assassinated)
Vice President: Hannibal Hamlin (1861-1865); Andrew Johnson 1865
Home State: Illinois
Political Party: Republican
First Lady: Mary Todd Lincoln

17. Andrew Johnson (1808-1875)
Years in Office: 1865-1869
Vice President: (none)
Home State: Tennessee
Political Party: Democrat
First Lady: Eliza McCardle Johnson

18. Ulysses S. Grant (1822-1885)
Years in Office: 1869-1877
Vice President: Schuyler Colfax 1869-1873; Henry Wilson 1873-1875, died
Home State: Illinois
Political Party: Republican
First Lady: Julia Dent Grant

19. Rutherford B. Hayes (1822-1893)
Years in Office: 1877-1881
Vice President: William A. Wheeler
Home State: Ohio
Political Party: Republican
First Lady: Lucy Webb Hayes

20. James A. Garfield (1831-1881)
Years in Office: 1881 (assassinated)
Vice President: Chester A. Arthur
Home State: Ohio
Political Party: Republican
First Lady: Lucretia Rudolph Garfield

21. Chester A. Arthur (1829-1886)
Years in Office: 1881-1885
Vice President: (none)
Home State: New York
Political Party: Republican
First Lady: (none)

(t)McGraw-Hill Education, (presidents)White House Historical Association

R3

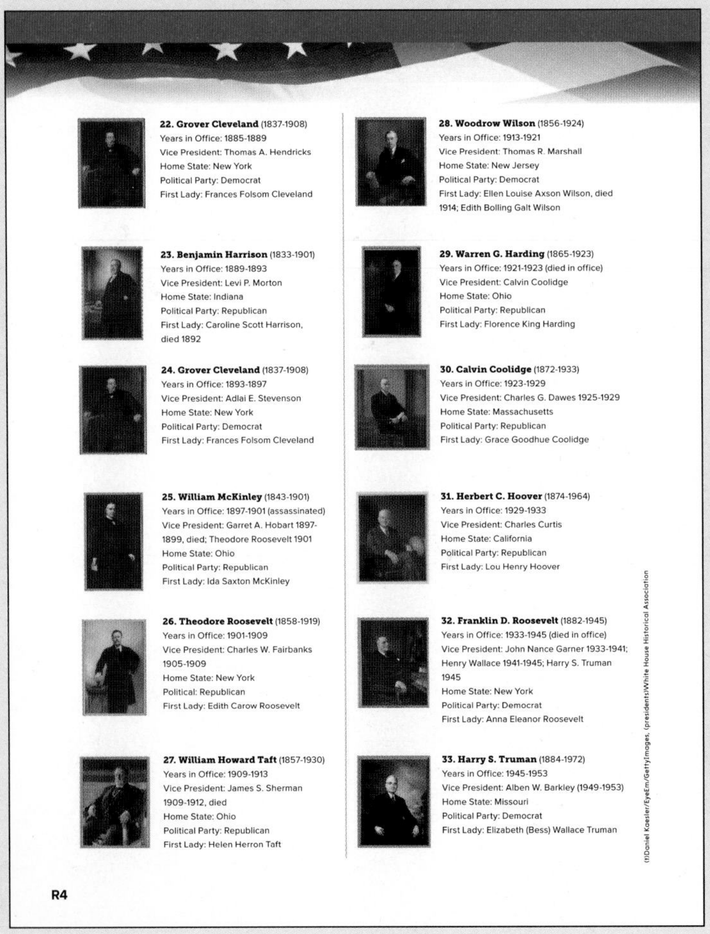

22. Grover Cleveland (1837-1908)
Years in Office: 1885-1889
Vice President: Thomas A. Hendricks
Home State: New York
Political Party: Democrat
First Lady: Frances Folsom Cleveland

23. Benjamin Harrison (1833-1901)
Years in Office: 1889-1893
Vice President: Levi P. Morton
Home State: Indiana
Political Party: Republican
First Lady: Caroline Scott Harrison, died 1892

24. Grover Cleveland (1837-1908)
Years in Office: 1893-1897
Vice President: Adlai E. Stevenson
Home State: New York
Political Party: Democrat
First Lady: Frances Folsom Cleveland

25. William McKinley (1843-1901)
Years in Office: 1897-1901 (assassinated)
Vice President: Garret A. Hobart 1897-1899, died; Theodore Roosevelt 1901
Home State: Ohio
Political Party: Republican
First Lady: Ida Saxton McKinley

26. Theodore Roosevelt (1858-1919)
Years in Office: 1901-1909
Vice President: Charles W. Fairbanks 1905-1909
Home State: New York
Political: Republican
First Lady: Edith Carow Roosevelt

27. William Howard Taft (1857-1930)
Years in Office: 1909-1913
Vice President: James S. Sherman 1909-1912, died
Home State: Ohio
Political Party: Republican
First Lady: Helen Herron Taft

28. Woodrow Wilson (1856-1924)
Years in Office: 1913-1921
Vice President: Thomas R. Marshall
Home State: New Jersey
Political Party: Democrat
First Lady: Ellen Louise Axson Wilson, died 1914; Edith Bolling Galt Wilson

29. Warren G. Harding (1865-1923)
Years in Office: 1921-1923 (died in office)
Vice President: Calvin Coolidge
Home State: Ohio
Political Party: Republican
First Lady: Florence King Harding

30. Calvin Coolidge (1872-1933)
Years in Office: 1923-1929
Vice President: Charles G. Dawes 1925-1929
Home State: Massachusetts
Political Party: Republican
First Lady: Grace Goodhue Coolidge

31. Herbert C. Hoover (1874-1964)
Years in Office: 1929-1933
Vice President: Charles Curtis
Home State: California
Political Party: Republican
First Lady: Lou Henry Hoover

32. Franklin D. Roosevelt (1882-1945)
Years in Office: 1933-1945 (died in office)
Vice President: John Nance Garner 1933-1941; Henry Wallace 1941-1945; Harry S. Truman 1945
Home State: New York
Political Party: Democrat
First Lady: Anna Eleanor Roosevelt

33. Harry S. Truman (1884-1972)
Years in Office: 1945-1953
Vice President: Alben W. Barkley (1949-1953)
Home State: Missouri
Political Party: Democrat
First Lady: Elizabeth (Bess) Wallace Truman

(t)Daniel Koesler/EyeEm/Getty Images, (presidents)White House Historical Association

R4

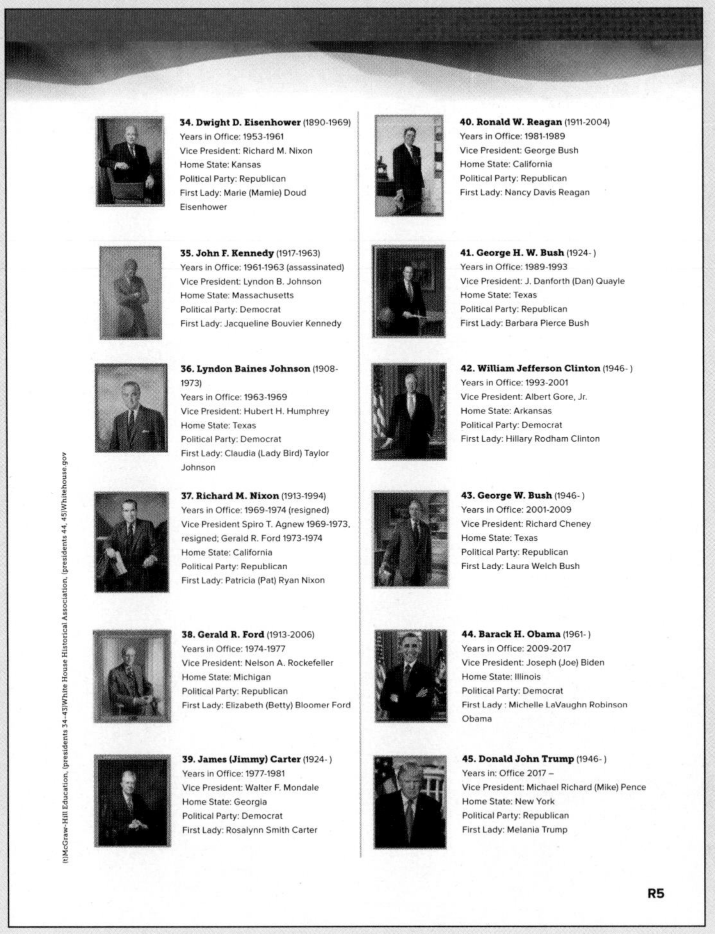

34. Dwight D. Eisenhower (1890-1969)
Years in Office: 1953-1961
Vice President: Richard M. Nixon
Home State: Kansas
Political Party: Republican
First Lady: Marie (Mamie) Doud Eisenhower

35. John F. Kennedy (1917-1963)
Years in Office: 1961-1963 (assassinated)
Vice President: Lyndon B. Johnson
Home State: Massachusetts
Political Party: Democrat
First Lady: Jacqueline Bouvier Kennedy

36. Lyndon Baines Johnson (1908-1973)
Years in Office: 1963-1969
Vice President: Hubert H. Humphrey
Home State: Texas
Political Party: Democrat
First Lady: Claudia (Lady Bird) Taylor Johnson

37. Richard M. Nixon (1913-1994)
Years in Office: 1969-1974 (resigned)
Vice President Spiro T. Agnew 1969-1973, resigned; Gerald R. Ford 1973-1974
Home State: California
Political Party: Republican
First Lady: Patricia (Pat) Ryan Nixon

38. Gerald R. Ford (1913-2006)
Years in Office: 1974-1977
Vice President: Nelson A. Rockefeller
Home State: Michigan
Political Party: Republican
First Lady: Elizabeth (Betty) Bloomer Ford

39. James (Jimmy) Carter (1924-)
Years in Office: 1977-1981
Vice President: Walter F. Mondale
Home State: Georgia
Political Party: Democrat
First Lady: Rosalynn Smith Carter

40. Ronald W. Reagan (1911-2004)
Years in Office: 1981-1989
Vice President: George Bush
Home State: California
Political Party: Republican
First Lady: Nancy Davis Reagan

41. George H. W. Bush (1924-)
Years in Office: 1989-1993
Vice President: J. Danforth (Dan) Quayle
Home State: Texas
Political Party: Republican
First Lady: Barbara Pierce Bush

42. William Jefferson Clinton (1946-)
Years in Office: 1993-2001
Vice President: Albert Gore, Jr.
Home State: Arkansas
Political Party: Democrat
First Lady: Hillary Rodham Clinton

43. George W. Bush (1946-)
Years in Office: 2001-2009
Vice President: Richard Cheney
Home State: Texas
Political Party: Republican
First Lady: Laura Welch Bush

44. Barack H. Obama (1961-)
Years in Office: 2009-2017
Vice President: Joseph (Joe) Biden
Home State: Illinois
Political Party: Democrat
First Lady : Michelle LaVaughn Robinson Obama

45. Donald John Trump (1946-)
Years in: Office 2017 –
Vice President: Michael Richard (Mike) Pence
Home State: New York
Political Party: Republican
First Lady: Melania Trump

(t)McGraw-Hill Education, (presidents 34-43)White House Historical Association, (presidents 44, 45)Whitehouse.gov

R5

All page numbers shown here are from the student Research Companion.

Geography Handbook

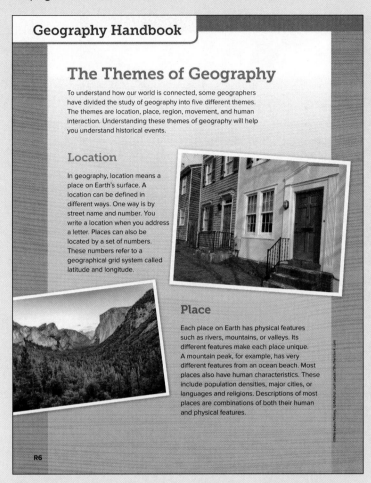

The Themes of Geography

To understand how our world is connected, some geographers have divided the study of geography into five different themes. The themes are location, place, region, movement, and human interaction. Understanding these themes of geography will help you understand historical events.

Location

In geography, location means a place on Earth's surface. A location can be defined in different ways. One way is by street name and number. You write a location when you address a letter. Places can also be located by a set of numbers. These numbers refer to a geographical grid system called latitude and longitude.

Place

Each place on Earth has physical features such as rivers, mountains, or valleys. Its different features make each place unique. A mountain peak, for example, has very different features from an ocean beach. Most places also have human characteristics. These include population densities, major cities, or languages and religions. Descriptions of most places are combinations of both their human and physical features.

R6

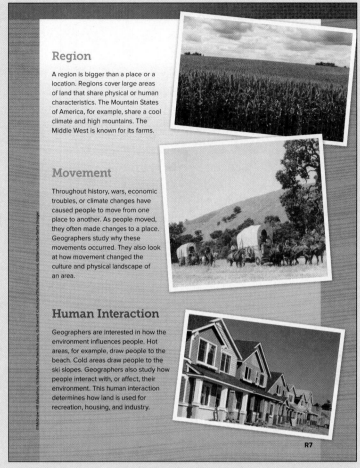

Region

A region is bigger than a place or a location. Regions cover large areas of land that share physical or human characteristics. The Mountain States of America, for example, share a cool climate and high mountains. The Middle West is known for its farms.

Movement

Throughout history, wars, economic troubles, or climate changes have caused people to move from one place to another. As people moved, they often made changes to a place. Geographers study why these movements occurred. They also look at how movement changed the culture and physical landscape of an area.

Human Interaction

Geographers are interested in how the environment influences people. Hot areas, for example, draw people to the beach. Cold areas draw people to the ski slopes. Geographers also study how people interact with, or affect, their environment. This human interaction determines how land is used for recreation, housing, and industry.

R7

Dictionary of Geographic Words

1. **CANAL** A channel built to carry water for irrigation or transportation
2. **CANYON** A deep, narrow valley with steep sides
3. **COAST** The land along an ocean
4. **DAM** A wall built across a river, creating a lake that stores water
5. **DELTA** Land made of soil left behind as a river drains into a larger body of water
6. **DESERT** A dry environment with few plants and animals
7. **GLACIER** A huge sheet of ice that moves slowly across the land
8. **GULF** Part of an ocean that extends into the land; larger than a bay
9. **HARBOR** A sheltered place along a coast where boats dock safely
10. **HILL** A rounded, raised landform; not as high as a mountain
11. **ISLAND** A body of land completely surrounded by water
12. **LAKE** A body of water completely surrounded by land
13. **MOUNTAIN** A high landform with steep sides; higher than a hill
14. **MOUNTAIN PASS** A narrow gap through a mountain range
15. **MOUNTAIN RANGE** A row or chain of mountains

R8

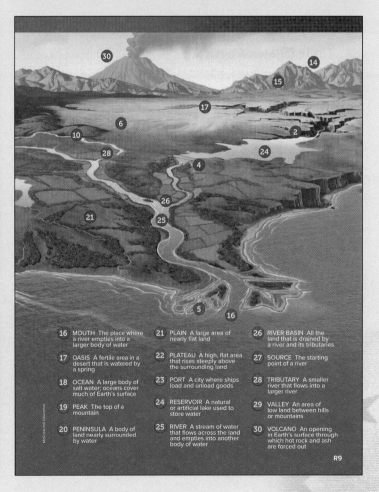

16. **MOUTH** The place where a river empties into a larger body of water
17. **OASIS** A fertile area in a desert that is watered by a spring
18. **OCEAN** A large body of salt water; oceans cover much of Earth's surface
19. **PEAK** The top of a mountain
20. **PENINSULA** A body of land nearly surrounded by water
21. **PLAIN** A large area of nearly flat land
22. **PLATEAU** A high, flat area that rises steeply above the surrounding land
23. **PORT** A city where ships load and unload goods
24. **RESERVOIR** A natural or artificial lake used to store water
25. **RIVER** A stream of water that flows across the land and empties into another body of water
26. **RIVER BASIN** All the land that is drained by a river and its tributaries
27. **SOURCE** The starting point of a river
28. **TRIBUTARY** A smaller river that flows into a larger river
29. **VALLEY** An area of low land between hills or mountains
30. **VOLCANO** An opening in Earth's surface through which hot rock and ash are forced out

R9

All page numbers shown here are from the student Research Companion.

Atlas

United States: Political

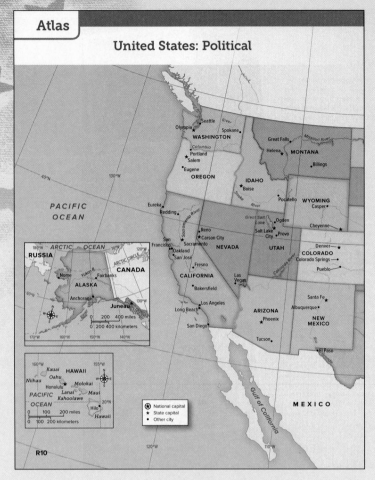

United States: Physical

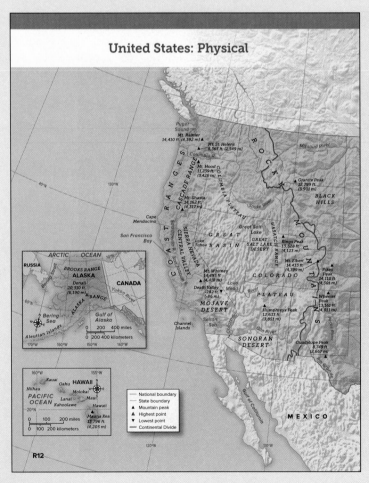

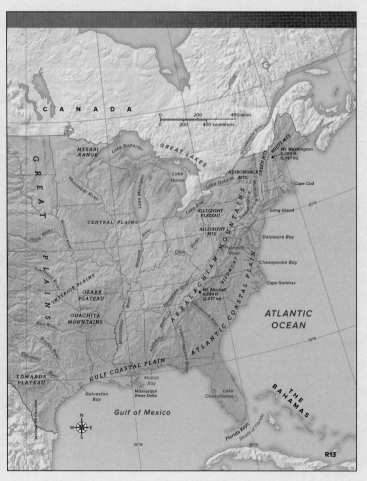

All page numbers shown here are from the student Research Companion.

World: Political

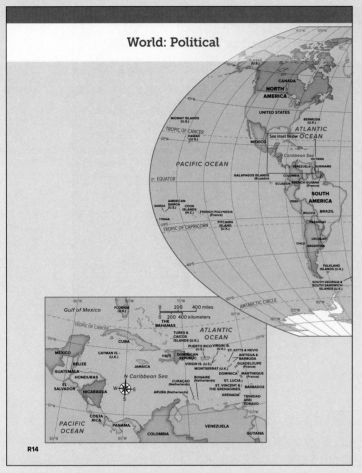

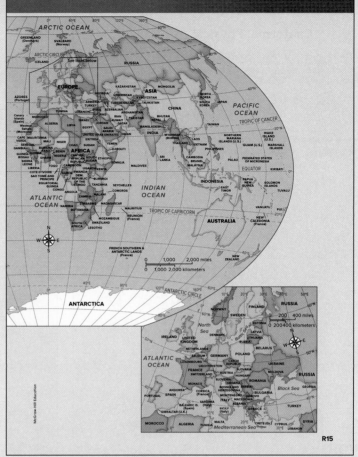

World: Physical

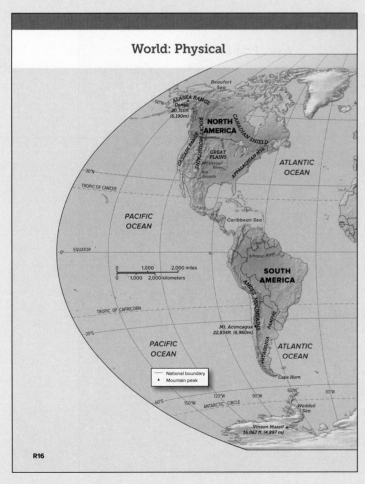

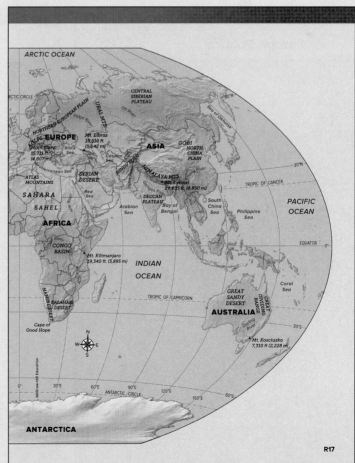

ATLAS

All page numbers shown here are from the student Research Companion.

California: Physical

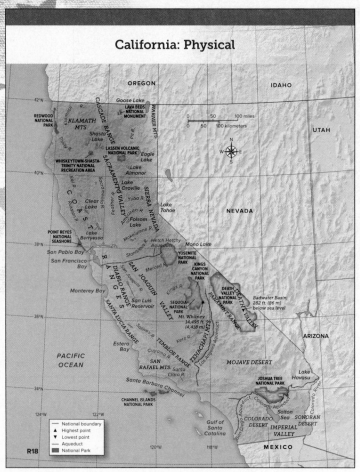

R18

North America: Political

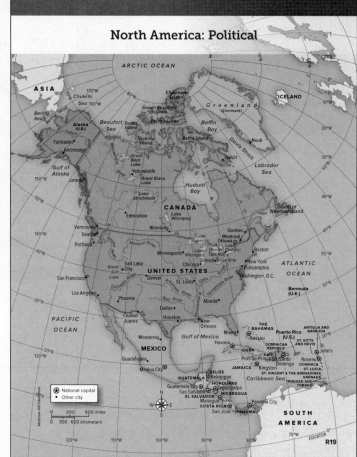

R19

Europe: Political

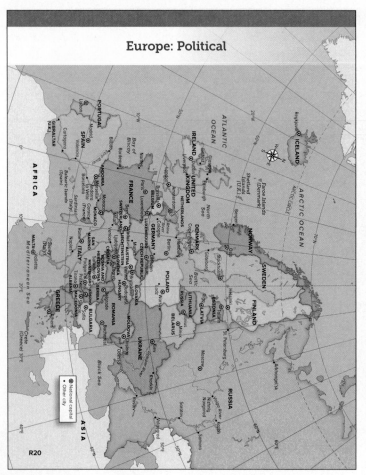

R20

Asia: Political

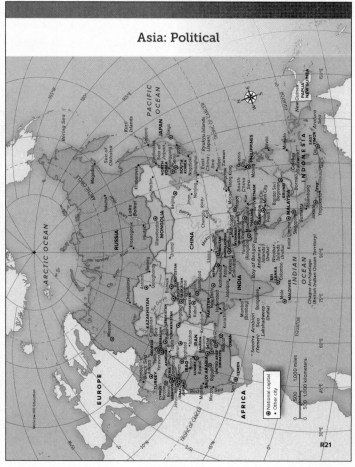

R21

McGraw-Hill Education

All page numbers shown here are from the student Research Companion.

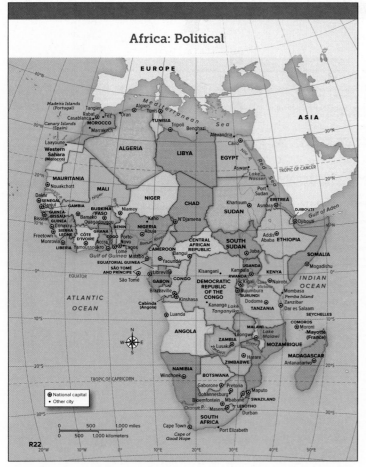

Africa: Political

South America: Political

GLOSSARY

All page numbers shown here are from the student Research Companion.

Glossary

A

amendment an addition to the Constitution

article a paragraph in a legal document

assembly a government legislature that represents the people of a particular place

B

bill a suggestion for a new law

blockade an obstacle preventing the movement of people or goods

boundary a line that marks where one area ends and another begins

boycott to refuse to do business or have contact with a person, group, company, country, or product

C

cash crop a plant that is grown for making money

cede to give up something to someone else

charter a document granting someone special legal powers

claim to declare that a place belongs to one's country upon arrival at the place

colony a territory settled by people from another place, usually far away

commerce the buying and selling of goods

composition the way in which something is put together

conquest victories by invading armies

corruption the use of government money for personal gain

covenant a contract, an agreement

currency the type of money used in a particular place

D

delegate a person who represents other people

demand the level of need for something

dissension disagreement between members of a group over an important issue

diverse containing many types of people or things

E

encomiendas system of forced labor in Spanish colonies

endeavor try hard to achieve a goal

environment the setting in which something takes place

H

habitat an environment that is favorable to the survival of a species

harvest to take and gather such crops as wheat and corn for use

hieroglyph a type of ancient writing that uses pictures for words

hostility opposition; ill will

hunter-gatherer Early humans who lived by gathering wild plants and hunting animals

I

immigrant a person who arrives in a new country after leaving his or her country of birth

imposing putting in place by a government order

inflation increase in the cost of goods and services

inland in an area that is away from oceans and coastal regions

interchangeable something that can be used in place of something else because it is identical

issue to give out or publish

J

jury a group of citizens that decides the outcome of a court case

L

loom a machine for making thread or yarn into cloth

M

manifest destiny the belief that it was divine will for the United States to expand westward to the Pacific Ocean

mercenary soldiers from a different country who are paid to fight in a war

merchants people who buy and sell goods

mesa a flat-topped hill with steep sides

militia a group of citizens organized for military service

missionary system of forced labor in Spanish colonies

monarch a king and queen who rules nations

monopoly complete control of something

musket long guns similar to rifles

N

navigation the art of guiding a boat, plane, or other transportation vehicle

negotiate to discuss and bargain for a solution

McGraw-Hill Education

O

oral history spoken records, including stories, that have been passed from one generation to the next

outpost a fort or other military structure established away from the main army to help guard against surprise attacks

oxen cattle that are used for doing work

P

physical relating to material objects; having actual form

policy an official position on an issue

potlatch a special feast given by American Indians of the Northwest Coast, in which the guests receive gifts

prairie flat or gently rolling land covered mostly with grasses and wildflowers

press the news media, including newspapers and magazines, websites, and TV and radio

profiteer people who take advantage of a poor economic situation, hoarding goods and selling them at high prices to make a large profit

proprietor the owners

R

reaping having to do with cutting down and gathering

rebel person who defies authority

recession a temporary downturn in business activity

reconcile to become friendly again after a disagreement; to make peace with

reconciliation returning to the previous friendly condition of a relationship after a disagreement

repeal cancelation or withdrawal

republic an area of land that has its own government and elected leaders

resistance defense to diseases developed by the immune system

S

settlement town created by people in an area previously uninhabited by that people

slash-and-burn a method of clearing land for farming by cutting and burning trees

sovereign having independent authority

surge sudden increase

survey to examine and measure

T

term the period of time during which an elected person is in office

territory an area of land that belongs to a government

totem pole a tall carved log used by American Indians of the Northwest Coast to honor an important person or to mark a special event

traitor someone who betrays his or her country

U

unconstitutional an action or policy that goes against the Constitution of the United States

V

vandalism destruction of property

veto to reject or prevent

W

warship ships mounted with cannons or other large guns

McGraw-Hill Education

INDEX

This index lists many topics along with the pages in this book on which they are found. Page numbers after a *c* refer you to a chart or graph; after an *m*, a map; after a *p*, a photograph or an artwork; and after a *q*, a quotation.

INDEX

INDEX

INDEX

F

INDEX

INDEX

INDEX

73, T672–73; Explore Main Idea and Details, T238–39, T262–63; Explore Making Inferences, T468–69, T568–69; Explore Maps, T180–81; Explore Motivations, T490–91; Explore Point of View, T728–29; Explore Problem and Solution, T98–99, T652–53; Determine Pros and Cons, T548–49; Summarize, T592–93

reaping machine, T657

rebels, T429

recession, T381

reconciliation, T451

Reconquista, T139

religion, T139; African American, T553; First Great Awakening and, T273, T297; freedom of, T265, T313; Native American, T29. *See also* African Methodist Episcopal (A.M.E.) Church; Anglican Church; Catholicism; Jew; Pilgrims; Puritans.

Resaca de la Palma, Battle of, *Tp753*

Research and Inquiry, project, T8, T122, T204, T338, T412, T536, T616, T698; Wrap-Up, T114, T194, T328, T404, T526, T608, T690, T766

reservations, T67, *Tp701*

resistance, T161

Revere, Paul, T397; ride of, T415, *Tp415*, T427, *Tp427*

Revolutionary War. *See* American Revolution.

Rhode Island, as absent from Constitutional Convention, T571; ratification of Constitution

by, T538, T597; settlement of, T208, T273

rice growth, T319

Rio Grande River, T755

Roanoke, T191, *Tp191*, T219

Robbins, John, T427

Rochambeau, Comte de, T517

Rochester, New York, T661

Rolfe, John, T221, T225

Ross, Betsy, T457

Ross, Betsy, House, T457, *Tp457*

Roundhouses, T65

Rousseau, Jean-Jacques, T449

Rubrics, California Smarter Balanced Assessment Connections, T33, T53, T73, T91, T113, T149, T173, T195, T231, T255, T279, T301, T325, T365, T385, T403, T439, T461, T483, T503, T525, T561, T585, T607, T645, T665, T687, T721, T741, T763; Inquiry Project (chapter), T5, T119, T201, T335, T409, T533, T613, T695; Performance Task Evaluation (lesson), T32, T52, T72, T90, T112, T148, T172, T194, T230, T254, T278, T300, T324, T364, T384, T402, T438, T460, T482, T502, T524, T560, T584, T606, T644, T664, T686, T720, T740, T762

Rush, Benjamin, T683, *Tp683*

S

Sacagawea, T620, *Tp620*, T637, T639, *Tp639*

St. Augustine, T167, T169, *Tm169, Tp169*

St. Clair Arthur, T553

St. Clement's Island, T313

St. Lawrence River, T245, T359

St. Louis, T661

Salem, Massachusetts, witchcraft in, T273

Salem, Peter, T416, *Tp416*, T497,

Salomon, Haym, T416, *Tp416*

Salt Lake City, T717

Sampson, Deborah, *Tp499*

San Diego, T167

San Jacinto, Battle of (1836), T702, T753

San Salvador, T143

Santa Anna, Antonio López de, T702, *Tp702*, T753

Santa Maria, T141, T143, *Tp141*

Saratoga, Battle of, T475–77, T479, *Tp475*

Savannah, T315, T513

Schuylkill River, T295

Scott, Winfield, Indian removal and, T735

Seattle, Chief, T67, *Tp67*

Second Amendment, T599

Second Continental Congress, T416, T431, *Tp431*, T451, T453, T471, T519, T551

Seminoles, T702

Seminole Wars, T702, T737

Senate. *See* U.S. Senate.

Senegal, T519

Separatists, T265

Sequoyah, T737, *Tp737*

Serrano, T65

settlements, T161. *See also* English explorations and settlements; specific settlements.

Seven Cities of Gold, T167

Seven Years' War. *See* French and Indian War.

sextant, T141, *Tp141*

Shawnee, T553, T679

Shays, Daniel, T540, *Tp540*; rebellion led by, T555–57, *Tp551, Tp555*, T571; views on rebellion of, T557

Sherman, Roger, T451, T575

"A Ship Called the Hamilton" (Calkins), T539

Shoshone, T39, T620

Siberia, T21

Silk Road, T139

Sioux, T85, T637; bison hunt by, *Tp701*; reservation of, *Tp701*

Sixth Amendment, T603

slash-and-burn, T101

Slater, Samuel, T655

slave codes, purpose of, T319

slavery, T227, *Tp227*, T243, *Tq319*; controversy over, T679–81; as cruel practice, T227; growth of, T247; as issue in Northwest Territory, T553; Massachusetts, legalization of, T271; movement to end, T297; plantations and, T317, *Tp317*; in Southern colonies, T451, T521; triangular trade and, T321, *Tp321*; working conditions and, T317, T319

INDEX

town meetings, T271

Townshend, Charles, T381

Townshend Acts (1767), T381, T397

trade, colonial trading posts and, *Tp249;* Columbian Exchange and, T159, T161; fur, T245, T249, T251, *Tp251,* T291, T353; in the Middle Ages, T137, T139, *Tp139;* Native American, T27, T28; Silk Road and, T139; slave, T187, T208, T225, T227, *Tp319,* T321; trading posts, *Tp249;* triangular, T321, *Tp321*

Trail of Tears, T735

traitors, T495

transportation, advances in, T659, *Tp659. See also* Railroad travel.

The Travels of Marco Polo, T137

Treasury, Department of, T631

triangular trade, T321, *Tp321;* slaves in, T321

Tuscaroras, T315, T497

Twenty-Fourth Amendment, T601

Twenty-Sixth Amendment, T601

Twenty-Third Amendment, T601

typhoid, T479

U

unconstitutional, T633

U.S. Constitution, T208, *Tp571, Tq581;* amendments to, T601; Bill of Rights and, T599, *Tp599;* checks and balances in, T579, *Tc579;* economic aspects of the, T581; executive branch in, T577, T579, *Tc579;* influence of Iroquois Confederacy on, T109; judicial branch in, T577, T579, *Tc579;* legislative branch in, T577, T579, *Tc579, Tq579;* Preamble in, T577; ratification of, T539, *Tp539,* T595–97; signing of, T577. *See also* Constitutional Convention.

U.S. House of Representatives, T579

U.S. President, T579

U.S. Senate, T579

U.S. Supreme Court, T579; *Marbury* v. *Madison* and, T633; Marshall, John, as Chief Justice of, T633, T735, *Tp633; Worcester* v. *Georgia* and, T735, *Tq735*

Utah, T27, T755

Uxmal, T25, *Tp25*

V

Vail, Albert, T661

Valley Forge, T479, *Tp479*

vandalism, T399

Vermont, T618

Verrazzano, Giovanni da, T185, *Tp185,* T189

Vespucci, Amerigo, T145

veto, T731

Victory Woods, *Tp475*

Virginia, crossing of Appalachian Mountains and, T355; ratification of Constitution and, T597; settlement of, T313. *See also* Jamestown.

Virginia Company, T219, T221, T227

Virginia Plan, T573

Vizcaíno, Sebastián, T167; route of, *Tm167*

Vocabulary Explore Academic/Domain-Specific Words, T9, T65, T123, T205, T413, T537, T617, T699; Develop Vocabulary, T20, T37, T46, T89, T224, T310, T450, T476, T498, T550, T674; WordBlast, T6, T120, T202, T410, T534, T614, T696. *See also* English Language Development (ELD).

voting rights for 18-year olds, T601; for African American men, T601; for residents of Washington, D.C., T601; for white males, T601, *Tp601;* for women, *Tp595,* T601

Voting Rights Act (1965), T601

vulcanization, T657

W

wagon trains, *Tp713,* T715–717, *Tp715, Tq717*

Wahunsonacock, Chief, T223, *Tp223*

"Walking Purchase," T295

Wampanoag, T267, T273, T275

wampum, *Tp105*

War, Department of, T631

War Hawks, T639

War of 1812, T620, T639–41, *Tp641, Tq641,* T679

Warren, James, T435

Warren, Mercy Otis, T416, *Tp416,* T435, T493,

Washington, American Indians in, T63, T67

Washington, D.C., attack on, in War of 1812, T620, T639, *Tp641;* design of, T633; voting rights for residents of, T601

Washington, George, T109, *Tq361, Tp399,* T416; cabinet of, T631, T633; as commander in American Revolution, T431, *Tp431, Tq431,* T473, *Tp473,* T479, T515, *Tp515,* T517; expansion of U.S. and, T635, *Tp635;* as Federalist, T595; in French and Indian War, T355, T357, T361, *Tp361;* as leader at Constitutional Convention, T573, *Tp573;* letter from Lee, Henry, to, T557, *Tq557;* letter to Cornwallis, Charles, *Tq513–15;* oath of office for, *Tp631;* portrait of, T639; presidency of, T631, T661; retirement of, T633

Western & Atlantic Railroad, T661

western settlement, T713, *Tp713,* T715–17, *Tm715, Tp717, Tq717;* California and, T753–55, T755, T757–59, *Tp757, Tp759;* Mormons and, T717, *Tp717;* Oregon Trail in, T715, T717; routes in, *Tm715, Tp713;* Texas and, T751, T753; wagon trains in, *Tp713*

Wheatley, Phillis, T493

"The Whistle" (Franklin), T207

White, John T191, *Tp191*

Whitefield, George, T297, *Tp297*

History-Social Science Content Standards for California Public Schools

Historical and Social Sciences Analysis Skills

The intellectual skills noted below are to be learned through, and applied to, the content standards for kindergarten through grade five. They are to be assessed only in conjunction with the content standards in kindergarten through grade five.

In addition to the standards for kindergarten through grade five, students demonstrate the following intellectual, reasoning, reflection, and research skills:

STANDARD	CITATIONS
Chronological and Spatial Thinking	
1. Students place key events and people of the historical era they are studying in a chronological sequence and within a spatial context; they interpret time lines.	**IJ:** 62–63, 70–71, 150–151, 159, 232–233, **RC:** 2–3, 9, 10–11, 19, 21–22, 27, 28, 35, 41, 47, 52–53, 59, 61, 65, 67, 69, 77, 81, 85, 87, 89, 92–93, 101, 109, 111, 113, 117, 123, 125, 133, 135, 138, 145, 147, 149, 151, 153, 155, 157, 159–161, 169, 179, 187, 194–195, 201, 211, 219, 221, 229, 239, 242, 247, 250–251, 259, 267, 279, 289–291, 301, 305, 309, 311, 315–316, 319, 324, 330, 332–333, 341, 345, 347, 348, 353, 355, 358, 363–367 **TE:** T10, T20, T124, T136, T158, T182, T218, T240, T264, T288, T310, T340, T352, T374, T390, T414, T424, T426, T454, T470, T490, T508, T512, T516, T538, T550, T570, T594, T618, T654, T674, T700, T728, T730, T750
2. Students correctly apply terms related to time, including *past, present, future, decade, century,* and *generation.*	**IJ:** 12–13, 60, 66–67, 248–249 **RC:** 7, 23, 31, 37, 39, 63, 79, 90–91, 121, 127, 130, 147, 159, 217, 219, 236, 274, 283, 285, 289, 306, 309, 313, 316, 327, 345, 348, 359 **TE:** T68, T158, T222, T242, T296, T307, T340, T356, T363, T432, T462, T596, T636, T680, T716, T758

3. Students explain how the present is connected to the past, identifying both similarities and differences between the two, and how some things change over time and some things stay the same.	**IJ:** 18, 65–66, 159, 174–175, 248–249
	RC: 2–3, 7, 22, 23, 31, 39, 49, 63, 67, 70, 79, 90–91, 97, 105, 109, 119, 121, 127, 130, 138, 143, 157, 161, 175, 191, 195, 205, 217, 219, 233, 236, 247–248, 274, 283, 288–289, 302, 306, 313, 316–317, 330, 333, 337, 345, 353, 362, 366–368
	TE: T68, T108, T186, T222, T224, T460, T462, T600, T708
4. Students use map and globe skills to determine the absolute locations of places and interpret information available through a map's or globe's legend, scale, and symbolic representations.	**IJ:** 8–9, 19, 41, 44–45, 62–63, 70–71, 92–93, 134–135, 200–201, 274–275
	RC: 3, 11, 15, 21–22, 28, 47, 53, 61, 65, 67, 75, 77, 87, 89, 93, 103, 113, 155, 157, 161, 170, 175, 195, 203, 209, 251, 261, 291, 302, 305, 324, 328–329, 333, 342, 358, 364–367
	TE: T10, T44, T64, T84, T100, T144, T106, T124, T138, T144, T154, T164, T166, T178, T180, T188, T190, T220, T240, T264, T288, T310, T320, T340, T354, T358, T414, T428, T434, T516, T538, T552, T618, T636, T678, T700, T714, T754
5. Students judge the significance of the relative location of a place (e.g., proximity to a harbor, on trade routes) and analyze how relative advantages or disadvantages can change over time.	**IJ:** 9, 28–29, 62–63, 70–71, 100–101, 102–103, 282–283
	RC: 3, 10–11, 15, 22, 23, 29, 51, 79, 83, 85, 89, 91, 93, 103–104, 117, 121, 127, 149, 153, 157, 159, 174, 219, 226, 242, 261, 302, 306, 315, 317, 320, 330, 337, 342, 344, 349, 358, 362, 364–365
	TE: T100, T102, T220, T236, T356, T434, T474, T656, T660, T706, T720

Research, Evidence, and Point of View

1. Students differentiate between primary and secondary sources.	**IJ:** 100–101, 230–231, 244–245, 252–253, 283–283
	RC: 159
	TE: T64, T130, T244, T260, T284, T292, T306, T318, T348, T360, T370, T378, T398, T422, T430, T442, T450, T454, T460, T494, T508, T512, T544, T546, T564, T566, T590, T596, T626, T636, T638, T650, T670, T676, T678, T716, T726

2. Students pose relevant questions about events they encounter in historical documents, eyewitness accounts, oral histories, letters, diaries, artifacts, photographs, maps, artworks, and architecture.	**IJ:** 6–7, 70–71, 84–85, 116–117, 214–215, 222–223, 230–231, 244–245, 252–253, 260–261, 282–283 **RC:** 3, 7, 11, 15, 21–22, 49, 55, 63, 87, 89, 103, 127, 155, 157, 183, 205, 215, 219, 271, 274, 277, 283, 288–289, 348 **TE:** T16, T38, T56, T60, T64, T68, T76, T78, T84, T94, T96, T106, T108, T130, T142, T152, T154, T162, T164, T166, T178, T180, T182, T188, T190, T212, T214, T218, T234, T244, T246, T260, T264, T266, T282, T284, T292, T306, T310, T318, T320, T340, T348, T352, T354, T358, T360, T370, T374, T378, T388, T398, T422, T426, T430, T442, T450, T454, T456, T460, T464, T466, T470, T472, T486, T488, T492, T494, T506, T512, T518, T544, T546, T556, T564, T566, T588, T590, T598, T602, T626, T636, T638, T648, T650, T670, T676, T678, T708, T710, T714, T716, T724, T726, T734, T738, T744, T746
3. Students distinguish fact from fiction by comparing documentary sources on historical figures and events with fictionalized characters and events.	**RC:** 7, 106, 159, 197 **TE:** T224, T492, T746

Historical Interpretation

1. Students summarize the key events of the era they are studying and explain the historical contexts of those events.	**IJ:** 110–111, 159, 232–233, 246–249, 254–255 **RC:** 2–3, 7, 10–11, 13, 15, 17, 23, 37, 47, 49, 50, 61, 63, 67, 70, 77, 79, 83, 87, 89–93, 104–106, 109, 113, 115, 117, 119, 121, 125, 127, 130, 133, 141, 143, 147, 149, 151, 155, 158–159, 165, 170–172, 174, 177, 180, 182, 184–185, 188, 190, 192–193, 203, 209, 213, 215, 223, 226–227, 229, 233, 235, 242, 245, 247–249, 255, 264–265, 271, 274–275, 277, 281, 283, 287–289, 295, 301–302, 306, 308–309, 313, 315, 317, 320, 326, 330–331, 337, 342, 348–349, 351, 353, 358–359, 362–363, 368–369 **TE:** T22, T24, T26, T30, T44, T46, T48, T62, T64, T66, T68, T82, T84, T86, T88, T98, T100, T102, T104, T106, T108, T136, T138, T140, T142, T144, T160, T162, T164, T166, T168, T170, T184, T190, T228, T238, T288, T290, T292, T294, T308, T312, T314, T316, T318, T320, T352, T354, T356, T358, T360, T390, T394, T396, T398, T476, T478, T490, T514, T520, T634, T640, T654, T656, T658, T660, T662, T730, T732, T736

2. Students identify the human and physical characteristics of the places they are studying and explain how those features form the unique character of those places.	**IJ:** 32–33, 180–181, 184–185, 252–253, 269, 280–283 **RC:** 7, 10, 13, 15, 17, 21, 23, 25, 29, 31, 37, 39, 43, 45, 47, 49, 50–51, 61, 65, 67, 70, 79, 85, 87, 89, 90–91, 93, 103, 105, 109, 113, 117, 119, 138, 143, 147, 149, 151, 153, 157–159, 170, 174, 193, 195, 219, 226, 261, 291, 302, 305–306, 317, 324, 330, 333, 337, 342, 344–345, 353, 362–367, 368–369 **TE:** T50, T82, T168, T246
3. Students identify and interpret the multiple causes and effects of historical events.	**IJ:** 56–57, 94–95, 152–155, 216–217, 224–225, 232–233, 246–249, 254–255, 292–293 **RC:** 7, 10–11, 23, 29, 37, 43, 45, 47, 61, 63, 67, 70, 75, 77, 85, 87, 89–91, 104–105, 109, 117, 119, 121, 125, 133, 147, 149, 151, 153, 159, 161, 165, 170, 172, 175, 177, 180, 182, 184, 190, 192–93, 197, 203, 213, 215, 219, 223, 226–227, 229, 232, 235–236, 240, 242, 245, 247–249, 255, 264, 271, 274, 277, 281, 283, 285, 287–289, 295, 302, 306, 308–309, 313, 315, 317, 320, 322, 330–331, 337, 342, 345, 349, 353, 358–359, 362, 368 **TE:** T132, T134, T136, T140, T154, T156, T158, T160, T162, T216, T250, T308, T350, T354, T356, T358, T360, T382, T392, T452, T464, T476, T494, T510, T514, T520, T638, T640, T656, T660, T746, T748, T760
4. Students conduct cost-benefit analyses of historical and current events.	**IJ:** 56–57, 79, 129, 146–147, 190–193, 198–19, 209 **RC:** 11, 15, 21–22, 37, 39, 45, 70, 77, 79, 83, 85, 87, 89–91, 97, 103, 109, 113, 115, 117, 119, 127, 130, 141, 147, 151, 153, 157–158, 191–192, 177, 182–184, 188, 193, 197, 203, 207, 213, 219, 226, 229, 235–236, 240, 242, 248–249, 261, 265, 271, 274, 277, 283, 285, 287–289, 302, 306, 309, 313, 315–316, 320, 324, 326, 327–329, 337, 342, 344, 349, 368 **TE:** T248, T376, T460, T498

CORRELATIONS

United States History and Geography: Making a New Nation

Students in grade five study the development of the nation up to 1850, with an emphasis on the people who were already here, when and from where others arrived, and why they came. Students learn about the colonial government founded on Judeo-Christian principles, the ideals of the Enlightenment, and the English traditions of self-government. They recognize that ours is a nation that has a constitution that derives its power from the people, that has gone through a revolution, that once sanctioned slavery, that experienced conflict over land with the original inhabitants, and that experienced a westward movement that took its people across the continent. Studying the cause, course, and consequences of the early explorations through the War for Independence and western expansion is central to students' fundamental understanding of how the principles of the American republic form the basis of a pluralistic society in which individual rights are secured.

STANDARD	CITATIONS
5.1 Students describe the major pre-Columbian settlements, including the cliff dwellers and pueblo people of the desert Southwest, the American Indians of the Pacific Northwest, the nomadic nations of the Great Plains, and the woodland peoples east of the Mississippi River.	
5.1.1 Describe how geography and climate influenced the way various nations lived and adjusted to the natural environment, including locations of villages, the distinct structures that they built, and how they obtained food, clothing, tools, and utensils.	**IJ:** 8–9, 18–19, 28–29, 32–33, 40–41 **RC:** 10, 11, 13, 15, 17, 21, 22–23, 25, 29, 31, 39, 43, 50–51 **TE:** T8, T14, T16, T18, T20, T22, T24, T26, T28, T30, T36, T38, T40, T41, T42, T44, T46, T48, T50, T56, T60, T62, T64, T66, T70, T76, T78, T82, T84, T88, T94, T98, T100, T102, T104, T100, T104, T110
5.1.2 Describe their varied customs and folklore traditions.	**IJ:** 16–17, 26–27, 32–33 **RC:** 7, 13, 15, 17, 21–23, 25, 31, 37, 39, 43, 50–51 **TE:** T8, T38, T44, T58, T60, T62, T64, T66, T68, T70, T78, T80, T84, T86, T96, T98, T102
5.1.3 Explain their varied economies and systems of government.	**IJ:** 28–29, 34–36, 40–41 **RC:** 11, 13, 15, 17, 21, 23, 25, 31, 37, 39, 43, 45, 47, 50–51 **TE:** T8, T84, T86, T106, T108
5.2 Students trace the routes of early explorers and describe the early explorations of the Americas.	
5.2.1 Describe the entrepreneurial characteristics of early explorers (e.g., Christopher Columbus, Francisco Vásquez de Coronado) and the technological developments that made sea exploration by latitude and longitude possible (e.g., compass, sextant, astrolabe, seaworthy ships, chronometers, gunpowder).	**IJ:** 52–53, 54–55, 56–57, 64–65 **RC:** 63, 64–65, 70, 75, 77 **TE:** T130, T132, T134, T136, 138, T140, T142, T144, T146, T154, T156, T158, T160, T164, T166, T170

5.2.2 Explain the aims, obstacles, and accomplishments of the explorers, sponsors, and leaders of key European expeditions and the reasons Europeans chose to explore and colonize the world (e.g., the Spanish Reconquista, the Protestant Reformation, the Counter Reformation).	**IJ:** 52–53, 64–65, **RC:** 53, 55, 60, 61, 65, 67, 70, 75, 77, 79, 83, 85, 87, 89–91, 104, 105, 109, 121 **TE:** T130, T138, T142, T144, T146, T152, T154, T156, T158, T160, T162, T164, T166, T168, T170, T176, T178, T180, T182, T184, T186, T188, T190, T192, T238, T240, T250
5.2.3 Trace the routes of the major land explorers of the United States, the distances traveled by explorers, and the Atlantic trade routes that linked Africa, the West Indies, the British colonies, and Europe.	**IJ:** 62–63, 70–71 **RC:** 53, 77, 87 **TE:** T178, T180
5.2.4 Locate on maps of North and South America land claimed by Spain, France, England, Portugal, the Netherlands, Sweden, and Russia.	**IJ:** 72–73 **RC:** 53, 59, 77, 79, 82, 85, 89, 93, 103, 113, 138, 141, 161 **TE:** T166, T180, T188, T190, T242
5.3 Students describe the cooperation and conflict that existed among the American Indians and between the Indian nations and the new settlers.	
5.3.1 Describe the competition among the English, French, Spanish, Dutch, and Indian nations for control of North America.	**IJ:** 70–71, 94–95, 134–139 **RC:** 90–91, 93, 106, 109, 113, 117, 119, 121, 138, 158–159 **TE:** T178, T180, T182, T184, T186, T188, T190, T192, T218, T234, T246, T252, T346, T348, T350, T352, T354, T356, T358, T360, T362
5.3.2 Describe the cooperation that existed between the colonists and Indians during the 1600s and 1700s (e.g., in agriculture, the fur trade, military alliances, treaties, cultural interchanges).	**IJ:** 74–75, 84–85, 94–95, 102–103, 106–107, 116–119 **RC:** 105–106, 109, 115, 119, 158–159 **TE:** T176, T186, T188, T190, T192, T216, T224, T244, T258, T266, T272, T274, T276, T282, T294, T314, T348, T350, T352, T356, T358, T360, T362
5.3.3 Examine the conflicts before the Revolutionary War (e.g., the Pequot and King Philip's Wars in New England, the Powhatan Wars in Virginia, the French and Indian War).	**IJ:** 84–85, 102–103, 134–139 **RC:** 109, 121, 133, 158–159, 170, 172, 174–175 **TE:** T214, T274, T346, T348, T350, T352, T354, T356, T358, T360, T362
5.3.4 Discuss the role of broken treaties and massacres and the factors that led to the Indians' defeat, including the resistance of Indian nations to encroachments and assimilation (e.g., the story of the Trail of Tears).	**IJ:** 262–265, 282–287 **RC:** 133, 158, 177, 322, 330, 349, 351 **TE:** T724, T726, T728, T732, T734, T736, T738
5.3.5 Describe the internecine Indian conflicts, including the competing claims for control of lands (e.g., actions of the Iroquois, Huron, Lakota [Sioux]).	**IJ:** 134–135, 262–265, 282–287 **RC:** 119, 158, 170, 363 **TE:** T248, T274, T348, T350, T352, T362, T732

5.3.6 Explain the influence and achievements of significant leaders of the time (e.g., John Marshall, Andrew Jackson, Chief Tecumseh, Chief Logan, Chief John Ross, Sequoyah).	**IJ:** 262–265, 282–287
	RC: 171, 322, 330, 348–349, 351, 353
	TE: T342, T620, T680, T682, T728, T730, T732, T734, T736, T738

5.4 Students understand the political, religious, social, and economic institutions that evolved in the colonial era.

5.4.1 Understand the influence of location and physical setting on the founding of the original 13 colonies, and identify on a map the locations of the colonies and of the American Indian nations already inhabiting these areas.	**IJ:** 100–105, 108–111, 116–121
	RC: 109, 125, 141, 147, 149, 156–158, 195
	TE: T212, T264, T274, T310, T312
5.4.2 Identify the major individuals and groups responsible for the founding of the various colonies and the reasons for their founding (e.g., John Smith, Virginia; Roger Williams, Rhode Island; William Penn, Pennsylvania; Lord Baltimore, Maryland; William Bradford, Plymouth; John Winthrop, Massachusetts).	**IJ:** 100–101, 102–103, 110–113, 116–119
	RC: 141, 158
	TE: T208, T220, T236, T264, T266, T270, T272, T282, T286, T290, T292, T294, T298, T312, T314, T320
5.4.3 Describe the religious aspects of the earliest colonies (e.g., Puritanism in Massachusetts, Anglicanism in Virginia, Catholicism in Maryland, Quakerism in Pennsylvania).	**IJ:** 100–101
	RC: 130, 141, 146–147, 159
	TE: T258, T260, T262, T264, T266, T270, T284, T292, T294, T296, T298, T320
5.4.4 Identify the significance and leaders of the First Great Awakening, which marked a shift in religious ideas, practices, and allegiances in the colonial period, the growth of religious toleration, and free exercise of religion.	**IJ:** 112–113
	RC: 142–143
	TE: T272, T296
5.4.5 Understand how the British colonial period created the basis for the development of political self-government and a free-market economic system and the differences between the British, Spanish, and French colonial systems.	**IJ:** 142–147
	RC: 109, 125, 127, 147, 158–159
	TE: T266, T268, T286, T288, T292, T296, T298
5.4.6 Describe the introduction of slavery into America, the responses of slave families to their condition, the ongoing struggle between proponents and opponents of slavery, and the gradual institutionalization of slavery in the South.	**IJ:** 114–121, 262–265
	RC: 109, 137, 151, 153, 155, 213, 217, 313, 324
	TE: T226, T242, T304, T306, T308, T316, T318, T320, T322
5.4.7 Explain the early democratic ideas and practices that emerged during the colonial period, including the significance of representative assemblies and town meetings.	**IJ:** 142–147
	RC: 109, 125, 127, 138, 141, 143, 158
	TE: T226, T266, T286, T288, T290, T292, T294, T296, T320

5.5 Students explain the causes of the American Revolution.

5.5.1 Understand how political, religious, and economic ideas and interests brought about the Revolution (e.g., resistance to imperial policy, the Stamp Act, the Townshend Acts, taxes on tea, Coercive Acts).	**IJ:** 142–147, 151–155
	RC: 180, 184, 190, 192–193, 215, 249
	TE: T368, T370, T372, T374, T376, T378, T380, T382, T388, T390, T392, T396, T398, T400

5.5.2 Know the significance of the first and second Continental Congresses and of the Committees of Correspondence.	**IJ:** 151–155, 166–167, 172–173 **RC:** 188, 190–191, 205, 219 **TE:** T388, T390, T392, T396, T398, T4~, T430, T458
5.5.3 Understand the people and events associated with the drafting and signing of the Declaration of Independence and the document's significance, including the key political concepts it embodies, the origins of those concepts, and its role in severing ties with Great Britain.	**IJ:** 172–173 **RC:** 213, 215, 217, 219 **TE:** T442, T450, T452, T454, T456, T458, T460, T464
5.5.4 Describe the views, lives, and impact of key individuals during this period (e.g., King George III, Patrick Henry, Thomas Jefferson, George Washington, Benjamin Franklin, John Adams).	**IJ:** 142–147, 151–155, 164–165, 172–173 **RC:** 165, 171, 183, 188, 197, 213, 223, 240, 245, 248–249, 265, 301, 306 **TE:** T208, T368, T370, T372, T374, T376, T378, T380, T382, T388, T390, T392, T396, T398, T422, T442, T450, T454, T456, T458, T468, T506, T508, T518, T546, T588

5.6 Students understand the course and consequences of the American Revolution.

5.6.1 Identify and map the major military battles, campaigns, and turning points of the Revolutionary War, the roles of the American and British leaders, and the Indian leaders' alliances on both sides.	**IJ:** 166–167, 182–185, 198–201 **RC:** 197, 203, 209, 223, 226–227, 229, 233, 235, 240 **TE:** T420, T426, T428, T430, T432, T434, T464, T466, T468, T470, T472, T474, T476, T478, T480, T486, T492, T494, T496, T500, T506, T508, T512, T514, T516, T518, T522
5.6.2 Describe the contributions of France and other nations and of individuals to the outcome of the Revolution (e.g., Benjamin Franklin's negotiations with the French, the French navy, the Treaty of Paris, The Netherlands, Russia, the Marquis Marie Joseph de Lafayette, Tadeusz Kosciuszko, Baron Friedrich Wilhelm von Steuben).	**IJ:** 166–167, 182–185, 200–201 **RC:** 242, 245, 229 **TE:** T468, T474, T476, T478, T518, T522
5.6.3 Identify the different roles women played during the Revolution (e.g., Abigail Adams, Martha Washington, Molly Pitcher, Phillis Wheatley, Mercy Otis Warren).	**IJ:** 188–189 **RC:** 232, 237 **TE:** T416, T488, T490, T492, T494, T498
5.6.4 Understand the personal impact and economic hardship of the war on families, problems of financing the war, wartime inflation, and laws against hoarding goods and materials and profiteering.	**IJ:** 166–167, 182–185, 192–193 **RC:** 232, 236 **TE:** T470, T498, T510, T520
5.6.5 Explain how state constitutions that were established after 1776 embodied the ideals of the American Revolution and helped serve as models for the U.S. Constitution.	**RC:** 260–261 **TE:** T510, T544, T546, T550, T554, T556, T558, T572, T574
5.6.6 Demonstrate knowledge of the significance of land policies developed under the Continental Congress (e.g., sale of western lands, the Northwest Ordinance of 1787) and those policies' impact on American Indians' land.	**IJ:** 216–219, 246–249, 282–287 **RC:** 261, 322, 330, 368–369 **TE:** T520, T552, T626, T628, T634, T642, T676, T684

...d how the ideals set forth in the Declaration of Independence ...ay people viewed slavery.	**IJ:** 172–177 **RC:** 302, 324, 330 **TE:** T456, T458, T678

5... ...nts describe the people and events associated with the development of the U.S. Constitution and analyze the ...tion's significance as the foundation of the American republic.

...7.1 List the shortcomings of the Articles of Confederation as set forth by their critics.	**IJ:** 214–219 **RC:** 264, 277 **TE:** T544, T550, T554
5.7.2 Explain the significance of the new Constitution of 1787, including the struggles over its ratification and the reasons for the addition of the Bill of Rights.	**IJ:** 222–227, 230–235 **RC:** 271, 277, 281, 288–289 **TE:** T588, T594, T596, T598
5.7.3 Understand the fundamental principles of American constitutional democracy, including how the government derives its power from the people and the primacy of individual liberty.	**IJ:** 222–227, 230–235 **RC:** 274–275, 277, 283, 287, 289 **TE:** T564, T566, T568, T570, T572, T574, T582, T588, T590, T598, T600
5.7.4 Understand how the Constitution is designed to secure our liberty by both empowering and limiting central government and compare the powers granted to citizens, Congress, the president, and the Supreme Court with those reserved to the states.	**IJ:** 222–227, 230–235 **RC:** 274–275, 277 **TE:** T564, T572, T574, T576, T578, T580, T582, T588, T594, T596, T598, T632
5.7.5 Discuss the meaning of the American creed that calls on citizens to safeguard the liberty of individual Americans within a unified nation, to respect the rule of law, and to preserve the Constitution.	**IJ:** 230–235 **RC:** 287–288 **TE:** T602
5.7.6 Know the songs that express American ideals (e.g., "America the Beautiful," "The Star Spangled Banner").	**IJ:** 244–245, 258–259 **TE:** T626, T628, T642, T668

5.8 Students trace the colonization, immigration, and settlement patterns of the American people from 1789 to the mid-1800s, with emphasis on the role of economic incentives, effects of the physical and political geography, and transportation systems.

5.8.1 Discuss the waves of immigrants from Europe between 1789 and 1850 and their modes of transportation into the Ohio and Mississippi Valleys and through the Cumberland Gap (e.g., overland wagons, canals, flatboats, steamboats).	**IJ:** 262–265 **RC:** 295, 317, 326, 330, 368–369 **TE:** T648, T650, T652, T656, T658, T660, T662, T668, T670, T672, T674, T678, T682
5.8.2 Name the states and territories that existed in 1850 and identify their locations and major geographical features (e.g., mountain ranges, principal rivers, dominant plant regions).	**IJ:** 276–282 **RC:** 333, 364–367 **TE:** T688, T708, T714, T716, T764
5.8.3 Demonstrate knowledge of the explorations of the trans-Mississippi West following the Louisiana Purchase (e.g., Meriwether Lewis and William Clark, Zebulon Pike, John Frémont).	**IJ:** 246–249, 276–282 **RC:** 358 **TE:** T628, T634, T636, T638, T642, T754

5.8.4 Discuss the experiences of settlers on the overland trails to the West (e.g., location of the routes; purpose of the journeys; the influence of the terrain, rivers, vegetation, and climate; life in the territories at the end of these trails).	**IJ:** 262–265, 276–282, 290–2 **RC:** 305, 306, 315, 320, 330, 342, 362, 368–369 **TE:** T706, T710, T712, T714, T716, T720
5.8.5 Describe the continued migration of Mexican settlers into Mexican territories of the West and Southwest.	**IJ:** 290–295 **RC:** 358 **TE:** T744, T746, T750, T752, T760
5.8.6 Relate how and when California, Texas, Oregon, and other western lands became part of the United States, including the significance of the Texas War for Independence and the Mexican-American War.	**IJ:** 276–282, 290–295 **RC:** 342, 344–345, 358, 362–363, 368–369 **TE:** T712, T744, T746, T748, T752, T754, T756, T758, T760
5.9 Students know the location of the current 50 states and the names of their capitals.	**RC:** 156–157, 328–329, 364–367 **TE:** T326, T688, T764